KU-850-417

Welcome to Greece

Ancient sun-bleached ruins pierce blue skies as the Aegean laps at the endless coastline. And Greek culture is alive with passionate music, inspired cuisine and thrill-seeking activities.

Cultural Treasure Chest

Standing in the shadow of the Acropolis feels otherworldly. Greece is full of such moments. Step into the ring where Olympians first competed. Climb steps hewn out of stone to Meteora's monasteries, perched atop towering rocks. Contemplate the oracle's insights from the grandeur of Delphi, take in a starlit drama at an ancient outdoor theatre and be stunned by massive marble sculptures dredged up from the Aegean. But then you'll encounter bold modern art, the melancholic throb of *rembetika* (blues songs) and artisans creating new work from traditional techniques. Greece has endless cultural pursuits and a calendar bursting with festivals, holidays and exhibits.

Local Flavours

The secret to Greek cooking is often found in the chef's garden – regional produce and cooking styles make travelling here a culinary adventure. Taste herbs and mountain greens you've never heard of, mussels steamed in ouzo, bread baked with olives, and fish straight from the sea. Taste-test regional cheeses: crumbling feta, honeyed soft cheeses and sharp, hard rounds. Find Italian influences in pastas or Turkish spices in delicate sweets. A traditional-cooking renaissance has chefs lifting time-honoured recipes to new heights.

Socially Spirited

Socialising is more than a pastime in Greece – it's a way of life. Cafes overflow with teenagers gossiping or older locals in heated debate. Restaurants are filled with long tables for big gatherings and friends amble arm in arm down the street. Squares are the focal point, where life unfolds collectively. Immerse yourself, whether it's a coffee, a shot of ouzo, a chorus on the bouzouki or a local celebration. Greeks are passionate and live life to the fullest, even at the most difficult times. The result is a country seemingly riddled with challenges, yet full of people loving life.

Wildly Natural

Whether you're a serious adrenalin junkie or dedicated beach bum, Greece will bewitch you. Days melt from one to the next under wide open skies and a sea speckled with islands that deliver the white-sand, palm-fringed beaches of your dreams. Wander along cobbled Byzantine footpaths, hike into volcanoes, watch for dolphins and sea turtles, and cycle through lush forests. Meander through olive groves, idyllic villages and petrified forests. Thrill seekers will discover world-class kitesurfing, wreck diving, and rock-climbing locations with dizzying views. Or simply hop on a boat and set sail into the glittering blue beyond.

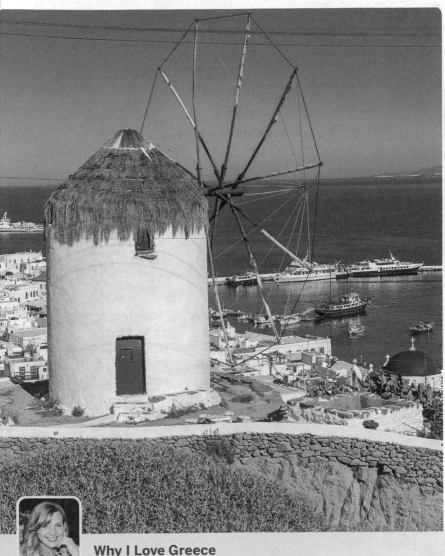

Why I Love Greece

By Korina Miller, Writer

I first visited Greece as an 18-year-old, sleeping on the decks of slow-moving ferries, living on olives and feta, and constantly salt-crusted from swimming in the deep-blue Aegean. I've returned many times since – to watch a starlit performance at a 3rd-century-BC theatre; to wander through mysterious Minoan ruins; or to drink ouzo with locals who declare me family. I love Greece because magical moments like these aren't so hard to find.

For more about our writers, see p784.

Above: Mykonos (p349)

Greece

Thessaloniki
Greece's dynamic
second city (p246)

Zagorohoria
Charming stone and slate
mountain villages (p300)

Corfu
Stunning multicultural
seaside architecture (p663)

Meteora
Soaring rock pinnacles topped
with monasteries (p237)

Ancient Delphi
Where mythology
and history meet (p201)

Acropolis
The most iconic monument
of ancient Greece (p67)

The Mani
Steeped in Maniot culture
and perfect for hiking (p168)

Samaria Gorge
Carved between unending
towering cliffs (p480)

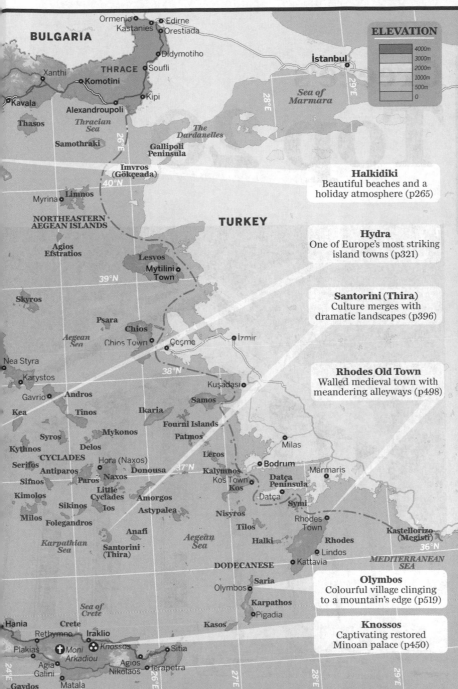

N
0 ———— 100km
0 ———— 50miles

ELEVATION

4000m
3000m
2000m
1000m
500m
0

Ormenio
Edirne
Kastanies
Orestiada
BULGARIA
Didymotiho
İstanbul
Xanthi
THRACE
Soufli
Komotini
Sea of
Marmara
Kavala
Kipi
Alexandroupoli
Thasos
Thracian
Sea
The
Dardanelles
Samothraki
Gallipoli
Peninsula
Imvros
(Gökçeada)

Halkidiki
Beautiful beaches and a
holiday atmosphere (p265)

Myrina
Limnos
NORTHEASTERN
AEGEAN ISLANDS

TURKEY

Agios
Efstratios

Hydra
One of Europe's most striking
island towns (p321)

Skyros

Lesvos
Mytilini
Town

Santorini (Thira)
Culture merges with
dramatic landscapes (p396)

Psara
Chios
Aegean
Sea
Chios Town
Çeşme
İzmir

Rhodes Old Town
Walled medieval town with
meandering alleyways (p498)

Nea Styra
Karystos
Kuşadası
Gavrio
Andros
Samos
Kea
Tinos
Ikaria
Fourni Islands
Syros
Mykonos
Patmos
Milas
Kythnos
Delos
Leros
Bodrum
Marmaris
Serifos
CYCLADES
Hora (Naxos)
Kalymnos
Antiparos
Donousa
Kos Town
Datça
Sifnos
Paros
Naxos
Kos
Peninsula
Kimolos
Little
Cyclades
Datça
Sikinos
Amorgos
Symi
Milos
Ios
Astypalea
Folegandros
Nisyros
Rhodes
Anafi
Tilos
Town
Aegean
Sea
Symi
Karpathian
Santorini
Halki
Rhodes
Sea
(Thira)
Kastellorizo
DODECANESE
Lindos
(Megisti)
Kattavia
MEDITERRANEAN
SEA

Olympos
Colourful village clinging
to a mountain's edge (p519)

Saria
Olympos
Karpathos
Pigadia

Knossos
Captivating restored
Minoan palace (p450)

Hania
Crete
Rethymno
Iraklio
Plakias
Moni
Knossos
Sitia
Arkadiou
Agia
Agios
Galini
Nikolaos
Ierapetra
Kasos
Gavdos
Matala

Sea of
Crete

Greece's
Top 20

1

Experiencing the Acropolis

1 Regal on its hilltop, the elegant Acropolis (p67) of Athens remains the quintessential landmark of Western civilisation. Explore it early in the morning or soak up the view from a dinnertime terrace; no matter how you experience the Acropolis, you will be mesmerised by its beauty, history and sheer size. Beyond the Parthenon (p69), you can find quieter spots such as the exquisite Temple of Athena Nike (p68) and the Theatre of Dionysos (p72). Nearby, the Acropolis Museum (p73) showcases the surviving treasures of the Acropolis. Parthenon (p69)

Meteora

2 Magnificent Meteora (p237) will leave you speechless. Soaring pillars of rock jut heavenward, a handful complete with monasteries perched on their summits. Built as early as the 14th century, these were home to hermit monks fleeing persecution. The rope ladders that once enabled the monks to reach the top have long been replaced by steps carved into the rock, and six of the 24 monasteries remain open to resident monks and visitors alike. Today this spectacular stone forest beckons pilgrims and rock climbers from around the world. Moni Agias Varvaras Rousanou (p238)

SAIKO3P/SHUTTERSTOCK ©

2

CGE2010/SHUTTERSTOCK ©

ANASTASIOS71/SHUTTERSTOCK ©

Ancient Delphi

3 Early morning is a magical time at Delphi (p201), as the sun's rays pour over the Sanctuary of Athena Pronea (p204; pictured). As you gaze out over the Bay of Corinth, it is easy to understand why the ancient Greeks chose this as the centre of their world. Today, only three columns remain of the magnificent sanctuary, but that's enough to let your imagination soar. Nearby, the Sacred Way meanders past the Temple of Apollo (p201) where prophecies were uttered that sent armies to battle and made lovers swoon.

Rhodes' Old Town

4 Getting lost in Rhodes' Old Town (p499) is a must. Away from the crowds, you'll find yourself meandering down twisting, cobbled alleyways with soaring archways and lively squares. In these hidden corners your imagination will take off with flights of medieval fancy. Explore the ancient Knights' Quarter, the old Jewish Quarter or the Hora (Turkish Quarter). Hear traditional live music in tiny tavernas or dine on fresh seafood at atmospheric outdoor restaurants. Wander along the top of the city's walls, with the sea on one side and a bird's-eye view into this living museum.

Santorini Sunsets

5 There's more to Santorini (p396) than sunsets, but this remarkable island, shaped by the fire of prehistoric eruptions, has made the celebratory sunset its own. On summer evenings, the clifftop towns of Fira (p398) and Oia (p406; pictured) are packed with visitors awed by the vast blood-red canvas of the cliff face as the sun struts its stuff. You can catch the sunset without the crowds from almost anywhere along the cliff edge. And if you miss sundown, you can always face east at first light for some fairly stunning sunrises.

Cutting-Edge Capital

6 Life in Athens (p60) is a magnificent mash-up of both the ancient and the contemporary. Beneath the majestic facades of the many venerable landmarks, the city is teeming with life and creativity. Galleries and clubs hold the exhibitions, performances and installations of the city's booming arts scene. Fashionable restaurants and humble tavernas rustle up plate after plate of satisfying fare. Soulful *rembetika* (blues songs) serenade the cobbled streets, while discos and bars abound and swing deep into the night.

BASILT/ALAMY ©

Cretan Cuisine

7 Waistlines be damned: Crete (p438) is the perfect place to indulge. The island's Mediterranean diet is known for its health benefits but the farm-fresh produce, aromatic herbs, straight-from-the-ocean seafood, soft, tangy cheese and some of the world's best virgin olive oil make it legendary. Whether it's a bowl of snails, fresh artichokes, mussels or figs, the essence of this rustic cuisine is a balance of flavours. It's hard to beat traditional hand-spun filo, a salad of *horta* (wild greens) picked from a backyard garden and red mullet just hauled in.

Easter Festivities on Patmos

8 The Greek calendar is chock-full of festivals and holidays, but the biggest event of the Greek Orthodox Church is Easter. And the best place to experience it is on Patmos (p560) in the Dodecanese. The island comes to life with fireworks, dancing in the streets, huge outdoor lamb roasts and plenty of ouzo shots. Begin by witnessing the moving, candlelit processions of flower-filled biers through the capital, marking the start of the celebration on Good Friday. By Saturday night you'll be shouting *Hristos Anesti* (Christ is Risen) and cracking vibrant red-dyed eggs.

7

8

Island Hopping in the Cyclades

9 From the spirited nightlife and celebrity hideaways of Mykonos and Ios, to the isolated sandy coasts of tiny, far-flung specks such as Anafi, hopping through the Cyclades (p331) is a Greek experience not to be missed. Peppered with ancient ruins (try Delos), mystical castles (head to Naxos), lush scenery and dramatic coastlines (visit Milos), the islands are spread like Greek jewels across the sea. Speed over the Aegean on catamarans and sway on old-fashioned ferry boats. You won't regret a single saltwater-splashed second of it.

Hora (Mykonos; p351)

Samaria Gorge

10 The dramatic gorge of Samaria (p480) is the most-trodden canyon in Crete – and with good reason. Starting at Omalos and running down through an ancient riverbed to the Libyan Sea, it's home to varied wildlife, soaring birds of prey and a dazzling array of wildflowers in spring. It's a full-day's walk (about six hours down) but the jaw-dropping views make it worth every step. To get more solitude, try lesser-known gorges such as Imbros Gorge (p479), which runs roughly parallel to Samaria.

Hydra

11 Everyone approaches Hydra (p321) by sea. There is no airport, there are no cars. The white-gold houses of the tiny island's stunningly preserved stone village fill a natural cove and hug the edges of the surrounding mountains. Below, sailboats, caïques (little boats) and megayachts fill Hydra's quays while locals and vacationers fill the harbourside cafes. Here, a mere hour and a half from Athens, you'll find a great cappuccino, rich naval and architectural history, and the raw sea coast beckoning you for a swim.

Vibrant Thessaloniki

12 Stylish Thessaloniki (p246) remains northern Greece's liveliest town, thanks to its universities, cultural scene, arts and nightlife. Explore the old quarter, a neighbourhood full of winding streets marked by white-plastered houses, lazy cats and Byzantine churches. Taste-test your way through the city's *zaharoplasteia* (patisseries) for Ottoman-inspired sweets. Drink up with throngs of students at bars and clubs. Tour the galleries of one of the country's most artistically fertile locations and save time for the first-rate museums. Thessaloniki has it all going on.
Church of Agios Dimitrios (p249)

Knossos

13 Rub shoulders with the ghosts of the mighty Minoans. Knossos (p450) was their Bronze Age capital more than 4000 years ago; from here they attained an astonishingly high level of civilisation and ruled vast parts of the Aegean. After mysteriously disappearing less than a thousand years later, their extraordinary wealth of frescoes, sculptures, jewellery and structures lay buried under the Cretan soil until the site's excavation in the early 20th century. Despite a controversial partial reconstruction, Knossos remains one of the most important archaeological sites in the Mediterranean.

Halkidiki & Mt Athos

14 Northern Greece's Halkidiki (p265) stretches out into the Aegean like three enticing escape routes into sand and sun-soaked bliss. Kassandra Peninsula buzzes in summer with open-air discos and umbrella-peppered beaches, while Sithonia Peninsula has sandy shores reserved for escapists. Meanwhile, Athos Peninsula offers stunning, family-friendly beaches and is home to the heavily forested Mt Athos (p269) with a monastic community that has preserved its Byzantine rituals for more than 1000 years. Sithonian Peninsula (p266)

Zagorohoria

15 After passing through a seemingly endless array of tunnels, the Egnatia Odos Hwy brings you into rugged Epiros, home of the Pindos Mountains and the Zagorohoria (p300) – an immaculately preserved region of traditional villages spread along the ridges of Europe's deepest canyon, the Vikos Gorge. Here, the air is clear, fresh and cool, and the views astounding. You can explore the region by hiking or mountain biking, or simply get cosy by the fire in one of the many rustic B&Bs dotting the region. Dilofo (p300), Zagorohoria

14

15

Olymbos

16 Let your mind drift from the sandy coast to the interior, where secluded mountaintop villages have developed unique cultures. Olymbos (p519) looks precarious at best, perched high above the plunging rocky shoreline. Once the day trippers leave, the village exudes a certain quietness. Along narrow, cobbled alleyways, women bake bread in communal ovens and men whittle on doorsteps. They're dressed the way they've dressed for centuries and speak a language nearly lost. In a shrinking world, there aren't many places like Olymbos left. Soak up some of the magic while it still survives.

Lesvos

17 Bulky and imposing, Lesvos (p605) does its size justice with its tremendously varied landscape. Rolling olive groves and cool pine forests stretch into grassy plains, where one of the world's few petrified forests stands. The island's coast is lined with beaches, many hardly touched by tourism. Lesvos' capital, Mytilini Town, is energised by a large student population and a busy cafe and bar scene aided by fine local ouzo and wine. Some exploration will reveal a medieval castle town and two exquisite Byzantine churches. The only thing you may be short of here is time.

Molyvos (p611)

Corfu

18 The story of Corfu (p663) is written across the handsome facades of its main town's buildings. This is a place that crams a remarkable mix of architecture into its small circumference. Stroll past Byzantine fortresses, neoclassical 19th-century British buildings, Parisian-style arcades, Orthodox church towers and the narrow, sun-dappled streets of the Venetian Old Town. Beyond the town, Corfu is lush green mountains, rolling countryside and dramatic coastlines. And if the architecture and scenery aren't enough, come to enjoy the Italian-influenced food. Corfu Town (p665)

Hiking the Mani

19 Although it can no longer be described as 'remote', the Mani (p168) holds a magic unlike anywhere else in Greece. For centuries, the feuding families here were literally a law unto themselves and this has contributed to the unique Maniot culture. The Mani's footpaths and landscape beckon hikers from around the world. With everything from rugged rocky highlands and hidden lush green oases to small fishing tavernas and severe rock-solid tower houses, this pocket of the Peloponnese is well worth exploring.

Ancient Olympia

20 The atmosphere at the site (p185) of the first Olympics is almost mythical. Feel the watchful eye of Zeus as you tour the ruins of the stadium, gymnasium and temples, imagining the thousands of men that gathered to compete with hands full of offerings. The games were held here for at least 100 years and the nearby museums offer a glimpse into the world of the long-ago athletes. The historical significance of this site is both humbling and inspiring. You may even be motivated to run a lap or two.

Need to Know

For more information, see Survival Guide (p747)

Currency
Euro (€)

Language
Greek

Visas
Generally not required for stays of up to 90 days; however, travellers from some nations may require a visa, so double-check with the Greek embassy.

Money
In cities, debit and credit cards are accepted but in out-of-the-way locations you'll need cash. Most towns have ATMs but they're often out of order.

Mobile Phones
Local SIM cards can be used in European and Australian phones. Most other phones can be set to roaming. US/Canadian phones need to have a dual- or tri-band system.

Time
East European Time (GMT/UTC plus two hours)

When to Go

Dry climate
Warm summer, mild winter
Mild summer, very cold winter

Thessaloniki
GO May–Nov

Corfu
GO May–Sep

Athens
GO May–Sep

Rhodes
GO Apr–Sep

Iraklio
GO May–Oct

High Season
(Easter & May–Aug)

➜ Sights, tours and transport are running full tilt.

➜ Accommodation prices can double.

➜ Both crowds and temperatures soar.

Shoulder
(Apr, Sep & Oct)

➜ Accommodation prices can drop by up to 20%.

➜ Temperatures are not as blazing.

➜ Internal flights and island ferries have reduced schedules.

➜ Crowds begin to thin.

Low Season
(Nov–Mar)

➜ Many hotels, sights and restaurants shut down, especially on the islands.

➜ Accommodation rates can drop by as much as 50%.

➜ Ferry schedules are skeletal.

➜ Temperatures fall; Athens and Crete may even see snow.

Useful Websites

EOT (Greek National Tourist Organisation; www.gnto.gr) Concise tourist information.

Greek Travel Pages (www.gtp.gr) Access to ferry schedules and accommodation.

Lonely Planet (www.lonelyplanet.com/greece) Destination information, hotel bookings and traveller forum.

Ministry of Culture (www.culture.gr) For cultural events and sights.

Important Numbers

In Greece, the area code must be dialled, meaning you always dial the full 10-digit telephone number.

Country code	☎30
International access code	☎00
Ambulance	☎166
Highway rescue (ELPA)	☎10400
Police	☎100
Tourist police	☎171

Exchange Rates

Australia	A$1	€0.69
Canada	C$1	€0.69
Japan	¥100	€0.77
New Zealand	NZ$1	€0.64
UK	£1	€1.12
US	US$1	€0.86

For current exchange rates see www.xe.com.

Daily Costs

Budget: Less than €100

➡ Dorm bed and domatio (Greek B&B): less than €60

➡ Meal at markets and street stalls: less than €15

Midrange: €100–180

➡ Double room in midrange hotel: €60–150

➡ Hearty meal at a local taverna: around €20

➡ Entrance fee for most sights: less than €15

Top End: More than €180

➡ Double room in top hotel: from €150

➡ Excellent dining, some accompanied by Michelin stars: around €60

➡ Activity such as diving: certification around €400

➡ Cocktail: around €12

Opening Hours

Opening hours vary throughout the year. We've provided high-season opening hours; hours decrease significantly in the shoulder and low seasons, when many places shut completely.

Banks 8.30am–2.30pm Monday to Thursday, 8am–2pm Friday

Restaurants 11am–2pm or 3pm and 7pm–1am

Cafes 10am–midnight

Bars 8pm–late

Clubs 10pm–4am

Post offices 7.30am–2pm Monday to Friday (rural); 7.30am–8pm Monday to Friday, 7.30am–2pm Saturday (urban)

Shops 8am–3pm Monday, Wednesday and Saturday; 8am–2.30pm and 5–8pm Tuesday, Thursday and Friday

Arriving in Greece

Eleftherios Venizelos International Airport (Athens) Express buses operate 24 hours between the airport, city centre and Piraeus. Half-hourly metro trains run between the city centre and the airport from 5.30am to 11.30pm. Taxis to the city centre cost €38 (closer to €50 at night) and take about 45 minutes.

Nikos Kazantzakis International Airport (Iraklio, Crete) Bus 1 runs every 10 minutes between the airport and the city centre from 6.15am to 10.45pm. Taxis to the city centre cost €20.

Diagoras Airport (Rhodes) Buses run between the airport and Rhodes Town from 6.30am to 11.15pm (from 11.45am Sunday). Taxis from the airport to Rhodes Town cost around €30.

Getting Around

Air Domestic flights are abundant and significantly cut down travel time. In high season, flights fill up fast so book ahead.

Boat Ferries link the islands to each other and the mainland, including catamarans, well-equipped modern ferries and overnight boats with cabins. Schedules can be unreliable. Book ahead in high season.

Bus Generally air-conditioned and frequent, buses are a good way to travel between major cities.

Car Rentals are reasonably priced and found on all but the tiniest islands. They give you the freedom to explore the islands, but you'll need a good dose of bravery and road smarts.

For much more on **getting around**, see p760

First Time Greece

For more information, see Survival Guide (p747)

Checklist

➡ Check your passport is valid for at least six months past your arrival date

➡ Make reservations for accommodation and travel, especially in high season

➡ Check airline baggage restrictions, including for regional flights

➡ Inform credit-/debit-card company of your travel plans

➡ Organise travel insurance

➡ Check if you'll be able to use your mobile (cell) phone

What to Pack

➡ Waterproof money belt

➡ Credit and debit cards

➡ Driving licence

➡ Phrasebook

➡ Diving qualifications

➡ Phone charger

➡ Power adapter

➡ Lock/padlock

➡ Lightweight raincoat

➡ Seasickness remedies

➡ Mosquito repellent

➡ Swimwear, snorkel and fins

➡ Clothes pegs and laundry line

➡ Earplugs

Top Tips for Your Trip

➡ If at all possible, visit in the shoulder seasons – late spring or early autumn. The weather is softer and the crowds are slim.

➡ Be sure to visit a few out-of-the-way villages where you can still find full-on, unselfconscious traditional culture. The best way to do this is to rent a car and explore. Stop for lunch, check out the local shops and test out your Greek.

➡ Go slowly. Greece's infrastructure doesn't befit a fast-paced itinerary. Visit fewer places for longer.

➡ Visit at least one local coffee shop, one seafood taverna next to a port and one traditional live-music venue. This is where you'll experience Greek culture at its most potent.

What to Wear

Athenians are well groomed and the younger crowd is trendy, so keep your most stylish clothes for the city. Nevertheless, in Athens and other big cities such as Rhodes and Iraklio, you'll still get away with shorts or jeans and casual tops. Bars or high-end restaurants require more effort – the scene is fashionable rather than dressy. Think tops and trousers rather than T-shirts and cut-offs. In summer, the heat will make you want to run naked so bring things such as quick-drying tank tops and cool dresses. Sturdy walking shoes are a must for the cobbled roads and ruins.

Sleeping

Reserving your accommodation out of season is important, as in some locations many hotels close for months on end. In high season it's equally essential as hotels can be fully booked well in advance.

➡ **Hotels** Classed from A through E, with A being five-star resort-style hotels and E having shared baths and unreliable hot water.

➡ **Domatia** The Greek equivalent of the British B&B, minus breakfast. Nowadays, many are purpose-built with fully equipped kitchens.

➡ **Campgrounds** Found in the majority of regions and islands and often include hot showers, communal kitchen, restaurants and swimming pools.

Money

ATMs are widespread in tourist areas, and can usually be found in most towns large enough to support a bank. Most are compatible with MasterCard or Visa, while Cirrus and Maestro users can make withdrawals in major towns and tourist areas. If travelling to smaller islands, you may want to take a backup supply of cash, as many ATMs can lose their connection or (in remote areas) run out of cash at the end of the day!

It's always wise to notify your bank of your travel plans before you leave, to avoid them blocking the card as an antifraud measure after your first withdrawal abroad.

For more information, see p752.

Bargaining

Bargaining is acceptable in flea markets and markets, but elsewhere you are expected to pay the stated price.

Tipping

➡ **Restaurants** If a service charge is included, a small tip is appreciated. If there's no service charge, leave 10% to 20%.

➡ **Taxis** Round up the fare by a couple of euros. There's a small fee for handling bags; this is an official charge, not a tip.

➡ **Bellhops** Bellhops in hotels and stewards on ferries expect a small gratuity of €1 to €3.

Language

Tourism is big business in Greece and being good businesspeople, many Greeks have learned the tools of the trade: English. In cities and popular towns, you can get by with less than a smattering of Greek; in smaller villages or out-of-the-way islands and destinations, a few phrases in Greek will go a long way. Wherever you are, Greeks will hugely appreciate your efforts to speak their language.

Etiquette

➡ **Eating and dining** Meals are commonly laid in the table centre and shared. Always accept a drink offer as it's a show of goodwill. Don't insist on paying if invited out; it insults your hosts. In restaurants, service might feel slow; dining is a drawn-out experience and it's impolite to rush waitstaff.

➡ **Photography** In churches, avoid using a flash or photographing the main altar, which is considered taboo. At archaeological sites, you'll be stopped from using a tripod which marks you as a professional and thereby requires special permissions.

➡ **Places of worship** If you visit churches, cover up with a shawl or long sleeves and a long skirt or trousers to show respect. Some places will deny admission if you're showing too much skin.

➡ **Body language** 'Yes' is a swing of the head and 'no' is a curt raising of the head or eyebrows, often accompanied by a 'ts' click-of-the-tongue sound.

Eating

Like much of Europe, the Greeks dine late and many restaurants don't open their doors for dinner until after 7pm. Outside of Athens, you will only need reservations for the most popular restaurants, and these can usually be made a day in advance.

➡ **Taverna** Informal and often specialising in seafood, chargrilled meat or traditional home-style baked dishes.

➡ **Estiatorio** More formal restaurant serving similar fare to tavernas or international cuisine.

➡ **Mezedhopoleio** Serves mezedhes (small plates); an ouzerie is similar but serves a round of ouzo with a round of mezedhes.

➡ **Kafeneio** One of Greece's oldest traditions, serving coffee, spirits and little else.

What's New

Stavros Niarchos Foundation Cultural Center

This recently opened development is just 4.5km south of Athens' city centre and houses the National Library, National Opera and a vast park with paths, playgrounds and a labyrinth. (p118)

Koules Fortress

Standing guard in Iraklion's harbour, this Venetian fortress has finally reopened. History buffs will love artefacts recovered from shipwrecks by Jacques Cousteau in 1976. Other rooms take you through the city's history. (p446)

Byzantine Museum of Argolis

Step into 4th-century-AD life in this museum, opened in 2017 in the Peloponnese. Experience church life, home life and markets in six evocative rooms housed in stunningly restored former soldiers' and horses' barracks. (p143)

9D: Throne of Helios

Journey through the birth of Rhodes, to the day of the Knights and on to the present day through this 3D experience with falling rain, bubbles and hydraulic chairs, guided by Helios, the Sun God and patron of Rhodes. (p507)

Paralia

One of Greece's oldest and most significant Paleolithic, Mesolithic and Neolithic sites, with finds showing the transitions between eras. Snorkel among a submerged Neolithic settlement in the Paralia underwater ruins. The shoreline was 7km further away back then. (p154)

Archimedes' Museum

This private museum displays the technological achievements of the Ancient Greeks. Marvel at the mechanics of the crane used to build the Parthenon, the *antikythera* (the 'first laptop') and a statue servant that serves holy water, touted as the 'world's oldest auto vending machine'. (p189)

Nafplio Bio-Farms

Cultural tours offering first-hand experience with centuries-old farming practices. The farm produces its own oranges, olives and organic flour. Sample farm-made treats such as *tiganites* (Greek pancakes) or try making local biscuits. (p149)

Graffiti Art

Since the economic crisis, Greek artists have responded to rough austerity measures through art, with challenging and thought-provoking graffiti on walls from quiet residential neighbourhoods (like the Exarchia district of Athens) to busy commercial districts. Ignore the hit-and-run tagging and watch for superb posters and portraits.

National Museum of Contemporary Art

Housed in a former brewery, Athens' recently renovated, prestigious contemporary museum shows exhibitions of Greek and international art. (p76)

For more recommendations and reviews, see lonelyplanet.com/greece

If You Like...

Ancient History

Ancient Akrotiri Phenomenal Minoan city that lay buried deep beneath volcanic ash from 1613 BC until 1967; on-site archaeologists continue to make discoveries. (p409)

Epidavros Catch a starlit performance from the well-worn stone seats at this theatre amid pine-clad hills, where Greek classics were first performed over 2000 years ago. (p153)

Heraklion Archaeological Museum Artefacts spanning 5500 years, but most famous for its Minoan collection, including the gob-smacking frescoes from Knossos. (p443)

Kos Town Step into the once-impregnable Castle of the Knights, check out 3rd-century-AD mosaics and rest under the plane tree where Hippocrates taught his students. (p538)

Moni Hozoviotissis Perhaps not as ancient as some sites but certainly dramatic, this monastery from 1017 clings to a cliff face high above the pounding sea. (p391)

Art

Byzantine iconography This art thrives in galleries around Greece where artists create exquisite, gold-hued creations; check out galleries at Ouranoupoli near Mt Athos, on Patmos and in Rhodes' Old Town. (p733)

National Museum of Contemporary Art A hub for the capital's flourishing modern-art scene, this museum hosts regular exhibits in a neighbourhood that's home to numerous art events and galleries. (p76)

Art Space An atmospheric gallery housed in the wine caverns of one of Santorini's oldest vineyards. Showing some of the country's top current artists, it's one of Greece's largest art galleries. (p409)

Museum of Islamic Art Be mesmerised by over 8000 pieces at one of the world's most significant collections of Islamic art, from tiles to carvings and prayer rugs. (p89)

Fish & Olive Tucked in the heart of Naxos, this gallery showcases the ceramic wizardry of local artists Katharina Bolesch and Alexander Reichardt, whose work has found its way to galleries in Helsinki and New York. (p378)

Beaches

Elafonisi Turquoise water and long, gentle dunes of pink sand await sun worshippers on Crete's southwest coast. (p483)

Lefkada's Wide stretches of uninterrupted soft sand on a quiet little island – one of Greece's best-kept secrets. (p683)

Sithonian Peninsula Head down dirt roads to find hidden coves, or stretch on a pretty, sandy bay backed by friendly tavernas and guesthouses. (p266)

Loutra Edipsou Take a dip at any time of year from this truly therapeutic beach where the bay is fed by thermal sulphur water. (p638)

Santorini Its volcanic past hasn't just left the island with gorgeous sunsets – beautiful beaches of red and black volcanic sand are easily reached and surprisingly quiet. (p396)

Regional Cuisine

Ottoman influence The Turkish influence is felt strongly in the kitchens of Thessaloniki and northern Greece, from *yiaourt-lou* (beef kebab on pitta with Greek yoghurt) to patisseries piled high with *loukoumi* (Turkish delight; p246).

Italian influence The Italians left behind pastas that the Greeks added to their own dishes; try *makarounes* (pasta with cheese and onions) and visit Corfu Town, where some of the finest homemade pasta is rolled out. (p665)

Seafood Harbourside kitchens land everything from mackerel to cuttlefish, squid and sea urchins; have yours grilled, fried, baked or stuffed with cheese and herbs. Fill yourself to the gills at 1500 BC on Santorini. (p396)

Wine The islands have a vibrant wine industry with crisp whites made from indigenous grapes, rich dessert wines and heady reds. Sample them in the Iraklio Wine Country on Crete. (p454)

Cheese Crafted mainly from goat's and sheep's milk, there's a world of Greek cheese beyond feta: ricotta-like *myzithra*, provolone-style *kaseri* and nutty, mild, gruyère-like *graviera*, best sampled on Naxos (p370) or Tinos (p338).

Walking

Crete's gorges Hikers flock to the spectacular Samaria Gorge, but its nearby cousins, the slender Imbros Gorge and lush Agia Irini Gorge, are equally breathtaking and less crowded. (p480)

Mt Olympus Follow trails from ancient times up thickly forested slopes towards the cloud-covered peak, once the lair of the Ancient Greek pantheon. (p273)

Pelion Peninsula Follow donkey trails that zigzag over rolling hills to quiet, sandy coves and quaint villages. (p223)

Homer's Ithaki Visit the homeland of Odysseus, hiking through dramatic island scenery and past archaeological sites. (p693)

Skopelos Wander deep into cool pine forests, through olive groves and clifftop plum and almond orchards. (p645)

Top: Lunch on Naxos (p370).
Bottom: Poros Beach (p682), Lefkada

Month by Month

TOP EVENTS

Orthodox Easter, April

Hellenic Festival, June to August

Carnival, February

Thessaloniki International Film Festival, November

August Moon Festival, August

January

Most islands snooze during winter. However, the capital and surrounding mainland are awake and welcome visitors with festivals that aren't really aimed at tourists. Expect local insight and warmth from hospitality (rather than the sun).

✦ Epiphany (Blessing of the Waters)

The day of Christ's baptism by St John is celebrated throughout Greece on 6 January. Seas, lakes and rivers are all blessed, with the largest ceremony held at Piraeus.

✦ Feast of Agios Vasilios (St Basil)

The first day of January sees a busy church ceremony followed by gifts, singing, dancing and feasting. The *vasilopita* (golden glazed cake for New Year's Eve) is cut; if you're fortunate enough to get the slice containing a coin, you'll supposedly have a lucky year.

✦ Gynaikokratia

The villages of the prefectures of Rodopi, Kilkis and Seres in northern Greece hold a day of role reversal on 8 January. Women spend the day in *kafeneia* (coffee houses) while the men stay at home to do the housework.

February

While February is an unlikely time to head to Greece, if you like a party and can time your visit with Carnival, it's well worth it.

✦ Carnival Season

Carnival starts three weeks before Lent, from mid-January to late February/early March. Minor events lead to a wild weekend of costume parades, floats, feasting and traditional dancing. There are regional variations: Patra's Carnival is the largest, while Skyros features men and their male 'brides' dressed in goatskins.

✦ Clean Monday (Shrove Monday)

On the first day of Lent (a day which is referred to as Kathara Deftera), people take to the hills throughout Greece to enjoy picnicking and kite-flying.

March

The islands are sleepy but the weather is warming up, making March a relaxed time to visit. Although the national calendar is quiet, there are countless religious festivals celebrated with great gusto in towns.

✦ Independence Day

The anniversary of the hoisting of the Greek flag by independence supporters at Moni Agias Lavras is celebrated with parades and dancing on 25 March. This act of revolt marked the start of the War of Independence.

April

The biggest religious celebration of the year is

Easter, when the country, particularly the islands, shakes off its winter slumber. The holiday weekend is busy with vacationing Greeks; be sure to reserve well in advance.

✹ Festival of Agios Georgios (St George)

The feast day of Agios Georgios (St George), the country's patron saint and the patron saint of shepherds, falls on 23 April or the first Tuesday following Easter. It's celebrated with particular exuberance in Arahova, near Delphi. Expect dancing, feasting and a general party atmosphere.

✹ Orthodox Easter

Communities celebrate Jesus' resurrection with candlelit processions on Good Friday. One of the best climbs Lykavittos Hill in Athens. The 40-day fast ends on Easter Sunday with red-dyed eggs, firecrackers, feasting and dancing. Patmos' Monastery of St John is a great place to witness it.

May

If you're planning to go hiking, May is a great time to visit. Temperatures are relatively mild and wildflowers create a huge splash of colour. Local greens, veggies and produce fill Greek kitchens.

✹ May Day

The first of May is marked by a mass exodus from towns for picnics in the country. Wildflowers

are gathered and made into wreaths to decorate houses. It's a day associated with workers' rights, so recent years have also seen mass walkouts and strikes.

June

For festival-goers looking for contemporary acts rather than traditional village parties, June is hopping on the mainland. Top national and international performers fill atmospheric stages with dance, music and drama.

☆ Classical Music Festival

Featuring Greek and international performers, this classical-music festival in the Peloponnese uses the Palamidi fortress as one of its atmospheric concert venues. Check out www.nafplionfestival.gr for dates and details.

✹ Feast of St John the Baptist

The country is ablaze with bonfires on 24 June as Greeks light up the wreaths they made on May Day.

☆ Athens & Epidaurus Festival

The most prominent Greek summer festival features local and international music, dance and drama at the ancient Odeon of Herodes Atticus on the slopes of the Acropolis in Athens and the world-famous Theatre of Epidavros, near Nafplio in the Peloponnese. Events run June through August. (p96)

✹ Miaoulia Festival

Hydra ignites in celebration of Admiral Miaoulis and the Hydriot contribution to the War of Independence. Witness a spectacular boat burning, fireworks, boat racing and folk dancing, held approximately the third weekend of June.

☆ Navy Week

Celebrating their long relationship with the sea, fishing villages and ports throughout the country host historical reenactments and parties in early June.

☆ Rockwave Festival

Rockwave has major international artists and massive crowds. It's held in late June on a huge parkland at the edge of Athens. (p96)

July

Temperatures soar and life buzzes on island beaches throughout Greece, while outdoor cinemas and giant beach clubs draw visitors to Athens' nightlife. If you're staying near the water, fill your belly with seafood that's hauled in daily.

☆ Delphi Cultural Festival

Every July the European Cultural Centre of Delphi hosts a 10-day cultural festival with fine arts, a sculpture park and drama performances at its own open-air theatre.

⭐ Wine & Cultural Festival

Held at Evia's coastal town of Karystos, this festival includes theatre, traditional dancing, music and visual-art exhibits as well as a sampling of every local wine imaginable. (p640)

August

Respect the heat of August: do a little bit less and relax a little more fully. If you're travelling midmonth, reserve well ahead as Greeks take to the roads and boats in large numbers.

⭐ August Moon Festival

Under the year's brightest moon, historical venues in Athens open with free moonlit performances. Watch theatre, dance and music at venues such as the Acropolis or Roman Agora. The festival is also celebrated at other towns and sites around Greece; check locally for details.

✨ Feast of the Assumption

Assumption Day is celebrated with family reunions on 15 August; the whole population is seemingly on the move on either side of the big day. Thousands also make a pilgrimage to Tinos to its

miracle-working icon of Panagia Evangelistria.

September

The sun is high though less and less blazing, especially on the islands. The crowds begin to thin and some ferry schedules begin to decline midmonth. Fresh figs and grapes are in season and plentiful.

✨ Gennisis Tis Panagias

The birthday of the Virgin Mary is celebrated throughout the country on 8 September with religious services and feasting.

October

While most of the islands start to quieten down, the sunny weather often holds in October. City life continues apace.

✨ Ohi Day

A simple 'no' (*ohi* in Greek) was Prime Minister Metaxas' famous response when Mussolini demanded free passage through Greece for his troops on 28 October 1940. The date is now a major national holiday with remembrance services, parades, feasting and dance.

November

Autumn sees temperatures drop. Olive-picking is in full swing in places such as Crete and feta production picks up, giving you the opportunity to taste some seriously fresh cheese.

⭐ Thessaloniki International Film Festival

Around 150 films are crammed into 10 days of screenings around the city in mid-November. The focus is on independent filmmakers – the festival (www.filmfestival.gr) is gaining increasing notoriety.

December

The islands may be quiet but Athens and Thessaloniki are still in full swing. Expect cooler temperatures and a chilly sea. With fewer tourists, you're likely to meet more locals.

✨ Christmas

Traditionally, Christmas marked the end of a 40-day fast with honey cookies and a roasted hog. Today you are more likely to see Christmas trees, fishing boats decorated with lights and children carolling. Families gather for a Christmas Day feast.

Itineraries

The Grand Tour

First trip to Greece? Here's a mixed bag of the country's top sights, most beautiful beaches, cultural highs, contemporary cities and laid-back island life.

Begin in **Athens**, visiting grand ancient sites and museums. Dive into the markets, contemporary-art scene and award-winning restaurants. Catch a ferry to chic **Mykonos**, with its fashionable bars and crowd-pleasing beaches. Day-trip to the sacred island of **Delos** for its fascinating ancient ruins. Hop a ferry to spectacular **Santorini** to watch the sun sink from the dramatic cliffs of its volcanic caldera.

Depending on your time, take a ferry or a flight to **Iraklio**, Crete's vibrant capital. Explore the nearby magnificent Minoan ruins of **Knossos**. Catch the bus to **Hania** with its charming harbour and labyrinth of backstreets, then discover the island's wild side on a trek through **Samaria Gorge**, which spills out on to a beach lapped by the Libyan Sea.

Return to Iraklio and hop a flight to cultured **Thessaloniki** to lose yourself in Ottoman-style architecture, Turkish sweets and a vibrant arts scene. Scale the slopes of **Mt Olympus** (2918m), Greece's highest peak, then visit the monasteries of **Meteora**, perched high on narrow pinnacles of rock. Your last stop is **Ancient Delphi**, former home of the mysterious Delphic oracle.

3 WEEKS Ionians & the Peloponnese

If you've a hankering for island life along with beautiful medieval towns, ancient historic sights and dramatic scenery, a tour of the Ionian Islands and the neighbouring Peloponnesian peninsula will more than satisfy you. This is doubly true if you're keen to toss some outdoor activities into your trip.

Begin on **Corfu**, spending a couple of days wandering through the amazing blend of Italian, French and British architecture in Corfu's Old Town, indulging in gourmet cuisine, exploring picturesque coastal villages and lounging on sandy beaches. Corfu is also great for windsurfing, or biking in the mountainous interior. From Corfu, hop on a ferry to **Kefallonia** to visit the picturesque village of Fiskardo, kayak to isolated beaches and sample the island's local wine.

From Kefallonia, it's a short ferry ride to Kyllini on the Peloponnesian peninsula. Visit the sanctuary of **Ancient Olympia** and stand in the stadium that hosted the first Olympic Games. Stay overnight in the town and take in some of the excellent museums. Head south to the captivating World Heritage–listed ruins of **Mystras**. This massive ancient fortress town was the last stronghold of the Byzantine Empire.

Continue south to the rugged and remote **Mani** region, to encounter villages filled with fascinating architecture and the remnants of the unique Maniot culture. This region is a haven for hikers with the dramatic Taÿgetos Mountains and tiny, isolated coves. It's also home to one of mainland Europe's most southerly points at **Cape Tenaro**, made famous in Homer's 'Iliad'. Follow the coast east to spectacular **Monemvasia** and spend at least a day exploring the medieval cobbled alleyways and a night staying in atmospheric lodgings within the walls of its medieval town.

Next head north to graceful **Nafplio** with its mansions, museums and lively port. From here, it's easy to do day trips to the impressive acropolis at **Tiryns** and the citadel of **Ancient Mycenae**. East of here is the ancient theatre of **Epidavros**, where it's well worth taking in some starlit classical performances. Then hop on a ferry from nearby Methana to end your journey in **Athens**.

Top: House of
Dionysos, Ancient
Delos (p360)

Bottom: Palace of the
Grand Master (p500)
Rhodes Old Town

IUSHAKOVSKY/SHUTTERSTOCK ©

Crete & the Dodecanese

Eastern Crete offers a tranquil side of the island with relaxed resorts and impressive sights. From here it's a short hop to the neighbouring Dodecanese, with their wealth of culture and speedy catamaran services that make island hopping a breeze.

Begin in **Iraklio**, taking in the excellent archaeological museum. Make a day trip to the captivating Minoan ruins of **Knossos** before sampling fine vintages in the Iraklio Wine Country, a mosaic of shapely hills, sun-baked slopes and lush valleys.

From Iraklio head east along the northern coast to the relaxed resort town of **Agios Nikolaos**, which radiates charm and chilled ambience. This makes a great base for exploring the surrounding region. Explore the massive Venetian fortress on **Spinalonga Island**, a leper colony until 1957 and just a short ferry ride across the Gulf of Mirabello. Visit the surrounding Minoan ruins, such as the **Palace of Malia**, still filled with mysteries, and rent a bike to explore the tranquil villages of the fertile **Lasithi Plateau**, lying snugly between mountain ranges and home to Zeus' birthplace.

Continue on to **Sitia**, from where you can head for the clear water and white sand of **Vaï**, Europe's only natural palm-forest beach. You can also head south from here to Zakros to hike through the dramatic, cave-honeycombed **Valley of the Dead** to Kato Zakros and its Minoan palace.

From Sitia, get settled on a twice-weekly, 12-hour ferry ride to **Rhodes**. Spend a couple of days exploring the atmospheric, walled medieval Old Town and checking out its burgeoning nightlife. Visit some of the surrounding beaches and stunning Byzantine chapels. Catch a catamaran to lush **Nisyros** to explore atop the alarmingly thin crust of its caldera and then carry on to **Patmos** to experience its artistic and religious vibe and to visit the cave where St John wrote the Book of Revelations. There are also some laidback beaches here and excellent restaurants. Backtrack to **Kos** to spend a final couple of days on gorgeous, sandy **Kefalos Bay** and to sip coffee and cocktails in Kos Town's lively squares. From Kos Town you can catch onward flights to **Athens**.

Plan Your Trip
Island Hopping

Whether you're sailing into a colourful harbour, listening to the pounding surf on a sun-drenched deck, or flying over azure waters in a propeller-driven plane, you'll be filled with a sense of adventure. In Greece, getting there is half the fun and island hopping remains an essential part of the experience.

Island Highlights

Best for Culture
Delos (p359) A stunning archaeological site.

Karpathos (p519) Experience Olymbos culture.

Patmos (p560) See the cave where St John wrote the Book of Revelations.

Naxos (p372) Roam around the Venetian Old Town.

Crete (p450) Explore the Minoan palace of Knossos.

Best for Low Season
Santorini (p396) Watch gorgeous sunsets.

Hydra (p321) Escape from Athens.

Crete (p438) Medieval cities and mountain villages.

Corfu (p663) Venetian and French architecture.

Best for Drinking & Dining
Santorini (p406) Taste-test local wine and beer.

Ikaria (p576) Have your fill of fresh lobster.

Crete (p438) Savour herb-rich Cretan specialities.

Samos (p587) Sample the famous sweet wine.

Best for Outdoors
Nisyros (p533) Explore inside the volcano.

Kefallonia (p685) Kayak to a remote cove or beach.

Lesvos (p613) Hike in a 20-million-year-old petrified forest.

Kos (p537) Ride bikes to long stretches of sand.

Planning Essentials

While the local laissez-faire attitude is worth emulating while island hopping, a little bit of planning can take you a long way. Deciding where and when you want to go and getting your head around routes and schedules before you go will take the work out of your holiday.

Travelling in Greece is that much more enjoyable when you have room to be flexible with your itinerary. Transportation schedules are always vulnerable to change, even after you've booked and paid for your ticket. Everything from windy weather to striking workers mean planes and boats are regularly subject to delays and cancellations at short notice. Ferry and airline timetables change from year to year and season to season, with ferry companies often 'winning' contracts to operate different routes annually. When island hopping, it's important to remember that no timetable is watertight.

When to Go
High Season

➡ Lots of ferries and transport links but book ahead.

➡ Water temperature is warm enough for swimming.

➡ The *meltemi* (dry northerly wind) blows south across the Aegean, sometimes playing havoc with ferry schedules.

GETTING YOUR SEA LEGS

Even those with the sturdiest stomachs can feel seasick when a boat hits rough weather. Here are a few tips to calm your tummy.

➡ Gaze at the horizon, not the sea. Don't read or stare at objects that your mind will assume are stable.

➡ Drink plenty and eat lightly. Many people claim ginger biscuits and ginger tea settle the stomach.

➡ Don't use binoculars.

➡ If possible stay in the fresh air – don't go below deck and avoid hydrofoils where you are trapped indoors.

➡ Try to keep your mind occupied.

➡ If you know you're prone to seasickness, consider investing in acupressure wristbands before you leave.

Shoulder Season

➡ Transport is less frequent but still connects most destinations.

➡ Water temperature can be chilly.

➡ The best time for sea-life spotting begins in May and runs through to September.

Low Season

➡ Planning ahead is essential as transportation can be limited.

➡ Swimming in the sea is only for those immune to cold water.

➡ Most businesses offering water sports are closed for the winter.

Travelling by Sea

With a network covering every inhabited island, the Greek ferry system is vast and varied. The slow rust buckets that used to ply the seas are nearly a thing of the past. You'll still find slow boats, but high-speed ferries are increasingly common and cover most of the popular routes. Local ferries, excursion boats and tiny, private fishing boats called caïques often connect neighbouring islands and islets to one another. You'll also find water taxis that will take you to isolated beaches and coves. At the other end of the spectrum, hydrofoils and catamarans can drastically reduce travel time. Hydrofoils have seen their heyday but continue to link some of the more remote islands and

island groups. Catamarans have taken to the sea in a big way, offering greater comfort and coping better with poor weather conditions.

For long-haul ferry travel, it's still possible to board one of the slow boats chugging between the islands and to curl up on deck in your sleeping bag to save a night's accommodation. Nevertheless, Greece's domestic ferry scene has undergone a radical transformation in the past decade and these days you can also travel in serious comfort and at a decent speed. Of course, the trade-off is that long-haul sea travel can be quite expensive. A bed for the night in a cabin from Piraeus to Rhodes can be more expensive than a discounted airline ticket.

Ticketing & Fares

As ferries are prone to delays and cancellations, for short trips it's often best not to purchase a ticket until it has been confirmed that the ferry is leaving. During high season, or if you need to reserve a car space, you should book in advance. High-speed boats such as catamarans tend to sell out long before the slow chuggers. For overnight ferries it's always best to book in advance, particularly if you want a cabin or particular type of accommodation. If a service is cancelled you can usually transfer your ticket to the next available service with that company.

Many ferry companies have online booking services or you can purchase tickets from their local offices and most

Boarding a ferry at the port of Iraklio, Crete

travel agents in Greece. Agencies selling tickets line the waterfront of most ports, but rarely is there one that sells tickets for every boat, and often an agency is reluctant to give you information about a boat they do not sell tickets for. Most have timetables displayed outside; check these for the next departing boat or ask the *limenarhio* (port police).

Ferry prices are determined by the distance of the destination from the port of origin, and the type of boat. The small differences in price you may find at ticket agencies are the results of some agencies sacrificing part of their designated commission to qualify as a 'discount service'. (The discount is seldom more than €0.50.)

High-speed ferries and hydrofoils cost about 20% more than traditional ferries, while catamarans are often 30% to 100% more expensive than their slower counterparts. Caïques and water taxis are usually very reasonable, while excursion boats can be pricey but useful if you're trying to reach out-of-the-way islands. Children under five years of age travel for free while those aged between five and 10 are usually half price.

Classes

On smaller boats, hydrofoils and catamarans, there is only one type of ticket available and these days, even on larger vessels, classes are largely a thing of the past. The public spaces on the more modern ferries are generally open to all. What does differ is the level of accommodation that you can purchase for overnight boats.

A 'deck-class' ticket typically gives you access to the deck and interior, but no overnight accommodation. Aeroplane-type seats give you a reserved, reclining seat in which you will hope to sleep. Then come various shades of cabin accommodation: four-berth, three-berth or two-berth interior cabins are cheaper than their equivalent outside cabins with a porthole. On most boats, cabins are very comfortable, resembling a small hotel room with private bathroom.

Unless you state otherwise, you will automatically be given deck class when purchasing a ticket. Prices quoted are for deck-class tickets, unless otherwise indicated.

ISLAND FINDER

ISLAND	FOOD	FAMILY FRIENDLY	OFF THE BEATEN TRACK	NIGHTLIFE	BEACHES	CULTURE	ACTIVITIES	EASY ACCESS
Aegina						x		x
Alonnisos						x	x	x
Amorgos			x			x	x	
Andros			x			x	x	x
Chios	x	x			x	x	x	x
Corfu	x	x			x	x		x
Crete	x	x			x	x	x	x
Evia	x				x	x	x	x
Fourni Islands			x		x	x		
Hydra		x		x		x	x	x
Ios	x			x	x		x	x
Kalymnos		x		x		x	x	x
Karpathos			x			x	x	
Kefallonia	x	x			x		x	x
Kos		x		x	x	x	x	x
Lefkada					x	x	x	x
Leros		x	x			x	x	
Lesvos	x	x			x	x	x	x
Milos		x			x	x	x	x
Mykonos				x	x			x
Naxos	x	x		x	x	x	x	x
Paros	x	x		x	x	x		x
Patmos	x	x			x	x	x	x
Paxi			x			x	x	x
Rhodes	x	x		x	x	x		x
Samos	x	x			x	x	x	x
Samothraki			x		x	x	x	
Santorini	x			x	x	x	x	x
Sifnos			x			x	x	
Skiathos				x	x		x	x
Skopelos	x	x			x			x
Skyros					x	x	x	x
Small Cyclades			x		x	x		
Symi						x		x
Thasos		x			x	x	x	x
Zakynthos					x	x		x

Taking a Car

While almost all islands are served by car ferries, they are expensive and, to ensure boarding, you'll generally need to secure tickets in advance. A more flexible way to travel is to board as a foot passenger and hire a car on each island. Hiring a car for a day or two is relatively cheap and possible on virtually all islands.

Resources

The comprehensive weekly list of departures from Piraeus put out by the EOT (known abroad as the GNTO, the Greek National Tourist Organisation) in Athens is as accurate as possible. While on the islands, the people with the most up-to-date ferry information are the local *limenarhio* (port police), whose offices are usually on or near the quayside.

You'll find lots of information about ferry services on the internet and many of the larger ferry companies have their own websites. Always check online schedules, or with operators or travel agencies for up-to-the-minute information.

A few very useful websites:

Danae Travel (www.danae.gr) A good site for booking boat tickets.

Greek Travel Pages (www.gtp.gr) Has a useful search program and links for ferries.

Greekferries (www.greekferries.gr) Allows you to search ferry schedules from countless providers, including accommodation options and multileg journeys.

Open Seas (www.openseas.gr) A reliable search engine for ferry routes and schedules.

Travelling by Air

A flight can save you hours at sea and offers extraordinary views across the island groups. Flights between the islands tend to be short and aeroplanes small, often making for a bumpy ride. The vast majority of domestic flights are handled by the merged Olympic Air and Aegean Airlines, offering regular domestic services and competitive rates. In addition to these national airlines, there are a number of smaller outfits running seaplanes or complementing the most popular routes.

Ticketing & Fares

The easiest way to book tickets is online, via the carriers themselves. You can also purchase flight tickets at most travel agencies in Greece. Olympic Air has offices in the towns that flights depart from, as well as in other major towns. There are discounts for return tickets when travelling midweek (Monday to Thursday), and bigger discounts for trips that include a Saturday night away. You'll find full details and information on timetables on the airlines' websites.

Resources

Up-to-date information on flight timetables is best found online. Airlines often have local offices on the islands.

Aegean Airlines (www.aegeanair.com) Domestic flights.

Astra Airlines (www.astra-airlines.gr) Thessaloniki-based carrier with domestic flights.

Olympic Air (www.olympicair.com) Aegean Airline's subsidiary with further domestic flights.

Sky Express (www.skyexpress.gr) Domestic flights based out of Crete.

3 WEEKS Island-Hopping Itinerary

For intrepid travellers without a tight time schedule, Greece's northeastern islands offer languid coasts, lush scenery and divine beaches, as well as some amazing historic sights. Scheduled ferries are regular but not always frequent – thankfully you won't be in any hurry to leave.

From **Athens**, hop a ferry for **Tinos** to visit the sacred Church of Panagia and explore marble-ornamented villages dotted across the terraced hillsides and misty mountaintops. Head east to **Ikaria** for isolated stretches of soft sand and lobster-rich menus. Join in the island culture of dancing, drinking and feasting during summer *panigyria* (all-night celebrations held on saints' days across the island). Afterwards take a short hop to the serene **Fourni Islands**, a former pirates' lair with surreal sunsets.

Ferry north to **Samos** where you can hike through lush forests to secluded waterfalls and laze on idyllic beaches. From Samos, head to **Chios** and get lost in the labyrinth of stone alleyways in the southern village of Mesta before venturing into the interior to hike through citrus groves under the shade of towering mountain peaks.

The next stop is **Lesvos** (Mytilini), birthplace of the poet Sappho and producer of some of Greece's finest olive oil and ouzo. Not surprisingly, it's also home to hopping nightlife. Visit the island's fantastic modern-art gallery and the hilltop Byzantine monastery of Moni Ypsilou. Lesvos' landscape, with salt marshes, gushing hot springs, dense forests and soft beaches, is as diverse as its cultural offerings.

From Lesvos, hop to **Limnos** to dine on the day's catch at Myrina's waterside seafood restaurants. Carry on to secluded **Agios Efstratios** to stretch out on volcanic-sand beaches. The village, flattened by an earthquake in 1968 and rebuilt by uninspired junta, draws few tourists meaning the beaches are yours to escape on.

Head to **Skyros** via Limnos, exploring the cobble-stoned village, Venetian fortress and many artist studios, watching for endangered Skyrian wild horses. Hop a ferry to **Evia** for a therapeutic dip in the thermal-fed bay at Loutra Edipsou before catching a final boat to Rafina on the mainland and returning to **Athens**.

Plan Your Trip
Cruising

The azure water stretches before you, punctuated by occasional dolphins and an endless scattering of palm-fringed islands. The Aegean will call to your seafaring spirit – thankfully, there are many cruising options. Cruising removes the stress of deciding an interisland itinerary, and gets you out on the sea with the breeze at your back.

Great Cruise Lines for...

Culture
Silversea Cruises (www.silverseacruises.com) Runs exclusive tours with language and cooking classes, guest lectures and entertainment from local ports.

Freedom
Azamara (www.azamaraclubcruises.com) Offers cruises at a slower pace, with top service and few organised activities.

Luxury
Seadream Yacht Club (www.seadream.com) Ultrapampering with nearly as many crew as guests.

Small & personalised trips
Variety Cruises (www.varietycruises.com) Has a maximum of 50 guests and the sea as its swimming pool.

Unconventional trips
Star Clippers (www.starclipperscruises.com) Runs cruises on the world's largest fully rigged tall ships.

Choosing a Cruise

Cruises aren't what they used to be and are certainly no longer the domain of blue rinses and slot machines. Catering to a discerning, ever-growing clientele, cruises are often geared to specific interests and niches. Greater competition also means better facilities, more varied excursions, worthwhile on-board diversions and increased dining options. Whether you're in the 30-something crowd, travelling with kids, after a little luxury or just want a no-frills adventure, if the idea of boarding a cruise ship appeals to you, chances are there's a perfect liner out there waiting.

Ship Size

Forget what you've heard, size does matter – at least when you're choosing a cruise ship. A ship's size says a lot about the experience it's offering: megaships can seem more like floating resorts, with a few thousand people on-board, while tiny liners cater to fewer than 50 passengers.

Large or Megaships
➡ Accommodate 1000-plus people.

➡ Nonstop activities and complete amenities.

➡ Casinos, restaurants, spas, theatres, children's clubs, discos, bars, cafes and shops.

➡ Often unable to squeeze into some of the smaller islands' harbours and so visit the largest, most popular ports.

CRUISE COMPANIES

COMPANY	CONTACT	SHIP SIZE	CRUISE LENGTH	DESTINATIONS	BUDGET
Azamara	www.azamaraclubcruises.com	medium	7-10 days	Greece, Turkey, Italy	$$$
Celebrity Cruises	www.celebrity.com	mega	10-13 days	Greece, Italy, Turkey, Croatia, France	$$
Celestyal Cruises	www.celestyalcruises.com	medium	3-7 days	Greece, Cyprus	$$
Costa Cruise Lines	www.costacruises.com	large	7-9 days	Greece, Italy, Turkey, Croatia, Israel	$
Crystal Yacht Cruises	www.crystalcruises.com	small	9-15 days	Greece, Italy, Turkey, Spain, Portugal	$$$
Cunard Line	www.cunard.com	large	7-14 days	Greece, Italy, Croatia, Turkey, France, Spain	$
Golden Star	www.golden-star-cruises.com	medium	3-8 days	Greece, Turkey	$
Holland America Line	www.hollandamerica.com	large	6-12 days	Greece, Italy, Spain, Croatia	$
MSC	www.msccruises.com	large	7-10 days	Greece, Turkey, Croatia, Italy, Egypt	$
Oceania Cruises	www.oceaniacruises.com	medium	10-12 days	Greece, Turkey, France, Italy, Spain	$$
Princess Cruises	www.princess.com	large & mega	7-21 days	Greece, Italy, Turkey	$$
Regent Seven Sea Cruises	www.rssc.com	medium	7-21 days	Greece, Italy, Turkey, France	$$$
Seadream Yacht Club	www.seadream.com	small	6-13 days	Greece, Turkey, Italy, Croatia	$$$
Silversea Cruises	www.silverseacruises.in	small & medium	7-12 days	Greece, Spain, Turkey, Italy	$$$
Star Clippers	www.starclipperscruises.com	small	7-14 days	Greece, Turkey, Italy	$$$

➡ Can seem to dwarf an island, with its passengers more than doubling the destination's population.

Medium or Midsized Ships

➡ Cater for 400 to 1000 passengers.

➡ Usually more focused on the destination, with more port stops, more excursions and fewer on-board activities.

➡ Spa, pool, restaurants and bars.

➡ More often able to dock in small island harbours.

Small Ships

➡ Itineraries are often more varied as they can stop at small, out-of-the-way ports.

➡ Often concentrate on a particular cruise niche, such as luxury or activity-based adventure.

➡ Don't expect a pool, spa, large cabin or plethora of dining options.

Local Cruise Lines

International cruises tend to visit Greece in combination with ports from other countries – usually Italy, Turkey and Croatia, often beginning at one port and ending at another. Greece-based cruises usually focus solely on ports within Greece and offer round-trips. These cruises are often more destination-focused, with one or two stops each day. The crew are usually Greek, adding to the feel of authenticity, and cuisine and entertainment is more locally based with a bit of international flavour thrown in.

There are some Greek-based cruise lines worth checking out.

Golden Star (www.golden-star-cruises.com) Mid-sized, short cruises taking in the Greek islands, Turkey and Italy.

Variety Cruises (www.varietycruises.com) Small, luxury cruises taking in some of the smallest Greek islands.

Celestyal Cruises (http://americas.celestyal cruises.com) Large cruises with on-board activities focusing on Greek culture and cuisine.

Excursions

Excursions are often what make cruises worthwhile and are designed to help you make the most of your sometimes-brief visits ashore. They are generally most valuable when sights are not near the port or if a cultural expert is leading the tour. Where all the sights are near the harbour, it's often just as worthwhile and more relaxing to go exploring on your own. If you plan to explore alone, it's worth double-checking before you book; some larger cruise boats dock at distant ports and it's difficult to reach the island's sights or main towns independently.

Excursions are usually booked before you depart or when you first board the ship. They are offered on a first-come, first-served basis and are generally very popular, so if you're choosing your cruise based on the excursions on offer, it's important to book as soon as possible. Tours generally range from €40 to €60 for a half-day, or €80 to €120 for a full day. Activity-based tours such as mountain biking or kayaking tend to be more, with a half-day around €100. Ensure that you factor in the cost of excursions from the get-go.

Budgeting

Cruise prices vary greatly depending on the time of year. Booking during the low season will get you good deals but it means you will probably only have the opportunity to visit the largest and busiest ports, as smaller islands virtually close out of season.

Budget cruises can be anywhere from €100 to €200 per day, midrange from €200 to €400, and luxury liners begin at around €400 and go up to as much as €650 per day. Prices on cruises include meals, on-board activities, entertainment, port fees and portage but there are sometimes additional fuel charges. You also need to budget for airfare, tips, alcohol, pre- and post-cruise accommodation and excursions. Deals to look out for include two-for-one offers, airfare- or hotel-inclusive deals, and early-bird rates.

Booking

If you know what you want from your cruise, booking online can be a straight-forward option, and certainly worth it for the virtual tours and reviews. But a knowledgeable travel agent can help you through the plethora of options available and advise you on extra excursion charges and surcharges that you may miss when booking online.

There are often great rates for booking early and this allows you more choice in choosing cabins, excursions, dining options and so forth. While you can get great last-minute deals, you need to be willing to be flexible about dates and options. Booking your airfare through the cruise line may also mean you're collected at the airport and taken to the ship and if your flight or luggage is delayed, they will wait or transport you to the first port.

Choosing a Cabin

Standard cabins are akin to very small hotel rooms, with fully equipped en suites, a double bed and somewhere to unpack. The cheapest option is an 'inside cabin' (ie no window). If you get claustrophobic, you can pay significantly more for

HAVOC/SHUTTERSTOCK ©

Top: Cruise ship off
the coast of Santorini
(p396)

Bottom: Day trip to
Shipwreck Beach
(p700), Zakynthos

CRUISING INDEPENDENTLY

Yachting is an amazing way to sail the seas, offering the freedom to visit remote and uninhabited islands. If you can't afford to buy a yacht, there are several other options. You can hire a bare boat (a yacht without a crew), if two of your party have sailing certificates. Prices start at €1930 per week; check out **Bare Boat Yacht Charters** (www.moorings.com). If you'd rather have someone else do the sailing for you, **Odyssey Sailing** (www.odysseysailing.gr) will add a skipper to your bare-bones boat for an additional €150 per day.

Hellenic Yachting Server (www.yachting.gr) has general information on sailing around the islands and lots of links, including information on chartering yachts.

The sailing season is from April to October, although July to September is most popular. Unfortunately, it also happens to be when the *meltemi* (dry northerly wind) is at its strongest. This isn't an issue in the Ionian Sea, where the main summer wind is the *maïstros*, a light to moderate northwesterly that rises in the afternoon and usually dies away at sunset.

an 'outside cabin' where you get either a window or porthole. Prices tend to climb with each floor on the ship but so does the ship's movement. If you suffer from seasickness, choose a lower deck where it's less rocky.

Cabin pricing is for double occupancy; if you're travelling solo you pay a surcharge, and if you're travelling as a group of three or four and willing to share a cabin, you can receive substantial discounts. Bunks are referred to as upper and lower berths, otherwise there is a double bed or twin beds that can be pushed together to make a double. Family rooms are sometimes available via connecting cabins.

Things to check are how close your cabin is located to the disco and, if you're paying extra for a window, whether or not your view is likely to be blocked by a lifeboat.

Life on Board

Embarking: What to Expect

➡ Check-in time will be two or three hours before sailing.

➡ Your passport will be taken for immigration processing.

➡ The first day's program and a deck map can be found in your cabin.

➡ You'll be offered a tour of the ship.

➡ A safety drill is legally required on all ships.

➡ You'll be able to set up an on-board credit account.

➡ Your dining-room table will be assigned.

Meals

Set mealtimes and seating assignments are still the norm on most ships and you will be able to choose your preferred dinnertime and table size when you book. Many ships continue to have formal dining evenings with dress codes. Some smaller ships have an all-casual policy, while others have alternative dining options for those not interested in attending the formal evenings.

Tipping

Firstly, don't tip the captain or officers; it would be akin to tipping your dentist or airline pilot. On the final day of your cruise, you'll likely find tipping guidelines in your cabin, usually around €8 per person per day. Tipping is not required but makes up a huge part of the wage of service staff, and is expected.

Plan Your Trip
Eat & Drink Like a Local

Greeks love eating out, sharing impossibly big meals with family and friends in a drawn-out, convivial fashion. Whether you're eating seafood at a seaside table or trying modern Greek fare under the floodlit Acropolis, dining out in Greece is never just about what you eat, but the whole sensory experience.

Food Experiences

Take a cue from the locals and go straight to the source, heading to seaside fishing hamlets for fresh fish or mountain villages for local meat. Seek out tavernas that produce their own vegetables, wine and oil, where the fried potatoes are hand-cut and recipes are passed down through generations.

Meals of a Lifetime

Koukoumavlos (p404) Modern Aegean cuisine in a spectacular caldera-edge Santorini setting.

Katogi (p395) Tantalising and inventive mezedhes (small plates) in lively and delightful garden surrounds on Ios.

Klimataria (p672) Stellar example of fresh, simple food from the humble taverna, in Corfu's fishing village of Benitses.

Thalassaki (p342) Artful use of local produce and outstanding seafood in a charming seaside setting on Tinos.

Hotzas Taverna (p599) Exquisite traditional and fusion dishes in a classic stone taverna on Chios.

Marco Polo Cafe (p505) Idyllic garden courtyard with an ever-changing menu of delicious Greek and Italian-influenced dishes in Rhodes.

Regional Cuisine

Crete
Thalassino Ageri (p472) From the superb setting just outside Hania, peruse the changing Cretan menu starring the day's catch.

Cyclades
Rambagas (p428) Celebrity chef pays homage to Sifnos' culinary heritage.

Northern Greece
Doltso (p281) Macedonian cuisine at its finest in an old-town tavern in Kastoria.

Peleponnese
Elies (p175) Lunch on Mani dishes in a private garden.

Cheap Treats

Souvlaki Greece's favourite fast food, both the *gyros* and skewered meat versions wrapped in pitta bread, with tomato, onion and lashings of tzatziki.

Pies Bakeries make endless variations of *tyropita* (cheese pie) and *spanakopita* (spinach pie), plus other pies.

Street food Includes *koulouria* (fresh pretzel-style bread) and seasonal snacks such as roasted chestnuts or corn.

Cooking Courses

Well-known Greece-based cooking writers and chefs run workshops on several islands and in Athens, mostly during spring and autumn.

Glorious Greek Kitchen Cooking School (www.dianekochilas.com) Diane Kochilas runs week-long courses on her ancestral island, Ikaria, in spring and summer, as well as 10-day culinary tours to Ikaria, Athens, Peloponnese and Corinthia.

Kea Artisanal (www.keartisanal.com) Aglaia Kremezi and her friends open their kitchens and gardens on the island of Kea for cooking workshops.

Crete's Culinary Sanctuaries (www.cookingin crete.com) Nikki Rose combines cooking classes, organic-farm tours and cultural excursions around Crete.

Cook It at Home

Leave room in your baggage for local treats (customs and quarantine rules permitting) such as olives and extra virgin olive oil from small, organic producers; aromatic Greek thyme honey; dried oregano, mountain tea and camomile flowers; or a jar of spoon sweets (fruit preserves).

The Greek Kitchen

The essence of traditional Greek cuisine lies in seasonal homegrown produce. Dishes are simply seasoned. Lemon juice, garlic, pungent Greek oregano and extra virgin olive oil are the quintessential flavours, along with tomato, parsley, dill, cinnamon and cloves.

Mayirefta Home-style, one-pot, baked or casserole dishes. Prepared early, they are left to cool to enhance the flavours. Well-known *mayirefta* include *mousakas* (eggplant, minced meat, potatoes and cheese), *yemista* (vegetables stuffed with rice and herbs), *lemonato* (meat with lemon and oregano) and *stifadho* (sweet stewed meat with tomato and onion).

Grills Greeks are masterful with grilled and spit-roasted meats. Souvlaki – arguably the national dish – comes in many forms, from cubes of grilled meat on a skewer to pitta-wrapped snacks with pork or chicken *gyros* done kebab-style on a rotisserie. *Païdakia* (lamb cutlets) and *brizoles* (pork chops) are also popular.

Fish & seafood Fish is often grilled whole and drizzled with *ladholemono* (lemon and oil dressing). Smaller fish such as *barbounia* (red mullet) or *maridha* (whitebait) are lightly fried. Octopus is grilled, marinated or stewed in wine sauce. Popular seafood dishes include *soupies* (cuttlefish), calamari stuffed with cheese and herbs, and *psarosoupa* (fish soup). The best way to avoid imports is to seek out tavernas run by local fishing families.

Mezedhes These small dishes (or appetisers) are often shared. Classics include tzatziki (yoghurt, cucumber and garlic), *melidzanosalata* (aubergine), *taramasalata* (fish roe), fava (split-pea purée with lemon juice) and *saganaki* (fried cheese). Also watch for *keftedhes* (meatballs), *loukaniko* (pork sausage), grilled *gavros* (white anchovies) and dolmadhes (rice wrapped in marinated vine leaves).

Greek salad This ubiquitous salad (*horiatiki* or 'village salad') is made of tomatoes, cucumber, onions, feta and olives; however, it's often garnished with local greens (*horta*), peppers, capers or nuts. Feta is sometimes replaced by a local cheese. Beetroot salad is also popular, often served with walnuts and cheese.

Cheese Greece's regions produce many different types of cheese, most using goat's and sheep's milk, with infinite variations in taste. Apart from feta, local cheeses include *graviera* (a nutty, mild

Top: *Gyros*

Bottom: *Mezedhes and ouzo*

RAWPE/SHUTTERSTOCK ©

> ### FETA
> ....
> Greece's national cheese has been produced for about 6000 years from sheep's and goat's milk. Only feta made in Greece can be called feta, an EU ruling giving it the same protected status as Parma ham and Champagne.

Gruyere-like sheep's-milk cheese), *kaseri* (similar to provolone), *myzithra* (ricotta-like whey cheese) and *manouri* (creamy soft cheese from the north).

Local Specialities

From cheese and olive oil to the raw ingredients on your plate, you will find many regional variations and specialities on your travels. Crete is a popular foodie destination with distinct culinary traditions, but the islands and mainland offer their own culinary treats. Be sure to ask about local dishes, cheese and produce.

Northern Greece Influenced by eastern flavours, there's less olive oil and more peppers and spices along with a strong mezes culture and Ottoman sweets.

Peloponnese Known for its herb-rich, one-pot dishes and *ladhera* (vegetarian, peasant-style dishes).

Cyclades A traditional reliance on beans and pulses led to the popularity of fava (split-pea purée) and *revythadha* (chickpea stew); you'll also find spaghetti with lobster and a strong sausage tradition.

Ionian Islands The Venetian influence is found in spicy braised beef, rooster *pastitsadha* (red-sauce pasta) and *sofrito* (braised veal with garlic and wine sauce).

Crete Herb-rich dishes include *anthoi* (stuffed zucchini flowers), *soupies* (cuttlefish) with wild fennel and *hohlioi bourbouristoi* (snails with vinegar and rosemary).

What to Drink

While there is coffee strong enough to stand a spoon in and ouzo that will knock you flat, thankfully Greece also has plenty of tamer options for quenching your thirst.

Coffee

The ubiquitous *kafeneio* (coffee house) is a time-honoured tradition, with older Greeks stationed over a cup of coffee, intensely debating local politics, football or gossip. They're often small and unchanged for generations, and it's well worth visiting at least one. The trendy cafes serving iced coffees are the modern answer to the *kafeneia* and are usually packed with a younger crowd.

Greek coffee is traditionally brewed in a *briki* (narrow-top pot), on a hot-sand apparatus called a *hovoli,* and served in a small cup. Order a *metrio* (medium, with one sugar) and sip slowly until you reach the mud-like grounds (don't drink them).

Ouzo

Ouzo – Greece's famous liquor – has come to embody a way of eating and socialising, enjoyed with mezedhes (small plates) during lazy, extended summer afternoons. Sipped slowly and ritually to cleanse the palate between dishes, ouzo is usually served in small bottles or *karafakia* (carafes) with a bowl of ice cubes to dilute it (turning it a cloudy white).

Ouzo is made from distilled grapes with residuals from fruit, grains and potatoes, and flavoured with spices, primarily aniseed, giving it that liquorice flavour. The best ouzo is produced on Lesvos (Mytilini).

Greek Wine

The Greek wine renaissance has been gaining international attention and awards, with first-class wines being produced from age-old indigenous varietals with unique character. The latest generation of internationally trained winemakers are producing great wines from Greece's premier wine regions, including Nemea in the Peloponnese, the vineyards of Santorini, the Iraklio Wine Country on Crete and Naoussa in the Cyclades.

Greek white varieties include *moschofilero, asyrtiko, athiri, roditis, robola* and *savatiano*; the popular reds include *xinomavro, agiorgitiko* and *kotsifali*.

House or barrel wine varies dramatically in quality (white is the safer bet), and is ordered by the kilo/carafe. Few places serve wine by the glass.

Greek dessert wines include excellent muscats from Samos, Limnos and Rhodes,

Santorini's Vinsanto, Mavrodafni wine (often used in cooking) and Monemvasia's Malmsey sweet wine.

Retsina, white wine flavoured with the resin of pine trees, became popular in the 1960s and retains a largely folkloric significance with foreigners. It does go well with strongly flavoured food (especially seafood) and some winemakers make a modern version.

How to Eat & Drink

Greece's relaxed and hospitable dining culture makes it easy to get into the local spirit.

When to Eat

Greece doesn't have a big breakfast tradition, unless you count coffee and a cigarette, and maybe a *koulouri* or *tyropita* eaten on the run. You'll find English-style breakfasts in hotels and tourist areas.

While changes in working hours are affecting traditional meal patterns, lunch is still usually the big meal of the day, starting around 2pm.

Greeks eat dinner late, rarely sitting down before sunset in summer. This coincides with shop closing hours, so restaurants often don't fill until after 10pm. Get in by 9pm to avoid the crowds. Given the long summers and mild winters, al fresco dining is central to the dining experience.

Most tavernas open all day, but some upmarket restaurants open for dinner only.

Vegetarian Friendly

While vegetarians are an oddity in Greece, they are well catered for, since vegetables feature prominently in Greek cooking – a legacy of lean times and the Orthodox faith's fasting traditions.

Look for popular vegetable dishes such as *fasolakia yiahni* (braised green beans), *bamies* (okra), *briam* (oven-baked vegetable casserole) and vine-leaf dolmadhes. Of the nutritious *horta* (wild greens), *vlita* (amaranth) is the sweetest, but other common varieties include wild radish, dandelion, stinging nettle and sorrel.

Festive Food

Greece's religious and cultural celebrations inevitably involve a feast and many have their own culinary traditions.

The 40-day Lenten fast spawned *nistisima,* foods without meat or dairy (or oil if you go strictly by the book). Lenten sweets include *halva,* both the Macedonian-style version (sold in delis) made from tahini and the semolina dessert often served after a meal.

Red-dyed boiled Easter eggs decorate the *tsoureki,* a brioche-style bread flavoured with *mahlepi* (mahaleb cherry kernels) and mastic. Saturday night's post-Resurrection Mass supper includes *mayiritsa* (offal soup), while Easter Sunday sees whole lambs cooking on spits all over the countryside.

A *vasilopita* (golden-glazed cake) is cut at midnight on New Year's Eve, giving good fortune to whoever gets the lucky coin inside.

Where to Eat

Steer away from tourist restaurants and go where locals eat. As a general rule, avoid places on the main tourist drags, especially those with touts outside and big signs with photos of food. Be wary of hotel recommendations, as some have deals with particular restaurants.

Tavernas are casual, good-value, often family-run (and child-friendly) places, where the waiter arrives with a paper tablecloth and plonks cutlery on the table.

SWEET TREATS

Greeks traditionally serve fruit rather than sweets after a meal, but there's no shortage of local sweets and cakes. Traditional sweets include baklava, *loukoumadhes* (spherical doughnuts served with honey and cinnamon), *kataïfi* (chopped nuts inside angel-hair pastry), *ryzogalo* (rice pudding) and *galaktoboureko* (custard-filled pastry). *Ghlika kutalyu* (syrupy fruit preserves, also known as 'spoon sweets') are served on tiny plates as a welcome offering but are also eaten over yoghurt.

ETIQUETTE & TABLE MANNERS

➡ Greek tavernas can be disarmingly and refreshingly laid-back. The dress code is generally casual, except in upmarket places.

➡ Service may feel slow (and patchy), but there's no rushing you out of there either.

➡ Tables generally aren't cleared until you ask for the bill, which in traditional places arrives with complimentary fruit or sweets or a shot of liquor. Receipts may be placed on the table at the start of the meal in case tax inspectors visit.

➡ Greeks drink with meals (the drinking age is 16), but public drunkenness is uncommon and frowned upon.

➡ Book for upmarket restaurants, but reservations are unnecessary in most tavernas.

➡ Service charges are included in the bill, but most people leave a small tip or round up the bill; 10% to 15% is acceptable. If you want to split the bill, it's best you work it out among your group rather than ask the server to do it.

➡ Greeks are generous and proud hosts. Don't refuse a coffee or drink – it's a gesture of hospitality and goodwill. If you're invited out, the host normally pays. If you are invited to someone's home, it is polite to take a small gift (flowers or sweets), and remember to pace yourself, as you will be expected to eat everything on your plate.

➡ Smoking is banned in enclosed public spaces, including restaurants and cafes, but this rule is largely ignored, especially on distant islands.

Don't judge a place by its decor (or view). Go for places with a smaller selection (where food is more likely to be freshly cooked) rather than those with impossibly extensive menus.

Restaurant Guide

Taverna The classic Greek taverna has a few specialist variations – the *psarotaverna* (serving fish and seafood) and *hasapotaverna* or *psistaria* (for chargrilled or spit-roasted meat).

Mayirio (cookhouse) Specialises in traditional one-pot stews and baked dishes *(mayirefta)*.

Estiatorio Serves upmarket international cuisine or Greek classics in a more formal setting.

Mezedhopoleio Offers lots of mezedhes (small plates).

Ouzerie In a similar vein to the *mezedhopoleio*, the *ouzerie* serves mezedhes (traditionally arriving with each round of ouzo). Regional variations focusing on the local firewater include the *rakadhiko* (serving raki) in Crete and the *tsipouradhiko* (serving *tsipouro*) in the mainland north.

Menu Advice

➡ Menus with prices must be displayed outside restaurants. English menus are fairly standard but off the beaten track you may encounter Greek-only menus. Many places display big trays of the day's *mayirefta* or encourage you to see what's cooking in the kitchen.

➡ Bread and occasionally small dips or nibbles are often served on arrival (you are increasingly given a choice as they are added to the bill).

➡ Don't stick to the three-course paradigm – locals often share a range of starters and mains (or starters can be the whole meal). Dishes may arrive in no particular order.

➡ Frozen ingredients, especially seafood, are usually flagged on the menu (an asterisk or 'kat' on Greek menu).

➡ Fish is usually sold per kilogram rather than per portion, and is generally cooked whole rather than filleted. It's customary to go into the kitchen to select your fish (go for firm flesh and glistening eyes). Check the weight (raw) so there are no surprises on the bill.

Plan Your Trip
Outdoor Activities

Greece is graced with blue water, warm winds, undersea life, dramatic cliff faces, flourishing forests and ancient walkways – but only recently have visitors looked up from their sunloungers to notice. If you're a novice kitesurfer or avid cyclist, if you want to hike deep gorges or ski from lofty heights, opportunities abound.

Water Activities

Diving & Snorkelling

Snorkelling can be enjoyed just about anywhere along the coast of Greece and equipment is cheaply available. Especially good spots to don your fins are Monastiri on Paros, Paleokastritsa on Corfu, Xirokambos Bay on Leros and anywhere off the coast of Kastellorizo (Megisti). Many dive schools also use their boats to take groups of snorkellers to prime spots.

Greek law insists that diving be done under the supervision of a diving school in order to protect the many antiquities in the depths of the Mediterranean and Aegean Seas. Until recently dive sites were severely restricted, but many more have been opened and diving schools have flourished. You'll find schools on the islands of Corfu, Evia, Leros, Milos, Mykonos, Paros, Rhodes, Santorini, Skiathos, Crete, in Glyfada near Athens, and in Parga and Halkidiki in northern Greece.

The **Professional Association of Diving Instructors** (PADI; www.padi.com) has lots of useful information, including a list of all PADI-approved dive centres in Greece.

Best Outdoors

Hiking

Samaria Gorge (p480) Trek among towering cliffs and wildflowers.

Andros (p337) Follow well-worn footpaths across hills to deep valleys.

Nisyros (p535) Hike amid lush foliage and down into the caldera.

Samos (p594) Wander through woods and swim under waterfalls.

Skopelos (p650) Walk around olive groves and pristine meadows.

Experts

Santorini (p400) Enjoy a pathway of canyons and swim-through sand caverns for divers.

Kalymnos (p553) Climb towering limestone cliffs.

Paros (p368) Shangri-La for kitesurfing.

Novices

Vasiliki (p683) Learn how to windsurf.

Ios (p393) Dive schools catering to first-timers.

Paxi (p676) Walks through ancient olive groves.

Kos (p538) Cycle on the flat.

Hiking Mt Olympus (p273)

Windsurfing

Windsurfing is a very popular water sport in Greece. Hrysi Akti on Paros and Vasiliki on Lefkada vie for the position of the best windsurfing beach.

There are numerous other prime locations around the islands and many water-adventure outlets rent equipment. Check out Kalafatis Beach on Mykonos, Agios Georgios on Naxos, Mylopotas Beach on Ios, Cape Prasonisi in southern Rhodes, around Tingaki on Kos and Kokkari on Samos.

You'll find sailboards for hire almost everywhere. Hire charges range from €15 to €30, depending on the gear and the location. If you are a novice, most places that rent equipment also give lessons. Sailboards can be imported into Greece freely (one per passenger) provided they will be taken out of the country on departure, but always check customs regulations for your country.

Kitesurfing & Surfing

With near-constant wind and ideal conditions, Paros' Pounta beach is a magnet for kitesurfing's top talent, attracting both the

Professional Kiteboard Riders Association and the Kiteboard Pro World Tour. With a shallow side, this is also a great place to learn surfing. Mikri Vigla on Naxos is also an excellent spot, with courses off the gorgeous white-sand beach.

Waterskiing

Given the relatively calm and flat waters of most island locations and the generally warm waters of the Mediterranean, waterskiing is a very pleasant activity. August is sometimes a tricky month, when the *meltemi* (dry northerly wind) can make conditions difficult in the central Aegean. Poros is a particularly well-organised locale, with Passage (p320) hosting a popular school and slalom centre.

White-Water Rafting

The popularity of white-water rafting and other river-adventure sports has grown rapidly in recent years as more and more urban Greeks, particularly Athenians, head off in search of a wilderness experience. While spring and autumn are the best times, with high water levels and decent weather, many operators offer trips year-round on the larger rivers.

Athens Extreme Sports (www.athens extremesports.com) offers rafting on several rivers including the Ladonas and Lusios Alfios. Compass Adventures (p302), based in northern Greece, guides rafting excursions from the Zagorohoria village of Aristi down the frothing Voïdomatis River.

Land Activities

Hiking

Much of Greece is mountainous and, in many ways, a hiker's paradise. Popular routes are well walked and maintained; however, the **EOS** (Greek Alpine Club; ⌨210

321 3255; www.eosathinon.gr; Lekka 23-25, Athens) is underfunded and consequently many lesser-known paths are overgrown and inadequately marked. You'll find EOS branches in Ioannina in Epiros, Litohoro by Mt Olympus, Crete (Greek Mountaineering Association) and Evia (Halkida Alpine Club).

Northern Greece has plenty of rugged hiking terrain, especially around the Zagorohoria in the Pindos Mountains and the hill trails around Prespa Lakes. Beyond the mainland, the Lousios Gorge and the Mani, both in the Peloponnese, are two of the best places in Greece to explore on foot. With the launch of the 75km **Menalon Trail** (www.menalontrail. eu), hikers can embark on newly certified short walks or even a five-day trek along the Lousios Gorge, Mt Menalon's western

TOP ISLAND HIKES

DESTINATION, ISLAND GROUP	SKILL LEVEL	DESCRIPTION
Alonnisos, Sporades	easy	A network of established trails that lead to pristine beaches
Hydra, Saronic Gulf Islands	easy	A vehicle-free island with a well-maintained network of paths to beaches and monasteries
Paxi, Ionian Islands	easy	Paths along ancient olive groves and snaking drystone walls; perfect for escaping the crowds
Samaria Gorge, Crete	easy to medium	One of Europe's most popular hikes with 500m vertical walls, countless wildflowers and endangered wildlife (impassable mid-October to mid-April)
Zakros & Kato Zakros, Crete	easy to medium	Passing through the mysterious Valley of the Dead, this trail leads to a remote Minoan palace site
Tragaea, Naxos, Cyclades	easy to medium	A broad central plain of olive groves, unspoiled villages and plenty of trails
Sifnos, Cyclades	easy to medium	Monasteries, beaches and sprawling views abound on this freshly updated network of trails, covering 200km of island terrain
Tilos, Dodecanese	easy to medium	Countless traditional trails along dramatic clifftops and down to isolated beaches; a bird-lover's paradise
Dimosari Gorge, Evia	easy to medium	A 10km trek through a spectacular gorge of shady streams and cobbled paths ending at a small bay
Ithaki, Ionian Islands	easy to medium	Mythology fans can hike between sites linked to the Trojan War hero Odysseus
Samos, Northeastern Aegean Islands	easy to medium	Explore the quiet interior of this island with its mountain villages and the forested northern slopes of Mt Ambelos
Nisyros, Dodecanese	medium to difficult	A fertile volcanic island with hikes that lead down steep cliffs to reach steaming craters
Steni, Evia	medium to difficult	Day hikes and more serious trekking opportunities up Mt Dirfys, Evia's highest mountain

slopes and scenic villages galore. Crete's Samaria Gorge is rightly a global favourite, but western Crete boasts many gorges suitable for hikers of different skill levels.

On small islands you will encounter a variety of paths, including *kalderimia,* which are cobbled or flagstone paths that have linked settlements since Byzantine times. Other paths include *monopatia* (shepherds' or monks' trails) that link settlements with sheepfolds or link remote settlements via rough unmarked trails. Shepherd or animal trails can be very steep and difficult to navigate.

If you're venturing off the beaten track, a good map is essential. Most tourist maps are inadequate; the best hiking maps for the islands are produced by **Anavasi** (www.anavasi.gr) and **Terrain** (www.terrainmaps.gr), both Greece-based companies. Be realistic about your abilities. Always inform your guesthouse or local hiking association of your planned route before setting out.

Spring (April to June) is the best time for hiking; the countryside is green and fresh from the winter rains, and carpeted with wildflowers. Autumn (September to October) is another good time, but July and August, when temperatures rise to around 40°C (104°F), are not much fun. Whatever the season, come equipped with a good pair of walking boots to handle the rough, rocky terrain, a wide-brimmed hat, a water bottle and a high-UV-factor sunscreen.

A number of companies run organised hikes. The biggest is **Trekking Hellas** (www.trekking.gr), which offers a variety of hikes ranging from a four-hour stroll through the Lousios Valley to a week-long hike around Mt Olympus and Meteora. The company also runs hikes in Crete and the Cyclades. Many of the treks require a minimum number of participants or the price hike is steeper than the trail.

Cycling

Greece has recently established itself as a cycling destination both for mountain bikers and novices yearning to take a spin on its coastal roads. Bicycles can usually be taken on trains for free, though you may need a ticket. On ferries, mention your bike when booking tickets.

Much of Greece is very remote. Be sure to carry puncture-repair and first-aid kits with you. Motorists are notoriously fast and not always travelling in the expected lane; extra caution on corners and narrow roads is well warranted. In July and August most cyclists break between noon and 4pm to avoid sunstroke and dehydration.

Cycle Greece (www.cyclegreece.gr) Runs road- and mountain-bike tours across most of Greece for various skill levels including some sail-and-cycle tours.

Hooked on Cycling (www.hookedoncycling. co.uk/greece) Offers boat - and bike - trips through the islands plus tours of the mainland.

Bike Greece (www.bikegreece.com) Specialises in mountain biking, with various weeklong tours for beginners and the experienced.

Skiing & Snowboarding

Greece's main skiing areas are Mt Parnassos (1600m to 2250m), 195km northwest of Athens, and Mt Vermio (1420m to 2005m), 110km west of Thessaloniki. The best action is in the north, with Metsovo, Konitsa or the Zagori villages all possible bases for snow sports around Vasilitsa in the Pindos Mountains.

Resorts are used mainly by Greeks and can be a pleasant alternative to western Europe's expensive resorts. If you want to combine city and snow, ski Vigla-Pisoderi as a day trip from Florina or head to Mt Vermio from Veria.

The season depends on snow conditions but runs approximately from January to the end of April. Get information from the **Hellenic Skiing Federation** (☎210 323 0182; www.eox.gr) and check conditions and ski centres at **Snow Report** (www.snowreport.gr).

Plan Your Trip
Travel with Children

While Greece doesn't cater to kids the way that some countries do, children will be welcomed and included wherever you go. Greeks generally make a fuss over children, who may find themselves receiving many gifts and treats. Teach them some Greek words and they'll feel even more appreciated.

Greece for Kids
Sights & Activities

While even the most modern Greek museums are often filled to the gills with relics and objects that not all children will appreciate, the ancient palace-like settings can be intriguing for kids to wander through. The stories behind the objects can also captivate their imaginations – ancient statues hauled up from the depths of the sea or helmets worn by gladiators. Generally more popular than the museums are the many ancient sights where kids enjoy climbing and exploring.

The beach is one of the best sources of entertainment for children in Greece. In summer, many of the larger, popular beaches have bodyboards, surfboards, snorkelling gear and windsurfing equipment for rent. Many also offer lessons or trips on boats or giant, rubber, air-filled bananas. While some beaches have steep drop-offs or strong currents, there is generally a calmer side to each island or a shallow, protected bay that locals can direct you to.

Most towns will have at least a small playground, while larger cities often have fantastic, modern play parks. In many cases, you can admire children's innate ability to overcome language barriers

Best Regions for Kids
Athens

With ruins to clamber over, plus museums and child-geared sights to explore, Athens is great for kids. You'll also find big parks and gardens, a variety of cuisines and family-friendly hotels.

Crete

The island's beaches are long and sandy, Knossos ignites kids' imaginations, and you can explore from a single base, side-stepping the need to pack up and move around.

Dodecanese

The magical forts and castles, glorious beaches, laid-back islands, and speedy catamarans linking the Dodecanese daily make it ideal for families. And the Italian influence means an abundance of kid-friendly pasta dishes.

Northern Greece

Offers slightly lower summertime temperatures, Ottoman patisseries and Halkidiki's beaches. Laid-back Ioannina makes a great base and Parga is popular with families. Sithonia is less crowded but also less family-friendly than the rest of Halkidiki.

through play while you enjoy a coffee and pastry at the park's attached cafe. Some of the larger and more popular locations (such as Rhodes, Crete and Athens) also have water parks.

Dining Out

Greek cuisine is all about sharing; ordering lots of mezedhes (small dishes) lets your children try the local cuisine and find their favourites. You'll also find lots of kid-friendly options such as pizza and pasta, omelettes, chips, bread, savoury pies and yoghurt.

The fast service in most restaurants is good news when it comes to feeding hungry kids. Tavernas are very family-friendly affairs and the owners will generally be more than willing to cater to your children's tastes. Ingredients such as nuts and dairy find their way into lots of dishes so if your children suffer from any severe allergies, it's best to ask someone to write this down for you clearly in plain Greek to show restaurant staff.

Accommodation

Many hotels let small children stay for free and will squeeze an extra bed in the room. In all but the smallest hotels, travel cots can often be found, but it's always best to check in advance. Larger hotels and resorts often have package deals for families and these places are generally set up to cater to kids with childcare options, adjoining rooms, paddling pools, cots and high chairs.

Safety

Greece is a safe and easy place to travel with children. Greek children are given a huge amount of freedom and can often be seen playing in village squares and playgrounds late into the night. Nevertheless, it's wise to be extra vigilant with children when travelling, and to ensure they always know where to go and who to approach for help. This is especially true on beaches or in playgrounds where it's easy for children to become disoriented. It's also prudent not to have your children use bags, clothing, towels etc with their name or personal information (such as national flag) stitched onto them; this kind of information could be used by

potential predators to pretend to know you or the child.

Dangers children are far more likely to encounter are heatstroke, water-borne bugs and illness, mosquito bites, and cuts and scrapes from climbing around on ancient ruins and crumbling castles. Most islands have a clinic of some sort, although hours may be irregular so it's handy to carry a first-aid kid with basic medicine and bandages.

Children's Highlights
Keep Busy

Boat trips Whether it's zipping over the sea in a catamaran, bobbing up and down in a fishing boat or sailing on a day trip to a secluded bay.

Kayaking Paddle alongside dolphins and visit pirate coves off Kefallonia.

Beach time Jump waves, build sandcastles and snorkel. Always ask locally for kid-friendly beaches; Patmos is a great place to start.

Cycling Use pedal-power along the flat, bike-friendly roads of Kos.

Playgrounds Every city has one and they are most often well maintained and shady.

Explore

Acropolis (p67) The home of the Greek gods is perfect for exploring early in the day.

Rhodes' medieval castles (p498) The island of Rhodes is packed with crumbling castles perched on cliffs above the sea – perfect for climbing and make-believe.

Knossos (p450) Young imaginations go into overdrive when let loose in this labyrinth.

Nisyros' volcano (p536) See it hiss and hear it bubble.

Eat Up

Yemista Veggies (usually tomatoes) stuffed with rice.

Pastitsio Buttery macaroni baked with minced lamb.

Tzatziki A sauce or dip made from cucumber, yoghurt and garlic.

Loukoumadhes Ball-shaped doughnuts served with honey and cinnamon.

Galaktoboureko Custard-filled pastry.

Politiko pagoto Constantinople-style (slightly chewy) ice cream made with mastic.

Cool Culture

Carnival season Fancy dress, parades and traditional dancing will keep even the oldest kids enthralled.

Football Snag tickets for a game to catch some national spirit. Athens and Thessaloniki stadiums draw the biggest crowds.

Hellenic Children's Museum (p88) Build, bake and investigate alongside Athenian kids in this museum's brand-new location.

Planning

The shoulder seasons (April to May and September to October) are great times to travel with children because the weather is milder and the crowds thinner.

An excellent way to prepare your kids for their holiday and to encourage an active interest in the destination is by introducing them to some books or DVDs ahead of time. Lots of younger children enjoy stories of Greek gods and Greek myths while slightly older kids will enjoy movies like *Mamma Mia* or *Lara Croft: Tomb Raider* for their Greek settings. You can also find children's books about life in Greece that include a few easy phrases that your kids can try out.

Fresh milk is available in large towns and tourist areas, but harder to find on smaller islands. Supermarkets are the best place to look. Formula is available almost everywhere, as is heat-treated milk. Disposable nappies are also available everywhere, although it's wise to take extra supplies of all of these things to out-of-the-way islands in case of local shortages.

Travel on ferries, buses and trains is free for children under four. For those up to age 10 (ferries) or 12 (buses and trains) the fare is half. Full fares apply otherwise. On domestic flights, you'll pay 10% of the adult fare to have a child under two sitting on your knee. Kids aged two to 12 travel with half-fare. If you plan to hire a car, it's wise to bring your own car seat or booster seat as rental agencies are not always reliable for these, particularly on small islands or with local agencies.

If your kids aren't old enough to walk on their own for long, consider a sturdy carrying backpack; pushchairs (strollers) are a struggle in towns and villages with slippery cobblestones and high pavements. Nevertheless, if the pushchair is a sturdy, off-road style, with a bit of an extra push you should be OK.

Online Resources

My Little Nomads (www.santorinidave.com/greece-with-kids) For plenty of recommendations and hearty discussion on visiting Greece with kids, visit David Hogg's site.

Travel Guide to Greece (www.greektravel.com) Matt Barrett's website has lots of useful tips for parents

Greece 4 Kids (www.greece4kids.com) Matt Barrett's daughter Amarandi has put together some tips of her own.

Regions at a Glance

Athens & Around

Ancient Ruins
Nightlife
Museums

Architectural Relics

For many, the Acropolis is the pinnacle of Western civilisation and their Greek holiday. The region is littered with other ruins to explore: watch a Greek drama unfold at the Odeon of Herodes Atticus, visit the Ancient Agora in the city's heart or see the Temple of Poseidon on Cape Sounion.

Bars & Clubs

This city refuses to snooze, with glamorous beachside clubs where thousands dance to international DJs, intimate *rembetika* clubs where you can soak up Greek blues and ouzo, and everything in between.

Ancient Treasures

Step into the Benaki Museum, filled with Bronze Age finds, works by El Greco and regional costumes. Explore the expansive collection at the Byzantine & Christian Museum and the floors of antiquities at the National Archaeological Museum. And don't miss the ultramodern Acropolis Museum housing long-lost treasures.

p60

Peloponnese

Ancient Ruins
Architecture
Activities

Citadels

The Peloponnese is packed with inspiring ancient sites. Visit the sanctuary of Ancient Olympia, explore the citadels of Mycenae and Tiryns, or take in a show at the Theatre of Epidavros.

Fortresses

From Byzantine cities to Venetian fortresses, this region is peppered with architectural gems. Cross the causeway to magical Monemvasia *kastro* (fort) or explore the Mani's tower houses from the 17th century.

Hiking Trails

The Mani, the peninsula's rugged and remote southern region, is a popular place to amble, with mountains tumbling down to gorgeous coastal views. Northwest of here, hike through the Lousios Gorge to find charming village monasteries.

p137

Central Greece

Ancient Sites
Activities
Beaches

Delphi & Meteora

Resting on the slopes of Mt Parnassos with views of the Gulf of Corinth, the sanctuary of Delphi has an almost magnetic pull and an atmosphere of awe. Nearby, Meteora's monasteries sit defiantly atop towering pinnacles of rock.

Trails & Waterways

Follow cobblestone trails past villages and through forests on the Pelion Peninsula; hug the coast in a kayak on the Aegean Sea; and follow in Hercules' footsteps, exploring the green depths of Iti National Park.

Sandy Coves

Central Greece keeps its beautiful beaches a secret. Low-key resorts dot the Gulf of Corinth and the Pelion Peninsula, where hidden, sandy coves and crystal-clear waters await the intrepid.

p198

Northern Greece

Food & Wine
Activities
Beaches

Eastern Spice

The strong mezedhes (appetisers) culture brings a spiciness from the Anatolian Peninsula in Turkey. You'll encounter mussel pilaf, crayfish, lots of cheese and Macedonian wine. Sample artful Ottoman sweets in Thessaloniki.

Mountain Hikes

The story of Zeus takes you hiking into the clouds atop Mt Olympus, Greece's highest peak. In Zagorohoria, hike between 46 preserved hamlets in the Pindos Mountains.

Resort Life

With sandy beaches, island getaways and strong Italian-village influences, Parga typifies the region's resorts – popular yet relaxed, good for families yet great for nightlife. Alternatively, head for the remote sandy coves of Halkidiki.

p244

Saronic Gulf Islands

Activities
Architecture
Museums

Diving & Hiking

Diving is magical in these waters. Dolphin safaris, sunken pirate ships and underwater caves are just the start. When dry land beckons, Poros, Hydra and Spetses have forests to explore and hilltops to climb.

Monasteries & Mansions

Tiers of traditional buildings sweep down to Hydra's pretty harbour, and serene, ancient monasteries dot nearby hilltops. Next door on Spetses, see traditional boatbuilding and impressive ancestral mansions.

Traditional Seacraft

Hydra's museums include a restored hilltop mansion and eclectic naval collections. At Spetses, see a traditional seafarer's home, and at Baltiza, a museum of sea craft, from caïques to yachts.

p311

Cyclades

Ancient Ruins
Cuisine
Nightlife

Delos & Akrotiri

One of the country's most important archaeological sites, the sacred relics of Delos are protected on their own private island. The Minoan city of Akrotiri on Santorini is equally atmospheric.

Traditional Meals

Sample smoked eel and ham, Mykonian prosciutto, handmade soft cheeses and local wild mushrooms. Kitchens are filled with creative culinary flair and modern takes on traditional foods.

Glamour Clubs

The legendary Mykonos nightlife is glamorous and always entertaining. Ios is less swanky but very full-on, with wall-to-wall clubs and nonstop beach parties. Quieter Santorini has cocktail bars over the caldera with unparalleled sunset views.

p331

Crete

Ancient Ruins
Activities
Beaches

Minoan Palaces

The ruins of the Minoan civilisation grace this island, including the spectacular restored palace of Knossos and the labyrinth referred to in Greek mythology. At remote sites, there's a lingering sense of mystery.

Gorge Hikes

The Samaria is Europe's longest gorge, and one of Crete's most popular draws. The island boasts other quieter, equally dramatic gorges for hiking and rock climbing, and a mountainous interior with caves and woodland to explore.

Sun Worship

Crete has some of Greece's top beaches, palm-fringed stretches of powder-soft sand. Others are lapped by the crystal-clear Libyan Sea or backed by charismatic old towns. All are worth sinking your toes into.

p438

Dodecanese

Architecture
Activities
Cuisine

Byzantine & Medieval

Architectural eye candy is everywhere. See fairytale hilltop castles, frescoed Byzantine churches and Rhodes' medieval Old Town. Visit mountain villages, the ruins of ancient temples and Italian-inspired harbour towns.

Outdoor Adventures

Some of the world's top rock climbing, kitesurfing, beachcombing, diving and walking are packed into the Dodecanese. Ancient footpaths, endangered birdlife, a bubbling volcano and surfing too.

Culinary Mix

Mix Greek cuisine with long-term Italian influences for scrumptious results: pizzas, pastas, stews, local cheeses, honey, wild greens and herbs, seafood and grilled meats.

p495

Northeastern Aegean Islands

Activities
Cuisine
Beaches

Great Outdoors

The clear water lapping these islands is perfect for diving into. You'll be beckoned to hike to wooded waterfalls, wade through rivers and explore oldgrowth forests on foot or bicycle.

Seafood & Wine

Dining daily on fresh seafood is a way of life. Venus clams, sea urchins, crayfish, grilled cod and lobster are all washed down with plenty of ouzo and Samos' sweet local wine.

Aqua Aegean

From the remote, white-pebbled coast on Ikaria to hidden coves on the Fourni Islands, pristine sandy stretches on Chios and seaside resorts on Samos, you're never far from a beach on the aquamarine Aegean.

p572

Evia & the Sporades

Activities
Cuisine
Nightlife

Seaside Meadows

Soak in thermal waters at local beaches or spas, watch for dolphins in the waters of a marine park, and hike through olive groves and meadows. The region is also renowned for its diving.

Sweet & Fresh

Don't miss the local honey, especially the *elatos* (fir) and *pefko* (pine) varieties. Select amazingly fresh fish directly from the nets and served on the dock. Locally pressed olive oil produces home cooking like *yiayia* (grandma) makes it.

Wine Bars

Nightlife isn't always about clubbing. Here it's about listening to some of the country's top bouzouki players and watching the sun sink over the horizon from lowkey wine bars.

p633

Ionian Islands

Architecture
Activities
Cuisine

Mansions & Windmills

Corfu Town is a symphony of pastel-hued Venetian mansions, French arcades and British neoclassical architecture. Corfu is dotted with other historic mansions and neighbouring islands have whitewashed villages and ancient windmills.

Kayak & Ramble

Kayak remote coves, sail the blue Aegean, wander ancient olive groves and hike the mountains. Continuous stretches of gorgeous coastline and quiet interiors lure the adventurous.

Italian-Inspired

Soft braised meat, plenty of garlic, homemade bread, seafood risottos and hand-rolled pasta allude to an Italian influence in the kitchen. Without a history of Turkish rule, Corfiot cuisine is distinctive and delicious.

p661

On the Road

Athens & Around

Best Places to Eat

→ Mani Mani (p101)

→ Ta Karamanlidika tou Fani (p107)

→ Telis (p106)

→ Mavro Provato (p110)

→ Funky Gourmet (p105)

Best Places to Stay

→ Grande Bretagne (p99)

→ NEW Hotel (p99)

→ Hera Hotel (p97)

→ Athens Was (p98)

→ City Circus (p100)

Why Go?

With equal measures of grunge and grace, Athens is a heady mix of history and edginess. Cultural and social life plays out amid, around and in ancient landmarks. The magnificent Acropolis, visible from almost every part of the city, reminds Greeks daily of their heritage and the city's many transformations.

Although individuals have endured difficult circumstances since the start of the economic crisis in 2009, the city is on the rise. There is crackling energy in galleries, political debates and even on the walls of derelict buildings. This creates a lively urban bustle, but at the end of the day, Athenians build their own villages in the city, especially in open-air restaurants and bars where they linger for hours.

Beyond Athens, down the Attica peninsula, are more spectacular antiquities, such as the Temple of Poseidon at Sounion, as well as very good beaches, such as those near historic Marathon.

When to Go
Athens

May Perfect weather for sightseeing and open-air attractions such as cinemas and restaurants.

Jun–Aug The Athens & Epidaurus Festival lights up venues with drama and music.

Sep–Oct Weather cools and the social scene heats up as residents return from the islands.

Athens & Around Highlights

1 Acropolis (p67) The awe-inspiring ancient site.

2 Acropolis Museum (p73) Enjoying the majesty of the Parthenon sculptures.

3 Ancient Agora (p76) Strolling in the historic centre.

4 Tailor Made (p111) Staying out till the wee hours at lively cafe-bars.

5 Benaki Museum (p89) Admiring superb antiquities and other legacies of Greece.

6 Odeon of Herodes Atticus (p73) Catching a summer festival show.

7 Monastiraki Flea Market (p122) Picking through flea-market antiques and finding a bargain.

8 Strofi (p101) Dining out at restaurants with views of the floodlit Acropolis.

9 Panathenaic Stadium (p92) Revelling in ancient feats of strength.

10 Cine Paris (p116) Watching a movie at a historic outdoor theatre with views of the Acropolis.

ATHENS ΑΘΗΝΑ

POP 3.1 MILLION

History

Early History

The archaeological record of Athens' early years is patchy. What is known is that the hilltop site of the Acropolis, with two abundant springs, drew some of Greece's earliest Neolithic settlers. When a peaceful agricultural existence gave way to war-orientated city states, the Acropolis provided an ideal defensive position.

By 1400 BC the Acropolis had become a powerful Mycenaean city. It survived a Dorian assault in 1200 BC but didn't escape the dark age that enveloped Greece for the next 400 years. Then, in the 8th century BC, during a period of peace, Athens became the artistic centre of Greece, excelling in ceramics.

By the 6th century BC, Athens was ruled by aristocrats and generals. Labourers and peasants had no rights until Solon, the harbinger of Athenian democracy, became *arhon* (chief magistrate) in 594 BC and improved the lot of the poor by establishing a process of trial by jury. Continuing unrest over the reforms created the pretext for the tyrant Peisistratos, formerly head of the military, to seize power in 560 BC.

Peisistratos built a formidable navy and extended the boundaries of Athenian influence. A patron of the arts, he inaugurated the Festival of the Great Dionysia, the precursor to Attic drama, and commissioned many splendid works, most of which were later destroyed by the Persians.

In 528 BC, he was succeeded by his son, Hippias, no less an oppressor. With the help of Sparta in 510 BC, Athens rid itself of him.

Athens' Golden Age

After Athens finally repulsed the Persian Empire at the battles of Salamis (480 BC) and Plataea (479 BC) – again, with the help of Sparta – its power knew no bounds.

In 477 BC Athens established a confederacy on the sacred island of Delos and demanded tributes from the surrounding islands to protect them from the Persians. The treasury was moved to Athens in 461 BC and Pericles, ruler from 461 BC to 429 BC, used the money to transform the city. This period has become known as Athens' golden age.

Most of the monuments on the Acropolis today date from this period. Drama and literature flourished due to such luminaries as Aeschylus, Sophocles and Euripides. The sculptors Pheidias and Myron and the historians Herodotus, Thucydides and Xenophon also lived during this time.

Rivalry with Sparta

Sparta didn't let Athens revel in its newfound glory. Cooperation gave way to competition

---

ATHENS IN...

Two Days

Climb to the glorious **Acropolis** (p67) in the early morning, then wind down through the **Ancient Agora** (p76), or pop in to the **Tower of the Winds** (p77). Explore **Plaka**, looping back to the **Acropolis Museum** (p73) for the Parthenon masterpieces. Complete your circuit along the **grand promenade** (p75), then up to **Filopappou Hill** (p75) and the cafes of **Thisio** before dinner at a restaurant with Acropolis views – or grab a souvlaki and head to an **outdoor movie** (p117).

On day two, watch the **changing of the guard** (p83) at Syntagma Sq before heading through the gardens to the **Temple of Olympian Zeus** (p75) or the **Panathenaic Stadium** (p92). Take a trolleybus to the **National Archaeological Museum** (p89), then catch an evening show at the historic **Odeon of Herodes Atticus** (p73), or head to the **Plateia Agia Irini** area in Monastiraki for dinner and nightlife.

Four Days

Visit the **Benaki Museum** (p89), the **Museum of Cycladic Art** (p89) and the **Byzantine & Christian Museum** (p90) before lunch in **Kolonaki**. Take the *teleferik* (funicular railway) or climb **Lykavittos Hill** (p90) for panoramic views. Hit a **rembetika club** (p117) in winter, or bar-hop around Exarhia in summer.

On day four explore the dynamic **central market** (p121) and **Kerameikos** (p85). Trip along the coast to Cape Sounion's **Temple of Poseidon** (p134), or save your energy for nightlife at Glyfada's **beach bars** (p111).

and the Peloponnesian Wars, which began in 431 BC and dragged on until 404 BC. Sparta gained the upper hand and Athens never returned to its former glory. The 4th century BC did, however, produce three of the West's greatest orators and philosophers: Socrates, Plato and Aristotle.

In 338 BC Athens, along with the other city-states of Greece, was conquered by Philip II of Macedon. After Philip's assassination, his son Alexander (soon to be known as the Great) favoured Athens over other city-states. But after Alexander's untimely death, Athens passed in quick succession through the hands of his generals.

Roman & Byzantine Rule

The Romans defeated the Macedonians, and in 186 BC attacked Athens after it sided against them in a botched rebellion in Asia Minor. They destroyed the city walls and took precious sculptures to Rome. During three centuries of peace under Roman rule, known as the 'Pax Romana', Athens continued to be a major seat of learning. The Romans adopted Hellenistic culture: many wealthy young Romans attended Athens schools and anyone who was anyone in Rome spoke Greek. The Roman emperors, particularly Hadrian, graced Athens with many grand buildings.

In the late 4th century, Christianity became the official religion of Athens and worship of the 'pagan' Greek gods was outlawed. After the subdivision of the Roman Empire into east and west, Athens remained an important cultural and intellectual centre until Emperor Justinian closed its schools of philosophy in AD 529. Athens declined and, between 1200 and 1450, was continually invaded – by the Franks, Catalans, Florentines and Venetians, all preoccupied with grabbing principalities from the crumbling Byzantine Empire.

Ottoman Rule & Independence

Athens was captured by the Turks in 1456, and nearly 400 years of Ottoman rule followed. The Acropolis became the home of the Turkish governor, the Parthenon was converted to a mosque and the Erechtheion became a harem.

On 25 March 1821, the Greeks launched the War of Independence, declaring independence in 1822. Fierce fighting broke out in the streets of Athens, which changed hands several times. Britain, France and Russia eventually stepped in and destroyed

CONTEST FOR ATHENS

The founding of Athens is enshrined in myth. Phoenician king Kekrops, the story goes, founded a city on a huge rock near the sea. The gods of Olympus proclaimed that it should be named for the deity who could provide the most valuable legacy for mortals. Athena (goddess of wisdom, among other things) produced an olive tree, symbol of peace and prosperity. Poseidon (god of the sea) struck a rock with his trident, creating a saltwater spring, to signify great maritime power. It was a close contest, but the gods judged that Athena's gift, which would provide food, oil and fuel, would better serve the citizens – though of course Athens today draws its wealth from Poseidon's domain as well.

the Turkish–Egyptian fleet in the famous Battle of Navarino in October 1827.

Initially the city of Nafplio was named Greece's capital. After elected president Ioannis Kapodistrias was assassinated in 1831, Britain, France and Russia again intervened, declaring Greece a monarchy. The throne was given to 17-year-old Prince Otto of Bavaria, who transferred his court to Athens. It became the Greek capital in 1834, though was little more than a sleepy town of about 6000, as so many residents had fled after the 1827 siege. Bavarian architects created imposing neoclassical buildings, tree-lined boulevards and squares.

Otto was overthrown in 1862 after a period of power struggles, including the British and French occupation of Piraeus, aimed at quashing the 'Great Idea' – Greece's doomed expansionist goal. The imposed sovereign was Danish Prince William, crowned as Prince George in 1863.

The 20th Century

Throughout the latter half of the 19th century and the beginning of the 20th, Athens grew steadily – and then quite suddenly in 1922 and 1923, when more than a million refugees arrived in the city, first from the burning of Smyrna (Izmir), then due to the population exchange mandated by the Treaty of Lausanne the next spring.

During the German occupation of WWII, Athens suffered appallingly. More Athenians

Greater Athens

Kitissos 🚌 Larissa Train Station 🚉
Terminal A (2.6km)
Gagarin 205
Club (1.5km);
Liossion 🚌
Terminal B (3.1km)

Enjoy Just Falafel (200m);
Victoria Square Project (200m)

Plateia
Petroula
Sot

Ioanninon

Argous

Lenorman

Ipirou

Aharnon

Aristotelous

28 Oktovriou-Patision

Plateia
Rampes

Palamidiou

Plateia
Vathis

METAXOURGIO

See Psyrri, Omonia & Exarhia Map (p108)

🅼 Metaxourghio

OMONIA

Agiou Konstantinou

Plateia
Eleotrivion

Leof Athinon

Ahilleos

Giatrakou

Plateia
Omonias

🅼 Omonia

Naousis

Thermopylon

Eolou

Kastorias 32

16

28

Stadiou

Halkidikis

27

Paramythias

14

21

Plateia
Kotzia

Meg Alexandrou

24

11

Pireos (Tsaldari Panagi)

KERAMIKOS

🅿

Plateia Eleftherias
(Koumoundourou)

Varvakios
Agora (Athens
Central Market)

🅼 **GAZI**
Kerameikos

Technopolis

Ermou

Plateia
Karamanou

Plateia
Karamanou

PSYRRI

Plateia
Koulouris

Pireos

Thisio
Park

Plateia Agion
Asomaton

See Syntagma, Plaka &
Monastiraki Map (p78)

Plateia
Agia Irini

Plateia
Thisiou

Plateia
Afea

Plateia Thissio 🅼

Plateia Avyssinias

19

Monastiraki 🅼

THISSIO

Apostolou Pavlou

MONASTIRAKI

Plateia Arhaia
Agoras

Hellenic
Cosmos (2km)

ROUF

Alsos
Petralonon

Hill
of the
Nymphs

Areopagus
Hill

ANAFIOTIKA

Acropolis

Hill of the
Pnyx

See Gazi, Keramikos & Thisio Map (p84)

See Akropoli & Makrygianni
Map (p74)

🅼 Petralona

3

Akropoli 🅼

9

MAKRYGIANNI

34

8

Dimofontos

4

6

13

Marble House Pension (200m);
National Museum of Contemporary
Art (350m); Figoures & Koukles (400m);
Hytra (1.5km); Onassis Cultural Centre (1.5km);
Panetarium (3km);
Glyfada (17km)

Leof Andreas

KOUKAKI

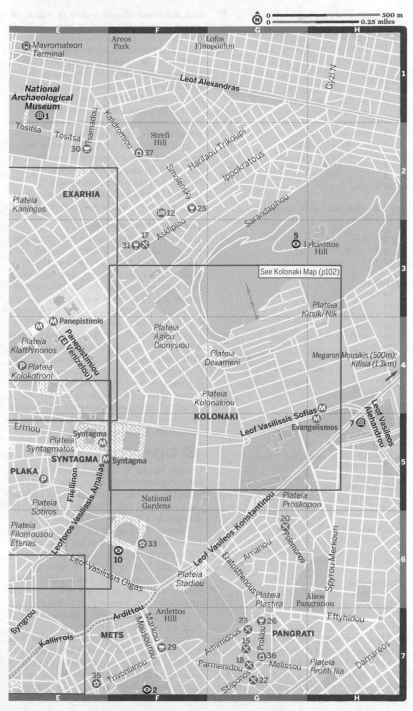

0 ———— 500 m
0 ———— 0.25 miles

E **F** **G** **H**

Mavromateon Terminal

Areos Park

Lofos Finopoulou

1

Leof Alexandras

Gyzi N

National Archaeological Museum ⊞1

Tositsa Tositsa 30

Tsamadou

Kalidromiou

Strefi Hill

🔒37

Harilaou Trikoupi

Ippokratous

2

EXARHIA

Plateia Kaningos

Smolensky

Asklipiou

🍴12 🛒25

Sarandapiliou

5
◉ Lykavittos Hill

31 ✕17

3

See Kolonaki Map (p102)

Ⓜ Panepistimio

Panepistimiou (El Venizelou)

Plateia Klafthmonos

Plateia Agiou Dionysiou

Plateia Dexameni

Plateia Kitsiki Nik.

Megaron Mousikis (500m); Kifisia (1.3km)

Ⓟ Plateia Kolokotroni

Plateia Kolonakiou

4

KOLONAKI

Leof Vasilissis Sofias Ⓜ

Leof Vasileos Alehandrou

Ermou

Syntagma Ⓜ

Plateia Syntagmatos

SYNTAGMA

Filellinon

Ⓜ Syntagma

Evangelismos

7 ⊞

5

PLAKA Ⓟ

Leoforos Vasilissis Amalias

Plateia Sotiros

National Gardens

Plateia Proskopon

Plateia Filomousou Eterias

⊙10 ⭐33

Leof Vasileos Konstantinou

20 ✕

Polemonos

Spyrou Merkouri

6

Leof Vasilissis Olgas

Plateia Stadiou

Arrianou

Eratosthenous

Plateia Plastira

Alsos Pangratiou

Eftyhidou

Syngrou

Kallirrois

Ardittou

Markou Mousourou

Ardettos Hill

Arhimidou

23 🍴26

PANGRATI

METS

🍴29

15 ✕

18 ✕

Proklou

🔒36

Melissou

Plateia Profiti Ilia

Damareos

7

35 ⭐

Trivonianou

Parmenidou

Stilponos

22 ✕

Plateia Profiti Ilia

◉2

E **F** **G** **H**

Greater Athens

died from starvation than were killed by the enemy. The suffering only continued during the bitter civil war that followed.

A '50s industrialisation program, launched with the help of US aid, brought another population boom, as people from the islands and mainland villages moved to Athens in search of work. The colonels' junta (1967–74) tore down many of the old Turkish houses of Plaka and the neoclassical buildings of King Otto's time, but failed to tackle the chronic infrastructure problems resulting from the rapid growth of the 1950s. The elected governments that followed didn't do much better, and by the end of the 1980s the city had a reputation as one of the most traffic-clogged, polluted and dysfunctional in Europe.

In the 1990s, as part of an initial bid to host the Olympics, authorities embarked on an ambitious program to drag the city into the 21st century. Athens finally won the competition to host the 2004 Olympics, a deadline that fast-tracked infrastructure projects.

The New Millennium
The 2004 Olympics legacy was a cleaner, greener and more efficient capital, and booming economic growth. But the optimism and fiscal good times were short-lived, as it became clear the country had overborrowed. In 2010, the Greek debt crisis set in, with strict austerity measures including cutting pensions by half. The unemployment rate hit 28% in 2014 and banks closed briefly in 2015 amid dramatic elections. That same year, Athens also welcomed hundreds of thousands of refugees from Syria, Afghanistan and elsewhere. The majority passed through to northern Europe, but a significant portion have stayed. The bounty represented by Athena's olive tree persists, despite this period of adversity.

◉ Sights

Central Athens is relatively small: you can walk a leisurely circuit around the base of the Acropolis in about an hour. However, because the city is quite hilly, what looks like a short distance on a map can be a hike in real life.

Plateia Syntagmatos (Syntagma Sq; translated as Constitution Sq) is considered the centre of modern Athens. A short walk south and west is the old Turkish quarter in **Plaka**, virtually all that existed when Athens was declared capital of Greece. This neighbourhood is ground zero for tourism, but lifelong residents and a splash of graffiti keep it from losing its character.

Due west from Syntagma is **Monastiraki** and just north, **Psyrri**. They're both very lively at night, but some emptier blocks can be a bit sketchy at night, especially in the northern fringes of Psyrri. West of the Acropolis, in **Thisio**, Apostolou Pavlou is a lovely green pedestrian promenade with a host of cafes and youth-filled bars, with residential blocks to either side. Further west, **Gazi** was for years the edgy neighbourhood; now it's decidedly the centre, mostly for nightlife and a strong gay scene. The urban fringes, where new bars and creative endeavours pop up, are now **Keramikos** and **Metaxourgio**, where car-repair shops mix with abandoned mansions.

East and north of Syntagma, **Kolonaki** is Athens' poshest central neighbourhood. Behind the Panathenaic Stadium, **Pangrati** and neighbouring **Mets** are unpretentious residential areas, with low-key-cool places to eat. The quiet neighbourhoods of **Makrygianni** and **Koukaki**, south of the Acropolis, are relatively untouristed as well.

Heading north from Syntagma, you pass the 'neoclassical trilogy' of elaborate, formal late-19th-century buildings on Stadiou. Up the hill behind, **Exarhia**, covered in more graffiti than the rest of the city, is known for its lively squat scene, with frequent rallies on Plateia Exarhia. **Omonia**, once one of the city's smarter areas, can be seedy at night – although the square itself, focus of police vigilance, is relatively fine. North from here, you reach **Viktoria**, **Kypseli** and **Plateia Amerikis**, all home to many recent immigrants.

Athens is somewhat constrained by the surrounding mountains, though it is eating its way up the slopes. Far to the north is Mt Parnitha; the northeast is marked by Mt Pendeli, the west by Mt Egaleo and the east by Mt Hymettos. Downtown Athens is dominated by its much smaller hills.

◎ Acropolis

★**Acropolis**   HISTORIC SITE
(Map p78; ☑210 321 4172; http://odysseus. culture.gr; adult/concession/child €20/10/free; ⊙8am-8pm Apr-Oct, to 5pm Nov-Mar, last entry 30min before closing; Ⓜ Akropoli) The Acropolis is the most important ancient site in the Western world. Crowned by the Parthenon, it stands sentinel over Athens, visible from almost everywhere within the city. Its monuments and sanctuaries of white Pentelic marble gleam in the midday sun and gradually take on a honey hue as the sun sinks, while at night they stand brilliantly illuminated above the city. A glimpse of this magnificent sight cannot fail to exalt your spirit.

Inspiring as these monuments are, they are but faded remnants of the city of Pericles, who spared no expense – only the best materials, architects, sculptors and artists were good enough for a city dedicated to Athena. It was a showcase of lavishly coloured colossal buildings and of gargantuan statues, some of bronze, others of marble plated with gold and encrusted with precious stones.

The Acropolis was first inhabited in Neolithic times (4000–3000 BC). The earliest temples were built during the Mycenaean era, in homage to the goddess Athena. People lived on the Acropolis until the late 6th century BC, but in 510 BC the Delphic oracle declared that it should be the province of the gods.

After all the buildings on the Acropolis were reduced to ashes by the Persians on the eve of the Battle of Salamis (480 BC), Pericles set about his ambitious rebuilding program. He transformed the Acropolis into a city of temples, which has come to be regarded as the zenith of Classical Greece.

Ravages inflicted during the years of foreign occupation, pilfering by foreign archaeologists, inept renovations following Independence, visitors' footsteps, earthquakes and, more recently, acid rain and pollution have all taken their toll on the surviving monuments. The worst blow was in 1687, when the Venetians attacked the Turks, opening fire on the Acropolis and causing an explosion in the Parthenon – where the Turks had been storing gunpowder – and damaging all the buildings.

Major restoration programs are continuing and most of the original sculptures and friezes have been moved to the Acropolis Museum (p73) and replaced with casts. The Acropolis became a World Heritage-listed site in 1987.

The one modern detail on the hill (aside from the ever-present scaffolding and cranes) is the large Greek flag at the far east end. From here, you can look down into the Temple of Olympian Zeus. In 1941, early in the Nazi occupation, two teenage boys climbed up here and pulled down the Nazi flag and raised the Greek one; their act of resistance is commemorated on a brass plaque nearby.

A combined ticket permits entry to the Acropolis and six other sites within five days. On the first Sunday of the month from November to March, admission is free.

Beulé Gate   ARCHITECTURE
(Map p78) Inside the main entrance of the Acropolis site, the path leads you up through the Beulé Gate, named after the French archaeologist Ernest Beulé, who uncovered

Acropolis

Roman Agora (270m);
Ancient Agora (320m);
Plaka (510m)

Areopagus Hill

Lift

Temple of Poseidon

Themistocles' Wall

Wheelchair Access

Athena Promachos Pedestal

Erechtheion

Porch of the Caryatids

Flag of Greece

Agrippa Pedestal

Propylaia

Panathenaic Way

Beulé Gate

Parthenon Columns

Parthenon

Parthenon Pediments

Thisio (750m)

Temple of Athena Nike

Metopes & Frieze

Wheelchair Access

Main Entrance

Parthenon Pediments

Panagia Hrysospiliotissa

Odeon of Herodes Atticus

Asclepion

Stoa of Eumenes

Theatre of Dionysos

East Entrance

Ticketed Area

Dionysiou Areopagitou

Rovertou Galli

Akropoli Metro Station (200m); Syntagma (750m)

Acropolis Museum

it in 1852. The 8m-high pedestal on the left, halfway up the stairs leading to the Propylaia, was once topped by the Monument of Agrippa, a bronze statue of the Roman general riding a chariot, erected in 27 BC after victory in the Panathenaic Games.

Propylaia   ARCHITECTURE

(Map p78) The Propylaia formed the monumental entrance to the Acropolis (p67). Built by Mnesicles between 437 BC and 432 BC, it ranks in architectural brilliance with the Parthenon. It consists of a central hall with two wings on either side; each section had a gate, and in ancient times these five gates were the only entrances to the 'upper city'. The middle gate, the largest, opened on to the Panathenaic Way, the route for the great Panathenaic Procession.

As you walk through on the central boardwalk, admire the thick panels of marble cladding, and as you pass the northeastern section (once used as a *pinakothiki*, or art gallery), look up to see the marble ceiling panels. These were once painted with gold stars on a blue field. Up ahead, beyond the Propylaia to the right, near the Parthenon, the path leads past (new) ceiling panels, stored upright. They are startlingly huge, giving a sense of the true height of the Propylaia's columns.

Temple of Athena Nike   TEMPLE

(Map p78) The small but exquisitely proportioned Temple of Athena Nike sits at the southwest edge of the Acropolis (p67), jutting in front and to the right of the Propylaia. Designed by Kallicrates, the temple was built of white Pentelic marble between 427 BC and 424 BC. The building is almost square, with four graceful Ionic columns at either end.

Only fragments remain of the frieze and relief sculptures, now replicas; the originals are in the Acropolis Museum (p73). The frieze shows scenes from mythology, the Battle of Plataea (479 BC) and Athenians fighting Boeotians and Persians. An additional relief sculpture shows Athena Nike fastening her sandal. The temple housed a wooden statue of Athena.

The temple was dismantled in 1686, when the Turks used its stones to build a bastion against the Venetians. From 1836–42, it was carefully reconstructed, but this and later interventions had to be corrected starting in 2003. The temple was once again dismantled, piece by piece, and painstakingly rebuilt without corrosive iron and using new marble from ancient quarries to fill in gaps; this gleams white in contrast with the old stones.

Statue of Athena
Promachos & Pedestals
RUINS

(Map p78) As you walk beyond the Propylaia into the Acropolis (p67) site, along the Panathenaic Way, you will see to your left the foundations of pedestals for the statues that once lined the path, including one that held Pheidias' 9m-high statue of Athena Promachos (*promachos* means 'champion'). Symbolising Athenian invincibility against the Persians, the helmeted goddess held a shield in her left hand and a spear in her right.

The statue was carted off to Constantinople by Emperor Theodosius in AD 426. By 1204 it had lost its spear, so the hand appeared to be gesturing. This led the inhabitants to believe that the statue had beckoned the Crusaders to the city, so they smashed it to pieces.

★ Parthenon
TEMPLE

(Map p78) More than any other monument, the Parthenon epitomises the glory of Ancient Greece. Meaning 'virgin's apartment', it's dedicated to Athena Parthenos, the goddess embodying the power and prestige of the city. The largest Doric temple ever completed in Greece, and the only one built completely of white Pentelic marble (apart from its wooden roof), it took 15 years to complete. It was designed by Iktinos and Kallicrates and completed in time for the Great Panathenaic Festival (p76) of 438 BC.

Designed to be the pre-eminent monument of the Acropolis (p67) and built on its highest ground, the Parthenon had a dual purpose: to house the great statue of Athena commissioned by Pericles and to serve as the new treasury. It was built on the site of at least four earlier temples dedicated to Athena.

The temple consisted of eight fluted Doric columns at either end and 17 on each side. To achieve perfect form, its lines were ingeniously curved to create an optical illusion – the foundations are slightly concave and the columns are slightly convex to make both look straight. Supervised by Pheidias, the sculptors Agoracritos and Alcamenes worked on the architectural sculptures of the Parthenon, including the pediments and friezes, which were brightly coloured and gilded.

The metopes (the decorative panels on the frieze) on the eastern side depicted the Olympian gods fighting the giants; on the western side they showed Theseus leading the Athenian youths into battle against the Amazons. The southern metopes illustrated the contest of the Lapiths and Centaurs at a marriage feast, while the northern ones depicted the sacking of Troy.

Much of the frieze depicting the Panathenaic Procession was either damaged in the Turkish gunpowder explosion of 1687 or later defaced by the Christians, but the greatest existing part (over 75m long) consists of the controversial Parthenon Marbles, taken by Lord Elgin and now in the British Museum in London. The British government continues to ignore campaigns for their return.

The ceiling of the Parthenon, like that of the Propylaia, was painted blue and gilded with stars. At the eastern end was the holy cella (inner room of a temple), into which only a few privileged initiates could enter. Here stood the statue for which the temple was built: the Athena Polias (Athena of the City), considered one of the wonders of the ancient world. Designed by Pheidias and completed in 432 BC, it was gold-plated over an inner wooden frame and stood almost 12m high on its pedestal. The face, hands and feet were made of ivory, and the eyes were fashioned from jewels. Clad in a long gold dress with the head of Medusa carved in ivory on her breast, the goddess held a statuette of Nike (the goddess of victory) in her right hand; in her left, a spear with a serpent at its base. On top of her helmet was a sphinx, with griffins in relief at either side.

Erechtheion
TEMPLE

(Map p78) Although the Parthenon was the most impressive monument of the Acropolis (p67), it was more showpiece than working sanctuary. That role fell to the Erechtheion. Named after Erechtheus, a mythical king of Athens, the temple housed the cults of Athena and Poseidon. It was here that, the myths told, the god and goddess had a contest for the city's affections. Poseidon struck the ground with his trident, making a salt spring, but Athena won by producing an olive tree.

The Erechtheion was part of Pericles' plan for rebuilding after the Persian attack, but the project was postponed after the outbreak of the Peloponnesian Wars. Work did not start until 421 BC, eight years after his death, and was completed around 406 BC.

It is the most unusual monument of the Acropolis, a supreme example of Ionic architecture ingeniously built on several levels to compensate for the uneven bedrock. The main temple is divided into two cellae – one dedicated to Athena, the other to Poseidon – representing a reconciliation of the two deities after their contest.

The Acropolis

A WALKING TOUR

Cast your imagination back in time, two and a half millennia ago, and envision the majesty of the Acropolis. Its famed and hallowed monument, the Parthenon, dedicated to the goddess Athena, stood proudly over a small city, dwarfing the population with its graceful grandeur. In the Acropolis' heyday in the 5th century BC, pilgrims and priests worshipped at the temples illustrated here (most of which still stand in varying states of restoration). Many were painted brilliant colours and were abundantly adorned with sculptural masterpieces crafted from ivory, gold and semiprecious stones.

As you enter the site today, elevated on the right perches one of the Acropolis' best-restored buildings: the diminutive ❶ **Temple of Athena Nike**. Follow the Panathenaic Way through the Propylaia and up the slope towards the Parthenon – icon of the Western world. Its ❷ **majestic columns** sweep up to some of what were the finest carvings of their time: wrap-around ❸ **pediments, metopes and a frieze**. Stroll around the temple's exterior and take in the spectacular views over Athens and Piraeus below.

As you circle back to the centre of the site, you will encounter those renowned lovely ladies, the ❹ **Caryatids** of the Erechtheion. On the Erechtheion's northern face, the oft-forgotten ❺ **Temple of Poseidon** sits alongside ingenious ❻ **Themistocles' Wall**. Wander to the Erechtheion's western side to find Athena's gift to the city: ❼ **the olive tree**.

TOP TIP

The Acropolis is a must-see for every visitor to Athens. Avoid the crowds by arriving first thing in the morning or late in the day.

Themistocles' Wall
Crafty general Themistocles (524–459 BC) hastened to build a protective wall around the Acropolis and in so doing incorporated elements from archaic temples on the site. Look for the column drums built into the wall.

Sanctuary of Pandion

Sanctuary of Zeus Polieus

Erechtheion

Temple of Poseidon
Though he didn't win patronage of the city, Poseidon was worshipped on the northern side of the Erechtheion, which still bears the mark of his trident-strike. Imagine the finely decorated coffered porch painted in rich colours, as it was in the past.

VWB PHOTOS / GETTY IMAGES ©

Porch of the Caryatids

Perhaps the most recognisable sculptural elements at the Acropolis are the majestic Caryatids (c 415 BC). Modelled on women from Karyai (modern-day Karyes, in Lakonia), the maidens are thought to have held a libation bowl in one hand, and to be drawing up their dresses with the other.

Parthenon Pediments, Metopes & Frieze

The Parthenon's pediments (the triangular elements topping the east and west facades) were filled with elaborately carved three-dimensional sculptures. The west side depicted Athena and Poseidon in their contest for the city's patronage, the east Athena's birth from Zeus' head. The metopes are square carved panels set between channelled triglyphs. They depicted battle scenes, including the sacking of Troy and the clash between the Lapiths and the Centaurs. The cella was topped by the Ionic frieze, a continuous sculptured band depicting the Panathenaic Procession.

Parthenon

Chalkotheke

Panathenaic Way

Sanctuary of Artemis Brauronia

Statue of Athena Promachos

Arrephorion

Propylaia

Pinakothiki

Entrance

Athena's Olive Tree

The flourishing olive tree next to the Erechtheion is meant to be the sacred tree that Athena produced to seize victory in the contest for Athens.

Parthenon Columns

The Parthenon's fluted Doric columns achieve perfect form. Their lines were ingeniously curved to create an optical illusion: the foundations (like all the 'horizontal' surfaces of the temple) are slightly concave and the columns arc slightly convex, making both appear straight.

Spring of Klepsydra

Temple of Athena Nike

Recently restored, this precious tiny Pentelic marble temple was designed by Kallicrates and built around 425 BC. The cella housed a wooden statue of Athena as Victory (Nike) and the exterior friezes illustrated Athenian battle triumphs.

In **Athena's cella** stood an olive-wood statue of Athena Polias holding a shield adorned with a gorgon's head. It was this statue on which the sacred *peplos* (shawl) was placed at the culmination of the Great Panathenaic Festival (p76). In front of the temple grows an olive tree, held to be a cutting of the one that sprang forth at Athena's behest when she won the contest against Poseidon. The current tree was planted in 1952, from a cutting made during WWII to protect the tree from the Germans.

The southern portico is supported by six larger-than-life maiden columns, the Caryatids, modelled on women from Karyai – modern-day Karyes, in Lakonia, hence the name. Those you see are plaster casts. The originals (except for one removed by Lord Elgin, now in the British Museum) are in the Acropolis Museum.

Poseidon's cella, the northern porch, is accessible by a small set of stairs against the boundary wall. It consists of six Ionic columns; the fissure in the floor is supposedly left either by Poseidon's trident in his contest with Athena, or by Zeus' thunderbolt when he killed the mythical king Erechtheus.

ℹ COMBINED TICKETS & ENTRY HOURS

➡ A €30 unified ticket covers entry to the Acropolis and Athens' other main ancient sites: Ancient Agora, Roman Agora, Hadrian's Library, Kerameikos, the Temple of Olympian Zeus and Aristotle's Lyceum. It pays off if you're planning to see the Acropolis (€20 alone) and at least two other sites. The ticket is valid for five days and can be purchased at any of the included sites.

➡ For museums, a €15 ticket covers the National Archaeological Museum, the Byzantine & Christian Museum, the Epigraphic Museum and the Numismatic Museum. It's valid for three days.

➡ Hours for many sites can be cut back in winter, closing sometimes as early as 2pm. Additionally, budget cuts have occasionally curtailed opening times. Be sure to double-check hours before making a special trip.

➡ Box offices close 15 to 30 minutes before the sites close. Check www.culture.gr for free-admission holidays.

★ Theatre of Dionysos · THEATRE
(Map p78; ☎ 210 322 4625; Dionysiou Areopagitou; adult/child €2/free, with Acropolis pass free; ⊙ 8am-8pm, reduced hours low season; Ⓜ Akropoli)
The tyrant Peisistratos introduced the annual Festival of the Great Dionysia during the 6th century BC, and held it in the world's first theatre, on the south slope of the Acropolis. The original theatre on this site was a timber structure, and masses of people attended the contests, where men clad in goatskins sang and danced, followed by feasting and revelry. Drama as we know it dates to these contests.

At one of the contests, Thespis left the ensemble and took centre stage for a solo performance, an act considered to be the first true dramatic performance – hence the term 'thespian'.

During the golden age in the 5th century BC, the annual festival was one of the state's major events. Politicians sponsored dramas by writers such as Aeschylus, Sophocles and Euripides, with some light relief provided by the bawdy comedies of Aristophanes. People came from all over Attica, with their expenses met by the state.

The theatre was reconstructed in stone and marble by Lycurgus between 342 BC and 326 BC, with a seating capacity of 17,000 spread over 64 tiers, of which about 20 survive. Apart from the front row, the seats were built of Piraeus limestone and occupied by ordinary citizens, with women confined to the back rows. The front row's 67 Pentelic marble **thrones** were reserved for festival officials and important priests. The grandest one – in the centre, with lion-paw armrests – was reserved for the Priest of Dionysos, who sat shaded from the sun under a canopy.

Stoa of Eumenes & Asclepion · RUINS
(Map p78) From the stage of the Theatre of Dionysos, the path leads uphill and west to the top of the long Stoa of Eumenes, a colonnade built by Eumenes II, King of Pergamum (197–159 BC), as a shelter and promenade for theatre audiences. Above the stoa, against the hillside, the Asclepion is a temple that was built around a sacred spring.

The worship of Asclepius, the physician son of Apollo, began in Epidavros and was introduced to Athens in 429 BC, when plague was sweeping the city.

Panagia Hrysospiliotissa · HISTORIC SITE
(Map p78) Above the Theatre of Dionysos, accessible by a path east from the Asclepion, is a grotto in the cliff face that Thrasyllos

❶ ACROPOLIS LOGISTICS

➜ The main entrance is at the southwest side of the hill. Tour groups enter here and if you have a large bag (or camera bag), you must check it at the cloakroom. You can also hire a tour guide here.

➜ The east entrance is by the Theatre of Dionysos and the Akropoli metro station. It's recommended for individuals as it's less crowded.

➜ Tour groups start massing around 9am; arrive earlier to get a head start. Or go in the last two hours, when crowds thin out.

➜ Sight clearance starts 15 minutes before closing. At this time, you must go out via the main (west) entrance.

➜ The site closes before sunset, but Aeropagus Hill, outside the main gate, is a nice (if busy) place to watch the light show.

➜ Wear shoes with grippy rubber soles, as the paths around the site are uneven and slippery.

➜ People with mobility issues can access the site via a cage-lift rising vertically up the rock face on the north side. It's best to call ahead (☑ 210 321 4172) to arrange. When you arrive, first go to the main entrance for guidance.

➜ There are restrooms near the main entrance (outside the ticket gate) and at the top of the hill, east of the Parthenon. Several water fountains are around the site.

➜ Phones get poor reception at the top. Take paper or download information.

---

converted to a Dionysian temple in 320 BC. In the Christian era, it became the Chapel of Our Lady of the Cavern; old pictures and icons cover the walls. Above the chapel, two slender Ionic columns are the remains of Thrasyllos' temple. It's open only on 15 August, the day of the Dormition of the Virgin.

◉ South Slope of the Acropolis & Makrygianni

★ **Odeon of Herodes Atticus**   THEATRE
(Map p78; ☑ 210 324 1807; Ⓜ Akropoli) This large amphitheatre was built in AD 161 by wealthy Roman Herodes Atticus in memory of his wife Regilla. It was excavated in 1857–58 and completely restored from 1950–61. The Athens & Epidaurus Festival (p96) holds drama, music and dance performances here in summer.

★ **Acropolis Museum**   MUSEUM
(Map p74; ☑ 210 900 0900; www.theacropolis museum.gr; Dionysiou Areopagitou 15, Makrygianni; adult/child €5/free; ⊙ 8am-4pm Mon, to 8pm Tue-Sun, to 10pm Fri Apr-Oct, 9am-5pm Mon-Thu, to 10pm Fri, to 8pm Sat & Sun Nov-Mar; Ⓜ Akropoli) This dazzling modernist museum at the foot of the Acropolis' southern slope showcases its surviving treasures still in Greek possession. While the collection covers the Archaic and Roman periods, the emphasis is on the Acropolis of the 5th century BC, considered the apotheosis of Greece's artistic achievement. The museum cleverly reveals layers of history, floating over ruins with the Acropolis visible above, showing the masterpieces in context. The surprisingly good-value **restaurant** has superb views; there's also a fine museum **shop**.

Designed by US-based architect Bernard Tschumi with Greek architect Michael Photiadis, the €130-million museum includes items formerly held in other museums or in storage, as well as pieces returned from foreign museums.

As you enter the museum grounds, look through the plexiglass floor to see the **ruins of an ancient Athenian neighbourhood**, which were artfully incorporated into the museum design after being uncovered during excavations.

Finds from the slopes of the Acropolis are on display in the **foyer gallery**, which has an ascending glass floor emulating the climb up to the sacred hill, while allowing glimpses of the ruins below. Exhibits include painted vases and votive offerings from the sanctuaries where gods were worshipped, and more recent objects found in excavations of the settlement, including two clay statues of Nike at the entrance.

Bathed in natural light, the 1st-floor **Archaic Gallery** is a veritable forest of

Akropoli & Makrygianni

Akropoli & Makrygianni

statues, mostly votive offerings to Athena. These include stunning examples of 6th-century *kore* – statues of young women in draped clothing and elaborate braids, usually carrying a pomegranate, wreath or bird. Most were recovered from a pit on the Acropolis, where the Athenians buried them after the Battle of Salamis. The 570

BC statue of a youth bearing a calf is one of the rare male statues found. There are also bronze figurines and artefacts from temples predating the Parthenon (destroyed by the Persians), including wonderful pedimental sculptures such as Hercules slaying the Lernaian Hydra and a lioness devouring a bull. Also on this floor are five **Caryatids**, the maiden columns that held up the Erechtheion (the sixth is in the British Museum).

The museum's crowning glory is the top-floor **Parthenon Gallery**, a glass atrium housing the temple's 160m-long frieze. It's mounted as it once was, following the layout of the building, and you can stroll along, as though atop the columns, and examine the fragments at eye level. The frieze depicts the Panathenaic Procession, starting at the southwest corner of the temple, with two groups splitting off and meeting on the east side for the delivery of the *peplos* to Athena. (It helps a bit to see the **movie** that is screened on this floor.) Interspersed between the golden-hued originals are stark-white plaster replicas of the missing pieces – the Parthenon Marbles hacked off by Lord Elgin in 1801 and later sold to the British Museum (more than half the frieze is in London).

Filopappou Hill   PARK

(Map p64; MAkropoli) Also called the Hill of the Muses, Filopappou Hill – along with the Hills of the Pnyx and the Nymphs – was, according to Plutarch, where Theseus and the Amazons did battle. Inhabited from prehistoric times to the post-Byzantine era, today the pine-clad slopes are a relaxing place for a stroll. They offer excellent views of Attica and the Saronic Gulf, well-signed ruins and some of the very best vantage points for photographing the Acropolis.

The hill, to the southwest of the Acropolis, is identifiable by the **Monument of Filopappos** (Map p64) crowning its summit; it was built between AD 114 and 116 in honour of Julius Antiochus Filopappos, a prominent Roman consul and administrator. The paved path to the top starts near the *periptero* (kiosk) on Dionysiou Areopagitou. After 250m, it passes the excellent **Church of Agios Dimitrios Loumbardiaris** (Map p64), which contains fine frescoes, and continues past **Socrates' prison** (Map p64), the **Shrine of the Muses** (Map p64) and on up to the top.

Areopagus Hill   PARK

(Map p78; MMonastiraki) This rocky outcrop below the Acropolis has great views over the Ancient Agora. According to mythology, it was here that Ares was tried by the council of the gods for the murder of Halirrhothios, son of Poseidon. The council accepted his defence of justifiable deicide on the grounds that he was protecting his daughter, Alcippe, from unwanted advances.

The hill became the place where murder, treason and corruption trials were heard before the Council of the Areopagus. In AD 51, St Paul delivered his famous 'Areopagus Sermon' here: 'As I...looked carefully at your objects of worship, I even found an altar with this inscription: to an unknown god. So you are ignorant of the very thing you worship.' (The words are in Greek on a brass plaque on the hillside.) From this St Paul gained his first Athenian convert, Dionysos, who became the city's patron saint.

Hill of the Pnyx   PARK

(Map p84; MThissio) North of Filopappou Hill, the Pnyx is a rocky outcropping that was the official meeting place of the Democratic Assembly in the 5th century BC – really, the first site of democracy. You can see the speakers' steps, where the great orators Aristides, Demosthenes, Pericles and Themistocles addressed assemblies. More generally, the hill is less visited than other central sites and a peaceful place to walk.

Hill of the Nymphs   PARK

(Map p84; MThissio) Northwest of Hill of the Pnyx, this hill is home to the **old Athens observatory**, built in 1842.

★ Temple of Olympian Zeus   TEMPLE

(Olympieio; Map p74; ☑210 922 6330; http://odysseus.culture.gr; Leoforos Vasilissis Olgas, Syntagma; adult/student/child €6/3/free, with Acropolis pass free; ⊙8am-3pm Oct-Apr, to 8pm May-Sep, final admission 30min before closing; MAkropoli,

ATHENS & AROUND ATHENS

ANCIENT PROMENADE

One major lasting benefit of the 2004 Olympics was the transformation of the once traffic-choked streets around Athens' historic centre into a spectacular 3km-long pedestrian promenade, one of Europe's longest. Locals and tourists alike come out in force for an evening *volta* (stroll) along the interesting heritage trail, which passes many of the best historic sites.

The grand promenade starts at Dionysiou Areopagitou, opposite the Temple of Olympian Zeus, and continues along the southern foothills of the Acropolis, all the way to the Ancient Agora, branching off from Thisio to Keramikos and Gazi, and north along Adrianou to Monastiraki and Plaka.

PANATHENAIC PROCESSION

The biggest event in ancient Athens was the Panathenaic Procession, the climax of the Panathenaic Festival held to venerate the goddess Athena. Colourful scenes of the Procession are depicted in the 160m-long Parthenon frieze in the **Acropolis Museum** (p73).

There were actually two festivals, a lesser one to mark Athena's birthdate every year, and the Great Panathenaic Festival, every fourth year. This began with dancing, followed by athletic, dramatic and musical contests. On the final day, the Panathenaic Procession began at **Kerameikos** (p85), led by men carrying animals sacrificed to Athena, followed by maidens carrying *rhytons* (horn-shaped drinking vessels) and musicians playing a fanfare for the girls of noble birth who held aloft the sacred *peplos,* a glorious saffron-coloured shawl. The parade followed the Panathenaic Way, which cuts across the middle of the Acropolis. In the festival's grande finale, the *peplos* was placed on the statue of Athena Polias in the **Erechtheion** (p69).

Syntagma) A can't-miss on two counts: it's a marvellous temple, the largest in Greece, and smack in the centre of Athens. The temple is impressive for the sheer size of its 104 Corinthian columns (17m high with base diameter of 1.7m), of which 15 remain – the fallen column was blown down in a gale in 1852.

Begun in the 6th century BC by Peisistratos, the temple was abandoned for lack of funds. Various other leaders took a stab at completing it, but it was left to Hadrian to finish the job in AD 131, thus taking more than 700 years in total to build. In typically immodest fashion, Hadrian built not just a colossal statue of Zeus in the cella, but also an equally large one of himself.

⭐**Hadrian's Arch**   MONUMENT
(Map p74; cnr Leoforos Vasilissis Olgas & Leoforos Vasilissis Amalias, Syntagma; Ⓜ Akropoli, Syntagma) FREE The Roman emperor Hadrian had a great affection for Athens. Although he did his fair share of spiriting its Classical artwork to Rome, he also embellished the city with many monuments influenced by Classical architecture. His arch is a lofty monument of Pentelic marble that stands on the edge of one of Athens' busiest avenues. Hadrian erected it in AD 132, probably to commemorate the consecration of the Temple of Olympian Zeus.

The inscriptions show that it was intended as a dividing point between the ancient and Roman city. The northwest frieze reads, 'This is Athens, the Ancient city of Theseus', while the southeast frieze states, 'This is the city of Hadrian, and not of Theseus'.

**National Museum of
Contemporary Art**   MUSEUM
(EMST; Ⓙ 211 101 9000; www.emst.gr; Kallirrois & Frantzi, Koukaki-Syngrou; adult/student/child €8/4/

free, 5-10pm Thu free; ☺ 11am-8pm Tue-Sun, to 11pm Thu; Ⓜ Sygrou-Fix) Set in the former Fix Brewery (though you'd never know it, following the flashy renovation unveiled in 2015), the city's most prestigious contemporary museum shows exhibitions of Greek and international art in all media, from painting to video to experimental architecture. The Greek scene is still evolving, so shows can be hit or miss. The building layout is not very welcoming, with each exhibit hall behind closed doors, and a rather too-accessible fire-escape stairwell.

Onassis Cultural Centre   CULTURAL CENTRE
(Ⓙ info & tickets 210 900 5800; www.sgt.gr; Leoforos Syngrou 107-109, Neos Kosmos; ☒ 10 or 550 to Panteio, Ⓜ Sygrou-Fix, ☒ Kassomouli) The eye-catching visual- and performing-arts centre livens up the dull urbanity of Leoforos Syngrou. Cloaked in a net of white marble, it glows at night when it hosts big-name productions, installations and lectures. Check the schedule for free events. It's 1.5km southwest of the Sygrou-Fix metro station.

⊙ Syntagma, Plaka & Monastiraki

⭐**Ancient Agora**   HISTORIC SITE
(Map p78; Ⓙ 210 321 0185; http://odysseus. culture.gr; Adrianou 24, Monastiraki; adult/student/ child €8/4/free, with Acropolis pass free; ☺ 8am-8pm daily May-Oct, to 3pm Nov-Apr; Ⓜ Monastiraki) The heart of ancient Athens was the Agora, the lively focal point of administrative, commercial, political and social activity. Socrates expounded his philosophy here, and in AD 49 St Paul came here to win converts to Christianity. The site today is a lush, refreshing respite, with beautiful monuments, the grand **Temple of Hephaistos** (Ancient Agora, Monastiraki), a fascinating **museum** (Map

p78) and the late-10th-century Byzantine **Church of the Holy Apostles**, trimmed in faux-Kufic brick patterns, in imitation of an Islamic style of decoration.

First developed as a public site in the 6th century BC, the Agora was devastated by the Persians in 480 BC, but a new one was built in its place almost immediately. It was flourishing by Pericles' time and continued to do so until AD 267, when it was destroyed by the Herulians, a Gothic tribe from Scandinavia. The Turks built a residential quarter on the site, but this was demolished by archaeologists after Independence and later excavated to Classical and, in parts, Neolithic levels.

⭐**Roman Agora & Tower of the Winds**　　　　HISTORIC SITE
(Map p78; ☑210 324 5220; http://odysseus. culture.gr; Dioskouron, Monastiraki; adult/student/ child €6/3/free, with Acropolis pass free; ⊘8am-5pm, reduced hours in low season; Ⓜ Monastiraki) The most dramatic remains of the **Roman Agora** (Map p78; cnr Pelopida & Eolou, Monastiraki; Ⓜ Monastiraki) are at the entrance,

ART GALLERIES

Get the 'Athens Contemporary Art Map', a list of art spaces and events, at www.athens artmap.net. Alternatively, pick up a paper copy at galleries and cafes around town.

Depot Gallery (Map p102; ☑210 364 8174; www.depotgallery.gr; Neofytou Vamva 5, Kolonaki; ⊘noon-9pm; Ⓜ Evangelismos) Located in Kolonaki, this is a newer gallery in the city's contemporary-art scene. The whitewashed space celebrates 'the line between art and design' and holds popular events. It features both Greek artists (including George Raptis, Vasilis Geros and Faye Tsakalides) and international names such as Frederic Bootz. Exhibitions change monthly.

Theocharakis Foundation for the Fine Arts & Music (Map p102; ☑210 361 1206; www.thf.gr; Leoforos Vasilissis Sofias 9, Kolonaki; adult/child €6/free; ⊘10am-6pm Mon-Wed & Fri-Sun, to 8pm Thu Sep-Jul; Ⓜ Syntagma) This excellent centre has three levels of exhibition space featuring local and international 20th- and 21st-century artists, a theatre, an art shop and a pleasant cafe. Music performances are held between September and May.

Metamatic:TAF (The Art Foundation; Map p78; ☑210 323 8757; www.theartfoundation.gr; Normanou 5, Monastiraki; ⊘noon-9pm Mon-Sat, to 7pm Sun, cafe-bar open late; Ⓜ Monastiraki) The central courtyard at TAF, surrounded by crumbling 1870s brick buildings, is a cafe-bar that fills with an eclectic young crowd. The surrounding space hosts art, music and theatre, often free.

CAN (Map p102; ☑210 339 0833; www.can-gallery.com; Anagnostopoulou 42, Kolonaki; ⊘11am-3pm & 5-8pm Tue-Fri, 11am-4pm Sat Sep-Jul; Ⓜ Syntagma) The brainchild of Christina Androulidaki, this entry on the Kolonaki gallery scene has a stable of emerging contemporary Greek artists.

A.antonopoulou.art (Map p108; ☑210 321 4994; www.aaart.gr; Aristofanous 20, 4th fl, Psyrri; ⊘2-8pm Wed-Fri, noon-6pm Sat; Ⓜ Monastiraki) One of the original galleries to open in Psyrri's warehouses, this impressive art space hosts exhibitions of contemporary Greek and international art, including installations, video art and photography.

Medusa Art Gallery (Map p102; ☑210 724 4552; www.medusaartgallery.com; Xenokratous 7, Kolonaki; ⊘11am-2.30pm & 6.30-9.30pm Tue-Fri, closed Aug; Ⓜ Evangelismos) Since 1979, this Kolonaki stalwart has shown excellent Greek contemporary painting, sculpture, installations and photography.

Qbox Gallery (Map p108; ☑211 119 9991; www.qbox.gr; Armodiou 10, Monastiraki; ⊘noon-6pm Tue-Fri, to 4pm Sat; Ⓜ Omonia, Monastiraki) Myrtia Nikolakopoulou directs this gallery, which promotes young, emerging local and visiting artists on the international scene. Great for a taste of Greece's cutting edge.

Bernier/Eliades (Map p84; ☑210 341 3935; www.bernier-eliades.gr; Eptachalkou 11, Thisio; ⊘10.30am-6.30pm Tue-Fri, noon-4pm Sat; Ⓜ Thissio) This well-established gallery showcases prominent Greek artists and an impressive list of international artists, from abstract American impressionists to British pop.

Syntagma, Plaka & Monastiraki

Mikonos
Esopou
Hristokopidou
Agias Theklas
Miaouli
Kakourgodikiou
Voreou

85 36 114

42
58
Karaiskaki
Pittaki

PSYRRI

90
88
Eolou
Vasilis Limbona
87 75
62
91
Klitiou
57
65
Skouze
89 79
Plateia
Agia Irini
80

Artemidos
Kevitos
Thermidos
Athinas
Agias Irinis
Karori
64
69
Athinaidos

Ermou
111 44
Ermou

Plateia
Kapnikareas
15

60
Agiou Filippou
112 77
86 22
115 113
Plateia
Avyssinias
43
93
Plateia
Monastirakiou
105
Plateia
Mitropoleos
55

Kynetou
Ifestou
Nisou
Monastiraki M
23
70 Plateia
Dimopratiriou
Pandrosou
Pandrosou
Hristopoulou
Kapnikareas
Mnisikleous
VlanouAng

**Ancient
Agora** 2
MONASTIRAKI
Adrianou
18

8
Vrysakiou
Kladou
Dexippou
Adrianou
Plateia Arhaia
Agoras
Kalogrioni
47
Adrianou

Aeos
Peikilis
Epaminonda
Pelopida
Eolou
25
Diogenous
107

**Roman Agora &
Tower of the Winds** 5
Taxiarhon
30
34
11 97
Kyrristou
Erehtheos

Athens
Archaeological
Service
Polygnotou
Dioskouron
Panos
Markou Aureliou
Lyssiou
Mnisikleous
94
Erotokritou
68

Mitrou
Thrasyvoulou
84
Theorias
Prytaniou
Stratonos
7

Dioskouron
Tholou
Aretousas
20
ANAFIOTIKA

Areopagus
Hill
Theorias
Klepsydras

9

17
1 **Acropolis**

12 29
31
4 **Parthenon**

33
Stratonos

27
6
**Theatre of
Dionysos**

3 **Odeon of
Herodes Atticus**
32

Theorias

**Fllopappou
Hill**
Dionysiou Areopagitou

Acropolis
East
Entrance
Thrasyllou

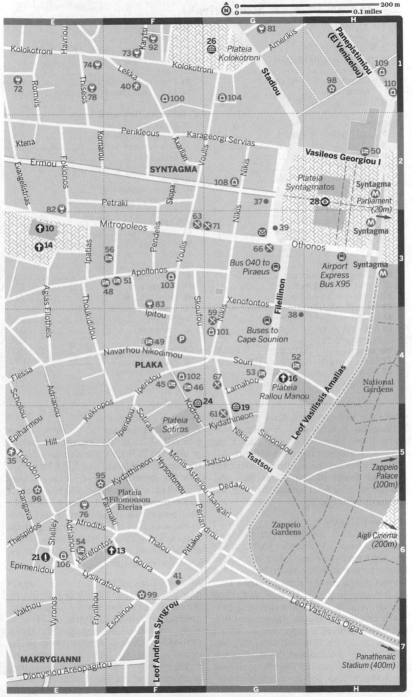

Syntagma, Plaka & Monastiraki

where the well-preserved **Gate of Athena Archegetis** is flanked by four Doric columns. It was financed by Julius Caesar and erected sometime during the 1st century AD. The real attraction here is the ingenious and beautiful **Tower of the Winds** (Map p78). You can see a lot from outside the fence, but it's worth going inside.

Hadrian's Library RUINS
(Map p78; ☑ 210 324 9350; http://odysseus. culture.gr; Areos 3, Monastiraki; adult/child €4/ free, with Acropolis pass free; ☉ 8am-3pm, reduced hours in low season; Ⓜ Monastiraki) North of the Roman Agora are the remains of the largest structure erected by Hadrian, in the 2nd century AD. The library, which also held music and lecture rooms, was set next to a courtyard bordered by 100 columns, with a pool in the centre. However, today only one restored wall remains and the site is dominated by an 11th-century church. If you have the Acropolis pass, pop in – but only specialists will make a special trip.

Museum of Greek Popular Instruments MUSEUM
(Map p78; ☑ 210 325 4119; http://odysseus.culture. gr; Diogenous 1-3, Plaka; ☉ 10am-2pm Tue & Thu-Sun, noon-6pm Wed; Ⓜ Monastiraki) ⒻⓇⒺⒺ More than 1200 folk instruments, most collected by a single avid ethnomusicologist, fill three floors of this museum. Some instruments date to the 18th century. Headphones let visitors listen to the sounds of the *gaida* (Greek goatskin bagpipes) and Byzantine mandolins, among others. Musical performances are held in the lovely garden in summer.

Athens Cathedral CHURCH
(Map p78; ☑ 210 322 1308; Plateia Mitropoleos, Monastiraki; ☉ 7am-7pm, Mass Sun 6.30am; Ⓜ Monastiraki) The ornate 1862 Athens Cathedral is the seat of the archbishop of the Greek Orthodox Church of Athens. However, far more significant, both historically and architecturally, is the small, 12th-century, cruciform-style marble church next to the cathedral, known as the **Little Metropolis**

(p87) built of bits and pieces of ancient temples and earlier Christian monuments.

Church of Kapnikarea
CHURCH

(Map p78; Ermou, Monastiraki; ⊗8am-2pm Tue, Thu & Fri; Ⓜ Monastiraki, Syntagma) This small 11th-century structure stands smack in the middle of the Ermou shopping strip. It was saved from the bulldozers and restored by Athens University. Its dome is supported by four large Roman columns.

Bath House of the Winds
MUSEUM

(Map p78; ☏210 324 4340; www.melt.gr; Kyrristou 8, Monastiraki; adult/child €2/free, free Sun Nov-Mar; ⊗8am-3pm Wed-Mon; Ⓜ Monastiraki) This 17th-century *hammam* (Turkish baths) is one of the few remnants of Ottoman times, and the only surviving public bath building in Athens. A helpful free audio tour takes you back to its glory days, through multiple levels, including the furnaces in the basement. It's beautiful, but of course it would be nicer if it were functional.

Kanellopoulos Museum
MUSEUM

(Map p78; ☏210 321 2313; http://odysseus.culture.gr; Theorias 12, cnr Panos, Plaka; adult/child €2/1; ⊗8am-3pm Tue-Sun, reduced hours in low season; Ⓜ Monastiraki) **FREE** In 1972, Paul and Alexandra Kanellopoulos bequeathed to the Greek state the jewellery, clay and stone figurines, weapons, Byzantine icons and assorted objets d'art they'd amassed in their lifetime. The mansion setting is lovely, and as it's often empty of other visitors, it can feel like you're touring your own private eclectic collection.

Agios Nikolaos Rangavas
CHURCH

(Map p78; ☏210 322 8193; Prytaniou 1, cnr Epiharmou, Plaka; ⊗8am-noon & 5-8pm; Ⓜ Akropoli, Monastiraki) This lovely 11th-century church was part of the palace of the Rangavas family, who counted among them Michael I, emperor of Byzantium. The church bell was the first installed in Athens after liberation from the Turks (who had banned them), and was the first to ring in 1833 to announce the freedom of Athens.

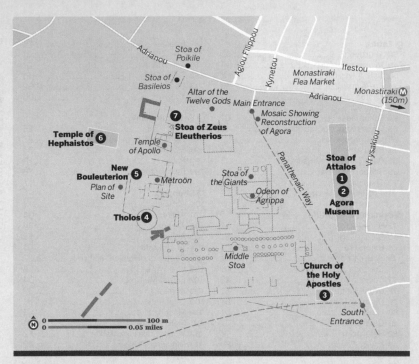

Stoa of Poikile
Adrianou
Agiou Filippou
Kynetou
Ifestou
Monastiraki Flea Market
Monastiraki (M) (150m)
Stoa of Basileios
Altar of the Twelve Gods
Main Entrance
Adrianou
Mosaic Showing Reconstruction of Agora
7 **Stoa of Zeus Eleutherios**
Temple of Hephaistos **6**
Temple of Apollo
Panathenaic Way
Vrysakiou
Stoa of Attalos
New Bouleuterion **5**
Metroön
Stoa of the Giants
Odeon of Agrippa
1
2
Agora Museum
Plan of Site
Tholos **4**
Middle Stoa
Church of the Holy Apostles
3
South Entrance
N
0 .... 100 m
0 .... 0.05 miles

Site Tour
Ancient Agora

LENGTH TWO HOURS

As you enter the Agora, make your way to the magnificent **1 Stoa of Attalos**, built by the king of Pergamum in the 2nd century BC. Originally its facade was painted red and blue. People gathered here to watch the Panathenaic Procession (p76). It was also the first-ever shopping arcade, for which the word stoa is still used today.

The excellent **2 Agora Museum**, inside the stoa, is a good place to make sense of the site. It holds a model of the Agora, and is surrounded by ancient statues of the gods.

Continue to the southern end of the site to the charming **3 Church of the Holy Apostles**, built in the early 10th century to commemorate St Paul's teaching in the Agora. From 1954–57 it was stripped of 19th-century additions and restored to its original form. It contains 17th-century frescoes. The exterior patterns are an imitation of Islamic Kufic-style decoration, showing the cross-pollination of style in this period.

Walking northwest across the site, you'll pass the circular **4 Tholos**, where the heads of government met, and what was the **5 New Bouleuterion**, where the Senate met.

On the Agora's western edge is the striking **6 Temple of Hephaistos**, god of the forge, which was surrounded by foundries and metalwork shops. It was one of the first buildings of Pericles' rebuilding program and is the best-preserved Doric temple in Greece. Built in 449 BC by Ictinus, one of the Parthenon architects, it has 34 columns and a frieze on the eastern side depicting nine of the Twelve Labours of Hercules. In AD 1300 it was converted into the Church of Agios Georgios. The last service held there was in 1834, to honour King Otto's arrival in Athens.

In 1922–23, the temple sheltered refugees from Asia Minor. Photos from that period show families hanging laundry among the pillars, and tents erected along the temple's base.

Northeast of the temple, you'll pass the foundation of the **7 Stoa of Zeus Eleutherios**, one of the places where Socrates expounded his philosophy.

Jewish Museum
MUSEUM

(Map p78; ☑210 322 5582; www.jewishmuseum. gr; Nikis 39, Plaka; adult/child €6/free; ⊙9am-2.30pm Mon-Fri, 10am-2pm Sun; Ⓜ Syntagma) This small museum traces the history of the Jewish community in Greece – starting with the deeply rooted Romaniote community established in the 3rd century BC, through the arrival of Sephardic Jews and beyond the Holocaust. The documents, religious art and folk objects are beautifully presented. It's worth visiting to learn the story of the bishop and the mayor of Zakynthos, the only Greek leaders who managed to save the Jewish community from Nazi round-ups.

Church of Sotira Lykodimou
CHURCH

(Map p78; Fillelinon, Plateia Rallou Manou, Plaka; Ⓜ Syntagma) First built in the 11th century and now the Russian Orthodox Cathedral, this is the only Byzantine church built to an octagonal plan. It's quite small but topped with a high dome, so the whole space, glittering with gold stars and icons, soars upward. It's open more frequently than other churches, so it's worth crossing the street to peek inside.

Lysikrates Monument
MONUMENT

(Map p78; cnr Sellei & Lysikratous, Plaka; Ⓜ Akropoli, Syntagma) FREE Chorus leader and musical patron Lysikrates built this tower in 334 BC to commemorate the victory of his sponsored chorus in the dramatic contests of the Dionysia. The trophy, a bronze tripod, was set atop the pedestal. It's the earliest-known monument using Corinthian capitals externally, a style that is imitated in many modern monuments. The reliefs depict the battle between Dionysos and the Tyrrhenian pirates, whom the god had transformed into dolphins.

Plateia Syntagmatos
SQUARE

(Syntagma Sq; Map p78; Ⓜ Syntagma) Generally considered the centre of Athens, this square is a transport hub and general hang-out spot, especially on warm summer evenings when young people and families lounge around the central fountain. Parliament, where the syntagma (constitution) was granted in 1843, is directly across the road, so the square is also the epicentre for any demonstrations or strikes.

★Parliament & Changing of the Guard
NOTABLE BUILDING

(Map p102; Plateia Syntagmatos; Ⓜ Syntagma) FREE In front of the parliament building on Plateia Syntagmatos, the traditionally costumed *evzones* (guards) of the Tomb of the Unknown Soldier change every hour on the hour. On Sunday at 11am, a whole platoon marches down Vasilissis Sofias to the tomb, accompanied by a band.

★National Gardens
GARDENS

(Map p102; cnr Leoforos Vasilissis Sofias & Leoforos Vasilissis Amalias, Syntagma; ⊙7am-dusk; Ⓜ Syntagma) FREE Formerly the royal gardens, designed by Queen Amalia in 1938, this park makes a delightful, shady refuge, especially when summer heat and traffic turn intense. Tucked among the trees is a cafe, a large playground and ponds for turtles and ducks, as well as a tiny, slightly dispiriting zoo.

Zappeio Gardens
GARDENS

(Map p64; Syntagma; Ⓜ Syntagma) FREE These gardens sit between the National Gardens and the Panathenaic Stadium (p92) and are laid out in a network of wide walkways around the grand Zappeio Palace. The palace was built in the 1870s and hosts conferences and exhibitions. A pleasant cafe, restaurant and the open-air Aigli Cinema (p116) are alongside the palace.

National Historical Museum
MUSEUM

(Map p78; ☑210 323 7617; www.nhmuseum. gr; Stadiou 13, Syntagma; adult/child €3/free, Sun free; ⊙8.30am-2.30pm Tue-Sun; Ⓜ Syntagma) Specialising in memorabilia from the War of Independence (1821–27), this museum houses Byron's helmet and sword, a series of paintings depicting events leading up to the war and a collection of photographs and royal portraits. The museum is housed in the old Parliament building, where Prime Minister Theodoros Deligiannis was assassinated on the front steps in 1905.

Church of Agii Theodori
CHURCH

(Map p108; cnr Dragatsaniou & Agion Theodoron, Syntagma; Ⓜ Panepistimio) FREE Even if it's locked, this church is worth a detour just to see it still existing, as it has since the 11th century, amid all the modern office buildings. If you get in, you'll see a tiled dome and walls decorated with a pretty terracotta frieze of animals and plants.

◉ Gazi, Keramikos & Thisio

★Benaki Museum Pireos Annexe
MUSEUM

(Map p84; ☑210 345 3111; www.benaki.gr; Pireos 138, cnr Andronikou, Rouf; €6-8; ⊙11am-9pm Tue-Sun, to 11pm Thu; Ⓜ Kerameikos) While the main

Gazi, Keramikos & Thisio

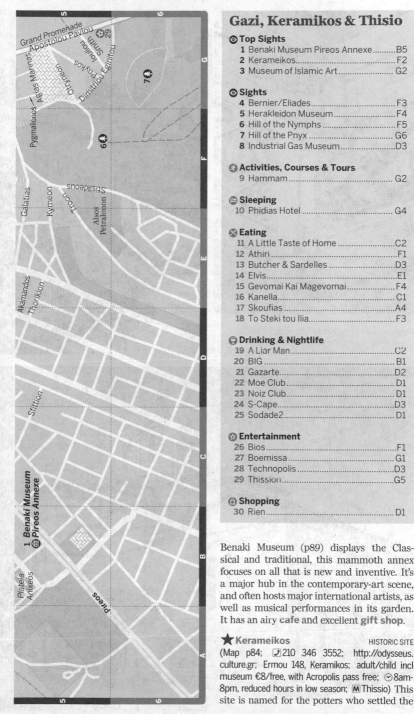

Gazi, Keramikos & Thisio

Benaki Museum (p89) displays the Classical and traditional, this mammoth annex focuses on all that is new and inventive. It's a major hub in the contemporary-art scene, and often hosts major international artists, as well as musical performances in its garden. It has an airy **cafe** and excellent **gift shop**.

★**Kerameikos**　　　HISTORIC SITE
(Map p84; ☎210 346 3552; http://odysseus.culture.gr; Ermou 148, Keramikos; adult/child incl museum €8/free, with Acropolis pass free; ⊗8am-8pm, reduced hours in low season; Ⓜ Thissio) This site is named for the potters who settled the

ADRIANA IACOB/SHUTTERSTOCK ©

1. Architectural details, Church of Eleftherios 2. Moni Kaisarianis
3. Church of the Holy Apostles 4. Mosaic, Moni Dafniou

Byzantine Athens

The city is dotted with churches that just happen to be a thousand years old, dating from the high point of the Byzantine Empire. Few churches open regularly, but the ones that do are gold-bedecked portals to the past. Don't miss the outstanding Byzantine & Christian Museum (p90), as well as the great icons at the Benaki Museum (p89).

Moni Dafniou

The area's most important Byzantine building is the World Heritage–listed 11th-century **Moni Dafniou** (☏210 581 1558; http://whc.unesco.org/en/list/537; Dafni; ☉9am-2pm Tue & Fri; 🚌811, 866 or A16 to Psychiatreion) FREE at Dafni, 10km northwest of Athens. Many of the church's elaborate mosaics, wrought by artisans from Constantinople, have been beautifully restored and more work is underway. The octagonal structure incorporates part of a wall from a 6th-century church.

Moni Kaisarianis

Nestled on the slopes of Mt Hymettos, 5km east of Athens, beautiful 11th-century **Moni Kaisarianis** (Monastery of Kaisariani; ☏210 723 6619; Mt Hymettos; adult/child €2/free; ☉8.30am-2.45pm, grounds to sunset, Tue-Sun) is a peaceful walled sanctuary. The domed *katholikon* (main church), supported by four columns from an ancient temple, has well-preserved frescoes from the 17th and 18th centuries.

Church of the Holy Apostles

One of the oldest churches in Athens is the late-10th-century Church of the Holy Apostles in the Ancient Agora (p77), a tribute to the place where St Paul once taught. It bears decorative details that are now seen as Islamic but were a product of artisans who worked across the eastern Mediterranean.

Church of Eleftherios (Little Metropolis)

Look closely at this 12th-century **church** (Plateia Mitropoleos, Monastiraki), and you'll see it's a historical collage of medieval stonework and ancient Pentelic marble. Its facade sports both medieval lions and Classical athletes, a portion of a delicate ancient marble frieze. It was even built on the ruins of an ancient temple.

area in around 3000 BC, then on the clay-rich banks of the Iridanos river. But its real finds come from its long later use as a cemetery, through the 6th century AD, under the Romans. Rediscovered in 1861 during the construction of Pireos St, the site is now lush and tranquil, with a small but excellent **museum** containing remarkable *stelae* (stone slabs) and sculptures, vases and terracotta figurines.

Once inside, head for the small knoll ahead to the right, where you'll find a **plan of the site**. A path leads down to the right from the knoll to the remains of the **city wall** built by Themistocles in 479 BC, and rebuilt by Konon in 394 BC. The wall is broken by the foundations of two gates; tiny signs mark each one.

The first, the **Sacred Gate**, spanned the Sacred Way and was the gate by which pilgrims from Eleusis entered the city during the annual Eleusian procession. To the northeast is the **Dipylon Gate** – the city's main entrance and where the Panathenaic Procession (p76) began. It was also where the city's prostitutes gathered to offer their services to travellers. From a platform outside the Dipylon Gate, Pericles gave his famous speech extolling the virtues of Athens and honouring those who died in the first year of the Peloponnesian Wars.

Between the Sacred and Dipylon Gates are the foundations of the **Pompeion**, used as a dressing room for participants in the Panathenaic Procession.

Leading off the Sacred Way to the left as you head away from the city is the **Street of Tombs**. This avenue was reserved for the tombs of Athens' most prominent citizens. The surviving *stelae* are now in the National Archaeological Museum, so what you see are mostly replicas. The astonishing array of funerary monuments and their bas-reliefs warrant close examination. Ordinary citizens were buried in the areas bordering the Street of Tombs. One well-preserved *stela* (up the stone steps on the northern side) shows a little girl with her pet dog. The site's largest *stela* is of sisters Demetria and Pamphile.

ATHENS WITH CHILDREN

Athens is short on playgrounds, but there's plenty to keep kids amused and children are welcome everywhere. The National Gardens (p83) has a playground, duck pond and small, somewhat dismal, zoo. There is also an enclosed, shaded playground in the Zappeio Gardens (p83). A tram ride south gets you to the much bigger facilities at Stavros Niarchos Park (p92) and **Flisvos Park** (Palaio Faliro; ▣; ▣ Parko Flisvou) FREE; the latter also has an outdoor cinema and an excellent shadow-puppet theatre (p118).

The **Museum of Greek Children's Art** (Map p78; ☑ 210 331 2621; www.childrens artmuseum.gr; Kodrou 9, Plaka; €3; ⊙ 9am-2pm Tue-Sat Sep-Jul; Ⓜ Syntagma) FREE has a room set aside where children can learn about Ancient Greece. The **Hellenic Children's Museum** (Map p102; ☑ 210 331 2995; www.hcm.gr; Vasileos Georgos II 17-19, Athens Conservatory; ⊙ 11am-7pm Wed, to 3pm Thu-Sun; Ⓜ Evangelismos) FREE was in the process of moving in 2017, and the new facility was developing exhibits.

Attica Zoological Park (☑ 210 663 4724; www.atticapark.gr; Yalou, Spata; adult/child €18/14; ⊙ 9am-sunset) has an expanding collection of big cats, birds, reptiles and other animals, including a monkey forest and 'Cheetahland'. It's near the airport.

Escape the heat and amuse the kids with a virtual-reality tour of Ancient Greece at the **Hellenic Cosmos** (Cultural Centre of the Foundation for the Hellenic World; ☑ 212 254 0000; www.hellenic-cosmos.gr; Pireos 254, Tavros; per show adult €5-10, child €3-8, day pass adult/child €15/12; ⊙ 10am-3pm Mon-Fri & Sun, earlier hours in winter, closed 2 weeks mid-Aug; Ⓜ Kallithea), or explore the universe at the impressive **Planetarium** (☑ 210 946 9600; www.eugenfound. edu.gr; Leoforos Syngrou 387, Palaio Faliro; adult €6-8, child €4-5; ⊙ 5.30-8.30pm Wed-Fri, 10.30am-8.30pm Sat & Sun late Aug–mid-Jul; ▣ 550 or B2 to Onassio, Ⓜ Sygrou-Fix). At the **War Museum** (Map p102; ☑ 210 725 2975; www.warmuseum.gr; Rizari 2, cnr Leoforos Vasilissis Sofias, Kolonaki; adult/child €4/2; ⊙ 9am-7pm Tue-Sun Jun-Aug, to 5pm Sep-May; Ⓜ Evangelismos), kids can climb into the cockpit of a WWII plane and other aircraft.

Head 6km west of Syntagma Sq for the enormous **Allou Fun Park & Kidom** (☑ 210 809 2888; www.allou.gr; cnr Leoforos Kifisou & Petrou Rali, Renti; passes from €12; ⊙ 5-10.30pm Mon-Fri, 10am-11.30pm Sat, to 11pm Sun; ▣ 21 or B19 to Kan Kan, 803 to Nekrotafeio, Ⓜ Egaleo), Athens' biggest amusement-park complex. Kidom is aimed at younger children.

Industrial Gas Museum NOTABLE BUILDING
(Technopolis; Map p84; ☑210 347 5535; www.
technopolis-athens.com; Pireos 100, Gazi; adult/
child €1/free; ☻10am-8pm Tue-Sun, to 6pm mid-
Oct–mid-Apr; ⓂKerameikos) A walking route
runs through the old gasworks in Gazi, a
complex of furnaces and industrial buildings
from the mid-19th century. The atmosphere
is cool, and so are the old photos and film
clips. There's a pleasant cafe, and the space
is often used for music and other events.

Herakleidon Museum MUSEUM
(Map p84; ☑210 346 1981; www.herakleidon-
art.gr; Iraklidon 16, Thisio; adult/child €6/free;
☻10am-2pm Sun for permanent exhibit; ⓂThis-
sio) This eclectic private museum examines
the interrelation of art, mathematics and
philosophy. The main building, a restored
mansion, holds a kid-oriented permanent
science exhibit. An annex, around the corner
at Apostolou Pavlou 37, is dedicated to eclectic rotating shows (with varied hours and
admission), on topics from shipbuilding to
printmaking. The museum also holds one of
the world's biggest collections of MC Escher
artworks (though it is not always on view).

⊚ Psyrri, Omonia & Exarhia

★**National
Archaeological Museum** MUSEUM
(Map p64; ☑213 214 4800; www.namuseum.
gr; 28 Oktovriou-Patision 44, Exarhia; adult/child
€10/free; ☻1-8pm Mon, 8am-8pm Tue-Sun Apr-Oct,
1-8pm Mon, 9am-4pm Tue-Sun Nov-Mar; ⓠ2, 3, 4, 5
or 11 to Polytechnio, ⓂViktoria) This is one of the
world's most important museums, housing
the world's finest collection of Greek antiquities. Treasures offering a view of Greek art
and history – dating from the Neolithic era
to Classical periods, including the Ptolemaic
era in Egypt – include exquisite sculptures,
pottery, jewellery, frescoes and artefacts found
throughout Greece. The beautifully presented
exhibits are displayed mainly thematically.
Allow plenty of time to view the vast and spectacular collections (more than 11,000 items)
housed in this enormous (8000-sq-metre)
19th-century neoclassical building.

A joint ticket with the Byzantine & Christian Museum (p90) and two others is €15.

★**Museum of Islamic Art** MUSEUM
(Map p84; ☑210 325 1311; www.benaki.gr;
Agion Asomaton 22 & Dipylou 12, Keramikos; adult/
student/child €9/7/free; ☻10am-6pm Thu-Sun;
ⓂThissio) This is one of the world's most

significant collections of Islamic art. Housed
in two restored neoclassical mansions near
Keramikos, it exhibits more than 8000
items representing the 12th to 19th centuries, including weavings, carvings, prayer
rugs, tiles and ceramics. On the 3rd floor is a
17th-century reception room with an inlaid
marble floor from a Cairo mansion. In the
basement, part of Athens' ancient Themis-
toklean wall is exposed.

⊚ Kolonaki & Around

★**Benaki Museum** MUSEUM
(Map p102; ☑210 367 1000; www.benaki.gr;
Koumbari 1, cnr Leoforos Vasilissis Sofias, Kolonaki;
adult/student/child €9/7/free, Thu free, pass to all
Benaki museums €20; ☻9am-5pm Wed & Fri, to
midnight Thu & Sat, to 3pm Sun; ⓂSyntagma, Evangelismos) Antonis Benakis, a politician's son
born in Alexandria, Egypt, in the late 19th
century, endowed what is perhaps the finest
museum in Greece. Its three floors showcase
impeccable treasures from the Bronze Age
up to WWII. Especially gorgeous are the
Byzantine icons and the extensive collection
of Greek regional costumes, as well as complete sitting rooms from Macedonian mansions, intricately carved and painted.

The variety of displays here, including
Classical Greek masterpieces, mean it's
great for a group with varied interests. Late
opening hours are another plus. Note also
(to avoid confusion) that there are two other
major branches: the Pireos Annexe (p83),
for contemporary art, and the Museum of
Islamic Art in Keramikos, as well as several
smaller museums; a €20 pass is valid for
three months.

★**Museum of Cycladic Art** MUSEUM
(Map p102; ☑210 722 8321; www.cycladic.gr;
Neofytou Douka 4, cnr Leoforos Vasilissis Sofias, Kolonaki; adult/child €7/free, Mon half-price, special exhibits €10; ☻10am-5pm Mon, Wed, Fri & Sat, to 8pm Thu,
11am-5pm Sun; ⓂEvangelismos) The 1st floor of
this exceptional private museum is dedicated
to the iconic minimalist marble Cycladic figurines, dating from 3000 BC to 2000 BC. They
inspired many 20th-century artists, such as
Picasso and Modigliani, with their simplicity and purity of form. Most are surprisingly
small, considering their outsize influence,
though one is almost human size. The rest of
the museum features Greek and Cypriot art
dating from 2000 BC to the 4th century AD.

Overall, there's an interesting focus on
how these objects were used, culminating in

the 4th-floor exhibit, *Scenes from Daily Life in Antiquity*, where objects are set in photo recreations of ancient scenes.

★ **Byzantine & Christian Museum**   MUSEUM
(Map p102; ☑ 213 213 9500; www.byzantine museum.gr; Leoforos Vasilissis Sofias 22, Kolonaki; adult/child €8/free; ⊙ 8am-8pm Apr-Oct, reduced hours Nov-Mar; Ⓜ Evangelismos) This outstanding museum – on the grounds of former Villa Ilissia, an urban oasis – presents a priceless collection of Christian art from the 3rd to 20th centuries. Thematic snapshots of the Byzantine and post-Byzantine world are exceptionally presented in expansive, well-lit, multilevel galleries, clearly arranged chronologically with English translations. The collection includes icons, frescoes, sculptures, textiles, manuscripts, vestments and mosaics.

Aristotle's Lyceum   RUINS
(Lykeion; Map p102; http://odysseus.culture.gr; cnr Rigillis & Leoforos Vasilissis Sofias; adult/child €4/free; ⊙ 8am-8pm Mon-Fri; Ⓜ Evangelismos) Unearthed when the site was cleared to build a museum of contemporary art, the Lyceum where Aristotle founded his school in 335 BC was excavated only in 2011. The Lyceum, which used to lie outside the city walls, was a *gymnasio* where Aristotle taught rhetoric and philosophy. It was also known as a Peripatetic School, because teacher and pupils would walk as they talked.

Lykavittos Hill   LANDMARK
(Map p64; Kolonaki; Ⓜ Evangelismos) The summit of Lykavittos – 'Hill of Wolves', from ancient times, when it was wilder than it is now – gives the finest panoramas of the city and the Attic basin, *nefos* (pollution haze) permitting. Perched on the summit is the little **Chapel of Agios Giorgios** (Map p102), floodlit like a beacon over the city at night. Walk up the path from the top of Loukianou in Kolonaki, or take the 10-minute funicular railway (p126), or *teleferik*, from the top of Ploutarhou.

National Sculpture & Art Gallery   MUSEUM
(National Glyptotheque; ☑ 210 723 5857; www. nationalgallery.gr; Army Park – Alsos Stratou, Goudi; adult/child €5/free; ⊙ 9am-8pm Mon & Wed-Fri, to 4pm Sat & Sun; Ⓜ Katehaki) While the more central building of the **National Gallery** (Map p64; ☑ 210 723 5937; Leoforos Vasileos Konstantinou 50, Kolonaki; Ⓜ Evangelismos) is being rebuilt, a portion of the collection has moved alongside the National Sculpture Gallery, in the former royal stables in Goudi. Although a

Museum Tour
National Archaeological Museum

LENGTH TWO HOURS

Straight ahead as you enter the museum is the ❶ **Prehistoric collection**, showcasing the fabulous collection of ❷ **Mycenaean antiquities** (gallery 4). The first cabinet holds the celebrated gold ❸ **Mask of Agamemnon**, unearthed at Mycenae, and bronze daggers with intricate representations of the hunt. The exquisite ❹ **Vaphio gold cups**, with scenes of men taming wild bulls, are regarded as among the finest surviving examples of Mycenaean art.

The ❺ **Cycladic collection** (gallery 6) includes superb figurines of the 3rd and 2nd millennia BC, which inspired modern artists such as Picasso.

The galleries to the left of the entrance house the oldest, most significant pieces of the sculpture collection. The colossal, Naxian marble ❻ **Sounion Kouros** (room 8), carved in 600 BC, stood before Poseidon's temple in Sounion. In artistic terms, it's a link between Ancient Egypt's rigid monumental statues and the Greeks' later life-size, naturalistic sculpture. Gallery 15 is dominated by the incredible 460 BC bronze ❼ **statue of Zeus or Poseidon**, found in the sea off Evia. It depicts one of the gods with his arms outstretched.

The 200 BC ❽ **statue of Athena Varvakeion** (gallery 20) is the most famous copy of the colossal statue of Athena Polias by Pheidias that stood in the Parthenon.

In gallery 21, the striking ❾ **statue of horse and young rider** (2nd century BC), recovered from a shipwreck off Cape Artemision in Evia, stands opposite exquisite works such as the ❿ **statue of Aphrodite**.

On the upper level, straight ahead from the stairs, are the spectacular ⓫ **Minoan frescoes** from Santorini (Thira). They were uncovered in the prehistoric settlement of Akrotiri, which was buried by a volcanic eruption in the late 16th century BC.

Also upstairs is a superb ⓬ **pottery collection**, from the Bronze Age through Attic red-figured pottery (late 5th to early 4th centuries BC). Among the treasures are six amphorae presented to the winners of the Panathenaic Games.

NATIONAL ARCHAEOLOGICAL MUSEUM

1st Floor

Pottery Collection

Cypriot Collection

Pottery Collection

12

Panathenaic Amphorae

Thira Gallery

Lift

Minoan Frescoes **11**

Ground Floor

Stathatos Collection

Egyptian Gallery

Lift

Temporary Exhibitions

Statue of Horse & Young Rider
9

10 **Statue of Aphrodite**

4 **Vaphio Gold Cups**

Statue of Zeus or Poseidon
7

8

Lift

Prehistoric Collection **1**

Statue of Athena Varvakeion

2 **Mycenaean Antiquities**

Mask of **3**
Agamemnon

5 **Cycladic Collection**

Sounion Kouros **6**

Entrance

Basement

Lift

Toilets

Cafe

Museum Shop

bit far from the centre, the museum is a nice break from the classics. The modern sculpture exhibit begins in the early 19th century, when figurative marble carving was taken up again. In the other building are the gallery's prize El Grecos, plus some compelling portraiture.

Pangrati & Mets

★ Panathenaic Stadium
HISTORIC SITE

(☑ 210 752 2984; www.panathenaicstadium.gr; Leoforos Vasileos Konstantinou, Pangrati; adult/student/child €5/2.50/free; ⊘ 8am-7pm Mar-Oct, to 5pm Nov-Feb; 🚋 2, 4, 11 to Stadio, Ⓜ Akropoli, 🚊 Zappeio) Originally built in the 4th century BC as a venue for the Panathenaic athletic contests, this stadium has had several lives. It's said that at Hadrian's inauguration in AD 120, a thousand wild animals were sacrificed in the arena. Later, the seats were rebuilt in Pentelic marble by Herodes Atticus. In 1895, after centuries of disuse, the stadium was restored by wealthy Greek benefactor Georgios Averof to host the first modern Olympic Games the following year.

This 19th-century rendition is a faithful replica of the original. It seats 70,000 spectators around the running track and field – which is not, unfortunately, modern Olympic-size, so the stadium could be used only for archery and the marathon finish in the 2004 games. Now it's occasionally used for concerts and public events. Morning joggers are welcome here from 7.30am to 9am.

Stavros Niarchos Park
PARK

(www.snfcc.org; Synggrou 364, Kallithea; ⊘ 6am-midnight Apr-Oct, to 8pm Nov-Mar; 🚋 550 to Onasseio, 10 to Epaminonda) FREE Athens is short on green spaces, so this vast park, opened in 2016, is a true breath of fresh air. A large central lawn hosts free dance and exercise classes (a fine way to learn some Greek!), while rambling paths cut through patches of lavender and rows of olive trees. A playground, interactive sound installations and rental bikes (€1 per hour) add to the fun.

Athens' First Cemetery
CEMETERY

(Map p64; Longinou, Mets; ⊘ 8am-5pm winter, 7am-8pm summer; Ⓜ Sygrou-Fix) FREE Under Ottoman rule, Greeks buried their dead at their local church. Only after independence in 1821 was this city cemetery established. It's a peaceful place to explore, with beautiful neoclassical sculptures, including *Sleeping Maiden* by Yannoulis Chalepas, the most admired Greek sculptor of the modern era. Famous people buried here include the Benaki family and the archaeologist Heinrich Schliemann (1822–90), whose mausoleum is decorated with scenes from the Trojan War.

🏃 Activities

For all the time its residents spend in cafes, Athens is a fairly active city and loves its sports. Visitors can also hit the streets with a number of good walking tours.

Beaches & Water Sports

Astir Beach
BEACH

(☑ 210 890 1621; www.astir-beach.com; Apollonus 40, Vouliagmeni; adult/child Mon-Fri €18/10, Sat & Sun mid-Jun–mid-Sep €28/15, reduced prices rest of year; ⊘ beach 8am-9pm, restaurants to midnight; 🚊 114 from Glyfada or Voula tram stops) Astir is the most exclusive summer beach playground (giveaway: there's a helipad, for the most elite Athenian commuters). It has all the water sports, shops and restaurants you could want (plus, oddly, a TGI Fridays). It's 19.5km south of Athens, 7.5km south of Glyfada. If it all gets too flashy for you, there's a nice public beach across the road.

Limanakia
BEACH

(🚊 117, 122) The rocky coves below the bus stop at Limanakia B (near Varkiza on the Apollo Coast) are a popular nudist hang-out with a slight gay slant. Take the tram or A2/E2 express bus to Glyfada, then bus 117 or 122 to the Limnakia B stop.

Yabanaki
BEACH

(☑ 210 897 2414; www.yabanaki.gr; Varkiza; adult/child Mon-Fri €5/3.50, Sat & Sun €6/3.50; ⊘ 8am-7pm Jun-Aug, 9am-5pm May; 🚊 122) Slightly less flashy than the beach clubs near Glyfada, Yabanaki (21km south of Syntagma) nonetheless has a full complement of entertainment options, from a restaurant to beach volleyball. Great if you're travelling with kids.

Limni Vouliagmenis
SWIMMING

(☑ 210 896 2239; www.limnivouliagmenis.gr; Leoforos Vouliagmenis; adult/child Mon-Fri €12/5.50, Sat & Sun €13/6; ⊘ 7.30am-8pm; ♿; 🚊 114, 115 or 149, 🚊 A2 or E2) This lightly salty lake, at the base of a huge cliff, is connected to the sea underground and fed by mineral-rich warm springs, so its temperature never falls below 21°C. This makes it a friendly habitat for fish that nibble the dead skin from your feet – an exfoliating treat for some, or a nightmare for the ticklish.

The loyal clientele of bathing-cap-clad elderly citizens tout the water's healing properties. There's a modern spa-cuisine cafe (lunch from €12) at the edge, where you can eat without paying the lake admission, plus sunbeds, a playground and showers. Take the A2 bus (E2 express in summer) to Plateia Glyfada, then take bus 114, 115 or 149.

Planet Blue Dive Centre   DIVING
(☑ 210 418 0174; www.planetblue.gr; Velpex Factory, Lavrio; PADI certification from €300, dives €35-80) Popular with seasoned divers, but caters to all levels at sites around Cape Sounion.

Hellenic Windsurfing Association   WINDSURFING
(www.speedslalom.gr) No offices in Athens, but can be reached via windsurfing spots around Athens, such as Loutsa.

Bathhouses

Al Hammam Baths   BATHHOUSE
(Map p78; ☑ 211 012 9099; www.alhammam. gr; Tripodon 16 & Ragava 10, Plaka; 45min bath €25, bath-scrub combos from €35; ☺ 11am-9pm; ⓜ Acropolis) Like the other two Turkish-style baths in Athens, this one is a bit small, but it is beautifully decorated, in marble and tile and coloured chandeliers, to conjure an old-Ottoman atmosphere. Moreover, it's set in a nice old house in Plaka, so after your steam and skin scrub, you can have tea on the terrace and admire the Acropolis.

Polis Hammam   BATHHOUSE
(Map p78; ☑ 210 321 2020; www.polis-hammam. gr; Avliton 6, Psyrri; 1½hr bath €20, bath-scrub combos from €27; ☺ noon-11pm Mon-Fri, from 11am Sat & Sun; ⓜ Thissio) The best value of Athens' three Turkish-style baths. There's also space for other treatments, such as Thai massage and cupping. The only complaint is the mood music. Look for it down a tiny alley, sharing with a theatre.

Hammam   SPA
(Map p84; ☑ 210 323 1073; www.hammam.gr; Melidoni 1, cnr Agion Asomaton, Thisio; 1hr €25, bath-scrub combos from €45; ☺ 12.30-10pm Mon-Fri, 10am-10pm Sat & Sun; ⓜ Thissio) The marble-lined Turkish-style steam room here is small; the real attraction is the added scrubs and massages. Tuesday is women only.

Cycling & Skating

Cycle Greece   CYCLING
(☑ 210 921 8160; www.cyclegreece.com; Aristotelous 13, Moschato) This excellent company, run by a husband–wife team, offers a great

BASKETBALL

'Basket' is one of Athens' most popular sports, with a number of men's and women's pro teams in Athens (Panathinaikos and AEK are the biggest) and Piraeus (Olympiacos). For schedules, see the website of the **Hellenic Basketball Federation** (EOK; www. basket.gr). Games are often at the 18,000-seat stadium at the **Athens Olympic Complex** (OAKA; ☑ 210 683 4777; www.oaka.com.gr; Marousi; ⓜ Irini).

range of trips, from day rides outside Athens, including a tour of Attica wineries, to multiday tours that combine biking and sailing. Very well-planned self-guided itineraries too.

Funky Rides   CYCLING
(Map p74; ☑ 211 710 9366; www.funkyride.gr; Dimitrakopoulou 1, Koukaki; 3hr/day €7/15; ⓜ Akropoli) Rents bikes near the Acropolis.

Solebike   CYCLING
(Map p74; ☑ 210 921 5620; www.solebike.eu; Lembesi 11, Makrygianni; 2hr from €12; ☺ 9am-5pm Mon-Sat Apr-Nov, 10am-4pm Mon-Sat Sep-Mar; ⓜ Akropoli) Hires out electric bikes, and offers tours (from €39).

Latraac   SKATING
(Map p64; www.facebook.com/latraac; Leonidou 63-65, Keramikos; ☺ skating noon-3pm & 5.30-10.30pm, cafe to 1am) **FREE** If you ever thought the problem with skateboarding was that there was nowhere to drink a coffee while you did it, the Greeks have solved this for you. A wooden skate bowl occupies one half of a city lot; picnic benches take up the other. The crowd skews adult and arty, but kids are welcome. Food is good too.

Outdoor Adventure

Alpin Club   ADVENTURE
(☑ 210 675 3514; www.alpinclub.gr) For kayaking, rafting, canyoning and mountain biking – just to name a few. In Athens but operates out of Karitena in the Peloponnese.

Trekking Hellas   OUTDOORS
(☑ 210 331 0323; www.trekking.gr; Gounari 96, Marousi) Array of activities tours ranging from Athens walking tours (€50) to caving, cycling, or trekking in the Peloponnese and the islands.

EOS
HIKING

(Greek Alpine Club; Map p78; ☑210 321 3255; www.eosathinon.gr; Lekka 23-25) The EOS runs weekly hiking trips outside the city (information only in Greek) and maintains trails on Mt Hymettos and around Attica. It's not really geared to tourists, but it is the place to ask for advice on longer trips and lesser-known trails.

Hellenic Skiing Federation
SKIING

(☑210 323 0182; www.eox.gr) Information about skiing in Greece.

✆ Tours

Three main companies run almost identical air-conditioned city coach tours, as well as excursions to nearby sights: **CHAT** (Map p78; ☑210 323 0827; www.chatours.gr; Xenofontos 9, Syntagma; 5hr tour €68; Ⓜ Syntagma), **GO Tours** (Map p74; ☑210 921 9555; www.gotours.com.gr; Kallirrois 12, Makrygianni; Ⓜ Akropoli) and **Hop In Sightseeing** (Map p78; ☑210 428 5500; www.hopin.com; Leoforos Vasilissis Amalias 44, Makrygianni; ☺6.30am-10pm; Ⓜ Akropoli).

Tours include a half-day sightseeing tour of Athens (from €78), usually doing little more than pointing out all the major sights and stopping at the Acropolis. There are also half-day trips to Ancient Corinth (€62) and Cape Sounion (€49); day tours to Delphi (€93), the Corinth Canal, Mycenae, Nafplio and Epidavros (€100); and **cruises** to Aegina, Poros and Hydra (including lunch €109). Hotels act as booking agents and often offer discounts.

CitySightseeing Athens
BUS

(Map p78; ☑210 921 4174; www.city-sightseeing.com; Plateia Syntagmatos, Syntagma; adult/child €20/8; ☺every 30min 9am-9pm Apr-Oct, to 6.30pm Nov-Mar; Ⓜ Syntagma) Open-top double-decker buses cruise around town on a 90-minute circuit starting at Syntagma. With the basic ticket, you can get on and off at 15 stops in 24 hours; add on Piraeus and/or the beaches, and extend duration to 48 or 72 hours.

Athens Walking Tours
TOURS

(☑210 884 7269; www.athenswalkingtours.gr; Heyden 2, Viktoria; Ⓜ Viktoria) Runs a full range of guided tours around and outside the city, but especially notable for its cooking class (€77) in a Thisio taverna, which cuts no corners and even shows you how to roll out your own filo for *spanakopita* (spinach pie) and other pies.

🏃 Walking Tour
Central Athens

START PLATEIA SYNTAGMATOS
END MONASTIRAKI FLEA MARKET
LENGTH 3.5KM; TWO HOURS

Start in ❶ **Plateia Syntagmatos** (p83). The square has been a favourite place for protests ever since the rally that led to the granting of a constitution on 3 September 1843. In 1944 the first round of the civil war began here after police, under British direction, opened fire on a communist rally. In 1954 it was the location of the first demonstration demanding the *enosis* (union) of Cyprus with Greece.

The historic Hotel Grande Bretagne, the most illustrious of Athens' hotels, was built in 1862. During WWII, the Nazis made it their headquarters, and the British moved in after. Resistance fighters laid dynamite to blow up the building, but the operation was halted when Winston Churchill arrived unexpectedly; the fighters weren't willing to assassinate him.

On the north side of the square is a section of the ❷ **Peisistratos aqueduct**, unearthed during metro excavations.

Across the road, in front of ❸ **Parliament**, the much-photographed *evzones* (presidential guards) stand sentinel at the Tomb of the Unknown Soldier. The changing of the guard takes place every hour.

Walk through the lush ❹ **National Gardens** (p83) and exit to the Zappeio Palace, opened in 1888 in preparation for the first modern Olympic games in 1896, for which part was used as a fencing hall. Follow the road south, passing the playground. Turn left and walk until you see the crossing to the ❺ **Panathenaic Stadium** (p92), the main site of the 1896 Olympic Games.

Walk back along the south edge of the gardens to the striking ❻ **Temple of Olympian Zeus** (p75), the largest temple ever built. Teetering on the edge of the traffic alongside the temple is ❼ **Hadrian's Arch** (p76), the ornate gateway erected to mark the boundary of Hadrian's Athens.

Cross Leoforos Vasilissis Amalias and head right towards Lysikratous, where you turn left into Plaka. Ahead on your right are the ruins of a Roman monument in the forecourt of the ❽ **Church of Agia Ekaterini**.

Ahead on the left is the **⑨Lysikrates Monument** (p83), built in 334 BC, the only remaining example of monuments that lined this street to the Theatre of Dionysos, site of dramatic contests. The monument commemorates one chorus's victory, with reliefs showing Dionysos battling the Tyrrhenian pirates, transformed into dolphins. It's the earliest-known monument using Corinthian capitals externally, a style imitated in many modern monuments.

Facing the monument, turn left and then right into Epimenidou. At the top of the steps, turn right into Stratonos, which skirts the Acropolis. Just ahead you'll see the **⑩Church of St George of the Rock**, which marks the entry to the **⑪Anafiotika quarter**. The picturesque maze of little white-washed houses is the legacy of stonemasons from the small Cycladic island of Anafi, who were brought in to build the king's palace after Independence. It's a peaceful spot, with brightly painted olive-oil cans brimming with flowers in the tiny gardens in summer.

Continue past the tiny **⑫Church of Agios Simeon**. The street looks like a dead end but persevere and you'll emerge at the Acropolis road. Turn right, then left into Prytaniou, veering right after 50m into Tholou. The yellow-ochre building at Tholou 5 is the **⑬old Athens University**, from 1837–41. Built by the Venetians, it was used by the Turks as public offices; it's now a history museum.

Continue down to the ruins of the **⑭Roman Agora** (p77). To the right of the Tower of the Winds on Kyrristou is the **⑮Bath House of the Winds** (p81), a historic (but nonfunctional) Turkish *hammam*. Meanwhile, the **⑯Museum of Greek Popular Instruments** (p80), on Diogenous, is filled with more than a thousand ways to make music. Turning on to Pelopida, you'll see on the right the gate of the 1721 Muslim Seminary, the only remains after the complex was destroyed in a fire in 1911. Ahead on the left, the 17th-century **⑰Fethiye Mosque** is on the site of the Agora.

Follow the road around the Agora to the ruins of **⑱Hadrian's Library** (p80). Next to them is the 1759 **⑲Mosque of Tzistarakis**, only very occasionally open as a ceramics museum; after Independence it lost its minaret and was used as a prison.

You're now in Monastiraki, the colourful, chaotic square teeming with street vendors. To the left is **⑳Monastiraki Flea Market** (p122).

Alternative Athens TOURS

(Map p78; ☑6951518589; www.alternative
athens.com; Karaiskaki 28) As the name promises, this company offers tours with less-
typical slants. There's a very good three-hour
street-art tour (€40), and another visiting
Athenian designers (€50), as well as an
LGBTQ bar crawl, food tours and even day
trips out of the city.

This Is My Athens TOURS

(http://myathens.thisisathens.org) **FREE** Excellent city-run program that pairs you with
a volunteer local to show you around for
two hours. You must book online 72 hours
ahead.

Athens Adventures TOURS

(Map p74; ☑210 922 4044; www.athensadvent
ures.gr; Veikou 3a, Makrygianni; walking tour €7;
⊙walking tour 10am Mon & Wed-Sat) Run by
the team at Athens Backpackers, this group
offers a very popular Athens walking tour,
departing from **Athens Sports Bar** (Map
p74; www.athenssportsbar.com; Veikou 3a,
Makrygianni; ⊙7.30am-late; Ⓜ Akropoli). In high
season, it also runs day trips to Nafplio, Delphi and Sounio.

Athens Happy Train TOURS

(Map p78; ☑213 039 0888; www.athenshappy
train.com; Plateia Syntagmatos, Syntagma; adult/
child €6/4; ⊙every 30min 9am-11pm Jun-Sep, to
9pm Oct-May; Ⓜ Syntagma) This little red train-
on-wheels is a bit goofy, but at least it's more
city-friendly than a massive double-decker
tour bus. Stops include the Acropolis,
Monastiraki and the Panathenaic Stadium.
Tours take one hour nonstop, or you can get
on and off over five hours. Trains leave from
the top of Ermou every 30 minutes.

Athens Segway Tours TOURS

(Map p74; ☑210 322 2500; www.athenssegway
tours.com; Eschinou 9, Plaka; 2hr tour €59; Ⓜ Akropoli) Zip through town on a Segway.

⭐ Festivals & Events

Athens & Epidaurus Festival PERFORMING ARTS

(Hellenic Festival; ☑210 928 2900; www.greekfesti
val.gr; ⊙Jun-Aug) The ancient Theatre of
Epidavros (p153) and Athens' Odeon of
Herodes Atticus (p73) are the headline
venues for Greece's annual cultural festival
featuring a top line-up of local and international music, dance and theatre.

Major shows in its **Athens Festival** take
place at the Odeon of Herodes Atticus (p73),
one of the world's prime historic venues,

with the Acropolis as a backdrop. Events are
also held in modern venues around town.

Its **Epidavros Festival** presents local and
international productions of Ancient Greek
drama at the famous ancient Theatre of Epidavros in the Peloponnese, two hours west
of Athens, on Friday and Saturday nights in
July and August. Check the festival website
for special KTEL buses (p123) to Epidavros.

As box-office queues can be long and events
often sell out, it's best to book tickets online,
by phone, at the **box office** (Map p108; ☑210
327 2000; Stoa Pesmatzoglou, Panepistimiou 39,
Panepistimio; ⊙10am-4pm Mon-Fri, to 3pm Sat;
Ⓜ Panepistimio), or at Public and Papasotiriou
stores. Half-price student discounts (with ID)
are available for most performances.

August Moon Festival PERFORMING ARTS

(⊙Aug) Every August on the night of the
full moon, major historic sites such as the
Acropolis and the Roman Agora are open all
night and host musical performances.

Athens International Film Festival FILM

(☑210 606 1413; www.aiff.gr; ⊙Sep) Features
retrospectives, premieres and international
art films and documentaries.

Rockwave Festival MUSIC

(☑210 882 0426; www.rockwavefestival.gr; ⊙late
May-Jul) Annual international rock show
held at Terra Vibe, a parkland venue on the
outskirts of Athens in Malakasa. Special
buses from town. Sometimes cheap camping is offered.

Athens Pride PARADE

(www.athenspride.eu; ⊙early Jun) Athens
Pride is an annual LGBTQ event, usually
celebrated in early June, culminating in a
parade that starts on Syntagma.

Athens Technopolis Jazz Festival MUSIC

(www.technopolisjazzfestival.com; ⊙late May-
early Jun) Annual early-summer jazz festival
at Technopolis (p119), the converted gasworks in Gazi, as well as at the Onassis Cultural Centre (p76).

🛏 Sleeping

Athens lodging covers the full range, from
hostels to five stars, but can be a bit basic for
the price, especially in the midrange. Nonsmoking rules are often laxly enforced. For
the best selection in July and August, book
several months ahead.

Boutique Athens (☑6985083556; www.
boutiqueathens.com; 1-/2-/4-bedroom apt from

IMMIGRANT ATHENS

Starting in the early 1990s, Greece saw an influx of immigrants, at least 600,000 people in a decade, most of whom came to Athens: migrant agricultural labourers from Punjab, domestic help from the Philippines, Albanians fleeing the postcommunist collapse, asylum seekers from all over. And since 2015, the city has been actively working to absorb another estimated 100,000 refugees from Syria, Afghanistan, Congo and other countries, from the sudden influx of people on boats from Turkey.

City government has embraced the change, stating that immigration is not a problem but an opportunity for growth. And indeed, it has reinvigorated previously tired neighbourhoods and brought new businesses – and foods. In the centre, **Psyrri**, just south of Omonia, has a few blocks of Pakistani and Bangladeshi businesses, established in the 1990s.

Newer arrivals have enlivened the squat scene in **Exarhia – Steki Metanaston** (Map p64; www.facebook.com/stekimetanaston; Tsamadou 13a, Exarhia; ☺late morning–midnight; Ⓜ Polytehnion) is a great social centre – as well as the **Viktoria** neighbourhood, where **Victoria Square Project** (www.facebook.com/victoriasquareproject; Elpidos 13, Viktoria; ☺9am-4pm Mon-Sat; Ⓜ Victoria) FREE is a good place to start exploring. Also don't miss **Enjoy Just Falafel** (p106) nearby. Further north, the blocks around **Plateia Amerikis** have attracted immigrants from West Africa and Eritrea.

€80/140/430; ✴ ⑧) rents renovated spacious apartments and whole houses all over town.

Akropoli, Makrygianni & Koukaki

★Athens Backpackers HOSTEL €
(Map p74; ☎ 210 922 4044; www.backpackers. gr; Makri 12, Makrygianni; dm incl breakfast €27-30; ✴ @ ⑧; Ⓜ Akropoli) The popular rooftop bar with cheap drinks and Acropolis views is a major draw at this modern and friendly Australian-run backpacker favourite. There's a barbecue in the courtyard, a well-stocked kitchen and a busy social scene. Spotless dorms with private bathrooms and lockers have bedding, but towel use costs €2. Management also runs well-priced Athens Studios (p98), with modern apartments nearby.

Marble House Pension PENSION €
(☎ 210 923 4058; www.marblehouse.gr; Zini 35a, Koukaki; d/tr €49/59, d/tr/q with shared bathroom €45/50/69; ✴ @ ⑧; Ⓜ Sygrou-Fix) In a quiet cul-de-sac is one of Athens' best-value budget hotels. Rooms have been artfully updated, with wrought-iron beds, and bathrooms are sleek marble. All rooms have fridge and ceiling fan and some have air-con (€9 extra). It's a fair walk from the tourist drag, but close to the metro. Breakfast available (€5).

Art Gallery Hotel PENSION €
(Map p74; ☎ 210 923 1933; www.artgallery hotel.gr; Erehthiou 5, Koukaki; s/d/tr/q from €70/75/100/120; ✴ ⑧; Ⓜ Sygrou-Fix) This family-run place is an ideal combo: close to

tourist zones, but set on a pretty residential block, so you feel you're in a home, inside and out. Some rooms are a bit small and can show their age, but the upstairs balcony is a fine breakfast spot. The cheapest rooms have bathrooms across the hall (private, though, not shared).

★Hera Hotel BOUTIQUE HOTEL €€
(Map p74; ☎ 210 923 6682; www.herahotel.gr; Falirou 9, Makrygianni; d incl breakfast €160-190, ste €250; ✴ @ ⑧; Ⓜ Akropoli) Behind its elegant neoclassical facade, this boutique hotel was totally rebuilt. But the formal interior design stays true to exterior style, with lots of brass and dark wood. It's a short walk to the Acropolis and Plaka, and the rooftop Peacock restaurant and bar have fine views and good service. North-side rooms, away from an adjacent music bar, are preferable.

★Herodion HOTEL €€
(Map p74; ☎ 210 923 6832; www.herodion.gr; Rovertou Galli 4, Makrygianni; d incl breakfast from €165; ✴ @ ⑧; Ⓜ Akropoli) This smart four-star hotel is geared towards the well-heeled traveller and business travellers. Rooms are small but decked out with all the trimmings and have supercomfortable beds. The rooftop spa and lounge have unbeatable Acropolis and museum views.

Philippos Hotel HOTEL €€
(Map p74; ☎ 210 922 3611; www.philipposhotel. com; Mitseon 3, Makrygianni; d incl breakfast from €145; ✴ @ ⑧; Ⓜ Akropoli) A popular favourite, under the same ownership as the larger

Herodion nearby, Philippos offers small, well-appointed rooms near the Acropolis. The double on the roof has a private terrace.

Athens Studios
APARTMENT €€

(Map p74; ☑210 923 5811; www.athensstudios. gr; Veïkou 3a, Makrygianni; apt incl breakfast €105; @ 🛜; Ⓜ Akropoli) Run by the folk from Athens Backpackers (p97), these relaxed apartments are spacious, with kitchenettes, colourful bathrooms and a lounge area with shared balcony (top-floor balconies are largest). The bedroom has either two beds or four bunks, making it a well-priced alternative to dormitory living. Another perk: a laundry on the ground floor.

Athens Was
BOUTIQUE HOTEL €€€

(Map p74; ☑210 924 9954; www.athenswas. gr; Dionysiou Areopagitou 31-39, Makrygianni; d €198-365, ste from €350; ✳ @ 🛜; Ⓜ Akropoli) The location, a three-minute walk to the Acropolis gate, couldn't be better. Staff is friendly, adding a warm touch to the minimalist decor, and standard rooms have big balconies overlooking the pedestrian street. Korres amenities are another plus. Breakfast is excellent and the terrace has a magnificent view. Suites on the 5th and 6th floors also have Acropolis views.

Athens Gate
BUSINESS HOTEL €€€

(Map p74; ☑210 923 8302; www.athensgate. gr; Leoforos Syngrou Andrea 10, Makrygianni; d incl breakfast €205-280; ✳ @ 🛜; Ⓜ Akropoli) With stunning views over the Temple of Olympian Zeus from the spacious front rooms, and a central (if busy) location, this old reliable hotel was improved with a 2007 renovation. The chic, stylish rooms are immaculate and have all the mod cons; staff are friendly and breakfast is served on the superb rooftop terrace with 360-degree Athens views.

🛏 Syntagma, Plaka & Monastiraki

Phaedra
HOTEL €

(Map p78; ☑210 323 8461; www.hotelphaedra. com; Herefontos 16, Plaka; s/d/tr from €60/80/90; ✳ @ 🛜; Ⓜ Akropoli) All the rooms at this small, family-run hotel have balconies overlooking a church or the Acropolis. The rooms are basic and range from small to snug; a few have private bathrooms across the hall.

Morning trash collection on the corner can be a bit noisy, but given the rooftop terrace, the friendly staff and the unbeatable location, it's still one of the better deals in Plaka.

Cecil
HOTEL €

(Map p108; ☑210 321 7079; www.cecilhotel.gr; Athinas 39, Monastiraki; s/d/tr/q incl breakfast from €60/75/120/155; ✳ @ 🛜; Ⓜ Monastiraki) This charming old hotel on busy Athinas has beautiful high, moulded ceilings, polished timber floors and an original cage-style lift. The simple rooms are tastefully furnished, but don't have fridges. Two connecting rooms with a shared bathroom are ideal for families.

Tony
APARTMENT €

(Map p64; ☑210 923 0561; www.hoteltony.gr; Zaharitsa 26, Koukaki; studios €65-130; ✳ @ 🛜; Ⓜ Sygrou-Fix) After a total renovation in 2015, Hotel Tony offers spacious, clean and modern studios, all with kitchenette. Great for groups as, for instance, the 'superior family room' has three balconies. Bathrooms boast walk-in showers and sleek tiles all around. It's about 1km southwest of the Acropolis. The only small shame is the treeless block, but Filopappou is just uphill.

Tempi Hotel
HOTEL €

(Map p78; ☑210 321 3175; www.tempihotel. gr; Eolou 29, Monastiraki; d/tr €59/72, s/d with shared bathroom €39/52; ✳ 🛜; Ⓜ Monastiraki) Location and affordability are the strengths of this older, family-run place on pedestrian Eolou. Front balconies overlook Plateia Agia Irini, the scene of some of Athens' best nightlife; side views get the Acropolis. Basic rooms have satellite TV, but bathrooms are primitive. Top-floor rooms are small and quite a hike. There is a communal kitchen.

InnAthens
BOUTIQUE HOTEL €€

(Map p78; ☑210 325 8555; www.innathens.com; Souri 3, Syntagma; d incl breakfast €165; ✳ @ 🛜; Ⓜ Syntagma) This 22-room hotel is minutes from Syntagma, but you'd never know it once you're inside this cocoon, down the end of a shopping arcade. All rooms look down on to a pretty interior courtyard, and the restfulness is reinforced with soothing grey-and-white decor and excellent Coco-Mat beds.

Sweet Home Hotel
BOUTIQUE HOTEL €€

(Map p78; ☑210 322 9029; www.sweethome hotel.com; Patroou 5, Plaka; s/d incl breakfast from €140/150; ✳ @ 🛜; Ⓜ Syntagma) Just a stone's throw from all the major Athens sights, this 15-room place in a converted old mansion has cosy, well-appointed rooms that are a good mix of old (wood floors, chandeliers) and new (sleek, if tiny, bathrooms). The attic room has a nice wood ceiling, and an Acropolis view if you stretch.

Central Hotel   BUSINESS HOTEL €€
(Map p78; ☑210 323 4357; www.centralhotel.
gr; Apollonos 21, Plaka; d/tr incl breakfast from
€135/160; ❄@❂; Ⓜ Syntagma) This low-key
stylish hotel has comfortable rooms done
in light, contemporary tones, with good
bathrooms. The roof terrace has the requisite Acropolis view (as do some rooms),
plus a small spa and sunloungers. As its
name suggests, Central Hotel is in a great
location between Syntagma and Plaka. The
cheapest rooms (from €111) look on to an
air shaft.

Adonis   HOTEL €€
(Map p78; ☑210 324 9737; www.hotel-adonis.
gr; 3 Kodrou St, Plaka; s/d/tr incl breakfast
€75/95/105; ❄@❂; Ⓜ Syntagma) This comfortable pension on a quiet pedestrian street
in Plaka has basic, clean rooms with TV.
Bathrooms are small but have been excel-
lently renovated. Take in great Acropolis
views from 4th-floor rooms and the rooftop terrace (where breakfast is served). No
credit cards.

Hermes   HOTEL €€
(Map p78; ☑210 323 5514; www.hermeshotel.
gr; Apollonos 19, Plaka; s/d/q incl breakfast
€104/150/251; ❄@❂; Ⓜ Syntagma) Hermes
offers modern amenities with snug but comfortable rooms, including two interconnect-
ing rooms for families. No real Acropolis
views, but sister hotel Plaka has them, and
guests are welcome to visit the rooftop bar
there.

Plaka Hotel   HOTEL €€
(Map p78; ☑210 322 2096; www.plakahotel.
gr; Kapnikareas 7, cnr Mitropoleos, Monastiraki; d
incl breakfast from €181; ❄❂; Ⓜ Monastiraki)
It's hard to beat the Acropolis views from
the rooftop garden, as well as those from
top-floor rooms. Tidy rooms have light timber floors and furniture, and satellite TV,
though bathrooms are on the small side.
Though called the Plaka, it's actually closer
to Monastiraki.

Adrian Hotel   HOTEL €€
(Map p78; ☑210 322 1553; www.douros-hotels.
com; Adrianou 74, Plaka; s/d/tr incl breakfast from
€120/145/160; ❄@❂; Ⓜ Monastiraki) This
tiny hotel right in the heart of Plaka serves
breakfast on a lovely shady terrace with
Acropolis views. The well-equipped rooms
are pleasant, if a bit worn. Third-floor rooms
are the best, with large balconies overlooking the square.

Acropolis House Pension   PENSION €€
(Map p78; ☑210 322 2344; www.acropolis
house.gr; Kodrou 6-8, Plaka; d/tr/q incl breakfast
from €89/119/149; ❄❂; Ⓜ Syntagma) This
family-run pension is in a beautifully preserved, 19th-century house, which retains
many original features and has lovely
painted walls. There are discounts for stays
of three days or more. The cheapest rooms
(from €83) have private bathrooms across
the hall. Avoid the street level, due to noise.

★Grande Bretagne   LUXURY HOTEL €€€
(Map p78; ☑210 333 0000; www.grande
bretagne.gr; Vasileos Georgiou I 1, Syntagma; r/
ste from €400/700; Ⓟ❄@❂❂; Ⓜ Syntagma)
If you aspire to the best, *the* place to stay
in Athens is – and always has been – the
Grande Bretagne, right on Syntagma Sq.
Built in 1862 to accommodate visiting heads
of state, it ranks among the grandest hotels
in the world. Though renovated some years
ago, it still retains its old-world grandeur.

There is a divine **spa**, and the rooftop
restaurant and **bar** are worth a visit, even
if you aren't a guest.

★Electra Palace   LUXURY HOTEL €€€
(Map p78; ☑210 337 0000; www.electrahotels.
gr; Navarhou Nikodimou 18, Plaka; d/ste incl breakfast from €270/375; Ⓟ❄@❂❂; Ⓜ Syntagma)
Plaka's smartest hotel is one for the roman-
tics – have breakfast under the Acropolis
on your balcony (in higher-end rooms) and
dinner in the chic rooftop restaurant. Completely refurbished with classic elegance,
the well-appointed rooms are buffered from
the sounds of the city streets. There's a gym
and an indoor swimming pool, as well as a
rooftop pool with Acropolis views.

★NEW Hotel   DESIGN HOTEL €€€
(Map p78; ☑210 327 3000; www.yeshotels.
gr; Filellinon 16, Plaka; d from €218; Ⓟ❄@❂;
Ⓜ Syntagma) Brazilian designers, the Cam-
pana designers, melded their signature
scraps-to-art style with Greek-folk touches
and old Athens photos, creating a space
that's full of fun eye candy. More practically,
the rooms are cushy (lots of pillow options)
and there's a good roof lounge. Location is
prime but loud; upper floors are better.

A for Athens   HOTEL €€€
(Map p78; ☑210 324 4244; www.aforathens.
com; Miaouli 2, Monastiraki; d from €213; ❄❂;
Ⓜ Monastiraki) Modern and simple, A for
Athens is a good, central base – and its loca-
tion just across from the Monastiraki metro

makes it a straight shot from the airport. The rooftop **cafe-bar** is grand, with sweeping 360-degree views that take in the Acropolis (as do some of the rooms). But it can get a bit rowdy on weekends.

360 Degrees
HOTEL €€€

(Map p78; ☑210 324 0034; www.360hotel athens.com; Plateia Monastirakiou, Monastiraki; d incl breakfast €190; ✳☎; Ⓜ Monastiraki) The raison d'etre of this hotel is in its name: the super roof restaurant gives a view around the whole city. The rooms are basic, with a light sprinkling of hipster-rustic wood and Edison light bulbs. The location on Monastiraki Sq is handy (especially for the metro from the airport), but potentially noisy. Request an upper floor, away from the square.

🛏 Thisio

Phidias Hotel
HOTEL €€

(Map p84; ☑210 345 9511; www.phidias.gr; Apostolou Pavlou 39, Thisio; s/d/tr incl breakfast from €170/180/190; ✳☎; Ⓜ Thissio) Midway along Thisio's grand pedestrianised promenade, this hotel is in a lovely location. A 2016 makeover to the rooms boosted prices substantially, but you can still find substantially better deals online. The cheapest rooms (single/double €105/115) have only windows on an air shaft – not as grim as it sounds, and cool in summer.

🛏 Psyrri, Omonia & Exarhia

★ City Circus
HOSTEL €

(Map p108; ☑213 023 7244; www.citycircus.gr; Sarri 16, Psyrri; dm incl breakfast €27-31.50, s/d from €47.50/95; ☺✳@☎; Ⓜ Thissio, Monastiraki) It's not the cheapest hostel going, but with its jaunty style and helpful staff, City Circus does lift the spirit more than most ultrabudget lodgings. Its bright, well-designed rooms have modern bathrooms; some have kitchens. Book at its website for free (and good) breakfast.

★ Athens Quinta Hostel
HOSTEL €

(Map p64; ☑213 030 5322; www.facebook. com/athensquinta; Methonis 13, Exarhia; dm €25; ☎; Ⓜ Panepistimio) Set in an old mansion, complete with velvet sofas and patterned tile floors, this friendly place is pleasantly homey and a nice change from slicker, busier hostels. There's a nice backyard for lounging. The location in cool Exarhia is a

plus for neighbourhood vibe, but it is far from the main sights.

Evripides
HOTEL €

(Map p108; ☑210 321 2301; www.evripideshotel. gr; Evripidou 79, Psyrri; s/d incl breakfast €65/75; ✳@☎; Ⓜ Monastiraki, Omonia, Thissio) Excellent and clean 62-room budget hotel on a somewhat divey block. Most rooms have a little balcony, and all have minifridges, handy for longer stays. Book early, and you might score a room with an Acropolis view and bigger balcony, for only a tiny bit more. Failing that, everyone can enjoy the view from the rooftop breakfast terrace and bar.

Exarchion
HOTEL €

(Map p108; ☑210 380 0731; www.exarchion. com; Themistokleous 55, Exarhia; s/d/q incl breakfast from €45/58/90; ✳@☎; Ⓜ Omonia) What this 1960s high-rise hotel lacks in character, the surrounding neighbourhood of Exarhia makes up for. Rooms are clean and comfortable, and some have balconies. There's a rooftop cafe-bar, though most guests will head straight out to the action of Plateia Exarhia out front, and the numerous nearby dining and entertainment options.

Fresh Hotel
BOUTIQUE HOTEL €€

(Map p108; ☑210 524 8511; www.freshhotel. gr; Sofokleous 26, cnr Klisthenous, Omonia; s/d/ ste incl breakfast from €160/180/310; ✳☎✳; Ⓜ Omonia) A hip hotel in the gritty south-of-Omonia area, this is a cool place so long as you're happy to ignore the working girls in the streets outside. Expect chic design and brightly coloured rooms plus a fantastic Acropolis-view rooftop with pool, bar and restaurant. Front rooms have balconies, but if you need quiet, go for the back.

Attalos
HOTEL €€

(Map p108; ☑210 321 2801; www.attalos hotel.com; Athinas 29, Psyrri; s/d/tr/q from €81/91/113/179; ✳@☎; Ⓜ Monastiraki) Decor can be an odd mix of antique and late-'90s-chain-hotel, but nonetheless this 78-room place is comfortable, clean and central. Its best feature remains the rooftop bar with wonderful views of the Acropolis. Rooms at the back have balconies with Acropolis views.

Ochre & Brown
BOUTIQUE HOTEL €€€

(Map p108; ☑210 331 2940; www.oandbhotel. com; Leokoriou 7, Psyrri; d/ste from €196/330; ✳☎; Ⓜ Thissio) As the name promises, this boutique hotel is all about the earth tones, with subdued, somewhat small rooms. They are quiet, however, and the style is not painfully trendy. Very friendly staff. A bit overpriced at the standard rate, but potentially excellent value if you score a deal on the website.

Kolonaki

Periscope
BOUTIQUE HOTEL €€

(Map p102; ☑210 729 7200; www.yeshotels.gr; Haritos 22, Kolonaki; s/d from €149/168; ✳🔊; Ⓜ Evangelismos) On a small street lined with tiny, creative boutiques, this sleek, greytone hotel is the essence of new Kolonaki. Clever gadgets are sprinkled throughout, including the lobby slide show and aerial shots of the city on the ceilings. Korres toiletries and the trendy **Pbox** restaurant add to the vibe. The penthouse's private rooftop spa has sensational views.

Coco-Mat
BOUTIQUE HOTEL €€€

(Map p102; ☑210 723 0000; www.cocomat athens.com; Patriarhou Ioakeim 36, Kolonaki; d incl breakfast from €195; ☀✳🔊✉; Ⓜ Evangelismos) A literal boutique hotel, this place adjoins the showroom for Coco-Mat beds, the excellent Greece-made all-natural mattresses. Tiny 'Sleep Tight' (appropriate!) rooms are suitable only for solo travellers; 'Urban' rooms have little balconies. There's a nice honour bar and good breakfast. Overall, rooms are small for the price – but, oh, those beds!

St George Lycabettus
BOUTIQUE HOTEL €€€

(Map p102; ☑210 741 6000; www.sglycabettus. gr; Kleomenous 2, Kolonaki; s/d from €157/201; ✳@🔊✉; Ⓜ Evgangelismos, Syntagma) A high-end clientele bunks here for excellent service and posh, if a bit staid, rooms. Newer 'eco-chic' rooms have organic bedding and comfy Coco-Mat beds. Up the hill in Kolonaki, it's a bit remote, but this pays off in views of the city and a good price for a pool. Plenty of promo rates online.

Eating

Eating, drinking and talking is the main entertainment for Athenians. The vibrant restaurant scene is marked by a delightful culture of casual, convivial al fresco dining. Many nouveau-Greek restaurants have real substance while neighbourhood tavernas have become less reliable, with quality sometimes compromised to keep prices low. *Ouzeries* and *mezedhopoleia,* serving small plates with drinks, are popular for those with limited budgets.

Reservations are essential on weekends for higher-end restaurants; book through E-table (www.e-table.gr).

Akropoli, Makrygianni & Koukai

Fresko Yogurt Bar
DESSERTS €

(Map p74; ☑210 923 3760; www.freskoyogurt bar.gr; Dionysiou Areopagitou 3, Makrygianni; yoghurt from €2.20; ⊙9am-9pm; Ⓜ Akropoli) Delicious Greek yoghurt is the base of all things here. Either fresh or in smoothie form, you can pair it with any number of toppings, from chocolate to black-cherry spoon sweets. A perfect cool-off after seeing the Acropolis.

★ Mani Mani
GREEK €€

(Map p74; ☑210 921 8180; www.manimani.com. gr/english.html; Falirou 10, Makrygianni; mains €15-20; ⊙2-11pm Mon-Sat, 1-6pm Sun; Ⓜ Akropoli) Head upstairs to the relaxing, cheerful dining rooms of this delightful modern restaurant, which specialises in herb-filled cuisine from the Mani region in the Peloponnese. Standouts include the ravioli with Swiss chard and the tangy sausage with orange. Good for a late lunch, as before 6pm weekdays dishes can be ordered as half portions, allowing you to sample widely.

★ Strofi
GREEK €€

(Map p74; ☑210 921 4130; www.strofi.gr; Rovertou Galli 25, Makrygianni; mains €11-15; ⊙noon-1am; Ⓜ Akropoli) Book ahead for a Parthenon view from the rooftop of this exquisitely renovated townhouse. Food is simple grilled meats and fish, but the setting, with elegant white linen and sweet service, elevates the experience to romantic levels.

Lebanese Chef
SYRIAN €€

(☑211 184 4606; Syngrou 184, Kallithea; mains €8-15; ⊙12.30pm-1am; 🚌10 to Sostis) The location on unscenic Sygrou is misleading, and so is the name: inside it's all warmth and hospitality, and excellent food by a recently arrived Syrian-refugee chef.

Fabrika tou Efrosinou
GREEK €€

(Zini 34, Koukaki; mains €8-17; ⊙1.30-11pm Tue-Thu, to midnight Fri & Sat, 1-10pm Sun; Ⓜ Sygrou-Fix, 🚇Fix) Named for the patron saint of cooks, this 'factory' is really a homey-feeling bilevel restaurant focusing on good ingredients and rarer Greek recipes. Service can

Kolonaki

be a little patchy (all those stairs), but when everything is swinging, it's the perfect combination of bountiful, healthy food, excellent wine (a co-owner is a winemaker) and great atmosphere. Book ahead on weekends.

Aglio, Olio & Peperoncino   ITALIAN €€
(Map p74; ☑210 921 1801; Porinou 13, Makrygianni; mains €15-25; ⊙8pm-12.45am Tue-Sat, 2-6.45pm Sun; ⓂAkropoli) The food at this cosy Italian trattoria is simple pastas and the like, satisfying and reasonably priced. It's enhanced by the satisfaction of evading all the restaurant touts facing the nearby Acropolis Museum and finding this place on a quiet side street.

Hytra   MEDITERRANEAN €€€
(☑210 331 6767, 217 707 1118; www.hytra.gr; Syngrou 107-109, Onassis Cultural Centre; mains €27-32, 8-course tasting menu €59; ⊙8pm-midnight Mon, Tue & Sun, to 1am Fri & Sat; ☐10, 550 to Panteio, ⓂSygrou-Fix, ☐Kassomouli) Head to Hytra

at the Onassis Cultural Centre (p76) for exquisitely presented Greek food with a modern twist. Though portions are small, flavours are large, which is how it earned its Michelin star. In summer, the restaurant moves to the 7th floor, for amazing Acropolis views.

✗ Syntagma, Plaka & Monastiraki

★Avocado   VEGETARIAN €
(Map p78; ☑210 323 7878; www.avocadoathens.com; Nikis 30, Plaka; mains €8-13; ⊙noon-11pm Mon-Fri, 11am-11pm Sat, noon-7pm Sun; 🛜✎; ⓂSyntagma) This excellent, popular cafe offers a full array of vegan, gluten-free and organic treats – a rarity in Greece. Next to an organic market, and with a tiny front patio, you can enjoy everything from sandwiches to quinoa with eggplant or mixed-veg coconut

Kolonaki

curry. Fresh juices and mango lassis are all made on the spot.

★ **Kalderimi** TAVERNA €

(Map p108; ☏ 210 331 0049; Plateia Agion Theodoron, cnr Skouleniou, Monastiraki; mains €5-8; ☺ 11am-7pm Tue-Sat; 🖱; Ⓜ Panepistimio) Look behind the Church of Agii Theodori for this open-air taverna offering Greek food at its most authentic. Everything is freshly cooked and delicious: you can't go wrong. Hand-painted tables edge a pedestrian street, for a feeling of peace in one of the busiest parts of the city. (It helps that it closes just before nearby bars get rolling.)

Thanasis KEBAB €

(Map p78; ☏ 210 324 4705; Mitropoleos 69, Monastiraki; gyros €2.50; ☺ 8.30am-2.30am; Ⓜ Monastiraki) In the heart of Athens' souvlaki hub, just off Plateia Monastiraki, Thanasis is a good place to settle in and watch the street parade. It's known for its kebabs on pitta with grilled tomato and onions.

Cremino ICE CREAM €

(Map p78; Nikis 50a, Plaka; scoops €1.50; ☺ 11am-11pm, to midnight Sat Jun-Aug, reduced hours Sep-May; Ⓜ Syntagma, Akropoli) The lovely proprietress at Cremino makes all the ice cream from scratch, using cow and buffalo milk and popular Greek recipes.

★ **Tzitzikas kai Mermigas** MEZEDHES €

(Map p78; ☏ 210 324 7607; www.tzitzikasmermigas.gr; Mitropoleos 12-14, Syntagma; mezedhes €6-12; ☺ noon-11pm; Ⓜ Syntagma) Greek merchandise lines the walls of this cheery, modern *mezedhopoleio* that sits smack in the middle of central Athens. It serves a tasty range of delicious and creative mezedhes (appetisers), such as honey-drizzled, bacon-wrapped Naxos cheese, to a bustling crowd of locals and tourists.

Meatropoleos 3 GREEK €

(Map p78; ☏ 210 324 1805; www.meatropoleos3.com; Mitropoleos 3, Syntagma; mains €6-12, souvlaki €1.50; ☺ noon-midnight; Ⓜ Syntagma) A blessing amid the multistorey fast-food joints on Syntagma, this sleek little restaurant does a great array of grilled meats, including good housemade sausage and a hefty burger, as well as the usual souvlaki to offset a night on the town. You'll also find good salads, seasonal pies and other Greek staples.

Palia Athina TAVERNA €

(Map p78; ☏ 210 324 5777; www.paliaathina.gr; Nikis 46, Syntagma; mains €6-12; ☺ noon-midnight; Ⓜ Syntagma) No muss, no fuss, no music or show: just a quiet little family-run taverna with excellent prices, especially for the area. The stews and casseroles are solid; if you can't read the menu, you can go to the kitchen and point. Also does delivery or takeaway, if you're too tired to leave the hotel room.

Mikro Politiko
FAST FOOD €

(Map p74; ☏210 321 7879; Dionysiou Areopagitou 8, Makrygianni; souvlaki €1.70; ☉11am-midnight; Ⓜ Akropoli) Just the thing to stave off post-Acropolis collapse: a quick souvlaki or falafel from this little takeout place. It's markedly better than other snack options in the area, with fresh ingredients and good salads too. Nowhere to sit, but the sweet staff can pack food to go. Order inside at the cash register.

Lukumades
SWEETS €

(Map p78; ☏210 321 0880; Eolou 21, Monastiraki; portion €2.70; ☉8am-1am, to 3am Fri & Sat; Ⓜ Monastiraki) What's not to love about fried dough? *Loukoumadhes* (from Arabic *lu'mat al-qadi*, 'the judge's morsel') are served here as crunchy round balls, doused either in traditional honey and cinnamon or with all manner of 'modern' innovations, such as chocolate, fruit or ice cream. You can even get them filled, for maximum morseliciousness. Open late, to bar-goers' delight.

Le Greche
ICE CREAM €

(Map p78; ☏216 700 6458; Mitropoleos 16, Syntagma; ice cream from €2.50; ☉8.30am-1am Mon-Thu, 8.30am-2am Fri, 10am-2am Sat, 10am-midnight Sun; Ⓜ Syntagma) Gem of a gelato shop, with espresso and little cakes as well. Gelato flavours mix traditional (intense, not-too-sweet pistachio) and novel (bergamot peel and Aperol).

Kallipateira
MEZEDHES €

(Map p108; ☏210 321 4152; www.kallipateira.gr; Astingos 8, Monastiraki; dishes €4-10; ☉lunch & dinner; Ⓜ Monastiraki) In a neoclassical building overlooking an archaeological dig, this restaurant is a good stop for mezedhes and carafes of ouzo – and live *rembetika* (Greek blues music) Saturday and Sunday afternoons starting at 2.30pm. Daily specials are a very good deal.

Kuzina
GREEK €€

(Map p64; ☏210 324 0133; www.kuzina.gr; Adrianou 9, Monastiraki; mains €12-25, set menu €20; ☉11am-late; Ⓜ Thissio) This comfortably elegant restaurant does upscale Greek, with novel creations and rarer traditional dishes such as Cretan pappardelle or chicken with figs and sesame. It's cosy in winter, as light streams in, warming the crowded tables. In summer, book ahead for a rooftop-terrace

table. A fine second choice is an outside table on the pedestrian street.

Manas Kouzina-Kouzina
GREEK €€

(Map p78; ☏210 325 2335; www.manaskouzina kouzina.gr; Aiolou 27a, Monastiraki; mains from €10; ☉8am-midnight; Ⓜ Monastiraki) 'Mother's kitchen' brings the slow-cooked, traditional Greek recipes called *magirefta* to the forefront. Incorporating locally sourced ingredients, lunch is a cafeteria-style selection of dishes from around the country. In the evening, the selection is à la carte, always seasonal and featuring some interesting rarer dishes.

Café Avyssinia
MEZEDHES €€

(Map p78; ☏210 321 7047; Kynetou 7, Monastiraki; mains €10-16; ☉11am-1am Tue-Sat, to 7pm Sun; Ⓜ Monastiraki) This antiques-bedecked place on Plateia Avyssinias, in the middle of the flea market, has been legendary since the 1980s for its boisterous live music and varied mezedhes. But on a slow day, it can feel a bit stuffy. Either take a midday break from the market, or go late on a weekend night. In summer, snag fantastic Acropolis views upstairs.

Black Duck Garden
CAFE €€

(Map p108; ☏210 325 2396; www.blackduck garden.gr; Paparigopoulou 5-7, Plateia Klafthmonos; mains from €10; ☉10am-1am; Ⓜ Panepistimio) The cafe at the **Museum of the City of Athens** (Map p108; ☏210 323 1397; www.athens citymuseum.gr; Paparigopoulou 7, Syntagma; adult/child €5/3; ☉9am-4pm Mon & Wed-Fri, 10am-3pm Sat & Sun; Ⓜ Panepistimio) occupies a lovely courtyard of potted plants, marble sculptures and shady trees. By day a full menu of brunch, Greek specialities, coffee and dessert is served. It's also an evening retreat for dinner or cocktails among the romantically lit greenery, often with live jazz.

Palia Taverna tou Psara
TAVERNA €€

(Map p78; ☏210 321 8734; www.psaras-taverna. gr; Erechtheos 16, Plaka; mains €12-24; ☉11am-12.30am Wed-Mon; Ⓜ Akropoli) Away from the main hustle of Plaka, this taverna is a cut above the rest and fills tables cascading across the street. It's known as the best seafood taverna in Plaka (fish €65 per kilogram).

School Pizza Bar
ITALIAN €€

(Map p78; ☏210 325 1444; Plateia Agia Irini 8, Monastiraki; pizzas from €10; ☉9am-4am; Ⓜ Monastiraki) Settle into a desk like the old days, and check out the chalkboard. This time round though, school is a party. Topping options for the thin-crust pizzas include good Greek products, such as cured pork from Crete. At night, it's the choice hang-out near trendy Plateia Agia Irini for excellent drinks and cocktails and lounge music by top local DJs.

✖ Gazi, Keramikos & Thisio

To Steki tou Ilia
TAVERNA €

(Map p84; ☑210 345 8052; Eptahalkou 5, Thisio; chops per portion/kg €9/30; ⊙noon-late; Ⓜ Thissio) It's worth joining the line to dine at this *psistaria* (restaurant serving grilled food) that's famous for its grilled lamb and pork chops. In summer, the operation moves across the street into a hidden garden over the train tracks. It's a no-frills place with barrel wine and simple dips, chips and salads.

Elvis
GREEK €

(Map p84; ☑210 345 5836; Plataion 29, Keramikos; skewers €1.50; ⊙noon-3am, to 5am Fri & Sat; Ⓜ Keramikos or Thissio) This souvlaki joint is mobbed, and not just because the counter staff slide you a shot of booze while you're waiting. The meat quality is high, the prices are right and the music is great. Souvlaki comes with good chewy bread (NYC style; an owner is from Queens). A branch in Pangrati, next to Chelsea Hotel (p116), applies the same winning formula.

Kanella
TAVERNA €

(Map p84; ☑210 347 6320; www.kanellagazi. gr; Leoforos Konstantinoupoleos 70, Gazi; dishes €7-11; ⊙1.30pm-late; Ⓜ Keramikos) Housemade village-style bread, mismatched retro crockery and brown-paper tablecloths set the tone for this modern taverna serving regional Greek cuisine. Friendly staff serve daily specials such as lemon lamb with potatoes, and an excellent zucchini and avocado salad.

Gevomai Kai Magevomai
TAVERNA €

(Map p84; ☑210 345 2802; Nileos 11, Thisio; mains €6-14; ⊙lunch & dinner; 🛜; Ⓜ Thissio) Stroll off the pedestrian way to find this small corner taverna with marble-topped tables. Neighbourhood denizens know it as one of the best for home-cooked, simple food with the freshest ingredients. Menu changes constantly.

Skoufias
TAVERNA €

(Map p84; ☑210 341 2252; Vasiliou tou Megalou 50, Rouf; mains €5-9; ⊙9pm-late Oct-May; Ⓜ Keramikos) This gem of a winter-only taverna

near the railway line is off the beaten track but worth seeking out. The menu has Cretan influences and an eclectic selection of regional Greek cuisine, including dishes you won't find in any tourist joint, from superb rooster with ouzo to lamb *tsigariasto* (braised) with *horta* (wild greens) and potato salad with orange.

★ Athiri
GREEK €€

(Map p84; ☑210 346 2983; www.athirirest aurant.gr; Plateon 15, Keramikos; mains €14-19; ⊙8pm-1am Tue-Sat, 1-5pm Sun; Ⓜ Thissio) Athiri's lovely garden courtyard is a verdant surprise in this pocket of Keramikos. The small but innovative menu plays on Greek regional classics, with seasonal specialities. This might include Santorini fava and hearty beef stew with *myzithra* (sheep's-milk cheese) and handmade pasta from Karpathos.

Butcher & Sardelles
INTERNATIONAL €€

(Map p84; ☑210 341 3440; Persefonis 19, Gazi; mains €10-17; ⊙7-11.30pm; Ⓜ Keramikos) Surf or turf? No need to choose at this modern restaurant where the menu is split between meat and seafood. It's in a scenic spot alongside the Gazi gasworks arts centre and has tables outside.

A Little Taste of Home
GREEK €€

(Map p84; ☑210 341 0013; www.facebook. com/alittletasteofhomeathens; Dekeleon 3, Gazi; mains €8-11; ⊙6pm-1am Mon-Thu, to 2am Fri & Sat, 2-10pm Sun) You might expect a restaurant owned by a Syrian refugee to serve Syrian food, but this is solid Greek, plus creative salads – all good and fresh, and indeed, a nice homey place in the middle of party-scene Gazi. Ahmed is an excellent host.

★ Aleria
MEDITERRANEAN €€

(Map p64; ☑210 522 2633; www.aleria.gr; Megalou Alexandrou 57, Metaxourgio; mains €20-28, set menus from €64; ⊙7.30-11.30pm Mon-Sat, closed late Aug; Ⓜ Metaxourghio) This contemporary, elegant restaurant in a restored mansion feels a bit out of place in the otherwise scruffy Metaxourgio neighbourhood. Still, it does lovely things with Greek ingredients.

★ Funky Gourmet
MEDITERRANEAN €€€

(Map p64; ☑210 524 2727; www.funkygourmet. com; Paramythias 13, cnr Salaminas, Keramikos; set menu from €145; ⊙7.30pm-1am Tue-Sat, last order 10.30pm; Ⓜ Metaxourghio) Greek food gets the molecular gastronomy treatment at this two-Michelin-star restaurant. The two chefs seem to take absolute glee in devising mind-bending versions of familiar flavours. It's most famous for its somewhat macabre 'Silence of the Lamb' presentation. A worthwhile stop for any foodie. Book ahead.

✕ Psyrri, Omonia & Exarhia

★ Telis
TAVERNA €

(Map p108; ☑ 210 324 2775; Evripidou 86, Psyrri; meal with salad €13; ☉ 8am-2am Mon-Sat; Ⓜ Thissio) A fluorescent-lit beacon of good food and kind service on a grimy block, Telis has been serving up simplicity since 1978. There's no menu, just a set meal: a small mountain of charcoal-grilled pork chops atop chips, plus a side vegetable. Greek salad is optional, as is rough house wine or beer.

★ Varvakios Agora
MARKET €

(Athens Central Market; Map p108; Athinas, btwn Sofokleous & Evripidou, Omonia; ☉ 7am-6pm Mon-Sat; Ⓜ Monastiraki, Panepistimio, Omonia) The streets around the colourful and bustling Varvakios Agora are a sensory delight. The meat and fish market (p121) fills the historic building on the eastern side, and the fruit and vegetable market (p121) is across the road. The meat-market **tavernas** are an Athenian institution. Clients range from hungry market workers to elegant couples emerging from nightclubs in search of hangover-busting *patsas* (tripe soup).

★ Diporto Agoras
TAVERNA €

(Map p108; ☑ 210 321 1463; cnr Theatrou & Sokratous; plates €5-7; ☉ 7am-7pm Mon-Sat, closed 1-20 Aug; Ⓜ Omonia, Monastiraki) This quirky old taverna is an Athens' dining gem. There's no signage – two doors lead to a rustic cellar where there's no menu, just a few dishes that haven't changed in years. The house speciality is *revythia* (chickpeas), usually followed by grilled fish and paired with wine from one of the giant barrels lining the wall.

Nikitas
TAVERNA €

(Map p108; ☑ 210 325 2591; Agion Anargyron 19, Psyrri; mains €7-10; ☉ noon-6.30pm Sun-Tue, to 11.30pm Wed-Sat; Ⓜ Monastiraki) Locals swear by this tried-and-true taverna that has been serving reasonably priced, refreshingly simple and tasty traditional food since well before Psyrri became a hotspot. It's the only place busy on weekdays.

Hypovrlhio
GREEK €

(Map p64; ☑ 210 409 0058; Asklipiou 53, cnr Arahovis, Exarhia; small plates €4-10; ☉ 4pm-4am Sun-Fri, noon-4pm Sun) The 'Submarine' is a typical

Exarhia hang-out, colourful and cramped. Raki (Cretan fire water) is encouraged, but the booze is offset with a big range of home-cooked Greek standards (pork chops, Cretan rusk salads, lots of veg options) and pastas that meet Italian standards of toothiness. Food comes in 'small' portions, great for solo diners or tasting a range of things.

Kimatothrafstis
TAVERNA €

(Map p108; ☑ 213 030 8274; Harilaou Trikoupi 49, Exarhia; small/large plate €4/7; ☉ 8am-11pm, closed dinner Sun; 🖥🅿; Ⓜ Omonia) This great-value, bright and casual little cafe dishes out a range of home-style Greek cooking and alternative fare. Choose from the day's offerings at the cafeteria-style display. Plates come in two sizes: big or small.

Nancy's Sweet Home
CAFE €

(Map p108; ☑ 210 321 1323; www.nancysweet home.gr; Plateia Iroön 1, Psyrri; cakes from €10; ☉ 9am-midnight; Ⓜ Monastiraki) Get your sugar fix at this place on a bustling *plateia*. It's famous for its extra-large cakes swimming in melted chocolate and giant dollops of ice cream. Also has syrup-soaked Greek pastries; a local favourite is the *kunefe*, a sweet cheese pastry served with a generous helping of mastic-flavoured ice cream.

Enjoy Just Falafel
SYRIAN €

(Aristotelous 98, Viktoria; sandwiches from €2; ☉ 8am-8pm Mon-Fri, 11am-7pm Sat; 🅿; Ⓜ Viktoria) Sweet little falafel-and-salad shop run by a Syrian immigrant who came to Greece in the late 1990s. Good food and information about this interesting neighbourhood.

Barbagiannis
TAVERNA €

(Map p108; ☑ 210 330 0185; Emmanuel Benaki 94, Exarhia; mains €5-8; ☉ lunch & dinner; Ⓜ Omonia) An Exarhia institution, this low-key *mayirio* (cookhouse) is popular with students and those wanting good-value, home-style Greek food.

Ivis
MEZEDHES €

(Map p108; ☑ 210 323 2554; Navarhou Apostoli 19, Psyrri; mezedhes €4-10; ☉ noon-2am Tue-Sat, to 8pm Sun; Ⓜ Thissio) This cosy corner *mezed-hopoleio*, with its bright, arty decor, has a small but delicious range of simple, freshly cooked mezedhes that change daily. A good ouzo and raki selection lights things up.

Rozalia
TAVERNA €

(Map p108; ☑ 210 330 2933; www.rozalia.gr; Valtetsiou 58, Exarhia; mains €5-11; Ⓜ Omonia) An Exarhia favourite on a lively pedestrian strip, this family-run taverna serves grills and home-style fare. Mezedhes are brought around on a tray, so you can point and pick. Pavement tables are tempting, but better to sit in the garden where the ground is level.

Oxo Nou
CRETAN €
(Map p108; ☑ 210 380 1778; www.facebook.com/oxonouathens; Emmanuel Benaki 63-65, Exarhia; mains €8-11; ⊙ 1pm-1.30am; 🛜; Ⓜ Omonia) This was one of the trailblazers for supercasual and superdelicious Cretan food and it still delivers, often with a free shot of island booze to start.

★ Akordeon
MEZEDHES €€
(Map p78; ☑ 210 325 3703; Hristokopidou 7, Psyrri; dishes €6-18; ⊙ 7pm-2am Tue-Sat, 1-7pm Sun Sep-May; Ⓜ Monastiraki, Thissio) Slide into this charming butter-yellow house across from a church in a quiet Psyrri side street for a warm welcome by musician-chefs Pepi and Achilleas (and their spouses), who run this excellent venue for local music and mezedhes. They'll help you order authentic Greek fare, then (at night and on weekends) surround you with their soulful songs.

★ Ta Karamanlidika tou Fani
GREEK €€
(Map p108; ☑ 210 325 4184; www.karamanlidika. gr; Sokratous 1, Psyrri; dishes €7-18; ⊙ 11am-midnight; Ⓜ Monastiraki) At this modern-day *pastomageireio* – a combo tavern-deli – tables are set alongside the deli cases, and staff offer tasty morsels while you're looking at the menu. Beyond the Greek cheeses and cured meats, there's good seafood, such as marinated anchovies, as well as rarer wines and craft beers. Service is excellent, as is the warm welcome from Fani herself.

★ Yiantes
TAVERNA €€
(Map p108; ☑ 210 330 1369; Valtetsiou 44, Exarhia; mains €10-18; ⊙ 1pm-midnight; ☑; Ⓜ Omonia) This lovely garden restaurant is upmarket for Exarhia, but the food is superb and made with largely organic produce. Expect interesting seasonal greens such as *almirikia,* perfectly grilled fish or delicious mussels and calamari with saffron.

✖ Kolonaki

★ Oikeio
MEDITERRANEAN €
(Map p102; ☑ 210 725 9216; Ploutarhou 15, Kolonaki; mains €8-12; ⊙ 12.30pm-midnight Mon-Thu, to 1am Fri & Sat, to 6pm Sun; Ⓜ Evangelismos) With excellent home-style cooking, this modern taverna lives up to its name (meaning

'homey'). It's decorated like a cosy bistro, and tables on the footpath allow people-watching without the normal Kolonaki bill. Pastas, salads and international fare are tasty, but try the daily *mayirefta* (ready-cooked meals), such as the excellent stuffed zucchini. Book ahead.

Mia Zoe tin Ehoume
MEZEDHES €
(Map p64; ☑ 6987854164; www.ikalizoi.gr/miazoitinehoume; Sfaktirias 20, Keramikos; ⊙ 5pm-late; Ⓜ Kerameikos, Thisso or Metaxourghio) 'We have but one life', as the name of this neighbourhood taverna says, and this is a fine place to enjoy it. The summer yard is a ramshackle mix of sofas, lanterns and rusting oddities. In winter, there's a cosy wood stove. Drink and snack till late, with live music on weekends.

Filippou
TAVERNA €
(Map p102; ☑ 210 721 6390; Xenokratous 19, Kolonaki; mains €8-12; ⊙ 1-5pm & 7-11pm Mon-Fri, 1-5pm Sat; Ⓜ Evangelismos) Why mess with what works? Filippou has been dishing out Greek goodness – heavy on the garlic and hearty meats – since 1923, and it's still a go-to for the neighbourhood. You can get this food elsewhere and for less, but here you get white linen and a gracious older long-lunching clientele, in the heart of Kolonaki.

Kalamaki Kolonaki
GREEK €
(Map p102; ☑ 210 721 8800; Ploutarhou 32, Kolonaki; mains €7; ⊙ 1pm-midnight; Ⓜ Evangelismos) Order by the *kalamaki* (skewer; €1.70), add some salad and pittas, and you have great quick eats at this standout souvlaki joint. It's small, but there's pavement seating, for the requisite people-watching. And because it's Kolonaki, it's just a little more chic than average.

Benaki Museum Cafe
GREEK €€
(Map p102; Koumbari 1, Kolonaki; mains €12-16; Ⓜ Evangelismos) Traditional Greek food gets dressed up to match the museum setting, with an open dining room and terrace with a view of the national gardens and the Acropolis. It feels a bit clubby, with older locals meeting for lunch, and it's open as late as the museum is, so you can have dinner or even just a late drink here.

Nice N' Easy
CAFE €€
(Map p102; ☑ 210 361 7201; www.niceneasy.gr; Omirou 60, Kolonaki; mains €8-18; ⊙ 9am-1.30am; ☑; Ⓜ Panepistimio) 🍴 Dig into organic, fresh sandwiches, salads and brunch treats such as huevos rancheros beneath images of

Psyrri, Omonia & Exarhia

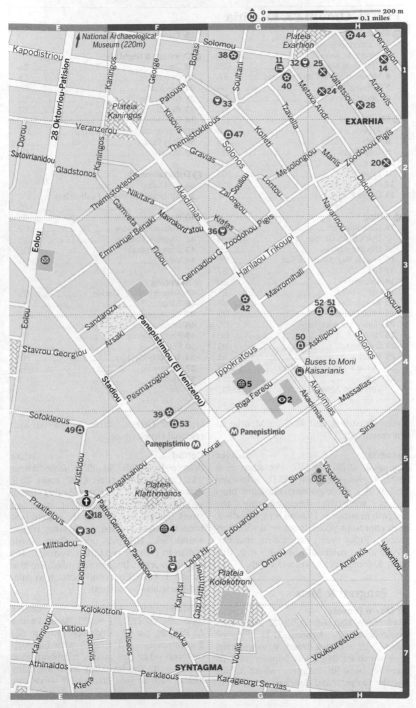

Psyrri, Omonia & Exarhia

Louis Armstrong and Marilyn Monroe at this casual cafe.

Capanna ITALIAN €€
(Map p102; ☎ 210 724 1777; Ploutarhou 38 & Haritos 42, Kolonaki; mains €10-17; ☉1pm-1am Tue-Sun; ☎; Ⓜ Evangelismos) Capanna hugs a corner, with tables wrapping around the footpath in summer. Cuisine is fresh Italian, from enormous pizzas to gnocchi with gorgonzola. Enjoy hearty eating with attentive service and a goblet of wine, although, this being Kolonaki, prices are a tad high.

🍴 Pangrati & Mets

★ Mavro Provato MEZEDHES €
(Black Sheep; Map p64; ☎ 210 722 3466; www.tomauroprovato.gr; Arrianou 31-33, Pangrati; dishes €5-12; ☉ lunch & dinner; Ⓜ Evangelismos) Book ahead for this wildly popular modern *mezedhopoleio* in Pangrati, where tables line the footpath and delicious small (well,

small for Greece) plates are paired with regional Greek wines.

Colibri PIZZA €
(Map p64; ☎ 210 701 1011; Embedokleous 9-13, Pangrati; small pizzas €6-12, mains €5-9; ☉ noon-late; ☒ 2, 4, 11 to Plateia Plastira) One of several fine cafes on this quiet, tree-lined street, but locals go here for the alleged best pizza in Athens, served to a low-key reggae soundtrack. The pies range from classic Italian to creative vegetarian (seriously, the yoghurt works!). Burgers and salads are also excellent. There's a second location at Anapafseos 9, also in Pangrati.

Kallimarmaro BAKERY €
(Map p64; ☎ 210 701 9062; Plateia Varnava 22, Pangrati; pita €2; ☉ 8am-8pm Mon-Sat; ☒) Exceptionally good *spanakopita* (spinach pie) and other pies at this neighbourhood bakery – it's the breakfast go-to for many locals. Fills all your cream-puff needs too.

There's a second one nearby in Mets, across from the Odeon Cafe (p116).

Vyrinis TAVERNA €
(Map p64; 210 701 2021; Arhimidous 11, Pangrati; mains €6-8; ⏰7-11pm Mon-Fri, noon-3pm & 7-11pm Sat & Sun; 2, 4, 11 to Plateia Plastira) Just behind the old Panathenaic stadium, this popular neighbourhood spot has been modernised a bit, but maintains its essential taverna-ness, with home-style Greek food and reliable house wine at reasonable prices. On warm nights, all activity moves to the lovely courtyard garden, just up the side street.

★**Spondi** MEDITERRANEAN €€€
(Map p64; 210 756 4021; www.spondi.gr; Pyrronos 5, Pangrati; mains €44-52, set menus from €73; ⏰8pm-late; 209 to Plateia Varnava, 2, 4 or 11 to Plateia Plastira) Athenians frequently vote two-Michelin-starred Spondi the city's best restaurant, and its Mediterranean haute cuisine, with a strong French influence, is indeed excellent. Visitors to the city might want something a bit more distinctly Greek, however. Either way, it's a lovely dining experience, in a relaxed setting in a charming old house with a bougainvillea-draped garden. Book ahead.

🍷 Drinking & Nightlife

In Athens, the line between cafe and bar is blurry. Most places serving coffee by day segue to drinks, and maybe music and a DJ, at night. Many cafes and bars also serve food – although places that serve only drinks are more common in the economic crisis (you can bring your own snacks).

🍸 Akropoli, Makrygianni & Koukaki

Tiki Athens BAR
(Map p74; 210 923 6908; www.tikiathens. com; Falirou 15, Makrygianni; ⏰6pm-late; M Akropoli) Kitschy bachelor-pad decor, a whole roster of live music, an Asian-inspired menu and an alternative young crowd make this two-storey spot a fun place for a drink.

Sfika BAR
(Map p74; 210 922 1341; Straligou Kontouli 15, Makrygianni; ⏰9am-late; M Akropoli) Glowing yellow inside (perhaps for its namesake; *sfika* means 'wasp'), this small neighbourhood cafe-restaurant-bar has an alternative/student vibe and occasional live music.

Duende BAR
(Map p74; Tzireon 2, Makrygianni; ⏰8pm-3am; M Akropoli) With the golden glow of a Parisian brasserie, this intimate pub is a good place for a grown-up glass of wine or whisky (though not so much for food or cocktails). It's especially welcome as a respite from the tourist bustle nearby.

🍷 Syntagma, Plaka & Monastiraki

The best central bars are around Kolokotroni St, north of Syntagma, and around Plateia Agia Irini in Monastiraki. Look especially at the ends of shopping arcades for old-style bars staffed with smart barkeeps and DJs. Multiuse spaces such as Metamatic:TAF (p77) and Six DOGS (p112) combine gallery, cafe and overflowing bar. Some hotel bars, such as Grande Bretagne (p99) and A for Athens (p99), have super Acropolis views.

★**Tailor Made** BAR
(Map p78; 213 004 9645; www.tailormade. gr; Plateia Agia Irini 2, Monastiraki; ⏰8am-2am; M Monastiraki) Arguably the best third-wave coffee operation in Athens, with its own microroastery and hand-pressed teas, this place has outdoor tables alongside the flower market. At night it turns into a happening cocktail and wine bar. Menu includes homemade desserts (€5) and sandwiches (€6) too.

★**Tall's Toy** COCKTAIL BAR
(Map p78; 210 331 1555; www.facebook. com/tallstoybar; Plateia Karytsi 10, Syntagma; ⏰noon-4am; M Syntagma) With jewel-toned walls, old-fashioned wood fittings, open windows to the street and a usually chill DJ, this might be the ideal small downtown bar. The crowd is usually 30-something and older.

ATHENS & AROUND ATHENS

Dude
BAR

(Map p78; ☎210 322 7130; www.facebook.com/thedudebar; Kalamiotou 14, Monastiraki; ◉2pm-5am, to 6am Sat & Sun; Ⓜ Monastiraki) Exceptionally good music – obscure funk and soul that makes you feel like you're living a Quentin Tarantino soundtrack – at this little bar on a pedestrian street. Moreover, the Dude abides till practically dawn.

Couleur Locale
BAR

(Map p78; ☎216 700 4917; Normanou 3; ◉10am-4am; Ⓜ Monastiraki) Tucked in a narrow pedestrian lane in Monastiraki, Couleur Locale is a great secret. At ground level, it's a pretty enough bar, but often completely empty. That's because everyone has taken the elevator to the 3rd-floor rooftop. It's a go-to spot for Athenians who love to sip a coffee or drink with a chill vibe and a view of their beloved Acropolis.

Baba Au Rum
COCKTAIL BAR

(Map p78; ☎211 710 9140; www.babaaurum.com; Klitiou 6, Monastiraki; ◉7pm-3am Sun-Fri, 1pm-4am Sat; Ⓜ Syntagma, Monastiraki) As the name implies, the focus here is on rum drinks, with an excellent selection of rarer Caribbean rums and a whole range of cocktails, from classic tiki drinks to new inventions. This is just one of a handful of good little bars in this strip.

Noel
BAR

(Map p78; ☎211 215 9534; www.noelbar.gr; Kolokotroni 59b, Monastiraki; ◉11am-4am; Ⓜ Monastiraki) The bar's slogan is 'where it's always

---

> ### ⓘ TOP NIGHTLIFE TIPS
>
> ➡ Bars begin filling after 11pm and uually stay open till 3am or 4am.
>
> ➡ Transit stops or slows after midnight, but cabs are very cheap.
>
> ➡ Athenians drink plenty, but public drunkenness is rarely seen. If you're visibly intoxicated, you're a clear target for pickpockets or worse.
>
> ➡ Gazi and Kolonaki tend towards slick and bigger-budget clubs. For cheaper drinks and live music, head for Keramikos or Exarhia. Monastiraki and north of Syntagma are the best central areas for more interesting bars.
>
> ➡ For the best dancing in summer, head to beach clubs (p111) along the coast near Glyfada – city locations close earlier.

Christmas' and Noel is going for the candle-lit cocktail-party kind of Christmas, no Santa suits required. The downright beautiful place is decked out with period furniture and softly glimmering chandeliers. Smartly suited bartenders serve some of the most creative cocktails in town. Music is a mix of '80s, '90s and jazz.

Barley Cargo
BAR

(Map p78; ☎210 323 0445; Kolokotroni 6, Syntagma; ◉11am-3am; Ⓜ Syntagma) If you think Greek beer stops at Alpha, head here to learn more. The big open-front bar stocks the products of many Greek microbreweries, as well as more than 100 international beers. Live music is a bonus.

Galaxy Bar
BAR

(Map p78; ☎210 322 7733; Stadiou 10, Syntagma; ◉1pm-late Mon-Sat; Ⓜ Syntagma) Once upon a time (the early 1970s, to be exact), this was a modern bar – the sort with an actual European-style *bar*. Now it's a beautiful, subdued time capsule with gallant bartenders who respect the spirit of the place, which can be summarised in the framed photos of the Rat Pack and Franz Kafka. At the end of the arcade.

Six DOGS
BAR

(Map p78; ☎210 321 0510; www.sixdogs.gr; Avramiotou 6-8, Monastiraki; ◉10am-late; Ⓜ Monastiraki) The core of this supercreative events space is a rustic back garden, a great place for quiet daytime chats over coffee or a relaxed drink. From there, you can head in to one of several adjoining buildings to see a band, art show or other general cool happening.

Klepsidra
CAFE

(Map p78; ☎210 321 2493; Klepsydras & Thrasyvoulou, Plaka; snacks €4; ◉9am-1am; Ⓜ Monastiraki) Tucked away in a delightfully quiet spot on the west end of Plaka, with shady outdoor tables and friendly service, Klepsidra is a favourite with locals before and after work and an ideal rest spot after serious sightseeing. It has a small selection of snacks, such as *spanakopites* (spinach pies), though it's really about the atmosphere.

Clumsies
BAR

(Map p108; ☎210 323 2682; www.theclumsies.gr; Praxitelous 30, Syntagma; ◉10am-2am, to 4am Fri & Sat; Ⓜ Syntagma) Look for the red neon in the hallway of this unsigned bar that fills your coffee and creative cocktail needs.

Founded by three award-winning bartenders, it is very serious about its drinks, but the atmosphere is definitely fun, and full of handsome types on the weekends.

Drunk Sinatra
COCKTAIL BAR
(Map p78; ☑210 331 3733; Thiseos 16, Syntagma; ⊙10am-late; Ⓜ Syntagma) Look for the movie marquee on a small side street to find this hipster hang. It serves a mean cocktail.

Brettos
BAR
(Map p78; ☑210 323 2110; www.brettosplaka.com; Kydathineon 41, Plaka; ⊙10am-3am; Ⓜ Akropoli) You won't find any happening bars in Plaka, but Brettos is a delightful old bar and distillery with a stunning wall of colourful bottles and huge barrels. Sample its home brands of wine, ouzo, brandy and other spirits.

Faust
BAR
(Map p78; ☑210 323 4095; www.faust.gr; Kalamiotou 11 & Athinaidos 12, Monastiraki; ⊙Sep-May; Ⓜ Monastiraki) Loud, raunchy, funny, just plain quirky – eclectic and popular bar Faust probably hosts it on its small stage.

Heteroclito
WINE BAR
(Map p78; ☑210 323 9406; www.heteroclito.gr; Fokionos 2, Monastiraki; ⊙12.30pm-midnight Mon-Thu, to 1.30am Fri & Sat, 6pm-midnight Sun; Ⓜ Monastiraki) This relaxed wine bar with a French bistro-like setting showcases the best of Greek wines. The petite, yet charming, venue has a vintage feel with mismatched period furniture and a mix of warm wood and cool marble details. The wines can be paired with Greek cheeses and cold cuts. Heteroclito periodically organises tasting events.

Booze Cooperativa
BAR
(Map p78; ☑211 405 3733; www.boozecooperativa.com; Kolokotroni 57, Monastiraki; ⊙11am-late; ⊗; Ⓜ Monastiraki) By day, this art mansion is full of young Athenians playing chess and backgammon and working on their Macs. Later it transforms into a happening bar that rocks till late. The basement hosts art exhibitions and there's a theatre upstairs.

Bartesera
BAR
(Map p78; ☑210 322 9805; Kolokotroni 25, Syntagma; ⊙10am-late, 6pm-late Sun; Ⓜ Syntagma) This casual bar-cafe with great music hides at the end of the narrow Praxitelous arcade.

Yiasemi
CAFE
(Map p78; ☑213 041 7937; www.yiasemi.gr; Mniskleous 23, Plaka; ⊙10am-3am; Ⓜ Monastiraki) Proof that Plaka is still very much a Greek neighbourhood, despite the tourists: this cafe attracts a good mix of young Athenians, who set up for hours in the big armchairs or out on the scenic steps. It's better by day and on weeknights, when it's not overwhelmed by the night scene at nearby restaurants.

Gin Joint
COCKTAIL BAR
(Map p108; ☑210 321 8646; Christou Lada 1, Syntagma; ⊙noon-2am; Ⓜ Syntagma) Just what the name promises: sample 60 gins or other fancy beverages, some with historical notes on their origin. It's a tiny place, but like so many downtown bars, the crowd can expand into the adjacent arcade.

Kiki de Grece
WINE BAR
(Map p78; ☑210 321 1279; www.facebook.com/kikidegrece; Ipitou 4; ⊙noon-1am; Ⓜ Syntagma) Man Ray's muse, Kiki de Montparnasse, declared that in hard times, all she needed was bread, an onion and a bottle of red wine. This pedestrian-street bar also takes her as its muse, and offers plenty more than a bottle of red. There's a huge range from Greece's vintners, paired with seasonal dishes from various regions in Greece.

Poems & Crimes Art Bar
CAFE
(Map p78; ☑210 322 8839; www.poemsandcrimes.gr; Agias Irinis 17, Monastiraki; ⊙9am-midnight; Ⓜ Monastiraki) Set in a 19th-century neoclassical building, Poems & Crimes is the local writers' and book lovers' haunt. The quiet bookshop is also the office for a Greek publishing house and a coffee shop. Various book and poetry readings are often scheduled, and a little backyard turns into a cafe and music performance space in summer.

Hitchcocktales
COCKTAIL BAR
(Map p74; ☑210 921 0023; www.facebook.com/hitchcock.athens; Porinou 10; ⊙9am-2am; Ⓜ Acropolis) Famous Hitchcock film scenes are spray-painted on the wall in front of this bar on a quiet street that gathers a crowd that loves creative drinks and candlelight. The bartenders are polished, and the soundtrack can be lively swing, jazz, soul and funk. The noise level, in the industrial-look raw-concrete space, can spike later in the night.

ATHENS & AROUND ATHENS

Gazi, Keramikos & Thisio

Once touted as the 'edgy' neighbourhood, Gazi is now fairly mainstream and particularly well known for its gay scene. In Thisio, cafes along the pedestrian promenade Apostolou Pavlou have great Acropolis views; those along pedestrianised Iraklidon pack 'em in at night. More creative, fringier bars are found in Keramikos and adjoining Metaxourgio – pedestrian-only Salaminos is especially nice.

★ Gazarte   BAR
(Map p84; ☑ 210 346 0347; www.gazarte.gr; Voutadon 32-34, Gazi; Ⓜ Kerameikos) At this varied arts complex, you'll find a cinema-sized screen playing videos, amazing city views taking in the Acropolis, mainstream music and a trendy 30-something crowd. At ground level is a large theatre that hosts music and comedy. There's occasional live music and a restaurant to boot.

Alphaville   BAR
(Map p64; ☑ 215 505 2001; Salaminos, cnr Sfaktirias, Metaxourgio; ⊘ 11am-3am; Ⓜ Thissio, Kerameikos or Metaxourghio) Just one in a strip of near-perfect bohemian bars on the pedestrian street of Salaminos, the heart of the cool Keramikos scene. All with a good mix of music, inexpensive drinks and loads of *kefi* (atmosphere), plus a dramatic graffiti backdrop on the derelict buildings. Start here and wander.

A Liar Man   BAR
(Map p84; ☑ 210 342 6322; www.facebook.com/aliarmanathens; Sofroniou 2, Gazi; ⊘ 5pm-2am Mon-Thu, to 4am Fri & Sat, 2pm-1am Sun mid-Sep–mid-Jun; Ⓜ Kerameikos) A tiny hideout with a more hushed vibe – a very nice antidote to other top-volume bars and clubs nearby. It closes in summer.

Laika   BAR
(Map p64; ☑ 215 501 3801; Pellis 30, Gazi; ⊘ noon-2am Tue-Sun; Ⓜ Kerameikos) Out on the fringes of Gazi, amid car workshops and the occasional experimental theatre, this hip little cafe-bar is a treat. There's a good food menu, and often music at night.

Psyrri, Omonia & Exarhia

Exarhia is a good bet for youthful, lively bars on Plateia Exarhion and side streets; many have live music. The cheap-bar precinct on nearby Mesolongiou is popular with students and anarchists. At night, the actual square of Omonia is less seedy than it was, but drug-dealing and the like have simply been pushed south into Psyrri, west of the market; stay alert here.

Veneti   CAFE
(Map p108; ☑ 210 523 0740; Plateia Omonias 7, Omonia; ⊘ 7am-11pm; Ⓜ Omonia) Legendary cafe Neon, famous haunt of Athens literati, fell victim to the crisis. But the cavernous space got a decent new tenant in Veneti (aka Beneth, if you read the letters in English), which has filled the lower level with good-quality pastries, cookies, pies and even hot meals. There's seating upstairs and out on the square. Excellent service.

There are several other branches of Veneti around town, including one on **Monastiraki** (Map p78; ☑ 210 323 3122; Monastiraki 10; ⊘ 7am-midnight; Ⓜ Monastiraki).

Little Kook   CAFE
(Map p78; ☑ 210 321 4144; www.facebook.com/littlekookgr; Karaiskaki 17, Psyrri; ⊘ 11am-midnight, from 10am Sat & Sun; ♿; Ⓜ Monastiraki) Nominally, this place sells coffee and cake. But it's really about its dazzling decor, which conjures an odd childhood fantasy. Precisely which one depends on the season, as the theme changes regularly. Everywhere are dolls, props, paintings and table decorations. You'll know you're getting close when you see party streamers over the street. Kids will be dazzled; Instagrammers will swoon.

Blue Fox   BAR
(Map p64; ☑ 6942487225; Asklipiou 91, Exarhia; ⊘ 9pm-3am Thu-Sat; Ⓜ Panepistimio) Athens supports a small but lively swing and rockabilly scene, and Blue Fox, with its big wooden dance floor, is one of its hubs. Weekend nights, you'll likely spot it from the Vespas parked outside.

Cinque   WINE BAR
(Map p108; ☑ 215 501 7853; www.cinque.gr; Agatharhou 15, Psyrri) Painted dark purple, this place feels like a jewel box, and the assorted Greek wines are the gems. Also a good place for light food, with platters of meats and cheeses.

Tralala   BAR
(Map p64; ☑ 210 362 8066; Asklipiou 45, Exarhia; ⊘ 11pm-3am; Ⓜ Panepistimio, Omonia) Actors frequent cool Tralala, with its original artwork, lively owners and gregarious atmosphere.

Revolt BAR
(Map p108; ☑ 210 380 0016; Kolleti 29, Exarhia; ⊙ 11am-2am; Ⓜ Omonia) This small, simple bar with tables spilling out on to a pedestrianised square anchors a few solid blocks of good nightlife. The vibrant murals out front are super. Start here and explore.

Tsin Tsin COCKTAIL BAR
(Map p108; ☑ 210 384 1460; Kiafas 6, Exarhia; ⊙ 7pm-late; Ⓜ Omonia) Teeny, tiny and a bit out of the way on a little lane. The bartender knows the craft and the loungey feel is relaxing.

Tranzistor BAR
(Map p108; ☑ 210 322 8658; Protogenous 10, Psyrri; ⊙ 9am-midnight; Ⓜ Monastiraki) Sidle up to the backlit bar or relax at tables outside at this small, cool spot. It's one of a few good mellow bars on this narrow street.

Spiti Mas CAFE
(Map p108; ☑ 210 331 4751; Navarhou Apostoli 10, Psyrri; ⊙ 9am-6pm; Ⓜ Thissio, Monastiraki) Fancy breakfast in bed? You can have it at 'Our House', a cafe set up like a hip apartment, complete with a single bed. The whole operation might be unbearably twee if it weren't for the good, fresh food and the genuinely sweet staff.

Ginger Ale BAR
(Map p108; ☑ 210 330 1246; Themistokleous 74, Exarhia; ⊙ 8am-late; Ⓜ Omonia) This place cultivates a poppy '60s kitsch vibe. By day, it's a good place to sip coffee and watch the

---

GAY & LESBIAN ATHENS

Athens' gay and lesbian scene is relatively low-key. **Athens Pride** (p96), held in June, has been an annual event since 2005; there's a march and a concert on Syntagma.

For nightlife, Gazi has become Athens' gay and lesbian hub. Gay and gay-friendly clubs around town are also in Plateia Agia Irinis, Metaxourgio and Exarhia. Check out www. athensinfoguide.com.

Rooster (Map p78; www.roostercafe.gr; Plateia Agia Irini 4, Monastiraki; ⊙ 9am-3am; Ⓜ Monastiraki) This wonderfully packed gay cafe on lively Plateia Agia Irini is straight-friendly, too, and so fills with chatting locals.

Loukoumi (Map p78; www.loukoumibar.gr; Plateia Avyssinias 3, Monastiraki; ⊙ 11am-2am; Ⓜ Monastiraki) This creative, gay-friendly cafe and arts space occupies two buildings facing each other across Plateia Avyssinias. It covers everything from daytime coffee and snacks to night-time DJs to drag queens, plus a vintage shop and gallery space.

S-Cape (Map p84; www.s-capeclub.gr; Iakhou 32, Gazi; ⊙ 11.30pm-5am; Ⓜ Kerameikos) Stays packed with the younger gay, lesbian and transgender crowd. Check theme nights online.

Trap (Map p64; ☑ 210 922 2248; Korytsas 15, Gazi; ⊙ 11pm-8am Mon & Wed Sun) This club is out on the fringes of Gazi and has a laid-back atmosphere to match.

Sodade2 (Map p84; ☑ 210 346 8657; Triptolemou 10, Gazi; ⊙ 11pm-6am; Ⓜ Kerameikos) Open since 2000, before Gazi was any kind of nightlife destination, this club remains superfun for dancing. Weeknights are pop, weekends are EDM. Mondays are Greek-music nights.

Noiz Club (Map p84; ☑ 210 346 7850; www.facebook.com/noizclubgaz; Konstantinoupoleos 78, Gazi; Ⓜ Kerameikos) Athens' main lesbian club has retro dance nights.

Myrovolos (Map p64; ☑ 210 522 8806; Giatrakou 12, Metaxourgio; ⊙ noon-4am Mon-Fri, 11am-4am Sat & Sun; Ⓜ Metaxourghio) Popular lesbian cafe-bar-restaurant on a vast and somewhat unkempt *plateia*, with a motorcycle clubhouse (unrelated) upstairs. Archetypal Metaxourgio, in other words.

BIG (Map p84; ☑ 6946282845; www.barbig.gr; Falesias 12, Gazi; ⊙ 10pm-3am Tue, Thu & Sun, to 5am Fri & Sat; Ⓜ Kerameikos) Cosy hub for Athens' lively bear scene.

Moe Club (Map p84; www.moeclub-gazi.blogspot.com; Keleou 5, Gazi; ⊙ 1am-6am; Ⓜ Kerameikos) After-hours hang-out with occasional special parties. Next door is the **Moe Bear Garage**, which opens earlier.

scene on Plateia Exarhia. By night, it's all tiki cocktails and rock music.

 Kolonaki

Kolonaki has two main nightlife strips: sprawling bar-cafes, most quite slick and sceney, around the north end of Skoufa, and a cluster of tiny, crowded bars along Haritos.

Rock'n'Roll   BAR

(Map p102; ☑ 210 722 0649; www.facebook.com/ rockathens; Plateia Kolonakiou, Kolonaki; ☺ Sep-Jun; Ⓜ Evangelismos) A Kolonaki classic, this upscale crowd-pleaser lives up to its name at night, when dance parties get wild. Popular with the trendy Kolonaki crowd, it has a good vibe, but 'face control' can be strict. During the day it's a busy, but more relaxed cafe lining Kolonaki's main square. In summer, it closes in favour of a beach location.

Filion   CAFE

(Map p102; ☑ 210 361 2850; Skoufa 34, Kolonaki; ☺ 8am-midnight; ☎; Ⓜ Syntagma) Holding strong against modern glitz in Kolonaki, Filion is a pleasantly dowdy old-school cafe, frequented by older members of the intellectual establishment and the occasional younger artist or writer.

Dark Side of Chocolate   CAFE

(Map p102; ☑ 210 339 2348; Solonos 49; ☺ 8am-11pm; Ⓜ Syntagma) This tiny cafe in Kolonaki has made a name for itself for its hot chocolate and handmade truffles, displayed like gems in a glass case. It's a tiny, cosy place for some restorative caffeine (there's coffee too) and a sweet to nibble.

Petite Fleur   CAFE

(Map p102; www.petite-fleur.gr; Omirou 44, Kolonaki; ☺ 8am-11pm; Ⓜ Panepistimio) Petite Fleur serves up large mugs of hot chocolate and speciality cappuccinos in a quiet, almost-Parisian ambience.

 Pangrati & Mets

Chelsea Hotel   BAR

(Map p64; ☑ 210 756 3374; Arhimidous 1, cnr Proklou, Pangrati; ☺ 9.30am-late; ☎; ☐ 2, 4, 11 to Plateia Plastira) When people talk about the cool but mellow scene in Pangrati, they're probably thinking of this busy cafe-bar on Plateia Plastira. By day, it's coffee, books and the occasional laptop. When the sun sets, every seat, inside and out, is filled with young Athenians aspiring to be as artistic and bohemian as residents of the bar's NYC namesake.

Odeon Cafe   CAFE

(Map p64; ☑ 210 922 3414; Markou Mousourou 19, Mets; ☺ 8.30am-late; Ⓜ Akropoli) This delightful slice of local Athens life is a simple corner cafe-bar where quietly chatting friends sit beneath ivy winding over the footpath. Extra-friendly staff, plus snacks and drinks, and occasional live music at night.

 Entertainment

English-language entertainment information appears daily in the *Kathimerini* supplement in the *International New York Times*. Athens' thriving multiuse art spaces host all manner of goings-on. For comprehensive events listings, with links to online ticket-sales points, try the following:

www.thisisathens.gr Athens tourism site.

www.elculture.gr Arts and culture listings.

www.tickethour.com Also has sports matches.

www.tickethouse.gr Rockwave and other festivals.

www.ticketservices.gr Range of events.

Cinema

★ **Cine Paris**   CINEMA

(Map p78; ☑ 210 322 0721; www.cineparis.gr; Kydathineon 22, Plaka; Ⓜ Syntagma) The Paris was the very first outdoor cinema in Athens, established in the 1920s. It's still a magical place to see a movie, on a rooftop in Plaka, with great views of the Acropolis from some seats.

Thission   CINEMA

(Map p84; ☑ 210 342 0864; www.cine-thisio.gr; Apostolou Pavlou 7, Thisio; Ⓜ Thissio) Across from the Acropolis, this is a lovely old-style outdoor cinema in a garden setting. Sit towards the back if you want to catch a glimpse of the glowing edifice.

Aigli Cinema   CINEMA

(Map p64; ☑ 210 336 9369; www.aeglizappiou.gr; Zappeio Gardens, Syntagma; €8.50; ☺ films at 9pm & 11pm; Ⓜ Syntagma) Historic open-air cinema in the verdant Zappeio Gardens (p83).

Vox   CINEMA

(Map p108; ☑ 210 331 0170; Themistokleous 82, Exarhia; Ⓜ Omonia) Vox open-air cinema on

Exarhia's main square rivals the Paris in Plaka as one of the older cinemas in the city. It has fortunately received historic-building designation. Still, it has the rough-and-ready vibe you'd expect in this neighbourhood.

Cine Athinaia
CINEMA
(Map p102; ☑ 210 721 5717; www.facebook.com/cineathinaia; Haritos 50, Kolonaki; Ⓜ Evangelismos) This summer-only open-air cinema in Kolonaki lists what's playing on its Facebook page.

Dexameni
CINEMA
(Map p102; ☑ 210 362 3942; www.facebook.com/cine-dexameni; Plateia Dexameni, Kolonaki; Ⓜ Evangelismos) This classic open-air cinema is in a lovely spot in the quieter reaches of Kolonaki, with a wall of cascading bougainvillea, deckchairs and little tables to rest your beer on.

Greek Music
Athens has some of the best *rembetika* in intimate, evocative venues. Performances usually include both *rembetika* and *laïka* (urban popular music), start at around 11.30pm and do not have a cover charge, though drinks can be more expensive than at bars. Most close May to September, so in summer try live-music tavernas around Plaka and Psyrri, or small bars in Exarhia.

Stoa Athanaton
TRADITIONAL MUSIC
(Map p108; ☑ 210 321 4362; Sofokleous 19, Central Market, Omonia; ☺ 3-6pm & midnight-6am Mon-Sat Oct-May; Ⓜ Monastiraki, Panepistimio, Omonia) This legendary club occupies a hall above the central meat market (p121). Popular for classic *rembetika* and *laïka* from a respected band of musicians, it often starts from midafternoon. Access is by a lift in the arcade. Food is not the attraction.

Perivoli tou Ouranou
TRADITIONAL MUSIC
(Map p78; ☑ 210 323 5517; www.perivolitouranou.gr; Lysikratous 19, Plaka; ☺ 9pm-late Fri & Sat, noon-6pm Sun Oct-Jun; Ⓜ Akropoli) A favourite rustic, old-style Plaka music haunt with dinner (mains €18 to €29).

Boemissa
TRADITIONAL MUSIC
(Map p84; ☑ 210 383 8803; www.boemissa.gr; Pireos 69, Thisio; ☺ 10pm-late Thu-Sat; Ⓜ Omonia) For decades in Exarhia, this budget-friendly music joint moved across town and lost some of its accumulated divey-ness. But the young audience, fuelled by a €15 'crisis special' meal and unlimited wine, makes up for lost time when singers belt the classic heart-rending *rembetika* and *laïka*.

SUMMER CINEMA

One of the delights of Athens is the enduring tradition of open-air cinema, where you can watch the latest Hollywood or art-house flick in the warm summer air. Many original outdoor cinemas have been refurbished and are still operating in gardens and on rooftops around Athens, with modern sound systems.

Plaka's rooftop **Cine Paris** and Exarhia's **Vox** both claim to be the oldest, though Cine Paris has an advantage with Acropolis views, as does **Thission**. **Aigli**, in the verdant Zappeio Gardens, is a bit away from traffic noise, and you can watch a movie in style with a glass of wine. Kolonaki's **Dexameni** is in a peaceful square.

Kavouras
TRADITIONAL MUSIC
(Map p108; ☑ 210 381 0202; Themistokleous 64, Exarhia; ☺ 11pm-late Thu-Sat Sep-Jun; Ⓜ Omonia) Above Exarhia's popular souvlaki joint, this lively club usually plays until dawn for a student crowd.

Mostrou
TRADITIONAL MUSIC
(Map p78; ☑ 210 322 5558; www.mostrou.gr; Mnisikleous 22, cnr Lyssiou, Plaka; ☺ 6pm-2am Thu-Sun; Ⓜ Monastiraki) This is the postcard scene of an Athens taverna, with tables set up on Plaka's famous stair-street, Acropolis views and a band playing all the bouzouki hits. As a result, it's thronged with tourists, but the music and food are still good. In winter, it's even rowdier, with a dance floor inside.

Rock & Jazz Music
Athens has a healthy rock-music scene and many European tours stop here. In summer, check Rockwave and other festival schedules.

★ Half Note Jazz Club
JAZZ
(Map p64; ☑ 210 921 3310; www.halfnote.gr; Trivonianou 17, Mets; Ⓜ Akropoli) Athens' most serious jazz venue is a stylish place that hosts Greek and international musicians. Check the schedule ahead of your trip, as it's not open every night and closes entirely in summer.

Gagarin 205 Club
LIVE MUSIC
(☑ 211 411 2500; www.gagarin205.gr; Liossion 205, Thymarakia; Ⓜ Agios Nikolaos) Friday- and Saturday-night gigs feature leading rock and underground bands.

AN Club
LIVE MUSIC

(Map p108; ☑ 210 330 5056; www.anclub.gr; Solomou 13-15, Exarhia; Ⓜ Omonia) A spot for lesser-known international and local rock bands.

Bios
LIVE MUSIC, GALLERY

(Map p84; ☑ 210 342 5335; www.bios.gr; Pireos 84, Gazi; ⊙ 11am-late; Ⓜ Thissio) Occupying a Bauhaus apartment building, this multilevel warren has a ground-floor bar, a basement club, a tiny art-house cinema and a roof deck. Expect live performances, art and new-media exhibitions, or at the very least a solid DJ and an Acropolis view.

Theatre & Performing Arts

Athens, as the birthplace of live theatre, has an excellent scene – but it's unfortunately accessible only to Greek speakers; subtitling and English performances are rare. In summer the main cultural happening is the Athens & Epidaurus Festival (p96), which includes dance and music programming.

Theatro Skion Tasou Konsta
PUPPET THEATRE

(☑ 6948852493; www.fkt.gr; Floibos Park, Palaio Faliro; €3.50; ⊙ 8.30pm Fri-Sun; ⓐ; ⓠ Park Flisvou) Greece's wise fool, Karagiozis, gave his name to the art of shadow puppetry (karagiozi), and they're on beautiful display in this tiny outdoor theatre every summer. Sure it's all in Greek, but the humour is slapstick and there's plenty of music in the various shows. After the 45-minute show, kids can file backstage to see how the magic happens.

Figoures & Koukles
PUPPET THEATRE

(Map p78; ☑ 210 322 7507; www.fkt.gr; Tripodon 30, Plaka; €3.50; ⊙ shows Sun morning) This puppet workshop gives weekly karagiozi shows in winter in its sweet 50-seat theatre. The husband-and-wife team are happy to show how the shadow-puppet set-up works and how the figures are made. Check the site for the winter schedule. In summer, they mount more frequent shows in the Theatro Skion Tasou Konsta, in the park in Palaio Faliro.

Treno sto Rouf
ARTS CENTRE

(☑ 210 529 8922; www.totrenostorouf.gr; Konstantinoupoleos, Rouf; ⊙ 8pm-late Tue-Sat Sep-Jul; ⓠ 21 or B16 to Rouf, Ⓜ Kerameikos) Look for the glowing headlight on a steam locomotive behind Rouf station. Attached is a string of old train cars converted into a restaurant, bar-cafe, music club and theatre. Even on a night when nothing's scheduled, it's a cool place to have a drink and a snack (€6 to €15) and imagine yourself on the Orient Express.

Stavros Niarchos Foundation Cultural Center
CULTURAL CENTRE

(☑ 216 809 1001; www.snfcc.org; Leoforos Syngrou 364, Kallithea; ⓠ 550 to Onasseio, 10 to Epaminonda) FREE Spreading its winged roof on a hill above Faliron Bay, this Renzo Piano building, surrounded by a vast park (p92), made a big splash on the Athens cultural scene when it opened in 2017. Architecture buffs will love seeing the structure. Otherwise, check the schedule for arts events by the grand pool or at the National Opera of Greece, inside the complex.

National Theatre
THEATRE

(Map p108; ☑ 210 528 8100; www.n-t.gr; Agiou Konstantinou 22-24, Omonia; Ⓜ Omonia) Performances of contemporary plays and ancient theatre in one of the city's finest neoclassical buildings, as well as in venues around town and, in summer, in ancient theatres across Greece. Happily for tourists, some of the productions are surtitled in English.

Pallas
THEATRE

(Map p78; ☑ 210 321 3100; www.ellthea.gr; Voukourestiou 5, Syntagma; Ⓜ Syntagma) One of Athens' premier theatres, the Pallas is centrally located and stages large productions, often in Greek. The Mikro Pallas is a smaller, basement theatre in the same complex, connected via an indoor strip of sleek bars and cafes.

Megaron Mousikis
PERFORMING ARTS

(Athens Concert Hall; ☑ 210 728 2333; www.megaron.gr; Kokkali 1, cnr Leoforos Vasilissis Sofias, Ilissia; ⊙ box office 10am-6pm Mon-Fri, to 2pm Sat, later on performance days; Ⓜ Megaro Mousikis) The city's state-of-the-art concert hall presents a rich winter program of operas and concerts featuring world-class international and Greek performers. In summer, it has shows in the back garden.

Dora Stratou Dance Theatre
DANCE

(Map p64; ☑ 210 921 4650; www.grdance.org; Filopappou Hill; adult/child €15/5; ⊙ performances 9.30pm Wed-Fri, 8.30pm Sat & Sun Jun-Sep; Ⓜ Petralona, Akropoli) Every summer this company performs its repertoire of Greek folk dances at its open-air theatre on the western side of Filopappou Hill. It also runs folk-dancing workshops in summer.

Greek National Opera
OPERA

(Ethniki Lyriki Skini; ☑ 210 366 2100; www.nationalopera.gr; Leoforos Syngrou 364, Kallithea) The season runs from November to June. Performances are usually held at the grand Renzo

Piano building at the Stavros Niarchos Foundation Cultural Center, plus the Odeon of Herodes Atticus (p73) in summer. The opera's former home, the Olympia Theatre, is also still used, and is a central place to buy tickets.

Olympia Theatre PERFORMING ARTS
(Map p108; 🖉 210 361 2461; Akadimias 59, Exarhia; Ⓜ Panepistimio) From November to June; ballet, symphony and some opera.

Technopolis PERFORMING ARTS
(Map p84; 🖉 210 346 7322; www.technopolis-athens.com; Pireos 100, Gazi; Ⓜ Kerameikos) There's always something on at the city's old gasworks, the impressively restored 1862 complex of furnaces and industrial buildings. It hosts multimedia exhibitions, concerts, festivals and special events and has a pleasant cafe.

🔒 Shopping

Central Athens is one big shopping hub, with an eclectic mix of stores, many still organised roughly by category – lace and buttons on one block, light bulbs on the next. The main (if generic) shopping street is pedestrianised Ermou, running from Syntagma to Monastiraki.

Books, Maps & Music

Politeia BOOKS
(Map p108; 🖉 210 360 0235; www.politeianet.gr; Asklipiou 1-3, Panepistimio; ⊙ 9am-9pm Mon-Fri, to 8pm Sat; Ⓜ Panepistimio) Large bookstore that occupies four storefronts. While it doesn't have a dedicated English section, it does stock English-language books, filed in the relevant sections. And because it's on the edge of Exarhia, it stocks communist theory in the impulse-buy section by the checkout.

Anavasi MAPS, BOOKS
(Map p78; 🖉 210 321 8104; www.anavasi.gr; Voulis 32, cnr Apollonos, Syntagma; ⊙ 9.30am-5.30pm Mon & Wed, to 8.30pm Tue, Thu & Fri, 10am-4.30pm Sat; Ⓜ Syntagma) Great travel bookshop with an extensive range of Greece maps and walking and activity guides.

Yiannis Samouelin MUSIC
(Map p78; 🖉 210 321 2433; www.musicshop.gr; Ifestou 36, Monastiraki; ⊙ 9am-7pm; Ⓜ Monastiraki) Wedged between more modern, generic shops on Ifestou, this shop is the place to buy the bouzouki of your dreams. It has been dealing in musical instruments from around the world since 1928.

Xylouris MUSIC
(Map p108; 🖉 210 322 2711; http://xilouris.gr; Stoa Pesmatzoglou, Panepistimiou 39, Panepistimio; ⊙ 9am-4pm Mon, Wed & Sat, to 8pm Tue, Thu & Fri; Ⓜ Panepistimio) Set in an arcade with several other music shops, this treasure trove is run by the family of legendary Cretan composer Nikos Xylouris. They can guide you through the comprehensive range of Greek music. Also has a branch at the Museum of Greek Popular Instruments (p80).

Comicon Shop COMICS
(Map p108; 🖉 213 008 0255; www.comicon-shop.gr; Solonos 128, Exarhia; Ⓜ Omonia) Browse a full range of Greek indie comics, graphic novels and zines.

Travel Bookstore BOOKS
(Map p108; 🖉 210 361 6943; www.travelbookstore.gr; Solonos 71, Panepistimio; ⊙ 8.30am-4.30pm Mon, Wed & Sat, to 8.30pm Tue, Thu & Fri) Good central place for maps.

Syd MUSIC
(Map p78; 🖉 210 321 8374; www.sydrecords.com; Protogenous 13, Monastiraki; ⊙ noon-8pm; Ⓜ Monastiraki) Not just vinyl records, but the whole 'vinyl culture' – whatever that entails. Lots of new and interesting stuff, plus tickets to local shows.

Tsigaridas BOOKS
(Map p108; 🖉 210 271 7521; www.tsigaridasbooks.gr; Alikarnassou 19, Panepistimio; ⊙ 8am-5pm Mon, to 8pm Tue-Fri, to 3pm Sat; Ⓜ Panepistimio) The best selection of English books – in fact, books in all languages – in central Athens.

Fashion & Jewellery

Korres COSMETICS
(Map p78; 🖉 210 321 0054; www.korres.com; Ermou 4, Syntagma; ⊙ 9am-9pm Mon-Fri, to 8pm Sat; Ⓜ Syntagma) Most pharmacies stock at least some of this popular natural-beauty-product line, but you can get the full range at the company's original homeopathic pharmacy – at a fraction of the price you'll pay in London or New York. There's also a branch at the airport and one near the Panathenaic Stadium.

Fanourakis JEWELLERY
(Map p102; 🖉 210 721 1762; www.fanourakis.gr; Patriarhou Ioakeim 23, Kolonaki; ⊙ 10am-5pm Mon, Wed & Sat, to 9pm Tue, Thu & Fri; Ⓜ Syntagma) One of the most creative Greek jewellers, Fanourakis designs delicate pieces of folded gold, encrusted rings, bows and other unique creations. The forms are sheer art, a factor that is

also reflected in the prices (though it now has a more inexpensive line as well).

El.Marneri Galerie
JEWELLERY, ART

(Map p74; ☑ 210 861 9488; www.elenimarneri. com; Lembesi 5-7, Makrygianni; ☺ 11am-8pm Tue, Thu & Fri, to 4pm Wed & Sat; Ⓜ Akropoli) Sample rotating exhibitions of local modern art and some of the best jewellery in the city. Handmade, unusual and totally eye-catching.

Lovecuts
CLOTHING

(Map p74; ☑ 215 501 1526; Veikou 2, Makrygianni; ☺ 10am-2pm Mon, 4-8pm Tue, noon-4pm Wed, 11am-2.30pm & 5.30-8.30pm Thu & Fri, 10am-3pm Sat; Ⓜ Akropoli) A young Greek designer makes all the cute, affordable cotton clothing here, such as reversible hoodies and skirts in fun prints. One of several creative, small-scale boutiques on this street.

Rien
FASHION & ACCESSORIES

(Map p84; ☑ 210 342 0622; www.rien.gr; Triptolemou 2-4, Gazi; ☺ 4-8pm Wed-Sat, or by appointment; Ⓜ Kerameikos) Penny Vomva designs stylish, sexy clothes with naturalistic lines. Her handbags are colourful leather fancies.

Melissinos Art
SHOES

(Map p78; ☑ 210 321 9247; www.melissinos poetsandalmaker.com; Agias Theklas 2, Psyrri; ☺ 10am-8pm, to 6pm winter; Ⓜ Monastiraki) Pantelis Melissinos continues the sandal-making tradition of his famous poet/cobbler father Stavros, who built his reputation by crafting Classical-inspired shoe designs for Hollywood stars. The shop can get a bit crowded, as people come for the character of Pantelis himself. But the prices are reasonable – and where else can you get sandals adjusted just to your feet?

Olgianna Melissinos
SHOES

(Map p78; ☑ 210 331 1925; www.melissinossandals.gr; Normanou 7, Monastiraki; ☺ 10am-6pm Mon, Wed, Sat & Sun, to 8pm Tue, Thu & Fri; Ⓜ Monastiraki) Another scion of the legendary Stavros Melissinos, Olgianna has a line of custom-fitted sandals as well as smart belts and bags. She can also make designs to order.

Vassilis Zoulias
CLOTHING

(Map p102; ☑ 210 338 9924; www.vassiliszoulias. com; Akadimias 4, Kolonaki; ☺ 10am-5pm Mon, Wed & Sat, to 9pm Tue, Thu & Fri; Ⓜ Syntagma) An exquisite range of elegant, feminine shoes can be found at the boutique store of Greece's Manolo Blahnik. Some of these designs are works of art inspired by '50s and '60s films, as is his couture line.

Lalaounis
JEWELLERY

(Map p78; ☑ 210 361 1371; www.iliaslalaounis. eu; Panepistimiou 6, cnr Voukourestiou, Syntagma; ☺ 10am-4.30pm Mon, Wed & Sat, to 8pm Tue, Thu & Fri; Ⓜ Syntagma) Leading Greek jeweller Lalaounis' exquisitely crafted creations reflect ancient Greek motifs and draw inspiration from other cultures, biology, nature and mythology. If you like his work, you may also appreciate his **museum** (Map p74; ☑ 210 922 1044; www.lalaounis-jewelrymuseum.gr; Kallisperi 12, cnr Karyatidon, Makrygianni; adult/child €5/free; ☺ 9am-3pm Tue-Sat, 11am-4pm Sun; Ⓜ Akropoli).

Actipis
JEWELLERY

(Map p78; ☑ 210 323 6907; www.actipis.com; Lekka 20, Syntagma; ☺ 11.30am-8pm Mon-Fri, to 5pm Sat Nov-Apr; Ⓜ Syntagma) Spiros Actipis designs elegant jewellery using smooth pebbles, gleaming silver and raw leather. The shop closes in summer.

Food

Bahar
FOOD

(Map p108; ☑ 210 321 7225; www.bahar.gr; Evripidou 31, Omonia; ☺ 7am-3pm Mon-Thu & Sat, to 6pm Fri; Ⓜ Omonia, Monastiraki) Evripidou, just south of the central market, is Athens' traditional street for spices, a couple of highly aromatic blocks of Mediterranean herbs and imported seeds, barks and other wonders. Bahar is just one of half a dozen shops here, all overflowing with hundreds of ways to add flavour and fragrance to your life.

Pantopoleion
FOOD & DRINKS

(Map p108; ☑ 210 323 4612; www.atenco.gr; Sofokleous 1, Omonia; ☺ 8am-7pm; Ⓜ Panepistimio) Enormous store selling traditional food products from all over Greece, from Santorini capers and boutique olive oils to Cretan rusks, jars of goodies for edible souvenirs and Greek wines and spirits.

Bakaliko
FOOD & DRINKS

(Map p64; ☑ 210 756 0055; Proklou 31, Pangrati; ☺ 9am-3pm Mon, Tue & Sat, to 6pm Wed, Thu & Fri; 🚌 2, 4, 11 to Plateia Plastira) One-stop shopping for the best Greek food products: the store has won awards for its dedication and stock of traditional oil, wine, cheese, yoghurt and honey. Herbs hang in bunches, lentils fill sacks, beans are dazzling in their freshness and variety.

Aristokratikon
FOOD

(Map p78; ☑ 210 323 4373; www.aristokratikon. com; Voulis 7, Syntagma; ☺ 8am-9pm Mon-Fri, to 4pm Sat; Ⓜ Syntagma) Since 1928, this shop has been making fine chocolates. One of its specialities is dried fruits and candied citrus peel dipped in dark chocolate. It's in the tiny nuts-and-sweets district on Karageorgi Servias; look for it just inside an arcade.

Gusto di Grecia
FOOD & DRINKS

(Map p102; ☑ 210 362 6809; Pindarou 16-20, Kolonaki; ⊙ 8am-9pm Mon-Sat, 10am-6pm Sun; Ⓜ Syntagma) Shop for the best treats from all over Greece, from cheese to local honeys, cold cuts, olive oil and wine.

Fine Wine
WINE

(Map p78; ☑ 210 323 0350; www.finewine.gr; Lysikratous 3, Plaka; ⊙ noon-9pm; Ⓜ Akropoli) In the winding streets of Plaka, the finest wines can be found in this small terracotta-hued building. It's a welcoming destination for the curious and for local wine lovers who come to browse the rows of vintage Greek wines.

Gifts & Souvenirs

★ Forget Me Not
GIFTS & SOUVENIRS

(Map p78; ☑ 210 325 3740; www.forgetmenot athens.gr; Adrianou 100, Plaka; ⊙ 10am-10pm May-Sep, to 8pm Oct-Apr; Ⓜ Syntagma, Monastiraki) This impeccable small store stocks supercool design gear, from fashion to housewares and gifts, all by contemporary Greek designers. Great for gift shopping – who doesn't want a set of cheerful 'evil eye' coasters or some Hermes-winged beach sandals?

Centre of Hellenic Tradition
ARTS & CRAFTS

(Map p78; ☑ 210 321 3023; www.kelp.gr; Pandrosou 36, Monastiraki; ⊙ 9am-8pm Apr-Nov, to 6pm Oct-Mar; Ⓜ Monastiraki) If you like traditional crafts, make this one of your first stops, to see the range and skill of Greek artisans. This organisation collects excellent work and stocks its shop with ceramics, sculpture and handicrafts from around the country. There's an old-style *kafeneio* (coffee house) upstairs (open till midnight) that makes a nice break from the Monastiraki shopping frenzy.

Mompso
ARTS & CRAFTS

(Map p102; ☑ 210 323 0670; www.mompso.com; Athinas 33, Psyrri; ⊙ 10am-6pm Mon-Sat; Ⓜ Monastiraki) The curators of Mompso have put a refined spin on all things rural, so it has the most elegant and excellent-quality equestrian supplies and traditional accessories for donkeys (beaded headdresses), shepherds (bronze bells) and country folk (walking sticks).

Mastiha Shop
FOOD, BEAUTY

(Map p78; ☑ 210 363 2750; www.mastihashop. com; Panepistimiou 6, Syntagma; ⊙ 9am-8pm Mon & Wed, to 9pm Tue, Thu & Fri, to 5pm Sat; Ⓜ Syntagma) Mastic, the medicinal resin from rare trees only on the island of Chios, is the key ingredient in everything in this store, from natural skin products to a liqueur that's divine when served chilled.

Amorgos
ARTS & CRAFTS

(Map p78; ☑ 210 324 3836; www.amorgosart.gr; Kodrou 3, Plaka; ⊙ 11am-8pm Mon-Fri, to 7pm Sat; Ⓜ Syntagma) Charming store crammed with wooden toys, *karagiozis* puppets, ceramics, embroidery and other folk art, as well as carved wooden furniture made by the owner.

Apivita
COSMETICS

(Map p102; ☑ 210 364 0560; www.apivita.com; Solonos 6, Kolonaki; ⊙ 10am-9pm Tue, Thu & Fri, to 5pm Mon, Wed & Sat, spa closed Mon & Sun; Ⓜ Syntagma) Honey, propolis and other bee-made stuff are the wonder ingredients in many of Apivita's natural beauty products. You can also try Greek herbal teas or head upstairs to the spa. There's also a branch at the airport.

Aidini
ARTS & CRAFTS

(Map p78; ☑ 210 323 4591; Nikis 32, Syntagma; ⊙ 10.30am-5pm Mon & Wed, to 9pm Tue, Thu & Fri, to 4pm Sat; Ⓜ Syntagma) Artisan Errikos Aidini's unique metal creations are made in his workshop at the back of this charming store, including small mirrors, candlesticks, lamps, planes and his signature bronze boats.

Markets

Athens Central Market
MARKET

(Varvakios Agora; Map p108; Athinas, btwn Sofokleous & Evripidou; ⊙ 7am-3pm Mon-Sat; Ⓜ Monastiraki, Panepistimio, Omonia) The hectic, colourful Athens *agora* (market; also referred to as the Varvakios Agora) is the highlight of the vibrant Athinas market district. It's a sensory and gastronomic delight, with an amazing range of olives, spices, cheeses and deli treats. The historic **meat market** (Map p108; ⊙ 7am-6pm Mon-Sat), with hanging carcasses illuminated by swinging light bulbs, is a highlight. **Fruits and vegetables** (Map p108; Athinas, btwn Sofokleous & Evripidou, Omonia; ⊙ 7am-6pm Mon-Sat) are across Athinas.

Kolonaki Weekly Market
MARKET

(Map p102; www.laikesagores.gr; Xenokratous, Kolonaki; ⊙ 7am-2pm Fri; Ⓜ Syntagma) Most Athens neighbourhoods have a weekly *laïki agora*, a street market for fruit, veg and household miscellany, and Kolonaki's is a good one. Leafy Xenokratous is blocked off to traffic from Friday morning to early afternoon. Local regulars come to buy fresh fruit, vegetables, fish, honey, handmade products and flowers.

Exarhia Weekly Market MARKET
(Map p64; www.laikesagores.gr; Kalidromiou, Exarhia; ⊘ 6am-2pm Sat; 🚌 026, Ⓜ Omonia) With rowdy traders working against lovely neo-classical buildings, this is one of the most atmospheric renditions of the *laïki agora*, the weekly market that takes over a street in each big neighbourhood every week. Visitors won't have much practical use for the produce and household goods, but look for the roving ouzo seller. Or camp at a cafe and spectate.

★ Monastiraki Flea Market MARKET
(Map p78; btwn Adrianou, Ifestou & Ermou, Monastiraki; ⊘ daily May-Oct, Sun-Wed & Fri Nov-Apr; Ⓜ Monastiraki) What's touted as a 'flea market' is now mostly souvenir shops, though there are still a few good artisans, as well as *palaiopoleia* ('old-stuff sellers'). For the best rummaging, come Sunday mornings, when dealers of jewellery, handicrafts and bric-a-brac set up tables on Plateia Avyssinias.

Eleonas Flea Market MARKET
(Pazari; Agias Annis, Eleonas; ⊘ dawn-2pm Sun; Ⓜ Eleonas) The so-called 'Gypsy market' is not for everyone. The city's trash-pickers and junk dealers, plus sellers of vegetables, new clothes and bulk items, lay out their wares in several warehouses and parking lots in this industrial part of town. The brave of heart can find some bargains, collectables and kitsch delights among the junk.

ⓘ Information

DANGERS & ANNOYANCES
During the financial crisis, crime has risen in Athens. But this is a rise from almost zero, and violent street crime remains relatively rare. Nonetheless, travellers should be alert. Stay aware of your surroundings at night, especially in streets around Omonia, where prostitutes and junkies gather, as well as by the Mavromateon bus terminal, as the adjacent park is a rather grim homeless encampment.

EMERGENCY
Athens' landline numbers begin with 210. Mobile phones begin with 6.

ELPA (Elliniki Leschi Aftokinitou kai Periigiseon; 🖉 210 606 8800, 24hr roadside assistance 10400; Leoforos Mesogion 541, Agia Paraskevi, Athens) Nationwide roadside assistance.

Police station (🖉 210 770 5711, emergency 100; www.astynomia.gr; Leoforos Alexandras 173, Ambelokipi; Ⓜ Ambelokipi); **Syntagma**

station (🖉 210 725 7000, emergency 100; Mimnermou 6-8; Ⓜ Syntagma)

Tourist Police (🖉 210 920 0724, 24hr 171; Veïkou 43-45, Koukaki; ⊘ 8am-10pm; Ⓜ Sygrou-Fix, Akropoli)

MEDICAL SERVICES
Check pharmacy windows for details of the nearest duty pharmacy, or call 🖉 1434 (Greek only). There's a 24-hour pharmacy at the airport.

SOS Doctors (🖉 210 821 1888, 1016; www.sosiatroi.gr; ⊘ 24hr) Pay service with English-speaking doctors.

MONEY
Major banks have branches around Syntagma. ATMs are plentiful enough in commercial districts, but harder to find in more residential areas.

National Bank of Greece (🖉 210 334 0500; cnr Karageorgi Servias & Stadiou, Syntagma; Ⓜ Syntagma) Has a 24-hour automated exchange machine.

Onexchange Currency and money transfers. Branches: **Syntagma** (🖉 210 331 2462; www.onexchange.gr; Karageorgi Servias 2, Syntagma; ⊘ 9am-9pm; Ⓜ Syntagma), **Monastiraki** (🖉 210 322 2657; www.onexchange.gr; Areos 1, Monastiraki; ⊘ 9am-9pm; Ⓜ Monastiraki).

POST
Athens Central Post Office (Map p108; Eolou 100; ⊘ 7.30am-8.30pm Mon-Fri, to 2.30pm Sat; Ⓜ Omonia)

Parcel Post Office (Map p78; Mitropoleos 60, Monastiraki; ⊘ 7.30am-8.30pm Mon-Fri; Ⓜ Monastiraki)

Syntagma Post Office (Map p78; Plateia Syntagmatos, Syntagma; ⊘ 7.30am-8.30pm Mon-Fri, to 2.30pm Sat, 9am-1.30pm Sun; Ⓜ Syntagma)

TOURIST INFORMATION
EOT (Greek National Tourism Organisation; Map p74; 🖉 210 331 0347, 210 331 0716; www.visitgreece.gr; Dionysiou Areopagitou 18-20, Makrygianni; ⊘ 8am-8pm Mon-Fri, 10am-4pm Sat & Sun May-Sep, 9am-7pm Mon-Fri Oct-Apr; Ⓜ Akropoli) Free Athens map, transport information and *Athens and Attica* booklet. There's also a desk at **Athens Airport** (⊘ 9am-5pm Mon-Fri, 10am-4pm Sat).

Athens Airport Information Desk (⊘ 24hr) This 24-hour desk has Athens info, booklets and the free Athens Spotlighted discount card for restaurants and attractions.

Athens City Information Kiosks Airport (🖉 210 353 0390; www.thisisathens.org; ⊘ 8am-8pm; Ⓜ Airport), **Acropolis** (Map p74; 🖉 210 321 7116; www.thisisathens.org; Dionysiou Areopagitou & Leoforos Syngrou; ⊘ 9am-9pm May-Sep; Ⓜ Akropoli) Maps, transport information and all Athens info.

ℹ Getting There & Away

AIR

Modern **Eleftherios Venizelos International Airport** (ATH; ☑ 210 353 0000; www.aia.gr), at Spata, 27km east of Athens, has all the modern conveniences, including 24-hour luggage storage in the arrivals hall, a children's playroom and even a small archaeological museum.It's served by many major and budget airlines as well as high-season charters.

Average domestic one-way fares range from €56 to €140, but vary dramatically depending on season. Between Aegean Airlines and Olympic Air (which have merged but still run separate routes), there are flights to all islands with airports.

Aegean Airlines (www.aegeanair.com)

Air Berlin (AB; ☑ 210 353 5264; www.airberlin.com)

Astra Airlines (☑ 800 700 7466, 2310 489 392; www.astra-airlines.gr) Thessaloniki-based, but with a few flights from Athens to Kozani/Kastoria, Chios and Samos.

British Airways (☑ from landline only 800 4414 6798; www.ba.com)

Olympic Air (☑ 801 801 0101, 210 355 0500; www.olympicair.com)

Sky Express (GQ; ☑ 28102 23800; www.skyexpress.gr) Crete-based. Beware harsh baggage restrictions.

BOAT

Most ferry, hydrofoil and high-speed catamaran services to the islands leave from the massive port at Piraeus, southwest of Athens.

Purchase tickets online at **Greek Ferries** (☑ 28105 29000; www.greekferries.gr), over the phone or at booths on the quay next to each ferry. Travel agencies selling tickets also surround each port; there is no surcharge.

BUS

Athens has two main intercity bus stations, 5km and 7km north of Omonia, plus a small bay for buses bound for south and east Attica. Pick up timetables at the tourist office, or see the relevant KTEL operator's website. Find a master list of KTEL companies at www.ktelbus.com; **KTEL Attikis** (☑ 210 880 8000; www.ktelattikis.gr) covers the Attica peninsula.

For international buses (from Bulgaria, Turkey etc), there is no single station; some come to Kifissos, while others stop at Plateia Karaïskaki or near Omonia.

Kifissos Terminal A (☑ 210 515 0025; Leoforos Kifisou 100, Peristeri; Ⓜ Agios Antonios) Buses to Thessaloniki, the Peloponnese, Ionian Islands and destinations in western Greece such as Igoumenitsa, Ioannina, Kastoria and Edessa. Local bus 051 goes to central Athens (junction of Zinonos and Menandrou, near Omonia) every 20 minutes from 5am to midnight. Local bus X93 goes to/from the airport. Local bus 420 goes to/from Piraeus (junction of Akti Kondili and Thermopilon). Taxis to Syntagma cost about €16 (€28 at night).

Liossion Terminal B (☑ 210 831 7153; Rikaki 6, Thymarakia; Ⓜ Agios Nikolaos, Attiki) Buses to central and northern Greece, such as Trikala (for Meteora), Delphi, Larissa, Thiva and Volos. To get here, take the metro to Attiki and catch any local bus north on Liossion. Get off the bus at Liossion 260 (stop labelled 'Stathmos Iperastikon Leof'), backtrack to Gousiou and turn left, and you'll see the terminal. Between 11.40pm and 5am, there are no buses to the centre; taxis to Syntagma cost about €15 (at night (€9 by day). Local bus X93 connects Kifissos Terminal A, Liossion Terminal B and the Athens Airport.

Mavromateon Terminal (Map p64; ☑ 210 822 5148, 210 880 8000; www.ktelattikis.gr; cnr Leoforos Alexandras & 28 Oktovriou-Patision, Pedion Areos; ☐ 2, 4, 5 or 11 to OTE, Ⓜ Viktoria) About 250m north of the National Archaeological Museum, with buses for around Attica. For Cape Sounion, look for the stop just north of Leoforos Alexandras. Ticket booths and buses for Rafina, Lavrio and Marathon are just north, on Mavromateon.

KTEL Buses to Epidavros (☑ 210 513 4588; www.ktelargolida.gr; 1-way €13)

Tourist Service (www.tourist-service.com) Buses from Piraeus and Athens to Bulgaria.

Key Buses From Kifissos Terminal A

DESTINATION	DURATION	FARE (€)	FREQUENCY
Alexandroupoli	11hr	77	5 daily
Corfu*	9hr	59	3 daily
Epidavros	2½hr	13	2 daily
Igoumenitsa	7½hr	49	3 daily
Ioannina	6¼hr	43	6 daily
Ithaki*	8½hr	52	1 daily
Kalavryta	3hr	18	1 daily
Kefallonia*	7hr	38	4 daily
Lefkada	5¼hr	37	4 daily (5 Jul-Aug)
Monemvasia	6hr	32	4 daily
Nafplio	2½hr	14	hourly
Olympia	5½hr	33	2 daily
Patra	3hr	22	half-hourly
Thessaloniki	7hr	45	9 daily
Zakynthos*	6hr	38	3 daily

* quoted price includes ferry ticket

Key Buses From Liossion Terminal B

DESTINATION	DURATION	FARE (€)	FREQUENCY
Agios Konstantinos	2½hr	17	8 daily
Delphi	2½hr	17	4 daily
Halkida	1¼hr	8	half-hourly
Karpenisi	4½hr	27	2 daily
Paralia Kymis	4½hr	23	2 daily (Jul-Aug)
Trikala (for transfer to Meteora)	4½hr	30	6 daily
Volos	4½hr	30	10 daily

Key Buses From Mavromateon Terminal

DESTINATION	DURATION	FARE (€)	FREQUENCY
Cape Sounion (coastal road)	2hr	6.90	hourly
Lavrio port	1½hr	5.30	half-hourly
Marathon	1½hr	4.10	half-hourly
Rafina port	1hr	2.60	half-hourly

CAR & MOTORCYCLE

Attiki Odos (Attiki Rd), Ethniki Odos (National Rd) and various ring roads facilitate getting in and out of Athens.

The airport has all major car-hire companies, and the top end of Leoforos Syngrou, near the Temple of Olympian Zeus, is dotted with firms. Local companies tend to offer better deals than multinationals. Expect to pay €45 per day, less for three or more days.

Avis (☑ 210 322 4951; www.avis.gr; Leoforos Syngrou 23, Makrygianni; ☉ 7.30am-9pm; Ⓜ Akropoli)

Budget (☑ 210 922 4200; www.budget.gr; Leoforos Syngrou 23, Makrygianni; ☉ 7.30am-9pm; Ⓜ Akropoli)

Europcar (☑ 210 921 1444; www.europcar-greece.gr; Leoforos Syngrou 25, Makrygianni; ☉ 8.30am-9pm; Ⓜ Akropoli)

Hertz (☑ 210 922 0102; www.hertz.gr; Leoforos Syngrou 12, Makrygianni; ☉ 8am-9pm; Ⓜ Akropoli)

Kosmos (☑ 210 923 4695; www.kosmos-carrental.com; Leoforos Syngrou 5, Makrygianni; ☉ 8am-8.30pm; Ⓜ Akropoli)

Motorent (☑ 210 923 4939; www.motorent.gr; Kavalloti 4, Makrygianni; ☉ 9am-6pm Mon-Fri, 9.30am-3pm Sat; Ⓜ Akropoli) From 50cc to 250cc (from €20 per day); must have motorcycle licence (and nerves of steel).

TRAIN

Intercity (IC) trains to central and northern Greece depart from the central **Larisis train station** (Stathmos Larisis; ☑ €1 per min 6am-11pm 14511; www.trainose.gr; Ⓜ Larissa Station), about 1km northwest of Plateia Omonias.

For the Peloponnese, take the **suburban rail** (☑ 14511; www.trainose.gr) to Kiato and change for a bus there. At time of research, the Patra train line was closed for repairs, so OSE buses replace its services. It's easier to just take a bus from Athens' Kifissos Bus Terminal A to your ultimate destination.

At the time of research, Greece's train system was in a state of flux due to the financial crisis. Domestic schedules/fares should be confirmed online or at **OSE** (☑ 210 362 4406, 210 362 4402, €0.99 per min 6am-11pm 14511; www.trainose.gr; Sina 6, Syntagma; ☉ 8am-3pm Mon-Fri; Ⓜ Panepistimio). Tickets can be bought online.

Consult www.seat61.com for tips on international trains to/from Greece; all service goes via Thessaloniki.

DESTINATION	DURATION	FARE (€)	FREQUENCY
Alexandroupoli	12¼hr	40	1 daily (overnight)
Alexandroupoli (IC)	11hr	65	1 daily (via Thessaloniki)
Corinth (suburban rail)	1hr 20min	8	13 daily
Kalambaka (for Meteora)	5hr	30	1 daily direct, 4 via Paleofarsalos (€18)
Kiato (suburban rail)	1hr 40min	8	13 daily
Thessaloniki	7hr	25	1 daily
Thessaloniki (IC)	5½hr	45	5 daily
Volos (IC)	5hr	30	6 daily (via Larissa)

❶ Getting Around

TO/FROM THE AIRPORT

The metro and suburban rail provide quick connections to central Athens. The bus is cheapest, though it takes longer. The suburban rail also goes to Piraeus and Larisis stations.

Bus

Express buses operate 24 hours between the airport and the city centre, Piraeus and KTEL bus terminals. At the airport, buy tickets (€6; not valid for other forms of public transport) at the booth near the stops.

Plateia Syntagmatos Bus X95 (Map p78; tickets €5; 1-1½ hours, every 30 minutes, ⊙24hrs). The Syntagma stop is on Othonos St.

Kifissos Terminal A bus station Bus X93 (1 hour; every 30 minutes by day, 60 minutes at night; ⊙24hrs).

Piraeus Bus X96 (1½ hours; every 20 minutes; ⊙24hrs). To Plateia Karaïskaki.

Metro

Metro line 3 goes to the airport. Some trains terminate early at Doukissis Plakentias; disembark and wait for the airport train (displayed on the train and platform screen). Trains run every 30 minutes, leaving Monastiraki between 5.50am and midnight, and the airport between 5.30am and 11.30pm, on the hour and half-hour.

Airport tickets cost €10 per adult or €18 return (return valid seven days). The fare for two/three or more passengers is €9/8 each, so purchase tickets together (same with suburban rail). Tickets are valid for all forms of public transport for 90 minutes (revalidate your ticket on the final mode of transport).

Suburban Rail

Take the suburban rail (one hour) from central Athens (Larisis train station), then change trains for the airport at Ano Liosia, or Neratziotissa (on metro line 1); it's the same price as the metro but the return ticket is valid for a month. The metro also connects with the suburban rail at Doukissis Plakentias (line 3). Trains to the airport run from 6am to midnight; trains from the airport to Athens run from 5.10am to 11.30pm; trains run every 15 minutes from Neratziotissa.

Suburban rail also goes from the airport to Piraeus (change trains at Neratziotissa) and Kiato in the Peloponnese (via Corinth).

Taxi

Fares are fixed between the airport and the centre (both directions): day/night (midnight to 5am) €38/54. For Piraeus, expect day/night €50/60 to Piraeus. It's around 30 to 45 minutes to the centre and an hour to Piraeus.

To prebook a taxi, contact **Welcome Pickups** (www.welcomepickups.com), at the same flat rate as regular taxis, with local English-speaking drivers.

BICYCLE

Even experienced cyclists might find Athens' roads a challenge, with no cycle lanes, often reckless drivers and loads of hills – but some hardy locals do ride. Work is progressing on a 27km bike route between Kifisia in the north and Faliro in the south, but only small stretches are open, south of Thisio. A few outfits offer bicycle hire, such as Funky Rides (p93).

CAR & MOTORCYCLE

Athens' notorious traffic congestion, confusing signage, impatient/erratic drivers and narrow one-way streets make for occasionally nightmarish driving.

Contrary to what you see, parking is actually illegal alongside kerbs marked with yellow lines, on footpaths and in pedestrian malls. Paid parking areas require tickets available from kiosks.

PUBLIC TRANSPORT

Athens has an extensive and inexpensive integrated public-transport network of metro, electric trolleybuses and regular buses. Visitors are most likely to use the metro and the trolleys, which run roughly north–south. Bus routes are extensive, but no printed maps exist; information is very well integrated with mobile-app trip planners, though. You can also use the trip planner at the website of bus company **OASA** (Athens Urban Transport Organisation; ✆11185; www.oasa.gr; ⊙6.30am-11.30pm Mon-Fri, from 7.30am Sat & Sun).

Tram and metro extensions are under way, but will likely not be used much by visitors; the waterfront tram will reach Piraeus by 2018, and metro line 3 will eventually reach the commercial port southwest of the city.

Tickets

In 2017, the Athens transport network was shifting away from paper tickets to stored-value swipe cards. But at the time of research, there was no date set for the transition.

In the meantime, paper tickets good for 90 minutes (€1.40) and a 24-hour/five-day travel pass (€4/10) are valid for all forms of public transport except for airport services. The three-day tourist ticket (€22) includes one round-trip airport ride. Children under six travel free; people under 18 and over 65 pay half-fare.

Buy tickets in metro stations or transport kiosks or most *periptera* (kiosks). Validate the ticket in the machine as you board your transport of choice.

Bus & Trolleybus

Local express buses, regular buses and electric trolleybuses operate every 15 minutes from 5am to midnight. The OASA website's trip planner shows routes.

Buses to Cape Sounion (Map p78; www. ktelattikis.gr)

Buses to Elefsina (Map p108)

Buses to Moni Kaisarianis (Map p108)

The metro is preferable, but after it stops at midnight, you can still get to Piraeus on the bus: **From Syntagma Bus 040** (Map p78). On Filellinon just south of Syntagma to Akti

Xaveriou (every 10 to 20 minutes 6am to midnight, half-hourly after).

From Omonia Bus 500 (Map p108) Opposite the town hall south of Omonia to Plateia Themistokleous (hourly midnight to 5am, starting in Kifisia).

Metro

The metro works well and posted maps have clear icons and English translations. Trains operate from 5am to midnight, every four minutes during peak periods and every 10 minutes off-peak. On Friday and Saturday, lines 2 and 3 run till 2am. Get information at www.stasy.gr. All stations have wheelchair access.

Line 1 (Green) The oldest line, Kifisia–Piraeus, known as the Ilektriko, is slower than the others and above ground. Transfer at Omonia and Attiki for line 2, Monastiraki for line 3 and Neratziotissa for suburban rail. The hourly all-night bus service (bus 500, Piraeus–Kifisia) follows this route, stopping outside the metro stations.

Line 2 (Red) Runs from Agios Antonios in the northwest to Agios Dimitrios in the southeast. Attiki and Omonia connect with line 1; Syntagma connects with line 3.

Line 3 (Blue) Runs northeast from Egaleo to Doukissis Plakentias, with airport trains continuing on from there. Transfer for line 1 at Monastiraki; for line 2 at Syntagma.

Train

Fast suburban rail (p124) links Athens with the airport, Piraeus, the outer regions and the northern Peloponnese. The airport–Kiato line (€14, 1½ hours) connects to the metro at Doukissis Plakentias and Neratziotissa. Two other lines cross the metro at Larissa station.

Funicular Railway (Teleferik; ☑ 210 721 0701; return/1-way €7.50/5; ☺ every 30min 9am-3am) For Lykavittos Hill.

Tram

Athens' **tram** (www.stasy.gr) offers a slow, scenic coastal journey to Faliro and Voula, via Glyfada.

Trams run from Syntagma, opposite the National Gardens, to the coast, then split: east to Voula (one hour) and west to Faliro (45 minutes). (The western line is being extended to Piraeus but most visitors will find the metro a faster option.) Service is from 5.30am to 1am Sunday to Thursday (every 10 minutes), and to 2.30am on Friday and Saturday (every 40 minutes). Ticket vending machines are on the platforms.

TAXI

Athens' taxis are excellent value and can be the key for efficient travel on some routes. But it can be tricky getting one, especially during rush hour. Thrust your arm out vigorously...you may still have to shout your destination to the driver to see if he or she is interested. Make sure the meter is on. It is better to use the mobile app **Taxibeat** (www.taxibeat.gr) – you can book from abroad and pay in cash. It also does deliveries. Uber also operates in Athens. Or call a taxi from dispatchers such as **Athina 1** (☑ 210 921 0417, 210 921 2800; www.athens1.gr), **Enotita** (☑ 6980666720, 18388, 210 649 5099; www.athensradiotaxienotita.gr) or **Parthenon** (☑ 210 532 3300; www.radiotaxi-parthenon.gr).

ATHENS PORTS

Piraeus   Πειραιάς

POP 163,688

Ten kilometres southwest of central Athens, Piraeus is dazzling in its scale, its seemingly endless quays filled with ferries, ships and hydrofoils. It's the biggest port in the Mediterranean (with more than 20 million passengers passing through annually), the hub of the Aegean ferry network, the centre of Greece's maritime trade and the base for its large merchant navy. While technically its own city, it melds into the Athens sprawl, with close to half a million people living in the greater area.

Shabby and congested, central Piraeus is not a place where visitors choose to linger. Beyond its shipping offices, banks and public buildings are a jumble of pedestrian precincts, shopping strips and rather grungy areas. The most attractive quarter lies east around **Zea Marina** and **Mikrolimano** harbours. The latter is lined with cafes, restaurants and bars often filled with people who've disembarked from cruise ships for the day.

◉ Sights

Electric Railways Museum   MUSEUM
(☑ 210 412 9503, 210 414 7552; www.museum-synt-isap.gr; Loudovikou 1; ☺ 9am-2pm Mon-Fri; Ⓜ Piraeus) FREE Tucked inside the Piraeus station, this museum is a trove of old switches, nifty models and cool machinery, including a gleaming old wooden train car. It's a passion project of a former railway employee, and he and the other staff are full of interesting facts.

Piraeus Archaeological Museum   MUSEUM
(☑ 210 452 1598; http://odysseus.culture.gr; Harilaou Trikoupi 31; adult/child €4/free; ☺ 8am-3pm Tue-Sun) The museum's star attraction is the magnificent **statue of Apollo**, the *Piraeus Kouros*, the larger-than-life, oldest hollow

Piraeus

Piraeus

bronze statue yet found. It dates from about 520 BC and was discovered buried in rubble in 1959. Other important finds from the area include fine tomb reliefs from the 4th to 2nd centuries BC.

Hellenic Maritime Museum   MUSEUM
(☏ 210 451 6264; http://hmmuseum.gr; Akti Themistokleous, Plateia Freatidas, Zea Marina; €4; ☺ 9am-2pm Tue-Sat) As nautical museums go, this unfortunately isn't one of the best,

despite Greece's long maritime history. Still, it does have all the requisite models of ancient and modern ships, seascapes by leading 19th- and 20th-century Greek painters, guns, flags and maps, and even part of a submarine.

🛏 Sleeping

If you're catching an early ferry, it can make sense to stay in Piraeus instead of central Athens, but be wary of the cheapest hotels, as they are often aimed at sailors and clandestine liaisons. Don't sleep outside: Piraeus is probably one of the most dangerous places in Greece to do so.

Piraeus Dream City Hotel   HOTEL €
(📞 210 411 0555; www.piraeusdream.gr; Notara 78; d/tr from €75/95; ❇@🌐; ⓂPiraeus) This renovated hotel is about a 10-minute walk from the metro; quiet rooms start on the 4th floor. It has a rooftop restaurant.

Hotel Triton   HOTEL €
(📞 210 417 3457; www.htriton.gr; Tsamadou 8; s/d/tr from €58/90/95; ❇@🌐; ⓂPiraeus) This simple, conveniently located hotel with helpful staff is a treat compared to some of the other run-down joints in Piraeus. Some rooms overlook the bustling market square. There's one family suite (€148).

Phidias Piraeus   HOTEL €€
(📞 210 429 6480; www.hotelphidias.gr; Kountouriotou 189, Zea Marina; s/d/tr from €49/79/119; ❇@🌐; 🚌040 to Terpsithea) A far cry from standard Piraeus grunge, this place is also a bit far from the metro (20-minute walk) and the ferry port. But it runs a free shuttle and you're close to the prettier leisure port, for an evening's stroll. Rooms are simple and new, with cute wallpaper. Full breakfast is an extra €7.

🍴 Eating

The Great Harbour is backed by lots of gritty cafes and fast-food joints; better food and ambience hide away in the backstreets – or further afield around Mikrolimano, Zea Marina and along the waterfront promenade at Freatida.

★Mandragoras   DELI €
(📞 210 417 2961; Gounari 14; ⊙7.45am-4pm Mon, Wed & Sat, to 8pm Tue, Thu & Fri; ⓂPiraeus) This superb delicatessen and spice shop offers a fine selection of gourmet cheeses, readymade mezedhes, olive oils and preserved

foods. It's a veritable museum of regional Greek foodstuffs.

Yperokeanio   MEZEDHES €
(📞 210 418 0030; Marias Hatzikiriakou 48; dishes €6-12; ⊙noon-11.30pm) Grab a cab to this fantastic seafood *mezedhopoleio,* where you can tuck into small plates of grilled sardines or steamed mussels. For dessert there's *kaimaki* ice cream – an old Asia Minor recipe made chewy with *sahlep* (orchid root) and flavoured with Chios mastic. Book ahead, if possible; it's often packed.

General Market   MARKET €
(Dimosthenous; ⊙6am-4pm Mon-Fri; ⓂPiraeus) With the sea breezes blowing over the morning hustle and bustle, the Piraeus market is an excellent slice of life. There's a broad range of food and bric-a-brac, as well as cheap bars and cafes around the periphery, especially in the back alley behind.

Captain's Grill   GREEK €
(📞 210 417 6242; Akti Poseidonos 8; mains €6-12; ⊙9.30am-11pm) A reputable place for an inexpensive and tasty lunch of Greek standards in central Piraeus. Nothing fancy, but very nice owners and superconvenient location.

To Kapileio Tou Zaxou   TAVERNA €€
(📞 210 481 3325; Komotinis 37; mains from €15; ⊙noon-1am; 🚌16) It may be a bit inland, but this family-run Greek fish taverna still conveys the spirit of the sea. Choose from grilled catches of the day, calamari and octopus. House wine comes from the big barrels shelved above the tables, as it ought to in a traditional place. A favourite among locals for its reasonable prices and generous portions.

Margaro   SEAFOOD €€
(📞 210 451 4226; Marias Hatzikiriakou 126; mains €6-21; ⊙noon-midnight Mon-Sat, to 5.30pm Sun Sep-Jul; 🚌904) This port restaurant is the picture of simplicity, with a menu that comprises exactly three things: salad, fried shrimp and fried red mullet. Although it's tucked away by the naval academy, it's no secret, and can be very crowded on weekends. Take the bus here from the Piraeus metro, or a taxi.

Rakadiko   TAVERNA €€
(📞 210 417 8470; www.rakadiko.gr; Karaoli kai Dimitriou 5, Stoa Kouvelou; mains €7-18; ⊙noon-midnight Mon-Sat, 1-6pm Sun; ⓂPiraeus) A spot of calm: head back into this renovated old shopping arcade to dine under grapevines on

mezedhes or classic dishes from all over Greece. There's live *rembetika* on weekends. If you're not hungry for a full meal, stop at the adjacent sweets shop for ice cream or very good orange-blossom-scented fried *loukoumadhes*.

★ **Varoulko** SEAFOOD €€€
(🖉 210 522 8400; www.varoulko.gr; Akti Koumoundourou 52, Mikrolimano; mains €45-65; ⊙1pm-1am) Chef Lefteris Lazarou, a Piraeus native, has been shaping Greek tastes since the 1980s, when he brought fish to the fine-dining menu. For years he had a Michelin-starred restaurant in Athens, but moved back to his roots in 2014. Michelin still approves, and his cooking remains elegant and creative. The setting in Mikrolimano, where sailboats bob, is lovely.

ℹ Information

There are luggage lockers at the metro station (€3 for 24 hours, maximum 15 days).

ATMs and money changers line the Great Harbour.

Alpha Bank (🖉 210 412 1721; Ethnikis Antistaseos 9; ⊙8am-2pm Mon-Fri)

National Bank of Greece (🖉 210 414 4311; cnr Antistaseos & Makras Stoas; ⊙8am-2.45pm Mon-Fri)

ℹ Getting There & Away

The metro and suburban rail from Athens terminate at the northeastern corner of the Great Harbour on Akti Kalimassioti. Airport bus X96 stops out front. A few ferry departure points are just across the road; for further gates, you'll need a port-run bus (free) or a taxi (cheap).

The Athens tramway is extending its line from Faliro to the harbour, with a terminus just south of the metro stop; it's expected to be completed in 2018.

BOAT

Piraeus is the busiest port in Greece, with daily service to most island groups. The exceptions are the Ionians, with boats only to Kythira (for the other islands, sail from Patra and Igoumenitsa) and the Sporades, plus Kea (Tzia) and Andros in the Cyclades (which sail from Rafina and Lavrio). Piraeus ferries also serve the Peloponnese (Methana, Ermioni, Porto Heli, Monemvasia and Gythio).

Always check departure docks with the ticketing agent.

Note that there are two departure points for Crete: ferries for Iraklio leave from the western end of Akti Kondyli, while ferries for other Cretan

ports occasionally dock there as well, or in other places.

Schedules & Tickets

Ferry schedules are reduced in April, May and October, and radically cut in winter, especially to smaller islands. Find schedules and buy tickets online (www.greekferries.gr, www.openseas.gr, www.ferries.gr or company websites), or buy in person at travel agents or at each ferry company's kiosk in front of the boat (open about two hours before sailing). **Piraeus Port Authority** (🖉 210 455 0000, €0.89 per 1min 14541; www.olp.gr) also has schedule information.

In this book, we list ferry schedules in the relevant island/destination chapters.

BUS

The **X96 Piraeus–Athens Airport Express** (Plateia Karaïskaki; tickets €5) stops in front of the metro. It runs around the outside of the port also, but stops rarely, so it's better to take the inside-port shuttle to your gate. Bus 040 goes to Athens from Lambraki at the corner of Vasileos Georgiou II. Arriving, you'll come down Polytehniou; get off at Plateia Korai.

METRO

The fastest and most convenient link between the Great Harbour and Athens is the metro (€1.40, 30 minutes, every 10 minutes, 5am to midnight), near the ferries at the northern end of Akti Kalimassioti.

SUBURBAN RAIL

Piraeus is connected to the suburban rail – the terminus is next to the metro station. To get to the airport or to Kiato in the Peloponnese, you need to change trains at Nerantziotissa.

ℹ Getting Around

The port is massive, so a free shuttle bus runs regularly along the quay inside the port from gate E7 to E1; cross over from the metro and you'll see it. For gate E9, look for buses outside the port, with route numbers starting with 8.

The Piraeus city buses most likely to interest travellers are 904 and 905 between Zea Marina and the metro station.

The continuing Athens tramway and metro extensions have made the port area a zoo of blocked streets and redirected traffic.

Rafina Ραφίνα

POP 13,091

Rafina, on Attica's east coast, is a port town with passenger ferries to the northern Cyclades. If this is your destination, it's a good alternative to Piraeus, as it's smaller (hence, less confusing), and fares are about

20% cheaper. It's also a pleasant place to spend a night if ferry schedules require it.

🛏 Sleeping

Avra   HOTEL €€

(☎ 22940 22780; www.hotelavra.gr; Arafinidon Alon 3; d from €90) Set on one end of Rafina's pretty crescent port, Avra is a big and functional hotel that helps make this town a pleasant stop midtransit. (It also runs a free shuttle to the airport, about 30 minutes away.) Rooms are modern and comfortable, with balconies for watching the ships come in.

❶ Getting There & Away

Rafina is close to Athens airport, so if you're headed to the northern Cyclades (Mykonos, Naxos etc), consider coming here directly, bypassing Athens and Piraeus completely.

BUS

Frequent KTEL buses (p123) run from Athens to Rafina (€2.60, one hour) between 5.45am and 10.30pm, departing from Athens' Mavromateon bus terminal. Buses from Athens airport (€3, 45 minutes) leave from in front of the arrivals hall near the Sofitel, between 4.40am and 10.20pm; buy tickets on board. Both stop on the Rafina quay.

BOAT

Rafina Port Authority (☎ 22940 28888; www. rafinaport.gr) and www.openseas.gr have information on ferries.

Lavrio   Λαύριο

POP 10.370

Lavrio, on the coast 60km southeast of Athens, is the port for ferries to Kea and Kythnos and high-season catamarans to the western Cyclades. It is, unfortunately, not an exciting place to spend the night. The long beach north of the ferry port is a bit of a windsurfing scene, but that same wind is somewhat wearing if you're not on the water. It has a grand industrial past – from silver mining in antiquity to massive late-19th-century steam-powered mining works – but there's not much happening now. (The sprawling ruins of the more recent industry are awesome, but open only to Athens Technical University students.)

◉ Sights

Mineralogical Museum   MUSEUM

(☎ 22920 26270; Iroön Polytehniou, Lavrio; adult/child €2/free; ⊙ 10am-noon Fri-Sun) If you happen to be in town during the museum's limited opening hours, peek in to see fabulous crystals and metals mined from the area, plus a bit about the region's rich mining history. Outside are the ruins of the town's old steam-powered ore-washing facility.

Archaeological Museum   MUSEUM

(☎ 22920 22817; http://odysseus.culture.gr; cnr Agias Paraskevis & Leoforos Souniou; adult/child €2/free; ⊙ 8am-3pm Tue-Sun) Lavrio's small

BOAT SERVICES FROM RAFINA

DESTINATION	COMPANY	DURATION	FARE (€)	FREQUENCY
Andros	Fast Ferries, Golden Star	2½hr	19	4-6 daily
Ios	Golden Star	6hr	48	6 weekly
Mykonos	Fast Ferries, Golden Star	4½hr	29	2-3 daily
Mykonos*	Sea Jets	2¼hr	33	2 daily
Naxos	Fast Ferries	6hr	30	6 weekly
Naxos*	Golden Star, Sea Jets	4hr	33	3 daily
Paros*	Golden Star, Sea Jets	3½hr	30	3 daily
Santorini (Thira)*	Golden Star	6¾hr	48	1 daily
Tinos	Fast Ferries, Golden Star	3¾hr	27	6-9 daily
Tinos*	Sea Jets	2hr	39	2 daily

*high-speed services

archaeological museum holds finds from the area – mostly stone carvings. Some date to 5000 BC. Entrance and parking is on the small branch of Agias Paraskevis on the south side of the building.

ℹ Getting There & Away

BUS

KTEL buses (p123) to Lavrio (€5.30, two hours, every 30 minutes) run from the Mavromateon terminal in Athens. Airport buses leave from the front of the arrivals hall near the Sofitel; you must change buses at Markopoulo. Both stop on the Lavrio quay.

BOAT

Lavrio Port Authority (☑ 22920 25249) and www.openseas.gr have ferry information.

TAXI

Taxi Posidon (☑ 22920 24200; www.taxi poseidon.gr) can run you to the airport (day/night €40/55, 30 minutes) and central Athens (€60/80, one hour); fares are higher for pick-up in Athens or the airport. Lavrio to Cape Sounion is €12.

AROUND ATHENS

An agricultural region with several large population centres, the southern Attica peninsula has some fine beaches, particularly along the Apollo Coast and at Shinias, near Marathon. It's also known for its wine production; a group of five **wineries** have information online (www.winesofathens. com), including a downloadable map. Cycle Greece (p93) runs an excellent day-trip bike ride to some.

Until the 7th century, Attica was home to a number of smaller kingdoms, such as those at Eleusis (Elefsina), Ramnous and Brauron (Vravrona). In pure visual terms, the remains of these cities pale alongside the superb Temple of Poseidon at Cape Sounion, but any of them can be nice to visit simply because you'll probably have the place to yourself.

Apollo Coast

Glyfada, about 17km southeast of Athens, is an upscale suburb of Athens that marks the beginning of the Apollo Coast (sometimes called the Athenian Riviera), a 48km stretch down to Cape Sounion of fine beaches, resorts and summer nightlife. It is

---

ℹ APOLLO COAST TOP TIPS

➡ To avoid heavy traffic on weekends in summer, set out by 9am; without much traffic, the drive from Glyfada to Sounion should take about an hour.

➡ Beaches closest to Glyfada can be reached from Athens by tram. To get further south, change in Glyfada or Voula for a coastal bus.

➡ Pack evening wear in your beach bag in case an all-day sun-fest leads to nightclubbing on the beach.

➡ There are free beaches and rocky coves near Palaio Faliro (Edem), Kavouri, Glyfada and south by Varkiza. Look for areas where locals have parked their cars by the side of the road.

---

a refreshing getaway from Athens and easily reached by bus.

The coast road (Poseidonos Ave, often just called *paraliaki*) leads from Glyfada to **Voula**, **Kavouri** and then bustling and popular **Vouliagmeni** and ritzy Astir Beach. In general, the coast is a bit expensive, but the further south you go, the cheaper and less built-up it becomes. Of note are the natural mineral waters at **Limni Vouliagmenis** and the gay and nudist beaches tucked into the rocky coves at **Limanakia**.

There is better (free) swimming northeast and east of Athens, at Shinias, Marathon and Vravrona, though these take longer to get to and are best reached by car.

🏃 Activities

Most of the Apollo Coast beaches are privately run and charge admission (€5 to €15 per adult). They're usually open from 8am to dusk, May to October (later during heatwaves), and have sunbeds and umbrellas (additional charge in some places), changing rooms, children's playgrounds and cafes. Many morph into summer nightclubs (p111) as well.

Akti tou Iliou　　　　　　　　　BEACH
(☑ 210 985 5169; www.aktitouiliou.gr; Leoforos Poseidonos, Alimos; adult/child Mon-Fri €5/3, Sat & Sun €6/3; ⊙ 8am-8pm; 🚋 Zefyros) Relatively laid-back, with a slew of sunloungers and some reed-roofed beach bars, it's one of the closer beaches to Athens (just 7.5km south).

Attica

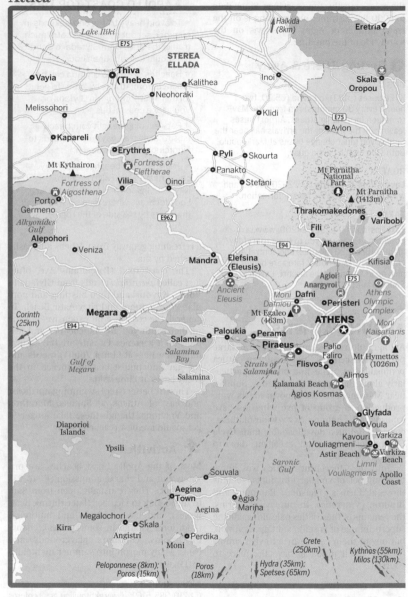

Lake Iliki

E75

Halkida (8km)

Eretria

STEREA ELLADA

Inoi

Skala Oropou

Vayia

Thiva (Thebes)

Kalithea

Neohoraki

Klidi

E75

Aylon

Melissohori

Kapareli

Erythres

Pyli

Skourta

Fortress of Eleftherae

Panakto

Mt Parnitha National Park

Mt Parnitha (1413m)

Mt Kythairon

Fortress of Aigosthena

Vilia

Oinoi

Stefani

Thrakomakedones

Varibobi

Porto Germeno

Alkyonides Gulf

Alepohori

Veniza

E962

Mandra

Elefsina (Eleusis)

Fili

Aharnes

Kifisia

E94

Ancient Eleusis

Agioi Anargyroi

E75

Athens Olympic Complex

Corinth (25km)

E94

Megara

Moni Dafniou

Dafni

Peristeri

Mt Egaleo (463m)

ATHENS

Moni Kaisarianis

Gulf of Megara

Salamina

Paloukia

Perama

Piraeus

Palio Faliro

Mt Hymettos (1026m)

Salamina Bay

Straits of Salamina

Flisvos

Alimos

Salamina

Kalamaki Beach

Agios Kosmas

Glyfada

Diaporioi Islands

Voula Beach

Voula

Kavouri

Varkiza

Ypsili

Saronic Gulf

Vouliagmeni

Astir Beach

Varkiza Beach

Limni Vouliagmenis

Apollo Coast

Souvala

Aegina Town

Agia Marina

Megalochori

Skala

Aegina

Kira

Angistri

Perdika

Moni

Crete (250km)

Kythnos (55km); Milos (130km)

Peloponnese (8km); Poros (15km)

Poros (18km)

Hydra (35km); Spetses (65km)

Asteras Beach   BEACH

(210 894 1620; www.asterascomplex.com; Glyfada; adult/child Mon-Fri €6/3, Sat & Sun €7/3; beach 8.30am-8pm; 790 from Syntagma, T5 to Asteria) Swanky Asteras, convenient to Glyfada and the tram, is a resort without the hotel: a complex of waterfront cafes, play zones, bars and the see-and-be-seen **Balux** (210 894 1620; www.baluxcafe.com; Leoforos Poseidonos 58, Glyfada; ; T5 to Asteria) restaurant. If the megabeach with sunloungers for thousands isn't enough, there's also a pool.

0 — 20 km
0 — 10 miles

Aliveri

Amarynthos

Gulf of Evia

Porto Boufalo

Kalamos

Ramnous

Lake Marathón

Agia Marina

Marathon

Evia (12km)

Shinias
Shinias Beach
Marathon Tomb
Petalia Gulf

Mt Pendeli ▲ (1107m)
Nea Makri

Evia (27km)

Rafina

Andros (60km)

Peania Spata
Vorres Museum
Koutouki Cave

Loutsa

Eleftherios Venizelos International Airport

Mykonos (120km)

Sanctuary of Artemis
Vravrona (Brauron)

Koropi

Porto Rafti
Markopoulo

Kalyvia

Keratea

Anavissos

Lavrio

Sounion
Kea (15km); Kythnos (35km)
Temple of Poseidon
Cape Sounion

The restaurants are expensive for Greece (coffee €4.50, mains from €15), but if you don't take a seat, you can order from a basic menu of coffee, water and toasted sandwiches for less than €2.

🛏 Sleeping

Spending the night along the Apollo Coast can be a bit pricey, and for this reason (and the proximity to Athens), visitors often limit themselves to day outings. But there are a couple of good-value options if you do want to stay the night as part of a road trip.

Villa Orion
HOTEL €

(📞 210 895 8000; www.villaorionhotel.gr; Ioanni Metaxa 4, Voula; d/tr incl breakfast €70/85; ❄ 🛜; 🚌 A1, A2, 122, 🚌 Asklipiio Voulas) This simple hotel has been dressed up with a bit of creative interior decor, but its real attraction is its great value. It's a few blocks inland, yes, but convenient to all the beaches. Rooms have little balconies and breakfast is served outside in a small garden.

Hotel Vouliagmeni Suites
HOTEL €€€

(📞 210 896 4901; www.vouliagmenisuites.com; Panos 8, Vouliagmeni; s/d incl breakfast from €172/183; 🚌 122 to Agia Pantelimon) This posh pad a bit back from the beach has quirkily decorated luxe rooms, some with sea views.

🍴 Eating

Trigono
TAVERNA €

(📞 22990 48540; Athinon 36, Kalyvia; mains €8-15; ⏰ lunch & dinner) At this casual grill house, the pork chops are flawless and flow nonstop – thanks to an in-house butcher, an exceedingly rare feature in Greece. As it's just off the highway back to Athens, it's a popular family pit stop on weekend afternoons. Go early to avoid the epic post-lunch lull, when it feels like an army has just marched out.

Family
AMERICAN €€

(📞 212 104 3411; www.family-voula.gr; Vasileos Pavlou 74, Voula; mains €9-15; ⏰ 9am-2am; 🚌 Asklipiio Voulas) The restaurant lives up to its name with affectionate service and a nice homey atmosphere in an old mansion. It has a wide-ranging, family-friendly menu: eggs, burgers, pizzas and plenty more. It's on Voula's pleasant little downtown strip, calmer than Glyfada. It's about a 20-minute walk from the last tram stop.

Moouu Quality Meats
STEAK €€

(📞 211 409 6295; Foivis 17, Glyfada; mains €10-25; ⏰ 12.30pm-2am; 🚌 Platia Espiridon) Dig in to grilled meats at this steakhouse du jour in the heart of Glyfada's restaurant and cafe district.

❶ Getting There & Away

The Athens tram (p126) runs all the way to Voula, via Glyfada. For Vouliagmeni and beyond, you can take buses from the end of the tram line or (faster but less scenic) buses direct from Athens.

Cape Sounion
Ακρωτήριο Σούνιο

The Ancient Greeks knew how to choose a site for a temple. At Cape Sounion, 70km south of Athens, the **Temple of Poseidon** (☑ 22920 39363; http://odysseus.culture.gr; Cape Sounion; adult/child €8/4; ☺ 9am-sunset) stands on a craggy spur that plunges 65m to the sea. Built in 444 BC – same year as the Parthenon – of marble from nearby Agrilesa, it is a vision of gleaming white columns. Sailors in ancient times knew they were nearly home when they saw the first glimpse of white, and views from the temple are equally impressive.

It is thought that the temple was built by Iktinos, the architect of the Temple of Hephaestus in Athens' Ancient Agora. Sixteen of the slender Doric columns remain. The site also contains scant remains of a propylaeum, a fortified tower and, on a lower hill to the northeast, a 6th-century temple to Athena.

As with all major sites, it's best to visit first thing in the morning, or head there for sunset to enact Byron's lines from *Don Juan*: 'Place me on Sunium's marbled steep/ Where nothing save the waves and I/May hear our mutual murmurs sweep.'

Byron was so impressed by Sounion that he carved his name on one of the columns (sadly, many other not-so-famous travellers followed suit).

There is a decent cafe-restaurant at the site, and from the parking lot at the Athena temple, a steep path leads down to a small beach. If you want more room or variety, you'll need a car, or a short bus ride, to reach the nearby bigger beaches and tavernas. (There is a pretty, if busy, beach near the site to the west, plus some nice wilder areas along the west-coast road towards Sounio town.)

The site is a common package day trip from Athens, and this is the easiest way to visit. KTEL also runs frequent buses from the Mavromateon Terminal (p123) in Athens; the buses also stop near Syntagma (p125). The ride along the coast road takes about two hours.

Mt Parnitha
Πάρνηθα

Mt Parnitha National Park (☑ 210 243 4061; www.parnitha-np.gr/welcome.htm; Aharnes), about 25km north of Athens, comprises a number of smaller peaks, the highest of which is Karavola (1413m), tall enough to get snow in winter. The forest was badly burned in 2007 but has rebounded well. There are many caves and much wildlife, including red deer. The park is criss-crossed by hiking trails, with two large, full-featured hiking lodges. It's popular for mountain biking as well.

The easiest way to explore is on the path (about a 45-minute walk) through **Tatoi**, the 4000-hectare grounds of the former summer palace (closed); follow Tatoi Rd out of Varibobi and look for a small trail sign on the right. For other common trails, see Activities on the park website, or contact EOS (p94) in Athens for more current advice (the site is not well maintained).

For a meal with a view, wind past the posh country estates of Varibobi and up the foothills of Mt Parnitha to reach busy taverna **Agios Merkourios** (☑ 210 816 9617; Varibobi; starters €4-6, lamb per kg €33; ☺ 1pm-midnight Tue-Sun). Weekends, it's packed with Athenians making the pilgrimage for a big family meal. You'll see all sorts of meat on the menu, but charcoal-grilled lamb chops are the order of the day.

Marathon & Around
Μαραθώνας

The town of Marathon, northeast of Athens, may be small and unremarkable, but in 490 BC the surrounding plain was the site of one of the most celebrated battles in world history. All over the area, you can see traces of the event – even in the road signs that mark the historic route of Pheidippides, the courier who ran to Athens to announce victory, and thus gave the name to the 42km race. The Marathon battlefield, directly south of town, is where the **Athens Marathon** (www.athensauthenticmarathon.gr) begins.

◉ Sights & Activities

Marathon Archaeological Museum   MUSEUM
(☑ 22940 55155; http://odysseus.culture.gr; Plataion 114; museum & Marathon Tomb site adult/child €6/3; ☺ 8.30am-3pm Tue-Sat) South of Marathon town, this excellent museum displays local

discoveries from various periods, including Neolithic pottery from the Cave of Pan and finds from the Tomb of the Athenians. The showpieces are several larger-than-life statues from an **Egyptian sanctuary** in nearby Brexiza. Next to the museum is a **prehistoric grave circle site**, which has been preserved under a hangar-like shelter, with raised platforms and walkways. Another hangar on the road to the museum contains an early Helladic **cemetery site**.

The admission fee covers entrance to the Marathon Battlefield & Tomb area, a few kilometres southeast.

Ramnous　　　　　　　　　　RUINS
(📌 22940 63477; http://odysseus.culture.gr; adult/child €4/2; ⊘ 8.30am-3pm Tue-Sun) The evocative, overgrown and secluded ruins of the ancient port of Ramnous, about 10km northeast of Marathon, stand on a picturesque plateau overlooking the sea. Among the ruins are the remains of the Doric **Temple of Nemesis** (435 BC). Another section of the site leads 1km down a track to a clifftop with the relatively well-preserved town **fortress** and the remains of the city, a temple, a gymnasium and a theatre. There is no public transport to the site.

Marathon Battlefield & Tomb　MONUMENT
(📌 22940 55155; http://odysseus.culture.gr; site & archaeological museum adult/child €6/3; ⊘ 8am-3pm Tue-Sat) This 10m-high tumulus, or burial mound, sits 4km south of the town of Marathon, just east of the Athens–Marathon road. Traditionally in Ancient Greece, bodies of those killed in battle were returned to their families for private burial. But after the Battle of Marathon, as a sign of honour, the 192 men who fell were cremated and buried in this collective tomb. The site has a model of the battle and historical information.

Shinias　　　　　　　　　　BEACH
A long, gold-sand beach, Shinias is backed by a brushy pine forest. There are sunloungers and a taverna, but no other major developments around, making it the most relaxed and prettiest place to swim in this part of Attica. It's very popular at weekends.

🛏 Sleeping & Eating

Ramnous Camping　　　CAMPGROUND €
(📌 22940 55855; www.ramnous.gr; Leoforos Poseidonos 174, Shinias; campsites per adult/child €6/4; ⊘ Apr-Oct; 🅿 🛜) About 1km south of Shinias Beach, this is the most pleasant campground in Attica, with sites nestled among shrubs and trees and long-stay residents who maintain a calm atmosphere. There's a minimarket, playground, laundry and a nice bar-restaurant, **Octopus** (mains €4 to €14). Casual campers can rent a tent (€6 per night). Buses to Athens go right by out front.

❶ Getting There & Away

Given that most of the traces of ancient Marathon are spread around the area, it is easiest to visit by car (and you can also pass by the large dam at Lake Marathon). But the tomb and museum, at least, are a short walk from bus stops. Service is hourly (half-hourly in the afternoon), from Athens' Mavromateon terminal (€4.10, 1¼ hours).

Vravrona　　　　　　Βραυρώνα

The **Sanctuary of Artemis** (Archaeological Museum at Brauron; 📌 22990 27020; http://odysseus.culture.gr; Vravron, Markopoulou; adult/child €6/free; ⊘ 8am-2.45pm Tue-Sun), a partially restored temple to the goddess of the hunt, dates from approximately 420 BC, with some earlier remains. Most remarkable is an ancient stone bridge over the river (now rerouted), cut through with wagon-wheel tracks. Entrance is via a very good museum, which shows remarkable votive gems and statues of children (Artemis was their protector). Then a pleasant path leads to the site through lush marshland with lots of birds. Another path leads to a quiet stretch of beach.

From Athens, take metro line 3 to Nomismatikopio, then bus 304 to Artemis (Vravrona). It's a 10-minute taxi ride from there.

Peania　　　　　　Παιανία

◉ Sights

Vorres Museum　　　　　　MUSEUM
(📌 210 664 2520; www.vorresmuseum.gr; Parodos Diadohou Konstantinou 4, Peania; adult/child €5/free; ⊘ 10am-2pm Sat & Sun; 🚌 125 or 308 to Koropi-Peania, Ⓜ Nomismatikopio) This hodgepodge of a museum is set on a rambling 32-hectare estate, once the home of Ion Vorres. Vorres migrated to Canada as a young man, but built his home here in 1963 and began collecting contemporary art, furniture, artefacts, textiles and historic objects from around Greece to preserve the national heritage. Like many personal collections, it's

a bit erratic, but a pleasant place to spend an hour or two.

Take bus 125 or 308 to Koropi-Peania from Athens' Nomismatikopio metro station.

Koutouki Cave
CAVE

(Σπήλαιο Κουτούκι Παιανίας; ☑ 210 664 2910; http://odysseus.culture.gr; Peania; adult/child €2/ free; ⊘ 8.30am-3pm Mon-Fri, to 2.30pm Sat & Sun) This cave is not particularly large, but the winding path goes past some interesting formations and the whole place is tinged rust-red from iron deposits. The guided tour takes about a half-hour.

The cave is best visited by car. Buses 125 and 308 from outside Athens' Nomismatikopio metro station can take you as far as Peania, but it's a further 4.5km to the cave.

Elefsina
Ελευσίνα

POP 29,902

◉ Sights

Old Oil Mill
ARTS CENTRE

(Palaio Elaiourgeio; Kanellopoulou 1, Paralia Elefsinas; ⊘ 5-9pm Mon-Fri, 10.30am-7pm Sat & Sun) FREE Elefsina's current culture revolves around this vast, ruined soap factory, a space constantly in flux as various arts and performance groups adapt it to their uses. The big event of the year is the summer **Aeschylia Festival** (☑ 210 556 5613; www.aisxlia.gr; ⊘ Jun & Jul); it's also a venue for some events in the Athens & Epidaurus Festival (p96).

Ancient Eleusis
RUINS

(☑ 210 554 6019; Sotiriou Gkioka; adult/child €6/ free; ⊘ 8am-8pm Tue-Sun; ☐ A16 or B16 from Plateia Eleftherias, Koumoundourou) Eleusis occupies a great site on the slopes of a low hill, close to the shore of the Saronic Gulf. Although little has been restored, the scale of its construction is impressive, as enormous pieces of columns and building blocks are scattered all over. The core of the site is the **Sanctuary of Demeter**, dating to Mycenaean times, when the goddess's cult was one of the most important in Ancient Greece.

By Classical times, until the 4th century AD, Demeter was celebrated with a huge annual festival that attracted thousands of pilgrims seeking initiation to the Eleusinian mysteries. They walked in procession from the Acropolis to Eleusis along the Sacred Way, which was lined with statues and votive monuments. Initiates were sworn to secrecy on punishment of death; during the 1400 years that the sanctuary functioned, its secrets were never divulged.

Peloponnese

Why Go?

The Peloponnese (Πελοπόννησος) is the stuff of legends. Literally. It is here that Hercules fought the Nemean lion and gods walked the earth, meddling in mortal affairs; it's from here that Paris of Troy eloped with Helen and the Argonauts set sail in search of the Golden Fleece. Celestial and mythological charms aside, this region bears tangible traces of the many civilisations that once called it home, witnessed in its classical temples, Mycenaean palaces, Byzantine cities, and Ottoman, Frankish and Venetian fortresses.

The very topography that kept invaders at bay for centuries – lofty, snowcapped mountains, vast gorges, sandy beaches and azure waters – now draws visitors of a very different kind. *Filoxenia* (hospitality) is as strong here as anywhere in the country; the food is among Greece's best; and the region's vineyards are contributing to Greece's wine renaissance. Locals claim to have the best of everything to give. And that's no myth.

Best Places to Eat

➡ Elies (p175)

➡ Kavalaris Corner Mezedopoleio (p151)

➡ Chromata (p164)

➡ Chrisovoulo (p167)

Best Places to Stay

➡ Antares (p172)

➡ Mazaráki Guesthouse (p164)

➡ Mpelleiko (p155)

➡ Pension Marianna (p150)

When to Go
Nafplio

Easter The pomp and ceremony of religious festivities during Orthodox Easter week are unforgettable.	**Apr–Jun** Perfect hiking and beach weather, without the summer crowds.	**Sep** Take part in the gruelling Spartathlon...if you think you're tough enough.

Peloponnese Highlights

1 Monemvasia
(p165) Soaking up the past and present of an ancient walled city.

2 Ancient Olympia
(p185) Marvelling at this sanctuary, the birthplace of the Olympic Games.

3 Mani (p168) Hiking one of Greece's most remote and rugged regions and spending a night in a traditional Maniot tower house.

4 Menalon Trail
(p156) Hiking this stunning trail through the Lousios Gorge and charming mountain villages Stemnitsa and Dimitsana.

5 Mystras (p161) Meandering through the magical World Heritage–listed ruins of the former Byzantine capital.

6 Ancient Mycenae (p145) Tapping into the ghost of Agamemnon at this incredible historic site.

7 Vouraïkos Gorge
(p196) Tackling the dramatic gorge via the unique rack-and-pinion train or on foot from the beautiful village of Kalavryta.

History

Since ancient times the Peloponnese (named after the mythical Pelops) has played a major role in Greek history. When the Minoan civilisation declined after 1450 BC, the focus of power in the ancient Aegean world moved from Crete to the hill-fortress palaces of Mycenae and Tiryns in the Peloponnese. As elsewhere in Greece, the 400 years following the Dorian conquests in the 12th century BC are known as the Dark Ages. When the region emerged from darkness in the 7th century BC, Athens' arch rival, Sparta, had surpassed Mycenae as the most powerful city in the Peloponnese, sparking the Peloponnesian Wars (431–404 BC).

A period of peace and prosperity ensued under Roman rule (146 BC to around AD 250), but was shattered by a series of invasions by Goths, Avars and Slavs.

The Byzantines were slow to make inroads into the Peloponnese, only becoming firmly established during the 9th century AD. In 1204, after the fall of Constantinople to the Crusaders, the Frankish Crusader chiefs William de Champlitte and Geoffrey de Villehardouin divided the region into 12 fiefs, which they parcelled out to various barons of France, Flanders and Burgundy. These fiefs were overseen by de Villehardouin, the self-appointed prince of the Morea, as the region was called in medieval times.

The Byzantines gradually won back the Morea and, although the empire as a whole was now in decline, a glorious renaissance took place in the area, centred on Mystras, which became the region's seat of government.

The Morea fell to the Turks in 1460, and hundreds of years of power struggles between the Turks and Venetians followed. The Venetians had long coveted the Morea and succeeded in establishing profitable trading ports at Methoni, Pylos, Koroni and Monemvasia.

The Greek War of Independence supposedly began in the Peloponnese, when Bishop Germanos of Patra raised the flag of revolt near Kalavryta on 25 March 1821. The Egyptian army, under the leadership of Ibrahim Pasha, brutally restored Turkish rule in 1825.

In 1827 the Triple Alliance of Great Britain, France and Russia – moved by Greek suffering and by the activities of philhellenes (the death of Lord Byron in 1824 was particularly influential) – came to the rescue of the Greeks by destroying the Turkish–Egyptian fleet at the Battle of Navarino, ending Turkish domination of the area.

The Peloponnese became part of the independent state of Greece, and Nafplio became the first national capital. Ioannis Kapodistrias, Greece's first president, was assassinated on the steps of Nafplio's Church of St Spyridon in October 1831, and the new king, Otto, moved the capital to Athens in 1834.

Like the rest of Greece, the Peloponnese suffered badly during WWII and the civil war (1944–49) that followed. During the 1950s many villagers migrated to Athens, and further abroad to Australia, Canada, South Africa and the USA.

❶ Getting There & Around

AIR

The Peloponnese has one airport, Kalamata International Airport. Many international flights also arrive at Athens International Airport (Eleftherios Venizelos).

BOAT

Domestic and international ferries service the region, the main ones being Patra (for Italy), Kyllini (for Kefallonia and Zakynthos), Gythio (for Crete), Neapoli (for Kythira), and from various ports in Argolis for the Saronic Gulf Islands. Note that ferries to Corfu depart from Igoumenitsa.

BUS

A good bus network services the region. Be aware of the difference between Corinth Isthmus (the canal) and Corinth (the city). Located on a main road on the Peloponnese side of the Corinth Canal, the **Corinth Isthmus (Peloponnese) KTEL bus station** (☑ 27410 75410, Athens 210 512 4919) is the spot to change for buses south to the rest of the Peloponnese. No formal timetables are available; most buses from Athens heading to the Peloponnese stop here. Meanwhile, for Ancient Corinth, you'll need to head to Corinth City's **KTEL Korinthos bus station** (☑ 27410 75410; www.ktelkorinthias.gr; Dimocratias 4).

CAR

Cars are a great way to get around the Peloponnese. Several major motorways have opened in the last few years in the Peloponnese and provide easy access along the northern coast and through the middle of the region. All require toll fees. The A8 links Athens with Patra along the Gulf of Corinth; the A7 links Corinth (north) with Tripoli (centre) and Kalamata (south). The 46km stretch linking Lefktro with Sparti is the most recent section to open and provides a less hilly access to the Mani.

If driving the winding, scenic minor roads across the peninsula, always allow yourself plenty of time. When going around sharp bends, watch out for oncoming drivers who tend to cut across your lane without sounding their horn.

TRAIN

Train ('OSE') services are limited. Only one line – Athens to Patra – still operates, with a replacement bus service between Kiato and Patra. The *proastiako*, Athens' suburban rail service, runs between Kiato, Corinth (city) train station and Athens International Airport (approximately €12, 1½ hours, around eight daily).

CORINTHIA   KOPINΘIA

Corinthia has had a rich and tumultuous history, owing largely to its strategic position adjoining the Corinth Isthmus. Throughout time several empires have wrestled here for dominance over the Peloponnese: the Romans constructed a vast wall across the isthmus; many centuries later the Turks overran it; and pretty much everyone else has attempted to carve a canal across it.

Once dominated by the mighty ancient city of Corinth, Corinthia is now the keeper of its remains.

In the pretty hinterland west of Corinth you can take part in the resurrected Nemean Games, or travel the Nemea region's wine route in search of Greece's best vintages.

History

Ancient Corinth was an affluent and powerful city during its first golden age. Earthquakes and centuries of pillage, however, have left only the remnants of once-grand buildings, 7km southwest of the modern city, surrounded by the village of Ancient Corinth and overlooked by the Acrocorinth fortress.

During the 6th century BC Corinth was one of Ancient Greece's richest cities, thanks to its strategic position on the Corinth Isthmus. Its twin ports, one on the Aegean Sea (Kenchreai, near Kechries) and one on the Ionian side (Lecheon), enabled it to trade throughout the Mediterranean. It survived the Peloponnesian Wars and flourished under Macedonian rule, but it was sacked by the Roman consul Mummius in 146 BC for rebelling against Roman rule. In 44 BC Julius Caesar began rebuilding the city and it again became a prosperous port.

◉ Sights

★ **Ancient Corinth**   ARCHAEOLOGICAL SITE
(✆27410 31207; adult/concession €8/4; ⏰8am-8pm) In the centre of a modern village loom the extensive yet compact ruins of this ancient (mostly Roman) city. Home to the legendary Jason of the Argonauts, stealer of the Golden Fleece, the streets of Ancient Corinth were once trodden by the likes of Pausanias, Roman traveller, and St Paul, who taught the gospel of Christ in vain here. You can follow in their footsteps by visiting the Temple of Apollo, the Peribolos of Apollo, the ancient theatre and other site highlights. The on-site museum puts everything into context.

An exception to the Roman ruins is the prominent 5th-century-BC Doric **Temple of Apollo**. To the south of this temple is a huge **agora** (market) bounded on its southern side by the foundations of a **stoa** (long colonnaded building). This was built to accommodate the bigwigs summoned here in 337 BC by Philip II to sign oaths of allegiance to Macedon. In the middle of the central row of shops is a **bema**, a marble podium from which Roman officials addressed the people.

At the eastern end of the *agora* are the remains of the Julian basilica. To the north is the **Lower Peirene fountain** – the Upper Peirene fountain is on Acrocorinth. According to mythology, Peirene wept so much when her son Kenchrias was killed by Artemis that the gods, rather than let all the precious water go to waste, turned her into a fountain.

West of the fountain, steps lead to the Lecheon road, once the main thoroughfare to the port of Lecheon. On the east side of the road is the **Peribolos of Apollo**, a courtyard flanked by Ionic columns, some of which have been restored. Nearby is a public latrine, where some seats remain.

South of the museum are the columns of **Temple E** (Pausanias describes it as being dedicated to Octavia, sister of Augustus).

The site's excellent **museum** is a must-see and a good way to begin and end your visit. It has five main rooms, the most impressive of which were opened in 2016. These contain finds from the area (including their prized pieces, two *kouroi* statues that were stolen and retrieved), dating to Archaic Greece and Classical Greece. The next two rooms exhibit fine Greek and Roman statues, mosaics, figurines, reliefs and friezes. The small fifth

CORINTH CANAL ΔΙΩΡΥΓΑ ΤΗΣ ΚΟΡΙΝΘΟΥ

The Corinth Canal is an engineering marvel. A project that spanned many centuries, it was conceived by a ruler of Ancient Corinth, begun by Roman emperor Nero, and completed in the 19th century by the French. Cut through solid rock, the canal is more than 6km long and 23m wide, its vertical sides rising 90m above the water. The canal did much to elevate Piraeus' status as a major Mediterranean port and is particularly impressive when a ship is passing through.

The concept of cutting a canal through the Corinth Isthmus to link the Ionian and Aegean Seas was first proposed by Periander, tyrant of Ancient Corinth at the end of the 7th century BC. The magnitude of the task defeated him, so he opted instead to build a *diolkos* (paved slipway), across which sailors dragged small ships on rollers, a method used until the 13th century.

In the intervening years many leaders, including Alexander the Great and Caligula, toyed with the canal idea, but it was Nero who struck the first blow himself, using a golden pickaxe in AD 67 before leaving it to 6000 Jewish slaves to do the hard work. The project was soon halted by invasions by the Gauls. Ironically, it was a French engineering company that finally completed the canal in 1893.

If you have your own transport, head to nearby Isthmia to the submersible bridge, one of two bridges crossing the canal. The nearby banks are great vantage points if you're lucky enough to be there when a ship passes over the submerged bridge.

For the adventurous, **Zulu Bungy Jump** (☑ 69327 02535; www.zulubungy.com; €80; ☺10am-6pm Wed-Sun Jun-Sep) offers the chance to see the canal walls from a unique angle.

All buses from Athens pass over the bridge and stop at the Corinth Isthmus KTEL bus station (p140), 200m from the canal.

---

room houses the finds of excavations at the nearby Sanctuary of Asklepios (500 BC).

Opposite the site entrance is the **ancient theatre**, constructed in the 5th century BC for up to 15,000 spectators, and the Roman **odeion** (indoor theatre), from the 1st century AD.

Acrocorinth FORTRESS

(☺8am-3pm) **FREE** High up above Ancient Corinth, crowning the sheer bulk of limestone known as Acrocorinth, are the ruins of one of the finest natural fortifications in Ancient Greece. Cast your eyes upwards and you'll give an involuntary gasp. Commanding wonderful views over the surrounding region, the fortress is a stiff but utterly worthwhile 4km uphill hike (or taxi ride) if you don't have your own wheels.

The original fortress has been modified many times over the centuries by a string of invaders. Passing through the three gates (Turkish, Frankish and Byzantine), you can explore the medley of imposing Roman, Byzantine, Frankish, Venetian and Turkish ramparts, harbouring remains of Byzantine chapels, Turkish houses and mosques.

From the main path, the right fork leads to the remains of a 14th-century Frankish **keep**. The central path leads you to the **Fountain of Peirene**, the favourite watering hole of Pegasus the winged horse. Accessible by the left-hand path, on the higher of Acrocorinth's two summits are the remains of the **Temple of Aphrodite**, where sacred courtesans catered to the desires of the insatiable Corinthians.

Wear sturdy shoes and take plenty of water.

Ancient Nemea ARCHAEOLOGICAL SITE

(☑ 27460 22739; €6/3; ☺8am-7pm Apr, to 8pm May-Oct, to 3pm Nov-Mar) Situated 31km southwest of Corinth, on the northeastern edge of modern Nemea, Ancient Nemea was once the venue for the biennial Nemean Games, held in honour of Zeus. Three original columns of the imposing 4th-century-BC Doric Temple of Zeus survive, and the on-site museum displays rich finds from the area. The stadium where the Games were held is nearby; once connected to the sanctuary by a sacred road, it plays host to the resurrected Games.

Like Ancient Olympia, Nemea was not a city but a **sanctuary of Zeus**. The Nemean Games were hosted by the nearby city of Kleonai and became one of the great Panhellenic festivals. There's a mythological side to Nemea as well: it was around here that Hercules carried out the first of his labours – the slaying of the lion that had been sent by Hera to destroy Nemea. After Hercules had killed the lion by lifting it off the ground and choking it to death, using his prodigious strength, the lion became the constellation Leo (each of Hercules' 12 labours is related to a sign of the zodiac).

It's worth visiting the site's **museum** before seeing the remains of the temple. It has two models of the ancient site – the first shows what it would have looked like in 573 BC, the second in AD 500 – as well as ancient paraphernalia from the Games and treasures from the area's Mycenaean tombs. The jewel of the collection, quite literally, is the Gold of Aidonia, an exquisite assortment of gold rings, seals and beads from the site of Aidonia, near Nemea. Don't miss the video that explains the extraordinarily advanced race-starting mechanism (English subtitles).

At the temple site, the three original columns of the 4th-century-BC **Temple of Zeus** have been joined by six more, reassembled by an American team; reconstruction is in progress. Other ruins include a bathhouse, probably used by athletes to oil up pre-competition, and a hostelry.

The **stadium** is 500m back along the road. There's a fantastic view of it in all its restored glory from the path that skirts it through the pine trees. Alternatively, enter it the way the athletes would have done, through the tunnel hidden behind the columns by the site entrance. The athletes' starting line is still in place, together with the distance markers. Look out for ancient graffiti in the tunnel. Resurrected in 1996, the two-day **Modern Nemean Games** (www.nemeangames.org) occur each Olympic year in June.

Buses to/from Corinth Isthmus (around €5, one hour, four to five daily, one Sunday) stop on request outside the site on the way to modern Nemea, about 4km northwest of the site.

❶ Getting There & Away

The KTEL Korinthos bus station (p140) in Corinth (city) is the departure point for buses to Ancient Corinth (€1.80, 20 minutes, regular Monday to Friday, eight Saturday), Nemea (€4.50, one hour, four to five daily Monday to Saturday, one Sunday) and Loutraki (for Corinth Isthmus; €1.70, 10 minutes, half-hourly).

Weekend bus services range from infrequent to non-existent.

A handy bus shuttles between Corinth city's Plateia Kentriki (20 minutes) and the train station.

ARGOLIS ΑΡΓΟΛΙΔΑ

The Argolis peninsula, which separates the Saronic and Argolic Gulfs, is steeped in legend and history. The town of Argos, from which the region takes its name, is thought to be the longest continually inhabited town in Greece. Argolis was the seat of power of the Mycenaean empire that ruled Greece from 1600 to 1100 BC. Traces of this mighty civilisation lie scattered across the region in the shape of *tholos* (tombs shaped like beehives), citadels and ancient theatres. The Venetian seafront town of Nafplio, the first ever capital of Greece, makes a handy base for ventures into the surrounding countryside.

❶ Getting There & Away

Both Argos and Nafplio are hubs for the region and are well serviced by regional KTEL Argolis buses, including those from Isthmus (a transport hub to the Peloponnese).

The ancient theatre of Epidavros (not to be confused with Archaea Epadavros, a village on the coast) can be most easily reached from Nafplio (€2.90, 45 minutes, six Monday to Friday, four Saturday, one Sunday). Buses for Ancient Mycenae (three Monday to Friday, two Saturday) run from both Nafplio (€2.90, one hour) and Argos (€1.80, 30 minutes).

While you can reach the ancient sites in a bus, your own wheels will give you far more flexibility.

Argos Αργος

POP 22,200

The ancient town of Argos has history stretching back an astonishing 6000 years, though today most vestiges of its past glory lie buried beneath the bustling modern town. Overshadowed by its neighbour, Nafplio (12km away), Argos is worth a detour for its fabulous and recently opened Byzantine museum and the nearby ruins and fortress.

⦿ Sights

★ **Byzantine Museum of Argolis** MUSEUM (www.byma.gr; Kapodistrias Barracks; adult/concession €4/2; ☻9am-2pm Tue-Sun) It's worth visiting Argos for this stunning museum alone. Opened in 2017, it provides an

NEMEA'S WINE ROUTE

In the rolling hills southwest of Corinth, the Nemea region is one of Greece's premier wine-producing areas, famous for its full-bodied reds, many produced from the local *agiorgitiko* grape. Look out also for wine made from *roditis*, a local variety of white grape.

Nemea has been known for its fine wines since Mycenaean times, when nearby Phlius supplied the wine for the royal court at Mycenae. Half a dozen or so wineries provide tastings for visitors (many free, some by appointment).

Domaine Spiropoulos (☑ 27960 61400; www.domainspiropoulos.com; Corinthos–Tripoli National Rd; ☺ by appointment) With two vineyards that have been in the family since 1860 – one near Nemea and the other on the Martinia plateau in the heart of the Peloponnese – Apostolos Spiropoulos is a pioneering figure in organic viticulture and produces *moschofilero*, *agiorgitiko*, merlot, cabernet sauvignon, cabernet franc, chardonnay, sauvignon blanc and syrah wines.

Domaine Helios (☑ 21062 16811; www.semeliwines.gr; ☺ by appointment) éNorth of Nemea is the dramatically located Domaine Helios, which produces several *agiorgitiko* reds, as well as other varietals. Whites include chardonnay and sauvignon blanc, and there's also a single rosé.

Gaia Wines (☑ 21080 55642; www.gaia-wines.gr; Koutsi; wine tastings €4-8; ☺ by appointment) North of Nemea in pretty hill country, Gaia Wines produces unfiltered wines, including *appellation d'origine contrôlée* (AOC) varieties. Its signature wine is the dry white *thalassitis*, made from the *asyrtiko* grape.

Lafkiotis Winery (☑ 27460 31000; www.lafkiotis.gr; Ancient Kleonai; ☺ 11am-4pm) The Lafkiotis family has been specialising in wines made from local grape varieties since 1963. Besides the *agiorgitiko*, *agionymo*, Nemea and *rodamos* reds, you can also sample the fruity *moschofilero* white.

Ktima Palivou (☑ 27460 24190; www.palivos.gr; Ancient Nemea; ☺ by appointment) Third-generation winemaker George Palivos specialises in *agiorgitiko* wines.

evocative insight into Byzantine history, within the context of the region of Argolis. Six rooms neatly showcase Byzantine life in Argolis from the 4th century AD onwards. 'An Empire is Born' explains the empire and then, through objects – mosaics to jewellery, household plates to smoking pipes – you follow themes: Middle Ages, Church life, home life, a market and a look at Argolis itself.

It's housed in the stunningly restored former soldiers' and horses' barracks of Ioannis Kapodistrias, Greece's first president.

Larissa Castle   CASTLE
(☺ 24hr) FREE Looming over Argos, Larissa Castle is a crumbling conglomeration of purple-flower-studded towers, bastions and wall sections – contributed by Roman, Frankish, Venetian and Ottoman Turk conquerors – that stands on the foundations of the city's principal ancient citadel. Much of the citadel has undergone restoration, with new signs and some rebuilding of turrets. Regardless, the all-encompassing views from the top are well worth the ascent.

Take Tsokri west from the centre and follow the signposts to the narrow road that winds around the back of the ruined keep (approximately 3km in total). Alternatively, and less congested, follow the signs from the north edge of town on the Korinthou road (road to Corinth).

Roman Ruins   RUINS
(☺ 8am-3pm) FREE Impressive Roman ruins straddle both sides of the Tripolis road. The star attraction is the half-crumbled **theatre**, which originally seated 20,000 people. Dating from the early 5th century BC, it was greatly modified by the Romans around 300 BC. Nearby are the remains of a 1st-century AD **odeion** (a smaller theatre) and **Roman baths**. Opposite is the **Ancient Agora**. Signs provide diagrams and contextualise the setting. From central Argos, head south along Danaou for about 500m and then turn right onto Theatrou.

Skouras   WINERY
(☑ 27510 23688; www.skouraswines.com; ☺ by appointment) FREE George Skouras has been

producing wines from local and international grape varieties since 1986. For wine tastings, reserve ahead on thei website.

ℹ Getting There & Away

On the southern end of Argos, the new **KTEL Argolis** (📞 27510 69323; www.ktelargolida.gr; Kapodistriou 8) bus station has services to Nafplio (€1.80, 30 minutes, hourly) and Mycenae (€1.80, 30 minutes, two to three Monday to Saturday).

There are also bus services to Athens (€13, two hours, 10 to 15 daily) via Corinth Isthmus (€5.70, 50 minutes), and to Tripoli (€7.70, one hour, two daily).

Ancient Mycenae
Αρχαία Μυκήνες

★ **Ancient Mycenae**   ARCHAEOLOGICAL SITE
(📞 27510 76585; adult/concession €12/6; ⊘ 8am-8pm Apr-Oct, to 3pm Nov-Mar) In the barren foothills of Mt Agios Ilias (750m) and Mt Zara (600m) stand the sombre and mighty ruins of Ancient Mycenae, home of the mythical Agamemnon. For 400 years (1600–1200 BC) this kingdom was the most powerful in Greece, holding sway over the Argolid and influencing other Mycenaean kingdoms.

Two to three daily buses (excluding Sundays) head to Mycenae from Nafplio (around €3, one hour) and Argos (€1.80, 30 minutes). Buses stop both in the village and at the ancient site.

World Heritage–listed Mycenae is synonymous with the names Homer and Schliemann. In the 9th century BC Homer told in his epic poems, 'Iliad' and 'Odyssey', of 'well-built Mycenae, rich in gold'. These poems were, until the 19th century, regarded as no more than gripping and beautiful legends. But in the 1870s the amateur archaeologist Heinrich Schliemann (1822–90), despite derision from professional archaeologists, struck gold, first at Troy then at Mycenae.

In Mycenae, myth and history are inextricably linked. According to Homer, the city of Mycenae was founded by Perseus, the son of Danae and Zeus. By Agamemnon's time the Royal House of Atreus was the most powerful of the Achaeans (Homer's name for the Greeks).

The historical facts are that Mycenae was first settled by Neolithic people in the 6th millennium BC. Between 2100 and 1900 BC, during the Bronze Age, Greece was invaded by people of Indo-European heritage who had crossed Anatolia via Troy to Greece. The invaders brought an advanced culture to then-primitive Mycenae and other mainland settlements. This new civilisation is now referred to as the Mycenaean, named after its most powerful kingdom. The other kingdoms included Pylos, Tiryns, Corinth and Argos, all in the Peloponnese. Evidence of Mycenaean civilisation has also been found at Thiva (Thebes) and Athens.

The city of Mycenae consisted of a fortified citadel and surrounding settlement. Due to the sheer size of the 'Cyclopean' walls (13m high and 7m thick), formed by stone blocks weighing 6 tonnes in places, legend has it that Perseus enlisted the help of a Cyclops, one of the one-eyed giants described in 'Odyssey' to build Mycenae.

Archaeological evidence indicates that the palaces of the Mycenaean kingdoms declined sometime around 1200 BC and the palace itself was destroyed around 1100 BC, possibly by fire. Whether the destruction was the work of outsiders or due to internal division between the various Mycenaean kingdoms remains unresolved.

Agamemnon's fortress is entered through the dramatic **Lion Gate**, a solid construction of massive stone blocks over which rear two large lionesses. This motif is believed to have been the insignia of the Royal House of Atreus.

Once inside the citadel, **Grave Circle A** is on the right. This was the royal cemetery and contained six grave shafts. Five shafts were excavated by Schliemann between 1874 and 1876, uncovering one of the richest archaeological hauls ever to be found, including a well-preserved gold death mask. Schliemann sent a telegram to the Greck king stating, 'I have gazed upon the face of Agamemnon', though the mask turned out to belong to an unknown king.

South of Grave Circle A are the remains of a group of **houses**. In one was discovered the famous Warrior Vase, regarded by Schliemann as one of his greatest discoveries because it offered a glimpse of what Mycenae's legendary warriors looked like.

Follow the main path up to **Agamemnon's Palace**, centred on the **Great Court**. The rooms to the north were private **royal apartments** where it is thought that Agamemnon was murdered. On the palace's southeastern side is the **megaron** (reception hall where the great hearth would have been), with the column bases remaining and, beyond this, the artisans' quarters.

Head down to the northeast extension, to find the entrance to the secret cistern in the corner. You can only go down 25 of the 100 or so steps but can get a good sense with a torch. The cistern itself was an ingenious piece of engineering, connected as it was to a spring, but the water has long run dry.

Follow the main path anti-clockwise and on the northern boundary of the citadel you'll come across the **Postern Gate**, through which, it is said, Orestes escaped after murdering his mother, Clytemnestra.

Until the late 15th century BC the Mycenaeans interred their royal dead in shaft graves; later they used a new form of burial – the beehive-shaped *tholos* tomb. Back outside the Lion Gate, head down to the *tholos* tombs of Aegisthus, with its collapsed roof, and **Clytemnestra's tomb**, with its dramatic entrance and restored dome roof.

Another Mycenae highlight, the **Treasury of Atreus**, also known as **Agamemnon's Tomb**, is found 500m down the road from the car park, beyond the main Mycenae site.

Treasury of Atreus (Agamemnon's Tomb)   ARCHAEOLOGICAL SITE

(adult/concession incl site €12/6; ☉8am-8pm Apr-Oct, to 3pm Nov-Mar) Dating back to around 1300 BC, this is the finest existing example of a domed *tholos*. It's wonderfully misnamed, since it has little to do with the mythical Atreus, or with his equally mythical son, Agamemnon, but the interior is truly awe-inspiring, with a 40m-long passage leading to the vast beehive-shaped chamber. Spot the original bronze nails that once held the door in place.

Ancient Mycenae Museum   MUSEUM

(adult/concession incl site €12/6; ☉8am-8pm Apr-Oct, to 3pm Nov-Mar) Part of the Ancient Mycenae (p145) complex, this museum is well worth visiting before seeing the rest of the site. It initiates you into the mysteries of Mycenae's construction, its various incarnations, and its excavation from 1841 onwards. The displays run the gamut from fine stirrup jars and fresco fragments to ritual objects, jewellery and bronze weaponry. Replicas of archaeologist Heinrich Schliemann's most spectacular Mycenae finds are also displayed; the originals are in Athens' National Archaeological Museum.

Audio guides – in English, Greek, French and German – are available on request; leave your passport or ID as security. These are a wonderful way to learn about exhibits in more detail and provide valuable context to the site and life in a Mycenaean community.

Nafplio   Ναύπλιο

POP 14,500

Nafplio, 12km southeast of Argos on the Argolic Gulf, is one of Greece's prettiest and most romantic towns. It occupies a knock-out location, on a small port beneath the towering Palamidi fortress, and is graced with attractive narrow streets, elegant Venetian houses, neoclassical mansions and interesting museums. It's also full of quayside cafes, posh boutiques and many comfortable hotels and guesthouses. Because it's a popular destination for locals from Athens, it fills up on weekends and gets overcrowded in high season.

Nafplio was the first capital of Greece after Independence (between 1833 and 1834) and has been a major port since the Bronze Age. So strategic was its position that it had three fortresses: the massive principal fortress of Palamidi, the smaller Akronafplia, and the diminutive Bourtzi on an islet west of the old town.

The town is an ideal base from which to explore many nearby ancient sites.

◉ Sights

★ Archaeological Museum   MUSEUM

(☑27520 27502; Plateia Syntagmatos; adult/child €6/3; ☉8am-3pm Tue-Sun) Inside a splendid Venetian building, this museum traces the social development of Argolis, from the hunter-gatherers of the Fracthi cave to the sophisticated Mycenaean-era civilisations, through beautifully presented archaeological finds from the surrounding area. Exhibits range from Paleolithic fire middens, dating from 32,000 BC, to elaborately painted amphorae (c 520 BC). You may also spot the only existing bronze armour from near Mycenae (3500 years old and complete with boar-tusk helmet), a wealth of funereal offerings and ceremonial clay masks.

★ Palamidi Fortress   FORTRESS

(☑27520 28036; adult/concession €8/4; ☉8am-8pm May-Oct, reduced hrs rest of year) This vast, spectacular citadel, reachable either by steep ascent on foot or a short drive, stands on a 216m-high outcrop of rock that gives all-encompassing views of Nafplio and the Argolic Gulf. It was built by the Venetians between 1711 and 1714, and is regarded as a masterpiece of military architecture in spite of being successfully stormed in one night by Greek troops in 1822, causing the Turkish garrison within to surrender without a fight.

Within its walls stands a series of independent, strategically located bastions. The most important, and best preserved, is the western **Agios Andreas Bastion**, which stands at the top of the steps from town. The former home of the garrison commander, it is named after the tiny church in the interior courtyard.

The **Miltiades Bastion**, to the northeast, is the largest of the bastions. It was used as a prison for condemned criminals from 1840 to 1920. War of Independence hero Theodoros Kolokotronis spent several years here after being condemned for treason.

There are two main approaches to the fortress. You can go via the road (a taxi one way will cost about €10) or tackle the steps that begin southeast of the bus station. It's 576 steps to the outer gate and 901 steps to the entrance to the castle (we've counted). Climb early and take water.

Church of Agios Spyridon CHURCH

This 18th-century church was the site of an assassination of great political significance to the Greeks. On 9 October 1831 Ioannis Kapodistrias, elected the first president of an independent Greece in 1828, was stabbed and shot near the door of the church by Konstantinos and Georgios Mavromichalis, brother and son of the leader of the Maniots. They had had a bitter disagreement with Kapodistrias over the spoils of victory.

Peloponnesian Folklore Foundation Museum MUSEUM

(☑ 27520 28379; www.pli.gr; Vasileos Alexandrou 1; adult/child €2/free; ☉ 9am-2.30pm Mon-Sat, 9.30am-3pm Sun) Established by its philanthropic owner, Nafplio's award-winning museum is a beautifully arranged collection of folk costumes and household items from Nafplio's 19th- and early-20th-century history. Be wowed by the intricate embroidery of traditional costumes and the heavy silver adornments; admire the turn-of-the-20th-century couture and look out for the cute horse-tricycle. The gift shop sells high-quality local crafts.

Bourtzi FORTRESS

(☑ 6977716998; return cruise €4.50) Odyssey Cruises runs boat excursions to this island fortress. Built in 1473, it lies about 600m west of the town's port and has served variously as a pirate deterrent, a home for executioners and a hotel. Note that the battlements are identical in design to Moscow's Kremlin; both were built by 15th-century Venetians. Boats leave from the northeastern end of Akti Miaouli. You can buy tickets from where the boats depart.

Komboloi Museum MUSEUM

(☑ 27520 21618; www.komboloi.gr; Staïkopoulou 25; adult/concession €2/free; ☉ 9.30am-8pm) Whether or not you wish to buy Greece's most popular souvenir item – *komboloï* (worry beads) – at the shop below, it's worth popping into the incense-scented museum upstairs to learn what distinguishes the *komboloï* from prayer beads and why the amber-mastic mix is so special. Among the collection of prayer beads belonging to assorted religions are tiny wooden skulls, and black coral beads inlaid with mother-of-pearl and carved ivory.

National Gallery – Alexandros Soutzos Museum GALLERY

(www.nationalgallery.gr; Sidiras Merarhias 23; adult/concession €3/1.50; ☉ 10am-3pm Mon, Thu & Sat, 10am-3pm & 5-8pm Wed & Fri, 10am-2pm Sun) This arm of the Athens National Gallery is housed in a stunningly restored neoclassical building (don't be deterred; the front door looks to be closed). It features numerous seascapes and different thematic takes on the 1821 Greek War of Independence, including paintings by Theodoros Vryzakis and Dionysios Tsokos, who are considered the most important Greek artists of the postwar years. Entry is free on Mondays.

Akronafplia Fortress FORTRESS

(☉ 24hr) **FREE** Rising above the old part of town, the Akronafplia fortress is the oldest of Nafplio's three castles. The lower sections of the walls date back to the Bronze Age; the most recent were built by the Venetians in the 15th century and the town was restricted to within its walls at the time. There's a lift up to the fortress from Plateia Politikou Nosokomeiou.

War Museum MUSEUM

(Amalias 22; adult/concession €3/1.50; ☉ 9am-7pm Tue-Sat, 9:30am-7pm Sun) This collection of paintings, uniforms, sketches, assorted

Nafplio

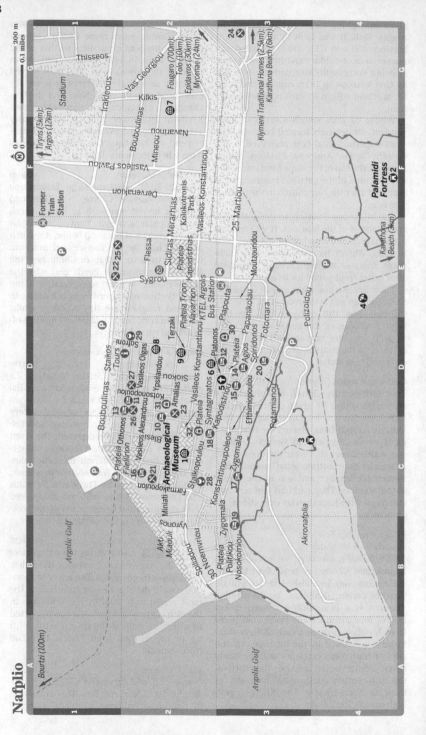

Nafplio

weaponry and photographs traces Greece's role in various battles, from the War of Greek Independence (1821–32) – a rebellion against the Ottoman Empire – to the Greek-Turkish War, the Balkans Wars, WWII and beyond. The suffering of the Peloponnese under the Nazis and the fierce resistance put up by Greek partisans is conspicuous by its near-absence.

🏖 Beaches

Karathona Beach   BEACH
A gorgeous pine-tree-lined 3km path runs from the car park next to Arvanitia Beach to the long, sandy Karathona Beach. It's a flat, easy walk, though the beach could be cleaner. Don't feel like walking? Head your car along 25 Martiou east of town to the end of the road.

Arvanitia Beach   BEACH
This small pebble beach is just five minutes' walk south of town, tucked beside the Akronafplia fortress, past the Land Gate. For a scenic stroll, take the blustery, cactus-adorned path that skirts the headland from the bottom of the promenade.

🏃 Activities

Nafplio Bio-Farms   FOOD
(📱6944184703; www.nafpliobiofarms.gr; 2-/3-hr tour per person €15/25) This fun, hands-on cultural experience is also tasty and inform-ative. Guests visit a small organic farm, located just outside Nafplio, that produces oranges and olives and makes its own organic flour. Owners Petros and Panagiota run through the history of farming techniques that follow centuries-old practices plus, depending on the tour, you may sample and/or make local goodies.

Pegasus Cruises   BOATING
(📱27250 59430; www.pegasus-cruises.gr; adult/child €35/17.50; ⏲late Apr–late Sep) Pegasus Cruises offers popular full-day trips to the islands of Hydra and Spetses from Tolo, 10km southeast of Nafplio. The tour stops for a couple of hours in each place. You can get to/from Tolo by taxi (around €12) or bus, depending on the schedule. There are at least two weekly departures (more in July and August).

Tickets are available at Staikos Tours (p152).

🎊 Festivals & Events

Nafplio is a good base for visits to Epidavros in July and August for performances at the famous ancient theatre (p153) during the Epidavros Festival, part of the larger cultural Hellenic Festival (p96).

Classical Music Festival   MUSIC
(www.nafplionfestival.gr; ⏲Jun or Jul) Nafplio hosts a classical-music festival, featuring Greek and international performers. Dates change annually.

PELOPONNESE NAFPLIO

🛏 Sleeping

Pension Eleni
PENSION €

(☑ 27520 27036; www.pensioneleni.gr; Zygomala 5; d/tr/ste incl breakfast €45/50/75; P❋🛜) One of Nafplio's oldest pensions, tucked away down a quiet street – nothing much has changed here, except the age of the (now elderly) owner. The 'superior' rooms come with thimble-sized balconies. Park in the nearby square.

★ Pension Marianna
HOTEL €€

(☑ 27520 24256; www.hotelmarianna.gr; Potamianou 9; s/d/tr/q incl breakfast €50/75/80/100; P❋🛜) Pension Marianna is one of our long-standing favourites. Its value for money, hospitality and setting are outstanding. Many of the bright and airy, squeaky-clean rooms provide superb vistas from the hilltop position. The welcoming Zotos family epitomises Greek *filoxenia* (hospitality), and serves up conviviality, good travel advice and delicious breakfasts (using their own farm produce).

For those who prefer cosy, romantic hideaways, ask for one of the stone rooms. Lemon trees and flowers release sweet aromas. Rates are €5 less per person without breakfast.

Nafplion 1841
PENSION €€

(☑ 27520 24622; www.nafplion1841.gr; Kapodistriou 9; s/d/tr incl breakfast from €50/55/95; ❋🛜) The five bright rooms (and steep stairs) are crammed into this converted 19th-century mansion. Rooms are very plain and very white, but expect good mattresses, superior bed linens, climate control, hydro-massage showers and flat-screen TVs. The hostess is a delight and so is the breakfast.

Klymeni Traditional Homes
APARTMENT €€

(☑ 27520 96194; www.klymeni.gr; studio/apt incl breakfast from €100/125; P🛜) On a hillside overlooking the peaceful countryside, these traditional stone houses are perfect for families. They have vast living areas, spa baths and respite from the hubbub of Nafplio, although the city is accessible by car. Helpful owner Alexander provides breakfast goodies. Take 25 Martiou out of town for 1.5km towards the Palamidi fortress.

It's only 1km from Karathona Beach.

Leto Nuevo
HOTEL €€

(☑ 27520 28093; www.letohotelnafplio.gr; Zygomala 28; d/tr incl breakfast from €65/90; ❋🛜) This revamped hotel on a quiet street overlooks much of the old town, with spacious rooms decked out in contemporary

---

NAFPLIO'S BOUTIQUE SLEEPS

Nafplio's streets burst with boutique hotels. These renovated former mansions vary in style, though most have four to eight (rather compact) rooms with contemporary, period or kitsch furnishings and steep internal stairs. Prices include cable TV.

Aetoma (☑ 27520 27373; www.nafplionhotel.com; Plateia Agios Spiridonos 2; d incl breakfast €75-120; ❋🛜) Intimate and comfortable, the five rooms in Aetoma, a classic mansion, have dark, heavy and stylish furnishings, and hospitable owners who go out of their way to be helpful. All rooms have balconies with views to a pretty, traditional alley below, or to the Palamidi. Generous traditional breakfast.

Grand Sarai (☑ 27520 22563; www.grandsarainafplio.com; cnr Fotomara & Potamianou 3; r incl breakfast from €120; 🛜) A beautifully renovated pink mansion over three floors that's sleek and modern on the inside. Rooms are very stylish, though may lack colour for some; they are decorated strictly in neutral tones. Most boast views, two rooms have spa baths. Extensive breakfasts using local produce are served in an intimate setting downstairs.

Adiandi (☑ 27520 22073; www.hotel-adiandi.com; Othonos 31; s/d/ste incl breakfast from €65/75/130; ❋🛜) Rooms in this fun place are individually decorated with bright colours, artistic door bedheads and marble sinks. One room is tiny, but there's more room in the funky cafe-meets-breakfast-room downstairs.

Amymone (☑ 27520 99477; www.amymone.gr; Othonos 39; s/d/ste incl breakfast €75/85/125; ❋@🛜) Amymone is all about stencilled art, faux graffiti and Blaxploitation silhouettes on funky door bedsteads. It will appeal to pop-art fans. Mod cons and an excellent breakfast included.

creams. It won't win design awards (it's a quirky shape), but the excellent location, general spaciousness and homemade jams at breakfast trump any glitches. It's a fair price for what you would otherwise get in Nafplio.

Room 121 is a standard double but has its own balcony that affords great views.

Hotel Byron
PENSION €€

(☑27520 22351; www.byronhotel.gr; Platonos 2; s/d/tr/q incl breakfast €60/70/100/120; ❋ 🛜) Occupying a fine Venetian building, the Byron is an older-style spot but a reliable favourite, with friendly management, neat rooms, iron bedsteads and period furniture.

Hotel Grande Bretagne
LUXURY HOTEL €€

(☑27520 96200; www.grandebretagne.com.gr; Plateia Filellinon; s/d/tr incl breakfast from €90/135/155; ❋ 🛜) Nafplion elegance – this is a plush, traditionally styled period hotel, right in the heart of the waterfront-cafe action.

3Sixty° Hotel & Suites
BOUTIQUE HOTEL €€€

(☑27525 00501; www.3sixtyhotel.gr; cnr Koletti & Papanikolau 26; ste incl breakfast €200-250; ❋ 🛜) Ascend the modern spiral staircase beneath the enormous chandelier, and you're faced with seven sumptuous suites of various sizes decked out in contemporary creams, charcoals and browns – the global trend (read, you could be anywhere). Oversized beds and bathrooms are top-notch, however, and a hot breakfast is included.

✖ Eating

Pidalio
GREEK €

(☑27520 22603; 25 Martiou 5; mains €7-9; ⊙12.30pm-midnight Wed-Mon) One of several excellent new spots in the 'new town' and frequented mainly by locals who might steer clear of those in the more touristy 'old town', this lovely taverna serves excellent Greek fare at fair prices. It's warm and lively, and you'll smell the aromas before you spot it.

Antica Gelateria di Roma
GELATO €

(☑27520 23520; www.anticagelateria.gr; cnr Farmakopoulou & Komninou; ice cream from €2.50; ⊙10am-11pm) The only 'true' gelato shop in Nafplio is still holding back the competition. Italian gelati maestros Marcello, Claudia and Monica Raffo will tell you: 'This is no fantasy – it's the real thing!' Only natural and local ingredients are used and it's all made on the premises.

Karamalis
GREEK €

(☑27520 97999; cnr Bouboulinas St & Syngrou St; mains €6-9; ⊙11am-midnight) You won't find many tourists here, at one of Nafplio's most long-standing stalwarts, possibly because of its location overlooking the port car park. Locals don't need the view. Their eyes are on the excellent price-to-quality ratio of the daily *mayirefta* (ready-cooked meals). You can also buy hefty portions to take away.

Fougaro
CAFE €

(www.fougaro.gr; Asklipiou 98; mains €8-12; ⊙6pm-midnight Wed-Sun) This lovely cafe-restaurant and cultural space sits 3km from Nafplio in a converted canning factory, on the road to Epidavros. Good coffee, light bites for lunch and a smarter dinner menu; particularly good during events. Look for the *fougaro* (chimney).

★ Kavalaris Corner Mezedopoleio
MEZEDHES €€

(☑27525 00180; cnr Amalias 2 & Koleti; mezedhes €3.50-7; ⊙noon-late Tue-Sun; 🗷) Just off Plateia Syntagmatos and nestled into a cosy corner, this delightful spot whips, tosses and fries up some of the best mezedhes (appetisers) around. You can watch the chef at work in the open kitchen, though our guess is you'll be too busy munching on everything from *spetsofaï* (sausage) to *apaki* (fried pork). Excellent veggie options, too. Traditional products but contemporary creations.

Scuola Pizza-bar
ITALIAN €€

(☑27520 99431; Bouboulinas 39; mains €7-13; ⊙1pm-1am) For a break from Greek cuisine, go Italian(ish). Scuola ('school' in Italian) teaches the locals, especially the younger crowd, a thing or two about good cuisine. Its quirky interior comprises a classroom setting, complete with a blackboard and books. Pasta and pizza with Greek twists break all the rules.

Taverna Aiolos
GREEK €€

(☑27520 26828; Olgas 30; mains €8-15) A warm and cosy traditional taverna where you come for a well-cooked and hearty Greek meal... and end up staying until three in the morning, such is the convivial atmosphere and hospitality. It serves up reliable Greek classics.

To Omorfo Tavernaki
GREEK €€

(☑27520 25944; Vasilissis Olgas 1; mains €8-15; ⊙noon-late; 🗷) Ample servings of homemade delights in a convivial restaurant adorned with antique oddments. The mezedhes – zucchini balls, feta with honey, tzatziki etc – are particularly good.

Drinking & Nightlife

Es Aei WINE BAR

(27520 22884; Staikopulou 8; noon-late) Mismatched furniture and bare light bulbs conjure up a hipster hang-out image, but the jazz playing and the candlelight transform this joint into something mellower. Sample from an extensive list of Greek wines, accompanied by a succinct selection of excellent tapas.

O Mavros Gatos BAR

(27520 26652; Sofroni 1; 8am-late) Chilled-out cafe by day, buzzy bar by night, with live performers and DJs on some nights. There are comfy seats outside and an eclectic vintage vibe inside and upstairs.

Shopping

Glykos Peirasmos FOOD

(Plapouta 10; 9am-10pm) *The* place for delicious chocolate, baklava, *loukoumi* (Turkish delight) and honey-sodden walnut cake.

Karonis WINE

(27520 24446; www.karoniswineshop.gr; Amalias 5; 8.30am-2pm & 5.30-9.30pm Mon-Sat) Wine enthusiasts can find a fine selection of wines from all over the country, including Nemean reds and spirits. Wine tastings offered. Well-read owner Ioannis has a wide range of interests, from grapes to politics.

Odyssey BOOKS

(27520 23430; Plateia Sytagmatos; 9am-midnight) This wonderful old-school bookshop stocks dusty relics and tourist paraphernalia and hasn't changed much since the '70s, it seems. It stocks some excellent guides and maps in English.

Information

Hospital (27523 61100; Kountouriotou 1) Nafplio's general hospital.

National Bank of Greece (Plateia Syntagmatos) Has ATMs.

Post Office (cnr Sygrou & Sidiras Merarhias; 7.30am-8pm Mon-Fri)

Staikos Tours (27520 27950; www.rentacar nafplio.gr; Bouboulinas 50; 8.30am-2.30pm & 5.30-9pm) Run by the personable, English-speaking Christos. Offers full travel services, including ferry tickets, plus Sixt rental cars.

Getting There & Away

The **KTEL Argolis bus station** (27520 27323; www.ktelargolida.gr; Syngrou) has buses to Athens (€13.10, 2½ hours, 11 to 13 daily) via Corinth Isthmus (Peloponnese) KTEL bus station (€6.50, 1½ hours). Other services include the following:

Argos (€1.80, 30 minutes, hourly)

Epidavros (around €3, 45 minutes, six Monday to Friday, four Saturday, one Sunday)

Galatas (€9, two hours, one to three daily)

Kranidi (€8.50, two hours, four Monday to Friday, three Saturday, two Sunday)

Mycenae (around €3, one hour, three Monday to Friday, two Saturday)

Tolo (€1.80, 15 minutes, nine to 12 daily)

Tripoli (€7.70, 1½ hours, two daily)

Getting Around

Call a **taxi** (6937194646) or head to the **rank** on Sygrou. Car-hire agencies include the following:

Hermes Car Rental (27520 25308; www.hermestravel.gr; Sygrou 18)

Sixt Rent a Car At Staikos Tours.

Tiryns Τίρυνθα

The unfairly underrated Mycenaean acropolis of **Tiryns** (27520 22657; adult/concession €8/4; 8am-3pm), 4km north of Nafplio, is the apogee of Mycenaean architectural achievement. Legend has it that its massive walls, 7m thick in parts, were built by a Cyclops. You can stroll around the immense stonework and explore the Upper and Lower Citadels, but the vaulted passageways, the secret stairway and the impressive gallery are off limits.

Built in the 13th century BC, this World Heritage site was, in its heyday, second only to Mycenae in terms of regional importance. The layout of some of the ruins is easy to make out, and there are few crowds. The site has little in the way of signs or descriptions, so it's worth buying *Tiryns*, by Dr Alkestis Papademetriou (€8), at the ticket office.

Any Nafplio–Argos bus can drop you outside the site.

Epidavros Επίδαυρος

⭐ **Epidavros** ARCHAEOLOGICAL SITE

(27530 22009; adult/concession €12/6; 8am-8pm Apr-Aug, reduced hrs rest of year; P) In its day Epidavros, 30km east of Nafplio, was famed and revered as far away as Rome as a place of miraculous healing. Visitors came great distances to the tranquil Sanctuary of Asclepius (god of medicine) to seek a cure for their ailments. Today the World Heritage site's amazingly well-preserved theatre remains a venue during the Hellenic Festival for Classical Greek plays, first performed here up to 2000 years ago.

Legend has it that Asclepius was the son of Apollo and Coronis. While giving birth to Asclepius, Coronis was killed by the jealous Apollo, who'd found out that she'd been unfaithful to him. Apollo took his son to Mt Pelion, where the physician centaur Chiron instructed the boy in the healing arts. Asclepius became a healer of such great renown that he brought a man back from the dead, which angered Hades, the god of the underworld, who asked Zeus to strike Asclepius down. Zeus did so, provoking, in turn, the wrath of Apollo, and Asclepius was eventually deified.

Apollo was worshipped at Epidavros in Mycenaean and Archaic times, but by the 4th century BC he had been superseded by his son. Epidavros became acknowledged as the birthplace of Asclepius. Although the afflicted worshipped Asclepius at sanctuaries throughout Greece, the two most important sites were at Epidavros and on the island of Kos. The fame of the Epidavros sanctuary spread, and when a plague raged in Rome, Livy and Ovid came to Epidavros to seek help.

It is believed that licks from snakes were one of the curative practices at the sanctuary. Asclepius is normally shown with a serpent, which – by renewing its skin – symbolises rejuvenation. Other treatments provided at the sanctuary involved diet instruction, herbal medicines and occasionally even surgery. The sanctuary also served as an entertainment venue and every four years, during the Festival of Asclepieia, Epidavros hosted dramas and athletic competitions.

There are buses from Nafplio to Epidavros (€2.90, 45 minutes, six Monday to Friday, four Saturday, one Sunday).

★ **Theatre of Epidavros** HISTORIC SITE
(adult/concession €12/6; ☺8am-8pm Apr-Aug, reduced hrs rest or year) Built of limestone, yet one of the best-preserved Classical Greek structures in existence, this 4th-century-BC theatre is the undisputed highlight of Epidavros. It's renowned for its amazing acoustics; a coin dropped in the theatre's centre

PEREGRINATIONS OF PAUSANIAS

Lonely Planet and its alternatives were beaten to the publishing of guidebooks by nearly 20 centuries. The traveller and geographer Pausanias wrote what is believed to be the first – and most definitive – 'guidebook' for tourists in the 2nd century AD. His work, *Description of Greece* (sometimes known as *Tour* or *Itinerary of Greece*), is a series of 10 volumes in which he describes most of Greece as seen at the time (between AD 143 and 161), covering the regions of Attica, Boeotia, Phocis and Ozolian Locris, plus the regions that make up much of the Peloponnese: Corinthia, Lakonia, Messinia, Elia, Achaïa and Arkadia. Classical Greek scholars, historians and archaeologists regard it as an extremely important historical work for its insight into places, people, monuments and sites, as well as associated facts and legends. Pausanias is believed to be from Lydia in Asia Minor and travelled extensively throughout Greece, Macedonia, Italy and parts of Asia and Africa.

can be heard from the highest seat. The theatre seats up to 14,000 people. Its entrance is flanked by restored Corinthian pilasters and the foundations of the ancient stage are beyond the circle. It's now used for performances of Ancient Greek drama during the annual Hellenic Festival (p154).

Sanctuary of Asclepius RUINS
(adult/concession €12/6; ☺8am-8pm Apr-Aug, reduced hrs rest or year) The Sanctuary of Asclepius was dedicated to the god of healing. The ruins include the huge **katagogeion**, a hostelry for pilgrims and patients; the large **banquet hall** in which the Romans built an **odeum** (a room for musical performances); and the **stadium** – the venue for the Festival of Asclepieia's athletic competitions. Just beyond is the remarkable **tholos** the **Temple of Asclepius** and the **abaton** (dormitory).

You first reach the large, square *katagogeion,* beyond which is the former-gymnasium-banquet-hall in which the Romans built an *odeum*. It was here that the Festival of Asclepieia took place.

The path meanders past the remains of the stadium on your left. Ahead is the circular *tholos* (built 360–320 BC and under heavy reconstruction at research time), originally surrounded by two circles of columns: Doric and Corinthian. In the centre there used to be a small labyrinth and one of the theories is that patients were put in there for a 'healing encounter' with snakes.

To the northeast are the foundations of the Temple of Asclepius and next to them is the *abaton*. The therapies practised here seemed to have depended on the influence of the mind upon the body. It is believed that patients were given a pep talk by a priest on the powers of Asclepius, then put to sleep in the *abaton* to dream of a visitation by the god. The dream would hold the key to the healing process.

East is the Sanctuary of Egyptian Gods, which indicates that the cult of Asclepius was an adaptation of the cult of Imhotep, worshipped in Egypt for his healing powers.

Epidavros Museum   MUSEUM
(adult/concession €12/6; ◷ 8am-8pm Apr-Aug, reduced hrs rest of year) Found between the Sanctuary of Asclepius and the Theatre of Epidavros, this museum houses statuary (mostly copies) that once adorned the Temple of Asclepius, stone inscriptions recording miraculous cures, alarming-looking surgical instruments, votive offerings and fragments of intricately carved reliefs from the ceiling of the sanctuary's *tholos*.

✱ Festivals & Events

Athens & Epidavros Festival   THEATRE
(☎ 21092 82900; www.greekfestival.gr/en; ◷ Jul & Aug) The Theatre of Epidavros stages both modern theatre and Ancient Greek dramas during the annual Athens and Epidavros Festival, part of the larger cultural Hellenic Festival (p96). Tickets can be bought in Epidavros at the theatre box office, online or from Athens' box office (p96). There are special bus services available from Athens (around €25, two hours) and Nafplio (around €10, 45 minutes).

Southwest Argolis

Very few travellers take the time to venture to the southwestern heel of the Argolis peninsula, yet the zigzagging drive along the east coast, past the pretty coastal town of Galatas and picturesque houses across the narrow bay that is Poros, is absolutely spectacular.

The western part of the peninsula, centred on the agricultural town of Kranidi, features the small resorts of Porto Heli, 4km south of Kranidi, and Ermioni, 4km east of Kranidi. Both offer convenient connections to the Saronic Gulf islands of Hydra and Spetses. Additional Hydra services fly across the water from Metochi, essentially a waterfront car park, around 10km east of Ermioni.

◉ Sights

Didyma Caves   CAVE
(◷ 24hr) **FREE** Off the main road between Kranidi and Epidavros, about 1km west of the village of Didyma, are the Didyma Caves – two extraordinary sinkholes. The caves collapsed thousands of years ago, leaving large crater-like holes. One hides an unexpected surprise – a tiny Byzantine church, Agios Georgios, constructed under a crevice. The caves are well signposted.

Frachti Cave & Paralia   CAVE
(Killada; ◷ 24hr) **FREE** Frachti Cave is one of Greece's oldest and most significant Paleolithic, Mesolithic and Neolithic sites; that equates to life up to 40,000 BC. The remarkable finds have revealed the transitions between all eras: the way hunter-gatherers lived as fishermen, then organised themselves in groups, and, later, as tool-using farmers. Many of the excavation's findings are in the archaeological museum (p146) in Nafplio. Offshore, you can snorkel among a submerged Neolithic settlement, Paralia; the shoreline was a further 7km away back then.

Signage in English is excellent and there's a small jetty. To get there, follow the signs to the cave for 4km (signs are 5km before Kranidi if coming from the north). You must walk along a trail over rocks for about 500m (these are marked by red painted arrows). At the time of research, however, you couldn't enter the cave without contacting the Municipality of Ermionida (☎ 27543 60028). Nevertheless, it's possible to peer through the security fencing.

ℹ Getting There & Away

BOAT
Regular **Hellenic Seaways** (☎ 21041 99000; www.hellenicseaways.gr) high-speed boats depart from Porto Heli to Piraeus via Spetses and Hydra, and from Ermioni to Piraeus via Hydra. The cheapest and most frequent boats to Hydra from Argolis are **Hydra Lines** (☎ 22980 52961; www.hydralines.gr; €6.50)

BOATS FROM SOUTHWEST ARGOLIS

DESTINATION	PORT	DURATION	FARE (€)	FREQUENCY
Hydra	Ermioni	20-40min	8	3 daily
Hydra	Poros	30min	13.50	5 daily
Hydra	Metochi	20min	6.50	6 daily
Spetses	Porto Heli	10min	6	3 daily
Spetses	Ermioni	25min	8	2 daily

and **Hydra Celebrity** (☑ 22980 53000, mobile 6981222550; www.hydracelebrity.gr; €6.50) from Metochi; park for free by the waterfront or leave your car in a secure, shaded car park. Caïques shuttle between Galatas and Poros (€1, five minutes). From Poros there are four daily fast boats to Piraeus (€24.50, 1¼ hours).

BUS

There are **bus services** (☑ 27540 21218; www. ktelargolida.gr) between Kranidi and Nafplio (€8.50, two hours, four weekdays, three on Saturday, one on Sunday), and local buses from Kranidi to Ermioni (€1.85, 10 minutes, several daily) and Porto Heli (€1.85, 10 minutes, several daily).

ARKADIA ΑΡΚΑΔΙΑ

The picturesque rural prefecture of Arkadia occupies much of the central Peloponnese. Its name evokes images of grassy meadows, forested mountains, gurgling streams and shady grottoes. According to mythology, it was a favourite haunt of Pan, the flute-playing, cloven-hoofed god of nature.

Almost encircled by mountain ranges, Arkadia was remote enough in ancient times to remain largely untouched by the battles and intrigues of the rest of Greece, and was the only region of the Peloponnese not conquered by the Dorians. The region is dotted with crumbling medieval villages, remote monasteries and Frankish castles, and is popular among fresh-air fiends.

The heart of Arkadia (to the west of the regional capital, Tripoli) comprises a tangle of precipitous ravines and narrow roads that wind their way through the medieval-village-speckled valleys of the Menalon Mountains. Think breathtaking mountainous scenery, along with some excellent hiking opportunities (and skiing in winter).

❶ Getting There & Away

Having your own wheels is advantageous here, as public transport to the main villages is limited to one or two buses per day.

KTEL Arkadia (☑ 27102 22560; www.ktel arkadias.gr; Nafpliou 141, Tripoli) in Tripoli is the departure point for buses to Stemnitsa (€4.50, one hour, one daily Monday, Thursday and Friday), Dimitsana (€7.10, 1½ hours, one to two daily) and Andritsena (€9.40, 1½ hours, one to two daily).

It also handles buses to Athens (via Corinth Isthmus, €16.50, almost hourly), Olympia (€13.50, one daily weekdays), Pyrgos (€15.50, one daily weekdays), Nafplio (€7.70, one to two daily) and direct to Patra (€19.80, one to two daily except Saturday).

Local buses run to Sparta (€5.90, nine daily) and Kalamata (€8.90, one daily on weekdays).

Stemnitsa Στεμνίτσα
POP 200

Stemnitsa, 26km northwest of Tripoli, is a striking village of stone houses and Byzantine churches. If you want to peek into any of the churches, ask around for the keys. There are several monasteries in the area, in the Lousios Gorge along the riverbank to/from the site of Ancient Gortys.

The starting (or finishing) point for the Menalon Trail (p156), Stemnitsa is a good base for hikers. It provides a useful base for a hike along the Lousios Gorge, accessed by Ancient Gortys and passing by monasteries including Prodomos, and the New and Old Philosophou.

Stemnitsa is also known for its silver and gold craftsmanship; even today, there is a silversmith school here.

🛏 Sleeping & Eating

★ **Mpelleiko** B&B €€
(☑ 6976607967, 27950 81286; www.mpelleiko. gr; s/d/tr incl breakfast €70/80/90; 🖥) The ultra-hospitable and knowledgable English-speaking owner, Nena, has converted her family home (dating from 1650) into a stylish guesthouse perched above the village. Each room's decor is unique and features tasteful, traditional local homewares.

You can even sleep in the former 'donkey basement'. Breakfast includes homemade organic produce and is served in a beautiful room with an open fireplace.

Xenonas Tsarbou
BOUTIQUE HOTEL €€

(☑ 27950 81406; www.xenonas-tsarbou.gr; s/d incl breakfast from €50/75; P ⑧) This slick-feeling place is a little incongruous in its converted historic stone building. But its rooms are pleasant, nonetheless, with gold and velvet trimmings. There's a cosy bar with fireplace for post-hike relaxation, and hospitable hostess Christina prepares an extensive breakfast spread.

I Stemnitsa
GREEK €

(mains €6-13; ⊘noon-late) It may be the only taverna open year-round in Stemnitsa, but you could do worse. Eat inside (enter off the alley to the left of the clock tower) or sit outdoors under giant umbrellas. The local butcher owns the establishment, so go for the grills and expect quality, hearty cuts of meat.

Gerousia
CAFE

(⊘7am-late) A *kafeneio* (coffee house) since 1870, this appealing cafe on the square is a good place to linger over a coffee or glass of wine.

❶ Getting There & Away

There is one bus in each direction between Tripoli and Dimitsana via Stemnitsa (€4.50, one hour, Monday, Thursday and Friday). A taxi to Dimitsana costs around €12, to Prodromos Monastery €15, Ancient Gortys €20, and the Philosophou Monasteries €25.

THE MENALON TRAIL

The well-signposted, 72.5km Menalon Trail (www.menalontrail.eu) stretches from Stemnitsa to Lagkadia, passing through the dramatic scenery of the Lousios Gorge, the western slopes of Mt Menalon, the Mylaon River valley and the Gortynian Mountains. Completed in May 2015 by a group of volunteers, the trail is divided into eight sections of varying difficulty; the Stemnitsa–Dimitsana section is the most popular; the website has a trail outline and maps. See also the Anavasi Topo 25 map, *Lousios 8.51 1:22,000*. You can also download the excellent Menalon Trail TopoGuide app for detailed offline maps and numerous points of interest.

Of the villages, Stemnitsa, Dimitsana, Valtesiniko and Lagkadia all have places to stay and eat, and you can pick up provisions at Vytina, Nymphasia and Magouliana.

There are eight trail sections:

Stemnitsa–Dimitsana (12.5km, 4½ hours) A picturesque descent into the Lousios Gorge past Prodromos Monastery, followed by an ascent to the Old and New Philosophou Monasteries. The trail then follows the course of the river before leading up to the Open Air Water-Power Museum. From the Prodromos Monastery there's a worthwhile detour south to Ancient Gortys.

Dimitsana–Zygovisti (4.2km, 1½ hours) A gentle ascent past St Apostoli Monastery, and along footpaths and dirt roads through fields.

Zygovisti–Elati (15km, five hours) This section ascends to the Bilali Pass over the Western Menalon massif, with some steep sections and an optional detour to Pliovouni Peak (1643m).

Elati–Vytina (8.5km, 2¼ hours) Partially paved, wooded trail that passes by some ancient ruins and abandoned windmills.

Vytina–Nymphasia (5.6km, 1½ hours) The trail descends to a short gorge before ascending gently through a rock-and-shrub landscape.

Nymphasia–Magouliana (9km, 3½ hours) Leading through oak and spruce forests, the trail descends to Kernitsas Monastery and passes by Sfyrida Hermitage and Gavros Spring.

Magouliana–Valtesiniko (7.5km, two hours) The path descends past an old sanatorium and follows a riverbed.

Valtesiniko–Lagkadia (13.9km, five hours) The path ascends to a Byzantine fortress, then passes through open country and traverses valleys before ending at a war memorial.

Dimitsana   Δημητσάνα

POP 350

Built like an amphitheatre on two hills at the beginning of the Lousios Gorge, Dimitsana, 11km north of Stemnitsa, is a delightful medieval village. This small place played a significant role in the country's struggle for self-determination. Its Greek school, founded in 1764, was an important spawning ground for the ideas leading to the uprisings against the Turks. Its students included Bishop Germanos of Patra and Patriarch Gregory V, who was hanged by the Turks in retaliation for the massacre in Tripoli. The village also had a number of gunpowder factories and a branch of the secret Filiki Eteria (Friendly Society), where Greeks met to discuss the revolution. Today, this sleepy village is hiker central in summer and full of skiing weekenders in winter.

◉ Sights & Activities

Open Air Water-Power Museum   MUSEUM
(☑ 27950 31630; www.piop.gr; adult/concession €3/1.50; ⊙ 10am-6pm Wed-Mon Mar–mid-Oct, to 5pm mid-Oct–Feb) This excellent little museum is an entertaining romp through the region's pre-industrial past. It occupies the old Agios Yiannis mill complex, 1.6km south of town (signposted), where a spring-fed stream once supplied power for a succession of mills spread down the hillside. The lush grounds are criss-crossed with channels alive with rushing water that power the fully operational fulling mill, flour mill and gunpowder mill (the last having provided ammunition during the Greek War of Independence).

Trekking Hellas   OUTDOORS
(☑ 6974459753, 27910 25978; www.trekkinghellas.gr) Trekking Hellas offers various activities, including white-water rafting (with lunch, €55) on the Lousios River and half-day guided treks along the Lousios Gorge (minimum four people, €50). Contact the company in advance.

🛏 Sleeping

Kazakou Guesthouse   B&B €
(☑ 27950 31660; www.xenonaskazakou.gr; d/tr/q incl breakfast €60/85/110; 🖥) This rambling stone house above central Dimitsana is one of the more casual options around. There's a hotchpotch of rooms with lots of wooden features and a vast breakfast is served in the

vaulted lounge. The location is either a boon or a bane, depending on whether you enjoy the sound of church bells. Would possibly appeal more to larger parties of travellers.

★ Amanites   BOUTIQUE HOTEL €€
(☑ 27950 31090; www.amanites.gr; d/tr incl breakfast from €75/90; P 🖥) This lovely place, a converted historic home, has seven elegant rooms with heavy drapes and tasteful fabrics. Four rooms have front-facing balconies overlooking the gorge. Delightful English-speaking owner Panos and his parents, Aris and Elena, go out of their way to be helpful.

Nerida   BOUTIQUE HOTEL €€
(☑ 27950 32700; www.nerida-hotel.gr; s/d/tr €65/85/100) Opened in 2013, this dwelling is run by its young owner. The 20 rooms look like they comprise a designer homeware collection and, as such, are more contemporary than the average mountain-village accommodation. Thankfully, the exterior is constructed in the obligatory stone to blend in. It's popular for romantic getaways for Greeks. Fine valley views from most rooms.

Enastron Guesthouse   B&B €€
(☑ 27950 31684; www.xenonasenastron.gr; d incl breakfast €65; 🖥) This appealing guesthouse with only three rooms is distinguished not just by the friendliness and helpfulness of its owners, but also by the meticulous attention to detail. The spacious wooden-beamed rooms come with contemporary fittings and excellent bathrooms, and the extensive breakfast buffet comprises fresh local produce. Rates are higher over weekends.

Tsiapa Guesthouse   PENSION €€
(☑ 27950 31583; www.xenonas-tsiapa.gr; d/tr €50/65; 🖥) One of the 'old school' budget options, with so-clean-you-could-eat-off-the-floor rooms that boast fridges and hotplates. The communal living room has a fireplace – perfect for a cold evening.

🍴 Eating & Drinking

Taverna Margarita   GREEK €€
(☑ 27950 31368; Zatouna; mains €7-12; ⊙ 1pm-10pm) This casual, ultra-typical, family-run taverna in the quaint village of Zatouna is a far cry from the tourist haunts of nearby Dimitsana. The pine decor and souvenir paraphernalia look likes they've been there since time immemorial. Don't expect silver service, but do expect some genuine kitchen

WORTH A TRIP

SUSTAINABLE FOOD SOJOURN

Tiny eatery **Zerzova** (☑6932847358, 27950 32452; Panaghia; mains €8-14; ⊙noon-8pm Fri-Sun, longer hours Jun-Aug; ☑), 14km southwest of Dimitsana in the village of Panaghia, ticks all the right boxes. Sustainable practices? Tick – the husband-and-wife team collects all wild herbs and cultivates its own produce. Home cooking? Tick – even Greek grandmothers are happy to come here. Traditional? Tick again – it's in a lovely old building with a cellar below.

cooking. It's known for its *pita* (pie), filled with fresh mountain *horta* (greens).

To Kapilio Ton Athonaton　　STEAK €€
(mains €6-15; ⊙10am-11pm Thu-Tue) The summer terrace overlooking the gorge, the Tavern of Immortals is sought out by discerning carnivores for its meaty specials – roast lamb, pork chops, locally made sausage...

Kato Apo To Roloi　　WINE BAR
(☑27950 32444; www.undertheclock.gr; ⊙10am-late; ☎) The Under the Clock cafe is *the* spot to unwind after a day's hiking. Look down at the gorge with a large glass of wine (€3.50) or an expertly mixed cocktail (from €8) in hand.

ⓘ Getting There & Away

There are two daily buses in each direction on weekdays only between Tripoli and Dimitsana (around €7, 1½ hours). A taxi to Stemnitsa costs around €12.50, to Monastery of Philosophou €16, and to Ancient Gortys €25.

Leonidio　　Λεωνίδιο
POP 3800

Leonidio, 76km south of Argos along a spectacular winding road, is dramatically located at the mouth of the Badron Gorge. In recent years the village has become a magnet for climbers who hang off the precipices and magnificent vertical rocks. Culturally, it's famous for its Tsakonian aubergines (eggplants) and summer Aubergine Festival, Melizazz. Its tiny Plateia 25 Martiou is an archetypal, unspoilt, whitewashed village square. There are still living locals who speak the local dialect, Tsakonica, said to date back to the time of Sparta. Five kilometres north of Leonidio, the tiny fishing village of **Plaka** is a drawcard for those after stunning clear waters and excellent beach-side tavernas.

✯ Festivals & Events

Melizazz　　CULTURAL
(Melijazz; www.melitzazz.gr; ⊙Jul) Combining a love of both *melitzana* (eggplant) and jazz music (as you would), this arts, food and cultural festival is a fun and colourful three-day annual event.

⨳ Sleeping

Semeli Camping　　CAMPGROUND €
(☑27570 22995; www.camping-semeli.gr; campsites per tent/person €6/6; ℗☎) Near the Badron Gorge and set amid trees, this is camping as nature intended. Oh, and the ocean and beach are a quick stroll away.

Agroktima Traditional Guesthouse　　APARTMENT €€
(☑6979400140; www.agroktima.com; apt from €65) A cluster of traditional stone houses 1km before Plaka. Quaint, self-contained and very comfortable. Surrounded by green lawn.

✕ Eating & Drinking

Delfinia　　GREEK €
(Dolphin; ☑27570 23036; Plaka; mains €7-10, fish per kilo €35-60; ⊙9am-late) The fresher the better. Owner Theodore's brother-in-law is the fisherman so you eat the catch of the day. Kids can run amok, you can sit on the terrace over the water.

Café Bar 2Porto　　CAFE
(☑27570 22255; www.2porto.gr/en; Thioporto) Run by a friendly, helpful owner, this trendy bar-cafe doubles as the KTEL bus office. It morphs into a bar in the evenings and is the frappé magnet for the village youth.

ⓘ Getting There & Away

Buses to/from Athens (€22, three daily); change at Astros.The friendly Café Bar 2Por doubles as the KTEL bus ticket office.

LAKONIA　　ΛΑΚΩΝΙΑ

The region of Lakonia occupies almost identical boundaries to the powerful mountain-skirted kingdom ruled by King Menelaus in Mycenaean times. It is home to legends, including the city of Sparta, plus the spectacular ruins of Mystras, the Byzantine Empire's last stronghold.

Dominating the landscape are two massive mountain ranges, the Taÿgetos Mountains in the west and the Parnonas Mountains in the east. These taper away to create the central and eastern fingers of the Peloponnese.

English speakers can thank the Lakonians for the word 'laconic'.

Sparta Σπάρτη

POP 17,000

Sparta, fearing no one, was without city walls or fortification, which is probably why so few traces are left of a remarkable people. At the height of their power, Greece's toughest, incorruptible, legendary warriors triumphed over Athens and the rest of Greece in the Peloponnesian Wars (431–404 BC). However, the decisive defeat by the Thebans in the Battle of Leuctra in 371 BC was the beginning of the end for Sparta, which was followed by successive subjugation by the Macedonians, Romans, Goths and Slavs.

The town was refounded in AD 1834 on the orders of King Otto. Mindful of history, Otto and his court felt that since Athens was to be rebuilt to reflect its former glory, so too should Sparta. He didn't succeed, though a few ruins attest to its ancient pre-eminence.

Most visitors pass through town on their way to and from the Byzantine glories of Mystras.

◉ Sights

★ Museum of the Olive & Greek Olive Oil MUSEUM

(☑ 27310 89315; www.piop.gr; Othonos Amalias 129; adult/concession €3/1.50; ⊙ 10am-6pm Wed-Mon) This beautifully designed museum initiates you into the mysteries of the olive from its initial appearance in the Mediterranean in 60,000 BC to the present day. Learn about its immense importance in millennia of Greek life. Immerse yourself in olive oil's many uses (cooking, fuel, ritual, perfume-making). Check out the magnificent reconstructions of olive presses in the courtyard, ranging from prehistoric to Byzantine. Finally, marvel at the minute working models (press the button) that demonstrate changes in pressing technology.

Ancient Sparta RUINS

(⊙ 8am-8pm, to 3pm winter) FREE Few buildings are standing that date back to the height of Sparta's greatness. This was when the acropolis and agora made up the religious and administrative centre (8th century BC until the Roman period). Recently, however, the area was restored to a formal site with paths and detailed English signs.

To get here, head to the King Leonidas statue that belligerently hefts its sword and shield at the northern end of Paleologou. West of here, signs point the way to the acropolis.

From the main cobbled road, signed paths head through olive groves. A highlight is the ancient theatre (2nd or 3rd century BC), a few steps and seats of which are still visible along the overgrown half-circle.

The main road leads north to the acropolis, passing the Byzantine Church of Christ the Saviour on the way to the 6000 BC Sanctuary of Athena Halkioitou on a small hillock. Some of the most important finds in the town's archaeological museum were unearthed here.

If you follow the Tripoli-bound road north of town, a signposted path leads downhill to the remains of the Sanctuary of Artemis Orthia; this is where Spartan boys were flogged till they bled, the bravest awarded bronze sickles which they dedicated to the goddess.

Koumantarios Gallery of Sparta GALLERY

(☑ 27310 81557; Paleologou 123; €3; ⊙ 8am-3pm, Wed-Mon) Part of the National Art Gallery, the quaint Koumantarios art gallery holds a rotating permanent collection plus wonderful temporary exhibitions. It's definitely worth popping in to see what's on.

Archaeological Museum MUSEUM

(☑ 27310 28575; cnr Lykourgou & Agiou Nikonos; adult €2; ⊙ 8am-3pm Tue-Sun Nov-May, 9am-4pm Tue-Sun Jun-Oct) Sparta's old-style archaeological museum hosts artefacts from Sparta's illustrious past, many unlabelled and most without any protective covering. Look for the votive sickle of the kind that Spartan boys dedicated to Artemis Orthia. There are also reliefs featuring Helen and Menelaus (and Helen with Paris), bronze and lead votive figurines, heads and torsos of various deities, a statue thought to be King Leonidas, votive terracotta masks and grave stelae. Fine mosaics from Hellenistic and Roman Sparta are also on show.

Sparta

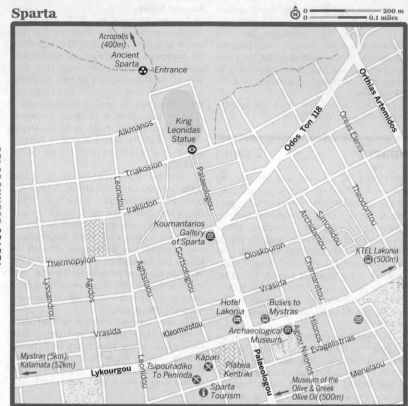

Acropolis
(400m)

Ancient
Sparta
Entrance

Alkmanos

King
Leonidas
Statue

Orthias Artemidos

Triakosion

Palaeologou

Oreas Elenis

Odos Ton 118

Leonidou

Iraklidon

Theodoritou

Koumantarios
Gallery
of Sparta

Dioskouron

Simonidou

Archidamou

Chamaretou

KTEL Lakonia
(500m)

Thermopylon

Aghsilaou

Gortsologou

Lyssandrou

Agidos

Vrasida

Vrasida

Kleomvrotou

Hotel
Lakonia

Buses to
Mystras

Archaeological
Museum

Agiou Nikonos

Hilonos

Evangelistrias

Menelaou

Mystras (5km);
Kalamata (52km)

Lykourgou

Leonidou

Kápari

Tsipouradiko
To Peninda

Plateia
Kentriki

Palaeologou

Sparta
Tourism

Museum of the
Olive & Greek
Olive Oil (500m)

✨ Festivals & Events

Spartathlon
SPORTS

(www.spartathlon.gr/en; ⊗ Sep) This gruelling
annual foot race takes place over the 246km
between Athens and Sparta. It follows in the
footsteps of Pheidippides, the messenger
who ran from Athens to Sparta in one day in
490 BC, to ask the Spartans for assistance in
the Battle of Marathon against the Persians.
The record currently stands at 20 hours and
25 minutes (set in 1984 by Yiannis Kouros).

🛏 Sleeping & Eating

Hotel Lakonia
HOTEL €

(☑ 27310 28951; www.lakoniahotel.gr; Palaeologou
89; s/d/tr incl breakfast €42/57/70; ✳ 🛜) The
rooms at the Lakonia are not hugely memorable, but far from spartan nonetheless.
Boons include a super-cental location and
double-glazed windows that cut out street
noise, and the service is friendly and helpful.

★ Tsipouradiko To Peninda
TAVERNA €

(☑ 27310 83585; Evangelistrias 50; €7-10; ⊗ lunch
Mon-Sat, dinner daily) This atmospheric spot
has been renovated to look like an old-style
shop and *tsipouradiko* (a taverna that specialises in selling *tsipouro*, the alcoholic
spirit) – barrels, china pieces and old cans
line the walls. There's an amazing backyard
and all sorts of nooks and crannies. As for
the food? Traditional *mayirefta* and grills.

Kápari
MEDITERRANEAN €€

(☑ 27313 00520; www.kaparirestaurant.gr; Gort-
soglou 77; mains €8-21; ⊗ noon-11.30pm) This
homey, friendly restaurant is a cut above
Sparta's largely uninspiring taverna scene,
though it is slightly pricier, too. Greek
standards are present and correct, but
there are also lovely salads and an extensive seafood menu; shrimp *saganaki*
(prawns in a savoury tomato sauce with
cheese) stands out.

ℹ Information

National Bank of Greece (cnr Paleologou & Dioskouron)

Police (📞 27310 89580; Episkopou Vresthenis 18)

Post Office (Archidamou 10; ⏱7.30am-2pm Mon-Fri)

Sparta Tourism (📞 27310 28166; Evangelistrias 83-91; ⏱ 8am-3pm Mon-Fri)

ℹ Getting There & Away

Sparta's **KTEL Lakonia bus station** (📞 27310 26441; www.ktel-lakonias.gr; cnr Lykourgou & Thivronos) has buses to Athens (€21.40, 3¼ hours, seven to nine daily) via Corinth (two hours, €14.10), and buses to Gythio (€4.70, one hour, six daily), Neapoli (€15.60, three hours, three daily), Tripoli (€5.90, one hour, nine daily) and Monemvasia (€10, two hours, two to three daily).

Buses run to Mystras (€2.80, 15 minutes, six daily except Sunday) from opposite the archaeological museum on Lykourgou; a taxi costs around €12.

Travelling by bus to Kalamata (€3.50, one hour, one to two daily) involves changing at Artemisia (€2.80, 40 minutes) on the Messinian side of the Langada Pass.

Departures to the Mani peninsula include buses to Gerolimenas (€11.30, 2¼ hours, three daily), Areopoli (€7.60, two hours, three daily) and a 9am service to Gythio with a 10.15am connection to the Diros Caves (€8.70); the return times change.

Mystras   Μυστράς
POP 850

The captivating ruins of churches, libraries, strongholds and palaces in the fortress town of Mystras, a World Heritage–listed site, spill from a spur of the Taÿgetos Mountains 7km west of Sparta. It's among the most important historical sites in the Peloponnese. This is where the Byzantine Empire's richly artistic and intellectual culture made its last stand before an invading Ottoman army, almost 1000 years after its foundation.

Traveller facilities are split between Mystras village, 1km or so below the main gate of ancient Mystras, and Pikoulianika village, 1.3km from Mystras' fortress gate.

GROWING UP SPARTAN

Maybe you saw the gory and highly imaginative film *300,* based (sometimes loosely) on the battle of Thermopylae in 480 BC, one of the most talked-about battles in history? Three hundred elite Spartan soldiers held an entire Persian army (whose force numbered several thousand) at bay at the pass ('hot gates') of Thermopylae (near today's Lamia). For three days, wave upon wave of Persian soldiers fell upon their deadly spears and unbridgeable tortoise-shell formation. What kind of soldiers could display such bravery? Ones raised in Sparta, where warfare was held to be the only occupation worthy of its men and where warriors embodied ferocious, self-sacrificing martial supremacy, living (and very often dying) by the motto 'return with your shield, or on it'.

If you were born male and deemed too weak and feeble to make it to adulthood, you would be left on the slopes of the Taÿgetos Mountains to die. Passed the first round? Then at the age of seven, you'd be plucked from the bosom of your family and sent to live in barracks with other boys, to undergo the military education system known as *agoge*, designed to build physical and emotional toughness. You'd be habitually underfed to encourage you to survive by living off the land and by stealing, but punished harshly if caught. You'd undergo brutal institutionalised beatings, which you'd be expected to bear without showing pain. At the age of 12, you'd form a sexual bond with an older mentor, who'd be responsible for your training. Upon turning 18, you'd become a member of the army until the age of 30, when you'd finally be granted Spartan citizenship, if you had proved yourself worthy.

Born a girl? Then you'd be better off than anywhere else in Greece at the time. You would eat the same food as your brothers, participate in sport and exercise nude. You'd be well educated and literate, and forbidden to marry until in your early 20s, which would spare you from teenage pregnancies and miscarriages. Then when you finally did marry, your husband-to-be would 'abduct' you, and you'd have your head shaved and be dressed in men's clothing before the marriage could be consummated. (That'd be to make your husband comfortable, since he wouldn't have spent much time around women.)

Mystras

History

The Frankish leader Guillaume de Ville-hardouin built the fortress in 1249. When the Byzantines won back the Morea from the Franks, Emperor Michael VIII Palae-ologos made Mystras its capital and seat of government. Settlers from the surrounding plains began to move here, seeking refuge from the invading Slavs. From this time until Dimitrios surrendered to the Turks in 1460, a despot of Morea (usually a son or brother of the ruling Byzantine emperor) lived and reigned at Mystras.

While the empire plunged into decline elsewhere, Mystras enjoyed a renaissance. Gemistos Plethon (1355–1452) founded a school of humanistic philosophy here and his enlightened ideas, including the revival of the teachings of Plato and Pythagoras, attracted intellectuals from all corners of Byzantium. Art and architecture also flourished, as seen in the town's buildings and frescoes.

Mystras declined under Ottoman rule, but thrived again after the Venetians captured it in 1687 and developed a flourishing silk industry. The population swelled to 40,000. The Turks recaptured the town in 1715 and from then it was downhill all the way; the Russians burnt it in 1770, the Albanians in 1780, and Ibrahim Pasha torched what was left in 1825. By the time of Independence it was a largely abandoned ruin. Much restoration has taken place since the 1950s (and continues to this day) and in 1989 it was declared a Unesco World Heritage site.

⊙ Sights

★Mystras   RUINS

(☎23315 25363; adult/concession €12/6; ⊙8am-8pm Apr-Aug, to 3pm Sep-Mar) Spread over a steep, verdant mountainside of the Taÿgetos ranges, this former capital of the Byzantine Empire is the single most compelling set of medieval ruins in Greece. A classic fortified city, Mystras is surrounded by verdant olive and orange trees. Treading the cobblestones, worn smooth by centuries of footsteps, you can walk with the ghosts, ducking into the ruins of palaces, monasteries and churches, most dating from between 1271 and 1460.

From the **upper-entrance** ticket office, the right-hand path (signposted 'Castle') leads up to the fortress; it's a 10-minute ascent. The fortress was built by the Franks and extended by the Turks; the views of the Lakonia plain, spread out below, are nothing short of fantastic. The left-hand path descends from the ticket office to **Agia Sofia**, which served as the palace church and burial ground for several emperors' wives; some frescoes survive in a side chapel. Steps descend from here to a T-junction.

A left turn leads to the **Nafplio Gate**. Near the gate is the huge **Palace of Despots**, restored over several years. The complex was started by the Franks and finished by the Byzantines; various buildings were constructed between 1250 and 1450 and the main palace was built between 1350 and 1400.

The right fork leads down to the **Monemvasia Gate**, the entrance to the lower town. Through the gate, turn right for the well-preserved 14th-century **Convent of Pantanassa**. This features a beautifully ornate stone-carved facade and is still maintained by nuns, Mystras' only inhabitants besides the motley crew of stray cats. The convent is an elaborate, perfectly proportioned building that's never overstated. The exquisite, richly coloured 15th-century frescoes here are among the finest examples of late-Byzantine art. Look out for the tiny stamped silver and gold votive offerings beneath the large icon of the Virgin. You'll find images of eyes, ears, legs, arms, breasts, babies, husbands and wives stamped onto these small tablets, depending on the problems (health or personal life) for which the faithful are hoping for supernatural help. The nuns ask that, before entering, you cover bare legs with the skirts provided.

The path continues down to the **Monastery of Perivleptos**, which is built into a rock and tucked away in a pine grove. Inside, the 14th-century frescoes, preserved virtually intact, equal those of Pantanassa. The church has a very high dome and in the centre you'll find the Pantokrator (the Byzantine depiction of Christ as the universal, all-powerful ruler) surrounded by the Apostles, and the Virgin flanked by two angels.

Continue down towards the Mitropolis and you'll pass **Agios Georgios**, one of Mystras' many private chapels. Further down, and above the path on the left, is the **Laskaris Mansion**, a typical Byzantine house.

The **Mitropolis (Cathedral of Agios Dimitrios)** is a complex of buildings enclosed by a high wall. The original church was built in the 1200s, but was greatly altered in the 15th century. The church stands in an attractive courtyard surrounded by stoas and balconies. Its impressive ecclesiastical ornaments and furniture include a marble iconostasis, an intricately carved wooden throne, and a marble slab in the floor featuring a two-headed eagle (the symbol of Byzantium) located on the exact site where Emperor Constantine XI was crowned. The church also has some fine frescoes. Exhibits at the small but modern museum upstairs include fragments of ancient cloth, buttons, jewellery and other everyday items of Mystras' inhabitants.

Beyond the Mitropolis is the **Vrontokhion Monastery**. This was once the wealthiest monastery of Mystras, the focus of cultural activities and the burial place of the despots. Of its two churches, **Agios Theodoros** and **Aphentiko**, the latter is the most impressive, with striking frescoes.

ⓘ TACKLING MYSTRAS

At least half a day is needed to do justice to the ruins of Mystras. Start early in the morning to beat the tour groups, wear sensible shoes and bring water (you can refill at the monastery). The site is divided into two interconnected sections – the *kastro* (the fortress on the summit) and the *hora* (upper town), accessible from the fortress gate; and the *kato hora* (lower town), accessible via the main gate.

If you don't have your own wheels, it makes sense to catch a taxi to the fortress gate and walk down. If you do have a car, you can cover the lower town first (enter and exit from the main gate) and then head separately up to the fortress gate to visit the fortress and the upper town ruins (or vice versa). You can use the same ticket to re-enter at either entrance.

🛏 Sleeping

There are some guesthouses around the village of Mystras and further out. Pikoulianika is an equally good village at which to base yourself.

Mystras Castle Town PENSION €
(📱 27310 20047; www.mystras-castle-town.com; d/tr/q €45/50/55; P 🛜) Run by a friendly English-speaking Russian-Greek couple, simple and spacious rooms in a converted house are just a stone's throw from Mystras' main square. Guests can use a communal kitchen.

Castle View CAMPGROUND €
(📱 27310 83303; www.castleview.gr; campsites per adult/tent/car €7/4/4, bungalow €45-50; ☺ Apr-Oct; 🛜 ♨) This campground, set among olive trees, is pleasant enough. It features a restaurant, pool and hot showers. It's about 1km before Nea Mystras village.

★ Mazaráki Guesthouse GUESTHOUSE €€
(📱 27310 20414; www.xenonasmazaraki.gr; Pikoulianika; d/ste/apt incl breakfast €85/120/190; P 🛜 ♨) 🅿 By far the most lovely accommodation for miles around, Mazaráki consists of four beautiful houses divided into individually decorated studios and apartments. Breakfast arrives on your doorstep in a basket, with produce from the owners' organic farm. The welcoming owners or managers are happy to advise about hiking and biking in the area (and to lend you mountain bikes).

Hotel Byzantion HOTEL €€
(📱 27310 83309; www.byzantionhotel.gr; s/d/tr incl breakfast €45/60/70; P ♨ @ 🛜 ♨) Located in the centre of the modern village of Nea Mystras, this appealing 26-room option is a good alternative to sleeping in Sparta itself. The management is helpful, there's a delightful garden in the rear of the property, and the bright rooms have balconies offering arresting valley or mountain views.

🍴 Eating

Taverna Pikoulianika GREEK €
(📱 27310 82403; Pikoulianika; mains €5-12; ☺ noon-midnight) The oldest taverna in Pikoulianika, this serves up quintesential 'home cooking'. It's a standard classic and the enthusiastic owner ensures you get a decent feed with hearty helpings of the likes of homemade meatballs and rabbit stew.

★ Chromata INTERNATIONAL €€
(www.facebook.com/Chromata.Mystras; Pikoulianika; mains €9-14; ☺ noon-late Jun-Sep, 7pm-late Wed-Fri, noon-late Sat & Sun Oct-May) Pikoulianika shows its true colours (chromata) at this wonderful spot, set high on a hill behind the village. The gorgeous garden patio (open in summer) has a 180-degree view over the Spartan plains. Nikos, the owner-chef, creates both Greek and modern dishes and a fusion of both. Think dishes such as handmade ravioli with pumpkin and smoked pork. The mantra he works by is 'local products only'.

ℹ Getting There & Away

Buses run in both directions between Sparta and Mystras (€2.80, 15 minutes, six daily except Sunday). A taxi between Sparta and Mystras costs around €12.

WORTH A TRIP

LANGADA PASS ΟΡΕΙΝΗ ΔΙΑΒΑΣΗ ΛΑΓΚΑΔΑ

If you have time and your own wheels, the 59km Sparta–Kalamata road is one of the most stunning, if time-consuming and winding, routes in Greece. The road crosses the Taÿgetos Mountains by way of the Langada Pass.

The climb begins in earnest at the village of **Trypi**, 9km west of Sparta, where the road enters the dramatic **Langada Gorge**. To the north of this gorge is the site where the ancient Spartans left to die those babies too weak or deformed to become good soldiers.

The road then follows the course of the Langada River before climbing sharply through a series of hairpin bends, fringed with plane trees and pines, to emerge in a sheltered valley. This is a good spot to stop for a stroll among the plane trees along the riverbank. The road then climbs steeply once more, to the high point of 1524m, crossing the boundary from Lakonia into Messinia on the way. The descent to Kalamata is equally dramatic.

Monemvasia Μονεμβασιά

POP 20

Surrounded by the teal waters of the Aegean Sea, vast, imposing, Monemvasia (moh-nem-*vah*-sia) is an iceberg-like slab of rock, with sheer cliffs rising hundreds of metres from the sea, linked to the mainland by a single, highly defendable causeway.

These days Monemvasia incorporates both the rock, with its medieval village enclosed within the walls of its *kastro* (fort), plus the modern mainland village of Gefyra, just across the causeway. 'You can find everything you want in this city – except water', observed an 18th-century Turkish traveller. Remarkably – given that for most of its existence Monemvasia's only source of drinking water came from the sky – Monemvasia has remained inhabited to this day. These days, though, only around 20 people live in the *kastro* permanently – the rest go home to Gefyra after a day's work. In spite of Monemvasia's immense popularity, the extraordinary visual impact of the medieval village – and the delights of exploring it – override the effects of mass tourism.

History

The rock island of Monemvasia was part of the mainland until it was cut off by an earthquake in AD 375. Its name means 'single entry' (*moni* – single, *emvasia* – entry), as there is only one way into the town.

During the 6th century, barbarian incursions forced inhabitants of the surrounding area to retreat to this natural rock fortress, where they eventually founded the upper town that eventually spread downwards. By the 13th century, if Mystras was the spiritual centre of the Byzantine Empire, then Monemvasia was one of its biggest trade centres. It was famous throughout Europe for its highly praised *malvasia*-grape Malmsey wine; George, Duke of Clarence, in Shakespeare's *Richard III*, drowned in a barrel of the stuff.

Monemvasia changed hands several times as the Franks, Venetians and Ottoman Turks all invaded in the following centuries, each adding their own elements to the architectural melange. During the War of Independence its Turkish inhabitants were massacred after their surrender, following a three-month siege; the fortress remained impregnable to the end, its only weakness being the food supply.

Falling into obscurity by the 18th century, Monemvasia is, these days, fast becoming something of a high-end tourist destination.

◉ Sights

★ **Kastro – Medieval Village**   HISTORIC SITE
FREE Almost wholly surrounded by ocean, Monemvasia's fortified medieval village is divided into the **lower town**, bisected by a main cobbled street lined with souvenir shops and tavernas that leads to the main square, and the **upper town**, with its ruins and **fortress**. The greatest pleasure of visiting the site comes from wandering the labyrinth: exploring the tiny alleyways and winding stairways that weave between a complex network of stone houses and walled gardens, and ducking into atmospheric nooks and crannies.

In the lower town, the central square is dominated by the **Cathedral of Christos Elkomenos**, dating from the 13th century. Head up through the stone archway opposite the bell tower and you come across the handsome 17th-century **Church of Myrtidiotissa**. Down near the waterfront fortifications is the whitewashed 16th-century **Church of Panagia Chrysafitissa**.

The path to the fortress and the upper town is signposted off the main street in several locations. A walking path (steep steps) skirts the edge of the upper-town ruins all the way to just above the main gate, affording great views of Monemvasia's cluster of rooftops against a cliff backdrop. Some of the upper town's extensive ruins – the central gate complex – have been restored and provide an evocative representation of how the entrance to the upper *kastro* operated (it's believed that the vaulted passages and spaces were used by the fort's garrison; excellent explanations in English). Don't miss the **Church of Agia Sofia**, which perches on the edge of a sheer cliff, whose interior and surviving frescoes have been restored. Take care and keep to the paths as the area is covered with overgrown cisterns.

Monemvasia Archaeological Collection   MUSEUM
(☑ 27320 61403; adult/concession €2/1; ⊙ 8.30am-3pm Tue-Sun) This small museum housed in a former temple, Agios Andreas (596 AD), displays finds unearthed in the course of old town excavations, such as pottery from Asia Minor, cementing Monemvasia's status as an important trading post. The star turn is the *templon* (chancel

screen) from an 11th-century church near the sea gate. Other objects of note include a marble door frame from the Church of Agia Sofia, coats of arms (the trend introduced by Frankish invaders) and well-heads of ancient cisterns.

🛏 Sleeping

There's limited budget accommodation in the *kastro* itself, and accommodation is cheaper in Gefyra. Prices fluctuate drastically depending on supply and demand.

A torch (flashlight) is a good idea for those staying in the cobbled, dimly lit *kastro*. Don't forget to plug in the mosquito repellent tablets (usually provided); mosquitoes seem to love this place.

Flower of Monemvasia   HOTEL €

(☑ 27320 61395; www.flower-hotel.gr; Gefyra; d/tr/ste incl breakfast from €53/106/131; 🅿 ❄ 🛜) Located in mainland Gefyra, opposite Monemvasia's *kastro*, this clean, modern spot is a far cry from the region's more traditional offerings. Nearly all 20 rooms have sea views and some have kitchenettes. The staff are very helpful.

Hotel Filoxenia   HOTEL €

(☑ 27320 61716; www.filoxenia-monemvasia.gr; Gefyra; d/tr €60/70; 🅿 ❄ 🛜) Spotless cheapie off Gefyra's main street. What it lacks in personality, it makes up for with its views of the Monemvasia rock from its balconies. Breakfast €5 per person.

Kellia   GUESTHOUSE €€

(☑ 27320 61520; www.keliamonemvasia.com; d/apt incl breakfast from €65/160) In a wonderful location, near the front sea wall with unimpeded views over a church and the sea. It's been recently renovated; rooms are simple and unfussy but atmospheric (some have fireplaces), and it's got a more laid-back air than most. The friendly, English-speaking owner adds to the experience.

Malvasia Traditional Hotel   HOTEL €€

(☑ 27320 61160; www.malvasiahotel-traditional.gr; d/tr/q incl breakfast from €65/100/165; ❄ 🛜) One of Monemvasia's oldest and most established hotels makes the most of traditional architecture. All rooms vary and it's pot luck what you get. Some of its renovated rooms feature heavy wooden beams and bright colour schemes; others are cosy, cave-like nooks with vaulted stone ceilings. Pricier rooms come with sea views; some have balconies overlooking the water. Wi-fi in lobby only.

Hotel Byzantino   HOTEL €€

(☑ 27320 61351; www.hotelbyzantino.com; d/tr/q incl breakfast from €65/95/115; ❄ 🛜) This range of atmospheric rooms offers a great experience of the traditional *kastro* – rooms occupy seven different buildings and come in varying shapes, sizes and prices (from cheaper rooms with no views to smarter digs with sea-facing balconies and vaulted stone ceilings); most are decked out in antiques. Wi-fi in cafe and reception only; full buffet breakfast.

Moni Emvasis
Luxury Suites   BOUTIQUE HOTEL €€€

(☑ 27320 62022; www.moniemvasis.gr; ste incl breakfast €235-315; ❄ 🛜) Consisting of just three individually conceived suites, Moni Emvasis doesn't hold back with luxurious touches, from rain shower heads and spa baths to oversized, sumptuous beds. The sea views from the balconies of the Junior and the Deluxe suites are the best, but the Moni Emvasis suite has a decadent, medieval ambience with vaulted ceilings and marble fireplace. Extensive breakfast showcases local produce.

🍴 Eating & Drinking

★ Voltes Mezedopolio
& Grocery   MEZEDHES €€

(☑ 27320 61919; mezes plates $2.50-7; ⏰ 6pm-3am Apr-Oct; 1pm-3am Thu-Sun Nov-Mar) Named after the switchback footpath leading to Monemvasia's upper *kastro* (the *voltes*), this wonderful eatery, run by two enthusiastic young brothers, manages to link modernity and tradition with ease. Choose from a fabulous array of fresh mezedhes. All fresh. All seasonal. The decor and dish presentation is contemporary, the flavours are still old-school.

Marianthi   TAVERNA €€

(☑ 27320 61371; mains €8-14; ⏰ noon-late) Run by 70-year-old Magda, who has been preparing and dishing up wonderful traditional cuisine for as long as she can remember. It doesn't have the outlook of the other restaurants as it's located on the main strip. Forget the views just this once and concentrate on what's on your plate: hearty, honest fare.

Matoula   TAVERNA €€

(☑ 27320 61660; mains €9-14; ⏰ noon-late Mar-Dec) Of all the tavernas on the main street, Matoula is the oldest and seems to boast a global profile. Perhaps because it has the best sea views (from its vine-shaded terrace), and after so many years has the art down pat: a reliable selection of classic dishes. Love 'em or hate 'em: the local cats love it, too.

★ **Chrisovoulo** INTERNATIONAL €€€
(☑ 27320 62022; www.chrisovoulo.gr; mains €14-30, set menu €30; ⊙1pm-midnight Apr-Oct; ☑) One of the newest restaurants to join the local scene, Chrisovoulo comes with attitude. But it delivers: it conjures up the likes of quinoa salad, veal with morel sauce, and risotto with *siglino* (salted) pork from the Mani, served in an intimate, stylish environment. Service is professional, the sea views fantastic, and there's a serious local wine list.

★ **Wine Tasting Kamara** WINE BAR
(☑ 27320 61704, 6972319434; ⊙varies) The home of Byron and Vivienne, this enchanting 11th-century wine cellar is decorated with souvenirs from a lifetime's travels. Get talking to the gregarious retired owners over a glass or two of Greek wine (from €4) and you may not want to leave. Follow the 'wine tasting' signs towards the waterfront. Hours can be a little unpredictable so just swing by.

❶ Information

Malvasia Travel (☑ 27320 61752; www. monemvasia.gr/en/malvasia-travel-3; Geyfra; ⊙7.30am-2.30pm & 5.15-8pm Mon-Sat) Just over the causeway in Gefyra.
Police (☑ 27320 61210)
Post Office (Geyfra; ⊙7.30am-2pm Mon-Fri)

❶ Getting There & Away

Buses leave from outside Malvasia Travel. There are buses to Athens (€32.50, six hours, at least four daily) via Sparta (€11, 2½ hours), Tripoli (€17, 3½ hours) and Corinth Isthmus (€25.20, 4½ hours).

❶ Getting Around

The medieval *kastro* of Monemvasia is pedestrianised, but cars and motorcycles can cross the causeway. Parking is available on the left-hand side of the narrow road skirting the rock. Alternatively, park in the waterfront car park in Gefyra.

Cross the causeway and follow the curving road that skirts the cliff to the official entrance, a narrow tunnel in a massive fortifying wall. The tunnel is L-shaped, so the magical town is concealed until you emerge on the other side.

A **shuttle bus** (€1.10; ⊙8am-midnight) ferries visitors between Gefyra and the *kastro* every 30 minutes.

Neapoli Νεάπολη
POP 2730

Neapoli (neh-ah-po-lih), close to the southern tip of the eastern prong of the Peloponnese, is the departure point for the Ionian Island of Kythira, clearly visible across the bay. You also pass through Neapoli to see the Kastania Cave.

Geologists, and anyone after quirky rocks, will appreciated the **petrified forest**, an expanse of trees that were fossilised possibly several million years ago. It's located on the coast around 16km southeast of Neapoli.

Gythio Γύθειο
POP 6000

Once the port of ancient Sparta, Gythio is the gateway to the Lakonian Mani. This pretty fishing town, with its 19th-century pastel houses, makes a pleasant stopover if you're travelling between the Mani and Sparta or Monemvasia, or if you're taking a ferry to Kythira. As well as a handful of things to see in the village, including a recently opened folkloric museum, there's **Mavrovouni Beach**, a long sandy stretch 2km south of Gythio, and pine-shaded **Marathonisi Islet**.

◉ Sights

Folkloric Museum MUSEUM
(www.kpmanis.gr; ⊙10am-1pm & 6-9pm) FREE
It may be compact, but this museum does a wonderful job of bringing to life the past

---

WORTH A TRIP

THE CAVE OF KASTANIA
ΣΠΗΛΑΙΟ ΚΑΣΤΑΝΙΑ

The extraordinary **Kastania Cave** (☑ 27343 60100; www.monemvasia.gr; adult/concession €7/3; ⊙10am-4pm Sat & Sun), located at the end of a spectacularly winding 17km route northeast of Neapoli, contains some of the best examples of rare stalactites and stalagmites in Europe, estimated to be around 3 million years old. Guided tours in English depart hourly; as you walk around a raised and lit 3km circuit, guides are quick to point out octopuses, exotic plants and otherworldly creatures cast in stone. Call ahead to check hours, as they can vary seasonally.

residents of Gythio and the surrounding Mani. Themed rooms exhibit everything from a historic classroom to objects relating to the trades, crafts and professions of the locals in what was a thriving port town. Music was particularly important to Gythio, thanks to visiting Italian musician Giocondo Moretti (1863–1941), who established a philharmonic society. Excellent English labelling. On the plaza at the northern end of town.

Shadow Theatre Museum MUSEUM
(☑ 27330 29128; www.hassanakos.gr; Larissiou 2) FREE This beautiful little studio-museum-shop is run by personable local artist Giorgos Hassanakos. The small upstairs gallery pays homage to traditional shadow puppets, plus has a range of the artist's own creations, including satirical puppets (Greek politicians). Mr Hassanakos will happily show you around.

Marathonisi Islet HISTORIC SITE
According to mythology, tranquil, pine-shaded Marathonisi, connected to Gythio by a thin causeway, is ancient Cranae, where Paris (prince of Troy) and Helen (wife of Menelaus) consummated the affair that sparked the Trojan War. A small 18th-century tower sits in the centre of the island; it houses the Mani Museum. We've yet to see it open, but we live in hope.

🛏 Sleeping & Eating

Domatia Matina PENSION €
(☑ 27330 22518; Pavlou 19; s/d €45/50) Clean and comfortable rooms and in a great location bang in the middle of town. Elderly owner Matina speaks no English but is very welcoming.

Saga Pension PENSION €
(☑ 27330 23220; www.sagapension.gr; Kranais; s/d/tr €40/50/55; ❄ 🛜) This is a good-value, comfortable place that overlooks Marathonisi Islet. The pleasant French owner speaks English and some rooms come with balconies. The upmarket Saga Restaurant specialises in seafood. Breakfast €5.

Camping Meltemi CAMPGROUND €
(☑ 27330 23260; www.campingmeltemi.gr; Mavrovouni; campsites per tent/adult €5/6, bungalows €30-60; ☻Apr-Oct; 🛜🏊) Very well organised and the pick of the three campgrounds at Mavrovouni. Three kilometres southwest of Gythio, it's right behind the beach and sites are set among 3000 well-tended olive trees.

The bungalows include kitchen, air-con and TV. Buses to Areopoli stop outside.

O!live GREEK €€
(☑ 27330 22009; www.facebook.com/OliveGytheio; Vassileos Pavlou 35; mains €8-13) An exception to the seafood eateries in Gythio, this small spot, right in the middle of the main strip, plates up modern Greek cuisine with flair. The most appealing seats are those on the water.

ℹ Getting There & Around

LANE Lines (www.lane.gr; per person/car €24/69) has one weekly ferry to Crete via Kythira and Antikythira. Check the schedule with **Rozakis Travel** (☑ 27330 22207; rosakigy@ otenet.gr; Pavlou 5), on the waterfront.

The **KTEL Lakonia bus station** (☑ 27330 22228; www.ktel-lakonias.gr; 55 Vasileos Georgios) is northwest along the waterfront. Services run north to Athens (€23.80, 4½ hours, six daily) or via Sparta (€4.70, one hour) and Tripoli (€10.60); and south to Areopoli (€2.90, 30 minutes, three daily), Gerolimenas (€6.60, 1¼ hours, three daily), the Diros Caves (€4, one hour, one daily in summer) and Vathia (€7.50, 1½ hours, Wednesday). For Kalamata or Monemvasia, change at Sparta.

Rozakis Travel has cars for hire. Taxis can be found opposite the bus station.

THE MANI   Η ΜΑΝΗ

Covering the central peninsula in the south of the Peloponnese, the Mani is a wild, rugged region. From the steep foothills of the snow-tipped Taÿgetos Mountains to the pristine coastal coves, and from the tiny villages nestling amid olive groves, connected by threads of walking trails, to the arid scenery in the south of peninsula, speckled with abandoned stone towers, the Mani has some of the most dramatic and varied scenery in the Peloponnese, much of it still wonderfully under-explored.

The Mani is generally divided into the Messinian Mani (or outer Mani) and the Lakonian Mani (or inner Mani). The Messinian Mani starts southeast of Kalamata and runs south between the coast and the Taÿgetos Mountains, while the Lakonian Mani covers the rest of the peninsula south of Itilo.

ℹ Getting There & Away

If driving, the recently opened motorway from Athens to Kalamata provides a handy link to the

Mani; follow the signs to skirt around Kalamata. If there's one place in the Peloponnese where your own car is a boon, it's here. Though it is still possible to take buses; these head east from Kalamata, via Kardymili.

To travel between Lakonian and Messinian Mani, you must change buses at Itilo. Itilo (*eet-ih-lo*), 11km north of Areopoli, was once the medieval capital of the Mani and traditionally regarded as the border between outer and inner Mani. There are buses to Areopoli (€1.80, 20 minutes, two Monday to Friday, one on Saturday) and Kalamata (€8.50, 2 hours, two daily). Areopoli–Itilo buses travel via Limeni.

Lakonian Mani

Grey rock, mottled with defiant clumps of green scrub, characterises the steep, forbidding mountains of Lakonian Mani. Cultivatable land is at a premium here, and supports little more than a few stunted olive and fig trees.

The indented coast's sheer cliffs plunge into the sea, and the rocky outcrops shelter pebbled beaches. This wild and barren landscape is broken only by the imposing stone towers (p172), which still stand sentinel over the region. In recent years, many of these have been restored and are no longer the crumbling sights you'll see in many photographs.

Long known to locals as Kakavoulia (land of evil counsel), this tough, mesmerising land makes for a fantastic road trip if you have your own wheels. You can follow the loop that runs south along the west coast from the main town, Areopoli, detouring en route along narrow lanes into semi-deserted villages. Stop to peek into family chapels (there are almost as many churches and chapels as there are towers, as you wouldn't worship with the enemy), and walk to Mani's southernmost tip before returning via the east coast (or vice versa). For detailed exploration, arm yourself with a copy of the Anavasi Topo 25 map, *Mani 8.4; 1:30,000*.

Areopoli   Αρεόπολη

POP 1100

Areopoli, capital of the Mani, is aptly named after Ares, the god of war. Dominating the main square, Plateia Athanaton, is a statue of Petrobey Mavromichalis, who proclaimed the Maniot insurrection against the Ottoman Empire in 1821. His brother and son,

Konstantinos and Georgios Mavromichalis, were responsible for the assassination of Ioannis Kapodistrias, the first president of independent Greece, in 1831. The town retains many other reminders of its rumbustious past.

Sights

There are some fine examples of Maniot architecture in the narrow, cobbled alleyways surrounding Plateia 17 Martiou, with most of the fortified towers built by the Mavromichalis clan.

Church of Taxiarhes   CHURCH
(Plateia 17 Martiou) On the southern side of Plateia 17 Martiou is this 18th-century church. Its four-storey bell tower marks it as the most important of Areopoli's many churches. The extremely well-preserved relief carvings above the main door look as if they belong to a much earlier era than the 18th century.

Church of Agios Ioannis   CHURCH
The Church of Agios Ioannis, built by the Mavromichalis family on a tiny square west of the main square, contains a series of well-preserved frescoes relating the life of Jesus.

Pikoulakis Tower House Museum   MUSEUM
(€2; ⊙8.30am-3pm Tue-Sun) Housed in a restored tower, this museum displays exquisite Byzantine pieces from Mani churches. These include a 12th-century marble *templon* (chancel screen) from the Church of Agios Ioannis in Mina, near Pyrgos Dirou. Upstairs is a clutch of well-preserved icons spanning five centuries. Take the westbound road from the southwest corner of the main square.

Activities

There is some rewarding walking in the area, with marked trails, though you'll still require a good map. A number of local guesthouse owners are happy to give walking tips.

Sleeping

Hotel Kouris   HOTEL €
(☑27330 51340; www.hotelkouris.gr; Plateia Athanaton; s/d/tr €40/50/65; P⊙) Right on the main square, this concrete and basic cheapie may lack ambience, but it's clean and central. Breakfast is €5 per person.

DON'T MISS

LIMENI · ΛΙΜΕΝΙ

The tiny village of Limeni, 3km north of Areopoli on the southern flank of aquamarine Limeni Bay, is well worth a stop for its stunning outlook, and for its two very good eateries. At **Takis** (27330 51327; Limeni; fish per kilo from €55; 10am-late Apr-Oct), you can enjoy grilled fish in a stunning setting, at a terrace overlooking the turquoise waters. Or head right next door to **Teloneio** (27330 52702; www.teloneio-limeni.gr; Limeni; mains €9-23; 10am-2am May-Oct;) for a more contemporary take on Greek cuisine. If you love it that much and want to stay, consider **Vasilios Apartments Hotel** (27330 51934; www.vasilioshotel.com; Limeni; studio/apt from €75/90; Mar-Oct;); set high on a hill overlooking the stunning bay, it's excellent value for money. Or splurge at the gorgeous **Pirgos Mavromichali Hotel** (27330 51042; www.pirgosmavro michali.gr; Limeni; d/ste incl breakfast from €120/250; Mar-Nov;).

Hotel Trapela
BOUTIQUE HOTEL €€
(27330 52690; www.trapela.gr; s/d/tr/f incl breakfast €70/80/100/120;) The rough-hewn stone rooms at this small hotel are each named after a Maniot settlement. They sport exposed stone, muted colours and wooden beams, coupled with comfortable furnishings. It's comfortable without being over-the-top luxurious. Some have balconies.

Areos Polis
BOUTIQUE HOTEL €€
(27330 51028; www.areospolis.gr; s/d/tr incl breakfast from €40/60/80;) This central option on the main square blends Old World decor (cast-iron bedsteads, exposed stone walls) with hydro-massage showers, and spa baths in some rooms. Slightly worn but good value. Extensive breakfast buffet included.

✖ Eating & Drinking

I Palaiopolis
GREEK €
(27330 51345; mains €6-10; 9am-late) I Palai-opolis (Old Town) is housed in a beautifully restored historic building that once housed an incense followed by a cigarette workshop. These days the aromas and flavours are equally diverse, thanks to the eclectic selection of modern Greek dishes: a salted pork salad, Mani spaghetti (local noodles), and more traditional vegetable concoctions. Has a lovely rear courtyard.

Barba Petros
TAVERNA €€
(27330 51205; mains €8-15; noon-11pm) This long-standing taverna has been in the same family since 1917. The current grand-child/owner and his son run the show. This is the place to pig out in every sense – the owner breeds his own pigs, and other meats are sourced locally. Local specialities include vegetable stew and piglet with plum sauce.

Bukka Home Bar
COCKTAIL BAR
A creeper-clad cafe by day, come evening this joint morphs into a sultry cocktail bar. Slip into the vaulted cavern and sip on a 'smoky margarita' or a 'porn-star Martini'.

🛍 Shopping

Adouloiti
BOOKS
(Invincible Mani; 27330 53670; Plateia Athana-ton; 9am-5pm) Has an excellent selection of hiking maps and books on the region.

ℹ Information

The town is split into two parts: the new upper town, around Plateia Athanaton, and the old lower town, around Plateia 17 Martiou. The two are linked by a pedestrian lane, Kapetan Matapa.
National Bank of Greece (Petrobey Mavromi-hali) The only bank in town; has an ATM. In the upper town.
Post Office (Petrobey Mavromihali; 7.30am-2pm Mon-Fri) At the northern edge of the upper town.

ℹ Getting There & Away

The **bus station** (27330 51229) is situated in the middle of the public car park at the town's northern end. Buses to Gythio (€2.90, 30 min-utes, three daily) then proceed to Athens via Sparta (€29).

Buses to Itilo (€1.80, 20 minutes, two daily except Sunday) run via Limeni. Other destina-tions include Gerolimenas (€3.70, 45 minutes, three daily), the Diros Caves (€1.80, 15 minutes, departs 10.15am and returns 12.45pm), and Lagia (€4.10, 40 minutes, two on weekdays).

Diros Caves · Σπήλαιο Διρού

These extraordinary **caves** (27330 52222; www.diroscave.gr; adult/concession €13/8; 8.30am-3.30pm), inhabited since Neolithic times and systematically explored from 1949, lie 11km south of Areopoli and are signposted near the village of Pyrgos Dirou. The entrance is on the beach.

Guides only speak Greek, so if your group doesn't you'll be treated to a half-hour's silent, eerie glide by boat through the cave's many passages, giving you time to admire the stalagmites and stalactites, many of the latter as fine as gossamer threads. You then walk the remaining 300m on foot.

Abandoned as human habitation in 4 BC after an earthquake, the caves weren't rediscovered until around 1895. Then in 1949 the local husband-and-wife speleology team of Anna and Yiannis Petrocheilou began to systematically explore the caves, now estimated to be around 14km long. Underwater exploration continues to this day.

Pyrgos Dirou to Gerolimenas
Πύργος Διρού προς Γερολιμένας

Journeying south down Mani's west coast from Pyrgos Dirou to Gerolimenas, you encounter a barren mountain landscape broken only by semi-deserted settlements with mighty towers. A left turn-off 3km south of Pyrgos Dirou heads up through the picturesque villages of **Drialos**, **Vamvaka**, **Briki** and **Mina**, which have fine examples of Maniot stonework, before depositing you back on the main road, 3km north of Kita. A right turn 9km south of Pyrgos Dirou leads down to the **Bay of Mezapos**, sheltered to the east by the frying-pan-shaped Tigani peninsula. The ruins on the peninsula are those of the **Castle of Maina**, built by the Frankish leader Guillaume de Villehardouin in 1248 and subsequently adapted by the Byzantines.

Kita, 13km south of Pyrgos Dirou, has the lion's share of the west coast's war towers and fortified houses. It was the setting for the last great inter-family feud recorded in the Mani, which erupted in 1870 and required the intervention of the army, complete with artillery, to force a truce. Just west of Kita, **Nomia** also bristles with some superb tower remains.

Gerolimenas
Γερολιμένας
POP 60

Gerolimenas is a tranquil fishing village built around a small, sheltered bay at the southwestern tip of the Mani peninsula. Its pebble beach overlooks teal waters and it's a popular weekend getaway for well-heeled Athenians.

🛏 Sleeping & Eating

Kyrimi B&B   B&B €€
(☏ 27330 53078; www.kyrimi.com; r incl breakfast €100-120; P ❄ 🛜) This intimate B&B, inside a traditional stone house, consists of just four luxurious rooms. Breakfast includes delicious homemade pies and produce. Each room has a patio overlooking the sea – perfect for sunbathing.

Hotel Kirimai   LUXURY HOTEL €€€
(☏ 27330 54288; www.kyrimai.gr; d/ste incl breakfast from €120/240; ❄ 🛜 ≋) In an idyllic setting at the far southern end of the harbour, Kirimai is a luxurious converted historic building with stone floors and timber beams. Rooms come in all shapes and sizes; some guests complain that the simple doubles are too small. Outside, however, there's a massive restaurant terrace overlooking the water. Substantial breakfast; the restaurant is open to non-guests.

Restaurant Akrotainaritis   GREEK €
(☏ 27330 54205; www.akrotainaritis.gr; mains €7-12; ⏰ 7am-midnight) One of several tavernas along the waterfront (none of which will knock your culinary socks off, but all have lovely settings overlooking the bay), we like this one for its reliability. It's been run since 1923 by several generations of one family. Today, with Vasiliki at its helm, it continues to serve up Greek standards with an honest, home-cooked touch.

❶ Getting There & Away

There are three buses daily from Gerolimenas to Areopoli (around €5, 45 minutes), which head on to Athens (around €30, five hours), Gythio (around €11, 1¼ hours) and Sparta (around €17, 2¼ hours). The bus stop is in the square.

Gerolimenas to Porto Kagio
Γερολιμένας προς Πόρτο Καγιο

South of Gerolimenas, the road continues 4km to the small village of **Alika**, where it divides. One road leads across the mountains to the east coast, and the other goes south to Vathia and Porto Kagio. The southern road follows the coast, passing pebbly beaches. It then climbs steeply inland to **Vathia**, the most photographed of the traditional Mani villages, comprising a cluster of closely packed tower houses perched on a rocky spur.

If you have nerves of steel and wish to see an equally impressive traditional village

TOWER HOUSES

Dotted around the Mani, particularly around Kakavoulia (or inner Mani), scores of stone towers rise eerily from the landscape. Some are solitary; some stand in clusters. Some are intact and fortress-like; others are crumbling. From the 17th century until well into the 19th century, the Mani was ruled by clans with chieftains, with bloody feuds constantly fought over what little fertile land there was. These towers were family fortresses. Feuds between warring clans were fought according to strict rules of engagement, the objective being the destruction of the rival's tower and the deaths of the male members of the rival's family. Male children were known as 'guns' (what else would they be useful for?) and women were exempt from the feuds; after all, someone had to till the fields and bury the dead.

Today, a growing number of towers are being restored to their former glory and turned into unique places to stay.

Antares (☎ 27330 51700; www.antareshotel.gr; Omales; d/ste incl breakfast €130/175; P ⊠) Run by the knowledgable Mina, this beautiful tower house, 1.5km south of Areopoli, seamlessly blends the historic (centuries-old vaulted ceilings, exposed stone walls) with the contemporary. Superbly appointed rooms look out over the lovingly tended herb garden. Breakfast is extraordinary and ingredients are hand-picked from local suppliers. The tranquillity and care that guests experience here inspire many to return.

Hotel Citta dei Nicliani (www.cittadeinicliani.com; Kita; d incl breakfast €90-160; P ⊠) The former stronghold of the namesake Mani clan is split between this uber-elegant hotel with an Italian medieval ambience and the tower house in nearby Stavri. Expect megalithic stonework (an ancient technique), exquisite beds and heavy wooden beams. The extensive breakfast makes great use of fresh local produce, and guests can engage in wine tasting from an extraordinary wine collection.

Sventoura Hotel (☎ 6975798180, 27330 53006; www.sventourahotel.com; Pyrgos Dirou; r incl breakfast €60-120; P ⊠) Tucked away en route from Pyrgos Dirou to the **Diros Caves** (p170), this handsome tower has just five unique, characterful and arty rooms. Vaulted ceilings, an antler chandelier, antique chests, wrought-iron bedsteads, and bathroom sinks hewn out of stone all conspire to give the lodgings that 21st-century-meets-Maniot vibe.

Tainaron Blue (☎ 27333 00461; www.tainaronblue.com; d/ste incl breakfast €260/340; P ✳ ⊠ ⊠) This lonely stone tower, 4km west of the turn-off to Porto Kagio, is a true retreat: there's nothing for miles around, except for breathtaking coastline views...which you can enjoy from the clifftop infinity pool. The project is a quirky one. Designed by the architect-owners, the three luxurious rooms were squeezed into the existing construction following strict planning requirements.

While it has won design awards, and the rooms comprise beautiful unadorned stone and vaulted ceilings, the sleeping experience might not be for everyone. Rooms in the top tower are reached by the original and extremely steep staircase (if you can even call it that). But every nook and cranny has been adapted ingeniously. An on-site chef is on hand to whip up gourmet cuisine at your whim.

---

with practically no visitors, take the road into the mountains from Alika and then the turn-off to **Mountanistika**. The road is very narrow, with a drop to one side and few places for passing, so pray for a lack of oncoming vehicles.

A turn-off to the right 3km south of Vathia splits in two. The right-hand road also splits in two: the right branch leads to **Marmari**, with its two sandy beaches, while the main

road heads as far south as you can go for 3km, to Kokinogia, where there's a taverna and little else.

The left-hand road from the turn-off south of Vathia cuts across the peninsula to the tiny east-coast fishing village of **Porto Kagio**, set on a perfect horseshoe bay, popular with the international yachting set. It's a very tranquil place to spend the night. Most of the waterfront tavernas there have similar menus (mains €8 to €17, fish per kilo €40 to €70) featuring seafood and local specialities, such as pie made with wild greens.

🛏 Sleeping

Akrotiri Domatia GUESTHOUSE €
(📞 27330 52013; www.porto-kagio.com; Porto Kagio; d incl breakfast €45-55; ☉ Mar-Oct; 🅿🛜) Set right on the waterfront – the best rooms are those at the front, which have balconies and overlook the glorious bay. Owner Nikos also runs boat trips.

Porto Kale GUESTHOUSE €
(📞 27330 54202, 6980755528; Porto Kagio; d/tr/f from €60/80/90; 🅿❄🛜) A good option in Porto Kagio – simple, snug rooms with stone walls and sun terraces. The young owner is very helpful and speaks English.

Messinian Mani

The Messinian Mani, or outer Mani, lies to the north of its Lakonian counterpart, sandwiched between the Taÿgetos Mountains and the west coast of the Mani peninsula. The rugged coast is scattered with small coves and beaches and backed by mountains that remain snowcapped until late May. Kardamyli features the region's best-organised hiking opportunities, and there are also some good options around Stoupa.

Kardamyli Καρδαμύλη

POP 350

It's easy to see why Kardamyli was one of the seven cities offered to Achilles by Agamemnon. This tiny village has one of the prettiest settings in the Peloponnese, nestled between the blue waters of the Messinian Gulf and the Taÿgetos Mountains. The **Vyros Gorge**, which emerges just north of town, runs to the foot of **Mt Profitis Ilias** (2407m), the highest peak of the Taÿgetos. Today the gorge and surrounding areas are very popular with hikers.

British writer Patrick Leigh Fermor lived in nearby Kalamitsi Bay for several decades until his death in 2011. Fermor wrote *Mani*, which is considered by many to be the definitive book on the region.

The surrounding mountain villages have wonderful nooks and crannies to explore, with ancient churches and excellent tavernas.

◉ Sights

Old Town Kardamyli RUINS
(📞 27210 73638; ☉ 8am-8pm) **FREE** Old Town Kardamyli consists of a fortified settlement with an 18th-century church, plus restored tower, oil press and three-storey building. You can poke around the fortifications and the building has basic exhibits with explanations in English of Maniot settlements including how people lived and worked. Follow the signs on the western edge of Kardamyli opposite the two supermarkets.

🏃 Activities

⭐ **2407 Mountain Activities** OUTDOORS
(📞 27210 73752; www.2407m.com) 🖉 Professional and friendly outfit offers a range of outdoor adventures, from half-day hikes (per person from €50) to full-day assaults on Taÿgetos peak (€100), rock climbing (with instructor €50), bicycle tours (from €60) and even a cultural event where you help prepare cuisine in a Maniot tower. Located halfway along the main street.

Chora–Saidona Trail WALKING
Follow the blue-and-white trail through Chora from Hotel Faraggi, then take the right-hand path (red with white cross), pass through Nikovo and follow the (green with white cross) trail, part dirt road, part old stone path, through the olive groves. The trail descends through lush vegetation

OFF THE BEATEN TRACK

CAPE TENARO
ΑΚΡΩΤΗΡΙΟΝ ΤΑΙΝΑΡΟ

From the car park below the taverna at Kokinogia, at the south of the Mani peninsula, it's a beautiful 30-minute walk along an uneven rocky path to one of Europe's southernmost points, Cape Tenaro (Cape Matapan), where a restored lighthouse stands. The cape has been an important location for millennia and was first mentioned in Homer's 'Iliad'.

At the beginning of the path are the ruins of ancient Tainaron, once a thriving Roman city (the entire area is buried ruins; look out for the stunning wave-patterned, circular mosaic), while another short path leads to the ruined church built on the foundations of Poseidon's Temple. Nearby is a cave rumoured to be the entrance to Hades.

I

PELOPONNESE MESSINIAN MANI

THE EAST COAST

The east coast of the Mani peninsula is even more rugged and barren than the west. The main town is the formidable-looking **Lagia**, 12km northeast of the Alika turn-off. Perched some 400m above sea level, it was once the chief town of the southeastern Mani, and some of its towers stand derelict.

From Lagia, the road winds down with spectacular views of the little fishing harbour of **Agios Kyprianos** – a short diversion from the main road. The next village is **Kokala**, a busy place with two pebbled beaches. The best beach is further north at **Nyfi**, where a turn-off to the right leads to sheltered **Alipa Beach**. Continuing north, a turn-off beyond tower-studded **Flomochori** descends east to **Kotronas**, while the main road cuts west across the peninsula to Areopoli.

to a dry river bed and then ascends gently to Saidona. The trail takes one hour 15 minutes.

Chora–Kardamyli Trail   WALKING
This four-hour walk starts at the village of Chora. Follow the blue-and-white trail markers down through the picturesquely ramshackle village; take the right fork where the trails divide and continue your gentle descent through the olive groves until the trail meets a road. Head right. Follow the dry riverbed left through the striking canyon all the way to Kardamyli.

It's well worth making the slight detour to see the frescoes of the Likaki Monastery, signposted halfway down the canyon. You can also take the gently ascending, signposted path up to Agia Sofia through the woods from the same spot; this path joins the yellow-and-black trail.

Kardamyli–Petrovouni Trail   WALKING
This is a gorgeous two-hour loop walk. Follow the signs to Old Town Kardamyli, then take the old stone path that leads up to the Agia Sofia church. Follow the path down through an enchanted forest section (tangled vegetation, scent of pine) towards Petrovouni, with a fantastic view of the coast en route. Descend to Kardamyli along a zigzagging stone path.

Kalamitsi–Kardamyli Trail   WALKING
From the Kardamyli–Stoupa road just east of pretty Kalamitsi Bay, take the stone path up towards Prastio, then follow the road as it passes through the village. Just north of Prastio, the white-with-red-dot trail meanders through olive groves before the footpath ascends gently to Petrovouni. Wander through the winding streets before descending to Kardamyli along a zigzagging stone path. Two hours.

Saidona–Prastio Trail   WALKING
Take the red-with-blue-dot trail from the church in Saidona. The minor road turns into a dirt-and-cobble footpath leading downhill through lush vegetation. It then alternates between sections of an old stone path, narrow footpath through olive groves, and a wide, zigzagging dirt road, with a beautiful view of the coastline ahead. Cross the stone bridge over the gorge to Prastio. One hour.

🛏 Sleeping

⭐ Olympia Koumounakou Rooms   PENSION €
(☏ 27210 73623; s/d €35/40; ※ 🛜) One of the Peloponnese's best budget options. Olympia loves her traveller guests (as they do her) and offers five clean rooms with bathrooms in the centre of the village. It's a stone's throw from the water, and has an appealing garden.

Y Volvere Studios   APARTMENT €
(Stratis Bravakos Rooms; ☏ 27210 73326; www.yvolvere.gr; d/tr €40/55) Y Volvere is great value for compact, spotless studio apartments with kitchenettes. It's at the south end of the village, along a street leading towards the water.

⭐ Elies   APARTMENT €€
(☏ 27210 73140; www.elieshotel.gr; studio/apt/maisonette €130/160/240; ⊙ Mar-Oct; ※ 🛜) Live out your image of quintessential Greece (dreamy sigh): tasteful provincial-style stone studios, apartments (sleep four) and maisonettes (sleep six), with stylish 'haven't-missed-a-beat' interiors, all nestled within an olive grove. Breakfast includes fresh fruit, bread and eggs. You can enjoy lunch at Elies' own taverna before wandering a few metres across the road – plop! – into the sea.

It's situated 1km north of the village, a pebble's throw from Ritsa Beach. Rates are significantly less outside of high season. Greece at its best.

Kalamitsi Hotel
HOTEL €€

(☑27210 73131; www.kalamitsi-hotel.gr; d/ste €110/160; P🐾) Situated 1km south of town, the Kalamitsi is a lovely, modern stone-built hotel with serene, well-appointed rooms. Family bungalows are also available for €220. Within its shady grounds are paths leading to a secluded pebbly beach. Home-cooked dinners and fresh buffet breakfasts are available to guests.

Hotel Vardia
HOTEL €€

(☑27210 73777; www.vardia-hotel.gr; studio €80, apt €115-165; ⊘Mar-Nov; P@🐾) This relaxing stone hotel (near a former sentry tower and situated high behind the village beyond Old Town Kardamyli) sits amid pretty grounds. All 18 studio-style rooms are simple and tasteful. Their main bonus is the exceptional views of the Messinian Gulf, and helpful staff. Vardia is signposted from the southern end of town.

Maison Viros
APARTMENT €€

(☑6972098289; www.maison-viros.com; studio/apt €120/170; P❄🐾🏊) On the Kalamata side of central Kardamyli, these spacious split-level apartments and studios are found inside pleasant stone houses arranged around a pool. They are not luxurious, but are spacious and comfortable. The apartments sleep up to six people, the studios four. Breakfast is not included. Minimum two-night stay.

✗ Eating

Lola Frozen Yogurt
ICE CREAM €

(yoghurt from €2; ⊘9.30am-late; 🐾) Right on the main street, sweaty hikers make a beeline for this frozen yoghurt (and sweets) joint that provides a cool, sweet balm. Gorgeous flower-filled garden out the back in which to rest, lick and munch.

Taverna Kiki
TAVERNA €

(☑27210 73148; mains €7-10; ⊘noon-10pm Apr-Oct) The kindly owners at this appealing taverna, tucked away off the main street, tell you the day's dishes on arrival. Although the choice is limited, the dishes tend to be more imaginative than usual; expect the likes of veal stew with shallots and cloves.

★ Elies
TAVERNA €€

(☑27210 73140; mains €8-14; ⊘1-6pm Apr, Sep & Oct, 1-10pm May-Aug; 🐾) Right by Ritsa Beach, 1km north of town, and nestled in an olive grove, Kardamyli's most popular and pretty eating venue has the atmosphere of a provincial Mediterranean private garden. Thanks to owner-chef Fani, it presents the best selection of top-notch Greek and Mani fare, including numerous scrumptious veggie dishes.

Kritamos
MEZEDHES €€

(☑27210 64102; www.kritamos-kardamili.com; mezhedes €3-7; ⊘lunch & dinner) At the northern end of the village, you don't come here for the view (it's of the road), but for a casual bar-restaurant experience and some fabulous mezedhes with a modern Greek twist.

Dioskouri
GREEK €€

(mains $8-15; ⊘1pm-midnight Mar-Sep) This long-standing spot on the hill, overlooking the bay and with a terrace filled with umbrella pines, is glorious on a moonlit evening. It's been infused with a bit of youthful flair as the next generation is involved in the business, though still serves the old-school Greek cuisine: simple and good quality, from calamari to excellent grilled seafood dishes.

🍷 Drinking & Nightlife

1866 Beer Bar
BAR

(☑27210 73479; ⊘6pm-late) This cosy bar, set back from the seafront, is renowned for its spirit shots and late nights. It's not raucous, but attracts a young local crowd who enjoy a chat, good company and a selection of the top-shelf stuff. And excellent beers.

ⓘ HIKING AROUND KARDAMYLI

To make sense of Kardamyli's colour-coded trails and to navigate your hike above Stoupa, invest in the excellent Anavasi Topo 25 map, *Mani: Kardamyli–Stoupa–Aghios Nikolaos 8.12/13; 1:25,000*, available from 2407 Mountain Activities (p173) and the local supermarkets. To avoid retracing your steps, you can get a taxi to drop you off in the village of your choice (book in advance via your lodgings) and walk back to Kardamyli or Stoupa.

Carry more drinking water than you think you'll need, a sun hat, a torch, and strong footwear to support your ankles on the uneven ground. Watch out for the odd scorpion and snake (most snakes are harmless).

Aquarella
COCKTAIL BAR

(☑27210 75010; www.facebook.com/aquarella.
kardamili; ☺8am-late) This gorgeous flower-
strewn spot is perched right over the bay
and is the picture-postcard spot for a sundowner. Decent nibbles, including salads,
are also served.

ⓘ Information

A useful website is www.kardamili-greece.com.

Post Office (☺7.30am-2pm Mon-Fri)

ⓘ Getting There & Away

Kardamyli is on the bus route between Kalamata
(around €4, one hour, four daily, one to two on
weekends) and Stoupa (€1.80, 15 minutes, three
daily); one bus daily (two in summer) continues
south to Itilo. The bus stops at the central square
at the northern end of the main thoroughfare,
and at the bookshop at the southern end.

Buses to the villages in the hills above Kardamyli are too infrequent and sporadic to be useful.
A taxi to Exohorio costs around €20.

MESSINIA ΜΕΣΣΗΝΙΑ

The southwestern corner of the Peloponnese
has many attractions, from the peninsula's
loveliest beaches to old Venetian towns,
impressive castles and even underwater
parks for divers.

Messinia's boundaries were established
in 371 BC following the defeat of Sparta by
the Thebans at the Battle of Leuctra. The
defeat ended almost 350 years of Spartan
domination of the Peloponnese – during which time Messinian exiles founded
the city of Messinia in Sicily – and meant
the Messinians were left free to develop
their kingdom in the region stretching
west from the Taÿgetos Mountains. Their
capital was Ancient Messini, about 25km
northwest of Kalamata on the slopes of Mt
Ithomi.

Kalamata Καλαμάτα
POP 70,000

Kalamata is Messinia's capital and the
second-largest city in the Peloponnese. Most
travellers blitz through. Give it a chance
and you'll discover decent restaurants, good
shopping and some excellent, easily 'doable'
museums.

Built on the site of ancient Pharai, Kalamata takes its modern name from a miracle-

working icon of the Virgin Mary known as
kalo mata (good eye). The icon now resides
inside the city's oversized cathedral, the
Church of Ypapantis.

Below the *kastro* is the small but attractive old town, which was almost totally
destroyed by the Turks during the War of
Independence, rebuilt by French engineers
in the 1830s, then levelled again by an earthquake in 1986.

◉ Sights

Archaeological Museum of
Messenia
MUSEUM

(☑27210 83485; www.archmusmes.gr; cnr Benaki
& Agiou Ioannou; €3; ☺1.30-8pm Mon, 8am-8pm
Tue-Sun) This partially interactive, child-
friendly museum focuses on treasures found
in four regions – Kalamata, Pylia, Messini
and Trifylia. Exhibits include everything
from sculpture, pottery and funereal objects
found in *tholos* at Nestor's Palace (p183),
to Roman mosaics, gold jewellery and votive
offerings. It provides wonderful context to
the surrounding areas.

Museum of Traditional Greek
Costumes
MUSEUM

(☑27210 86923; www.vgkareliascollection.com/
en; Stadiou 64; adult/concession €5/3; ☺9am-
2pm Tue-Sat, plus 5.30-8.30pm Wed & Sat,
10am-1pm Sun) Opened in 2017, this stunning
museum is thanks to one individual, Victoria Karelia, who donated her remarkable
collection of Greek costumes to a group
known as the 'Lyceum of Hellenic Women
of Kalamata'. Far from moth-eaten old
hand-me-downs, the clothing showcases
male and female folk dress from the 18th to
20th centuries in beautifully curated, dramatically lit exhibits.

History & Folklore Museum of
Kalamata
MUSEUM

(☑27210 28449; Ioannou 12, cnr Kyriakou; €3;
☺9am-1pm Wed-Sat, 10am-1pm Sun) This quaint
eggshell-blue building holds an exquisite
collection of donated local artefacts – from
tools and looms to household items and
clothes – that offer a thorough insight into
Kalamata's bygone era.

Church of Ypapantis
CHURCH

Kalamata's massive cathedral (constructed
in 1839) is home to the icon after which
Kalamata takes its modern name. Pilgrims
visit for its miracle-working icon of the Virgin Mary known as *kalo mata* (good eye).

Kalamata

Kalamata

◎ Sights

1 Archaeological Museum of Messenia	A2
2 History & Folklore Museum of Kalamata	B1
3 Kastro	B1
4 Museum of Traditional Greek Costumes	B2

🛏 Sleeping

5 Hotel Haikos	B7
6 Hotel Rex	A2

🍴 Eating

7 Food Market	B1
8 Kardamo	A3

The icon was discovered in the stables of the Ottoman *aga* (governor), who converted to Christianity as a result of the miracles it was believed to have performed.

Kastro FORT

(Vilardouinou; adult/concession €2/1; ⊘ 8am-8pm Tue-Sun, to 3pm Oct-Mar) Looming over the town is the 13th-century *kastro*. Remarkably, it survived the powerful 1986 earthquake that levelled the city. The entry gate is its most impressive feature. Inside, the *kastro* is a lush haven of tranquillity and there are excellent views over Kalamata and beyond from the battlements.

Military Museum MUSEUM

(🖉 27210 21219; Mitropolitou Meletiou 10; ⊘ 9am-2pm Tue-Sat, plus 6-8pm Wed, 11am-2pm Sun) **FREE** One for war buffs, this museum's displays depict Greek military history from the Turkish occupation to the Greek Resistance to Nazi occupation and 21st-century peacekeeping efforts through grisly paintings, photos, and ample displays of (sometimes hilarious) uniforms and weaponry. Most of the signs are in Greek, but national servicemen are on hand to give tours in basic English.

✨ Festivals & Events

Kalamata International Dance Festival MUSIC, DANCE

(www.kalamatadancefestival.gr; ⊘ Jul) This annual festival draws crowds to its quality performances of traditional music and dance. Venues include the amphitheatre of the *kastro*. See the website for dates and prices.

🛏 Sleeping & Eating

Hotel Rex
HOTEL €€

(📞27210 22334; www.rexhotel.gr; Aristomenous 26; s/d/tr/ste incl breakfast from €80/120/136/220; ❄️🛜) The Rex has a superb central location and will appeal if you like unapologetically retro decor, a Fawlty Towers–esque attitude from some staff and a touch of faded grandeur (it's been here since 1899). The rooms are reasonably modern but the air-con struggles in the summer heat. The corner rooms (ending in 03) are good choices.

Hotel Haikos
HOTEL €€

(📞27210 88902; www.haikos.gr; Navarino 115; s/d incl breakfast from €50/75; 🅿🛜) If you can look past the stained hall carpets, the rooms at this business-like modern hotel are fine, with funky wallpaper and balconies. Rooms at the front catch the sea breeze (and street noise). There's private parking; rare along this beachfront section.

Kardamo
INTERNATIONAL €

(📞2721 098091; Sidirodromikou Stathmou 21; mains €6.50-9; ⏲1pm-1am; 🛜🍴) Kardamo offers a tasty alternative to traditional Greek cuisine, without straying too far from its roots. The result? Greek dishes with a contemporary twist: the likes of spinach salad with *manouri* (soft cheese) and cranberries. The good price-to-quality ratio pulls in a younger crowd who seek modern alternatives. The setting is pretty in a tasteful taverna with a twist.

KALAMATA OLIVES

Kalamata gives its name to the prized Kalamata olive, a plump, purple-black variety found in delicatessens around the world. The region's reliable winter rains and hot summers make for perfect olive-growing conditions.

The Kalamata tree is distinguished from the common olive (grown for oil) by the size of its leaves. Like its fruit, the leaves of the Kalamata are twice the size of other varieties and a darker shade of green.

Unlike other varieties, Kalamata olives can't be picked green. They ripen in late November and must be hand-picked to avoid bruising. You can buy and sample these famous olives at the markets in Kalamata.

Food Market
MARKET €

(Nedontos; ⏲8am-2pm) This large food market across the bridge from the KTEL Messinia bus station stocks some of Kalamata's best-known products, including olives, olive oil and figs.

ℹ Information

National Bank of Greece (cnr Akrita & Navarinou) Also has branches on Aristomenous and Central Sq.

Police (📞27210 44653; Iroon Polytechniou)

Post Office (Andreas Skia; ⏲7.30am-2pm Mon-Fri)

Tourist Support Office (📞27213 60749; 28 Aristomenous St; ⏲9am-9pm)

ℹ Getting There & Away

AIR

Kalamata International Airport is 10.5km west of the city, near Messini, and served by various airlines from Nuremburg, Amsterdam, Barcelona and London Gatwick in summer. Aegean Airlines (www.aegeanair.com) operates daily flights between Kalamata and Athens and Thessaloniki from June through September.

BOAT

Between mid-June and September, a weekly ferry service operated by LANE Ferries (www.lane.gr) runs on Sundays from Kalamata to Kissamos, Crete (per person/car €26/69, 9¾ hours) via Kythira (per person/car €17/45, 5½ hours). Contact **SMAN Travel/Maniatis** (📞27210 20704; cnr Likourgou & Psaron 148), by the port, for the schedule and tickets.

BUS

KTEL Messinia bus station (📞27210 28581; www.ktelmessinias.gr; Artemidos) has buses to Athens (€24.30, 4½ hours, 11 daily) via Corinth Isthmus (€17.30, 2½ hours). It also has buses to Tripoli (€8.90, 1¼ hours) and Patra (€24.90, four hours, two daily) via Kyparissia (€7.70, 1¼ hours) and Pyrgos (€14, two hours).

Heading west, there are buses to Koroni (€5.50, 1½ hours, four to six daily), Methoni (€6.70, 1½ hours, three to five daily) and Pylos (€5.50, 1¼ hours, one to three daily).

Heading east across the Langada Pass, buses run to Sparta (€6.30, 1¾ hours, one to two daily) with a change at Artemisia. Four daily buses head to Kardamyli (€4, one hour) and Stoupa (€4.90, 1¼ hours), with some continuing to Itilo (€8.20, 2¼ hours). There are also direct buses to Thessaloniki (€71.30, three weekly, 11 hours).

❶ Getting Around

Local buses leave from the KTEL Messinia bus station. The most useful service is bus 1, which goes south to the seafront and then east along Navarinou as far as the Filoxenia Hotel. Buy tickets (€1.30) from kiosks or the driver.

Recommended car-rental options:

Avis (☑ 27210 28869; www.avis.gr; Aristomenous 107)

Verga Rent a Car (☑ 27210 95190; www.car-rental-kalamata.gr; Faron 202)

Ancient Messini
Αρχαία Μεσσήνη

The name Ancient Messini is used to refer to both the historic site and the village, a geographical and literal gateway to the ruins. Locals lobbied to drop the original name of Mavromati, which derives poetically from the fountain in the central square whose water gushes from a hole that resembles a black eye *(mavro mati)*. Many, including bus schedules, still refer to its original name. This cluster of attractive houses and a taverna, 25km northwest of Kalamata, overlook the extensive, and very impressive, site of Ancient Messini itself.

◉ Sights

★**Ancient Messini**　　HISTORIC SITE
(☑ 27240 51201; www.ancientmessene.gr; adult/concession €12/6; ☺ 8am-8pm) The remains of this vast ancient city are as extensive as those of Olympia and Epidavros, yet Ancient Messini receives only a fraction of their visitors. Picturesquely situated on a hillside below the village of Mavromati and still undergoing excavation, the site comprises a large theatre, an *agora* (marketplace), a vast Sanctuary of Asclepius and the most intact and impressive of all Ancient Greek stadiums.

Ancient Messini was founded in 371 BC after the Theban general Epaminondas defeated Sparta at the Battle of Leuctra, freeing the Messinians from almost 350 years of Spartan rule. Built on the site of an earlier stronghold, the new Messinian capital was one of a string of defensive positions designed to keep watch over Sparta. Epaminondas himself helped to plan the fortifications, which were based on a massive wall that stretched 9km around the surrounding ridges and completely enclosed the town.

Apart from its defensive potential, Ancient Messini was also favoured by the gods. According to local myth, Zeus was born here – not in Crete – and raised by the nymphs Neda and Ithomi, who bathed him in the same spring that gives the modern village its name.

The first construction you come across is the large **amphitheatre**, reconstructed for contemporary use. The path leads past the **Fountain of Arsinoe** building, which supplied the ancient city with water. The columned remains next to it are the **agora** with the **treasury** in its southwest corner. The Greek general Philopoemen was held prisoner by the Messinians here in 183 BC and dispatched to the other world with poison.

Beyond is the **Sanctuary of Asclepius**, the spiritual centre that lay at the heart of the ancient city, consisting of a rectangular courtyard fringed with Corinthian columns. This extensive complex was centred on a Doric temple that once housed a golden statue of Ithomi. The modern awning west of the temple protects the **artemision**, where fragments of an enormous statue of Artemis Orthia were found. The structures to the east of the *asclepion* include the **ekklesiasterion**, which looks like a small amphitheatre but once acted as an assembly hall. Nearby are the remains of a **Roman villa**, the steel roof protecting the mosaic remains.

Head downhill to the large **stadium**, which is surrounded by a forest of columns. You can see where the Romans closed off part of the athletics track, turning it into a gladiator arena. On the left-hand side, near the arena, are the **VIP seats** – the ones with backs and with lion paws for legs. On the right-hand side, near the intact gate of the enormous gymnasium, are round holes in stone slabs – these are ingenious **Roman public toilets** positioned over a now dry stream.

The cube-like building near the toilets is a **grave memorial** to an important Messinian family, and the Doric temple at the far end of the stadium is a **mausoleum** of the Saithidae, a prominent Roman family.

Excavations and improvements are ongoing – including partial recreations of buildings – so you might be lucky enough to have a more expansive experience.

Arcadian Gate ARCHAEOLOGICAL SITE

It's well worth heading 800m along the road from Mavromati village, past the museum to the celebrated Arcadian Gate. This unusual stone portal with a circular courtyard between the double gates and an immense, half-collapsed gatepost guarded the ancient route to Megalopoli – now the modern road north to Mcligalas and Zerbisia – which runs through the gate. Running uphill from the gate is the finest surviving section of the mighty defensive wall built by Epaminondas.

Museum of Ancient Messini MUSEUM

(adult/concession €12/6; ⊘8am-8pm Apr-Sep, 9am-4pm Nov-Mar) The compact museum, by the turn-off for Ancient Messini, houses some wonderful statuary from the site – including one of the most important and best-known statues in antiquity, *Doryphoros of Polykleitu*, and the fine specimen of manhood that is Hermes. Those of Machaon and Podaleiros are assumed to be the work of Damophon, who specialised in oversized statues of gods and heroes and was responsible for many of the statues that once adorned Ancient Messini. Ticket covers entry to Ancient Messini.

🛏 Sleeping & Eating

Likourgos Rooms GUESTHOUSE €

(🕿27240 51297; roomslykourgos@yahoo.gr; s/d/tr €35/45/55) This simple budget spot has clean and spacious rooms. Front rooms afford glimpses of the ruins. The helpful owner, Victoria, speaks English.

★Messana Hotel BOUTIQUE HOTEL €€

(🕿6974906832, 27240 51000; www.messana-hotel.gr; d incl breakfast €60; ❄🛜) A new hotel and welcome addition, Messana successfully blends the traditional elements of stone, wood and clay with modern decor including contemporary coloured-glass screens and brightly painted walls. It has all the mod cons yet maintains a traditional and very romantic feel. All rooms have balconies. A perfect option for those who enjoy a remote village experience.

Taverna Ithomi TAVERNA €

(🕿27240 51298; www.ithomi.gr; Ancient Messini; mains €7-12; ⊘9am-late) The pick of a handful of local *kafeneia* (coffee houses) and tavernas, this one offers traditional cuisine with a superb view over the ruins. Friendly owner Nikos is the local 'man in the know'

for travel information, and besides grilled meats, he makes a mean *briam* (oven-baked vegetable casserole).

ℹ Getting There & Away

Getting here without your own transport is difficult; there are only two weekly buses that run between the village and Kalamata (Monday and Thursday at 5.30am and 2pm). You'll want some independence to explore the area.

Koroni Κορώνη

POP 1700

Koroni is a lovely Venetian port town on Messinia Bay, 43km southwest of Kalamata. Medieval mansions and churches line the town's quaint, narrow and winding streets. These lead to a promontory, on which perches an extensive castle and convent.

◎ Sights & Activities

Castle CASTLE

(⊘24hr) FREE The castle crowns a bluff overlooking the town. Much of it is occupied by the **Timios Prodromos Convent**, so a strict dress code applies. You can enter via the castle's impressive Gothic entrance. The small promontory beyond the castle is a tranquil place for a stroll, with lovely views over the Messinian Gulf to the Taÿgetos Mountains.

Zaga Beach BEACH

Koroni's main attraction is Zaga Beach, a 2km sweep of golden sand just south of town. It takes about 20 minutes to walk to here – you can cut through the castle or go via the road.

Koroni also sees loggerhead turtles, which lay their eggs near Zaga.

🛏 Sleeping & Eating

Hotel Diana HOTEL €

(🕿27250 22312; www.dianahotel-koroni.gr; d €40; ❄🛜) This place is blessed (or otherwise) with Byzantine gold-plated bar stools, icons and the like. Rooms are not quite as glossy – they are simple and very compact. But it's bang in the centre, just off the central square, almost on the harbour. Breakfast costs €5.

Camping Koroni CAMPGROUND €

(🕿27250 22119; www.koronicamping.com; campsites per adult/car/tent €8/4/5; P🛜🏊) Located only 200m from Koroni, near the beach.

On-site restaurant, washing machines and supermarket; popular with families.

Colonides Beach Hotel
HOTEL €€

(☑ 27250 41200; www.colonides.gr; d/f incl breakfast from €130/160; P🅿️🛜♨️) Situated 10km northwest of Koroni, near the village of Vounaria, this small family-run resort has clean and spacious apartments. They are a little minimalist, but who needs colour inside when you're looking out over greenery, the hotel's swimming pool and, in the distance (a three-minute walk), the ocean? Rates drop enormously outside of high season.

Peroulia Restaurant
GREEK €€

(☑ 27250 41777; www.peroulia.gr; mains €8-15, fish per kilo from €55; ⊙9am-late May–mid-Oct; 🛜) Overlooking the teal waters of the gorgeous Peroulia Beach, 6km north of Koroni, this waterfront restaurant has earned a loyal local following for its traditional Greek cuisine and fresh seafood. As the owner's son (the manager) says, 'My father catches the fish; my mother cooks it.' And, by all accounts of satisfied clients, they are a good team.

Kaggelarios
SEAFOOD €€

(☑ 27250 22648; http://kaggelarios-koroni. com; mains €8-15, fish per kilo €35-55) One of a clutch of seafood eateries in Koroni, this ultra-popular, atmospheric spot churns out Greek standards. With its setting over the harbour, it's hard to go past a fresh seafood dish.

❶ Getting There & Away

Buses will drop you in the central square outside the Church of Agios Dimitrios, one block back from the harbour. There are services to Kalamata (€5.50, 1½ hours, six daily) and one to Athens (€28, four hours, daily). For Pylos you must change at Rizomilos (two daily), waiting for around 45 minutes at changeover. Buy tickets on the bus.

Methoni
Μεθώνη

POP 1170

Methoni, 12km south of Pylos, was one of the seven cities offered to Achilles by Agamemnon. Homer described it as 'rich in vines'. Today it's a pretty seaside town with a popular beach, next to which looms the most impressive example of a 15th-century Venetian fortress in the Peloponnese.

◉ Sights

Kastro
FORT

(adult/concession €2/1; ⊙8am-8pm Apr-Sep, to 3pm Oct-Mar) FREE This vast, crumbling *kastro*, a great example of 15th-century Venetian military architecture, is built on a promontory south of Methoni. It's surrounded on three sides by the sea and separated from the mainland by a dry moat. Enter the inner keep through the mighty gateway to discover a Turkish bath, a cathedral, a house, a cistern and underground passages. A short causeway leads from the fortress to the diminutive octagonal Bourtzi fortress on an adjacent islet.

The medieval port town, which was located within the fortress walls, was the Venetians' first, and their longest-held, possession in the Peloponnese. It was also a stopover for pilgrims en route to the Holy Land.

🛏️ Sleeping & Eating

★ Apartments Melina
APARTMENT €

(☑ 27230 31505; www.methoni-apartments.gr; d & tr apt €60, f apt €100) This charming little gem speaks for itself – recently modernised yet still appealingly rustic apartments across from the beach, with a perfumed garden of roses (over 300 varieties) and ultra-friendly English-speaking owners, Kathy and Spiros. Perfect for families and longer stays.

Hotel Aris
HOTEL €

(☑ 27230 31125; Plateia Sigrou; d/tr €60/70; P❄️🛜) Two blocks from the sea and overlooking a tree-lined square, this immaculately clean but very basic place is run by kind owners who don't speak English. Rates are lower outside June to August.

Hotel Achilles
HOTEL €€

(☑ 27230 31819; www.achilles-hotel.com; Plateia Eleftherias; d €80; P❄️🛜) The smartest of a range of small family hotels in town, Achilles has 13 comfortable, modern rooms and a pleasant outdoor terrace. There's a light, airy dining area, too. Breakfast costs €7. Prices are much cheaper outside of high season.

Taverna Alector
TAVERNA €

(☑ 27230 31838; mains €7-11; ⊙6-11pm mid-Feb–Dec) Traditional Greek dishes are served with aplomb by the friendly and accommodating multilingual husband-and-wife team, Andreas and Irini, at this central taverna. Often there's live music on Sundays; linger with a beer or carafe of house wine. (If you turn up during the day when it's closed, you might be served nevertheless.)

Taverna Klimataria
TAVERNA €€

(☑ 27230 31544; Miaouli; mains €9-13; ⊕ noon-11pm May-Oct) Locals are in agreement: this is the place to head to for traditional dishes. It's in an old home, with seating on the porch and in the courtyard. Typical choices include onion pie and stuffed zucchini flowers.

ℹ️ Getting There & Away

Buses depart from Methoni from the fork at the Pylos end of town where the two main streets meet. Buses travel to Pylos (€1.80, 15 minutes, one to six daily) and Kalamata (€6.80, 1½ hours, three daily). Services also run to Finikounda (€2.60, 15 minutes, five to six Monday to Saturday, one on Sunday); change there for Koroni, though connections may not match up. The bus to Kalamata stops at Harakopio, 4.5km from Koroni. For bus information contact KTEL in Kalamata (p178).

Pylos
Πύλος

POP 2700

Coastal Pylos, 51km southwest of Kalamata, presides over the southern end of an immense bay. With its huge natural harbour that's formed by the Sfaktiria Islet, its castle and surrounding pine-covered hills, Pylos is not just picturesque, but is also one of the region's most historically significant towns.

'Sandy Pylos', the Mycenaean kingdom mentioned by Homer, lay a short distance from here, near Gialova Lagoon, and was one of the few places where the Spartans suffered defeat at the hands of the Athenians. On 20 October 1827, the British, French and Russian fleets, under the command of Admiral Codrington, fired at point-blank range on Ibrahim Pasha's combined Turkish, Egyptian and Tunisian fleet, sinking 53 ships and killing 6000 men, with negligible losses on the Allies' side. The attack, the Battle of Navarino (Navarino being the town's former name), was a decisive moment in the War of Independence.

◉ Sights & Activities

René Puaux Exhibition
MUSEUM

(adult/concession €2/1; ⊕ 8am-8pm Tue-Sun May-Oct) Housed in a red mansion on the seafront, this collection of pictures depicts the War of Independence with a focus on the Battle of Navarino. It was donated by René Puaux (1878–1937), who bequeathed porce-lain, engravings and lithographs on condition that they be exhibited at Pylos, near the battle's location.

Neo Kastro
CASTLE

(☑ 27230 22955; adult/concession €3/2; ⊕ 8am-8pm Tue-Sun, to 3pm Nov-Mar) The more intact and accessible of two castles that lie on either side of Navarino Bay, Neo Kastro was built by the Turks in 1573 on the hilltop at the southern edge of town, off the road to Methoni. It affords excellent views of the bay. Within its formidable walls is a mosque converted into a church plus former dungeons, used as a prison for warring Maniots until the 1900s. It now houses now houses Pylos' impressive archaeological museum.

Club Boats
BOATING

(☑ 6945034205; www.pyloscruises.gr; ⊕ Jun-Sep) Runs boat tours around the Bay of Navarino and to Sfaktiria Islet, where silt-covered wrecks of sunken Turkish ships are discernible in the clear waters. The price depends on the number of passengers, but reckon on about €15 per person (minimum numbers apply). Tours generally last around two hours (with one hour for swimming). Has a kiosk on the quay.

🛏️ Sleeping & Eating

Karalís Beach Hotel
HOTEL €€

(☑ 27230 23021; www.karalisbeach.gr; Paralia; d/tr/f incl breakfast from €135/155/190; ❇️ 🅿️) Pylos' clear winner in the hotel stakes is this intimate little place with 14 compact, stylish rooms, all with wooden floors and decorated in tranquil cream tones. Those at the front have balconies. It's hard not to like this place for the setting alone – under the castle walls, clinging to a cliff over the water. Rates are significantly lower outside high season.

To Kastro
APARTMENT €€

(☑ 27230 28292; www.hotelkastro-pylos.gr; d & tr from €60; ⊕ Mar-Oct) These delightful, spotless, simple studio apartments are run by Panagiotis. In his words, he likes his guests to feel like they are 'in a small house'. He's referring to the sense of family and hospitality, though the apartments themselves are large enough to be a home, too. These are for longer-term stays (in high season there's a three-night minimum).

Hotel Miramare
HOTEL €€

(☑ 27230 22751; www.miramarepylos.gr; Tsamadou 3; s/d/tr/f incl breakfast €50/80/90/100; 🅿️ 🛜) With smallish rooms and low pine beds,

GIALOVA ΓΙΑΛΟΒΑ

The village of Gialova lies 8km north of Pylos on the northeastern edge of Navarino Bay and is well worth a trip. There's a fine sandy beach and safe swimming in the sheltered waters of the bay. As well as the Giavola Lagoon which is the region's best birdwatching site, only 5km away is the spectacular Voidokilia Beach (p148), a stunning arc of turquoise water, as well as a Franks castle, Paleokastro, and Nestor's Cave, where Hermes allegedly hid Apollo's cattle. These last two sites are a scramble from both Voidokilia Beach and the lagoon.

When you're hungry, head back to Gialova and choose from a waterfront full of fabulous eateries such as **Elia** (☑ 27230 23503; www.elia-gialova.gr; mains €8-16; ☺ 4-10pm Feb & Mar, noon-midnight Apr-Oct; 🐾 ☑), that serves modern Greek, or **La Cucina Italiana** (☑ 27230 23301; mains €7-17; ☺ 6pm-late; ☑), whose second storey affords views across the bay.

If you fall in love with the place and want to stay, the ever-expanding **Zoe Resort** (☑ 27230 22025; www.zoeresort.com; r/apt incl breakfast from €75/110; P 🅿 🐾 🖥 🌊) offers both beachfront rooms and apartments. Campers should opt for the well-organised **Camping Erodios** (☑ 27230 23269; www.erodioss.gr; campsites per adult/tent/car €7/5/4, 1-/2-bed cabins €55/65; 🐾).

There are four buses a day south to Pylos (around €2, 15 minutes) and two to four daily north to Kyparissia via Nestor's Palace and Chora. A taxi between Gialova and Pylos costs around €13.

rooms here are a little dated and bathrooms a squish. But add the position, the light (all have sea-facing balconies) and the extensive buffet breakfast, plus helpful English-speaking owners, and you can hardly complain.

En Plo
SEAFOOD €€

(☑ 27230 23306; Tsamadou; mains €7-11; ☺ Mar-Oct) We'll be upfront: there's no fancy contemporary setting, no white cloths, no candelabra. Which is exactly why the locals go here: for no-nonsense, unfussy, honest fare. This fisherman's hut, with harbour-front seating, is best known for its grills and calamari. On the seafood front, Nikos will be open about what's fresh and what's not (if it's out of season).

Koukos
TAVERNA €€

(☑ 27230 22950; mains €8-15; ☺ 1pm-late) The Cuckoo is a plain, unpretentious, good old-fashioned taverna, serving hearty portions of grills and oven-baked dishes on a changing menu to a loyal local clientele. It's about 100m up the coastal hill from the plaza – ask for directions in the plaza.

ⓘ Information

Banks with ATMS include **Alpha Bank** (Plateia Trion Navarhon) and **National Bank of Greece** (Plateia Trion Navarhon).

Police (☑ 27230 23016; Plateia Trion Navarhon)

Post Office (Nileos; ☺ 7.30am-2pm Mon-Fri)

ⓘ Getting There & Away

The **KTEL Messinia bus station** (☑ 27230 22230; www.ktelmessinias.gr; Plateia Trion Navarhon) is on the inland side of the central square. From the bus station, there are services to Kalamata (€5.50, 1¾ hours, four to seven daily), Kyparissia (€6.50, 1¼ hours, two to four daily) via Nestor's Palace (€2, 30 minutes) and Chora (€2.30, 35 minutes), Methoni (€1.80, 20 minutes, three to five daily) and Athens (€30, five hours, one daily). For Patra you must catch a connection from Kalamata or Kyparissia.

Four daily buses (sometimes more in summer) ply the route between Pylos and Gialova (€1.80, 15 minutes).

Around Pylos

Nestor's Palace
RUINS

(☑ 27630 31437; ☺ 8am-3pm Tue-Sun) The best preserved of all Mycenaean palaces lies 17km north of Pylos. It's described in Homer's 'Odyssey' as the court of the mythical hero Nestor, who took part in the voyage of the Argonauts and sent 90 ships to fight in the Trojan War. Originally a two-storey building, the palace's walls stand 1m high, and from the raised walkways and explanatory text you get a good idea of the layout of a Mycenaean palace complex.

The main palace was a building of many rooms. The largest, the throne room, was

INERY STOP

Mercouri Estate (☑ 26210 41601; www.
mercouri.gr; tastings €10; ⊙ 9am-3pm
Mon-Sat), 1km north of Korakohori village and about 15km from Pyrgos, is a
worthwhile winery for a stop-off. This
handsome estate produces a dry white
foloi, and a prize-winning rich red – its
flagship Domaine Mercouri. It also runs
tours of the grounds (reservations
required).

where the king dealt with state business. In
its centre was a large, circular hearth surrounded by four ornate columns that supported a balcony. Surrounding the throne
is the sentry box, pantry, waiting room,
a vestibule and, most fascinating, a bathroom with a terracotta tub still in place.
In this tub, according to legend, Polycaste,
Nestor's youngest daughter, bathed the hero
Telemachus.

After several years of excavations and
cleaning the site was reopened in 2016,
which explains its new roof, raised walkways
and small information kiosk. In the kiosk a
soundless 3-D screening is high on special
effects and low on information, although
it succeeds in depicting what the frescoes
would have looked like.

Many of the finds, including fragments of
the palace frescoes and some of the Linear B
script tablets – the first to be discovered on
the mainland – are housed in the museum
in the nearby village of Chora.

Opening hours may be extended in summer months; check before visiting.

Paleokastro & Nestor's Cave   RUINS
The ruins of this ancient castle, built by the
Franks in the 13th century on the site of the
acropolis of Ancient Pylos, lie 5km west of
Gialova on rugged **Koryphasion Hill**, a formidable natural defensive position overlooking the northern entrance to Navarino Bay.

The castle (officially closed) can be
explored, but with care; avoid falling down
cisterns hidden by overgrowth. The views
from the top are magnificent. The road to
the castle is signposted on the northern edge
of the village.

Follow signs to Paleokastro, where the
road ends in a little car park. From there
you'll find two ways of reaching the castle:
the left-hand path (20 minutes) skirts Kory-

phasion Hill and gradually leads up to the
entrance. The other route (40 minutes) is
signposted 'Nestor's Cave'; the path skirts
the lagoon before leading towards **Voidokilia Beach** through the sand dunes; a fork
in the path leads up towards **Nestor's Cave**
where, according to legend, Hermes hid
Apollo's cattle. From the cave, it's a tough
scramble up to the castle's crumbling battlements, rewarded by views of the perfect
crescent of Voidokilia Beach.

Chora Archaeological Museum   MUSEUM
(☑ 27632 31358; €2; ⊙ 8am-3pm Tue-Sun) This
little museum, 4km northeast of Nestor's
Palace in the village of Chora, houses finds
from the palace site and other Mycenaean
weaponry, jewellery and pottery from tombs
around Messinia. The prize pieces are the
large oil vat, fragments of frescoes from the
throne rooms at Nestor's Palace, and the
Linear B tablets (the tablets are copies).

Buses from Pylos to Kyparissia stop at
Chora. If driving, follow signs for Kalamata.

Ionian Dive Center   DIVING
(☑ 27630 61551; www.ioniandivecenter.com; 1-/2-
/3-dive packages €45/90/130) Based in Mar-
athopoli, this reputable outfit offers dives in
coastal sites in Messinia. PADI courses are
also offered.

OLYMPIA   ΟΛΥΜΠΙΑ

Most people come to Olympia for one reason: to visit the historically important and
impressive site of Ancient Olympia, birthplace of the Olympic Games. Otherwise the
surrounding region of Elia (Ελιά) is largely
agricultural.

Ancient Elia took its name from the
mythical King Helios. Its capital was the
city of Elis, now a forgotten ruin on the road
from Gastouni to Lake Pinios. When the
Franks arrived, they made Andravida the
capital of the principate of Morea. Pyrgos is
the region's underwhelming modern capital.

❶ Getting There & Around

From the **KTEL bus terminal** (☑ 26210 20600;
www.ktelileias.gr; Erithrou Stavrou 6) in Pyrgos,
there are services to Athens (€27.70, four hours,
up to 10 daily), Tripoli (€15.50), Patra (€9, two
hours, up to 10 daily), Andritsena (€6.20, two
hours, two daily except Friday and Sunday),
Kalamata (€13.10, two hours, two daily) and
Olympia (€2.20, 30 minutes, eight to 13 daily).

There's also a small train that runs on the branch line from Pyrgos to Olympia.

Ionian Ferries (☑ 26102 40000; www.ionian ferries.gr) runs to Zakynthos (per adult/car €7.50/28.50, 1¼ hours, four daily in summer) and to Poros (per adult/car €8.80/37.90, 1½ hours, one to two daily in summer) on Kefallonia.

Olympia Town   Ολυμπία

POP 1020

The compact village of Olympia, lined with souvenir shops and eateries, caters to the coach-loads of tourists who pass through on their way to the most famous sight in the Peloponnese: Ancient Olympia. This is where myth and fact merge. According to one (of many different) legends, Zeus held the first Olympic Games to celebrate beating his father Cronos at wrestling. This is the birthplace of the ideal that still brings states together, differences aside, for the sake of friendly athletic competition, just as it did more than 4000 years ago.

Just 500m south of the village, across the Kladeos River, are the remains of Ancient Olympia. As you walk around, or stand at the starting line of the ancient stadium, contemplate the influence of this site through millennia. This is where they light the Olympic flame every four years. This is where the Games began.

◉ Sights

★**Ancient Olympia**   HISTORIC SITE
(☑ 26240 22517; adult/concession €12/6; ⊙ 8am-8pm, to 3pm Nov-Mar) The Olympic Games took place here every four years for at least 1000 years, until their abolition by Emperor Theodosius I in AD 393. The Olympic flame is still lit here for the modern Games. Thanks to the destruction ordered by Theodosius II and various subsequent earthquakes, little remains of the magnificent temples and athletic facilities, but enough exists to give you a hint of this World Heritage–listed sanctuary's former glory. It's a signposted five-minute walk from the modern village.

Wandering amid the tree-shaded ruins, you can almost picture the blood and smoke of oxen sacrificed to Zeus and Hera, the sweaty, oiled-up athletes waiting inside the original stadium, the jostling crowds, and the women and slaves watching the proceedings from a nearby hill. It's worth remembering that some buildings precede others by centuries; a visit to the archaeological museum (p189) beforehand or afterwards (as heading into the site before the crowds on opening is something you'll never forget) will provide context and help with visualising the ancient buildings.

The first ruin encountered is the **gymnasium**, which dates from the 2nd century BC. South of here are the columns of the partly restored **palaestra** (wrestling school), where contestants practised and trained. The next building was the **theokoleon** (priests' house). Behind it is **Pheidias' workshop**, where the gargantuan ivory-and-gold Statue of Zeus, one of the Seven Wonders of the Ancient World, was sculpted. The workshop was identified by archaeologists after the discovery of tools and moulds. Beyond the *theokoleon* is the **leonidaion**, an elaborate structure that accommodated dignitaries.

PELOPONNESE OLYMPIA TOWN

Ancient Olympia

The Olympic Games

The Olympic Games were undoubtedly the ancient world's biggest sporting event and remain for most athletes today the ultimate dreams. Then, as now, the Games made warring states temporarily halt their squabbles, and victorious competitors won great fame and considerable fortune.

Origins of the Games

Some Ancient Greek texts attribute the founding of the Games to the hero Pelops; others name Hercules as the founder who made Zeus the patron god of the Olympic sanctuary. The first official quadrennial Olympic Games were declared in 776 BC by King Iphitos of Elis, took place around the first full moon in August, and reached the height of their prestige in 576 BC.

During the ancient Games, writers, poets and historians read their works to large audiences; traders clinched business deals; and city-state leaders attempted to resolve differences through diplomacy.

Olympic Qualifications

In Ancient Greece only free-born Greek males were allowed to compete in the Games; the Romans changed the rules to include Roman citizens. Slaves and women were not allowed to enter the Olympic sanctuary even as spectators; women trying to sneak in were thrown from Mt Typaion. Today's Summer Olympics include athletes from 204 countries, with 88 countries competing in the Winter Olympics.

Demise & Rebirth

During Roman times the Games declined. Held for the last time in AD 393, they were banned by Emperor Theodosius I as part of a purge of pagan festivals.

1. Ancient pottery depicting Olympic wrestlers
2. Ruins of the Temple of Hera (p188), Olympia Town
3. Statue of a discus thrower

The modern Olympic Games were instituted in 1896 and, except during WWI and WWII, have been held every four years around the world ever since. The Olympic flame is lit at the ancient site and carried by runners to the city where the Games are held.

Scandal & Controversies

Throughout history the Olympics have been marred by scandals. These range from the farcical – Emperor Nero entering the chariot race in AD 67 with 10 horses, ordering that other competitors could only have four, falling off and still being declared winner – to the serious, including Israeli athletes being murdered by Palestinian group Black September in 1972, and Hitler refusing to award gold medals to African American sprinter Jesse Owens in 1936.

ANCIENT OLYMPICS VS MODERN OLYMPICS

➡ Contemporary opening ceremonies may involve such displays as James Bond parachuting in. In Ancient Greece, it was all about sacrificing oxen to Zeus.

➡ Ancient Greek events included wrestling, chariot and horse racing, the pentathlon (three foot races, the long jump and the discus), javelin, boxing and pankration (few-holds-barred fighting). Today's Summer Olympics have been joined by the Winter Olympics; a total of 56 events across both games include modified sprinting, equestrian, boxing and wrestling.

➡ Victorious ancient Olympians were crowned with sacred olive branches and enjoyed tax exemption and other privileges. Modern Olympians receive medals, TV fame and sponsorship fortune.

The Altis, or **Sacred Precinct of Zeus**, lies east of the path. Its most important building was the immense 5th-century Doric **Temple of Zeus**, which enshrined Pheidias' statue, later removed to Constantinople by Theodosius II (where it was destroyed by fire in AD 475). One column of the temple has been restored and re-erected, and helps put into perspective the sheer size of the structure.

South of the Temple of Zeus is the **bouleuterion** (council house), which contains the **altar of oaths**, where competitors swore to abide by the rules decreed by the Olympic Senate and not to commit foul play.

East of the temple is the **echo portico**, with a Doric colonnade leading towards the stadium. Its remarkable acoustics meant that a sound uttered within was repeated seven times. Just east of the portico are the remains of a lavish **villa** used by Emperor Nero during his participation in the Games in AD 67; it replaced the original Sanctuary of Hestia.

The **stadium** lies to the east of the Altis and is entered through a stone archway. It's rectangular, unlike today's stadiums, and the stone start and finish lines of the 120m sprint track and the judges' seats still survive. The stadium could seat at least 45,000 spectators. Slaves and women spectators, however, had to be content to watch from outside on the Hill of Kronos.

KLIO'S HONEY FARM

A massive departure from the reason you have probably come to Olympia, nonetheless, **Klio's Honey Farm** (☑ 6977714530; www.klioshoneyfarm. com; Ancient Olympia 270 65; ⊙ 11am-4pm Mar-May & Sep-Nov, 10am-6pm Jun-Aug) is a quaint experience. Enterprising Klio, a professional beekeeper, has opened up the family home to educate visitors not only about bees and honey, but to provide a very local experience. Sit at one of the lace-cloth-covered tables in the flower-filled garden, converse with Klio's mother and help make *diplas* (fried dough dusted in icing sugar).

In short, Klio wants people to merely 'taste and enjoy'. Entry is free; jams and sweets for sale.

To the north of the Temple of Zeus was the **pelopion**, a small, wooded hillock with an altar to Pelops, the first hero of the Olympic Games. It was surrounded by a wall containing the remains of its Doric portico. Many artefacts now displayed in the museum were found on the hillock.

Further north is the 6th-century Doric **Temple of Hera**, the site's most intact structure. Hera was worshipped along with Rea until the two were superseded by Zeus. The Hermes statue was found here.

To the east of this temple is the **nymphaeum** (AD 156–60), erected by the wealthy Roman banker Herodes Atticus. Typical of buildings financed by Roman benefactors, it was grandiose, consisting of a semicircular building with Doric columns flanked at each side by a circular temple. The building contained statues of Herodes Atticus and his family, though Zeus took centre stage. Despite its elaborate appearance, the nymphaeum had a practical purpose; it was a fountain house supplying Olympia with fresh spring water.

Just in front of the nymphaeum is the spot where the altar of Hestia would have maintained a continuous **fire** during the Games, symbolising the fire stolen from the gods by Prometheus; fires were also lit in the temples of Zeus and Hera. Today, the **Olympic flame** is lit where the Temple of Hestia once stood.

Beyond the nymphaeum and up a flight of stone steps, a row of 12 **treasuries** stretched to the stadium, each erected by a city-state for use as a storehouse for offerings to the gods; these were mainly used to advertise the city-state's prestige and wealth.

At the bottom of these steps are the scant remains of the 5th-century-BC **metroön**, a temple dedicated to Rea, the mother of the gods. Apparently the ancients worshipped Rea in this temple with orgies.

The foundations of the **philippeion**, west of the Temple of Hera, are the remains of a circular construction with Ionic columns built by Philip of Macedon to commemorate the Battle of Chaironeia (338 BC), where he defeated a combined army of Athenians and Thebans. The building contained gold-and-ivory-covered statues of Philip and his family, including his son, Alexander the Great.

North of the *philippeion* was the **prytaneum**, the magistrate's residence. Here, winning athletes feasted and were entertained.

★ **Archaeological Museum** MUSEUM
(adult/concession incl site €12/6; ⊙ 8am-8pm, to 3pm Nov-Apr) This superb museum features finds from the archaeological site. Visiting it before or after touring the ruins helps to put the ancient site and its buildings into perspective. The museum's exhibits span the Olympic sanctuary's history, from the prehistoric to the Roman periods. Artefacts include increasingly sophisticated ceramics, votive offerings to Zeus and Hera, sacrificial cauldron adornments and statuary from the Temple of Hera.

The main hall dramatically displays the biggest highlight: reassembled pediments and metopes from the Temple of Zeus.

The eastern pediment of the Temple of Zeus depicts the chariot race between Pelops and Oinomaos, while the western pediment shows the fight between the centaurs and Lapiths at the wedding feast of Pirithous (the centaurs got drunk and tried to abduct the women). The metopes depict the Twelve Labours of Hercules; half the fun is trying to work out which is which from the remains alone.

Another highlight, in a room of its own, is 4th-century Parian marble statue of Hermes of Praxiteles. Other treasures include the votive offering (look out for the tiny helmet), a bronze arm protector decorated with the face of the Gorgon Medusa, a tiny bronze figure of Silenus (tutor to Dionysis, the god of wine) featuring optimistically proportioned genitalia, and a masterpiece of classical sculpture from the Temple of Hera.

Museum of the History of the Olympic Games in Antiquity MUSEUM
(adult/concession €12/6; ⊙ 8am-3pm Tue-Fri) Beautifully presented displays depict the history of the world's most prestigious sporting competition. Learn about its core original events (foot racing, wrestling, boxing and chariot racing), why it's associated with Hercules (or Pelops), and what fate befell women who tried to watch the Games despite prohibitions. The sculptures, mosaics, pottery art and votive offerings all pay tribute to athletes and athleticism. Other Games – Heraean, Nemean, Panathenaic, Pythian and Isthmian – also get a mention. Ticket includes entry to Ancient Olympia.

★ **Archimedes' Museum** MUSEUM
(www.kotsanas.com; Praxitelous Kondyli; by donation; ⊙ 10am-8pm) This extraordinary private collection is generously on display courtesy of the collector, mechanical engineer Kostas Kotsanas. It gets to the literal nuts and bolts behind the technological achievements of the Ancient Greeks. Marvel at the mechanics of the crane used to build the Parthenon, the *antikythera* (the 'first laptop'), and a statue servant that serves holy water, touted as the 'world's oldest auto vending machine'. Fascinating and educational, and marvellous for kids, both young and old. Excellent English explanations.

It's next to the National Bank of Greece.

☞ Tours

To really make the Ancient Olympia site come alive, it's well worth considering hiring a guide, especially if there are a few of you. Tours usually include both the site and the Archaeological Museum, but any preference will be catered for. Tours start at around €100 for two or three people. Recommended guides include **Panagiota Karachaliou** (☑ mobile 6975820655; karachaliou panagiota@yahoo.com), who speaks English, **Marieta Kolotourou** (☑ mobile 6977526146), who speaks English and Spanish, and **Niki Vlachou** (☑ 6972426085; www.olympictours.gr), who speaks English and French.

🛏 Sleeping

★ **Hotel Pelops** HOTEL €
(☑ 26240 22543; www.hotelpelops.gr; Varela 2; s/d/tr incl breakfast €45/60/80; ❄ @ 🛜) This is among the town's best contenders, with comfortable rooms (many with balconies) and a delightful, sunny lounge. The Greek-Australian owners, Susanna and Theo, provide friendly, knowledgable service and a decent breakfast. And, hurrah, there are tea and coffee facilities in each room. Guests also have free use of the swimming pool at Best Western Europa (p190).

Hotel Kronio HOTEL €
(☑ 26240 22188; www.hotelkronio.gr; Tsoureka 1; s/d/tr incl breakfast €40/49/64; P ❄ @ 🛜) The helpful, multilingual owner, Panagiotis, is a bonus at this pleasant spot, which has 23 excellent-value bright and airy rooms.

Pension Posidon PENSION €
(☑ 26240 22567; www.pensionposidon.gr; Stefanopoulou 9; s/d/tr incl breakfast €35/40/45; ❄) A helpful couple runs this centrally located, cosy spot where rooms are simple but pleasant and have balconies. Snug roof terrace, too.

Best Western Europa
HOTEL €€

(☑ 26240 22650; www.hoteleuropa.gr; Drouva 1; s/d/tr incl breakfast €75/94/105; P❉@ⓢ⊠) This family-run franchise is popular with groups and families. Rooms have blond wood and mod cons; the larger rooms with balcony vistas are more luxurious. A bar, swimming pool, a lovely poolside taverna surrounded by roses and under the shade of olive trees, and excellent service seal the deal.

Arty Grand Hotel
HOTEL €€

(☑ 26240 26000; www.artygrandhotel.gr; d/tr/ste incl breakfast & dinner €125/150/155; P❉ⓢ⊠) Though its hilltop location, 1.5km from the ruins, means that the hotel is somewhat isolated, its spacious rooms are comfortable, the service is pleasant and the pool and spa are nice luxury touches. Though meals are included, the restaurant is nothing special. Popular with tour groups.

✖ Eating

Anesi
GREEK €

(☑ 26240 22644; cnr 13 Avgerinou & Spiliopoulou; mains €6.50-8; ☉ 7pm-midnight mid-May–mid-Sep) No-frills grills. And excellent ones at that. Run by a hard-working family, it's a fabulous budget option. They'll even deliver to your hotel (no charge). Also does hearty homemade dishes including *pastitsio* (a pasta-based baked dish) and stuffed tomatoes. We love the *kontosouvli* (spit-roasted pork).

★ The Garden Taverna
GREEK €€

(☑ 26240 22650; Best Western Europa; mains €9.50-15; ☉ 7-11pm May-Sep plus 1-3.30pm & 7-11pm Jun-Aug; ⓢ) Nestling under olive trees in a tranquil rose garden overlooking the valley below, this restaurant is the most original in Olympia. Alongside the excellent grilled meats you'll find the likes of pasta in vodka cream sauce with smoked salmon and dill. The service is prompt and attentive. Lunch is light bites only. A great spot to come for sunset drinks.

Aegean
GREEK €€

(☑ 26240 22540; G Doyma 4; mains €8-15; ☉ noon-11pm; ✐) One of a cluster of tavernas on the main square, Aegean distinguishes itself by its extensive array of vegetarian dishes served alongside Greek favourites. Only local produce is used. Don't miss the baklava, possibly the best we've had in Greece.

❶ Information

National Bank of Greece (Praxitelous Kondyli)

❶ Getting There & Away

Buses depart from the train station, in the middle of town one block east of the main street. There are services to Pyrgos (€2.30, 30 minutes, eight to 13 daily), with three handy Athens connections (€30.10, four hours), and to Tripoli (around €15, three hours). Note that for tickets to Tripoli, you should reserve your seat with **KTEL Pyrgos** (☑ 26210 20600; www.ktelileias.gr; Erithrou Stavrou 6, Pyrgos) one day prior to travel; hotels will call on your behalf.

Andritsena
Ανδρίτσαινα

POP 580

The birthplace of Panayotis Anagastopoulos, one of the leaders in the War of Independence, Andritsena sits on a hillside overlooking the valley of the Alfios River, 65km southeast of Pyrgos. Crumbling stone houses, some with rickety wooden balconies, flank the village's narrow cobbled streets and a stream bubbles its way through the central square, Plateia Agnostopoulou. (Keep an eye out for the fountain emerging from the trunk of a huge plane tree.) Andritsena is a handy springboard for visiting the magnificent Temple of Epicurean Apollo at Vasses, a World Heritage–listed site, located 14km south.

⊙ Sights

★ Temple of Epicurean Apollo at Vasses
HISTORIC SITE

(☑ 26260 22275; adult/concession €6/3; ☉ 8am-8pm) Situated 14km southwest of Andritsena, on a wild, isolated spot overlooking rugged mountains and hills, the World Heritage–listed Vasses with its Temple of Epicurean Apollo is one of Greece's most atmospheric archaeological sites. The striking, well-preserved temple is robbed of some of its splendour and immediate visual impact by the giant steel-girded tent that's been protecting it from the elements since 1987 (for restoration purposes), but it's magnificent all the same.

The temple was built in 420 BC by the people of nearby Figalia, who dedicated it to Apollo Epicurus (the Helper) for delivering them from the plague. Designed by Iktinos, the architect of the Parthenon, the temple combines Doric and Ionic columns and a single Corinthian column – the earliest example of this order.

The temple's most prominent decoration, a marble frieze depicting battles between Greeks and Amazons, and between Lapiths and Centaurs, was spirited away in 1814 by 'archaeologists' who procured it from Greece's Ottoman rulers and sold it to the British Museum, where it is currently displayed.

No public buses run to Vasses. A return taxi from Andritsena, including waiting time, costs around €40.

Nikolopoulos
Andritsena Library   LIBRARY, MUSEUM
(☑ 2626022242; www.andritsainalibrary.gr; ⊙ 8am-2pm Tue-Sat) FREE In 1838 Konstantinos Nikolopoulos, a composer, archaeologist and member of the Greek Resistance looking to liberate Greece from the Turks, donated 4000 rare books to his father's home town to establish a school. It was one of Europe's largest private book collections at the time. Displayed along with manuscripts from Greece's 1821 Independence movement is a cast of a frieze from the Temple of Epicurean Apollo at Vasses. Explanatory English video. Located behind Hotel Theoxenia.

🛏 Sleeping

Archontico Hotel   HOTEL €€
(☑ 26260 22401; www.archontiko-andritsenas.gr; d incl breakfast €65; P �🛜) Complete with terraces and artfully scattered amphorae, this fine historic building at the western end of the village offers snug rooms with exposed stone walls and mod cons.

Epikourios Apollon   HOTEL €€
(☑ 26260 22840; Plateia Agnostopoulou; s/d/tr incl breakfast €40/60/75; 🛜) This guesthouse-cum-hotel has simple but cheerful rooms overlooking the central square or the valley behind.

ℹ Getting There & Away

Buses run to Athens (€25.90, two hours, one daily) via Megalopoli, Tripoli and Corinth Isthmus. Buy tickets from the *kafeneio* (coffee house) near the tiny main square.

ACHAÏA   AXAÏA

The northern region of Achaïa comprises some high and skiable mountain country (reached via a historic rack-and-pinion rail-

way), a swathe of small coastal resorts (popular with Greeks), and a bustling port, Patra.

Achaïa owes its name to the Achaeans, an Indo-European branch of migrants who settled on mainland Greece and established the mighty Mycenaean civilisation. When the Dorians arrived, the Achaeans were pushed into this northwestern corner of the Peloponnese, displacing the original Ionians.

Legend has it that the Achaeans founded 12 cities, which later developed into the powerful Achaean Federation that survived up until Roman times. Principal among these cities were the ports of Patra and Egio (located on the coast of the Gulf of Corinth).

ℹ Getting There & Away

Formerly a very dangerous road known for its high accident rate, the Corinth–Patra motorway that spans the northern Peloponnese has been completely overhauled; the new and much-improved road was inaugurated in 2017. It provides excellent access across northern Achaïa. From the road, there are turn-offs to both Diakofto **train station** (☑ 26910 43206) (for the **rack-and-pinion train** (p196) to Kalavryta) and Kalavryta. Public buses are more reliable and frequent than trains (many trains use bus replacement services in any case).

Patra   Πάτρα
POP 168,000

Most travellers head to Patra for the ferry port only. But there's worse things you could do than spend a night here.

The largest city in the Peloponnese, Patra is named after King Patreas who ruled Achaïa around 1100 BC. Little is evident of this busy port's 3000 years of history, during which it was an important trade centre under the Mycenaeans and the Romans. Although there's a gritty element to the city, it has attractive squares and lively pedestrian streets, and bars and restaurants filled with the young and the trendy.

Before you depart by boat or via the Rio–Andirio suspension bridge, an engineering feat that links the city with western continental Greece, it's worth visiting Patra's wonderful castle and making the most of the diverse eating and nightlife scene, helped by the presence of Patra's 20,000 university students.

Patra

◉ Sights

★ Archaeological Museum of Patras
MUSEUM

(☏26136 16100; www.patrasmuseum.gr; Patras-Athens National Rd 38-40; adult/concession €6/3; ⊙8am-8pm) This fabulous museum, the country's second largest, should be shouting its existence from its space-age rooftop. Its exhibits comprise regional objects from prehistoric to Roman times arranged across three vast themed halls: Private Life, Public Life and Cemeteries. The mosaics, the best around, are simply extraordinary. There are barnacle-encrusted amphorae, duck-shaped vessels, coin hoards, a gold ring decorated with a tiny phallus, oil lamps featuring erotic scenes, Mycenaean bronze swords from warrior burials and four skulls with funereal wreaths intact.

Explanations are in English. The museum is 4km northeast of the centre.

Kastro
CASTLE

(⊙8.30am-5pm Tue-Sun, reduced hrs in winter) **FREE** Patra's castle stands on the site of the acropolis of ancient Patrai. The Romans were the first to build a fort here around AD 550, but the present structure is of Frankish origin, remodelled many times over the centuries by the Byzantines, Venetians and Turks. Set in an attractively maintained pencil-pine park, it is reached by climbing the 190-plus steps at the southeastern end of Agio Nikolaou. Great views of Zakynthos and Kefallonia are the reward.

Church of Agios Andreas
CHURCH

(Agiou Andreou) Seating 5500 people, this church is one of the largest in the Balkans. It houses religious icons and paintings, plus St Andreas' skull, along with part of the cross on which he was crucified.

✷ Festivals & Events

Patras Carnival
CARNIVAL

(www.carnivalpatras.gr; ⊙Feb/Mar) Patra's citizens party hard during the annual Patras Carnival. The program features a host of minor events leading up to a wild weekend of costume parades, colourful floats and celebrations in late February or early March. The event draws big crowds, so hotel reservations are essential if you want to stay overnight. Dates change annually, so check the website.

⊨ Sleeping

Hotels are surprisingly limited here and the best seem to be those catering to businesspeople. Prices double at Carnival time; book well in advance.

Pension Nicos
HOTEL €

(✆26106 23757; cnr Patreos 3 & Agiou Andreou 121; s/d/tr €25/30/40, without bathroom €22/25/35; ✳🛜) One of the few good budget options, this 1960s-style home on a busy street has flaking shutters on the outside, but inside Nicos runs a tight ship with clean rooms on several floors, plus a roof terrace.

★City Loft Boutique Hotel
APARTMENT €€

(✆26102 23552; www.cityloft.gr; Valtetsiou 6; 1-/2-/3-person apt incl breakfast €80/115/135; 🅿✳🛜) Nine sleek and stylish apartments in white or black, on a quiet side street several blocks north of the main square, are slightly incongruous compared with the surrounding grittiness. Perks include high-quality bed linens, king-sized beds with orthopaedic mattresses, balconies and a small, attractive garden.

Castello City Hotel
BUSINESS HOTEL €€

(✆26102 25000; www.castellocityhotel.gr; cnr Agios Andreou 118 & Filopoimenos 3; s/d/tr incl breakfast €56/67/83; ✳🛜) The 17 rooms in this central business-style hotel are compact, but they are ultra-modern and decked out in lots of taupes and greys. As such, it lacks any real Greek 'person-ality', but it's a drink's spit from the bars on the main drags and is convenient to everything. Has cable TV with programs in lots of languages.

There's no parking but it's only a block back from the parking on the nearby port.

Maison Grecque
BOUTIQUE HOTEL €€

(✆26102 41212; www.mghotels.gr; 25 Martiou 116; s/d/ste incl breakfast €60/85/180; ✳🛜) This smart boutique spot has a touch of 'sleek Greek' pretension. Each room is decked out uniquely (with an original ceil-ing fresco or two thrown in) – think dark hues with metallic touches. A couple of the rooms have very small windows. The rest, however, are sophisticated and smart. It's a five-minute walk from the pedestrianised centre.

✗ Eating & Drinking

Trendy cafes, bars and restaurants line the pedestrianised Riga Fereou, Patanas-sis, Agiou Nikolaou and surrounding alleys. Cheap student eateries are along Gerokostopoulou.

Labyrinthos
GREEK €

(✆26102 26436; Poukevil 44; mains €6.50-11; ⏰noon-5.30pm & 8.30pm-1am Mon-Sat Sep-Jun; 🛜🍴) Inside the rough stone walls of this 80-year-old family restaurant (one of the oldest in Patra), you can expect classics such as *briam* (oven-baked vegetable casserole), dolmadhes and beef casserole in *tentoura* (Patras' traditional sauce), as well as roasted lamb sweetbreads and intestines for the adventurous epicurean. Plus plenty of hos-pitality; the owners want the best for their guests.

Terra Bistro
INTERNATIONAL €€

(✆26103 13000; cnr Riga Feraou & Kanari; mains €9-18; ⏰8am-midnight Mon-Sat) The floors – modern, Spanish tiles – are not the only striking things here. This modern, minimalist spot has excellent pita breads with toppings (€7 to €10) plus a range of international dishes including salmon with couscous and Black Angus steaks. It draws in the locals in cooler weather, too, for its sun-filled front, unique for a (usually dark) city building.

Salumeria
FUSION €€

(✆2610 225 930; Pantanassis 27; mains €9-14; ⏰1pm-1am, closed Sun mid-Jun–Aug; 🛜🍴) On a pedestrian street, this is one of many chi-chi bistros on the strip. It describes itself as modern Greek with an Italian influence, serving the likes of risotto with roasted pear and chicken with honey and sesame. In the evenings it's a popular wine bar.

Bodegas Wine Bar
WINE BAR

(✆26102 21113; Riga Feraou 147; ⏰noon-1am) Whether you're nursing a margarita or a glass of wine from over 300 Greek vintages, this stylish bar is a spot worth lingering. Sal-ads come in an enormous bowl. It's a popu-lar 'it' spot to be seen; expect to see lots of business suits, too. Opens for coffee at 7am.

ℹ Information

General University Hospital Patras (✆26136 03000; www.pgnp.gr; Rio; ⏰24hr) Patras' public hospital.

National Bank of Greece (Plateia Trion Syma-hon; ⏰8am-2pm Mon-Fri) Opposite the train station.

Olympion S.A (✆26104 64100; www. olympion-sa.gr/olympionpatras; Volou; ⏰24hr). A private clinic.

Police (✆2610 695000; Ermou 95)

Post Office (cnr Zaïmi & Mezonos; ⏰7.30am-8:30pm Mon-Fri)

❶ Getting There & Away

BOAT

The passenger port is 1km south of town. Ferry offices are located at the port, and a few agencies that sell ferry tickets are sprinkled along Othonos Amalias and Iroön Polytehniou. Ferry schedules and prices change seasonally; call ahead. Note that there are no ferries directly to Corfu from Patra; ferries to Corfu depart from Igoumenitsa only.

Domestic

Kyllini, 76km southwest of Patra, is the departure point for domestic ferry services to Kefallonia and Zakynthos. But check: combinations change like the tides. At the time of writing, ferries to Ithaki departed from Astakos in Sterea Ellada.

Ionian Group (☑ 26102 40000; www.ionian group.com/en) has services from Kyllini to Sami on Kefallonia (per person/car €9.90/38.70, 1¼ hours, four daily). **Kefalonian Lines** (https:// kefalonianlines.com) heads to Poros on Kefallonia (per person/car €9.50/39.20, three to four daily) and Zakynthos (per person/car €8.40/27.50, three to four daily).

International

Patra is Greece's main port for ferry services to Italy, with departures to Ancona, Bari and Venice. Note that, while some ferries may stop at Igoumenitsa and Corfu en route, you cannot disembark.

The **ANEK/Superfast Ferries** (☑ 21041 97400; www.anek.gr; cnr Othonos Amalias & Aratou) conglomeration runs trips to Ancona (from €67, 21 to 24 hours), Bari (from €84, 15½ hours) and Venice (from €95, 31 hours), while **Minoan Lines** (☑ 26104 26000; www.minoan. gr/en) heads to Ancona (from €89, 21 hours) and Venice (from €67, 31 hours).

Prices given here are for deck seats; rates are higher for airline seats and cabins. Check up-to-date schedules on websites.

BUS

The **KTEL Achaia bus station** (☑ 26106 23886; www.ktelachaias.gr; Othonos Amalias 4) has services to the following places:
Athens (€20.70, three hours, every 30 minutes) and Corinth Isthmus (€14, 1½ hours)
Ioannina (€25.30, 4½ hours, two daily)
Kalamata (€25, four hours, two daily)
Kalavryta (€8.60, two hours, two to four daily)
Pyrgos (€10.60, two hours, hourly)
Thessaloniki (€48.50, seven hours, two to three daily)

Buses link the KTEL Achaia bus station in Patra with Terminal A (aka Kifissos) in Athens,

from where there are frequent buses to/from the international airport.

The **KTEL Kefallonia bus station** (☑ 26102 74938; www.ktelkefalonias.gr; Othonos Amalias 58) has services to the Ionian islands of Lefkada (€17.60, three hours, twice weekly) and Kefallonia (€22.10, three daily). To reaxh Argostoli, travel by bus from KTEL Kefallonia bus station to the port of Kyllini, from where you catch a ferry to Poros (1½ hours) and continue again by road to Argostoli (one hour). Buses also depart KTEL Kefallonia bus station to Amfissa for Delphi (€15, three hours, one daily) and Tripoli (€19.80, one daily).

The **KTEL Zakynthos bus station** (☑ 26102 20993; www.ktel-zakynthos.gr; Othonos Amalias 84) has services to Zakynthos, via the port of Kyllini (including ferry €18, 3½ hours, three daily).

TRAIN

Trains depart from the centrally located **Patra train station** (☑ 26102 74180; www.trainose.gr; ☺ 6am-10pm). There are 10 trains a day to Athens (€17). At the time of writing, a replacement bus goes as far as Kiato, from where you take the *proastiako*, Athens' local train service. On arrival in Athens you can use your *proastiako* ticket for 1½ hours on the metro (validate it first).

Kalavryta   Καλάβρυτα

POP 1800

Perched 756m above sea level, Kalavryta is a delightful little town with fresh mountain air, gushing springs and a square that nestles under giant plane trees. Though in existence for centuries, the present-day town came into being on the ruins of ancient Kinaitha in the mid-19th century. The town is a popular ski-season destination among Athenians, who also come for weekend getaways year-round. In spring and summer, visitors from abroad come here to hike and visit the nearby monasteries.

◉ Sights

★**Museum of the Kalavryta Holocaust**   MUSEUM
(☑ 26920 23646; www.dmko.gr; 1-5 Syngrou; €3; ☺ 9am-4pm Tue-Sun) The country's only Holocaust museum, this is a powerful tribute to the residents of Kalavryta who perished in the 13 December 1943 slaughter perpetrated by the Nazis. It's a dignified, understated, yet extremely evocative account of the struggle between the occupying forces and partisan fighters in the area, and the events running up to the massacre – an atrocity reported to

be partly put in motion by the partisans' execution of a group of German prisoners.

Located inside the rebuilt old schoolhouse that was set on fire with women, children and the elderly inside, the museum depicts the history of 19th- and 20th-century Kalavryta, the advent of the rack-and-pinion railway and the region's suffering during WWII through evocative photographs and personal effects.

ELAS, the Greek resistance movement, was very active in the Kalavryta region during WWII. On 17 October 1943 partisans captured a German battalion. Negotiations stalled when the Nazis launched 'Operation Kalavryta', designed to crush the resistance. The partisans killed the German prisoners and in retaliation, on 13 December 1943, the Nazis herded almost 500 men and boys over the age of 13 to the nearby Kappi Ridge and gunned them down. The women and children who managed to break out of the burning schoolhouse were left with the task of gathering and burying the dead, as commemorated by the statues behind the schoolhouse.

Whatever you do, don't pass by the videos on continuous loop dotted throughout the exhibition. These are the accounts of surviving townspeople who escaped death, some of whom were children at the time. The walls covered with pictures of the dead Kalavryta villagers and the names of the dead is an especially stark memorial.

Martyrs' Monument　　　MONUMENT
A huge white cross on a cypress-covered hillside just east of town marks the site where the Nazis machine-gunned almost 500 men and boys from Kalavryta on 13 December 1943. Only 13 survived the massacre. Beneath this imposing monument is a poignant little shrine to the victims. It's signposted off Konstantinou.

🛏 Sleeping

While ski lodges abound on the outskirts, good hotel options are in the village. Peak period is the ski season (December to April), when reservations are essential. Prices are slashed on weekdays. Alternatively, look inside the kiosk signed 'Hotel i' in front of the train station where accommodation options are listed; those with vacancies are lit up. Budget options are in the streets behind the railway station. Also check www.kalavrita-hotels.gr.

> ### ⓘ KALAVRYTA CITYPASS
> For bargain sightseeing in and around Kalavryta, the Kalavryta CityPass discount card (www.trainose.gr) covers a return trip on the Diakofto–Kalavryta railway and entrance to the Cave of the Lakes, the Kalavryta Holocaust Museum, and either Kalavryta Ski Centre or the Tetramythos Winery, saving you 40% overall. The card costs €24.80, is valid for a month and can be purchased at Kalavryta, Diakofto and Patra train stations.

Tsovolos Apartments　　　PENSION €
(☑26920 22292; Kosta Fassou 14; d/tr/apt incl breakfast €30/45/55; 🖥) Towards the west end of town, near the EKO petrol station, these rooms are basic but offer good value (contrary to their name, they're not apartments per se). It's a bit of a 'hey-it's-a-bed' experience, but fine if your budget is stretched.

⭐**Archontiko Zafeiropoulou**　APARTMENT €€
(☑26920 24500; www.archontiko.gr; Striftompala; d/tr/ste incl breakfast €65/95/120; P🖥) All options are essentially spacious, spotless studios and apartments, all with kitchenettes. The real treasure here is the friendly South African–Greek owner, George, who has an outstanding knowledge of the town and surrounding attractions, and useful maps to hand. The excellent breakfast includes local sheep's milk yoghurt, honey, preserves and cheeses.

Hotel Filoxenia　　　HOTEL €€
(☑26920 22422; www.hotelfiloxenia.gr; Ethnikis Andistasis 10; d/tr incl breakfast €70/120; P🅰🖥) Kind of like an old-fashioned ski lodge with its handsome stone exterior, the long-running Filoxenia has had a recent modern spruce-up. Its 28 rooms are individually decorated with bright, fresh colours and contemporary fabrics. A definite plus is that it's open all year and prices are significantly cheaper on weekdays. It offers an expansive buffet breakfast.

Rates include a sauna, hammam or hydromassage session per day.

Hotel Kynaitha　　　HOTEL €€
(☑26920 22609; www.kynaitha.com; Ethnikis Andistasis 11; d/tr/ste incl breakfast €100/120/150; P🖥) Modern and comfortable with spacious and attractively furnished

RIDING THE MOUNTAIN RAILS

One of the unmissable journeys to make in the Peloponnese is aboard the tiny **Diakofto–Kalavryta Railway** (☑ OSE customer information 14511; www.odontotos.com; one way/return €9.50/19) running along the vintage rack-and-pinion railway between Diakofto and Kalavryta. It takes travellers on a remarkably scenic ride through the dramatic **Vouraïkos Gorge**, its reddish cliffs seemingly closing in on the train. The line switches back and forth under a leafy canopy of plane trees, clinging to a narrow ledge overhanging the rushing rapids below, and passing through seven curving tunnels along the way.

To reach Kalavryta, the train climbs over 700m in 22.5km, using a rack-and-pinion (cog) system for traction on the steep sections, effectively clamping itself to the notched girder you can see running between the rails. Built by an Italian company between 1889 and 1895, the railway was a remarkable feat of engineering for its time, with only a handful of equivalents around the world (most notably in the Swiss Alps). Between 2007 and 2009 the entire rails and cog sections were completely replaced, and four new modern trains were constructed to replace the former carriages. The original steam engines that first plied the route can still be seen outside Diakofto and Kalavryta stations.

The journey takes just over an hour, and stops en route at the picturesque hamlet of Zahlorou and two other tiny stations on demand, in case you want to be dropped off at one and walk to another. The railway makes an even more scenic hike, as you have more time to appreciate your surroundings.

Hiking the 22km down from Kalavryta to Diakofto takes around five hours; train drivers are used to hikers along the tracks and give them plenty of warning. Take a torch for the tunnels.

At the time of writing there were three departures on weekdays and five on weekends in each direction; confirm times at respective train stations.

Kalavryta is linked by regular buses to Athens and Patra. To get to Diakofto, catch the only 'working' train line, Corinth–Patra, with OSE replacement buses running in place of trains along the Diakofto–Kiato section. On leaving Diakofto, you can catch the same replacement bus service west to Patra or, to head east, take this service to Kiato, from where you catch the *proastiako* train (Athens suburban train line), either to Corinth or as far as Athens airport.

rooms. Think exposed stone walls, gleaming white bathrooms and posh toiletries. Low-season prices are nearly half those listed here.

✗ Eating

Gri Gri Café   SWEETS €
(25 Martiou; snacks €2-4; ⊙ 8am-8pm) This good family-run spot is renowned for its local specialities and sweet and savoury homemade snacks, such as cheese pie, baklava and tasty *crèma* (sweet, set custard).

To Spitikou   TAVERNA €€
(☑ 26920 24260; Vasileos Constantinou; mains €8-15; ⊙ 10am-late; 🛜 🅿) This cosy place with a ski-lodge feel serves up great-quality traditional taverna meals and fabulous mezedhes. Expect the likes of veal with tomato sauce, chicken baked with vegetables, spinach and feta soufflé and scrummy tzatziki. Mihaela is a delightful, multilingual host.

ℹ Information

The train station is on the northern edge of town, opposite the Holocaust museum. To the right of the museum is Syngrou/25 Martiou, a pedestrian precinct. To the left of the museum is Konstantinou.

The central square, Plateia Kalavrytou, is two blocks up from the train station.

There is no formal year-round tourist office.
National Bank of Greece (25 Martiou) Just before Plateia Kalavrytou.

Post Office (⊙ 7.30am-2pm Mon-Fri) Behind Plateia Kalavrytou.

ℹ Getting There & Away

The rack-and-pinion train to/from Diakofto via Zahlorou runs to a changing timetable.

There are buses to Patra (€8.60, two hours, three to four daily on weekdays, two on weekends) and Athens (€18.40, three hours, two Monday to Saturday, one Sunday). The **bus** station (☎ 26920 22224) is 200m before the entrance to town (from the Diakofto approach road), beside the Shell petrol station.

Kalavryta's **taxi rank** (☎ 26920 22127) is in front of the train station.

Most of the attractions are out of town, so it's very handy to have your own transport.

Around Kalavryta

Kalavryta and its surrounding mountains feature several varied and interesting sites. While some are just outside the town, others are further afield but doable in a car.

◎ Sights & Activities

★ Cave of the Lakes   CAVE

(☎ 26920 31588; www.kastriacave.gr; adult/ concession €9/4.50; ☉ 9am-4.30pm, to 5.30pm summer) The remarkable Cave of the Lakes lies 16.5km south of Kalavryta near the village of Kastria. A 500m boardwalk snakes its way through the cave, through the vast entrance chamber (home to five species of bats) past spectacular cauliflower-like rock formations, and over the deep, crystal-clear subterranean pools – the 13 stone basins formed by mineral deposits over the millennia. The most impressive formations are in the final chamber, where delicate, ribboning curtains cascade down the wall.

The cave features in Greek mythology and is mentioned in the writings of the ancient traveller Pausanias, but its whereabouts remained unknown in modern times until 1964 when locals investigated, having noticed water pouring from the roof of a smaller cave. They discovered a large bat-filled cavern at the start of a 2km-long cave carved out by a subterranean river.

Access is by guided half-hour tour (in Greek) only. Foreign visitors are provided with a booklet in English; the sight at each designated stop along the boardwalk corresponds to the letter in the booklet.

A taxi from Kalavryta costs around €45 return (the taxi will wait for you for about one hour). There's a good taverna right next to the cave entrance.

Moni Mega Spileo   MONASTERY

(Monastery of the Great Cavern; ☎ 26920 23130; ☉ 8am-1pm & 2pm-sunset) FREE Moni Mega Spileo is believed to be one of the oldest monasteries in Greece (though the current building dates from the 20th century). The original monastery was destroyed in 1943 when Nazis executed all the monks. Its prized relic is the miraculous icon of the Virgin Mary, said to have been painted by St Luke and supposedly discovered in the nearby cavern by St Theodore and St Simeon in AD 362 (though it most likely dates to around AD 1000). it's popular with pilgrims; strict dress code.

Many people, especially those on the train, hike the pretty, if steep, 3km walk from Zahlorou, the village stop on the Diakofto–Kalavryta railway. You can also arrive by car (there's parking). A taxi from Kalavryta costs around €30 (including a 30-minute wait time).

Moni Agias Lavras   MONASTERY

(☎ 26920 22363; ☉ 10am-1pm & 4-5pm) FREE The original 10th-century monastery that stood here was burnt down by the Nazis, and its monks killed. The chapel of the new monastery is where Greece's War of Independence was allegedly launched; the banner standard from the war is displayed alongside monastic memorabilia. The monastery is around 5km southwest of Kalavryta. A taxi from Kalavryta costs around €20 return. Call ahead for winter hours.

Ski Centre   SKIING

(☎ 26920 24451; www.kalavrita-ski.gr; half/full day €18/25; ☉ 9am-4pm Dec-Apr) Head 14km east of Kalavryta on Mt Helmos (2355m) to the Ski Centre (elevation 1700m to 2340m), which has 12 runs and seven lifts (two chairlifts). There's no overnight accommodation but it rents skis and snowboard equipment (€20 for boots and skis or a snowboard). The season lasts from December to April, snow permitting. A taxi costs around €45 return.

Tetramythos Winery   WINE

(☎ 26910 97500; www.tetramythoswines.com; ☉ 9am-4pm) Located in Ano Diakofto village (not to be confused with Diakofto town), 5km along the road from Diakofto to Kalavryta, this winery, one of Greece's most prolific, is run by two local brothers who take a lot of pride in their *agiorgitiko*, cabernet sauvignon, *malagousia* and other varietals. There are tours and free wine-tasting sessions but the staff's English is limited.

Central Greece

Best Places to Eat

➜ Taverna Vakhos (p207)

➜ Taverna To Paramithi (p241)

➜ Taverna Angelika (p230)

➜ Taverna Niki (p227)

➜ Brighton Food & Wine (p221)

➜ Kritsa Hotel Restaurant (p224)

Best Places to Stay

➜ Lost Unicorn Hotel & Restaurant (p230)

➜ Old Silk Store (p229)

➜ Doupiani House (p243)

➜ Alsos House (p240)

➜ Hotel Alexakis (p218)

➜ Iliovolo Guesthouse (p232)

Why Go?

Delphi – Ancient Greece's centre or 'navel' of the earth – is these days among Greece's most visited places for its archaeological site, ancient footpaths and vistas of the Corinthian Gulf. Delphi is rivalled in popularity only by Meteora, the breathtaking outcrops of rocky towers topped by teetering monasteries (and rock climbers).

The central Greece (κεντρική Ελλάδα) region also holds many underrated surprises. Alpine meadows and valleys cover the Evritania mountain range, making it perfect for breezy summer hikes and winter skiing. And it doesn't get much better than the beautiful Pelion Peninsula, home to Jason and the Argonauts, and criss-crossed with historic cobblestone paths linking lush mountain hamlets with coves and beaches that rival the best islands.

And speaking of 'good, better, best'... The region's good-natured people serve up hospitality, superb experiences and great cuisine. There's no better place to navel-gaze.

When to Go
Delphi

Apr & May Wild chamomile and red poppies mingle in alpine meadows.

Sep Warmer seas, sunny weather and fewer crowds.

Orthodox Easter Villages follow traditional customs, with parades, dancing and copious food.

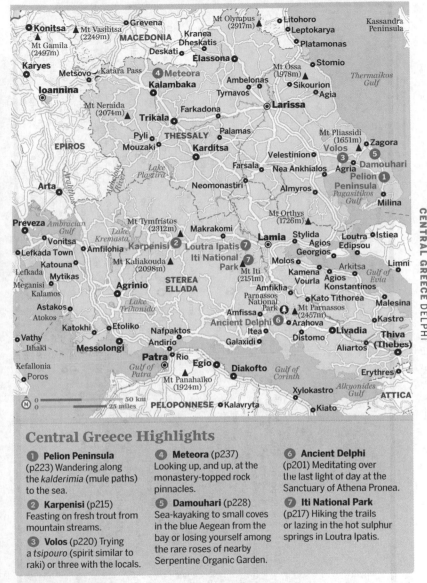

Central Greece Highlights

1 Pelion Peninsula
(p223) Wandering along
the *kalderimia* (mule paths)
to the sea.

2 Karpenisi (p215)
Feasting on fresh trout from
mountain streams.

3 Volos (p220) Trying
a *tsipouro* (spirit similar to
raki) or three with the locals.

4 Meteora (p237)
Looking up, and up, at the
monastery-topped rock
pinnacles.

5 Damouhari (p228)
Sea-kayaking to small coves
in the blue Aegean from the
bay or losing yourself among
the rare roses of nearby
Serpentine Organic Garden.

6 Ancient Delphi
(p201) Meditating over
the last light of day at the
Sanctuary of Athena Pronea.

7 Iti National Park
(p217) Hiking the trails
or lazing in the hot sulphur
springs in Loutra Ipatis.

DELPHI & STEREA ELLADA

Greek mythology and history mingle in the
rugged landscape of Sterea Ellada. On the
slopes of Mt Parnassos is the famous site of
Ancient Delphi. The land stretches east to
Attica, where legendary King Oedipus met his
fate, and west to Messolongi, where bard Lord
Byron died of fever during the Greek War of
Independence. The region acquired its name,
meaning 'Mainland Greece', in 1827, as part of
the newly formed nation.

Delphi   Δελφοί

22650 / POP 2370

If the Ancient Greeks hadn't chosen Delphi
(from *delphis,* womb) as their navel of the
earth and built the Sanctuary of Apollo here,

Sterea Ellada

Map scale: 50 km / 25 miles

EPIROS

Ioannina (45km)
Filippiada
Parga (45km)
Preveza
Aktion
Lefkada Town
Limni Voulikarriá
Lefkada
Nydri
Meganisi
Kalamos
Atokos
Vathy
Ithaki
Kefallonia (8km)
Poros
Kefallonia

Arta
Vonitsa
Monastirakion
Paleros
Mytikas
Astakos
Oxia
Cape Araxos

Ambracian Gulf
Lake Amvrakia
Lake Ozeros

DYTIKI ELLADA
Amfilohia
Katouna
Fitiai
Stratos
Agrinio
Lake Lisimahia
Etoliko
Matarariga
Messolongi
Klisova Lagoon
Kato Achaia
Lapas
Vardha

ETOLO AKARNANIA
Lake Trihonida
Thermo
K Makrinou
Nafpaktos
Andirio
Rio
Gulf of Patra
Paralia
Tourlida

Thessaloniki (165km)
Loutraki (Glossa Port)
Skopelos
Skiathos
Skiathos Town
Skyros

Mt Pelion (1455m)
Pelion Peninsula
Agria
Milina
Palio Trikeri (Nisos)
Sourpi
Volos
Nea Ankhialos
Almyros

Pagasitikos Gulf
Larissa (45km)

THESSALY
Sofades
Anavra
Neomonastiri
Farsala
Paleofarsalos

Trikala (30km);
Kalambaka (50km)
Agrafa
Fourna
Lake Plastira
Lake Kremasta
Achelóos River

Karpenisi
Koryshades
Fidakia
Gavros
Megalo Horio
Mikro Horio
Mt Kaliakouda
Prousos
Moni Panagias Proussiotissas
Mt Velouchi (2315m)
Tymfristos

Makrakomi
Sperkhias
Krikello
Ano Hora
Thermo

Mt Orthys (1726m)
Stylida
Glyfa

Agios Georgios
Molos
Kamena Vourla
Agios Konstantinos

Lamia
Loutra
Ipatis
Ipati
Mt Iti (2151m)
Iti National Park
Pavliani

Thermopylae

Amfiklia
Ancient Delphi
Mt Parnassos (2457m)
Parnassos National Park
Delphi
Kirra
Itea
Galaxidi
Agios Nikolaos
Amfissa
Lidhorikion
Monastiraki
Trizonia
Kamares
Spilia

PELOPONNESE
Egio
Diakofto
Zahlorou
Kalavryta
Aigeria
Xylokastro

Gulf of Corinth

Skiathos
Strofylia
Psahna
Nea Artaki
Halkida
Eretria
Skala Oropou

Evia
Limni
Loutra Edipsou
Ilstiea
Ilsitea

Gulf of Evia
Skeathos Strait

Theologos
Malesina
Martinon
Cape Ghaidhoros
Atalandi
Livanatai
Kato Tithorea
Davlia
Orhomenos
Livadia
Distomo
Arahova
Dhestina
Moni Osiou Loukas
Kyriaki
Domvraina
Saranti
Melissohori
Kaparelli

Mt Kythairon
Plataea
Porto Germeno
Alepohori
Vayia
Yeoriyos
Allartos
Thiva (Thebes)
Neohoraki
Pyli
Erythres
Elefsina (Eleusis)

Parilimni Limni
Lake Iliki
Kifissos River
Maliakos Gulf

ATTICA
Inoi
Kalithea
Klidi
Skourta
Mt Parnitha (1413m)
Aharnes

Alkyonides Gulf
Ionian Sea

E75 E65 E951 E962 E55

someone else would have thought of a good reason to make this eagle's nest of a village a go-to attraction. Its cliffside location is spectacular and, despite its commercialism and the constant passage of tour buses through the modern village, it still has a special feel. Ancient Delphi (and the adjoining village of Delphi) is 178km northwest of Athens.

History

Delphi reached its height between the 6th and 4th centuries BC, when multitudes of pilgrims came to the sanctuary to consult the oracle (p205).

Delphi was protected by the Amphictyonic League, a federation of 12 tribal states (that unified most of southern Greece), which took control of the sanctuary following the First Sacred War (595–586 BC), making Delphi an autonomous state that enjoyed great prosperity from numerous benefactors, including the kings of Lydia and Egypt, and Hadrian.

The influence of the oracle had a major impact on political and intellectual life, determining – directly or otherwise through the prophecies – such decisions as the establishment of colonies and wars.

The sanctuary survived fire (548 BC) and earthquake (373 BC) and in the 3rd century BC it was conquered by the Aetolians, and then by the Romans in 191 BC. Although the Roman Sulla plundered the sanctuary in 86 BC, other emperors, fascinated by its reputation, kept the rituals at Delphi alive well into the 2nd century AD, when the oracle's influence began to dwindle. The sanctuary was finally abolished by the Byzantine emperor Theodosius in the late 4th century AD. By the 7th century a new village, Kastri, had appeared over the ancient site. Much of what is known about Delphi today comes from the detailed travel journals of 2nd-century-AD Athenian geographer Pausanius.

◎ Sights

★ **Ancient Delphi**   ARCHAEOLOGICAL SITE
(☎22650 82312; http://ancient-greece.org/history/delphi.html; combined ticket for site & museum adult/student/child, €12/6/free; ⊙8am-8pm Apr-Oct, to 3pm Nov-Mar) Of all the archaeological sites in Greece, Ancient Delphi is the one with the most potent spirit of place. Built on Mt Parnassos, overlooking the Gulf of Corinth and extending into a valley of olive trees, this World Heritage Site's allure lies both in its setting and its inspiring ruins.

Check ahead for hours as these are subject to change. In summer, visit the archaeological site early to avoid the crowds and the heat. But if you go in the afternoon, arrive at least half an hour before closing to allow time to walk around and not be ushered out by staff. The combined ticket allows entry to the Delphi Archaeological Museum (p204).

➡ **Sanctuary of Apollo**
The Sanctuary of Apollo is considered the heart of the Delphic oracle. From the main entrance, the Sacred Way gradually winds up to the Doric Temple of Apollo. In ancient times the Sacred Way was lined with treasuries and statues given by grateful city-states – Athens, Sparta, Marathon, Siphnos and Thiva (Thebes) etc – not only as thanks to Apollo, but as a kind of PR machine to show their wealth and might.

Entering the site, you pass several stone bases. The first, on your right, is the pedestal that held the **statue of the Bull of Kerkyra** (Corfu). Just beyond it, on the left, are the remains of the **Spartan Victory Monument** (a votive, or offering, to the admiral Lysander). The next two semicircular structures on either side of the Sacred Way were erected by the Argives (people of Argos). To their right stood the **Kings of Argos Monument**. Further on sits the **Omphalos**, the navel of the Ancient Greek world; the museum houses a second omphalos.

To the northeast of the reconstructed **Athenian Treasury** is a portion of the column which supported the **Sphinx of Naxos**, on view in the museum. Near it, find the **Rock of the Sibyl**, where Delphi's earliest sibyl made her predictions. A few steps away are three columns from the **Stoa of the Athenians**, behind which is the remarkable **Polygonal Wall**, a retaining wall supporting the terrace of the second Temple of Apollo (548 BC).

The 4th-century-BC **Temple of Apollo** dominated the entire sanctuary with a statue of Apollo and a hearth where an eternal flame burned. It was here that the Pythia, the mouthpiece of Apollo, delivered her pronouncements. On the temple vestibule were inscriptions from Greek philosophers, such as 'Know Thyself' and 'Nothing in Excess', known as the Delphic Maxims, and mentioned by Socrates in Plato's *Protagoras*.

Above the temple is the well-preserved 4th-century-BC **theatre**, which was restored by Pergamene king Loukumenes II in the 2nd century BC (160–155 BC), yielding magnificent views from the top row. Plays were

Ancient Delphi

A PILGRIM'S WALKING TOUR

The pretty, hillside-strewn ruins of Delphi were in use for more than 1200 years (8th century BC to 4th century AD), but the period from the 6th to the 4th century BC was particularly active. Visitors can still walk in the footsteps of past pilgrims and, with a bit of imagination, re-create the experience of this ancient place.

The sanctuary was adorned with many buildings and dedications to Apollo erected by Greek city-states. Worshippers purified themselves in the Castalian Spring (now closed to the public), paid a *pelanos* (tribute) and, if they hadn't brought one with them, purchased a votive offering from ❶ **The Roman Market**. Then they wandered up the ❷ **Sacred Way** towards the Temple of Apollo.

En route they passed thousands of dedications, including templelike buildings (treasuries), statues and sculptures. Treasuries, including the ❸ **Athenian Treasury**, were constructed by victorious city-states and filled with the spoils of war. The nearby ❹ **omphalos** (navel stone), a symbol of the centre of the earth, was left by archaeologists where it was found.

Next, visitors would pass the ❺ **Rock of the Sibyl** before arriving at the Stoa of the Athenians, behind which is an extraordinary ❻ **polygonal wall**. Finally, they arrived at the ❼ **Temple of Apollo** in the centre of the sanctuary, where consultations with the oracle took place and the chants of the Pythia (priestess of Apollo) were interpreted by the priests of Apollo. The ❽ **theatre** behind the temple held drama, music and poetry competitions.

TOP TIPS

➡ Visit in the morning or late afternoon to beat the heat and crowds.

➡ Allow time to visit the stadium, which is located further uphill.

➡ Wear comfortable shoes and a hat, and bring drinking water.

➡ Opening hours are subject to change, so check ahead.

➡ Don't miss the Delphi Museum, which helps to contextualise the site.

Athenian Treasury

The impressive Athenian Treasury is one of many important treasury buildings here. Built to commemorate the Athenians' victory against the Persians at the battle of Marathon in 490 BC, it was reconstructed in the early 1900s.

Omphalos

Delphi was considered the *omphalos* (navel) of the world. There was also an omphalos in the *adyton* (temple chamber) where the Pythia pronounced her oracles.

Siphnian Treasury

The Bouleuterion

The Sacred Way

The Sacred Way (so-named in modern times by archaeologists) leads to the Temple of Apollo. It was lined with thousands of monuments, statues and treasuries that commemorated victories (usually in war, sometimes the Pythian Games).

To Delphi Museum

Temple of Apollo

The most sacred building in the sanctuary, this is the third temple constructed on this site (4th century BC). A large ramp leads to its interior, from where the Pythia delivered her pronouncements.

Theatre

The Pythian Games, held in Delphi every four years, were not just about athletics – they also included music and drama contests (Apollo is the god of music). The original theatre was built in the 4th century BC; the current one dates fom the 1st century BC and could seat 5000 spectators.

To Stadium

Acanthus Column of Dancers

Sphinx of the Naxians

King of Argos Monument

Votive Offering of Lacedaemon

Stoa of the Athenians

Bull of Kerkyra

To Castalian Spring and Sanctuary of Athena Pronea

Polygonal Wall

This extraordinary retaining wall comprises interlocking polygonal stones. It features around 800 inscriptions that relate to the emancipation of slaves.

The Roman Market (Agora)

Pilgrims could buy small votives and offerings here. Wealthier and more powerful visitors, however, brought statues and valuable items from afar. The remains of many of these are in the Delphi Museum.

Rock of the Sibyl

Legend has it that this marks the spot where the first sibyl (an elderly prophetess, not to be confused with the Pythia) stood and pronounced Delphi's first oracle.

KRECHET/GETTY IMAGES ©

SANTI RODRIGUEZ/SHUTTERSTOCK ©

CONSTANTINOS ILIOPOULOS/SHUTTERSTOCK ©

performed here during the Pythian Festival, held, like the Olympic Games, every four years. From the theatre the path continues to the **stadium**, the best preserved in all of Greece. Unfortunately, stadium access is currently limited because of possible rockslides. A highlight of the roughly 200m track used by the sprinters are the etched-in-stone starting blocks at the eastern end.

The archaeological site's newest addition (2015), is a precise replica of the **Serpentine Column**, aka the Tripod of the Plataeans, located immediately to the right of the Temple of Apollo, as you face north. The original bronze column was plucked by Constantine the Great in AD 324, and today resides at the Hippodrome of Constantinople, now modern İstanbul. It was built to commemorate the Greeks who fought and defeated the Persian Empire at the Battle of Plataea (479 BC).

From the Sanctuary of Apollo, a paved path towards Arahova runs parallel to the main road and leads to the **Castalian Spring** on the left, where pilgrims cleansed themselves before consulting the oracle.

➡ Sanctuary of Athena Pronea

The Sanctuary of Athena Pronea is the site of the 4th-century-BC *tholos* (rotunda). This much-photographed spot is often wrongly interpreted by tourists as the place the Pythia (priestess of Apollo) was located. Pilgrims usually began their visit here, before proceeding to the Temple of Apollo. The graceful circular structure comprised 20 columns on a three-stepped podium; three of its columns were re-erected in the 1940s. The white portions of each column are the original marble; the darker portions are new material. Parts of the Tholos are on display in the museum (room 10).

To its west, the foundations of the **Temple of Athena Pronea** are all that remain of a rectangular structure that was heavily damaged by the same rockslides and earthquake that levelled much of the *tholos*.

★ Delphi Archaeological Museum   MUSEUM

(🖉 22650 82313; www.culture.gr; combined ticket for site & museum adult/student/child €12/6/free; ⊘8am-8pm summer, to 2.45pm winter) From around the 8th century BC, Ancient Delphi managed to amass a considerable treasure trove, much of it reflected in its magnificent museum. Opinions vary about whether to visit the museum or the site first, where the sense of place is unmistakably powerful. On the other hand, the museum helps construct

(or complete) an image of what the site must have looked like with its wealthy buildings, statues and other valuable offerings.

Upon entering the museum, you'll first notice (in room 5) the **Sphinx of the Naxians**, dating from 560 BC. Also here are well-preserved parts of the **frieze from the Siphnian treasury**. This depicts the battle between the gods and the giants, and also the Judgment of Paris. In room 3 are two fine examples of 6th-century-BC *kouroi* (statues of young men), the **'twins of Argos'**.

In the rooms to the left are fragments of **metopes** (figures within the frieze) from the Athenian treasury depicting the Labours of Hercules, the Exploits of Theseus and the Battle of the Amazons (room 7). Further on you can't miss the tall **Acanthus Column of Dancers** (room 11), with three women dancing around its top. Next to it is the **omphalos**, a sculpted cone, one of which stood at what was considered the centre of the world. In the end room (13) is the celebrated, life-size **Bronze Charioteer**, which commemorates a victory in the Pythian Games of 478 or 474 BC.

Folklore Museum of Chrisso   MUSEUM

(🖉 22650 83203; Chrisso; ⊘Tue-Sun 9am-3pm) **FREE** The Delphi region's newest museum is set in the traditional village of Chrisso, about 4km south of Delphi towards Itea. The former mansion shows off costumes dating from the 19th century, including a man's skirt with 400 pleats symbolising 400 years of Ottoman rule. Other displays include jewellery, pistols, period paintings and photographs.

Sikelianos Museum   MUSEUM

(Delphic Festivals Museum; 🖉 22650 82173; cnr Sikelianos & Diakou; €1; ⊘Thu-Mon 9am-2pm; 🅿) Fans of Greek drama should head to this intimate 1927 mansion-turned-museum, overlooking both modern and ancient Delphi. It is dedicated to Greek poet Angelos Sikelianos and his American-born wife Eva Palmer, who together established Delphi as a modern Greek centre for drama and the arts.

🏃 Activities

Three popular day hikes, all part of the E4 European long-distance path, start and end at Delphi. Keen walkers should see www.delphi walkingtours.com/korykion-cave.

Contact local and multilingual hiking expert Girogos Korodimo at **Trekking Hellas** (🖉 6981114041; www.trekking.gr; Arahova) in

THE DELPHIC ORACLE

The Delphic oracle was considered one of the most important religious (and political) sanctuaries in Greece. Worshippers flocked here from far and wide to consult the god Apollo on serious decisions. Apollo's instrument of communication was the Pythia (priestess) usually an older woman, who sat on a tripod in the Temple of Apollo.

During visitations and consultations, the priestess chewed laurel leaves and entered a trance after inhaling vapours from a chasm below. Archaeologists believe this could have been ethylene wafting through a crack from a fault line (carried by water running underground). Her vapour-inspired, if somewhat vague, answers were spoken in tongue then 'translated' by the priests of Apollo. In fact, the oracle's reputation for infallibility may have rested with the often-ambiguous or cryptic answers. Wars were fought, marriages sealed, leaders chosen and journeys begun on the strength of the oracle's visions. After all, the prophecies were the will of a god, so the oracle's reputation remained throughout antiquity.

Legend holds that one priestess suffered for her vagueness. When Alexander the Great visited, hoping to hear a prophecy that he would soon conquer the ancient world, the priestess refused direct comment, instead asking that he return later. Enraged, he dragged her by the hair out of the chamber until she screamed, 'Let go of me; you're unbeatable'. He quickly dropped her, saying, 'I have my answer'.

Arahova for guided treks around Parnassos, including the Korykeon Cave.

Korykeon Cave Walk   HIKING

The wonderful Korykeon Cave walk connects two ancient sites: the Temple of Apollo (p201) and Korykeon Cave, a sacred mountain cave-shrine for Pan, companion of nymphs. The cavern comprises a natural amphitheatre filled with stalactites and stalagmites. You can walk 80m inside (caution: it can be slippery). Many hikers hire a taxi in Delphi or Arahova to take them about 2km from the cave entrance (around €30), and hike down to Delphi along the well-marked E4 path in about four hours.

Delphi to Kroki View Point Walk   HIKING

(Kroki Observatory Walk) The Delphi to Kroki View Point walk goes along the same E4 trail which eventually reaches the Korykeon Cave. This shorter hike takes about 90 minutes each way (4km up and 4km down). Begin at the grassy trailhead opposite the Sikelianos Museum in upper Delphi, and follow the yellow and black E4 signposts up the *kako skala* (evil steps) which soon give way to a more gradual climb with superb views over the archaeological site and beyond. Carry water.

Delphi to Ancient Kirra Walk   HIKING

The Delphi to Ancient Kirra hike meanders through shady olive groves – the largest continuous olive grove in Greece – and takes three to four hours to cover the 14km downhill trail. After lunch or a swim, return by bus (around €2) to Delphi. The E4 trailhead is marked 100m east of the Hotel Acropole.

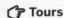 Tours

The best way to get your head around the Ancient Delphi site is to do a tour with a knowledgable and licensed guide.

Penny Kolomvotsos   WALKING

(☏6944644427; kpagona@hotmail.com) Excellent English-language tours of Delphi are offered by the charismatic and ultrapassionate Penny Kolomyotsos; also speaks German.

Christina Stolis   WALKING

(☏6944987411; xristolh@gmail.com) English-speaking guide for tours of Delphi.

George Malissos   WALKING

(☏6948181084; malissosg@hotmail.com) Recommended guide for tours of Delphi; also speaks French.

🛏 Sleeping

★Hotel Sibylla   HOTEL €

(☏22650 82335; www.sibylla-hotel.gr; Vasileon Pavlou & Friderikis 9; s/d/tr €26/30/40; ❄ 🌐) A gem of a budget choice, cosy and central Sibylla has gracious and helpful owners along with eight light and tidy rooms, all with overhead fans and several with views across to the gulf. Book early.

Arion Hotel   HOTEL €

(☏22650 82097; www.ariondelphihotel.com; Syngrou 29; s/d/tr/q incl breakfast from €30/40/50/60; ❄ @ 🌐) Basic with apricot-coloured decor,

Delphi Town

European Culture Centre of Delphi (400m);
Itea (18km); Amfissa (21km)
Trans-European
Diakou E4 Trail
Osiou Loukas
Syngrou
Apollonos
Fragou
Filellinon
Vasileon Pavlou & Friderikis
Syngrou
Sikelianos
Chrisso (4km);
Kirra (10km)
Bus Stop
Kroki Observatory (4.3km);
Korykean Cave (9km)
Delphi Archaeological Museum
Ancient Delphi (500m);
Sanctuary of Athena Pronea (1.5km);
Arahova (8km)

Delphi Town

⊙ Top Sights
1 Delphi Archaeological Museum D1

⊙ Sights
2 Sikelianos Museum D2

⊕ Activities, Courses & Tours
3 Delphi to Ancient Kirra Walk C2
4 Delphi to Kroki View Point Walk D2

⊜ Sleeping
5 Arion Hotel A1
6 Fedriades Hotel B2
7 Hotel Acropole C2
8 Hotel Hermes B2

9 Hotel Sibylla C2
10 Kastalia Hotel C2
11 Nidimos Hotel A1
12 Rooms Pitho B2

⊗ Eating
13 In Delphi C2
14 Taverna Gargadouas A1
15 Taverna To Patriko Mas A2
16 Taverna Vakhos B2

⊝ Drinking & Nightlife
17 Café Agora B2
18 Club Katoi A2
19 Melopoleio Cafe C2

Arion offers value in a quiet, higher location at the back of town, with rear rooms overlooking the Gulf of Corinth.

Chrissa Camping   CAMPGROUND €
(📞22650 82020; www.chrissacamping.gr; campsites per person/tent/car €6.50/6/3.50, bungalows from €30; 🅿🌑🛜🏊) Welcoming and well situated spot, about 7km west of modern Delphi, with great views to the gulf.

Rooms Pitho   PENSION €
(📞22650 82850; www.pithohotel.gr; Vasileon Pavlou & Friderikis 40a; s/d/tr incl breakfast €45/55/70; ⊜🌑🛜) Pitho's eight spotless, modern rooms (some on the small side), excellent service, extremely friendly owners and location – about halfway along the street above the family's handsome gift shop – make it a good choice. Because it's incorporated into a home-style lodging, it's quieter than some larger hotels.

Hotel Hermes   HOTEL €
(📞22650 82318; www.hermeshotel.com.gr; Vasileon Pavlou & Friderikis 27; s/d/tr incl breakfast €35/45/55; 🌑🛜) The family-run Hermes is in the heart of Delphi. All of the wood-shuttered and marble-floored rooms have balconies facing the gulf. Views from the breakfast lounge are splendid. Attentive staff, and satellite TV a plus.

Delphi Camping   CAMPGROUND €
(📞22650 82209; www.delphicamping.com; campsites per person/tent/car €7.20/5/4.20; 🅿🌐🛜🏊) About 4km from Delphi towards Itea, this well stocked camp occupies a pretty setting with safe playground equipment, but mind the killer entrance on a sharp corner.

Kastalia Hotel   BOUTIQUE HOTEL €€
(📞22650 82205; www.kastaliahotel.gr; Vasileon Pavlou & Friderikis 13; s/d/tr/ste incl breakfast from €50/70/85/110; 🌑🌐🛜) Named for the ancient spring nearby, the Kastalia is the

most recent addition to Delphi's upscale lodging scene following a thorough renovation in 2016. Rooms are large, light and smartly decorated, with comfortable beds, modern bathrooms, and balconies overlooking the gulf. The hotel has its own restaurant as well (Elia) where the owner's Cypriot roots show up in several recipes.

Nidimos Hotel
HOTEL €€

(☑ 22650 82056; www.nidimoshotel.gr; D Fragou 10; s/d/tr from €44/64/78; P ⊕ ❄ 🛜) Among Delphi's sleekest options, this recently renovated spot is for those who want modern – there are lots of contemporary taupes and whites. The rooms at the front boast massive terraces and cost slightly more, though those at the back look out onto wall art and are much quieter.

Fedriades Hotel
HOTEL €€

(☑ 22650 82370; www.fedriades.com; Vasileon Pavlou & Friderikis 46; s/d/tr/ste incl breakfast €45/62/75/130; ❄ @ 🛜) The Fedriades is a reliable bet with small and neat, but bright, modern rooms, plus a suite, and extra-friendly staff. Enthusiastic owner Babis will help with onward routes. Breakfast includes homemade treats, and bicycles are free for peddling around. The lobby is a pleasant place to lounge after a site visit.

Hotel Acropole
HOTEL €€

(☑ 22650 82675; www.delphi.com.gr; Filellinon 13; s/d/tr incl breakfast €55/70/89; ❄ 🛜) On a quieter street below the main drag, the Acropole has a ski-lodge ambience, with recently renovated bathrooms and attractive chalet-style rooms with wood and wrought-iron fittings. Top-floor rooms have angled ceilings and great views across to the gulf. A stone's throw to the hiking path leading downhill to Ancient Kirra.

✕ Eating

In Delphi
TAVERNA €

(☑ 22650 82230; Apollonos 8; mains €5-9; ⊙ breakfast, lunch & dinner; ❄ 🛜) This reliable and cosy eatery is a local favourite for its good grills and oven-ready dishes. Next to the bus station, with summer seating under a shady plane tree.

Taverna Gargadouas
TAVERNA €

(Vasileon Pavlou & Friderikis; mains €8-10; ⊙ 1-11pm) Easily the local favourite for grilled meats. The house summer speciality is *pro-vatina* (slow-roasted lamb), with pork chops a close second. You can tuck into a combo of pasta, meat, salad and wine for about €12. Good value, friendly, cosy atmosphere.

★ Taverna Vakhos
TAVERNA €€

(☑ 22650 83186; www.vakhos.com; Apollonos 31; mains €8-15; ⊙ noon-late; 🛜 🍴) Take the steps above the National Bank to this exceptional family taverna featuring traditional local fare and herbs gathered from the mountainside. Along with traditional *mayirefta* (ready-cooked meals) and hearty lamb and rooster recipes, Vakhos has a wide assortment of generous salads and veggie dishes ranging from *horta* (wild greens) *to trachanopita* (savoury pie of cracked wheat, zucchini and feta).

Taverna To Patriko Mas
MEDITERRANEAN €€

(☑ 22650 82150; Vasileon Pavlou & Friderikis 69; mains €8-15; ⊙ lunch & dinner; ❄ 🛜) Set in a 19th-century stone building, this swank taverna is decidedly upscale and features unusual salads, generous mezedhes (appetisers) and local favourites like a savoury pie with leek and pork, boar soup, grilled meats and fresh fish in summer, along with a fine all-Greek wine list.

🍷 Drinking & Nightlife

Melopoleio Cafe
CAFE-BAR

(☑ 22650 83247; Vasileon Pavlou & Friderikis 14; ⊙ 7am-11pm; 🛜) Go-to place for oven-baked savoury pies, fresh juices and espresso drinks, plus teas from local herbs. Melopoleio morphs into an afternoon sandwich and ice-cream stop, then into an evening wine bar with signature cocktails.

Club Katoi
CLUB

(☑ 6932526578; Vasileon Pavlou & Friderikis; €5-10; ⊙ 9pm-3am; 🛜) Delphi's only late-night DJ and music spot to let your hair down. Price includes a drink, or two. Opposite the BP petrol station.

Café Agora
CAFE

(☑ 22650 83116; www.agoracafe.gr; Vasileon Pavlou & Friderikis; 🛜) Along with the panoramic verandah views of the gulf, Agora serves up Delphi's best pizza and crêpes.

☆ Entertainment

European Cultural
Centre of Delphi
ARTS CENTER

(ECC; ☑ 22650 82731; www.eccd.gr; ⊙ 8am-3pm daily spring & summer) **FREE** This handsome facility in a garden setting comes to life in the spring and summer with photography and art exhibitions, lectures and open-air theatre events.

❶ Information

Almost everything you'll need in Delphi is on Vasileon Pavlou & Friderikis. Delphi's other through roads are Apollonos, which runs north of and parallel to Vasileon Pavlou & Friderikis, and Filellinon, which runs south and parallel to the main drag. Four steep stairways connect all three roads. Several ATMs are on Pavlou & Friderikis.

There is no tourist office, aside from a staffed exhibition space at the town hall. A useful website for information on the area is www.ancient-greece.org.

Amfissa Hospital (☑ 22650 72010, 22650 22222; Gidhogiannou 35) For serious medical matters, it's best to head to Amfissa, 20km from Delphi.

Pharmacy (☑ 22650 82700; Apollonos 18; ⊘ 9am-1.30pm & 6-9pm) For first aid and minor medical matters you can head here.

Post Office (Vasileon Pavlou & Friderikis; ⊘ 7.30am-2pm Mon-Fri)

❶ Getting There & Away

Buses (☑ 22650 82317; www.ktel-fokidas.gr; Vasileon Pavlou & Friderikis) depart from the eastern end of Vasileon Pavlou & Friderikis, next to the In Delphi restaurant, where tickets can be purchased between 9am and 8pm (the bus system's closing time). If you're taking an early bus, plan ahead and buy tickets the day before. The same especially applies in high season when buses fill up quickly. Travellers to Kalambaka/Meteora should find better connections via Lamia and Trikala, rather than Larissa.

Bus Services from Delphi

DESTINATION	DURATION	FARE (€)	FREQUENCY
Amfissa	30min	2.10	6 daily
Arahova	20min	1.80	4 daily
Athens	2½hr	16.40	4 daily
Galaxidi	45min	3.80	2-3 daily
Itea	30min	2	5-6 daily
Lamia	2hr	9.90	1 daily
Larissa	3½hr	23.70	1 daily
Livadia	55min	4.50	4-5 daily
Nafpaktos	2½hr	11.80	3 daily
Patra	3½hr	14.80	1-2 daily
Thessaloniki	4½hr	38	1 daily
Thiva	1hr	8.60	4 daily

Around Delphi

Olive groves and clear skies mark the road south from Delphi, which stretches 18km to the Gulf of Corinth before branching east to Kirra (2km). This was Ancient Kirra, the port of Delphi, now a quiet suburb of the market town of Itea, with a long sand-and-pebble beach, very clean sea and good beachside camping.

Amfissa   Άμφισσα

☑ 22650 / POP 6850

The town of Amfissa (the capital of the new Municipality of Delphi) sits in the foothills 21km from Delphi on the road to Lamia. The village was sacked in 338 BC by Philip of Macedon and, more recently, it played a crucial role at the beginning of the Greek War of Independence against Ottoman rule.

◉ Sights

Amfissa Castle   RUINS

Also known as the Castle of Salona, the Castle of Amfissa dominates the hill behind the village. Around 600m of the castle's fortified wall remains and you can wander through the castle grounds.

Believed to have been constructed under the orders of Thomas I d'Autremencourt, the first Lord of Salona, after division of the Byzantine Empire following the Fourth Crusade, it was the fort for subsequent invaders, including the Romans, Catalans, Franks and Turks. All left their mark, as shown in the melange of architectural elements that survive today, especially those from Byzantine and Frankish times.

Archaeological Museum of Amfissa MUSEUM

(☑ 22650 23344; http://odysseus.culture.gr; 2 Kechagia St; adult/child €2/free; ⊘ 9am-4pm Wed-Sat; ℗) This handsome museum, housed in a former bank and a police station, is home to a wonderful collection of local finds dating from the Bronze Age to the early Byzantine period. Highlights include rare idols purchased by pilgrims in Ancient Kirra and taken to Delphi, miniature marionettes, coin and pre-coin exchange displays, and a bronze helmet circa 300 BC.

Moni Profiti Ilia   CONVENT

(⊘ 8am-2pm & 4pm-sunset; ℗) **FREE** East of Amfissa towards Delphi, the 19th-century convent of Moni Profiti Ilia rests on a hillside with superb views of the Gulf of Corinth and

PARNASSOS NATIONAL PARK ΕΘΝΙΚΟΣ ΔΡΥΜΟΣ ΠΑΡΝΑΣΣΟΥ

Established in 1938, **Parnassos National Park** (☑22340 23529; http://en.parnassosnp. gr), to the north of Delphi and Arahova, has three peaks over 2300m: Parnassos (2457m), the highest; Tsarkos (2416m); and Gerondovrachos (2396m). Kouvelos (1882m) is a popular rock-climbing face. Mt Parnassos is part of the elaborate E4 European long-distance path (orivatiko monopati) from Gibraltar to Cyprus organised by the European Ramblers Association (www.era-ewv-ferp.com); see http://en.parnassosnp.gr for details.

The slopes of Parnassos support Kefallonian fir, spruce and juniper, interspersed with yellow-flowered shrubs, plum trees and the rare purple-flowered Daphne jasminea.

The **Parnassos Ski Centre**, 24km from Arahova, handles ski and snowboard operations on Kelaria (1950m; 13 lifts). For accommodation, it's best to stay in Arahova. Adjacent to Kelaria are the steeper slopes of **Fterolakkas** (six lifts), popular with extreme skiers. For more information, see www.snowreport.gr/parnassos/indexen.html and www.skiresort.info/ski-resorts/mount-parnassus.

There is no public transport between Arahova and the ski centre. A taxi from Delphi or Arahova costs around €45.

Amfissa olive groves. This is where Essaeas, the bishop of Salona (Amfissa), raised the flag of revolution on 24 March 1821. The turn-off is marked with a small cross and '3KM' sign, which also serves as a makeshift bulletin board. Sunday-morning services are highlighted by the nuns singing mass.

Note: the convent has a strict dress code. Definitely no shorts for men or women.

🛏 Sleeping & Eating

Amfissaeum Hotel HOTEL €
(☑22650 22161; www.amfissahotel.gr; Ioannou Gidogiannou 18; s/d/tr from €38/48/58; ❄🕏) This brightly painted 40-room hotel is welcoming, clean, carpeted and comfortable, if a bit dated in decor. Breakfast is €6 per person.

Steki tou Kalofaga TAVERNA €
(☑22650 23123; Plateia Kehagia; pitta snacks €2-7.50; ☉6-11pm; ❄) Popular eatery on the upper square (Plateia Kehagia) for tasty souvlaki, gyros (meat slivers cooked on a vertical rotisserie) and salads.

Kaisaras GREEK €
(Caesar's; ☑22650 22007; Salonon 2, Plateia Isaia; souvlaki, snacks €2-7; ☉lunch & dinner) The go-to place in Amfissa for souvlaki, chargrilled meat, fresh potatoes and salads. Half a block west of the taxi rank at the main square.

🍷 Drinking & Nightlife

Ouzeri Hamouzas CAFE-BAR
(Χαμούζας; ☑22650 28463; Plateia Kehagia; ☉8am-11pm) Amfissa's more laid-back upper square, Plateia Kehagia, is surrounded by several low-key cafes and ouzeries (place that

serves ouzo & light snacks), among them the traditional Hamouzas, good for a morning coffee or afternoon beer or glass of tsipouro (distilled spirit similar to raki), always served with a small plate of something tasty.

Art Cafe CAFE-BAR
(☑22650 22300; Salonon 16; ☉7am-2am; 🕏) This smart-looking cafe 150m east of the main square (Plateia Isaia) features original artwork, strong coffee, sturdy drinks and mellow music.

❶ Getting There & Away

The **bus stop** (KTEL; ☑22650 28226; www. ktel-fokidas.gr; Karaogiorgou at Karamanli) connects Amfissa to Delphi (€2.10, 30 minutes, six daily), Athens (€16.90, three hours, four daily), Lamia (€9.10, 1½ hours, one daily) and Patra (€14.20, three hours, one to two daily).

Arahova Αράχωβα

☑22670 / POP 3470

Arahova, only 8km from Delphi, rests on a rocky spur of Mt Parnassos at an altitude of 960m. While it's easy to stick to the main drag, the stepped alleyways of the mountain town are also charming and include the historic 'clock on the rock', an impressive stone clock tower overlooking the village. As well as a side trip from Delphi, the town is a winter resort for skiers who hit the slopes of Parnassos National Park.

Arahova's more touristy shops sell embroidery, hand-woven bags and flokati (shaggy woollen rugs) and traditional products, but it's also noted for its formaela cheese, honey, hilopites (fettuccine-style pasta) and red wine.

◉ Sights

Arahova Folklore Museum MUSEUM
(Ethonographic Museum; ✍22670 31630; www.
arachovamuseum.gr; Delphon; ⊙8am-3pm Tue-Fri,
9am-5pm Sat & Sun) **FREE** Housed in the former town hall, this little spot houses some
lovely old photos and temporary exhibitions;
poke your nose in when you're passing by.

✯✯ Festivals & Events

Festival of Agios Georgios CARNIVAL
(✍22670 32091; ⊙Apr) Held in town around
23 April (if this date falls during Lent, the
festival is postponed until the following
Easter Tuesday), this is a joyous three-day
celebration with virtually the entire village
in costume. There's dancing and singing, a
tug-of-war contest and, on the last day, feasting on roasted lamb, all compliments of the
town, wine included.

⨭ Sleeping

Hotel Likoria HOTEL €€
(✍22670 31180; www.likoria.gr; s/d/tr incl breakfast from €60/75/95; P✽@🛜) Off the main
road, 250m northwest of Plateia Xenias, the
low-key Likoria feels more like a country inn.
Rooms are quite traditional, with carpeting,
huge soft beds and shuttered doors opening
to large balconies. The quiet location, countryside views, major breakfast spread and
friendly English-speaking staff are pluses.

Pension Maria HERITAGE HOTEL €€
(Xenonas Maria; ✍22670 31803, 6976879205; Solomou; d €50-70, tr €70; 🛜) Atmospheric, old-
style *arhontiko* (traditional mansion) with
split-level rooms and lots of red carpets,
antiques and stonework, and a warm welcome from Yiannis and Nikos, Maria's sons.
Behind the town hall, near Ouzeri Zambas.
Open all year.

✕ Eating

Dasayiris Taverna TAVERNA €
(✍22670 31291; Delphon 56; mains €6.50-11;
⊙lunch & dinner) Outstanding traditional
taverna, with food and ambience to match.
House favourites include *hilopites, horta*,
eggplant with garlic, rooster in red wine
sauce, and slow-roasted lamb. Nothing is
frozen. Park near the taxi rank 150m west.

Parnassos Taverna TAVERNA €
(✍22670 32569; Plateia Xenias; dishes €7-10.50;
⊙lunch & dinner; P✽) Reliable local go-to
taverna on Plateia Xenias, just above the taxi

rank. Open year-round, with well-prepared
mayirefta, good grills and jug wine.

▼ Drinking & Nightlife

Sehre All Day Cafe CAFE-BAR
(✍22670 31518; Plateia Lakka; ⊙8am-2am; 🛜)
Reliable all-purpose, all-day spot on the main
square that opens earlier than most, and
closes late. Great for coffee, wine, cocktails,
plus outdoor seating.

Bonjour Cafe Snack Bar CAFE-BAR
(✍22670 32330; Plateia Lakka; ⊙8am-midnight;
🛜) Local favourite for espresso drinks,
cocktails, homemade croissant sandwiches
and desserts, plus breakfast any time.

ⓘ Information

The **post office** (Plateia Xenias; ⊙7.30am-2pm
Mon-Fri) has ATMs are at Plateia Xenias.

ⓘ Getting There & Away

The daily buses that run between Athens' Liasion
station and Delphi stop at Arahova's **KTEL Bus
Station** (Plateia Xenias); they cost €16.80 and
take 2½ hours.

Galaxidi Γαλλαξίδι

✍22650 / POP 2010
The prettiest of the low-key resorts on the
Gulf of Corinth, Galaxidi is graced with narrow cobblestone streets, handsome stone
mansions and two small harbours. It's a
good, and cooler, alternative to staying in
Delphi during midsummer. A forested headland, opposite the waterfront, is fringed by a
1.5km walking path and pebbled coves popular with swimmers. The town is reasonably
tranquil except during summer and holiday
weekends, when its charm is tested by car-
loads of Athenians.

Galaxidi's most prosperous period was
between 1830 and 1910 when it was a major
maritime power, playing an important role
in the Greek War of Independence against
Ottoman rule. When the maritime industry
failed to keep pace with modern shipbuilding trends, the town became a centre for
building caïques (small fishing boats).

◉ Sights

Nautical Historical Museum MUSEUM
(✍22650 41795; Plateia; adult/student/child
€3/1/free; ⊙9am-4pm Tue-Sun Jun-Sep, 9.15am-
3pm Tue-Sun Oct-May; ♿) The excellent Nautical Historical Museum documents Greece's

MONI OSIOS LOUKAS

The World Heritage–listed monastery **Moni Osios Loukas** (Μονή Οσίου Λουκά; Monastery of St Luke; ☑ 22670 22228; €4; ⊕ 9am-5.30pm) is 23km southeast of Arahova, between the villages of Distomo and Kyriaki. Its principal church contains some of Greece's finest Byzantine frescoes. Modest dress is required (no shorts). Nearby is the smaller 10th-century **Agia Panagia** (Church of the Virgin Mary).

The monastery is dedicated to a local hermit who was canonised for his healing and prophetic powers. The monastic complex includes two churches.

The interior of the larger, **Agios Loukas**, is a glorious symphony of marble and mosaics, with icons by Michael Damaskinos, the 16th-century Cretan painter. In the main body of the church, the light is partially blocked by the ornate marble window decorations, creating striking contrasts of light and shade. Walk around the corner to find several fine frescoes that brighten up the crypt where St Luke is buried.

To get here from Delphi, you'll need your own transport or a taxi. Buses do not go to Osios Loukas from Delphi. Taxis will get you to the monastery from Delphi (€50 return, 20 minutes each way), Distomo (€20 return) or Livadia (€30 return). Taxis normally will wait for an hour; arrange the price before you go.

Coming from Livadia, one daily bus heads to Moni Osios Loukas (€3.70, 30 minutes).

maritime history and Galaxidi's unique shipbuilding lore, and includes several miniature models along with splendid carved wooden figureheads from mid-19th-century clipper ships.

Moni Metamorfosis of Sotiras   MONASTERY
The little 13th-century Byzantine-era Moni Metamorfosis of Sotiras stands amid olive groves and cypress trees, 4km inland from Galaxidi. From this vantage point there are terrific views down to the Gulf of Corinth. To reach it, go under the flyover and take the road opposite.

Church of Agios Nikolaos   CHURCH
The carved-wood iconostasis in the Church of Agios Nikolaos is one of Greece's finest. Follow the English signs for the museum and church.

🛌 Sleeping

In summer, several of the waterfront cafes have rooms to let, though they're not great value, nor the quietest place to spend a night. On busy weekends, you might check out the places around the bend at the low-key old harbour known as Hirolakas, Greek for 'Widows' Port', named for the wives who waited in vain for their seamen husbands whose ships never returned to port.

Hotel Galaxidi   HOTEL €
(☑ 22650 41850; www.hotelgalaxidi.gr; Sigrou 11; s/d/tr incl breakfast €40/60/70; 🅿 ❄ 🛜) Renovated 32-room hotel in quiet spot, but just 60m from the port. Friendly service, decent

breakfast with homemade extras, plus balconies and basin sinks.

★ MiraMare Hotel   APARTMENT €€
(☑ 6937154567, 22650 41328; www.ganimede.gr/services/hotel-miramare; Platoni & Piniatidou, waterfront; s/d studios incl breakfast €55/75; ⊕ ❄ 🛜) These five bright and airy studios, equipped with small kitchenettes and balconies, are a pebble's throw from the waterfront action, including sea views from the upper balconies and the same lavish breakfasts as their sister **Hotel Ganimede** (p212).

Nostos Hotel   BOUTIQUE HOTEL €€
(☑ 22650 41266, 6937064188; www.nostoshotel.com; Plateia Iroon & Papapetrou; s/d/tr from €60/70/80; 🅿 ❄ 🛜) A neoclassical sea-captain's gem, this recently renovated six-room lodging manages handsome and frilly at the same time. Think pastels, wood floors with area rugs, lace, modern bathrooms and a traditional breakfast. It faces Plateia Iroon (aka Plateia Manousakia), a short 300m to the waterfront.

Galaxa Mansion   BOUTIQUE HOTEL €€
(☑ 22650 41620, 6946437772; www.galaxamansion.com; 8 Eleftherias & Kennedy; s/d/tr incl breakfast €50/65/85; ❄ 🛜) Housed in a former shipowner's residence, this historic house at the old port has been smartly refurbished, and the bathrooms updated. Each of the nine rooms – named after Greek mythological characters – is light and airy with antique-style touches as testimony to its maritime days. Stunning views of the old

port from some of the rooms, plus a rose-filled terrace for breakfast or afternoon drinks.

Hotel Ganimede
BOUTIQUE HOTEL €€

(☑ 22650 41328, 6937154567; www.ganimede. gr; Nikolaou Gourgouris 20; s/d/tr incl breakfast €55/75/90, studios from €90; ❋ @ 🞸) This cosy courtyard hotel in a 19th-century captain's house offers a range of pastel-shaded rooms with panelled ceilings and period furniture. What it's best known for, however, are owner Chrisoula's gut-busting breakfasts – think homemade jams, chutneys, cheeses, fresh-squeezed juices and pastries from the family bakery. Also has studios with kitchenettes, and on-site cooking classes, complete with takeaway caps and aprons.

✖ Eating

Skeletovrachos Taverna
TAVERNA €

(☑ 22650 41303, 6987877263; Akti Oianthis; mains €6-11; ☉ lunch & dinner) A low-key eatery further along the waterfront, featuring excellent grilled fish, fairly priced by the kilo, along with great side dishes like fava and *taramasalata* (a thick pink or white purée of fish roe, potato, oil and lemon juice). Ask Dinos, the convivial and philosophical owner, about cooking lessons, too.

Zygos
TAVERNA €

(☑ 22653 01071, 6945171359; Akti Oianthis 115; mains €6.50-12; ☉ 11am-late) The German beer mugs seem a little incongruous until you realise this small and inviting taverna, towards the end of the 'new harbour', offers over 40 beers, plus a range of *tsipouro*. Beer aside, the cuisine is excellent, with fresh fish always on offer, along with generous salads and upstairs balcony seating overlooking the harbour.

Albatross
TAVERNA €

(☑ 22650 42233; Konstadinou Satha 36; mains €6-8; ☉ lunch & dinner) We love this little place opposite the Church of Agios Nikolaos, run by a long-standing, elderly-if-young-at-heart couple. Prices haven't changed in years and the generous offerings of mezedhes (try the dolmadhes, and *taramasalata*), along with a few oven-ready dishes, are always tasty.

★ Bebelis
GREEK €€

(☑ 22650 41677; Nikolaou Mama 20-22; mains €7-16.50; ☉ 5.30-11pm Dec-Oct) Fresh flowers, lace curtains and its location – a couple of blocks from the 'new harbour' – add a touch of taverna class to Galaxidi. Proud

and convivial owner Bebelis (the owner Nikos' nickname) offers a lovely go-slow dinner experience. A full bar, good wine and exceptional mezedhes and local recipes like *lavraiki* (sea bass) and *kelemnia* (stuffed onions).

Maritsa Restaurant
GREEK €€

(☑ 6947842009, 22650 41059; Eolida, main port; mains €10-18; ☉ lunch & dinner; P 🞸) First-rate kitchen in upscale atmosphere, specialising in fresh fish, veggie and fish soups, along with good pasta dishes. Maritsa moved in 2017 from its 30-year old location on the waterfront, to just opposite the narrow inlet, where it now faces the waterfront, a five-minute walk away.

🍷 Drinking & Nightlife

To Kioski
COCKTAIL BAR

(☑ 6979978455; cnr Akti Oianthis & Nikolaou Mama; ☉ 8am-midnight; 🞸) Classy waterfront spot under the shade of a mulberry tree, with excellent coffee, teas and a full bar. Also a destination for desserts, like homemade ice cream and cheesecake.

Absinthe
BAR

(Ouzerie; ☑ 22650 41220; Nikolaou Mama 33; ☉ 11am-5pm Thu-Tue; 🞸) Chill main-street dive, opposite a bakery shop, with excellent homemade mezedhes to accompany ouzo and other drinks, plus live music on weekend nights to help make the heart grow fonder.

❶ Getting There & Away

There are **buses** (☑ 22650 42087; Plateia Iroon/Manousakia) to Delphi (€3.80, 45 minutes, two to three daily), Athens (€20.30, 3½ hours, two to three daily) and Patra (€10.80, 1¾ hours, one to two daily). For Delphi and Athens, you must change bus in Itea, but ticket prices cover the entire journey.

Nafpaktos   Ναύπακτος

☑ 26340 / POP 23,800

West of the small town of Galaxidi, and only 9km after the bridge crossing (Rio–Andiro) from Patras that joins the Peloponnese with Sterea Ellada, is the delightful, bustling town of Nafpaktos. It spreads out from a handsome circular-walled harbour dotted with plane trees, trendy cafes and a good **swimming beach** (Psani). Above it looms a Venetian *kastro* (castle). Nafpaktos is a pleasant en-route stop to Delphi or Lamia, if coming from the Peloponnese. A market takes place every Saturday.

History

Nafpaktos was known as Lepanto in medieval times, and it was here on 7 October 1571 that the naval battle of Lepanto took place between the Ottoman Empire and the combined navies of the Vatican, Spain and Venice. The decisive victory over the Turks temporarily ended the Ottoman's naval domination of the Mediterranean.

The Spanish author Cervantes fought in the battle of Lepanto (and lost an arm). A small, dramatic statue on the waterfront honours him, along with a Greek hero, Giorgos Anemogiannis (1796–1821), who, during the Greek War of Independence, tried to burn the Turkish fleet that was moored in the harbour (he failed and was killed by the Turks).

◉ Sights

Castle _CASTLE_
(Kastro; ⊙8am-3pm Tue-Sun) The well-preserved fortress and Venetian *kastro* overlooking Nafpaktos consist of a series of five terraced stone walls, built by a succession of conquerors (Doric, Roman, Byzantine, Venetian and Turk), that end at the town's waterfront. The walk and views alone are well worth checking out. Note: if you drive, turn uphill at the Shell petrol station.

Fethiye Mosque _MOSQUE_
(Fethiye Tzami; ⊙7-9pm Fri, Sat & Sun) FREE Look for the domed roof on the eastern (lighthouse and jetty) side of the port to find this stunning Ottoman mosque, named Fethiye Mosque (Conquest Mosque) because it was built after the conquest of the city by Sultan Beyazid II, who ruled the Ottoman Empire between 1481 and 1512. Hours vary, though summer exhibitions expand opening times.

Botsari Tower Museum _MUSEUM_
(✆26340 29779; Botsareon; ⊙9am-1pm Mon-Fri) FREE Battle aficionados must head to the Venetian-style Tower of Botsaris, currently a small museum which houses a collection of replicas of paintings and engravings – the originals made by the most famous artists of that era (Vasari, Tintoretto and the like) – recording the Battle of Lepanto. Ring the bell during opening hours; ring ahead for weekend visits. Look for the white structure 400m northwest of the port square.

⌂ Sleeping & Eating

Hotel Akti _HOTEL €€_
(✆26340 28464; www.akti.gr; Grimbovo Beach; s/d/tr €45/60/75, ste €100-120; P❄☎) The Akti's exterior looks like a pastel colour chart with balconies. Inside this delightful surprise are beautiful rugs and antiques galore and rooms that are spacious and comfortable. Delightful English-speaking owner Giorgos offers continental breakfast with homemade produce. The hotel is set in leafy surrounds opposite the beach. Note the owner's dog, Morpheus, named for the god of dreams.

Perigiali Mezedopoleio _GREEK €_
(Ouzerie Perigiali; ✆26343 03454; Navmahias 20, Psani Beach; small plates €4-7.50) Put together several small plates of Greek mezedhes, add wine, ouzo or *tsipouro*, and you've got a meal on the beach. Perigiali's menu is simple, with typical mezedhes like *taramasalata,* grilled sardines and grilled squid. It's on the boardwalk near the Plaza Hotel.

Evinos _MEDITERRANEAN €_
(✆26340 28266; Sismani 3, Stenopazaro; mains €6.50-10.50; ⊙noon-midnight & 6pm-1am summer) A twist of gourmet hits at this pleasant spot, the name of which translates as 'good wine'. The cuisine is a Mediterranean-Greek fusion – pastas and risotti – plus traditional dishes with a twist, such as *haloumi torta* (briny fried cheese sandwich). A lovely setting, though not by the sea.

▬ Drinking & Nightlife

Suita Cafe-Bar _CAFE-BAR_
(✆6947683599; Formionos 8; ⊙8am-2am; ☎) Busy and swanky portside destination with sturdy drinks, good espressos and frappes, all overlooking the medieval harbour.

The Bar _BAR_
(✆6933118686; Botsari 3; ⊙9pm-3am; ☎) Strictly a late-evening affair; arrive at 9pm and you'll be the first one there on most nights. Cocktails, coffee, beer on draught, plus good and loud DJ music and space to dance, a stone's throw from the port.

❶ Getting There & Away

Nafpaktos has two bus stations. The **KTEL Nafpaktos station** (Aitoloakarnania long-distance station; ✆26340 27224; Megalou Alexandrou & Athinon) is 1.5km east of the port and past the Church of Agios Georgios. The **KTEL Fokida station** (✆26340 27241; Asklipiou 1, cnr Kefalourisou) is 400m further east.

CENTRAL GREECE NAFPAKTOS

KTEL Bus Services from Nafpaktos

DESTINATION	DURATION	FARE (€)	FREQUENCY
Athens (via Rio–Andirio bridge)*	3hr	22.60	2 daily
Delphi (via Itea)**	3hr	11.60	3-4 daily
Galaxidi**	1½hr	7.80	3-4 daily
Lamia*	3½hr	15.80	2-3 daily
Messolongi*	50min	5.30	3 daily
Patra*	30min	3.70	2-8 daily Mon-Sat
Thessaloniki*	6hr	45	3 daily

*service departs from Nafpaktos
**service departs from Fokida

Messolongi   Μεσολόγγι

📱 26310 / POP 18,400

From a distance, Messolongi's flat landscape lacks the siren's irresistible draw. The town skirts the motionless **Klisova Lagoon**, the largest natural wetland in Greece, a favourite winter stopover for migrating birds and an important breeding ground for the endangered Dalmatian pelican – not to mention a pilgrimage site for birdwatchers and photographers, thanks to the remarkable *pelades* (stilt huts) in the water. The town centre is anything but motionless, however, with the pedestrian and bicycle lanes around the central square, Plateia Markou Botsari, lined with lively bars and tavernas. Though it has been hit hard by the economic crisis, Messolongi's character and vitality are hard to miss.

History

During the War of Independence (1821–30), Lord Byron, Britain's philhellenic bard, arrived in Messolongi with the intention of organising the troops and supporting the Greek war effort. After months of vain attempts, Byron contracted a fever and died on 19 April 1824, his immediate aims unfulfilled.

Byron's death, however, spurred international forces to hasten the end of the War of Independence, making him to this day a Greek national hero. Many men bear the name Byron (Vyronas in Greek) and most Greek towns have a street named after him. Messolongi is home to the Byron Society, an active international research group (www.messolonghibyronsociety.gr).

In the spring of 1826, under the helm of Egyptian general Ibrahim, Messolongi was captured by the Turks. Their year-long siege drove 9000 men, women and children to escape on the night of 22 April 1826 through what is now called the Gate of Exodus. Many took refuge on nearby Mt Zygos, only to be caught or killed by an Albanian mercenary force. A smaller group remained behind to detonate explosives as the Turks approached. This tragic exodus was immortalised in Dionysios Solomos' epic poem 'I Eleftheri Poliorkimeni' (The Free Besieged).

⊙ Sights

Garden of the Heroes   GARDEN
(⊘8am-8pm) **FREE** Just beyond the Gate of Exodus (a stone archway where Ottoman forces massacred Greeks trying to escape on 10 April 1826) is this memorial garden, which contains a prominent statue of Lord Byron. When Byron died, the Greeks were heartbroken at the loss of a British nobleman who had given his life for their freedom. At the end of a national 21-day mourning period, Byron's embalmed body was returned to England, but his heart was kept and is buried beneath the statue.

To identify Byron's statue, look for the Greek word, BYPΩNA, in the top right of the inscription. The English authorities at the time refused Byron's burial at Westminster Abbey, though in 1969 a memorial was installed there. He is buried at St Mary Magdalene church, in Hucknall, Notts.

The Garden of the Heroes was established by the first governor of Greece following independence, Ioannis Kapodistrias, who issued the following decree (the Greek text of which is on the marble slab to the right as you enter the garden): '...within these walls of the city of Messolongi lie the bones of those brave men, who fell bravely while defending the city...it is our duty to gather together, with reverence, the holy remains of these men and to lay them to rest in a memorial where our country may, each year, repay its debt of gratitude'.

Diexodos Museum of
Literature & Art   ARTS CENTRE
(Centre of Culture & Art; 📱 26310 51260; www.diexodos.com.gr; Razi-Kotsika 25; ⊘11am-1pm Wed-Sun) **FREE** A labour of love for a local lawyer, who restored the 19th-century mansion, this beautiful gallery houses a private collection of rare paintings and hosts exhibitions and cultural events throughout the year.

Museum of History & Art   MUSEUM
(Municipal Art Gallery; ☑26310 22134; Plateia Markou Botsari; ⊗9am-1.30pm & 4-6pm) FREE
This intimate neoclassical house museum off the main square is dedicated to the Greek War of Independence and features a fine collection of Byron memorabilia and paintings. The passionate and informative overseer, Dimitris Paraskevas, has clocked up over 30 years in his chair.

🛏 Sleeping & Eating

Hotel Liberty   HOTEL €
(☑26310 28050; www.hotelliberty.gr; Iroon Politechniou 41; s/d/tr/ste from €30/35/45/65; 🅿✳@🛜) Ignore the drab exterior of this central Messolongi lodging so as not to miss the '70s-era time warp that awaits inside. In its favour are spotless rooms (1st-floor rooms are the most up to date), funky wood decor, breakfast buffet, bicycle rental and small gym.

Hotel Theoxenia   HOTEL €
(☑26310 22493; Tourlidos 2; s/d/tr incl breakfast from €35/50/65; 🅿✳@🛜✳) You can't get much closer to the water than at this grassy perch just before the causeway over Klisova Lagoon. The hotel itself is a rambling relic, but with clean rooms, friendly staff and many rooms with a sunset view over the lagoon. Be prepared, as summer mosquitoes can arrive by dusk.

To Avgo tou Kokora   TAVERNA €€
(Egg of the Rooster; ☑26310 24377; Razi Kotsika 15; mains €7-15; ⊗lunch & dinner; ✳🛜) Friendly taverna near the main square (Plateia Markou Botsari), serving up the day's catch, well-prepared salads and pasta dishes.

ℹ Getting There & Away
The **KTEL Messolongi station** (☑26310 22371) is outside the walled town, near the arched Gate of Exodus. There are regular buses to Athens (€25.30, 3½ hours, nine or 10 daily) via the Rio–Andirio bridge, as well as buses to Patra (€6.30, one hour, eight daily), Nafpaktos (€5.40, 30 minutes, two daily) and Mytikas (€9.50, 1½ hours, one daily).

Karpenisi   Καρπενήσι
☑22370 / POP 8575
Karpenisi, the underrated capital of the mountainous prefecture of Evritania, lies in the well-wooded foothills of Mt Velouchi (2315m, also identified as Mt Tymfristos on some maps), between Lamia and Lake

WORTH A TRIP

TOURLIDA   ΤΟΥΡΛΙΔΑ
From Messolongi you can drive, walk or cycle across the surreal **Klisova Lagoon** on the 5km-long causeway to visit the sandy hamlet of Tourlida. Besides the scenery afforded by the fishing huts scattered on stilts over the still lagoon, the main reason to be here is to wile away a few hours at the **Tourlida Restaurant** (☑26310 25360; Tourlida; mains €6-11; ⊗9am-11pm), a light and airy spot with multicoloured rush-seated chairs, a 180-degree view of the water and fishing boats, and plenty of locals lapping up the atmosphere and tucking into hearty helpings of Greek seafood delights.

Kremasta. Not surprisingly, given its billing as the 'Switzerland of Greece', the town has an alpine feel, with chalet-style lodgings and bars with fireplaces. There are lovely walks around the area. For the less action-oriented, driving through the forests to villages and monasteries is equally rewarding.

🛏 Sleeping & Eating

City Hotel Apollonion   HOTEL €
(☑22370 25001; www.hotelapollonion.gr; Athanasiou Karpenisioti 4; s/d/tr incl breakfast from €30/45/55; ✳🛜) This attractive and updated hotel is great value, and you can't miss its massive mural just off the central *plateia* (square); bold colours and more murals await in the lobby. Rooms are smartly decorated in pastel shades, well lit, with area rugs. An excellent Greek breakfast starts the day.

Deluxe Hotel Anesis   HOTEL €€
(☑22370 80700; www.anesis.gr; Zinopoulou 50; s/d/tr incl breakfast €65/80/95; 🅿✳🛜) The nearest thing to a Swiss chalet without the snow, this slightly tired lodging sports a welcoming lobby and friendly staff, though the quiet, carpeted rooms are on the small side.

Taverna Folia   TAVERNA €
(☑22370 24405; Kosma Etolou 12; mains €5.50-11; ⊗lunch & dinner) Tucked down a small stair between two streets 50m south of the central *plateia*, this welcoming *psistaria* (taverna that specialises in char-grilled or spit-roasted meat) serves traditional *mayirefta* like *mousakas* along with meaty grills and good house wine. Weekend evenings usually feature a low-key guitar duo.

From the central *plateia*, walk 50m south on Zinopoulou, and opposite the Vodafone shop, look for a hand-painted sign with a guitar and red arrow pointing down the steps.

ℹ️ Information

Several banks around the central square have ATMs.

Hospital (☑ 22373 50100; Pavlou Bakagianni 2)
Police (☑ 22370 22966; Anistastis 9)
Post Office (Athanasiou Karpenisiotou 8; ⊙ 7.30am-2pm)

ℹ️ Getting There & Away

Karpenisi's **KTEL bus station** (☑ 22370 80013; Harilaou Trikoupi) is 1.5km southeast of town. Buses run to Athens (€27.50, four hours, two daily) and Lamia (€7.80, 1½ hours, three daily).

Lamia   Λαμία

☑ 22310 / POP 52,000

Lamia is the capital of the prefecture of Fthiotida, midway between Delphi and Meteora. Lamia rarely figures on travellers' itineraries, but it's a vibrant and lively place year-round. Life here revolves around the town's rambling squares and it's famous for its *kokoretsi* (lambs' intestines), *kourabiedes*

(almond shortcake) and *xynogalo* (sour milk). It's the gateway to Iti National Park.

⊙ Sights

Gorgopotamos Railway Bridge   BRIDGE
The original Gorgopotamos Railway Bridge, 7km south of Lamia, was blown up by a coalition of Greek and British guerrilla forces on 25 November 1942, in order to delay the German advance, and is considered one of the greatest acts of sabotage of the time. The spectacular attack put the Greek underground on the map and forced the Germans to divert resources away from the Russian front. The reconstructed bridge spans a deep ravine.

Thermopylae   HISTORIC SITE
About 20km southeast of Lamia is the narrow pass of Thermopylae where, in 480 BC, Leonidas and a band of 300 brave Spartans managed to temporarily halt the invading Persian army of Xerxes. A detailed Greek-English signboard and a huge statue of Leonidas honour the heroic battle site where the Spartans ultimately perished against overwhelming odds.

A stone's throw south is the most recent addition to Leonidas' legacy, a small **museum** (sign in Greek). At the time of research, there was little to see aside from

---

WORTH A TRIP

MICRO HORIO & MEGALO HORIO

Just 14km south of Karpenisi are the twin villages of Mikro Horio (Little Village), with a couple of good tavernas, and scenic Megalo Horio (Big Village). This latter village boasts traditional stone houses, a nice **cafe** (Kafeneio Karveli; ☑ 22370 41339, 6978773969; Megalo Horio; ⊙ 8am-midnight; 🛜) and a charming **Folklore Museum** (☑ 6948295141, 22370 41502; Megalo Horio; €2; ⊙ 10.30am-2.30pm Fri, Sat, Sun; 🅿️).

Megalo Horio is also the starting point for the all-day hike to **Mt Kaliakouda** (2098m) and back. If you fancy something more level, you can take a satisfying stroll along the banks of the Karpenisiotis River on a footpath that begins opposite the village bus terminal.

Back on the main road, at the foot of Megalo Horio, the riverside **Gavros** attracts Karpenisi families in search of a good meal in the countryside, such as at **Taverna To Spiti tou Psara** (Fisherman's Taverna; ☑ 22370 41202; Gavros; mains €6-10; ⊙ lunch & dinner; 🅿️🛜), or a stroll along the Karpenisiotis River among fir, pine and chestnut trees. You can overnight here at **Pension Agrambeli** (☑ 22370 41148; www.agrampeli.gr; Gavros; d/tr incl breakfast from €45/55, ste €95; 🅿️@🛜❄️).

With your own transport, you can visit the restored village of **Koryshades**, reached through a marked turn-off about 4km southwest of Karpenisi.

Without your own transport, getting around is tricky. A single local bus does a morning return circuit between Karpenisi and Megalo Horio, Mikro Horio and Gavros twice a week (€2.25, 25 minutes). The schedule changes by the season, so first check with the **Municipality of Karpenisi** (☑ 22373 50000; Ydras 6, Karpenisi). From Karpenisi's central *plateia* (square), a taxi costs about €15 to Gavros, Megalo Horio or Mikro Horio.

a short video and a couple of temporary displays, and T-shirts and historical maps on sale.

Nearby, a rushing sulphur **hot spring** fills a small natural pool where you can relax in water that reaches up to 40°C. A sign cautions bathers to limit their dips to 10 minutes. Drive north about 200m to an abandoned petrol station, turn left and go another 150m to find the spring.

Archaeological Museum　　MUSEUM
(☑ 22310 29992; €2; ⊘ 8am-3pm Tue-Sun; [P]) Lamia's *frourio* (fortress) is worth the hike just for the views. Within it is the Archaeological Museum, chock-a-block with amazing finds from Neolithic to Roman times, including some c 2nd-century-BC Hellenistic children's toys.

🏃 Activities

Lamia Mountaineering Club　　OUTDOORS
(EOS Lamia, Hellenic Federation of Mountaineering; ☑ 22310 26786, 22310 59007, 21036 45904; www.eooa.gr) For information about hikes on Mt Iti and in Iti National Park, contact this Lamia- and Athens-based organisation.

🛏 Sleeping & Eating

Hotel Athina　　HOTEL €
(☑ 22310 27700; www.hotelathinalamia.gr; Rozaki Angeli 41; s/d/tr incl breakfast from €40/50/70; [P]❄️🛜) The efficient, friendly and family-managed Athina has tile-floored rooms, large modern bathrooms, comfortable beds and, remarkably, its own free parking. It's handy to Plateias Laou and Eleftherias.

Fitilis Restaurant　　TAVERNA €
(Plateia Laou 6; mains €6-12; ⊘ lunch & dinner) On a lovely square, Fitilis serves classic *mayirefta* dishes at value-for-money prices. If you're lucky, there might be slow-cooked goat, which sizzles over an open, antique wood oven.

🍷 Drinking & Nightlife

Dégagé　　CAFE-BAR
(☑ 22310 51300; Plateia Eleftherias 15; ⊘ 9am-2am; 🛜) Hip, modern, friendly and swanky cocktail bar on the square of Plateia Eleftherias.

ℹ️ Information

Banks, all with ATMs, are adjacent to both Plateia Parkou and Plateia Laou.
Police Station (☑ 22310 56865; Leoforos Athinon 188) Located on the southern edge of Lamia.

ℹ️ Getting There & Away

BUS
All buses depart from the **KTEL bus station** (☑ 22310 51345; www.ktelfthiotidos.gr; Taygetou 74), 2.4km southeast of the centre. A taxi between the centre and the bus station costs around €5.

For Iti National Park, go to Ipati (€2.40, 40 minutes, five to seven daily) via Loutra Ipatis (€1.90).

Bus Services from Lamia

DESTINATION	DURATION	FARE (€)	FREQUENCY
Agios Konstantinos	50min	5.20	hourly
Amfissa	1½hr	7.70	2 daily
Athens	3hr	22.30	hourly
Delphi*	2hr	9.90	1 daily
Karpenisi	1¾hr	7.90	2-3 daily
Larissa	1½hr	13.90	1-5 daily
Patra	3hr	20.50	2-3 daily
Thessaloniki	4hr	28.10	4-7 daily
Trikala**	2hr	12.90	6 daily
Volos	2hr	13.90	2 daily

* change in Amfissa
** change for Meteora and Kalambaka

TRAIN
Lamia's main train station is 6km west of the town centre at Lianokladi. But train tickets should be purchased in Lamia from the **OSE ticket office** (☑ 22310 44883; www.trainose.gr; Konstadinopoleos, Kon/Poleos), where an OSE shuttle bus links with the Lianokladi train station. Normal and Intercity (IC) trains run to Athens (€15.30 to €25, 2½ to three hours) and Thessaloniki (€21 to €33, 3½ to 4½ hours).

Iti National Park
Εθνικός Δρυμός Οίτης

Iti is one of Greece's most beautiful but least developed national parks, anchored by graceful Mt Iti (2151m). It's a verdant region with forests of fir and black pine, upland meadows, wild mushrooms and snow-melt pools fringed by marsh orchids, and is home to butterflies, woodpeckers, eagles, deer and boar. According to mythology, Hercules built his own funeral pyre on Mt Iti, near the village of Pavliani, before joining his divine peers on Mt Olympus.

The bordering village of **Ipati**, 22km west of Lamia and 8km south of the Karpenisi–Lamia road, has the remains of a fortress and is (along with Pavliani to the south) a starting point for hikes on Mt Iti. The hub of the village is the tree-shaded central square, Plateia Ainianon, flanked by a few traditional *kafeneia* (coffee houses).

Loutra Ipatis, a sweet and low-key village on the approach to Ipati, is home to a year-round thermal spa, a few hotels and tavernas.

◎ Sights & Activities

Agathon Monastery   MONASTERY
(☉sunrise-sunset) Just 7km past the village of Ipati is the lovely Byzantine Agathon Monastery in a stunning setting at over 550m above sea level, clinging to the slopes of Mt Iti. A **natural-history museum** is housed here, among other relics.

Loutra Ipatis Thermal Spa   SPA
(☑22310 59526; Loutras Ipati; €4; ☉7am-8pm summer, 9am-5pm winter) The gorgeous and shady village of Loutras Ipati is the year-round home to a low-key and well-managed thermal sulphur spa. You can see the 'eye' of the source in the adjacent park, plus there are mineral baths.

Hiking
Trails criss-cross Iti National Park. A good day hike begins clearly at Ipati; the four-hour (8km) trek reaches an often-locked refuge (**Trapeza** at 1850m) near the Pyrgos summit (2151m). Other day hikes reach the villages of **Kastania** and **Kapnohori**. For shorter strolls from Ipati, take the 2.4km **Farmakides Path** to the **Kremastos Waterfall**, or the 4.4km trail to **Arsali monastery**.

ⓘ FERRIES FROM ASTAKOS TO IONIAN ISLANDS

Otherwise unremarkable, Astakos is a convenient stepping stone for access to the Ionian Islands from Central Greece, via the daily ferry (the *Ionio Pelagos*) to/from the port of Sami on Kefallonia (per person/car €11/45, three hours), and Pisa Aetos on Ithiki (per person/car €9.20/36, two hours) in summer. For both crossings, there are one or two ferries daily, but check ahead with **Ionian P. Lines** (☑26460 38020; www.ionionpelagos.com; Astakos) as days and hours vary seasonally. In Astakos, a few cafes and tavernas line the small waterfront so you can get your fill while waiting.

Try *Anavasi Map No 2.3, Central Greece: Giona, Iti, Vardhousia*; or *Map of Mt Olti – Routes & Paths*, available in Lamia and Loutra Ipatis, published by the Mt Iti National Park administration, or *Road Editions Map No 43, Iti*. Keen hikers can check out www.oiti.gr/?q=en/content/hiking-routes-footpaths. Further information can be obtained through the Lamia Mountaineering Club (p217).

⊨ Sleeping & Eating

★Hotel Alexakis   HOTEL €
(☑22310 59380; www.alexakis.gr; Loutra Ipatis; s/d/tr incl breakfast €35/50/60; P❋❆@☎) The immaculate, newly renovated Alexakis boasts contemporary rooms, a lovely terrace with breakfast to match, and broad views of Mt Iti. The delightful, friendly owners, Julia and Sofia, epitomise *filoxenia* (hospitality).

★I Mouries   TAVERNA €
(Mulberry; ☑22310 59488; www.lymouries.gr; Loutra Ipatis; mains €6-10; ☉lunch & dinner; P✍) Traditional village taverna with fabulous *mayirefta* and daily grills (each day a different meat, though it's lamb more often than not) along with *horta* and *briam* (oven-baked veggies). Ingredients are always locally sourced, and mountain mushrooms are often featured.

ⓘ Information

Check out the city of Lamia's useful website: www.lamia.gr/en/content/mountain-trails-ipatis.

ⓘ Getting There & Away

With your own transport, it's easy to move among the small villages that border Mt Iti, as well as driving into the park as far as Neochori. There are frequent local buses from Lamia to Ipati via Loutra Ipatis (€2.20, 35 minutes, four or five daily).

METEORA & THESSALY

The region of Thessaly (Θεσσαλία) occupies much of east-central Greece between the Pindos Mountains and the Aegean Sea. The fertile and river-fed Thessalian plain supported two of the earliest Neolithic settlements, Sesklo and Dimini, on the continent. Today it boasts two of Greece's most extraordinary natural phenomena: the lofty, monastery-capped rock pinnacles of Meteora, and the

THIVA   ΘHBAI

Thiva, the birthplace of Hercules and Dionysos, was a powerful city-state in 400 BC during Greece's golden age, occupying a strategic position between northern Greece and the Peloponnese. The tragic fate of its royal dynasty, centred on the myth of Oedipus, rivalled that of ancient Mycenae. After the Trojan War in the 12th century BC, Thiva became the dominant city of the Boeotia region. Thiva's glorious run ended in 335 BC, however, when it was sacked by Alexander the Great for siding with the Persians.

Present-day Thiva has few vestiges of its past glory – except for exhibits in a wonderfully restored **archaeological museum** (☑22620 23559, 22620 27913; www.mthv.gr; Threpsiadon 1, Plateia Keramopoulou; adult/student/child under 18 €6/3/free; ◷8am-8pm Tue-Sun mid-Apr–Oct, to 3pm Tue-Sun Nov–mid-Apr; ℗) that reopened in 2016. Greek history fans might head here for posterity, and the town centre, filled with cafes, is worth a wander.

Buses operate to Athens (€8.80, one hour, hourly until 8.30pm) from Thiva's **central bus station** (☑22620 27511; www.ktelthivas.gr; Estias 10), 500m south of Plateia Agios Kalotinis. Trains from **Thiva station** (☑22620 27531; www.trainose.gr; Tiresiou & Kiriakou; ◷7am-11pm), 500m north of the museum, depart for Athens (normal/Intercity €7.30/13.70, 70/65 minutes, eight or nine daily) and Thessaloniki (€22.30/37.90, 5½/4½ hours, five or six daily).

---

lush Pelion Peninsula. The mountains and alpine meadows around Elati are destinations for outdoor enthusiasts.

Larissa   Λάρισα
☑2410 / POP 144,650

◉ Sights

You can gaze at the ongoing archaeological excavation of a well-preserved 3rd-century-BC **theatre** (☑24135 08234; Venizelou) FREE in the city centre, 100m north of Plateia Sapka. Nearby, the **acropolis** on Agios Ahillios hill dates from Neolithic times (6000 BC).

Diachronic Museum of Larissa   MUSEUM
(Archaeological Museum; ☑24135 08242; Karampilia 12; adult/student/child €4/2/free; ℗) The region's newest museum, with an eye towards ancient cultures, is exceptional, with detailed displays from the Larissa area, from the Middle Palaeolithic to the late Byzantine times, including discoveries from the Neolithic period. It's on the southwest side of Larissa.

Municipal Art Gallery of Larissa   GALLERY
(Katsigras Museum; ☑2410621205; www.katsigras museum.gr; Papandreou 2; €3; ◷10am-2pm & 6-9pm Tue-Fri, 10am-2pm Sat & Sun; ℗) Houses a superb private collection of Greek art from 1850 to 1950 (said to rival the National Art Gallery in Athens) in a stunning contemporary building, plus temporary exhibitions.

⌑ Sleeping

Hotel Metropol   BUSINESS HOTEL €
(☑24105 37161; www.hotelmetropol.gr; Rousvelt 14; s/d/f incl breakfast €41/48/90; ℗❄@☏) Should you linger in Larissa, you'll find large rooms decorated with the owner's paintings at this dated, but adequate, business-style hotel. Remarkably for Larissa, the hotel has parking.

❶ Information

There are several banks around Plateia Mihail Sapka and Plateia Laou.
Hospital (☑24102 30031; Tsakalof 1)
Police Station (☑100; Papandreou 14)
Post Office (cnr Papanastasiou & Athanasiou Diakou)

❶ Getting There & Away

BUS

Buses leave Larissa's **KTEL station** (☑24105 67600; www.ktellarisas.gr; cnr Georgiadou & Olympou) for Athens (€32, four hours, nine daily), Thessaloniki (€15.50, two hours, nine daily) and Volos (€5.60, one hour, hourly until 9pm).

From the branch **KTEL Trikalon station** (☑24106 10124; Iroön Polytechniou), near the junction with Gazi Anthimou, buses run hourly to/from Trikala (€6.90, one hour, hourly until 9.30pm). For Meteora, take the Trikala bus, then change for Kalambaka.

TRAIN

Trains pass daily through Larissa's **train station** (☑24102 36250; www.trainose.gr; cnr 28 Octovriou & Iroön Polytechniou) to/from Athens

AROUND LARISSA

If you have time and transport, it's an easy drive 28km northeast of Larissa to the **Vale of Tembi**, a dramatic gorge cut by the Pinios River between Mt Olympus and Mt Ossa that was sacred to Apollo in ancient times. A small bridge connects the car park with 13th-century **Agia Paraskevi** church and, 2km further on, the ruins of a **medieval fortress**.

The picturesque village of **Ambelakia**, 5km up a winding road from the village of Tembi, was a prosperous textile centre in the 18th century. A few of the original 600 mansions remain, and walking the cobbled streets is a delight. There is a pleasant cafe and taverna on the small square shaded by a large plane tree. From the square it's a short walk to a colourful **folklore museum**, and the remarkable **Georgios Schwartz museum** which chronicles the destruction of the village by Nazi troops during WWII.

(Intercity €35, four hours, five daily), Thessaloniki (express €14.80, 1¾ hours; Intercity €19.80, 1½ hours, hourly) and Volos (normal €4, one hour). You can buy tickets at the **OSE office** (☑ 24105 90239; Papakyriazi 35-37; ☉ 9am-2pm Tue & Thu, 9am-2pm & 5-9pm Wed & Fri).

Volos   Βόλος

☑ 24210 / POP 131,000

Known as Iolkos in Ancient Greece, Volos was the mythic home of Jason and his band of Argonauts. These days, Volos is a large and bustling university city on the northern shores of the Pagasitikos Gulf, and its function as the gateway to the Pelion Peninsula and the Sporades draws travellers to the city.

◉ Sights

Archaeological Museum   MUSEUM
(☑ 24210 25285; Athanasaki 1; €3; ☉ 8am-3pm Tue-Sun summer, to 3pm winter; [P]) This excellent museum is set in a pretty rose garden and houses finds from Dimini (p223) and Sesklo (p223), along with an impressive collection of painted grave stelae from the nearby Hellenistic site of Dimitrias. Recorded commentaries are available.

Tsalapatas Brickworks Museum   MUSEUM
(☑ 24210 29844; Notia Pyli, Palaia; €3; ☉ 10am-6pm Wed-Mon Mar–mid-Oct, to 5pm Wed-Mon mid-Oct–Feb) From 1926 until 1975, Tsalapatas Rooftile and Brickworks was part of the cultural fabric of Volos. In 2006 the restored plant opened as the handsome Tsalapatas Brickworks Museum, with brick-making machinery, grinding mills and massive kilns on display and frequent art exhibits. It's at the South Gate in the Old Town.

Volos Museum of the City   MUSEUM
(☑ 24210 29878; http://volosinfo.gr/en/item/the-museum-of-volos-city; Feron 15; €2; ☉ 10.30am-1.30pm & 6-9pm Tue-Sun; [P]) This smart new museum, in an old tobacco warehouse in the Palaia district, focuses specifically on the history of Volos through a beautiful collection of black-and-white photos from the 1800s to the present day, including a riveting section on the population exchange in 1923 between Greece and Turkey. A swanky cafe adjoins the museum.

🛏 Sleeping

Hotel Jason   HOTEL €
(☑ 24210 26075; www.jason-hotel.gr; cnr Pavlou Mela 1 at Argonauton; s/d/tr €40/50/60; ❄ 🛜) One of Volos' few real budget hotels, it offers simple rooms with few frills. The upsides are attentive staff and its close proximity to the port. Rooms at the rear are €10 less.

Hotel Argo   HOTEL €
(☑ 24210 25372; www.hotelargovolos.gr/en; Dimitriados 165; s/d/tr from €35/45/55; ❄ 🛜) A very good budget option in central Volos, the Argo has been recently renovated. Rooms are basic, but spotless, and staff attentive.

★ **Hotel Aegli**   BOUTIQUE HOTEL €€
(☑ 24210 24471; www.aegli.gr; Argonafton 24; s/d/tr/q incl breakfast from €70/100/130/140; ❄ ❄ 🛜) This 80-year-old hotel on the boardwalk has a modern face. It's well-managed, sleek, swanky and comfortable in every respect. High-ceilinged rooms are austere with modern, spacious bathrooms and elegant touches throughout, and most have views of the port. Professional staff can help with all Volos and Pelion plans. Excellent value; ask about off-season deals.

Hotel Domotel Xenia Volou   HOTEL €€
(www.domotel.gr/hotel/4/Xenia-Volos; Plastira 1; s incl breakfast from €80, d €100-120; [P] ❄ @ 🛜 ❄) Volos' most upmarket place appeals to

Greek visitors because of its sleekness. We like it more for its position on the water and looking back at town. Smart rooms, half facing the sea, the other half the city, a spa, two pools, a *hammam* (Turkish baths) and lavish breakfast make it a reliable stay.

✗ Eating

★ Brighton Food & Wine   GREEK €

(Krokiou 34, Palaia; mains €6-11; ⊗8pm-late Tue-Fri, lunch & dinner Sat & Sun; ❄🛜) The old Palaia warehouse district is home to this handsome, open-kitchen eatery started by two Greek friends who met at university in Brighton, England. Elias and Dimitris use organic produce, serve local craft beer, Greek wine and cocktails. Expect a subtle twist on old favourites, like fava dip with leek, braised octopus, and pasta with zucchini and goat cheese.

Palios Fournos   BAKERY €

(Palaia Bakery; ☑ 24210 33703; Krokiou 56; breads, pastries €1.50-5; ⊗7am-midnight) The best bakery for miles. Pelion residents think nothing of driving here from their villages to get authentic village breads and pastries. In the Palaia district. Open late.

Kavouras Tsipouradhiko   GREEK €

(Gatziagiri 8; drink & mezedhes plate €4-5; ⊗11am-5pm Mon-Sat) Believed to be one of Volos' oldest *tsipouradika* (place that serves ouzo and light snacks), up a tiny street between Dimitriados and Iasonos, this is a no-nonsense, no-frills, hard-drinking and eating experience. *Tsipouro* is poured from bottle to glass as per the old days. It bustles with locals and there's a heavy dose of testosterone, but all are welcome.

Kerasia Tsipouradhiko   GREEK €

(Cherry Tree; Papakiatzi 40; drink & mezedhes €4-5; ⊗9am-6pm) For nearly 30 years, a husband and wife team have kept their heads down and clients happy at this traditional *tsipouradiko*. Locals are known to traipse across town for their Greek coffee. Old photos on the establishment's wall attest to former times, though thankfully little has changed.

Stafylos   GREEK €€

(☑ 6970668344; Melounas 6; mains €8-12; ⊗lunch & dinner; ❄🛜) Your welcome is a small glass of *tsipouro* and some olives and a tomato dip before you've even ordered. There are lovely dishes from all over Greece, Crete in particular, including a delicious *apaki* (Cretan cured pork), snails and much more. In the Palaia district, towards the old train station.

CENTRAL GREECE VOLOS

Thessaly

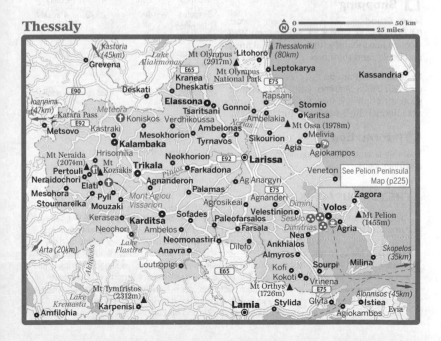

🍷 Drinking & Nightlife

For a night of music, drinking and dancing, head to the revitalised old industrial district known as the Palaia, the hang-out for nearby university students. On warm evenings, the narrow lanes of the Palaia around Krokiou, and the city centre around Koumoundourou and Kontaratou, and also Ermou west of Agios Nikolaos church, swarm with cafes, live-music and jazz bars.

MeZen Tsipouradhiko   OUZERIE, BAR
(📞 24210 20844; Alonissou 4; ⏰ noon-midnight) The name MeZen is a hip pun, combining zen and mezed, short for mezedhes, which they do exceptionally well at this snappy *tsipouradhiko* in the heart of Volos, with small bottles of *tsipouro*, either anise-flavoured or *choris* (without). Like ouzo, the flavoured version of *tsipouro* turns milky when poured over ice.

Poco Pico Cafe Bar   BAR
(📞 24210 22922; Koumoundourou; ⏰ 7am-late) This tiny spot – a hole-in-the-wall cafe-bar – is the nearest thing you'll get to a street party with good espresso. Everyone, it seems, especially university students, gathers here for an evening drink, but it's also great for early risers who need their java fix.

🛍 Shopping

News Stand   BOOKS
(📞 24210 23200; Iasonos 84; ⏰ 8am-8pm) Well stocked news-stand with international press and books, and souvenirs.

Ekonomou O Papous   FOOD
(📞 24210 34606; Anthimou Gazi 135) Charming shop with only one item for sale: *loukoumi*, a traditional Greek version of Turkish delight.

ℹ Information

There are several ATMs on Argonafton, Iasonos and Dimitriados.

Tourist Police (📞 24210 39057; 28 Octovriou 179) For crime-related issues, head here.

Volos General Hospital (📞 24210 94200; Polymeri 134) Near the Archaeological Museum.

Volos Tourist Information Centre of Magnesia (📞 24210 30940; http://volosinfo.gr/en; cnr Grigoriou Lambraki & Sekeri; ⏰ 8am-4pm Mon-Fri) Just opposite the KTEL bus station, this modern facility offers hotel information, town maps and bus, train and ferry schedules, along with helpful travel tips for the Pelion Peninsula.

ℹ Getting There & Away

BOAT

Volos is a gateway to the northern Sporades isles of Skiathos, Skopelos and Alonnisos. Ferries arrive at and depart from the far end of the dock; hydrofoils from the near end. In July and August there is often a biweekly ferry service from Alonnisos to Skyros. Check in advance.

Boat Services from Volos

The following are high-season schedules which change regularly.

DESTINATION	DURATION	FARE (€)	FREQUENCY
Alonnisos	5hr	26	1-2 daily
Alonnisos*	3¼hr	52	1 daily
Skiathos	2¾hr	22	1-2 daily
Skiathos*	1½hr	41	1-2 daily
Skopelos (Skopelos Town)	4hr	25.70	3-4 weekly
Skopelos (Skopelos Town)*	3hr	52	1 daily
Skopelos (Glossa)	3½hr	23	3-4 weekly
Skopelos (Glossa)*	2¼hr	43.50	1 daily

* high-speed service

THE TSIPOURADHIKA

Volos is famous throughout Greece for its *ouzeries* and *tsipouradika*. If you have not already come across one, an *ouzerie* (strictly speaking, called a *tsipouradiko*) is a type of small restaurant serving various plates of mezedhes (appetisers) and tiny bottles of *tsipouro*, a distilled spirit, like ouzo but stronger. You can pour it over ice or dilute it with water if you prefer it weaker. When you've finished one round of mezedhes or *tsipouro*, you keep ordering until you've had your fill (or can't stand up). The basic rule: don't expect a drink without a plate. Typical mezedhes include grilled *ohtapodi* (octopus), *saredeles* (grilled sardines) and fried calamari. Traditional *tsipouradhika* were open during the day only. Some of our old-time favourites in Volos: Kerasia (p221), Kavouras (p221) and MeZen .

BUS

From the **KTEL Volos bus station** (🖉 24210 33257; www.ktelvolou.gr; cnr Zachou & Almyrou), opposite the tourist info centre, buses depart for Athens (express, €30, 4½ hours, five daily), Larissa (€5.90, one hour, 12 daily), Thessaloniki (€20.20, 2¼ hours, eight daily), Trikala (€14.90, 2½ hours, four daily) and Ioannina (€26.10, 4½ hours, three daily). If you don't want to traipse to the station, you can buy tickets in advance at **Amygdalo Sweet Shop** (🖉 24210 22375; Dimitriados 84b; ☉ 9am-2.30pm & 5.30-10pm Mon-Fri, 9am-3pm Sat) in central Volos.

TRAIN

The atmospheric Volos **train station** (🖉 24210 24056; www.trainose.gr; Papadiamanti) is 200m northwest of Plateia Riga Fereou. Seven trains run daily to Larissa (€3.90, one hour), which is the place to catch connections to Athens (normal/express €19/31, six daily) and Thessaloniki (normal/express €14/17, hourly). You can also check schedules and buy tickets at the **OSE outlet** (Dimitriados 186; ☉7.30am-2pm Wed & Fri, to 8.30pm Tue, Thu & Fri, 8am-2pm Sat, closed Sat Jun-Aug) near the university.

❶ Getting Around

Cars can be hired from **Hertz** (🖉 24210 22544; stvolos@herz.gr; Port K-27), at the port next to the fish market, and **Avis** (🖉 24210 22880; avisvolos@otenet.gr; Argonafton 41).

Parking in Volos can be tricky. Head straight for a parking lot: the one on the quay (€1.50 per hour, with price decreasing to €1 after two hours) is the most convenient.

Around Volos

Just west of Volos are two major archaeological sites, both dating from early Greek civilisation in Thessaly. The architecture at both sites typifies the complex agrarian communities that could sustain much larger populations than those of their Palaeolithic hunter-gatherer ancestors.

◉ Sights

Seseklo   ARCHAEOLOGICAL SITE
(adult/child €2/1; ☉8am-3pm Tue-Sun) Features the remains of the oldest acropolis in Greece (6000 BC). Once believed to have had a population of up to around 5000. To reach Sesklo from Volos, head due west via Eparciaki Odos Volou-Paliouriou for 11km, a drive of about 20 to 25 minutes.

Dimini   ARCHAEOLOGICAL SITE
(adult/child €2/1; ☉8am-3pm Tue-Sun) A late-Neolithic site (4800–4500 BC) inhabited through to the Bronze Age, complete with traces of streets and houses and a wonderful *tholos* (Mycenaean tomb shaped like a beehive). To reach the site, drive west from Volos about 5km via Eparciaki Odos Volou-Paliouriou, turning right at the modern village of Dimini.

Pelion Peninsula
Πήλιον Ορος

The Pelion Peninsula lies to the east and south of Volos. It's formed by a dramatic mountain range, where the highest peak is Mt Pliassidi (1651m). The largely inaccessible eastern flank consists of high cliffs that plunge into the sea. The gentler western flank coils around the Pagasitikos Gulf. The interior is a green wonderland where trees heavy with fruit vie with wild olive groves and forests of horse chestnut, oak, walnut, fir and beech to reach the light of day. The villages tucked away in this profuse foliage are characterised by whitewashed, half-timbered houses with overhanging balconies, grey slate roofs and old winding *monopati* (footpaths) and cobbled *kalderimia* (mule paths). In Greek mythology, the Pelion was the summer home of the 12 gods of Mt Olympus.

History

In mythology the Pelion was inhabited by *kentavri* (centaurs) – half-man, half-horse creatures who took delight in drinking wine, deflowering virgins and generally ripping up the countryside. Not all were random reprobates, however – Chiron, considered the wisest of the group, was renowned for his skill in medicine.

The Turkish occupation did not extend into the inaccessible central and eastern parts of the Pelion and, as a result, the western coastal towns were abandoned in favour of mountain villages. In these remote settlements, culture and the economy flourished – silk and wool were exported to many places in Europe. The Orthodox Church at the time was instrumental in maintaining Kryfa Skolia (Hidden Schools). Like many remote areas in Greece, the Pelion became a spawning ground for ideas that culminated in the War of Independence.

CENTRAL GREECE PELION PENINSULA

❶ Getting There & Away

Buses to villages throughout the Pelion leave from the Volos bus station. Trains from Athens and Thessaloniki reach Volos via a local link at Larissa. There are regular domestic and charter flights to the island hub of Skyros, a two-hour ferry ride away from Volos and the Pelion. Additionally, charter flights to Volos from London, Paris, Munich and Amsterdam have started to appear.

Bus Services from Volos to the Pelion

The following buses service villages in the Pelion Peninsula from Volos:

DESTINATION	DURATION	FARE (€)	FREQUENCY
Agios Ioannis	2hr	7.30	1-2 daily
Kala Nera	50min	1.90	15 daily
Makrinitsa (via Portaria)	45min	1.80	6-8 daily
Milina (via Argalasti & Horto)	1½hr	5	3-5 daily
Pinakates	1hr	2.60	3 daily (weekdays)
Platanias	2hr	7.10	2-3 daily
Pouri	1¾hr	5.40	2-3 daily
Trikeri	3hr	8.30	1-2 daily
Tsagarada	1½hr	5.60	1-3 daily
Vyzitsa (via Milies)	1¼hr	3.10	4-6 daily
Zagora (via Hania)	1½hr	4.70	1-2 daily

Northwest Pelion
VOLOS TO MAKRINITSA

Volos has its port, and also its *balkoni* (balcony), the nickname for the striking village of Makrinitsa, and the frequent destination for escapees from Volos' hot summer days. The mountainside is popular for hiking and gathering wild herbs used in local recipes.

Taking the northeastern route from Volos to Makrinitsa, the road climbs 6km to the village of **Anakasia** (just after Ano Volos), home to the fascinating Theophilos Museum.

True to Pelion form, the *plateia* in **Portaria** has a splendid old plane tree, and the little 13th-century **Church of Panagia of Portaria** has fine frescoes. Portaria is 2km east of Makrinitsa and 12km northeast of Volos.

◉ Sights

Theophilos Museum   MUSEUM
(☑24210 47340; www.diki.gr; Anakasia; ⊙8am-2.30pm Mon-Fri; ℗) **FREE** This inconspicuous and faded mansion in Anakasia village features the fanciful and colourful work of Theofilos Hatzimihail (1866–1934), a wandering self-taught artist from Lesvos who earned his food and keep painting the interior walls of houses and cafes and, in 1912, this mansion. The rooms are a riot of whimsical and even humorous figures – modern, mythological and historical.

🛏 Sleeping

Dryanoubaina   GUESTHOUSE €
(☑6979333492; www.dryanoybaina.gr; Portaria; d incl breakfast from €50; ℗❄🛜) Little English is spoken here, but it doesn't much matter thanks to the enthusiasm of the owner, Dina. She runs a tight ship with three rooms, communal sitting room and kitchen. There are lots of fluffy carpets and embroidered pictures (done by Dina).

Anna's Home   GUESTHOUSE €
(☑6978556347; www.annashome.gr; Portaria; d incl breakfast from €50; ℗❄🛜🏊) These apartments in Portaria have traditional wood and stone touches, plus modern bathroom, and a garden pool. The main building where breakfast is served has a small bar, all part of Anna's homey hospitality.

Hotel Despotiko   BOUTIQUE HOTEL €€€
(☑24280 99042; www.despotiko.gr; Portaria; r incl breakfast from €80, ste €200; ❄@🛜🏊) For an upmarket experience, try this handsomely converted mansion. Significantly cheaper outside high season. Over 30 rooms are spread among four buildings, amid immaculate grounds.

🍴 Eating & Drinking

⭐**Kritsa Hotel Restaurant**   RESTAURANT €
(☑24280 99121; www.hotel-kritsa.gr; Portaria; mains €7.50-12; ⊙12.30pm-late; ℗❄🛜🍴🛗) Head to the Portaria *plateia* to find this welcoming spot under plane trees that serves outstanding Pelion favourites such as slow-cooked lamb, grilled mushrooms and roasted wild greens with egg. It's popular for its delicate and savoury pies with zucchini, leek, pepper or cheese. An all-Greek wine list to boot. Summer cooking classes also available at the family's nearby farm.

Pelion Peninsula

Aeriko Café-bar　　　　CAFE €
(☑ 6978556347; www.aeriko-pelion.gr; Portaria; drinks & snacks €3-5; ⊗ 10am-late, from 5pm Jun & Jul; ℗ ❋ 🛜) Between Makrinitsa and Portaria, worthy of an ice-cream stop to take in the wonderful view. Music in the evening.

Me Mostra　　　　BAR
(☑ 6944477683; Portaria; ⊗ noon-midnight; 🛜) This sharp little *tsipouradiko* in Portaria serves great mezedhes and *tsipouro*. Easy parking, about 200m east of main square.

MAKRINITSA　　　　ΜΑΚΡΙΝΙΤΣΑ
From a distance, the traditional houses of Makrinitsa give the impression that they're stacked on top of one another. Up close, the whitewashed structures are threaded with steep stairs crowded with flowers. Further up, the path leads to more than 50 stone water fountains. It is one of the loveliest of the Pelion villages and, because of its proximity to Volos, also the most visited.

The village is a pedestrian zone; a bus terminus and shaded car park mark the entrance. The central square is anchored by a massive plane tree with a kid-friendly hollow, a marble fountain and the tiny chapel of **Agia Panagia**.

👁 Sights

Museum of Folk Art　　　　MUSEUM
(☑ 24280 99505; €2; ⊗ 9am-2.30pm Wed-Sat, 11am-2.30pm Sun; ℗) This restored 1844 mansion, Arhontiko Topali, has well-displayed relics, including an old *tsipouro* still, a Victrola phonograph 'talking machine' and a hidden water fountain built into a stone wall.

🛏 Sleeping

Sisilianou Guesthouse　　　　GUESTHOUSE €
(Arhontiko; ☑ 24280 99556; sisilianou@gmail.com; s/d/tr/f incl breakfast from €45/55/65/70; ℗ ❋ 🛜) Just above the central square, this eight-room traditional mansion is the bargain *arhontiko* of the village. Rooms are

basic with old wood floors, high ceilings and a nice airy feeling throughout. Manager Anna makes a spectacular breakfast as well, served on a small terrace overlooking the village.

Melanthi Traditional Hotel GUESTHOUSE €€
(☑ 24280 99977; www.melanthi.gr/en; d/ste incl breakfast from €50/140; P ✳ ☎) Dating from 1858, this mansion has been decorated with atmosphere in mind and a view-from-the-bed focus. Traditional Greek fittings and outdoor terrace add charm to the 17 rooms (four with squeezy bathrooms). The comfortable beds, quieter village location and energetic and helpful owner Kiki are all pluses.

Arhontiko Repana GUESTHOUSE €€
(☑ 24280 99067; www.arhontikorepana.gr; s/d/tr incl breakfast from €45/60/70; P ✳ ☎) For hospitality and value, we love this friendly, family-run converted mansion (built in 1858). Each of the five rooms is homey, comfortable and decked out with wood and red carpets (only one is a bit squeezy). Gut-busting breakfasts, courtesy of Dimi and crew, are worth the stay alone. At the beginning of the village.

✗ Eating

A-B Taverna TAVERNA €
(☑ 24280 99355; mains €7-10.50; ☺ lunch & dinner; P ✳ ☎) A-B Taverna, a longtime favourite in Makrinitsa, has reopened 30m east of village car park in a handsome old village house. Sit outside or find a table upstairs overlooking the mountainside and Volos below, and sample traditional Greek appetisers (they make their own cheese), and *vetouli* (kid goat with zucchini or eggplant).

Kardomo TAVERNA €
(Cardomom; ☑ 24280 90131; mains €6.50-12; ☺ lunch & dinner; P ☎ ✐) Makrinitsa's newest eatery sits on a beautiful perch at the end of the village, after the Art Cafe. Solid Greek grills, rooster in wine sauce, pastas and well-prepared veggie dishes, plus very good house wine, and a Greek wine list.

Apolafsi GREEK €
(☑ 24280 90085; €8-12; ☺ 1pm-late Thu-Mon; P ☎) The most beautiful of the restaurant settings on a terrace under the canopy of the ancient plane tree in the *plateia*, it wouldn't matter what this place served up it's so beautiful. Luckily, however, it also does a great selection of traditional Greek dishes.

🍷 Drinking & Nightlife

Art Cafe CAFE-GALLERY
(Spiros; ☑ 6974384488; ☺ 10am-midnight; ☎) A delightful spot with outdoor tables overlooking the gulf. Very good coffee and sweets. Ask the gracious owner Spiros to show you the adjacent c 1830 stone building, and its (very) unusual door lock designed to foil intruders. Artwork by local painters, including *marioneta* (porcelain puppets). Not to be confused with nearby Paschalis Art House Cafe.

Northeast Pelion

Mountain and sea combine dramatically in the northeast Pelion, where rocky hillside villages seem to watch over the blue Aegean, connected by twisty roads and steep mule paths ending at small bays with the best beaches on the peninsula.

ZAGORA ΖΑΓΟΡΑ
Zagora is the largest of the Pelion villages and a major fruit-growing centre – it's the apple capital of Greece. The town exported fine silk around the continent until blight ruined the silk industry in 1850. Two War of Independence landmarks – the **museum** (☑ 24260 23708; Plateia Agios Georgios; by donation; ☺ 10am-2pm & 6-9pm Tue-Sun; P) and library – have their roots in Zagora. If you are coming from Hania, the road zigzags down through chestnut trees to a junction leading to the village.

◉ Sights

Library of Zagora LIBRARY
(☑ 24260 22591; www.library-zagora.gr; ☺ 9am-3pm Mon-Sat; P) **FREE** Starting with just 48 schoolbooks in 1767, the fascinating Library of Zagora is now home to one of Greece's largest collections of rare books and manuscripts, including 10th-century publications. Ask to see the exhibits. The website is in Greek only.

🛏 Sleeping & Eating

Arhontiko Dhrakopoulou PENSION €
(☑ 24260 23566, 24260 23460; Plateia Agios Georgios; r incl breakfast €40; P ✳ ☎) The local women's agritourism cooperative manages this homey lodging, next to charming and cobblestoned Plateia Agios Georgios. A local flower designates each of five simply furnished rooms.

★ **Arhontiko Stamou** GUESTHOUSE €€
(☑ 24260 23880; www.stamou-hotel.com; s/d/tr/q incl breakfast from €55/65/80/90; P @ ☎)

Arhontiko Stamou, a handsome and spacious nine-room villa (c 1863), shares a summertime courtyard with the mellow Café Anemella (Greek for 'silkworm'), just up the garden steps to your left. The gracious and knowledgable owner, George, will point you in the right direction. Excellent value with a quiet location that's still near the centre.

★**Taverna Niki**　　　　　　　　TAVERNA €
(Meintani; www.meintani.gr; mains €6.50-10; ☺noon-late; P🔊) In Plateia Sotira, flower-draped Taverna Niki excels for *mayirefta,* fresh seafood, and local delicacies like *kolokythoanthi* (stuffed zucchini flowers), and *kritama* (sea herbs) salad, hand-picked from the rocks along the Pelion coast. Convivial atmosphere, and good local wine and *tsipouro* to accompany the views to nearby Alonnisos and Skopelos islands.

🛍 Shopping

**Women's Agritourism
Cooperative Zagora**　　　　FOOD & DRINKS
(📋24260 23566; www.agrosweet.gr; Plateia Agios Georgios; ☺11am-7pm) A women's cooperative, the oldest in Greece, that makes a range of delicious jams and sweet products. Stop in for a coffee and see what's available, including a jam made from the small local *firiki* apple, found only in the Pelion.

❶ Information

Zagora Health Centre (📋24260 22591) For medical emergencies in the Pelion.

KISSOS　　　　　　　　　　ΚΙΣΣΟΣ

The hydrangea-draped village of Kissos is built on steep terraces surrounding the 18th-century **Church of Agia Marina** (☺8am-2pm) FREE, where the frescoes are considered the finest in the Pelion. It's a pleasant stop for a coffee or meal.

　　Taverna Klimataria (mains €6.50-9.50; ☺lunch & dinner; P) is a pretty spot on the square, near the historical church of Agia Marina, and the place to try *spetzofai* (a spicy sausage dish).

　　Nearby, picturesque villages adorn the road from to Tsagarada, one of the most scenically spectacular in the Pelion. The village of **Anilio** ('sunless') rests in the shadow of a ridge of chestnut and walnut trees.

HOREFTO　　　　　　　　　ΧΟΡΕΥΤΟ

Eight kilometres downhill from Zagora, Horefto is a low-key resort with palm trees

and a long sandy beach. It's also the mythical home of Chiron, a roving centaur who healed the sick in the days when doctors still made house calls. The main beach is sandy and very decent, while isolated **Agioi Seranta beach** fills a beautiful cove 2km south. Summer weekends can fill up fast.

🛏 Sleeping & Eating

Camping Horefto　　　　　　CAMPGROUND €
(📋6973209525; campsites per adult/tent/car €6/4/4; ☺May-Sep; P🔊) Long closed, this beachside campground has reopened with a shaded, clean and roomy site, with full facilities and a canteen.

★**Hotel Aeolos**　　　　　　　　HOTEL €€
(📋24260 22910; www.aeolos.com.gr; studios/apt from €110/160; ☺May-Sep; P❄🔊❄🏊) An elegant in-town spot near the beach with split-level studios and apartments, large pool, smart and comfortable rooms with modern bathrooms, and helpful staff. The hotel is actually a half-dozen buildings dotted around a 2-acre garden, enclosed by an old stone wall. Prices lower in the off season.

Hotel Cleopatra　　　　　　　HOTEL €€
(📋24260 22606; www.hotelcleopatra.gr; s/d €40/60; ☺Apr-Oct; P❄🔊) This vine-adorned hotel has simple, spacious tile-and-wood rooms, balconies and overhead fans,

WORTH A TRIP

POURI   ΠΟΥΡΙ

The laid-back village of Pouri, 3km down the hill from Zagora, spills down a steep mountainside to a small bay. It's home to a few tavernas clustered beneath the church. Downhill from Pouri, find two fine swimming beaches, pebbly **Elitsa** and **Analipsi**. Enjoy a meal at the delightful **Taverna Plimari** (✆6977706151; Analipsi beach; mains €7-12; ⊙Easter-Oct; P🖥), where the road ends.

making it good value. It's opposite the beach as you enter Horefto.

Taverna O Petros   TAVERNA €
(✆24260 22666; mains €5-9; ⊙May-Oct; P🖥) This reliable seaside eatery starts you out with a complimentary shot of local *tsipouro* and mezedhes, and serves up fine fish grills and a variety of traditional *ladera* dishes (with olive oil, oven-baked) like okra, zucchini and leeks, including cheesy local favourite *hortopita* (pie made with greens and cheese).

AGIOS IOANNIS   ΑΓΙΟΣ ΙΩΑΝΝΗΣ

Agios Ioannis is the busiest of the eastern coastal resorts, but there's still plenty of room. Small hotels, tavernas and pizzerias line the waterfront, and two sandy beaches are just a short walk north (Plaka) and south (Papa Nero).

🛏 Sleeping

★Katerina's Apartments   APARTMENT €
(✆6945762183, 24260 31159; www.pilio-katerina.gr; d/tr/f from €45/55/85; ⊙Apr-Oct; 🖼🖥) A narrow lane just north of Papa Nero beach opens up to a cosy courtyard anchored by a lemon and orange tree at this welcoming, family-run gem. Rooms are light, tidy and charming and have small kitchenettes. Katerina herself epitomises *filoxenia*.

Camping Papa Nero   CAMPGROUND €
(✆24260 31319; www.campingpapanero.com; campsites per adult/tent/car €5.50/5/4; ⊙May-Oct; P@🖥) Clean and tidy spot, attractive and shaded, with a cafe-bar, 200m south of the waterfront.

★Hotel Anesis   HOTEL €€
(✆24260 31123; www.hotelanesis.gr; s/d/tr incl breakfast €60/75/90; 🖼@🖥) Along with its appealing location set back from the street, the Anesis has pleasant pastel-toned rooms,

modern if smallish bathrooms, and a great breakfast with fresh juice, fruit, homemade yoghurt and jam, all served on a vine-shaded terrace overlooking the sea. Best of all, ever-helpful owner Miltos can lead you on a lovely three-hour walk to Tsagarada.

To Pelagos Studios   APARTMENT €€
(✆24260 31404; www.topelagos.gr; Papa Nero; d & tr €90; ⊙May-Oct; 🖼🖥) This perfect spot sits alone in front of Papa Nero beach, with standout features that include light, breezy rooms with small kitchenettes, all overlooking the sea. You need only enough energy to cover around 100m from the balcony, then down the stairs, over the green lawn, across the road and – plonk – into the water. The website is in Greek only.

🍴 Eating

O Christos   TAVERNA €
(O Xristos; ✆24260 31227; mains €7.50-11; ⊙11am-midnight; P) O Christos, a smart and friendly little *psarotaverna* (fish taverna) and *ouzerie*, is worth finding at the north end of the waterfront for its superior quality and seashell decorations, just opposite the beach. Choose from fresh red mullet, grilled squid and sardines. You can also buy fish by the kilo.

Taverna Akrogiali   SEAFOOD €
(✆24260 31112; www.akrogialipelion.gr; mains €7.50-12, fish per kg €30-50; ⊙noon-late May-Oct; P🖼🖥) A favourite of Volos locals, who love its seafood dishes, including *rizi tou psara* (seafood risotto, or a Greek version of paella; €8.50). Owner Apostolos says 'our food is honest' – think Greek produce (cooked by the matriarch, Eleftheria, for over 40 years) and realistic prices.

★Taverna Orea Ammoudia   TAVERNA €€
(✆24260 31219; mains €8-15; ⊙9am-late May-Sep; P🖥) Spread out under lush foliage at the southern end of Papa Nero beach, this breezy open-air taverna does excellent oven-ready mains such as baked cod, and unusual salads like *kritama* – tomatoes with sea herbs gathered in small rocky coves. An outdoor bar serves up drinks and ice cream in summer.

DAMOUHARI TO MOURESSI

Picturesque **Damouhari** is next to a rambling grove of olive trees bordering a pebble beach and protected cove that once shielded the hamlet from passing pirate ships. According to local lore, the village got its name from the expression *dos mou hari* (give me grace). Damouhari enjoyed brief fame from the 2008 movie *Mamma Mia!* (with Meryl Streep), which borrowed the secluded port for two weeks of filming. Damouhari is also the starting point for a beautiful 4km walk to **Fakistra Beach**.

Nestled off the main road, 3km north of Tsagarada, is the mellow village of **Mouressi**, known for its cherries, chestnuts and *mouries* (mulberries). There are great views of the Aegean from the lime-tree-shaded *plateia*.

◎ Sights & Activities

Agios Nikolaos
CHURCH

(Damouhari) Don't miss (as it's a bit hidden) the gorgeous, but sadly crumbling, little church of Agios Nikolaos. The interiors are covered in fine frescoes by an unknown artist. See the folks at the sea-kayaking company in the Ghermaniko building at the entrance to the village for the key.

Sea Kayaking Damouchari
KAYAKING

(✒6938491283, 24260 49872; www.shakayak.gr; Damouhari; short/half-day/full-day tour €18/25/45; ⊙Apr–Oct; ⊞) The small natural harbour of Damouhari is the perfect spot from which to launch kayaks and stand-up paddleboards (SUPs). Excellent guided trips (by Tomas and Odysseas, both superexperienced) range from short jaunts to full-day journeys to hidden coves, caves and beaches, including Fakistra, Mylopotamos, Limniounas or Lambinou.

🛏 Sleeping & Eating

★ Old Silk Store
GUESTHOUSE €

(✒24260 49086, 6937156780; www.pelionet.gr; Mouressi; d from €50; ⊙mid-May–mid-Oct; ⓅⓇ) The historical Old Silk Store, a 19th-century neoclassical gem properly managed by personable owner and British transplant Jill Sleeman, has a range of five traditional-style rooms in a leafy garden setting complete with cherry tree. There's an on-request breakfast (€8) including homemade goodies. And Jill has loads of information, maps too, on Pelion hikes and excursions.

Hotel Damouhari
HOTEL €€

(✒24260 49840; www.damouchari.gr/index.php/en/; Damouhari; r from €60, apt €100; ⓅⓇ⊞⊞) Hotel Damouhari is right on the beach and its range of unique stone rooms, which face a garden, are quaint, creaky and filled with quirky antiques and paraphernalia. The eye-catching Kleopatra Miramar bar brims

with nautical finds and is the spot for a post-beach drink.

Victoria Guesthouse
GUESTHOUSE €€

(✒6938491283, 24260 49872; www.gopelion.com; Damouhari; d/apt incl breakfast €60/90; ⓅⓇⓇ) One of three very decent domatia in Damouhari (the owners are related). Has a cafe below with fresh lemonade and smoothies and up-close views of the bay. Book early, only three rooms.

Taverna Karagatsi
TAVERNA €

(✒24260 49841; Damouhari; mains €7-9; ⊙lunch & dinner; Ⓡ) Apostolis serves up wonderful Pelion taverna standards but the fresh fish is the thing here, plus big Greek salads and tasty mezedhes such as *taramasalata,* all overlooking the tiny bay.

TSAGARADA   ΤΣΑΓΚΑΡΑΔΑ

Tsagarada (sometimes written as Tsangarada) nestles in oak and plane forests. This rambling and spread-out village comprises the four semiseparate communities of **Agio Taxiarhes**, **Agios Stefanos**, **Agia Kyriaki** and **Agia Paraskevi**, the largest of the group, just north of the main Volos–Milies–Tsagarada road. The plane tree in Agia Paraskevi's *plateia* is said to be one of the largest and oldest in Greece.

◎ Sights

Serpentine Organic Garden
GARDENS

(✒24260 49060; www.serpentin-garden.com; Agio Taxiadhes; by donation; ⊙by appointment) Serpentine Organic Garden is a one-woman one-of-a-kind labour of love, the inspiration of Doris Schlepper, who, over 30 years, has created a virtual museum of all things green and flowering, including rare trees and scented roses, along with sustainable vegetable, berry and herb gardens. Call ahead. Seeds for planting and yummy homemade jams available.

✯ Festivals & Events

Tsagarada Escape Festival
SPORTS

(Outdoor Activities Festival; ✒6975322472.; www.tsagarada-pelion.com; ⊙Jun & Jul) **FREE** Billed as a combination 'Sea & Mountain Sports Festival' with music concerts, this mostly free prefecture-sponsored four-day event kicks off the summer in Tsagarada with organised hiking, archery, horseback riding, mountain biking, rock climbing and even lifeguard seminars. There are even outdoor music concerts! It's on the last week of June and the first week of July.

🛏 Sleeping & Eating

Hotel Filoxenia
HOTEL €

(☑ 6995192135, 24260 49392; filoxeniapilio@gmail.com; Agia Paraskevi; s/d/tr incl breakfast from €35/45/55, apt €80; ⊙ year-round; P ❀ 🛜) Head down a few flowery steps when you see the hand-painted sign to find this attractive, efficient and comfy 10-room lodging in the heart of Tsagarada. Rooms tend to pastel with high ceilings and large, bright and airy bathrooms. Daniella is the hospitable and hands-on manager. Good value, and open year-round.

Villa Ton Rodon
GUESTHOUSE €

(☑ 24260 49340; Agia Paraskevi; s/d/tr incl breakfast €35/55/65; ⊙ May-Oct; P 🛜) This simple, unpretentious but comfortable pine-clad spot is surrounded by the friendly owners' garden. It's 50m down a small path off the main road, which continues all the way to Damouhari (signed in Greek).

★ Lost Unicorn Hotel & Restaurant
HOTEL €€

(☑ 6979795252, 24260 49930; www.lostunicorn.com; Agia Paraskevi; s/d incl breakfast from €50/90; ⊙ Apr-Oct; P ❀ @ 🛜) Lost Unicorn Hotel features Persian carpets, slow-swirling fans and antique-outfitted rooms in an elegant and well-appointed 19th-century mansion set in a beautiful glade. The Greek and English owners, Christos and Clare, make a breakfast worthy of the scenery, complete with singing nightingales.

Aleka's House
GUESTHOUSE €€

(☑ 24260 49380; www.alekas-house.gr; Agia Paraskevi; d/tr incl breakfast €65/75; P ❀ 🛜) Attractive Aleka's House features 10 very comfortable rooms with wood and stained-glass touches and modern bathrooms, and is one of the few accommodation options in the region to open all year. It has an upstairs cafe-bar and lovely restaurant with local produce, and popular daily specials like Aleka's chicken with a touch of spice (mains €7 to €12).

Taverna To Agnanti
TAVERNA €€

(☑ 24260 49210; Agio Taxiarches; mains €8-14; ⊙ lunch & dinner May-Oct; P 🛜 ♫) This atmospheric eatery cooks up the likes of pork leg, slow-cooked lamb and risotto with shrimps. Located in Plateia Taxiarhes, opposite the church and under the massive cover of the plaza's ancient plane tree.

MYLOPOTAMOS ΜΥΛΟΠΟΤΑΜΟΣ

Scenic Mylopotamos is divided by a rocky outcrop, with a natural tunnel connecting two small, beautiful beaches. It's 7km along the road from Tsagarada's Agia Paraskevi.

🛏 Sleeping & Eating

Hotel Faros
HOTEL €€

(☑ 6946897965, 24260 49994; d incl breakfast €75-85; ⊙ May-Oct; P ❀ 🛜) The Greek word *faros* means 'lighthouse' and this place is a shining beacon. For those who like seclusion, this quiet but dramatic spot, overlooking the Aegean Sea and surrounded by olive groves, is the place. There are 17 simple and spotless rooms, but it's all about the location. Easiest access is from Xourichti along a 3km road. Significant price reduction outside high season.

Diakoumis Rooms
GUESTHOUSE €€

(☑ 24260 49203; www.diakoumis.com; s/d/tr from €45/65/75, apt €85; P ❀ 🛜) At Diakoumis Rooms, just 1km before the village and beach at Mylopotamos, energetic and welcoming owners Stathis and Athina have made the most of the dramatic cliffside setting. All eight light and airy stone-floored rooms have clear views of the bay and Skiathos beyond, plus there are four self-catering apartments.

★ Taverna Angelika
TAVERNA €

(Aggelika; ☑ 24260 49588; mains €7-14; ⊙ daily May-Oct, Sat & Sun winter; P ❀ 🛜) Taverna Angelika is a highlight for many Pelion residents, as it should be. A 2017 expansion to the upper terrace has kept the same warm atmosphere, exceptional seafood, mezedhes and salads, and the breezy view over Mylopotamos beach is better than ever. This family affair includes the owners' own boat to provide the daily catch.

West-Central Pelion

VOLOS TO PINAKATES, VYZITSA & MILIES

The west-central region is easily the most developed on the entire peninsula, especially between Volos and Kala Nera where coastal traffic is a fact of life. With the exception of good camping there, it's best to head inland to a classic string of handsome village squares.

From Volos, the west-coast road heads south through the touristy villages of **Agria** and **Ano Lehonia**, where a branch road leads inland to **Agios Vlasios, Agios Georgios, Pinakates, Vyzitsa** and **Milies**, while the main road continues to neighbouring **Kato Gatzea, Ano Gatzea** and **Kala Nera**. After the tortuous roads of the eastern Pelion villages, this stretch of road is a blessing.

Olive Museum of Pelion　　　MUSEUM
(☑24230 22009; www.mouseioelias.gr; Ano Gatzea, rail station square; ⊙8am-5pm, or on train arrival) FREE Set in an old stone mansion, this inviting little spot is dedicated to the olive and its oil. It has detailed displays of picking tools and ladders, presses and storage vessels, plus a small shop. Ano Gatzea is a stop on the To Trenaki (p232) train ride.

PINAKATES　　　ΠΙΝΑΚΑΤΕΣ
An old plane tree anchors Plateia Agios Dimitrios, home to the church, a couple of tavernas, a small fountain, ceramic shop and wood-oven bakery. Pristine Pinakates only acquired electricity in 1973 and, from the looks of it, things haven't gotten out of hand.

🛏 Sleeping & Eating

Hotel Ta Xelidonakia　　　HOTEL €€
(Little Swallows; ☑24230 86920, 6976215187; www.pinakates.com; d/tr incl breakfast €100/120; P@🛜🏊) This restored mid-19th-century mansion balances history and comfort in grand fashion (read plush rooms, each named for a mythical Greek god). The verandah is anchored by a 3000L chestnut wine barrel.

Mansion Sakali　　　BOUTIQUE HOTEL €€€
(☑24230 86560, 6932429150; www.sakalihotel.gr/en; d incl breakfast from €150; P❄🛜🏊) Old-world charm meets contemporary conveniences. This atmospheric restored mansion has a touch of the perfect honeymoon spot about it (it offers spa treatments too), and offers a Pinakates upmarket experience.

Taverna Drosia　　　TAVERNA €
(mains €7-10; ⊙noon-late) This eatery is an extension of the family's house, and is one of the few places in Pinakates open all year. Look for Pelion favourites like baked goat and *spetzofaï* (stewed pork with peppers), with good local wine always on hand.

O Pileas　　　TAVERNA €
(☑24230 86873; mains €5.50-9; ⊙lunch & dinner; P) Best of the village tavernas, popular with locals and Volos folks for traditional village fare, *mayireftal,* grills and good *tsipouro* and regional wine.

VYZITSA　　　ΒΥΖΙΤΣΑ
Handsome Vyzitsa's cobbled pathways wind between traditional slate-roofed *arhontiko* (mansions). To reach its shady central square and two tavernas, walk up the cobbled path beside Cafe Baraki behind the clock tower.

🛏 Sleeping & Eating

Mansion Karagiannopoulou　　　GUESTHOUSE €€
(☑24230 86717, 6945479570; www.karagianno poulou.com; d incl breakfast €60-80, tr from €70; P❄🛜) Built in 1791 with the extraordinary architecture of the region, this beautiful guesthouse with garden ingeniously combines traditional and modern and boasts a range of stunning sitting rooms and bedrooms, elaborate ceilings included.

Hotel Stoikos　　　HOTEL €€
(☑24230 86406; www.hotelstoikos.gr; d/tr incl breakfast from €60/70; P❄🛜) The well-managed Stoikos has a traditional look, with beamed ceilings, handsome furnishings and stained glass adorning the spacious rooms. But what sets it apart, aside from the great views of the gulf, is the helpful and energetic owner Stella, who prepares a breakfast of local and homemade goodies.

Georgaras Restaurant　　　GREEK €
(☑24230 86359; mains €8-12; ⊙9am-late May-Sep, 6pm-late Sat & Sun Oct-Apr; P❄) One of Vyzitsa's oldest eateries, with a mountain menu featuring salads, stews and rich soups, along with stuffed pork with orange, and *kouneli stifadho* (rabbit stew).

🛍 Shopping

Esperides　　　FOOD
(Women's Agrotourism Cooperative; ☑24230 86838; ⊙10am-2pm & 5-7pm Mon-Fri, 10am-7pm Sat & Sun) The place for edible souvenirs. It comprises a group of 13 women who hand-make traditional jams, biscuits, baklava and other (very irresistible) sweet delights. By the car park. Call ahead as hours vary each year.

MILIES　　　ΜΗΛΙΕΣ
Beautiful Milies is anchored by a shady square and a plethora of fountains. The village played a major role in the intellectual and cultural awakening that led to Greek independence. It was the birthplace of Anthimos Gazis (1761–1828), who organised revolutionary forces in Thessaly in 1821 and toured mountain villages of the Pelion inspiring local resistance and leadership.

CENTRAL GREECE PELION PENINSULA

Milies is the start/end point for scenic rail To Trenaki. The walk down to the old station is very pretty and well worth doing (note: there are many steps).

Milies is also the trailhead for a marvelous three-hour, 11km circular hike to coastal Kala Nera and back, mostly following the old *kalderimia*.

◎ Sights

Agioi Taxiarhes   CHURCH
This church with 18th-century frescoes is on the central square. It's extraordinary for the 48 internal ceramic 'jars' that enhance acoustics, and for the unique frescoes, completed over 33 years by one monk.

Library of Milies   LIBRARY
(☑ 24230 86260; ⊙ 10am-2pm Mon-Fri, to 4pm Sat & Sun) FREE The Library of Milies is home to an extraordinary display of 3000 books (of a collection of around 10,000) printed between 1498 and 1899.

Museum of Milies   MUSEUM
(☑ 24230 86602; ⊙ 10.30am-2.30pm Wed-Sun) FREE The quaint Milies Museum houses a display of local crafts and costumes, along with the history of the area. Call ahead for changes in hours.

🛏 Sleeping

★ Iliovolo Guesthouse   GUESTHOUSE €
(Hliovolo; ☑ 24230 86777; www.iliovolo.gr; Milies; d/tr incl breakfast from €55/70; P ✳ �) In a lovely setting with traditional and modern amenities galore, Iliovolo's 10 rooms, all with superb balcony views, are great value. Add owners Maria and Andreas' sweet hospitality and homemade breakfast, and this is a great spot from which to explore the Pelion.

Palios Stathmos Hotel & Restaurant   GUESTHOUSE €
(Old Station; ☑ 24230 86425; www.paliosstathmos. com; s/d/f incl breakfast from €40/50/70; P ✳ framedsymbol) Named for the narrow-gauge railway station opposite, and nestled among a grove of plane trees, Palios Stathmos is a wood-and-stone pension built in 1903 that recalls a bygone era on the outside. Balconied rooms are simple but comfortable, and the resourceful manager Sofia can help with local info.

Sikia Camping   CAMPGROUND €
(☑ 24230 22279; www.camping-sikia.gr; campsites per adult/car/tent €7/3.50/4; ⊙ year-round; P @ framedsymbol) Well-managed and welcoming facility, with restaurant, minimarket and beach bar. Located 17km southeast of Volos, between Kato Gatzea and Kala Nera.

Camping Hellas   CAMPGROUND €
(☑ 24230 22267; www.campinghellas.gr; campsites per adult/tent/car €7/4/3; P @ framedsymbol) Attractive and shady campground located 17km southeast of Volos, just east of Kato Gatzea, fronting a pretty swimming beach on the west coast of the Pelion Peninsula.

(margin text, vertical) CENTRAL GREECE PELION PENINSULA

THE LITTLE TRAIN

Even if you have a car, it's well worth the effort to coordinate a ride on the quaint scenic rail To Trenaki (Little Train; ☑ 6948182800, 24210 39723; www.trainose.gr; Ano Lehonia & Milies stations; adult/child 4-14 one way €10/6, return €18/10; ⊙ daily Aug, Sat & Sun Apr-Jul & Sep-Oct). It will have you choo-choo'ing all the way home.

In 1895 a 13km narrow-gauge (60cm) railway line was built between Volos and Ano Lehonia and, by 1903, to Milies, making the town a prosperous centre of commerce. To Trenaki, the steam train that used to chug along this route, retired formally in 1971, but was revived in 1997 as a tourist attraction.

A restored Belgian coal-burning locomotive pulled the train when the route first reopened. But in 2000 a new diesel engine went into service after the train operators grew tired of following the smoke-belching original with a water tanker to put out the frequent grass fires started by airborne sparks. Despite the environmental upgrade, To Trenaki is still called Moudzouris, an affectionate term meaning 'the Smudger'.

The popular four-carriage train leaves Ano Lehonia at 10am and returns around 3pm, leaving you time to stroll around Milies. Check schedules and departure times as these change annually.

✖ Eating

Taverna Panorama　　　　　TAVERNA €
(☑ 24230 86128; mains €7-9.50; ⊙ lunch & dinner; �ⓢ) This cosy grill serves up Pelion favourites such as *spanikopita* (spinach pie), wild pork chops with potatoes, and *dolmadakia* (rolled grape leaves stuffed with rice and herbs). In summer sit across the narrow road at the terrace tables. Look for the climbing roses out front, about 200m north of the central square.

Anna Na Ena Milo　　　　　CAFE €
(☑ 2423086889; drinks, snacks €4-6; ⊙ 9am-late; ⓢ) A cosy crêpe-and-jam cafe with a quirky interior of old posters and children's book covers (like *Anna Na Ena Milo;* Anna Have an Apple). It's a wonderful spot to watch the world go by, possibly with a slice of owners Nicoletta and Nikos' homemade cheesecake.

Korbas Bakery　　　　　BAKERY €
(snacks €1.50-4) Head here for good pastries and savoury pies like the *tyropsomo* (cheese bread) and *eliopsomo* (olive bread). It's located at the junction of the main road and a smaller road which drops down to the little train station.

South Pelion
SOUTH TO TRIKERI

The south Pelion has an otherworldly feel as the landscape stretches out, with long vistas, straight roads and small fishing harbours, like picturesque Agia Kyriaki at the southernmost point of the peninsula. Sparsely forested hills, olive groves and lovely beaches line the road.

Before heading inland after **Kala Nera**, the road skirts the little coastal fishing village of **Afissos**, winds up to the attractive farming community of **Argalasti** and then forks – the left fork continues inland, the right goes to the coastal resorts of Horto and Milina. From Milina the road branches southwest to Trikeri, and southeast towards Platanias.

HORTO & MILINA　　ΧΟΡΤΟ & ΜΗΛΙΝΑ

Milina is the larger of these two coastal villages and sees many package tourists. Both are on a quiet part of the peninsula with pristine water and a few inviting pebble beaches and cafes.

There is an end-of-the-world feel about this part of the Pelion, as the road from Milina to Trikeri becomes more and more desolate. Residents pride themselves on their tradition as seafarers, fighters against the Turks in the War of Independence and upholders of traditional customs and dress.

◉ Sights

Old Radio Museum　　　　　MUSEUM
(☑ 6970374922; Lafkos; ⊙ daily 16 May-14 Sep, Sat & Sun 15 Sep-15 May; Ⓟ) **FREE** If you're one of those people who think nostalgia isn't what it used to be, turn your dial to this spot, in the village of Lafkos, 5km east of Milina, to check out one collector's pre-digital love affair with the original wireless. Hours can be unpredictable, call ahead.

🛏 Sleeping & Eating

Hotel Nicolas　　　　　GUESTHOUSE €
(☑ English 6932689782, German & Greek 24230 65296; www.nicolaspelion.gr; Horto; d/tr from €40/45; ⊙ May-Oct; Ⓟⓢ) Okay, the rooms are of the no-frills variety, but request front-facing rooms which seem to dangle over the turquoise water below. Superb location, friendly hosts, German spoken. Just outside Horto towards Milina.

Argentina　　　　　TAVERNA €
(☑ 6971912110; Milina; mains €6-10.50, fish by the kilo; ⊙ 8am-late; Ⓟ✱ⓢ) Popular eatery on the main road in town, with well-priced fresh fish specials, rabbit, *kleftiko* (slow-cooked lamb) and pasta dishes, plus plenty of veggies and salads. Breakfast features omelettes and fresh orange juice. Cheerful service, and open late.

The owners have three simple and spotless rooms upstairs for about €30.

Gibraltar　　　　　TAVERNA €
(Marianthi; ☑ 24230 65033; Milina; mains €7-11; ⊙ 8am-11pm; Ⓟ✱) Originally aimed at feeding the region's shipbuilders, these days the Gibraltar serves visitors and locals, who enjoy good Greek *fagito* (food), usually two or three daily dishes, wine and *tsipouro* 'from our vineyard'. It's located 1.5km south of Milina.

◉ Drinking & Nightlife

★ Casablanca　　　　　CAFE-BAR
(☑ 24230 65250; Horto; ⊙ 8am-11pm; ⓢ🖶) Look for the small hand-painted sign by the road, pointing the way to this delightful cafe with a tropical feel and slow-turning overhead fans, all the inspiration of charming French-German-Moroccan expat Marie, who makes perfect sweet and savoury crêpes, along with fresh juices and a full bar.

ℹ Information

Four-ways Travel (☑ 6972624653; Platanias; ☺ Jun-Sep) Volos travel agency's summer office, with info on transfers, lodging and area excursions.

Milina Holidays (☎ 24230 65020, 6932391592; www.milina-holidays.com; Milina; ☺ 9am-2.30pm & 6-9pm May-Oct) Resourceful George Fleris of Milina Holidays, on the waterfront, can help with accommodation, as well as arranging bike hire and day cruises to nearby Palio Trikeri for adult/child €30/15.

AGIA KYRIAKI   ΑΓΙΑ ΚΥΡΙΑΚΗ

This is the last stop on the Pelion Peninsula, a steep 4km drive off the main road, or a quick 1.5km walk down a cobblestone path. This fishing village sees few tourists and the bright, orange-coloured boats are put to good use by a hard-working population of around 200. A good footpath leads past tiny **Milos** to a **lighthouse**, about a 20-minute stroll. Another trail ascends gradually 10km east from Agia Kyriaki to Mt Tiseo (644m), with views of both the Aegean to the south and Trikeri Bay to the north.

🛏 Sleeping & Eating

Agia Kyriaki Guesthouse   GUESTHOUSE €
(☑ 6978771831, 24230 91112; http://agiakyriaki.gr; Agia Kyriaki; s/d incl breakfast €35/50; ☺ May-Sep; P ✳ 🛜) Just what you need for a quaint stay in a quaint spot, this top place has a stunning setting just behind the main strip, plus clean doubles and a friendly owner.

Taverna Athanassia   TAVERNA €
(Agia Kyriaki; mains €6.50-10; ☺ 8am-midnight) Small and excellent *psarotaverna* (fish taverna), much favoured by the locals. Open all day with coffee, wine, *tsipouro* and, best of all, well-prepared fresh fish and mezedhes. On the west side of the harbour.

O Manolas   GREEK €
(Agia Kyriaki; mains €7-10; ☺ 8am-late 15 Mar-28 Oct, Sat & Sun rest of year; P) Of Agia Kyriaki's three fish tavernas in a row, all facing the opposite shore of Evia, this one is popular with travellers for the lobster and spaghetti (among other fresh-fish delicacies).

PALIO TRIKERI   ΠΑΛΙΟ ΤΡΙΚΕΡΙ

If you really must go that one step further to get away from it all, then head for this little island, just off the coast, with a year-round population of 15 – it's often called I Nisos (The Island) for short. To reach I Nisos from the fishing village of **Alogoporos**, you need to take a taxi for the five-minute boat ride (around €2 per person). Several water-taxi signs are on the beach. Alternatively, telephone Nikos at **Taverna Diavlos** (☑ 6976851056; Palaio Trikeri; mains €5-10; ☺ Feb-Nov) on the island or take a cruise with Milina Holidays.

There are a couple of basic domatia at the taverna. The main activities on Palio Trikeri are explaining to locals why you're there, and then explaining to yourself why you're leaving.

PLATANIAS ΠΛΑΤΑΝΙΑΣ

Platanias' natural harbour was used as a base by the Persians. More recently, it was a popular resort, until the hydrofoil service stopped in 2001. Since then, it's returned to its low-key roots. There's a good sand-and-pebble beach, a campground and a few tavernas and domatia. Pretty **Mikro Beach** is a 10-minute walk southwest.

🛏 Sleeping

Studios Charoula   APARTMENT €
(☑ 6948179977, 24230 65020; www.charoula.com; Platanias; d/tr from €55/75; P ✳ 🛜) Welcoming and comfortable whitewashed studios and fully outfitted apartments, all with balconies overlooking pool and deck in a garden setting.

Hotel des Roses   HOTEL €
(☑ 24230 71268; www.peliondesroses.gr; Platanias; s/d/tr/q incl breakfast €30/50/55/62; ☺ year-round; ✳ 🛜) Platanias' first-ever hotel, and one that put the small resort on the map, is quiet, spotless, affordable and framed by rose bushes. Owner Nikos also makes soaps (from olive oil and donkey milk), and you can learn the art at an on-site class; milking optional. There are also regular 'eco-walking' and wild-herb-collecting excursions.

Olive Store Cottage   GUESTHOUSE €€
(☑ 6945575360; www.holidaylettings.co.uk/rentals/pelion/347420; Platanias; 2-person cottages €100; P 🛜) Head 4km north of Platanias for this beautiful self-catering cottage run by two enthusiastic expats and keen walkers.

🍴 Eating

Drosero Akrogiali   TAVERNA €
(Platanias; mains €5.50-9; ☺ lunch & dinner; P 🛜) The place to eat in Platanias with fresh fish, grilled meat and *mayirefta*.

Taverna Ondas   GREEK €€
(Promiri; mains €6-10; ☺lunch & dinner; 🅿🛜)
Seven kilometres northeast of Platanias, in
the mountaintop village of Promiri, is this
quaint, family-run taverna on the village
square with great cooking. The owners are
real hunter-gatherers so the products are
simple, but as fresh as can be. Forget the
menu, just ask them to recommend whatever is going. Guaranteed hearty and tasty.

Trikala   Τρίκαλα
☑24310 / POP 62,150
Roughly halfway between Karditsa and Kalambaka is Trikala, an attractive and bustling
agricultural centre straddling the narrow,
tree-lined Lithaios river. The first thing
you might notice about the town are the
bicycles. Many souls, young and old, pedal
around on their two-wheeler 10-speeds and
fixies. Trikala was once ancient Trikki, and
home to Asclepius, the god of healing. A
statue honouring the mythic doctor stands
on a small bridge by the main square where,
coincidentally, the city loans bikes for free.

👁 Sights

Tsitsani Museum   MUSEUM
(☑24310 77977; www.mouseiotsitsani.gr; Karditsis
1; ☺9am-3pm; 🅿) FREE Trikala's homage to
its musical heritage and composer Vassilis
Tsitsanis, in a modern setting with interactive displays. Worth the trip alone for the old
78 rpm record labels. The old prison building setting lends an extra high note to it all.

Varousi   AREA
The old Turkish quarter of Varousi, just east
of the fortress, is a fascinating area of narrow streets and fine old houses with overhanging balconies. At the corner of Anagiron
and Virvou, peek at the fine murals within
the 16th-century church of **Agioi Anargiri**.
Another 200m up the hill from Varousi is
the **Chapel of Profitis Ilias**.

Sanctuary of Asclepius   RUINS
Asclepius' sanctuary ruins are located before
the turn to the Fortress of Trikala.

Koursoun Tzami   MOSQUE
(Osman Sah; cnr Davaki & Kavrakou; ☺8am-2pm
Mon-Fri) The Koursoun Tzami was built in
the 16th century by Sinan Pasha, the same
architect who built the Blue Mosque in
İstanbul. The Unesco-designated mosque
was restored in the mid-1990s with EU

funding. From the central bus stop in town
head south and follow the river for 300m.

Fortress of Trikala   FORT
(Frourio) It's worth a wander up to the gardens
surrounding the restored Byzantine fort.
An adjacent cafe-bar overlooks the town.
Walk 400m up Sarafi, west from the central
square, and look for the sign pointing right.

🛏 Sleeping

Hostel Meteora   HOSTEL €
(☑6975949554; www.hostelmeteora.com; Tiouson
51, cnr Papagou; dm/d €10/30; 🌐🛜) This corner
hostel just east of the Varousi district is a welcome addition to the accommodation scene,
with three dorm rooms and four private doubles with small balconies. The friendly owner
Dimitris was born and raised in Trikala, and
is full of tips on getting around, and can
arrange tours. Free bikes to use, too.

Hotel Panellinion   HOTEL €€
(www.hotelpanellinion.com; Plateia Riga Fereou; s/d
incl breakfast from €45/60; 🌐🛜) Dating from
1914, this restored and spacious neoclassical
beauty is filled with traditional memorabilia, including old telephones and beautiful rugs. It's just opposite the river, on Riga
Fereou square.

🍴 Eating

Trikala's cafe life centers on the northern
end of Asklipiou and across the river in the
old Manavia district. Ypsilanti is flanked by
tavernas and *tsipouradhika*.

Taverna Kapileio   GREEK €
(☑6986954156; Pangalou 14; mezedhes €3-7;
☺lunch & dinner) This hole-in-the wall
tsipouradiko and part-time taverna serves
beautifully prepared mezedhes, and fine
grills too. Opposite a small park above the
river and the Manavika district.

Kebab Karthoutsos   KEBAB €
(Ioulietas Adam 5, Plateia Riga Fereou; mains €3-7.50;
☺6pm-late) With nearly 40 years standing,
this is the place for grills, including great pork
kebab (served on paper), *horta,* feta and local
wine, all for around €10 per head. In summer,
sit outside on the square.

Taverna Katogi   TAVERNA €€
(☑24310 20150; Kariskaki 58, cnr Ypsilantou; mains
€8-15; ☺12.30pm-late; 🌐) A smart place with
wooden interiors and beams in the Manavika district, that attracts businesspeople
and families alike. All want what this spot

WORTH A TRIP

DRIVING ROUTES FROM PYLI

About 18km southwest of Trikala is the village of Pyli (Πύλη; 'gate' in Greek), opening to a spectacular gorge and one of Greece's more inviting wilderness areas in the southern Pindos Range. It is home to the stunning little 13th-century **Church of Porta Panagia** (Pyli; ⊙8am-3pm). To reach it, cross the bridge from Pyli and follow the signs to the left. Five kilometres from Pyli is the **Moni Agiou Vissarion** (Dousikou; Pyli), a 16th-century monastery that stands on a slope of Mt Koziakas. Only men are permitted to enter. To get here, cross the bridge over the river, take the first turn left (annoyingly the sign, in Greek, is 20m after the left turn so don't expect a clear indicator). From here, you must wind your way up the hill for another 4.2km.

From Pyli, you can do three driving routes. The first is a half-day circuit around each side of the gorge. The route goes via **Elati**, a mountaintop village and something of a hill station for Trikala. Elati was called Tierna before the Germans burned it to the ground for harbouring Greek resistance fighters in WWII. After Elati you then head around the gorge in an anticlockwise direction.

The second circuit heads from Pyli all the way to Kalambaka, a route that climbs steadily through breathtaking alpine scenery, passing Elati with an optional detour via the smaller alpine outposts of **Neraidochori** and **Pertouli** (also a ski centre). Back on the main road, continue to head north, passing several mountain villages, before coming out at Kalambaka. Allow a leisurely day.

A third route takes you south from Trikala via Pyli to beautiful **Lake Plastira**, home to a fascinating **botanical garden** (☑ 24413 52200; www.plastiras-ota.gr/en/content/botanical-garden; Neochori; ⊙10am-1pm & 5-8pm; P ☒) **FREE** at **Neohori**.

---

does best: grills. There's roast pork, chicken, lamb and *loukaniko*, a village sausage comprising leek and fat. Lots of it, plus wine to wash it down.

🍷 Drinking & Nightlife

On weekend nights, the idea in Trikala seems to be to tank up on coffee along Asklipiou until midnight, then cross the bridge to the humming Manavika district for mojitos, mezedhes and music. This three-block maze of narrow passageways and outdoor tables jumps with lamp-lit music bars, small *ouzeries* and all-night cafes.

Klimataria   TAVERNA
(Rembetika mezedhopoleio; ☑ 24311 01576; Asklipiou 46; ⊙noon-2am; ☎) The Greek blues *(rembetika)*, once reserved for underground hideaways and speakeasies, is alive and well at this late-night Trikala hang-out. Live music, good food (perfect mezedhes) and plenty of spirits to go around.

❶ Information

Banks with ATMs ring the squares on either side of the river.
Police Station (☑ 24310 63013; cnr Yiannitson & Farmaki)
Post Office (Sarafi 13) Next to Plateia Riga Fereou.

❶ Getting There & Away

BUS

Buses depart from Trikala's **KTEL bus station** (☑ 24310 73130; www.ktel-trikala.gr; Rizargio; ⊙6.30am-10.30pm), 4km south of town. A shuttle (€0.60) runs from the **ticket office** (☑ 24310 73130; www.ktel-trikala.gr; cnr Othonos & Garivaldi) in town. Travellers for Delphi should change buses in Lamia. For the bus to Kalambaka, you can depart from the central bus stop (and ticket office) at the corner of Othonos and Garivaldi (thereby skipping the KTEL station south of town).

Bus Services from Trikala

DESTINATION	DURATION	FARE (€)	FREQUENCY
Athens	4hr	30.50	7 daily
Elati	1hr	3.90	1-2 daily
Ioannina	2½hr	15.90	2 daily
Kalambaka	35min	2.60	hourly
Lamia	2hr	12.90	7 daily
Larissa	1hr	6.90	hourly
Patra	5hr	33	3 weekly
Thessaloniki	3hr	20.40	5 daily
Volos	2hr	14.90	4 daily

TRAIN

From Trikala **train station** (☑ 24310 27529; www.trainose.gr; ⊙ 5am-9pm) there are trains to Kalambaka (€1.80, 15 minutes, four to five daily), Larissa (€8.10, one hour, three daily), Athens (Intercity €19.10, 4½ hours, two daily) and Thessaloniki (€22.60, four hours, two daily).

Meteora   Μετέωρα

The World Heritage–listed Meteora is an extraordinary place and one of the most visited in all of Greece. The massive pinnacles of smooth rock could be the setting for a futuristic science-fiction tale, or an ancient one. The monasteries atop them add to the strange and beautiful landscape.

The geological heart of Meteora is the **Adrachti**, or obelisk, a striking column visible from anywhere in Kastraki. Nearby, on the east-facing side of the Pixari rock face, closer to Kastraki, look for the colourful cave chapel of **Agios Andonios**. To the left of the chapel, in the hollows and cavities of the rock face, are the Askitaria (Cave Hermitages), complete with hanging ladders and nesting doves. The Askitaria were occupied until the early 20th century by solitary monks, and they remain a testament to the original spirit of Meteora.

History

The name Meteora derives from the Greek adjective *meteoros,* which means 'suspended in the air' (the word 'meteor' is from the same root).

The jutting pinnaclesof the Meteora were once sediments of an inland sea. About 10 million years ago, tectonic movements pushed the entire region out of the sea at a sloping angle. The same movements caused the flanking mountains to move closer, exerting extreme pressure on the hardened sedimentary deposits. The Meteora developed netlike fissures and cracks. The weathering and erosion that followed formed the towering outcrops of rock that now vault heavenwards.

From the 11th century, hermit monks lived in the scattered caverns of Meteora. By the 14th century, the Byzantine power of the Roman Empire was on the wane and Turkish incursions into Greece were on the rise, so monks began to seek safe havens away from the bloodshed. The inaccessibility of the rocks of Meteora made them an ideal retreat.

The earliest monasteries were reached by climbing removable ladders. Later, windlasses were used so monks could be hauled up in nets. A story goes that when curious visitors asked how frequently the ropes were replaced, the monks' straight-faced reply was 'when the Lord lets them break'.

These days, access to the monasteries is by steps that were hewn into the rocks in the 1920s and by a convenient access road.

◉ Sights

The monasteries and the towering rocks that support them seem impossibly suspended in air, bending the mind's eye to contemplate how either was formed. As you walk, climb and take pictures, let your imagination be your guide.

Each monastery is built around a central courtyard surrounded by monks' cells, chapels and a refectory. In the centre of each courtyard is the *katholikon* (principal church).

Moni Megalou Meteorou   MONASTERY
(Grand Meteoron; €3; ⊙ 9am-5pm Wed-Mon Apr-Oct, 9am-4pm Thu-Mon Nov-Mar) The best known of the Meteora monasteries, Moni Megalou Meteorou is an imposing form built on the highest rock in the valley, 613m above sea level. Founded by St Athanasios in the 14th century, it became the richest and most powerful monastery thanks to the Serbian emperor Symeon Uros, who turned all his wealth over to the monastery and became a monk. Its *katholikon* has a magnificent 12-sided central dome.

Moni Agias Triados   MONASTERY
(Holy Trinity; €3; ⊙ 9am-5pm Fri-Wed Apr-Oct, 9am-12.30pm & 3-5pm Fri-Tue Nov-Mar) Of all the monasteries at Meteora, Moni Agias Triados has the most remote feel, plus the longest approach. It was featured in the 1981 James Bond film *For Your Eyes Only.* The views here are extraordinary, and the small 17th-century *katholikon* is beautiful, in particular the *Judgement of Pilate* and the *Hospitality of Abraham* frescoes. A well-marked 1km *monopati* leads back to Kalambaka.

Moni Agiou Nikolaou   MONASTERY
(Monastery of St Nikolaou Anapafsa; €3; ⊙ 9am-3.30pm Sat-Thu Apr-Oct, 9am-2pm Nov-Mar) Moni Agiou Nikolaou is the nearest *moni* to Kastraki, just 2km from the village square to the steep steps leading to the *moni*. The monastery was built in the 15th century and

Meteora, Kastraki & Kalambaka

its exceptional frescoes were painted by the monk Theophanes Strelizas from Crete. Especially beautiful is the 1527 fresco *The Naming of Animals by Adam in Paradise.*

Moni Varlaam   MONASTERY
(€3; ⊙9am-4pm Sat-Thu Apr-Oct, 9am-3pm Sat-Wed Nov-Mar) About 700m down from Moni Megalou, Moni Varlaam has a small museum, an original rope-basket (until the 1930s, the method for hauling up provisions and monks) and fine late-Byzantine frescoes by Frangos Kastellanos. The mural *The Blessed Sisois at the Tomb of Alexander the Great* shows the

great conqueror as a humble skeleton. Look just above the door, past the candles.

Psaropetra Lookout   VIEWPOINT
For a panoramic break from visiting the monasteries, visit the rambling Psaropetra lookout, 300m east of the signposted fork northeast of Moni Varlaam.

Moni Agias Varvaras Rousanou   MONASTERY
(€3; ⊙9am-5.45pm Thu-Tue Apr-Oct, 9am-2pm Nov-Mar) Access to Moni Agias Varvaras Rousanou is via a small wooden bridge. The beautiful coloured-glass *katholikon* is the highlight here, with superb frescoes of the

Meteora, Kastraki & Kalambaka

Resurrection (on your left as you enter) and *Transfiguration* (on your right). The imposing structure of Rousanou is itself a stunning accomplishment and is today home to an order of around 15 nuns. If you're here near closing, listen for the call to vespers, made with the wooden *talando* (an oblong board struck with a small hammer or stick).

Moni Agiou Stefanou MONASTERY
(St Stephen's; €3; ⊙ 9am-1.30pm & 3.30-5.30pm Tue-Sun Apr-Oct, 9am-1pm & 3-5pm Tue-Sun Nov-Mar) Moni Agiou Stefanou was built in 1798 and is dedicated to St Charalambos. In recent years, Greek hagiographer Vlassios Tsotsonis has been repainting the *katholikon* – depicting the life of Christ – with beautiful results. Efficient nuns do a thriving trade selling religious souvenirs. The monastery is at the very end of the road, 1.5km beyond Agias Triados.

🏃 Activities

Walking

Walkers will be in their element exploring several days' worth of *monopatia* that thread through the region (about 800 at last count).

Lovely walks head along the path above Alsos House (p240) to the monasteries of Agias Triados (p237) and Agiou Stefanou.

Once at the top, from the side of Varlaam (p238), you can head back into Kastraki on foot or with a returning bus.

To head further off piste to some 'secret' locations, Visit Meteora (p240) offers some fabulous half-day walks (from €25 per person), or an adrenalin-pumping hiking and scrambling tour.

Two good maps (by Anavasi and Gecko) on walking the Meteora are available from Petraikis News & Maps (p241) in Kalambaka.

Rock Climbing

The area is a rock-climbers' mecca, and people from around the world head here to tackle these extraordinary peaks and towers. Beginners, too, can have a go at some of the smaller rocks, such as **Doupiani Rock**. Visit Meteora offers some excellent opportunities with professional guides Lazaros Botelis and Kostas Liolios.

ⓘ Getting There & Away

For those without a car, a bus (one way €1.80, 20 minutes up or down, or all-day Flex ticket €5.50) departs from Kalambaka and Kastraki at 9am, 11am, 1pm and 4pm and returns to Kalambaka at 10am, noon, 2pm and 5pm. That's enough time to explore at least three monasteries – Megalou Meteorou, Varlaam and Rousanou, for example.

A popular option is to take the bus one way to the top and then work your way down and around on foot, finishing at either Moni Agiou Nikolaou on the Kastraki side, or at Moni Agios Triados on the Kalambaka side.

There's a useful **bus stop** on the Kalambaka–Kastraki road close to **Vrachos Camping** (p243) for the route between Kalambaka, Kastraki and Meteora.

❶ Getting Around

Before setting out to the area's monasteries, decide on a route. If you start early, you can see several, if not all, *mones* (monasteries) in one day. The main sealed road surrounding the entire Meteora complex of rocks and monasteries is about 15km in length.

Keen walkers should definitely explore the area on foot on the old and once-secret *monopatia*.

Kalambaka   Καλαμπακά

📞 24320 / POP 8320

Kalambaka is the gateway to Meteora. It's almost entirely modern, having been burned to the ground by the Nazis in WWII. It takes at least a day to see all of the monasteries of Meteora, so you'll need to spend a night or two either in Kalambaka or the village of Kastraki (p242).

◉ Sights

As well as the rocks, Kalambaka boasts some new museums, an interesting change of pace to the monasteries. A bustling market (p242) takes place every Friday.

Museum of Hellenic Culture   MUSEUM
(📞 6973338270; www.bookmuseum.tr; cnr M Alexandros & Chatzipetrou; adult/student €5/4; ⊙ 9am-7pm Mon-Fri, 11am-7pm Sat & Sun) A passionate local collector has amassed a collection of rare antiquarian books, from *Aesop's Fables* to a 1567 Homer text, all beautifully displayed. This is no dull exhibit, but a delightfully colourful journey through the world of literature. Other books relate to Greek education since 1830, with children's readers, school desks and quills.

**Natural History
& Mushroom Museum**   MUSEUM
(📞 24320 24959; www.meteoramuseum.gr; Pildou 20; adult/child €5/4; ⊙ 10am-8pm Mon-Sun summer, 9am-5pm Mon-Fri, 10am-6pm Sat & Sun winter) To give the kids, or yourself, a nature-based break from the Meteora monasteries, this museum with a quirky collection of dioramas with animals and birds from around the globe might appeal. If taxidermy isn't your thing, head upstairs to view the extraordinary collection of copies of over 250 Greek mushroom species, including free tastings.

**Church of the Assumption
of the Virgin Mary**   CHURCH
(€2; ⊙ 8am-1pm & 3-8pm) It's worth finding your way to this 7th-century Byzantine cathedral (near Alsos House and Koka Roka Rooms), a three-aisle basilica with superb frescoes dating to the 14th century. At 6.30pm you can hear the vespers.

🏃 Activities

Visit Meteora   ADVENTURE SPORTS
(📞 24320 23820; www.visitmeteora.travel; Patriarchou Dimitriou 2; ⊙ 8am-9pm) Most of Meteora's tours and guided activities are run through this sharp crew. Guides are professional and very experienced. Guided activities and tours include hiking and walking for the most part, and even rock climbing. The tours around Meteora are good value; most run about €30 per person, including hotel pick-up and drop-off.

Hobby Shop   CYCLING
(📞 24320 25262, 6973743747; www.meteorabike-rentals.gr; Patriarhou Dimitriou 28; per day bike €8, motorcycle €18-20; ⊙ 8am-9pm Mon-Sat, to 2pm Sun) Efficient service for bicycle and motorcycle hire (helmets included), next door to Visit Meteora.

🛏 Sleeping

Rooms are plentiful in Kalambaka at all budget levels, though it's best to avoid noisy Trikalon.

★ Alsos House   PENSION €
(📞 24320 24097; www.alsoshouse.gr; Kanari 5; s/d/tr incl breakfast €35/45/65, f incl breakfast €75-80, apt €80-100; 🅿✳@🛜) The well-managed Alsos House has a communal kitchen, laundry service and great views of the rocks from the massive terrace and rooms. It's 500m from the centre and a stone's throw from wonderful walking paths. Welcoming and multilingual owner Yiannis Karakantas wants the best for his guests; he knows as much about Meteora as the monks do about prayers.

Meteora Central Hostel   HOSTEL €
(📞 6977809016, 24320 77395; meteoracentral@gmail.com; Trikalon 86; dm €15; 🅿✳🛜) Very

sharp and well-managed spot, one of the best we've come across. The owners are welcoming and superhelpful. Four dorm rooms (one with 10 and three with six beds) are spotless, with good lockers. The common kitchen is well-stocked, and there's even a slim view of the rocks.

Hotel Meteora
PENSION €
(☑ 6981405444, 24320 22367; http://hotel-meteora.blogspot.com.au/; Ploutarhou 14; s/d/tr incl breakfast €30/40/50; P ✳ @ 🛜) On a nearly hidden, quiet cul-de-sac below the rocks, this ten-room budget gem offers a great breakfast for early starters, compliments of hospitable Dimitris and Victoria. Moni Agios Triados is a one-hour walk from the nearby path. Guests have use of a swimming pool at a relative's large hotel.

Guest House Elena
BOUTIQUE HOTEL €
(☑ 24320 77789, 6976562529; www.elenaguesthouse.com; Kanari 3; s/d/tr incl breakfast from €40/50/70, ste €100; P ✳ 🛜) Period furnishings in five lovely rooms, balconies, an intimate atmosphere, and ot's itadjacent to a footpath to Meteora. The multilingual owner, Elena, is full of tips.

Monastiri Guest House
BOUTIQUE HOTEL €€
(☑ 24320 23952; www.monastiri-guesthouse.gr; cnr Agios Kostantinos & Elenis; s/d/tr/q/ste incl breakfast €50/70/80/85/120; P ✳ @ 🛜 ⊠) Behind the railway station, this converted stone mansion has colourful decorations, long poster-beds and light and airy bathrooms. The handsome wood-and-stone lobby sports a fireplace and bar. There are panoramic views of the rocks, and a small pool ringed by the owner Dita's well-tended rose bushes. Service is outstanding.

✗ Eating

The restaurant scene won't blow your culinary mind. Most places are tavernas that serve up hearty *mayirefta,* grilled meat and generous salads.

★ Taverna To Paramithi
TAVERNA €
(☑ 24320 24441; Patriarhou Dimitriou 14; mains €5.50-9; ⊗ lunch & dinner Mar-Dec; ✳ 🛜 👪) Along with excellent grills and fresh pasta served in a convivial environment, owner-cooks Makis and Eleni bring in fresh seafood daily and cook up classic dishes. Local musicians often end the night here, with guitar or bouzouki in hand (plus a glass of the house wine or *tsipouro*). Good service, good value.

Koka Roka Taverna
TAVERNA €
(☑ 24320 24554; www.kokaroka.com; Kanari 21; mains €2.50-8; ⊗ breakfast, lunch & dinner; P 🛜) This cosy taverna (and domatia) tucked away beneath the rocks is perfect for a low key meal, afternoon beer or traditional Greek coffee. A small menu includes breakfast made to order, with tea or coffee on the house; afternoons and evenings feature traditional salads and char grills.

Taverna Archontariki
RESTAURANT €
(☑ 24320 22449; Trikalon 13, Plateia Riga Fereou; mains €5.50-9; ⊗ lunch & dinner; ✳) A traditional and roomy taverna, featuring the handy kitchen work of Kostas and Sotiris, with seasonal veggies and local meat. *Mayirefta* like *mousakas* are the mainstay, plus pasta, lamb chops and grilled feta. Just opposite Plateia Riga Fereou.

Taverna Panellinion
TAVERNA €
(☑ 24320 24735; Plateia Dimarhiou; mains €6-11.50; ⊗ lunch & dinner) Next to the fountain at Plateia Dimarhiou, and filled with antique bric-a-brac, the popular Panellinion serves mezedhes, such as roasted feta and red peppers, and fine versions of traditional dishes such as *pastitsio* (macaroni and meat bake), *briam* and chicken fillet. It's open all year.

🍺 Drinking & Nightlife

★ Fortounis
BAR, OUZERIE
(☑ 24320 22555; Vlahavas 26; ⊗ noon-midnight; 🛜) A favourite for ouzo and low-key music most evenings, this long-standing *ouzerie* attracts a young crowd that stays late.

Rapsody
CAFE-BAR
(☑ 24320 22470; Trikalon 25, Plateia Dimola; ⊗ 7.30am-midnight; 🛜) Inviting and comfortable espresso and wine bar with indoor/outdoor seating, and decent prices for good coffee drinks, wine and sandwiches.

Kafeneio Mikas
CAFE-BAR
(☑ 24320 22048; Vlahavas 32; ⊗ noon-midnight; 🛜) An attractive *ouzerie* with black-and-white photos of old times inside. A younger crowd can be found congregating over coffees and good *tsipouro* at this characteristic, friendly spot.

🔒 Shopping

Petraikis News & Maps
BOOKS
(☑ 6937238718; Patriachou Dimitriou 1, Plateia Dimarhiou; ⊗ 8am-10pm) Efficient and friendly corner store on the traffic circle at Plateia

Dimarhiou (the town-hall square) carrying good maps, international press and souvenirs.

Morning Market
MARKET

(To Pazari; Plateia Dimarhiou; ⏱8am-2pm Fri) Kalambaka's busy little fruit-and-vegetable market is on every Friday, at Plateia Dimarhiou, the town-hall square.

ⓘ Information

Banks with ATMs surround the central Plateia Riga Fereou on Trikalon. There is a currency exchange window next to the post office on Pindou.

Health Care Centre (☎24320 22222; Ioninon) At the western entrance to town.

Info Tourist Centre (☎24323 50245; www. infotouristmeteora.gr; Plateia Dimarhiou; ⏱8am-9pm) Helpful for maps, recommendations for lodging and transport.

Visit Meteora (☎24320 23820, 6989626382; www.visitmeteora.travel; Dimitriou 2; ⏱9am-9pm; 📶) Run by a young crowd, this well-organised private tourist office is the information hub for the region. It provides maps, information on opening hours and coordinates most of the area's guided tours, transport and activities (climbing, hiking, walking).

Post Office (Trikalon 24; ⏱7.30am-2.30pm)

Tourist Police (☎24320 76100; cnr Ipirou & Pindou)

ⓘ Getting There & Away

BUS

Kalambaka's **KTEL bus station** (☎24320 22432; www.ktel-trikala.gr; Ikonomou) is 50m down from Plateia Dimarhiou (the town-hall square) and large fountain, and is the arrival/departure point for regular Trikala bus connections. For Delphi, travellers should go via Trikala (not Larissa). The trip requires three bus changes: Kalambaka to Trikala, Trikala to Lamia, Lamia to Amfissa, and finally Amfissa to Delphi. Enquire at the station.

Bus Services from Kalambaka

DESTINATION	DURATION	FARE (€)	FREQUENCY
Athens	4½hr	31.50	6 daily
Ioannina	2hr	13.60	2 daily
Lamia (change in Trikala)	2hr	15.30	5 daily
Thessaloniki	2½hr	21.40	5 daily
Trikala	30min	2.60	hourly
Volos (change in Trikala)	2hr	17.50	4 daily

TRAIN

Trains depart from the Kalambaka **train station** (☎24320 22451; www.trainose.gr). For trains to Athens and Thessaloniki you may need to change at Paleofarsalos. For Volos you must change at Larissa.

Train Services from Kalambaka

DESTINATION	DURATION	FARE (€)	FREQUENCY
Athens normal	7hr	23	1 daily
Athens Intercity	5hr	19.60	2 daily
Thessaloniki	3-4½hr	16-24.10	3 daily
Volos (via Larissa)	3hr	13.20	3 daily

ⓘ Getting Around

BUS

Every two hours, buses for Kastraki (€1) leave from beside the **Plateia Dimarhiou fountain**. Four daily Meteora-bound buses (one way/return/day €1.60/3/5) depart from the KTEL station , also picking tourists up at the fountain and bus stops en route, between May and September. Ask at the KTEL office or Visit Meteora office for the schedule.

TAXI

Taxi stations are at each of the town's four squares. Taxis go to Kastraki (€4) and all the monasteries (for example, Moni Megalou Meteorou for €9 to €10). Some drivers speak English, German or Italian, and you can arrange a taxi tour from about €20 per hour.

Kastraki   Καστράκι
☎24320 / POP 1600

The village of Kastraki is an integral part of Meteora, and feels like a low-key extension of busier Kalambaka, although it's less than 2km further on. But its location adjacent to the rocks gives it an otherworldly feel and its small central square has a relaxed vibe. For those after a more peaceful sleep, Kastraki is a good bet.

◎ Sights

Meteora Geological History Museum
MUSEUM

(☎24323 50245; www.infotouristmeteora.gr/main-menu/sights/museums; Plateia Pavlou & Petrou) This long-anticipated museum, opposite the main church in Kastraki, had yet to open at the time of research. It promises to showcase the Meteora's rocky emergence over a period of 10 million years. Check at the municipality's Info Tourist Centre in Kalambaka for details.

🛏 Sleeping

★ Hotel Tsikeli   HOTEL €
(☑ 6974414913, 24320 22438; www.tsikelihotel.gr; s/d incl breakfast from €35/50; P ❋ 🛜) The Tsikeli's recent renovation included smartly decorated rooms and modern bathrooms to complement large balconies and a lovely and inviting grassy front garden to enjoy a drink. Excellent service, good value.

Vrachos Camping   CAMPGROUND €
(☑ 24320 22293; www.campingkastraki.com; campsites per person/tent €8/3; ◷ Mar-Oct; P ❋ 🛜) *Mouries* (mulberry trees) provide the shade at this well-run campground on the Kalambaka–Kastraki road with excellent facilities, including BBQ and nightly movies. Owner George also cooks up a great grill outside the shop and taverna (open to the public; mains €6–€9.50).

★ Doupiani House   PENSION €€
(☑ 24320 77555; www.doupianihouse.com; s/d/tr incl breakfast from €50/60/75; P ❋ @ 🛜) The delightful Doupiani House has the lot: spotless, comfortable, tastefully decorated rooms with balconies or garden access. Its location – just outside the village – provides a window to Meteora, boasting one of the region's best panoramic views. There's a super breakfast on the terrace, birdsong and helpful hosts Toula and Thanasis.

Pyrgos Adrachti   BOUTIQUE HOTEL €€
(☑ 24320 22275; www.hotel-adrachti.gr; s/d/tr/apt incl breakfast from €50/60/80/90; P ❋ 🛜) Slick and cool sums up this place – think subtle designer-style touches throughout the 14 rooms, bar and common areas, and an up-close-and-personal rock experience. Plus there's a tidy garden to relax in post-activities. It feels remote, but in fact it's a short stroll to the village square. A boutique hotel for real. Follow the signs.

Hotel Kastraki   HOTEL €€
(☑ 24320 75336; www.hotelkastraki.gr; s/d/tr/ste incl breakfast from €45/70/90/100; P ❋ @ 🛜) Smart and updated hotel on the main road, with large rooms and updated bathrooms, good service and a handsome lobby bar. Popular with package groups. Prices vary with the view.

🍴 Eating

Taverna Gardenia   TAVERNA €
(☑ 6972700698; mains €7-11.50; ◷ lunch & dinner; ❋ 🛜) Popular taverna for excellent *mousakas, yemista* (stuffed peppers and tomatoes) and other filling *mayirefta,* along with great grilled and spit-roasted meats which you can watch being prepared at the patio entrance. Just steps from the adjacent church square (Plateia Pavlou & Petrou).

Taverna Harama   GREEK €
(Xarama; ☑ 24320 23976; mains €5-10; ◷ lunch & dinner; P ❋ 🛜) Very good traditional eatery with reliable taverna standards baked and grilled, and a lovely setting down a few steps off the main Kalambaka–Kastraki road, near Vrachos Camping.

Taverna Batalogianni   TAVERNA €
(☑ 24320 23253; mains €7-12; ◷ 8am-late; ❋ 🛜) You know the type of place you wouldn't look twice at 'cos it's slightly off the road and you don't realise it has an oasis of a garden terrace and serves up delicious 100% homemade *mayirefta?* This charming little spot is all that, plus welcoming chief cook and owner Zoe. It's located next to the pharmacy.

Taverna Paradisos   TAVERNA €
(☑ 24320 22723; mains €6.50-9; ◷ noon-4pm & 6pm-late; P 🛜) The traditional meals at roomy Paradisos will have you exclaiming '*nostimo!*' (delicious!), thanks to local and high-quality ingredients and locally loved owner-chef Koula's magic touch. Excellent starters (like *taramasalata*), and good Greek basics from baked pastas to juicy grills and chops, plus good house wine.

ⓘ Getting There & Away

It's easy to reach Meteora by car, bus or rapid intercity train service from either Athens or Thessaloniki. With exception of the tortured alpine roads that thread north from the Gulf of Corinth, the Thessaly region is criss-crossed with up-to-date highways, including the national toll road.

Northern Greece

Best Places to Eat

➡ Mourgá (p258)

➡ Extravaganza (p258)

➡ I Nea Follia (p258)

➡ Sempriko (p259)

➡ Taverna Sopotseli (p303)

➡ Palaia Polis (p286)

Best Places to Stay

➡ Trilogy House (p256)

➡ Primoula (p303)

➡ Kokkino Spiti (p275)

➡ Caravan (p257)

➡ Boutique Hotel 1905 (p286)

Why Go?

Diversity should be northern Greece's second name – the region stretches across more cultures and terrains than any other in the country. Mighty civilisations, including Macedonians, Thracians, Romans, Byzantines, Slavs and Turks, have left traces here. this is nowhere more apparent than in Greece's second city, Thessaloniki – a magnetic place that breathes history and character, and has the best food in the country.

Border influences from Albania, the Former Yugoslav Republic of Macedonia, Bulgaria and Turkey add to the region's distinctive flair. Northern Greece boasts beautiful beaches, too – especially in popular Halkidiki and around Parga, along the golden Ionian coast. The plains and woodlands of Thrace offer rich birdlife. Ruins at Ancient Dion and the archaeological site at Vergina will leave you breathless, and if they don't, Epiros, to the west, will, with its perfect mountain life, mysterious villages and one of Europe's biggest canyons.

When to Go
Thessaloniki

May–Aug Sizzle on beaches and swim in perfect waters in Parga and Halkidiki.

Sep–Nov Bask in lower coastal prices then hit Thessaloniki's restaurants and film festivals.

Dec–Apr Snuggle into a ski lodge near Florina or explore the villages of Zagorohoria.

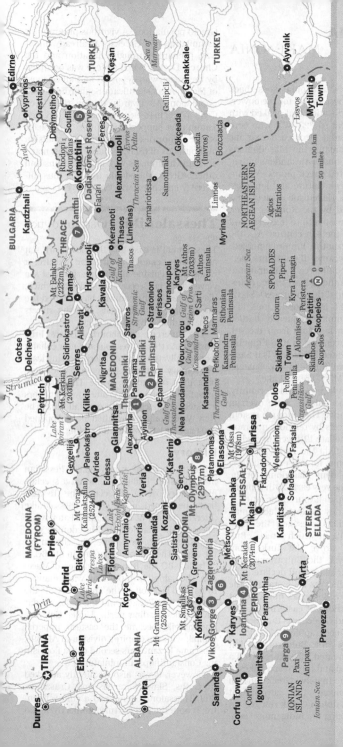

Northern Greece Highlights

1 Thessaloniki (p246)
Experiencing the city's cuisine, history and nightlife.

2 Halkidiki Peninsula (p265) Swimming in clear waters and mountain biking verdant interiors.

3 Vikos Gorge (p301)
Feeling your jaw drop in one of Europe's grandest canyons.

4 Ioannina (p295)
Strolling around the relaxed old quarter and taking a ferry ride to tranquil To Nisi (The Island).

5 Dadia Forest Reserve (p291) Pointing your binoculars at birds of prey.

6 Zagorohoria (p300)
Village-hopping between ancient settlements in a breathtaking mountain setting.

7 Xanthi (p284) Roaming Old Xanthi's winding streets.

8 Mt Olympus (p273)
Reaching Greece's highest peak.

9 Parga (p308) Relaxing and swimming in this picture-perfect town.

MACEDONIA

ΜΑΚΕΔΟΝΙΑ

History

Although life in Macedonia goes back 700,000 years, it's best known for the powerful Macedonian civilisation that peaked with Alexander the Great (d 323 BC), who conquered as far as India. Deemed barbarians by cultivated Athenians, the Macedonians subjugated Greece under Alexander's father, Philip II, yet adopted Greek mores. Alexander spread the Greek culture and language widely, creating a Hellenistic society that would be absorbed by the Romans. Later, after their empire split into eastern and western halves in the 4th century AD, the Greek-speaking Byzantine Empire emerged.

Thessaloniki became Byzantium's second city, a vital commercial, cultural and strategic centre on the Balkan trade routes. However, 6th- and 7th-century-AD Slavic migrations brought new populations and challenges. The empire frequently battled with the Bulgarian kingdom from the 9th century to the 11th century. In 1018 Emperor Basil II finally defeated Bulgarian Tsar Samuel, who had ruled much of the Balkans from Macedonia's Mikri Prespa Lake.

After Serbian rule in the 14th century, Macedonia and the Balkans were overrun by the Ottoman Turks. The Ottoman system distinguished subjects by religion, not race, causing strife in the late 19th century, when guerrillas arose to fight the Turks, pledging to annex Macedonia for Greece, Bulgaria or even an independent 'Macedonia for the Macedonians'; in the very early 20th century, powers such as Britain favoured the latter.

Ottoman atrocities against Macedonia's Christian populations presaged the First Balkan War of 1912, in which Greece, Bulgaria and Serbia drove the Turks from Macedonia; however, the Bulgarians were unhappy with their share, and declared war on their former allies in 1913, starting the Second Balkan War. Bulgaria's quick defeat lost it allotted portions of eastern Macedonia and Thrace, and Greece was the big winner, taking half of geographical Macedonia, with Serbia taking 38%. Bulgaria was left with 13%. Newly created Albania received a sliver around Ohrid and the Prespa Lakes.

In 1923, with the massive Greek–Turkish population exchanges, the government resettled many Anatolian Greek refugees in Macedonia, displacing the indigenous (non-Greek) populations. A vigorous program for assimilating non-Greeks was already under way, primarily through education and the Church. During WWII Greece was occupied by the Nazis, who deported and killed most of Macedonia's significant Sephardic Jewish population. Afterwards, during the Greek Civil War (1944–49), authorities targeted 'communist supporters' – often a label for ethnic minorities – causing the expulsion of thousands of (Slavic) Macedonians, many of them children, as well as Bulgarians and others. Greek Macedonia today is thus different from what it was even 60 years ago.

Thessaloniki Θεσσαλονίκη

POP 325,200

Thessaloniki is easy to fall in love with – it has beauty, chaos, history and culture, a remarkable cuisine and wonderful, vast sea views. This is Greece's second city, which, like the rest of the country, has suffered the hit of the economic crisis, but the streets remain full of life and vibrancy.

The different neighbourhoods are little worlds unto themselves. Old and new cohabit wonderfully: the Arch of Galerius, an intricate 4th-century monument, overlooks the shopping drag of Egnatia, while Thessaloniki's most famous sight, the White Tower, anchors a waterfront packed with cocktail bars. The New Waterfront has breathed life and opened up space for long walks and cycling.

History

With the help of remarkable Thessalian horsemanship, Philip II achieved a spectacular victory over a Phoecian tribe. To celebrate, he named his daughter Thessalonike (literally, 'victory of Thessalians'). Later, when Thessalonike married the Macedonian general Kassandros, her name was chosen for the city of Thessaloniki, founded in 315 BC.

In 168 BC the Romans conquered Macedon. Thessaloniki's importance was enhanced by its ideal location on the Thermaic Gulf, the east–west Via Egnatia and the Axios/Vardar River valley leading north. Under Galerius, Thessaloniki became the eastern imperial capital; with the empire's division in AD 395, it became Byzantium's second city, a flourishing Constantinople in miniature.

However, it was also frequently attacked by Goths, Slavs, Saracens and Crusaders. Still, Thessaloniki remained a cultural centre. It bore the 9th-century monks Cyril and

Macedonia

50 km
25 miles

Rhodopi Mountains
Mt Koula (1827m)
Smoljan
Paranesti
Xanthi
Keramoti
Nestos
Limnos (25km)
Thasos (Limenas)
Skala Prinou
Thasos
Karadere Forest
Skaloti
Elatia
Stavroupoli
Gulf of Thasos
Nestos
Potamoi
Drama
Kavala
Kalabakion
Adriani
Kato
Nevrokopi
Mt Falakro (2232m)
Hrysoupoli
Gotse Delchev
Exohi
Philippi
Agora
Proti
Mt Symvolon
BULGARIA
Mt Vrontous (1888m)
Sidirokastro
Khimaros
Lailias
Serres
Prosotsani
Nea Zikhni
Alistrati
Elevtheroupoli
See Thrace Map (p285)
Strymonic Gulf
Mt Athos (2033m)
Karyes
Promahonas
Neon
Petritsion
Khrison
Stavros
Stratonion
Mt Athos
Gulf of Agion Oros
Mt Kerkini (2031m)
Lake Kerkinis
Lakhanas
Nigrita
Ampholis
Lake Volvi
Arnea
Ierissos
Athos Peninsula
Ammouliani
Ouranoupoli
See Athos Peninsula Map (p269)
Strumica
Lake Doiran
Pondokerasea
Khimaros
Langadas
Lake Koronia
Hortiatis
Galatista
Polygyros
Vrastama
Ormilia
Vourvourou
Panagias
Neos Marmaras
Sarti
Sithonian Peninsula
Kalamitsi
Strumica
Evzoni
Skra
Kilkis
Nea Magnisia
Vasilika
Epanomi
Olynthos
Nikiti
Neos
Paradisos
Polyhrono
Kallithea
Pefkohori
Loutra
Gevgelija
Paleokastro
Goumenissa
Vardar
Nea
Panorama
Thessaloniki
Ancient Olynthos
Nea Moudania
Gulf of Kassandra
Kassandria
Possidi
Nea Skioni
MACEDONIA (FYROM)
Giannitsa
Skidhra
Pella
Halkidona
Alyzion
Eleohora
Petralona Cave
Krini
Nea Fokaia
Kassandra Peninsula
Kallithea
Prilep
Aridea
Edessa
Alexandria
Agia Triada
Faros Beach & Potamos Beach
Gulf of Thessaloniki
Skathos (90km)
Skathos (150km), Lesvos (230km)
Bitola
Mt Voras (Kaimaktsalan) (2524m)
Arnissa
Naoussa
Pella Nera
Filotas
Vergina
Kolindros
Velvendos
Litohoro
Castle of Platamonas
Platamonas
Limnos (150km), Lesvos (230km)
Prespa Lakes
Agios Germanos
Pisoderi Pass
Florina
Amyntaio
Mt Vermic (320m)
Veria
Ancient Dion
Palouri
MACEDONIA (FYROM)
Niki
Aetos
Nymfeo
Ptolemaida
Kozani
See Epiros Map (p294)
Servia
Mount Olympus National Park
Mt Olympus (2917m)
Leptokarya
Kastoria
Mt Vernon
Mt Vitsi (2128m)
Lake Orestiada
Lake Himadhitis
Eratira
Siatista
E65
Elassona
ALBANIA
Krystallopigi
Vrondero
Vigla
Psarades
Agios Achillos
Nestorio
Neapoli
Pendalofos
Grevena
Zakas
Vovousa
Korçë
Mt Grammos (2520m)
Agia Paraskevi
Eptahori
Mt Smolikas (2637m)
Mt Vasilitsa (2497m)
Mt Gamila (2249m)
Karperon
Deskati
Aoös River

Methodius (creators of Glagolitic, precursor to Cyrillic), who expanded Orthodox Byzantine literary culture among the Slavs. The city also nurtured great 14th-century theologian St Gregory Palamas, who became Archbishop of Thessaloniki.

In 1430 the Ottoman Turks captured Thessaloniki; after 1492 they resettled Sephardic Jews fleeing the Inquisition to here, adding to the city's diversity.

With the 1821–27 War of Independence only a partial success, 19th-century Thessaloniki became a lurid hub for intrigue, secret societies and mutually antagonistic rebels and reformers. Along with Greek revolutionaries, these included the pro-Bulgarian Internal Macedonian Revolutionary Organisation (IMRO), and the Young Turks, who wanted Western-style reforms for the empire. Indeed, one Young Turk and Thessaloniki native, Mustafa Kemal (Atatürk), would become modern Turkey's founding father.

Thessaloniki suffered successive tragedies over the following four decades. The August 1917 fire burned two-thirds of it, and ethnic diversity shrank with the 1923 population exchanges. During the WWII Nazi occupation, Thessaloniki's Jews were deported to concentration camps and other non-Greeks were expelled following the Greek Civil War.

Recent decades have brought cultural acclaim, including the city's 1997 reign as European Capital of Culture and its hosting of sporting events during the 2004 Athens Olympics. In 2014 Thessaloniki was European Youth Capital, thanks to one of the largest student populations in Southern Europe.

◉ Sights

◉ White Tower & Waterfront

White Tower   HISTORIC BUILDING
(Lefkos Pyrgos; ☑ 2310 267 832; www.lpth.gr; Nikis; adult/student Apr-Oct €8/4, Nov-Mar €4/2; ⊙ 9am-4pm Tue-Sun, to 8pm in summer) Thessaloniki's top landmark, the 34m-high White Tower has a harrowing history as a prison and torture chamber. In 1826 Ottoman sultan Mahmud II massacred rebellious janissaries (elite troops of forcibly Islamicised Christian boys) here. The story goes that the structure was known as the Tower of Blood until a prisoner painted the tower white in exchange for his liberty in 1890, when it was renamed Lefkos Pyrgos (White Tower). Others say that the name was changed after the 1913 Greek reconquest.

★ **Archaeological Museum**   MUSEUM
(☑ 2310 830 538; www.amth.gr; Manoli Andronikou 6; adult/concession €8/4; ⊙ 8am-8pm daily) Macedonia's major prehistoric and ancient Macedonian and Hellenistic finds are housed in this museum (except for Vergina's gold tomb finds, which are exhibited in Vergina). Highlights include the **Derveni Crater** (330–320 BC), a huge, ornate Hellenistic bronze-and-tin vase. Used for mixing wine and water, and later as a funerary urn, it's marked by intricate relief carvings of Dionysos. The Derveni Treasure contains Greece's oldest surviving papyrus piece (320–250 BC).

★ **Museum of Byzantine Culture**   MUSEUM
(☑ 2313 306 400; www.mbp.gr; Leoforos Stratou 2; adult/student Apr-Oct €8/4, Nov-Mar €4; ⊙ 8am-8pm Apr-Oct, 9am-4pm Nov-Mar) This fascinating museum has plenty of treasures to please Byzantine buffs, plus simple explanations to introduce the empire to total beginners. More than 3000 Byzantine objects, including mosaics, intriguing tomb paintings, jewellery and glassware, are showcased with characterful asides about daily life. You'll be confidently discerning early-Christian from late-Byzantine icons in no time.

Museum of the Macedonian Struggle   MUSEUM
(☑ 2310 229 778; www.imma.edu.gr; Proxenou Koromila 23; €2; ⊙ 9am-2pm Tue-Fri, 10am-2pm Sat) Ground zero for Greek nationalism, this museum recounts how Hellenes wrested Macedonia from both Turks and Bulgarians. Housed in Greece's former Ottoman consulate, the museum has hard-to-find maps, old firearms, photos, uniforms and more.

New Waterfront   WATERFRONT
(Nea Paralia) Thessaloniki's New Waterfront is evidence that architecture can change the world by changing public space and improving daily urban life. The secret is to implement intelligent, citizen-oriented design that enables local people to meaningfully inhabit their cities. Recipient of numerous architectural awards, this 3.5km walkway that extends from the White Tower to the Thessaloniki Concert Hall, was designed by architects Prodromos Nikiforidis and Bernard Cuomo. Completed in 2013, it has been embraced by Thessalonikians with absolute delight.

Thessaloniki Concert Hall   ARCHITECTURE
(Megaro Mousikis (M1 & M2); ☑ 2310 895 800; www.tch.gr; 25 Martiou, cnr Paralia) **FREE** Japanese architect Arata Isozaki created the M2, one

of two buildings that house Thessaloniki's live music scene. The M2 is a contemporary structure with impeccably simple geometry, using glass, stone and steel, making the most of the city's sea views and natural light. The neighbouring M1 is a red-brick structure, and the two work oddly together, the M1 solid and dense and the M2 transparent and light.

⊙ Egnatia & Central

This is the central street that cuts across Thessaloniki, and much of the city is divided as above and below Egnatia. Three major Roman monuments of early-4th-century emperor Galerius spill across Egnatia at Plateia Navarinou: the ruined Palace of Galerius, the Arch of Galerius and the now renovated Rotunda to its north. This central Thessaloniki neighbourhood also has some of the city's most fascinating churches.

Rotunda of Galerius   HISTORIC BUILDING

(☑2310 204 868; Plateia Agiou Georgiou; adult €2; ⊙9am-5pm daily Nov-Mar, 8am-7pm daily Apr-Oct) FREE In AD 306 Roman emperor Galerius built this stocky 30m-high brick structure as his future mausoleum. But instead of being laid to rest within the 6m-thick walls of the Rotunda, he was buried in today's Serbia after succumbing to an unpleasant disease that still puzzles historians. Later, Constantine the Great made the Rotunda Thessaloniki's first church (Agios Georgios; observe dragon-slaying St George above the door). The Ottomans made it a mosque (note the restored minaret).

Arch of Galerius   HISTORIC SITE

FREE The Arch of Galerius (AD 303) celebrates a victory over the Persians with carved, lunging soldiers. It's south of the Rotunda of Galerius on Egnatia. Known locally as Kamara, this landmark is also the city's main meeting spot. The Arch originally had four main and four supporting pillars, with eight gates and arches, and a dome – only two of the central arches and one supporting arch can be seen today.

Palace of Galerius   RUINS

(Plateia Navarinou; ⊙8.30am-3pm Tue-Sun) FREE The ruined Palace of Galerius sprawls east-west across Plateia Navarinou. You can descend into it, or just peer over the handrail. Pieces of floor mosaic, columns and a few walls survive.

Roman Agora   RUINS

(Plateia Dikastirion; ⊙8am-3pm Tue-Sun) FREE The 1st-century-AD *agora* (forum) lies north of Plateia Aristotelous, on Plateia Dikastirion. In the 3rd century BC, the Macedonians had made it a commercial centre and the Romans maintained this function. An English-language placard explains the site, which contains clustered shop walls and mosaic floor remnants.

★ Church of Agios Dimitrios   CHURCH

(☑2310 270 008; www.inad.gr; Agiou Dimitriou 97; ⊙8am-10pm) This enormous 5th-century structure honours Thessaloniki's patron saint. A Roman soldier, Dimitrios was killed around AD 306 at this former Roman bath

NORTHERN GREECE THESSALONIKI

JEWISH THESSALONIKI

Thessaloniki's Jewish community swelled following the arrival of exiled Sephardic Jews from Spain in the 15th century. The city enjoyed a golden age of Jewish industry and culture, including crafts such as weaving and silk dyeing, in the 16th century.

The flourishing Jewish community was brutally cut down in 1943 when 43,850 Jews were deported to their deaths at Auschwitz. The history is movingly conveyed at the city's Jewish Museum (p253).

In the city centre, find Thessaloniki's principal synagogue, **Monastirioton** (☑2310 275 701; www.jmth.gr; Sygrou 35; ⊙10am-3pm Mon-Fri, 10am-3pm & 5-8pm Wed, 10am-2pm Sun, closed Sat), used as a Red Cross centre during the WWII Nazi occupation and therefore spared. Services are held at **Yad Lazikaron** (Vassiliou Irakliou 24).

Find other traces of this rich history at 19th- and 20th-century former Jewish mansions **Villa Allatini** (Olgas 198), **Casa Bianca** (Municipal Art Gallery; ☑2310 427 555; Olgas 214; ⊙10am-5pm Tue-Sat, 1am-8pm Thu) – now the Centre for Contemporary Art – and **Villa Mordoch** (Olgas 162), a 15-minute bus ride along Leoforos Vasilissis Olgas. To dig deeper into Thessaloniki's Jewish heritage, buy a copy of *Jewish Sites in Thessaloniki: Brief History and Guide* by Rena Molho and Vilma Hastaoglou-Martinidi (Lycabettus Press) from bookshops or the Jewish Museum.

Thessaloniki

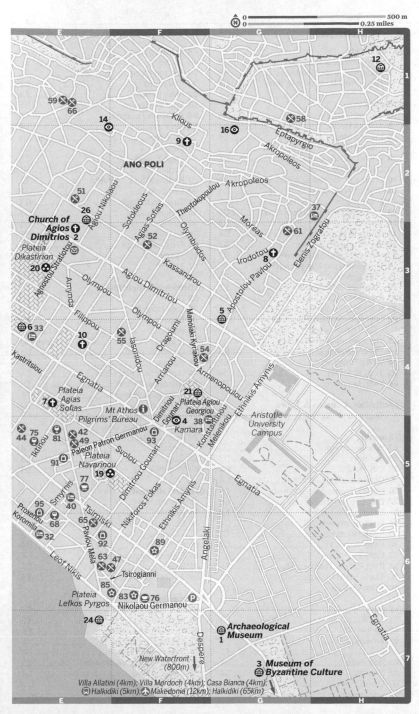

N 0 _____ 500 m
0 _____ 0.25 miles

ANO POLI

12

59 66

14

Klious

16

58

Eptapyrgio

9

Akropoleos

51

Akropoleos

26

Church of
Agios
Dimitrios 2

Sofokleous

Agias Sofias

Theotokopoulou

Moreas

37

52

Olymbiados

Elenis Zografou

61

Plateia
Dikastirion

20

Agnostou Stratiotou

Olympou

Agiou Dimitriou

Kassandrou

Irodotou

8

6 33

Amynda

Filippou

Olympou

Arrianou

Dragoumi

Manolaki Kyriakou

Apostolou Pavlou

5

10

55

Iasonidou

54

Armenopoulou

Kastritsiou

Egnatia

21

Plateia
Agias
Sofias

7

Mt Athos
Pilgrims' Bureau

Dimitriou
Gounari

Plateia Agiou
Georgiou

Ethnikis Amynis

Aristotle
University
Campus

44 75

Iktinou

81

42

49

Paleon Patron Germanou

93

38

Kamara

4

Konstantinou

Melenikou

91

Svolou

Plateia
Navarinou

19

Dimitriou Gounari

Egnatia

77

Smyrnis

40

Tsimiski

Nikiforos Fokas

Ethnikis Amynis

95

68

32

Proxenou
Koromila

65

Pavlou Mela

92

63

47

89

Tsirogianni

Leof Nikis

85

Plateia
Lefkos Pyrgos

83

76

Nikolaou Germanou

Angelaki

P

24

Despere

Archaeological
Museum
1

New Waterfront
(800m)

Museum of
Byzantine Culture
3

Villa Allatini (4km); Villa Mordoch (4km); Casa Bianca (4km);
Halkidiki (5km); Makedonia (12km); Halkidiki (65km)

Thessaloniki

site by order of Emperor Galerius, infamous persecutor of Christians. The martyrdom site is now an underground **crypt**. Dimitrios' relics occupy a silver reliquary inside. The Ottomans made Agios Dimitrios a mosque, and plastered over frescoes that were again revealed after the 1913 Greek reconquest. While the city's devastating fire of 1917 was very damaging, five 8th-century mosaics survive, spanning the altar.

Church of the Panagia Achiropiitos CHURCH
(Odos Agias Sofias 56; ☉ 7am-noon & 4.30-6.30pm)
This basilica-style 5th-century Byzantine church has notable mosaics and frescoes. The name, meaning 'made without hands', refers to a miraculous 12th-century appearance of an icon of the Virgin. It was the first of Thessaloniki's churches to be transformed into a mosque under Ottoman rule.

Atatürk House HISTORIC BUILDING
(☑ 2310 248 452; Apostolou Pavlou 75; ☉ 10am-5pm Tue-Sun) **FREE** Modern Turkey's illustrious founder, Mustafa Kemal, was born here in 1881. Bring your identity card or passport for this three-floor museum within the Turkish consulate and be prepared for security checks. Along with numerous original furnishings and memorabilia, you'll see Atatürk paraphernalia, such as dapper suits, white gloves and a cane.

Church of Agia Sofia CHURCH
(Plateia Agias Sofias; ☉ 7am-1pm & 6-7.30pm)
Candlelight twinkling from gold chandeliers pierces the gloom in this 8th-century church, modelled on its İstanbul namesake. The dome has a striking mosaic of the Ascension of Christ. Built over a previous 3rd-century church, it's notable for the cross-basilica style associated with middle-Byzantine architecture. The narthex and south aisle were used as a burial place for dignitaries from the 10th century. Like many Thessaloniki churches, it spent a period as a mosque (1535–1912) before returning to Christian worship.

Bey Hammam HISTORIC BUILDING
(Paradeisos Baths; ☑ 2313 310 400; cnr Egnatia & Plateia Dikastirion) **FREE** Stocky Bey Hammam was built in 1444, making it Thessaloniki's oldest Turkish bathhouse. Currently these former 'Baths of Paradise' only open on request.

Yeni Hammam HISTORIC BUILDING
(☑ 6946688588; cnr Kassandrou & Agiou Nikolaou; ☉ 11am-5pm) An atmospheric 16th-century structure, this former Turkish bath has great

acoustics. Today it hosts occasional exhibitions and a restaurant.

◉ Ladadika & Port

Former bazaar neighbourhood Ladadika has Thessaloniki's favourite eateries and nightlife, and is bordered to its east by the former Jewish neighbourhood along Mitropoleos. Opposite, the pier area hosts two hip museums and is a favourite evening haunt for students.

Thessaloniki Museum of Photography MUSEUM
(☑ 2310 566 716; www.thmphoto.gr; Warehouse A, Port; adult/student €2/1; ☉ 11am-7pm Tue-Sun, to 10pm Fri) This 1910 port warehouse is home to thought-provoking exhibitions of historic and contemporary Greek photography. The sea views from the cafe are fantastic, too.

Thessaloniki Centre of Contemporary Art MUSEUM
(☑ 2310 593 270; www.cact.gr; Warehouse B1, Port; adult/child €3/1.50; ☉ 10am-6pm Tue-Sat) The wonderful programming at this old harbour space features fine art, video, installations, photography and all other forms of expression, and the exhibitions range from reflections on John Berger, the economic crisis, gender and identity issues, and many more burning contemporary issues.

Jewish Museum of Thessaloniki MUSEUM
(☑ 2310 250 406; www.jmth.gr; Agiou Mina 13; ☉ 11am-2pm Tue, Fri & Sun, 11am-2pm & 5-8pm Wed & Thu) **FREE** This touching museum is housed in one of the few Jewish buildings to survive the great fire of 1917, the former office of Jewish newspaper *L'Independent*. The museum traces the city's Jewish heritage through the 15th-century Sephardic immigrations and its peak period of creativity in the 16th century, before the community was brutally annihilated during the Holocaust.

Modiano Market MARKET
(btwn Ermou & Vassiliou Irakliou; ☉ 8.30am-2.30pm Mon, Wed & Fri, 8.30am-1.30pm & 5.30-8.30pm Tue, Thu & Sat, closed Sun) The city's largest indoor market sits on the ashes of former Jewish neighbourhood Kadi, which burned down in the 1917 fire. The architect Eli Modiano designed the market, which opened in 1930 and has carried his name ever since. Covered by a glass roof, there are several shops and tavernas here, and it's a charming place to wander around.

Cinema Museum
MUSEUM

(☑2310 508 398; www.cinemuseum.gr; Warehouse A, Port; adult/student €2/1; ⊙9am-3pm Mon-Wed, to 7pm Thu & Fri) Delve into the history of the silver screen via realism, musicals and modern Greek cinema at this well-executed small museum inside the fantastic old port complex.

◉ Ano Poli

The labyrinthine, steep streets of Ano Poli, Thessaloniki's upper town, have magnificent ruins and lesser-visited churches, and a wonderful atmosphere. Only Ano Poli largely survived the city-wide devastation of the 1917 fire – although the fire originated here, the wind swept the flames towards the sea.

Kastro
HISTORIC SITE

FREE The *kastro* (castle) encloses Byzantine churches and timber-framed houses with overhanging upper storeys. Enjoy panoramic views from the tower by the eastern edge of the **Byzantine Walls**, built to survive sieges in the late 4th century BC. Emperor Theodosius fortified the walls; in places they were 10m high and 5m thick. They stood until the 19th century when the Ottomans demolished large stretches. Enjoy the views of the sunset over the city, along with students and locals.

Monastery of Vlatadon
MONASTERY

(cnr Eptapyrgiou & Agathangelou; ⊙7.30am-5pm & 5.30-8pm, museum 10am-noon Sun) **FREE** Near Ano Poli's Byzantine Walls, this secluded monastery has both a tonne of fascinating history and the best views of the city. Believed to have been founded around 1351 by the pious brothers Vlatades, this monastery is a Unesco heritage site. It is thought to have been significant for Hesychasm, a controversial movement based around solitary spiritual reflection. Its foremost 14th-century proponent, St Gregory Palamas, is depicted in a fresco here.

Church of Nikolaos Orfanos
CHURCH

(Irodotou 20; ⊙hours vary) This early-14th-century church has superb (though age-darkened) frescoes. The 'orphan' in the church's name remains a mystery: it may be a nod to an anonymous benefactor or be linked to a former orphanage nearby.

Church of Osios David
CHURCH

(Vlatadon 1; ⊙10am-5pm Tue-Sat) This little 5th-century church was allegedly built by the orders of Theodora, daughter of anti-Christian Galerius, who was baptised in

🏃 City Walk
Thessaloniki

START ANO POLI
END PORT
LENGTH 8KM; FOUR HOURS

Start around 9am, as many churches close by noon. Avoid Mondays, when most sites are closed.

Begin at Ano Poli's tower by the easternmost end of the **1 Byzantine Walls**. Follow the walls west on the main road Eptapirgiou; turn left onto Akropoleos (becoming narrow walkway Agathaggelou) to find the church and museum at the **2 Monastery of Vlatadon**. This 14th-century edifice has well-preserved frescoes and a calm, leafy setting.

Double back to Eptapirgiou and continue west, following more ragged Byzantine walls. Turn left and follow the stairs on Sthenonos along pastel-painted walls and houses with blooming window boxes. At the bottom of the stairs, veer right along Dimitriou Poliorkitou. Look out for the easy-to-miss stairway that doubles backwards; follow it down to Unesco-listed **3 Church of Osios David** – a sign for the church marks the stairway – which is resplendent with rare frescoes.

From here, wander labyrinthine Ano Poli eastwards along the small streets. The most direct route follows Fotiou across Akropoleos, turning left onto Krispou. The road wiggles into Eolou, and then hits Moreas. Follow Moreas to the left, then find 14th-century **4 Church of Nikolaos Orfanos** by turning right onto Amfitryonos. Burnished angels blaze from the walls of this intimate Byzantine church.

Returning to Moreas, go southwest to leave behind Ano Poli's steep streets. Once you cross Olymbiados and reach Kassandrou, you're back in the big city.

Dodge the pedestrian bustle for a few blocks west along Kassandrou and turn south on Agiou Nikolaou. You'll see the bulging red-domed roof of **5 Yeni Hammam** (p253), a restored 17th-century Turkish bath, in front of you. A few steps south of Yeni Hammam is the burly brick **6 Church of Agios Dimitrios** (p249), occupying its own square and sheltering relics of St Dimitrios within.

Venture south on Agnostou Stratiotou across Olympou and you'll see the ruin of the ⑦ **Roman Agora** (p249), with a backdrop of modern tower blocks. After marvelling at the contrast of ancient and new, double-back to Agiou Dimitriou and proceed east 10 blocks to ⑧ **Atatürk House** (p253) on your left, inside the Turkish consulate.

A block further east on Agiou Dimitriou, hike right on Dimitriou Gounari; at the end you'll find the imposing and newly renovated ⑨ **Rotunda of Galerius** (p249). This squat, rounded building has been a mauseoleum, temple, church and mosque. Amble downhill along the path towards the statue-studded 3rd-century ⑩ **Arch of Galerius** (p249), created to commemorate Galerius' victory over the Persian army. After crossing busy Egnatia, meander down the pedestrianised street until you see excavated walls. The ruins may look scant, but they are remnants of the once-vast ⑪ **Palace of Galerius** (p249).

Continue following gravity's pull downhill. Cross Tsimiski and, at Plateia Fanarioton, arc left to see the iconic ⑫ **White Tower** (p248). Thessaloniki's waterfront icon was once a notorious prison, but now harbours a multimedia museum. Next wander west for a waterside

stroll on Leoforos Nikis. Some of the city's most effervescent nightlife is along this road.

Leave the water by turning right up Agias Sofias towards the impressive ⑬ **Church of Agia Sofia** (p253). If your energy is low after craning your neck at its mosaic-decorated inner dome, pause for a quick sugar rush at ⑭ **Blé** (p259) before returning to Tsimiski to proceed west. Soon you'll hit Aristotelous; ⑮ **Plateia Aristotelous** is to the left. Follow your rumbling belly to the right; between Irakliou and Ermou you'll discover ⑯ **Modiano Market** (p253), full of fish on ice and trays of olives and cheese.

Nibble your way through Modiano before rejoining Ermou. You'll cross busy Venizelou. Next turn towards the sea once more by pacing down Ionos Dragoumi. If your feet are sore, end here with a visit to the excellent ⑰ **Jewish Museum** (p253); or quench your thirst by returning to Leoforos Nikis' waterfront bars.

Further down Ionos Dragoumi note the splendid ⑱ **National Bank of Greece** building; after it, turn right onto Mitropoleos and head into the ⑲ **Ladadika district**, once full of olive-oil warehouses. Finish with sea views, walking south to Kountouriotou towards the beautified ⑳ **port**.

secret. It contains well-preserved mosaics and rare 12th-century frescoes.

Eptapyrgion
HISTORIC BUILDING

(Yedi Kule) **FREE** A prison from Ottoman times until 1989, the Eptapyrgion, or Yedi Kule in Ottoman Turkish (in both languages, 'Seven Towers'), is a grim reminder of Thessaloniki's penal past, recounted in *rembetika* (Greek blues) songs. It's in Ano Poli, behind the Byzantine Walls.

☞ Tours

Thessaloniki Walking Tours
WALKING

(☑6798186900; www.thessalonikiwalkingtours. com) Started by a Thessaloniki journalist, who enlisted architect, archaeologist and historian friends to work as guides, this is a great opportunity to go on specialised walks with expert locals. There are themed tours, such as a sailing tour exploring the city's bay as well as specific buildings, or a music tour that takes you around famous *rembetika* bars. Call for details.

Free Walking Tours
WALKING

(☑6936896280; https://thessalonikifreewalking tours.wordpress.com) Well-informed free walking tours run on most days during the high season. They're led by energetic local enthusiasts in multiple languages (with advance notice). Find 'Thessaloniki Free Walking Tours' on Facebook for details or email the address on its website.

Thessaloniki Sightseeing
BUS

(☑2310 515 944; www.thessaloniki-sightseeing. com; White Tower; adult/child €10/5; ☺10am-8pm Jun-Sep, to 5pm Oct, to 6pm Mar-May; ⊞) While a walking tour is the best way to see Thessaloniki's sights, hop-on, hop-off bus and miniature train tours also zigzag through the city's major sights, starting from the White Tower. If you stay seated, bus tours take about 70 minutes, while the train completes a short circuit in 45 minutes.

⚹ Festivals & Events

Festivals in Thessaloniki are youth-focused, vibrant and often provocative. Book accommodation far in advance if your visit coincides with HelExpo (www.helexpo.gr; ☺Sep) or Reworks International Music Festival. The two film festivals – Thessaloniki Documentary Festival and the Thessaloniki International Film Festival – are also worth attending if you're in town for their eclectic programming and showcasing local talent.

Thessaloniki International Film Festival
FILM

(☑2310 378 400; www.filmfestival.gr; ☺Sep-Nov) This popular film festival unfurls alongside a calendar of concerts, exhibitions and theatrical performances.

Thessaloniki Documentary Festival
FILM

(☑2310 378 400; www.filmfestival.gr; ☺Mar) A rich program of documentary film events are screened at various Thessaloniki venues.

PicNic Urban Festival
CULTURAL

(☑2310 273 660; www.urbanpicnic.gr; ☺end Aug) On the festival scene since 2012, Urban Picnic reconnects the community with archaeological sites by hosting concerts and short film screenings at Thessaloniki's Roman Agora.

Reworks International Music Festival
MUSIC

(☑2310 266 648; www.reworks.gr; ☺Sep) Three days of DJ sets, music concerts and live events across the city's many squares.

🛏 Sleeping

🏚 White Tower & Waterfront

★ **Trilogy House**
BOUTIQUE HOTEL €€

(☑2310 232 305; www.thetrilogyhouse.gr; Tsimiski 97; d €65-90; ⊞☎) Trilogy House gets all the top marks for, well, everything design and comfort-oriented. The nine rooms are stunning – chic messed-up walls, designer furniture, banana plants, espresso machine (in each room), wooden floors, incredibly comfortable beds. All affordable, and central. It's hard to find a more sumptuous place in town.

City Hotel
BUSINESS HOTEL €€

(☑2310 269 421; www.cityhotel.gr; Komninon 11; d/tr/ste incl breakfast from €70/90/110; ⊞@☎) This four-star near Plateia Eleftherias balances elegant rooms with friendly, cheerful service. There's a big American-style breakfast and a spa centre with gym and *hammam* (Turkish baths).

★ **Daios Luxury Living**
BOUTIQUE HOTEL €€€

(☑2310 250 200; www.daioshotels.com; Leoforos Nikis 59; s/d/ste from €145/165/190; ⊞☎) Close to the White Tower, this boutique hotel has spacious, opulent rooms at a glorious seafront location. The suites have enormous soundproofed windows and balconies. The hotel's waterfront cafe is just as sophisticated, with an excellent range of cocktails. Enter on side street Smyrnis.

Electra Palace Hotel
HOTEL €€€

(☑2310 294 000; www.electrahotels.gr; Plateia Aristotelous 9; d incl breakfast €130-275; ❀🛜🏊) Even if just coming to gaze at the harbour from the rooftop garden cafe, you can't miss the appeal of this fabulous five-star city landmark, standing splendidly over Plateia Aristotelous. The renovated rooms are spacious, with ornate furnishings, and there's a mosaic-tiled indoor pool, a rooftop outdoor pool and a *hammam*.

🛏 Egnatia & Central

★ Caravan
HOTEL €€

(☑2313 062 780; www.thecaravan.gr; cnr Rebelou & Vamvaka; d/ste €70/150; 🛜) This beautiful hotel is a mix between a travellers' haven and contemporary design – with a bit of luxury thrown in. Opened by three friends from Thessaloniki who love travel, the aim here is to make guests feel at home. Therefore, you get smart rooms in cool colours, a friendly common area and plenty of advice on where to go.

Rent Rooms Thessaloniki
HOSTEL €€

(☑2310 204 080; www.rentrooms-thessaloniki.com; Konstantinou Melenikou 9; dm/s/d/tr/q incl breakfast €25/55/70/90/115; ❀🛜) This excellent-value hostel and apartment accommodation has a charming back-garden cafe, where you can tuck into a choice of filling breakfasts with views of the Rotunda of Galerius. Some dorms and rooms have mini-kitchens; all have fridges and bathrooms. Security lockers and luggage storage available. The friendly staff is brimming with local info.

Egnatia Palace Hotel
HOTEL €€

(☑2310 222 900; www.egnatia hotel.gr; Egnatia 61; s/d/ste €50/100/120; ❀🛜🏊) This four-star hotel offers bright, individually decorated rooms and suites. It's well located on central Egnatia.

🛏 Valaoritou & Western Egnatia

Blue Bottle Hotel
BOUTIQUE HOTEL €

(☑2310 520 090; www.bluebottlehotel.gr; Amvrosiou 1; s/d/tr/f from €47/50/63/70; ❀🛜) A newly opened hotel with more style than it knows what to do with – the differently sized rooms cater to all kinds of travel groups, but all are equally hip. There is a mix of modern and sleek with details of dishevelled vintage, walls are painted in geometric multi-coloured patterns, and the beds are very, very comfortable indeed.

Colors Rooms & Apartments
APARTMENT €

(☑2310 502 280; www.colors.com.gr; Valaoritou 21; s/d/ste from €45/52/60; ❀🛜) Valaoritou party people: finally you have somewhere suitably hip to crash. These 15 sparkling apartments (some self-catering) rival more expensive hotel rooms, with cool lighting and minimalist decor. At weekends they're perfect for night owls exploring the surrounding bars (but bring ear plugs if you plan to tuck up in bed early).

Hotel Aegeon
HOTEL €

(☑2310 522 921; www.aegeon-hotel.gr; Egnatia 19; s/d incl breakfast €40/50; ❀🛜) Although rooms are simple and somewhat cramped, the Aegeon is a budget godsend by western Egnatia standards, surrounded as it is by pricey chain hotels and sordid cheap digs. The train station is a 10-minute walk away, and the popular Valaoritou bars are just behind Egnatia opposite.

Thess Hostel
HOSTEL €

(☑2310 554 120, 6937320162; http://thesshostel. gr; Ag Panton 12; dm/apt €18/49; 🛜) This hostel, behind the train station, has all the backpacker essentials (good wi-fi, 24-hour reception, a quirkily decorated hang-out area), clean rooms and friendly staff. Thess is well situated if you have an early start at the train or main bus station.

🛏 Ladadika & Port

Colors Central Ladadika
BOUTIQUE HOTEL €€

(☑2316 007 676; www.colorscentral.gr; Oplopiou 1, cnr Katouni; s/d/ste €70/80/100; ❀🛜) This stylish boutique hotel, sister to the Colors hotel in Valaoritou, occupies a grand heritage house with 12 uniquely decorated rooms. The modern pop-art decor and vibrant tones give it an uplifting, contemporary feel, and its location in the heart of Ladadika's restaurant quarter couldn't be better.

Met Hotel
HOTEL €€€

(☑2310 017 000; www.themethotel.gr; 26 Oktovriou 48; s/d incl breakfast from €110/150; P❀🛜🏊) Near the port and train stations, the Met is a posh, minimalist luxury hotel with sleek modern bathrooms, a spa centre and an outdoor pool. Amenities include designer soaps, flat-screen TV and some seriously comfortable mattresses. There's a complimentary shuttle service to the city centre.

Ano Poli

Little Big House
HOSTEL €

(📱 2313 014 323; www.littlebighouse.gr; Andokidou 24; dm/d €17/48; ✲ 🕏 🐼) This clean and friendly hostel, run by the uproarious Vicky and her brother Harry, is an ideal base for exploring the charismatic upper town. There are kitchenettes, a garden, a common room, and a choice of shared dorms and private rooms. From the train station, take bus 23 to Agios Pavlos. The hostel is north of Plateia Kallithea.

Hostel Arabas
HOSTEL €

(📱 6944466897; www.hostelarabas.gr; Sachtouri 28; dm/d/tr €12/40/51; ✲ 🕏) Located up a hill, hard to find, with a warm welcome and a washing machine: this is hostelling as it used to be. This simple place has spartan dorms, plus private doubles and triples. There's a relaxing front garden for coffee (and sometimes barbecues) plus free luggage storage. The staff enthusiastically helps arrange tours and activities.

✗ Eating

✗ White Tower & Waterfront

To Etsi
GREEK €

(📱 2310 222 469; Nikoforos Fokas 2; grills €2.80-4; ⏰11am-1am) This bawdily decorated, iconic eatery near the White Tower is a local institution offering refreshingly light souvlaki and *soutzoukakia* (meat rissoles in tomato sauce) with vegetable dips, in Cypriot-style pitta bread. Look for the neon sign.

To Mikraki
TAVERNA €

(📱2310 270 517; Proxenou Koromila 2; mains €4-7.50; ⏰12.30-6pm Mon-Sat) This friendly shopfront in a bastion of chic cafes offers top home-cooked Greek fare with smiling familiarity. A true neighbourhood hang-out. Look behind the counter to see the day's specials.

Dore Zythos
MEDITERRANEAN €€

(📱2310 279 010; http://zithos.gr; Tsirogianni 7; mains €8-16; ⏰lunch & dinner) With their view of the White Tower, Zythos' outside tables are a scenic spot to enjoy a fava bean purée topped with capers or feast on beautifully smoked pork.

Agioli
SEAFOOD €€

(📱2310 262 888; www.agioli.gr; Leoforos Nikis 15, cnr Ploutarhou; mains €7-15; ⏰noon-1am) Just the right mix of rustic and modern, this waterfront restaurant has catch-of-the-day specials and boards of fresh salads, including Florina sweet peppers and tzatziki. The garlic hanging from the rafters and the murals give you something to admire while digesting squid and sausage linguine.

✗ Egnatia & Central

★ Mourgá
GREEK €

(📱2310 268 826; Christopoulou 12; mains €4-10; ⏰1pm-late) This has got to be the place that will linger in your sensory memory for decades – elegant and relaxed, Mourgá will make you fall in love with Greek food, Thessaloniki style. Taste the buttery pan-fried shrimp, fava bean purée with preserved caper leaves that melt on your tongue, incredible local seaweed, fantastic cheese selection and local wine.

Bombidia
STREET FOOD €

(Modiano Market, cnr Platia Aristotelous & Ermou; mains from €3; ⏰noon-5pm) Bombidia specialises in street food, serving meatballs on sticks, on a piece of paper – cheap, a bit messy and authentic, plus it's in the lively Modiano Market area, giving it a vibrant outdoor atmosphere.

Giannoula
GREEK €

(📱2310 263 928; Kassandrou 50; mains €10; ⏰noon-late Mon-Sat Sep-Jun) This is grandmother's cooking in a very literal way. Simple Greek classics from grills to salads to cheese-stuffed meats have been served with the same simple expertise for decades in this tiny taverna above the Roman Agora. Kyria Giannoula's sons run the taverna now, but her cooking wisdom has been well preserved.

★ I Nea Follia
GREEK €€

(📱2310 960 383; cnr Aristomenous & Haritos; mains €9-14; ⏰noon-late; 🖊) I Nea Follia is nothing special to look at, but once you sit down to a table and get served a beetroot and pistachio salad, an excellent veal steak or a juicy set of shrimp, you'll be coming back over and over again. It's the baby of three young chefs who specialise in classic Greek fare with a contemporary twist.

★ Extravaganza
MEDITERRANEAN €€

(📱2310 529 791; Stoa Ptolemaion 29a, cnr Avramou; mains €6-14; ⏰lunch & dinner) Three friends and an abandoned space near the Roman Agora resulted in this fantastic restaurant. The food is as innovative as it is sensual – the strawberry and sausage risotto may sound unusual, but once you taste it you'll wonder why it's not on *all* menus. Try the lamb with cumin and spiced yoghurt and the hand-cut chips with truffle oil.

✕ Ladadika & Port

★ Sempriko
GREEK €

(☑ 2310 557 513; Fragkon 2; mains €7-11; ☉ 9am-midnight Tue-Fri, 2pm-midnight Sat & Sun) Near the western Byzantine Walls, Sempriko has become a classic thanks to its consistent quality. Steaks immersed in truffle oil are enormous and absolutely divine, salads are imaginative, shrimp is sizzled in butter, and there are excellent risottos with seasonal mushrooms or seafood. An excellent variety of cheese completes the experience, as does the fantastic selection of Greek wine.

Zythos
TAVERNA €

(Katouni 5; mains €8-12; ☉ noon-3pm & 7pm-midnight) Popular with locals, this excellent taverna with friendly staff serves up delicious standards, interesting regional specialities, good wines by the glass and beers on tap. Its second outlet is Dore Zythos, near the White Tower.

Athivoli
CRETAN €

(☑ 2310 508 509; www.athivoli.gr; Katouni 15; mezedhes €5-8; ☉ lunch & dinner) Ladadika's Cretan restaurant is enlivened by traditional music, an amiable background to platefuls of plump mussels and flaky cheese pies. Look for the neon outline of Crete to spot the restaurant.

Pizza Poselli
PIZZA €

(☑ 2314 019 687; Vilara 2; pizza slices €2.30; ☉ 1pm-4am) Many locals will agree that this is the best pizza place in town. Simple decor, with chic touches in the way of elegant wooden tables and vintage lamps, Poselli has mozzarella and truffle-oil pizzas, margheritas and the classic standards done to perfection. It also does a roaring trade in pizza by the slice with the Valaoritou bar crowd.

Omikron
GREEK €

(☑ 2310 532 774; Oplopiou 3; mains €7-10; ☉ 1pm-late) This neat and tidy local favourite does excellent fresh fish and inventive grills, and

---

SWEET INDULGENCES: THE BEST THESSALONIKI DESSERT STOPS

Thessaloniki's historic ties with the Ottoman East have bequeathed it a rich tradition of sweets. In between traditional Greek pastries, fire your taste buds with *soutzouk loukoum* (aromatic rolls of Turkish delight and pistachio), as well as halva and refreshing gelato.

Chatzis (☑ 2310 221 655; http://chatzis.gr; Mitropoleos 24; sweets €1.40-4; ☉ 8am-late) Glistening syrup-soaked treats have been luring dessert fans into Chatzis since 1908, back when Thessaloniki was still an Ottoman city. Try the sugar-rush-inducing *revani* (syrupy semolina cake), chickpea and raisin halva, or *rizogalo* (rice pudding) scented with cinnamon.

Terkenlis (☑ 2310 271 148; www.terkenlis.gr; Aristotelous 4; ☉ 8am-8pm) This upmarket patisserie chain has temptations including freshly baked *tzoureki* (brioche-style bread) and macarons, as well as confectionery and honey-glazed fruit salads.

Trigona Elenidis (☑ 2310 257 510; www.elenidis.gr; cnr Dimitriou Gounari & Tsimiski; trigones from €1.40; ☉ 8am-5pm) A veritable institution since 1960, Elenidis specialises in Thessaloniki's favourite pastry, the *trigona*. This sweet, flaky triangular cone filled with tasty custard cream is legendary. Locals emerge with 2kg boxes, but you might want to save room for the Greek halva (made with semolina) or homemade ice cream.

Blé (☑ 2310 231 200; www.ble.com.gr; Agias Sofias 19, cnr Georgiou Stavrou; cakes €2-5; ☉ 24hr) This chic patisserie chain (the name is French for 'wheat') has a tooth-tingling range, from traditional Cretan baked goods to dainty cupcakes. The Thessalonikians crowd here in the afternoons, choosing from creamy millefeuille or small bites of chocolate cake topped with berries. Get a coffee, too, and watch the world go by through the large windows.

Fregio (www.fregio.gr; Kouskoura 7; ice cream from €1.50; ☉ 10am-midnight) This wickedly indulgent ice-cream parlour is a local favourite; its gelato-topped waffles are spoken of in rapturous whispers. We love the gourmet choc ices, dipped in toasted nuts.

Kokkinos Fournos (☑ 2310 206 337; www.kokkinosfournos.gr; Apostolou Pavlou 1; ☉ 8am-8pm) Just above the Rotunda of Galerius, this classic bakery does great breads as well as Thessaloniki's best *koulourakia vanilias* – crunchy, slightly sweet golden cookies perfect for dipping in Greek coffee.

the superb daily specials are scribbled out on the chalkboard by the door – you'll often find oysters, market fish and herb-strewn salads on the list.

Paparouna GREEK €€

(☑2310 510 852; www.paparouna.com; Pangaiou 4, cnr Doxis; mains €9-14; ⊙11am-3am) An all-time local favourite, Paparouna has dishes as vibrant as its interior design. Bright primary-coloured walls and a checkerboard floor set the tone for bold flavours, such as thyme-infused cocktails, salads of sea fennel and spice-crumbed seafood.

Full tou Meze MEZEDHES €€

(☑2310 524 700; www.fullmeze.gr; Katouni 3; mains €4-12; ⊙1pm-midnight) This packed Ladadika favourite piles plates high with towers of veal and aubergine, vast seafood risottos and inventive creations, such as its magenta beetroot, yoghurt and walnut salad. In prime position on Plateia Katouni, this is an excellent spot to let the hours drift past between jugs of wine.

Kitchen Bar INTERNATIONAL €€

(☑2310 502 241; Warehouse B, Port; mains €11-17; ⊙9am-midnight) Brilliantly located at the port, with views of the Gulf of Thessaloniki (Thermaïkos Kolpos) from its outdoor tables. Order a cocktail and risotto and people-watch the trendy clientele. Team it with one of the port's late-opening museums for an offbeat evening out.

✖ Ano Poli

★ Taverna to Igglis GREEK €

(Irodotou 32; mains €7; ⊙noon-2am; ☎) Sister to Sempriko and I Nea Follia, this neighbourhood taverna's ordinary looks hide some of the best food in town. Slow-cooked pork in thyme, ever-changing daily specialities and marinated meat grills are simply fantastic. Don't forget the salads whose ingredients vary with the seasons. Have some local beer and/or *tsipouro* (distilled spirit similar to raki) and enjoy life.

Radikal MEDITERRANEAN €

(☑2130 202 007; Stergiou 61; mains €5-12; ⊙noon-late) Up in the heights of Ano Poli, this place makes the best of the rich quality of local ingredients. Radikal is set in an elegant space, pays very careful attention to its wine list and serves immaculately cooked food – try the oxtail, slow-baked veal and any of the salads.

Rediviva Cucina Povera GREEK €

(☑2313 067 400; Papadopoulou 70; mains from €4; ⊙noon-midnight) In the delightful Tsinari part of Ano Poli, this earthy restaurant sources many of its ingredients from its back garden, serving a diverse range of Greek dishes that focus on specialities from Crete and Lesvos islands – try the Cretan herb pita, sun-dried fish and fantastic salads. You can also buy some of its preserves, such as marmalades and chutneys.

Tsinari GREEK €

(☑2310 284 028; Papadopoulou 72; mains from €4; ⊙noon-midnight) One of the most picturesque tavernas in town, it sits on a corner in Ano Poli and serves simple mezedhes (appetisers) and ouzo to a loyal local clientele.

☕ Drinking & Nightlife

🍷 White Tower & Waterfront

West of the White Tower, pedestrianised Iktinou is bursting with boutique bars and charismatic cafes. Along the waterfront, most bars offer little to distinguish between them, though several have stylish interiors and excellent cocktails.

Vogatsikou 3 COCKTAIL BAR

(☑2310 222 899; Vogatsikou 3; ⊙6pm-late) Locals consider this place to be the best cocktail bar in town, so if you're a lover of mixed-up drinks, head here and choose from the carefully prepared menu. If you're a whisky connoisseur, there's a good selection too. It's an officially nonsmoking bar, which is much appreciated by many travellers.

Iktinou au Trottoir COCKTAIL BAR

(☑2310 283 133; www.iktinouautrottoir.gr; Iktinou 10; cocktails €9; ⊙noon-late) Tucked away on pedestrian alley Iktinou, this bar sparkles at night with cocktails as rainbow-coloured as the fairy lights strung around the outdoor area. Generous free snacks accompany the cocktails and the open-air seating is plush and romantic.

Slag BAR

(☑2313 040 747; Zefxidos 2; ⊙10am-late) Brits may blush at the name, but this small, quirky bar is as good for coffees as it is for beers after sundown. Nestled into a pedestrianised alley off Iktinou, it's a superb location to nibble biscotti with a frappé (Greek-style iced coffee). Alternatively, arrive after 11pm when the real fun begins.

Kafeneion Giasemi
CAFE
(☑ 2315 316 300; Tsopela 4; ⊙ 11am-2am) The cosy interior cheerfully blends classic countryside Greece and colourful retro, with space for just a few tables. Along with coffees and drinks, Giasemi offers small mezedhes (the menu entries are carefully handwritten in pencil). Sometimes there's live music in summer.

Palermo Coffee Shop
CAFE
(☑ 2310 279 958; Plateia Aristotelous 8; ⊙ 10am-midnight) On the 1st floor inside a pretty building on busy Plateia Aristotelous, this is a cosy haven – there's good music, delicious cake, great tea and coffee, all in a vintage setting that features kaleidoscopic floor tiles, old typewriters and radios.

Berlin
BAR
(Smyrnis 10; ⊙ midnight-7am Mon-Fri, 10.30pm-9am Sat & Sun) Berlin has operated since 1979, and still welcomes a crowd of bleary-eyed party people seeking a grunge or Gothic fix to see them through until morning. The music is as alternative as the clientele.

Loxias
CAFE
(☑ 2310 233 925; Isavron 7; ⊙ 11am-late Mon-Sat, 8pm-late Sun) Fuel your philosophising with ouzo and snacks at this bookshop-cafe, where literary bar talk gets more animated as the sun goes down. It's decorated with wine casks, bursting with bookshelves and full of historic photos and prints.

Cafe Nikis 35
CAFE
(☑ 2310 230 449; Leoforos Nikis 35; ⊙ 10am-late; ☎) This snug waterfront cafe sits just under street level. It's perfect for a Sunday-morning coffee (€3) or afternoon beer (€4), or come here in the evening if you fancy a place that's quieter than many of the other bars on Nikis. It's a great place for sea views and people-watching.

⬢ Valaoritou

The last decade has seen this former commercial district metamorphose into an alternative nightlife district. Graffiti and dive bars sit next to mushrooming cocktail bars.

★Coo
BAR
(☑ 2311 274 752; Vassiliou Irakliou 4; ⊙ 7pm-late) What started as a venue to promote the musical creations of a few friends has become an alternative bar, and a great one

at that – Coo often hosts live events, dancing and exhibitions. The top floor is open for drinks and coffee, and the basement hosts experimental theatre, photo exhibits and summer concerts.

La Doze
BAR
(☑ 2310 532 986; Vilara 1; ⊙ 8pm-late) Skate-boarding students and sports-car collectors mingle for cocktails and freestyle-DJ action at this legendary Valaoritou hang-out. Put your trust in La Doze's mixology magic: with more than 100 cocktails and rare ingredients, the bar staff delights in new creations.

Fragile
BAR
(☑ 2310 547 443; Valaoritou 29; ⊙ 11am-late) Surrounded by the neighbourhood's dark office blocks and dive bars, this rooftop bar has views that are more Gotham City than postcard-pretty, but no matter – it's a fun spot that broadcasts an eclectic mix of pop, rock and electronica into the night. Tip: locals also call it Taratsa.

Partizan Bar
BAR
(☑ 6944767374; Valaoritou 29; ⊙ 10am-late) Bohemian Partizan is open for coffee by day, unlike most of Valaoritou's drinking haunts. But it's best by night, when revellers crowd its industrial-themed bar to gulp down one of 20 whiskies.

Enola
BAR
(www.enola.gr; 2nd fl, Valaoritou 19; ⊙ 11pm-3am) Anything from 1980s to karaoke to thumping dance music can be danced to at Thessaloniki's liveliest gay bar. Enter from the Valaoritou side and take the elevator to the 2nd floor.

Gambrinus
BAR
(☑ 2310 512 876; Sygrou 7; ⊙ noon-late) If your love of guitar music is matched only by your devotion to beer, step into the darkness of this Czech-inspired place. Central European beers abound, with hefty carb and sausage snacks to keep you sober enough to sample another ale.

⬢ Ladadika & Port

Competition from Valaoritou inspired a comeback for Ladadika, a historic quarter of old tobacco houses and brothel buildings. Facing it, the port area has trendy cocktail bars and student-driven cafes, and several art venues.

NORTHERN GREECE THESSALONIKI

Gorilla
COCKTAIL BAR

(☑6977590306; Verias 3; ⊙6pm-late) A new and ultra-popular cocktail bar, Gorilla is all industrial interiors and serious attitudes – when it comes to cocktails. The music is eclectic and always good. Check out its special cocktail mixes, which change seasonally.

High School Pizza Bar
COCKTAIL BAR

(☑2310 286 161; Leoforos Nikis 9a; ⊙9am-2am) This nostalgic bar and pizzeria has some of the best cocktails in Thessaloniki's port area. The decor evokes school days past with pencil candleholders, exam-room chairs and arithmetic on the walls, and the drinks are truly top of the class.

Sinatra
BAR

(☑2310 223 739; Mitropoleos 20, cnr Komninon; ⊙7am-4am) Espresso and wine, together at last. While you might not want both in a single sitting, the quality coffee and breathtaking wine selection make this a sophisticated choice. Sinatra gets quite busy at night, so head here if you want an upbeat vibe.

☆ Entertainment

City-centre cinemas include **Olympion** (☑2310 378 400; Plateia Aristotelous 10) and **Plateia Alpha Odeon** (☑2310 290 290; Tsimiski 43), where the film festivals are also held. Live music can be found in Ladadika, and if your Greek is decent, several theatres – such as **Aristotelion** (☑2310 262 051; http://aristoteleion.gr/; Ethnikis Amynis 2) – stage interesting plays.

Rover
LIVE MUSIC

(☑2310 544 304; Salaminos 6, Ladadika) Live music and arts events form an eclectic calendar at Rover bar. But while the soundtrack could be anything from Slovenian dubstep to rock 'n' roll, the cocktail quality is thirst-quenchingly consistent.

Kismet
LIVE MUSIC

(☑2310 548 490; Katouni 11; ⊙10pm-4am) Set right among Ladadika's restaurants, Kismet is a fine, though crowded, spot for live bands, ranging from rock and pop to Greece's most popular *rembetika* acts.

National Theatre of Northern Greece
THEATRE

(☑info & bookings 2315 200 000; www.ntng.gr; Ethnikis Amynis 2) Offers opera, classical Greek drama and modern theatre, in Greek.

Ticket House
BOOKING SERVICE

(☑2310 253 630; cnr Ethnikis Amynis & Tsimiski) Book tickets for music and theatre performances through this agency.

🔒 Shopping

Modiano Market is excellent for food shopping. West Egnatia has bargain-basement shopping, while Tsimiski has more upscale clothing and electronics stores.

★ From Thessaloniki
ARTS & CRAFTS

(☑2310 272 298; www.fromthessaloniki.gr; Dimitriou Gounari 21) Architect Evangelia and set designer Athanasia, two wonderfully creative and warm women, started this little shop that makes and sells the most original and beautiful souvenirs in town. Choose from painted tiles, Greek god and goddess pillows, T-shirts, tote bags, mugs, jewellery, notebooks – all original and locally produced, and all useful objects that you can enjoy for years.

★ 2 Concept Store
ARTS & CRAFTS

(☑2310 265 999; Ioustinianou 6; ⊙9am-midnight) It's difficult to categorise this place – it includes a workshop, a shop, an exhibition space and a cafe. Run by agriculturist Christos and the graphic designer Nikos, who is also a marvellous carpenter, the pair find old furniture and decoration and turn them into something new and original.

★ Votanopoleio
SPICES

(Aghiou 18, cnr Venizelou; ⊙9am-2pm & 5-8pm Mon-Sat) A fantastic place to shop and learn – Alkiviadis Grigoriadis, the store owner and botanist, will give you an insight into all the properties of the herbs, spices and essential oils you want to buy. He also makes herbal drinks and oregano oil.

Agora Products
FOOD

(☑2310 223 550; www.ergonproducts.gr; Kouskoura 5; ⊙9am-7pm) Located beside **Agora restaurant** (☑2310 284 224; Pavlou Mela 42; mains €8-15; ⊙noon-midnight), this shop extols the rich variety and health-giving properties of traditional Greek food and sells several hundred delicacies. Test your luggage-weight limits with olive oils, wines, traditional seasonings, jams and honey.

Salami, Feta & Krasi
FOOD

(Ermou 33; ⊙9am-8pm) This family-run deli is a great place to stock up on Greek produce. The owners also sell their own preserves, such as cabbage pickled in wine.

Travel Bookstore Traveller
BOOKS

(☑2310 275 215; www.traveler.gr; Proxenou Koromila 41; ☉10am-9pm) Satiate your wanderlust at this delightful bookshop that sells maps, travel souvenirs and stationery, as well as Lonely Planet and other guidebooks.

Medusa Handmade
JEWELLERY

(☑2310 270 401; Egnatia 142; ☉9am-9pm) Opposite the Arch of Galerius, this inventive shop has handmade jewellery and accessories, including unique pendants, vintage-inspired scarves and Mary Poppins brooches.

❶ Information

INTERNET ACCESS

Free wi-fi zones abound, and many cafes and restaurants offer wi-fi for customers.

MEDICAL SERVICES

Whenever closed, Thessaloniki pharmacies must list nearby working pharmacies.

If going to hospital, bring an ID card/passport and insurance information (if possible). If you are an EU citizen, bring your EU health card.

Farmakeio Gouva-Peraki (☑2310 205 544; Agias Sofias 110, Ano Poli; ☉8am-8pm) Pharmacy in Ano Poli with experienced staff.

Farmakeio Sofia Tympanidou (☑2310 522 155; Egnatia 9; ☉8am-8pm) Well-stocked pharmacy on west Egnatia.

Ippokration (☑2310 837 921; Kostantinoupoleos 49; ☉24hr) Some 2km east of the city centre, this is Thessaloniki's largest public hospital.

MONEY

Except in Ano Poli, banks and ATMs are widespread. Commission-hungry exchange offices line western Egnatia.

POLICE

Tourist Police (☑2310 554 871; 5th fl, Dodekanisou 4; ☉7.30am-11pm)

POST

Find post-office branches on www.elta.gr.

Central post offices include **Agiou Dimitriou** (☑2310 231 579; Agiou Dimitriou 98; ☉7.30am-2.30pm Mon-Fri) and **Irakliou** (☑2310 277 434; Vassiliou Irakliou 38; ☉7.30am-8.30pm Mon-Fri, 7.30am-2.30pm Sat, 9am-1.30pm Sun). The train station has a post window.

TOURIST INFORMATION

For local happenings and other info, visit the frequently updated www.enjoythessaloniki.com website, run by local enthusiasts.

Mt Athos Pilgrims' Bureau (☑2310 252 575; www.agioritikiestia.gr; Egnatia 109; ☉9am-4pm Mon-Sat) Issues permits for Mt Athos monasteries to male pilgrims.

Tourism Office (☑2310 229 070; www.thessaloniki.travel; Plateia Aristotelous; ☉10am-5pm) The tourism office on Plateia Aristotelous can assist with hotel bookings, local information, and arranging tours and excursions beyond Thessaloniki.

❶ Getting There & Away

AIR

Besides Greece's **Aegean Airlines** (www.aegeanair.com), many foreign carriers use Thessaloniki for domestic and international flights. Prices and routes are fluid, so ascertain which companies are currently flying from the **Makedonia International Airport** (SKG; ☑2310 985 000; www.thessalonikiairport.com) website. Then visit a travel agent or book online.

If you're visiting Thessaloniki briefly, you can store luggage with Sky Bag at the airport.

BOAT

From Thessaloniki port, you can get to the Sporades Islands only, within Greece, and you can sail to Italy, Turkey and Albania.

Karacharisis Travel & Shipping Agency (☑2310 513 005; b_karachari@tincewind_techpath.gr; Navarhou Koundourioti 8; ☉8am-8.30pm) Also books ferry tickets.

NEL Lines (☑2810 346 185; www.ferries.gr; Ferry Port) The website has details and booking options for ferries from Thessaloniki, and you can pick up your ticket at the port.

BUS
Domestic

Thessaloniki's main bus station, **KTEL Makedonia** (☑2310 595 400; www.ktelmacedonia.gr; Giannitson 244), is 3km west of the city centre. Each destination has its own specific ticket counter, signposted in Greek and English.

For Athens only, avoid the trip by going instead to **Monastiriou bus station** (☑2310 500 111; http://ktelthes.gr; Monastiriou 67) – an easy-to-miss office opposite the train station – where Athens-bound buses start before calling in at KTEL Makedonia. Additional discounts to regular fares apply for kids, students, special-needs travellers, retirees and soldiers (well, Greek ones, anyway). Travellers can leave luggage at KTEL Makedonia (€1 to €7 for 24 hours).

Buses leave for Halkidiki from the eastern Thessaloniki **Halkidiki bus terminal** (☑2310 316 555; www.ktel-chalkidikis.gr; Km 9 Thessaloniki-Halkidiki road). The terminal is out towards the airport, reached via city buses 45A or 45B. From the main bus station, buses stop en route at the train station and Plateia Aristotelous. With waiting time and traffic, this 'express' service to the bus terminal can take more than an hour. Then there's the trip to Halkidiki itself. The whole production can take three to six hours. It's wiser to rent a car for your entire Halkidiki trip or at least take a taxi (€10 to €15) to Halkidiki bus terminal.

International

KTEL offers international services to Bulgaria and Albania. Direct services reach Tirana (€32, nine hours, twice weekly), Sofia (€20 to €25, five hours, four daily), Plovdiv (€27, 7½ hours, one daily, or transfer via Sofia) and Blagoevgrad (€20, four hours, four daily).

Weekly overnight buses set out to the Slovak and Czech Republics on Wednesdays (€70 to €90, 19½ hours), through Bratislava, Brno and Olomouc.

Small bus companies, such as **Simeonidis Tours** (☑ 2310 540 970; www.simeonidistours. gr; 26 Oktovriou 14; ☺ 9am-9pm Mon-Fri, to 2pm Sat), opposite the courthouse, serve Turkey, Romania, Hungary, Serbia, the Czech and Slovak Republics, and Germany. **Crazy Holidays** (☑ 2310 237 696; www.crazy-holidays.gr; 1st fl, Aristotelous 10) operates daily buses to İstanbul departing at 10am and 10pm. It also goes to Skopje, Belgrade, Budapest and Tirana.

Bus Services from KTEL Makedonia

DESTINATION	DURATION	FARE (€)	FREQUENCY
Alexandroupoli	4hr	29	7 daily
Arta	4½hr	36.80	2 daily
Athens	6hr	39	9 daily
Didymotiho	5½hr	37.60	5 daily
Drama	2hr	13	10 daily
Edessa	1¾hr	8.40	14 daily
Florina	2½hr	15.60	4 daily
Igoumenitsa	4hr	34.30	2 daily
Ioannina	3½hr	28	6 daily
Kastoria	2½hr	17.60	7 daily
Kavala	2¼hr	15	4 direct daily
Komotini	3hr	25.30	7 daily
Litohoro	1¼hr	8.50	12 daily
Orestiada	6½hr	39.50	5 daily
Pella	45min	3.30	18 daily
Serres	1½hr	8.20	15 daily
Veria	1hr	6.80	20 daily
Volos	2hr	18.40	8 daily
Xanthi	2½hr	19	9 daily

TRAIN

Domestic

Direct trains serve Athens (€55.40, 5¼ hours, seven daily), Litohoro (€9, one hour, 10 daily)

and Larissa (€14 to €21, two hours, 15 daily). Several daily trains serve Veria, Edessa and Florina (mostly via Platy). Only two daily trains currently serve Xanthi, Komotini and Alexandroupoli in Thrace.

Thessaloniki's train station has ill-kept downstairs toilets, ATMs, a post office, card phones and small modern eateries, plus an Orthodox chapel. Self-serve luggage storage lockers start from €3. Additionally, a staffed luggage storage room (€3 per item per day) operates until 10pm daily – show your train ticket when depositing luggage.

International

Daily international trains serve Sofia (€17, six hours) and Blagoevgrad (€12, 4½ hours) in Bulgaria, as well as Skopje (€13, six hours) and Belgrade (€34, 14 hours). Check ahead at Thessaloniki **train station** (☑ 2310 599 421; www. trainose.gr; Monastiriou) or consult the OSE website (www.trainose.gr).

Trains are regular or intercity (IC or ICE). If possible, book a day ahead, as long lines are common.

❶ Getting Around

TO/FROM THE AIRPORT

Bus 78 runs half-hourly from the airport (17km southeast of town), heading west through the city to the main bus station (KTEL Makedonia) via the train station. Tickets cost €2 from the airport to the bus station; €1.10 for short journeys.

Taxis to the airport cost €15 to €20 – much depends on your luck with the taxi driver. Call in advance if you need them to pick you up from town; the operator speaks English.

BUS

Dependable city buses have electronic rolling signs listing the next destination, accompanied by an audio announcement in Greek and English. Screens above most bus stops note how many minutes until the next buses.

Bus 1 connects the main bus station (KTEL Makedonia) and the train station, while buses 45A and 45B stop at both (plus Plateia Aristotelous and Kamara) en route to the Halkidiki bus terminal. From the train station, major points on Egnatia are served by buses such as Nos 10 and 14.

Buy tickets at *periptera* (street kiosks) for €1, or from on-board blue ticket machines (€1.10). Validate the former in the orange machines. Machines neither give change nor accept bills; when boarding, be sure you have the right change and buy your ticket immediately. Thessaloniki's ticket police pounce at any sign of confusion. If they nab you, you'll pay €60.

CAR

If driving, take note that Ano Poli's streets are steep and can be rather narrow, so avoid driving

PETRALONA CAVE   ΣΠΗΛΑΙΟ ΠΕΤΡΑΛΩΝΩΝ

Some 50km southeast of Thessaloniki on the main road is the stalagmite-rich **Petralona Cave** (☑ 6936705100; www.petralona-cave.gr; €7; ☉ 9am-4pm) . Discovered by Petralona village locals in 1959, it became famous when a prehistoric man's skull (dubbed Arhanthropos; in Greek, the 'first' or 'original man') was found; scientists have dated it as 700,000 years old, making Arhanthropos Europe's oldest known man.

Fossils of extinct species, including lions, panthers, bears, rhinoceroses, elephants, bison, deer, numerous birds and bats, have been found here. The most intriguing objects discovered, the so-called Petralonas Hoard, are kept at Thessaloniki's Archaeological Museum. The ticket price includes a cave tour and visit to the adjacent anthropological museum. Photos aren't allowed, and the cave closes one hour before sunset.

there if you're not used to such conditions. If you can't find free parking (a common problem in hectic Thessaloniki), try the municipal parking at the port (per hour €2).

For rental cars try the following:

Avance Rent a Car (☑ 2310 279 888; www. avance.gr; Agelaki 7)

Budget Rent a Car (☑ 2310 819 990; Km 15 Thessaloniki-Peraia road)

TAXI

Thessaloniki's blue-and-white taxis carry multiple passengers, and only take you if you're going the same way. The minimum fare is €3.40. A more expensive 'night rate' takes effect from midnight until 5am. To book a cab for an airport transfer, try **Taxi Way** (☑ 2310 214 900, 2310 866 866; www.taxiway.gr).

Halkidiki   Χαλκιδική

The popular Halkidiki Peninsula has three tendrils stretching into the Aegean Sea. Kassandra and Sithonia draw crowds to their blissful beaches and growing adventure travel scene. Meanwhile, Athos is the mysterious monks' republic.

Being closest to Thessaloniki, Kassandra is more built up with better nightlife (though it has good beaches, too). More subdued Sithonia has campgrounds, hidden coves and clear waters. Both are popular with Greek and foreign holidaymakers (most from Eastern and Central Europe). Most of the easternmost peninsula belongs to the Mt Athos monastic community. Active for well over 1000 years, it's accessible by boat and open to male pilgrims (with advance reservations).

Kassandra and Sithonia are mostly populated along the coasts, the interiors of both being rugged, with thick pine forests. The main roads, therefore, hug the coasts. Many Halkidiki beach villages were settled by ref-ugees during the 1923 population exchanges with Turkey; the government gave the 'useless' coastal land to these newcomers, and their descendants would have the last laugh when beach tourism took off in the 1970s.

In high summer, traffic can be exasperating and finding accommodation tough. For those after beach-bar parties and nightclubs, July and August are best; families and solitude seekers will prefer September when waters are warmest and the crowds disappear.

Kassandra Peninsula   Χερσόνησος Κασσάνδρας

Sublime beaches bring no shortage of tourists to Kassandra; its roads are clogged with Thessaloniki weekenders, Balkan families and Australian backpackers during the summer. But its rippling forested interior is a delight for road trips; mountain-bike tours draw visitors away from the shade of their beach umbrellas; and unfussy thermal baths are an antidote to the resort gloss.

Kallithea is a great base if you want nightlife. **Polyhrono** is crammed with fast-food places and souvenir stands but has great beaches. **Pefkohori** is quieter with even more resplendent sands. You'll find the less-busy south coast has more cultural draws, such as snoozy villages and a thermal spa near **Loutra**.

🏃 Activities

⭐ **Poseidi Cape**   BEACH

(Poseidi) An absolute beauty of a beach lies hidden at Poseidi Cape. Kilometres of sand are lapped by crystal-clear waters, and it's a rare place to find peace and quiet (though little shade) in the summer months. It's a joy year-round, though, backed as it is by a lighthouse and a pine forest.

Agia Paraskevi Thermal Baths SPA

(☑ 23740 71358; Loutra; from €5; ☺ 9am-9pm summer) This bathing complex near Loutra on the south coast has a large swimming pool of thermally heated water as well as private bathing areas, a *hammam*, a sauna and other soothing amenities. The restorative properties of the mineral waters may linger as long as the sulphurous whiff in your swimsuit. Towel rental is €1 extra.

Break Free MOUNTAIN BIKING

(☑ 23103 48073; www.breakfreemtb.com; ☺ Apr-Oct) See a more rugged side of Halkidiki with guided mountain-biking excursions arranged through this safety-conscious outfit, based in Thessaloniki.

🛏 Sleeping

Polyhrono, Afytos and Pefkohori all have a wealth of hotels to stay in, but expect them to be very busy indeed in the summer months.

Hotel Odysseas HOTEL€

(☑ 23720 51923; www.odysseas.net; Polyhrono; d incl breakfast €40-80, tr incl breakfast €45-90; P ✳ 🛜 🌊) Moments from Polyhrono beach, Odysseas has clean, roomy digs and a small pool. Good for families on a budget.

Poseidi Camping CAMPGROUND€

(Camping Kalandra; ☑ 23740 41123; www.posidicamping.gr; Possidi; campsites adult/tent from €6/7; ☺ May-Sep; P) This well-equipped campground is on Kassandra's south coast, five minutes' drive from Kalandra, and is a great base for water sports. There are also log cabins on-site from €30 per night.

Blue Bay Hotel HOTEL€€

(☑ 23740 91645; www.bluebayhotel.com.gr; Afytos; d/ste from €95/125; ☺ May-Oct; @ 🌊) This serene hotel, five minutes' drive north of Kallithea, has lively modern decor on the inside, and a delightful blue mosaic pool outside. With beach access, a Greek and international breakfast spread, and a lavish *hammam*, it's family-friendly and a lovely spot to unwind.

Akrogiali Boutique Hotel BOUTIQUE HOTEL€€

(☑ 23740 51500; www.hotelakrogiali.com; Polyhrono; d €40-140; P ✳ 🛜) All 10 of the modern, comfortable rooms at this romantic hotel, 60m from sandy Polyhrono beach, have balconies with wonderful sea views.

Flegra Palace Hotel HOTEL€€€

(☑ 23740 61702; www.flegrahotels.com; Pefkohori; d from €150; P ✳ 🛜 🌊) Spacious doubles and suites surround a refreshing pool at this

family-friendly four-star hotel with breezy charm, just north of Pefkohori on Kassandra's north coast. Sister to Flegra Beach.

Flegra Beach APARTMENT€€€

(☑ 23740 61832; www.flegrahotels.com; Pefkohori; d/ste from €100/215) The opulent Flegra Beach in Pefkohori village has luxury apartments with nautical and modern trimmings and a dazzling beach bar and restaurant.

🍴 Eating

There are waterfront tavernas and restaurants in Polyhrono, Afytos and Pefkohori, all catering to tourists and serving fish and seafood.

Bakalis Taverna TAVERNA€€

(☑ 23740 63060; www.bakalis-restaurant.com; Pefkohori; mains from €8; ☺ 11am-late) A good seafood taverna with tables on the waterfront, just above the beach. Try the grilled octopus, big refreshing salads and ask about the fish of the day. It's a busy place in the summer, but the service is always attentive.

ℹ Getting There & Away

Kassandra by bus from Thessaloniki can feel like a slog. Take city bus 45A or 45B to Thessaloniki's KTEL Halkidiki bus terminal (p263). Connections run to Kallithea (€8.80, 1½ hours, 10 daily), Pefkohori (€11.80, two hours, eight daily) and Polyhrono (€11, 2¼ hours, 10 daily) on the north coast, via Kryopigi and Hanioti (€10.60 and €11.50, 2½ hours). Buses also reach Agia Paraskevi spa near Loutra (€12.60, 2½ hours, three daily) and Nea Skioni (€11.90, two hours, three daily) on the south coast. Discounts apply for 15-day open-return tickets.

To return from Kassandra, check timetables with **KTEL Kallithea** (☑ 23740 23714).

Sithonian Peninsula
Χερσόνησος Σιθωνίας

Of the two touristic 'fingers' of Halkidiki, the Sithonian Peninsula is one that is loved by families and those in search of a more low-key summer option – though the beaches get rather packed in the high season and on weekends. Pine forests crowd a wild interior, fringing cliffsides that plummet towards tranquil coves. Sunsets are remarkable; diving and water-sports opportunities are excellent; and dozing on a beach might seem a little enticing after all.

Along the west coast you'll find Sithonia's largest resort, **Neos Marmaras**. The east coast's beaches have a little more sparkle;

further south the terrain gets wilder. If you don't rate total seclusion, hang your sunhat at **Sarti** for a 1970s vibe, an escapist feel and good nightlife. **Kalamitsi**, at Sithonia's southernmost tip, is also an excellent base: it's a good starting point for diving excursions and water sports.

🏃 Activities

Along the west coast you'll find well-loved beaches, including **Paradisos**, **Kalogria** and **Lagomandra**. On the east coast, **Karydi** beach has ruggedly rocky views (though it's sometimes not the cleanest), and **Zografou** has stunning sands.

Sarti-based **Sithon Travel** (⌨ 23750 94066, Oct-Apr 23104 25921; www.sarti.gr; Sarti; ⊙ 10am-2pm & 6-10pm) can assist with arranging excursions and activities.

Dolphin Diving Centre
DIVING
(⌨ 23750 41346; www.kalamitsi.com; Kalamitsi) Right at the tip of the Sithonian Peninsula, Dolphin offers twice-daily dives from May to mid-October. Prices start at €35 for accomplished divers with their own kit or €60 if you need to hire gear. It's adjoined by Camping Porto Kalamitsi.

Atlantis Diving Center
DIVING
(⌨ 6978165361; www.atlantis-scubadiving.com; Nikiti) Let the safety-conscious diving experts at Atlantis guide you to an underwater wonderland. The range of diving programs at this PADI member outfit includes dives for absolute beginners and children. A one-day boat diving trip including transport and refreshments costs €150.

🛏 Sleeping

On the east coast the range of lodgings is more glamorous. In the south there are fantastic campgrounds tucked into hidden bays. Kalamitsi has comfortable guesthouses and campgrounds.

★ Porto Elea Camping
CAMPGROUND €
(⌨ 6984625581; www.portoelea.com; Zografou; campsites per adult/child/tent €8/4/10; ⊙ May-Sep) Porto Elea is nestled in woodland shade by a glowing cove, down a dirt road 9km east from Vouvourou. The luminous water, fancy beach bars and excellent taverna explain why it's the favourite place of Balkan celebs. Apart from caravans, there is also the converted convent of Porto Elea, which is now a hotel featuring minimalist rustic rooms.

Camping Porto Kalamitsi
CAMPGROUND €
(⌨ 23750 41565; Kalamitsi; campsites per adult/tent €6/8) This campground has sunshades, washing machines and a superbly shady location, and it adjoins Dolphin Dive Centre.

Camping Armenistis
CAMPGROUND €
(⌨ 23750 91487; www.armenistis.com.gr; Sarti; campsites per person/tent €7.80/8.80; ⊙ May-Sep; P) Large and very popular Camping Armenistis near Sarti enjoys a fantastic setting between forest and beach, and is outfitted with services including a restaurant and crêperie, a cinema, sportsgrounds and a medical centre. Summer sees frequent concerts and DJ parties. You can also rent a caravan or mobile home (from €60).

O Giorgakis
PENSION €
(⌨ 23750 41013; Kalamitsi; studios €55-85; ⊙ May-Sep) Tucked away from the harbour above the eponymous seafood tavern, this great-value family-run guesthouse in Kalamitsi offers pleasant sea-facing studios. The taverna has a lavish menu, warm service and soothing views of the water.

Hotel Vergos
HOTEL €€
(⌨ 23750 91379; www.hotelvergos.com; Vourvourou; s/d/studio/apt incl breakfast €65/77/90/120; ❄ 🛜 🏊) Spacious Hotel Vergos offers well-furnished rooms in a relaxed setting, a pool and a big lawn for kids.

Ekies All Senses Resort
RESORT €€€
(⌨ 23750 91000; http://ekies.gr; Vourvourou; d/ste from €140/160; ⊙ end Apr–mid-Oct; ❄ 🛜) This sumptuous resort is a fantasy land of sculpted grounds and spa amenities, just steps from a private beach. Themed rooms give a modernist nod to local nature and myth. Honeymooners and hedonists will delight in the shady alcoves and hammocks.

🍴 Eating & Drinking

Navagos
SEAFOOD €
(⌨ 6977193183; Vourvourou; mains from €6; ⊙ lunch & dinner May-Nov) Yorgos, the local fisherman who runs this beach bar and restaurant, lives here year-round, but in the summer he prepares his catch for guests on an open fire on the beach. It's really quite spontaneous – you can visit and see what he's got, or call him in advance. He catches fish, octopus, you name it.

Kivotos
SEAFOOD €€
(Noah's Ark; ⌨ 23750 94143; waterfront, Sarti; mains €10-12; ⊙ 10am-1am May-Oct) This

NORTHERN GREECE HALKIDIKI

gloriously situated taverna in Sarti has tables right on the sand and a menu of excellent seafood specialities. Choose from the day's catch and don't skimp on the mouthwatering mezedhes. Effusive owner Daniel is a rich source of local information.

Orange Cafe Beach Bar
CAFE

(waterfront, Sarti; ⊙9am-2am; 🛜) This beachfront bar has free wi-fi and relaxing couches under gauze curtains, plus loungers for a quick siesta.

Goa Beach Bar
BAR

(🗷6977995220; Sarti; ⊙Jun-Sep) This famed long-time beach bar 4km south of Sarti pours drinks day and night. Check ahead for DJ sets and themed parties.

🛈 Getting There & Away

Driving is the best way to navigate around Halkidiki in general, and that includes Sithonia. Budget plenty of time to account for transfers and traffic if travelling from Thessaloniki to Halkidiki by public transport. Buses to the peninsula depart from Thessaloniki's Halkidiki bus terminal (p263), reached via city bus 45A or 45B.

Buses serve Nikiti (€10.60, 1¼ hours, three daily), Neos Marmaras (€13, two hours, three daily), Sarti (€17.40, three hours, three daily) and Kalamitsi (€17.40, 3½ hours, three daily). Check at the bus station for other villages served en route. The discounted return ticket is valid for 15 days.

Crossing to Sithonia from Kassandra by bus requires changing at Nea Moudania, at Kassandra's northern foot. Halkidiki's buses do not go east to Kavala (or anywhere else); it's back to Thessaloniki for everyone.

Athos Peninsula
Χερσόνησος του Αθω

Athos offers an unforgettable, immersive experience into a 1000-year-old spiritual tradition – if you're male, that is. While main town **Ouranoupoli** is open to all, just south is a border enclosing the all-male monastic community of Mt Athos from the rest of the world.

Land entry is prohibited between secular and monastic Athos. Boats from Ouranoupoli to the 'monks' republic' are carefully guarded, with thorough checks for customs (and forbidden women).

Male visitors hoping to bunk with monks must apply for permits well in advance, the reward being access to the peninsula's rugged terrain and dazzling religious architecture. Meanwhile, women travellers in Ouranoupoli might feel alienated or bemused by the whirl of spiritual activity. Women and mixed groups can take boat trips to get a glimpse of Athos.

OURANOUPOLI   ΟΥΡΑΝΟΥΠΟΛΙ

A thriving tourist industry has sprung up around Athos' monks. Consequently the pretty seaside town of Ouranoupoli feels rather commercial: expect souvenir stands overflowing with monk-made soaps, high-end jewellery shops and steep cafe prices. It's a dramatic contrast to the untouched terrain and ongoing spiritual activity across the border in monastic Athos. Nonetheless, it's a pleasant, friendly place with a lively centre and some excellent tavernas and guesthouses.

⊙ Sights

Pyrgos Prosforeiou
HISTORIC BUILDING

(Ouranoupoli Tower) The Byzantine tower by Ouranoupoli's harbour dates to the 14th century and is the town's most distinctive landmark. The tower has been restored but is still closed to the public.

🛏 Sleeping

Camping Ouranoupoli
CAMPGROUND €

(🗷23770 71171, Nov-Apr 23770 71165; www.camping-ouranoupoli.gr; campsites per adult/tent €9/9; ⊙late May-Oct) A solid campground on Ouranoupoli's northern beach side, with on-site supermarket and restaurant. 'Glamping' packages and bungalows are offered for nature seekers averse to pitching their own tent.

Lazaros Andonakis Rooms
PENSION €

(🗷23770 71366; s/d €45/55; ❄🛜) These airy, pine-furnished rooms, some with harbour views, are 50m from the Pilgrims' Office. Walk north from the White Tower past the harbourside restaurants to find them.

Hotel Filoxenia
HOTEL €€

(🗷23770 71158; www.filoxenia-r.gr; s/d/tr incl breakfast €52/75/81; 🅿❄🛜) Perched in a tranquil location at the top of Ouranoupoli, this hospitable hotel has well-kept rooms and satisfying breakfasts, as well as beautiful views of the Aegean from its terrace. Look out for signs for Filoxenia shortly after entering Ouranoupoli; it's left, up a steep driveway, 1km before you reach central Ouranoupoli.

Athos Peninsula

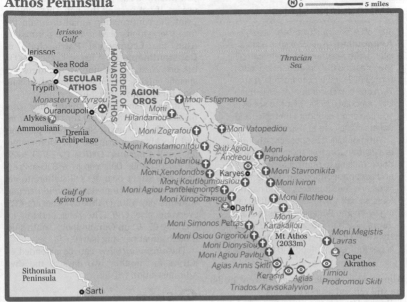

🍴 Eating

Lemoniadis　　　　　　　　　　　TAVERNA €€
(☑23770 71355; mains €10-14; ⊘lunch & dinner)
This waterside taverna has been sizzling
sensational seafood since 1957. With a rous-
ing *rembetika* soundtrack and outdoor
seating with views of the Aegean, an atmospheric feast is assured.

Kritikos　　　　　　　　　　　　SEAFOOD €€
(☑23770 71222; www.okritikos.com; mains €12-15;
⊘lunch & dinner) Whether you're looking to
celebrate a 'last supper' before visiting Mt
Athos or just a leisurely dinner, this bright
place on a central side street offers some of
Ouranoupoli's best fresh fish.

Mt Athos　　　　　　　　Αγιον Ορος

This isolated peninsula has seen unbroken
spiritual activity unfold for over a millennium. Access is granted to male visitors only,
on whom traipsing the quiet Athonite forest
paths and marvelling at monastic architecture will leave a strong impression.

An enormous World Heritage site, 56km
long and 8km wide, Mt Athos is formally
Greek, though ecclesiastically it's under the
Orthodox Patriarchate of Constantinople
(İstanbul). Athos has 20 working monasteries, and *skites* (monastic dependencies),
plus *kelli* (ascetic hermitages). The north is
thickly forested, and the more inaccessible
south is dominated by soaring Mt Athos
(2033m). With neither industry nor hunting
in the region, it's essentially a nature reserve.

Legend attests that the Virgin Mary visited
and blessed Athos; considered the Garden of
the Virgin, it's dedicated to her – there's no
room for other women. Though controversial to European human-rights activists and
frustrating to would-be women visitors, the
1000-year-old decree has stood firm.

History

Unorganised ascetic life is thought to have
begun on Athos as early as the 5th and 6th
centuries. It was consolidated by Emperor
Basil I's AD 885 *chrysobull* (sealed decree)
and the 958 arrival of the monk Athanasios.
He brought organisation to Athos' spiritual
activity by framing daily life around communal food, work and prayer. In 963 the Holy
Mountain was formally dedicated when
Emperor Nikoforos II Fokas funded Megistis
Lavras, still Athos' biggest monastery.

In response to fears that Athos' traditions
were being diluted, in 1060 Constantine IX
Monomahos banned women, female domestic animals, beardless persons and eunuchs.

WORTH A TRIP

AMMOULIANI ISLAND

Just off Athos' northwestern coast, **Ammouliani** (Αμμουλιανή) is a small island with beaches, pensions, camping, tavernas and 600 inhabitants. Six daily ferries (€2) travel here from **Trypiti**, 7km north of Ouranoupoli; while there isn't much of a ticket office to speak of, you can enquire about timetables and tickets in the cafe at Trypiti dock.

Ammouliani's best beach, **Alykes**, is a 20-minute stroll southwest of the dock. Walking to more distant beaches and accommodation can take over an hour, and the shadeless island has no taxis, so call ahead for a free lift if staying overnight. Waterfront **Restaurant Janis** (☑ 23770 51322; fish €6-12; ⊙ 9am-11pm May-Oct) is an excellent excuse to linger for fresh seafood and fine sunsets.

Women and female animals (except birds) are still refused access to Athos.

By the 11th century, 180 monasteries had been built on Athos, though periodic pillaging and burnings by pirates necessitated ongoing investment and repair.

When the Ottomans arrived in 1430, Athonites pledged allegiance to Murad II in return for retaining their semi-independent status. During the War of Independence (1821–29), Turks plundered and burned monasteries and their libraries. During the WWII Nazi occupation, Hitler agreed to place Athos under his personal protection. It survived the war unscathed.

Athos' 1927 Constitution was guaranteed in Greece's 1975 Constitution. Each of the 20 surviving monasteries has one representative on the Holy Council (Iera Synaxis), which oversees Athos' 2300 monks. The Julian calendar is still followed by most monasteries.

Getting a Permit

Male visitors should book up to six months ahead for summer and Orthodox holidays. Only 10 non-Orthodox and 100 Orthodox men are admitted daily. Those under 18 years must be accompanied by their father or, if with a group or guardian, need their father's written permission.

First call Thessaloniki-based Mt Athos Pilgrims' Bureau (p263) before emailing or faxing them a copy of your passport and your preferred visit dates. They will inform you when you can pick up your permit. Otherwise, if not passing through Thessaloniki, print the confirmation email or retain the fax. Clergymen need written permission from the **Ecumenical Patriarchate of Constantinople** (☑ in Turkey 90 21253 49037; İstanbul). Next, phone monasteries to reserve specific nights; free accommodation and food is generally offered for one night.

Finally, take your written/printed confirmation to Ouranoupoli for the *diamonitirion* (final permit). Show your passport and booking confirmation at Ouranoupoli's small **Pilgrims' Office** (☑ 23770 71422; fax 23770 71450; Ouranoupoli; ⊙ 8.10am-2pm), on a side street near Jet Oil station, to get the three-night (four-day) *diamonitirion:* students pay €10, Orthodox believers €25, everyone else €30. There's a parking lot (per day €7.50) on Ouranoupoli's south side, though street parking is free.

The *diamonitirion* can be extended in Karyes for another two days at the Civil Administration Office.

◉ Sights

Dress modestly; don't take photos during church services; and if you must bathe, do it out of sight of monasteries.

KARYES TO THE SOUTHEAST COAST MONASTERIES & MT ATHOS

From Karyes, walk southeast through the **Kapsala** woods to coastal **Moni Stavronikita** (☑ tel/fax 23770 23255; ⊙ noon-2pm) or, just under it, **Moni Iviron** (☑ 23770 23643; fax 23770 23248; ⊙ noon-2pm). This Georgian-founded monastery contains more than 2000 manuscripts, including 100 rare Georgian-language parchments.

From Iviron, coastal paths reach hospitable **Moni Filotheou** (☑ 23770 23256; fax 23770 23674), also accessible from Karyes along a shady path with spring water (3½ hours). Beyond **Moni Karakallou** (☑ 23770 23225; fax 23770 23746) the Byzantine-era path becomes a road leading (after 5½ hours) to Moni Megistis Lavras. Alternatively, buses from Karyes go there.

Magnificent **Moni Megistis Lavras** (Great Lavra; ☑ 23770 23754; fax 23770 23013) is Athos' biggest monastery and houses founder St Athanasios' tomb. From here, a small boat sometimes serves the hospitable west-coast **Agias Annis Skiti** (☑ 23770 23320).

A very tough trail leads around the peninsula's southern tip; it passes the Romanian **Prodromou Skiti** (☑ 23770 23294), then coastal **Agias Kavsokalyvion** (☑23770 23319).

KARYES TO THE SOUTHWEST COAST MONASTERIES

If heading southwest from Karyes, you will first encounter **Moni Koutloumousiou** (☑23770 23226; fax 23770 23731). Further west, coastal **Moni Xiropotamou** (☑23770 23251; fax 23770 23733; ☉12.30-2.30pm) is said to hold the largest-known fragment of the True Cross. The path southward accesses Dafni; either walk the coastal path or take the boat, which leaves at 12.30pm, calling at Simonos Petras, Osiou Grigoriou, Dionysiou and Agiou Pavlou.

Spectacular **Moni Simonos Petras** (Simopetra; ☑23770 23254; fax 23750 94098; ☉1-3pm), fronted by wooden balconies over a cliff, is Athos' most-photographed monastery. From here the coastal path branches off towards the *arsanas* (monastery port/dock) at a small shrine, accessing **Moni Osiou Grigoriou** (☑23770 23668; fax 23770 23671), Athos' most inhabited monastery with a community of 100 monks.

The hilly coastal path south reaches **Moni Dionysiou** (☑23770 23687; fax 23770 23686), another tranquil cliff-hanging monastery. Dionysiou's *katholikon* (principal church) contains a unique wax-and-mastic icon of the Virgin and Child.

After Dionysiou, the coastal path continues to the architecturally magnificent **Moni Agiou Pavlou** (☑23770 23741; fax 23770 23905) and Agias Annis Skiti.

KARYES TO THE NORTHERN MONASTERIES

Northward from Karyes, the road passes sprawling **Skiti Agiou Andreou** (☑23770 23810). The main route continues to coastal **Moni Pandokratoros** (☑23770 23880; fax 23770 23685); an alternative two-hour forest path reaches coastal **Moni Vatopediou** (☑23770 41488; fax 23770 41462; ☉9am-1pm), the only monastery to follow the modern Gregorian calendar.

From Vatopediou, a coastal path leads to **Moni Esfigmenou** (☑23770 23229), and further on is **Moni Hilandariou** (☑23770 23797; fax 23770 23494), a hospitable Serbian monastery (also accessible from Dafni by a south-coast boat, and then a connecting bus ride). The UK-based Friends of Mt Athos (www. athosfriends.org) donated towards rebuilding structures here that were destroyed in a 2004 fire. The FOMA website has detailed information in English on the monasteries, their history and tips on visiting them.

The humble, pretty **Moni Konstamonitou** (☑tel/fax 23770 23228) is worth visiting, as is the Bulgarian **Moni Zografou** (☑tel/fax 23770 23247) further north. Its name, meaning 'painter', comes from a miraculous icon believed not to have been painted by human hands. The northernmost west-coast monastery, **Moni Dohiariou** (☑tel/fax 23770 23245), slopes towards the sea and boasts remarkable architecture.

Next down the coastal path, venerable **Moni Xenofondos** (☑23770 23633; fax 23770 23631) was first mentioned in 998, but probably dates to the 6th century. Although loot-seeking pirates often plundered it, impressive mid-Byzantine marble and wood-carved iconostases survive in its 10th-century *katholikon*. Finally, **Moni Agiou Panteleimonos** (☑tel/fax 23770 23252; ☉10am-noon), further on, is a typically grand and friendly Russian monastery.

ℹ Information

Karyes has an ATM. Both Dafni and Karyes have a post office.

Civil Administration Office (☑23770 23314) In Karyes, oversees local matters (including extensions of official visitors' permits).

Police Station Dafni (☑23770 23222; Dafni)
Police Station Karyes (☑23770 23212; Karyes)

ℹ Getting There & Away

If you have arranged an Athos pilgrimage, either take the first bus (5.30am) from Thessaloniki to Ouranoupoli on the date you'll enter Athos, or stay over the night before in Ouranoupoli, which lets you rest, buy supplies and store unnecessary luggage. Get your *diamonitirion* and ticket before the next morning's 9.45am boat.

Boats leave Ouranoupoli for Dafni on weekdays at 8am, 9.45am and 11.45am; get tickets in advance from the **ticket office** (☑23770 71248; Ouranoupoli) on the waterfront. In Dafni a bus serves Karyes, the administrative capital (€2.60). For monasteries further down the coast, change boats at Dafni.

The Athos–Ouranoupoli ferry leaves Dafni at noon, after a customs check to prevent antiquities theft. The morning boat from monasteries south of Dafni is timed to catch this ferry, which also collects passengers from the coastal monasteries north of Dafni.

ℹ Getting Around

Twice-daily boats from Dafni (around €2.50) serve west-coast monasteries such as Dionysiou,

ATHOS DAY TRIPS BY BOAT

Regular boat trips from Ouranoupoli skirt Athos, allowing both male and female visitors a peek at Athos' spectacular clifftop monasteries – while carefully keeping to the legal 500m distance from shore, of course.

Athos Sea Cruises (☑ 23770 71370, 23770 71071; www.athos-cruises.gr; Ouranoupoli; adult €30-20, child 7-12yr/under 7yr €10/free; ☺ 10.30am Apr-Oct, 10.30am & 1.45pm mid-May–mid-Oct) runs daily three-hour excursions, passing major west-coast monasteries and giving good views of Athos' peak. There's a recorded running commentary in English, German and Greek, which explains Athos' turbulent history and the monks' unchanged lifestyle: work, prayer, sleep (and, occasionally, wine).

If you're based on Halkidiki's Sithonian Peninsula, similar tours run from Ormos Panagias – try **Ormos Travel** (☑ 23750 31522; http://halkidiki.com/ormos-travel), whose cruises depart around 9.30am and return by 5pm. A lunch stopover in Ouranoupoli is often included.

Simonos Petras, Agiou Pavlou and Agias Triados/Kavsokalyvion.

While monastic vehicles, buses and boats operate, walking is ideal for experiencing Athos' serenity. Paths can be overgrown and ravines steep, so watch your step and prepare as you would for any hike (wear decent boots, bring water and use a map).

Litohoro & Plaka Litohorou
Λιτόχωρο & Πλάκα Λιτοχώρου

POP 7260 / ELEV 293M

Litohoro sits on the mountainside and looks onto beaches and the snow-kissed peaks of Mt Olympus. It's a great hiking base. The town itself has a small centre with brick bell towers and wooden-balconied houses, and steep, winding streets.

Six kilometres east, **Plaka Litohoro's** stretch of coastal hotels and campgrounds springs to life during summer. The general area is known as Pieria, and nearby beaches such as **Leptokarya** and **Skotina** are very popular with Greek and foreign tourists.

Both Litohoro and Plaka Litohoro are well positioned for trips to Mt Olympus, mystical Ancient Dion and Platamonas Castle. If you don't have a car, think carefully about where to base yourself; public transport is scant between town and coast, so you'll be reliant on taxis.

🏃 Activities

EOS　　　　　　　　　　　　　　CLIMBING
(Greek Alpine Club; ☑ 23520 82444, 23520 84544; http://eoslitohorou.blogspot.com; ☺ 9.30am-12.30pm & 6-8pm Mon-Sat Jun-Sep) Hikers and climbers should head to EOS, below the public parking lot, which distributes pamphlets with hiking information, and runs mountain refuges. Take Ithakisiou from the square; turn left after 100m. Noticeboards detail the locations of emergency huts and general hiking conditions.

SEO　　　　　　　　　　　　　　CLIMBING
(Association of Greek Climbers; ☑ 23520 84200; ☺ 6-10pm) This place is informative for hikers and rock climbers and runs an Olympus refuge. Walk down Ithakisiou, turn left and then left again.

🎉 Festivals & Events

Festival Olympou　　　　　　　CULTURAL
(www.festivalolympou.gr; ☺ Jul-Aug) During this summer festival, concerts, plays and artistic events unfold at venues around Litohoro.

🛏 Sleeping

★**Xenonas Papanikolaou**　　GUESTHOUSE €
(☑ 23520 81236; www.xenonas-papanikolaou.gr; Nikolaou Episkopou Kitrous 1; s/d €45/50; P ✳ @) This romantic guesthouse in a flowery back-street garden has spacious self-catering rooms, with uplifting views of Litohoro's terracotta rooftops. The downstairs lounge has a fireplace and couches. From the square, take 28 Oktovriou uphill and turn left on Nikolaou Episkopou Kitrous. Breakfast is an extra €4.

Olympos Beach　　　　　　CAMPGROUND €
(☑ 23520 22112, 23520 22111; www.olympos-beach.gr; Plaka Litohorou; campsites per adult/tent €7.50/7.50; P ☎) This leafy, well-run camping option on the Plaka Litohorou strand has a restaurant, minimart, well-stocked bar and bungalows with wi-fi.

Hotel Olympus Mediterranean
HOTEL €€

(📞 23520 81831; www.mediterraneanhotels.gr; Dionysou 5; d/tr incl breakfast €70/90, luxury ste €100; 🅿️❄️@⌘) This four-star hotel occupies a neoclassical building with ornate balconies, and has 20 luxurious rooms and three suites, plus an indoor pool and sauna. Some rooms have fireplaces and spas.

Olympios Zeus
BUNGALOW €€

(📞 23520 22115; www.olympios-zeus.gr; Plaka Litohorou; bungalows from €78; 🅿️❄️📶) This Plaka Litohorou beachfront bungalow-hotel has simple but smart huts, a beach bar and it's right on the sands.

Cavo Olympo Luxury Resort & Spa
RESORT €€€

(📞 23520 22222; www.cavoolympo.gr; Plaka Litohorou; d/ste from €210/250; 🅿️❄️@📶⌘) On Plaka Litohorou's seafront, this minimalist masterpiece consists of 49 rooms and suites overlooking either Mt Olympos or the sea, some with spas or private pools. All are airy, spacious and relaxing, with big balconies. The hotel's centrepiece is an enormous infinity pool sloping towards the bluff overlooking the water.

✕ Eating

Meze Meze
GREEK €

(📞 23520 82271; Agiou Nikolaou 40; mains €6-8; ⏱️6-10.30pm Tue-Fri, noon-3pm & 6-10.30pm Sat, noon-3pm Sun; 📶) Mussels on rice, grilled meats and the catch of the day are very good indeed at this simple taverna near Litohoro's bus station. Rotating daily specials keep things fresh and interesting, salads are generous and the service is attentive.

Damaskinia
TAVERNA €

(📞 23520 81247; Vasileos Konstandinou 4; mains €6-11; ⏱️10am-11pm) A popular upper-town taverna, no-frills Damaskinia does tasty *mousakas* (baked layers of eggplant or zucchini, minced meat and potatoes topped with cheese sauce) and *kokoretsi* (spit-roasted lamb offal, wrapped in intestines). There's a garden at the back.

★ Gastrodromio
GREEK €€

(📞 23520 21300; Agiou Nikolaou 36; mains €10-15; ⏱️noon-late) If Gastrodromio was around in Olympian times, Zeus and co would have dined here. There's fantastic truffle-laced risotto, lamb stewed in rosemary and tomato, and 30 different cheese options.

Erato
MEDITERRANEAN €€

(📞 23520 21100; Agiou Nikolaou; mains €8-15; ⏱️lunch & dinner) Tuck into seafood, baked cheeses and classic Greek grills at this chic restaurant near the Agiou Nikolaou church by the main square. The mountain views are as glorious as the wine list.

ⓘ Information

Plateia Eleftheria and Ithakisiou have ATMs.

Katerini Hospital (📞 23510 57200) is the nearest hospital with an accident and emergency department.

Medical Centre (📞 23520 22222; Plaka Litohorou)

Police (📞 23520 81100; cnr Ithakisiou & Agiou Nikolaou)

Tourist Information Booth (Agiou Nikolaou; ⏱️9am-6pm Jun-Sep) In a white building with a tiled roof, by the municipal park.

ⓘ Getting There & Away

From the **bus station** (📞 23520 81271; Agiou Nikolaou) in Litohoro town, buses serve Katerini (€2.30, 25 minutes, 14 daily), Thessaloniki (€8.50, 1¼ hours, 13 daily) and Athens (€33, 5½ hours, two daily via Katerini). Buses from Thessaloniki to Volos and Athens drop you on the highway to catch a Katerini–Litohoro bus.

Litohoro's **train station** (📞 23520 22522) is 4km north of Plaka Litohorou and serves Thessaloniki (€9, one hour, 10 daily). For Florina and Edessa, change at Platy (€6, 30 minutes, 10 daily).

Around Litohoro

★ Mt Olympus
MOUNTAIN

(Όρος Όλυμπος) The cloud-covered lair of the Ancient Greek pantheon, awe-inspiring Mt Olympus is simply spectacular. It fires visitors' imaginations today, just as it did for the ancients who venerated it. Greece's highest mountain, Olympus hosts more than 1700 plant species, some rare and endemic, as well as wolves, jackals, deer and more than 100 bird species. Its slopes are thickly forested and its peaks often shrouded in fog.

The first known mortals to reach **Mytikas** (2918m), Olympus' highest peak, were Litohoro local Christos Kakalos and Swiss climbers Frédéric Boissonnas and Daniel Baud-Bovy in August 1913. Olympus became Greece's first national park in 1938.

Although you can drive up Olympus, many people hike; consult the Litohoro-based hiking associations for maps and current conditions, or check with the

Management Agency of Olympus National Park (☑ 23520 83000; www.olympusfd.gr; Litohoro), which also lists the hiking routes and the regulations for visitors. Both provide info on the mountain's 15 refuges, where hikers can sleep.

Ancient Dion   HISTORIC SITE

(Δίον; ☑ 23510 53484; www.ancientdion.org; Dion; adult/student €8/4, incl Archaeological Museum; ☺ 8am-8pm) Dion was sacred for ancient Macedonians worshipping the Olympian gods, especially Zeus. Before his epic eastern adventures, Alexander the Great made sacrifices here. A path leads through more than a dozen clearly labelled sites, including sacred springs and the ruins of a Roman theatre. This wooded area is also rich in wildlife: look out for frogs tumbling into often-flooded sanctuaries and kingfishers diving with a sapphire flash.

The ruins of the 6th-century-BC **Sanctuary of Demeter** are the first you'll see and are the site's oldest. Further along is the leafy **Sanctuary of Zeus Hypsistos**, which bears copies of statues and column bases (the originals are in the on-site museum). Other replicas adorn the remnants of Dion's (usually flooded) **Sanctuary to Isis**, goddess of childbirth, across a small bridge. As elsewhere in the Hellenistic world, worship of this Egyptian goddess was merged with that of Artemis and Aphrodite. Later constructions include 4th-century-AD Christian **basilica ruins** and **public baths** once paved with mosaics.

The park has a small visitor centre with cafe. Entry includes the **Archaeological Museum of Dion** (☑ 23510 53206; www.ancientdion.org; adult/student €8/4, incl Ancient Dion site; ☺ 8am-8pm), a 10-minute walk from the site. Taxis from Litohoro to Dion cost from €12.

Castle of Platamonas   CASTLE

(Κάστρο Πλαταμώνα; ☑ 23250 44470; Platamonas; adult/child €2/free; ☺ 8am-3pm) Looming from a coastal bluff near Platamonas village, 20km south of Plaka Litohorou, this well-preserved 11th-century castle was once defended by brave Byzantines, safeguarding trade routes and scanning for pirates. Today, however, the only *stratiotes* (soldiers) you're likely to see are handymen with weed whackers and the occasional lumbering turtle. Taxis from Litohoro town cost about €22.

From the parking area, pass the (unstaffed) booth and take the hilly path 150m to the castle and ticket booth. From here, follow the walls counterclockwise to understand the development of the fortress over time. The first small tower on the right dates from the 6th-century emperor Justinian, and predates much of the existing structure. The ruined Byzantine **Church B** was rebuilt in the 17th century.

The more extensive **Church A** ruins, protected by a wooden enclosure, were built over a 2nd-century-AD Hellenistic warehouse. Squint through the gloom to see faint fresco remains. At the castle's nearby northeastern edge, drink in magnificent views of sandy **Skotina Beach** below and Mt Olympus in the distance.

Veria   Βέροια

POP 48,300

Around 75km west of Thessaloniki, Veria is a small city that merits a exploration – the old Jewish quarter, Barbouta, is atmospheric and its history fascinating, and the small but lush Tripitamos River that runs through it is a beauty. The two town museums are well presented, and Veria is en route to the magnificent Vergina tombs (p276). Add to that some fantastic accommodation options and some decent restaurants, plus the ski areas at Mt Vermio, and you have a real little treat.

◉ Sights & Activities

Archaeological Museum   MUSEUM

(☑ 23310 24972; Leoforos Anixeos 45; €2, combined ticket incl Byzantine Museum & Vergina €8; ☺ 8am-8pm) Browse an impressive haul from Neolithic figurines to Vergina tomb findings at this museum, located at Anixeos' northern end. You'll find iron swords, delicate jewellery, doe-eyed portrait heads and a charming statue of Aphrodite slipping out of her sandals. A combined ticket (€8) for Veria's Archaeological and Byzantine Museums, plus the royal tombs at Vergina, saves €4.

Byzantine Museum   MUSEUM

(☑ 23310 25847; Thomaidou 26; €2, combined ticket incl Archaeological Museum & Vergina €8; ☺ 8am-4pm Tue-Sun) This museum in a restored mill will turn you from novice to nerd in all things Byzantine. Splendorous Madonnas, huge 5th-century floor mosaics and ornate sarcophagi fill all three floors of the beautifully lit space. A film on the bottom floor gives the history of the mill and Veria's Barbouta quarter.

Barbouta
AREA

Walk from Plateia Antoniou down Vasileos Konstandinou to find Veria's atmospheric former Jewish quarter. The synagogue (with the bright blue and yellow facade) dates back to 1850 and it is the region's oldest. It's not normally open, except for when used for worship by visiting groups. The area around Tripitamos River is leafy and lush, beautiful for a stroll.

Mt Vermio
SKIING

(☑ info 23310 49226) Some 22km northwest of Veria, Mt Vermio has three small ski areas with a total of 585m of vertical slopes. It's a good spot for beginners, but check conditions in advance. Visit from December to March.

🛏 Sleeping

★ Kokkino Spiti
BOUTIQUE HOTEL €€

(☑ 23310 74440; www.kokkinospiti.gr; Olganou 10, Barbouta; s/d €60/75; P🅿❄🛜) This is an absolute gem – a restored 1840 mansion with six uniquely decorated bedrooms in its main room and three more in the adjacent building. Wrought-iron bed frames, wood-beamed ceilings, fantastic details and mesmerising river views. It's nestled in the heart of Veria's old Jewish quarter, and is as comfortable as it is elegant.

Olganos VL
BOUTIQUE HOTEL €€

(☑ 23310 72226; www.olganos.com; Merarchias 7, Barbouta; apt €80-120) In the old Jewish quarter, this is a beautiful place to stay – a family-run boutique hotel with eight luxurious, spacious rooms. The suites have Jacuzzis in the bathroom, and a glass fireplace that you can watch as you bubble in the bath. There are lovely views of the neighbourhood, and one room has a terrace.

Hotel En Eari
HOTEL €€

(☑ 23310 75788; www.eneari.gr; Leoforos Anixeos 82; s/d/tr €80/89/90; P🅿❄🛜) En Eari has homey rooms and friendly service. This simple and unfussy hotel is a short walk from the nightlife on Elias, and just a few paces from the Archaeological Museum, facing the new church.

✖ Eating & Drinking

★ Eleas Gi
TAVERNA €€

(☑ 23310 23053; Anixeos 65, cnr Koundouriotou; mains €8-10; ⊙ lunch & dinner; 🛜) Feast on home-cooked Macedonian fare in this lively taverna. Tangy pomegranate chicken is cooked to perfection; smoky cheeses

demand attention among mouthwatering salads and appetisers; and there's always a tempting aroma from the grill. The service is friendly and efficient.

12 Grada
MEDITERRANEAN €€

(☑ 23311 00112; Dimosthenous; mains €12-15; ⊙ noon-midnight) There's no more picturesque spot to clear a plate of grilled vegetables and juicy meatballs than this riverside taverna and wine bar.

Vergiotiko
GREEK €€

(☑ 23310 74133; www.vergiotiko.gr; Thomaidou 2; mains €8-15; ⊙ lunch & dinner) This grotto-like restaurant serves generous servings of oregano pork, chicken schnitzel and cheese-stuffed peppers. You can have a real feast. Find it near the Byzantine Museum.

Batrahos
CAFE

(☑ 23310 20282; Karakosti 13; ⊙ 7am-1am) Follow the scent of freshly brewed coffee to this little brunch place. There is a range of chocolate-slathered cakes and cookies; night-time is all about beers and spirits.

Coin Cafe-Bar
BAR

(☑ 23310 71727; Elias 14; ⊙ 7am-1am; 🛜) This cafe-bar spills onto the pavement of lively Elias, and has decent coffees and a range of cocktails. The hanging bare light bulbs and verandah seating give it a modern, unfussy vibe. Coffees from €3 and cocktails from €7.

❶ Information

ATM-equipped banks line Venizelou and Mitropoleos.

Police (☑ 23310 22391; Mitropoleos)

Post Office (Mitropoleos 39; ⊙ 8am-6pm) In the centre of town.

❶ Getting There & Away

BUS

Veria's two central adjoining **bus stations** (☑ 23310 26100, 23310 22342; Iras) serve Thessaloniki (€6.80, one hour, 14 daily), Athens (€35, 6½ hours, two daily), Edessa (€4.70, one hour, one daily) and Vergina (€1.60, 20 minutes, six daily).

TRAIN

The **train station** (☑ 23310 24444), 2km north of town, has trains for Thessaloniki (€5, one hour, six daily) and Florina (€9, two hours, three daily).

❶ Getting Around

Veria is walkable and has **taxis** (☑ 23310 26049).

WORTH A TRIP

SPLENDOURS OF ANCIENT MACEDON: VERGINA & PELLA

Northern Greece boasts two remarkable sites of the ancient Macedonia dynasty. The royal burial site at **Vergina** lies 11km southeast of Veria. Between Thessaloniki and Edessa lies Alexander the Great's birthplace, the former royal capital **Pella**.

With a car, it's possible to see both sites in a single day trip from Thessaloniki. Matching up bus connections can be a jigsaw, so if you don't have wheels consider exploring Pella and Vergina on separate days or staying overnight: hospitable **Olympia Guesthouse** (☑ 23310 68052; www.xenonasolympia.gr; Aristotelous, Vergina; s/d/tr €35/45/60; Ⓟ🖵) is five minutes' walk from Vergina's archaeological site.

Buses from Thessaloniki to Palia Pella (€3.30, 45 minutes, seven daily) stop by the main road, 20 minutes' walk from the museum. From Thessaloniki to Vergina, take the bus to Veria (€6.80, one hour, 14 daily), from where you can then catch a bus to Vergina (€1.60, 20 minutes, six daily).

Vergina Royal Tombs Museum (☑ 23310 92347; www.aigai.gr; Vergina; adult/child €8/4; ⊙ 8am-8pm) A grass-covered *tumulus* (burial mound) has been converted into a truly spine-tingling museum where visitors can descend to the entryways of royal tombs and admire treasures unearthed at this very site. The showpiece is the 336 BC tomb of Philip II: the monarch was buried with silver chalices, an ivory and gold shield, a gold-plated quiver and his full suit of armour, all on display here.

Elsewhere in the museum, Tomb I and Tomb IV boast mythic friezes, while Tomb III, the prince's tomb, is thought to be the final resting place of the son of Alexander the Great. About 400m past the Royal Tombs lie extensive palace ruins of 3rd-century-BC king Antigonos Gonatas.

Archaeological Site of Pella (☑ museum 23820 31160; www.pella-museum.gr; Thessaloniki-Edessa national hwy; adult/child €8/4, incl museum admission; ⊙ 8am-8pm, closed various public holidays) Pella rose to fame when King Archelaos (413–399 BC) made it a capital of the ancient kingdom of Macedon. This atmospheric archaeological site, with re-erected columns and black-and-white geometric mosaics, fires the imagination about the city's glory days. Don't miss 300 BC Dionysus House, the largest in Pella, and the splendid stag-hunting mosaics.

Archaeological Museum of Pella (☑ 31160 23820; www.pella-museum.gr; Thessaloniki-Edessa national hwy; adult/child €8/4, incl entrance to archaeological site; ⊙ 8am-8pm, closed various public holidays; Ⓟ) This airy two-floor museum on Pella's western edge unravels the city's history, from Bronze Age bones in urns to well-preserved 300 BC mosaics and phallic drinking vessels. Burial treasures include helmets, swords, and the mauve garb and remarkable gold jewellery of 'The Lady of Aigai', wife of Amyntas I.

Edessa   Εδεσσα

POP 18,200

The town's long-existing Slavic name, Voden ('Place of Water'), reveals the essence of Edessa – it's woven through with water, be it in the form of rivers, streams, fountains or the famous waterfalls on the edge of town. The old quarter and a handsome Byzantine bridge add a further touch of charm to this generally pleasant town, where you can spend a night resting if you've been hiking or exploring archaeological parks in the surrounding area.

Until the 1977 discovery of Vergina's royal tombs, Edessa was thought to have been ancient Macedonian Aigai. With the government's Hellenisation project following the 1923 Greek–Turkish population exchanges, the town's name was changed back to the archaic Edessa.

⊙ Sights

Edessa's old quarter, **Varosi**, lies south of Waterfalls Park. Brightly coloured traditional houses and churches make it a lovely area for a stroll. Edessa's **Byzantine Bridge** is beautiful; take Ir Polytechniou from central Plateia Timenidon until you reach the river fork.

Waterfalls Park   WATERFALL
(☑ info 23810 20300) **FREE** Several viewing points around Waterfalls Park allow you to gaze at Edessa's star attraction. The larger of the two falls, **Karanos**, is quite impressive

at 70m high. A path winds downwards to a second, smaller waterfall.

The **cave** (€0.50) is worth a peep for its fang-like stalactites, though the narrow grotto is sadly scarred by graffiti. Through the cave you can stand behind Karanos' curtain of falling water. A short walk away from the watery action, towards Varosi, lie family-friendly attractions, including an open-air **Water Museum** (☉11am-4pm Wed-Mon) FREE and a small aquarium and reptile house.

Folkloric Museum MUSEUM
(Meg Alexandrou, Varosi; adult €2; ☉9am-4pm Tue-Sun) Written explanation is scant at this small museum in the Varosi quarter, but there are plenty of embroidered rugs, farming implements and looms across the three floors to satisfy fans of folk history.

🛏 Sleeping

Hagiati PENSION €
(📞23810 51501; www.hagiati.gr; Makedonomahon 40, Varosi; s/d incl breakfast €50/60; P❄☎) This wonderfully tranquil guesthouse in the old quarter has a tasteful, traditional feel with wooden furnishings, a rustic lounge room and a serene open courtyard.

★Varosi Four Seasons BOUTIQUE HOTEL €€
(📞23810 51440; www.varosi4seasons.gr; Arhiereos Meletiou, Varosi; s/d incl breakfast €70/90; P❄☎) This boutique hotel sits 50m away from its related pension, Varosi Guesthouse. Six of the 10 rooms overlook the outstretched Edessa plain (as does the outdoor verandah cafe). Rooms are pristine and sumptuously decorated, and service is friendly. Book in advance, especially if you plan to stay on a weekend.

Varosi Guesthouse PENSION €€
(📞23810 21865; www.varosi.gr; Arhiereos Meletiou 45-47, Varosi; s/d incl breakfast €55/70; P❄☎) This gorgeous pension occupies a restored traditional wood-and-stone house in Edessa's old quarter. Rooms have double-wood doors, fine linen, colourful embroidery and antique brass beds. In winter a fireplace heats the lounge room, while the flower-filled balcony is superb for a relaxing coffee in summer.

🍴 Eating & Drinking

Ousies GREEK €
(📞23815 02414; 25th Martiou 4; mains €5-8; ☉noon-1am) Ousies serves mezedhes, such as dolmadhes and fish, and roast lamb and

simple but delicious salads. It's all accompanied by fiery *tsipouro* (distilled spirit similar to raki), the best being from the local grape variety *opsimo*. There is a traditional ambience and decor, with historic photos and hanging instruments, and wonderful *rembetika* music.

Katarraktes Edessas TAVERNA €
(📞23810 27810; Kapetan Gareti-Perdika 1; mains €5-9) Publicly owned Katarraktes Edessas, before the waterfalls, is an old-school restaurant serving standard but dependable fare. Hearing the rushing of the stream water from your outdoor table is quite a treat.

Irtha & Edessa TAVERNA €€
(📞23813 00660; cnr Karaoli & Tsmiski; mains €12; ☉lunch & dinner; ☎📶) A short walk from the waterfalls, this local favourite, set in a glass construction, has spit-roasted lamb and grilled meat specialities, as well as a great choice of vegetable dishes and innovative, heaped salads. The locals pour in on weekend evenings, making for a lively atmosphere full of families.

Jam CAFE
(📞6973775100; Thessalonikis 2, Varosi; coffees €2; ☉10am-3pm & 6pm-late) One of Edessa's livelier drinking spots, in Varosi, you can enjoy coffee frappés in the morning and beers in the evenings, and mingle with the locals.

ℹ Information

ATM-equipped banks line Dimokratias.

Police (📞23810 23333; Iroön Polytehniou) A centrally located station.

Post Office (Pavlou Mela; ☉8am-6pm) In the town centre.

Tourist Information Office (📞23810 20300; www.edessacity.gr; ☉10am-6pm) Good for maps and advice for activities.

ℹ Getting There & Away

Edessa bus station (KTEL Pellas; 📞23810 23511; www.ktelpellas.gr; Pavlou Mela 13) serves Thessaloniki (€12, two hours, hourly), Veria (€4.70, one hour, five daily) and Athens (€45.60, eight hours, three daily). The bus to Florina (€8.10, 1½ hours, two daily) departs from 30m away.

The **train station** (📞23810 23510; Leoforos Nikis) is on the Thessaloniki–Athens line and also serves Florina (€7, one hour, three daily).

Find **taxis** (📞23810 22904, 23810 23392) on the corner of Dimokratias and Monastiriou.

Florina Φλώρινα

POP 20,000

Florina is a springboard to remarkable natural spaces to its west, including Mt Vigla 15km away and the wild Prespa Lakes 45km away. Snug within a lush valley, Florina itself is a student town, with a lively local life, and it's a base for hikers and winter-sports fans.

Florina also serves as a crossroad for further Balkan travel: south of Prespa Lakes lies Krystallopigi, the border crossing into Albania, and lively Bitola in the Former Yugoslav Republic of Macedonia (FYROM) is only 35km north of Florina.

Florina was the northernmost town occupied and annexed by Greek troops during the Balkan Wars of 1912–13; its location just south of the mountains kept it near the front in subsequent wars. The existence of Greece's (Slavic) Macedonian minority, denied outright by the government and Greece's latter-day fascists, has always been sensitive in the Florina, Edessa and Prespa regions, where the Macedonian language is still spoken by many Greek people despuite pressure from Greek society, media and government.

◉ Sights & Activities

Archaeological Museum MUSEUM

(✆23850 28206; Sidirodromikou Stathmou 3; €2; ◷8am-3pm Tue-Sun) This museum near the train station paints a picture of the verdant Florina region across millennia, with detailed exhibits on daily life and traditions in ancient Macedonia. Look out for stone reliefs adorned with Macedonian horsemen and haunting 1st-century-BC graves, carved with the faces of those buried inside.

Vigla-Pissoderi Ski Area SNOW SPORTS

(✆23850 45800; www.vigla-ski.gr; Vigla-Pissoderi; ◷9am-4pm Dec-Mar) This small ski area is nestled between the Varnous and Verno mountain ranges, 19km west of Florina. With 11km of pistes and five lifts, it has enough terrain to keep skiers of most levels happy for a weekend. Obviously, check snow conditions before you go.

⌯ Sleeping

Hotel Hellinis HOTEL €

(✆23850 22671; www.hotel-hellinis.gr; Pavlou Mela 31; s/d €35/40; ☏) If you're looking for a cheap place in the centre of town, Hellinis will do. The rooms are clean, basic and somewhat cosy, there is wi-fi and the location

– five minutes' walk from the bus and train stations – works well for further travels.

Pleiades BUNGALOW €€

(✆23850 44070; www.pleiadesflorina.gr; Papathanasiou; s/d/tr €80/90/100; ℗❋☏) Set on a kind of promontory overlooking the Florina valley, 2km north of town, this self-enclosed stone village of cottages and suites fuses Macedonian architecture with modern amenities. There's a summer pool and a beach volleyball area, and breakfast with the views of the valley on the restaurant terrace is a treat.

Hotel Veltsi HOTEL €€

(✆23850 46555; www.hotel-veltsi.gr; Km 6 Florina-Prespes Rd; d €70; ℗❋☏☼) A boutique hotel, 6km west of Florina, Veltsi has woodland views, well-furnished rooms, a pool and a playground. It is perfectly positioned for winter adventures at Vigla-Pissoderi Ski Area, 13km further west.

✗ Eating & Drinking

Prespa TAVERNA €

(✆23850 23973; Tirnavou 12; mains €5-8; ◷dinner) A proper local taverna that is as frill-free as it is authentic – go for the beetroot salad with feta, grilled peppers, shrimp *saganaki,* or any of the grilled meats.

Sakoulevas Cafe Restaurant CAFE €

(✆23850 25580; Eleftherias 68; mains €8; ◷lunch & dinner) Feast on traditional Florina specialities at this agreeable cafe right next to the rushing Sakoulevas River. Hearty favourites such as Prespa beans, grilled trout and 'grandma's meatballs' keep a bustling clientele fed at this scenic spot.

Koukoutsi GREEK €

(✆23850 46010; Stoa Spyraki 6; mezedhes €3-6; ◷11am-1am) Koukoutsi serves refreshing mezedhes, steamed mussels, and famous Florina red peppers with garlic and tomato, as well as a range of grilled meats.

Women's Cafe CAFE

(✆23850 24647; Kallergi 4; cakes from €1.50; ◷lunch & dinner) A superfriendly cake shop run by the wonderful Flora, where you can sip tea and coffee by day and enjoy drinks by night, and eat homemade sweets. The decor is homey and rustic, and occasionally there are live music events and book readings.

El Greco CAFE

(Pavlou Mela 62; ◷10am-late; ☏) This a superpopular spot on Pavlou Mela, with

GREECE'S FORGOTTEN WATERWAYS: THE PRESPA LAKES

West of Florina, the twin Prespa Lakes are a breathtaking beauty spot, rich in wildlife and history. **Megali Prespa** and **Mikri Prespa** (Great Prespa and Small Prespa) are the Balkans' highest tectonic lakes and among Europe's most ancient, at one million years old. Once a single lake, today they are separated by a narrow isthmus formed by sediment churned up over centuries. Greece shares Megali Prespa with the Former Yugoslav Republic of Macedonia (FYROM) and Albania, and Mikri Prespa with Albania.

The wildlife is extraordinary too, with brown bears, wolves and wild pigs skulking around the lakes. The region is also aflutter with more than 260 types of birds, including the world's largest colony of Dalmatian pelicans at Mikri Prespa, as well as great white pelicans, great white egrets and the EU's largest colony of pygmy cormorants. A clutch of sleepy villages act as springboards to this majestic wilderness.

Driving allows you to make the most of Prespa Lakes, and it's quite hard to explore the area without your own wheels. Once-weekly buses from Florina take a circuitous route each Wednesday at 7am (€5.20, 1½ hours), returning the same day at 2pm. Mention to the driver which village you want to get to. Taxis from Florina cost €60 to €80.

Agios Germanos

With its stone houses and well-preserved churches, Agios Germanos is the region's most visually appealing town. The highlight is 11th-century **Agios Germanos church**, an extraordinary work of ecclesiastic mid-Byzantine architecture with a domed brick structure and separate bell tower. This tiny town makes a good base because of its homey accommodation and tavernas, and its helpful **information centre** (Prespa National Forest Management Body; ☑ tel/fax 23850 51870; ☉ 9.30am-3pm) that advises on hiking, birdwatching and wildlife. For emergencies, there's a **police station** (☑ 23850 51202) in the village and a **health centre** (☑ 23850 46284) further south in Lefkonas.

From Agios Germanos, cross the connecting strip between the two lakes and turn immediately left onto a 1km-long wooden bridge. A signposted path to the left hugs the east coast and leads to the basilica and other church ruins. Alternatively, turn right off the bridge for the shop and taverna. Agios Ahillios is sparsely inhabited, though August's Prespes Festival features a headlining concert in the amphitheatre-like basilica.

Agios Ahillios

The semidetached island of Agios Ahillios is Prespes' main attraction and its surrounds are excellent for birdwatching. The grand, concave outer wall of the ruined **Basilica of Agios Ahillios** stands on its eastern shore, with some half-toppled walls, columns and a stone floor. It's a legacy of the 10th-century Bulgarian tsar Samuel, who expanded his empire across much of the southern Balkans, chronically sparring with Byzantium.

Psarades

Out on Lake Megali Prespa's promontory, friendly Macedonian-speaking villagers inhabit Psarades (population 144), while 1m-tall dwarf cattle meander in its surrounds. Fishers offer boat trips to Megali Prespa's isolated Byzantine *askitiria* (hermitages). These include the 13th-century **Metamorfosi**, where scant remnants survive of paintings and two sections from a wood-carved *temblon* (votive screen); the 15th-century **Mikri Analipsi**; and the 14th-century old rock **Church of Panagia Eleousa**, tucked above a ravine and boasting beautiful frescoes.

Vrondero

South of Psarades and close to the Albanian border, ramshackle farming village Vrondero has little to detain you other than access to excellent walking trails. **Kokkalis Cave**, used as a partisan hospital during the Greek Civil War, is a 30-minute hike from Vrondero or a short drive if you have a 4WD. For maps and information, contact the **Society for the Protection of Prespa** (☑ 23850 51233; www.spp.gr) in **Lemos** village, just west of Agios Germanos.

comfortable sofas facing the street so that you can keep an eye on all the people walking up and down the street. Coffee-sipping students gather here morning and evening.

ℹ Information

ATM-equipped banks are near the square, on Stefanoi Dragoumi.

Police (☎ 23850 22222; Saggariou 24)

Post Office (Plateia Giorgiou Modi; ⊙ 8am-6pm) In the centre of town.

ℹ Getting There & Away

BUS
Domestic

Florina bus station (KTEL Florinas; ☎ 23850 22430; www.ktelflorinas.gr; Makedonomahon 10) serves Athens (€50.50, nine hours, one daily) and Thessaloniki (€15.60, 2¾ hours, eight daily). Two serve Thessaloniki direct via the Egnatia Odos Hwy, the others go through Edessa (€8, 1½ hours, three daily).

For Prespa, buses leave only on Wednesdays at 7am, returning at 2pm. Tell the driver your destination when you board, as they may skip some villages. For Kastoria, head to Amyntaio (€3.70, 30 minutes, eight daily) and change buses there. Amyntaio has daily buses for Kastoria (€9, 1½ hours). Twice-weekly Florina buses also reach Ioannina (€30, three hours).

International

The Greece–FYROM border is served by buses to Niki (€1.80, 30 minutes) twice daily during the school year and at other times once a week on Wednesdays. The Greece–Albania border crossing at Krystallopigi (€5.40, one hour) is served once weekly by the Prespa-bound bus.

TAXI

A taxi trip to Bitola (40km) in the FYROM costs around €50 one way, or €60 return including two hours for shopping and sightseeing. Florina cabbies also drive to the Prespa Lakes villages; Agios Germanos costs around €60, Psarades €80.

TRAIN

Florina's **train station** (☎ 23850 22404) connects with Edessa (€7, 1¼ hours, three daily) and Thessaloniki (€10, 2½ hours, three daily).

Kastoria   Καστοριά

POP 17,000

Kastoria is a wonderfully quiet town on Lake Orestiada, with a pretty old town jutting from the hilltop. Enveloped by the lake, most activities naturally happen on and around its still waters – locals power walk (or cycle) the 9km circuits of the lake, and you can admire preening pelicans and darting ferruginous ducks (no binoculars required) as you have a coffee or drink in one of Kastoria's lakeshore bars.

Climb up and around Kastoria's steep and winding old town lanes and you'll find a surprising wealth of post-Byzantine churches. You might have to ask the tourist information kiosk to allow you to go inside.

◎ Sights & Activities

Most charismatic is Kastoria's historic Doltso neighbourhood. This romantically creaky quarter has several restored 18th- and 19th-century mansions housing museums and tavernas. Admire colourful and timbered *arhontika* (mansions), including the splendid **Skoutaris** and **Picheon** mansions. Signposting around the old town explains the former resident families.

Byzantine Museum   MUSEUM
(☎ 24670 26781; Plateia Dexamenis; adult €4; ⊙ 8am-3pm Tue-Sun) **FREE** This museum, home to a rich collection of icons, was recently restored, and holds some 400 Byzantine and post-Byzantine icons. A handful is on display. There are also frescoes and mosaics from local churches, as well as pottery and coins from the Byzantine period, excavated in the Kastoria region.

Taxiarhia of the Metropolis   CHURCH
(Plateia Pavlou Mela) South of Plateia Omonias, note the 13th-century **fresco of the Madonna and Child** above this church's entrance. Inside is the sacrosanct **tomb of Pavlos Melas**, leader of the 1904–08 'Macedonian Struggle' against the Ottomans.

Kastorian Museum of Folklore   MUSEUM
(☎ 24670 28603; Kapetan Lazou; adult/child €2/free; ⊙ 10am-5pm Tue-Sat, 11am-5pm Sun) In the Nerantzis Aïvazis family's former 530-year-old mansion, this museum displays ornaments, utensils and tools.

O Podilatis   CYCLING
(☎ 24670 23834; www.yellowbike.gr; Leoforos Megalou Alexandrou 119; ⊙ 10am-8pm Mon-Sat, 11am-4pm Sun) This southern waterfront shop rents mountain bikes, regular bicycles and tandem fun bikes. The staff can explain local routes and arrange guided mountain-biking trips. Bike prices are €3 for the first hour and €1 every subsequent hour, or €8 for 24-hour rental.

✦ Festivals & Events

Ragkountsaria Festival DANCE, CULTURE
(⊙6-10 Jan) This winter festival harks back to its pagan roots and features traditional dancing, costumed partying and a lot of eating and drinking.

Nestorio River Festival MUSIC, ARTS
(http://riverparty.org; ⊙late Jul-early Aug) This popular five-day summer festival features Greek and international musicians and DJs, as well as art, games and parties into the early hours. Four camping areas are designed to suit different hedonism tolerance thresholds. KTEL Kastoria runs special festival buses to Nestorio.

🛏 Sleeping

Alexios Vergoulas Traditional Hotel B&B €
(✐24670 23415; www.vergoulasmansion.gr; Aidistras 14; s/d/tr incl breakfast €40/50/60; 🛜) Restored, but still rustic, this 150-year-old Doltso mansion comes with soothing lake views, while its traditional rooms, with some stunning wood carving decorations, plus cosy breakfast/dinner salon, make it a great choice.

Anesis Hotel HOTEL €
(✐24670 83908; www.anesishotelkastoria.gr; Grammou 10; s/d incl breakfast €40/50; ♒❄🛜) If you're travelling car-free or have an early start at the bus station, Anesis' location can't be beaten. Rooms are comfortable, the breakfast is filling and the service friendly.

★ Doltso Hotel BOUTIQUE HOTEL €€
(✐24670 22022; www.doltsohotel.gr; Riga Fereou 7; d from €65; ❄🛜) In a renovated Doltso mansion, this 10-room hotel has an intimate atmosphere, plus rooms with grandiose double beds and spacious bathrooms. Upstairs rooms have balconies. The service is friendly and the breakfast plentiful.

Esperos Palace Hotel HOTEL €€
(✐24670 24670; www.esperospalacekastoria.gr; Fountoukli; s/d/tr from €60/85/115; ❄🛜♒) If you don't mind a short drive to the quiet northwestern coast, the Esperos spa hotel represents excellent value: spacious, gleaming rooms, a spa centre with pool and *hammam*, and fine dining in its elegant restaurant.

Katerina APARTMENT €€
(✐24670 24645; www.katerinastudioskastoria.com; Leoforos Megalou Alexandrou 127; s/d €70/80) These modern, family-friendly studios lie 15 minutes' walk from the bus station, east along the waterfront. Panoramic lake views unfurl from the balconies. The thoughtful owners can provide baby cots, a laundry service and even a boat tour on the lake.

🍴 Eating & Drinking

Palia Poli TAVERNA €
(✐24670 21401; Orestiados 51; mains from €5; ⊙lunch & dinner; 🍴) A lovely restaurant inside a waterfront mansion and with a spacious courtyard, where you can spend hours over your food and wine; the offer is classic Greek fare, done artfully – try the meatballs, prawn *saganaki* (a tomato and onion-based sauce) or the lamb souvlaki (barbecued). The service is attentive and friendly.

Kratergo TAVERNA €
(✐24670 22981; Oresteion 19; mains €6-9; ⊙8pm-late) This lakefront taverna is worth a short drive north of town. Featuring well-prepared Greek specialities, it has impressive stone arches, ambient lighting, lake views and wistful *rembetika*.

★ Doltso TAVERNA €€
(✐24670 23377; www.ntoltso.gr; Plateia Doltso; mains €9-13; ⊙lunch & dinner) From melt-in-the-mouth pork with prunes to fantastic aubergine and feta, every local speciality is cooked with panache (and served in generous portions) at Doltso. This restored 1860 mansion's stone walls and wooden ceilings infuse the experience with romance, which is assisted by warm hosts and a good wine list. Wild boar is available from November to March.

Grada BISTRO €€
(✐24670 29615; www.grada-bistrot.gr; Oresteion 37; mains €8-17; ⊙1-5pm & 8pm-midnight Tue-Sun) This stylish northwest waterfront bistro

---

GREECE'S ELUSIVE BROWN BEAR

The brown bear, Europe's largest land mammal, still manages to survive in very small numbers in the Pindos Mountains, the Peristeri Range that rises above the Prespa Lakes and in the mountains that lie along the Bulgarian border. It's estimated that only around 200 survive; if you want to see a bear in Greece nowadays, you're better off heading for the **Arcturos Bear Sanctuary** (www.arcturos.gr; Nymfeo) in the village of Nymfeo in Macedonia.

has some seriously inventive cuisine – the shrimp and melon risotto will befuddle your taste buds while Britain's own fish and chips also grace this menu of marvels. Should you wish a change from traditional Greek food, this is the place to go.

Ta Kymata   TAVERNA €€
(☑ 24670 28887; Thimados 7; fish €9-13; ☺ lunch & dinner) Kymata's seafood, some from the Aegean and some sourced right from the lake, is bewitchingly succulent and well presented. Proximity to the fishmongers in the adjacent market hall carries a reassuring guarantee of freshness. The clacking pelicans from the waterside terrace make for extra entertainment.

Zaza   BAR
(☑ 24670 24016; Leoforos Megalou Alexandrou 61; ☺ 10am-3am) Friendly service, good cocktails and an easygoing vibe draw the crowds at weekends, but it's just as amiable a stop for mid-morning coffee.

❶ Information

Municipal Tourist Kiosk (☑ 24670 26777; ☺ 8am-3pm Mon-Fri) Brochures, maps and information in the lakeside Park of the Olympic Flame.
Police Station (☑ 24670 21551; Grammou 25) Near the bus station.
Post Office (Leoforos Megalou Alexandrou; ☺ 8am-6pm) Centrally located.

❶ Getting There & Away

Kastoria bus station (KTEL Kastorias; ☑ 24670 83454; www.ktel-kastorias.gr; Athanasiou Diakou 14) is on the southern waterfront, facing the Park of the Olympic Flame. Buses serve Thessaloniki (€17.60, 2½ hours, six daily), Ioannina (€19.60, 3½ hours, four weekly) and Athens (€48.50, nine hours, two weekly).
  Taxis (☑ 24670 21222) are available from the waterfront.

Kavala   Καβάλα
POP 58,800
Port city Kavala, often used as a gateway to the northeastern Aegean Islands, is hitting its stride as a destination in its own right. Cultural highlights include the aqueduct of Sultan Süleyman the Magnificent, quality museums of history and industry, and fascinating Ottoman buildings scattered through its pastel-hued old town, Panagia.

Sheer relaxation can be found at nearby beaches and bustling harbourfront eateries.
  Modern Kavala was once ancient Philippi's port. More infamously, Ottoman Pasha Mehmet Ali (1769–1849), eventual founder of Egypt's last royal dynasty, ruled here. He ordered his fleet to slaughter tens of thousands of Christian Greeks on islands such as Kassos and Psara during Greece's independence struggle. Islanders still commemorate these events annually.

◎ Sights & Activities

A 280m-long aqueduct, **Kamares**, overlooks central Kavala at Ethnikis Dimokratias. For swimmable shores, **Rapsani Beach**, 1.5km west of town, is popular, while young people flock to **Batis Beach**, an additional 3km southwest on the coastal road. For something quieter and more family-friendly, continue for another 2km to **Tosca Beach**.

Panagia Quarter   HISTORIC SITE
Panagia's narrow, tangled streets are lined by pretty pastel houses. A calf-stiffening walk leads up to the castle. Highlights include the restored ruby **Halil Bey Mosque** and **Mehmet Ali House**. The enormous 18-domed **Imaret** (1817), now a hotel, was Ottoman ruler Pasha Mehmet Ali's hostel for Islamic theology students.

Mehmet Ali House   HISTORIC BUILDING
(☑ 25106 20515; Pateia Mehmet Ali; adult/student €3/2; ☺ 10am-2pm Tue-Sun) This superb example of late-Ottoman architecture was once home to Pasha Mehmet Ali and displays the way the Pasha would have lived across the two floors. There is a women's room, Pasha's own quarters, plenty of swords and knives, and lovely Ottoman wood carvings and rugs.

Tobacco Museum   MUSEUM
(☑ 25102 23344; www.tobaccomuseum.gr; Konstantinou Palaeologou 4; adult/student €2/1; ☺ 8am-3pm Mon-Fri, 9am-1pm Sat) This surprisingly interesting museum whirls through the history of tobacco cultivation and production in eastern Macedonia and Thrace. Bright murals, old photographs, a curious collection of pipes and a tobacco press enliven plenty of description (in Greek and English). The tang of tobacco and wood in the air adds to the ambience.

Castle   CASTLE
(☑ 25108 31388; www.castle-kavala.gr; Panagia; adult/child €2.50/1.50; ☺ 8am-9pm May-Sep, to 8pm Apr, to 6pm Oct, to 4pm Nov-Mar; ⛽) Built

on the ruins of a Byzantine acropolis, most of this looming fortress dates to the 15th century. Panoramic views of the city are fantastic for climbing the circular tower. There's a small cafe in the grounds.

Archaeological Museum MUSEUM
(☑ 25102 22335; Leoforos Erythrou Stavrou 17; adult €2; ☉ 8am-3pm Tue-Sun; ℗) Sculpture, jewellery, grave stelae, terracotta figurines and vases from ancient Amfipoli are found in this well-lit, elegant museum. The permanent exhibition traces the city's turbulent transition from ancient Neapolis to Byzantine Christoupolis and finally, modern Kavala.

🛏 Sleeping

Hotels can be found along the seafront, but most Kavala accommodation is of the business variety. For a fee of €1, the tourist office can arrange accommodation for you – sometimes getting you discounts.

Hotel Esperia HOTEL €
(☑ 25102 29624, 25102 29621; www.esperiaka vala.gr; Leoforos Erythrou Stavrou 44; s/d/ste €55/65/115; ℗ ❄ 🖥) Esperia soars above the ranks of Kavala's midrange business hotels with exemplary service and simple, smart rooms.

Batis Multiplex Camping CAMPGROUND €
(☑ 25102 45918; www.batis-sa.gr; Km 4 Kavala-Thessaloniki road; campsites per adult/tent €4/10, caravans 2 adults & 2 children €80; 🖥) Four kilometres west of the city centre, this campground is right next to Kavala's best beach. Apart from tents, you can stay in caravans that have wooden hut-like structures in the front, with charming living areas and kitchens.

Galaxy Hotel HOTEL €€
(☑ 25102 24812; www.airotel.gr; Venizelou 27; s/d incl breakfast €59/69; ❄ 🖥) The Galaxy is a big block of a hotel with pleasant, roomy digs with balconies, many boasting splendid port views. A traditional Greek breakfast is served from the 7th-floor restaurant.

★ Imaret BOUTIQUE HOTEL €€€
(☑ 25106 20151; www.imaret.gr; Poulidou 30-32; s/d/ste incl breakfast €200/300/550; ❄ 🖥 🏊) This luxurious and absolutely stunning hotel complex in Panagia complements the original stone architecture devised by Pasha Mehmet Ali, with modern comforts and elegant lighting. The huge rooms have some

original features, vaulted ceilings and often large fireplaces. The restored Turkish *hammam,* a muscle-melting array of spa treatments and a candlelit indoor pool complete an exceedingly decadent picture.

✗ Eating & Drinking

To Araliki TAVERNA €
(☑ 6984718521; Poulidou 33; mains from €4; ☉ lunch & dinner) A cheap and cheerful family-run taverna that is all about the souvlaki – locals come for the barbecued lamb chops, kebabs, meatballs, and the jolly atmosphere.

Panos Zafira SEAFOOD €€
(☑ 25102 27978; cnr Plateia Karaoli & Dimitriou; fish €9-15; ☉ 10am-1am) This friendly eastern waterfront taverna has been serving fresh fish dishes and good grills since 1965.

Wood & Rock BAR
(☑ 6931309300; Poulidou 19; ☉ 11am-4am) From chamomile teas to Campari and everything in between, this cafe-bar at the bottom of Panagia is housed in one of the quarter's most historic buildings. The light pop-rock soundtrack intensifies as the sun sets.

ⓘ Information

Post Office (cnr Hrysostomou Kavalas & Leoforos Erythrou Stavrou; ☉ 8am-6pm) Near the Kavala bus station.
Tourist Office (☑ 25102 31011; www.kavala greece.gr; Filikis Eterias; ☉ 8am-9pm Mon-Fri) Helpful English- and German-speaking staff provides maps, plus transport and events information and hotel bookings.

ⓘ Getting There & Away

AIR
Alexander the Great Airport (☑ 25910 53119) is 30km east of Kavala and 44km southwest of Xanthi. **Aegean Airlines** (☑ 25102 29000; Leoforos Erythrou Stavrou 1) offers two daily Athens flights (€60). Island flights go via Athens or Thessaloniki.

BOAT
Ferries serve Skala Prinos in Thasos (adult/child/car €4.70/2.40/19, 1½ hours, five daily during summer) from Kavala's eastern waterfront. From the bus station, it's a brisk 15-minute walk along the waterfront to get here. A small building on the left sells tickets for Thasos; tickets for other islands are sold by **Euro Kosmos Travel Agency** (☑ 25102 21960; www.eurokos mos.gr; Leoforos Erythrou Stavrou 1; ☉ 9am-6pm) and **Maritime Agency Miliadis** (☑ 25102 26147; www.miliadou.gr; Karaoli-Dimitriou 36).

Ferries to Limenas in Thasos (adult/child/car €3/1.50/16, 45 minutes) depart from Keramoti, 12km from Kavala's Alexander the Great Airport. Ferries from Kavala to Limnos run weekly during summer.

Timetables for ferry routes and information about weather-related route suspensions are available from the **Port Authority** (☎ 25102 23716; cnr Ethnikis Andistasis & Averof).

BUS

Kavala bus station (☎ 25102 22294; www. ktelkavalas.gr; cnr Filikis Eterias & Hrysostomou Kavalas) serves Athens (€55, 8¾ hours, two daily), Xanthi (€5.40, one hour, 14 daily), Keramoti (€4.70, one hour, 17 daily), Serres (€9.30, two hours, four daily), Alexandroupoli (€14.90, two hours, five daily) and Thessaloniki (€15, 2¼ hours, 15 daily). The *apothiki* (store-room) stores luggage.

ⓘ Getting Around

Taxis wait near the bus station.

THRACE ΘΡΑΚΗ

Thrace is among Greece's least visited areas, but it hides unique natural gems and cultural idiosyncrasies. In the north, the Rhodopi Mountains demarcate the Bulgarian border, and are home to the wonderful Pomak villages, whose minarets glisten on the rolling green hills. Eastward, towards the Turkish border, significant migratory bird populations stop at the Dadia Forest Reserve and the Evros Delta on the Aegean, delighting nature- and bird-loving travellers.

Once home to a powerful, non-Greek ancient Thracian civilisation, Thrace's agricultural traditions are attested today by tobacco crops, rolling wheat fields and vivid plains of sunflowers.

The region is notably influenced by its neighbours, Bulgaria and Turkey. Its unique Muslim minorities have roots in Ottoman times, and pockets of Thrace are dotted with mosques, Turkish-style houses and traditional sweet shops.

The largest town, Alexandroupoli, is also the jumping-off point for ferries to Samothraki.

History

The ancient Thracians spoke a now-lost language. Greek-language sources, myth and supposition depict them as warlike sorts, devoted to mystery religions such as the Great Gods cult, which influenced Greek pagan religion, too. At the Thracians' supreme temple on Samothraki island, ancient Macedonian, Roman and Egyptian rulers were initiated. Secret rituals were associated with Orpheus, the mythical, tragic Thracian father of music.

Powerful Greek city-states vied with the Persians for Thrace's coast. Athens prevailed at the Battle of Plataea, though Philip II of Macedon took over in 346 BC. Later, with the Roman Empire's AD 395 division, Thrace's strategic positioning on the Via Egnatia trade route made it important.

Constantinople's defensive zone was the Thracian plain, though its flatness made it vulnerable to marauding Goths, Huns, Vandals, Bulgars, Pechenegs, Cumans and poorly behaved Latin Crusaders – relatively few historic structures predating the Ottomans' 14th-century invasion thus remain.

In the 19th century Thrace's turbulent past reawakened. The 1877 Russo–Turkish War, the 1912–13 Balkan Wars, WWI and finally Greece's failed 1922 invasion of Anatolia saw the territory change hands frequently. A mess of treaties and tragedies resulted in its final tripartite division.

The Turks of Greek Thrace were exempt during the 1923 population exchanges. While İstanbul's Greek population was largely expelled after a 1955 pogrom, the Turks of Greek Thrace remain.

Xanthi Ξάνθη

POP 65,100

Xanthi is by far the most attractive Thracian town, with its winding historic streets, natural setting, great restaurants, fun nightlife and good places to stay. It's worth settling here for a couple of days and exploring the old quarter's tilting timbered Ottoman houses, most of them formerly owned by tobacco barons. Some now house museums, others friendly bars and tavernas. Make sure you taste Xanthi's traditional sweets, famous throughout Greece.

South of Xanthi, the ports of Keramoti and Kavala have ferries to Thasos and other islands. North, the rippling Rhodopi Mountains offer forest hikes and thermal baths, and to the east the Nestos River provides kayaking and birdwatching opportunities. Don't miss the fantastic Pomakohoria region, with its curious border villages and unique culture.

Thrace

TURKEY

Kesan

Edirne

Uzunköprü

Pythio

Svilengrad

Kastanies

Dikea

Orestiada

Valtos

Lepti

Didymotiho

Petrota

Ormenio

Fylakio

Plati

Pendalofos

Kyprinos

Ivaylovgrad

Mikri Doxipara
Mikri Doxipara

Metaxades

Mikro

Ladi

Erythropotamus

Mandra

Soufli

Dadia

Dadia Forest
Reserve

Tyhero

Kipi

Malko
Gradishte

Roussa
Sidiro

Derio

Megalo
Derio

Feres

Loutra

Esymi

Leptokarya

Alexandroupoli

Demir Ali
Beach

Samothraki
(40km)

Evros
Delta

Byal

Goniko

Roussa

Krumovgrad

Rhodopi Mountains

Arriana

Filouri River

Sapes

Maronia

Agia Paraskevi
Beach

Kardzhali

Yazovir-Studen
Kladenets

Momchigrad

Makaza

Gratini

Komotini

Xilagani

Adriani

Thracian Sea

Ardino

Nedelino

Zlatograd

Mt Papikio
(1460m)

Polyantho

Egiros

Limni
Mitrikou

Lagos

Fanari

Komiatos
River

Sounio

Loket
Vistonida

BULGARIA

Arda

Rodopi Mountains

Thermes

Dimari

Melivia

Echinos

Stavroupoli

Xanthi

Mandra

Mangana

Mt Koula
(1827m)

Toxotes

Hrysoupoli

Nestos

Keramoti

Smoljan

Ustovo

See Macedonia Map (p247)

Paranesti

Thasos
(Limenas)

Thasos

Thasos Strait

Skala
Prinou

Gulf of
Kavala

Dospat

Yazovir
Dospat

Elatia

Skaloti

Agora

Adriani

Drama

Kalabakion

Elevtheroupolis

Mt Symvolon

Limnos
(110km)

Kavala

MACEDONIA

Nestos

50 km

25 miles

N

Tundzha

Maritsa

Maritsa

Arda

Ebros

◉ Sights & Activities

Old Xanthi
HISTORIC SITE

On a serene hillside above town, Old Xanthi features pastel-coloured timber-framed houses on narrow, winding lanes and grand neoclassical mansions once inhabited by tobacco barons. Though some of its structures could benefit from further restoration, this grand neighbourhood has been enlivened by a vibrant nightlife scene along Orfeas.

House of Shadow
GALLERY

(☑6977612726; www.vaitsis.com; Orfeus 33; €2; ⊙10am-2pm Mon & Wed, 10am-2pm & 6-8.30pm Tue & Thu-Sun) Now in a new location, this rather eccentric gallery works with shadow art to reveal that which we apparently cannot see. The local artist Triandafyllos Vaitsis does his best to provoke thought with tin sculptures that create two different shadows. It's worth a peek mostly for a bit of local flavour.

Folk Museum
MUSEUM

(☑25410 25421; www.fex.org.gr; Antika 7; €2; ⊙8.30am-2.30pm Wed-Fri, 10.30am-3pm Sat & Sun) Stroll through the former mansion of the Kougioumtzolgou brothers, made rich by the region's flourishing tobacco trade, for a nostalgic glimpse of Xanthi's past. This museum features folk costumes and farming tools, and you can admire the original decorated ceilings. Labels are in Greek only, but helpful staff can explain the exhibits.

Riverland Outdoor Activities
OUTDOORS

(☑25410 62488; www.riverland.gr; Toxotes village) In Toxotes village, southwest of Xanthi, Riverland runs kayaking, rafting and other water sports on the Nestos River, plus ziplining, mountain biking, birdwatching tours and other local outdoor activities.

✦✧ Festivals & Events

Winter Carnival
MUSIC, CULTURE

(http://carnivalofxanthi.gr; ⊙Feb) This nationally famous celebration in mid- to late February features colourful floats accompanied by music and masked merrymaking.

Xanthi Old Town Festival
PERFORMING ARTS

(⊙early Sep) Festival featuring theatre, music, book fairs and art exhibitions, all set in Xanthi's beautiful old town.

🛏 Sleeping

Hotel Xanthippion
HOTEL €

(☑25410 77061; www.hotelxanthippion.gr; 28 Oktovriou 212; s/d/tr incl breakfast €50/60/70;

※�no) A short walk from the old town, this agreeable midrange hotel gets all the basics right: great breakfasts, ample space in its clean, well-kept rooms, good wi-fi signal and enormously helpful staff.

Happy Living
HOSTEL €

(☑25410 73547; Vasilissis Sofias 1a; dm from €12) This is a colourful hostel in the middle of Xanthi. Bright murals and a friendly cafe contribute to the eclectic vibe. Think twice if you're not the sociable type: dorms are intimate and even the private double is fairly open.

Hotel Elisso
BOUTIQUE HOTEL €€

(☑25410 84400; www.hotelelisso.gr; Vas Sofias 9; d/ste from €85/180; P※@no) This chic hotel has pleasant suites and very comfortable double rooms, two of them equipped for people with disabilities. Decor is minimalist yet bright, characterised by geometric patternwork and big beds.

★ Boutique Hotel 1905
BOUTIQUE HOTEL €€€

(☑25410 77362; Chasirtzoglou 3; ste €100-140) This former house of Hilmi Pasha (a local functionary), built in 1905, now houses a delightful hotel with six suites, all of which are kitted out in luxurious detail. The pillows and mattresses are made in a local factory that produces only natural fibres. There are original frescoes in some of the rooms, marble bathrooms, wood floors and generous service.

✕ Eating & Drinking

★ Palaia Polis
TAVERNA €

(☑25410 68685; www.palaiapolis.net; Chasirtzoglou 7; mains €7-9; ⊙lunch & dinner) This wood-and-brick taverna has some of the most sumptuous cuisine around – try the fantastic *hunkar bejendi* (tender beef pieces on a bed of mashed aubergine and cheese) and its lush salads. The wine list is extensive and well chosen, the service excellent, and the exposed stone and wood interior stylish and pleasant. Don't miss it.

★ Paparaskeva
SWEETS €

(☑25410 22677; www.papaparaskevas.gr; 28 Oktovriou 186; sweets from €1.50; ⊙10am-6pm) Locally recommended and famous Greece-wide, Paparaskeva has been selling Xanthi's sweets for over 80 years. Try the *karioka* – a spongy chocolate and nut cake – which is one of the best souvenirs you can take home (if you don't eat it along the way).

POMAKOHORIA ΠΟΜΑΚΟΧΩΡΙΑ
••

For a wonderful road trip far from the tourist track, drive north of Xanthi to the fascinating Pomakohoria (Pomak villages), tucked into the forested Rhodopi Mountains near Bulgaria.

The 25 or so Pomak villages are inhabited by Muslims speaking Greek, Bulgarian and Turkish. Spread across the borders, their ethnic identity is a subject of some uncertainty (even to themselves). In Greece, they are officially classified as 'Greek Muslims'. During the Cold War, this border area was off limits and tourists are still rare.

The villages, accessible via winding and sometimes steep roads, aren't rich in major sights but the villagers are welcoming and the views spectacular.

Echinos village, 30km north of Xanthi, has remarkable mountain views, a striking minaret that seems to glow across the valley and a fascinating multicultural cemetery. Best known are the **mineral baths of Thermes**. The main bath, in a building opposite the church, charges for entry (€3 for 30 minutes), while the outdoor bath (100m to the right-hand side of the village shop, and below the entry road) costs €1. Ask the man who tends the village baths for a key. The main bath has the temperature of 42°C, while the outdoor is over 60°C .

The Xanthi–Thermes bus (€3.80, 90 minutes) departs at 6.30am daily and returns at 3.30pm. A later bus runs at 2.10pm, meaning you must stay overnight in Thermes.

Taverna To Perasma TAVERNA €
(☑ 25410 78014; Ikoniou 16; mains €5-9; ☺ lunch & dinner) Facing Megalou Alexandrou park near the bus station, local secret To Perasma serves huge portions of satisfying Greek specialities. Try the aubergine and feta salad, zucchini balls or beef kebabs, and taste the fiery raki (Cretan fire water).

★ **Ntili Ntili** BAR
(☑ 25415 50575; Pygmaliona; ☺ 8am-late) A really popular, vintage-laden bar painted in bright colours and hosting all kinds of cultural events and parties. One of the local favourites.

Ermis BAR
(☑ 25410 83514; Orfeos 37-39; ☺ 10am-3am) This bar in a restored old-town mansion has a fun vibe, an old *avli* (courtyard) with secluded tables and a colourful upstairs for winter. The owners, siblings Theodota and Georgios, serve homemade Greek-meets-international mezedhes and good cocktails.

ℹ Information

ATM-equipped banks line 28 Oktovriou and Plateia Antiko.
Police Station (☑ 25410 24900; 28 Oktovriou)
Post Office (behind Plateia Kentriki; ☺ 8am-6pm)

ℹ Getting There & Away

AIR

Xanthi shares **Alexander the Great Airport** (☑ 25910 53119), 44km southwest, near Hrysoupoli, with coastal Kavala.

BUS

The **bus station** (KTEL Xanthis; ☑ 25410 22684; www.ktelxanthis.gr; Dimokritou 6) is 700m south of Kentriki Plateia. Dimokritou (later Karaoli) leads to Kentriki Plateia from the bus station.

Buses travel to Komotini (€5, one hour, eight daily), Thessaloniki (€19, 2½ hours, nine daily), Athens (€61, nine hours, one daily) and Alexandroupoli (€8, one hour, eight daily). Buses also serve northern Pomakohoria villages (€3.80, 1½ hours, two daily) and Stavroupoli to the west.

Buses (€90) leave daily at 9.30am and 5.30pm for Bulgarian destinations Svilengrad, Harmanli, Haskovo and Plovdiv (Philippopouli in Greek).

TRAIN

Xanthi's **train station** (☑ 25410 22581; Terma Kondyli) connects Alexandroupoli and Komotini with Thessaloniki twice daily.

ℹ Getting Around

Only **taxis** (☑ 25410 72801) serve the airport (€35) from Xanthi. Alternatively, take a Kavala-bound bus to Hrysoupoli and from there take a taxi 12km to the airport.

Abdera Άβδηρα

For an easy, culture-packed day trip, head to the excellent museum and archaeological site at Abdera, 24km north of Xanthi.

◉ Sights

Archaeological Museum of Abdera MUSEUM
(☑ 25410 51003; €2; ☺ 8.30am-3pm, to 7.30pm summer) This splendid museum paints a vivid picture of ancient Abdera, from daily

life to the region's luminaries. Most interesting is the detail about Abdera's defence against incursions by the Thracians, with rich exhibits including swords, sling bullets and other weapons.

Archaeological Site of Abdera
ARCHAEOLOGICAL SITE

(🏛museum 25410 51003; Abdera-Nea Kessani road; ⏰8.30am-3pm) A 20-minute drive northeast of modern Abdera (and 28km from Xanthi) lie the ruins of the ancient town. Outdoor exhibitions display stone sarcophagi, huge urns and other imagination-spurring remnants of the town, while the foundations of temples and houses can be explored around the site.

Komotini
Κομοτηνή

POP 60,600

The draw for a curious visitor in Komotini is the town's multicultural character and the vibrant Turkish and Muslim street life. The tall minarets, piles of sugary *soutzouk loukoum* and the waft of flame-seared kebabs, and shopkeepers who lure passers-by with bright silks and silverware, make Komotini quite distinct from the surrounding towns of Thrace. It's a workaday place, but it has a pleasant and particular ambience.

The town is spread quite wide, but the central neighbourhood around Yenii Cami (New Mosque) is walkable and the most interesting, with some good places to eat, and plenty of coffee roasters and sellers. It's a lovely place to spend a day or stop for an afternoon.

◉ Sights

Turkish Quarter
HISTORIC SITE

Just behind Plateia Eirinis, Komotini's relaxing Turkish quarter has old houses, barber shops and teahouses. Sights include the 1884 **Clock Tower** (Orologio), **Yeni Camii** (New Mosque, in Turkish) and **Eski Camii** (Old Mosque) from 1608 and still operational.

Archaeological Museum
MUSEUM

(🏛25310 22411; Simeonidou 4; adult/child €2/1; ⏰8.30am-3pm) Significant archaeological finds, accompanied by English-language wall texts, detail ancient Thracian history within this elegant building. Roman coins, clay figurines, delicate gold wreaths and glazed ceramics illuminate the region's history from the Neolithic to Byzantine periods.

Ecclesiastical Museum
MUSEUM

(Imaret; 🏛25310 34177; Xenofontos 8; €3; ⏰10.30am-1pm Tue, Thu, Sat & Sun, 5-8pm Wed & Fri) This museum occupies Komotini's early Ottoman *ptohokomeio* (almshouse), inside a courtyard. The structure's brickwork and design resemble a Byzantine church. It exhibits post-Byzantine icons, 500-year-old printed gospels, silver ceremonial crosses, gold embroidery and 18th-century Hebrew scrolls.

Byzantine Fortress
RUINS

Komotini's 4th-century-AD Byzantine fortress was built by Emperor Theodosius, near today's Plateia Eirinis. Remnants include one of 16 original towers.

Church of the Assumption of Mary
CHURCH

(🏛25310 22827; Eleftheriou Venizelou) Built in 1800 on a Byzantine shrine site, the church contains 16th-century icons and wood carvings.

🛏 Sleeping

Orpheus Hotel
HOTEL €

(🏛25310 37180-5; www.hotelorfeas.gr; Parasiou 1; s/d/tr €35/45/55; ❄) Well positioned on the *plateia,* Orpheus occupies a characterless block but has 78 tidily furnished and comfortable rooms.

Chris & Eve Mansion
BOUTIQUE HOTEL €€

(🏛25310 33560; www.chris-eve.com; Km 4 Komotini-Alexandroupoli road; s/d/ste from €45/65/100; 🅿❄🅦🐾) For a touch of quirky glamour, drive east of Komotini for the plush Chris & Eve Mansion. Away from the dust and bustle of central Komotini, its balconied rooms with bright satiny fittings overlook a pool.

Anatolia Hotel
HOTEL €€

(🏛25310 36242; www.anatoliahotels.gr; Agchialou 53; s/d €55/65; ❄🐾) The large block Anatolia combines simple, clean rooms with glossy decor. It's in northeastern Komotini, near Parko Agogis.

Hotel Astoria
HOTEL €€

(🏛25310 35054; www.astoriakomotini.gr; Plateia Eirinis 28; s/d €76/101; ❄@) Slightly concealed by the square's side cafes, Astoria has attractive rooms with small balconies overlooking Plateia Eirinis.

🍴 Eating & Drinking

★Petrino
GREEK €

(🏛25310 73650; Serron 25; mains €7-9; ⏰lunch & dinner) Under a creeper-strewn canopy just off pedestrianised Ermou, Petrino's dishes are as enticing as its shaded location. Try the wonderfully garlicky aubergine mezedhes and generous portions of mussels on rice.

To Sokaki tis Lakokolas
TAVERNA €

(☑25310 81800; Parasiou 5; mains €5-7; ☺noon-midnight) In an underpass opposite Emboriki Bank, this lively taverna has simple and succulent grills and excellent salads.

Nedim's
SWEETS €

(☑25310 22036; cnr Leoforos Orfeos & Syntagmatos Kriton 15-17; sweets €2-4; ☺10am-6pm) Nedim has been serving what is perhaps the best baklava this side of İstanbul since 1950. Try your teeth on *kadayif* (sweet bird's nests of pistachio and pastry), Turkish delight ranging from mint to orange and cocoa flavours, and sausage-shaped *soutzouk loukoum* (aromatic rolls of Turkish delight and pistachio).

Kaffeine
COFFEE

(☑25310 84933; Eleftheriou Venizelou 50; ☺8am-1am; ☺) Coffee is a big deal in Komotini – this is an immensely popular place, and it's packed with students who swear by the quality of their cup of joe here. It's a great place to people-watch.

El Clasico
BAR

(☑25310 70007; www.el-clasico.gr; Zoidi 52-54; ☺8am-3am) Sip coffee or wine to a light jazz soundtrack at this somewhat American-themed cafe-bar. El Clasico's cavernous interior is a popular place for locals and has a lively atmosphere.

ⓘ Information

Hospital (☑25313 51100; Sismanogleio 45) The hospital is 1km southeast of Plateia Eirinis.

ⓘ Getting There & Away

BUS

From **Komotini bus station** (KTEL Rodopis; ☑25310 22912; www.ktelrodopis.gr; Geor Mameli 15) buses serve Xanthi (€5.30, one hour, five daily) and Alexandroupoli (€4.80, one hour, eight daily). Buses also serve Thessaloniki (€25.30, 2½ hours, eight daily) and Athens (€63, 8¾ hours, one daily).

TRAIN

The **train station** (☑25310 22650; Anapafseos) connects Komotini with Xanthi (€4.70, 30 minutes, twice daily) and Alexandroupoli (€6.10, 80 minutes, twice daily). The train station is 1km southwest of town parallel to Sidirochoriou.

ⓘ Getting Around

Komotini sprawls, but the town centre is walkable. There are **taxis** (☑25310 37777; http://radiotaxikomotini.gr) available, and **Evros Car Rental** (☑25510 3699; www.evroscar.gr; Toutsas 1; ☺9am-7pm) has cars (from €45) and jeeps (€60) for hire.

Alexandroupoli
Αλεξανδρούπολη
POP 61,700

Alexandroupoli is eastern Thrace's largest town, an axis for travel to Turkey, Bulgaria and (in summer) Samothraki island. Alexandroupoli is also a gateway to adventures in the wildlife-rich Evros Delta and beguiling Dadia Forest Reserve.

ⓞ Sights

Drive 10km west of Alexandroupoli for sandy **Demir Ali Beach**, popular for swimming and known for the **Agios Giorgios Church** by its shore. **Agia Paraskevi Beach**, 3km further west, is even better, with beach bars and clubs.

Cathedral of Agios Nikolaos
CHURCH

(Plateia Agiou Nikolaou) This cathedral houses the miracle-working 13th-century **icon of the Panagia Trifotissa**, from Aenos (Enez in Turkish) across the Evros River. Villagers with eyes damaged by the reflected glare of the sun on the salt marshes around Aenos are said to have had their vision restored by praying before it.

Ethnological Museum of Thrace
MUSEUM

(☑25510 36663; www.emthrace.org; 14 Maiou 63; adult/child €2/free; ☺9am-3pm Tue-Sat, 10am-3pm Sun Oct-Feb, 9am-3pm Tue, Wed & Sat, 10am-3pm & 6-9pm Thu & Fri, 10am-3pm Sun Mar-Sep) Inside a grand sandstone mansion, this museum with backyard cafe packs its displays with colourful Thracian costumes, musical instruments, oil presses, and exhibitions on traditional occupations such as beekeeping and tobacco production. You'll learn how many silkworms are needed to make 25g of silk and which Greek sweet is made by slamming the ingredients against a wall.

Ecclesiastical Art Museum
MUSEUM

(☑25510 82282; Plateia Agiou Nikolaou; adult/student €3/2; ☺9am-2pm Tue-Fri, to 1pm Sat) Opposite the custard-coloured Agios Nikolaos cathedral, this excellent museum contains priceless icons, many brought by refugees in 1923, plus early printed Greek books. Look for the heart-rending realism of the lamenting Mary paintings in between embroidered priestly vestments, dragon-dispatching St Georges and delicate silverwork. English-language guide pamphlet on request.

📷 Sleeping

Camping Alexandroupoli
CAMPGROUND €
(☑ 25510 28735, 25510 26055; www.ditea.gr; Leoforos Makris 1; campsites per tent/car €4.50/5; ☺ summer; 🅿 🛜) This large, well-run campground has water sports and beach volleyball, plus basketball and tennis courts. It's 2km west of Alexandroupoli; take local bus 7 from Plateia Eleftherias.

Apartment Hotel Athina
HOTEL €
(☑ 25510 34492; Paleologou 53; d/tr incl breakfast €50/60; ❄ 🛜) Central Athina has large, clean and simple rooms with mini-kitchens and balconies. The service is friendly. First child (under four years) stays free.

Hotel Erika
HOTEL €
(☑ 25510 34115; www.hotel-erika.gr; Dimitriou Karaoli 110; s/d €40/50; 🅿 ❄ 🛜) Well-located Erika has waterfront views and is only 100m from Alexandroupoli's lighthouse and nearby slew of restaurants and bars. The rooms are clean and comfortable, but without much personality.

Hotel Santa Rosa Beach
HOTEL €€
(☑ 25510 25551, 25510 33895; www.santa-rosa.gr; Km 1 Alexandroupoli-Chili road; s/d/tr incl breakfast €51/72/88; 🅿 ❄ 🛜) This family-run beach hotel 3km west of the town centre assures a warm welcome. The roar of the sea is audible from Santa Rosa's well-kept but somewhat boxy rooms, and a relaxing lounge overlooks the private beach.

Astir Egnatia Alexandroupolis
RESORT €€€
(☑ 25510 38000; www.astiregnatia.com; Egnatia Park; s/d/apt €120/140/170; 🅿 ❄ @ 🛜 🏊) This 200-room shoreside resort, just west of Alexandroupoli, is a behemoth of a hotel with spacious rooms, impeccably helpful staff and several pools. Check ahead out of season as some leisure facilities may not be available.

🍴 Eating

Ai Giorgis
TAVERNA €
(☑ 25510 71777; www.aigiorgis.com; Agios Georgios Makris; mains €7-13; ☺ 10am-1am) Overlooking Demir Ali Beach, Ai Giorgis sizzles

up shrimp *saganaki* and expertly steams cockles, while guests sip ouzo and enjoy the sea breeze.

I Love Gelato
ICE CREAM €
(☑ 25510 24832; cnr Megalou Alexandrou & Karaïskaki; double scoop €2.50; ☺ 10am-midnight) This quality gelateria opposite the lighthouse has a dilemma-inducing rainbow of flavours, but we can never say no to pistachio.

Nisiotiko
SEAFOOD €€
(☑ 25510 20990; Zarifi 3; mains €8-16; ☺ lunch & dinner) Try the grilled octopus and mullet and some of the fresh, simple salads at this fish taverna. Starfish ornaments and nautical miscellany decorate the space. It's tucked away off the waterfront.

🍷 Drinking & Nightlife

SoHo Absolutely Fabulous
BAR
(☑ 25510 80134; www.sohocafe.gr; Leoforos Dimokratias 300; cocktails €7; ☺ 9am-late) If you want to see how the locals live it up, have a drink or two at this bar – neon pinks, UFO-shaped tables and a fashionable crowd: SoHo is busy and popular. Squeeze in among the glamorous crowds and go for one of the signature cocktails while nibbling on complimentary snacks.

Outopia
CAFE
(Nikiforou Foka; coffee €2; ☺ hours vary) A really popular place for morning coffees and evening drinks, with a nostalgic pop soundtrack and vintage-inspired furnishings that give it an uplifting air. The outdoor seating offers ample opportunity to people-watch.

NOA
BAR
(Naftikos Omilos Alexandroupoleos; ☑ 25510 53226; Port; ☺ 9am-2am; 🛜) If you like smooth, nautical and posh places to drink, go for Alexandroupoli's 'yacht club' on the central ferry pier. Dress smart and don't forget your shades.

🛍 Shopping

⭐ Myrsini
ARTS & CRAFTS
(☑ 25510 31205; www.silkyhouse.gr; Plateia Polytehniou; ☺ 10am-6pm) This treasure trove of original Soufli silks has scarves from €5 as well as flamboyant table runners, jewellery and voluminous spreads (€300). Step inside to see silk being snipped and shelves that are packed with shimmering fabric.

Souvenirs such as tote bags and discounted scarves can be found at the entrance.

ℹ Information

Leoforos Dimokratias has ATM-equipped banks.

Kassapidis Exchange (☑ 25510 80910; www.kasslinetravel.gr; Leoforos Dimokratias 307; ☺ 8am-8.30pm Mon-Sat, 10am-2pm Sun) Changes 115 currencies, including Balkan currencies, plus handles Western Union transfers.

Leon Tours (☑ 25510 27754; www.leontours.gr; 14 Maiou 51; ☺ 9am-3pm & 6-9.30pm Mon-Sat) Helpful Maria Karakampatzaki and the team at Leon sell plane, bus and ferry tickets, including ferries for Kavala, Samothraki and other islands. They also offer international tours, including weekly trips to İstanbul, a combo trip to Cannakale and Ayvalik in Turkey, and Lesvos island.

Police (☑ 25510 37440, 25510 66103; Karaïskaki 6) In the town centre.

Post Office (cnr Psaron & Megalou Alexandrou; ☺ 8am-6pm) Alexandroupoli's waterfront post office.

ℹ Getting There & Away

AIR

Alexandroupoli's **Dimokritos Airport** (☑ 25510 89300; www.alxd.gr) is 7km east. **Aegean Airlines** (☑ 25510 89150; www.aegeanair.com), based at the airport, serves Athens (from €69). **Sky Express** (www.skyexpress.gr) serves Sitia in Crete (from €99, three flights weekly).

BOAT

Ferries serve Samothraki only. There is usually one boat daily, but schedules and times can change; always check locally, at the portside SAOS kiosk, or through travel agencies such as Leon Tours, and book in advance.

BUS
Domestic

From **Alexandroupoli bus station** (KTEL Evrou; ☑ 25510 26479; www.ktelevrou.gr; Eleftheriou Venizelou 36) frequent buses ply the northeastern line to Soufli (€6, 1½ hours), Didymotiho (€8.60, 1½ hours) and Orestiada (€10.60, two hours); some continue to Kastanies, for the border crossing with Turkey. Another bus terminates at Kipi, the main Turkish border crossing (€3.90, 35 minutes, five daily), east of Alexandroupoli.

Buses serve Athens (€63, 10 hours, one daily) and Thessaloniki (€29, 3¾ hours, nine daily). For Kavala (€14.90, two hours, 14 daily), buses travel via Komotini (€6.30, 70 minutes) and Xanthi (€10.60, 1¾ hours).

International

Leon Tours can assist with bus travel to Turkey.

TRAIN

The **train station** (☑ 25510 26395; www.trainose.gr) connects Alexandroupoli Port with Thessaloniki (€22.50, seven hours, two daily) and Xanthi (€9.80, 1½ hours, two daily).

ℹ Getting Around

Central Alexandroupoli is walkable but you'll need a car if you're based at the campground, beach resorts or plan to explore the Evros Delta. For the airport, take a Loutra-bound bus from Plateia Eleftherias, or a **taxi** (☑ 25510 33500; www.alexpolistaxi.gr). Some buses plying the Alexandroupoli–Orestiada route stop at the airport.

Around Alexandroupoli

★ **Dadia Forest Reserve**   NATURE RESERVE
Bird and nature lovers will delight in this beautiful reserve, situated on one of Europe's major bird migration routes. The 73-sq-km reserve has 203 bird species, including three types of vulture. Visits are best in May, before migration begins, or in July, when baby vultures hop out of their nests. The **Ecotourist Centre** (☑ 25540 32202; www.dadia-np.gr; Dadia; ☺ 8am-4pm) has detailed bilingual wall displays and trail maps to the bird of prey observatory; it's an hour's hike – the orange trail up, the yellow trail down.

The observatory does not contain binoculars and telescopes, so bring your own. The hike is light and goes through a lovely oak forest. The itinerant WWF scientist, whose office adjoins the Ecotourist Centre, can give in-depth information.

These enchanting forests deserve a couple of days. **Forest Inn** (☑ 25540 32263; www.forestinn.eu; Dadia; d from €50; P ❋ 🛜) 🐾 is an amiable guesthouse only a short walk from bird hides and has Dadia's nature unfolding right from its doorstep.

★ **Art of Silk Museum**   MUSEUM
(☑ 25540 22371; www.artofsilkmuseum.gr; Vasilis Georgiou 199, Soufli; ☺ 9am-9pm) **FREE** Located in Tsiakiri House, a silk producer of 60 years pedigree, this museum beautifully illuminates the region's sericultural history. Incredibly enthusiastic, multilingual staff take you through the history and the process of silk production, from the tiny, hardly visible worms munching on mulberry leaves, to the soft cocoon that produces the actual thread. It is curious to learn that silk worms can no longer survive without human interference. The front has a shop where you can buy silk products.

Displays include hand looms and silk-reeling machines, as well as elaborate traditional costumes. The village of Soufli was once a wealthy cultural centre, fuelled largely by silk production in the 19th century. When the borders shifted in 1923, the vital mulberry orchards (silkworms' food source) were lost to Turkey and silk production declined. Today Soufli has only three functioning silk-weaving units, with only Tsiakiris processing it from start to finish.

Look out for impostor 'silk museums' around Soufli; the signs are often a ploy to lure visitors into shops. Soufli is a 66km drive north of Alexandroupoli or 30km south of Didymotiho.

Orestiada   Ορεστιάδα

POP 23,600

With wide boulevards and a tidy grid layout, Orestiada has a different feel to most other Greek cities. Other towns boast of their ancient roots, but Orestiada was created after the 1923 Greek–Turkish population exchanges (then Nea Orestiás).

While the border history of barely centennial Orestiada intrigues, the town doesn't brim with attractions. Visitors from countries other than Bulgaria and Turkey may be greeted with a mix of astonishment and delight by down-to-earth locals. It is an agreeable stopover on your way from or to

DON'T MISS

BIRDWATCHING WONDER OF EVROS DELTA

Just 20km southeast of Alexandroupoli, the **Evros Delta** (Δέλτα Εβρού) is among Europe's most important wetlands, comprising 188 sq km of coastal lakes, lagoons, interior rivers, sand dunes, swamps and reed beds. Half of the area is protected, allowing an incredible richness of wildlife to thrive. When road-tripping around the area, be wary where you point your camera lens; this is a militarised border zone.

The delta is formed where the Evros River reaches the Aegean. Gushing from Bulgaria's Rila Mountains, the 530km-long Evros (Maritsa) winds through Turkey into Greece's Evros prefecture, where it forms part of the Greece–Turkey border. The delta came under threat in the 1950s due to drainage works that attempted to prepare the land for cultivation. Fortunately, since 1974 half of the delta has come under Ramsar protection, allowing its fauna to flourish.

The wildlife of the Evros Delta has the power to leave you slack-jawed. An incredible 325 bird species have been observed here, and the number is increasing. The possibility of spotting a glossy ibis has many twitchers scrambling for their binoculars. Most impressive are the spring migrations, where thousands of wader birds pause to guzzle in the nutrient-packed waters of the delta. Three species of European swan glide through these waters, while geese forage through meadows, including endangered lesser white-fronted geese, who winter here. Meanwhile eagles (spotted, white-tailed and imperial) wheel overhead along with more common buzzards and hen harriers.

There's more to the delta than just feathered friends, too. Forty species of mammal live around the delta, including prowling wild cats and boar in winter, and sousliks (European ground squirrels) scamper along the banks in summer. The waters are also home to 28 reptile species, including terrapins and water snakes.

The western part of the delta, including the **Anthia Marshes** and **Drana Lagoon**, is readily accessible via dirt roads navigable by most (sturdy) cars. The most fascinating eastern section, near Turkey, requires a police and army permit, arranged for free by the **Evros Delta Visitor Centre** (☑ tel/fax 25510 61000; www.evros-delta.gr; Traianoupolis; ☺ 8am-4pm). Fax or email 14 days ahead with your full name, date of birth, passport number and expiry date. It's a a 20km-drive east of Alexandroupoli.

The visitor centre is also a good place to gather maps and wildlife-spotting tips. Call ahead to book into a group guided tour (€10 per person, €30 if you're the only visitor) comprising minibus and boat excursions. A tour is vastly preferable to attempting the delta's pothole-ridden roads in a hire car. In late spring and summer, tours run at 9am, 11am and 1pm. If you don't have your own car to reach the delta, bus 5 runs from Alexandroupoli to the visitor centre.

Bulgaria or Turkey – the latter is accessible from nearby Kastanies village.

◉ Sights

Orestiada's streets are brightened by buildings such as the striking brick **Church of the Sts Theodoros**. Most of the action in this quiet town is found around Emmanouil Riga, between Konstantinopoleos and Pantazidou.

Historical and Folklore Museum   MUSEUM
(☑25520 28080; www.musorest.gr; Agion Theodoron 103; €2; ☉10am-1pm Tue-Sun) This fascinating museum exhibits Thracian furniture, costumes and old weaponry. Most moving are graphic displays about the Greek–Turkish population exchanges, which detail the tumult experienced by displaced communities and highlight stories of their pluck and ingenuity in rebuilding their lives anew.

🛏 Sleeping & Eating

Hotel Elektra   HOTEL €€
(☑25520 21110; www.hotelelectra.gr; Athanasiou Pantazidou 52; s/d incl breakfast €46/65; P❋🛜) This friendly and well-kept hotel in a restored neoclassical mansion is just off Plateia Dasiou.

Safran   MEDITERRANEAN €
(☑25520 29088; http://safran.com.gr; Lochagou Diamanti 17; mains €5-12; ☉lunch & dinner; ☑) Long-time favourite Safran does international-style taverna cuisine. Perch at one of the outdoor tables for ouzo-marinated tenderloin, flamed *saganaki*, or vegetarian burgers with mushroom and Florina peppers.

Sapore Cucina Italiana   ITALIAN €€
(☑6932385040; cnr Athanasiou Pantazidou & Emmanouil Riga; mains €8-13; ☉10am-11pm) This Italian restaurant features a short but excellent seasonal menu. Try the tasty bruschetta, lasagne with goat's cheese or ravioli in wine sauce, accompanied by rich local wines.

❶ Information

ATM-equipped banks hug Plateia Dasiou.

Hatzigiannis Tours (☑25520 28333; Konstantinoupoleos 216, cnr Emmanouil Riga; ☉9am-6pm) Sells plane, boat and train tickets.

Police (☑25520 29644; Vasileos Konstantinou 4)

Post Office (☑25520 22435; Athanasiou Pantazidou; ☉8am-6pm) In the centre of town.

❶ Getting There & Away

From Orestiada's **bus station** (☑25520 22550; www.ktelevrou.gr; Andrianoupoleos 164), buses serve Didymotiho (€1.80, 20 minutes, hourly), many continuing to Alexandroupoli (€10.60, 1¼ hours, 13 daily). Other buses go northward to Dikea (€5.70, 45 minutes, four daily) and Ormenio (€5.50, 40 minutes, two daily) for Bulgaria. The Turkish border crossing at Kastanies is also served (€1.80, 20 minutes, six daily).

The **train station** (☑25520 22328) connects Orestiada with Thessaloniki direct (€25.20, 8½ hours, one daily) or via Alexandroupoli (€6, two hours, two daily). **Taxis** (☑25520 25025; Plateia Dasiou) can be found near the train station.

EPIROS   ΗΠΕΙΡΟΣ

The Epiros region boasts one of the most stunning natural settings in Northern Greece, the magnificent 12km-long Vikos Gorge – among the world's deepest (900m) – a national park in the Pindos Mountains, filled with forests, waterfalls and ice-cold mountain lakes. It is surrounded by the Zagorohoria's immaculate stone-and-slate villages that will keep nature-loving visitors returning for years.

South of these mountains sits beautiful Ioannina, a youthful town on a picturesque lake where days can be spent enjoying local life. The Ionian coast has long sandy beaches punctuated by archaeological sites. Don't miss the beautiful, and touristy, Parga, with its Venetian legacy. North of Parga, Igoumenitsa's ferries access Italy.

Reaching Epiros is an event in itself. The road from Kalambaka in Thessaly winds over the Pindos Mountains; from Macedonia, the marvellous Egnatia Odos Hwy cuts straight through them, into massive tunnels.

History

The Dorian invasion (1100–1000 BC) left three main Greek-speaking tribes: the Thesproti, the Chaones and the dominant Molossi. The marriage of Molossi princess Olympias to powerful Macedonian king Philip II brought conflict with emerging Rome. King Pyrrhus (319–272 BC) famously defeated the Romans at Ausculum, at a heavy cost; hence the concept of a 'Pyrrhic victory'.

After the Roman Empire split in AD 395, Epiros was ruled from Constantinople. Centuries later, it became important after

Epiros

the 1204 Latin sack of Constantinople; Byzantine nobles escaping here established a key successor state. Eminent Byzantines again fled to Epiros' mountain fastnesses after the Ottomans conquered Constantinople in 1453.

Infamously linked with Epiros is 18th-century Albanian despot Ali Pasha, who ransacked much of Albania and western Greece, while wheeling and dealing with Turks, Brits and even Napoleon. Ali's remorseless mass killings and torture made him infamous, while Europeans were titillated by rumours of his harem of hundreds

of women. Ottoman troops finally killed him in 1822, on Ioannina's lake island. Nevertheless, Ali had tacitly aided Greek freedom fighters elsewhere by wearing down and distracting the Turks.

Epiros was divided after 1912 when the newly created Albania was given a northern chunk. Mussolini's 1940 invasion was repelled in Epiros, which became a communist resistance stronghold, first against the Nazis and then against the right-wing army in the Greek Civil War (1944–49). Although the communists lost, Epiros remains generally leftist.

Ioannina   Ιωάννινα

POP 80,400

Ioannina is one of Northern Greece's most atmospheric cities. It is set on the western shore of the lovely Lake Pamvotis, and framed by the impressive mountain range that turns lilac at sunset. The walls of the Kastro enclose an atmospheric, tranquil old quarter, and the lakeside area is lined by opulent plane trees that let in dappled afternoon sunlight. Together with jutting minarets, the fantastic fortress and the unique appeal of To Nisi (The Island), Ioannina makes a beautiful place to spend at least a couple of days.

The large student population means that bars far outnumber any other entertainment option – there is a lively atmosphere here year-round. Ioannina's rich history as an arts and culture centre is still keenly felt throughout the town.

History

Byzantine emperor Justinian founded Ioannina in the 6th century, and it became an important commercial and cultural outpost. In 1204, when Latin Crusaders sacked Constantinople and dismembered Byzantium, Ioannina became a key city of Michael I Komnenos Doukas' Byzantine successor state. Ottomans conquered in 1430, a Sephardic Jewish population arrived after 1492, and despite the disarray of the early Ottoman period (including a peasant revolt in 1611) Ioannina became a leading cultural and artistic centre. Ioannina was (and still is) known for its silver craftsmanship and, through the 16th and 17th centuries, an 'Epirot School' of religious painting also blossomed.

Albanian warlord Ali Pasha (1740–1822) capitalised on Ottoman decline to vie for Ioannina. In 1789 Ali made it the capital of his far-ranging fiefdom. His cruelty was known to sicken pious philhellene and poet Lord Byron, who visited Ioannina and even attended Ali's court. But Ali enforced the law and Ioannina flourished – albeit with brutal mass drownings and torture along the way. In 1822, trapped at the Agios Panteleimon monastery on To Nisi (The Island) in Lake Pamvotis, octogenarian Ali was killed by the Ottomans.

Greeks liberated Ioannina in the 1912–13 Balkan Wars. The 1923 population exchanges saw Turks replaced by Anatolian Greek refugees. In 1943 the Nazis deported the Jewish population to concentration camps.

◎ Sights & Activities

The relaxing one-hour lake cruise (p296) departs from near the ferry quay.

For Anavasi's *Pindus-Zagori* 1:50,000 hiking map (€8), inquire at local *periptera* (kiosks) or Public (p298). Hikers should consult EOS about mountain conditions.

Its Kale   FORTRESS

(Kastro; ◎8am-5pm & 8-10pm Tue-Sun) **FREE**
Kastro's sublime citadel, including a Middle Byzantine tower, rises over a long bluff overlooking lake and mountain. The outer ramparts are cluttered with cannon balls and elegant Ottoman carvings. Within, it holds the restored **Fetiye Cami** (Victory Mosque), built in 1611 after a failed Greek uprising that saw Christians expelled from the citadel, and the **Tomb of Ali Pasha**. The decorative iron railing is a copy of the original, which was removed during WWII.

Byzantine Museum   MUSEUM

(⌨26510 25989; Kastro; €3; ◎8am-3pm Tue-Sun) This museum presents early Christian and Byzantine art, pottery, coins and silverware, plus post-Byzantine icons and manuscripts, early Venetian-produced Greek books and ornate silver jewellery boxes with cloisonné enamel. Textual accompaniments detail Ioannina's history from the 4th to the 17th century. There's a separate silverware hall; buy tickets at the main counter.

Municipal Ethnographic Museum   MUSEUM

(⌨26510 26356; Kastro; adult/student €2/1; ◎8am-8pm summer, 8.30am-4.30pm winter) Set inside the erstwhile Aslan Pasha Mosque (1619), the museum exhibits local costumes and period photographs, along with tapestries and prayer shawls from Ioannina's former synagogue (Ioustinianou 16). The area around the museum is really quite idyllic, elevated as it is atop Ioannina, amid quiet ruins.

Archaeological Museum   MUSEUM

(⌨26510 01051; www.amio.gr; Plateia 25 Martiou 6; adult/child €2/1; ◎8.30am-3pm Tue-Sun) This top-notch museum contains more than 3000 Epirot finds, including Neolithic items and antiquities from Dodoni, Vitsa and Efira. Note, the museum website is in Greek only.

Ioannina

NORTHERN GREECE IOANNINA

Ioannina

◎ Sights
1 Archaeological Museum B3
2 Byzantine Museum D2
3 Its Kale D2
4 Municipal Ethnographic Museum C1

✈ Activities, Courses & Tours
5 Lake Cruise C1

🛏 Sleeping
6 Filyra & Platanos C2
7 Hotel Astoria B3
8 Hotel Kastro D1
9 Traditional Hotel Dafni C2

✗ Eating
10 Ippotes B2
11 Mystagogia B2
12 Seirios A1
13 Stoa Louli B2

🍷 Drinking & Nightlife
14 Blue Gin Bar C2
   Byzantine Museum Cafe .... (see 2)
15 Denoar B2
16 Mpizisten B3

🔒 Shopping
17 Public A4

Lake Cruise   CRUISE
(☎ 6944470280; cruise €5; ⏰ 10am-midnight daily summer, Sat & Sun winter) Regular one-hour cruise on Lake Pamvotis, leaving from near the ferry quay.

🛏 Sleeping

The best sleeping options are inside the Kastro, where there are small, atmospheric and quiet hotels.

Hotel Astoria HOTEL €

(☑ 26510 20755; http://hotelastoria.gr; Paraskeuopoulou 2, cnr Averof; s/d €45/60; P ✳ 🛜) Very much a basic, clean rooms sort of place, with no frills. It's a few paces from the laneway nightlife on Lord Byron and Stoa Liampei, on the main artery of Ioannina.

Limnopoula Camping CAMPGROUND €

(☑ 26510 25265; off lot Merarchias; campsites per tent/adult €4/8; ☺ Apr-Oct; P 🛜) This breezy lakeside campground is 2km from the centre on Lake Pamvotis' northwestern shore. It has a kitchen, a laundry and a restaurant. Don't swim in the lake (note the algae) and do bring mosquito repellent.

★**Hotel Kastro** PENSION €€

(☑ 26510 22866; www.hotelkastro.gr; Andronikou Paleologou 57; d from €60; P ✳) This restored Kastro mansion overlooking Its Kale citadel is immaculately decorated, with antique brass beds, stained-glass windows and a tranquil courtyard. It's a very quiet place, where rest is guaranteed. Follow signs for the Byzantine Museum after you enter the Kastro.

Filyra & Platanos BOUTIQUE HOTEL €€

(☑ 6932601240; www.hotelfilyra.gr; Andronikou Paleologou 18; d/studio €65/75; P ✳ 🛜) These flower-bedecked boutique hotels face each other on different sides of Paleologou, in the centre of the Kastro neighbourhood. The 1st-floor rooms have more natural light than the ground-floor ones; there are rooms and self-catering suites. Note, the website is in Greek only.

Traditional Hotel Dafni HOTEL €€

(☑ 6932601240; Ioustinianou 12; d/q €65/90; P ✳ 🛜) Set inside the Kastro's enormous outer walls, Dafni offers rooms combining traditional and modern amenities. There's one grand, well-decorated family room (€90). Reception is at nearby sister establishments, Filyra & Platanos.

✖ Eating

Ioannina has good eating options, but keep in mind that some of the best places only open for dinner and many more get busy from 9pm.

Mystagogia TAVERNA €

(☑ 26510 65325; www.mystagwgia.gr; Koundouriotou 44; mains €6; ☺ dinner; 🖉) A popular *tsipouradhiko* (ouzerie) set in an old mansion, Mystagogia has nourishing mezedhes,

juicy grills and an occasionally raucous ouzo-fuelled late-night ambience.

Ippotes MEDITERRANEAN €

(☑ 6932358223; Soutsou 7; mains €7-11; ☺ 8pm-2am) Greek grills and rock music combine in this inventive stone-walled restaurant with a relaxing backyard – note that the backyard is open in summer only.

★**Stoa Louli** TAVERNA €€

(☑ 26510 71322; www.stoa-louli.gr; Anexartisias 78; mains €7-12) Built in 1875, Stoa Louli has been an inn, a trade centre for Jewish leather merchants and an Ottoman Bank. Fronted by grand arches, this friendly place serves delicious Greek favourites, some with a contemporary twist. Try the beetroot salad bejewelled with pistachio, roast aubergine with feta and garlic, and *hunkar bejendi* – tender pieces of beef on a bed of aubergine mash.

Seirios GREEK €€

(☑ 26510 77070; www.seirioskouzina.gr; cnr Georgiou Papandreou & Evanggelidi; mains €8-12; ☺ noon-11pm) Locally recommended Seirios has excellent and imaginative specials. Try the sausage in Greek yoghurt, stuffed pork shoulder blade or mushrooms in oil and lemon.

🍷 Drinking & Nightlife

Popular student bars are found in Skala, opposite the Kastro's southern stretches. Off Anexartisias, check out Stoa Liampei, an arched laneway with a checkerboard pavement packed with bars, and backstreets Lord Byron and Katsantoni. Southwest from here Plateia Pargis has scenic outdoor drinking spots in the shade of a lovely ochre-tiled Orthodox church.

★**Byzantine Museum Cafe** CAFE

(☑ 26510 64206; Kastro; ☺ 8am-5pm & 8-10pm Tue-Sun) On Its Kale, the museum cafe is popular with locals and visitors alike, with its big grassy grounds and beautiful views. It serves food too, but most come for a coffee and chat in the gorgeous setting.

Blue Gin Bar BAR

(☑ 6932020361; Ethnikis Antistaseos 46; ☺ 8am-2am) An atmospheric bar on two floors, with live music, DJ parties and, well, gin. A great place to drink and talk into the wee hours.

Mpizisten CAFE

(☑ 26510 27369; cnr Lord Byron & Katsantoni; ☺ 10am-late) Beer-bottle vases and vintage styling give a quirky feel to this cafe in the laneways off Averof. Imaginative bar snacks, such as roasted feta and miniature omelettes, are a good snack between drinks or coffees.

Denoar BAR
(☑ 6984766894; www.denoar.de; Anexartasias 41-42; ☺ 9pm-late) This bar occupies a beautifully arching 200-year-old former *agora* (market). It has friendly people, twinkling lights, strange curvy stairs and an interesting musical mix.

🛍 Shopping

Public BOOKS
(☑ 26510 70087; cnr Melanidi & Pirsinela; ☺ 9am-8pm) This chain bookshop is good for maps and travel guides for Zagorohoria or the rest of Greece and beyond.

**Centre of Traditional
Handcrafts of Ioannina** HANDICRAFTS, JEWELLERY
(☑ 26510 27650; www.kepavi.gr; Arhiepiskopou Makariou 1; ☺ 9.30am-2.30pm & 5.30-8.30pm) You'll need to get out of the centre and into the Anatoli neighbourhood to see Ioannina's centuries-old silverwork tradition at this collective artisans' workshop and store. Pieces range from intricate jewellery to enormous silverware sets.

ℹ Information

Plateia Pyrrou and Averof have banks and ATMs.
EOS (Greek Alpine Club; ☑ 26510 22138; www.orivatikos.gr; Smyrnis 15; ☺ hours vary) Good for basic maps, info on Ioannina, and hiking information for Zagorohoria.
EOT (Greek National Tourist Organisation; ☑ 26510 41142; Dodonis 39; ☺ 7.30am-2.30pm Mon-Fri) Hiking information on the surrounding mountain region.
Post Office (☑ 26510 76880; 28 Oktovriou 9; ☺ 7.30am-2pm Mon-Sat) Post office branch in central Ioannina.

ℹ Getting There & Away

AIR

Aegean Airlines (☑ 26510 64444) serves Athens. The **airport** (☑ 26510 83600; Km 4 Ioannina-Kozani road) is 4km northwest of town.

**BUS
Domestic**

Ioannina bus station (KTEL Ioanninon; ☑ 26510 25014; www.ktelioannina.gr; Georgiou Papandreou 45) serves Athens (€39, 6½ hours, seven daily), Konitsa (€6.20, 1¼ hours, five

daily), Thessaloniki (€32, 3½ hours, six daily), Arta (€7.10, two hours, six daily) and Metsovo (€5.80, one hour, four daily). In summer buses sometimes serve Parga (€12, 1½ hours); alternatively, travel via Igoumenitsa (€9.80, 1¼ hours, seven daily) or Preveza (€10.40, two hours, eight daily). Buses also serve Dodoni (€2, 40 minutes). Zagorohoria buses are irregular, so check ahead.

International

Buses from Ioannina serve Albanian border post Kakavia (€6, one hour, eight daily).

ℹ Getting Around

BUS

Buses to the airport run from the **clock tower** (Plateia Dimokratis) every 20 minutes.

CAR

The following car-rental agencies have offices in Ioannina, as well as branches at the airport.
Auto Union Car Rental (☑ 25610 67751; Dodonis 66; ☺ 9am-7pm)
Avis (☑ 26510 46333; Dodonis 71; ☺ 9am-1.30pm & 6-8.30pm)
Budget Rent a Car (☑ 26510 43901; Dodonis 109; ☺ 9am-7pm) Call ahead to check opening hours.

TAXI

Taxi (☑ 26510 46777) Taxis wait near Plateia Pyrrou and the lake.

To Nisi   Το Νησί

To Nisi (The Island) lies opposite Ioannina, amid woods and wildflowers in Lake Pamvotis. It's a wonderful place to spend a few hours, strolling around the peaceful island and having a coffee or some food on its squares.

In the 17th-century, refugees from Peloponnesian Mani built its portside village, where around 200 people still live. The island's secluded monasteries are significant for their unusual frescoes and book collections, while the laneways with their old, white-plastered houses lend atmosphere.

It was here that the last act in despot Ali Pasha's grand drama unfolded. After years of double-dealing and challenges the Ottomans decided to eliminate the 82-year-old 'Lion of Ioannina' in 1822. Falsely assured of a pardon, Ali withdrew with his guard to the island's Moni Panteleimon. There he was trapped and Ottoman soldiers shot him; note the fatal bullet hole in the floorboards at the Ali Pasha Museum.

WORTH A TRIP

METSOVO ΜΕΤΣΟΒΟ

Metsovo is a ski town – it clings to the Pindos Mountains at 1156m, and the three ski areas – Profitis Ilias, Karakoli and Zigos – lure winter sports fans come snowfall. Fresh alpine air, lofty views and traditional wooden architecture make it a relaxing stop – as well as a potentially gluttonous one. Bulging sausages dangle in shop windows and huge rounds of smoky cheese beg to be melted. Out of season, it can make a nice stopover on your way further north or south.

Ski Centre (☑ 26560 41095; ⊙ 9.30am-3.45pm winter) In winter, Metsovo's ski centre can advise on conditions, gear hire and skiing or snowboarding lessons.

Averoff Gallery (☑ 26560 41210; www.averoffmuseum.gr; adult/student €3/2; ⊙ 10am-4pm Wed-Mon, to 6.30pm mid-Jul–mid-Sep) Founded by Evangelos Averoff-Tositsa to fulfil a long-held wish to crown his home town with a quality gallery, the Averoff exhibits the works of 19th- and 20th-century Greek painters and sculptors.

Folk Museum (☑ 26560 41084; adult/student €3/2; ⊙ 9am-1.30pm & 4-6pm Fri-Wed) The Tositsas mansion hosts Metsovo's folk museum, recreating a typical wealthy 19th-century Metsovite household, with hand-crafted furniture, artefacts and utensils. Guided tours run every half an hour.

Hotel Egnatia (☑ 26560 41900; Tositsa 19; s/d/studios incl breakfast €40/70/90) Egnatia offers doubles and spacious studios with handsome bathrooms. The hotel is marked by its wooden fixtures and the friendly, knowledgeable owner can provide info about outdoor activities. The mountain views are superb.

Metsovitiko Saloni (☑ 26560 42142; Tositsa 10; mains €12; ⊙ lunch & dinner) Tuck into aubergine and smoked cheese, or some hearty grills in the cosy salon or on the flower-draped wooden balcony, and taste the decent local wines. Follow a creaking wooden staircase from the main street.

Metsovo is a 45-minute drive from Ioannina. **Metsovo bus station** (☑ 26560 42646) serves Ioannina (€10, 1½ hours, two daily).

NORTHERN GREECE ΤΟ ΝΙΣΙ

◉ Sights

Information about Lake Pamvotis can be found at the stand near the Ali Pasha Museum.

Just off Plateia Alieon there are souvenir stands packed with decorative weapons and jewellery.

Moni Filanthropinon MONASTERY
(Μονή Φιλανθρωπινών; ⊙ 9am-6pm) FREE Moni Filanthropinon looks unassuming from the outside. But after entering the monastery courtyard, the caretaker will usher you through a wooden door for you to see unflinchingly macabre frescoes of the fates of the saints. No detail of amputations, skin peelings and torture by wheel is left unrendered. Just as intriguing (and easier on the eye) are the 16th-century frescoes of Greek philosophers Plato, Aristotle and Plutarch sitting alongside more suitably Christian personalities.

Built in the 13th century by the Filanthropini, a leading Constantinopolitan family who fled the Crusaders in 1204,

Moni Filanthropinon became a secret school for Christians during the Ottoman Muslim domination. Follow the right-hand path along the island's western edge to reach this well-signposted monastery. Continue along the trail for what is the island's oldest monastery, **Moni Diliou** (less well preserved than Filanthropinon) and **Moni Eleousis**.

Ali Pasha Museum MUSEUM
(adult €2; ⊙ 8am-10pm Jun-Sep, 10am-9pm Oct-May) This island museum commemorates Ioannina's former despot, Ali Pasha. There's a printed narrative (in English) recounting the heady events of Ali's last days, plus various personal effects and etchings of the portly Pasha in full repose, sitting fat and happy with his consort, beard and hookah. To get there, walk the hill from the dock into town and turn left.

✖ Eating & Drinking

The small, shady Plateia Alieon has restaurants and cafes.

Propodes
SEAFOOD €

(☑ 26510 81214; fish €4-6; ⊙ noon-11pm) Simple fish and grills are served at this humble island eatery.

Kafeteria Ta Bakakakia
CAFE

(☑ 6947135096; ⊙ 9am-9pm daily May-Sep, Sat & Sun Oct-Apr) This charming cafe, run by young islander Marina Vakatsa, has juices, milkshakes and other drinks, and a lovely view across the lake to the northern hills.

ℹ Getting There & Away

Ioannina's ferry quay has ferries (€2, 10 minutes, every 15 minutes) from 7am to 11.30pm in high season (from June to September). Out of season, ferries run hourly from 8am to 10pm (October to May). Summer services run every 15 minutes; in winter, every 30 minutes.

Around Ioannina

Epiros' rocky scenery lends a dramatic quality to the setting for the sights around Ioannina, from crowd-pleasing Perama Cave to sacred spots such as Dodoni. Each can be achieved in half a day if you're short on time.

Perama Cave
CAVE

(Σπήλαιο Περάματος; ☑ 26510 81521; www.spilaio-perama.gr; Perama; adult/child €7/3.50; ⊙ 9am-9pm summer, to 5pm winter) Stalactite-rich Perama Cave, 4km from Ioannina, is among Greece's largest and most impressive. Discovered by accident in 1940 by residents fleeing bomb attacks, 1100m of its fairy-tale passageways can be explored on hourly guided tours (45 minutes, in Greek and English). Knowledgeable guides come armed with fascinating facts about geology and unique cave fauna. The cave is several degrees colder than outside, so dress accordingly.

Buses 8 and 16 from Ioannina's clock tower run regularly to Perama, 250m south of the cave.

Dodoni
RUINS

(Δωδώνη; ☑ 26510 82287; adult €2; ⊙ 8am-3pm) Flanked by mountains and meadows, the colossal 3rd-century-BC Theatre of Dodoni, 21km southwest of Ioannina, is Epiros' most imagination-firing ancient site. The north-side acropolis has wall remnants. East of the theatre are **bouleuterion** (council house) foundations and the small **Temple of Aphrodite**. Nearby, Zeus' sanctuary once stood. Dodoni is 30 minutes' drive from central

Ioannina. Buses from Ioannina serve Dodoni twice daily. Taxis cost about €35 return.

From around 2000 BC, the earth goddess worshipped here spoke through Greece's oldest oracle. Around 400 BC a temple to Zeus was built here, too, and oracles interpreted his messages through the rustling of an ancient oak tree's leaves and the movements of birds nesting in its branches.

Zagorohoria
Τα Ζαγοροχώρια

Zagorohoria is one of Northern Greece's most attractive and mysterious regions and a real must-explore, with 46 traditional stone-and-slate villages, tucked into the Pindos range. If you like silence, quality hiking and nature, plus breathtaking mountain views at each turn, you'll never want to leave.

Each village has its own character, but all are tranquil and beautiful – romantic **Dilofo** has only a handful of inhabitants and an uncanny silence, and the region's loveliest restaurant; the charming and rugged **Monodendri** is the most popular, while **Kato Pedina**, **Ano Pedina** and **Aristi** are the outdoor activities hubs. The **Papingo** villages are reached by precipitous mountain roads, while traditional **Kipi** is slightly livelier.

Once connected only by mountain paths and stone bridges, the villages are now connected by paved roads, some of which enjoy spectacular twists and turns. Hikers also come for the immediate proximity to the Vikos Gorge and other mountain routes.

Vikos-Aoös National Park
Εθνικός Δρυμός Βίκου-Αώου

Vikos-Aoös National Park bursts with pristine rivers and forests, flowering meadows, and shimmering lakes that reflect jagged mountains and endless blue sky. Almost one-third of Greece's flora (some endemic) lives here, along with native fish, foxes and chamois, rare hawks, otters and bears. The park's Tymfi Massif contains numerous ear-popping peaks, including Mt Trapezitsa (2022m), Mt Astraka (2436m) and Mt Gamila (2497m). Beneath them lies 12km-long Vikos Gorge.

Whether for the adrenaline rush of hiking, biking and rafting, or to seize some binoculars and admire its fauna, the park is a huge draw for travellers wending their way through the steep Zagorohoria. While hik-

Zagorohoria

Map scale: 0—5 km / 0—2.5 miles

Locations shown on map: Iliorahi, Bourazani (2km), Mazi, Konitsa, Elefthero, Palloseli, Padhes, Voïdomatis-Aoös Valley, Aoös River, Konitsa Bridge, Mt Trapezitsa (2022m), Moni Stomiou, Aoös River Gorge, Aoös River, Mt Vasilitsa (30km); Grevena (71km), Kallithea, Drakolimni (Dragon Lake), Mt Gamila (2497m), Vrisohori, Klidonia, Ano Klidonia, Papingo Rock Pools, Lake Xeroloutsa, Iliohori, Megalo Papingo, Mikro Papingo, Mt Astraka (2436m), Klidoniavista Bridge, Voïdomatis River, Vikos, Vikos-Aoös National Park, Mesovouni (8km), Voïdomatis Springs, Aristi, Tsuka Rosa (2377m), Vikos Gorge, Klima Spring, Beloi Lookout, Skamneli, Oxya Lookout, Skala Vradetou, Tsepelovo, Elafotopos, Vradeto, Paliogefyro Bridge, Ano Pedina, Monodendri, Kapesovo, Hatsi Bridge, Kato Pedina, Moni Agia Paraskevi, Vitsa, Koukouli, Kipi, Negades, Karyes (12km); Ioannina (30km), Dilofo (1km); Elati (8km); Ioannina (36km)

NORTHERN GREECE ZAGOROHORIA

ers comprise the majority of visitors, semi-nomadic Vlach and Sarakatsani shepherds still take their flocks up to high grazing ground in summer, returning to the valleys in autumn.

★ Vikos Gorge
CANYON

The Voïdomatis River, a tributary of the Aoös, carved the 12km-long, 900m-deep Vikos Gorge over millions of years, leaving stark cliffs and yawning depths. According to Guinness, it's the world's deepest canyon in proportion to its width. It begins south of Monodendri, running north until the Papingo villages. Trail maps and signs for hikes can be found in most major villages. Check routes and get guidance on hikes suitable for your experience level at EOS (p298) in Ioannina.

From Monodendri, you can survey the gorge from Moni Agia Paraskevi. A steep, marked path into the gorge begins a chal-lenging four-hour walk; at canyon's end a right-hand trail leads to Mikro Papingo (2½ hours). Megalo Papingo is a further 2km west, but the track splits at the hike's base. The only water is at Klima Spring, halfway along the gorge.

Oxya Lookout, 5km beyond Monodendri on a dirt road, has fantastic gorge views, as does Beloi Lookout opposite. To get there, drive 9km along a winding road from Kapesovo to Vradeto, and hike 1.5km along a marked trail after the dirt road (it's a bumpy drive). Vradeto is set along striated lime-stone cliffs. For the Beloi Lookout, climb the rock stairway, Skala Vradetou, signposted outside Tsepelovo, another relaxing base for hiking northern Zagorohoria sites such as the Drakolimni (Dragon Lake).

Check the weather forecast and kit your-self out with sturdy hiking boots and drink-ing water. Always let someone local (such as your guesthouse) know your departure time and planned route, so they can raise the alarm if necessary.

Rafting Athletic Center OUTDOORS
(☑ 26530 41888, 6942015143; www.rafting-athletic-center.gr; Hotel Taxiarches, Aristi; per person €25)
A great opportunity to raft down Voïdomatis River, inside Vikos Gorge; the level is pretty basic, and great fun. The centre is inside Hotel Taxiarches, in Aristi.

Monodendri   Μονοδένδρι

Around 38km north of Ioannina, Monodendri is among Zagorohoria's most-visited villages. Superb hiking trails lead from here to Papingo through Vikos Gorge (about six hours). This village of slate-roofed houses also has a cluster of great tavernas and some fascinating churches, notably the triple-bell **Church of Agios Athanasios** and charismatic 17th-century **Church of Agios Minas**.

Moni Agia Paraskevi MONASTERY
A short path leads from Monodendri's northeastern edge to Moni Agia Paraskevi, a monastery with spectacular views over Vikos Gorge. Agia Paraskevi has the oldest preserved church in Zagorohoria. According to legend, Michael Voevodas Therianos founded it in 1413 to thank God for healing his daughter of an incurable illness. The church's frescoes partially date to the 15th century.

Rizarios Centre CULTURAL CENTRE
(☑ 26530 71573; www.rizarios.eu; ◌ 9am-4pm)
This cultural centre with an adjoining handicrafts school is housed in a renovated manor. Rizarios shines a light on Zagorohoria history with exhibitions of photos and artworks. Coffee-table books and embroidered souvenirs are for sale here.

Kato Pedina & Ano Pedina   Κάτω Πεδινά & Ανω Πεδινά

Until the middle of the 20th century, Kato Pedina was the wheat-winnowing capital of Zagorohoria, producing the majority of the region's grain. Today it's an ideal departure point for adventure travellers to mountain bike, trek or ski the Pindos Mountains. Drive 4km east and you'll find Ano Pedina (population 170) perched at an altitude of 960m on Mt Tymfi. This village charms with 18th-century churches and exhilarating mountain views.

Moni Evaggelistria MONASTERY
(Ano Pedina) This wonderfully well-preserved monastery, founded in the late 18th century, has a wealth of 200-year-old icons and frescoes that will leave you breathless.

Compass Adventures OUTDOORS
(☑ 6978845232; www.compassadventures.gr; Elati Zagoriou) Compass Adventures runs outdoor excursions and activities in the Zagorohoria wilds. Adventures range from one-day mountain-biking tours and guided family hikes (from May to October) to multiday ski touring in the Pindos Mountains (from December to April).

Aristi   Αρίστη

Picturesque Aristi is tucked into the Pindos Mountains at an altitude of 650m. The village has ancient roots, evidenced by Paleolithic remnants discovered nearby. Today, a clutch of guesthouses snoozes along Aristi's cobblestoned streets and adrenaline junkies descend here to raft and hike. Its most arresting sight is **Moni Panagia Spiliotissa**; this arched, frescoed spiritual site stands aside a boulder by the Voïdomatis River and dates from 1665.

If you're driving from Ioannina, Aristi is the last village before Papingo. After Aristi, prepare for white-knuckle driving as the road winds upwards. If you aren't venturing further than Aristi, take the Papingo road as far as **Voïdomatis Bridge**, a beautiful stone span over bright cerulean water.

Papingo   Πάπιγκο

The road ribboning north from Aristi to Papingo offers Zagorohoria's most breathtaking views. **Megalo Papingo** and **Mikro Papingo** – respectively, the large and the small – are two villages tucked into the Vikos-Aoös National Park at a dizzying altitude of 960m. The most distinctive element of Papingo's setting is the looming rock formations known locally as the **Towers**. The tallest is 1788m high. A 2km trail separates the two villages, along which you can find two **natural pools** fed by the Rogovo River. These rock pools are swimmable in summer.

Agios Vlasios CHURCH
(Megalo Papingo) The most striking of Papingo's churches is Agios Vlasios (1852) with its separate 15m-high hexagonal bell tower (1887).

🛏 Sleeping

★ Arhontiko Dilofo   GUESTHOUSE €

(📞26530 22455; www.dilofo.com; Dilofo; d incl breakfast from €60; P) One of Zagorohoria's finest guesthouses, this restored 1633 mansion in placid Dilofo village is ideal for anyone seeking peace and natural harmony. Each of its nine rooms features traditional decor, furnishings and ornate painted window shutters. There's a charming courtyard and views over Dilofo's cluttered slate rooftops. The hosts are friendly and helpful.

Arhontiko Zarkada   PENSION €

(📞26530 71305; Monodendri; d incl breakfast from €45; P🛜) Enjoy the views of Vikos Gorge from your balcony at this lovely old stone house with clean, snug rooms. Some rooms have spa baths.

★ Primoula   BOUTIQUE HOTEL €€

(📞26530 71133; www.primoula.gr; Ano Pedina; d incl breakfast from €75; P❄🛜) 🐾 This exceptional guesthouse in central Ano Pedina has uniquely designed rooms, some glowing in warm pastel tones and others retaining traditional stone walls. The helpful staff assists with organising outdoor activities, and a lavish, locally sourced breakfast kickstarts each day. A recently added outdoor (and indoor) spa (€25 per person for two hours) means vast views while you soak. Unmissable.

Zagori Suites   BOUTIQUE HOTEL €€

(📞6944342739, 26530 71076; www.zagorisuites.gr; Vitsa; ste from €85; P🛜) With ornately decorated suites and chalets, this boutique hotel at the entrance to Vitsa village is one of Zagorohoria's most sumptuous choices. In summer there's a closed playground and games for children, while adults can clink glasses at the well-stocked bar.

Arhontiko Aristis   B&B €€

(📞26530 42210, 6945676261; www.arhontiko-aristis.gr; Aristi; s/d/tr from €70/80/110; P🛜) Set in an 1800 stone mansion, this Aristi guesthouse offers spectacular views and has exposed stone walls inside the cosy rooms, and fireplaces, too – what more do you need for a perfect mountain stay?

Papaevangelou   GUESTHOUSE €€

(📞26530 41135; www.hotelpapaevangelou.gr; Megalo Papingo; d/studio incl breakfast from €75/120; 🛜) This popular Papingo guesthouse has four studios and 10 rooms with outstanding views and traditional trimmings galore:

ℹ️ NAVIGATING THE ZAGOROHORIA ZIGZAGS

Zagorohoria's vertiginious views are guaranteed to tighten your grip on the steering wheel. These challenging mountain roads are steep, often narrow, and with frequent hairpin bends. Debris from hillsides sloughs onto the road surface and even short drives are likely to be interrupted by herds of goats, dazed dogs and even lumbering tortoises. Check weather conditions before you set out; nervous drivers should avoid driving by night when roads are unlit.

dark wooden floors, lace curtains and (in some spaces) fireplaces.

Mikro Papigo 1700   BOUTIQUE HOTEL €€

(📞26530 41179; www.mikropapigo.gr; Mikro Papingo; d incl breakfast from €90; P🏊) 🐾 Fifteen handsome rooms and suites vary in styles from minimalist to rustic, while gorge views from the restaurant delight. Reward yourself for the steep uphill climb (cars aren't allowed in the village centre) by unwinding in the small sauna and steam room; there is also a small swimming pool.

Porfyron   B&B €€

(📞26530 71579; http://porfyron.gr; Ano Pedina; d from €65; P) This red-painted 19th-century mansion has individually decorated rooms with antique furnishings and soft-coloured walls. Porfyron arranges occasional workshops on cookery, liqueurs and yoga, plus excursions covering rafting to fly-fishing. Half-board with tasty home cooking is available from €100.

🍴 Eating

Each village has a taverna or a restaurant, and since the distances are so short between the villages, it's quite easy to drive out for lunch or dinner. Game and meats are omnipresent, as are wonderful vegetable dishes and plentiful salads.

★ Taverna Sopotseli   TAVERNA €

(📞26530 22629, 6942785095; Dilofo; mains €7-10; ⏰lunch & dinner) Dilofo's little taverna has a beautiful terrace and a calm, relaxed interior. It has wonderful salads, excellent grilled meat and game, and tasty local pies. There is also a good Greek wine list, and the service is just wonderful. It's a place to come for a morning coffee or an afternoon mug of mountain herb tea, too.

O Dionysos
TAVERNA €

(☑ 26530 71366; Monodendri; pites €5-6; ☺ lunch & dinner) Along upper Monodendri's main street, Dionysos serves tasty *fakopita* (lentil pie) among other traditional Epirot pies – a great place to explore seasonal pies too.

Konaki
GREEK €

(☑ 26530 42238; www.papigo-konaki.gr; Megalo Papingo; mains €8; ☺ lunch & dinner Mon-Sat, lunch Sun) Tuck into spit-roasted lamb, Epirot pies and lovingly simmered stews at this welcoming restaurant in Megalo Papingo. Konaki also has a five-room guesthouse in Zagorohoria's traditional stone-and-wood style.

Restaurant Tsoumaniskos
TAVERNA €

(☑ 26530 41893; www.tsoumanisnikos.gr; Vikos; mains €6-9; ☺ lunch & dinner) Excellent Greek pies and hearty local meats grilled to perfection are a real treat at this Vikos taverna. Try some of the local wine or have a shot of *tsipouro* (distilled spirit similar to raki) as an aperitif. There's a charming guesthouse above.

Sta Riza
GREEK €€

(☑ 26530 71550; Elati; mains €9-13; ☺ 12.30-10pm) It's hard to disagree with the locals – Sta Riza, overlooking rolling hills, is the place for hearty country cooking, such as *manitaria fournitsa* (baked mushrooms in red wine, tomato, feta and herbs) and *arnakia vlahika* (soft baked lamb with yoghurt). Elati is in the southernmost Zagorohoria; it's a very narrow village, so park 30m before the restaurant.

Aris Journeys of Flavors
CAFE €€

(☑ 26530 41411; Megalo Papingo; mains €8-12; ☺ lunch & dinner) This friendly cafe-bar has a rotating selection of main dishes and plenty of homemade desserts to enjoy after a long walk.

ⓘ Information

Vikos-Aoös Geopark Information Centre (Megalo Papingo; ☺ 9am-6pm) Great for local information on hiking and rafting.

WWF Information Centre (☑ 26530 41071; wwf-ppg@otenet.gr; Mikro Papingo; ☺ 10.30am-5.30pm Sun-Thu, 11am-6pm Fri & Sat) In Mikro Papingo, this centre looks at the area's unique wildlife and fauna.

ⓘ Getting There & Away

To really see Zagorohoria, you should drive. Limited bus services operate from Ioannina but they are geared towards local residents' needs, rather than those of visitors. These services tend to run only one day per week, departing very early in the morning with return journeys in the afternoon of the same day.

Buses serve Megalo Papingo and Mikro Papingo (€5.10, two hours, Tuesdays), Ano Pedina and Kato Pedina (€4.30, 1½ hours, Mondays) and Monodendri (€4.30, one hour, Mondays) in summer.

Taxis from Ioannina to various villages cost €20 to €55; try negotiating.

Konitsa
Κόνιτσα

POP 4630

Along the trails that flow from Konitsa (*ko-nit-sah*), only the crunch of hiking boots interrupts birdsong and rushing water. This sprawling village is carved into a hillside 60km north of Ioannina. It's where trekkers return to share tales of bird sightings and gorge views over a chilled Mythos beer. Greek hunters also use Konitsa as a sort of cowboy depot.

Beyond Konitsa, the road arcs northeast to Kastoria. While still passable, this road can be tricky to navigate, especially at night.

⚡ Activities

At Konitsa's southern entrance is a 4.5km **river hike** along the Aoös River Gorge to strikingly situated monastery **Panagia Stomiou**. Begin at the elegant 20m-high, 40m-long single-arched stone **Konitsa Bridge**, dating from 1870, which straddles the river. After it, a signposted trail becomes a narrow path between the water and a steep bank, and turns upwards through thick forests.

No Limits
OUTDOORS

(☑ 26550 23777; www.nolimits.com.gr; Konitsa) This local company provides equipment and experienced guides for kayaking, horseback riding, rafting, climbing and mountain biking. Guided hikes range from four hours in Vikos Gorge to multiday adventures. You'll have a greater choice in spring through to autumn, but ask in advance for out-of-season activities.

🛏 Sleeping & Eating

Gefyri
HOTEL €

(☑ 26550 23780; www.gefyri.gr; Konitsa; d from €50; 🅿 ❄ 🛜 🐾) Right next to the stone bridge, this hospitable family-run hotel has comfortable rooms, a playground and an outdoor pool (open from May to September). It also organises activities in the surrounding area.

Grand Hotel Dendro
HOTEL €

(☑ 26550 29365; www.grandhoteldentro.gr; per person €25; P✱🛜) This luxurious place offers attic suites with hydromassage showers, spacious living rooms and a fireplace.

Konitsa Mountain Hotel
HOTEL €€

(☑ 26550 29390; www.konitsahotel.gr; d/tr/ste incl breakfast €70/80/105; P✱🛜) A great place to treat yourself to some luxury, this palatial hotel on the hill behind town offers spacious rooms with fireplaces and beautifully seasoned wooden floors. The hotel has a sauna, Turkish baths and a gym. Take the road behind the town centre uphill for 2km. Taxis go from the *plateia* (about €3).

To Dendro Restaurant
TAVERNA €

(☑ 26550 22055; mains €10; ⊙ lunch & dinner; ☑) Follow the scent of traditional roasted lamb to the taverna of innkeeper Yiannis Mourehidis. Quality Greek food is prepared here, and the atmosphere is warm. If you've been hiking, rest your weary feet, seize some grilled feta, and swap stories about trekking the Konitsa wilds.

⊙ Information

Pharmacies, post office and ATM-equipped banks can be found near the main square.
Health centre (☑ 26550 23111) Small but OK for minor emergencies.

⊙ Getting There & Away

Konitsa bus station (☑ 26550 22214) serves Ioannina (€6.20, two hours, five daily on weekdays). Buses reach Mertziani (€1.60, 30 minutes, two daily) for Albania.
Taxis (☑ 26550 22500) can be found near the main square.

Preveza
Πρέβεζα

POP 22,900

Preveza is a good stopover destination for lunch on your way to the Ionian Islands or the vast ruins of Nikopoli and the Nekromanteio of Afyra. The town itself has a large harbour and a long beach, and a small old quarter with some decent restaurants.

⊙ Sights & Activities

A couple of blocks from the waterfront, a maze of backstreets bursts with lively tavernas. Preveza's **Venetian clock tower**

(1792) and several fine churches distract visitors from the forest of yachts lining the waterfront.

Eco Cruising
CRUISE

(☑ 26820 41992; www.eco-cruising.gr; Akragantos 5; dolphin cruises adult/child 6-12yr/0-5yr €45/20/ free) On the central waterfront, Eco Cruising offers sailboat cruises on the Amvrakikos Gulf and to the islands. Tours include sunset cruises, birdwatching trips in protected wetlands, and dolphin-spotting with guaranteed sightings.

🛏 Sleeping & Eating

Camping Kalamitsi
CAMPGROUND €

(☑ 26820 22192; www.campingkalamitsi.eu; Kalamitsi; campsites per adult/child/tent €6.50/4/4.50; P🛜⛱) This large beach campground, 4km northeast of Preveza on the road to Parga, operates from May to mid-September. It has a pool and restaurant, and bungalows that sleep four people (from €65).

Hotel Urania
HOTEL €

(☑ 26820 89570; www.hotelurania.gr; Leoforos Irinis 33; s/d/tr €40/55/65; 🛜) Hospitable Hotel Urania is on busy main road Leoforos Irinis, which leads towards the bus station, Nikopoli and the road to Parga. Elegant and comfortable, this hotel is well positioned for a quick stopover.

Dioni Boutique Hotel
BOUTIQUE HOTEL €€

(☑ 26820 27381; www.masthotels.gr/boutique hoteldioni; cnr Kalou & Parthenagogiou; s/d/ste incl breakfast from €70/90/130; 🛜) 🍴 If you need to stay in central Preveza, Dioni is the best you'll find. The rooms are comfortable, the service friendly and breakfast is served with sea views in the rooftop cafe.

★Amvrosios
SEAFOOD €

(☑ 26820 27192; near Andrianoupoleos; fish €7-11; ⊙ 11am-2pm Tue-Sun) This well-loved taverna spills onto a flowering side lane off the waterfront. A local favourite, Amvrosios whips up some of the town's best seafood – the battered squid is perfectly crunchy on the outside, the grilled sardines are sprinkled with fragrant parsley, and you're guaranteed to walk away licking your fingers. The house white is great too.

Taverna O Kaixis
SEAFOOD €

(☑ 6947899404; Parthenagogiou 7; fish €5-9; ⊙ dinner) The friendly 'mermaid' taverna on a side street near the water prepares excellent fresh fish dishes and grills.

ℹ️ Information

Busy Leoforos Irinis, two blocks up from the waterfront, has banks and ATMs.

ℹ️ Getting There & Away

An underwater car tunnel (€3) links Preveza with Aktion; no passenger ferry exists. Cyclists and pedestrians can be transported through for free.

AIR

Preveza airport (Aktio Airport; ✆26820 26113) Also known as Lefkada or Aktio, this is a summer-only charter flight airport for European destinations.

Sky Express (✆28102 23835; www.skyex press.gr) An airline that serves domestic flights from Preveza. Book online.

BUS

Prevesa bus station (✆26820 22213; Km 2 Preveza-Parga road) serves Ioannina (€10.40, two hours, eight daily), Parga (€7.10, two hours, five daily), Igoumenitsa (€9.80, 2½ hours, one daily), Thessaloniki (€38, eight hours, two daily) and Athens (€37.30, six hours, five daily).

Nikopoli   Νικόπολη

Nikopoli was built in 31 BC by Octavian (later Emperor Augustus) to commemorate defeating Marc Antony and Cleopatra in the naval Battle of Actium (present-day Aktion). After 5th- and 6th-century barbarian raids, Emperor Justinian rebuilt it. But the 11th-century Bulgarians sacked it for good. The ruins that remain require a pinch of imagination to conjure the fabled 'City of Victory', but their scale is breathtaking.

◉ Sights

Nikopoli   RUINS
(City of Victory; ✆26820 41336; Preveza-Ioannina national road, E951; ⊘8.30am-8pm high season) FREE The ruins of Nikopoli include scant Roman walls, better-preserved Byzantine walls and churches, and a theatre, all spread across a vast site. Stairs lead to the top of the Byzantine walls in some places (such as by Church B) but ascend these crumbling steps at your own risk. Allow an hour or two to hike the site, which is 6km from Preveza. Large stretches of the walls are parallel to major roads, so beware of traffic when crossing to admire temples and towers.

Museum of Nikopoli   MUSEUM
(✆26820 89892; Preveza-Ioannina national road, E951; adult/child €3/free; ⊘8.30am-3pm Mon-Fri; 🅿) This museum brims with fascinating funerary monuments and statues in an airy, naturally lit exhibition space. Abundant English-language explanations enliven the collection.The eager museum staff members may follow your every step. The museum is 5km from Preveza.

Arta   Άρτα

POP 27,300

Arta's main draw is its medieval stone bridge, spanning the Arahthos River, at the entrance into town – its elegant arches step delicately over the often dry riverbed, making a lovely sight.

The city's sights are scattered among Arta's workaday urban-sprawl appearance. If you have time to spare, you will enjoy checking out the Roman ruins and Byzantine walls, as well as the unique structure of the Parigoritissa church, and the interesting archaeological museum.

Arta owes its ruins to the ancient city of Ambracia, founded in 625 BC. Ambracia once vibrated with music and art as the capital of Pyrrhus' kingdom. Its population relocated to Nikopolis (now Nikopoli) in 168 BC after vicious sackings.

◉ Sights

Ancient sights around Arta include the remains of a **Temple of Apollo** (Pyrrhou 3) and Greece's smallest **ancient theatre**. There's also a **cemetery** dating from the 6th to the 1st centuries BC. The walls of a 13th-century **Byzantine castle** can be admired around the city; there are impressive views from the Makrygianni area, near the clock tower.

Old Bridge   BRIDGE
(Gefiri tis Artas; Thiakogianni) This graceful stone bridge loops 20m high over the Arahthos River. A bridge has spanned this spot since Roman times; the version you see today is thought to be Ottoman. Folk ballads tell of a woman walled into its foundations, to banish a curse that saw the bridge crumble each time it was built. Take the best pictures from the New Bridge opposite, a hectic artery into the city.

Church of Parigoritissa Byzantine Museum   MUSEUM
(✆26810 28692; cnr Tzoumerkon & Parigoritras; adult/senior €2/1; ⊘8am-3pm) This multistorey marvel with intricate brick domes is quite

unique in the region. Craftspeople from Thessaloniki and Constantinople poured their hearts into the frescoes of this 13th-century edifice. Today it's billed as a museum of Byzantine culture – don't miss the lavish upper floors and gilt Christ on the top dome.

Archaeological Museum   MUSEUM
(📷 26810 71700; Trigono; €3; ⊙ 8am-3pm Tue-Sun; 🅿) This wonderful museum wrapped around a central courtyard tells the story of the ancient city of Ambracia from its foundation in 625 BC through its indigenous settlements right up to the foundation of Nikopolis (now Nikopoli), where Ambracia's citizens relocated. The ancient city's musical traditions and burial practices – including

elaborately carved *stelae* (pillars) – are illustrated with plenty of clear explanations in Greek and English.

🛏 Sleeping & Eating

Hotel Cronos   HOTEL €
(📷 26810 22211; www.hotelcronos.gr; Plateia Kilkis; s/d €40/55; 🅿 ✳ 🛜) If you need to stay in central Arta, this faded but functional hotel is comfortable. Ask for a room looking onto the *plateia* with a view of the fearsome Pyrrhus statue.

Arta Palace   HOTEL €€
(📷 26810 61530; www.artapalace.gr; Km 5 Arta-Agriniou road; s/d/tr €55/60/75; 🅿 ✳ 🛜 🖥) An easy 10-minute drive out of town, this

---

ℹ SAILING TO ITALY: FERRY FROM IGOUMENITSA

If you're heading to Italy by ferry, you'll have to pass through Igoumenitsa, in Epiros' far northwest. This port city also serves Ionian islands such as Corfu (Kerkrya) and Paxi. Igoumenitsa itself is not very attractive and there's little to draw you here other than the promise of sailing to lovelier shores.

Ferries leave from three adjacent quays on the waterfront. Just show up in Igoumenitsa to buy deck-class passenger tickets to Italian ports; the waterfront kiosks clearly signpost ferry destinations and departure times. Book ahead for car tickets or sleeping cabins. Be at the port two hours before departure, and check at the shipping agent's office for your boarding pass. On-board 'camping' is allowable for those with campervans (bring your own oxygen).

At the time of research, passenger deck-class tickets cost around €60 to Brindisi (six to 9½ hours), €62 to Bari (8½ to 10½ hours), €75 to Ancona (15 hours) and €80 to Venice (24 hours). A passenger ticket in a four-bed cabin with shower is generally twice as expensive. Vehicle prices for Bari and Brindisi start from €59, and from €90 to €114 for Ancona and Venice. Each destination has from two to four sailings per day during summer.

Different ferry companies charge similar prices and return tickets are sometimes cheaper than one-way; call local ferry offices or check the websites. They include **ANEK Lines** (📷 26650 29274, 26650 29063; www.anek.gr), **Endeavor Lines** (📷 26650 26833), **Grimaldi Lines** (📷 26650 23077, 26650 24404; www.grimaldi-lines.com), **Minoan Lines** (📷 26650 26715, 26650 22952; www.minoan.gr), **Superfast Ferries** (📷 26650 29200; www.superfast.com) and **Ventouris Ferries** (📷 26650 26670, 26650 23565; www.ventourisferries.gr). The central **Milano Travel** (📷 26650 24237; milantvl@otenet.gr; Agion Apostolon 11; ⊙ 9am-7pm) also sells tickets. If you're planning ahead from Parga, **International Travel Services** (p310) can find hidden discounts and cabin upgrades. For Corfu ferry information, call the automated **Igoumenitsa Port Authority information line** (📷 26650 99460).

If you need to stay over, the **Angelika Pallas Hotel** (📷 26650 26100; www.angelikapallas. gr; Agion Apostolon 63; d/tr incl breakfast from €64/96; ✳ 🛜) is Igoumenitsa's best: it's friendly, comfortable and close to the quays. Travellers sleeping in rooms with dock views endure a wake-up call of honking ferries; ask if you want a quieter room. Slightly cheaper, less attractive places line the waterfront. **Jolly Hotel** (📷 26650 23971; jollyigm@otenet.gr; Ethnikis Antistasis 14; d incl breakfast from €40; @) is faded, but OK if you need a budget place close to the ferry terminals. The waterfront has some eateries that are not far from the ferry port.

From **Igoumenitsa bus station** (KTEL Thesprotias; 📷 26650 22309; www.ktel-thes protias.gr; 49 Martiron), two blocks behind the Corfu ferry docks, buses serve Ioannina (€9.80, two hours, seven daily), Parga (€5.90, one hour, three daily), Athens (€44.50, eight hours, three daily), Preveza (€13, 2½ hours, one daily) and Thessaloniki (€34, eight hours, one daily). Buses are less frequent from October to May.

hotel isn't quite as grand as the name promises. Nonetheless, it's a slightly more glamorous choice than the digs in central Arta due to its smart rooms, large balconies and zany pastel-coloured pool areas.

Synousies TAVERNA €

(☑ 26810 26566; Karaiskaki 20; mains €7-10; ☺ dinner) There's a heartily old-time feel to this local favourite with a robust menu of Greek cuisine.

❶ Getting There & Away

Direct buses from the **main bus station** (☑ 26810 26374; www.ktelartas.gr; Kristalli) connect Arta with Thessaloniki (€37, 4½ hours, two daily), Athens (€34, 5½ hours, six daily), Preveza (€5.20, one hour, four daily) and Ioannina (€7, 1½ hours, six daily).

Parga Πάργα

POP 3900

If there is a picture-perfect town in northern Greece, Parga is it – the hollow castle perches above a sandy bay, rock islets stick out of the sea sporting slanting pines, and the surrounding beaches and coves are as inviting as the transparent turquoise waters. Add to it a labyrinthine and charming old quarter, and you have the ideal Greek seaside town. Yes, it's a little on the touristy side (quite a lot in high summer), but it's a beauty.

This former Venetian possession is an excellent base for swimming, historic sites and excursions to the Ionian Islands. After the sun sets, a slew of seafront tavernas and bars give Parga plenty of fizz. Outside May to September, Parga snoozes: expect shutdowns of some restaurants and activities if you visit during the low season.

❍ Sights & Activities

Several interesting churches are scattered around Parga. The **Church of the Dodeka Apostoli** (1780) seems bare at first glance, but it has lovingly painted frescoes of Christ's last supper and crucifixion. A few paces away, peer through the gloom in the **Church of Agios Dimitrios** (1850) at numerous depictions of the eponymous saint spearing a Christian-slaying gladiator from his horse. The largest is the **Church of Agios Nikolaos**, dedicated to Parga's patron saint.

Krioneri Beach is the main town beach, sandy with shallow waters, opposite a small island, Panagia. A 15-minute walk over the castle hill (well signposted from the upper town) leads to the 2km-long **Valtos Beach**. Alternatively, 4km east of Parga, **Lichnos Beach** is more relaxed, with a small, shady campground and clear waters.

Parga Tour Train offers an edifying, child-friendly two-hour diversion that takes you around some of the local sights.

Venetian Castle CASTLE

(Kastro) FREE Centuries of turbulent history have taken their toll on Parga's castle, now a romantic ruin with remarkable sea views. Dating to the 11th century, the castle passed from Venetian to Ottoman control with numerous invasions and bouts of rebuilding in between. The ramparts are uneven, so wear sturdy shoes and hang on to the kids. Pause for a drink in the cafe (open from 11am until late) to watch ferries, rather than invading pirate ships, ply the shore.

Paragaea Olive Oil Museum MUSEUM

(☑ 26840 32889; www.paragaea.gr; Tzavella 19; €3.50; ☺ 10am-11pm, by request low season) This fascinating old-town museum in Parga's erstwhile olive-oil factory, operational from 1929 until 1974, unlocks the history of Parga's major pre-tourist industry. There's a sampling of bread and oils (with flavours from oregano to orange) and a museum shop with olive-themed goodies from salad dressings to soaps.

Tickets include a guided tour, which enriches the displays of original machinery and documents found during renovations.

Parga Tour Train RAIL

(☑ 6944624155, 6945793049; waterfront; per person €10; ☺) This open-air tourist train departs every morning and evening from Parga waterfront from May to mid-October for a two-hour historical tour. Starting from the waterfront at 9.30am, it chugs up the coast road, veers into olive groves and stops at Anthousa village's forested Watermill Museum. The evening train visits Anthousa village (800m up) and its ruined Castle of Ali Pasha.

Buy tickets at the small train stop at the waterfront.

🛏 Sleeping

Valtos Camping CAMPGROUND €

(☑ 26840 31287; www.campingvaltos.com; Valtos Beach; campsites per adult/tent €7/6; ℗ ❄) This campground set amid orange trees beside busy Valtos Beach has a restaurant, supermarket and – for the tent-averse – bungalows with kitchenette, TV and air-con. It's a steep 15-minute walk from central Parga (or a five-minute drive).

Enjoy Lichnos Beach Camping
CAMPGROUND €

(✆26840 31171; www.enjoy-lichnos.net; Lichnos Beach; campsites per adult/tent €6/4, d €55; P🐾) This mellow campground near Lichnos Beach is 2km away from Parga town. Hidden in the shade of olive trees, you can hire water-sports gear and enjoy drinks and food in the taverna. The beach is a short walk from the campsites. Studios with wi-fi and fridges are also available.

★Utopia
APARTMENT €€

(✆26840 31133; www.utopia.com.gr; Agiou Athanasiou 5; apt from €70; ❄🐾) With perfect views of Krioneri Beach, these seven studio apartments couldn't be better located – you can go for a swim before breakfast! The furnishings are simple and the balconies huge. There is a kitchenette and a fridge, perfect for a breakfast overlooking the bay. The friendly owner runs a cafe below, where you can get breakfast and good coffee.

Bella Vista Studios & Apartments
APARTMENT €€

(✆26840 31457, 26840 31834; www.bellavista. com.gr; Lichnos Beach; studio/apt €80/100; P❄🐾) Above Lichnos Beach, these modern studios and apartments encircle an inviting pool set amid citrus trees. The apartments sleep up to five, and the upper rooms have large balconies overlooking the beach and hills. It's a steep downhill walk to the beach, but the views are excellent.

Hotel Acropol
HOTEL €€

(✆26840 31239; www.acropol.biz; Agion Apostolon 4; s/d €60/90; ❄🐾) Tucked in among the shady alleyways of Parga's old town, Hotel Acropol has an old-world glamour that suits its surroundings. From fine wrought-iron balconies to rooms decked out in handmade Italian furniture, its comfortable beds and kindly owner ensure a relaxing stay. Hotel Acropol is well signposted within the old quarter and it also hosts the fabulous Castello Restaurant.

Salvator Villas & Spa Hotel
HOTEL €€€

(✆26840 32910; www.salvator.gr; Kyperi; deluxe apt/villa incl breakfast €200/700; P❄🐾) Friendly, luxurious Salvator overlooks Parga

and the coast from the main road, 2.5km east of town. Villas have two bedrooms, kitchenette and terrace, and some have private pools (there's also a central outdoor pool). Free shuttle buses go into town throughout the day, though it's best to have a car if you stay here.

✖ Eating

Tzimaz
GREEK €

(✆26840 32337; Parga-Perdikas road; mains €6-10; ⊙noon-late; 🅿🖶) A great little taverna a few metres up from the supermarket, Tzimaz comes recommended by the locals for the quality of its food. Traditional Greek cuisine is done to perfection – roast aubergine with feta, beetroot salad, meatballs – the service is friendly, and the flower-laden terrace is shady and pleasant. You'll have to make do without a sea view.

Motley Coffeesweet
SWEETS €

(✆26840 32115; waterfront; desserts €3-5; ⊙8am-late) There's a dizzying range of sweet-toothed temptations at this late-opening cafe right by Krioneri Beach. Chocolate-drizzled waffles and ice creams make for a good any-time-of-day indulgence.

★Castello Restaurant
GREEK €€

(✆26840 31239; www.castello-restaurant.com; Hotel Acropol, Agion Apostolon 4; mains €8-14; ⊙noon-late; ❄🅿) Local favourite Castello whips up a creative menu of Mediterranean and Asian cuisine. Fish brochettes and steaks keep the grill smoking, while homemade pasta dishes burst with fresh seafood and herbs. The owners are especially proud of the well-stocked wine cellar, visible through a glass panel beneath your feet. Service is attentive, and soft music rounds off the elegant atmosphere.

★Eden
BISTRO €€

(✆26840 31409; nastast@otenet.gr; V Vasila 26; mains around €9; ⊙9am-2pm) An array of Italian-inspired dishes are served with a smile at this refreshing bistro in Parga's old town. Try the seafood risotto with fresh tomato and parsley, or grab crêpes and juices for a quick bite.

Taverna Arkoudas
SEAFOOD €€

(✆26840 32553; waterfront; fish €8-15; ⊙noon-1am) Amid a swarm of waterfront eateries, Arkoudas excels in all things tentacled, and charms with traditional music and sea views.

🍷 Drinking

Sugar Bar BAR

(www.sugarbar.gr; waterfront; cocktails around €7; ☺10am-late; ☎) Fancy starting the evening with a Champagne Pick Me Up or a Devil's Kiss? You'll find a drink to suit your mood on Sugar Bar's staggering cocktail menu. If you overdo it, return the following morning for a cappuccino at adjoining Spice Cafe.

Antico BAR

(☑26840 32713; Anexartisias 4; ☺noon-late) The logo – a guitar swirling in a shot glass – gives you a fine idea of what to expect from Parga's rock bar, located on an old-town side street moments from Krioneri Beach. It's a lively, unpretentious joint, with friendly staff.

ℹ️ Information

Parga has several ATM-equipped banks. There are pharmacies on Spyrou Livada and in the old town.

Dr Spiros Padiotis (☑26840 32450, 6944162261; Alexandrou Baga 1; ☺9am-2pm & 6-10pm) Private, 24-hour medical help.

International Travel Services (ITS; ☑26840 31833; Spyrou Livada 4; ☺9am-5pm Apr-Sep) Helpful for all kinds of travellers' needs, including excursions and maps.

Police (☑26840 31222; Alexandrou Baga 18) Near the post office.

Post Office (Alexandrou Baga 18; ☺8am-6pm)

ℹ️ Getting There & Away

BUS

Parga bus station (☑26840 31218; Spyrou Livada) serves Igoumenitsa (€5.90, 1½ hours, four daily on weekdays), Preveza (€7.10, two hours, four daily), Thessaloniki (€44, seven hours, one daily) – or travel via Preveza for more services – and Athens (€41.20, seven hours, three daily).

CAR

Europcar (☑26840 32777; Spyrou Livada 19; per day from €45) If you need car rental, this is the place to go.

International Travel Services also arranges car rental.

WATER TAXI

During the summer, water taxis serve Valtos Beach (€2) every half-hour from 9.30am to midnight and Lichnos Beach (€7) from 11am to 5pm.

ℹ️ Getting Around

The main road between Preveza and Igoumenitsa runs just north of Parga. Take the northern exit for the bus stop and central Parga (down Spyrou Livada) or the southeasterly exit for Krioneri Beach and the waterfront. Parking becomes difficult as you drive into the narrow streets, so grab a space as soon as you see one.

Nekromanteio of Afyra

Who would have imagined the gate of Hades, god of the underworld, to be fringed by cypress glades and flower-strewn meadows? The late-4th-century-BC site **Nekromanteio of Afyra** (☑26840 41206; adult/child €2/free; ☺8.30am-3pm; P) near Mesopotamo, 20km from Parga, was once famed as a place to commune with the dead. The Romans burned down the site in 167 BC but an evocative ruin remains, with limestone walls enclosing the main sanctuary, labyrinth and pilgrims' purification room.

Ancient Greek pilgrims brought offerings (and substantial payment) to this site on the north bank of the Acheron River, hoping the *nekromanteio* (oracle) would channel mystical powers to help them contact long-dead ancestors. The dead were thought to hold powers of clairvoyance, so priests eagerly cashed in by selling showy rituals to dazzle and disorientate. It is thought the thickness of the sanctuary walls (more than 3m) was to allow secret passageways for priests to slip through. To purify themselves ahead of rituals, pilgrims ate a diet only of beans and lupins, and made sacrifices of blood and honey (for a good price). Tiptoe down the narrow ladder to a womb-like underground chamber where dazed pilgrims would be led for a grand finale of supernatural showmanship.

By car head southeast towards Mesopotamo (20km); the Nekromanteio is on the opposite side of the village to the entrance from the main road. Park your car a few hundred metres downhill of the sanctuary; a cobbled path leads up to the ticket office. Alternatively, book a guided excursion through International Travel Services in Parga, or negotiate with a taxi driver in town – return trips, including waiting time, should cost around €40.

Saronic Gulf Islands

Includes →

Best Places to Eat

→ On the Verandah (p330)

→ Techne (p327)

→ Oraia Hydra (p325)

→ Aspros Gatos (p321)

→ Miltos (p317)

→ Akrogialia (p330)

Best Places to Stay

→ Poseidonion Grand Hotel (p329)

→ Hydra Hotel (p323)

→ Rosy's Little Village (p317)

→ Orloff Resort (p330)

→ Sirene Blue Resort (p320)

Why Go?

The Saronic Gulf Islands (Νησιά του Σαρωνικού) dot the waters nearest Athens and offer a fast track to Greek island life. As with all Greek islands, each of the Saronics has a unique feel and culture, so you can hop between classical heritage, resort beaches, exquisite architecture and remote escapism.

Aegina is home to a spectacular Doric temple and ruined Byzantine village, while nearby pine-clad Angistri feels protected and peaceful outside of the booming midsummer months. Further south, Poros, with its forested hinterland, curves only a few hundred metres from the Peloponnese. The Saronic showpiece, Hydra, is a gorgeous car-free island with a port of carefully preserved stone houses rising from a chic, history-charged harbour. Deepest south of all, pine-scented Spetses also has a vibrant nautical history and pretty town architecture, plus myriad aqua coves only minutes from the Peloponnese.

When to Go
Hydra

Apr & May The islands awaken after winter; come for flower-filled Easter.

Jun Celebrate Miaoulia in Hydra with sparkling waters and warm weather.

Sep The best-kept secret: clear skies, thinning crowds and Spetses' Armata celebration.

Saronic Gulf Islands Highlights

1 Hydra (p321) Bouncing between the gorgeous port, with its excellent museums and stylish scene, and the island's deserted trails and ubiquitous swimming rocks.

2 Aegina (p313) Delving into ancient history at the beautiful Temple of Aphaia and

Byzantine village, Paleohora, then sipping seaside cocktails.

3 Spetses (p327) Taste testing your way through top restaurants, tracing the region's history in the town's museums, or cycling the island's ring road to dip into sparkling bays.

4 Angistri (p317) Getting away from it all in the low season, when the beaches are most tranquil.

5 Poros (p318) Exploring the peaceful, forested interior and strolling the cafe-lined quay in town, or trying out the family-run tavernas.

AEGINA ΑΙΓΙΝΑ

POP 13,056

Beyond its bustling port, Aegina has the seductive, easygoing character of a typical Greek island, but with the added bonus of more than its fair share of prestigious ancient sites. Weekending Athenians spice up the mix of laid-back locals and island-dwelling commuters who use the island like an Athens suburb. Unique Aegina treats include a special – and delicious – pistachio nut, the splendid 5th-century Temple of Aphaia and the magical Byzantine Paleohora ruins.

Aegina was the leading maritime power of the Saronic Gulf during the 7th century BC, when it grew wealthy through trade and political ascendancy. The island made a major contribution to the Greek victory over the Persian fleet at the Battle of Salamis in 480 BC. Despite this solidarity with the Athenian state, the latter invaded in 459 BC out of jealousy of Aegina's wealth and status, and of its liaison with Sparta. Aegina never regained its glory, although in the early 19th century it played a bold part in the defeat of the Turks and was the temporary capital of a partly liberated Greece from 1827 to 1829.

🛈 Getting There & Away

Aegina's main port, Aegina Town, has conventional ferries that you book online at www.saronicferries.gr. They are operated by **Hellenic Seaways** (☑ conventional ferry 22970 22945, high-speed ferry 22970 26777; www.hsw.gr), **Nova Ferries** (☑ 22970 24200; www.novaferries.gr), **Agios Nektarios** (ANES Ferries; ☑ Aegina 22970 25625, Piraeus 21042 25625; www.anes.gr), 2wayferries and Leves Lines. Book high-speed hydrofoils with Hellenic Seaways and **Aegean Flying Dolphins** (☑ 22970 25800) to/from Piraeus and Angistri. Ferries

dock at the large outer quay, with hydrofoils at the smaller inner quay.

Evoikos Lines (☑ Agia Marina 22970 32234, Piraeus 21048 21002, Souvala 22970 52210; www.evoikoslines.gr) serves Aegina's smaller ports Agia Marina and Souvala, and Piraeus in high season only.

Even in winter, high-speed ferries from Piraeus get fully booked for weekends: book ahead.

Angistri Express (p318) makes several daily trips in high season to Skala and Mylos on Angistri. It leaves from midway along Aegina harbour, where timetables are displayed.

Water taxis (☑ 6944535659, 6972229720, 22970 91387) to Piraeus cost about €40 one way, regardless of the number of people.

🛈 Getting Around

BUS

Buses from Aegina Town run several times a day on three routes across the island. Departure times are displayed outside the ticket office on Plateia Ethnegersias (Ethnegersias Sq); you must buy tickets there. Visit www.aeginagreece.com for details.

Agia Marina (€2, 30 minutes), via Paleohora (€2, 15 minutes) and Temple of Aphaia (€2, 25 minutes)

Perdika (€1.80, 15 minutes)

Vagia (€1.80, 25 minutes) via Souvala (€1.80, 20 minutes)

CAR, MOTORCYCLE & BICYCLE

Numerous outfits hire out vehicles. Prices start from €35 per day for cars, €17 for a 50cc motorcycle and €8 for bicycles.

Karagiannis Travel (☑ 22970 28780; www.aeginatravel.gr; Pan Irioti 44; ⊙ 9am-2pm & 5-9pm) Rents vehicles and arranges tours and tickets.

Sklavenas Rent A Car (☑ 22970 22892; Kazantzaki 5; ⊙ 9am-2pm & 5-9pm) For cars,

SARONIC GULF ISLANDS AEGINA

BOAT SERVICES FROM AEGINA

DESTINATION	PORT	DURATION	FARE (€)	FREQUENCY
Angistri (Skala)	Aegina Town	20min	2.80	1-2 daily
Angistri (Skala)*	Aegina Town	10min	6	4-6 daily
Angistri (Mylos)*	Aegina Town	10min	6	5 daily
Methana	Aegina Town	40min	5.70	2-3 daily
Piraeus	Aegina Town	1hr 10min	8-10	hourly
Piraeus*	Aegina Town	40min	14	6 daily
Piraeus	Agia Marina	1hr	10	3-4 daily, summer
Piraeus	Souvala	1hr 35min	8	3-4 daily, summer
Poros	Aegina Town	1hr 50min	8.50	2-3 daily

*high-speed services

Aegina & Angistri

4WDs, scooters, quads and bikes. In Aegina Town, located on the road near the Temple of Apollo. Also has a branch in Agia Marina.

TAXI

Taxi (☑ Aegina Town 22970 22010, Agia Marina 22970 32107) Taxis around Aegina island.

Aegina Town   Αίγινα

POP 8905

Aegina Town's sparkling harbour is backed by a buzzing promenade of people, motorbikes, cafes and restaurants. As you wander back into the narrow town streets, with kids riding bikes and laundry strung from balconies, small-town Greek life takes over again.

The parallel streets backing the harbour, Irioti and Rodi, are crammed with shops of every kind and a few 19th-century neoclassical buildings intermix with whitewashed houses. Ancient Greece is represented by the impressive ruins of the Temple of Apollo, just north of the harbour.

◉ Sights

Temple of Apollo   RUINS

(Kolona; ☑ 22970 22248; http://odysseus.culture. gr; adult/child €3/free; ⊘ 8.30am-3pm Tue-Sun May-Oct, reduced hours Nov-Apr) Northwest of the port, ruined walls, cisterns and broken pillars in honey-coloured stone are lorded over by a solitary surviving column. It's all that's left of a 5th-century-BC temple that was once part of an ancient acropolis (built on a prehistoric site). The informative Sanctuary Museum has translations in English and German.

Folklore Museum MUSEUM
(☑ 22970 26401; http://laografiko.gr; S Rodi; €2; ☉10am-12.30pm & 5.30-8.30pm Fri & Sat) Peruse historic clothing, housewares and artwork re-creating the mood of old-time island life.

✯✯ Festivals & Events

Aegina Fistiki Fest FOOD & DRINK
(www.aeginafistikifest.gr; ☉ Sep) *Fistiki* means 'pistachio' and this three-day brouhaha celebrates Aegina's famous Protected Designation of Origin (PDO) pistachio through music, art and culinary contests.

🛏 Sleeping

Aegina offers a range of solid, simple guesthouses, apartment complexes and a handful of hotels. Book ahead at weekends.

Electra Pension PENSION €
(☑ 22970 26715; www.aegina-electra.gr; Leonardou Lada 25; r €45; ❄ 🛜) There are no views from this small whitewashed pension, but rooms are impeccable and comfy in a quiet corner of the town centre. It outclasses nearby hotels by a long way.

Marianna Studios PENSION €
(☑ 22970 25650; www.aeginastudiosmarianna.com; Kiverniou 16-18; s/d €35/40, d/tr with kitchen €40/45; ❄) Simple, basic rooms and very friendly owners create a top-notch budget choice. Some rooms have balconies or overlook a quiet, leafy garden alongside an interior courtyard. One room has a kitchen.

★ Hotel Rastoni HOTEL €€
(☑ 22970 27039; www.rastoni.gr; Odos Stratigou Dimitri Petriti 31; d/tr/q €80/120/130; 🅿 ❄ @ 🛜) Spacious rooms have balconies overlooking a lovely garden and the Temple of Apollo. Generous breakfasts and friendly staff round out the experience. Find it in a residential neighbourhood a few minutes north of the harbour.

Aegina Hotel HOTEL €€
(☑ 22970 28501; www.aeginahotel.gr; Stratigou Dimitriou Petriti 23; d/tr from €60/70; ❄ 🛜) This 19-room hotel sits about 500m back from the harbour and has clean, well-appointed rooms with refrigerators and TVs.

Aeginitiko Archontiko PENSION €€
(☑ 22970 24968; www.aeginitikoarchontiko.gr; cnr Ag Nikolaou & Thomaidou 1; s/d/tr/ste incl breakfast from €50/60/70/100; ❄ 🛜) The rich character of this centrally located old mansion translates through period 19th-century features, a charming salon and courtyard and a splendid breakfast. Rooms, however, are a bit cramped and worn, and bathrooms are basic. Sea views from the rooftop terrace.

Fistikies Holiday Apartments APARTMENT €€
(☑ 22970 23783; www.fistikies.gr; Logiotatidou 1; studios €90, 4-person apts €120; 🅿 ❄ 🛜 ❄) This complex of tidy, family-friendly apartments was built in 2007 on the southern edge of town, inland from the football field. Spacious apartments have DVD players and terraces overlooking the pool.

🍴 Eating

The harbourfront restaurants make for lazy world-watching, but are not outstanding, unless you hit the unvarnished *ouzeries* (places serving ouzo and light snacks). Aegina's pistachio nuts are on sale everywhere (from €7 for 500g, depending on quality).

Elia MEDITERRANEAN €
(☑ 22975 00205; Koumoundourou 4; mains €6-9; ☉noon-4pm & 6-11pm, hours reduced winter) Burrow into the backstreets to find this excellent restaurant that's popular with locals. Imaginative, fresh specialities include its pistachio pesto and the pittas of the day.

Gelladakis MEZEDHES €
(☑ 22970 27308; Pan Irioti 45; dishes €7-12; ☉lunch & dinner) Ensconced behind the noisy midharbour fish market, this vibrant joint is always thronged with people tucking into charcoal-fired octopus or sardines, plus other classic mezedhes (appetisers).

Tsias TAVERNA €
(☑ 22970 23529; Dimokratias 47; mains €7-10; ☉lunch & dinner) Harbourside eating at its best. Try shrimps with tomatoes and feta, or one of the daily specials.

Kriton Gefsis CRETAN €€
(☑ 22970 26255; www.facebook.com/kritongefsis; cnr Pan Irioti & Damanos; dishes €5-15; ☉10am-2am) Cretan ingredients and flavours are the order of the day at this lively taverna, with fresh seafood featuring; also has live music.

Bakalogatos MEZEDHES €€
(☑ 22975 00501; cnr Pan Irioti & Neoptolemou; mains €7-13; ☉lunch & dinner Tue-Sun) Fresh, well-crafted mezedhes in an elegant setting,

with faux-finished tables and traditional products on the walls.

Drinking & Nightlife

International Corner
BAR

(☑ 22970 26564; cnr I Katsa & S Rodi; ☺ noon-late) Get off the main strip and head to this character-filled, wood-panelled bar room. The gregarious owner takes requests, from top 40 to fantastic Greek music.

Avli
BAR

(☑ 22970 26438; Pan Irioti 17; ☺ 9am-late) This lively restaurant and bar plays tunes from '60s to Greek pop, and has a covered garden that bubbles with activity.

Remvi
BAR

(☑ 22970 28605; Dimokratias 51; ☺ 8am-late; ☎) A popular music cafe-bar that hops day and night.

ⓘ Information

Harbour-front banks have ATMs. Aegina has no tourist office. Check Karagiannis Travel (p313) for car hire, tours and non-Aegina boats.

Hospital (☑ 22970 24489, emergency 22970 22251; Agios Dionisios Nosokomeiou 4)

Port Authority (☑ 22970 22328; Dimokratias) At the entrance to the ferry quays.

Tourist Police (☑ 22970 27777; Leonardou Lada) Up a lane opposite the hydrofoil dock.

ⓘ Getting There & Away

Aegina's main port is located in Aegina Town: it's served by both conventional ferries (book online at www.saronicferries.gr) and high-speed hydrofoils operated by Hellenic Seaways (p313) and Aegean Flying Dolphins (p313).

ⓘ Getting Around

There is a hub of local buses and water taxis at the main port.

ⓘ ISLAND HOPPING

No direct ferries connect Aegina and Angistri with Hydra and Spetses; go via Piraeus or Poros. For day trips, take the Hydra–Poros–Aegina cruise from Piraeus with **Athens One Day Cruise** (☑ 210 451 6106; www.athensonedaycruise.com; cruise adult/child €99/56, with transfers €109) or **Evermore Cruises** (☑ 211 188 2220; www.evermorecruises.com; cruise adult/child €99/56, with transfers €109). Pegasus Cruises (p149) goes from Nafplio to Spetses and Hydra.

Around Aegina Town

Aegina is lush and wildflower-laden in spring, and year-round offers some of the best archaic sites in the Saronic Gulf. The interior hills and mountains add drama to the small island, but beaches are not its strongest suit. The east-coast town of Agia Marina is the island's main package resort. It has a shallow-water beach that is ideal for families, but it's backed by a fairly crowded main drag. A few thin, sandy beaches, such as Marathonas, line the roadside between Aegina Town and Perdika.

⊙ Sights

★ Paleohora
CHURCH, RUIN

(Παλαιοχώρα) **FREE** This enchanting remote hillside is dotted with the remains of a Byzantine village. More than 30 surviving churches punctuate the rocky heights of the original citadel, and several have been refurbished. They are linked by a network of paths, carpeted with wildflowers in spring. The ancient town of Paleohora was Aegina's capital from the 9th century through the medieval period and was only abandoned during the 1820s.

Paleohora is 6.5km east of Aegina Town, near enormous modern church Moni Agiou Nektariou. Buses from Aegina Town to Agia Marina stop at the turn-off to Paleohora (10 minutes); taxis cost €8 one way.

★ Temple of Aphaia
TEMPLE

(☑ 22970 32398; http://odysseus.culture.gr; adult/child €4/free; ☺ 9.30am-4.30pm, museum 10.30am-1.30pm Tue-Sun) The well-preserved remains of this impressive temple stand proudly on a pine-covered hill with far-reaching views over the Saronic Gulf. Built in 480 BC, it celebrates a local deity of pre-Hellenic times. The temple's pediments were originally decorated with splendid Trojan War sculptures, most of which were stolen in the 19th century and now decorate Munich's Glyptothek. Panels throughout the site are also in English.

Aphaia is 10km east of Aegina Town. Infrequent buses to Agia Marina stop here (20 minutes); taxis cost about €12 one way.

Christos Capralos Museum
MUSEUM

(☑ 22970 22001; Nikou Kazantzaki (Coast Rd), Livadi; €2; ☺ 10am-2pm & 6-8pm Tue-Sun Jun-Oct, 10am-2pm Fri-Sun Nov-May) The home and studio of acclaimed sculptor Christos Capralos (1909–93), on the coast near Livadi, 1.5km north of Aegina Town, has been made into a

PERDIKA ΠΕΡΔΙΚΑ

The quaint fishing village of Perdika lies about 9km south of Aegina Town on the southern tip of the west coast and makes for a relaxed sojourn.

Perdika's harbour is very shallow so, for the best swimming, catch one of the regular caïques (little boats; return adult/child €5/free) to the small island of Moni, a few minutes offshore. A nature reserve, it has a tree-lined beach and summertime cafe.

Tavernas line Perdika's raised harbour-front terrace, and sultry sunset relaxation makes way for buzzing nightlife when late-night music bars rev into gear during summer.

Villa Rodanthos (☑6944250138, 22970 61400; www.villarodanthos.com; studios from €55; ❇☎) is a gem of a place, not least because of its charming owner. Each room has its own colourful decor and a kitchen.

The most locally popular of Perdika's quayside tavernas, **Miltos** (☑22970 61051; mains €12-15; ☺noon-4pm & 6pm-late) is known for the highest-quality seafood and no-nonsense Greek staples.

museum displaying many of his fluid, powerful works. Monumental sculptures include the 40m-long *Pindus Frieze*.

ANGISTRI ΑΓΚΙΣΤΡΙ

POP 1142

Tiny Angistri lies a few kilometres off the west coast of Aegina and, out of high season, its mellow lanes and azure coves make a rewarding day trip or longer escape.

The port-resort village of **Skala** is crammed with small hotels, apartments, tavernas and cafes, but life, in general, still ticks along gently. A right turn from the quay leads to the small harbour beach and then to a church on a low headland. Beyond lies the best beach on the island, but it disappears beneath sun loungers and broiling bodies in July and August. Turning left from the quay at Skala takes you south along a dirt path through the pine trees to the pebbly and clothing-optional Halikadha Beach.

About 1km west from Skala, Angistri's other port, Mylos (Megalochori), has an appealing traditional character, rooms and tavernas, but no beach.

Aponissos has turquoise waters, a small offshore island and a reliably tasty taverna. Limenaria has deeper green waters. The entire island is supersleepy in low season.

🛏 Sleeping & Eating

Book ahead, especially for August and summer weekends. A board on Skala's quay lists a range of small guesthouses and hotels.

Alkyoni Inn PENSION €
(☑22970 91378; www.alkyoni-agistri.com; s/d/ maisonettes from €30/45/60; ☺Easter-Sep;

❇☎) This recently refurbished pension offers some sea-facing rooms with fabulous, unobstructed views. Two-storey family maisonettes sleep up to four. Its taverna is very popular too.

★**Rosy's Little Village** PENSION €€
(☑22970 91610; www.rosyslittlevillage.com; s/d/tr/q from €65/73/83/108; ❇☎) A complex of simple Cycladic-style cubes steps gently down to the sea, a short way east of Skala's quay. Full of light and colour, with built-in couches and tiny balconies with sea views, Rosy's also offers mountain bikes, summer courses, weekly picnics and live-music evenings. Its restaurant (mains €8 to €18, open lunch and dinner) emphasises organics.

Akrogiali Hotel HOTEL €€
(☑22970 91354; www.akrogiali-agistri.gr; Skala; d from €65; ☺Apr-Oct; ❇☎) Just a quick hop from the ferry dock, this modern beachfront hotel has tidy rooms with colourful, tasteful decor.

Nontas Hotel HOTEL €€
(☑22970 91212; www.facebook.com/NontasHotel Agistri/; Mylos; d from €65; ☺Apr-Oct; ❇☎) This space-age-looking hotel is best for its sea-facing modern rooms and proximity to local cafes and tavernas.

Alkyoni Inn TAVERNA €
(☑22970 91378; www.alkyoni-agistri.com; mains €7-15; ☺8am-10pm Easter-Sep; ❇☎🍴) The welcoming, family-run Alkyoni is a 10-minute stroll southeast of Skala's quay. The popular taverna dishes up well-prepared fish and meat, while the refurbished pension offers sea-facing rooms and family maisonettes.

❶ Information

There's a bank with ATM on Skala's main street. Visit www.agistri.com.gr for island information.

❶ Getting There & Away

Fast Aegean Flying Dolphins (p313) and Hellenic Seaways (p313) hydrofoils and car ferries (www.saronicferries.gr) come from Piraeus (hydrofoil/ferry €14.50/10.90, 55 minutes/1½ hours) via Aegina (hydrofoils €6, 10 minutes, four to six daily; ferry €2.80, 20 minutes, one to two daily) to either Skala or Mylos. **Angistri Express** (☎ 6934347867) serves Aegina several times daily, Monday to Saturday.

Water taxis (p313) cost €45 one way between Aegina and Angistri.

❶ Getting Around

Several **buses** (☎ 6973016132, 22970 91244; Skala) a day during summer run from Skala and Mylos (Megalochori) to Limenaria and Dhragonera Beach. It's worth hiring a scooter (€15) or sturdy bike (€7) to explore the coast road.

You can also follow tracks from Metohi overland through cool pine forest to reach Dhragonera Beach. Take a compass; tracks divide often and route-finding can be frustrating.

Kostas Bike Hire (☎ 22970 91021; Skala)

Takis Rent a Bike & Bicycles (Logothetis; ☎ 22970 91001; www.agistri.com.gr/logothetis; Mylos)

Taxi (☎ 6977618040, 22970 91455; Skala)

POROS   ΠΟΡΟΣ

POP 3800

Poros is separated from the mountainous Peloponnese by a narrow sea channel, and its protected setting makes the main settlement of Poros Town seem like a cheery lakeside resort. Its pastel-hued houses stack up the hillside to a clock tower and make a vibrant first impression.

Poros is made up of two land masses connected by a tiny isthmus: Sferia, which is occupied mainly by the town of Poros; and

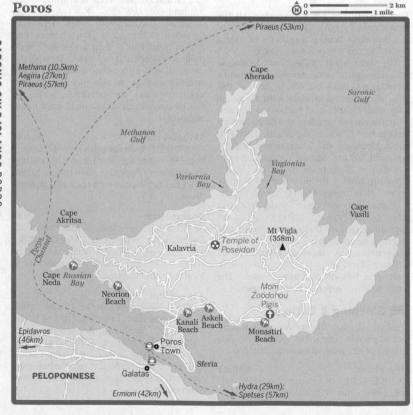

Poros

0 ——— 2 km
0 ——— 1 mile

Piraeus (53km)

Methana (10.5km);
Aegina (27km);
Piraeus (57km)

Cape Aherado

Saronic Gulf

Methanon Gulf

Vagionias Bay

Variarnia Bay

Cape Vasili

Cape Akritsa

Poros Channel

Mt Vigla (358m) ▲

Kalavria

Temple of Poseidon

Cape Neda

Russian Bay

Neorion Beach

Moni Zoödohou Pigis

Epidavros (46km)

Kanali Beach

Askeli Beach

Monastiri Beach

Poros Town

Sferia

PELOPONNESE

Galatas

Ermioni (42km)

Hydra (29km);
Spetses (57km)

the much larger and mainly forested Kalavria, which has the island's beaches and seasonal hotels scattered along its southern shore. Poros still maintains a sense of remoteness in its sparsely populated, forested interior.

The Peloponnesian town of Galatas lies on the opposite shore, making Poros a useful base from which to explore the ancient sites of the Peloponnese. For example, the exquisite ancient theatre of Epidavros (p153) is within reach by car or **taxi** (⏺in Galatas 22980 42888).

❶ Getting There & Away

Daily ferries (www.saronicferries.gr) connect Piraeus to Poros in summer (reduced timetable in winter). High-speed Hellenic Seaways (p313) ferries continue south to Hydra, Spetses, Ermioni and Porto Heli. Conventional ferries connect Aegina to Poros and Methana on the mainland. Travel agents (p320) sell tickets.

Caïques shuttle constantly between Poros and Galatas (€1, five minutes). They leave from the quay opposite Plateia Iroön, the triangular plaza near the main ferry dock in Poros Town. Hydrofoils dock about 50m north of here. Car ferries to Galatas (per person/car €1/6, from 7.30am to 10.40pm) leave from the dock several hundred metres north again, on the road to Kalavria.

You can also do a one-way rental between branches of **Pop's Car** (⏺in Galatas 22980 42910; www.popscar.gr) at Athens Airport and Galatas (or Ermioni).

❶ Getting Around

BOAT
Caïques go to beaches around the island during summer.

BUS
A bus (€3) operates mid-June to October every hour from 7am until midnight on a route that starts next to the kiosk at the eastern end of Plateia Iroön. It crosses to Kalavria and goes east along the south coast for ten minutes as far as Moni Zoödohou Pigis (p320), then turns around and heads west to Neorion Beach (15 minutes). Buy tickets from the kiosk.

MOTORCYCLE & BICYCLE
Several places on the road to Kalavria rent out bicycles, scooters and all-terrain vehicles (ATVs; per day from €6/20/30).
Moto Fotis (⏺22980 25873; www.motofotis-poros.gr; Kanali; ☺9am-9pm) Rents bicycles, motorbikes and ATVs.
Moto Stelios (⏺22980 23026; www.moto stelios.gr; Harbour, Poros Town; ☺9am-9pm) Rents ATVs, scooters and bicycles in Poros harbour and Askeli beach.

TAXI
Taxi (⏺22980 23003) Standard taxi fares are posted at the main stand on the quay.

Poros Town   Πόρος
POP 3651

Zippy Poros Town is a mishmash of charming ice-cream-coloured houses that look out across the narrow channel at Galatas and the shapely mountains of the Peloponnese. Sailing boats bob along the lengthy quay, while ferries glide through the channel and smaller vessels scurry to and fro. Behind the harbour, *plateies* (squares) and tavernas hide from view and a rocky bluff rises steeply to a crowning clock tower.

◉ Sights

Archaeological Museum of Poros   MUSEUM
(⏺22980 23276; http://odysseus.culture.gr; Harbourfront, Plateia Koryzi; €2; ☺8.30am-3pm Tue-Sun) This small museum on the waterfront shows a beautiful collection of classic Greek sculpture from the area.

Citronne   GALLERY
(⏺22980 22401; www.citronne.com; Leof Papadopoulou; ☺10am-3pm Mon-Sat Jun-Aug) This bright and cheerful local gallery shows artists from around Greece.

⛱ Sleeping

⭐**Seven Brothers Hotel**   HOTEL €
(⏺22980 23412; www.7brothers.gr; Poros Harbour; s/d/tr €50/55/60; ❄⏺) Conveniently close to the hydrofoil quay, this modern hotel has bright, comfy rooms with superduper bathrooms. Some have small balconies, some sea views.

Georgia Mellou Rooms   PENSION €
(⏺22980 22309; http://porosnet.gr/gmellou; Plateia Georgiou; d/tr €40/45; ❄⏺) Simple, old-fashioned rooms tucked into the heart of the old town, next to the cathedral, high above the harbour. The charming owner keeps everything shipshape. Book ahead for fantastic views from the west-side rooms.

Hotel Manessi   BUSINESS HOTEL €
(⏺22980 22273; www.manessi.com; Harbourfront; d from €55; ❄@⏺) Well placed at the midpoint of the harbour, the Manessi is a bit worn in places, but offers clean business-style rooms, some with sea views.

Sto Roloi   APARTMENT €€
(⏺6932427267, 22980 25808; www.storoloi-poros.gr; studio/apt/houses from €63/105/155; ❄)

Roloi is a good source for tidy apartments and houses around Poros Town.

✕ Eating

Dimitris Family Taverna
TAVERNA €

(☎22980 23709; www.dimitrisfamily-poros.gr; mains €6-14; ☺6-10pm or 11pm) Renowned for its meat, this taverna's owners have a butchering business, so cuts of pork, lamb and chicken are of the finest quality. It's up the hill in the centre of town; ask a local for directions.

Taverna Karavolos
TAVERNA €

(☎22980 26158; www.karavolos.com; mains €6-12; ☺7-11pm) Karavolos means 'big snail' and snails are a house speciality at this quaint eatery on a backstreet. Friendly proprietors also offer classic Greek meat dishes and some fish, as well as **rooms** (double/triple €35/45) upstairs.

Poseidon
SEAFOOD €€

(☎22980 23597; www.poseidontaverna.gr; Harbourfront; mains €7-15; ☺9.30am-12.30am Easter-Oct) A quayside favourite for delicious seafood, friendly service and occasional Greek dancing.

Oasis
TAVERNA €€

(☎22980 22955; Harbourfront; mains €7-14; ☺10am-1am) Hang out harbourside and feast on home-cooked Greek staples and seafood.

❶ Information

Banks on Plateia Iroön have ATMs. Poros has no tourist office. Harbour-front agencies arrange accommodation, car hire, tours and cruises.

Family Tours (☎22980 23743; www.family tours.gr; Harbourfront; ☺9am-2pm & 5-10pm) Sells conventional-ferry tickets.

Marinos Tours (☎22980 23423; www.marinos tours.gr; Harbourfront; ☺7am-9.30pm Apr-Oct, to 7pm Nov-Mar) Across from the hydrofoil quay; sells hydrofoil tickets.

Tourist Police (☎22980 22256; Dimosthenous 10) Behind the high school.

Around Poros

◉ Sights & Activities

Poros' best beaches include the pebbly Kanali Beach, on Kalavria islet 1km east of the bridge, and the long, sandy Askeli Beach, about 500m further east.

Neorion Beach, 3km west of the bridge, has waterskiing, and banana-boat and air-chair rides. The best beach is at Russian Bay, 1.5km past Neorion.

Temple of Poseidon
RUINS

(☎22980 23276; ☺8.30am-3pm) **FREE** There's very little left of this 6th-century temple. Once it was a magnificent building giving sanctuary to fugitives and wrecked sailors, but in the 18th century it was mostly dismantled and the materials used to build a monastery on Hydra. Still, the walk or drive to the site gives superb views of the Saronic Gulf and the Peloponnese.

With your own wheels, from the road near Moni Zoödohou Pigis, head inland to reach the ruins. Then you can continue along the road and circle back to the bridge onto Sferia. It's about 6km in total.

Moni Zoödohou Pigis
MONASTERY

(☺9am-noon & 2.30-6pm) The 18th-century 'Monastery of the Life-giving Spring', well signposted 4km east of Poros Town, has a beautiful gilded iconostasis (a screen bearing icons) from Asia Minor.

Passage
WATER SPORTS

(☎22980 42540; www.passage.gr; Neorion Bay; lesson from €45) A popular waterskiing school and slalom centre.

🛏 Sleeping & Eating

★ Sirene Blue Resort
RESORT €€

(☎22980 22741; www.sirenebluresort.gr; Monastiri Beach; d/tr incl breakfast from €120/150; ❋☎☒) Sirene Blue Resort offers a deluxe

BOAT SERVICES FROM POROS

DESTINATION	DURATION	FARE (€)	FREQUENCY
Aegina	1¼hr	8.50	2-5 daily
Hydra*	30min	13.50	4-5 daily
Methana	30min	4.30	2-3 daily
Piraeus	2½hr	11.50-14	2-3 daily
Piraeus*	1hr	24.50	4-5 daily
Spetses*	1½hr	16	4 daily

*high-speed services

seaside vacation, from sparkling pool to crisp linens. Find it at Monastiri Beach, near Moni Zoödohou Pigis.

Hotel New Aegli　　　　　　　HOTEL €€
(☑ 22980 22372; www.newaegli.com; Askeli Beach; d from €95; ☉ Apr-Oct; ❄@🛜🌊) Poros' best beaches include the long, sandy Askeli Beach. Hotel New Aegli, across the road from the beach, is a decent resort-style hotel and offers good, modern rooms, many with sea views.

★**Aspros Gatos**　　　　　SEAFOOD, TAVERNA €€
(☑ 22980 24274; Labraki 49; mains €6-15; ☉ noon-11pm Easter-Oct) A short walk from town, 400m west of the bridge on the road to Neorion Beach, Poros' best seafood taverna sits smack out over the water. Watch the local kayaking team do its thing as the jolly owner provides anything from bolognese to the catch of the day.

HYDRA ΥΔΡΑ
POP 1966

Hydra is truly the gem of the Saronic Gulf and stands alone among Greek islands as the one free of wheeled vehicles. No cars. No scooters. Just tiny marble-cobbled lanes, donkeys, rocks and sea. Artists (Brice Marden, Nikos Chatzikyriakos-Ghikas, Panayiotis Tetsis), musicians (Leonard Cohen), actors and celebrities (Melina Mercouri, Sophia Loren) have all been drawn to Hydra over the years. In addition to the island's exquisitely preserved stone architecture, criss-crossing rural paths and clear, deep waters, you can find a good cappuccino along the harbour, which is great for people-watching.

History

Hydra was sparsely populated in ancient times and is just mentioned in passing by Herodotus. The most significant evidence of settlement dates from Mycenaean times. But in the 16th century, Hydra became a refuge for people fleeing skirmishes between the Venetians and the Ottomans. Many hailed from the area of modern-day Albania.

By the mid-1700s the settlers began building boats and took to the thin line between maritime commerce and piracy with enthusiasm. They travelled as far as Egypt and the Black Sea and ran the British blockade (1803–15) during the Napoleonic Wars. As a result of steady tax paying, the island experienced only light interference under the Ottoman Empire. By the 19th century,

Hydra had become a full-blown maritime power, and wealthy shipping merchants had built most of the town's grand mansions. At its height in 1821, the island's population reached 28,000. Hydra supplied 130 ships for a blockade of the Turks during the Greek War of Independence and the island bred such leaders as Admiral Andreas Miaoulis, who commanded the Greek fleet, and Georgios Koundouriotis, president of Greece's national assembly from 1822 to 1827.

❶ Getting There & Away

High-speed **Hellenic Seaways** (www.hsw.gr) ferries link Hydra with Poros, Piraeus and Spetses, and Ermioni and Porto Heli on the Peloponnese. Service is greatly reduced in winter. Buy tickets from **Hydreoniki Travel** (☑ 22980 54007; www.hydreoniki.gr; ☉ 7am-10pm or around ferry departures), up the lane to the right of the Alpha Bank in Hydra Town.

　Freedom (☑ 6947325263, 6944242141; www.hydralines.gr) boats run between Hydra and Metohi (little more than a car park) on the mainland (€6.50, 15 minutes, five to 11 daily). The schedule is posted on the quay and online.

❶ Getting Around

Generally, people get around Hydra by walking.

　The island is vehicle-free, and mules and donkeys are the main means of heavy transport. Donkey owners are clustered around the port; they transport luggage to the hotels and provide quick donkey rides around the port. Note that animal rights groups urge people to consider whether the animals are maltreated before deciding to take a ride.

　In summer, caïques (little boats) from Hydra Town go to the island's beaches. **Water-taxi** (☑ 22980 53690) fares are posted on the quay (Kamini €10, Vlyhos €15).

Hydra Town Υδρα
POP 1900

Life in Hydra centres around the gorgeous port. Whether you sail or ferry in, the sparkling boat-filled harbour and the bright light striking the tiers of carefully preserved stone houses make a lasting impression. The harbour in high season is an ecosystem of its own, with yachts, caïques (little boats) and water taxis zipping in and out. The marble quay is a surging rhythm of donkeys, visitors, cafe denizens and boat-taxi hawkers. By night the scene becomes a promenade: grab a chair, order a drink and watch the world go by.

Hydra

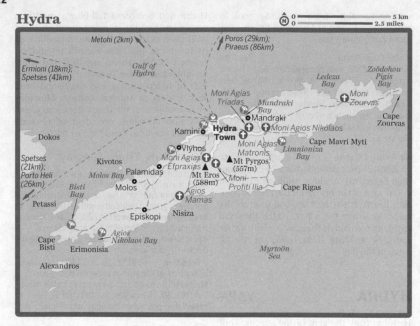

If you head back into the warren of portside houses, to the steep slopes banking away from the town centre, you get a different view on Hydriot life. Grandmothers chat in quiet lanes about what's for dinner, and roads peter out into dirt paths that head into the mountains, ever-changing in colour, depending on the time of day.

◉ Sights

Melina Mercouri Exhibition Hall and Deste Foundation host high-season art shows.

★ Kimisis Tis Theotokou
Cathedral   CHURCH
(Metropolis; Harbour; ⊙7am-7pm) Housed in the peaceful monastery complex on the harbour, this lovely cathedral dates from the 17th century and has a Tinian-marble bell tower. Its **Ecclesiastical Museum** (⊉22980 54071; www.imhydra.gr/mouseio_main.htm; adult/child €2/free; ⊙10am-5pm Tue-Sun Apr-Nov) contains a collection of icons and vestments. The monastery complex is also known as Faneromeni. Dress appropriately (covered shoulders, long skirts or pants) to enter.

★ Deste Foundation   GALLERY
(www.deste.gr) FREE Deste Foundation hosts an annual Hydra exhibit at the small former slaughterhouse on the sea.

★ Lazaros Koundouriotis
Historical Mansion   MUSEUM
(⊉22980 52421; www.nhmuseum.gr; adult/child €4/free; ⊙10am-4pm Tue-Sun Mar-Oct) Hydra's star cultural attraction is this handsome ochre-coloured *arhontiko* (stone mansion) high above the harbour. It was home to one of the major figures in the Greek independence struggle and is an exquisite example of late 18th-century traditional architecture, featuring original furnishings, folk costumes, handicrafts and a painting exhibition.

Historical Archives
Museum of Hydra   MUSEUM
(⊉22980 52355; www.iamy.gr; Harbour; adult/child €5/3; ⊙9am-4pm) This fine harbourfront museum houses an extensive collection of portraits and naval artefacts, with an emphasis on the island's role in the War of Independence. It hosts temporary exhibitions in summer, and concerts on the rooftop terrace.

🏃 Activities

Harriet's Hydra Horses   HORSE RIDING
(⊉6980323347; www.harrietshydrahorses.com; 1/2/8hr tour €25/55/175) Harriet, a friendly, bilingual British-Greek local, guides licensed horse-riding tours (from one to eight hours) around the island, to the monasteries and to the beaches.

Vasilis Kokkos BOATING
(☑ 6977649789; bkokkos@yahoo.com) Vasilis Kokkos, proprietor of Caprice (p325) restaurant and boat captain, rents speedboats (per day €80 to €250) and a sailing boat (by prior arrangement; one-week minimum from €900). Licence required.

✻✥ Festivals & Events

Miaoulia Festival CULTURAL
(◷ weekend around 21 Jun) Celebration of Admiral Miaoulis and the Hydriot contribution to the War of Independence, with a spectacular boat burning (with fireworks) in Hydra harbour.

🛏 Sleeping

Accommodation in Hydra is of a high standard, but you pay accordingly. Most owners will meet you at the harbour and organise luggage transfer.

Piteoussa PENSION €
(☑ 22980 52810; www.piteoussa.com; Kouloura; d €50-70; ❄🛜) Jolly owners maintain beautiful rooms in two buildings on a quiet, pine-tree-lined street. Rooms in the restored corner mansion have period character and all the modern amenities you need, while the smaller rooms in the second building were renovated in 2010 and have a mod feel.

Pension Erofili PENSION €
(☑ 22980 54049; www.pensionerofili.gr; Tombazi; s/d/tr from €45/55/97; ❄🛜) Tucked in the inner town, these pleasant, unassuming rooms are a good deal for Hydra. Also has a studio with kitchen.

Hotel Sophia BOUTIQUE HOTEL €€
(☑ 22980 52313; www.hotelsophia.gr; Harbourfront; d incl breakfast €85-115; ◷ Apr-Oct; ❄🛜) Gorgeous small rooms sit right on the harbour and some have balconies. Each has been painstakingly outfitted with all the mod cons, and bathrooms are luscious marble. Some rooms are two storeys.

Angelica Hotel BOUTIQUE HOTEL €€
(☑ 22980 53202; www.angelica.gr; Miaouli; d/tr/q incl breakfast from €130/180/220; ❄🛜) An attractive boutique hotel in a quiet location, the Angelica is popular for its comfortable, luxurious rooms and spacious, impeccable bathrooms. Superior rooms have balconies. Relax in the spa or courtyard.

Mastoris Mansion BOUTIQUE HOTEL €€
(Ξενώνας Αρχοντικό του Μάστορη; ☑ 22980 29631; www.mastoris-hydra.gr; d/tr from €100/150) One of the most recent entries on Hydra's hotel scene, this renovated stone building in the centre of town offers plush doubles and triples. While convenient to harbour action, rooms don't have views.

Nereids PENSION €€
(☑ 22980 52875; www.nereids-hydra.com; Kouloura; d from €70; ❄🛜) This carefully restored stone house contains lovely rooms of exceptional value and quality. Spacious, peaceful and with beautiful decor, rooms have open views to Hydra's rocky heights and top-floor rooms have sea views.

Amaryllis Hotel HOTEL €€
(☑ 22980 53611; www.amarillishydra.gr; Tombazi 15; s/d €45/60; ❄🛜) Simple rooms, a friendly owner and a super location right in the heart of town make this a safe midrange bet. Shared kitchen too.

★ Cotommatae BOUTIQUE HOTEL €€€
(☑ 22980 53873; www.cotommatae.gr; d/f incl breakfast from €170/250; ❄) This restored mansion has retained the character and some of the memorabilia of the original family while adding impeccable modern touches. Some suites have private terraces or a spa.

★ Hydra Hotel APARTMENT €€€
(☑ 6985910717, 22980 53420; www.hydra-hotel.gr; Petrou Voulgari 8; studio incl breakfast €175-265, maisonettes €255; ❄🛜) Climb high on the south side of the port to swishy, top-of-the-line apartments in an impeccably renovated ancient mansion with kitchenettes and

BOAT SERVICES FROM HYDRA

DESTINATION	DURATION	FARE (€)	FREQUENCY
Ermioni*	20-40min	8	3 daily
Piraeus*	1¾hr	28	4-6 daily
Poros*	30min	13	4 daily
Porto Heli*	1hr	16.50	4 daily
Spetses*	40min	11.50	4-5 daily

*high-speed services

Hydra Town

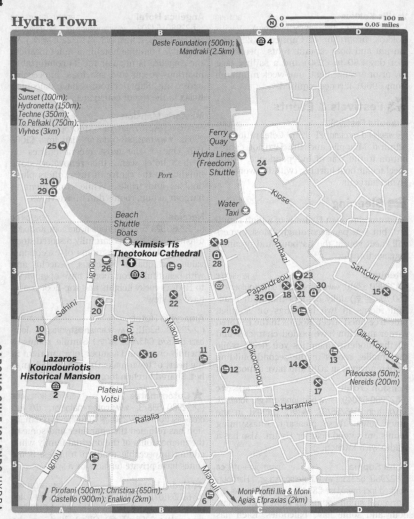

Port

Kimisis Tis Theotokou Cathedral

Lazaros Koundouriotis Historical Mansion

Sunset (100m); Hydronetta (150m); Techne (350m); To Pefkaki (750m); Vlyhos (3km)

Deste Foundation (500m); Mandraki (2.5km)

Ferry Quay

Hydra Lines (Freedom) Shuttle

Water Taxi

Beach Shuttle Boats

Kiose

Tombazi

Sahtouri

Papandreou

Sahini

Votsi

Miaouli

Oikonomou

Gika Kouloura

Piteoussa (50m); Nereids (200m)

S Haramis

Lignou

Plateia Votsi

Rafalia

Lignou

Miaouli

Pirofani (500m); Christina (650m); Castello (900m); Enalion (2km)

Moni Profiti Ilia & Moni Agias Efpraxias (2km)

SARONIC GULF ISLANDS HYDRA

sweeping views. Get room 202 for a tiny balcony with panoramas to die for.

Leto Hotel
HOTEL €€€

(☎22980 53385; www.letohydra.gr; Rigillis 8; d/ste from €177/485) This proper hotel is family-owned with formal rooms and all the services. It also offers a rarity in Greece: a wheelchair-accessible room, served by ramps all the way from the harbour.

Douskos Guest House
PENSION €€€

(☎22980 53845; www.douskosguesthouse.gr; d/tr from €180/190) Clean lines and clock-tower views are part of this new guesthouse just back from the harbour. Bathrooms are top-

notch and owners also operate a popular local restaurant.

✗ Eating

Flora's
SWEETS €

(Anemoni; ☎22980 53136; Plateia Votsi; sweets from €1; ⊙9am-late) Flora's sweet shop on inland Plateia Votsi makes *galaktoboureko* (custard slice), rice pudding and ice cream from local goats' milk.

Zefyros
TAVERNA €

(☎22980 52008; Miaouli; mains €5-9; ⊙noon-10pm) Lovely Amalia and her family serve up classic Greek dishes in a low-key dining room

Hydra Town

◎ **Top Sights**
1 Kimisis Tis Theotokou Cathedral B3
2 Lazaros Koundouriotis Historical
   Mansion A4

◎ **Sights**
3 Ecclesiastical Museum B3
4 Historical Archives Museum of Hydra ..C1

🛏 **Sleeping**
5 Amaryllis Hotel C3
6 Angelica Hotel B5
7 Cotommatae A5
8 Douskos Guest House B4
9 Hotel Sophia B3
10 Hydra Hotel A4
11 Leto Hotel B4
12 Mastoris Mansion C4
13 Pension Erofili D4

🍽 **Eating**
14 Barba Dimas C4
15 Caprice D3

16 Flora's B4
17 Il Casta D4
18 Ke Kremmidi C3
19 Oraia Hydra C3
20 Ostria A3
21 Paradosiako C3
22 Zefyros B3

🍷 **Drinking & Nightlife**
23 Amalour C3
24 Isalos C2
25 Papagalos A2
26 Pirate A3

🎭 **Entertainment**
27 Cinema Club of Hydra C4

🛍 **Shopping**
28 Elena Votsi C3
29 Sirens A2
30 Sugarfree D3
31 Svoura A2
32 Turquoise C3

just back from the port. Look in the glass case to see the day's specials. German expats also say it's got the best schnitzel on the island.

Ke Kremmidi GREEK €
(☑ 22980 53099; Tombazi; gyros €2.50, mains €6-9; ⊙ noon-late) This friendly souvlaki joint has tables spilling out onto a busy pedestrian way and offers up good salads and grilled-meat plates as well.

Ostria TAVERNA €
(Stathis & Tassoula; ☑ 22980 54077; mains €5-8; ⊙ noon-4pm & 6.30pm-late) Often referred to by just the gregarious owners' names 'Stathis & Tassoula', this year-round taverna serves only what's fresh: put the menu to one side and ask. You might be served chicken cutlets or fava or zucchini balls. Stathis catches his own sweet and delicious calamari.

Paradosiako TAVERNA €
(☑ 22980 54155; Tombazi; mains €5-15; ⊙ noon-11.30pm Easter-Nov) This little streetside spot is traditional Greek personified. Sit on the corner terrace to watch the people parade as you dig into classic mezedhes – perhaps beetroot salad with garlic dip – or meats and seafood, such as fresh, filleted and grilled sardines.

★ **Oraia Hydra** GREEK €€
(☑ 22980 52556; Harbourfront; mains €9-18; ⊙ noon-midnight) Oraia Hydra translates as 'Beautiful Hydra' and this small bistro lives right up to its name. You'll dine on the harbour with sailboats bobbing alongside and

enjoy Greek dishes elevated by top ingredients and creative twists.

★ **Il Casta** ITALIAN €€
(☑ 22980 52967; Tombazi; mains €10-22; ⊙ noon-11pm) Dine al fresco and enjoy authentic Italian food like owner Pietro's Neapolitan grandmother used to make. Menus change daily. Reserve in high season.

★ **Sunset** MEDITERRANEAN €€
(☑ 22980 52067; mains €9-25; ⊙ noon-11pm Easter-Oct) Famed for its splendid panoramic spot near the cannons to the west of the harbour, Sunset has fine, fresh cuisine. Tasty salads, inventive pastas and local fish are prepared with flair and a hint of elegance.

Barba Dimas MEZEDHES €€
(☑ 22980 52967; Tombazi; small dishes €4-12; ⊙ 6-11pm) Tables line a small lane, back from the portside fray, and dishes run the gamut of Greek mezedhes, from tender calamari to greens picked from the mountains.

Caprice ITALIAN €€
(☑ 22980 52454; Sahtouri; mains €9-15; ⊙ 6pm-midnight Apr-Oct) A chance for romantic candlelit dining with a solid repertoire of Italian dishes, some using freshly made pasta.

🍸 Drinking & Nightlife

Prices are high, but lively people-watching comes with your coffee or cocktail. The harbour revs up after midnight.

SARONIC GULF ISLANDS HYDRA

★ Pirate
CAFE

(☑22980 52711; www.thepiratebar.gr; Harbourfront; ☺8am-late) Friendly Wendy and Takis and their kids, Zeus and occasionally Zara, run this daytime cafe with first-rate coffee, some of the island's most delicious breakfasts and home-cooked lunches (9am to 5pm), then morph it into a raging party place at night. Music changes with the crowd and the mood.

★ Hydronetta
BAR

(☑22980 54160; www.hydronetta.gr; ☺noon-11pm Easter-Oct) You can't beat this gorgeous waterfront location on the swimming rocks to the far west of the harbour. Brothers Andreas and Elias provide snazzy cocktails and lunch (high season only) with a smile.

Papagalos
BAR

(☑22980 52626; Harbourfront; ☺9am-late) Papagalos is just that bit away from the madding crowd, on the quieter side of the harbour. By day, it offers coffee and basic food, and by night, cocktails and a clear view of the moonrise.

Isalos
CAFE

(☑22980 29661; www.isaloshydra.gr; Harbourfront; ☺7am-late) Isalos makes exceptional coffee and a solid run of sandwiches and pastas.

Amalour
COCKTAIL BAR

(☑22980 53800; Tombazi; ☺7pm-late Jun-Aug, reduced hours Sep-May) A lively line in cocktails, relaxed outdoor seating and dancing inside after midnight.

☆ Entertainment

Cinema Club of Hydra
CINEMA, THEATRE

(☑22980 53105; http://cineclubhydras.blogspot.com; Oikonomou) In July and August the open-air cinema screens blockbusters and indie flicks. It also organises excursions to plays at the ancient theatre of Epidavros (p153).

🔒 Shopping

Sirens
CLOTHING

(☑22980 53340; Harbourfront; ☺10am-10pm Easter-Oct) Charming owner Elena offers unique island-friendly, high-end fashion and Greek-designed jewellery.

Sugarfree
CLOTHING

(☑22980 53352; www.sugarfreeshops.com; Tombazi; ☺11am-11pm May-Nov) Youthful beach- and loungewear created by Greek designers fill this sparkling white shop just back from Amalour bar, on the way to the Bratsera Hotel. Prices are reasonable by local standards and the colours dazzling.

Svoura
ARTS & CRAFTS

(☑22980 29784; Harbourfront; ☺10am-11pm Apr-Oct) Carefully curated ceramics from all over Greece plus a smattering of fashion make this one of Hydra's top shops.

Elena Votsi
JEWELLERY

(☑22980 52637; www.elenavotsi.com; Harbourfront; ☺10am-11.30pm) Hydra native Votsi is renowned for her original, bold designs using exquisite semiprecious stones, which sell in New York and London. She designed the Athens Olympic Games medal.

Turquoise
FASHION & ACCESSORIES

(☑22980 54033; www.turquoise.gr; ☺10am-10pm Jun-Aug, reduced hours Sep-May) Local designer Dimitris creates an annual line of womenswear and accessories using intricate Indian block prints.

ℹ Information

ATMs are at harbour-front banks. There's no tourist office on Hydra.

Hospital (☑22980 53150; Votsi) Basic hospital with an X-ray machine.

Post Office (☺7.30am-2pm Mon-Fri) On the small, internal market square.

Tourist Police (☑22980 52205) Shares an office with regular police.

Around Hydra

Hydra's mountainous, arid interior makes a robust but peaceful contrast to the clamour of the quayside. A useful map for walkers is Anavasi's *Hydra* map. A map is posted on the quay, and several marked trails extend across the island. Once you leave the villages of Hydra/Kamini/Vlyhos there are no services. Take plenty of water.

An unbeatable experience is the long haul up to Moni Profiti Ilia. The wonderful monastery complex contains beautiful icons and boasts super views. It's a solid hour or more through zigzags and pine trees to panoramic bliss on top.

A smaller monastery, Moni Agias Efpraxias, sits just below Profiti Ilia and is run by nuns.

Other paths lead to Mt Eros (588m), the island's highest point, and east and west along the island spine, but you need advanced route-finding skills or reliable directions from knowledgable locals.

The coastal road turns into a partially cobbled, beautiful trail about 1.5km west of the port, after Kamini. Kamini has a tiny fishing port, several good tavernas, swimming rocks and a small pebble beach. In fact, Hydra's shortcoming – or blessing – is its lack of sandy beaches to draw the crowds. People usually swim off the rocks, but if you go as far as Vlyhos, 1.5km after Kamini, this last little hamlet before the mountains offers two slightly larger pebble beaches (one called Vlyhos and the other, the more pristine Plakes), tavernas and a restored 19th-century stone bridge.

The coastal road leads 2.5km east from the port to a pebble beach at Mandraki.

Boats run from the harbour to all of these places, and you certainly need them to reach Bisti Bay or Agios Nikolaos Bay, in the island's southwest, with their remote but umbrella-laden pebble beaches and green waters.

✕ Eating

Christina TAVERNA €
(☎22980 53516; Kamini; mains €6-12; ⊙noon-4pm & 6-10pm Thu-Tue Easter-Oct) Just inland from the port in Kamini, Mrs Christina and her kids dish out some of the island's best Greek dishes and fresh fish.

To Pefkaki SEAFOOD, MEZEDHES €
(☎6973535709; Kamini; dishes €5-10; ⊙noon-4pm & 6.30-10pm Thu-Tue Easter-Oct) Worth the short walk along the coast to Kamini for a laid-back lunch of mezedhes and fresh seafood (delicious fried anchovies).

★Techne INTERNATIONAL €€
(☎22980 52500; www.techne-hydra.com; Coast Rd, Avlaki; mains €13-23; ⊙10am-midnight) Spread across several terraces and overlooking a broad sweep of sea and sunset, this elegant cafe and restaurant serves lighter fare by day and full, well-conceived, delicious and thoughtfully served meals at night. Book ahead on weekend evenings to nab a table, perfect for date night.

Four Seasons TAVERNA €€
(☎22980 53698; www.fourseasonshydra.gr; Plakes Beach; mains €6-15; ⊙noon-10pm Easter-Oct; ☎) This tasty seaside taverna offers a different face of Hydra: the sound of the breeze and the waves instead of the portside buzz. Don't miss the *taramasalata* (fishroe dip) with bread and whatever else tickles your fancy. It also has handsome suites (from €240, including breakfast).

Enalion TAVERNA €€
(☎22980 53455; www.enalion-hydra.gr; Vlyhos; mains €6-12; ⊙noon-10pm Easter-Oct) Perhaps the best seaside option at Vlyhos Beach, with traditional Greek fare.

Pirofani INTERNATIONAL €€
(☎22980 53175; www.pirofani.com; Kamini; mains €10-16; ⊙7.30pm-midnight Wed-Sun late May-Sep) Gregarious Theo creates an eclectic range of dishes, from a beef fillet with rose-pepper sauce to a spicy Asian curry.

Castello MEDITERRANEAN €€€
(☎22980 54101; www.castellohydra.gr; Kamini; snacks €7-15, mains €15-30; ⊙1pm-late Jun-Sep) In a renovated 18th-century bastion and spilling onto the beach, Castello offers waterfront snacks at its daytime beach bar, gourmet seaside dining at its refined restaurant and sunset cocktails at its bar. Amazing views.

SPETSES ΣΠΕΤΣΕΣ

POP 4027

Spetses stands proudly just a few kilometres from mainland Peloponnese, but there is a stronger sense of carefree island Greece here than in other Saronic Gulf destinations. The lively, historic old town is the only village on the island; the rest, ringed by a simple road, is rolling hills, pine forests and crystal-clear coves. Relaxed Spetses Town has great nightlife, some of the Saronic's best restaurants and gorgeous, easily accessible swimming spots. With a rich naval history, it is still incredibly popular with yachties, and with its vibrant culture, it attracts artists, intellectuals and lovers of a good island party.

History

In Spetses Town there's evidence of early Helladic settlement near the Old Harbour and around the Dapia Harbour. Roman and Byzantine remains have been found in the area behind Moni Agios Nikolaos, halfway between the two.

From the 10th century, Spetses is thought to have been uninhabited for almost 600 years, until the arrival of Albanian refugees fleeing the fighting between Turks and Venetians in the 16th century.

Spetses, like Hydra, grew wealthy from shipbuilding. Island captains busted the British blockade during the Napoleonic Wars and refitted their ships to join the Greek fleet during the War of Independence. In the process they immortalised one local woman (albeit originally from Hydra) the formidable Laskarina Bouboulina, ship commander and fearless fighter.

The island's hallmark forests of Aleppo pine, a legacy of the far-sighted philanthropist Sotirios Anargyros, have been devastated

Spetses

by fires several times in the past 20 years. The trees are steadily recovering.

ⓘ Getting There & Away

High-speed ferries link Spetses with Hydra, Poros and Piraeus, and Ermioni and Porto Heli on the Peloponnese. In summer caïques (per person €4) and a car ferry (€2) go from the harbour to Kosta on the mainland. Note: only locally owned cars are allowed on Spetses. Park yours in Kosta. Get tickets at Bardakos Tours (p330).

ⓘ Getting Around

BICYCLE

Bike Center (☑ 22980 72209; http://spetses bikecenter.blogspot.com; ⓧ 10am-3.30pm & 5.30-10pm) Behind the fish market; rents out bikes (per day €8), including baby seats.

BOAT

In summer caïques serve the island's beaches (return €13). **Water-taxi** (☑ 22980 72072; Dapia Harbour; ⓧ 24hr) fares are displayed on a board at the quay. All leave from the quay opposite Bardakos Tours (p330).

BUS

Two routes start over Easter and increase in frequency to three or four daily from June to September. Departure times are displayed on boards by the bus stops and around town.

One goes from Plateia Agiou Mama in Spetses Town to Agia Paraskevi (€6, 40 minutes), travel-ling via Agia Marina and Agii Anargyri. The other leaves from in front of Poseidonion Grand Hotel, going to Vrellos (€4) via Ligoneri.

CAR & MOTORCYCLE

Only locally owned autos are allowed on Spetses, and those are not permitted in the centre of town. The transport of choice tends to be scooters. Motorbike- and quad-bike-hire shops abound (per day €15 to €35). Taxis are another option.

Spetses Town   Σπέτσες

POP 4001

Bustling Spetses Town stretches along a meandering waterfront encompassing several quays and beaches. The main Dapia Harbour, where ferries arrive, and the area around adjacent Plateia Limenarhiou and inland Plateia Orologiou (Clocktower Sq) teem with chic tourist shops and cafes.

As you head further inland on the quieter lanes, or go left along the harbour-front road of Sotiriou Anargyriou, past the town beach and Plateia Agiou Mama, impressive old arhontika (mansions) illustrate Spetses' historic (and ongoing) wealth.

Passing the church of Moni Agios Nikolaos you arrive at the attractive Old Harbour (Palio Limani) and the interesting Baltiza yacht anchorage and boat-building area.

From the north side of Dapia Harbour a promenade and road lead through the seafront Kounoupitsa area.

◉ Sights

Bouboulina's Museum MUSEUM
(☑22980 72416; www.bouboulinamuseum-spetses. gr; adult/child €6/2; ⊘tours daily Apr-Oct) The mansion of Spetses' famous daughter, the 19th-century seagoing commander Laskarina Bouboulina, has been converted into a museum. Entry is via 40-minute guided tours (billboards around town advertise starting times, also posted online). The museum hosts occasional concerts. There's an impressive **statue** of Bouboulina on the harbour, opposite the Poseidonion Grand Hotel.

Spetses Museum MUSEUM
(☑22980 72994; http://odysseus.culture.gr; adult/ child €3/free; ⊘8am-3pm Tue-Sun) Small, fascinating collections are housed in the old mansion of Hatzigiannis Mexis (1754–1844), a shipowner who became the island's first governor. They include island artefacts, traditional costumes and portraits of the island's founding fathers.

✯ Festivals & Events

★Armata CULTURAL
(⊘early Sep) This week-long celebration culminates on 8 September in a commemoration of Spetses' victory over the Turks in a key 1822 naval battle, with an enormous water-borne re-enactment and fireworks.

⌂ Sleeping

Villa Christina Hotel PENSION €
(☑22980 72218; www.villachristinahotel.com; s/d/ tr/f incl breakfast from €50/55/70/90; ❋🗐🤶) Located about 200m uphill on the main road inland from the harbour, these well-kept rooms and lovely garden are back from the worst traffic noise.

Villa Marina PENSION €
(☑22980 72646; www.villamarinaspetses.com; Agios Mamas; d €55-60; ❋🗐) Superbasic, clean rooms have refrigerators and there is a well-equipped communal kitchen downstairs. Just to the right of Plateia Agiou Mama.

Hotel Kamelia PENSION €
(☑6939095513; http://hotelkamelia.gr; Agias Mamas; s/d from €40/45; ⊘Easter-Oct; ❋🗐) Good-value airy rooms are tucked away from the busy seafront in the Agios Mamas area, with a bougainvillea-draped terrace.

Economou Mansion PENSION €€
(☑22980 73400; www.economouspetses.gr; d incl breakfast from €130; ❋🗐≋) This beautiful pension on the ground floor of a restored captain's mansion sits right on the waterfront, about 500m north of Dapia Harbour, and offers a homey, relaxed hideaway combining antique decor and modern amenities such as swimming pool, TV, hairdryer and safe. Breakfast is bountiful.

Kastro Hotel APARTMENT €€
(☑22980 75319; www.kastrohotel-spetses.gr; studios/4-person apt incl breakfast €120/165; ❋🗐🤶) A private, quiet complex encloses these studios and apartments close to the centre of town. Low-key decor and modern amenities combine with extensive terraces.

Klimis Hotel HOTEL €€
(☑22980 73725; www.klimishotel.gr; Dapia Harbour; s/d/apt incl breakfast from €75/95/170; ❋🗐) Sleek rooms, some with seafront balconies, at this standard hotel sit above a ground-floor cafe-bar and patisserie.

★Poseidonion Grand Hotel LUXURY HOTEL €€€
(☑22980 74553; www.poseidonion.com; Dapia Harbour; d/ste incl breakfast from €280/670; ❋🗐🤶) Here's your chance to live like a wealthy dame or gent in the roaring '20s. This grand old hotel has been totally renovated and every centimetre, from the chic rooms to the gracious lobby bar and grand

BOAT SEVICES FROM SPETSES

DESTINATION	DURATION	FARE (€)	FREQUENCY
Ermioni*	20-30min	8	2 daily
Hydra*	40min	11.50	4-5 daily
Piraeus*	2hr 10min	38.50	5 daily
Poros*	1½hr	16	4-5 daily
Porto Heli*	15min	6	3-4 daily

*high-speed services

pool, drips with luxury. Oh, and it also has one of the island's best restaurants.

★ Orloff Resort
BOUTIQUE HOTEL €€€

(☑ 22980 75444; www.orloffresort.com; Old Harbour; d/studios/apt incl breakfast from €210/225/410; ☉ Mar-Oct; ❈ 🅟 🅢) On the edge of town, along the road to Agia Marina and near the old port, the pristine Orloff hides behind high white walls. Enjoy stylish rooms and a crystal-clear pool.

✖ Eating

★ Akrogialia
SEAFOOD, TAVERNA €€

(☑ 22980 74749; www.akrogialia-restaurant.gr; Kounoupitsa; mains €9-17; ☉ 11am-midnight) This superb restaurant is on the Kounoupitsa seafront and matches its delicious food with friendly service and a bright setting. Tasty options include oven-baked *melidzana rolos* (eggplant with creamy cheese and walnuts). Enjoy terrific fish risotto or settle for a choice steak. All are accompanied by a thoughtful selection of Greek wines. Book ahead on weekends.

To Nero tis Agapis
MEDITERRANEAN €€

(☑ 22980 74009; www.nerotisagapis.gr; Kounoupitsa; mains €9-22; ☉ 11am-midnight) The sweetly named 'Water of Love' offers gourmet meat as well as fish dishes. The crayfish tagliatelle is worth every bite, as is the *zarzuela* (fish stew). There's a selection of creative salads. Book ahead for the romantic tables with the best sea views.

Patralis
SEAFOOD €€

(☑ 22980 75380; www.patralis.gr; Kounoupitsa; mains €7-15; ☉ 10am-midnight Jan-Oct) Operating for more than 70 years and known islandwide for its outstanding seafood, Patralis sits smack on the seafront in Kounoupitsa.

Orloff
MEDITERRANEAN €€

(☑ 22980 75255; www.orloffrestaurant.com; Old Harbour; mains €14-21; ☉ 6.30pm-1am Jun-Sep, 6.30pm-1am Fri, 12.30pm-1am Sat, 12.30-6pm Sun May & Oct) Fresh fish and specialities such as seafood linguine or pork fillet with aubergine purée are hallmarks of the popular Orloff. The terrace sits above the water at a bend in the road just north of the Old Harbour.

★ On the Verandah
MEDITERRANEAN €€€

(☑ 6957507267; www.poseidonion.com/en/Dining-On-the-Verandah; Poseidonion Hotel; 4-course dinner €38; ☉ 7.30pm-midnight Jul & Aug, reduced hours May, Jun & Sep) One of the Saronic Gulf's top dining experiences, the Verandah at the Poseidonion Hotel is the dining space for the high-concept cuisine of chef Stamatis

Marmarinos. Ingredients are locally sourced and comprise exquisitely presented, creative Mediterranean dishes. Book ahead.

★ Tarsanas
SEAFOOD €€€

(☑ 22980 74490; www.tarsanas-spetses.gr; Old Harbour; mains €17-26; ☉ 11am-midnight) A hugely popular *psarotaverna* (fish taverna) on the water at the Old Harbour, this family-run place deals almost exclusively in fish dishes. It can be pricey, but the fish soup (€7) alone is a delight and other starters, such as anchovies marinated with lemon, start at €6.

🍷 Drinking & Nightlife

Mourayo
BAR

(☑ 22980 73700; Old Harbour; ☉ 8pm-2am) You can come for the food, but be sure to stay for a sunset or late-night waterfront cocktail and dancing.

La Luz
BAR

(☑ 22980 75024; www.laluzspetses.gr; Old Harbour) La Luz often has live music and always sports super sea views in the Old Harbour area of Spetses.

Ariston
CAFE

(☑ 22980 73803; Dapia Harbour; ☉ 9am-late; 🛜) A touch of class on the waterfront, with coffee by day and sundowners by evening.

Bar Spetsa
BAR

(☑ 22980 74131; www.barspetsa.org; Agios Mamas; ☉ 8pm-late Mar-Oct) One of life's great little bars, this Spetses institution never loses its easygoing atmosphere. Find it 50m beyond Plateia Agiou Mama, on the road to the right of the kiosk.

Roussos
CAFE

(☑ 22908 72819; Dapia Harbour; ☉ 7.30am-late) Old-time Spetsiot coffee house with pastries, on the harbour.

ℹ Information

Banks at Dapia Harbour have ATMs.

Bardakos Tours (☑ 22980 73141; hswbarda@ yahoo.gr; Dapia Harbour; ☉ 8am-9pm Jun-Aug, reduced hours Sep-May) Sells ferry tickets and assists with other arrangements.

Municipal Information Kiosk (www.spetses. com.gr; ☉ 10am-9pm May-Sep) On the quay; seasonal staff provide answers to general questions about the island.

Port Authority (☑ 22980 72245; Dapia) Just inland from the cafe terrace overlooking Dapia Harbour.

Tourist Police (☑ Police 22980 73100, Tourist Police 22980 73744; Dapia; ☉ mid-May–Sep) Housed with the port authority.

Cyclades

Best Places to Eat

➡ Doukato (p376)

➡ M-Eating (p355)

➡ Captain Dimos (p389)

➡ Cayenne (p428)

➡ Theoni's Kitchen (p403)

➡ O Ntinos (p343)

Best Places to Stay

➡ Red Tractor Farm (p435)

➡ Pension Sofi (p375)

➡ Windmill of Karamitsos (p422)

➡ Stelios Place (p409)

➡ Francesco's (p394)

Why Go?

On a quest to find the Greek islands of your dreams? Start, here, in the Cyclades (Κυκλάδες). Rugged, sun-drenched outcrops of rock, anchored in azure seas and liberally peppered with snow-white villages and blue-domed churches, this is Greece straight from central casting, with stellar archaeological sites and dozens of postcard-worthy beaches. Throw in a blossoming food scene, some renowned party destinations and a good dose of sophistication, and you really do have the best of Greece's ample charms.

The biggest surprise may be the variety found within this island group. Chase hedonism on Mykonos or Ios, history on Delos, hiking trails on Andros or Amorgos. Want a romantic break? Try Santorini. To escape reality? Pick Donousa or Anafi. You can ferry-hop to your heart's content, enjoy long, lazy lunches at waterside tavernas, or simply lay claim to a sunbed by a spectacular beach. You're living the dream.

When to Go
Mykonos Town

Apr–Jun Catch the early-season sun without overheating, and boats without overcrowding.

Jul & Aug Pros: sun, sea and sand, plus balmy nights and lively company. Cons: peak crowds and prices.

Sep & Oct Quieter beaches, open spaces, the sweet scent of herbs, and great walks on island hills.

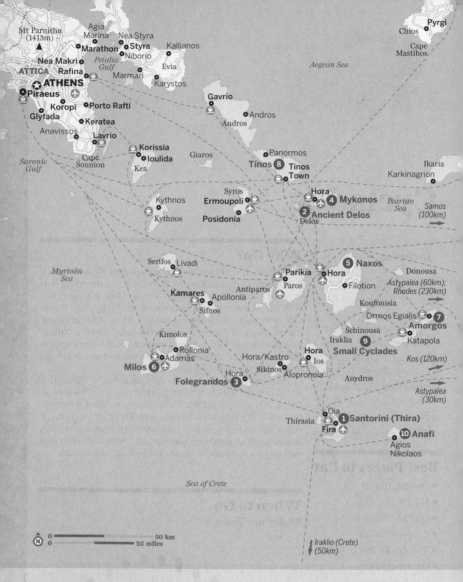

Cyclades Highlights

1 **Santorini (Thira)** (p396) Being mesmerised by the dramatic volcanic cliffs.

2 **Ancient Delos** (p359) Immersing yourself in history on this sacred island.

3 **Folegandros** (p413) Wandering the streets of Hora.

4 **Mykonos** (p349) Partying until dawn.

5 **Naxos** (p370) Exploring quaint villages.

6 **Milos** (p417) Sunning yourself on stone cliffs or lazing in sandy coves.

7 **Amorgos** (p387) Marvelling at the dazzling cliffside monastery.

8 **Tinos** (p338) Exploring

marble villages and gorgeous dovecote valleys.

9 **Small Cyclades** (p381) Slipping away to serenity on these remote-feeling islands.

10 **Anafi** (p410) Enjoying a slow-paced traditional lifestyle on this far-flung isle.

History

The Cyclades are said to have been inhabited since at least 7000 BC. Around 3000 BC there emerged a cohesive Cycladic civilisation that was bound together by seagoing commerce and exchange. During the Early Cycladic period (3000–2000 BC), the tiny but distinctive Cycladic marble figurines, mainly stylised representations of the naked female form, were sculpted. Recent discoveries on Keros, an uninhabited island near Koufonisia in the Small Cyclades, indicate that the island was a possible pilgrimage site where figurines that had been broken up as part of rituals were deposited.

During the Middle Cycladic period (2000–1500 BC), many of the islands were occupied by the Minoans, who probably colonised from Crete. At Akrotiri, on Santorini, a Minoan town has been excavated, and artefacts from the site have all the distinctive beauty of those from Crete's Minoan palaces. At the beginning of the Late Cycladic period (1500–1100 BC), the archipelago came under the influence of the Mycenaeans of the Peloponnese, who were supplanted by northern Dorians in the 8th century BC.

By the mid-5th century BC the Cyclades were part of a fully fledged Athenian empire. In the Hellenistic era (323–146 BC), they were governed by Egypt's Ptolemaic dynasties, and later by the Macedonians. In 146 BC the islands became a Roman province, and lucrative trade links were established with many parts of the Mediterranean.

The division of the Roman Empire in AD 395 resulted in the Cyclades being ruled from Byzantium (Constantinople), but after the fall of Byzantium in 1204, they came under a Venetian authority that doled out the islands to opportunistic aristocrats. The most powerful of these was Marco Sanudo (the self-styled Venetian Duke of Naxos), who acquired a dozen of the larger islands – including Naxos, Paros, Ios, Sifnos, Milos, Amorgos and Folegandros – introducing a Venetian gloss that survives to this day in island architecture.

The Cyclades came under Turkish rule in 1537, although the empire had difficulty in managing, let alone protecting, such scattered dependencies. Cycladic coastal settlements suffered frequent pirate raids, a scourge that led to many villages being relocated to hidden inland sites. They survive as the 'Horas' (capitals, also often written as 'Chora') that are such an attractive feature of the islands today. Ottoman neglect, piracy and shortages of food and water often led to wholesale depopulation of more remote islands, and in 1563 only five islands were still inhabited.

The Cyclades played a minimal part in the Greek War of Independence, but became havens for people fleeing from other islands where insurrections against the Turks had led to massacres and persecution. Italian forces occupied the Cyclades during WWII. After the war, the islands emerged more economically deprived than ever. Many islanders lived in deep poverty, while many more gave up the struggle and headed to the mainland, or to America and Australia, in search of work.

The tourism boom that began in the 1970s revived the fortunes of the Cyclades. The challenge remains, however, of finding alternative and sustainable economies that will not mar the beauty and appeal of these remarkable islands.

❶ Getting There & Away

AIR

Of the 24 Cyclades islands, six have airports – Mykonos, Syros, Paros, Naxos, Santorini and Milos – all with daily links to Athens. Some have direct links with European cities in summer (charter flights, plus scheduled services to Mykonos and Santorini). There are rarely direct links between islands, so to fly from Mykonos to Santorini, you'll almost certainly need to go via Athens.

BOAT

The key to sculpting an itinerary through the islands is knowing which ferries go where – and when they're going. The peak ferry services run in July and August, but in winter services are reduced or nonexistent on some routes.

A host of companies offer connections throughout the Cyclades. They depart from the main ports of Attica: Piraeus (the largest port, with services to most islands), Rafina (particularly good for Mykonos, Andros and Tinos) and Lavrio (for Kythnos and Kea).

Three extremely useful websites are:

http://ferries.gr For checking dates and times, and buying tickets online.

www.ferriesingreece.com/live-boat-traffic. htm See ferry locations in real time and check if they are likely to turn up on time.

www.vesselfinder.com If you know your ferry's name, check here to see where it is.

ANDROS ΑΝΔΡΟΣ
POP 9221

Andros, the second-largest island of the Cyclades, has a long and proud seafaring tradition and is also a walker's paradise. Its wild mountains are cleaved by fecund valleys with bubbling streams and ancient stone mills. A lush island, springs tend to be a feature of each village, and waterfalls cascade down hillsides most of the year. It's worth renting a car to get out to the footpaths, many of them stepped and cobbled, which will lead you through majestic landscapes, wildflowers and archaeological remnants. The handsome main town of Hora, also known as Andros, is a shipowners' enclave packed with neoclassical mansions.

ℹ Getting There & Away

Reach Andros from the mainland port of Rafina via regular ferries that continue south to Tinos and Mykonos. Direct services run to/from Syros a few times a week, from where easy onward links can be made (or you can reach Syros daily, by changing ferry in Tinos).

Buy tickets at Ploes Travel (p337) in Hora or Batsi Travel in Gavrio.

Boat Services from Andros

DESTINATION	DURATION	FARE (€)	FREQUENCY
Kea	6hr	13	Thu
Kythnos	4¾hr	18	Thu
Mykonos	2½hr	18-19	2-4 daily
Naxos	3¾-4hr	26-28	daily
Rafina	2hr	22-23	2-4 daily
Syros	2hr	12	Thu
Tinos	1½-2hr	12-17	2-4 daily

ℹ Getting Around

KTEL Andros (☑ 22820 22316) has up to nine buses daily (fewer on weekends) linking Gavrio and Hora (€4, 55 minutes) via Batsi (€2, 15 minutes), and Gavrio and Korthi (€5, 1¼ hours, two to three daily). Schedules are posted at the bus stops in Gavrio and Hora. Low-season buses are usually timed to meet Rafina ferries.

Taxis (☑ Batsi 22820 41081, Gavrio 22820 71561, Hora 22820 22171) from Gavrio to Batsi cost about €12, and to Hora €40.

Roads can be rough and narrow, but many walking paths and sights are only accessible by car. **Escape in Andros** (☑ 22820 29120; www.escapeinandros.gr) can arrange to meet you at the port with a rental car (from about €40 per

day in August, €25 in low season). There are a couple of scooter and ATV rental agencies on the waterfront in Gavrio.

Gavrio Γαύριο
POP 1199

Sleepy Gavrio on the west coast is the main port of Andros. The waterfront is lined with services (ATMs, ticket agencies, car and scooter hire), but the town isn't the most interesting part of the island to base yourself – there are some stretches of beach to the south (en route to Batsi) that are more appealing.

🛏 Sleeping & Eating

Standard tavernas line Gavrio's waterfront. Gavrio is used as the jumping-off point to visit Andros' most celebrated restaurant in the north part of the island.

Andros Camping CAMPGROUND €
(☑ 22820 71444; www.campingandros.gr; campsite per adult/tent/car €7/4/4; ☺ May-Sep; ⊛) A rustic site set among olive trees about 400m behind the harbour. Follow the signs from the road to Batsi, turning at the Escape in Andros travel agency.

Allegria Family Hotel HOTEL €€
(☑ 22820 72110; www.allegria-andros.com; Agios Petros Beach; d/f €75/85; ☺ Apr-Sep; ⊛ 🛜) Nicely geared to families and close to the beach at Agios Petros, a few kilometres south of Gavrio. Studios have kitchenettes, and some have bunks for kids, all set in a pretty garden.

ℹ Information

There's a full range of services along the waterfront, including three ATMs and two banks.
Kyklades Travel (☑ 22820 72363; ☺ 9am-9pm) and **Batsi Travel** (☑ 22820 71489; ☺ 9am-9pm) sell ferry tickets and can arrange accommodation.

Batsi Μπατσί
POP 957

Batsi lies 7km southeast of Gavrio on the over-built shores of a handsome bay with a long beige-sand beach. The island's main resort, it revs up through July and August. A couple of good, short hiking trails start from town.

🛏 Sleeping & Eating

Cavo D'Oro GUESTHOUSE €
(☑ 22820 41776; www.andros-cavodoro.gr; d €50; ⊛ 🛜) The handful of simple, pleasant rooms

Andros

0 — 10 km
0 — 5 miles

Cape Kampanos
Cape Fasa
Hartes
Zorkos Beach
Aegean Sea
▲716m
Vitali Beach
Amolohos
Vitali
Gulf of Vitali
Vori Beach
Fellos Bay
Agios Petros Beach
Gavrio
Ateni
Cape Gria
Ahla Beach
Rafina (65km)
Golden Beach
Agios Kyprianos Beach
Batsi
Remata
Vourkoti
Stenies
Delavoia Beach
Katakilos
Arni
Apikia
Gialia Beach
Anerousa Beach
Stivari
Mesathouri
Niborio Beach
Paraporti Beach
Green Beach
Mt Petalo (910m)
Hora (Andros)
Menites
Mesaria
Paleopoli Bay
Paleopoli
Sineti
Dipotamata Gorge
Pitrofos
Exo Vouni
Mesa Vouni
Kochilou
Halkolimionas
Piskopio
Ormos Korthiou
Cape Orginos
Kapparia
Aidonia
Batsilianos
Korthi
Mousionas
Pera Horio
Piso Meria
648m
Syros (30km); Tinos (30km); Mykonos (45km)
Cape Steno
Tinos

at Cavo D'Oro are excellent value. It's located above a restaurant across the road from the beach.

Krinos Suites Hotel BOUTIQUE HOTEL €€€
(22820 42038; www.krinoshotel.com; ste incl breakfast from €180; ⊙ late May–Sep; ❉ 🐾) One of Andros' high-end entries, housing nine well-kitted-out suites and a smart 'art cafe'. Some rooms have sea-view balconies.

★**Themelos** CYCLADIC €
(22820 29426; www.facebook.com/themelos andros; Dionisou; dishes €5-8; ⊙ 12.30-11pm; 🐾) Head up the stairs from the waterfront to find this delightful little cafe tucked away on a tiny pedestrian street. Works by local artists liven up the interior, and the menu is full of local mezedhes – smoked baby mackerel, slightly fermented local *kopanisti* cheese, locally made sausage, wild artichokes. Wash it down with a sour cherry juice.

Stamatis Taverna GREEK €€
(22820 41283; mains €7-17; ⊙ noon-11pm; 🐾) Next to the harbour, this restaurant's interior is a charming time warp, and the food is renowned for its authenticity: Andros lamb and stuffed chicken are specialities, as is the fresh fish. Reserve ahead for the Wednesday night slow-cooked lamb.

❶ Information

Greek Sun Holidays (22820 41198; www. andros-greece.com) Arranges accommodation, car hire, ferry tickets and island walks and excursions.

Hora (Andros)
Χώρα (Ανδρος)

POP 1665

Hora perches dramatically on a rocky promontory and has surprising views through the neoclassical mansions to two vibrant bays on either side: Niborio and Paraporti. The peninsula is tipped by the remains of a Venetian fortress, and the town itself owes its grand mansions and squares to both the Venetian settlement and the shipowners who came to inhabit it. Hora's cultural pedigree is burnished by its Museum of Contemporary Art, an impressive archaeological museum and several important churches.

Sights

★ Museum of Contemporary Art   MUSEUM
(✉22820 22444; www.moca-andros.gr; summer/rest of year €5/3; ⊙11am-3pm & 6-9pm Wed-Sun, 11am-3pm Mon Jul-Sep, 10am-2pm Wed-Mon Apr-Jun & Oct, 10am-2pm Sat-Mon Nov-Mar) MOCA has earned a reputation in the international art world for its outstanding summer exhibitions of world-famous artists. Split across two buildings, exhibits have included Picasso, Matisse, Toulouse-Lautrec and Miró. The sculpture gallery features prominent Greek artists, and a summertime sea-view cafe offers homemade sweets. Find it down the steps (signposted) from Plateia Kaïri.

Andros Archaeological Museum   MUSEUM
(✉22820 23664; Plateia Kaïri; adult/child €3/free; ⊙9am-4pm Tue-Sat) Here you can peruse the exquisite 2nd-century BC marble copy of the bronze *Hermes of Andros* by Praxiteles, and impressive finds from the 9th- to 5th-century BC settlements of Zagora and Paleopoli on Andros' west coast.

Afanis Naftis   MONUMENT
(Plateia Riva) The huge bronze sailor, donated by the Soviet Union, stands in the square at the tip of the promontory and celebrates Hora's seagoing traditions.

Venetian Fortress   RUINS
The picturesque ruins of a Venetian fortress stand on an island linked to the tip of the headland by the worn remnants of an arched stone bridge. Don't attempt to scramble over in the manner of locals.

Sleeping

★ Anemomiloi Studios   APARTMENT €€
(✉22820 24084; www.anemomiloi.gr; d/q from €95/105; ❄❀☎) This popular complex of bright, spic-and-span studios, split between two buildings, sits at the southern end of town enjoying views over green fields from all its balconies. There's friendly, helpful service from the owners, and a quiet poolside patio. Off-peak rates drop considerably.

Camara Homes   APARTMENT €€
(✉6972028853; Empeirikou; apt from €60; ❄☎) Towards the Venetian fortress along the main drag, this is an attractive handful of apartments, with sea views and spyglasses for peering at the horizon. The split-level ones with roof terraces are the most appealing.

Micra Anglia   BOUTIQUE HOTEL €€
(✉22820 22207; www.micra-anglia.gr; Goulandri 13; d/tr/ste incl breakfast from €117/198/270; ⊙May-Oct; ❄☎) Hora's five-star offering has a raft of chic amenities and stylish decor in neutral shades, as well as Hora's most imaginative restaurant. Discounts available online.

Archontiko Eleni   BOUTIQUE HOTEL €€
(✉2282022270;www.archontikoeleni.gr;Empirikou 9; s/d incl breakfast €85/100; ❄☎) Snuggle into comfy beds in this eight-room neoclassical mansion, which boasts high ceilings and classy decor, including original timber floors from the 1890s.

Eating

Hora's main street is lined with a dazzling array of *zaharoplasteia* (patisseries) and traditional tavernas, with a couple more by the sea. The town's high-end fusion restaurant is inside the Micra Anglia hotel.

Ta Skalakia   TAVERNA €
(✉22820 22822; mains €8-12; ⊙6-11pm Mon-Sat; ☎) Tables spill down the eponymous stairs from this buttercup-yellow restaurant. Inside feels more like a bistro, with quaint bric-a-brac. There's a short, tasty menu offering the likes of oregano-flavoured pork, meatballs and roasted feta.

I Parea   TAVERNA €
(✉22820 23721; Plateia Kaïri; mains €7-13; ⊙noon-10pm; ☎) Long-established and popular with locals, central Parea boasts a super terrace overlooking Paraporti Beach. Head inside to see what's been freshly cooked.

★ Dolly's Bar Restaurant   FUSION €€
(✉22820 22207; Goulandri 13; mains €16-25; ⊙7.30pm-late; ❄☎) In the basement of the Micra Anglia hotel, this is the most stylish and imaginative restaurant in town. Go for tabbouleh topped with grilled giant prawns or the impeccably grilled steak.

Endochora   CYCLADIC €€
(✉22820 23207; www.endochora.com; Empirikou; mains €9-17; ⊙noon-10pm May–mid-Sep, weekends only rest of year; ☎) Endochora is a stylish

hotspot on the main drag, offering a fresh twist on Greek classics and a great vantage point for people-watching. Salads showcase prime local produce like capers, tomatoes, figs and cheeses. It was under refurbishment on our last visit.

ℹ Information

The pedestrianised marble main street, leading downhill to the Venetian *kastro* (fortress), is lined with numerous banks.

See http://andros.gr/en for more info.

Ploes Travel (☑ 22820 29220; Empirikou; ☺ 9am-1pm & 3-9pm) Can arrange guided hikes and scooter and car rental. Also sells ferry tickets.

Around Andros

It's well worth renting a car or scooter to explore Andros' vast mountains and sprinkling of picturesque villages. Its mountain drives are panorama-filled.

The north of the island, with the lush watershed around **Arni**, gives way to raw, windswept hills as the road zigzags to **Vourkoti** and **Agios Nikolaou** with its sweeping views.

Paleopoli, 7km south of Batsi on the coast road, is the site of Ancient Andros and its sunken harbour. Only rubble remains but the small roadside **Archaeological Museum of Paleopoli** (☑ 22829 41985; ☺ 9am-4pm Tue-Sun) **FREE** displays finds.

The island is cleaved by a sweeping agricultural valley, and loads of small villages with springs, often marked by marble lions' heads and the like, surround Hora. The road winds through **Sariza, Stenies, Mesathouri, Strapouries** and **Menites** – all fun to explore.

In the south, visit quaint agricultural villages like **Livadia, Kochilou, Piskopio,** and **Aidonia**, which has ruined tower houses. The area's charming landscape of fields and cypresses encircle **Ormos Korthiou,** an uninspiring bayside village.

◉ Sights & Activities

Walking

There are 18 wonderful waymarked trails criss-crossing Andros, which range in duration from 30 minutes to six hours, and are labelled in difficulty level from easy to average. Wear hiking boots and trekking pants, as there are some (shy) snakes.

The best investment you can make is the *Andros Hiking Map* (€6) published by the marvellous **Andros Routes** (www.androsroutes.gr) project, in conjunction with Anavasi mapping company. It's available at bookshops and gift shops on the island. The Andros Routes website outlines the paths they maintain and has good advice for hiking on the island.

Locals recommend the areas north of Hora for great walks, including the villages of Stenies and Apikia. For a lovely short walk, **Pithara** is a shady glade of streams accessed from Apikia. For a longer ramble, hike up the dramatic **Dipotamata Gorge,** signposted as you drive inland, after Sineti (southeast of Hora). The trail is cobbled part of the way and leads past ancient bridges and water mills and through vivid foliage, water burbling below.

Better yet, book a guided walk with **Trekking Andros** (☑ 22820 61368; www.trekkingandros.gr; guided walk per person from €20), a company that arranges and guides a menu of activities on the island, including hiking, mountain biking, boat trips, yoga, cooking or painting classes.

🐾 Beaches

Between Gavrio and Paleopoli Bay excellent beaches include **Golden Beach** (Hrisi Ammos), **Delavoia** (one half of which is naturist), **Anerousa,** and **Green Beach.** Near Hora, check out lovely Gialia Beach.

Spectacular **Halkolimionas** – with tawny sand and a tiny church – sits 2km down a stone-terraced valley near the junction for Hora. A small beach bar sets up here in summer.

Many of the best beaches, such as **Ahla, Vori** and **Vitali** (all in the northeast), are only reached by 4WD, ATV or boat. Boat trips can usually be arranged (or boats hired) in Batsi and Nimborio.

🛏 Sleeping

Perrakis HOTEL €€
(☑ 22820 71456; www.hotelperrakis.com; Chrissi Ammos; s/d incl breakfast from €75/100; ❄ 🤖 🏊) Across the road from the sweep of Golden Beach, about 3km south of Gavrio, are super views and swell rooms – the superior rooms are lovely and have big balconies. A dive centre is based here, and there's a restaurant. Off-peak rates can drop by 50%.

★ **Onar Residence** COTTAGE €€€
(☏ 210 625 1052, 6932563707; www.onar-andros.gr;
Ahla Beach; 3-/5-/7-person cottage €220/370/680;
☉ May-Oct; ❄🛜) ⊘ Ecofriendly, unique and
luxurious secluded cottages in wetlands
behind the stunning remote beach at Ahla.
The resort has an organic restaurant for
guests. Details on how to reach the resort
are on the website (access road is 4WD only;
transfers can be arranged).

✖ Eating

Gialia
GREEK €
(☏ 22820 24452; mains €8-12; ☉ noon-10pm Apr-
Oct; 🛜) A few kilometres from Hora is the
delightful crystal-clear blue of Gialia Beach,
where this excellent restaurant serves snacks
and Greek classics to hungry beachgoers or
island explorers. There's no English menu,
but the waiter can give you the rundown.
Try the delicious (and ample) Andros salad
topped with local *kopanisti* cheese.

Tou Josef
TAVERNA €
(☏ 22820 51050; Pitrofos; mains €7-12; ☉ noon-
3pm & 6-10pm) Gregarious Katerina Remoun-
dou welcomes you to her sitting room or her
tree-lined courtyard like she's your long-lost
auntie. She chats with guests as they dine on
seasonal Andriot fare like cheese and onion
pie or stewed kid. Meals are rustic and delicious, and ingredients all sourced locally.
The restaurant is in Pitrofos village, about
7km southwest of Hora; call ahead.

A BENT FOR CYCLADIC TRAVEL

Long before the hip lotus-eaters of the
1960s discovered their dream world in
the Greek islands, a redoubtable pair of
travellers had been thoroughly 'doing'
the Cyclades during the late 19th century. James Theodore Bent and his wife,
Mabel, travelled extensively throughout
the Aegean, 'researching' the cultural
life of the islands as much as their
archaeology. J Theodore's 1885 island-
by-island book, *The Cyclades, Or Life
Among the Insular Greeks*, is a quirky
masterpiece that describes the sights
and cultural realities of the islands in the
late 19th century – along with Bent's
often eccentric reflections. Look for
it online, and in bookshops on bigger
islands such as Santorini.

★ **O Kossis** CYCLADIC €€
(☏ 6972002975; Gavrion; mains €9-17; ☉ noon-
11pm; 🛜) Renowned throughout Andros
as the island's best 'meatery', O Kossis is
located in the middle of nowhere, in the hills
above Gavrio, signposted beyond Epano Fellos. Attached to stables and festooned with
vines, this family-run taverna's speciality
is melt-in-your-mouth lamb chops, though
diners swear by their other meaty delights as
well. Complimentary ouzo shot. Call ahead.

Sea Satin Nino
CYCLADIC €€
(☏ 22820 61196; www.facebook.com/Sea.Satin.
Nino.Andros; Ormos Korthiou; mains €8-17; ☉ 7am-
2am; 🛜) Shaded by overhanging vines on a
tiny square, this place uses local ingredients
to great effect. Homemade pasta, fish dishes
and a smattering of beautifully done Greek
standards grace the short but sweet menu.

TINOS ΤΗΝΟΣ

POP 8636

Tinos is one of those sleeper hit islands. It's
known widely for its sacred Greek Orthodox
pilgrimage site: the Church of Panagia Evangelistria, in the main town, Hora. But as soon
as you leave the throngs in town, Tinos is a
wonderland of natural beauty, dotted with
more than 40 marble-ornamented villages
found in hidden bays, on terraced hillsides
and atop misty mountains. Also scattered
across the brindled countryside are countless
ornate dovecotes, a legacy of the Venetians.

There's a strong artistic tradition on
Tinos, especially for marble sculpting, as in
the sculptors' village of Pyrgos in the north,
near the marble quarries. The food, made
from local produce (cheeses, sausage, tomatoes and wild artichokes), is some of the best
you'll find in Greece.

❶ Getting There & Away

Year-round ferries serve the mainland ports of
Rafina and Piraeus and the islands Syros, Andros
and Mykonos. Summer high-speed services
include Tinos on their passage south from Rafina
to major islands such as Mykonos, Paros, Naxos,
Ios and Santorini. Get tickets at Malliaris Travel
(p341), on the waterfront in Hora.

Hora has two ferry departure quays. The New
(or Outer) Port is located 300m to the north of
the main harbour and serves conventional and
larger fast ferries. The Old (or Inner) Port, at the
northern end of the town's main harbour, serves
smaller fast ferries.

Boat Services from Tinos

DESTINATION	DURATION	FARE (€)	FREQUENCY
Andros	1½-2hr	12-17	up to 3 daily
Ios	3½hr	54	1-2 daily
Kea	8hr	16	Thu
Mykonos	20-40min	11-25	2-6 daily
Naxos	2hr-2hr 20min	24-52	1-2 daily
Paros	1hr-1hr 20min	12-53	1-3 daily
Piraeus	1¾-4¾hr	31-39	daily
Rafina	1¾-4¾hr	31-39	2-4 daily
Santorini	4½hr	52	1-2 daily
Syros	30min	12	4 weekly

❶ Getting Around

Between May and September, **KTEL Tinos buses** (☑ 22830 22440; www.kteltinou.gr) run from Hora to nearby Kionia (€1.80, 10 minutes, frequent), and northwest to Panormos (€4.50, one hour, several daily) via Kambos (€1.80, 15 minutes) and Pyrgos (€3.60, 50 minutes). The Hora bus station is on the harbour near the port. Buy tickets on board.

Hire motorcycles (€15 to €20 per day) and cars (€40 per weekday, €60 on weekends in high season) along the Hora waterfront. **Vidalis Rent a Car & Bike** (☑ 22830 23400; www.vidalis-rentacar.gr) has four outlets in Hora.

Phone for a **taxi** (☑ 22830 22470).

Hora (Tinos) Χώρα (Τήνος)

POP 4762

Hora, also known as Tinos, is the island's welcoming capital and port. Though the harbourfront is lined with cafes and hotels, and the narrow backstreets are packed with restaurants, Hora's crowning glory is its Church of Panagia Evangelistria, perhaps the most important pilgrimage site for the Greek Orthodox religion.

Two main streets lead up to the church. Evangelistria is lined with shops and stalls crammed with souvenirs and religious wares, while Leoforos Megalocharis has a carpeted strip down the side, used by pilgrims crawling towards the church and pushing long candles before them. Religion certainly takes centre stage in Hora (woe betide the tourist looking for a room on one of the high holy days), but the town still hums with the vibrancy of a low-key island port.

◎ Sights

★ Church of Panagia Evangelistria CHURCH

(Church of the Annunciation; ☑ 22830 22256; www.panagiatinou.gr; ⊙ 8am-8pm) FREE Tinos' religious focus is this neoclassical church and its icon of the Virgin Mary. The hallowed icon was found in 1822 on land where the church now stands, after a nun in Tinos, now St Pelagia, was visited by visions from the Virgin instructing her where to find it. From the start, the icon was said to have healing powers, thus encouraging mass pilgrimage. Our Lady of Tinos became the patron saint of the Greek nation.

As you enter the church, the icon is on the left of the aisle, and is totally draped in jewels. Hundreds of silver lamps hang from the ceiling, each dangling a votive offering: a ship, a cradle, a heart, a pair of lungs, a chainsaw.

The church, built of marble from the island's Panormos quarries, lies within a pleasant courtyard flanked by cool arcades. The complex has sweeping views all around and museums (with variable hours) that house collections of religious artefacts, icons and secular art.

Respectful attire must be worn.

Cultural Foundation of Tinos GALLERY

(☑ 22830 29070; www.itip.gr; adult/child €3/free; ⊙ 9am-3pm Mon-Thu, 10am-2pm & 5-8.30pm Fri, 10am-2pm Sat) This excellent cultural centre in a handsome neoclassical building on the southern waterfront houses a superb permanent collection of the work of famous Tinian sculptor Yannoulis Chalepas. A second gallery has rotating exhibitions. Musical events are staged in summer, and there's a gift shop and harbourfront cafe.

Archaeological Museum MUSEUM

(☑ 22830 29063; Leoforos Megalocharis; adult/child €2/free; ⊙ 8am-3pm Tue-Sun) Just downhill from the Church of Panagia Evangelistria, this museum has a collection that includes impressive clay *pithoi* (large Minoan storage jars).

Sanctuary of Poseidon & Amphitrite ARCHAEOLOGICAL SITE

(€2; ⊙ 8.30am-3pm Tue-Sun) Kionia, 3km northwest of Hora, has the remains of the 4th-century BC Sanctuary of Poseidon and his wife Amphitrite, a once-enormous complex that drew pilgrims with the deities' healing powers.

Tinos

Activities

KTEL Tours BUS

(22830 22440; www.poseidontravel-tinos.com; full-day tour €12) In summer, ask at the bus station about the daily tour that takes in a number of the island's villages, including Volax, Loutra, Pyrgos, Panormos and Tarambados. It's a great way to see the sights in a day. Tours departs the bus station at 11am, returning around 5pm.

Festivals & Events

Assumption of the Virgin Mary RELIGIOUS
(Feast of the Assumption) On 15 August the town is beyond full for the Virgin's feast day.

Sleeping

Hora is overcrowded on 25 March (Annunciation), Greek Easter, 15 August (Feast of the Assumption) and 15 November (Advent).

Book months ahead or join devotees sleeping in the street.

Nikoleta PENSION €
(22830 25863; www.nikoletarooms.gr; Kapodistriou 11; s/d from €35/45;) Little Nikoleta is a short walk inland from the southern end of town, but it's one of the best-value options. There's a lovely garden, and some rooms have kitchens.

★ **Studios Eleni II** GUESTHOUSE €€
(22830 24352; www.studio-eleni.gr; Ioannou Plati 7; d/tr €90/120;) A stone's throw from the Church of Panagia Evangelistria, pocket-rocket Eleni runs this beautiful guesthouse, all whitewashed walls, pale linen and a supremely photogenic Cycladic courtyard. Rooms each have a fridge, and share a small kitchenette.

Eleni also runs Studios Eleni I, which is of an equally high standard at the southern end of town, close to Agios Fokas Beach. Port transfer is offered by both properties.

Hotel Tinion
HISTORIC HOTEL €€

(☑ 22830 22261; www.tinionhotel.gr; Eleftherias Sq; s/d/tr incl breakfast €60/75/90; ❋ 🕙) This old-school central hotel dates from the 1920s, and has a broad verandah and sweeping stairs leading to comfortable, high-ceilinged rooms. They are a little dated in decor but not without charm, especially for the price; try to score a balcony with sea views. Breakfast is bumper.

Altana Hotel
BOUTIQUE HOTEL €€

(☑ 22830 25102; www.altanahotel.gr; s/d/ste incl breakfast from €80/90/120; 🕙 May-Oct; ❋ 🕙 💺) Located about a 10-minute walk north of the town centre en route to Kionia Beach, this agreeable hotel has a modernist Cycladic style, with snow-white walls and cool interiors incorporating distinctive Tinian motifs.

✖ Eating

Tinian food tends to be fresh and creative, using local products. Beer lovers should look for Tinos' own artisanal Nissos beer (p343). Hora may have the widest range of restaurants, but some of most celebrated tavernas are found in remoter parts of the island.

Mesklies
CAFE €

(☑ 22830 22151; www.mesklies.gr; snacks €3.50-7; 🕙 9am-late) This harbourfront cafe does a fine line in breakfasts, but it's the patisserie's delectable sweets that catch most people's eyes. From the homemade ice cream (try the bitter chocolate) to traditional sweets like *liknaraki* (sweet cheese cupcakes) and almond cookies, you'll find something to like.

★ Marathia
CYCLADIC €€

(☑ 22830 23249; www.marathiatinos.gr; Ir Politechniou; mains €10-25; 🕙 noon-midnight; 🕙) Grilled red mullet with capers and lemon. Wild artichokes, baked on coals. A glass of crisp white. Waves lapping at the beach. Pretty flawless, as far as combinations go. Super-fresh ingredients, family recipes and a deep appreciation for Tinian cuisine make this seafront restaurant a special place.

San To Alati
CYCLADIC €€

(☑ 22830 29266; www.facebook.com/santoalati; Ir Politechniou; mains €10-17; 🕙 noon-midnight; 🕙) Meaning 'like salt', this cute seaside taverna takes its name from a royal-themed fairy tale (hence the crowns and salt shakers). The place lives up to its Aegean cuisine

label, with extensive use of local produce, from local cheeses to just-out-of-the-sea *kalamari*, octopus and catch of the day.

Tarsanas
SEAFOOD €€

(☑ 22830 24667; Kazanova 5; mains €9-20, fish by kg; 🕙 noon-11pm; 🕙) The owner grills out front of this friendly, rustic spot, tucked away at the southern end of the harbour. It specialises in seafood: try smoked fish dip and anchovies wrapped in vine leaves, or splurge on lobster spaghetti.

Itan Ena Mikro Karavi
MEDITERRANEAN €€

(☑ 22830 22818; Trion Ierarchon; mains €13-27; 🕙 lunch & dinner; 🕙) Named for the opening line of a children's tale ('There was a little boat...'), this elegant indoor-outdoor eatery serves Greek fare with creative Mediterranean flair. Dishes like slow-cooked pork and rabbit ravioli are made with impeccably sourced local ingredients, and the setting and service are first-class.

To Koutouki Tis Elenis
TAVERNA €€

(☑ 22830 24857; G Gagou 5; mains €9-22; 🕙 noon-11pm; 🕙) This colourful, rustic little place is on the narrow taverna-packed lane veering off the bottom of Evangelistria. The menu bursts with local flavours. Try fresh cheeses, fish soup, artichoke pie or the delicious fritters made from fennel leaf.

ⓘ Information

Malliaris Travel (☑ 22830 24242; www.malliaristravel.gr; 🕙 9am-9pm) Sells ferry tickets.

Around Tinos

The countryside of Tinos is a glorious mix of broad terraced hillsides, mountaintops crowned with crags, unspoiled villages, fine beaches and fascinating architecture that includes picturesque dovecotes. Rent wheels to see it all.

Kionia, 3km northwest of Hora, has several small beaches and the scant remains of the 4th-century BC Sanctuary of Poseidon & Amphitrite (p339), a once-enormous complex that drew pilgrims.

First along the way north of town, beautiful **Ktikados** perches in a hanging valley and has a matched set of blue-topped church and campanile. **Drosia** is tops for local lunches and magnificent views.

Kambos sits on the top of a scenic hill surrounded by fields and is home to the **Costas Tsoclis Museum** (☑ 22830 51009;

DON'T MISS

MARVELLOUS MARBLE

On the slopes above Pyrgos is the outstanding **Museum of Marble Crafts** (☑ 22830 31290; www.piop.gr; adult/child €3/free; ☉ 10am-6pm Mar–mid-Oct, to 5pm mid-Oct–Mar, closed Tue year-round), a modern, well-curated complex that creatively explains quarrying and sculpting techniques. It includes films and beautifully illustrated displays with English translations, along with top examples of artefacts and architectural features shaped from Tinian marble. The films of some of the last living quarrymen plying their trade are fascinating.

Kambos; ☉ 10am-1.30pm & 6-9pm Wed-Mon Jun-Sep) **FREE**, home to works by the renowned contemporary artist.

Don't miss **Tarabados**, a fun maze of small streets decorated with marble sculptures and leading to a breezy valley lined with dovecotes (look for the sign 'Pigeon Houses' Area'). Explore!

About 17km northwest of Hora, lovely **Kardiani** perches on a steep cliff slope enclosed by greenery. Narrow lanes wind through the village, and the views towards Syros are exhilarating.

Pyrgos is a stunning, church-dotted hamlet where even the cemetery is a feast of carved marble, and the perfect village square looks like a film set. During the late 19th and early 20th centuries, Pyrgos was the centre of a remarkable sculpture enclave sustained by the supply of excellent local marble.

At the main entrance to Pyrgos, the fascinating **Museum House of Yannoulis Chalepas** (adult/child €3/free; ☉ 11am-3pm & 5.30-7.30pm Apr–mid-Oct) preserves the sculptor's humble rooms and workshop.

Further north of Pyrgos the main road ends at **Panormos**, a popular excursion destination for its photogenic fishing harbour lined with fish tavernas.

About 12km north of Hora on the north coast is emerald **Kolymvythra Bay**, where **Tinos Surf Lessons** (www.tinossurflessons. com; surfing lesson from €20 per person; ☉ 10am-9pm) takes advantage of the breaks at two excellent sandy beaches. It offers surf tuition, plus rentals of surfboards, bodyboards, kayaks and canoes.

A worthwhile detour inland takes you to **Agapi**, in a lush valley of dovecotes. Ethereal

and romantic, it lives up to its name (meaning 'love' in Greek).

Pass eye-catching **Krokos** with its Evangelismou tis Panagias, an enormous Catholic church, to reach **Volax**, about 6km directly north of Hora. This hamlet sits at the heart of an amphitheatre of low hills festooned with hundreds of enormous, multicoloured boulders.

The ruins of the Venetian fortress of **Exobourgo** lie 2km south of Volax, on top of a mighty 640m rock outcropping.

The northeast coast beach at **Livada** is spectacular, but the ones east of Hora, like Porto and Pahia Ammos, can seem comparatively built-up.

🛏 Sleeping & Eating

★ **Tinos Habitat** COTTAGE €€€
(☑ 22830 41907; www.tinos-habitat.gr; Triantoros; 4-person house from €200; 🅿 ≋) The cleverly designed complex lies in a village 6km northeast of Hora, and gives you a taste of traditional island life. Five houses incorporate local stone and marble and are fully equipped with kitchen, living spaces and outdoor areas (most with private pool). Our favourite is the dovecote irresistibly transformed into a three-bedroom villa.

Volax TAVERNA €
(☑ 22830 41021; mains €7-12; ☉ noon-3pm & 6-10pm) Volax is a scenic hamlet about 6km directly north of Hora, surrounded by low hills festooned with hundreds of enormous, multicoloured boulders. The taverna Volax serves reliable Tinian favourites like wild artichokes with lemon.

Drosia TAVERNA €
(☑ 22830 21807; Ktikados; mains €9-13; ☉ noon-3pm & 6-10pm Easter-Oct; 🅿) At Drosia, in the pretty village of Ktikados, you can dine on fish or lamb and take in the magnificent views.

★ **Thalassaki** GREEK €€
(☑ 22830 31366; Ormos Isternia; mains €9-18, fish by kg; ☉ noon-10pm Easter-Oct; 🅿) Come to Ormos Isternia, a stony beach set among plunging hills south of Pyrgos, on a foodie pilgrimage. The seafront taverna crafts local cheese, tomatoes, wild artichokes and the like into veritable works of art and has outstanding seafood prepared in deliciously creative fashion (eg octopus baked in grape molasses, mussels with wine and fennel). Book ahead in high season.

★ O Ntinos   CYCLADIC €€

(☑22830 31673; mains €8-16; ☎) Superlative home-cooked island specialties, served on a sunny terrace overlooking Giannaki Bay.

🍷 Drinking & Nightlife

Nissos Cyclades Microbrewery
at Tinos Island   MICROBREWERY

(☑22830 26333; http://nissos.beer; ⊙ tours mid-Jun–mid-Sep on Mon, Thu & Sat) It's well worth visiting this microbrewery to familiarise yourself with the mysteries of brewing and to sample Nissos' beer collection.

SYROS   ΣΥΡΟΣ

POP 21,507

Endearing little Syros merges traditional and modern Greece. One of the smallest islands of the Cyclades and relatively rural outside the capital, it nevertheless has the highest population since it's the legal and administrative centre of the entire archipelago. It's also the ferry hub of the northern islands and home to Ermoupoli, the grandest of all Cycladic towns, with an unusual history. As the Cyclades' capital, it pays less heed to tourism, and its beaches never get as crowded as those of the neighbouring islands. It buzzes with life year-round, boasts great eateries and showcases the best of everyday Greek life.

History

Excavations of an Early Cycladic fortified settlement and burial ground at Kastri in the island's northeast date from the Neolithic era (2800–2300 BC).

During the 17th and 18th centuries, Capuchin monks and Jesuits settled on the island. Becoming overwhelmingly Catholic, Syros even called upon France for help during Turkish rule.

During the War of Independence, thousands of Orthodox refugees from islands ravaged by the Turks fled to Syros. They brought an infusion of Greek Orthodoxy and a fresh entrepreneurial drive that made Syros the commercial, naval and cultural centre of Greece during the 19th century. Syros' position declined in the 20th century, but you still see shipyards, textile manufacturing, thriving horticulture, a sizeable administrative sector, a university campus and a continuing Catholic population.

ℹ Getting There & Away

AIR

Sky Express (☑28102 23800; www.sky express.gr) flies daily from Athens (€90, 35 minutes) to Syros airport (JSY; ☑22810 81900), 5km south of Ermoupoli.

BOAT

Year-round ferries serve the mainland port of Piraeus. As the island group's capital, Syros theoretically has fair to good year-round ferry links with all the Cyclades islands. Check www. openseas.gr due to ever-changing schedules.

Most boats leave from the **main ferry quay**. There's a weekly **Blue Star** (www.bluestarfer ries.com) ferry linking Syros with each of the Small Cyclades islands and then Amorgos (Aegiali port). A few times a week, Blue Star links Syros with Dodecanese islands, including Patmos, Leros, Kos and Rhodes. There are weekly **Hellenic Seaways** (www.hellenicseaways.gr) links with the northeastern Aegean islands, including Patmos, Ikaria, Samos, Lesvos and Limnos. **Sea Jets** (www.seajets.gr) serve Kea, Kythnos and Lavrio.

Buy tickets at **Teamwork Holidays** (p348) or **Vassilikos** (p348) in Ermoupoli. Ask where your ferry will depart from, as it may dock anywhere on the western part of the port. Both agencies have the week's ferry schedule on their websites.

Boat Services from Syros

DESTINATION	DURATION	FARE (€)	FREQUENCY
Chios	8½hr	55	Tue
Ios	6½hr	21	Fri
Kos	6hr	47	Mon, Wed & Fri
Leros	5½hr	42	Mon & Wed
Mykonos	45-75min	11-17	1-3 daily
Naxos	4½hr	13	1-4 weekly
Paros	1hr-10½ hr	11-17	5-6 weekly
Patmos	4hr	39	Mon & Wed
Piraeus	3¼-5hr	24-37	1-3 daily
Rhodes	9-11hr	52	Mon, Wed & Fri
Santorini	9½hr	24	Tue & Sat
Tinos	30min	8-12	4 weekly

ℹ Getting Around

Regular **buses** (☑22810 82575; www.ktel-syrou.gr) loop from Ermoupoli bus station beside the ferry quay, taking in Galissas, Finikas,

Syros

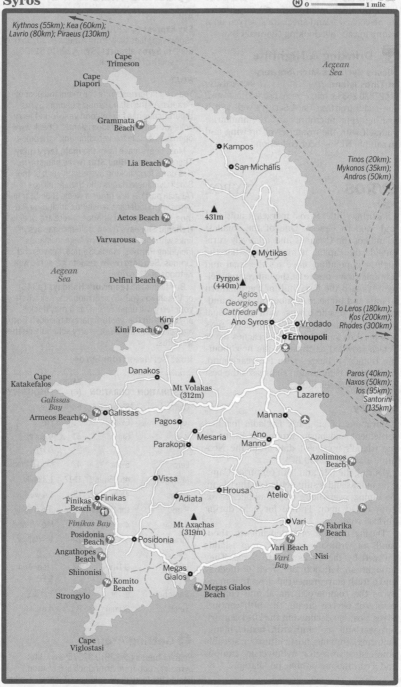

N

0 — 2 km
0 — 1 mile

Kythnos (55km); Kea (60km);
Lavrio (80km); Piraeus (130km)

Cape
Trimeson

Cape
Diapori

Aegean
Sea

Grammata
Beach

Kampos

Lia Beach

San Michalis

Tinos (20km);
Mykonos (35km);
Andros (50km)

Aetos Beach

431m

Varvarousa

Aegean
Sea

Delfini Beach

Mytikas

Pyrgos
(440m)

Agios
Georgios
Cathedral

Kini

Ano Syros

Vrodado

Kini Beach

Ermoupoli

To Leros (180km);
Kos (200km);
Rhodes (300km)

Cape
Katakefalos

Danakos

Mt Volakas
(312m)

Lazareto

Paros (40km);
Naxos (50km);
Ios (95km);
Santorini
(135km)

Galissas
Bay

Galissas

Pagos

Manna

Armeos Beach

Mesaria

Parakopi

Ano
Manno

Azolimnos
Beach

Vissa

Adiata

Hrousa

Atelio

Finikas
Beach

Finikas

Finikas Bay

Mt Axachas
(319m)

Vari

Fabrika
Beach

Posidonia
Beach

Posidonia

Vari Beach

Nisi

Angathopes
Beach

Vari
Bay

Shinonisi

Megas
Gialos

Komito
Beach

Megas Gialos
Beach

Strongylo

Cape
Viglostasi

Posidonia, Megas Gialos and Vari. The full loop takes about an hour, and buses run hourly in both directions, with a maximum fare of €1.70. About five buses go to Kini (€1.60, 35 minutes) or to Ano Syros (€1.60, 15 minutes) every day except Sunday. Schedules are posted at the waterfront bus station.

A free bus traverses the harbour between the car parks at the northern and southern ends of Ermoupoli (half-hourly 7am to 10pm Monday to Friday, to 4pm Saturday and Sunday).

You can hire cars (from €40 per day) and scooters (from €15) at waterfront agencies. Avoid driving in central Ermoupoli, as it's mostly stairs or pedestrianised ways.

From the port, **taxis** (☑ 22810 86222) charge around €4 to Ano Syros, €12 to Galissas and €12 to Vari.

Several rental agencies along the waterfront rent scooters (€18) and cars (€35).

Ermoupoli   Ερμούπολη

POP 11,407

As you sail into striking Ermoupoli, named after Hermes and formerly Greece's main port, its peaked hilltops emerge, each topped by a dazzling church. The Catholic settlers built on high ground, and the 19th-century Orthodox newcomers built from below. Now buildings spread in a pink and white cascade over it all, and the centre is a fun maze of stairways, pedestrianised shopping streets and neoclassical mansions all radiating out from the grand Plateia Miaouli, with its impressive town hall.

Catholic **Ano Syros** and Greek Orthodox **Vrodado** spill down from high hilltops to the northwest and northeast of town, with even taller hills rising behind.

◉ Sights

★ Industrial
Museum of Ermoupoli   MUSEUM
(☑ 22810 84762; www.ketepo.gr; George Papandreou 11; €3; ◷ 9am-5pm Mon-Fri Oct-Mar, 10am-3.30pm Mon-Fri, 10am-3.30pm & 6-8pm Sat, 10am-3pm Sun Apr-Sep) This excellent chronicle of Syros' industrial and shipbuilding traditions occupies a restored factory packed with more than 300 well-labelled items relating to sewing, printing, spinning, engines, ships and more. Ask if the Aneroussis lead shot factory is open – it's fascinating. Find the museum about 1km south of the centre, opposite the hospital on the road to Kini. At research time, there was talk about moving to a new location.

Apollo Theatre   THEATRE
(☑ 2281085192; www.facebook.com/apollontheater; Plateia Vardaka; €2; ◷ 10am-4pm & 6-10pm Mon, 10am-10pm Tue-Sat, 10am-2pm & 6-10pm Sun) Built in the 1860s, this venerable theatre was partly modelled on La Scala in Milan. Keep an eye out for regular theatre performances (in Greek), or pop in to take a look around.

Vaporia   AREA
Stroll the Vaporia district, east and northeast of Plateia Miaouli, for palm-lined squares and elegant shipowners' mansions (some now home to boutique hotels). The shipowners' wealth is evident in the grand Orthodox **Agios Nikolaos** (Vaporia District) loaded with fine murals, icons, gilt and chandeliers.

Plateia Miaouli   SQUARE
This great square is perhaps the finest urban space in the Cyclades. Once situated immediately upon the seashore, today it sits well inland and is dominated by the dignified neoclassical **town hall** (Plateia Miaouli), designed by Ernst Ziller. Flanked by palm trees and lined along all sides with cafes and bars, the square and accompanying statue are named for Hydriot naval hero Andreas Miaoulis.

The town's small, unremarkable **archaeological museum** (☑ 22810 88487; Benaki; adult/child €2/free; ◷ 8.30am-8pm) is housed in the rear of the town hall. A couple of elegant old-world cafes are found in the hall's wings, with al fresco seating for great people-watching.

🛏 Sleeping

Most budget options cluster above the ferry quay, while boutique hotels in renovated mansions dot the Vaporia district. Much accommodation is open year-round, with discounts in low season.

Hermoupolis Rooms   PENSION €
(☑ 22810 87475; www.hermoupolis-rooms.gr; Naxou; s/d/tr from €35/40/50; ❋ 🤶) There's a cheerful welcome at these well-kept self-catering rooms, a short climb from the waterfront. Front rooms open onto tiny, bougainvillea-cloaked balconies.

★ 1901
Hermoupolis Maison   BOUTIQUE HOTEL €€
(☑ 22810 84680; www.1901.gr; Palaion Patron Germanou 37-39; r from €75; ❋ 🤶) Housed in a 19th-century stone mansion, this delightful boutique hotel comprises just five rooms,

presided over by the ever-helpful Konstantinos and his wife. Rooms come with super-comfortable beds and free-standing tubs with Molton Brown toiletries, with quirky objects scattered throughout – antique telephones, an olive press, a Singer sewing machine. Terrific breakfast too.

Lila Guesthouse GUESTHOUSE €€

(☑22810 82738; www.guesthouse.gr; Kosma; s/d/tr incl breakfast €80/100/120, ste from €160; ❄✿🖥) In the former French consulate, these elegantly renovated rooms and suites are kitted out with impeccable modern decor and top-notch bathrooms. Suites are spacious, with dining tables and antiques. A bumper breakfast is served by the genial proprietors in the airy common area. Port pick-ups available.

Ethrion HOTEL €€

(☑22810 89066; www.ethrion.gr; Kosma 24; r €90-135; ❄🖥) The eight rooms and studios at family-run Ethrion are comfortable and well equipped. Opt for the ones with sea view if you can, and bear in mind that the ground-floor studio is on the dark side.

★**Wind Tales** BOUTIQUE HOTEL €€€

(☑6946771400; www.windtales.gr; Agiou Aloisiou; r from €150; ❄🖥) If you wish to linger after the madding crowd has gone and wander Ano Syros' labyrinthine lanes at your leisure, then try the Wind Tales' three gorgeous, individually designed rooms, one of them carved into natural rock. The service is wonderfully personalised, breakfast makes extensive use of local produce, and sipping cocktails on the terrace overlooking Ermoupoli is pure magic.

★**Ploes Hotel** BOUTIQUE HOTEL €€€

(☑22810 79360; www.hotelploes.com; Apollonos 2; d from €200, ste €600; ⊙Apr-Oct; ❄🖥) Unremitting elegance and attention to detail are hallmarks of this boutique beauty, inside a restored banker's mansion. Soaring ceilings, original artworks and designer furniture make the seven rooms here shine, and there's a private pavilion giving direct sea access to swimmers.

🍴 Eating & Drinking

Restaurants and cafe-bars throng the waterfront, especially along Akti Petrou Ralli – these fire up late, full of party people. Another great area for dining is the bougainvillea-bedecked laneways of Emmanouil Roidi and Kyparissou.

★**Kouzina** MEDITERRANEAN €€

(☑22810 89150; Androu 5; mains €12-26; ⊙7pm-12.30am Wed & Thu, 1pm-12.30am Fri & Sat, 1-6pm Sun; 🖥) In this colourfully lit, intimate dining room, fresh local ingredients are the building blocks of creative Mediterranean cuisine, from slow-cooked baby goat and smoked *mousakas* to *kalamari* with Cretan smoked pork. Decent wine list and craft beer to boot.

Sta Vaporia CAFE

(☑22810 76486; ⊙10am-3am) Down a signposted set of stairs behind Agios Nikolaos is this perfectly positioned all-day cafe. It's a cruisy terrace with postcard panoramas and a menu of coffee, cocktails, homemade lemonade and sangria, and snacks, large and small. Down below are popular seaside swimming platforms (so bring your swimsuit).

Kouchico COCKTAIL BAR

(☑22813 00880; www.facebook.com/kouchico; Ioannou Lavrentiou Ralli 15; ⊙7.30am-3am; 🖥) A hip spot to sip a coffee by day, Kouchico turns into a buzzy cocktail bar at night, with a trendy young crowd spilling out of its doors. The signature cocktails are not all to our taste, but involve quality ingredients.

DON'T MISS

ANO SYROS ΑΝΩ ΣΥΡΟΣ

The narrow lanes and whitewashed houses of Ano Syros, originally a medieval Catholic settlement, tower above Ermoupoli. From the bus terminus, head into the delightful maze and search out the finest of the Catholic churches, the 13th-century **Agios Georgios Cathedral**, with its star-fretted barrel roof and baroque capitals (still under renovation at the time of research). Continue past stunning viewpoints to reach the main street; the sweet **Our Lady of Mt Carmel**; the **Vamvakaris Museum** (€2; ⊙12.30-6.30pm Sat & Sun), celebrating locally born patriarch of *rembetika* (blues) Markos Vamvakaris; and the **monasteries** of the Jesuits and the Capuchins. Prepare to get lost, but try to find your way back to the view-enriched terraces of the handful of cafes and taverna along the main laneway.

Ermoupoli

Ermoupoli

◎ Sights
1 Agios Nikolaos	D1
2 Apollo Theatre	C1
3 Archaeological Museum	B2
4 Plateia Miaouli	B2
5 Town Hall	B2
6 Vaporia	C2

🛏 Sleeping
7 1901 Hermoupolis Maison	A1
8 Ethrion	A3
9 Hermoupolis Rooms	B4
10 Lila Guesthouse	A3
11 Ploes Hotel	D2

🍴 Eating
12 Kouzina	C3

🍷 Drinking & Nightlife
13 Kouchico	C2
14 Sta Vaporia	D1

WORTH A TRIP

SAN MICHALIS
ΣΑΝ ΜΙΧΑΛΗΣ

If you have your own wheels, don't miss the drive to the northern village of San Michalis, along the spine of Syros, with spectacular views of unspoilt valleys and neighbouring islands on either side. Famous for its cheese, San Michalis is now a small hamlet of stone houses and vineyards.

Walk the winding rock path to the hilltop church and get Syran food at its best at **Plakostroto** (☑ 6973980248; www.plakostroto.gr; mains €9-16; ☺ lunch & dinner May-Oct, Sat & Sun Nov-Apr; ☎). It serves local cheese plus rooster, lamb or rabbit grilled on the open wood fire. Views sweep down the hillside to Kea, Kythnos and beyond.

ⓘ Information

Alpha Bank (El Venizelou)

Eurobank (Akti Ethnikis Antistasis)

Piraeus Bank (Akti Petrou Ralli)

Information Booth (☑ 22810 80485; Akti Ethnikis Antistasis; ☺ hr vary)

Post Office (Protopapadaki; ☺ 9am-5pm Mon-Fri)

Teamwork Holidays (☑ 28810 83400; www.teamwork.gr; Akti Papagou 18; ☺ 9am-9pm) Arranges accommodation and excursions and sells ferry tickets.

Vassilikos (☑ 22810 84444; www.vassilikos.gr; Akti Papagou 10; ☺ 9am-9pm) Ferry tickets.

Around Syros

Outside Ermoupoli, Syros comprises a series of hills and valleys folding down to small bays and beaches, most well served by buses.

The old resort town **Galissas** has seen better days, but it has an appealing beach and is still popular with French travellers, and has a couple of excellent tavernas. Behind the Dolphin Bay Hotel is **Armeos**, the nudist beach.

South of Galissas, reachable via a short bus ride or a 40-minute walk, **Finikas** has a long, narrow strip of sand against a backdrop of tamarisk trees. South of the headland is **Posidonia**, another narrow, sandy beach, beyond which lies the delightful and popular **Agathopes** beach, with calm waters and a smattering of tavernas. Another 10-minute

walk south brings you to **Komito**, a sheltered bay backed by olive groves.

The beaches south of Galissas all have domatia, and some have hotels. It takes only about an hour to do a loop drive from Galissas around the south coast, so go exploring with your own wheels.

The south-coast town of **Megas Gialos** has a couple of roadside beaches with pedal boats for hire, but they are rather exposed when the *meltemi* (dry northerly wind) sweeps in in the summer. Gorgeous (and sheltered) **Vari Bay**, further east, is the better bet with its light grey sandy beach, though the waterfront and tavernas get packed with families in high season.

Kini Beach, on the west coast, has a long, thin stretch of beach popular with families due to its shallow waters.

🏃 Activities & Courses

Omilo   LANGUAGE
(☑ Athens 210 612 2896; www.omilo.com/syros) Offers summertime Greek language and culture courses on Syros and Andros. Courses take place in Azolimnos, 4km south of Ermoupoli.

Syros Windsurfing School   WINDSURFING
(☑ 6936713547;www.facebook.com/SyrosWindsurfingSchool; stand-up paddleboarding per hr €25) Organises windsurfing and stand-up paddleboarding for all ages and levels. Based at Finikas.

Cyclades Sailing   BOATING
(☑ 22810 82501; www.cyclades-sailing.gr) Large yacht-charter company, based at Finikas marina. See the website for the huge range of vessels and potential sailing areas. A week-long four-berth yacht in peak season costs from €1420.

🛌 Sleeping & Eating

Krinakia Agathopes   APARTMENT €
(☑ 22810 42375; apt from €50; ☺ May-Sep; ❄☎) Quiet, spacious, well equipped apartments overlooking Agkathopes Beach. Popular with families.

Hotel Alkyon   HOTEL €€
(☑ 22810 61761; www.alkyonsyros.gr; r from €60; ☺ Apr-Oct; ❄☎☒) Inland and about 1.5km from Megas Gialos is peaceful Hotel Alkyon, run by a charming French-Greek couple, with a large pool and spotless rooms. Hosts arrange seminars and activities that include painting and Greek gastronomy.

Blue Harmony Hotel　　　　HOTEL €€
(☑22810 71570; www.blueharmony.gr; r/tr from €126/135; ❋🛜) This waterfront hotel at Kini Beach makes a fine choice, with bright, well equipped rooms and a funky slate facade.

Hotel Benois　　　　HOTEL €€
(☑22810 42833; www.benois.gr; s/d/tr/f incl breakfast €70/77/90/121; ⊙Easter-Oct; ❋🛜🏊) A well-run hotel at the northern entrance to the village, the Benois has spick-and-span rooms that are all minimalist charm and neutral shades. It has relaxing and spacious public areas and an inviting swimming pool.

Allou Yialou　　　　SEAFOOD €€
(☑22810 71196; Kini Beach; mains €8-22; ⊙noon-10pm May-Sep; 🛜) Tops for eats on Kini Beach is Allou Yialou, absolutely waterfront and with excellent fish stew and other seafood. It's a prime sunset spot.

Iliovasilema　　　　CYCLADIC €€
(☑22810 43325; mains €8-16; ⊙noon-10pm Apr-Oct; 🛜) The name means sunset, and this west-coast fish-heavy restaurant is a fine choice for watching it. The menu is an ode to local produce. Try the *kakavia* (traditional fish soup) or the fennel pie.

MYKONOS　　ΜΥΚΟΝΟΣ

POP 10,134

Mykonos is the great glamour island of Greece and happily flaunts its sizzling St-Tropez-meets-Ibiza style and party-hard reputation.

The high-season mix of hedonistic holiday-makers, cruise-ship crowds and posturing fashionistas throngs Mykonos Town (aka Hora), a traditional whitewashed Cycladic maze, delighting in its authentic cubist charms and its chichi cafe-bar-boutique scene.

The number of tourists (and cashed-up A-listers) visiting Mykonos is booming, and hip new hotels, beach bars and restaurants are mushrooming. In July and August, come only if you are prepared to pay and are intent on joining the jostling street crowds, the oiled-up lounger lifestyle at the packed main beaches and the relentless party. Out of season, devoid of gloss and preening celebrities, find more subdued local life, the with occasional pelican wandering the empty streets and beaches that you will have largely to yourself.

Mykonos is also the jumping-off point for the archaeological site of the nearby island of Delos.

ⓘ Getting There & Away

BOAT
Year-round ferries serve mainland ports Piraeus and Rafina (the latter is usually quicker if you are coming directly from Athens airport), and nearby islands Tinos and Andros. In the high season, Mykonos is well connected with all neighbouring islands, including Paros and Santorini. Hora is loaded with ticket agents.

Mykonos has two ferry quays: the Old Port, 400m north of town, where some smaller fast ferries dock, and the New Port, 2km north of town, where the bigger fast ferries and all conventional ferries dock. When buying outgoing tickets, double-check which quay your ferry leaves from.

Excursion boats for Delos depart from the quay just off the waterfront of Mykonos Town.

Boat Services from Mykonos

DESTINATION	DURATION	FARE (€)	FREQUENCY
Andros	2hr 20min	18-19	1-2 daily
Folegandros	3½-6½	18-63	daily
Ios	2-3hr	52-57	3 daily
Iraklio	5hr	89	2 daily
Naxos	1hr 20min-3hr	13-53	3 daily
Paros	45-50min	35-53	up to 3 daily
Piraeus	2½-4½	32-63	2-3 daily
Rafina	2½-4½hr	32-52	3-4 daily
Santorini (Thira)	2½-4hr	52-71	up to 4 daily
Syros	45min-75min	11-17	1-2 daily

AIR
Mykonos Airport (☑22890 79000; www.mykonos-airport.com), 3km southeast of the town centre, has flights year-round to Athens with Sky Express (www.skyexpress.gr) and Aegean Airlines (www.aegeanair.com), among others, and to Thessaloniki with Astra Airlines (www.astra-airlines.gr) and Aegean Airlines.

From May to mid-September, direct European connections are plentiful, including easyJet flights from London, Geneva, Paris, Rome and Milan, and Air Berlin flights from German and Austrian hubs.

Mykonos

Tinos (15km);
Syros (30km);
Andros (70km);
Rafina (135km);
Piraeus (175km)

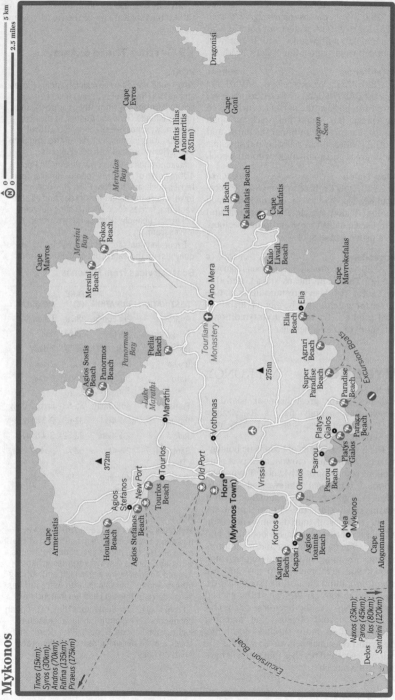

Dragonisi

Cape Evros

Cape Goni

Aegean Sea

Profitis Ilias Anomeritis (351m) ▲

Merchias Bay

Lia Beach

Kalafatis Beach

Cape Kalafatis

Cape Mavtos

Mersini Bay

Fokos Beach

Mersini Beach

Kalo Livadi Beach

Cape Mavrokefalas

Ano Mera

Tourliani Monastery

Elia Beach

Elia

Agios Sostis Beach

Panormos Beach

Panormos Bay

Ftelia Beach

Lake Maruthi

Marathi

▲ 275m

Agrari Beach

Super Paradise Beach

Paradise Beach

Excursion Boats

Vothonas

Platys Gialos

Paraga Beach

Cape Armenistis

372m ▲

Tourlos

Tourlos Beach

Old Port

New Port

Agios Stefanos

Houlakia Beach

Agios Stefanos Beach

Vrissi

Hora (Mykonos Town)

Psarou

Psarou Beach

Platys Gialos

Ornos

Nea Mykonos

Cape Alogomandra

Korfos

Kapari Beach

Kapari

Agios Ioannis Beach

Naxos (35km);
Paros (45km);
Ios (80km);
Santorini (120km)

Delos

Excursion Boat

ℹ️ Getting Around

TO/FROM THE AIRPORT

Buses from the southern bus station serve Mykonos' airport (€1.60). Some hotels and guesthouses offer free airport and port transfers. Otherwise, arrange airport transfer with your accommodation (around €7) or take a taxi to town (€10).

BOAT

Mykonos Cruises (📞 22890 23995; www. mykonos-cruises.gr; ⊙8am-7pm Apr-Oct) An association of sea-taxi operators offering services to the island's best beaches. See the timetables online. The main departure point is Platys Gialos, with drop-offs and pick-ups at Ornos, Paraga, Paradise, Super Paradise, Agrari and Elia beaches (return trip costs between €5 and €7). Cruises and personalised itineraries can also be arranged.

Sea Bus (📞 6978830355; www.mykonos-seabus.gr; one-way €2.50) This water-taxi service connects the New Port with Hora, running hourly from 9am to 10pm (more frequently when a cruise ship is in port).

BUS

The **KTEL Mykonos** (📞 22890 23360, 22890 26797; www.mykonosbus.com) bus network has two main terminals plus pick-up points at the Old and New Ports.

Low-season services are much reduced, but buses in high season run frequently; the fare is €1 to €2 depending on the distance travelled. Timetables are on the website. In July and August, some bus services run until 2am or later from the beaches.

Terminal A, the **southern bus station** (Fabrika Sq), known as Fabrika, serves Ornos and Agios Ioannis Beach, Platys Gialos, Paraga and Super Paradise Beaches.

Terminal B, the northern bus station, sometimes called Remezzo, is behind the OTE office and has services to Agios Stefanos via Tourlos, Ano Mera, and Kalo Livadi, Kalafatis and Elia beaches. Buses for Tourlos and Agios Stefanos stop at the Old and New Ports.

A regular bus connects the New Port with the southern bus station, and there are buses running between the southern bus station and the nearby airport. In summer there's a bus to Paradise Beach from the Old Port.

Private transfer buses operate in summer's peak every hour (11am to 11pm) from the Old Port to Paradise Beach (via Fabrika). There are also frequent shuttles to Super Paradise Beach.

CAR & MOTORCYCLE

Cars start at €45 per day in high season and €30 in low season. Scooters/quads are around €20/40 in high season and €15/30 in low season.

Avis and Sixt are among the agencies at the airport, and there are dozens of hire places all over the island, particularly near the ports and bus stations (which is where the large public car parks are found – you can't drive into Hora proper). You can rent from Mykonos Accommodation Centre (p357).

Apollon (📞 22890 24136; www.apollonrentacar.com; Epar. Od. Mikonou; ⊙9am-8pm) One of several agencies near Hora's southern bus station.

OK Rent A Car (📞 22890 23761; www. okmykonos.com; Agios Stefanos) Near New Port.

TAXI

Taxis (📞 22890 23700, 22890 22400) queue at Hora's Plateia Manto Mavrogenous (Taxi Sq), bus stations and ports, but waits can be long in high season. All have meters, and the minimum fare is €3.50 (plus €0.50 per bag, €3.30 for phone booking).

Approximate fares from Hora include New Port (€6), Ornos (€10), Platys Gialos (€10), Paradise (€11), Kalafatis (€18) and Elia (€18).

Hora (Mykonos)
Χώρα (Μύκονος)

POP 8397

Hora (also known as Mykonos), the island's well-preserved port and capital, is a warren of narrow alleyways and whitewashed buildings overlooked by the town's famous windmills. In the heart of the waterfront Little Venice quarter, which is spectacular at sunset, tiny flower-bedecked churches jostle with glossy boutiques, and there's a cascade of bougainvillea around every corner. High-season streets are crowded with chic stores, cool galleries, jangling jewellers and both languid and loud music bars – plus a catwalk cast of thousands.

⊙ Sights

★ **Aegean Maritime Museum**   MUSEUM
(📞 22890 22700; Enoplon Dynameon 10; adult/student €4/2; ⊙10.30am-1pm & 6.30-9pm Apr-Oct) Amidst the barnacle-encrusted amphorae, ye olde nautical maps and navigation instruments, there are numerous detailed models of various famous sailing ships and paddle steamers. You can also learn the difference between an Athenian trireme, a Byzantine dromon and an ancient Egyptian

seagoing ship. There's an enormous Fresnel lighthouse lantern in the courtyard.

★ Panagia Paraportiani CHURCH

(Paraportianis) Mykonos' most famous church, the whitewashed, rock-like Panagia Paraportiani, comprises four small chapels – plus another on an upper storey reached by an exterior staircase. It's usually locked but the fabulously photogenic whitewashed exterior is the drawcard.

Rarity Gallery GALLERY

(✆22890 25761; www.raritygallery.com; Kalogera 20; ⏰10am-midnight) FREE This little gallery is well worth a peek for its temporary exhibitions that showcase paintings, sculpture and photography by the likes of Paul Rousso, Yigal Ozeri and George Pousenkoff.

Windmills LANDMARK

(off Plateia Alefkandra) Constructed in the 16th century by the Venetians for the milling of wheat, seven of Mykonos' iconic windmills are picturesquely situated on a small hill overlooking the harbour.

Archaeological Museum MUSEUM

(✆22890 22325; Agiou Stefanou; adult/child €4/ free; ⏰9am-4pm Tue-Sun) Peruse pottery from Delos, dating back to the 9th century BC, and grave *stelae* (pillars) and jewellery from the island of Renia (Delos' necropolis). Chief exhibits include a statue of Hercules in Parian marble.

Lena's House MUSEUM

(✆22890 22591; Enoplon Dynameon 10; ⏰6-9pm May–mid-Oct) FREE This charming late-19th-century, middle-class Mykonian house (with furnishings intact) takes its name from its last owner, Lena Skrivanou. It's next door to the Aegean Maritime Museum.

---

❶ NAVIGATING HORA (MYKONOS)

Without question, you will soon pass the same junction twice. It's entertaining at first, but can become frustrating amid throngs of equally lost people and fast-moving locals. For quick-fix navigation, familiarise yourself with Plateia Manto Mavrogenous (Taxi Sq), and the three main streets of Matogianni, Enoplon Dynameon and Mitropoleos, which form a horseshoe behind the waterfront.

Mykonos Folklore Museum MUSEUM

(✆22890 22591; Paraportianis; ⏰10.30am-2.30pm & 5.30-8.30pm Jun-Sep) FREE This folklore museum, housed in an 18th-century sea captain's house, features a large collection of furnishings and other artefacts, including old musical instruments.

🏃 Activities & Tours

Mykonos Accommodation Centre (p357) organises excursions and guided tours, and arranges private tours and charters. Tours go to Delos (adult/child €50/25), including the return boat trip, admission fee and guide, and Tinos (€70/45) to see its holy church and island sights. It also organises a walking tour of Hora and a bus tour around the island (€40/25). A full-day island cruise along the south coast (€70/40), a sunset cruise (€45/30) and a 4WD safari to isolated beaches (€65/35) are also available.

Mykonos Cruises (p351) runs sea-taxis to various south-coast beaches and can arrange fishing trips and private cruises.

Mykonos Tour & Excursions WALKING

(✆22890 79376; www.mykonos-web.com; €69) This four-hour tour of the island takes in a couple of beaches and the monastery of Ano Mera by bus, and the highlights of Mykonos Town – Little Venice, the windmills, Paraportiani church – on foot. Knowledgeable guides.

Mykonos On Board Sailing SAILING

(✆6932471055; www.mykonosonboard.com) Highly recommended private and semi-private yachting excursions around Mykonos and to nearby islands Delos and Rhenia.

🛏 Sleeping

MyCocoon Hostel HOSTEL €

(✆22890 23168; www.hostelmykonos.com; Kaminaki; dm/q €50/350; ✴🛜) A lot of thought has gone into this stylish new hostel, from the custom-made bunks which are like Cycladic houses in miniature, allowing dorm guests some privacy, to ample storage space for luggage and a good ratio of guests per bathroom. It's a block from the Old Port.

Andriani's Guest House GUESTHOUSE €€

(✆22890 23091; www.andrianis.com.gr; d/apt €108/152; 🅿✴🛜) This clutch of typical Cycladic rooms and studios sits above the School of Fine Arts a few minutes' walk from the heart of Hora. There's a peaceful garden, and free pick-up and drop-off.

Hotel Jason HOTEL €€
(✆22890 23481; www.hoteljason-mykonos.gr; d/
tr €130/110; P❄🖂) With spotless, tiled
rooms, some with heavy wooden beams,
some with kitchenettes, this friendly budget
hotel is an easy walk from Ornos Beach and
a short ride from Hora. Doubles are nicer
than the triple rooms.

Town Suites APARTMENT €€
(✆22890 23160; www.mykonos-accommodation.
com; d/tr €240/315; ❄🖂) Owned by John, the
man behind the info-rich Mykonos Accommodation Centre (p357), this hidden complex of six bright, high-beamed suites and
apartments makes a splendid choice. Each
has well-equipped kitchen and sunny outdoor space. Gay-friendly, and in a quiet area.
Check in at MAC and you'll be guided to the
unsigned complex. Low-season rates are a
marvellous €70.

Fresh Hotel BOUTIQUE HOTEL €€
(✆22890 24670; www.hotelfreshmykonos.com;
Kalogera 31; s/d incl breakfast €160/170; ⊙mid-
May–Oct; ❄🖂) In the heart of town, with a
lush and leafy garden and highly regarded
on-site restaurant, Fresh is indeed very
fresh, with compact and stylishly minimalist rooms. Rates fall to €70/80 in the low
season.

Hotel Lefteris PENSION €€
(✆22890 23128; www.lefterishotel.gr; Apollonas
9; d from €130; ❄🖂) Tucked uphill and away
from the crowds, a colourful entrance-way
leads to pristine, compact rooms and a
warm welcome. A young family now runs
this eight-room guesthouse (established by
the owner's grandfather in the 1970s). Individually styled rooms have TV and air-con,
and there's a roof terrace with views. Winter
prices drop to €35.

★ Semeli Hotel HOTEL €€€
(✆22890 27466; www.semelihotel.gr; off Rohari;
d incl breakfast from €460; ❄🖂) Expansive
grounds, a glamorous restaurant terrace
and swimming pool, and stylish, contemporary rooms combine to make this one of
Mykonos' loveliest (and more affordable)
top-end hotels. Low-season rates make it
considerably more accessible.

**Portobello
Boutique Hotel** BOUTIQUE HOTEL €€€
(✆22890 23240; www.portobello-hotel.gr; Kaminaki; s/d/ste €169/289/589; ❄🖂) In an
elevated location on the edge of Mykonos

> **ℹ SLEEPING ON MYKONOS**
>
> In July and August, a no-frills double
> room with private bathroom in Hora
> costs about €100; midrange options
> cost €100 to €250. The sky's the limit
> for the top-end category. It's best not to
> arrive in July or August without a reser-
> vation, as there will be few vacancies.
> Some places insist on a minimum stay
> during the peak period. Noise levels in
> Hora and popular resorts are high in
> summer.

Town overlooking a ruined windmill, this
welcoming hotel is a prime sunset-viewing
spot. Delicious breakfast includes homemade yoghurt, and the staff are more than
happy to help you plan your stay.

✘ Eating

Sakis Grill House KEBAB €
(✆22890 24848; Grecia; mains from €5; ⊙24hr)
Sometimes you want a fancy meal, and sometimes there's nothing better than tucking into
a heaped portion of lamb or chicken souvlaki, or a bounty of doner kebab spilling out
of pitta bread. Caters to clubbing night owls.

Taste Diaries CRÊPES €
(✆22890 29117; www.facebook.com/TheTaste
Diaries; mains €6-10; ⊙24hr; 🖂) Sandwiches
and crêpes are served at all hours on the
waterfront. Build your own from gourmet
ingredients, or go with fab menu suggestions like a sweet crêpe of white praline,
almond slices, caramel and kiwi.

Nice n Easy FUSION €€
(✆22890 25421; www.niceneasy.gr; Little Venice; mains €12-25; ⊙9am-1am; 🖂) With a
great view of Mykonos' windmills from its
seafront terrace, this Athenian outpost specialises in organic fusion dishes. The chef
has spent time in California, and as a result
healthy options like egg-white omelettes,
quinoa salad and various vegan offerings
appear on the menu.

Joanna's Nikos Place Taverna GREEK €€
(✆22890 24251; mains €8-17; ⊙10am-11pm; 🖂)
Run by the delightful Joanna herself and
overlooking the beach just a few minutes'
walk south of Mykonos Town, this taverna
focuses on Greek standards and it does
them very well, particularly the meze and
the mixed grill.

Hora (Mykonos)

N 0 ——————— 100 m

Aegean Sea

Old Port (350m);
Tourlos (1.5km);
New Port (2km);
Agios Stefanos (4km)

Agiou Stefanou

3

8

Northern
Bus Station

Peristeronas Village (3km);
Mykonos (4km)

25

Port

Old
Jetty

Agia
Anna

Polikandrioti

Excursion
Boats for
Delos
Delos Boat
Ticket Kiosk   Sea Bus

Plateia
Karaoli
Dimitriou

Plateia Manto
Mavrogenous
(Taxi Sq)

21

18

4

Paraportianis

Panagia
Paraportiani

2

10   15

Akti Kambani

Platia
Kyriakis

7

Apollonos

33   17

Drakopoulou

Agios Vlassos   Kambani   32

Mavrogenous

Agias Annis

Inglesi

24

23

Sotiros

Agias Kyriakis

28

Portobello
Boutique
Hotel (40m)

36

Agion Saranta

Zouganeli

LITTLE
VENICE

22

34

K Georgouli

Panteleimonos

Ag Gerasimou

31

5

Matogianni

Plateia
Goumenou

13

11

35

20   26

Katsoni

Paneraki

Meletopoulou

Mitropoleos

Kalogera

6

Plateia
Alefkandra

14

27

Aegean
Maritime
Museum

19

1

16

30

37

Litous

Panahrantou

Malamatenias

Windmills

Baou

Legko Steno

Agias Paraskevis

Tria Pigadia
(Three Wells)

Enoplon Dynameon

Touliani

Eterias

Rohari

K Milon

Basoula

Ipirou

9

Laka

D Koutsi

Semeli Hotel (40m);
Hotel Elysium (300m)

Mirodiou

12

Sourneli

Aghios Efthimiou

Artakinou

Southern (Fabrika; 80m);
Joanna's Nikos Place Taverna (500m)

Andriani's Guest
House (300m)

Hora (Mykonos)

◎ **Top Sights**

◎ **Sights**

🛏 **Sleeping**

🍴 **Eating**

🍸 **Drinking & Nightlife**

🎭 **Entertainment**

🛍 **Shopping**

Eva's Garden   GREEK €€
(☎22890 22160; www.evas-garden.gr; Plateia Goumenou; mains €12-19; ⊙6.30pm-midnight; 🖥) Its patio shaded by hanging vines, this tempting corner of Eden focuses on traditional Greek specialities, such as *spaniko-pita* (spinach pie), moussaka and plenty of grilled fish.

Nikos Taverna   GREEK €€
(☎22890 24320; www.tavernanikos.gr; Mavrou Markou; mains €13-20; ⊙11.30am-1.30am) Still going strong after more than 40 years, this casual taverna serves heaped platters of seafood, as well as Greek standards, such as lamb *kleftiko*. Great value, and there's a semi-resident pink pelican who hangs around in hope of fish.

⭐**Funky Kitchen**   FUSION €€€
(☎22890 27272; www.funkykitchen.gr; mains €18-31; ⊙6pm-1am; 🖥) The open kitchen of this contemporary restaurant brings forth beautifully presented Mediterranean fusion dishes such as seared tuna with smoky aubergine mousse, octopus carpaccio with pink peppercorns and rack of lamb with cumin fava, the likes of which will tempt you back until you drift into insolvency. The chocolate nirvana is orgasm on a plate. Book ahead.

⭐**M-Eating**   MEDITERRANEAN €€€
(☎22890 78550; www.m-eating.gr; Kalogera 10; mains €17-38; ⊙7pm-1am daily; 🖥) Attentive service, soft lighting and relaxed luxury are the hallmarks of this creative restaurant specialising in fresh Greek produce prepared with flair. Sample anything from sea bass tartare to rib-eye veal with honey truffle. Don't miss the dessert of Mykonian honey pie.

Daniele & Alessandro   ITALIAN €€€
(☎22890 25852; Agia Moni Square; mains €15-39; ⊙noon-11pm; 🖥) After the runaway success of their **restaurant** (☎22890 71513; mains €16-39; ⊙noon-midnight; 🖥) in Ano Mera, this Italian couple have brought their superlative Italian cuisine to Hora. The menu is short and sweet – standouts include penne with homemade pesto and tender beef tagliata.

🍷 **Drinking & Nightlife**

Night action in town starts around 11pm and warms up by 1am. Hora's Little Venice is a swath of colourful bars; behind them are some excellent clubs. Another prime spot is the Tria Pigadia (Three Wells) area on Enoplon Dynameon.

⭐**Popolo**   COFFEE
(☎22890 22208; www.popolomykonos.com; Drakopoulou 18; ⊙8.30am-2.30am; 🖥) Hidden in Hora's labyrinthine depths, this tiny cafe

has gained a reputation as the best place for coffee on Mykonos. Freshly cooked breakfasts, plus salads, sandwiches and juices throughout the day seal the deal.

Galleraki
BAR

(☑22890 27188; www.galleraki.com; Little Venice; ☺8am-late; ☎) Choose plum waterfront seating or the upstairs balcony at this friendly cafe-bar, and order one of its ace fresh-fruit cocktails (like the signature 'katerinaki', made with melon) or a champagne mix.

Piano Bar
COCKTAIL BAR

(☑22890 23719; www.thepianobar.com; Agion Anargyron 24; ☺7pm-3am; ☎) With the sunset lighting up Mykonos' windmills, this Little Venice bar is a perfect place for watching the greatest free show on earth while sipping a reasonably priced cocktail. Cabaret and live music take over once the sun goes down.

Cosi
BAR

(☑22890 27727; Matoghiannia; ☺10am-6am; ☎) This, erm, cosy nook with bohemian lampshades is a cafe by day with a few al fresco tables. By night it morphs into a lively little bar with occasional DJ sets.

Semeli
COCKTAIL BAR

(☑22890 26505; http://semelithebar.gr; Little Venice; ☺9am-late) Recently refurbished by renowned Greek architect Pavlos Ninios, this funky cocktail bar in the heart of Little Venice draws the bold and the beautiful with its signature cocktails and DJ sets.

Remezzo
CLUB

(☑22890 25700; https://remezzo-mykonos.com; Polikandrioti; ☺6pm-4am) International hits pump until the wee hours of the morning, with plenty of beautiful people burning up the dance floor.

☆ Entertainment

★Cine Manto
CINEMA

(☑22890 26165; www.cinemanto.gr; Meletopoulou; adult/child €8/6; ☺9pm & 11pm Jun-Sep) Need a break from the bars and clubs? Seek out this gorgeous open-air cinema, in a perfect garden setting. There's a cafe here too. Movies are shown in their original language; view the program online.

🔒 Shopping

Fashion boutiques and art galleries vie for attention. Mavrogenous St is good for art, Matogliani is best for luxe brands and excellent Greek designers, while the streets of

Little Venice mix fashion with jewellery and tat. Most stores close in the winter (November to March).

★Eliza's Art Gallery
ARTS & CRAFTS

(☑22890 24461; www.elizasgallery.com; Mavrogenous 15; ☺10am-10pm) Gorgeous glass creations, quirky lamps, jewellery and works by renowned Naxos sculptor Yiannis Nanouris.

★iMuseum Shop
ART

(☑22890 77370; www.i-museumshop.com; Dilou 8; ☺10am-10pm) An elegant and innovative boutique, selling approved hand-crafted replicas of pieces showcased in the most important museums of Greece – including classic art, jewellery, ceramics and figurines.

HEEL Athens Lab
FASHION & ACCESSORIES

(☑22890 77166; www.heel.gr; Panahrantou; ☺11am-2am) ✍ Ecologically friendly garments made from organic cotton and other sustainable fibres, as well as one-of-a-kind jewellery made from recycled materials.

Mayonaisa Darling
JEWELLERY

(☑6975592478; www.mayonaisadarling.com; Drakopoulou 6; ☺10am-9pm) Worth buying for the designer's name alone, this collection of original handmade jewellery uses hypoallergenic materials, semi-precious stones and recycled pieces, such as gears from vintage clocks.

Delaros Fashion D-Tales
FASHION & ACCESSORIES

(☑22890 79359; www.delaros.gr; Matheou Andronikou 9; ☺10am-midnight) Gladiator sandals, handmade loom bags, wrap jumpsuits, beachwear, butterfly air maxi dresses, geometric Grecian-style jewellery and more by Greek designers such as Nadia Rapti, Milk & Honey, Monochrome, Park House, Noilence, Most Chic, Kyma Sandals and Thalatta.

Olive Oil Shop
GIFTS & SOUVENIRS

(☑22890 23598; Matogianni 15; ☺10am-midnight) Going strong for more than 20 years, this cute shop specialises in all things olive oil – soap, skincare products, the oil itself, plus olivewood kitchen implements and locally produced honey and herbs.

TЯUE Image
FASHION & ACCESSORIES

(☑22890 24432; Kalogera 11; ☺10am-11.30pm) These hand-printed T-shirts with a design of your choice are a good alternative to the corny, mass-produced tat sold nearby. Funky hand-printed shoes too.

Mykonos
Leather Shop FASHION & ACCESSORIES
(☑22890 78660; K Georgouli 37; ☺9.30am-10pm)
Gorgeous, colourful handmade leather
purses, bags, belts and accessories.

Mykonos Sandals SHOES
(☑22890 22451; www.mykonos-sandals.gr; Little
Venice; ☺10am-10pm) Come for the sunset
cocktails and stay for the handmade leather
sandals.

International Press BOOKS
(Kambani 5; ☺10am-9pm) International newspapers, magazines and books.

ℹ Information

Mykonos has no tourist office; visit travel agencies instead. Online, visit www.inmykonos.com
and www.mykonos.gr for more information.

There is information online at www.inmykonos.
com and www.mykonos.gr.
Mykonos Accommodation Centre (MAC;
☑22890 23408; www.mykonos-accommoda-
tion.com; 1st fl, Enoplon Dynameon 10; ☺9am-
1pm & 4-9pm) Helpful for all things Mykonos.
Sea & Sky (☑22890 22853; www.seasky.gr;
Akti Kambani; ☺9am-9pm) Sells ferry tickets.
Delia Travel (☑22890 22322; Akti Kambani;
☺9am-9pm) Ferry tickets.
Police Station (☑22890 22716) On the road
to the airport.
Post Office (☺9am-5pm Mon-Fri)

Around Mykonos

Aside from Hora, the island's only other village of any size is Ano Mera, which has the
attractive **Tourliani Monastery** (Ano Mera;
€1; ☺9am-1pm & 3.30-7pm Mon-Sat, 11am-1pm &
3.30-7pm Sun) on its taverna-lined square.

🏖 Beaches

Mykonos' golden-sand beaches in their
formerly unspoilt state were the pride of
Greece. Now most are jammed with umbrellas and backed by beach bars, but they do
make for a hopping scene that draws floods
of beachgoers. Moods range from the simply hectic to the outright snobby, and nudity
levels vary.

Without your own wheels, catch buses
from Hora or caïques from Ornos and Platys
Gialos to further beaches. Mykonos Cruises
(p351) has an online timetable of its sea-
taxi services.

The nearest beaches to Hora were over-
taken by the construction of the New Port.

That leaves little **Agios Stefanos** (4km
north of Hora), within sight of docking
cruise ships. There's a tiny strip of sand in
town, **Agia Anna**.

About 5km southwest of Hora are family-
oriented **Agios Ioannis** (where *Shirley Valentine* was filmed) and **Kapari**. The nearby
packed and noisy **Ornos** and the package-
holiday resort of **Platys Gialos** have boats for
the glitzier beaches to the east. In between
these two is **Psarou**, a magnet for the Greek
cognoscenti.

Approximately 1km south of Platys Gialos
you'll find **Paraga Beach**, which has a small
gay section. Party people should head about
1km east to famous **Paradise**, which is not
a recognised gay beach but has an action-
packed younger scene, a camping resort
(www.paradisemykonos.com) and nightlife
that doesn't quit. Down a steep access road,
Super Paradise (aka Plintri or Super P) has
a fully gay section (including the JackieO'
beach club) and a huge eponymous club.

Mixed and gay-friendly **Elia** is a long,
lovely stretch of sand and is the last caïque
stop. A few minutes' walk west from here is
the secluded **Agrari**.

Further east, **Kalafatis** is a hub for water
sports (including diving and windsurfing),
and **Lia** has a remote, end-of-the-road feel.

North-coast beaches can be exposed to the
meltemi, but **Panormos** and **Agios Sostis**
with their golden sand are fairly sheltered
and less busy than the south-coast beaches.

For out-of-the-way beaching you'll need
tough wheels to reach the likes **Fokos** and
Mersini on the northeast coast.

🏊 Activities

There's good diving around Mykonos, with
wrecks, caves and walls to explore, and
scuba diving operators on Paradise Beach
and Lia Beach. Kalafatis Beach and Ftelia
Beach are good for windsurfing, while Platys
Gialos is the place to try flyboarding or rent
a stand-up paddleboard or kayak.

⭐**Yummy Pedals** MOUNTAIN BIKING
(☑6972299282, 22890 71883; www.yummy
pedals.gr; 2hr tour from €40) A world away from
the beach bars, multilingual Dimitra offers
you guided mountain-biking tours through
the backroads of Mykonos. The duration
and route is personalised to fit your skill
level, but may take in farms, villages and
quiet beaches (with swimming and snack-
ing stops). Tours begin and end at Dimitra's

family's vineyard, with the option of food and wine.

★Platys Gialos Watersports   WATER SPORTS
(☑6977279584; www.mykonoswatersports.gr; Platys Gialos Beach; stand-up paddleboard 1hr €30; ☺9am-9pm) This operator specialises in adrenalin-packed water sports and arranges wakeboarding, wakeskating, waterskiing and wakesurfing sessions. They can also introduce you to the new flyboard craze, and rent sea kayaks and stand-up paddleboards.

GoDive Mykonos   DIVING
(☑6942616102; www.godivemykonos.com; Lia beach; 1-/2-tank dives €70/115; ☺9.30am-6pm; ⊕) This highly professional operator is based on Lia beach and offers a full range of activities below the waves, from multi-day scuba safaris to night dives, PADI courses, snorkelling trips and Bubblemaker inductions for kids over eight.

Mykonos Diving Centre   DIVING
(☑22890 24808; www.diveadventures.gr; Paradise Beach; 1-/2-tank dive €65/115; ⊕) Based at Paradise Beach, this reputable operator offers a range of PADI courses, as well as night dives, Discover Scuba outings and Bubblemaker for kids over eight.

Windsurf Centre Mykonos   WINDSURFING
(☑22890 72345; www.pezi-huber.com; Kalafatis Beach; 1hr/day windsurf rental €35/90, 1hr private lesson €65; ☺mid-May–Sep) Offers windsurf rental and private lessons at Kalafatis Beach.

🛏 Sleeping

Peristeronas Village   HOTEL €
(☑22893 00408; http://mykonos-pv.gr; r from €55; P ❄ 🐾 🛜 ☲) Around 2km from Mykonos Town and by the turn-off for Agios Sostis and Panormos beaches, this is a self-contained place that's equally popular with the young and the beautiful lying around the gorgeous pool or sipping cocktails by the bar, and holidaying middle-aged couples. Friendly young staff and free pick-up and drop-off are all boons.

Paradise Beach Camping   CAMPGROUND €
(☑22890 22852; www.paradisemykonos.com; campsites per tent/adult/child €5/10/5; @ 🛜 ☲) There are lots of options here, including camping, beach cabins and apartments, as well as bars, a swimming pool, games and so on. It is skin-to-skin mayhem in summer, with a real party atmosphere.

Artemoulas Studios Mykonos   APARTMENT €€
(☑22890 22174; www.artemoulas-mykonos.gr; 2-/3-/4-person apt €180/210/270; P ❄ 🛜 ☲) Funky decor and a hillside location a few minutes' walk from two of Mykonos' most popular beaches. The spacious, self-contained apartments make this a solid midrange choice.

MYKONOS' GAY SCENE

Mykonos is a gay travel mecca. Most gay-centric bars and hang-outs welcome a mixed crowd too. The waterfront area, between the Old Harbour and the Church of Paraportiani, is a focus for the late-night gay scene.

Check out coverage of the island's many hotspots (including beaches) on www.gay guide.gr.

Party people should visit in mid-August for Xlsior (www.xlsiorfestival.com), a huge gay clubbing festival that draws some 30,000 partiers.

Hotel Elysium (☑22890 23952; www.elysiumhotel.com; School of Fine Arts District; d from €260; ☺Apr-Oct; ❄ 🛜 ☲) Probably the most famous gay property on the island, this flash hotel sits high above the main town of Hora. Its high-camp sunset cabaret shows by the pool bar are an essential start to a night of partying (book a table). It's uphill from the Belvedere Hotel, in the town's southwest.

Porta (☑22890 27807; Ioanni Voinovich; ☺8pm-4am) Porta's cruisey ambience fills small-scale rooms where things get crowded and close towards midnight.

JackieO' (☑22890 77168; www.jackieomykonos.com; Old Harbour; ☺from 8pm) One of Mykonos' main gathering points for gay and straight alike. Throngs circulate from the retro-chic interior to the harbourfront, starting in early evening. There is a fab all-day outpost at Super Paradise Beach featuring restaurant, bar, pool and Jacuzzi.

Babylon (☑22890 25152; Old Harbour; ☺7.30pm-5.30am) Gay-friendly masses party pier-side next to JackieO'.

★ Nissaki

Boutique Hotel BOUTIQUE HOTEL €€€
(✆22890 27666; www.hotelnissaki.gr; Platys Gialos beach; d/ste from €600/750; [P][❄][☷]) With its pool overlooking the bay, this is one of the loveliest Mykonos retreats. Whitewashed rooms are livened up with touches of contemporary art, floor-to-ceiling windows let in plenty of light, and suites come with hot tubs. A spa, romantic dining and the pearly light dancing on the water after sunset make this an ideal place to canoodle with your sweetie.

✕ Eating

★ Kiki's Taverna

CYCLADIC €€
(✆6940759356; Agios Sostis Beach; mains €8-22; ☉1-7pm; ☏) Every day around noon customers begin lining up outside Kiki's, helping themselves to complimentary wine spritzers as they wait. Their prize? Enormous portions of solid local food off the grill: pork chops, octopus, swordfish, feta cheese, accompanied by epic salads and served beneath a shady vine trellis on a terrace overlooking the sea.

Indian Palace

INDIAN €€
(✆22890 78044; Paradise Beach; mains €12-20; ☉12.30pm-midnight; [❄][☏][✎]) Athens' loss is Mykonos' gain. Chef Manu Bhai abandoned the capital's renowned Jaipur Palace to open his own place overlooking Paradise Beach. Beachgoers and clubbers find it hard to resist the siren song of curries and crispy naan bread after a diet of grilled fish and tzatziki.

Kalosta

MEDITERRANEAN €€
(✆22890 78589; www.facebook.com/Kalosta RestaurantPanormos; Panormos Beach; mains €9-22; ☉noon-10pm; ☏) Drunk with sunshine and skin tangy with sea salt, beachgoers make their way up to Kalosta's shady terrace overlooking the Aegean. Bask in the afterglow of a long, lazy day at the beach and feast on its seafood-heavy mix of Mediterranean and local dishes.

★ Buddha Bar

JAPANESE €€€
(✆22890 23220; www.buddhabarbeachmykonos. gr; Ornos; mains €16-28; ☉1-6.30pm & 7pm-1am; ☏) On the premises of the luxurious Santa Marina resort, this elegant beachfront rèstaurant and bar is hands down the best place in Mykonos for refined takes on Japanese food and fishy delights such as ceviche. Portions are dainty, the service seamless and the wonderful signature cocktails an expensive temptation. Reservations recommended.

🍷 Drinking & Nightlife

Super Paradise

CLUB
(✆22890 24702; http://superparadise.com.gr; ☉9am-late; ☏) Dominating its namesake beach, this beach bar and club is synonymous with hedonism. Celebrity sightings, a crush of scantily-clad young bodies heaving to the DJs' beats, cocktails by the sea – yep, it's got all that. Music kicks off in the afternoons and pumps until the wee hours. Numerous free shuttle buses from Hora.

Paradise Club

CLUB
(✆6949468227; www.paradiseclubmykonos.com; Paradise Beach; ☉8pm-5am) Big-name international DJs and white-on-white decor that sets off all that bronzed skin in the island's biggest club.

Cavo Paradiso

CLUB
(✆22890 26124; www.cavoparadiso.gr; Paradise Beach; ☉11.30pm-7am) When dawn gleams just over the horizon, hard-core bar-hoppers move from Hora to Cavo Paradiso at Paradise Beach, the open-air clifftop mega-club that has featured top international DJs since 1994.

Kalua Beach Bar

CLUB
(✆22890 23397; https://kalua.gr; Paraga Beach; ☏) Originally made famous by the 1970s hippie generation and renowned for its beach parties that carry on until sunrise, this bar pretty much takes over Paraga Beach after sundown. During the day, it's a chilled-out cocktail haunt.

DELOS ΔΗΛΟΣ

The Cyclades fulfil their collective name (*kyklos* means circle) by encircling the sacred island of **Delos** (✆22890 22259; museum & site adult/child €12/free; ☉8am-8pm Apr-Oct, to 3pm Nov-Mar). The mythical birthplace of twins Apollo and Artemis, splendid Ancient Delos was a shrine turned sacred treasury and commercial centre. This Unesco World Heritage Site is one of the most important archaeological sites in Greece. Cast your imagination wide to transform this sprawling ruin into the magnificent city it once was.

The island, just 5km long and 1300m wide, has no permanent population, so it offers a soothing contrast to Mykonos, from where Delos can be visited. Overnight stays are forbidden, and boat schedules allow a maximum of four hours at Delos. Wear a hat, sunscreen and walking shoes.

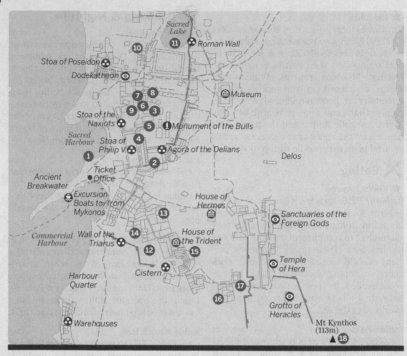

Site Tour
Ancient Delos

START & END BOAT DOCK
LENGTH THREE HOURS

Excursion boats from Mykonos dock on a bay south of the tranquil ❶ **Sacred Harbour**. The narrow spit dividing the two bays was man-made. Follow the arrowed path past the ruins of the ❷ **South Stoa**, or portico, built after the mid-3rd century BC with 28 Doric columns, and used to house shops and workshops. Continue to the ❸ **Sanctuary of Apollo**, northeast of the harbour. The Sacred Way (a wide, paved path used by ancient pilgrims) enters the complex through the ❹ **Propylaia**, to a compound of magnificent temples and treasuries. Three were dedicated to Apollo: ❺ **Temple of the Delians**, ❻ **Temple of the Athenians** and ❼ **Poros Temple**. The Sanctuary also housed the classical ❽ **treasuries** and the ❾ **Artemision**, a sanctuary of Artemis.

North of the sanctuary is the much-photographed ❿ **Terrace of the Lions**. To the northeast, the now-empty ⓫ **Sacred Lake** is where Leto gave birth to Apollo and Artemis.

Next, head south to the ⓬ **Theatre Quarter**, where Delos' wealthiest inhabitants lived in houses surrounded by peristyle courtyards, with intricate, colourful mosaics. The most lavish include the ⓭ **House of Dionysos**, named after its mosaic depicting the wine god riding a panther, and the ⓮ **House of Cleopatra**.

The ⓯ **theatre** dates from 300 BC and had a large cistern which supplied much of the town's water.

The ⓰ **House of the Masks** has another mosaic of Dionysos astride a panther between two centaurs. The extraordinary mosaic at the ⓱ **House of the Dolphins** incorporates lions, griffins and dolphins.

⓲ **Mt Kynthos** (113m) rises to the southeast of the harbour. It's worth the steep climb: on clear days there are terrific views of the encircling islands. It also has monuments such as the Sanctuaries of Zeus Kynthios and Athena Kynthia, and the Temple of Hera.

History

Delos won early acclaim as the mythical birthplace of the twins Apollo and Artemis, and was first inhabited in the 3rd millennium BC. From the 8th century BC it became a shrine to Apollo, and the oldest temples on the island date from this era. The dominant Athenians had full control of Delos – and thus the Aegean – by the 5th century BC.

In 478 BC Athens established an alliance known as the Delian League, which maintained its treasury on Delos. A decree ensured that no one could be born or die on Delos, strengthening Athens' control over the island by expelling the native population.

Delos reached the height of its power in Hellenistic times, becoming one of the three most important religious centres in Greece and a flourishing centre of commerce. Many of its inhabitants were wealthy merchants, mariners and bankers from as far away as Egypt and Syria. They built temples to their homeland gods, but Apollo remained the principal deity.

The Romans made Delos a duty-free port in 167 BC. This brought even greater prosperity, due largely to a lucrative slave market. During the following century, as ancient religions diminished and trade routes shifted, Delos began a long decline. By the 3rd century AD there was only a small Christian settlement on the island, and in the following centuries the ancient site was a hideout for pirates and was looted of many of its antiquities. It wasn't until the Renaissance that its antiquarian value was recognised.

Every now and then fresh discoveries are unearthed: in recent years a gold workshop was uncovered alongside the Terrace of the Lions.

The ticket office sells detailed Delos guidebooks, and Mykonos bookshops sell some with reconstructions which are helpful for picturing the ruins in their heyday.

Visitors are given a map of the site with three self-guided walking tours marked on it, taking from 1½ to five hours, depending on the route.

☞ Tours

It pays to tour the site with a guide, to give context to the various neighbourhoods and buildings. Mykonos Accommodation Centre (p357) in Hora (Mykonos) organises multilingual guided tours to Delos (adult/child €50/25) including boat, entrance fee and guide. Licensed guides may tout for

---

SANCTUARIES OF THE FOREIGN GODS

Delos was a place of worship for many cultures beyond the Greeks, and their temples are concentrated in the area called the Sanctuaries of the Foreign Gods.

Shrine to the Samothracian Great Gods Here people worshipped the Kabeiroi (twins Dardanos and Aeton).

Sanctuary of the Syrian Gods There are remains of a theatre used for mystical rites (some say ritual orgies) here.

Shrine to the Egyptian Gods Honoured deities including Serapis and Isis.

---

business as you disembark the boat; they charge around €10 per person.

❶ Getting There & Away

Boats for Delos (return adult/child €20/10, 30 minutes) leave Hora (Mykonos) four times daily in high season starting around 9am, with the last outward boat about 5pm. Boats return between 12.15pm and 8pm. There are fewer boats from November to March.

Departure/return times are posted at the **Delos Boat Ticket Kiosk** (☑ 22890 23051; www.delostours.gr; adult/child return ticket €20/10), located at the foot of the jetty at the southern end of the old harbour, as well as online. Buy tickets online or from the kiosk or various travel and transport agencies. When buying tickets, establish which boat you can return on.

PAROS ΠΑΡΟΣ

POP 14,920

Paros rests nonchalantly in the shadows of the limelight. Long tagged as primarily a ferry hub, its stylish capital, fashionable resort towns and sweet rural villages are all the more charming for their relative lack of crowds and tourist kudos. For holidaymakers looking for Mykonos without the hype and price tag, this might be the spot. But word is spreading. There's plenty to do, with good walks, plus excellent windsurfing, kite-surfing and diving.

Geologically speaking, Paros has long been a Greek star; white marble drawn from the island's interior made the island prosperous from the Early Cycladic period onwards. Most famously, the *Venus de Milo* was carved from Parian marble, as was Napoleon's tomb.

The smaller island of Antiparos, 1km southwest of Paros, is easily reached by car ferry or excursion boat. To Paros' east is Naxos, separated by an 8km channel.

❶ Getting There & Away

Paros is a major ferry hub for onward travel to other islands in the Aegean. It is well-served by regular ferries from Piraeus and by connections to most of the other islands of the Cyclades, and also to Thessaloniki, Crete and the Dodecanese.

New Paros Airport opened in 2016, a few kilometres north of the old airport (south of Parikia). Despite 'I'll believe it when I see it' comments from locals, scheduled international flights appear to be on the horizon. There are daily flights from Athens to Paros (€95, 40 minutes) with **Olympic Air** (www.olympicair.com).

Boat Services from Paros

DESTINATION	DURATION	FARE (€)	FREQUENCY
Amorgos	3hr-4hr	19	1 daily
Anafi	4hr 50min	20	2 weekly
Astypalea	4hr 50min	34	5 weekly
Donousa	2¼hr	14	4 weekly
Folegandros	4½hr	18	1 weekly
Ios	2¼hr	16	2-4 daily
Ios*	1-1½hr	29	2-3 daily
Iraklia	2hr	16	3 weekly
Iraklio*	3¾hr	69	1 daily
Koufonisia	3hr	19	3 weekly
Koufonisia*	1hr 20min	28	1 daily
Mykonos	1hr 20min	16	1 daily
Mykonos*	40-50min	29	3 daily
Naxos	45-50min	10	4-5 daily
Naxos*	30min	18	3 daily
Piraeus	4-5hr	33	2-5 daily
Piraeus*	2¾hr	51	1 daily
Rafina	5hr	30	1 daily
Rafina*	3¼hr	50	2 daily
Santorini (Thira)	3-3½hr	20	1-2 daily
Santorini (Thira)*	2-2¼hr	46	2-3 daily
Schinousa	2hr 20min	13	3 weekly
Syros	1½hr	12	3 weekly
Tinos*	1hr 20min	28	2 daily

* high-speed services

❶ Getting Around

BOAT

Sea-taxis leave from the Parikia quay for beaches around Paros and to Antiparos. Tickets range from €8 to €15 and are available on board.

BUS

Frequent **buses** (⌨ 22840 21395; http://ktelparou.gr) link Parikia and Naoussa (€1.80) directly. Buses also run from Parikia to east-coast beaches such as Piso Livadi (€2.40), Hrysi Akti (Golden Beach; €3) and Dryos (€3). Some of these services run via Naoussa, some via Lefkes (€1.80).

There are frequent buses to Pounta (for the Antiparos ferry; €1.80) and Aliki (€1.80).

Tickets can be purchased from machines at the bus terminals, and at kiosks and minimarkets island-wide, or from the driver at a slightly higher rate.

CAR & MOTORCYCLE

There are rental outlets along the waterfront in Parikia and all around the island. In high season the minimum cost is about €45 per day for car hire and €20 for a motorbike. A good outfit is **Acropolis** (⌨ 22840 21830; www.acropolisparos.com; Waterfront, Parikia).

TAXI

Taxis (⌨ 22840 21500) gather beside the roundabout in Parikia. Fares include the airport (€20), Naoussa (€13), Pounta (€12), Lefkes (€14) and Piso Livadi (€22). Add €1 if going from the port. There are extra charges for booking ahead, and for luggage.

Parikia   Παροικιά

POP 6100

For its small size, Parikia packs a punch. Its labyrinthine old town is pristine and filled with boutiques, cafes and restaurants. You'll also find a handful of impressive archaeological sites, a waterfront crammed with tavernas and bars, first-class midrange accommodation, and sandy stretches of beach – particularly popular is Livadia, a short walk north of town.

◉ Sights

★ Archaeological Museum   MUSEUM

(⌨ 22840 21231; €2; ⊙ 8am-3pm Tue-Sun) Behind the Panagia Ekatontapyliani, this museum is a cool escape into the island's past. It harbours some marvellous pieces, including a 5th-century BC Nike on the point of alighting and a 6th-century BC Gorgon also barely in touch with the earth. A major exhibit is a fragment slab of the 3rd-century BC Parian Chronicle, which lists the most outstanding personalities and events of Ancient Greece.

Panagia Ekatontapyliani   CHURCH
(www.ekatontapyliani.gr; ⊙8am-9pm) The Panagia Ekatontapyliani, which dates from AD 326, is one of the finest churches in the Cyclades. The building is comprised of three distinct churches: Agios Nikolaos, the largest, with superb columns of Parian marble and a carved iconostasis in the east of the compound; the ornate Church of Our Lady; and the ancient Baptistery. The name translates as Our Lady of the Hundred Doors. The **Byzantine Museum** (€2; ⊙9am-10pm Apr-Oct), within the compound, has a collection of icons and other artefacts.

Frankish Kastro   RUINS
Check out the outer walls of this fortress, built by the Venetian Duke Marco Sanudo of Naxos in AD 1260. Built with the stones from ancient buildings that once stood on this site, you can find remnants from the archaic temples of Athena and an Ionic temple from the 5th century BC.

Ancient Cemetery   RUINS
North along the waterfront is a fenced ancient cemetery dating from the end of the 8th century BC. It was in use until the 3rd century AD. Excavations in 1983 discovered graves, burial pots and sarcophagi.

🏃 Activities & Tours

Paros Hikes   HIKING
(☏6972288821; www.paroshikes.com) Chris guides ecotours to explore the lesser-known sides of Paros and Antiparos, from countryside walks to mountain hiking adventures. Tours can be tailor-made, or you can join

Paros & Antiparos

Parikia

Parikia

◎ Top Sights
1 Archaeological Museum C2

◎ Sights
2 Ancient Cemetery....................................C1
3 Byzantine Museum C2
4 Frankish Kastro A2
5 Panagia Ekatontapyliani......................B2

◈ Activities, Courses & Tours
6 Travel to Paros A2

🛏 Sleeping
7 Angie's Studios.......................................B3
8 Hotel Dina...A3

9 La Selini...D1
10 Pension Sofia..D1
11 Rooms Mike...B1

⊗ Eating
12 Cafe Distrato B2
13 Levantis.. A2
14 Little Green Rocket..............................C1
15 Ragoussis... A2
16 Symposium B2

⊖ Drinking & Nightlife
17 Bebop.. A2
18 Koukoutsi... A2
19 Pirate... A3

him for scheduled walks. Upcoming events are outlined on the website, along with routes, departure info and prices. There are also Bike & Hike and Sail & Hike combos.

Travel to Paros TOURS
(☑22840 24245; http://traveltoparos.gr) Opposite the bus terminal, this efficient company can book bus tours of Paros (€37), cruises around Antiparos (€50-100) and full-day excursions to Mykonos and Delos (€50), Santorini (€65), and the beaches of Iraklia and Koufonisia (€45).

🛏 Sleeping

Rooms Mike PENSION €
(☑22840 22856; http://roomsmike.com; r from €60; ❋🛜) A popular and friendly place, Mike's offers a great location within view of the ferry quay, and good local advice. Options range from shared facilities to self-contained units with kitchens. Mike's sign is easy to spot from the quay – away to the left. A decent budget option, if a tad dated.

Koula Camping CAMPGROUND €
(☑22840 22081; www.campingkoula.gr; Livadia Beach; campsite per adult/child/tent €8/3/4, tent rental €7; ☺May-Oct; ☎) With plenty of trees and just footsteps from the sea, this is a decent (if slightly ramshackle) place to pitch your tent. It's at the northern end of the Parikia waterfront on Livadia Beach. Free transfers to/from town are available, though it's only a 10-minute walk. There's a cafe and minimarket.

★Pension Sofia PENSION €€
(☑22840 22085; http://pension-sofia.gr; d/tr €80/120; ☺Apr-Oct; ❋☎) A few blocks behind the waterfront, Sofia's verdant garden alone makes it worth the stay. Rooms are immaculate, and some are decorated with the owner's artwork. Breakfast is available for €8; take it on your balcony or in the garden. Sofia is inland, 400m east of the ferry quay.

La Selini GUESTHOUSE €€
(☑22840 23106; www.laselini.com; s/d/tr €70/90/110; ☺Apr-Oct; ❋☎) La Selini shines under the care of its North American owner, Lou Ann. A short walk from Livadia Beach, the cheerful complex offers bright, comfy rooms and studios sleeping up to four. Upper rooms have a sea view.

Hotel Dina HOTEL €€
(☑22840 21325; www.hoteldina.com; Agora (Market St); s/d €70/80; ☺May-Oct; ❋☎) Smackbang in the heart of the Old Town, these eight family-run rooms are a find. With whitewashed walls and wrought-iron beds, they are spotless and comfortable. Each room has a small balcony, some looking out over Market St, with shared courtyards and verandahs in the traditional building's centre. Hostess Dina is a mine of information.

Angie's Studios APARTMENT €€
(☑22840 23909; www.angies-studios.gr; Makedonias; d €90; ☺Apr-Oct; ❋☎) South beyond the Old Town, but just a short walk to Market St, Angie's is a worthwhile place to lay your head. Spacious, immaculate rooms with flagstone floors and lots of local touches are set within a garden glowing with bougainvillea. Each room has a private balcony and a kitchenette, and the staff are warm. Call ahead for pick-up from the dock.

✗ Eating

★Symposium CAFE €
(☑22840 24147; http://cafesymposium.gr; mains from €8; ☺9am-3.30pm & 6pm-midnight) A gorgeous location under a massive bougainvillea tree adds to the delicious light meals, sophisticated atmosphere and tasteful jazz and classical music to make this a top place to hang out in Parikia. Head into the back of town to find this haven away from the full-on hustle and bustle.

★Cafe Distrato CAFE €
(☑22840 25175; G Gravari; mains €3-10; ☺8am-late) Dine outside under a leafy canopy at this friendly place that will draw you back time and again. This casual all-day cafe exudes wholesomeness, and is attached to a shop selling local food products. The crowd-pleasing menu lists crêpes, sandwiches, burgers, pastas and salads, plus coffee, cocktails and local wines. Look for the huge tree over the street.

Ragoussis BAKERY €
(☑22840 21573; https://ragoussisbakery.com; Plateia Mavrogenous; ☺8am-11pm) An ode to deliciousness, this bakery-patisserie just off the main square and next to Hotel Argonauta has cabinets full of baklava, cake and traditional biscuits, plus perfect beach picnic fodder like sandwiches. So, so much to choose from.

Little Green Rocket INTERNATIONAL €€
(☑2284027560; www.facebook.com/thelittlegreen rocket; mains €10-15; ☺6pm-late) Fresh and fun waterfront restaurant-bar, with a small but varied menu grabbing influences from all over (yakitori, curry, burritos). It's a good spot for a lazy drink too. Panos and his team have got things working well. Just past the post office on the way to Livadia Beach.

Ephessus GREEK €€
(☑22840 22520; www.parosweb.com/ephessus; Livadia Beach; mains €7-15; ☺10am-late) Sit in the beachfront, lantern-filled garden, then dig into a dish of Greek or Anatolian cuisine from Ephessus' wood-fired oven, and you'll understand why this restaurant is so popular. Setting, service and food are tops. Try the *manti* (Anatolian ravioli), the *peinirli* (traditional pizza) or take a look at the specials the chef has cooked up for the day.

Levantis GREEK €€
(☑22840 23613; www.levantisrestaurant.com; Agora (Market St); dishes €13-22; ☺dinner May-Oct) A vine-covered courtyard and simple, whitewashed interior with splashes of modern art create a polished setting for some of the Cyclades' finest contemporary Greek

cuisine. The menu makes for hungry reading – choose from inspired flavour combinations like chicken and pistachio dolmades, slow-braised honey-spiced lamb and dark chocolate mocha soufflé.

Drinking & Nightlife

The southwestern waterfront is peppered with bars, popular with both locals and visitors. Old Town also has its fair share of drinking holes.

Bebop
BAR

(22840 28075; ⊙9am-4am) Climb the steps up to this cool-cat waterfront spot with no shortage of outdoor areas, including a sunset-primed rooftop terrace. There's a long list of coffee and cocktail options, as well as fine sangria. Keep an eye out for live-music events, especially jazz. Look up as you head down the waterfront passing the *kastro*.

Koukoutsi
BAR

(6933020592; Plateia Mavrogenous; ⊙8am-late) On the inland back corner of the main square, this local hangout is a gem. Small and lively, with walls covered in posters and wooden benches filled with cushions, come here to mix with locals, nibble on mezedhes and sip juices, coffees, beer or a shot of ouzo.

Pirate
BAR

(6970024122; Agora (Market St); ⊙9am-late) Ultracool and cave-like, Pirate is an ideal refuge within the Old Town. It's been a favourite with locals since 1983.

ℹ Information

On the waterfront opposite the bus terminal, **Travel to Paros** (p364) sells ferry tickets, can advise on accommodation and car hire, and has luggage storage. You can also book various tours here.

Post Office Located 400m east of the ferry quay.

Naoussa
Ναούσα

POP 2870

Naoussa has gradually turned from a quiet fishing village into an increasingly stylish resort and visitor destination. Perched on the shores of the large Plastira Bay, there are good beaches nearby, excellent restaurants and an ever-expanding number of chic beachside hotels, cafes and bars. Behind the waterfront is a maze of narrow, white-washed streets.

◉ Sights & Activities

The fun of Naoussa is to get lost wandering the streets of Old Town, and admire the crumbling remains of the 15th-century Venetian *kastro* guarding the port area.

The best beaches in the area are **Kolimbythres**, set among fabulous rock formations, and **Monastiri**, which has some good snorkelling. Low-key **Lageri** is also worth seeking out. **Santa Maria**, on the other side of the eastern headland, is ideal for windsurfing. These beaches can all be reached by road, but caïques go from Naoussa to each of them during July and August.

Paros Park
PARK

(22840 53573; www.parospark.com; Agios Ioannis Detis Peninsula) This 80-hectare park north of Naoussa features impressive rock formations, caves, hidden coves and gorgeous beaches. There's three established walking trails, a museum, a monastery, a cafe and the extremely popular open-air Cine Enastron. There's also a lot of history – the Russian fleet was based here during the Russo-Turkish War (1768–74). The park is a 10-minute drive west, then north from Naoussa on the Agios Ioannis Detis Peninsula.

★ Moraitis Winery
WINERY

(22840 51350; www.moraitiswines.gr; tastings from €5; ⊙10am-3pm, to 8pm in summer) Pressing grapes since 1910, the Moraitis family has it down to a fine art. Wander the original stone cellars before sidling up to the bar for a taste of up to 14 wines. Anything made with the island's indigenous grape, Monemvasia, is particularly worth a try. The winery is an easy walk southeast of the centre.

Michael Zeppos
BOATING

(6947817125; www.mzeppos.gr) Operating primarily from Naoussa (and also from Aliki), this company offers full-day sailing itineraries taking in the beaches of Paros, Antiparos and potentially calling at Naxos. There are also sunset and fishing options. See the website for details; prices depend on numbers.

Kokou Riding Centre
HORSE RIDING

(22840 51818; www.horseridingparos.com) The well-established Kokou has 2½-hour morning rides (€60), venturing into the sea, and 1½-hour evening rides (€40). Pick-up is available from Naoussa's main square for €3.

🛏 Sleeping

Hotel Kalypso   HOTEL €€
(☑ 22840 51488; www.kalypso.gr; Agii Anargiri
Beach; r from €110; ⊗Apr-Oct; 🏵@🛜) This
cheerful complex has a fresh feel thanks to
attentive care and upgrades from its owners.
Inside there's a surprisingly chic lounge and
simple, spotless rooms, studios and apartments with colourful touches. Outside is the
winner, though: a sunlounger-filled garden,
right on the beach.

Katerina Mare   APARTMENT €€
(☑ 22840 51642; www.katerinamare.com; d/tr
incl breakfast €130/150, apt from €170; 🏵🛜) In
a word: lovely. Light-filled suites are classy
and pristine, each with a great view and
every convenience, including kitchenette.
Service is stellar. It's on a hillside southwest
of the town centre, with many accommodation options as neighbours.

Hotel Galini   HOTEL €€
(☑ 22840 51210; www.hotelgaliniparos.com; d €80-
90, tr €100; 🏵🛜) Run by a local family for
three generations, this spic-and-span hotel
has simple, comfortable rooms. Ask for
a balcony and a sea view. It's opposite the
blue-domed local church, on the main road
into town from Parikia. Rooms cost €50 outside July and August.

Lilly Residence   BOUTIQUE HOTEL €€€
(☑ 22840 51377; www.lillyresidence.gr; r incl breakfast from €285; ⊗May-Oct; 🅿🏵🛜🏊) Naous-
sa's most stylish hotel, where stone, wood
and wicker combine to great effect and
white is the unifying theme. The place is discreetly luxurious (eg Hermes toiletries) and
grown-up (no kids under 12). Just back from
the water, all 11 suites have sea views, or you
can enjoy the eye-candy pool area.

🍴 Eating

Naoussa knows how to do waterfront dining. Tables fill every waterfront spot, creating a superbly convivial atmosphere just
inches from moored boats or the beach.

★Sousouro   CAFE €
(☑ 22840 53113; www.facebook.com/Sousouro
CafeBar; breakfast €4-6; ⊗9am-3am) Occupying a small corner in the Old Town, this cafe
is big on flavour. It has one of the islands'
best breakfasts: superfood smoothies and
shakes, homemade granola with sheep's-
milk yoghurt and thyme honey, and toast
topped with avocado or cacao hazelnut

butter and banana. At night the wholesomeness makes way for killer cocktails.

To Paradosiako   SWEETS €
(loukoumadhes €4-5; ⊗6pm-midnight) An
essential evening stop for a serve of To Paradosiako's legendary fresh doughy balls of
goodness known as *loukoumadhes* (Greek
doughnuts). It's a self-service operation: add
honey, chocolate sauce and/or ice cream.

Glafkos   MEDITERRANEAN €€
(☑ 22840 52100; mains €8-16; ⊗lunch & dinner)
With tables practically on the sand on Agios
Dimitrios Beach, it's not surprising that this
tucked-away place specialises in seafood. Try
steamed mussels and grilled calamari, or dig
into shrimp *saganaki* or black risotto with
cuttlefish – all are great paired with local
white wine.

🍷 Drinking & Nightlife

★Sommaripa Consolato   BAR
(☑ 22840 55233; www.facebook.com/Sommaripa
Consolato; ⊗10am-late) The owner opened
this elevated cafe-bar in the former home
of his grandparents – how fortunate that
it's right in the hub of Naoussa's small port
(above Mario's restaurant), making for great
people-watching from the terraces. First-
class drinks, snacks and service too.

To Takimi   BAR
(Music Cafe; ☑ 22840 55095; ⊗5pm-late) Just
south of the main square, this is where
locals come to drink beer or ouzo and listen
to live music, often played on the traditional
string instruments waiting on the walls.
Everything from *rembetika* (blues) to rock
goes down here.

☆ Entertainment

Cine Enastron   CINEMA
(☑ 22840 53573; www.parospark.com/cine-enastron;
Paros Park; free; ⊗9.30pm Jul-Sep) As good as
it gets! Watch retro movies under the stars
by the sea in this classic open-air cinema in
Paros Park, a 10-minute drive around the
coast, north of Naoussa. You'll want a rental
car to get here. Check the website for a
schedule of what's on. Movies are in English
with Greek subtitles.

ℹ Information

The bus from Parikia terminates some way
inland from the waterfront, where there's a large
public car park (most of the Old Town area is
pedestrian-only). The Old Town is east of here.

Erkyna Travel (📋 22840 53180; www.
erkynatravel.com) Sells ferry tickets and can
help with accommodation, car hire, excursions,
water sports and boat trips to other islands. It's
on the main road into town.

Around Paros

On the southeast coast is Paros' top beach,
Hrysi Akti (Golden Beach), with good swimming, windsurfing and diving operations.

Paros' west coast, around **Pounta**, is
the hub for top water sports activities:
a long shallow-water shoreline and perfect sideshore wind conditions make it
perfect for all skill levels of kiteboarder or
windsurfer.

🏃 Activities

Walking

Paros is popular with walkers, and there
are excellent tracks all over the island. See
www.parosweb.com/guide for more information. One particularly popular trail is
the **Byzantine path** from Lefkes to Prodromos to Marpissa, taking a bit over an
hour. In places, the path is paved with marble as it heads out west from Lefkes in the
mountains.

Terrain (http://terrainmaps.gr) has an
excellent Paros/Antiparos map which covers
both islands, including walking tracks.

Water Sports

Force7 Surf Centre   WINDSURFING
(📋 22840 41789; www.force7paros.gr) Force7
Surf Centre is a well-run centre on Hrysi
Akti offering windsurfing courses and rental
(including classes for kids), plus kayaking, stand-up paddleboard and catamaran
rentals.

Paros Kite   KITESURFING
(📋 22840 93018; www.paroskite.gr; 90min intro
€90) At this slick, professionally run complex
at Pounta it's all about the wind: kitesurfing
and windsurfing instruction and gear rental
are offered, plus there's a surf shop, beach
bar-cafe, massage and yoga. Local accommodation can be arranged.

Aegean Diving College   DIVING
(📋 22840 43347; www.aegeandiving.gr; shore dive
from €80) At Hrysi Akti, the Aegean Diving
College offers a range of dives to places of
archaeological and ecological interest. Dive
courses are also available.

🛏 Sleeping

Golden Beach Hotel   HOTEL €€
(📋 22840 41366; www.goldenbeach.gr; Hrysi Akti;
d incl breakfast €125, 4-person apt €250; ☾ Apr–
mid-Oct; ❄ 🐾) Right on Hrysi Akti, this top
spot offers simple, appealing rooms and
apartments in pastel colours. More important is what's outside the rooms: a splendid
grassy lawn down to the shore, plus restaurant, beach bar and oodles of beach activities. Lots of fun to be had on Paros' east
coast.

ANTIPAROS ΑΝΤΙΠΑΡΟΣ

POP 1200

Antiparos lies dreamily offshore from Paros.
As soon as your ferry docks, you feel a distinct
slowing down in the pace of things. The main
village and port (also called Antiparos) are
relaxed. There's a touristy gloss around the
waterfront and main street, but the village
runs deep inland to quiet squares and alleyways that give way suddenly to open fields.

The rest of the island runs to the south of
the main settlement through quiet countryside. There are several decent beaches, especially at Glyfa and Soros, and one of Greece's
most celebrated caves. There's also a 'secret
getaway' factor to the island that puts it on
the radar of those who don't like to be disturbed: Euro royalty, Hollywood stars (Tom
Hanks has a villa on the island) and A-list
rock stars holiday here.

👁 Sights & Activities

Antiparos Town   VILLAGE
The main town is well worth a wander. Its
long pedestrianised main street is lined with
services and a whole lot of stylish boutiques,
bars and restaurants. Follow it to the end,
to the distinctive, giant plane tree of Plateia
Agios Nikolaou. From here, a narrow lane
leads to the intriguing remnants of the old
Venetian *kastro*, entered through an archway. This old fortified settlement dates from
the mid-15th century.

★ Cave of Antiparos   CAVE
(http://antiparos.gr; adult/child €5/2.50; ☾ 10am-
6pm Jul & Aug, to 5pm Jun, to 4pm May & Sep, to
3pm Apr) About 10km south of the port, this
huge and atmospheric cave remains impressive despite much looting of stalactites and
stalagmites in the past (check out the ancient
graffiti from past visitors; one dates from

1776). Descending the 400-plus concrete steps into the well-lit cave is an enthralling experience – beware the climb out! To get to the cave, follow the coastal road south until you reach a signposted turn-off. A bus runs here from the port (€1.80).

Anti Art Gallery GALLERY
(☑ 22840 61544; https://antiartgallery.gr; ⊙ 7pm-12.30am Jun-Sep) In true Antiparos fashion, the 'anti' Art Gallery has late hours and an excellent run of scheduled exhibitions, detailed on its website. The brainchild of curator Mary Chatzaki, it plays an entertaining, educational role in island life.

Historical & Folklore Museum of Antiparos MUSEUM
(☑ 22840 61417; €3; ⊙ 10am-9pm summer) This tiny new museum on the main street shows off intriguing old photographs, maps, manuscripts and all sorts of bits and pieces associated with life on the island.

🏃 Activities

Captain Sargos Boat Trips BOATING
(☑ 6973794876; www.sargosantiparos.gr; per person €25) Operating out of Agios Georgios, Yorgos runs three-to-four-hour boat trips that include a visit to the archaeological site on nearby Despotiko island, time to swim or laze on the island's spectacular beach, and a cruise through local sea caves. Also available for local charters.

Blue Island Divers DIVING
(☑ 22840 61767; www.blueisland-divers.gr; dives from €60, PADI certification from €240) On the northern waterfront is this operator, offering fun dives, PADI courses, and information on the island.

🛏 Sleeping

Camping Antiparos CAMPGROUND €
(☑ 22840 61221; www.camping-antiparos.gr; campsite per adult/child/tent €8/4/3; ⊙ May-Sep; 🛜) This chilled-out beachside campground is planted with bamboo 'compartments' and cedars. There's a bar, minimarket and free wi-fi. It's 1.5km north of the port (pick-up is available).

Artemis Hotel HOTEL €€
(☑ 22840 61460; www.artemisantiparos.com; d incl breakfast €80-90; ⊙ Apr–mid-Oct) The elegant, marble-lined rooms at Artemis (at the far northern end of the harbour) are compact but well priced, and have lovely private terraces (opt for a sea-view room). The common areas are stylishly appealing, and rates include a good breakfast. Family-run and friendly, rates halve out of the high season.

Beach House Antiparos RESORT €€€
(☑ 22840 64000; http://beachhouseantiparos.com; ste from €220; ⊙ mid-May–Sep; 🅿🛜) This is a glossy boutique resort on Apandima beach, with a 'beach house' housing nine suites (some family-sized). There's an upmarket beachside restaurant serving brunch, lunch and dinner, a beach bar and sunbeds, all open to nonguests. From the beach, arrange a massage, charter a boat or peek in the concept store.

🍴 Eating

Elia Kafenes CAFE €
(☑ 22840 61704; mains from €7; ⊙ 9am-2am) A handwritten menu details the day's offerings at this cool little cafe-bar just back from the waterfront on the main street. Stop by for a tasty breakfast or for tapas and drinks.

★ Margarita Cafe CAFE €€
(☑ 22840 61491; www.facebook.com/margarita antiparos; mains from €10; ⊙ 9am-late; 🛜) Strolling down Antiparos' main street, you'll find it hard to continue on past the Margarita Cafe – shaded seating both on the street and on the verandah under a huge palm tree make this spot. There are snacks and sandwiches during the day, pastas, risottos and seafood for dinner, plus a good range of beer and wine. Free wi-fi and extremely friendly service.

★ Captain Pipinos TAVERNA €€
(☑ 22840 21823; http://captainpipinos.com; mains €6-15, fish by kg; ⊙ lunch & dinner) In the island's south, right on the water at Agios Georgios and with panoramas of neighbouring uninhabited Despotiko, Captain Pipinos is a gloriously old-school fish taverna. Octopus dishes are a top pick (you'll see them drying), as is anything with fresh fish.

ℹ Information

From the ferry quay, go right along the waterfront. The main street, Agora, heads inland just by the Anarghyros Restaurant, and you'll find most services you need here, including groceries and banks. To reach the central square turn left at the top of the main street and then right. See www.antiparos.gr for more information.

There are several tour and travel agencies, including **Oliaris Tours** (☑ 22840 61231; www.

WORTH A TRIP

LEFKES ΛΕΥΚΕΣ

Lovely Lefkes clings to a natural amphitheatre amid hills whose summits are dotted with old windmills. Siesta is taken seriously here and the village has a general air of serenity. Just 9km southeast of Parikia on the cross-island road, it was the capital of Paros during the Middle Ages. The village's main attraction is wandering through its pristine alleyways. Consider walking here on the Byzantine path (p368) east to Marpissa.

The **Cathedral of Agia Triada** is an impressive structure with unique bell towers. On the square in front of the cathedral is **Kafeneio tis Marigos** (☑ 22840 44014; Lefkes; snacks from €4; ☺ 9am-late), a delightfully retro cafe run by Kostas serving up mama-made meatballs and cakes. The old photos inside are fascinating.

Out on the main road, the **Lefkes Ceramic Workshop** (☑ 22840 43255; ☺ 10am-midnight) features Kostas Fifas and his award-winning crackle-style ceramics. The style, passed down by Kostas' father, is unique and you can watch him at work and purchase his finished products.

antiparostravel.gr), where you can ask about the local bus.

❶ Getting There & Away

In summer, frequent small passenger boats depart for Antiparos from Parikia (€5), and numerous operators offer day cruises taking in the beaches of both islands, departing from Parikia, Pounta, Aliki and Naoussa.

There's also a regular car ferry that runs from Pounta on the west coast of Paros to Antiparos (one-way €1.10, per scooter €1.40, per car €5.90, one or two services hourly, 10 minutes). You can take a car rented on Paros to Antiparos on this ferry.

❶ Getting Around

A bus service runs from the port to the cave, and another services the east-coast beaches as far as Agios Georgios; tickets cost €1.80. The schedule varies with the season; in theory, buses run from April to September.

Wheels can be hired from **Aggelos** (☑ 22840 61626; http://antiparosrentacar.com), the first office as you come from the ferry quay. Cars start at about €40 per day (high season), scooters €15 and bicycles €5.

NAXOS ΝΑΞΟΣ

POP 18,900

The largest of the Cyclades, Naxos packs a lot of bang for its buck. Its main city of Hora (known also as Naxos) has a gorgeous waterfront and a web of cobbled alleys below its hilltop *kastro*, all filled with the hubbub of tourism and shopping. You needn't travel far, though, to find isolated beaches, atmospheric mountain villages and ancient sites.

Naxos was a cultural centre of Classical Greece and Byzantium, and Venetian and Frankish influences also left their mark. Its high mountains form rain clouds, and consequently Naxos is more fertile and green than most of the other Cyclades islands. It produces olives, grapes, figs, citrus fruit, corn and potatoes. Mt Zeus (also known as Mt Zas; 1004m) is the Cyclades' highest peak and is the central focus of the island's mountainous interior, where you will find enchanting villages such as Halki and Apiranthos.

❶ Getting There & Away

BOAT

Like Paros, Naxos is something of a ferry hub in the Cyclades, with a similar number of conventional and fast ferries making regular calls to/from Piraeus, plus links to/from the mainland port of Rafina via the northern Cyclades.

AIR

There are daily flights to/from Athens (€95, 45 minutes) with **Olympic Air** (www.olympicair.com).

❶ Getting Around

TO/FROM THE AIRPORT

The **airport** (JNX; www.naxos.net/airport) is 3km south of Hora. There's no shuttle bus, but buses to Agios Prokopios Beach and Agia Anna pass close by. A taxi costs €10 to €15 depending on the amount of luggage you have, the time of day and if booked.

BUS

Frequent buses run to Agios Prokopios Beach (€1.60) and Agia Anna (€1.60) from Hora. Seven buses daily serve Filoti (€2.30) via Halki

(€2); five serve Apiranthos (€3.10) via Filoti and Halki; and at least two serve Apollonas (€6.20), Pyrgaki (€2.30) and Melanes (€1.60). There are less frequent departures to other villages.

Buses leave from the end of the ferry quay in Hora; timetables are posted outside the **bus information office** (☏ 22850 22291; www.naxosdestinations.com; Harbour), diagonally left and across the road from the bus stop. You have to buy tickets from the office or from the machine outside (not from the bus driver).

CAR & MOTORCYCLE

August rates for hire cars range from about €45 to €65 per day, and quad bikes from €30. Hire from **Naxos Auto Rent** (☏ 22850 41350; http://naxosautorent.com), **Rental Center** (☏ 22850 23395; www.rentalcenter.com.gr; Plateia Evripeou), **Auto Tour** (☏ 22850 25480; www.naxosrentacar.com) or **Fun Car** (☏ 22850 26084; www.funcarandrides.com).

TAXI

Due to its large size, most visitors to Naxos rely on buses or their own wheels to travel around.

BOAT SERVICES FROM NAXOS

DESTINATION	DURATION	FARE (€)	FREQUENCY
Amorgos	2-6hr	11	2-5 daily
Amorgos*	1hr-1½hr	24	2 daily
Anafi	3¾hr	19	2 weekly
Astypalea	3¾hr	34	5 weekly
Donousa	1-4hr	7	7 weekly (note: not daily)
Folegandros	3hr 10min	17	1 weekly
Folegandros*	2½hr-4hr	49	6 weekly
Ios	1-2hr	14	1-2 daily
Ios*	50min	25	1-2 daily
Iraklia	1-1½hr	7	1-2 daily
Iraklio*	3hr 40min	70	1 daily
Kimolos	4hr 40min	17	1 weekly
Koufonisia	2½hr	8	1-2 daily
Koufonisia*	40-50min	19	1-2 daily
Milos	6hr	21	1 weekly
Milos*	3½hr-5½hr	59	6 weekly
Mykonos	2½hr	18	1 daily
Mykonos*	40min-1½hr	29	4-5 daily
Paros	50hr	10	4-5 daily
Paros*	30min	16	3 daily
Piraeus	5¼hr	34	2-4 daily
Piraeus*	3½hr	57	2 daily
Rafina	6hr	32	1 daily
Rafina*	4hr	52	2 daily
Santorini (Thira)	2hr	19	1-2 daily
Santorini (Thira)*	1hr 35min	38	4-5 daily
Schinousa	1¼hr-2hr	7	1-2 daily
Sikinos	2hr 20min	13	1 weekly
Syros	3h 10min	15	1 weekly
Tinos*	2hr	29	2 daily

* high-speed services

Note: journey times vary with vessel type and routing.

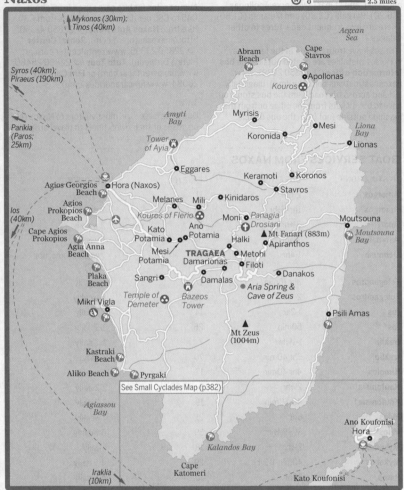

Map labels:

Mykonos (30km);
Tinos (40km)

Aegean
Sea

Abram
Beach

Cape
Stavros

Apollonas

Kouros

Syros (40km);
Piraeus (190km)

Myrisis

Mesi

Liona
Bay

Koronida

Lionas

Parikia
(Paros;
25km)

Amyti
Bay

Tower
of Ayia

Eggares

Keramoti

Koronos

Agios Georgios
Beach

Hora (Naxos)

Melanes

Mili

Kinidaros

Stavros

Agios
Prokopios
Beach

Kouros of Flerio

Moni

Panagia
Drosiani

Moutsouna

Ios
(40km)

Cape Agios
Prokopios

Kato
Potamia

Ano
Potamia

Halki

Mt Fanari (883m)

Moutsouna
Bay

Agia Anna
Beach

Mesi
Potamia

TRAGAEA

Damarionas

Metohi

Apiranthos

Filoti

Plaka
Beach

Sangri

Damalas

Danakos

Mikri Vigla

Temple of
Demeter

Bazeos
Tower

Aria Spring &
Cave of Zeus

Kastraki
Beach

Psili Amas

Aliko Beach

Pyrgaki

Mt Zeus
(1004m)

See Small Cyclades Map (p382)

Agiassou
Bay

Ano Koufonisi
Hora

Iraklia
(10km)

Cape
Katomeri

Kalandos Bay

Kato Koufonisi

Taxis (☑ 22850 22444) are an option for shorter trips (eg Hora to Agios Prokopios Beach or Agia Anna for around €10). Taxis cluster at the port, or you can call one.

Hora (Naxos) Χώρα (Νάξος)

POP 6700

Hora has the colour and bustle you'd expect of the island's port and capital. Settled on the west coast, the old town is a tangle of steep footpaths and is divided into two historic Venetian neighbourhoods: Bourgos,

where the Greeks lived, and the hilltop Kastro, where the Roman Catholics lived.

Despite being fairly large, Hora can still be easily managed on foot. It's almost impossible not to get lost in the old town, however, and maps are of little use.

◉ Sights

★ Kastro

AREA

The most alluring part of Hora is the 13th-century residential neighbourhood of Kastro, which Marco Sanudo made the capital of his duchy in 1207. Behind the waterfront, get lost in the narrow alleyways scrambling up to its spectacular hilltop location. Venetian mansions survive in the centre of Kastro, and you can see the remnants of the castle, the **Tower of Sanoudos**. To see the Bourgos area of the old town, head into the winding backstreets behind the northern end of Paralia.

★ **Temple of Apollo** ARCHAEOLOGICAL SITE
(The Portara) FREE From Naxos Town harbour, a causeway leads to the Palatia islet and the striking, unfinished Temple of Apollo, Naxos' most famous landmark (also known as the Portara, or 'Doorway'). Simply two marble columns with a crowning lintel, it makes an arresting sight, and people gather at sunset for splendid views.

**Della Rocca-Barozzi
Venetian Museum** MUSEUM
(☑ 22850 22387; www.naxosfestival.com; €5; ◷ 10am-10pm) This atmospheric museum is in a handsome old tower house of the 13th century, within the *kastro* ramparts (by the northwest gate). Wander through the rooms to see how the original Italian aristocrat owners lived, what they wore and how they furnished their rooms. There are changing art exhibitions in the vaults. Concerts (p377) and other events are frequently staged in the museum and its grounds.

Agios Georgios Beach BEACH
Conveniently just south of the waterfront is sandy Agios Georgios, Naxos' town beach. It's backed by hotels and tavernas at the town end (where it can get crowded), but it runs for some way to the south, where you can spread out a little. Its shallow waters make it great for families.

Mitropolis Museum MUSEUM
(☑ 22850 24151; Plateia Mitropolis; ◷ 8.30am-3pm Tue-Sun) FREE Behind the northern end of the waterfront are several churches and chapels, as well as the Mitropolis Museum. It features fragments of a Mycenaean city (13th–11th centuries BC) that was abandoned because of the threat of flooding. Glass panels underfoot reveal ancient foundations.

Archaeological Museum MUSEUM
(☑ 22850 22725; Kastro; adult/child €3/free; ◷ 8.30am-3pm Tue-Sun) This museum in Kastro is housed in the former Jesuit school where novelist Nikos Kazantzakis was briefly a pupil. It's slightly musty but contains fascinating finds from the Ionic

and Doric eras, and some splendid Early Cycladic marble figurines.

Folk Museum Collection MUSEUM
(☑ 22850 25561; www.naxosfolkmuseum.com; Old Market St; €3; ◷ 10am-2pm & 7-10pm) This small but well-curated collection gives a digestible account of the elements that make Naxos' history special: succinct displays cover farming, bee-keeping, weaving, bread-making, winemaking and cheese production. It's a privately owned collection and worth a stop.

🏃 Activities & Tours

★ **Naxos Bike** CYCLING
(☑ 22850 25887, 6932795125; www.naxosbikes.com; bike hire per day from €10) Get all of your equipment here, from electric-, road-, mountain- and trekking-bikes to children's seats. Local expert Giannis knows everything there is to know about bikes, and can set you up with maps to get you exploring. He also leads three-hour tours (per person €30, minimum two people).

Flisvos Sport Club WINDSURFING
(☑ 22850 24308; www.flisvos-sportclub.com; Agios Georgios Beach) Well-organised beach club offering a range of windsurfing courses (one-hour private lesson from €40), catamaran sailing (one-hour rental from €40) and mountain-bike rental (from €15 per day). It also has a cool cafe, accommodation and the options of beach volleyball, a fitness centre and yoga.

Naxos Horse Riding HORSE RIDING
(☑ 6948809142; www.naxoshorseriding.com; 2/3hr ride €45/55; ◷ Mon-Sat) Organises daily morning, afternoon and sunset horse rides inland and on beaches. Staff can arrange pick-up and return to and from the stables. Beginners, young children and advanced riders are all catered for.

Naxos Tours TOURS
(☑ 22850 24000; www.naxostours.net; island bus tour adult/child €30/15; ◷ 8am-10pm) Call into this agency on the waterfront to find out about its array of tours and excursions, including an island tour by bus, guided walks and daily cruises. There are frequent excursion boats to Delos and Mykonos (adult/child €45/20), Santorini (€55/30), and Iraklia and Koufonisia (€40/20), plus sailing explorations of various parts of Naxos.

Hora (Naxos)

N 0 ————————— 100 m

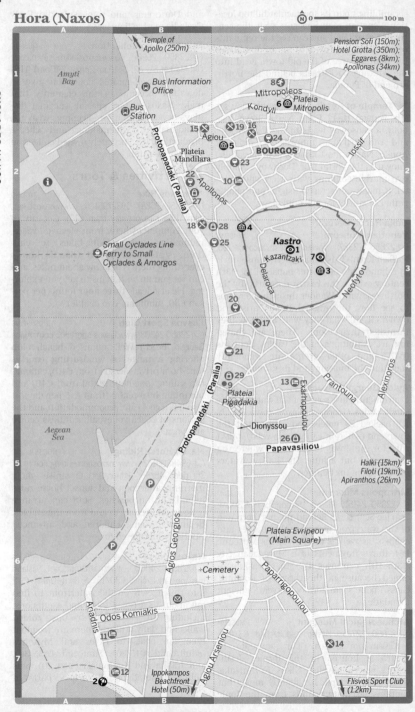

Temple of
Apollo (250m)

Pension Sofi (150m);
Hotel Grotta (350m);
Eggares (8km);
Apollonas (34km)

Amyti
Bay

Bus Information
Office

Bus
Station

Mitropoleos

8

Plateia
Mitropolis

6

Kondyli

Protopapadaki (Paralia)

15 Agiou 19 16

5

Plateia
Mandilara

24

BOURGOS

23

22 Apollonos

10

27

18 28 4

25

Small Cyclades Line
Ferry to Small
Cyclades & Amorgos

Kastro

1

Kazantzaki

7

3

Delaroca

Neofytou

Iossif

20

17

21

29

9

Plateia
Pigadakia

13 Exarhopoulou

Prantouna

Alexinoros

Protopapadaki (Paralia)

Dionyssou

26

Papavasiliou

Halki (15km);
Filoti (19km);
Apiranthos (26km)

Aegean
Sea

Plateia Evripeou
(Main Square)

Anadnis

Agios Georgios

Cemetery

Paparrigopoulou

Odos Komiakis

11

Agiou Arseniou

12

14

2

Ippokampos
Beachfront
Hotel (50m)

Flisvos Sport Club
(1.2km)

CYCLADES NAXOS

Hora (Naxos)

🛏 Sleeping

Hora has plenty of accommodation places (the majority open year-round), including numerous options backing the town beach, Agios Georgios. Book early for July and August.

The best campgrounds are at the beaches south of Hora (Agia Anna and Plaka); minibuses from these grounds will meet the ferries.

Despina's Rooms PENSION €
(☑ 22850 22356; www.despinarooms.gr; Kastro; d €60; ❄ 🀢) Despina has been renting simple, comfy rooms for more than 50 years, and they're a steal. Tucked away in the heart of Kastro (reached with a climb), some have sea views. Rooms on the roof terrace are popular despite their smaller size. There's a communal kitchen.

★ **Pension Sofi** PENSION €€
(☑ 22850 23077; www.pensionsofi.gr; r €90; 🅿 ❄ 🀢) Run by members of the friendly Koufopoulos family, guests at Pension Sofi are met with family-made wine or cake and immaculate rooms, each with a freshly renovated bathroom and a basic kitchen. Sofi is a short walk back from the waterfront. Let them know your arrival details for a complimentary pick-up at the port. Rates halve out of high season.

★ **Hotel Grotta** HOTEL €€
(☑ 22850 22215; www.hotelgrotta.gr; off Kontoleontos; d incl breakfast €110-135; ❄ 🀢) Located on high ground overlooking the *kastro* and main town, this excellent hotel has immaculate rooms, great sea views from the front, spacious public areas and a cool indoor Jacuzzi area. It's made even better by the cheerful, attentive atmosphere. A rooftop garden bar and complimentary port and airport transfers make Hotel Grotta a top choice.

Ippokampos Beachfront Hotel BOUTIQUE HOTEL €€
(☑ 22850 24648; www.ippokampos-naxos.com; Agios Georgios Beach; r incl breakfast from €105; ☺ mid-Apr–mid-Nov; 🅿 ❄ 🀢) Part of a stylish all-white beachfront complex that includes a restaurant-bar, this nine-room hotel offers accommodation kitted out with a dash of panache. Cheaper economy rooms are smaller. All share a fab terrace, and the gorgeous beach is right outside your door.

Nikos Verikokos Studios HOTEL €€
(☑ 22850 22025; www.nikos-verikokos.com; Naxos Town; s/d/tr €90/100/120; ❄ 🀢) Friendly Nikos maintains these immaculate rooms in the heart of the old town. Some have balconies and sea views, most have little kitchenettes. They offer port pick-up with pre-arrangement.

DRINKING IN THE HISTORY

It was on Naxos that an ungrateful Theseus is said to have abandoned Ariadne after she helped him escape the Cretan labyrinth. She didn't pine long, and was soon entwined with Dionysos, the god of wine and ecstasy, and the island's favourite deity. Naxian wine has long been considered a useful antidote to a broken heart.

Hotel Galini
HOTEL €€

(☑ 22850 22114; www.hotelgalini.com; d incl breakfast from €90; ❄ 🛜) A nautical theme lends this super-friendly place loads of character. Updated, spacious rooms have small balconies and wrought-iron beds, plus great decor creatively fashioned from seashells and driftwood. The location is first-rate – close to the old town and the beach – and the breakfast is hearty.

Hotel Glaros
BOUTIQUE HOTEL €€€

(☑ 22850 23101; www.hotelglaros.com; Agios Georgios Beach; d €150-180; ☺ Apr-Oct; ❄ @ 🛜) Edgy yet homey, simple yet plush, this well-run and immaculate 13-room hotel has a seaside feel in its boutique fit-out. Service is thoughtful, there's an indoor Jacuzzi, the beach is only a few steps away and it's adults only. Breakfast is €10.

✗ Eating

Hora has fantastic dining. For the freshest seafood, head to the tavernas on the waterfront where the fishermen hang out and sample their catch. Naxian cheeses, sausages and potatoes are also well worth taste-testing.

★ Doukato
GREEK €

(☑ 22850 27013; www.facebook.com/doukato naxos; Old Town; mains from €8; ☺ 6pm-late) In a magical setting that has been a monastery, church and a school, Doukato is capturing plenty of attention on the Naxos dining scene. Its award-winning chef produces top Naxian specialities such as *gouna* (sun-dried mackerel), *kalogeras* (beef, eggplant & cheese) and their unbelievably delicious Doukato 'Special' souvlaki. A lot of pride at the heart of the Old Town.

Anna's Garden Café
CAFE €

(☑ 22850 26774; http://annasorganicnaxos.blog spot.com; Paparrigopoulou; dishes €5-10; ☺ 9am-2pm & 6-9pm May-Sep; ☑ 🌱) Entirely earthy feeling and 100% organic, Anna's creates a lunchtime dish of the day, driven by local, seasonal produce. Breakfasts are good: think homemade muesli and yoghurt, spelt bread or omelettes. Anna's also supplies picnic baskets if ordered a day in advance.

Labyrinth
GREEK €€

(☑ 22850 22253; mains €10-17; ☺ lunch & dinner) It's a toss-up as to which is more welcoming here: the warm interior or the pretty, private courtyard. Munch through marinated veggies with grilled *manouri* (soft cheese from the north), swordfish with herbs, or seafood risotto with ouzo sauce. The name is apt: it has a sign, but is easiest to find if you enter the winding alleys from the north.

L'Osteria
ITALIAN €€

(☑ 22850 24080; www.osterianaxos.com; mains €10-16; ☺ 7pm-midnight) This authentic Italian eatery is tucked away in a small alley uphill from the harbour, beneath the *kastro* walls. Grab a table in the cute courtyard and prepare to be impressed: the appetising menu changes daily, but there's also an unchanging list of bruschetta, salads and delectable antipasti.

O Apostolis
GREEK €€

(☑ 22850 26777; Old Market St; mains €8-15; ☺ lunch & dinner) Right at the heart of labyrinthine Bourgos, O Apostolis serves up tasty dishes in its pretty flagstone courtyard. The *kleftiko* (lamb wrapped in filo pastry), with sautéed vegetables and feta cheese, is delicious.

Meze 2
SEAFOOD €€

(☑ 22850 26401; mains €6-15; ☺ lunch & dinner) It would be easy to dismiss this waterfront restaurant at the harbour as a tourist trap, but don't. Its Cretan and Naxian menu and fantastic service make it stand out from the bunch. The seafood is superb – try squid stuffed with local cheese, grilled sardines, or mussels in ouzo and garlic.

🍷 Drinking & Nightlife

There are a few large, louder clubs at the southern end of the waterfront, and some great bars offering big views and cocktails from upper floors along the waterfront.

★ The Rum Bar
BAR

(☑ 6948592718; ☺ 8pm-late) Perched upstairs above Hora's busy waterfront, this newbie has lovely sunset views looking out over the yacht harbour. Open year-round, Rum Bar plays rock classics and occasionally features live music. Original cocktails are the name of the game here – try the Isla Tropical, which includes a healthy dose of Naxos *kitron*.

Naxos Cafe BAR
(☑22850 26343; Old Market St; ☺8pm-2am) If you want to drink but don't fancy the club scene, here's your answer. This atmospheric, traditional bar is small and candlelit and spills into the cobbled Bourgos street. Drink Naxian wine with the locals.

520 BAR
(☑6976251135; ☺9am-late) With a deck overlooking the harbour, this cool, comfortable bar whips up the most divine cocktails. Have breakfast, read a newspaper or party – it's all possible in this chic, cushioned interior.

La Vigne WINE BAR
(☑22850 27199; www.lavignenaxos.com; ☺7pm-1am) For a relaxed take on Naxian nightlife, head for this cheerful wine bar just behind Plateia Mandilara. It's run by two French expats who know more than a thing or two about fine wines and good conversation. Excellent fusion food too.

Citron Cafe CAFE
(☑22850 27055; Protopapadaki; ☺8am-late) You can begin your day on a sofa here, with coffee and a harbour view, and end it with a glass of local wine or *kitron* (liqueur made from the leaves of the citron tree) from Halki's distillery (p378). Check out the *kitron*-based cocktails (€6) for local flavour.

DaCosta CLUB
(☑6975939104) Right behind the port police, this sleek club brings well-known guest DJs from Athens to play dance music into the wee hours. All white and wood and chic, it has a loungy feel, which gives you somewhere to relax while you contemplate the well-stocked bar.

☆ Entertainment

★ Della Rocca-Barozzi Venetian Museum LIVE MUSIC
(☑22850 22387; www.naxosfestival.com; Kastro; event admission €15-20; ☺8pm Apr-Oct) Special evening cultural events are held outside at the museum, almost nightly in summer. Posters around town advertise what's on the horizon. It may be traditional music and dance concerts, classical piano recitals, bouzouki, or jazz and blues. There may even

be screenings of *Zorba the Greek*. There's an inside venue on the off-chance it rains.

🛍 Shopping

Kohili Jewels GIFTS & SOUVENIRS
(☑22850 22557; ☺10am-11pm) Hidden in the maze of small streets behind the waterfront, Kohili is chock-full of goodies. This is a good spot to purchase jewellery made from the Eye of Naxos, the hard shell that develops in the hole of a shellfish. The eye in the beautiful rings, necklaces, earrings and bracelets is said to bring good luck and fortune.

Papyrus Jewellery & Used Books BOOKS
(☑22850 23039) What began as a box of books left by a traveller has turned into a shockingly organised collection of over 10,000 second-hand books, covering multiple languages and genres. It's uphill from the port, behind Meze 2.

Kiriakos Tziblakis FOOD & DRINKS
(☑22850 22230; Papavasiliou) The pungent aromas will bowl you over as soon as you get through the door of this colourful wonderland, a family store dating from 1938. It's where locals come to buy bulk spices, olives, honey and cheese, and it's crammed with a photogenic jumble of local produce and goods, from pots to brushes, soaps to ouzo and raki.

Zoom BOOKS
(☑22850 23675; Paralia; ☺10am-10pm) A large, well-stocked newsagent and bookshop that has most international newspapers the day after publication and perhaps the best collection of postcards in Greece.

ℹ Information

There's no official tourist office on Naxos. Travel agencies can deal with most queries. Handy online resources include www.naxos.gr.

Alpha Bank (cnr Paralia & Papavasiliou) Has an ATM.

Hospital (☑22850 23550; Prantouna) On the eastern edge of town.

Information Booth At the ferry quay in summer. Opens when ferries arrive.

National Bank of Greece (Paralia) Has an ATM.

Naxos Tours (☑22850 24000; www.naxostours.net; Paralia; ☺8am-10pm) Sells ferry tickets and organises accommodation, excursions and car hire.

Police Station (☑22850 22100; Paparrigopoulou) Southeast of Plateia Evripeou.

Post Office (Agios Georgios) Go past the OTE, across Papavasiliou, and left at the forked road.
Zas Travel (☑22850 23330; www.zastravel. com; ⊗9am-9pm) Sells ferry tickets and organises accommodation, tours and car hire. Shorter hours in winter. Located on the harbourfront.

Around Naxos

Southwest Beaches

Beaches south of Agios Georgios (Hora's town beach) include beautiful **Agios Proko-pios**, which is sandy and shallow and lies in a sheltered bay to the south of the headland of Cape Mougkri. It merges with **Agia Anna**, a stretch of white sand, quite narrow but long enough to feel uncrowded. Development is fairly solid at Prokopios and the northern end of Agia Anna.

Sandy beaches continue as far as Pyrgaki, passing the beautiful turquoise waters of the long, dreamy **Plaka Beach** and gorgeous sandy bays punctuated with rocky outcrops. You'll find plenty of restaurants, accommodation and bus stops along this stretch – it's an idyllic place for a chilled-out beach stay. **Maragas Beach Camping** (☑22850 42552; www.maragascamping.gr; Agia Anna Beach; campsites per adult/tent €9/2, d/studio from €40/€60) has a good set-up across from a long sandy

---

DON'T MISS

LOCAL LIQUEUR

The citron fruit (Citrus medica) looks like a very large, lumpy lemon and is barely edible in its raw state. The rind is quite flavoursome when preserved in syrup, however, and *kitron,* a strong liqueur made from citron leaves, has been a hallmark of Naxos since the late 19th century.

Leaves are collected from October to February, dried, dampened and distilled up to three times with water and sugar. Dye is then added to mark its strength: yellow is the strongest and green is the lightest and sweetest. Clear is somewhere in the middle.

Visit the **Vallindras Distillery** (☑22850 31220; ⊗10am-10pm Jul & Aug, to 6pm May-Jun & Sep-Oct) in Halki to sample all three, or try **Citron Cafe** (p377) in Hora.

---

strand south of Agia Anna: camping, studios and rooms, a supermarket and a taverna. There's a regular bus from Hora that stops out front.

At **Mikri Vigla** (http://mikrivigla.com), golden granite slabs and boulders divide the beach into two. This beach is becoming an increasingly big fish on the kitesurfing scene, with reliable wind conditions. **Flisvos Kite Centre** (☑6945457407; www. flisvos-kitecentre.com) offers kite- and windsurfing classes and rents equipment to certified surfers. You can stay next door at **Orkos Beach Hotel** (☑22850 75194; www.orkosbeach. gr; s/d/apt incl breakfast €75/105/166; ⊗mid-May–Sep; ❋�🛜⛱), where rooms are clean and comfy but will hardly see you as you'll be too busy on the beach.

Halki   Χάλκη

POP 480

This village is a vivid reflection of historic Naxos, with the handsome facades of old villas and tower houses a legacy of its wealthy past as the island's long-ago capital. Today it's home to a small but fascinating collection of shops and galleries, drawing artists and culinary wizards. Halki lies at the heart of the Tragaea mountainous region, about 20 minutes' drive (15km) from Hora.

The main road skirts Halki, with parking areas near the entry (from Hora) and exit of town (the latter by the schoolyard). Pedestrian lanes lead off the main road to the picturesque square at the heart of Halki.

Paths radiate from Halki through peaceful olive groves and flower-filled meadows. The atmospheric 11th-century **Church of St Georgios Diasorites** lies a short distance to the north of the village. It contains some splendid frescoes.

⊙ Sights

Fish & Olive   GALLERY
(☑22850 31771; www.fish-olive-creations.com; ⊗May–mid-Oct) This gallery displays the exquisite work of Naxian potter Katharina Bolesch and her partner, artist and craftsman Alexander Reichardt. Each piece of work reflects ancient Mediterranean themes of fish and olives, motifs that frame the edges of shining plates, tumble down the sides of elegant jugs and bowls and dart across platters. The artists' work has been exhibited nationally and internationally. There's also a boutique selling their works a few metres from the gallery.

TRAGAEA & MT ZEUS

Naxos' lovely inland Tragaea (Τραγαία) region is a vast plain of olive groves and unspoilt villages high in the mountains, harbouring numerous little Byzantine churches. The Cyclades' highest peak, Mt Zeus (1004m; also known as Mt Zas), dominates the landscape. Filoti, on the slopes of Mt Zeus, is the region's largest village.

To climb Mt Zeus from Filoti, walk 40 minutes up to Aria Spring, a verdant fountain and picnic area, carry on another 20 minutes to the Cave of Zeus, and then climb to the summit in another 45 minutes.

Alternatively, if you have a car and want to shorten the walk, there's a junction signposted to Aria Spring and Zas Cave, about 800m up from Filoti on the main road. This side road ends after 1.3km. From the road-end parking it's a short walk to Aria Spring, and you can carry on to the cave and summit from there.

An option for the descent, if you hike up via the cave, is to walk down via the little chapel of Agia Marina to Filoti. You can walk down this route on waymarked track Number 2 in about 1½ hours.

Make sure to take good walking shoes, water and sunscreen.

Phos Gallery   GALLERY
(☑ 22850 31118; www.phosgallery.gr; ☺ May-Oct) See the island through the lens of talented photographer Dimitris Gavalas. Stunning landscapes – mostly of Naxos – grace the walls of this gallery, along with a handful of conceptual prints.

 Eating

Dolce Vita   BAKERY, CAFE **€**
(☑ 6981467240; snacks €3-7; ☺ breakfast, lunch & dinner) Cool and inviting, with dark wood and a gramophone daring to be wound, this is the place to lounge over homemade baking, coffee and ice cream.

Giannis Taverna   TAVERNA **€**
(☑ 22850 31214; dishes €5-12; ☺ lunch & dinner) With tables filling Halki's pretty central square under a leafy overhang, Giannis is well known for traditional fare. Try moussaka, pork souvlaki, savoury pies or village sausage.

Il Basilico   ITALIAN **€€**
(☑ 22859 31140; mains €10-25; ☺ dinner Jun-Sep) Near the entrance to Halki coming from Hora, this lively restaurant offers an excellent, changing menu, sourcing ingredients daily. The garden patio and colourful tiles add to the atmosphere (as do the excellent Italian wines).

🔒 Shopping

Penelope   ARTS & CRAFTS
(☑ 22850 31754) The know-how has been passed down to Penelope through at least four generations, and her fingers and feet fly on the loom. Watch her incorporate traditional designs into hats, scarves, bags and tablecloths that make fab souvenirs. You'll notice a lot of red and blue – the traditional colours of Naxos.

Era Jam Workshop   FOOD
(☑ 22859 31009) A visit to this shop gives you a peek into the open workshop where more than 20kg of delicious marmalade, jam and spoon desserts are made every day. This stuff is only sold on the island; taste it while you can!

Panagia Drosiani
Παναγία Δροσιανή

Located 2.5km north of Halki, just below Moni, the small, peaceful **Panagia Drosiani** (donations appreciated; ☺ 10am-7pm May–mid-Oct) is among the oldest and most revered churches in Greece. Inside is a series of cavelike chapels. In the darkest chapels, monks and nuns secretly taught Greek language and religion to local children during the Turkish occupation. Several frescoes still grace the walls, and date from the 7th century. Look for the depiction of Mary in the eastern chapter; the clarity and expression is incredible.

Sangri   Σαγκρί

Temple of Demeter   TEMPLE
(Dimitra's Temple) About 2km south of the village of Sangri is the 6th-century BC Temple of Demeter. The ruins and reconstructions are not large, but they are historically interesting. Demeter was the goddess of grain,

and temples were built to her in fertile areas such as the valley running south from Sangri; the remains were discovered in 1949. Signs point the way from Sangri.

Bazeos Tower
TOWER

(☑ 22850 31402; www.bazeostower.gr) The handsome Bazeos Tower stands prominently in the landscape about 2km east of Sangri. It was built in its original form as a monastery during the 17th century, and was later bought by the Bazeos family, whose modern descendants have refurbished the building with skill and imagination. The castle now functions as a cultural centre and stages art exhibitions and the annual Naxos Festival in July and August, when concerts, plays and literary readings are held.

Melanes   Μέλανες

◎ Sights

Marble Quarries
LANDMARK

The area between Melanes and Kinidaros has been the island's marble quarry since ancient times. Marble is still collected from this region, and you'll see sides of the mountains sliced open and looking like huge slabs of feta.

Kouros of Flerio
MONUMENT

In Flerio, near Mili, is an ancient marble-working area. There remain two examples of *kouroi*, large marble statues created in the 7th and 6th centuries BC. Each measures about 5.5m and both are in a broken state (the theory being that they were damaged during transportation or were simply left unfinished by dissatisfied sculptors). The first *kouros* you come to is lying on its back under a tree; the second is on a hillside about 800m away.

Eggares Olive Press
MUSEUM

(☑ 22850 62021; www.olivemuseum.com; ☺ 9am-6pm May-Sep) FREE A worthy side-trip is to this sweet set-up in the village of Eggares, 7km from Hora. A guide explains the workings of this small olive press (in operation from 1850 to 1960), and there are free tastings of olive-based products. The store here sells oil, pastes, soaps and unguents, plus cake and coffee.

Apiranthos   Απείρανθος

Apiranthos seems to grow out of the stony flanks of rugged Mt Fanari (883m), about 25km east of Hora (or 10 winding kilometres from Halki). The village's unadorned stone houses and marble-paved streets reflect a rugged individualism that is matched by the villagers themselves. Many of them are descendants of refugees who migrated from Crete, and today the village's distinctive form of the Greek language has echoes of the 'Great Island'. Apiranthos people have always been noted for their spirited politics and populism, and the village has produced a remarkable number of academics. These days, the village is peppered with quirky shops, galleries and cafes, and it's a lovely place to spend an afternoon.

✖️ Eating

Taverna O Platanos
GREEK €

(☑ 22850 61192; mains €6-13; ☺ lunch & dinner) Set beneath the shade of its namesake plane tree, this lively family restaurant serves up everything from yoghurt and homemade cheeses to grilled local meat. Try the hearty traditional dish of 'rosto' pork in tomato sauce. They've also got seating on a terrace with glorious views out over the valley – and some intriguing old weaponry on display.

Lefteris
GREEK €€

(☑ 22850 61333; www.stoulefteri.gr; mains €10-22; ☺ lunch & dinner May-Oct) With a deck taking in a phenomenal view, this charming, well-regarded place has the look and feel of an old country kitchen. Not much has changed here in a while! The short menu homes in on local cheeses and grilled meats – try lamb, steak or a burger stuffed with cheese and tomato.

The North

Heading north from the mountains inland, the roads wind and twist like spaghetti, eventually taking you to the somewhat scrappy seaside village of **Apollonas**. In an ancient quarry on the hillside above the village is a colossal 7th-century BC **kouros**, much larger and easier to find than the Kouros of Flerio. Follow the small signs to get here.

Apollonas' beach isn't great but the seafood is. Tavernas line the waterfront and serve the freshest of fish.

A worthy side-trip is to **Lionas**, where a scenic 8km drive past old emery mines leads you to a lovely stony beach and a couple of tavernas. **Delfinaki** (☑ 22850 51290; www.delfinaki.gr; Lionas; mains from €8) is super-friendly, serving up great home cooking and farm-fresh ingredients. Vassiliki, the hostess, sells homemade jams, 'spoon sweets' and wines.

With your own transport you can return to Hora via the northwest-coast road, passing through wild and sparsely populated country with awe-inspiring sea views. En route, stop for a look at the **Tower of Ayia**, the majestic ruins of a castle with a spectacular ocean backdrop.

SMALL CYCLADES
ΜΙΚΡΕΣ ΚΥΚΛΑΔΕΣ

The tiny islands that lie between Naxos and Amorgos are like miniature outposts of calm. In the days of antiquity, all were densely populated, revealed by the large number of ancient graves that have been uncovered. During the Middle Ages, only wild goats and even wilder pirates inhabited these islands. Post-independence, intrepid souls from Naxos and Amorgos recolonised the Small Cyclades, and today four have permanent populations – Iraklia, Schinousa, Ano Koufonisi and Donousa. Recently, the islands have welcomed a growing number of independent-minded tourists.

The Small Cyclades are officially under the administration of Naxos. Donousa is the northernmost of the group and the furthest from Naxos; the others are clustered near the larger island's southeast coast.

ℹ Getting There & Away

There are several connections a week between Piraeus and the Small Cyclades via Naxos, and daily connections to/from Naxos. The Small Cyclades are off most tourists' radars, and unplanned old-fashioned island-hopping is still possible here outside high season; you'll have no problem finding a room at a reasonable rate. Make sure to book ahead for high season, though. For ferry schedules, visit http://ferries.gr.

Blue Star Ferries (www.bluestarferries.gr) serves the Small Cyclades year-round. It has two routes, both beginning in Piraeus and calling at Paros and Naxos. From Naxos, three times a week the ferry calls at Donousa, then Amorgos (Aegiali) and terminates at Astypalea (in the Dodecanese). Three times a week, from Naxos the ferry stops at Iraklia, Schinousa and Koufonisia before terminating at Amorgos (Katapola).

The **Small Cyclades Line** runs the mainstay service, weather permitting in winter. Their sturdy little *Express Skopelitis* has been plying these waters for 35 years and is due for retirement. It is expected a new vessel will be ready

for the 2018 season, but don't be surprised to see the *Skopelitis* back. It leave from Naxos in the afternoon daily Monday to Saturday, and calls at the Small Cyclades and Amorgos (often to both ports, Aegiali and Katapola). It then returns to Naxos early the following morning.

Iraklia   Ηρακλεία
POP 140

Iraklia is only 19 sq km in area, a little Aegean gem dozing in the sun. Dump the party gear and spurn the nightlife, the sightseeing and the souvenir shops. Instead, brace yourself for a serene and quiet life, and Iraklia will not disappoint. Only in July and August will you have to share the idyll with like-minded others.

The port and main village of Iraklia is **Agios Georgios**. It has an attractive covelike harbour, complete with a sandy beach.

Boat Services from Iraklia

DESTINATION	DURATION	FARE (€)	FREQUENCY
Amorgos	1¾-4¾hr	8	1-2 daily
Donousa	2¼hr	8	3 weekly
Koufonisia	55min	5	1-2 daily
Naxos	1hr-1½hr	7	1-2 daily
Paros	2¼hr	12	3 weekly
Piraeus	8hr	35	3 weekly
Schinousa	10min	4	1-2 daily

◉ Sights & Activities

A surfaced road leads off to the left of the ferry quay, and after about 1km you'll reach **Livadi**, the island's best beach. A steep 2.5km further on is **Hora** (also called Panagia). From Hora, a surfaced road carries on to **Tourkopigado Beach**.

Walking

There are well-marked hiking trails of varying length all over the island. Get a map, make sure to take plenty of water.

Follow tracks 7, 4 and 3 from Agios Georgios to get to the **Cave of the Sacred Icon of Agios Giannis** in about two hours. Alternatively, follow track 3 from Hora to get there in one hour.

Beyond the cave, a path leads to the beach at Alimina, which is also served by **boat** (☑ 22850 71145; ◷ Jun-Sep) from Agios Georgios in summer (offering a shortcut to the cave).

Small Cyclades

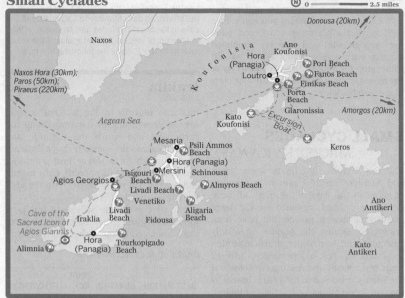

For a shorter walk from Agios Georgios, take track 8 for 30 minutes to reach the gorgeous cove of **Vorini Spilla** and a refreshing swim.

🛏 Sleeping

Maïstrali   ROOMS €
(☑22850 71807; www.bluehotels.gr; r from €60; 🛜) In Agios Georgios, a few hundred metres up from the port, Maïstrali offers a range of simple, good-value rooms and apartments with rates that tumble to €30 out of high season. It also features a shady elevated terrace **taverna** that has all the Greek standards covered and is open for breakfast, lunch and dinner. A good budget option.

Anna's Place   PENSION €
(☑22850 74234; www.annasplace.gr; d/q €60/80; 🌀🛜) Located on high ground above the port is this lovely, well-run complex, set in pretty gardens and with balconies taking in sweeping views. Inside, each super-clean, comfortable room has a kitchenette; some are well suited to families. Transfers from and to the port are complimentary.

Speires Hotel   BOUTIQUE HOTEL €€
(☑22850 77015; www.speires.gr; d incl breakfast €125; 🌀May-Oct; 🌀🛜) This stylish boutique is a short walk uphill from the port, with

white decor and flash bathrooms with all the mod-cons. Superior double rooms can fit a family. The terrace at the elegant on-site **cafe** and **wine bar** is a fine place to engage in a toast to holidaymaking.

🍷 Drinking & Nightlife

★En Lefko   CAFE
(☑22850 77027; www.facebook.com/en.leuko. iraklia; 🕘9am-late May-Sep) This rooftop bar on top of Perigiali Supermarket is lovingly run by a local couple. There are brunch menus plus cocktails, drinks and snacks until the wee hours. One of few options in Iraklia if you feel the urge to have a late night.

ℹ Information

There is an ATM by the harbour beach.

Schinousa   Σχοινούσα

POP 250

Like its neighbours, Schinousa has an easygoing pace and a sense of timelessness, although high season can be lively. With an area of only 8.5 sq km, it has a gentle landscape and is known for its beaches.

The major settlement **Hora (Panagia)** has a long, narrow main street lying along the breezy crest of the island. Ferries dock at the fishing harbour of **Mersini**. Hora is a 1km walk uphill from there.

Boat Services from Schinousa

DESTINATION	DURATION	FARE (€)	FREQUENCY
Amorgos	1½-4½hr	7	1-2 daily
Donousa	2hr	7	3 weekly
Iraklia	10min	4	1-2 daily
Koufonisia	30min	5	1-2 daily
Naxos	1hr 20min	7	1-2 daily
Paros	2hr 35min	13	3 weekly
Piraeus	8½hr	35	3 weekly

◉ Sights & Activities

Dirt tracks lead from Hora to beaches around the coast. The nearest are sandy **Tsigouri** and **Livadi**, both uncrowded outside August. Haul a little further southeast to decent beaches at **Almyros** with its shallow water and the small bays of **Aligaria**. Tsigouri, Livadi and Almyros have tavernas and/or beach bars. Just east of Mesaria in the north is **Psili Ammos** beach, good when a southerly is blowing.

Aeolia   BOATING
(☑ 6979618233; boat trip €15-35) From June to September, the Aeolia tour boat runs various daily trips, including around the beaches of the island, or to Iraklia and Koufonisia. Private trips can also be arranged. Ask about the week's schedule where you are staying.

🛏 Sleeping & Eating

There are rooms down at Mersini (the port) and plenty of options in Hora. Domatia owners, with transport, meet ferries from about May onwards and will always meet booked guests. Book ahead in July and August.

★Meltemi   PENSION €€
(☑ 22850 71947; www.pension-meltemi.gr; d €70-80; ❋ 🛜) Warm hospitality is the hallmark of this family-run pension and restaurant in the heart of Hora. Rooms are comfy and simple. You have a choice between older rooms in the Meltemi 1 building or newer rooms in Meltemi 2. Both are good. The on-site restaurant serves up delicious homemade meals. Free port and beach transfers too!

Iliovasilema   HOTEL €€
(☑ 22850 71948; www.iliovasilemahotel.gr; Hora; d incl breakfast €80; ☉ mid-May–Sep; ❋ 🛜) In

Hora, but perched at the port end of town with king-of-the-castle sunset views (*iliovaselima* means sunset), rooms here are small, simple and spotless. The views out towards Iraklia from the balconies are fab, and the service is warm. Rates include a good buffet breakfast.

Kafe stou Peri   CAFE €
(☑ 22850 76030; dishes €2-8; ☉ 7am-late) Open year-round, this colourful and friendly little cafe on the main street of Hora has crêpes, waffles, sandwiches and fresh salads, as well as breakfast options. There is also a well-stocked bar that keeps things pumping in the evening.

★Fish Tavern & Rooms Mersini   SEAFOOD €€
(☑ 22850 71159; www.mersini.gr; mains €8-18; ☉ May-Sep; ❋ 🛜) Down at the port, Mersini woos diners with a stylish white fit-out, in a garden setting with great harbour views. It seals the deal with excellent seafood (especially squid). The five chic all-white rooms behind the taverna are some of the nicest on the island (double €80 to €100). Straight ahead 200m from the quay.

Deli Restaurant & Cafe-Bar   GREEK €€
(☑ 22850 74278; restaurant mains €15-25; ☉ lunch & dinner Mar-Oct) Deli's upper floor features a top-notch restaurant with views out to Ios and Iraklia, while the ground floor houses a cool cafe-bar. On offer upstairs is a gourmet menu from the Cretan owner-chef using locally sourced ingredients, plus a wine list boasting some fine Greek vintages. Downstairs you'll find homemade sweets, coffees, drinks and cocktails and a cool crew.

❶ Information

For more information see www.schinousa.com and www.naxos.gr.

There's an ATM outside Hora's Paralos Travel. **Paralos Travel** (☑ 22850 71160; sparalos@otenet.gr) Halfway along Hora's main street. It sells ferry tickets and also doubles as the post office and newsagent in season.

Koufonisia   Κουφονήσια
POP 400

Koufonisia's star is on the rise; it is becoming a fashionable island for in-the-know visitors and is referred to by locals as 'the Mykonos of the Small Cyclades'.

BOAT SERVICES FROM KOUFONISIA

DESTINATION	DURATION	FARE (€)	FREQUENCY
Amorgos	40min-3½hr	7	1-2 daily
Amorgos*	25min	14	1-2 daily
Donousa	1hr 10min	6	3 weekly
Folegandros*	2¼-5½hr	69	6 weekly
Iraklia	50min	5	1-2 daily
Milos*	3¼hr-6½hr	69	6 weekly
Mykonos*	1hr 40min	55	3 weekly
Naxos	2-2½hr	7	1-2 daily
Naxos*	40-50min	19	1-2 daily
Paros	3hr 20min	19	3 weekly
Paros*	1hr 25min	30	1 daily
Piraeus	9hr	35	3 weekly
Piraeus*	4¼hr-5hr	59	1-3 daily
Santorini*	1-4hr	50	6 weekly
Schinousa	30min	5	1-2 daily
Serifos*	2hr	48	1 daily
Sifnos*	1½hr	45	1 daily

* high-speed services

It's made up of three main islands, two of which, Kato Koufonisi and Keros, are uninhabited. The three cover a total of 26 sq km. You'll arrive at the populated, low-lying **Ano Koufonisi**. It sees a flash-flood of tourism each summer thanks to its superb beaches, good hotels and chic restaurants, and it welcomes a growing number of summer high-speed ferries from other Cycladic islands. The main street is a joy to wander along.

Still, the island retains its low-key charm, and a substantial fishing fleet sustains a thriving local community outside the fleeting summer season.

Sights

Koufonisia's only settlement spreads out behind the ferry quay. The older part of town, the **Hora**, sprawls along a low hill above the harbour, parallel to the coast, and is one long whitewashed main street lined with restaurants and cafes.

At the western end of the main street, you'll reach **Loutro**, with a stony cove, small boatyard, windmill and whitewashed church.

Other Islands

The flat profile of uninhabited **Kato Koufonisi** is just to the south of Ano Koufonisi and a short caïque ride away. If you've come by ferry from Schinousa, you'll have passed its entire length on your way to Ano Koufonisi. Kato Koufonisi has some beautiful beaches and a lovely church.

East of here is the dramatic **Keros**, a rugged mountain of an island with towering cliffs. Archaeological digs on Keros have uncovered more than 100 Early Cycladic figurines, including the famous harpist and flautist now on display in Athens' National Archaeological Museum.

Beaches

An easy 2km walk along the sandy coast road east of the port leads to **Porta**, **Finikas** and **Fanos** beaches. All tend to become swamped with grilling bodies in July and August, and nudity becomes more overt the further you go.

Beyond Fano, a walking path leads to several rocky swimming places, including the glorious **Piscina**, a swimming hole surrounded by rock that is linked to the sea. The path then continues to the great bay at **Pori**, where a long crescent of sand slides effortlessly into the dreamy clear sea. Pori can also be reached by an inland road from Hora.

🏃 Activities & Tours

Bike Hire CYCLING
(☑ 6989637046; per day €4-10) Bike hire is available from this shop at the eastern end of the town beach. Koufonisia is relatively flat, so cycling is a good option. Look for the sign on the end of the building.

Captain Kostas BOATING
(☑ 22850 71438, 6945042548; www.roussetos hotel.gr; ⊙ Jun-Sep) Head to the marina and hop on Captain Kostas' boat to transfer to/from various beaches around the island (€3-5 return depending on the beach) and Kato Koufonisi (€5 return). There's a ticket kiosk at the port, or inquire at Prasinos travel agency.

Koufonissia Tours BOATING
(☑ 22850 74435; www.koufonissiatours.gr; Villa Ostria) Based at Villa Ostria, Koufonissia Tours organises sailing, diving and sea-kayaking trips around Koufonisia and the Small Cyclades.

🛌 Sleeping

★ Ermis Rooms PENSION €€
(☑ 22850 71693, 6972265240; www.koufonisia. gr/?page_id=1255&lang=en; 🖼 🛜) These immaculate rooms are in a quiet location, behind a pretty white-and-lilac exterior and a flowering garden. Ask Sofia for a balcony with sea view. At the port end of the beach, take the road uphill to the left of Roussetos Hotel. Ermis Rooms is next to the pale green post office, also run by Sofia.

Anna Villas PENSION €€
(☑ 22850 71697; www.annavillas.gr; d incl breakfast €100; 🖼 🛜) In a quiet location, these fresh, bright studios are charming and run with warmth. All have balconies and kitchen-ettes. It's a family-friendly spot, with a lovely reading nook and summertime cafe. Take the first left after the rental bike sign at the eastern end of the beach and climb the hill. On the left immediately after Villa Ostria.

Villa Ostria HOTEL €€
(☑ 22850 71671; www.ostriavilla.gr; r/studio €75/95; 🖼 🛜) One of several hotels on the high ground east of the beach, colourful Ostria has attractive rooms and studios with some quirky decor made from seashells and driftwood. Rooms have kitchenettes; spacious studios have kitchens. Take the first left after the rental bike sign at the eastern end of the beach and climb the hill.

🍴 Eating & Drinking

Gastronautis MEDITERRANEAN €
(☑ 22850 71468; mains €5-10; ⊙ lunch & dinner May-Sep) Found on the narrow, whitewashed main street, this is one of a new breed of fashionable eateries. There's a beachside-chic interior and a well-priced fusion menu. Try tuna tartar, zucchini cake or pork chops in barbecue sauce.

Karnagio TAVERNA €
(Loutro; mains from €8; ⊙ dinner Jun-Sep) This tiny taverna at Loutro, where the tables skirt the small harbour, has a magical setting. *Karnagio* means 'boatyard', and the taverna is owned by the same guy who fixes the boats. Expect good local food and a convivial atmosphere right on the water.

Capetan Nikolas SEAFOOD €€
(☑ 22850 71690; Loutro; mains €5-18; ⊙ dinner May-Oct) One of the best seafood places around, this cheerful restaurant overlooks the harbour at Loutro. Let the welcoming owners show you what's been freshly cooked, or help you select a fish for grilling. The lobster salad is famous and the seafood pasta delicious. Locally caught fish, such as red mullet and sea bream, are priced by the kilogram.

Scholio BAR
(☑ 22850 71837; ⊙ 7pm-3am; 🛜) A cosy bar and crêperie, Scholio plays to the crowd with jazz, blues or rock. It's at the western end of the main street above Loutro. The owners are accomplished photographers and often have exhibitions of their work on show.

ℹ Information

The post office has an ATM; it's up the road to the left of Roussetos Hotel.

For more information, check out www.koufo nisia.net and www.naxos.gr.

Prasinos (☑ 22850 71438; ⊙ 7am-11pm in summer) sells ferry tickets and tours on Hora's main street.

Donousa Δονούσα

POP 160
Donousa is the wonderfully out-on-a-limb island where you stop bothering about which day it is. In late July and August the island can be swamped by holidaymaking Greeks and sun-seeking northern Europeans, but out of season be prepared to linger – quietly.

Stavros is Donousa's main settlement and port. It's a cluster of whitewashed buildings around a handsome church, overlooking the ferry quay and a small sandy bay. Little has changed here over the years. There's an excellent **beach**, which also serves as a thoroughfare for foot traffic to a clutch of homes, rental rooms and a taverna on the far side of the sands.

For active types, Donousa offers up plenty to do, with good walking trails and attractive beaches.

Boat Services from Donousa

DESTINATION	DURATION	FARE (€)	FREQUENCY
Amorgos	40min-2¼hr	8	1-2 daily
Astypalea	2hr 20min	14	3 weekly
Iraklia	2hr	7	3 weekly
Koufonisia	1hr	5	3 weekly
Naxos	1hr 10min-3hr 40min	7	1 daily
Paros	2hr 25min	16	3 weekly
Piraeus	9hr 10min	35	3 weekly
Schinousa	1hr 50min	7	3 weekly

◉ Sights

Kendros, 1.25km southeast of Stavros, best reached by a stepped track, is a sandy and secluded beach with a seasonal taverna and free camping. **Livadi**, an hour's hike further east, sees even fewer visitors. A steep 20-minute walk up from Livadi is the excellent taverna I Kori tou Mihali in the village of Mersini. Both Kendros and Livadi are popular with naturists.

At the end of the road on the northeast coast, the tiny village of **Kalotaritissa** boasts three gorgeous little beaches and a seasonal taverna. Get here by minibus or the boat *Margissa* in summer – or hike over the hill from Stavros in 90 minutes.

🛏 Sleeping & Eating

Aposperitis Rooms PENSION €
(✆22850 51586; www.aposperitis-rooms.com; d/tr/apt €45/60/65; ◷mid-May–Sep; ❄🤶) Super-central to the beach and village (right on the town beach!), this guesthouse has a range of simple double rooms, triple studios (with kitchen) and family-sized apartments. Decor is dated, but balconies with sea views compensate.

★**Makares** APARTMENT €€
(✆22850 79079; www.makares-donoussa.gr; r & apt €80-140; ◷May-Oct; ❄🤶) Loukas is an excellent host at Makares, a complex of self-catering studios and apartments at the end of Stavros bay (across the beach from the port). It's a short walk to the beach and village, the views are fabulous, the decor simple and elegant, and the feeling of seclusion (with the required luxuries) is first-rate.

Captain George Restaurant GREEK €
(✆22850 51867; mains from €7.50; ◷lunch & dinner) A mainstay in Stavros as it's open year-round, this taverna above the port serves up Greek staples with everything from *gyros* to Greek salads to fish. The outlook is superb and, out of season, locals hang out here, eating and chatting. In high season you might be battling for a table. Nothing flashy, but it's a solid place to eat.

★**I Kori tou Mihali** TAVERNA €€
(✆22851 00006; mains €8-17; ◷lunch & dinner) At this welcoming taverna in Mersini village, 6km from Stavros by road, Koula conjures up excellent Greek cuisine with a modern twist: wild goat from the island, pork in honey and yoghurt, and smoky eggplant dip. It's worth the visit, for the food and the knockout views. Bathers at Livadi Beach hike 20 minutes up to eat here.

★**Skantzoxiros** CAFE-BAR
(✆22850 51880; ◷9am-late Jun-Sep) Up the stone steps at the port, this cafe-bar serves the younger crowd year-round. Out of season, it opens at 5pm, has Monday night movies and various locals' nights. In high season, it opens at 9am and is raging until the wee hours. Snacks, coffees, drinks and cocktails in a very convivial setting.

❶ Information

There's an ATM next to a small shop on the harbour road (it's sometimes hidden behind a blue shutter for protection from blown sand), but be sure to bring sufficient cash in high season.

There's good information online at www. donoussa.gr and www.naxos.gr.

Medical Centre (✆22850 51506) Just below the church.

Sigalas Travel (✆22850 51570) is the ticket agency for all ferries, with a main office in Stavros (behind the bakery) and a branch at the Iliovasilema restaurant complex on the far side of the town beach. The main office opens most evenings, plus 40 minutes before ferry arrivals.

AMORGOS ΑΜΟΡΓΟΣ

POP 1980

Dramatic Amorgos is shaped like a seahorse swimming its way east towards the Dodecanese. As you approach by sea, its long ridge of mountains appears to stretch ever skyward.

Amorgos is just 30km from tip to toe but reaches more than 800m at its highest point. The southeast coast is unrelentingly steep and boasts an extraordinary monastery built into the base of a soaring cliff. The opposite coast is just as spectacular, but softens a little at the narrow inlets where the main port and town of Katapola and the second port of Aegiali lie. The enchanting Hora (also known as Amorgos) lies amid a rocky landscape high above Katapola. All three towns have plenty of appeal as a base.

Amorgos is more about archaeology and activities than beach-going – there's great walking, diving and a burgeoning rock-climbing scene.

❶ Getting There & Away

Connections from Naxos are good, with the **Small Cyclades Line** (www.ferries.gr/small cycladeslines) operating each day (except Sunday), connecting Naxos with the two Amorgos ports by way of the Small Cyclades.

Blue Star Ferries (www.bluestarferries.gr) has three useful routes: two run regularly from Piraeus via Paros, Naxos and the Small Cyclades, ending at either Aegiali or Katapola port. The third route sails weekly from Piraeus to Katapola and eastwards to Patmos, Leros, Kos and Rhodes.

Ferries dock at either Katapola or Aegiali (sometimes both) so it's important to check both port schedules and to know which port you're arriving at or departing from.

Purchase your tickets from **Nautilos** (☑ Aegiali 22850 73032, Katapola 22850 71201), a ticket agency with offices close to both harbours.

❶ Getting Around

The **Amorgos Bus Company** (☑ 6936671033; http://amorgosbuscompany.com) has timetables and ticket prices online. Summer buses go regularly from Katapola to Hora (€1.80) and Moni Hozoviotissis and Agia Anna Beach (€1.80), and less often to Aegiali (€2.80, 30 minutes). There are also buses from Aegiali up to Langada (€1.80).

Without doubt, the easiest way to get around is by rental car. Cars and motorcycles are available for hire from **Thomas Rental** (☑ Aegiali 22850 73444, Katapola 22850 71777; www.thomas-rental.gr) or **Evi's Cars** (☑ 22850 71066; www.eviscars.gr). Expect to pay from €40 per day for a small car in August. There are only two petrol stations: one 1.5km inland from Katapola, the other in Aegiali.

Amorgos

BOAT SERVICES FROM AMORGOS

DESTINATION	DURATION	FARE (€)	FREQUENCY
Astypalea	1½hr	12	4 weekly
Donousa	2½hr	6	1 daily
Folegandros*	2hr 35min	69	5 weekly
Ios	5hr 20min	12	1 weekly
Iraklia	1¾-4½hr	8	1-2 daily
Kos	5hr	8	1 weekly
Koufonisia	40min-3½hr	6	1-2 daily
Koufonisia*	25min	14	1-2 daily
Leros	3hr 10min	2	1 weekly
Milos*	3¾hr	69	5 weekly
Mykonos*	2¼hr	55	3 weekly
Naxos	2-6hr	11	1-3 daily
Naxos*	1hr 20min	24	1-2 daily
Paros	3½-4½hr	19	7 weekly (note: not daily)
Paros*	2hr	29	1 daily
Patmos	2hr	21	1 weekly
Piraeus	8-10hr	35	7 weekly (note: not daily)
Piraeus*	5-6hr	62	1-3 daily
Rhodes	8hr	31	1 weekly
Schinousa	1½-4¼hr	7	1-2 daily
Santorini (Thira)	3¼hr	14	1 weekly
Santorini (Thira)*	1-4hr	50	5 weekly

* High-speed services

Katapola   Κατάπολα

POP 620

Katapola sprawls round the curving, yacht-filled shoreline of a picturesque bay in the most verdant part of the island. It's a bustling port town and there is a lot of activity around the ferry quay.

The remains of the ancient city of Minoa lie above the port and can be reached by footpath or a steep, concrete road, although there is no information. Amorgos has also yielded many Cycladic finds: the largest figurine in the National Archaeological Museum in Athens was found in the vicinity of Katapola.

🛏 Sleeping

★ Pension Amorgos   PENSION €€

(☑ 22850 71013; www.pension-amorgos.com; d €70; ❈ 🛜) There's a good deal of character in this traditional guesthouse, with bright and well-kept rooms right on the waterfront. It has the same owner as Emprostiada (p389) in Amorgos' Hora, and a similarly high quality. Very reasonable, Katapola's tavernas are only a short stumble away. You won't miss the morning ferry staying here – it parks up right outside.

Villa Katapoliani   PENSION €€

(☑ 22850 71664; www.villakatapoliani.gr; d €80-85, q €120; ❈ 🛜) Owner Stamatia has a high-quality collection of rooms, studios and apartments, handily located behind the waterfront and ferry quay. The balconies at Villa 1 overlook a garden filled with bougainvillea and the scattered ruins of the ancient temple of Apollo. Or scoot upstairs to the rooftop terrace for sea views. Apartments sleep up to four.

Minoa Hotel   HOTEL €€

(☑ 22850 74055; www.hotelminoa.gr; d/tr €90/100; ❈ 🛜) On the waterfront, this family-run place couldn't be more convenient for early-morning ferries. Service is friendly, and the sweet, neat rooms have tidy bathrooms and balconies overlooking a tree- and bird-filled garden. The lobby shares space with the family's Sweets by Pothiti cafe and patisserie.

✗ Eating

Honey & Cinnamon BAKERY €
(☑ 22850 71485; Katapola; ⊙ 8am-11pm) Look for the bright red window shutters and follow your nose. This tiny patisserie, a block back from the waterfront, bakes up cakes, pastries and lots of local cookies. Try the ones made with the local liquor, *psimeni raki,* or simply grab a coffee or a gelato.

★ Captain Dimos GREEK €€
(☑ 22850 71020; mains €6-16; ⊙ lunch & dinner) The captain, who is seriously into food, whips up mouthwatering dishes on his convivial harbourside patio. Crowding the tempting menu are dishes like octopus cooked in ouzo with lemongrass and ginger, and pork cooked with beer, apples and prunes. Creative pastas and pizza too. Sit back, enjoy and watch the world go by.

Karamel MEDITERRANEAN €€
(☑ 22850 71516; dishes €4-12; ⊙ lunch & dinner) Pass the beach and head to the far side of the harbour from the ferry quay to find some enticing dining options, including this colourful, French-run bistro. Sip wine at the waterfront tables and choose between daily dishes like chicken à la marocaine, carrots caramélisées and juicy octopus, which deliciously marry Greek and French flavours.

ℹ Information

Boats dock right on the waterfront. The bus station is a few minutes' walk inland along the water.

A bank (with ATM) is mid-waterfront.

N Synodinos (☑ 22850 71201; synodinos@nax. forthnet.gr) Sells ferry tickets and has a money exchange on the waterfront.

Hora (Amorgos)
Χώρα (Αμοργός)

The old capital of Hora sparkles like a snowdrift across its rocky ridge. It's capped by a 13th-century *kastro* and guarded by windmills that stand sentinel on the surrounding

cliffs. There's a veneer of sophistication in the handful of fashionable bars and stores that enhance Hora's appeal without eroding its timelessness. The main activity here is wandering, rewarded with beautiful village settings around each corner.

The bus stop is on a small square at the edge of town, with car parking. There's also an ATM next to a minimarket right at the entrance to Hora and a post office.

◎ Sights

Archaeology Collection MUSEUM
(⊙ 9am-1pm & 6-8.30pm Tue-Sun) **FREE** Hora's Archaeology museum has some interesting pieces excavated on the island, including remnants of the Minoan civilisation which existed here more than 4000 years ago.

⊨ Sleeping & Eating

Pension Ilias PENSION €
(☑ 22850 71277; www.iliaspension.gr; d/apt €60/100; ❄ 🕾) Tucked away amid a jumble of traditional houses not far from the bus stop is this friendly family-run place with pleasant, comfortable rooms. The apartments can accommodate four people.

★ Emprostiada GUESTHOUSE €€
(☑ 22850 71814; http://emprostiada.gr; d €100, ste €130-150; ⊙ Mar-Nov; ❄ 🕾) There's charm in abundance at this traditional guesthouse, where private, characterful suites are housed in an old merchant's home. It's a postcard scene in a peaceful setting at the back of the village. Choose from spacious doubles, maisonettes and suites. Doubles are a bargain €50 outside the July and August peak. Free port transfers from Katapola or Aegiali.

Jazzmin CAFE €
(☑ 22850 74017; breakfast €6-13, snacks €3-6; ⊙ 9am-late) Down some stairs from the main pedestrian street, Jazzmin spreads through the cosy rooms of a traditional home. Perch in a window seat or lounge on the roof deck. Breakfast choices are good, as are smoothies, juices and herbal teas. The list of cocktails hints at the impressively stocked bar, and jazz and other smooth tunes provide a chilled-out soundtrack.

Triporto CAFE €
(☑ 22850 73085; breakfast €8, snacks €3-5; ⊙ 9am-late) Once the village bakery, this cafe has a strong traditional feel, plumped up with some colourful, hip decor. Come for breakfast to create an omelette from

ingredients like olive sauce and hot paprika cream, or snack on salads, sandwiches and sweets. The friendly owner is a virtual encyclopaedia of local knowledge.

Kath Odon
GREEK €

(✐ 22850 74148; mains €5-10; ☺ lunch & dinner) The setting is idyllic: tables under trees in a lovely little *plateia* at the top end of the main street, nestled between whitewashed churches. The menu of this unpretentious bistro presents tasty Amorgon produce, including goat, sausage, cheese, and some excellent zucchini balls.

Aegiali
Αιγιάλη

POP 520

Aegiali is Amorgos' second port and sees fewer yachts and a bit more of the holidaymaker scene. It's a vibrant village with plenty going on. A sweep of sand lines the inner edge of the bay on which the village stands.

🏃 Activities & Tours

Amorgos Diving Center
DIVING

(✐ 6932249538, 22850 73611; www.amorgos-diving.com) Enthusiastic and friendly instruction can be had at this well-run centre on the beach. Dives (with equipment) start at €50, with night dives, wreck dives and PADI courses available. It also offers a Bubblemaker class for kids, and snorkelling tours (€20).

Special Interest Holidays
WALKING

(www.walkingingreece.com) Based at Langada, this outfit organises walking holidays (guided or self-guided) with experienced, knowledgeable hosts: Paul and Henrietta Delahunt-Rimmer, an English couple who have written the excellent resource *Amorgos: A Visitor's and Walker's Guide*. See the website for full details.

🛏 Sleeping

Apollon Studios
GUESTHOUSE €

(✐ 22850 73297; www.apollon-amorgos.com; studio d/q €55/85; ❈ 🗑) With a nautically themed lobby, this guesthouse in the heart of the village has studios with well-equipped kitchens and harbour-view balconies. Rooms aren't fussy, but they're comfortable and reasonably priced. This place draws lots of repeat guests and families. Lots of places to eat right out the front door.

Aegiali Camping
CAMPGROUND €

(✐ 22850 73500; www.aegialicamping.gr; campsite per adult/child/tent €5.50/2/4; ☺ May–mid-Oct; 🅿 🗑) Basic facilities a block back from the beach, with tents under the vines. There are showers, toilets and free wi-fi. Rent a tent for €6. On-site taverna and bar, too.

Yperia
HOTEL €€

(✐ 22850 73084; www.yperia.com; d €105-115, f €168, all incl breakfast; ☺ Apr-Oct; ❈ 🗑 ❈) Yperia's modern rooms have warm, artsy touches, handmade wood and iron furnishings, big bathrooms and excellent sea views. The pool overlooks the ocean, and the hotel is just a block from the beach. Staff are friendly and accommodating.

Aegialis Hotel & Spa
HOTEL €€€

(✐ 22850 73393; www.amorgos-aegialis.com; d from €195; ❈ 🗑 ❈) High on a hill and with magical views over Aegiali Bay and village, this is one of the island's smartest options. Rooms are good, but it's the facilities that make this place shine: pool and pool bar, a bliss-out day spa and indoor pool, restaurants – oh, and did we mention the view? Decent off-peak rates; book online.

🍴 Eating

★ Amorgis
CAFE €

(✐ 22850 73606; meals €3-10; ☺ 9am-late; 🗑) On the steps leading up from the ferry quay, Amorgis is open from morning until late. Sunset drinks here are a fine idea. Family-friendly, it's as pretty as a picture, full of pastel colours and hanging pot plants. The menu offers enticements like fresh juices, cool cocktails, baguettes, salads and tortillas. A lovely place to relax and stare out to sea.

Falafel
INTERNATIONAL €

(✐ 6936808038; dishes €4-12) Up an alley from the waterfront, Falafel is a fresh-faced, laid-back eating and drinking venue with a menu that's a grab-bag of world cuisines (spring rolls, falafel, summer salads, curries). It's an easy place to while away some time away from the main street.

To Limani
TAVERNA €€

(✐ 22850 73269; http://tolimani.weebly.com; dishes €5-15; ☺ breakfast, lunch & dinner) This popular restaurant carries its traditional atmosphere comfortably, up from the main street. Using home-grown produce, the cooks whip up hefty portions of great local dishes: try the fish soup, *patatao* (lamb with potatoes in tomato sauce), or anything with local cheese. And save room for some home-made orange pie.

❶ Information

Aegialis Tours (☑ 22850 73393; http://amorgos-aegialis.com/services), based at Aegialis Hotel & Spa, can help arrange local tours and experiences (hiking, cultural excursions, cooking classes etc).

Around Amorgos

Agia Anna Beach is the nearest beach to Hora, but it's tiny and rocky; the car park is bigger. It's popular for its starring role in the French film *Le Grand Bleu*, and is known for its dramatic location and photogenic whitewashed chapel. There's a small cantina next to the car park on the clifftop, selling food and drinks.

Amorgos is a popular walking destination, and the island has a selection of well-marked numbered walking tracks. Check these routes out online at www.amorgos.gr. Cartography company Terrain (http://terrainmaps.gr) produces an excellent hiking map for Amorgos.

The lovely villages of **Langada** and **Tholaria** nestle amid the craggy slopes above Aegiali, each about 3km from the town. The two are linked to each other, and to Aegiali, by a signposted 9km circular path that takes 2½ to three hours to walk.

🛏 Sleeping & Eating

Pagali Hotel   HOTEL €€
(☑ 22850 73310; www.pagalihotel-amorgos.com; Langada; d €73-110; ❄ �🛜) Pagali Hotel is tucked away in Langada village, with superb views. Rooms and studios are comfortable, and the year-round hotel offers alternative agritourism activities like grape or olive harvesting and winemaking, and activities including rock climbing, hiking, yoga and art workshops. The hotel sits in a cute family-run pocket of Langada, next to the excellent Nikos Taverna and Vassalos Bakery.

IOS   ΙΟΣ

POP 2030

Ios' image has long been linked to holiday sun, sea and sex, with a reputation for non-stop booze-fuelled partying. It's partly true: there's no denying that from June to August, the island is the much-loved stomping

MONI HOZOVIOTISSIS

The iconic 11th-century monastery **Moni Hozoviotissis** (Μονή της Χοζοβιώτισσας; donations appreciated; ⊙ 8am-1pm & 5-7pm) is a dazzling white structure seemingly embedded into the cliff-face high above the sea on the precipitous east coast below Hora. It's also high above the car park, with 350 steps to get to it. With any luck, a custodian will be there to explain the significance of the monastery and its icons. The dress code is modest and strict. No shorts, no mini-skirts, no bare shoulders and no women in trousers. No exceptions.

ground of youth and hedonism. But it's so much more – if you want it to be – and the partying doesn't infiltrate every village or beach.

Spend your days exploring the winding footpaths of the traditional hilltop old town or ensconced on a sandy beach. Discover the isolated interior or sandy beaches such as Manganari in the south, and then return to town in time for the party. Or visit in the shoulder season for a quieter pace, when Ios draws families and more mature travellers. It's pretty easy to escape the crowds: simply rent a car and venture into the countryside of goat farms, honey boxes and dramatic views.

❶ Getting There & Away

Ios lies conveniently on the Mykonos to Santorini ferry axis and has regular connections with Piraeus. Purchase tickets at **Acteon Travel** (p396) in Ormos, or its smaller branch in Hora.

❶ Getting Around

In summer crowded **buses** (☑ 22860 92015; www.ktel-ios.gr) run between Ormos, Hora and Mylopotas Beach (all fares €1.80) about every 20 minutes. Schedules are posted at the main village bus stops and online. In summer, additional buses run frequently to Koubara, and less frequently to beaches at Agia Theodoti, Psathi and Manganari. For taxis call **Ios Taxi Service** (☑ 6977760570); it's €5 from the port to Hora, €5 from Hora to Mylopotas.

Summertime caïques travel from Ormos to Manganari via Mylopotas and cost about €12 per person for a return trip.

BOAT SERVICES FROM IOS

DESTINATION	DURATION	FARE (€)	FREQUENCY
Amorgos	3hr	12	1 weekly
Anafi	2hr 25min	11	2 weekly
Folegandros	1hr 20min	10	4 weekly
Folegandros*	25min	44	2 weekly
Iraklio*	2hr 40min	64	2 daily
Kimolos	2hr 50min	16	3 weekly
Milos	3-4hr	16	2 weekly
Milos*	1¾hr	49	1 daily
Mykonos	4hr	24	1 daily
Mykonos*	1hr 50min-3hr 50min	48	4 daily
Naxos	1-1¾hr	14	1-3 daily
Naxos*	45min	25	1-2 daily
Paros	2hr 20min	16	1-3 daily
Paros*	1-1½hr	28	3 daily
Piraeus	7hr	36	6 weekly
Piraeus*	3hr 40min-5hr	59	2 daily
Rafina	7½hr	35	1 daily
Rafina*	5-6hr	62	2 daily
Santorini (Thira)	1-1½hr	12	6 weekly
Santorini (Thira)*	40-50min	29	4-7 daily
Serifos	4hr 50min	19	1 weekly
Sifnos	4-5½hr	18	3 weekly
Sifnos*	3hr	54	1 daily
Sikinos	25min	5	4 weekly
Syros	5hr 10min	18	1 weekly
Tinos*	3-4½hr	38	2 daily

* high-speed services

Ormos, Hora and Mylopotas Beach all have car, motorcycle and four-wheeler hire. You can book through Acteon Travel (p396).

Hora, Ormos & Mylopotas
Χώρα, Ορμός & Μυλοπότας

Ios' three main centres sit nearly on top of one another on the west coast. The port, Ormos, is lined with tavernas and cafes and stretches out into sandy **Gialos Beach**, backed by beach bars. Just 2km uphill (or 1.2km up a stone staircase) sits the capital of Hora, a stunning traditional village and nightlife hub. From here, the road winds south to the brown-sugar sand of **Mylopotas Beach**, with upscale and backpacker-style resorts. You'll find places to eat, sleep, drink and dance in all three

settlements. Grocery stores are also found in each.

Hora's central square is Plateia Valeta, buried deep in the old town. The road straight ahead from Hora's bus stop leads 3km to Mylopotas Beach.

◉ Sights & Activities

Hora is a charming Cycladic village with a labyrinth of narrow lanes and cubist houses. Visit during the day and wander from the main streets into the quiet residential quarters to get a glimpse of village life that carries on behind the tourist hype scene.

Skarkos   ARCHAEOLOGICAL SITE
(The Snail; €4; ⊙8am-3pm Tue-Sun May-Sep) Crowning a low hill just north of Hora, this Early to Late Bronze Age settlement has restored walled terraces and the low

ruins of several Cycladic-style buildings to explore. A small visitor centre and interpretation boards in Greek and English help out. If driving, take the signed turn-off between Ormos and Hora. To walk, follow the traditional stone footpath from the back of Hora, passing goats and farmhouses. The pleasant walk takes around 15 minutes.

Archaeological Museum
MUSEUM
(22860 91246; Hora; €2; ⏰8.30am-3pm Tue-Sun) Finds from Skarkos are displayed at this thorough, if slightly dry, museum in the town hall next to the bus stop in Hora. There are also exhibits from island excavations in general.

Mylopotas Watersports & New Dive
WATER SPORTS, DIVING
(22860 92340; http://mylopotas-watersports.gr; Mylopotas; ⏰May–mid-Oct) A thousand ways to fill your day: try a discover scuba-diving session (€55) or more intensive PADI courses

from €270. There are also wreck dives and night dives. Join a three-hour boat snorkelling trip for €35, or rent a long list of gear: windsurfing kit, kayaks, sailboats and more. Take a tube ride or do some waterskiing. Sea-taxi services too.

Meltemi Watersports & Dive Centre
WATER SPORTS, DIVING
(6980386990; www.meltemiwatersports.com; Mylopotas) Based at the Far Out Beach Club (p394), with a ready flow of keen customers, Meltemi has a smorgasbord of ways to get wet: try out a diving sampler (€55) or full PADI courses, then check out wreck, cave and night dives. Learn to windsurf, waterski and wakeboard, hire a stand-up paddleboard, join a canoe safari or take a boat excursion.

Yialos Watersports
WATER SPORTS
(22860 92463, 6974290990; www.yialoswatersports.com; Gialos Beach) Mylopotas isn't the

Ios

only beach full of activity. At Gialos Beach, this company can get you afloat with wind-surfing (lessons and gear), stand-up pad-dleboarding, waterskiing, wakeboarding, banana rides, canoes, snorkelling gear – you name it. There are mountain bikes for the landlubbers, too, or simply sunbeds if you're worn out from all the activities.

🛏 Sleeping

Ormos is considerably quieter than Hora or Mylopotas. If you're here to party, Hora is the best place to stay. Book early for July and August. Outside those months, prices fall by 50% or more.

🛏 Ormos

Yialos Ios Hotel   HOTEL €€
(📞22860 91421; www.yialosioshotel.gr; Ormos; s/d €80/100, studio €130-170, all incl breakfast; ☺May-Sep; ❄🛜🏊) Just a block back from the port, this newly restored, 200-year-old stone building feels like the home you wish you had. Crisp, characterful rooms, beamed ceilings, traditional beds and a flower-filled poolside give it the edge. The owners are attentive, and the breakfast room is just like your Greek grandma's kitchen. Off-peak rates are excellent (doubles around €50).

Avra Pension   PENSION €€
(📞22860 91985; www.avrapension.gr; Ormos; r €65; ☺Apr–mid-Oct; ❄🛜) Down a lane behind the yacht marina at the port, Kat-erina runs this delightful guesthouse with warmth and efficiency, and at bargain prices (outside the short summer peak, rooms fall to €30). Colourful potted plants, a restful terrace, homey common areas and fresh, appealing rooms add up to super value.

Pension Irene   PENSION €€
(📞22860 91023; www.iosirene.gr; r from €80; ☺Jun-Oct; ❄🛜🏊) Just back from the yacht marina in Ormos, with double rooms right through to a two-bedroom apartment. Quiet location with a sparkling swimming pool; ask for the top view to get a massive shared terrace. Reception is like a small museum, with some great old photos of Ios.

🛏 Hora

⭐Francesco's   HOSTEL €€
(📞22860 91223; www.francescos.net; Hora; dm/d/tr/q €20/70/105/140; ☺Apr–mid-Oct; ❄@🛜🏊) Former backpackers are now sending their own 18-year-olds to Francesco's, which is still going strong. Rooms are spotless, views are dreamy and it's within stumbling distance of Hora's nightlife. There's a global feel and a roll-call of happy-traveller features: terrace bar, pool and cheap breakfast menu. Head towards the main square and turn left down Odos Scholarhiou for 200m. Or ask anyone.

Pavezzo   GUESTHOUSE €€
(📞6977046091; www.iospavezzo.com; Hora; d €70-100; P🛜) This place is just steps from Hora but away from the night-time noise, on a quiet side road to Kolitsani Beach. The seven rooms are a steal; clean and comfort-able, they feature country-style decor and private, sea-view patios. Suites have well-stocked kitchens, and the hosts are welcom-ing and attentive.

Avanti Hotel   HOTEL €€
(📞22860 91165; www.avanti-hotelios.com; Hora; d incl breakfast €130-150; ☺mid-Apr–mid-Oct; ❄@🛜🏊) These fresh, sparkling rooms are a short stroll out of Hora, but far enough away to offer a little peace. Private balconies and a beautiful pool and outdoor area are the icing on the cake. Rates halve outside the summer peak.

⭐Liostasi   BOUTIQUE HOTEL €€€
(📞22860 92140; www.liostasi.gr; Hora; d/ste incl breakfast from €150/280; ☺May-Sep; ❄@🛜🏊) Step into the lobby of this place and you may never want to leave. A con-temporary Greek design blends chic and comfy in just the right proportions. The on-site spa, restaurant and pool area are top quality, and the rooms are crisp with splashes of colour and gorgeous sea views. Service is impeccable. It's halfway between Ormos and Hora.

🛏 Mylopotas

Far Out Beach Club & Beach Resort   HOSTEL, CAMPGROUND €
(📞22860 91468; www.faroutclub.com; Mylopotas; campsite per person €10, dm €15, d/q €90/180; P@🛜🏊) Nearly on top of the beach is this backpacker party haven with poolside bars, restaurants and everything from laundry to tattooing, a sushi bar, yoga and gym. There's an enormous array of sleeping options, from tents to dorm beds, including en-suite rooms. Far Out even has a hotel and luxury villas nearby.

✕ Eating

✕ Ormos

La Randa
ITALIAN €

(✆ 22860 92448; www.facebook.com/larandaios; Ormos; mains €7-14; ⊙9am-1am; 🐾) Right on the port where the ferries dock, this place is fabulous for Italian cuisine. The owner has shipped an authentic oven over from Italy and makes drool-worthy pizzas and pasta dishes in homemade tomato sauce.

Akrogiali
TAVERNA €€

(✆ 22860 91096; Ormos; mains from €8; ⊙lunch & dinner) In the complex across the road from the ferry quay, Akrogiali is a superb, well-priced seafood taverna. The locals eat here, which gives it a tick from the start. Try the *salatouri* (stingray salad) or the octopus in red wine sauce.

✕ Hora

★ Katogi
MEZEDHES €

(✆ 6983440900; www.facebook.com/katogios; Hora; dishes €4-11; ⊙dinner) Full of life, entering Katogi feels like you've walked into a party in someone's living room, where bright, homey decor flows into a gorgeous garden and the music selection rocks. More importantly, the food is divine. Try haloumi bites with cherry tomatoes, pork bites in whisky sauce or pasta purses filled with cheese and pear.

Thai Smile
THAI €

(✆ 22860 91925; Hora; mains €7-12; ⊙dinner) Ignore the international dishes and go for the authentic Thai flavours, created by the Thai owner-chef. A backstreet spot with plenty of atmosphere, serving plates overflowing with phad thai noodles, Massaman curry and tom yum soup.

The Nest
GREEK €€

(✆ 22860 91778; www.facebook.com/thenestios; Hora; mains €6-18; ⊙lunch & dinner) The Nest feels authentic, right down to the *rembetika* music and the tables of older men deep in discussion over rounds of raki. Local garlic sausage, chicken souvlaki, stuffed eggplant and lamb *kleftiko* are served with bowls of tzatziki, olives and fresh bread. Wine is served by the jug, and the veggies come from the owner's garden.

Lord Byron
MEDITERRANEAN €€

(✆ 22860 92125; www.lordbyronios.gr; dishes €7-14; ⊙dinner) An explosion of colour and quirky decor near the square in Hora, this laid-back, lively restaurant is as pleasing to the stomach as it is to the eye. Enjoy huge portions of creative salads and mains, with dishes like cheese pies with orange and honey mustard dip, or barbecued crab. Service gets five stars.

✕ Mylopotas

Cantina del Mar
CAFE €

(✆ 22860 91016; http://cantinadelmar.gr; Mylopotas; sandwiches & salads €2-8; ⊙breakfast, lunch & dinner) Come here, at the entrance to Mylopotas, to chill out next to the beach over bumper brunches, sandwiches and wraps. Choose from a long, healthy-sounding list of juices and smoothies (can the hangover juice of lemon, orange and carrot really do the trick?) or wine and cocktails for when you're feeling well again. The music selection soothes.

🍸 Drinking & Nightlife

Nightlife at the heart of Hora is full-on and radiates from the tiny main square, where it gets so crowded by midnight that you won't be able to fall down, even if you need to.

There's everything from jazz bars to frantic backpacker bars that dole out cheap shooters, though venues open and close regularly.

★ Blue Note Club
CLUB

(✆ 22860 92271; www.facebook.com/bluenote official; ⊙11.15pm-late May-Oct) This Hora favourite has been thumping for decades and is still the hottest spot on the island. Catering to a young crowd, if you were under the impression Ios was a party island before you came, Blue Note will reinforce those thoughts. Head straight through the square and turn left at Katogi.

Free Beach Bar
BAR

(✆ 22860 28357; http://freebeachbar.gr; ⊙10am-1am May-Sep) Offering dozens of colourful, ways to lounge and recline, this beach bar sits in the middle of Mylopotas Beach and sends a siren call via its beach cabanas and pool, surrounded by hanging beds and cushioned pods. Aside from all-day drinks, snacks are on offer (club sandwich, pizza). Chill out or dig the DJ-fired action.

Fun Pub   PUB

(📞 22860 92022; www.facebook.com/funpubios; ⏱ 11am-late Apr-Oct) If you can't find your tribe on Hora's main square, they might be here – at the Irish-owned Fun Pub, on the main road through the town. It does what it says on the label, with fun in various guises: music, dancing, food, live sports, pool tables and plenty of mingling. Pub grub and a Sunday roast.

Foiniki Art Cafe   BAR

(📞 22860 92247; Hora; 9am-late) It's easy to settle into this funky little bar, with its friendly owners, rich colours, stacks of magazines and hand-crafted beer from around Greece. Tucked behind Lord Byron (p395), it's a great spot for a morning coffee or pre-dinner tipple.

Ios Club   COCKTAIL BAR

(📞 6985720049; www.iosclub.gr; ⏱ 7pm-3am Apr-Oct) A deliciously sophisticated cocktail bar that's perfect for sunset cocktails and sweeping views on the chic terrace. It's along the pathway by Sweet Irish Dream, on the right as you head into Hora from Ormos.

☆ Entertainment

★ Cine Liostasi   CINEMA

(📞 22860 92140; www.liostasi.gr/cine-liostasi) **FREE** Outside at Liostasi Hotel & Suites, halfway between Ormos and Hora, this lovely setting hosts nightly outdoor cinema under the stars. The aim is to become the top outdoor cinema in Greece and, indeed, this spot is hard to beat. Watch classic and modern movies in loungers while sipping signature cocktails with a gorgeous view as background to the screen.

ℹ Information

There's an ATM right by the kiosks at the ferry quay in Ormos. In Hora, the National Bank of Greece, behind the church, has an ATM.

In Hora there is a seasonal information kiosk at the bus stop, across the road from the big cathedral. Online, check out http://ios.gr for more info.

Acteon Travel (📞 22860 91343; www.acteon.gr; ⏱ 8am-10pm) Purchase ferry tickets at Acteon Travel in Ormos, or its smaller branch in Hora.

Hospital (📞 22863 60000) On the way to Gialos, 250m northwest of the quay.

Dr Yannis Kalathas (📞 6932420200, 22860 91137; ⏱ 24hr) Your best contact in case of medical emergency.

Around Ios

Head to Cape Gero Angeli, at the northernmost tip of the island and 12km from Hora, to the believed site of **Homer's Grave**. There's nothing much to see here but the panoramic sea views are fabulous.

En route to Psathi is **Paleokastro**, the remains of a Byzantine castle perched atop a seaside cliff. Follow the stone pathway from the roadside; it'll likely just be you and the goats here.

Ios is well known for its beaches. Vying with Mylopotas for first place is **Manganari**, a long swath of fine white sand on the south coast, reached by bus or by caïque in summer. **Agia Theodoti** has the bluest of blue water and is favoured by Greek families in summer. Nearby **Psathi** is quieter.

SANTORINI (THIRA)
ΣΑΝΤΟΡΙΝΗ (ΘΗΡΑ)

POP 15,550

With multicoloured cliffs soaring above a sea-drowned caldera, Santorini looks like a giant slab of layered cake. The main island of Thira will take your breath away with its snow-drift of white Cycladic houses lining the cliff tops and, in places, spilling like icy cornices down the terraced rock. When the sun sets, the reflection on the buildings and the glow of the orange and red in the cliffs can be truly spectacular.

Santorini is no secret and draws crowds for much of the year, yet it wears its tourism crown well. The island's intrigue reaches deep into the past, with the fascinating Minoan site of Akrotiri and the gorgeous traditional hilltop village of Oia. It also glides effortlessly into the future with accomplished artists, excellent wineries, a unique microbrewery and some of the Cyclades' finest accommodation and dining experiences. The multicoloured beaches are simply the icing on the cake.

History

Minor eruptions have been the norm in Greece's earthquake-prone history, but Santorini has a definite history of overachieving – eruptions here were genuinely earth-shattering, and so wrenching they changed the shape of the island several times.

Dorians, Venetians and Turks have occupied Santorini, but its most influential early

Santorini (Thira)

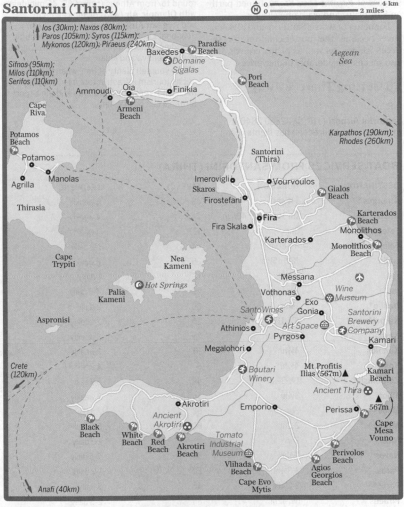

N · 0 ————— 4 km
0 ————— 2 miles

Ios (30km); Naxos (80km);
Paros (105km); Syros (115km);
Mykonos (120km); Piraeus (240km)

Sifnos (95km);
Milos (110km);
Serifos (110km)

Baxedes ● ● Paradise
Beach

Domaine
Sigalas

Pori
Beach

Aegean
Sea

Ammoudi ● Oia ● Finikia
Armeni
Beach

Cape
Riva

Karpathos (190km);
Rhodes (260km)

Santorini
(Thira)

Potamos
Beach
● Potamos

Agrilla ● ● Manolas

Thirasia

Imerovigli ● ● Vourvoulos
Skaros
Firostefani

Gialos
Beach

Karterados
Beach
Monolithos

Fira Skala ● ● Fira

Karterados ●

Monolithos ●
Monolithos
Beach

Cape
Trypiti

Nea
Kameni

Palia
Kameni

Hot Springs

Messaria ●
Vothonas ●
Exo
Gonia ●

Wine
Museum

Santorini
Brewery
Company

Aspronisi

Santo Wines

Athinios ●

Art Space

Pyrgos ●

Kamari ●

Megalohori ●

Crete
(120km)

Boutari
Winery

Mt Profitis
Ilias (567m) ▲

Kamari
Beach

Ancient Thira

● Akrotiri

Ancient
Akrotiri

Emporio ●

Perissa ● 567m ▲

Cape
Mesa
Vouno

Black
Beach

White
Beach Red
Beach

Tomato
Industrial
Museum

Akrotiri
Beach

Perivolos
Beach

Vlihada
Beach

Agios
Georgios
Beach

Anafi (40km)

Cape Evo
Mytis

inhabitants were Minoans. They came from Crete some time between 2000 BC and 1600 BC, and the settlement at Akrotiri dates from the peak years of their great civilisation.

The island was circular then and was called Strongili (Round One). Thousands of years ago, a colossal volcanic eruption caused the centre of Strongili to sink, leaving a caldera with towering cliffs along the east side – a truly dramatic sight. The latest theory, based on carbon dating of olive-oil samples from Akrotiri, places the event 10 years either side of 1613 BC.

Santorini was recolonised during the 3rd century BC, but for the next 2000 years sporadic volcanic activity created further physical changes that included the formation of the volcanic islands of Palia Kameni and Nea Kameni at the centre of the caldera.

As recently as 1956, a major earthquake devastated Oia and Fira, yet by the 1970s the islanders had embraced tourism as tourists embraced the island, and today Santorini is a destination of truly spectacular global appeal, drawing honeymooners, backpackers, the jet set, cruise-boat passengers, Chinese bridal parties (in part due to the success of *Beijing Love Story,* filmed partly on Santorini) and everyone else too.

For better or worse, Santorini and Mykonos have become the poster-children for the Greek islands. As well as bigger crowds, that also means considerably higher prices.

❶ Getting There & Away

AIR

Santorini Airport (JTR; ☎ 22860 28400; www.santoriniairport.com) has flights year-round to/from Athens (from €65, 45 minutes) with **Olympic Air** (www.olympicair.com) and **Aegean Airlines** (www.aegeanair.com). Seasonal European connections are plentiful, including, among others, easyJet from London, Rome, Geneva and Milan.

Give yourself plenty of time when flying back out as tourism infrastructure hasn't kept up with the island's growing popularity and the airport terminal can be mayhem.

BOAT SERVICES FROM SANTORINI (THIRA)

DESTINATION	DURATION	FARE (€)	FREQUENCY
Amorgos*	1-4¼hr	49	6 weekly
Anafi	1hr 10min-1hr 40min	7	4 weekly
Folegandros	3hr	12	3 weekly
Folegandros*	45-80min	44	1-2 daily
Halki	12½-15½hr	26	2 weekly
Ios	1-2hr	12	1 daily
Ios*	35-45min	29	4-6 daily
Iraklio*	1¾hr	60	2 daily
Karpathos	8½-11½hr	25	2 weekly
Kasos	6¾-9½hr	25	2 weekly
Kimolos	4½hr	16	2 weekly
Kos	4½hr	34	4 weekly
Koufonisia*	1½-3½hr	49	6 weekly
Milos	3½hr	17	2 weekly
Milos*	2hr	52	2 daily
Mykonos*	2-3hr	60	5-6 daily
Naxos	2hr	19	1-2 daily
Naxos*	1½hr	38	4-5 daily
Paros	3-3½hr	20	1-2 daily
Paros*	2-2¼hr	46	3 daily
Piraeus	5½-12hr	36	2-3 daily
Piraeus*	4½-6hr	59	3-4 daily
Rafina*	5¾hr	64	2 daily
Rethymno (Crete)*	2hr 20min	65	2 weekly
Rhodes	8-17¾hr	27	5 weekly
Serifos	6½hr	19	1 weekly
Sifnos	5-7¼hr	18	3 weekly
Sifnos*	3-4hr	54	1-2 daily
Sikinos	2hr	9	3 weekly
Sitia (Crete)	6hr	26	1 weekly
Tinos*	3½-4hr	40	2 daily

* high-speed services

Note: differences in durations are on account of vessel type and/or route.

BOAT

There are plenty of ferries each day to and from Piraeus and many Cyclades islands.

Thira's main port, Athinios, stands on a cramped shelf of land at the base of sphinx-like cliffs and is a scene of marvellous chaos that always seems to work itself out when ferries arrive. Buses (and taxis) meet all ferries and then cart passengers up the towering cliffs through an ever-rising series of S-bends to Fira. Accommodation providers can usually arrange transfers (to Fira per person is around €10).

❶ Getting Around

TO/FROM THE AIRPORT

There are frequent bus connections between Fira's bus station and the airport, located 5km east of Fira (€1.80, 20 minutes, 7am to 9pm). Most accommodation providers will arrange paid transfers.

Bus

KTEL Santorini Buses (☑ 22860 25404; http://ktel-santorini.gr) has a good website with schedules and prices. Tickets are purchased on the bus.

In summer buses leave Fira regularly for Oia, with more services pre-sunset (€1.80). There are also numerous daily departures for Akrotiri (€1.80), Kamari (€1.80), Perissa and Perivolos Beach (€2.40), and a few to Monolithos (€1.80).

Buses leave Fira for the port of Athinios (€2.30, 30 minutes) a half-dozen times per day, but it's wise to check times in advance. Buses for Fira meet all ferries, even late at night.

Car & Motorcycle

A car is the best way to explore the island during high season, when buses are intolerably over-crowded and you'll be lucky to get on one at all. Be very patient and cautious when driving – the narrow roads and heavy traffic, especially in and around Fira, can be a nightmare.

There are representatives of all the major international car-hire outfits, plus dozens of local operators in all tourist areas. A good local hire outfit is **Damigos Rent a Car** (☑ 22860 22048; www.santorini-carhire.com). You'll pay from around €50 per day for a car and €25/30 for a scooter/four-wheeler in high season, but it pays to shop around. Note: scooter hire requires you to have a motorbike licence, while four-wheelers require just a car licence. Check this website for details: www.santorini.com/rentals/motorbikes.

Taxi

Fira's **taxi stand** (☑ 22860 23951, 22860 22555) is on Dekigala just around the corner from the bus station. A taxi from the port of Athinios to Fira costs €10 to €15, and a trip from Fira to Oia about €15. Expect to add €2 if the taxi is booked ahead or if you have luggage. A taxi to Kamari is about €15, to Perissa €18 and to Ancient Thira about €25 one-way.

Santorini Transport (☑ 6984637383; www.santorinitransport.com) is a good option for arranging fixed-price transfers to/from the airport or Athinios port.

Fira   Φήρα

POP 2300

Santorini's main town of Fira is a vibrant, bustling place, its caldera edge layered with hotels, cave apartments, infinity pools and swish restaurants, all backed by a warren of narrow streets full of shops and even more bars and restaurants. A multitude of fellow admirers cannot diminish the impact of Fira's stupendous landscape; this is one of the few places in the world that actually looks better than the postcards! Views over the multicoloured cliffs are breathtaking, and at night the caldera edge is a frozen cascade of lights.

While Fira's population is only a tad over 2000, it sprawls north and merges into two more villages: **Firostefani** (about a 15-minute walk from Fira) and **Imerovigli** (the highest point of the caldera edge, about a half-hour walk from Fira). A path runs through these villages and is lined with glorious hotels, restaurants and endless photo opportunities.

◉ Sights

★ **Museum of Prehistoric Thera**   MUSEUM
(☑ 22860 22217; www.santorini.com/museums; Mitropoleos; adult/child €3/free; ⊘8.30am-3pm Wed-Mon) Opposite the bus station, this well-presented museum houses extraordinary finds excavated from Akrotiri and is all the more impressive when you realise just how old they are. Most remarkable is the glowing gold ibex figurine, dating from the 17th century BC and in mint condition. Also look for fossilised olive tree leaves from within the caldera, which date back to 60,000 BC.

Archaeological Museum   MUSEUM
(☑ 22860 22217; M Nomikou; adult/child €3/free; ⊘8.30am-3pm Tue-Sun) Near the cable-car station, this museum houses impressive finds from Akrotiri and Ancient Thira, such as unbelievably detailed clay statuettes from the latter site, including a donkey, pig, ram

Fira

and birds. Check out the chariot-racing images on some of the pottery. The content is strong, though the museum itself is in need of a little TLC.

Santozeum
MUSEUM

(📞22860 21722; www.santozeum.com; Ypapantis; adult/child €5/3; ☺10am-6pm May-Oct) Around the corner from the Archaeological Museum, this modern cultural centre is home to the 'Wall Paintings of Thera' exhibition, a collection of life-size reproductions of the finest Akrotiri murals. Be sure to watch the short video on the work of

conservators – it is fascinating. There's no labelling, so be sure to ask for the information sheet for context.

Megaro Gyzi Cultural Centre
MUSEUM

(📞22860 23077; www.megarogyzi.gr; Erythrou Stavrou; adult/child €3/free; ☺10am-9pm Mon-Sat, 10.30am-4.30pm Sun May-Oct) Escape the crowds to this quiet museum in the town's north to take in fascinating before-and-after photographs of the 1956 earthquake in Fira, along with a collection of maps, engravings, paintings and 15th-century manuscripts.

Fira

🏃 Activities

Walks in and around Fira are spectacular, particularly heading north to Firostefani and Imerovigli along the caldera-edge pathway. This is about a 30-minute walk, one-way. If you want to keep walking, you can eventually reach **Oia**, but be aware that this is no small undertaking, and the trail beyond Imerovigli can be rough. It's about 9km in all, and a good three to four hours' walk one-way. It's best not to undertake it in the heat of the day.

Other options include walking down to (or up from) the small port known as **Fira Skala**, from where volcanic island cruises leave (and where cruise-ship passengers come ashore). It's around 600 steps each way. You can make a more leisurely, and aromatic, upward trip by donkey (€5) – although animal-rights groups strongly urge travellers not to, due to the cruelty involved. You can also go by the **Santorini Cable Car** (https://scc.gr/cablecar.htm; one-way €6; ⊙ 7am-10pm May-Sep; reduced hr Oct-Apr) that hums quickly and smoothly (every 20 minutes 6.30am to 11pm June to August) between Fira and Fira Skala. Less frequent services operate outside the peak season; there is an additional charge to take luggage (€2.50).

From Imerovigli, a sign at Mezzo restaurant leads west to Skaros, a rocky headland with great views and a perfectly situated church. From Imerovigli it's about 20 minutes one-way.

👣 Tours

Any tour your heart desires can be organised on Santorini – there are dozens of agencies primed and ready to help with winery visits, archaeology tours, traditional villages, sunset-watching and other activities.

Another option is a cruise, and the most popular itinerary takes in the caldera's volcanic islands of Nea Kameni and Palia Kameni, including a stop at the former's crater and the latter's hot springs. Some tours will also call at Thirasia, and/or a port below Oia. Sunset-watching from a boat, drink in hand, is also in demand.

Departures are from Fira Skala, below Fira. Book with one of the agencies around town. Vessels vary, from replica schooners to sleek catamarans and yachts – therefore prices vary wildly.

The starting rate for a basic full-day excursion is around €30. Before booking, ask about the itinerary, inclusions (eg lunch or drinks) and the number of fellow passengers.

🛏 Sleeping

Pension Petros　　　　　　　PENSION €

(☑ 22860 22573; www.hotelpetros-santorini.gr; r from €90; ❄ 🛜 🏊) Three hundred metres east of the square in Fira, Petros offers decent rooms at good rates, but no caldera views. This is a friendly, family-run operation and makes an affordable option, especially outside high season, when rates are less than half. Cute pool too!

Santorini Camping　　HOSTEL, CAMPGROUND €

(☑ 22860 22944; www.santorinicamping.gr; Fira; dm/d €25/70, campsite per person €12.50; ☺ Mar-Nov; 🅿 ❄ @ 🛜 🏊) On the eastern outskirts of town, this hostel and campground has some shade and decent facilities. You get what you pay for with the rooms, which are clean but quite basic. There's a self-service restaurant, minimarket, bar and pool.

Villa Roussa　　　　　　　　HOTEL €

(☑ 22860 23220; www.villaroussa.gr; Dekigala; s/d/tr from €80/100/120; 🅿 ❄ 🛜 🏊) This place is all about location. Minutes from the caldera (without the prices to match) and seconds from the bus station (but thankfully out of earshot), it has fresh, immaculate rooms and helpful staff.

Hotel Sofia　　　　　　　　　HOTEL €

(☑ 22860 22802; www.sofiahotelsantorini.com; Firostefani; d €110; ☺ May-Oct; ❄ 🛜 🏊) Comfortable, with a touch of character, these half-dozen petite rooms at the heart of Firostefani are a great alternative to the bustle of Fira. There's no caldera view, but it's literally outside your door. The rates are a near-steal (book early) and the small, lovely pool and verandahs are a bonus. Fira's centre is about 800m south.

★ Aroma Suites　　　BOUTIQUE HOTEL €€

(☑ 22860 24112; www.aromasuites.com; Agiou Mina; d from €240; ❄ @ 🛜) Overlooking the caldera at the quieter southern end of Fira, and more accessible than similar places, this boutique hotel has charming service and six plush, beautiful suites. Built into the side of the caldera, the traditional interiors are made all the more lovely with monochrome decor, local art, books and stereos. Balconies offer a feeling of complete seclusion.

Kavalari Hotel　　　　　　　HOTEL €€

(☑ 22860 22455; www.kavalarihotel-santorini.com; r from €180; ⊝ ❄ 🛜) One of Fira's top-value hotels, Kavalari is at the heart of the action and offers standard rooms and cave

apartments. The central location, views and spotless rooms make this an affordable option when surrounding hotel rates are taken into consideration. An excellent breakfast is included.

Pelican Hotel　　　　　　　　HOTEL €€

(☑ 22860 23113; www.pelicanhotel.gr; Danezi; s/d/tr €90/110/130; ❄ 🛜) There's no caldera view, but you're just metres from the heart of the action in this long-standing hotel with a homey feel. Two of its best attributes are the restaurant next door and the delightful garden setting.

Hotel Keti　　　　　　　　　　HOTEL €€

(☑ 22860 22324; www.hotelketi.gr; Agiou Mina, Fira; d from €170; ❄ 🛜) Hotel Keti is one of the smaller 'sunset view' hotels in a peaceful caldera niche. Its attractive traditional rooms are carved into the cliffs, half of which have Jacuzzis. Two-night minimum in high season.

Villa Soula　　　　　　　　　HOTEL €€

(☑ 22860 23473; www.santorini-villasoula.gr; Fira; r from €100; ❄ 🛜 🏊) Cheerful and spotless, this hotel is a great deal. Rooms aren't large but are freshly renovated with small, breezy balconies. Colourful public areas and a small, well-maintained undercover pool give you room to spread out a little. It's a short walk from the town centre.

★ Mill Houses　　　BOUTIQUE HOTEL €€€

(☑ 22860 27117; www.millhouses.gr; Firostefani; d incl breakfast from €350; ❄ 🛜 🏊) Built right into the side of the caldera at Firostefani, down a long flight of steps, these superb studios and suites are chic and plush. Lots of white linen and whitewashed walls fill them with light. King-sized beds, Bulgari toiletries and private patios looking out over the Aegean are just a few of the lavish touches.

Anteliz Suites　　　BOUTIQUE HOTEL €€€

(☑ 22860 28842; www.anteliz.gr; r from €285; ⊝ ❄ 🛜 🏊) North of Fira on the path that runs to Firostefani, Anteliz offers an amazing pool, sun terrace and oh, those views. Relax in the open-air hot tub and take it all in. The suites feature white-marble floors and a high degree of elegance and style – definitely one of Fira's top places to stay.

🍴 Eating

Overpriced, indifferent food geared towards tourists is still an unfortunate feature of summertime Fira; thankfully, there are many excellent exceptions.

ℹ️ SLEEPING ON SANTORINI

There's so much to choose from in Fira and Oia that confusion can set in. Away from these main towns, the biggest concentration of rooms can be found in and around Kamari and Perissa. The latter is a good option if you are on a budget. High-season rates are as follows:

€ less than €100

€€ €100-250

€€€ over €250

Things to know about Santorini accommodation:

➡ Few of Fira's sleeping options are cheap. For a caldera view, expect to pay a premium.

➡ The sky is the limit here and in Oia: luxury accommodation is everywhere, with all the trimmings (private terrace, plunge pool etc).

➡ Consider accommodation in Firostefani and Imerovigli if you don't mind a walk into Fira. There are plenty of quality hotels and restaurants with caldera views here too.

➡ Many hotels on the caldera rim cannot be reached by vehicle and may involve several flights of steps. Many hotels have porters who can help with luggage.

➡ Some domatia touts at the port may claim that their rooms are in town, when they're actually a long way out; ask to see a map showing the exact location.

➡ Some places may offer free transfer to the port or airport; other places may charge €12 upwards for a transfer.

In general, there's a price hike for a caldera view, while cheap eats surround the central square. Book ahead in July and August.

⭐ **Theoni's Kitchen**　　　　　GREEK €
(☑ 22860 25680; www.theoniskitchen.com; Dekigala; mains from €7; ⊙ noon-midnight) Theoni's isn't fancy and you won't be gazing out over the caldera, but this is the best 'momma's kitchen' home-cooked Greek food you'll find, with smiling, friendly owners and good service. Expect decent-sized portions of Greek classics and daily specials that may well have you returning for more. The Greek salad here is exceptional.

Galini Cafe　　　　　　　　　CAFE €
(☑ 22860 22095; www.galinicafesantorini.com; mains €6-14; ⊙ 8am-midnight) Just as you reach Firostefani, this breezy cafe welcomes you with brightly coloured flowerpots and a hand-crafted school of fish swimming overhead. Chilled out and friendly, with unparalleled caldera views, it's a great place for breakfast or a light meal and cocktail at sunset. Gorgeous views.

To Ouzeri　　　　　　　　　TAVERNA €
(☑ 22860 21566, 6945849921; http://ouzeri-santorini.com; Fabrika Shopping Centre; mains €7-15; ⊙ lunch & dinner) Central and cheerfully dressed in red gingham, this terrace restaurant has surprisingly reasonable prices. It's a long-standing favourite with locals and tourist alike, with top traditional dishes like mussels *saganaki,* baked feta and stuffed calamari.

Cacio e Pepe　　　　　　　ITALIAN €€
(☑ 22860 24971; www.cacioepepe.gr; 25 Martiou; mains from €10; ⊙ noon-midnight) You're up for pizzas, pastas, meats, seafood and all kinds of Italian favourites at this proud place out on 25 Martiou. There's a full-on Italian wine list and they're especially proud of the signature dishes – the ravioli tartufo and the cacio e pepe (cheese and pepper) spaghetti.

Fanari　　　　　　　　　　　GREEK €€
(☑ 22860 25107; www.fanari-restaurant.gr; dishes €7-20) Tasty traditional Greek dishes and superlative views are on offer at this place overlooking the caldera on the steps down to the Old Port. Along with unique local recipes, seafood and fresh fish, there are local dessert favourites such as Santorini pudding and *meletinia,* made of skimmed-milk cheese and scented with mastic and vanilla.

Assyrtico Wine Restaurant　　GREEK €€
(☑ 22860 22463; www.assyrtico-restaurant.com; Fira; mains €15-30; ⊙ lunch & dinner) Settle in on this terrace above busy Ypapanti for polished

local flavours accompanied by caldera views. Start with, say, the *saganaki* wrapped in a pastry crust, and follow with the deconstructed *gyros* or the white eggplant moussaka. Service is relaxed and friendly; the wine list is big.

⭐ **1500 BC**   SEAFOOD €€€
(☑22860 21331; www.1500bc.gr; mains €22-39; ☺lunch & dinner) With top views south across the caldera, this elegant patio serves top-quality food. Braised lobster, royal crab legs with green olive oil, and chateaubriand veal fillet are just a few of the mouthwatering choices. Service is impeccable – they'll debone the fish at your table and bring you a shawl if you're chilly.

⭐ **Koukoumavlos**   GREEK €€€
(☑22860 23807; www.koukoumavlos.com; mains €28-34; ☺dinner Apr–mid-Oct) This terrace is filled with gleeful diners partaking of award-winning fresh, modern Aegean cuisine (including a worthwhile degustation at €74). Creativity reigns and the menu is poetic, elevating dishes to new heights: 'slow-cooked shoulder of lamb with potato mousseline flavoured with jasmine, fig and Greek coffee sauce'. Look for the pink building and wooden doorway. Book ahead.

Mylos   GREEK €€€
(☑22860 25640; www.mylossantorini.com; Firostefani; mains €22-26; ☺lunch & dinner) Located in a converted windmill on the caldera edge in Firostefani, this uber-glam venue has upscale food that's ambitious in its techniques and beautifully presented. Try crispy fish 'covered with sea snow', or Greek black pork with Romesco sauce. Book ahead.

🍷 Drinking & Nightlife

After midnight, Erythrou Stavrou fires up as the clubbing caldera of Fira, while Marinatou is lined with fabulously chic drinking spots.

Kira Thira   BAR
(☑22860 22770; Erythrou Stavrou; ☺9pm-6am Wed-Sun) The oldest bar in Fira and one of the best. Dark wood and vaulted ceilings give it an intimate, cave-like atmosphere, with smooth cocktails and smoother jazz. With a huge viola hanging on the ceiling, this tiny bar is so popular it often gets swamped, especially when there is live music on offer.

Crystal Cocktail Bar   COCKTAIL BAR
(☑22860 22480; www.loucashotelsantorini.com; ☺10am-1am) With views to die for, relax at Crystal with coffee in the morning and cocktails as your day evolves. This is one of those spots that you won't want to leave. Part of Loucas Hotel, Crystal is a top spot for romance, with stupendous sunsets.

Two Brothers Bar   BAR
(☑22860 23061; www.2brothersbarsantorini.com; ☺10am-6am) Originally started by brothers Dimitris and Giannis in 1983, this Fira institution is now run by their sons, Jack and Leuteris. Expect a party vibe and when things really wind up, little room to move. Two-for-one cocktails from 4pm to 7pm and 9pm to midnight at this island favourite.

MoMix Bar Santorini   BAR
(☑6974350179; www.facebook.com/MoMixBar Santorini; Marinatou; ☺8pm-5am) It might take a minute to get your head around this, but MoMix is short for Molecular Mixology. This popular party spot offers innovative

cocktails (to help your mind travel) and cool interior colours in its cave-like bar. Head outside for stunning caldera views.

Tango Champagne & Cocktail Bar BAR
(📱6947453999; www.tangosantorini.gr; Marinatou; ⊗8pm-5am) This is edge-of-the-caldera stuff, with stupendous views, delicious cocktails, a fashionable crowd and brilliant tunes that get louder and funkier as the sun goes down. Come for sunset and stay for hours – or until your wallet is empty.

Koo Club CLUB
(📱22860 22025; www.kooclub.gr; Erythrou Stavrou; ⊗10pm-5am Jun-Sep) Hang out with your new best friends on the sofa-strewn, multi-tiered outdoor balconies while sipping cocktails to live DJs.

☆ Entertainment

The White Door Theatro THEATRE
(📱22860 21770; www.whitedoorsantorini.com; €49; ⊗May-Oct) Fira's popular *Greek Wedding Show* is a hit with visitors, featuring lots of traditional music, dance, fun and audience participation. Small plates (mezedhes) and local wine are included in the ticket, which can be booked online – advisable in the high season. The show is in an atmospheric open-air courtyard surrounded by whitewashed buildings.

Casablanca Soul Bar LIVE MUSIC
(📱6977575191; www.facebook.com/casablanca soul; Ypapantis; ⊗9.30pm-5.30am) This cocktail and absinthe bar is a Fira, hotspot with live bands, visiting DJs and soul well into the wee hours. Expect tasty cocktails and a relaxed vibe.

🔒 Shopping

Mati Art Gallery ARTS & CRAFTS, JEWELLERY
(📱22860 23814; www.matiartgallery.com; Cathedral Plateau) The installation pieces outside are sure to catch your attention before you even step inside this gallery. This is the main exhibition space of Yorgos Kypris, an internationally celebrated artist who takes much of his inspiration from Santorini. Take in his larger sculptures (incredible fish) and then consider home items, pendants and jewellery that are hard to resist.

Orion Art Gallery ART
(📱22860 21616; www.artoftheloom.gr; Kamares; ⊗9am-10pm) This new gallery and shop next to the Megaro Gyzi Cultural Centre (p400) at the northern end of town displays

gorgeous pieces by some of the island's top artists. Expect everything from fusion glass to modern bronze statues, handmade jewellery and colourful ceramics. Everything can be packed and sent overseas.

AK Art Gallery ART
(📱22860 23041; www.ak-galleries.com) AK, Santorini's first art gallery, was founded in 1980 by local artists, painter Christopher Asimis and his wife, Eleni Kolaiti, who specialises in jewellery and sculptures. The stunningly white gallery, near the Orthodox Cathedral, was formerly a flour mill and features impressive art inspired by the beauty of the island. AK also has galleries in Oia and on the Fira–Pyrgos road.

Greco Gold Santorini JEWELLERY
(📱22860 22460; http://grecogoldsantorini.gr; ⊗10am-11pm) Just north of the cathedral, Greco Gold has been around for over four decades, selling the well-known Greek brand Konstantino, handmade Byzantine-style jewellery and contemporary pieces designed and made by Greco Gold itself.

the White, Santorini FASHION & ACCESSORIES
(📱22860 36217; www.thewhitesantorini.com) This small fashion boutique, run by designer Sophia Hatzigeorgiou, draws inspiration from Santorini's unique landscapes, colours and lifestyle. The clothing is hand-sewn in Greece and, as the name suggests, collections feature plenty of options in white. There's a second store out at Kamari Beach.

Theta 8 FASHION & ACCESSORIES
(📱22866 72935; Marinatou; ⊗9am-midnight) The new kid on the block is a chic boutique in a white-cave shop on the steps down to the Old Port. It offers colourful leather bags handmade in Greece, plus appealing accessories. Owned and operated by three local women, expect friendly smiles and service.

ℹ️ Information

There are numerous ATMs scattered around town.

Alpha Bank (Plateia Theotokopoulou) Has an ATM.

Central Clinic of Santorini (📱22860 21728; www.santorinicentralclinic.gr) Health clinic just east of the town centre. Open 24 hours for emergencies.

Dakoutros Travel (📱22860 22958; www.dak outrostravel.gr; Fira; ⊗8.30am-10pm) Travel agency on the main street, just before Plateia Theotokopoulou. Ferry and air tickets sold;

SAMPLING SANTORINI

Beyond caldera views, infinity pools and black-sand beaches, Santorini is cultivating a reputation for wine and food tourism. It's a side of the island well worth exploring.

Food

Food-wise, the island is best known in Greece for its white eggplants, capers, cherry tomatoes and fava (yellow split peas, not unlike lentils). Cooked and puréed, the popular fava dish is traditionally eaten warm, as an appetiser (or dip), or accompanying a main course of meat or fish. Santorini was 'tomato island' before the tourism boom, though only one of 13 former tomato processing factories is still in operation.

Tomato Industrial Museum (☑ 22860 85141; www.tomatomuseum.gr; Vlihada; €5; ☉ 10am-6pm Tue-Sun) Despite the dry-sounding name, this is a unique look inside an old tomato factory in Vlihada. Tomato processing was a major industry on the island, and the video interviews of elderly former factory workers is fascinating. The seaside museum is part of the cool **Santorini Arts Factory** (www.santoriniartsfactory.gr), which hosts exhibitions, concerts and theatre; check its program online.

Selene (☑ 22860 22249; www.selene.gr; Pyrgos) Acclaimed restaurant **Selene** (☑ 22860 22249; www.selene.gr; Pyrgos; mains restaurant €30-40, bistro €9-16; ☉ restaurant dinner, bistro lunch & dinner) offers a program of cooking demonstrations, wine-tasting and hands-on cooking courses, with plenty of opportunity for sampling the wares. Courses include a tour of the on-site **Cultural Village** (☑ 22860 31101; www.santorinimuseum.com; Pyrgos; €4; ☉ 10am-4pm & 6-8pm Mon-Sat), which explores culinary, agricultural and other island traditions. See the website for details.

Wine

Santorini's lauded wines are its crisp dry whites, and the amber-coloured, unfortified dessert wine known as Vinsanto. Both are made from the indigenous grape variety, Assyrtiko. Most local vineyards host tastings (usually for a small charge), and some offer food, with scenery and local produce combining to great effect.

---

assistance with excursions, accommodation and transfers.

Information Kiosk (☉ 9am-8pm Mon-Fri May-Sep) Seasonal information kiosk.

National Bank of Greece (Dekigala) South of Plateia Theotokopoulou, on the caldera side of the road. Has an ATM.

Police Station (☑ 22860 22649) In the centre of Fira.

Post Office (Dekigala)

Oia   Οία

POP 670

Perched on the northern tip of the island, the village of Oia reflects the renaissance of Santorini after the devastating earthquake of 1956. Restoration work has whipped up beauty, and you will struggle to find a more stunning Cyclades village. Built on a steep slope of the caldera, many of its dwellings nestle in niches hewn into the volcanic rock.

Not surprisingly, Oia draws enormous numbers of tourists, and overcrowding is the price it pays for its good looks. Try to visit in the morning or spend the night here; afternoons and evenings often bring busloads from the cruise ships moored in the bay. At sunset the town feels like a magnet for every traveller on the island.

◉ Sights & Activities

★ **Ammoudi** PORT
This tiny port full of colourful fishing boats lies 300 steps below Oia. It's a hot haul down and up again but the effort is well worth it for the views of the blood-red cliffs, the harbour and back up to Oia. Once you're down there, have lunch at one of the excellent, if pricey, fish tavernas right on the water's edge. In summer, boats and tours go from Ammoudi to Thirasia daily; check with travel agencies in Fira for departure times.

Santorini Wine Adventure (☑22860 34123; www.winetoursantorini.com; half-day tours from €100) Runs wine- and food-focused tours, including Santorini Wine Adventure, Wine & Food Lover Tour and Trails of History & Wine Tour.

Santorini Wine Tour (☑22860 28358; www.santoriniwinetour.com; ☺half-day tour from €100) Food- and wine-focused tours of Santorini.

SantoWines (☑22860 22596; www.santowines.gr; tours & tastings from €12.50; ☺9am-9pm) The best place to start your wine adventure is at Santorini's cooperative of grape growers, a large tourist-focused complex on the caldera edge near the port. It has short tours of the production process and lots of tasting options. There are also superb views, a wine bar with food and a shop full of choice vintages as well as gourmet local products.

Domaine Sigalas (☑22860 71644; www.sigalas-wine.com; Oia) A polished, peaceful patch not far from Oia, with wine samples and platters among the vines. On the road between Finikia and the coast, you'll want to join a tour or use rental wheels to get here.

Boutari (☑22860 81011; www.boutari.gr; Megalohori; ☺10am-7pm) A relaxed winery on the way south to Akrotiri with 40 great wines to sample in a number of packages. Simple local dishes on offer too. This is one of seven Boutari wineries around Greece.

Wine Museum (☑22860 31322; www.winemuseum.gr; €9.50; ☺10am-5pm Apr-Oct, 9am-4.30pm Mon-Sat Nov-Mar) At the Koutsoyannopoulos Winery en route to Kamari, this heavily promoted attraction has a pricey, slightly kitsch museum in a traditional *canava* (winery). Admission includes tastings of four wines.

Beer

Santorini Brewery Company (☑22860 30268; www.santorinibrewingcompany.gr; ☺11am-5pm Mon-Sat summer, shorter hr rest of year) The home of the island's in-demand Donkey beers (you may have seen the eye-catching logo on your travels) is well worth a stop. Sample the Yellow Donkey (golden ale), Red Donkey (amber ale), the Crazy Donkey (IPA) and the White Donkey (wheat with a touch of orange peel). All are unfiltered, unpasteurised and extremely palatable. Free tastings, plus cool merchandise that makes a fun souvenir.

Maritime Museum   MUSEUM
(☑22860 71156; €3; ☺10am-2pm & 5-8pm Wed-Mon) This museum is located along a narrow lane that leads off north from Nikolaou Nomikou. It's housed in a renovated and converted 19th-century mansion and has endearing displays on Santorini's maritime history. Oia's prosperity was based on its merchant fleet, which serviced the eastern Mediterranean, especially between Alexandria and Russia.

🛏 Sleeping

Oia is known for its glorious luxury villas and suites cascading down the caldera. Book well ahead. If you're on a budget, consider staying elsewhere.

Maria's Place   HOTEL €€
(☑22860 71221; www.mariasantorini.com; d studio €120; ❄ 🙼 ❄) Excellent midrange option, inland from town on the road to Finikia and a 10-minute walk to the caldera. Peaceful (no kids under 16), great hosts, lovely pool and very reasonable off-peak rates.

Zoe Houses   APARTMENT €€
(☑22860 71466; www.zoe-aegeas.gr; studio/apt €190/260; ❄ @ ❄) Traditional houses built into the caldera's edge with all the comforts of home. Classy decor, amazing views and unrivalled hospitality mean that this place gets a lot of happily returning guests. Book ahead. Each suite is different; some can sleep up to six.

**Chelidonia
Traditional Villas**   APARTMENT €€
(☑22860 71287; www.chelidonia.com; Nikolaou Nomikou; studio €215, villa from €245; ❄ ❄) Traditional cliffside dwellings that have been in the owner's family for generations and offer a grand mix of old and new. Modern niceties are offset with traditional wooden furniture, and private patios offer uninterrupted caldera views.

CINEKAMARI

After the caldera sunset, **CineKamari** (☑ 22860 33452; www.cinekamari.gr; Kamari; €8; ☉ 9.30pm) is one of the finest ways to spend a Santorini evening. On the road into Kamari, this tree-surrounded, open-air cinema screens movies in their original language throughout the summer. Pull up a deckchair, request a blanket if you're feeling chilly, and relax. Drinks and snacks available.

✕ Eating

Lolita's Gelato   ICE CREAM €
(☑ 22860 71279; www.lolitasgelato.com; cones €3-6) Near the bus station, Lolita's sells scoopfuls of homemade heaven, including classics like blueberry or pistachio, plus original flavours like rosewater and red pepper. Take a break while you wait for the bus.

Krinaki   TAVERNA €€
(☑ 22860 71993; www.krinaki-santorini.gr; Finikia; mains €12-22; ☉ noon-late) All-fresh, all-local ingredients go into top-notch taverna dishes at this homey spot in tiny Finikia, just east of Oia. Local beer and wine, plus a sea (but not caldera) view looking north to Ios.

Karma   GREEK €€
(☑ 22860 71404; www.karma.bz; mains €11-17; ☉ dinner) With fountains, flickering candles, golden-coloured walls and wine-coloured cushions, this courtyard restaurant feels rather royal and august. The food is traditional and hearty, and as Karma is away from the caldera, the prices are considerably more relaxed.

Skala   GREEK €€
(☑ 22860 71362; www.facebook.com/skalarestaurantoia; Nikolaou Nomikou; dishes €8-18; ☉ lunch & dinner) Watch life pass up and down to Armeni Bay from the high ground of Skala's relaxed terrace. Traditional dishes like souvlaki, baked eggplant and cheese pies fill the crowd-pleasing menu.

1800   GREEK €€€
(☑ 22860 71485; www.oia-1800.com; Nikolaou Nomikou; mains €13-35) Housed in a restored sea captain's mansion, the artistically prepared modern Greek cuisine has won this restaurant accolades for years. Sea bass with an aromatic spell of quinoa, artichoke and fennel purée or grilled lamb with sweet-and-

sour green apple sauce give you a glimpse at the creative menu. Dine inside or on the caldera-view rooftop.

🔒 Shopping

Iatis Workshop   JEWELLERY, CERAMICS
(☑ 22860 72127; www.facebook.com/IatisWorkshop; Nikolaou Nomikou) With his studio at the back of the gallery, Christos Papageorgiou wows passers-by with his contemporary designs. Stunning silver and gold jewellery is professionally crafted and shimmers next to the artist's striking pottery.

Atlantis Books   BOOKS
(☑ 22860 72346; www.atlantisbooks.org; Nikolaou Nomikou; ☉ 11am-8pm) This amazing little bookstore is a destination in itself. Follow quotes and words that wind their way down the stairs into a hobbit hole that appears to be held up by row upon row of books. Staff are friendly and knowledgeable, and musicians and other events are hosted on the rooftop.

ℹ Information

ATMs can be found on Nikolaou Nomikou and also by the bus terminus.

Travel agencies such as **NS Travel** (☑ 22860 71199; www.nst-santorinitravel.com) are found by the bus area.

Around Santorini

There's more than just the spectacular caldera and sunset views to keep visitors busy on Santorini. Head out to visit impressive ancient sites, black-sand beaches, wineries (and a brewery) or take a boat tour to an active volcanic island in the caldera.

⊙ Sights & Activities

Santorini's best beaches are on the east and south coasts. Sunbeds, beach bars and water sports operators are here to serve.

The long stretch of black sand, pebbles and pumice stones at **Perissa**, **Perivolos** and **Agios Georgios** is backed by bars, tavernas, hotels and shops and remains fairly relaxed.

Red (Kokkini) Beach, near Ancient Akrotiri in the south, has impressive red cliffs. Caïques from **Akrotiri Beach** can take you there and on to **White (Aspri)** and **Black (Mesa Pigadia) Beaches** for about €5 return.

Vlihada, also on the south coast, has a beach backed by weirdly eroded cliffs as well as tavernas; it also has a photogenic fishing harbour.

Kamari is Santorini's best-developed resort, with a long beach of black sand. The beachfront road is dense with restaurants and bars, and things get extremely busy in high season. Boats connect Kamari with Perissa in summer.

Note: at times, Santorini's black-sand beaches become so hot that a sunlounge or mat is essential.

★ **Ancient Akrotiri** ARCHAEOLOGICAL SITE
(🖉 22860 81366; http://odysseus.culture.gr/h/3/eh351.jsp?obj_id=2410; adult/child €12/free; ⊙ 8am-8pm Apr-Oct, 8am-3pm Nov-Mar) In 1967, excavations uncovered an ancient Minoan city buried deep beneath volcanic ash from the catastrophic eruption of 1613 BC. Housed within a cool, protective structure, wooden walkways allow you to pass through the city. Peek inside three-storey buildings that survived, and see roads, drainage systems and stashes of pottery. The vibe of excitement still courses through the site, with continued excavations and discoveries. Guided tours are available (per person €10) and help to give context.

Ancient Thira ARCHAEOLOGICAL SITE
(🖉 22860 23217; http://odysseus.culture.gr/h/3/eh351.jsp?obj_id=2454; adult/child €4/free; ⊙ 8am-3pm Tue-Sun) First settled by the Dorians in the 9th century BC, Ancient Thira consists of Hellenistic, Roman and Byzantine ruins and is an atmospheric and rewarding site to visit. The ruins include temples, houses with mosaics, an *agora* (market), a theatre and a gymnasium. Views are splendid. If you're driving, take the narrow, switchbacked road from Kamari for 3km. From Perissa, a hike up a dusty path takes a bit over an hour to reach the site.

★ **Art Space** GALLERY
(🖉 22860 32774; www.artspace-santorini.com; Exo Gonia; ⊙ 11am-sunset) FREE This unmissable, atmospheric gallery is on the way to Kamari, in Argyros Canava, one of the oldest wineries on the island. The atmospheric old wine caverns are hung with superb artworks, while sculptures transform lost corners and niches. The collection features some of Greece's finest modern artists. Winemaking is still in the owner's blood, and part of the complex produces some stellar vintages under the Art Space Wines label. Tastings (€5) enhance the experience.

🛏 Sleeping

🛌 Karterados

★ **Karterados Caveland Hostel** HOSTEL €
(🖉 22860 22122; www.cave-land.com; Karterados; dm/d incl breakfast €25/90; ⊙ Mar-Oct; 🅿 ❄ 🛜 🏊) This fabulous, chilled-out hostel is based in an old winery complex in Karterados about 2km from central Fira (see website for directions). Accommodation is in the big old wine caves, all of them with creative, colourful decor and good facilities. The surrounding garden is relaxing, and there are weekly barbecues, tennis courts, a swimming pool and yoga too.

🛌 Kamari

Narkissos Hotel HOTEL €
(🖉 22860 34205; www.narkissoshotel.com; Kamari; r incl breakfast €75; ⊙ Apr-Nov; ❄ 🛜) A decent budget option at the southern end of Kamari, close to the beach and with well-kept rooms. Outside the summer peak, room prices tumble (€30).

Hippocampus Hotel HOTEL €€
(🖉 22860 32050; www.hippocampus-hotel.gr; Kamari; d/tr/q €140/160/180; ⊙ May-Oct; ❄ 🛜 🏊) Just steps from Kamari's beachfront, this friendly place has a sparkling collection of rooms and studios, with added extras like hand-painted wall murals and a commitment to ecopractices. Good family-sized studios too.

🛌 Perissa

★ **Stelios Place** HOTEL €
(🖉 22860 81860; www.steliosplace.com; Perissa; d/tr/q €88/110/130; ❄ @ 🛜 🏊) This small, family-run hotel has a great position set

---

DISAPPEARING ACT

No one knows what happened to the Minoan people of Akrotiri as no human remains have been found at the site. Some believe that residents fled the city following the earthquake that took place two or three weeks before the volcanic eruption and are buried elsewhere on the island, beneath tonnes of ash. Others speculate that they recognised signs of impending doom and fled by boat towards Crete.

THIRASIA & VOLCANIC ISLETS
ΘΗΡΑΣΙΑ & ΗΦΑΙΣΤΕΙΑΚΕΣ ΝΗΣΙΔΕΣ

Relatively untouched in terms of tourism, **Thirasia** (population 160) was separated from Santorini by an eruption in 236 BC. Clifftop **Manolas**, the main town, has tavernas and domatia. It's an attractive place, noticeably more relaxed and reflective than Fira could ever be. Thirasia is a stop on a couple of ferry routes to/from Athinios a few times a week, or take one of the regular boats from Ammoudi, below Oia (€5). Ask at central travel agencies for the schedule.

The unpopulated islets of **Palia Kameni** and **Nea Kameni** in the middle of the caldera are still volcanically active and can be visited on various boat excursions from Fira Skala and Athinios. A day's excursion taking in Nea Kameni, the **hot springs** on Palia Kameni (more lukewarm than hot), Thirasia and Oia starts at about €30.

back from the main drag in Perissa, one block from the beach. Well-equipped rooms sparkle with cleanliness, as does the swimming pool. Breakfast is available. Free airport or port transfers for those staying three nights or longer; note that off-peak rates fall to a bargain €35.

Zorzis Hotel　　　　BOUTIQUE HOTEL €
(☑22860 81104; www.santorinizorzis.com; Perissa; d incl breakfast from €90; ❉☎✆) Behind a huge bloom of geraniums on Perissa's main street, Hiroko and Spiros (a Japanese-Greek couple) run an immaculate 10-room hotel. It's a pastel-coloured sea of calm (no kids), with delightful garden, pool and mountain backdrop.

✖ Eating

Brusco　　　　CAFE €
(☑22860 30944; Pyrgos; mains from €7) In Pyrgos, Brusco offers coffee, wine and local flavours in a sweet rustic cafe-deli, with plenty of outdoor space. Stop by for the warm welcome, homemade cakes (including baklava) and platters of great Santorini produce (fava, tomatoes, eggplant, capers and more).

★ Metaxi Mas　　　　TAVERNA €€
(☑22860 31323; www.santorini-metaximas.gr; Exo Gonia; mains €8-19; ☉lunch & dinner) The raki flows at this convivial taverna, a favourite among locals and authenticity-seeking travellers. In the central village of Exo Gonia (on the steep winding road between Pyrgos and Kamari), park by the large church and walk down some steps to reach it. Enjoy sweeping views and a delicious menu of local and Cretan specialities.

ANAFI　　　　ΑΝΑΦΗ
POP 270

Anafi lies a mere 22km east of Santorini, a tiny island perched on a distant horizon, with a slow-paced traditional lifestyle and striking Cycladic landscapes. There are few visitors outside high summer, which is a big part of its charm. Come to Anafi if you're looking for a quiet Greek island escape.

The port of **Agios Nikolaos** is on the south coast, with the main town of **Hora** a steep 2km by road above to the north.

❶ Getting There & Away

Anafi is out on a limb and you may face challenges getting there, but in July and August the island has reasonable ferry connections. Plan well, especially outside the high season, and consult http://ferries.gr for up-to-date ferry information. Because of its proximity to Santorini, to visit Anafi you will in all likelihood take a ferry from there. Don't make travel connections that are too tight as ferries from Anafi are notoriously late.

Buy ferry tickets at **Roussou Travel** (☑22860 61220) in Hora's main street or at an office on the harbourfront one hour before ferries are due.

❶ Getting Around

The island's port is Agios Nikolaos. From here, the main village, Hora, is a 10-minute bus ride (€1.80) up a winding road, or a 1km hike up a less winding but steep walkway. In summer a bus runs regularly and usually meets boats; buses also run east to the monastery (€2.60).

Summertime caïques serve various beaches and nearby small islands.

In Hora, **Manos** (☑22860 61430; www.rentacarmanos.com) has cars, scooters and four-wheelers for rent.

◎ Sights & Activities

The monastery **Zoodochos Pigi** is 9km from Hora by road, or reached by a 7km walk along the south-coast trail. The monastery lies in the east of the island, on the isthmus connecting Anafi to the imposing 463m **Kalamos** (or Monastery Rock), which has the uninhabited **Kalamiotissas Monastery** at its peak. Locals claim Kalamos as the second-largest rock in the Mediterranean after the Rock of Gibraltar.

There are several lovely beaches near Agios Nikolaos. **Klissidi**, a 1.5km walk east of the port and visible from the ferry when you arrive, is the closest and most popular. The south-coast walking trail that goes to Zoodochos Pigi Monastery gives access to more strands, including the long, sandy **Roukounas Beach**.

🛏 Sleeping

Many of the rooms on Hora's main pedestrian street have good views across Anafi's rolling hills to the sea and to the great summit of Kalamos. Beachgoers should stay at Klissidi Beach. Book early for July and August; outside these two months, accommodation is cheap.

★ Margarita's Rooms   PENSION €
(☑ 22860 61237; www.margarita-anafi.gr; d from €60; 🕿) Just above Klissidi beach, these simple, beloved family-run rooms hark back to the Greek island life of quieter times. Nothing luxurious here, but if you're after an affordable island escape next to a lovely beach, you can't really go wrong. It's a tad isolated, but all you need is here, including Margarita's taverna. Port transfers included.

Villa Kalamiotissa   APARTMENT €€
(☑ 22860 61415; www.villakalamiotissa.gr; d €100; ☺ Apr-Oct; ❃🕿) A handsome complex of rooms and studios, all white and pale blue with lovely stonework. It sits on a quiet edge of Hora, with spectacular views south from each verandah. Studios sleep three and have kitchens. Entry is from the ring road around Hora.

Apollon Village Hotel   APARTMENT €€
(☑ 22860 28739; http://apollonvillagehotel.com; d/studio/apt from €70/95/120; ☺ May-Sep; ❃🕿) Rising in tiers above Klissidi Beach, these individual rooms, studios and apartments with glorious views are each named after a Greek god and remain outstanding value. The Blue Cafe-Bar is a cool adjunct to the

hotel, with homemade sweets and pastries. Entry is from the port to Hora road.

🍴 Eating & Drinking

★ Margarita's   TAVERNA €
(☑ 22860 61237; www.margarita-anafi.gr; Klissidi; mains €6-12; ☺ breakfast, lunch & dinner; 🕿) A sunny little terrace overlooking the bay at Klissidi makes for an idyllic dining experience. Margarita's fresh-baked bread, handmade pasta and meatballs are staples; fava, goat stew and cheese pies are all full of local flavour. There are rooms here too.

Armenaki   TAVERNA €€
(☑ 22860 61234; mains €7-15; ☺ lunch & dinner Jun-Sep) Tuna and swordfish are the go-to dishes at this traditional taverna in Hora, enhanced by an airy terrace, splendid views and occasional live music. Head down the small street opposite the bakery in central Hora to find it.

Liotrivi   TAVERNA €€
(☑ 22860 61209; www.facebook.com/liotrivirest; mains from €7; ☺ lunch & dinner May-Oct) A classy old-school taverna on the main street in Hora, where fresh fish is brought in from the family's boat, while just about everything else, from eggs to vegetables and honey, comes from their garden. Huge views from the terrace seating.

Glaros   BAR
(☺ Jun-Sep) In Hora, be sure to stop for a drink at this local institution. If you're lucky, you'll stumble across some live music – if not, the views won't disappoint. Carry on down the main street past the market to find it.

ℹ Information

Find more information online at www.anafi.gr.

SIKINOS   ΣΙΚΙΝΟΣ
POP 280

A stone's throw from Santorini, Sikinos is really worlds away – and decidedly off the tourist radar. Quiet and remote, this is the place to come if you want to experience traditional island life at its least commercial. With a charming old town and terraced hills that sweep down to sandy beaches, Sikinos offers a true escape.

The main clusters of habitation are the port of Alopronia and the linked inland villages of Horio and Kastro (collectively known as the Hora). Kastro has homes and businesses, Horio is purely residential. They are reached by a 3.4km road winding up from the port. There's a post office at the eastern edge of Kastro, and an ATM in Kastro's central square.

July and August see lots of Greek visitors turn up, but if you arrive before mid-May, don't expect there to be much going on.

ℹ️ Getting There & Away

Ferry tickets can be bought at the port at **Kountouris Travel** (☑ 6981594106, 22860 51232). Out of high season, boat services are skeletal.

Boat Services from Sikinos

DESTINATION	DURATION	FARE (€)	FREQUENCY
Folegandros	45min	5	4 weekly
Ios	25min	5	4 weekly
Kimolos	2¼hr	13	4 weekly
Milos	3hr 25min	13	2 weekly
Naxos	2hr 25min	12	1 weekly
Paros	3hr 50min	14	1 weekly
Piraeus	7½-9½hr	39	4 weekly
Serifos	4¼hr	18	1 weekly
Sifnos	2¾hr-5hr	16	4 weekly
Santorini (Thira)	2hr	7	3 weekly
Syros	6hr	13	1 weekly

ℹ️ Getting Around

The local bus meets ferry arrivals and runs between Alopronia and Horio/Kastro (€1.80) every half-hour in August, but less frequently at other times. A timetable is posted at the terminus, just inland from the port. If you're out of season and nothing is going on, talk to English-speaking Flora in the minimarket at Alopronia – she'll call the bus driver, who'll come to get you in his car and take you to Hora for the same price as the bus!

There is a small agency at the port, **RaC** (☑ 21040 80300; www.rentacar-sikinos.gr), hiring out cars and scooters.

⊙ Sights & Activities

The beach at the port of **Alopronia** is lovely – sandy, with some shade and a children's playground. It looks straight out at Santorini.

A narrow, dramatic bay with a small sandy patch, **Agios Nikolaos Beach** is a 20-minute walk through the countryside from the port. To find it, follow signs to Dialiskari. A path leads further on to **Agios Georgios**, or you can reach it by sealed road (7km).

Summertime caïques (about €6) run to beaches, including **Malta** in the north (which boasts ancient ruins on the hill above) and **Kara** in the south.

Sikinos is popular with walkers, and the island has set up seven **Paths of Culture**, a network of well-signposted paths all over the island. Keen walkers should purchase Terrain's (http://terrainmaps.gr) excellent hiking map for Sikinos.

★**Moni Zoödohou Pigis**　　　MONASTERY
(☑ 6975743928; ⊙10am-noon & 4-6pm) FREE
A flight of whitewashed steps leads to the fortified monastery of Moni Zoödohou Pigis, high above the Kastro. Originally built as a women's monastery in 1690, this is where the nuns and villagers would hide out during pirate attacks. The monastery has recently opened to the public, and you can go into the church and the visitors' room, or check out the amazing views. Don't miss the nuns' emergency escape route, by rope down the cliffs out the back.

Kastro　　　VILLAGE
A Venetian fortress that stood here in the 13th century gave Kastro its name. Today it is a charming, lived-in place, with winding alleyways between brilliant white houses. At its heart is the main square and the Church of Pantanassa. Check out the buildings surrounding the church, which were homes to the town's wealthy merchants: two-storey affairs with remnants of ornate stonework around the windows.

Horio　　　VILLAGE
Just west of Kastro, above steeply terraced fields and reached by a flight of whitewashed steps, is the reclusive, beautiful Horio. Still home to a dozen or so residents, it's a patchwork of derelict and well-tended houses and is definitely worth a wander.

Moni Episkopis　　　MONASTERY
FREE From the saddle between Kastro and Horio, a surfaced road leads southwest to Moni Episkopis. The remains here are believed to be those of a 3rd-century AD Roman mausoleum that was transformed into a church in the 7th century and a monastery 10 centuries later.

Manalis Winery
WINERY

(☑ 6932272854; www.manaliswinery.gr; ☺ 6pm-late summer) On the road to Moni Episkopis, Manalis Winery produces Sikinos wine using self-sustaining, traditional methods. You can easily spend an hour or two here nibbling on snacks, sipping wine and trying out the traditional menu on the view-filled patio.

🛏 Sleeping

Rooms Kaminia
PENSION €

(☑ 22860 51304; Kastro; d €60; ❀ 🗅) A whitewashed staircase next to the post office in Kastro leads up to this complex of four simple studios – large and spotless, with kitchen facilities, new bathrooms and splendid views. It's open year-round, with low-season prices a steal at €30.

Stegadi Apartments
APARTMENT €€

(☑ 22860 51305; www.stegadi.com; Kastro; d €90; ❀ 🗅) Near the heart of Kastro, these traditional apartments sleep up to four and are individually decorated with modern furnishings and splashes of vibrant colour. The balconies have views across to the sea.

Ostria Studios
PENSION €€

(☑ 22860 51062; www.ostriastudios-sikinos.gr; Alopronia; d from €75; ❀ 🗅) These comfy rooms and studios are lovingly decorated. Margarita has three sets of rooms – Ostria Studios Spilia, Agnanti and Molos; Spilia is on the far side of the bay from the ferry quay. The rooms are right on the water, and you can swim below your room. They have seaview balconies and plenty of peace.

🍴 Eating

★ Anemelo
CAFE €

(☑ 22860 51216; Kastro; mains €4-8; ☺ 10am-3pm & 5pm-late) This is Kastro's most atmospheric place to grab a local tea, beer or simple crêpe-and-salad lunch. Locals chat at the tables over chess games or lounge over coffee at the tables outside. Take the *tiny* staircase up to the terrace for ace views. The killer Traditional Sandwich (€5) features olive paste, feta, capers and tomato.

Kapari
GREEK €

(☑ 22860 51070; Kastro; mains from €7.50; ☺ 8am-2.30am) Your go-to place if you arrive out of season or are staying at Alopronia and absolutely nothing is open. It's on the main road in Hora – Flora at the minimarket in Alopronia will figure out how to get you here if you're stuck. These guys have good solid

Greek staples, including their own uniquely named 'beer salad' and 'sinful meatballs'.

Klimataria
GREEK €€

(☑ 22860 51065; Kastro; mains €8-13; ☺ lunch & dinner May-Oct; 🗅) A cute leafy laneway shades a couple of traditional eateries, including this friendly spot, where you can indulge in platters heaped with mixed grills.

FOLEGANDROS
ΦΟΛΕΓΑΝΔΡΟΣ

POP 765

Folegandros lies on the southern edge of the Cyclades, with the Sea of Crete sweeping away to its south. The island has a bewitching beauty that is amplified by its alluring clifftop Hora, perhaps the most appealing village in the Cyclades.

Folegandros is barely 12km by 4km but shoulders a somewhat dark past. The remoteness and ruggedness of the island made it a place of exile for political prisoners from Roman times to the 20th century, as late as the military dictatorship of 1967–74. Today the seductive charm of Folegandros has left its grim history behind.

Boats dock at the little harbour of **Karavostasis**, on the east coast. Aside from it and Hora, the only other settlement of any size is **Ano Meria**. There are some good beaches, but be prepared for strenuous walking to reach some of them (or the easy option: take a boat).

ℹ Getting There & Away

Once poorly served by ferries, Folegandros has good connections (at least in summer) with Piraeus through the western Cyclades route. It has connections to Santorini and is part of a Ios-Sikinos-Folegandros link, with regular ferries passing through.

ℹ Getting Around

The local bus meets all ferry arrivals and takes passengers to Hora (3km; €1.80). From Hora there are buses to the port one hour before ferry departures. Buses from Hora run hourly in summer to Ano Meria (€1.80) and divert to Angali Beach (€2.20). The bus terminus is at the entrance to Hora from the south, behind the post office.

There is a **taxi service** (☑ 6944693957) on Folegandros. Fares to the port are about €7 to €10, to Ano Meria €10 and to Angali Beach €10 to €14.

BOAT SERVICES FROM FOLEGANDROS

DESTINATION	DURATION	FARE (€)	FREQUENCY
Amorgos*	2-5½hr	69	6 weekly
Ios	1hr 20min	10	4 weekly
Ios*	20min	44	2 weekly
Kimolos	1¼hr-2¾hr	13	4 weekly
Koufonisia*	1¾hr-5hr	69	6 weekly
Milos	2½hr	13	2 weekly
Milos*	1hr	39	1-2 daily
Mykonos*	3-3½hr	59	6 weekly
Naxos*	2hr 40min	49	6 weekly
Piraeus	6½hr-9hr	36	4 weekly
Piraeus*	3½hr-5hr	59	1-2 daily
Santorini (Thira)	3hr	12	3 weekly
Santorini (Thira)*	40-70min	44	1-2 daily
Serifos	3hr 20min	18	1 weekly
Sifnos	2-4hr	16	4 weekly
Sifnos*	2hr	49	3 weekly
Sikinos	45min	7	5 weekly
Syros	6¾hr	18	1 weekly

* high-speed services

You can hire cars/motorbikes from a number of outlets in high season for about €60/25 per day. Rates can drop by half outside high season. **Tomaso** (☑ 22860 41600; www.tomaso.gr) in Hora is a good option.

In summer, small boats regularly run between beaches.

Karavostasis Καραβοστάσις

POP 90

Folegandros' port is a sunny place with a pleasant pebble beach. Within a kilometre north and south lie a series of other beaches, all enjoyable and easily reached by short walks. In high season, boats leave Karavostasis for beaches further afield. If beaches are your allure, stay here – for our money, however, Hora, 3km up the road, is where the magic is.

🛏 Sleeping & Eating

Aeolos Beach Hotel   HOTEL €€
(☑ 22860 41205; www.aeolos-folegandros.gr; s/d €70/100; ⊗May-Sep; 🅿🛜) Settle in right on the beach here at Aeolos. Rooms have sea or mountain views and are each unique, with varying degrees of character. There's

a minimum three-night stay in July and August; breakfast costs €8.

★**Anemi**   LUXURY HOTEL €€€
(☑ 22860 41610; www.anemihotel.gr; d/ste incl breakfast from €275/430; ⊗late May–Sep; 🅿🛜🏊) Oh so modern and entirely luxurious, this is a place for pampering. Rooms are plush but sleek, brought to life by modern artwork that doubles as headboards. The pool is a large, beckoning sheet of blue (some of the suites have a private pool) and there's an enviable roll-call of extras, including family-friendly ones.

Meltemi   TAVERNA €
(☑ 22860 41287; mains from €7; ⊗9am-late Apr-Oct) Perched above the port with lovely views, Meltemi stands out with its lovely terrace with blue balustrades. This is a mama's cooking, family-run place with Greek staples, seafood and grilled meats.

Hora (Folegandros)
Χώρα (Φολέγανδρος)

POP 425

Hora (Folegandros) has had some high-profile television coverage of late, and the secret is now out – this village is probably the most charming in the Cyclades. Its meandering main street, winding happily from leafy square to leafy square, where al fresco tables buzz with life, is a joy to behold. Its marvellous natural stone buildings, mixed among those in Cycladic white and blue, stylishly impress.

◎ Sights

The village proper starts at **Plateia Pounta**; on its north side, it stands on the edge of a formidable cliff. Just west of here is the medieval **kastro**, a small tangle of narrow alleys spanned by low archways. It dates from when Marco Sanudo ruled the island in the 13th century. The balconies of the traditional houses blaze with bougainvillea, and a few whitewashed chapels add charm.

Panagia   CHURCH
(⊙6-9pm) From Plateia Pounta, a zigzag path leads up to the large Church of the Virgin, Panagia, which sits perched on the side of a hill above the town and acts as a mecca for sunset-watchers. It's an easy 20-minute walk without steps on a wide concrete path, offering spectacular views down to Hora, cliffs and pounding waves along the way.

☞ Tours

Given the tough-to-access nature of many beaches, a popular excursion is the six-hour boat trip around the island (adult/child €40/15). The price includes lunch and plenty of swimming stops. The tour leaves Karavostasis at 11am, and can be booked through Diaplous Travel (p416). Private boat trips can also be arranged.

🛏 Sleeping

In July and August, most domatia and hotels will be full, so book well in advance. Free port transfers (3km to the port) are generally included with most sleeping options.

★Ampelos   BOUTIQUE HOTEL €€
(☏22860 41544; http://ampelosresort.com; s/d/tr €100/110/120; ⊙May-Oct; ❈ �864 ⊛) Theo and Areti's place is a gorgeous family-run operation with a sparkling pool, tasteful colours and lovely rooms. It's an easy 10-minute stroll into the centre of Hora from just south of town. There are free port transfers, complimentary coffee, rates that halve outside the peak season and friendly smiles.

Hotel Odysseus   HOTEL €€
(☏22860 41276; www.hotelodysseus.com; s/d €85/110; ⊙mid-May–Sep; ❈ 864 ⊛) Tucked away in a quiet corner of town with some

Folegandros

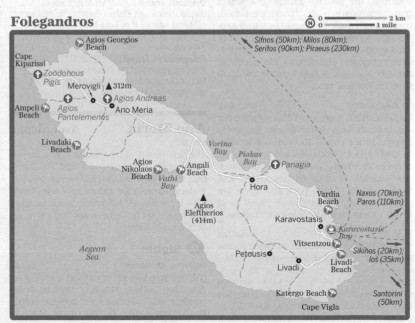

N ⊙   0 ——————— 2 km
        0 ——————— 1 mile

Agios Georgios Beach

Cape Kiparissi

Zoódohous Pigis

Merovigli ▲312m

Ampeli Beach

Agios Andreas

Agios Pantelemenos

Ano Meria

Livadaki Beach

Vorina Bay

Agios Nikolaos Beach

Vathi Bay

Angali Beach

Piakas Bay

Panagia

Hora

Vardia Beach

Karavostasis

Karavostasis Bay

Agios Eleftherios (414m)

Vitsentzou

Petousis

Livadi

Livadi Beach

Aegean Sea

Katergo Beach

Cape Vigla

Sifnos (50km); Milos (80km); Serifos (90km); Piraeus (230km)

Naxos (70km); Paros (110km)

Sikinos (20km); Ios (35km)

Santorini (50km)

dramatic views and colourful green doors, Odysseus has pretty, compact rooms with sweet terraces, and a lovely pool area that's shared with Aria Boutique Hotel next door. Low-season prices are ace (doubles €60) but breakfast is an additional €12.

Folegandros Apartments
APARTMENT €€
(☑ 22860 41239; www.folegandros-apartments. com; d from €140; ☺ May-Sep; ✲ 🗑 🌊) This lovely complex of studios and apartments (the largest can sleep seven) is set in well-kept gardens around a pristine pool just above Plateia Pounta in Hora. It's only a couple of minutes' stroll into the village.

Anemomilos Apartments
HOTEL €€€
(☑ 22860 41309; www.anemomilosapartments. com; d incl breakfast from €270; ☺ May-Sep; ✲ 🗑 🌊) A prime clifftop location just above Plateia Pounta in Hora grants awesome views from this stylish complex and its lovely terraces. Rooms are elegant and embellished with antiques. The pool is divine, and service comes with wonderful attention to detail.

✗ Eating & Drinking

★ Chic
GREEK €
(☑ 22860 41515; mains €6.50-13; ☺ dinner Easter-Oct; ☑) Chic is perfectly placed for watching the passing parade, but what's more impressive is the flavoursome food: everything is made from scratch, with gluten-free, dairy-free and vegan options (a rarity in Greece). Veggie dishes (featuring home-grown veggies and herbs) are plentiful; carnivores should plump for goat and lamb from the owners' farm.

To Asygkrito
TAVERNA €
(☑ 22860 41266; mains from €7.50; ☺ lunch & dinner) It would be a shame to miss this lovely taverna in a restored 300-year-old building in central Hora, with avocado-green tables and chairs spilling out into the surrounding square. Oven-baked vegetables and home-produced lamb, pork and rabbit are specialities at this family-run place. Head inside to admire the building restorations.

Pounta
TAVERNA €€
(☑ 22860 41063; www.pounta.gr; Plateia Pounta; mains €6-12; ☺ 8am-3pm & 6pm-midnight Easter–mid-Oct) A family business for 20 years, Pounta is the work of a creative Danish-Greek couple – dishes are served on Lisbet's handmade ceramics (also for sale), in a large, lush garden. The menu ranges from breakfast yoghurt to grilled octopus by way of rabbit *stifadho* (meat with onions in a tomato purée) and baked eggplant. Right on Plateia Pounta in Hora.

Eva's Garden
MEDITERRANEAN €€€
(☑ 22860 41110; www.facebook.com/evasgarden folegandros; mains €10-25; ☺ dinner May-Sep) Eva's is a sophisticated spot that puts a gourmet spin on Greek cuisine (with portions that may seem small if you've been eating at tavernas!). Starters include octopus carpaccio or sautéed shrimp, while mains tempt with sea bass fillet or rib-eye on the grill. Turn left after Plateia Piatsa.

★ Rakentia
BAR
(☑ 22860 41581; www.rakentia.gr; ☺ 10.30am-3pm & 6.30pm-1am May-Sep) Head west and look for a signed laneway beside the Anemousa Hotel to find this gem, a cafe-bar with cool music and cooler views. Watch birds soar at dusk over cocktails and creative tapas dishes.

❶ Information

ATMs are at the post office (as you reach town from the port) and on Plateia Dounavi.

Travel agencies are good sources of information. There's information (and a downloadable app) at www.folegandros.com.

Diaplous Travel (☑ 22860 41158; www. diaploustravel.gr; Plateia Pounta) Helpful and efficient agency that sells ferry tickets and arranges boat trips. There's also an office at Karavostasis.

Folegandros Travel (☑ 22860 41273; www. folegandros-travel.gr; Plateia Dounavi) Sells ferry tickets and exchanges money. There's also an office at the port.

Ano Meria
Ανω Μεριά

POP 240

The settlement of Ano Meria is a scattered community of small farms and dwellings that stretches along the road for several kilometres, virtually on the crest of the island. This is traditional Folegandros, where tourism makes no intrusive mark and life wanders happily along.

◉ Sights

Folklore Museum
MUSEUM
(€2; ☺ 5-8pm Jul–mid-Sep) At the Hora end of Ano Meria village, this tiny museum is up a side road, indicated by a peeling, faded, hand-painted sign on the main road. It

provides a glimpse of Folegandros village life. Ask the bus driver to drop you off nearby. If no one is there, an old woman may mysteriously appear and open up for you.

✗ Eating

★ I Synantisi
TAVERNA €

(☑22860 41208; mains from €6; ☉lunch & dinner May-Sep) Also known as Maria's, I Synantisi is at the far end of the strung-out village, so much so that you may think you've missed it. With pale blue colours, it was originally opened in 1920 by the proprietor's grandfather. This is a great spot to try *matsata* (local pasta) and Greek salad with local Folegandros cheese.

Mimis
TAVERNA €

(☑22860 41377; ☉lunch & dinner May-Sep) Towards the far end of Ano Meria village, Mimis specialises in *matsata*, the local hand-made pasta dish, but everything else on the menu is good too.

Around Folegandros

For **Livadi Beach**, 1.2km southeast of Karavostasis, take the 'bypass' road just past the Anemi Hotel and follow it around the coast. There is camping here (see www.folegandros. org).

Katergo Beach is on the southeastern tip of the island and is best reached by boat from Karavostasis. Boats leave regularly (weather permitting), for €8 return.

The sandy and pebbled **Angali** beach, on the central coast opposite Hora, is a popular spot. There are some rooms here and reasonable tavernas; buses run here regularly in summer from Hora. About 750m west of Angali over the hill along a footpath is **Agios Nikolaos**, a clothes-optional beach.

A number of beaches can be reached from where the road ends beyond Ano Meria: **Livadaki Beach** is a 1.5km hike from the bus stop near the church of Agios Andreas at Ano Meria. **Agios Georgios Beach** is north of Ano Meria and requires another demanding walk (about 40 minutes). Have tough footwear and sun protection – and, because most beaches have no shops or tavernas, make sure you take food and water.

Boats connect some west-coast beaches in high season: excursion boats make round trips from Angali to Agios Nikolaos (€5), and from Angali to Livadaki Beach (€10).

MILOS
ΜΗΛΟΣ

POP 4977

Volcanic Milos arches around a central caldera and is ringed with dramatic coastal landscapes of colourful and surreal rock formations. The island's most celebrated export, the iconic *Venus de Milo*, is far away in the Louvre, but dozens of beaches (the most of any Cycladic island) and a series of picturesque villages contribute to its current, compelling, attractions.

The island has a fascinating history of mineral extraction dating from the Neolithic period when obsidian was exported to the Minoan world of Crete. Today Milos is the biggest bentonite and perlite centre in the EU.

A substantial western chunk of Milos (and part of the east coast) is off-limits to rental vehicles due bad roads and a proliferation of the Milos viper, but the beaches are reachable by boat tour.

❶ Getting There & Away

BOAT

Milos is on the same western Cyclades ferry routes as Sifnos and Serifos. Buy tickets at Riva Travel (p422) or Milos Travel (p422) in Adamas.

Boat Services from Milos

DESTINATION	DURATION	FARE (€)	FREQUENCY
Anafi	6½hr	22	Fri
Folegandros	1-2½hr	12-45	1-2 daily
Ios	2-4hr	20-53	1-2 daily
Kea	9	18	Mon
Kimolos	30min-1hr	8-10	6 weekly
Koufonisia	4½-6¾hr	74	6 weekly
Kythnos	3¾-12½hr	10-16	6 weekly
Mykonos	6-8¾hr	24-74	6 weekly
Naxos	5¼-6hr	22-63	6 weekly
Paros	3¼hr	17	4 weekly
Piraeus	3-5¾hr	43-61	1-3 daily
Santorini (Thira)	2-5¼hr	22-51	1-2 daily
Serifos	1¼-3hr	12-22	1-2 daily
Sifnos	45min-2hr	11-21	1-3 daily
Sikinos	3-3½hr	16-17	4 weekly
Syros	5½-10hr	17-18	4 weekly

AIR

Sky Express (www.skyexpress.gr) has one or two flights daily between Athens and Milos airport (€80, 45 minutes).

ⓘ Getting Around

No buses serve the airport. Taxis to Adamas cost about €13, plus a token extra charge for bags.

Milos Buses (www.milosbuses.com) handily places updated timetable info on its website. Frequency of service varies with season, but in July and August buses leave Adamas for Plaka and Trypiti about every hour. Buses run to Pollonia every two hours, hourly to Paleohori and to Achivadolimni (Milos) Camping. Most fares are €1.80.

Hire cars, motorcycles and mopeds along the waterfront, at Riva Travel (p422), **Giourgas Rent a Car** (☑ 6937757066, 22870 22352; www.milosgiourgas.gr), or at **Milos Rent** (☑ 22870 41473; www.milosrent.gr), which has offices at the airport, Adamas and Pollonia.

Taxis (☑ 22870 22219) from the taxi station on Adamas' main square to Plaka are about €8, and to Pollonia €15; add €1 from the port.

Adamas
Αδάμας

POP 1347

Fishermen sell their wares in the early morning at the lively port of Adamas (also Adamantas). Loaded with accommodation, shops and general services, the modern village also has a diverting waterfront scene. Popular boat tours around the island depart from the yacht quay.

⊙ Sights

Milos Mining Museum   MUSEUM

(☑ 22870 22481; www.milosminingmuseum.gr; adult/child €4/2; ⊙10am-2pm & 5-10pm Jun-Sep, shorter hr Oct-May) This excellent small museum details Milos' mining history. It's about 600m east of the ferry quay.

Milos & Kimolos

Ask here about the **Miloterranean Geo Experience** (www.miloterranean.gr) project, a series of maps that outline great half-day 'geo walks' through Milos. The maps detail the island's geology and volcanic origin, mining history and natural environment, and can be purchased at the museum.

Ecclesiastical Museum of Milos MUSEUM
(☑ 22870 23956; www.ecclesiasticalmuseum.org; ⊙ 9.15am-1.15pm & 6.15-10.15pm May-Sep) FREE
Tucked in where the waterfront road turns inland, this collection in the Church of the Holy Trinity boasts rare icons and artefacts crafted by 18th-century Cretan icon-makers, a father-and-son team.

☞ Tours

Tour boats line Adamas' waterfront in the evening, touting their daily cruises. These leave every morning (weather permitting) to explore the impressive coastline, bizarre rock formations and beaches not reachable by road. **Kleftiko** in Milos' southwest, with its beautiful rocks and coves, is a prime destination. A number of cruises also visit Kimolos.

There are large and small boats, private charters, and speedboats, wooden-hulled boats, catamarans and sailboats. Check out what takes your fancy. It may be worth asking about group sizes, itineraries, lunch arrangements and swimming time.

Prices generally start from about €35. Most travel agencies can book you on a cruise; note that in summer's peak you can usually find departures from Pollonia.

🛏 Sleeping

There's a good range of hotels, apartments and domatia. In summer, lists of available domatia are usually kept at the quayside tourist kiosk.

Tassoula Rooms GUESTHOUSE €
(☑ 22870 22674; www.tassoularooms.eu; d €50; ❄ 🛜) Run by a friendly family, this budget pick is great value. Some of the spacious, bright rooms have tiny balconies overlooking the flowering inner courtyard, and the owner is the epitome of helpfulness. Free pick-up offered from the port.

Aeolis Hotel HOTEL €€
(☑ 22870 23985; www.hotel-aeolis.com; d/tr incl breakfast €94/120; ❄ 🛜) Inland from the harbourfront, this sweet, neat 12-room hotel is

peaceful and calm, its white rooms given a pop of colour here and there. Open year-round, with prices diving in low season (double €35).

Villa Helios Studios APARTMENT €€
(☑ 22870 22258; www.milos-island.gr/rooms-apartments/helios; studio €100; ⊙ May-Oct; ❄ 🛜) Rising high above the port, these large self-catering studios are neat as a pin and decorated in attractive traditional style, with sea-view balconies.

🍴 Eating & Drinking

⭐ **O! Hamos** CYCLADIC €
(☑ 22870 21672; www.ohamos-milos.gr; Papikinou Beach; dishes €7-12; ⊙ noon-11pm Easter-Oct; 🛜) In this rustic taverna across the road from the beach, sit in the garden and choose from an array of traditional recipes, such as goat baked in parchment. The best picks are cheeses and grilled meats, served with warmth and flair (and on cool branded ceramics), alongside craft beers and local wines. Located on Papikinou Beach, 2km southeast of Adamas.

Barko TAVERNA €
(☑ 22870 22660; http://barkotavern-milos.com; dishes €7-14; ⊙ 7pm-late; 🛜) This classic taverna on the road to Plaka, near the outskirts of town, serves local dishes such as chickpea fritters and oven-baked lamb in a sheltered garden setting.

Flisvos TAVERNA €€
(☑ 22870 22275; dishes €9-16; ⊙ noon-11pm; 🛜) This place has pedigree: it's the oldest waterfront restaurant in town. Choose from grilled meats (for which it's known), fish by the kilo or traditional specialities like lamb in lemon sauce.

Akri BAR
(☑ 22870 22064; www.facebook.com/akrimilos; ⊙ 9am-late; 🛜) Opposite Villa Helios, Akri is in a beautiful location with a fine terrace overlooking the port. Music favours ethnic, funk and easy listening. It's also open for breakfast. Upstairs is an elegant gallery selling superb glass jewellery, paintings, pottery and sculpture, many by island artists.

ℹ Information

Municipal Tourist Office (☑ 22870 22445; www.milos.gr; ⊙ 9am-5pm & 7-11pm Jun-Sep) Helpful kiosk opposite the quay, with maps and general info.

MILA ATKOVSKA/SHUTTERSTOCK ©

1. Ancient Delos (p359)

Once home to a magnificent city, Delos is now one of Greece's most important archaeological sites.

2. Naxos (p370)

A colourful, lively island with a strong cultural heritage.

3. Oia (p406), Santorini

Postcard-perfect Cycladic scenery.

4. Kleftiko (p419), Milos

A stunning coastline of rock formations and beaches.

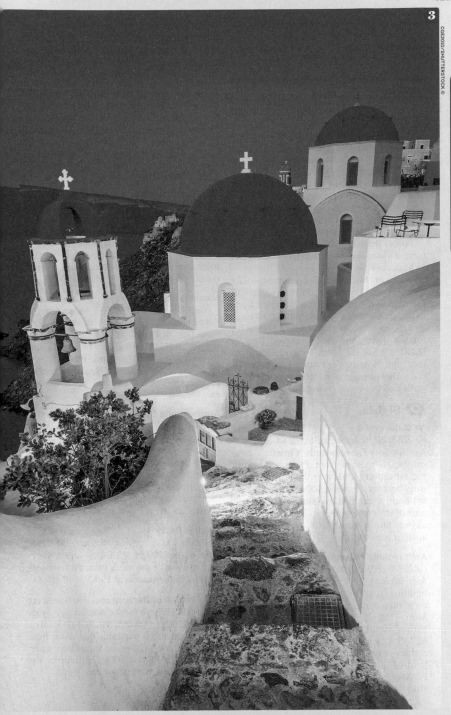

Milos Travel (☑22870 22000; www.
milostravel.gr; ⊙9am-9pm) Books ferry
tickets.

Riva Travel (☑22870 24024; www.rivatravel.
gr; ⊙9am-9pm) Car hire, ferry tickets.

Plaka & Trypiti
Πλάκα & Τρυπητή

POP 1,289

Supercharming Plaka (population 749), 5km
uphill from Adamas, embodies the Cycladic
ideal, with its white houses and labyrinthine
lanes perching along the edge of an escarp-
ment. Plaka was built on the site of Ancient
Milos, which was destroyed by the Athenians and rebuilt by the Romans. It meanders
straight into the settlement to the south,
Trypiti (population 540).

Plaka's **main church courtyard** has spectacular views and gets packed out for sunset
in high season.

Walks in this area are popular, especially
from Plaka to Trypiti and down to Klima. Off
the road to the catacombs, a dirt track leads
to the spot where a farmer found the *Venus
de Milo* in 1820; it's marked by a sign. A bit
further along, the well-preserved **Roman
theatre** hosts the Milos Festival each summer, and footpaths lead down to Klima or
onto the promontory with ancient stone
walls and two small churches.

◉ Sights

★Catacombs   MONUMENT
(☑22870 21625; Trypiti; adult/child €4/2; ⊙9am-
7pm Tue-Sun) Greece's only Christian catacombs, signposted from Plaka, date from
the 1st century and were the burial site for
early believers. Around 5000 people are buried here; a guide takes you on a 15-minute
tour of the eerie depths to let you see the lit
alcoves and to explain the workings of the
ancient cemetery.

Archaeology Museum   MUSEUM
(☑22870 28026; Plaka; adult/child €2/1; ⊙9am-
4pm Tue-Sun) This handsome neoclassical
building contains some riveting exhibits,
including a plaster cast of the *Venus de
Milo* – the original was likely carved from
Parian marble around 100 BC, was found
on Milos by a local farmer in 1820 and now
resides in the Louvre in Paris. A perky little
herd of tiny bull figurines comes from the
Filakopi settlement and dates from 1400 to
1100 BC.

Kastro   FORTRESS
(Plaka) Signs mark the path climbing to the
hilltop fortress, built on the ancient acropolis and offering panoramic views of the
island. The 13th-century church, Thalassi-
tras, lies inside the walls.

Milos Folk & History Museum   MUSEUM
(☑22870 21292; Plaka; adult/child €4/2; ⊙11am-
1pm & 7-10pm Tue-Sun) Peruse traditional
costumes, woven goods and household artefacts in a series of traditionally furnished
rooms, right by the main church courtyard.

⨴ Sleeping

★Vaos Windmill   APARTMENT €€
(☑26103 21742; Trypiti; apt €80; 🕸) An unpaved
path behind and above Trypiti's main church
leads to this converted windmill. Views from
the its terrace are nothing short of stupendous; the double and the twin sleep four in
total and there's a fully-equipped kitchen a
couple of steps out the front door.

Mimallis Houses   APARTMENT €€
(☑6972808758, 22870 21094; www.mimallis.gr;
Plaka & Klima; Plaka d €90-95, Klima d/q €200/220;
⊙Apr-Oct; 🕸🕸) Mimallis rents two small
houses in Plaka (sleeping two), and one
in precious Klima (sleeping up to five) –
each different, comfortable and packed
with amenities. Low-season discounts are
excellent.

Archondoula Studios   APARTMENT €€
(☑22870 23820; www.archondoula-studios.gr;
Plaka; r/studio €70/100; ⊙Mar-Nov; 🕸🕸)
Cheerful Stavros runs sleek, white-on-white
rooms and studios. Rooms are compact,
while the studios give more breathing space.
Take in spectacular sunset views from terraces and balconies, and enjoy the peace of
Plaka after dark.

Studios Betty   APARTMENT €€
(☑22870 21538; www.studiosbetty-milos.com;
Plaka; studio €100; 🕸🕸) Enjoy sunset views
as glorious as Santorini's from this complex
of four simple studios at Plaka's cliff edge.

★Windmill of Karamitsos   APARTMENT €€€
(☑6945568086; www.windmillmilos.gr; Trypiti;
windmill €200; ⊙Apr-Oct; 🕸) Bed down in a
unique converted windmill that dates from
1859 and now sleeps four in creative quarters over three levels. It's on a hilltop on the
edge of Trypiti, with panoramic views.

✗ Eating

Palaios CAFE €

(📞 22870 23490; Plaka; snacks from €3.50; ⏰9am-9pm; 🛜) This old-world cafe is a perfect pit stop for breakfast or coffee, but it's mostly worth stopping by to try some local specialities: *karpouzopita* (watermelon cake or pie), unique to Milos and Folegandros, and *ladenia* (not unlike a flatbread pizza).

★ Archondoula CYCLADIC €€

(📞 22870 21384; Plaka; dishes €6-17; ⏰noon-10pm Easter-Nov; 🛜) The whole cheerful family is involved at this top-notch taverna in a picturesque laneway setting. Classic Greek dishes have an assured touch and range from grilled vegetables with *manouri* (soft cheese) to grilled swordfish to lamb with tomato and artichoke.

Barrielo CYCLADIC €€

(📞 6984218360; www.barriello.com; mains €9-38; ⏰7pm-3am; 🛜) 🍴 Every evening, diners are lured to the little square below Trypiti's church by the wafting smells of sizzling meat on the grill. It's all organic and raised on the owner's farm; choose from sausage, beef with figs or chicken shashlik.

Pollonia Πολλώνια

POP 272

Pollonia, on the north coast, is a low-key fishing village with azure waters that transforms into quite a chic (albeit petite) summer resort.

The town is also the jumping-off point for Kimolos; note that it's sometimes mapped as Apollonia.

🏃 Activities

Milos Diving Center DIVING

(📞 22870 41296, 6976114846; www.milosdiving.gr; 1-tank dive €50; ⏰9.30am-3pm) Dives (from €50, including equipment) and PADI courses, based at Pollonia. Reputable operator, around for more than 20 years.

🛏 Sleeping

Zoe Rooms GUESTHOUSE €

(📞 22870 41235; www.zoe-milos.gr; Pollonia; d from €45; ❄🛜) This friendly little guesthouse is the pick of the budget spots, with large, spotless rooms, an extensive breakfast spread and an on-site restaurant that serves dinner on the cliff overlooking the waves.

DON'T MISS

KLIMA ROCK DWELLINGS

Tiny, photogenic Klima clings to the beachfront cliff face below Trypiti. It's the best example of Milos' *syrmata* (traditional fishermen's encampments), where the downstairs, with brightly painted doors, are used for rough-weather boat storage, and the upstairs are used for family life.

The homes, most still in use today, are incorporated into the rocks. A unique experience is to rent *syrmata* for your stay; a few of these are available via home-sharing services. You'll need your own wheels.

Nefeli Sunset Studios APARTMENT €€

(📞 22870 41466; www.milos-nefelistudios.gr; studio from €140; ⏰Apr-Oct; ❄🛜) Whitewashed cubes combine modern design with traditional touches, in a bay-front property with a delightful garden, on the northwest edge of the village.

★ Salt BOUTIQUE HOTEL €€€

(📞 22870 41110; www.salt-milos.com; d/ste incl breakfast from €200/380; ⏰Apr-Oct; ❄🛜) Sparklingly minimal, white-on-white sophistication, with all the luxuries and views to the sea. Low-season rates drop by almost 50%.

✗ Eating

★ Armenaki SEAFOOD €€

(📞 22870 41061; www.armenaki.gr; dishes €7-15, fish by kg; ⏰noon-11pm Apr-Oct; 🛜) Armenaki is revered for its fishy business – this place is all about seafood (in fact, there's little else on the menu). Seafood in all its guises is cooked to perfection, and service is first-rate (including the filleting of fish at your table). *Kakavia* (traditional fish stew) comes recommended, and there's an extensive wine list.

Jordan's Meat...ing Steak House STEAK €€

(📞 6972869333; www.jordansmeating.gr; mains €11.50-28; ⏰noon-3pm & 6-11pm; 🛜) Just imagine: you spent the day at the beach. You come here, suntanned, salty, ravenous. Then comes the moment of ecstasy: a giant slab of perfectly grilled T-bone or rib-eye or tenderloin placed in front of you, along with the cold fizz of beer in your frosted glass. For the carnivorously inclined only.

Hanabi
SUSHI €€

(☑ 22870 41180; Pollonia; mains €12-20; ⊘ noon-11pm; 🛜) Chic new Japanese restaurant, complete with ambient beats on the stereo, waterside terrace and funky wicker furniture. The sushi roll combos are imaginative and well-executed, and the spicy tuna sashimi stands out.

Gialos
SEAFOOD €€

(☑ 22870 41208; www.gialos-pollonia.gr; mains €8-20; ⊘ noon-11pm Easter-Oct) Watch port life while digging into fresh seafood and yummy pastas. Bustling Gialos has a creative menu bursting with fresh local flavour, including tuna tataki, salmon with nettle and sour-cheese patties. Save room for dessert.

❶ Information

Travel Me to Milos (☑ 22870 41008; www.travelmetomilos.com) Books activities, excursions and ferry tickets.

Around Milos

Milos and its offshore islets boast more than 70 splendid beaches in different-coloured sands and stone. Rent wheels or take a cruise to compare.

In the north, **Plathiena** is a fine sandy beach beyond Plaka, and on the way you can visit fishing villages Areti and Fourkovouni. **Firopotamos** is a delightful little sandy cove with a taverna, while **Mandrakia** is a tiny fishing outpost with a practically deserted sweep of sand and calm waters. Also in this area, **Sarakiniko** is a must, with its snow-white rock formations for sunbathing, a tiny sand beach and a deep channel for swimming. In the very north, if you have an ATV, you'll have the **Nerodafni** and **Trachilas** beaches almost to yourself.

On the south coast, golden-sanded **Provatas** feels remote but has a couple of tavernas. **Kyriaki** is backed by otherworldly grey-, rose- and rust-coloured hills and has soft, grey sand. The long taupe arch of **Paleohori** is backed by banded cliffs and has beach bars, water sports and hot sand, thanks to thermal springs in the area.

◉ Sights & Activities

Filakopi
HISTORIC SITE

(€2; ⊘ 8am-3pm Tue, Thu & Sat) This ancient Minoan city in the island's northeast (close to Pollonia) was one of the earliest settlements in the Cyclades. Now it's not much more than rubble, but the seaside setting is great, with cavelike rock formations all around.

★ Sea Kayak Milos
KAYAKING

(☑ 22870 23597; www.seakayakgreece.com; Triovasalos; sea kayak trip €75 per person; ⊘ 9am-5pm Apr-Oct) A superb way to explore the coastline. Australian Rod and his team lead highly regarded day trips, with no experience required. Itineraries depend on weather conditions. Multi-day kayaking and camping tours are also available.

🛏 Sleeping & Eating

Achivadolimni (Milos)

Camping
CAMPGROUND €

(☑ 22870 31410; www.miloscamping.gr; Achivadolimni; campsite per person/tent €7/5, bungalows incl breakfast €85-115; ⊘ mid-May–Sep; 🛜🏊) Beautiful oleander-filled grounds, with excellent facilities and high-standard rooms. Has a pool, minimarket, restaurant and bar. It's 6km south of Adamas, with regular bus connections. Also does port pick-ups.

Scirocco
TAVERNA €€

(☑ 22870 31201; www.restaurantsirocco.gr; Paleohori Beach; mains €7-16; ⊘ noon-10pm Apr-Oct; 🛜) Popular eatery smack-bang on the shore, with a novel hook: 'volcanic food' (ie dishes slow-cooked underground using the sand's thermal heat). There's also a full menu of Greek favourites, and a breezy view.

KIMOLOS ΚΙΜΩΛΟΣ

POP 910

Exquisite Kimolos, perched off the northeast tip of Milos, feels like a step back in time. Barely a trickle of visitors get the chance to take in its fantastical sienna-coloured walls hand-hewn from volcanic stones, or its sparkling bays and picturesque *syrmata*. It's an easy day trip from Milos; consider taking a car, bike or scooter on the ferry to make getting around easier.

The boat (from Pollonia in Milos' north) docks at **Psathi**, from where it's 1.5km to the pretty capital, Hora. Wander the maze of streets to reach Hora's central cafes and a semi-crumbling medieval *kastro*. The *kastro* holds the **Church of the Nativity** (from the late 16th century) and the petite **Folk & Maritime Museum of Kimolos** (☑ 22870 51118; ⊘ hr vary) FREE.

Caïques from Psathi buzz out to beaches, the best of which is magnificent, white-sand **Prassa** (also reachable by car/scooter/ATV along the partially sealed road). You can walk there from Hora in about two hours.

🛌 Sleeping & Eating

Meltemi Rooms   HOTEL €
(📞22870 51360; http://kimolos-meltemi.gr; d incl breakfast €55; 🅿️🅿️) Rooms perch on the edge of Hora with views to the sea. One has a kitchen.

★ The Windmill Kimolos   BOUTIQUE HOTEL €€
(📞22870 51554; www.kimoloshotel.com; r from €105; 🅿️🅿️) The most atmospheric abode in Kimolos, this converted windmill looks down on the island from its lofty hilltop position. The whitewashed rooms are cosy and comfortable.

Raventi   CAFE €
(📞22870 51212; snacks from €3.50; ⊙9am-late) On the beach at Psathi, this fashionable cafe has a comfy terrace, a display full of delicious cakes and ice cream, and disorganised service.

To Kyma   TAVERNA €€
(📞22870 51001; dishes €7-20; ⊙noon-11pm Easter-Oct; 🅿️) The taverna To Kyma, right on the beach at Psathi, is good for seafood and for trying the local specialities such as *ladenia* (similar to pizza, topped with tomato sauce).

ℹ️ Information

There's an ATM at the port and a petrol station.

ℹ️ Getting There & Away

Some Milos long-distance ferries stop at Kimolos. **Kimolos Travel** (📞22870 51219; ⊙9am-1pm & 4-8pm) in Hora sells tickets. A small **car ferry** (📞6948308758; www.kimolos-link.gr; per adult/child//scooter/car €2.10/1/5/8.70) connects Pollonia (Milos) with Psathi (Kimolos) up to eight times daily in high season, three times in low season (30 minutes).

ℹ️ Getting Around

Buses connect Psathi and Hora in high season only; infrequent services also visit beaches. A couple of rental agencies in Kimolos offer scooters and ATVs, or else you can call for a **taxi** (📞6945464093).

SIFNOS   ΣΙΦΝΟΣ

POP 2625

Sifnos has a dreamlike quality. Three white-washed villages, anchored by the capital Apollonia, sit like pearls on a string along the crest of the island. The changing light kisses the landscape, and as you explore the flanking slopes of the central mountains you'll discover abundant terraced olive groves, almond trees, oleander and aromatic herbs. Each of the island's bays harbours a spectrum of aqua waters and offers breath-taking vistas.

During the Archaic period (from about the 8th century BC), Sifnos was enriched by its gold and silver deposits, but by the 5th century BC the mines were exhausted. Sifnos is now known for pottery, basket weaving and cookery. Visitors flock to the southern half of the island, served by good bus links, but it's worth getting your own wheels and driving to the remote beaches of the north, where the main road culminates in – you guessed it! – a church.

ℹ️ Getting There & Away

Sifnos is on the Piraeus to western Cyclades ferry route, with good summer connections across the Cyclades. Get tickets at **Aegean Thesaurus Travel** (📞22840 33151; www.thesaurus.gr), **Xidis Travel** (📞Apollonia 22840 32373, Kamares 22840 31895; www.xidis.com.gr; ⊙9am-9pm) or the tourist office (p427).

Boat Services from Sifnos

DESTINATION	DURATION	FARE (€)	FREQUENCY
Folegandros	1¼-4¼hr	13-53	up to 3 daily
Kea	7hr	20	Mon
Kimolos	30min-2½hr	10-18	1-2 daily
Kythnos	2¼hr	13	5 weekly
Ios	1¼hr-5¾hr	16-58	daily
Lavrio	8hr	30	Mon
Milos	50min-2hr	11-20	up to 3 daily
Naxos	5¾hr	66	6 weekly
Paros	5½hr	9	Tue, Wed & Sat
Piraeus	2½-4½hr	30-55	up to 3 daily
Santorini (Thira)	2-7¼hr	18-58	1-2 daily
Serifos	20-40min	10-19	1-2 daily
Sikinos	2-5hr	14-41	4 weekly
Syros	3hr-4½hr	13	3 weekly

Sifnos

Serifos (25km); Kythnos (80km); Piraeus (170km)

Cape Heronisos
Heronisos
Heronisos Beach
Aegean Sea
Vroulidia Beach
Agios Dimos
476m
Kamares Bay
Poulati
Kamares
Artemonas
Ano Petali
Kato Petali
Apollonia
Kastro
Katavati
Seralia
Milos (45km); Santorini (110km)
680m
Exambelas
Moni Profiti Ilia
Acropolis of Agios Andreas
Moni
Faros
Vathy Bay
Vathy
Chrysopigi
Platys Gialos
Chrysopigi Beach
201m
Platys Gialos Bay
Fasolou Beach
Cape Kondou
Kitriani

ℹ Getting Around

Bus timetables are posted around the island, and frequent buses connect Kamares with Apollonia and Artemonas. Buses also link Apollonia with Kastro, Vathy, Faros and Platys Gialos. Fares are generally €1.80.

Car rental costs from €45 per day. Companies will deliver to the port or your hotel. Try **Apollo Rent a Car** (☑ 22840 33333; www.automoto apollo.gr; Apollonia; ☺ 9am-9pm) or **Proto Moto Car Rental** (☑ 22840 33791; www.protomoto car.gr; Kamares).

Taxis (☑ 6944761210, 6932403485) hover around the port and Apollonia's main junction. At bus stops you'll find a list of taxi numbers and indicative fares. Fares from Kamares include Apollonia €9, Platys Gialos €20 and Vathy €20.

Kamares

Καμάρες

POP 245

Scenically hemmed in by steep mountains, the port of Kamares has a holiday atmosphere, with its large beach and waterfront cafes, tavernas and shops. It makes a decent base, though it's not as convenient for exploring Sifnos as the very central Apollonia.

🛏 Sleeping

Kamares has the largest selection of accommodation in Sifnos. Domatia owners rarely meet boats; book ahead in high season. On the northern side of the bay, Agia Marina has plenty of hotels and domatia.

Camping Makis   CAMPGROUND €
(☑ 6945946339; www.makiscamping.gr; campsite per adult/child/tent €7/4/4, d €70, studio & apt €75-100; ☺ Apr-Nov; ✻ 🛜) Pitch your tent behind the beach in a basic lot with attractive olive trees (or hire a tent with mattresses for €25). There are well-equipped studios and apartments (sleeping up to five), a cafe, barbecue, communal kitchen, minimarket and laundry.

★ Aglaia Studios   GUESTHOUSE €€
(☑ 22840 31513; www.aglaiastudios.gr; Ag. Marina; d from €55; ✻ 🛜 🏊) In the evenings, you can sit on your balcony and watch the lights of Kamares across the bay. By day, a few steps take you down to the swimming platform, from which you can launch yourself into the Aegean. The studios themselves are snug and comfortable.

Hotel Kamari   HOTEL €€
(☑ 22840 33383; www.sifnostravel.com; d/apt €70/80; ✻ 🛜) Kamari provides spacious doubles and fully equipped studios, with plant-festooned balconies and very helpful staff. Sea views cost a little extra. Steep discounts outside peak season.

Stavros Hotel   HOTEL €€
(☑ 22840 33383; www.sifnostravel.com; d/q €80/120; ✻ 🛜) Main street's Stavros Hotel offers good service and excellent, spacious studios with kitchenettes and sea views. A bonus: flexible room configurations work to accommodate families. The info desk downstairs can help with car hire.

🍴 Eating

Cafe Folie   CAFE €
(☑ 6936519006; www.cafefolie.gr; mains €6-12; ☺ 8am-late; 🛜) Cafe Folie makes it far too easy to be a beach bum: it's a fun, decked area right on the sea (towards Agia Marina), with sunbeds, a ladder into the water, and a menu that allows you to slip from morning coffee to a salad lunch, and then on to dinner, and finally cocktails.

★ Absinthe   FUSION €€
(mains €8-19) This new kid on the block has been wowing Sifnos with its blend of

EXPERIENCING SIFNOS

Walking

Sifnos is justifiably proud of its excellent network of more than a dozen signposted walking trails, some 98km in all, ranging from 20-minute rambles to four-hour hikes. A great investment is the €4 info pack from **Aegean Thesaurus Travel** (p425), on the main square in Apollonia or else in Kamares; it includes the Terrain map of Sifnos, an overview of the island's walking trails, plus the current bus and ferry timetables.

There are some wonderful short walks: Apollonia to Artemonas (15 minutes) is worthwhile, as is the loop around Kastro. Our favourite is the 40-minute walk from Faros to **Moni Chrysopigi** (p429). Longer trails link major settlements via beaches, monasteries and great scenery – Apollonia to Vathy is about four hours.

Water Sports

Sheltered Vathy is a good spot for stand-up paddleboarding, while Platys Gialos has caught the flyboarding bug. **Vathi Sea Sports** (22840 36002; stand-up paddleboarding per hour €23; 10am-8pm May-Sep) and **Calypso Boat Rental** (6970424004; www.boatrental.gr; Platys Gialos; 8am-8pm) are the main water sports operators.

Cooking Classes

A big drawcard for travellers is Sifnos' culinary heritage. The island was the birthplace of Nikolaos Tselementes (1878–1958), author of the first (and best-known) Greek cookbook, published in 1910. Since then, Sifnos has enjoyed a reputation for producing excellent chefs. Engaging cooking classes are available with **Sifnos Farm Narlis** (6979778283; www.sifnos-farm-narlis.com; class €60-80; 9am-1pm). Book direct, or via **Aegean Thesaurus Travel** (p425).

Cycladic and fusion offerings, using the best of fresh local ingredients. Their standout dish is hot and spicy goat with rice, and there are plenty of daily specials, from stir-fried chanterelles to fish carpaccio. Don't miss the desserts!

O Argiris GREEK €€
(22840 32352; mains €6-16; 9am-11pm Apr-Oct;) It's well worth the walk around the bay to Agia Marina. Sure, the view looking back to Kamares is wonderful, but it's equalled by the top-notch food. You can't go wrong with Sifnos specialities (helpfully indicated on the menu); try *revithada* (baked chickpeas), *mastelo* (lamb in wine) and caper salad.

Information

An ATM is just a few metres from the ferry quay.
Aegean Thesaurus (22840 33151; www.thesaurus.gr; 9am-9pm) Books ferry tickets and provides a €4 Sifnos welcome pack (hiking info, bus timetables and more).
Municipal Tourist Office (www.sifnos.gr) Very helpful, with ferry tickets, accommodation and bus timetables.

Apollonia Απολλωνία
POP 869

Labyrinthine, church-studded Apollonia comes alive in high season with its parade of well-dressed Athenians strutting their stuff along the Steno – Odos Prokou, known as Steno (meaning 'narrow') because of its slenderness. Cafes, bars, clubs, shops and eateries buzz with life.

The quirky **Museum of Popular Art** (22840 31341; €1; 9.30am-2pm & 6-10pm) at the central junction contains a fun confusion of old costumes, textiles and photographs. Hours are erratic.

The main vehicular road cuts right through the centre of town, but park at the large free car park downhill from the village and walk up and into the warren of streets. At the central junction you'll find all the services: banks, post office, pharmacy, bookshop, taxis and so on.

Sleeping & Eating

Eleonas Apartments & Studios APARTMENT €€
(22840 33383; www.sifnostravel.com; apt from €160;) An idyllic complex tucked away

in an olive grove, Eleonas offers gloriously roomy apartments that sleep five, with kitchen, living space and terrace. Studios are slightly smaller, but still very spacious. It feels peaceful and rural, but it's just a few minutes' walk from the Steno.

Hotel Anthousa
HOTEL €€

(☑ 22840 31431; www.hotelanthousa-sifnos.gr; s/d/tr €55/70/90; 🕸🐾) Behind a pretty, vine-covered facade, this year-round hotel has fresh, appealing rooms set around an inner courtyard. Sweet in decor and sweet in intent: downstairs are a cafe (where breakfast is served) and a patisserie.

Drimoni
MEDITERRANEAN €

(☑ 22840 31434; www.drimoni.gr; mains €9-13; ⊙ 6pm-late; 🐾) Look out over the countryside or lounge by the pool (yes, pool!) at this contemporary restaurant with funky decor. Chef Giorgos does the Sifnian culinary tradition proud with the likes of *mastelo* (goat slow-cooked in wine with rosemary and dill), imaginative salads, risottos and pastas.

★Cayenne
CYCLADIC €€

(☑ 22840 31080; www.facebook.com/Cayenne RestaurantSifnos; mains €14-25; ⊙ 12.30pm-late; 🐾) Shaded by a fig tree and drowning in a riot of herbs just off the Steno, Cayenne affirms its strong commitment to Cycladic ingredients through such dishes as lemon-on-caper risotto, Byzantine meat patties and smoked eel with Santorini fava beans. The art gallery upstairs hosts events.

★Rambagas
GREEK €€€

(☑ 22840 32215; www.kikladonxoros.gr; mains €14-29; ⊙ 9am-late; 🐾) It's easy to succumb to celeb-chef hype when the setting is as beautiful as this – a tree-shaded terrace off the Steno, with artwork adding stylish appeal. Well-known chef Yiannis Loucacos (a *MasterChef* judge in Greece) designs the dinner menu, which pays homage to Sifnos' culinary traditions. Expect char-grilled octopus, smoked eel and ravioli filled with local *anthotiro* cheese for dinner.

Ano Petali & Artemonas
Άνω Πετάλι & Αρτεμώνας

POP 800

After crossing the main road from Apollonia, the string of houses continues north into Ano Petali and reaches Artemonas with its grand mansions. Walk the pedestrian-only streets to take it all in, stopping at one of the fashionable cafes.

Artemonas has a central square off the winding main road as well, with a bus stop and some appealing eateries.

🛌 Sleeping

Windmill Bella Vista
BOUTIQUE HOTEL €€

(☑ 22840 33518; www.windmillbellavista.gr; apt from €115, windmill €180; 🕸🕸) If you've never stayed in a converted Cycladic windmill, here's your chance! It's the atmospheric pick of the spacious, high-beamed apartments and studios clustered around the infinity pool en route from Artemonas to Poulaki.

Pension Geronti
PENSION €€

(☑ 22840 31473; www.gerontisifnos.gr; d €65; 🕸🐾) Opposite Petali Village Hotel, on the walkway between Apollonia and Artemonas, is this gem of a pension, with spotless rooms, sweeping views, sweet hosts and excellent rates.

Petali Village Hotel
HOTEL €€

(☑ 22840 33024; www.petalihotel.gr; Ano Petali; d/ste incl breakfast from €136/190; 🕸🐾🕸) Suspended on a walking street between Apollonia and Artemonas, this four-star terraced array of rooms and apartments has sweeping views to Apollonia and the sea, and an inviting kidney-shaped pool. Low-season discounts are decent. Port pick-up offered.

Around Sifnos

On the southeast coast, the fishing hamlet of **Faros** has fish tavernas and a couple of nice beaches nearby, including **Fasolou**, reached up steps and over the headland from the bus stop.

Platys Gialos, 10km south of Apollonia, has a big, generous beach entirely backed by tavernas, hotels and shops. **Vathy**, on the southwest coast, is a low-key resort village on an almost circular bay of aquamarine beauty.

Not to be missed is the walled village of **Kastro**, 3km east from Apollonia. The former medieval capital is a magical place of buttressed alleyways and whitewashed houses surrounded by valleys and sea. It has a modest archaeological museum, and the small port and pebble beach of **Seralia** is nestled below.

⊙ Sights

★**Moni Chrysopigi** MONASTERY

The handsome whitewashed monastery of Chrysopigi dates back more than 600 years and perches on an islet connected to the shore by a tiny footbridge. There is a superb walk to Chrysopigi from the village of Faros (about 40 minutes one-way); en route you'll go along beautiful, azure **Chrysopigi Beach**, home to two excellent tavernas.

Acropolis of Agios Andreas MONUMENT

(☑22840 31488; €2; ⊙8.30am-3pm Tue-Sun) At the heart of the island, 2km south of Apollonia, this well-excavated hilltop acropolis dates from the Mycenaean period (13th century BC). Take in extensive views of interior valleys and neighbouring Paros from above the intact defensive wall. The adjacent **Church of Agios Andreas** dates from about 1700.

🛏 Sleeping & Eating

🛏 Platys Gialos

Hotel Efrosini HOTEL €€

(☑22840 71353; www.hotel-efrosini.gr; d incl breakfast €80-90; ⊙Easter-Sep; ❋ 🛜) This well-kept, family-run hotel is one of the best on the Platys Gialos strip. Small balconies overlook a leafy courtyard with the sea lapping just in front.

Verina Suites APARTMENT €€€

(☑22840 71525; www.verinahotelsifnos.com; d/apt from €170/210; ⊙May-Oct; ❋ 🛜 ☷) Effortlessly chic, Verina rents minimalist suites and villas at outposts in Platys Gialos, Vathy and above Poulati (north of Kastro). Verina Suites lies behind the beach at Platys Gialos, but try dragging yourself from the gorgeous pool and cafe-bar area.

★**Nero & Alati** CYCLADIC €€

(☑22840 71208; www.facebook.com/neroalati; mains €8-15; ⊙1-10pm; 🛜) The seafront terrace of 'Water & Salt' serves lovingly prepared, slow-cooked local dishes using ingredients sourced by chef Alexander from his grandparents' farm, along with foraged mountain herbs. Okra *plaki,* wild goat and lamb *mastelo* are standout dishes.

Omega 3 SEAFOOD €€

(☑22840 72014; www.facebook.com/omega3greece; Platys Gialos; mains €9-23; ⊙noon-11pm May-Sep) The cute name (Ω3) hints at the treats on offer at this small, casual beach-front spot. There's a fresh-faced menu of fab fishy flavours, grabbing techniques from around the globe (sashimi, ceviche) but staying true to its roots too, with slow-cooked octopus and orzo with crayfish.

🛏 Vathy

Aerides Boutique Rooms BOUTIQUE HOTEL €€

(☑22840 36093; www.aerides-sifnos.com/en; studio from €60; ❋ 🛜) Run by a friendly young couple and artfully decorated with bits of flotsam and jetsam, this converted *syrma* (boat shed) comprises three spacious studios. The sea is right under your window.

🛏 Kastro

Antonis Rooms PENSION €

(☑22840 33708; http://sifnosholidays.gr; d €50; ❋ 🛜) Brilliant value. On the road as you head to Kastro, these simple, spotless rooms beckon. There's a communal kitchen and a terrace with splendid valley views. It's open year-round.

Aris & Maria Traditional Houses APARTMENT €€

(☑22840 31161; www.arismaria-traditional.com; d/tr/q €85/100/130; ❋) For an authentic Kastro experience, rent one of these six traditional Sifnian houses. Some have sea views.

Leonidas TAVERNA €€

(☑22840 31153; Kastro; mains €8-16; ⊙noon-10pm Easter-Sep; 🛜) At the northern edge of the village, this popular place offers tasty local dishes, including Sifnian appetisers like chickpea croquettes and cheese patties with honey and sesame seeds.

SERIFOS ΣΕΡΙΦΟΣ

POP 1420

Serifos has a raw, rugged beauty, with steep mountains plunging to broad ultramarine bays. Relatively deserted outside the quaint hilltop capital of Hora or the dusty port of Livadi down below, the island feels like it's gone beautifully feral. All that you find are the occasional remnants of past mining enterprises (rusting tracks, cranes) and the whoosh of the wind (which can be fierce). Rent wheels to make the most of it. Serifos is one of the few islands where locals drink the water.

In Greek mythology, Serifos is where Perseus grew up, bringing back the Medusa's head to save his mother from the unwanted romantic attentions of Polydectes, and where the Cyclopes were said to live. There's some fine walking on Serifos, and plenty to explore below the waves too.

❶ Getting There & Away

Serifos is on the Piraeus to western Cyclades ferry route and has reasonable summer connections (or travel to Sifnos for more options). Buy tickets at **Kondilis** (☑ 22810 52340; www.kondilis.gr; ⊙ 9am-9pm) on Livadi's waterfront.

Boat Services from Serifos

DESTINATION	DURATION	FARE (€)	FREQUENCY
Folegandros	2½-41½hr	15-53	3 weekly
Ios	4¼-6hr	18-62	2 weekly
Kimolos	1¾-3½hr	13-22	6 weekly
Kythnos	1½-4¾hr	12	6 weekly
Milos	1¼-2½hr	12-22	1-2 daily
Mykonos	7hr	74	Wed & Sun
Paros	6¼hr	13	2-3 weekly
Piraeus	1¾-4¾hr	35-51	1-2 daily
Santorini (Thira)	3½-7¾hr	23-63	daily
Sifnos	25-50min	10-18	1-2 daily
Sikinos	2½-5½hr	17-42	3 weekly
Syros	2¼-4¼hr	12	3 weekly

❶ Getting Around

Buses connect Livadi and Hora (€1.80, hourly, 15 minutes); the timetable is posted at the bus stop by the yacht quay. In high season, a circular bus route takes in Panagia, Galani, Kendarhos and Agios Ioannis Beach (up to six daily), with a couple of daily buses to Megalo Livadi and Koutalas.

Rent cars (per day from €45), scooters (€18) and quads (€25) at **Blue Bird** (☑ 22810 51511; www.rentacar-bluebird.gr), **Poseidon Rent a Car** (☑ 6974789706, 22810 52030; www.serifosisland.gr/poseidon) or **Serifos Travel** (☑ 22810 51463; www.serifostours.gr) just off the waterfront.

Taxis (☑ 6944473044, 6932431114) to Hora cost €8, Psili Ammos €8, Sykamia €22, Vagia €12 and Megalo Livadi €22.

Livadi   Λιβάδι

POP 605

The port town of Serifos is a fairly low-key place, popular with yachties and handy as a base for exploring the island. In spite of growing numbers of tourists, there's still a

reassuring feeling that the modern world has not entirely taken over.

Just over the headland that rises from the ferry quay lies the fine, tamarisk-fringed beach at **Livadakia**.

🛏 Sleeping

Much of the accommodation clusters at Livadakia Beach. Most lodgings can pick up at the port by arrangement.

Alisachni   APARTMENT €
(☑ 22810 51914; d from €50; ❈ 🎧) Friendly owner Giorgios runs a clutch of spacious, spotless rooms with kitchenettes and bug netting on the windows, just a couple of minutes' walk from the beach.

Coralli Camping & Bungalows   CAMPGROUND, APARTMENT €
(☑ 22810 51500; www.coralli.gr; Livadakia Beach; campsite per adult/child/tent €8/4/5, bungalow d/tr/q €75/90/110; ❈ 🎧 🏊) Right behind Livadakia Beach, this well-equipped and well-run eucalyptus-shaded campground also has 'bungalows' (rooms) with mountain or sea views. The complex includes a cool pool and bar, a restaurant, minimarket, kitchen and barbecue. Nearby self-catering apartments are of an equally high standard.

Alexandros-Vassilia   APARTMENT €
(☑ 22810 51119; www.alexandros-vassilia.gr; Livadakia Beach; d/tr/q from €35/55/85; ⊙ Easter-Sep; ❈ 🎧) Best known for its beachfront taverna in a flowering garden, this friendly Livadakia compound also has a big range of rooms and apartments. They range from decent-value economy rooms (no sea view) to family-sized, sea-view suites.

★ Studios Niovi   APARTMENT €€
(☑ 22810 51900; www.studiosniovi.gr; Livadi; apt incl breakfast €90-140; ❈ 🎧) On the furthest eastern curve of Livadi's bay, these immaculate apartments look at the broad expanse of the bay, bustling Livadi, towering Hora and the mountains beyond. The owner makes a super breakfast spread. You're about a 20-minute walk from Livadi itself. Your own wheels are an advantage. Good low-season rates.

🍴 Eating

Kali's   SEAFOOD €€
(☑ 22810 52301; mains €9-18; ⊙ noon-11pm Mar-Oct; 🎧) White tables on the water's edge with gregarious waiters and delicious home-cooking, much of it with a fresh-fish focus.

Metalleio MEDITERRANEAN €€
(☑22810 51755; www.facebook.com/Metalleio;
Livadi; mains €8-16; ⊙8.30pm-late; �ම) On
the road behind the waterfront, Metalleio
dishes up quality cuisine from a short menu
emphasising local flavours: risotto with local
goat's cheese, veal in local wine sauce, and
locally-made ice cream. Come midnight, the
action moves upstairs and Metalleio doubles
as the island's main live-music venue and
dance club (particularly in July and August).

Anemos Café BAR
(☑22810 51783; ⊙9am-late; ම) Above the Car-
refour supermarket, Anemos' broad terrace
offers top views of the marina and distant
Hora. The proprietors are friendly, snacks
and coffees are good and cheap, and it gets
hopping around boat arrivals.

Yacht Club Serifos BAR
(☑22810 51888; ⊙8am-4am; ම) Livadi's original waterfront cafe-bar (going back to 1938)
maintains a cheerful buzz. Lounge music
plays by day for coffee drinkers, with mainstream rock, disco and funk late into the
night.

ⓘ Information

There are two ATMs along the waterfront.

Hora (Serifos)
Χώρα (Σέριφος)

POP 364

This tiny town cascades down the summit of
a rocky hill above Livadi, putting it among
the most dramatically striking (and loftiest)
of all the Cycladic capitals.

Hora's bus terminus and main car park
are on its upper side, near some windmills,
as is its **archaeological collection** (☑22810
51138; €2; ⊙8.30am-4pm Tue & Thu-Sun) which
displays fragments of mainly Hellenic and
Roman sculpture excavated from the *kastro*. From there, steps climb into the maze of
Hora proper and lead to the **main square**,
watched over by the lovely neoclassical
town hall.

From the square, narrow alleys and more
steps lead upwards to churches like **Agios
Ioannis Theologos**, carved into the rock
and built on the site of an ancient temple
to Athena, and the remnants of the ruined
15th-century **Venetian Kastro**, from where
the views are spectacular.

🛏 Sleeping & Eating

Accommodation options are found east of
upper Hora. Head down the road opposite
Cuckoo cafe-bar, close to the bus terminus.

I Apanemia PENSION €
(☑22810 51517, 6971891106; www.apanemia.com.
gr; s/d €40/45; ⊛ම) This excellent-value,
family-run place has decent, well-equipped
rooms with front balcony views to the distant sea and side views towards Hora. It's
old-school in decor, but well cared for.

Anemoessa Studios APARTMENT €€
(☑22810 51132; www.serifos-anemoessa.gr; apt
€90-130; ⊛ම) Pretty, modern studios sleep
four in whitewashed Cycladic splendour.

Stou Stratou CAFE €
(☑22810 52566; Plateia Ag Athanasiou; dishes €4-9;
⊙9am-late Easter-Oct) Sitting postcard-pretty
in the main square, Stou Stratou has a menu
full of art and poetry (literally), plus it serves
good breakfasts and light snacks such as
fennel pie or a mixed plate of cold cuts and
cheese. Cocktails and coffee too.

★Aloni CYCLADIC €€
(☑22810 52603; mains €9-18; ⊙7pm-late Jun-Oct,
Sat & Sun Nov-May) Halfway up the hill between
Livadi and Hora, signposted on the right,

Aloni gives splendid panoramas. Islanders rate it among Serifos' best, with local produce (roasted meat, rabbit in lemon sauce, fennel pie) proudly showcased.

Around Serifos

About 1.5km north of Livadi, pretty little **Psili Ammos Beach** offers the best swimming close to Livadi, and has two excellent tavernas. **Platys Gialos Beach** in the north has a good summer-only taverna of the same name.

Sykamia is one of the island's best beaches, with a dramatic approach along a steep, windy road through terraced hills. The beach itself is grey-brown sand full of stones, with an excellent tavern above it. To reach Sykamia you will pass through the quaint village of Panagia, or on the east coast, Kendarhos (also known as Kallitsos, the 'most beautiful').

Tiny **Megalo Livadi**, on the southwest coast, is a fun visit for its sparkling bay, crumbling neoclassical buildings (remnants of the mining era), shallow, calm waters and two seaside taverns. The cave where the Cyclops was said to dwell is near here.

The best beaches on the south coast tend to be broad and sandy, and deserted out of high season. It's a wild landscape, punctuated by derelict mining machinery. Stop for a swim at sheltered **Vagia**, long and narrow **Ganema** and **Koutalas fishing bay**.

🏃 Activities

Serifos Scuba Divers　　　　　DIVING
(🖉6932570552; www.serifosscubadivers.gr; 1-tank dive/snorkelling €50/30) Based in Livadi, this recommended scuba operator takes divers to a dozen sites around the island, including wrecks, flooded mines and more. Day-long snorkelling trips can be arranged in July and August, and they also rent boats and arrange adrenalin-packed flyboard sessions.

🛏 Sleeping & Eating

★Coco-Mat Eco Residences　　BOUTIQUE HOTEL €€€
(🖉22877 72977; http://serifos.coco-mat-hotels. com; apt €460; 🌐🛜) Overlooking Vagia beach, this cluster of miners' houses has been turned into a trendy little hotel. Its split-level residences (with bedrooms on the cooler level) come with coarse whitewashed walls, heavy wooden beams, sea views, super-comfy beds and kitchenettes, with a great little restaurant on-site serving fusion dishes.

To Akrogiali tou Vitou　　　　TAVERNA €
(🖉22810 51289; mains €7-11; ⊗noon-10pm Jun-Aug; 🛜) To Akrogiali, just above one of Serifos' best beaches and one of the only signs of development for miles, serves delicious fish and excellent takes on Greek standards.

KYTHNOS　　ΚΥΘΝΟΣ

POP 1456

Low-key Kythnos is a series of rolling hills punctuated by stone huts and bisected by ancient walls, green valleys and some wonderful beaches. Port life in Merihas and village life in beautiful Hora and Dryopida remain easygoing, and foreign tourists are few, although the ease of access from Athens sees locals filling the island's beaches and marinas on summer weekends.

ℹ Getting There & Away

Ferries serve Piraeus and Lavrio on the mainland, Kea to the north (services are infrequent, so it's usually easier to travel via Lavrio), and in high season, islands to the south. Out of season it's hard to connect to the south. In Merihas buy tickets at **Anerousa Travel** (🖉22810 32372; ⊗9am-9pm) or **Larentzakis Travel Agency** (🖉22810 32104; ⊗9am-9pm).

There's a twice-weekly service with Hellenic Seaways (www.hellenicseaways.gr) that connects Kythnos and Syros, with some services continuing on to central Cyclades islands including Paros, Naxos and Ios.

Boat Services from Kythnos

DESTINATION	DURATION	FARE (€)	FREQUENCY
Kea	1hr 20min	11	Mon & Thu
Kimolos	3½-5¼hr	15	Tue & Fri
Lavrio	1¾-2½hr	21	1-2 daily
Milos	4hr-7¾hr	16	Tue, Fri & Sun
Piraeus	3¼hr	29	4-6 weekly
Serifos	1½hr	12	Tue, Fri & Sat
Sifnos	2½hr	13	Mon & Thu
Syros	2½hr	9	Tue & Fri

ℹ Getting Around

In July and August, buses go from Merihas to Dryopida, continuing to Kanala or Hora. Less regular services run to Loutra. There aren't any services outside these months, meaning that the best way to see the island is by car or scooter. Rentals are available at Larentzakis Travel Agency, among others.

Taxis ([📱] 69442 71609) cost about €10 to Hora and €8 to Dryopida. A **sea-taxi** ([📱] 6944906568) to/from the beaches in summer costs about €10 return; this is the easiest option to reach Kolona.

Merihas   Μέριχας

POP 369

Tiny Merihas is home to much of the island's low-season life. Cafes and restaurants line the small harbour, and rooms for let dot its hills. The town beach is uninspiring but good beaches are within walking distance, north of the quay at **Martinakia** and **Episkopi**.

🛏 Sleeping & Eating

★**Kontseta**   APARTMENT €€
([📱] 22810 33024; www.kontseta.gr; d €90-120; ⊗Apr-Oct; ❄🛜) Easily the nicest option in town, these modern studio apartments are a cut above, with fresh decor and fine views. They are high above the ferry quay, with steps signposted next door to the Alpha Bank.

Foinikas Studios   APARTMENT €€
([📱] 22810 32203; d/tr €90/100; ❄🛜) There are no harbour views, but you're well placed (just a few metres from the waterfront) and the studios and apartments are simple and appealing.

Molos   KEBAB €
([📱] 22810 32455; Merihas; mains €2.50-15; ⊗noon-11pm) Quick, delish souvlaki, kebabs and burgers stuffed with cheese from a sweetly unassuming spot just where the ferries dock.

Kantouni   TAVERNA €€
([📱] 22810 32220; mains €8-18; ⊗noon-11pm; 🛜) On the southern bend of the waterfront, Kantouni offers a menu of classic, meat-centric Greek hits in a delightful setting decked in creeping roses. There's also waterside seating.

Ostria   SEAFOOD €€
([📱] 22810 33017; Merihas; mains €8-25; ⊗noon-midnight; 🛜) Ostria is the place for seafood: grilled snapper, scorpion fish, grouper, calamari and lobster spaghetti all get the thumbs-up. Funny how seafood

Kythnos

tastes better when you're seated by moored yachts...

ℹ Information

There is one bank, plus two ATMs in Merihas.
Police Station ([📱] 22810 31201) For emergencies.

Hora (Kythnos)
Χώρα (Κύθνος)

The distinctively charming capital, Hora (also known as Kythnos or Messaria) nestles in the lap of rolling agricultural fields and preserves an inherent Greek character.

The long main street makes for a great stroll through a cute central square to a series of colourful cafes, restaurants, ceramicists and sweet shops. Traditional village lanes are tucked behind here, still populated by grannies hanging out the laundry.

VILLAGE LIFE

Loutra is a low-key resort and fishing village, 3km north of Hora. Sitting on a windy bay, its large marina is full of yachts and its harbourfront lined with high-standard eateries.

Loutra's claim to fame is its **hot springs**. You can access the water for free on the beachfront, where a rockpool marks the entry point of the hot water into the sea, or else visit the nearby **Hydrotherapy Centre** (☑22810 31217; €3.50; ☺Jun-Sep).

Maroula, a short coastal walk north, is the site of ancient Mesolithic graves.

Dryopida, a picturesque town of red-tiled roofs and winding streets clustered steeply on either side of a ravine, is connected to Hora by a footpath. It has a cluster of pretty eateries around the main church.

🛏 Sleeping & Eating

Filoxenia APARTMENT **€€**
(☑22810 31644; www.filoxenia-kythnos.gr; d €70; P⚒☎) Well-priced, fully equipped apartments and studios behind flower-bedecked walls.

Messaria GREEK **€€**
(☑22810 31672; www.messaria.gr; mains €9-17; ☺noon-10pm; ☎) At the entrance to Hora and inside the hotel of the same name, this cellar restaurant specialises in carnivorous delights, such as rooster cooked in wine, lamb *kleftiko* and rabbit stew.

Around Kythnos

Ten minutes' walk north of Merihas lies the pretty sandy cove of **Martinakia**. Half an hour further north is **Episkopi**, a wide swath of grey sand. Reachable via an hour's coastal walk (or via paved road) further northwest is the golden-sand **Apokrousi**, with two tavernas and a beach bar. From Apokrousi, a rutted road leads over the hill to the exquisite double-bay of **Kolona**, a sand spit joining the peninsula to the Aylos Loukas islet, with a high-season cafe above the beach. It's easiest to reach Kolona via sea-taxi from Merihas, or else by ATV or a hot 20-minute walk.

From Dryopida, the main road runs all the way south to **Agios Dimitrios**, a grey-sand beach with placid waters. Of the half-dozen east-coast beaches, mostly reachable by unpaved minor roads, the most accessible (and loveliest) is the sandy cove next to Kanala village.

◉ Sights & Activities

With more than 30 dive sites to choose from, from wrecks and caves to drift dives, Kythnos is a great destination for underwater explorers. **Aqua Team** (☑22810 31333; www.aquakythnos.gr; 1-/2-tank dive €50/90; 👣) arranges a full range of courses, including beginners' scuba for children.

Kastro Orias RUINS
Located on Cape Kefalos, a 90-minute picturesque ramble northwest from Loutra, these beautifully situated ruins are all that remains of a medieval city of around 5000 people.

🛏 Sleeping & Eating

Porto Klaras APARTMENT **€€**
(☑22810 31276; www.porto-klaras.gr; d/q €100/140; ☺Apr-Oct; ⚒☎) Impeccable studios with kitchens have modern baths and tons of amenities; apartments sleep four. Some have balconies with harbour views.

★Archipelagos CYCLADIC **€€**
(☑22810 32380; www.archipelagos-kythnos.com; mains €8-25; ☺noon-10pm; ☎) Come to this friendly, low-key taverna for grilled sardines, scorpion fish, red mullet and other bounty from the sea, as well as Greek salad topped with local cheese, kid and rabbit stew and oven-baked lamb.

KEA (TZIA) KEA (TZIA)

POP 2455

Kea, though naturally beautiful with cliffs, spectacular coastline and fecund hillsides, has been almost overrun by vacation homes. The island closest to Attica, it's just too easy to reach; but this is only evident on summer weekends, and in August. Rent wheels to get off the beaten path and find the island's charms: rocky spires, verdant valleys filled with orchards, olive groves and oak trees, and excellent walking trails.

The main settlements are the port of Korissia and the attractive capital, Ioulida, about 5km inland. Local people call the island Tzia.

❶ Getting There & Away

Kea's only mainland service is to Lavrio; connections to other islands are few. Weekend boats are packed. There are twice-weekly services, on Tuesdays and Fridays, with Hellenic Seaways (www.hellenicseaways.gr) that connect Kea with Kythnos (€7, one hour 20 minutes) and Syros (€11, four hours), Kimolos (€17, 13½ hours), Milos (€14, 14½ hours) and destinations in central Cyclades, such as Paros (€17, 7¼ hours), Naxos (€22, 8½ hours) and Ios (€24, 10½ hours). Tuesday services also stop at Serifos (€16, 8¼ hours) and Sifnos (€17, nine hours). There are one to three daily services to Lavrio (€12, one hour) between mid-June and mid-August; there are fewer services the rest of the year.

Book ahead with the **Stegadi** (☑ 22880 21435; http://praktoreiokeas.gr) ticket agent on the Korissia waterfront for **Marmari Express** (☑ Kea 22880 21435, Lavrio 22920 26200), **Makedon** (☑ Kea 22880 21435, Lavrio 22920 26777) and Hellenic Seaways.

❶ Getting Around

In July and August, regular buses go from Korissia to Vourkari, Otzias, Ioulida and Poisses Beach; fewer services run out of season. **Taxis** (☑ 6932669493, 6932418821) to Ioulida cost around €10, Otzias €8 and Poisses €25.

Leon Rent A Car (☑ 22880 21898; www.rentacarkea.gr; scooters/cars per day from €20/45), on the harbourfront, is the only place in Kea to rent scooters/cars (€25/50). In high season it's worth bringing your own from Athens.

Korissia   Κορησσία

POP 711

The little port of Korissia may not be quite as picturesque as the island's capital, but it makes an excellent base for exploring the island. The north-facing beach tends to catch the wind, but you're about a 15-minute walk from small but popular **Gialiskari Beach**, backed by eucalypts.

🛌 Sleeping

Koralli Studios   APARTMENT €
(☑ 22880 21268; www.kea-rooms.gr; studios from €45; ❄️📶) Run by the helpful Aristoteles, these spotless, well-equipped, bougainvillea-and-jasmine-clad studios are just 150m from the beach. The owner can meet the ferry and goes out of his way to assist his guests.

★ **Red Tractor Farm**   GUESTHOUSE €€
(☑ 22880 21346; www.redtractorfarm.com; Korissia; d €100, studio €140-180; ❄️📶) The outstanding Red Tractor Farm lies inland from

Kea (Tzia)

Korissia harbour, just a stone's throw from the town beach, among serene vineyards and olive groves. Kostis Maroulis and Marcie Mayer operate this sustainable, creative agritourism farm, with beautiful Cycladic buildings combining traditional and modern style and comfort. Rooms, studios and larger cottages are available.

Kostis and Marcie can advise on the best hiking routes; they also produce olive oil, wine, marmalade and chutney, plus unique acorn cookies. During business hours, visitors can stop by the farm to make purchases. The farm is open year-round.

Aegean View   GUESTHOUSE €€
(☑ 22880 22046; www.roomsinkea.gr; d €65-75; ❄️Mar-Dec; ❄️📶) On the harbourfront, just metres from the ferry dock, this guesthouse has a handful of bright, modern rooms and studios with funky bathrooms. Some have small private balconies; all share a lovely communal deck.

🍴 Eating & Drinking

★ **Rolando's**   CYCLADIC €€
(☑ 22880 22224; mains €8-17; ❄️noon-11.30pm; 📶) Ioulida's loss is Korissia's gain. Since moving, Rolando's continues to serve some of Kea's best food, from killer meatballs, *katsiki*

(goat) and moussaka to super-fresh fish and boiled courgettes smothered in garlic.

Magazes MEDITERRANEAN €€
(☑22880 21104; www.kearestaurant.gr; mains €9-17; ⊙noon-11.30pm; 🕿) Run by Greek-Californian Stefanos, Magazes is in a stylishly restored warehouse, producing high-quality local flavours. It's recommended for its fresh seafood, including lobster pasta, which comes from local fishermen, and *raga-salata* (traditional herring salad).

Kea Events CAFE
(☑22880 21841; www.keaevents.gr; ⊙9am-10pm May-Sep; 🕿) If you feel like a change from the beach, this large event complex has a big blue swimming pool open to the public free of charge, provided you buy something from the cafe menu (not hard, given it's loaded with snacks, coffee and beer). Find it 1.5km inland from Korissia (near the Eko petrol station).

❶ Information

Korissia has two banks and one ATM.

Ioulida   Ιουλίδα

POP 633

Ioulida is Kea's gem. Its pretty scramble of narrow alleyways and buildings drapes across two hilltops. Once a substantial settlement of Ancient Greece, it now has a distinctly cosmopolitan feel at weekends.

The bus turnaround is on a square just at the edge of town, from where an archway leads into the labyrinthine village. (Park in the car park below the square.) Beyond the archway, turn right and uphill along Ioulida's main street for its shops and cafes and to reach the famed Kea Lion.

◉ Sights

★**Kea Lion** MONUMENT
The enigmatic Kea Lion, chiselled from slate in the 6th century BC, lies across a small valley beyond the last of Ioulida's houses. The 15-minute walk to reach it is fantastic: follow small wooden signs reading Αρχαίος Λέων from the top of the main street until the path leads you out of town. If you look closely, you'll see the lion across the valley – the surrounding stones are painted white.

The footpath curves past a cemetery, and the lion, with its smooth-worn haunches and Cheshire-cat smile, is reached through a gate on the left. The path continues to Otzias.

Archaeological Museum MUSEUM
(☑22880 22079; adult/child €3/1; ⊙8am-3pm Tue-Sun) Find intriguing artefacts from Kea's four ancient city-states, including some superb terracotta figurines, many from excavations at Agia Irini. Thirteen Minoan-style statues are the museum's pride. It's just before the post office on the main thoroughfare.

🛏 Sleeping & Eating

Hotel Serie HOTEL €€
(☑22880 22355; www.serie.com.gr; d/tr €75/85; ❄🕿) Just a few minutes' walk from labyrinthine Ioulida, this compact hotel offers a cluster of light, brightly painted rooms with hilly views from the balconies.

★**Kea Villas** HOTEL €€€
(☑6972243330; www.keavillas.gr; ste €145-250, villa €700; ⊙Mar–mid-Nov; ❄🕿⛳) Gorgeously situated at the highest point of Ioulida, this complex with sweeping views offers a variety of suites and villas that sleep you and up to nine of your dearest friends in style. All have full kitchen and verandah.

To Spiti Sti Hora CYCLADIC €€€
(☑6972243330; mains €18-27; ⊙noon-3pm & 7-11pm Jun-Sep; 🕿) Elaborate takes on seasonal Kea dishes, with local ingredients put to excellent use. Expect the likes of suckling pig with pear, cuttlefish risotto, grilled meats and awesome sunset views over Ioulida to go with your cocktails. At Kea Villas.

Around Kea

Kea's northern half is more popular with visitors than the southern half.

The beach road from Korissia leads past the appealing **Gialiskari Beach** for 2.5km to tiny **Vourkari**, a favourite with yachties, where the waterfront is lined with sailboats and fashionable cafes.

Four kilometres to the northeast, **Otzias** has a large, sandy beach, though it does get rather windy. From Otzias, a 12km road runs inland to Ioulida, connected to the east coast's finest beach, **Spathi**.

Eight kilometres southwest of Ioulida is the unfortunately named **Pisses** (also spelled Poisses), a small, sandy beach with a taverna and beach bar, backed by orchards, olive groves and rugged hills. Four kilometres south along the coast is **Kondouros**, a playground for moneyed Athenians, with a number of small sandy coves. A little further south, **Kambi** is an inviting swimming spot with a waterfront taverna.

Sights

Karthea
RUINS

Accessible only by boat or walking path (about one hour, one-way) from Kato Meria is the bay of Poles in the southeast, home to the ancient city of Karthea. It's a walk with a spectacular destination: ancient ruins by a remote beach. For route details, buy a good map such as Terrain's *Tzia* map.

Moni Panagias Kastrianis
MONASTERY

(☉ sunrise-sunset Jun-Sep) FREE From Otzias, a spectacular coastal road runs for 6.5km to this clifftop, 18th-century monastery. If you're circling back to Ioulida, the road from here is equally gorgeous, along the crest of hills with valleys plunging to either side.

Activities

Kea has a dozen picturesque walking trails of varying length and difficulty. Check out http://praktoreiokeas.gr for trail descriptions and pick up a Terrain *Tzia* hiking map to hit the trails.

Kea has some of the best diving in Greece, with more than a dozen varied and challenging dive sites that include walls, ship and plane wrecks and underwater caves. Vourkari-based **Kea Divers** (☎ 22880 22280, 6973430860; www.keadivers.com; 1/2 dives incl equipment €50/90) is a reputable scuba-diving outfit that also runs snorkelling trips.

Sleeping & Eating

Camping Kea
CAMPGROUND €

(☎ 22880 31302; campingkea@yahoo.gr; campsite per adult/tent/car €7/7/5, bungalows €55; ☉ May-Sep; P 🐾 🛜) Well-kept Camping Kea, under thick eucalyptus, has a shop and cafe just off Poisses, a wide strip of white sand against a backdrop of greenery-clad hills.

Anemousa Studios
APARTMENT €€

(☎ 22880 21335; www.anemousa.gr; studio/apt from €90/110; ☉ Apr-Oct; ❄ 🛜 ☕) These white-washed, spacious, family-friendly studios and apartments curve around the pool 50m inland from the beach in Otzias.

I Taverna tou Simou
CYCLADIC €

(☎ 22880 24280; mains €6-15; ☉ noon-10pm May-Sep) In this traditional taverna in Kato Merias, proprietor Simos recreates a mix of traditional Kea and family recipes using local ingredients. Signature dishes include rabbit slow-cooked in a clay pot, parchment-wrapped goat, and chicken with homemade pasta.

I Strofi tou Mimi
SEAFOOD €€

(☎ 22880 21480; www.istrofitoumimi.com; mains €12-18; ☉ 7pm-midnight Apr-Oct; 🛜) On the far side of Vourkari Bay, this is one of Kea's most celebrated seafood restaurants. The bay laps at the tables, which are positioned as close to the sea as possible without actually being in the water.

Crete

Best Places to Eat

➔ Thalassino Ageri (p472)

➔ Peskesi (p448)

➔ Taverna Panorama (p466)

➔ Hope (p487)

Best Places to Stay

➔ Enagron Ecotourism Village (p464)

➔ Serenissima (p471)

➔ Villa Olga (p485)

➔ Eleonas Country Village (p455)

➔ Plakias Youth Hostel (p465)

Why Go?

Crete (Κρήτη) is the culmination of the Greek experience. Nature here is as prolific as Picasso in his prime, creating a dramatic quilt of big-shouldered mountains, stunning beaches and undulating hillsides blanketed in olive groves,vineyards and wildflowers. There are deep chiselled gorges,including one of Europe's longest, and crystal-clear lagoons and palm-tree-lined beaches that conjure up the Caribbean.Crete's natural beauty is equalled only by the richness of a history that spans millennia. The Palace of Knossos is but one of many vestiges of the mysterious ancient Minoan civilisation. Venetian fortresses, Turkish mosques and Byzantine churches bring history alive all over Crete, but nowhere more so than in charismatic Hania and Rethymno. Crete's hospitable and spirited people uphold their unique culture, cuisine and customs. Local life and traditions remain a dynamic part of the island's soul

When to Go
Crete (Iraklio)

Jul & Aug High season. Queues at big sights, busy beaches. Hot days, balmy evenings, warm waters.

Apr–Jun & Sep–Oct Moderate temperatures, smaller crowds. Best time for hiking and outdoor activities.

Nov–Mar Low season. Sights and restaurants scale back hours; beach resorts close. Major sights uncrowded.

History

Although inhabited since Neolithic times (7000–3000 BC), Crete is most famous for being the cradle of Europe's first advanced civilisation, the Minoan. Traces of this enigmatic society were only uncovered in the early 20th century, when British archaeologist Sir Arthur Evans discovered the palace at Knossos and named the civilisation after its ruler, the mythical King Minos.

Minoans migrated to Crete in the 3rd millennium BC. Their extraordinary artistic, architectural and cultural achievements culminated in the construction of huge palace complexes at Knossos, Phaestos, Malia and Zakros, which were all levelled by an earthquake around 1700 BC. Undeterred, the Minoans built bigger and better ones over the ruins, while settling more widely across Crete. Around 1450 BC, the palaces were mysteriously destroyed again, possibly by a tsunami triggered by a volcanic eruption on Santorini (Thira). Knossos, the only palace saved, finally burned down around 1400 BC.

Archaeological evidence shows that the Minoans lingered on for a few centuries in small, isolated settlements before disappearing as mysteriously as they had come. They were followed by the Mycenaeans and the Dorians (around 1100 BC). By the 5th century BC, Crete was divided into city-states but did not benefit from the cultural glories of mainland Greece; in fact, it was bypassed by Persian invaders and the Macedonian conqueror Alexander the Great.

By 67 BC Crete had become the Roman province of Cyrenaica, with Gortyna its capital. After the Roman Empire's division in AD 395, Crete fell under the jurisdiction of Greek-speaking Constantinople – the emerging Byzantine Empire. Things went more or less fine until 824, when Arabs appropriated the island. In 961, though, Byzantine general emperor Nikiforas Fokas (912–69) won Crete back following a nine-month siege of Iraklio (then called El Khandak by the Arabs). Crete flourished under Byzantine rule, but with the infamous Fourth Crusade of 1204 the maritime power of Venice received Crete as part of its 'payment' for supplying the Crusaders' fleet.

Much of Crete's most impressive surviving architecture dates from the Venetian period, which lasted until 1669 when Iraklio (then called Candia) became the last domino to fall after a 21-year Ottoman siege. Turkish rule brought new administrative

organisation, Islamic culture and Muslim settlers. Cretan resistance was strongest in the mountain strongholds but all revolts were put down brutally, and it was only with the Ottoman Empire's disintegration in the late 19th century that Europe's great powers expedited Crete's sovereign aspirations.

Thus, in 1898, with Russian and French consent, Crete became a British protectorate. However, the banner under which future Greek Prime Minister Eleftherios Venizelos and other Cretan rebels were fighting was Enosis i Thanatos (Unity or Death) – unity with Greece, not mere independence from Turkey. Yet it would take the Greek army's successes in the Balkan Wars (1912–13) to turn Crete's de facto inclusion in the country into reality, with the 1913 Treaty of Bucharest.

Crete suffered tremendously during WWII, due to being coveted by Adolf Hitler for its strategic location. On 20 May 1941 a huge flock of German parachutists quickly overwhelmed the Cretan defenders. The Battle of Crete, as it would become known, raged for 10 days between German and Allied troops from Britain, Australia, New Zealand and Greece. For two days the battle hung in the balance until the Germans captured the Maleme Airfield, near Hania. The Allied forces fought a valiant rearguard action, enabling the British Navy to evacuate 18,000 of the 32,000 Allied troops. The harsh German occupation lasted throughout WWII, with many mountain villages bombed or burnt down and their occupants executed en masse.

ℹ Getting There & Away

AIR

Most travellers arrive in Crete by air, often with a change in Athens. Travellers from North America need to connect via a European gateway city such as Paris, Amsterdam or Frankfurt and sometimes again in Athens. To reach Crete by air from other Greek islands also requires a change in Athens, except for some flights operated by Crete-based airline Sky Express (p760).

Iraklio's Nikos Kazantzakis International Airport (p449) is Crete's busiest airport, although Hania (p473) is convenient for travellers heading to western Crete. Sitia (p490) only receives a handful of domestic and summertime international charter flights.

Between May and October, European low-cost carriers and charter airlines like easyJet (to Iraklio) and Ryanair (to Hania) operate direct flights to Crete, mostly from the UK, Poland, Sweden and Italy. Ryanair also offers domestic flights to Hania from Athens and Thessaloniki.

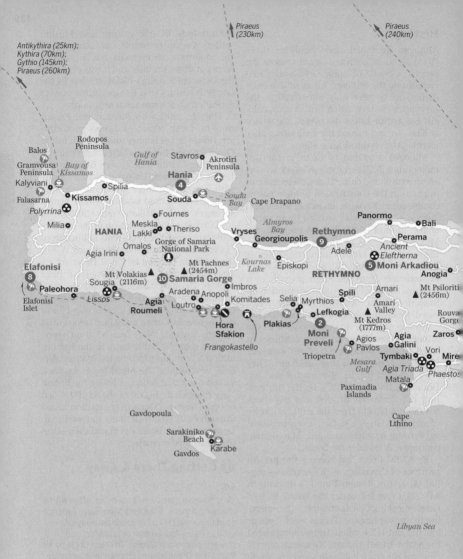

Crete Highlights

① Palace of Knossos (p450) Rubbing shoulders with the ghosts of the Minoans.

② Moni Preveli (p466) Absorbing lofty views from this 17th-century monastery above the magical Preveli Beach.

③ Iraklio Wine Country (p454) Exploring Minoan ruins and sampling the local tipple.

④ Hania (p467) Embarking on a wander around the evocative Venetian quarter.

⑤ Moni Arkadiou (p462) Being moved by the beauty and tragedy of this 16th-century stone church.

Antikythira (25km); Kythira (70km); Gythio (145km); Piraeus (260km)

Piraeus (230km)

Piraeus (240km)

Balos
Gramvousa Peninsula
Kalyviani
Falasarna
Polyrrina
Milia

Rodopos Peninsula
Spilia
Kissamos
Bay of Kissamos

Gulf of Hania
Stavros
Hania ④
Souda
Akrotiri Peninsula
Souda Bay
Cape Drapano

HANIA
Fournes
Meskla
Lakki
Theriso
Agia Irini
Omalos
Gorge of Samaria National Park

Mt Pachnes (2454m)
Mt Volakias (2116m)
Samaria Gorge ⑩
Aradena Anopoli
Sougia
Agia Roumeli
Loutro
Imbros
Komitades
Hora Sfakion
Frangokastello

Elafonisi ⑧
Paleohora
Elafonisi Islet
Lissos

Vryses
Georgioupolis
Almyros Bay
Kournas Lake
Episkopi
Rethymno ⑨
Panormo
Bali
Perama
Ancient Eleftherna
Moni Arkadiou ⑤
Anogia

RETHYMNO
Adele
Spili
Selia
Myrthios
Lefkogia
Plakias
Moni Preveli ②
Triopetra
Agios Pavlos
Amari
Amari Valley
Mt Kedros (1777m)
Mt Psiloriti (2456m)
Agia Galini
Tymbaki
Agia Triada
Matala
Mesara Gulf
Paximadia Islands

Cape Lthino

Rouva Gorge
Zaros
Vori
Mire
Phaestos

Gavdopoula

Sarakiniko Beach
Karabe
Gavdos

Libyan Sea

Sea of
Crete

Santorini
(70km)

N   0 ──────────────── 50 km
    0 ──────────── 25 miles

Dia

Kasos (55km);
Karpathos (100km);
Halki (185km);
Rhodes (250km)

Cape
Stavros

Iraklio
Bay

Cape Sideros

Fodele

Gournes

Hersonisos

Plaka

Cape Agios
Ioannis

6 **Spinalonga Island**

Mon
Toplou

Vaï

ylisos

Iraklio

1

Skalani

**Palace
of Malia**

Elounda

Kolokytha Peninsula

**Palace
of Knossos**

Malia

Gulf of
Mirabello

Myrtia

Tzermiado

**Agios
Nikolaos**

Arhanes

3

Peza

**Iraklio Wine
Country**

Alagni

**Lasithi
Plateau**

Neapoli

Psyhro

7

**Agios
Georgios**

Lato

Kri-Kri

Mohlos

Sitia

Palekastro

Dikteon Cave

Kritsa

Istron

LASITHI

Agia
Varvara

IRAKLIO

Arkalokhorion

▲ Mt Dikti
(2148m)

Zakros

Ziros

Kato
Zakros

Gortyna

Ano Viannos

Kalamafka

Gournia

Xerokampos

Pyrgos

Anatoli

Ierapetra

Koutsouras

endas

Arvi

Myrtos

Koufonisi

Gaïdouronisi
(Hrysi)

BOAT

Crete is well served by ferry with at least one daily departure from Piraeus (near Athens) to Iraklio and Hania year-round and several per day in summer. There are also ports in Sita in the east and Kissamos in the west, which have slow-ferry routes. Services are considerably curtailed from November to April. Timetables change from season to season, and ferries are subject to delays and cancellations at short notice due to bad weather, strikes or mechanical problems.

Getting Around

BUS

Buses are the only form of public transport in Crete, but in most regions a fairly extensive network makes it relatively easy to travel around the island. Fares are government regulated and quite reasonable by European standards. For the latest timetable, check www.bus-service-crete-ktel.com for western Crete and www.ktelherlas.gr for central and eastern Crete.

BOAT SERVICES FROM CRETE

Schedules and fares change all the time, so the following is merely a guideline of what to expect during the peak summer months. Fares listed are for the cheapest option (usually a deck chair). For current routes and timetables, consult the ferry company's website or go to www.gtp.gr, www.openseas.gr, www.ferries.gr and www.greekferries.gr.

ROUTE	COMPANY	FARE (FROM €)	DURATION (HOURS)	FREQUENCY
Hania-Piraeus	Anek	38	9	daily
Iraklio-Halki	Anek	22	12	2 weekly
Iraklio-Ios	Hellenic Seaways	70	2½	daily
Iraklio-Ios	Sea Jets	70	2½	daily
Iraklio-Karpathos	Anek	19	8	2 weekly
Iraklio-Kasos	Anek	20	6	2 weekly
Iraklio-Milos	Anek	23	11	weekly
Iraklio-Mykonos	Hellenic Seaways	84.50	4½	daily
Iraklio-Mykonos	Sea Jets	84.30	4½	daily
Iraklio-Paros	Hellenic Seaways	74.50	3¾	daily
Iraklio-Naxos	Sea Jets	77.80	3½	daily
Iraklio-Piraeus	Minoan	46	8½	daily
Iraklio-Piraeus	Anek (Bluestar)	38	9	daily
Iraklio-Rhodes	Anek	29	14½	2 weekly
Iraklio-Santorini (Thira)	Anek	28	4¼	2 weekly
Iraklio-Santorini (Thira)	Sea Jets	68.80	2	daily
Iraklio-Santorini (Thira)	Hellenic Seaways	69	1¾	daily
Iraklio-Sitia	Anek	16	3	2 weekly
Kissamos-Antikythira	Lane	11	2¼	2 weekly
Kissamos-Gythion	Lane	27	8	weekly
Kissamos-Kythira	Lane	18	5	4 weekly
Kissamos-Piraeus	Lane	28	13	2 weekly
Sitia-Iraklio	Anek	16	3	2 weekly
Sitia-Karpathos	Anek	19	4½	2 weekly
Sitia-Kassos	Anek	12	2¾	2 weekly
Sitia-Milos	Anek	26	15	weekly
Sitia-Piraeus	Anek	44	18	weekly
Sitia-Rhodes	Anek	28	11¼	2 weekly
Sitia-Santorini (Thira)	Anek	28	8	weekly

CAR

Having your own wheels is a great way to explore Crete if you can brave the roads and drivers. Although distances are often not that great, travelling on narrow and winding mountain roads will seriously slow you down, so factor that into your day's itinerary. In remote areas (particularly the south), you'll still find unpaved roads that are only suitable for 4WDs.

CENTRAL CRETE

Central Crete comprises the Iraklio prefecture, named after the island's booming capital, and the Rethymno prefecture, named after its lovely Venetian port town. Along with its dynamic urban life and Venetian remnants, the region is home to the island's top-rated tourist attraction, the Palace of Knossos, as well as other major and minor Minoan sites.

Even if the coastal stretch east of the city of Iraklio is one continuous band of hotels and resorts, just a little bit inland villages sweetly lost in time provide a pleasing contrast. Taste the increasingly sophisticated tipple produced in the Iraklio Wine Country, walk in the footsteps of Nikos Kazantzakis and revel in the rustic grandeur of the mountain village of Zaros.

Rethymno is a fascinating quilt of bubbly resorts, centuries-old villages and energising towns. Away from the northern coast, you'll quickly find yourself immersed in endless tranquillity and natural beauty as you drift through such villages as Anogia, where locals cherish their timeless traditions and their music. The southern coast is a different animal altogether – a wild beauty with steep gorges and bewitching beaches in seductive isolation, along with the relaxed resort of Plakias and the old hippie cave and beach hang-out of Matala.

Iraklio Ηράκλειο

POP 140,730

Crete's capital city, Iraklio (also called Heraklion), is Greece's fifth-largest city and the island's economic and administrative hub. It's also home to Crete's blockbuster sights: the must-see Heraklion Archaeological Museum and the nearby Palace of Knossos, which both provide fascinating windows into Crete's ancient past.

Though not pretty in a conventional way, Iraklio can grow on you if you take the time to explore its layers and wander its back-

streets. You'll discover a low-key urban sophistication with a thriving cafe and restaurant scene, good shopping and bustling nightlife. A revitalised waterfront invites strolling and the newly pedestrianised historic centre is punctuated by bustling squares flanked by buildings from the time when Christopher Columbus first set sail.

◉ Sights

★ Heraklion Archaeological Museum MUSEUM

(✆2810 279000; http://odysseus.culture.gr; Xanthoudidou 2; adult/concession/child €10/5/ free; ⊙8am-8pm daily Apr-Oct, 11am-5pm Mon, 8am-3pm Tue-Sun Nov-Mar) This state-of-the-art museum is one of the largest and most important in Greece. The two-storey revamped 1930s Bauhaus building makes a gleaming showcase for artefacts spanning 5500 years from Neolithic to Roman times, including a Minoan collection of unparalleled richness. The rooms are colour coded and displays are arranged both chronologically and thematically, and presented with descriptions in English. A visit here will greatly enhance your understanding of Crete's rich history. Don't skip it.

The museum's treasure trove includes pottery, jewellery, sarcophagi, plus famous frescoes from the sites of Knossos, Tylissos, Amnissos and Agia Triada. The pieces are grouped into comprehensive themes such as settlements, trade, death, religion and administration. Along with clear descriptions, these bring to life both the day-to-day functioning and long-term progression of societies on Crete and beyond. Budget at least two hours for this extraordinary collection, if necessary taking a break in the on-site cafe.

➡ Ground Floor

Rooms I to III focus on the Neolithic period to the Middle Bronze Age (7000 BC to 1700 BC), showing life in the first settlements in Crete and around Knossos. In Room II don't miss the golden pendant with bees from Malia, a sophisticated jeweller's masterpiece, and the extensive jewellery collection. The undisputed eye-catcher in Room III is the elaborately embellished Kamares tableware of red, black and white clay, including a 'royal dinner service' from Phaestos.

Rooms IV to VI illustrate life in the Late Bronze Age (1700 BC to 1450 BC). This is when Minoan culture reached its zenith, as reflected in the foundation of new palaces,

Iraklio

Sea of Crete

Old Harbour

Sofokli Venizelou

17 ✕

Plateia
18 Anglon

Mitsotaki

22

Theotokopoulou

Lahana

Vyronos

Epimenidou

9

4

Chortaki

P

12

25 Avgoustou

Almyrou

25

13

Koroneou

Koroneou

18 ✕

14 Kalimeraki

Grevenon

Paleologou

Arkoleondos

19

El Greco
Park

Plateia
Agiou
Titou

3

Agiou Titou

Hortatson

23

1878

Handakos

21

Agiostefaniton

Milatou

Idaiou Antrou

Psaromiligkon

Plateia
Venizelou

5

6

Perdikari

Korai

24

20

15 ✕

Dedalou

Station B
(750m)

Kalokerinou

Monis Odigitrias

Dikeosynis

8

7

Katehaki

1821

16 ✕

Odos 1866

Evans

Koziri

Zografou

Agiou Mina

Grave of Nikos
Kazantzakis
(900m)

P

elaborate architecture and prolific trading practices. Not surprisingly, these are among the most visited rooms and the collection is vast. Highlights include the small clay house from Arhanes, a stunning ivory-and-crystal inlaid draughts board and a scale model of Knossos. Most home in on the Phaistos disc, a stunning clay piece embossed with 45 signs, which has never been deciphered. Nearby, the massive copper ingots from Agia Triada and Zakros Palace demonstrate important units of economic exchange. Other gems include the bull-leaping fresco and incredible bull-leaper sculpture (Room VI) that show daring sporting practices of the time.

Rooms VII and **VIII** reveal the importance of Minoan religion and ideology with cult objects and figurines. Room VII houses the Chieftain's cup from Agia Triada that portrays two men, one holding a staff, the other a sword. In Room VIII, the snake goddesses and stone bull's head (inlaid with seashell and crystal) are two stunning ceremonial items from Knossos.

Rooms IX and **X** are dedicated to the palace of Knossos and its emergence as a centralised state (after the administrative collapse of other palaces) along with evidence of the Mycenaeans. Linear B clay tablets reveal the first 'Greek' script and indicate Knossos' complex administrative system and bureaucratic processes. In Room X, look for the extraordinary boar's helmet and gold-handled swords, displaying the importance of the aristocratic warrior status.

Rooms XI and **XII** highlight settlements, sanctuaries and graves of the Late Bronze Age, including fascinating visual representations of death. The extraordinary sarcophagus from Agia Triada (Room XII) is presumed to be that of a ruler, given its detailed, honorific fresco-style scenes.

➡ **1st Floor**

Room XIII showcases Minoan frescoes (1800 BC to 1350 BC), including Evans' famous (or infamous) recreations. The paintings reflect the interest in art and nature at the time. All are highlights, but for your at-a-glance reference, it's home to the Prince of the Lilies, the Ladies in Blue, the Cupbearer, La Parisienne and the Dolphin Fresco.

Rooms XV to **XIX** focus on the Geometric and Archaic periods (10th to 6th century BC), the transition to the Iron Age and formation of the first Greek cities. The Apollonian Triad, bronze statues from Deros, are the earliest known Greek hammered bronze statues,

CRETE IRAKLIO

Iraklio

while the bronze shields of the Ideon Cave are extravagant votive offerings to Zeus.

Rooms XX to XXII move to the Classical, Hellenistic and Roman periods (5th to 4th century BC), where utensils figurines and stunning mosaic floors and amphorae set the scene for the foundation of the autonomous Greek city-states, followed by civil wars and, finally, the Roman period. The huge Phalagari hoard of silver coins (Room XXI) is thought to be a military state fund. The cemetery finds of these periods are especially fascinating: look out for the skull with the gold wreath (Room XXII).

Room XXIII exhibits two private collections donated to the museum.

➡ **Ground Floor – Part II**
Rooms XXVI and **XXVII** (7th to 4th century BC), on the ground floor, house the museum's sculpture collection. Architectural reliefs from Gortyna exhibit the role of Crete in the development of monumental sculpture, while Roman sculptures and copies of heroes and Gods of the preceding Classical era highlight the type of art during the Roman period.

★ **Koules Fortress**   FORTRESS
(Rocca al Mare; ☎ 2810 288484; http://koules. efah.gr; Venetian Harbour; adult/concession €2/1; ☺ 8am-8pm Apr-Oct, to 3pm Nov-Mar) After six years of restoration, Iraklio's symbol, the 16th-century fortress called Rocca al Mare by the Venetians, reopened in August 2016 with a brand-new exhibit. It tells the story of the building, zeroes in on milestones in city history and displays ancient amphorae, Vene-

tian cannons and other finds recovered from shipwrecks around Dia island by Jacques Cousteau in 1976. The presentation is insightful and atmospheric thanks to muted light filtering in through the old cannon holes.

Visits conclude on the rooftop with panoramic views over the sea and the city.

Historical Museum of Crete   MUSEUM
(☎ 2810 283219; www.historical-museum.gr; Sofokli Venizelou 27; adult/student/child under 12yr €5/3/free; ☺ 9am-5pm Mon-Sat Apr-Oct, to 3.30pm Mon-Sat Nov-Mar) If you're wondering what Crete's been up to for the past, say, 1700 years, a spin around this engagingly curated museum is in order. Exhibits hopscotch from the Byzantine to the Venetian and Turkish periods, culminating with WWII. Quality English labelling, interactive stations throughout and an audio guide (€3) greatly enhance the experience.

The Venetian era gets special emphasis and even a huge model of the city circa 1650 prior to the Turkish occupation. Start in the introductory room, which charts the major phases of history through maps, books, artefacts and images. First-floor highlights include the only two El Greco paintings in Crete, 13th- and 14th-century frescoes, exquisite Venetian gold jewellery and embroidered vestments. A historical exhibit charts Crete's road to independence from the Turks in the early 20th century. The most interesting rooms on the 2nd floor are the recreated study of Cretan-born author Nikos Kazantzakis and those dramatically detailing aspects of the WWII Battle of Crete in 1941, including the Cretan resistance and the role of the Allied Secret Service. The top floor features an outstanding folklore collection.

Morosini Fountain
FOUNTAIN

(Lion Fountain; Plateia Venizelou) Unfortunately, water no longer spurts from the four lions that make up this charming fountain, which is the most beloved Venetian vestige around town. Built in 1628 by Francesco Morosini, it once supplied Iraklio with fresh water. Flanked by bustling cafes and fast-food joints, it's a fun spot to spend an hour resting and people-watching.

Municipal Art Gallery
GALLERY

(☑ 2810 3992089; 25 Avgoustou & Plateia Venizelou; ⊘ 9am-2pm & 5-8pm) FREE The three-aisled 13th-century Agios Markos Basilica was reconstructed many times and turned into a mosque by the Turks. Today it's an exhibit space showcasing Greek and foreign artists.

Church of Agios Titos
CHURCH

(☑ 2810 346079; Plateia Agiou Titou; ⊘ usually 7.30am-8pm) This majestic church dominates the eponymous, palm-studded square. It had Byzantine origins in AD 961, was converted to a Catholic church by the Venetians and turned into a mosque by the Ottomans, who used the bell tower as a minaret. It has been an Orthodox church since 1925. Since 1966, its most revered possession is once again the skull relic of St Titus, returned here after being spirited to Venice for safe-keeping during the Turkish occupation.

🏖 Beaches

Ammoudara, about 4km west of Iraklio, and **Amnisos**, 2km east, are the closest beaches to town; the latter is just past the airport and gets quite a bit of noise. The strands in **Agia Pelagia**, some 20km west of town, are nicer.

🏃 Activities

Mountaineering Club of Iraklio
HIKING

(☑ 2810 227609; www.eos-her.gr; Dikeosynis 53; ⊘ 8.30-10.30pm Mon-Fri) The local chapter arranges hiking trips across the island most weekends (trip programs are published on its website). Anyone is welcome to join.

Cretan Adventures
OUTDOORS

(☑ 2810 332772; www.cretanadventures.gr; 3rd fl, Evans 10; ⊘ 9am-5pm Mon-Fri) 🖉 This well-regarded local company run by friendly and knowledgeable English-speaking Fondas

organises hiking tours, mountain biking and extreme outdoor excursions. It also coordinates fabulous week-long self-guided hiking tours including detailed hiking instructions, accommodation with breakfast and luggage transfer from €740. Fondas' office is up on the 3rd floor and easy to miss.

🛏 Sleeping

Rea Hotel
HOTEL €

(☑ 2810 223638; www.hotelrea.gr; Kalimeraki 1; d €43-68; ⊘ Mar-Nov; ❄️🔌) Family-run Rea has an easy, friendly atmosphere with 16 compact but neat-as-a-pin rooms dressed in shades from vanilla to chocolate. There's a book exchange and a communal fridge. Optional continental breakfast costs €3.

Hotel Mirabello
HOTEL €

(☑ 2810 285052; www.mirabello-hotel.gr; Theotokopoulou 20; d €50-55; ❄️@🔌) Despite its dated Plain-Jane looks, this friendly and low-key hotel offers excellent value for money. Assets include squeaky-clean rooms with modern bathrooms, beds with individual reading lamps, a fridge and kettle plus a location close to, well, everything. The nicest units have a balcony.

Capsis Astoria
HOTEL €€

(☑ 2810 343080; www.capsishotel.gr; Plateia Eleftherias 11; r incl breakfast €100-140; 🅿️❄️@🔌) Not of the latest vintage, but with a handy location next to the Archaeological Museum and the bus stop to Knossos, this hulking city hotel has compact rooms decked out in neutral tones and accented with historic black-and-white photographs. The cheapest have windows but no views, the nicest private balconies. In summer, the rooftop pool is a big selling point.

Kastro Hotel
HOTEL €€

(☑ 2810 284185; www.kastro-hotel.gr; Theotokopoulou 22; d incl breakfast €65-100; ❄️🔌) Clearly plenty of thought has gone into the design of the smartly renovated Kastro, even though not all choices may be equally eye-pleasing (floral wallpaper meets faux-leather headboard). Still, good-quality mattresses, strong hot showers, a good breakfast buffet and the rooftop terrace are all welcome aspects of this central city hotel.

Atrion Hotel
HOTEL €€€

(☑ 2810 246000; www.atrion.gr; Chronaki 9; d incl breakfast €80-130; ❄️🔌) Although this modern, streamlined 60-room hotel was designed with the business brigade in mind, it's also a handy launch pad for city explorers. The carpeted rooms in shades of white and cinnamon come with a balcony (ask for a sea-facing one) and squeaky clean bathrooms. Breakfast is served in the light-filled central atrium.

GDM Megaron HOTEL €€€
(📞 2810 305300; www.gdmmegaron.gr; Doukos Beaufort 9; d incl breakfast €130-190; 🅿 @ 🛜 🎱) Built as a residence for Iraklio's power players in the 1930s, this hulking harbour-front landmark became a hotel in 2003. It sports all the expected mod cons of a traditional five-star property, including luxury mattresses, fine bath amenities and blackout drapes. Unwinding stations include a gym, a glass-sided pool and a panoramic rooftop restaurant and bar.

✖ Eating

Fyllo...Sofies CAFE €
(📞 2810 284774; www.fillosofies.gr; Plateia Venizelou 33; snacks €2.70-8.50; ⏰ 6am-late; 🛜) With tables sprawling out towards the Morosini Fountain, this is a great place to sample *bougatsa* (creamy semolina pudding wrapped in a pastry envelope and sprinkled with cinnamon and sugar). The less-sweet version is made with *myzithra* (sheep's-milk cheese).

They're traditionally eaten for breakfast but, quite frankly, taste good any time of day. If you can't decide whether to go sweet or savoury, ask for a combination of the two.

★ Peskesi CRETAN €€
(📞 2810 288887; www.peskesicrete.gr; Kapetan Haralampi 6-8; mains €8-13; ⏰ 10am-2am; 🛜 🍴) This foodie hotspot oozes rustic sophis-

---

DON'T MISS

IRAKLIO MARKET

An Iraklio institution, if slightly touristy these days, this busy narrow market along Odos 1866 (1866 St) is one of the best in Crete and has everything you need to put together a delicious picnic. Stock up on the freshest fruit and vegetables, creamy cheeses, honey, succulent olives, fresh breads and whatever else grabs your fancy. There are also plenty of other stalls selling pungent herbs, leather goods, hats, jewellery and some souvenirs. Cap off a spree with a coffee at one of the quaint *kafeneia* (coffee houses).

---

tication from every nook and cranny of its maze of stone rooms lidded by woodbeam ceilings. Chefs use heirloom produce and organic meats from their own farm to revive ancient recipes in progressive ways. Killer dish: *kreokakavos*, a Minoan roast pork. The all-Cretan wine list is tops and the complimentary appetiser and dessert a nice touch.

It's located in a tiny lane off the northwest corner of El Greco Park. Worth reserving ahead if busy.

★ Parasties GREEK €€
(📞 2810 225009; www.parasties.gr; Historical Museum Sq, Sofokli Venizelou 19; mains €7-24; ⏰ noon-midnight) Parasties' owner Haris is Iraklio's answer to a restaurateur who is genuine about serving great-quality local produce and top Cretan wines. And his passion shows in his small but gourmet menu of inventively updated traditional fare, including several daily specials, all prepared by a fleet of cooks in the open kitchen.

Decor is stylish and you can eat al fresco or indoors and watch the chef toss her snails and other delights in the open kitchen.

Giakoumis TAVERNA €€
(📞 2810 284039; Theodosaki 5-8; mains €6-13; ⏰ 7am-11pm) The oldest among the row of tavernas vying for business in a quiet passageway off Odos 1866, Giakoumis offers myriad *mayirefta* (ready-cooked meals) and grills. Don't go past the lamb chops; the cook has been grilling them for over 40 years and has perfected the seasoning and method. Giannis the owner says, 'Local servings for everyone!' In other words, generous.

Ippokambos SEAFOOD €€
(Sofokli Venizelou 3; mains €6-13; ⏰ noon-late Mon-Sat; 🛜 🚼) This long-running *ouzerie* (place that serves ouzo and light snacks) specialises in fish – freshly caught, simply but expertly prepared and sold at fair prices. In summer, park yourself on the covered waterfront terrace.

🍸 Drinking & Nightlife

Hipsters congregate around Korai and Perdikari while El Greco Park has a more mainstream feel. West of here, Handakos, Agiostefaniton and Psaromiligkon are more alternative-flavoured hang-outs. Nearby, there's a lively local cafe scene in the tiny lanes of Zampeliou and Kagiampi.

Utopia
CAFE

(☑2810 341321, 6936341321; www.facebook.com/
OutopiaCafeBeerOutopia; Handakos 51; ⊘9am-
2am) The Aztecs called it the 'elixir of the
gods' and if you too worship at the cocoa
altar, make a beeline for this been-here-
forever cafe for the best hot chocolate in
town. Add a side of decadence with an order
of ice cream or delectable pastry or skip the
sweet stuff altogether and order from the
extensive craft beer menu.

Mare Cafe
CAFE, BAR

(☑2810 241946; Sofokli Venizelou; ⊘9am-late;
☎) In an enviable location on the beautified
waterfront promenade opposite the Historical Museum, contempo Mare is great for
post-culture java and sunset drinks. If you've
got the munchies, there's an extensive menu
of burgers, salads, pasta and other staples to
choose from.

Jailhouse Bar
BAR

(☑6978090547; Agiostefaniton 19a; ⊘5pm-4am)
Rock, metal, punk and country, from
Johnny Cash to Johnny Rotten, is the ammo
at this dimly lit pub in a barrel-vaulted
Venetian-era building. Has a good selection
of beers.

Bar Blow-Up
BAR

(http://barblowup.blogspot.de; Psaromiligkon 1;
⊘1.30pm-late; ☎) This alt-flavoured lair
draws unpretentious types for beer, beats
and bands. There's an alchemy of electro,
funk and new wave on the turntable and the
occasional indie band on stage.

🛍 Shopping

Roadside Travel
BOOKS

(☑2810 344610; 25 Avgoustou 48; ⊘9am-9pm
Mon-Sat) This travel specialist bookshop has
an impressive selection of guidebooks and
maps plus good publications on Crete and
its ancient sites.

Aerakis Music
MUSIC

(www.aerakis.net; Koraï Sq 14; ⊘9am-9pm Mon-Fri,
to 5pm Sat) An Iraklio landmark since 1974,
this little shop stocks an expertly curated
selection of Cretan and Greek music, from
old and rare recordings to the latest releases,
many on its own record labels, Cretan Musical Workshop and Seistron.

There's also a small selection of musical
instruments, books and Cretan products
such as knives and woven bags. All can also
be ordered online.

ℹ Information

Banks with ATMs are plentiful, especially along
25 Avgoustou.

Main Post Office (☑2810 289994; www.elta.gr;
Plateia Daskalogianni; ⊘7.30am-8.30pm Mon-Fri)

Paleologos (☑2810 346185; www.paleologos.
gr; 25 Avgoustou 5; ⊘9am-8.30pm Mon-Fri,
to 4pm Sat) Useful full-service travel agent for
ferries, flights, car rentals, accommodation and
excursions. Also a shipping agency.

Tourist Police (☑2810 283190, emergency
171; Dikeosynis 10; ⊘7am-10pm) In the Halikar-
nassos suburb near the airport.

ℹ Getting There & Away

AIR

About 5km east of Iraklio, **Nikos Kazantzakis
International Airport** (HER; ☑general 2810
397800, info 2810 397136; www.heraklion-airport.
info) has an ATM, a duty-free shop and a cafe-bar.

BOAT

The ferry port is 500m to the east of the Koules
Fortress and old harbour, and the bus terminal is
right outside the port entrance. Iraklio is a major
port for access to many of the islands, though
services are spotty outside high season. Tickets
can be purchased online or through local travel
agencies, including central Paleologos. Daily
ferries from Iraklio's port include services to
Piraeus and faster catamarans to Santorini and
other Cycladic islands. Ferries sail east to Rhodes via Sitia, Kasos, Karpathos and Halki.

BUS

Iraklio has two major long-distance bus stations.
For details on services, see www.ktelherlas.gr.
Buses are wi-fi equipped.

Iraklio Bus Station A (Central Station; ☑2810
246530; Leoforos Nearchou; ☎) Near the
waterfront east of Koules Fortress, this depot
serves major destinations in eastern and
western Crete, including Hania, Rethymno,
Agios Nikolaos, Sitia and the Lassithi Plateau.
City bus 2 to Knossos leaves from the adjacent
local bus station.

Iraklio Bus Station B (Chanioporta Station;
☑2810 255965; Machis Kritis 3; ☎) Just
beyond Hania Gate, west of the centre, this
station serves Anogia, Phaestos, Agia Galini,
Gortyn, Zaros and Matala.

LONG-DISTANCE TAXI

For destinations around Crete, you can order a
cab from **Crete Taxi Services** (☑6970021970;
www.crete-taxi.gr; ⊘24hr) or **Heraklion Taxi**
(www.heraklion-taxi.com). There are also
long-distance cabs waiting at the airport, at
Plateia Eleftherias (outside the Capsis Astoria
hotel) and at Bus Station A. Sample fares for

up to four people include Agios Nikolaos (€85), Hersonisos (€39), Malia (€50), Matala (€101) and Rethymno (€108).

❶ Getting Around

TO/FROM THE AIRPORT

The airport is just off the E75 motorway, about 5km east of the city centre. City bus 10 connects it with the city centre, including the port, bus stations A and B and Plateia Eleftherias, every few minutes. The bus stop is to the left as you exit the terminal.

Taxis wait outside the departures terminal with official fares posted. The fare into town is about €11.

CAR & MOTORCYCLE

Iraklio's streets are narrow and chaotic so it's best to drop your vehicle in a car park (about €6 per day) and explore on foot.

All the international car-hire companies have branches at the airport. Local outlets line the northern end of 25 Avgoustou and include **Caravel** (☑ 2810 300150; www.caravel.gr; 25 Avgoustou 39; car per day from €42; ☺8am-11pm), **Motor Club** (☑ 2810 222408; www.motorclub. gr; Plateia 18 Anglon 1; per day/week car from €34/145, scooters from €30/175; ☺7am-10pm) and **Sun Rise** (☑ 2810 221609, 6981761340; www.sunrise-cars.com; 25 Avgoustou 46; per day car from €40; ☺8am-9pm).

TAXI

There are small taxi stands all over town but the main ones are at Bus Station A, on Plateia Eleftherias and at the northern end of 25 Avgoustou. You can also phone for one on ☑ 2814 003084.

Around Iraklio

Knossos   Κνωσσός

★ **Palace of Knossos**   ARCHAEOLOGICAL SITE
(☑ 2810 231940; http://odysseus.culture.gr; Knossos; adult/concession €15/8, incl Heraklion Archaeological Museum €16/8; ☺8am-8pm Apr-Oct, to 5pm Nov-Mar; P; ⊒2) Crete's most famous historical attraction is the Palace of Knossos, the grand capital of Minoan Crete, located 5km south of Iraklio. The setting is evocative and the ruins and recreations impressive, incorporating an immense palace, courtyards, private apartments, baths, lively frescoes and more. Excavation of the site started in 1878 with Cretan archaeologist Minos Kalokerinos, and continued from 1900 to 1930 with British archaeologist Sir Arthur Evans, who controversially restored parts of the site.

Evans' reconstructions bring to life the palace's most significant parts, including the columns, which are painted deep brown-red

---

MINOAN PALACES

In addition to the great Palace of Knossos, the Minoans left other remarkable sites:

Phaestos (☑ 28920 42315; http://odysseus.culture.gr; Iraklio-Phaestos Rd; adult/concession/under 18yr €8/4/free; ☺8am-8pm Apr-Oct, 8am-3pm Nov-Mar; P) Phaestos was the second-most important Minoan palace-city after Knossos and enjoys an awe-inspiring setting with panoramic views of the Messara Plain and Mt Psiloritis. Like Knossos, Phaestos (fes-tos) was built atop a previously destroyed older palace and laid out around a central court. In contrast to its bigger cousin, though, this site had fewer frescoes as walls were likely covered with white gypsum. Good English panelling and graphics stationed in key spots help demystify the ruins.

Agia Triada (☑ 28920 91564; www.interkriti.org; off Phaestos-Matala Rd; adult/concession/under 18yr €4/2/free; ☺9am-4pm; P) In an enchanting spot 3km west of Phaestos, Agia Triada encompasses vestiges of an L-shaped royal villa, a ramp once leading out to sea and a village with residences and stores. Built around 1550 BC, Agia Triada succumbed to fire around 1400 BC but was never looted. This accounts for the many Minoan masterpieces found here, most famously the Agia Triada Sarcophagus, now a star exhibit at the Heraklion Archaeological Museum.

Palace of Malia (☑ 28970 31597; adult/concession/child €6/3/free; ☺8.30am-3pm; P) The Palace of Malia, 3km east of Malia, was built at about the same time as the great Minoan palaces of Phaestos and Knossos. The First Palace dates back to around 1900 BC and was rebuilt after the earthquake of 1700 BC, only to be levelled again by another temble around 1450 BC. Most of what you see today are the remains of the Second Palace where many exquisite Minoan artefacts, including the famous gold bee pendant, were found. Buses from Iraklio stop on the main road, 250m from the site.

Palace of Knossos

with gold-trimmed black capitals and taper gracefully at the bottom. Vibrant frescoes add dramatic flourishes. The advanced drainage system and a clever floor plan that kept rooms cool in summer and warm in winter are further evidence of Minoan high standards.

There is no prescribed route to explore the palace, but the following tour takes in all the key highlights. Entering from the **West Court**, which may have been a marketplace or the site of public gatherings, you'll note a trio of circular pits on your left. Called **kouloures**, they were used for grain storage. From here, continue counterclockwise, starting with a walk along the **Processional Walkway** that leads to the **South Propylaion**, where you can admire the **Cup Bearer Fresco**. From here, a staircase leads past giant storage jars to an upper floor that Evans called **Piano Nobile** because it reminded him of Italian Renaissance palazzi and where he supposed the reception and staterooms were located. On your left, you can see the **west magazines** (storage rooms), or storage rooms, where giant *pithoi* (clay jars) once held oil, wine and other staples.

The restored room at the northern end of the Piano Nobile houses the **Fresco Gallery**, with replicas of Knossos' most famous frescoes, including the Bull-Leaper, the Ladies in Blue and the Blue Bird. The originals are now in the Heraklion Archaeological Museum. From the balcony, a great view unfolds of the **Central Court**, which was hemmed in by high walls during Minoan times. Rooms facing the western side of the courtyard had official and religious purposes, while the residential quarters were on the opposite side.

Follow the stairs down to the courtyard and then turn left to peek inside the beautifully proportioned **Throne Room**, with its simple, alabaster seat and walls decorated with frescoes of griffins, mythical beasts regarded as sacred by the Minoans. To the right of the stairs is a three-sectioned room that Evans called **Tripartite Shrine**. Areas behind it yielded many precious finds, including the famous Snake Goddess statue.

Crossing the central court takes you to the east wing where the **Grand Staircase** drops down to the royal apartments. Get there via the ramp off the southeast corner but not without first popping by the south entrance to admire a replica of the **Prince of the Lilies fresco**. Down below you can peek inside the **Queen's Megaron** (bedroom) with a copy of the Dolphin Fresco, one of the most exquisite Minoan artworks. The small adjacent chamber (behind plexiglass) may have

Palace of Knossos

THE HIGHLIGHTS IN TWO HOURS

The Palace of Knossos is Crete's busiest tourist attraction, and for good reason. A spin around the partially and imaginatively reconstructed complex (shown here as it was thought to be at its peak) delivers an eye-opening glimpse into the remarkably sophisticated society of the Minoans, who dominated southern Europe some 4000 years ago.

From the ticket booth, follow the marked trail to the ❶ **North Entrance** where the Charging Bull fresco gives you a first taste of Minoan artistry. Continue to the Central Court and join the queue waiting to glimpse the mystical ❷ **Throne Room**, which probably hosted religious rituals. Turn right as you exit and follow the stairs up to the so-called Piano Nobile, where replicas of the palace's most famous artworks conveniently cluster in the ❸ **Fresco Room**. Walk the length of the Piano Nobile, pausing to look at the clay storage vessels in the West Magazine. Circle back and descend to the ❹ **South Portico**, beautifully decorated with the Cup Bearer fresco. Make your way back to the Central Court and head to the palace's eastern wing to admire the architecture of the ❺ **Grand Staircase** that led to what Sir Arthur Evans imagined to be the royal family's private quarters. For a closer look at some rooms, walk to the south end of the courtyard, stopping for a peek at the ❻ **Prince of the Lilies Fresco**, and head down to the lower floor. A highlight here is the ❼ **Queen's Megaron** (Evans imagined this was the Queen's chambers), playfully adorned with a fresco of frolicking dolphins. Stay on the lower level and make your way to the ❽ **Giant Pithoi**, huge clay jars used for storage.

JOHN COPLAND/SHUTTERSTOCK ©

South Portico
Fine frescoes, most famously the Cup Bearer, embellish this palace entrance anchored by a massive open staircase leading to the Piano Nobile. The Horns of Consecration recreated nearby once topped the entire south facade.

Fresco Room
Take in sweeping views of the palace grounds from the west wing's upper floor, the Piano Nobile, before studying copies of the palace's most famous artworks in its Fresco Room.

West Court

West Magazines

❹ Horns of Consecration

FOOD TIP

Save your appetite for a meal in the nearby Iraklio Wine Country, amid sunbaked slopes and lush valleys. It's just south of Knossos.

MICHAEL RUNKEL/GETTY IMAGES ©

Prince of the Lilies Fresco
One of Knossos' most beloved frescoes was controversially cobbled together from various fragments and shows a young man adorned in lilies and peacock feathers.

PLANNING

To beat the crowds and avoid the heat, arrive before 10am. Budget one or two hours to explore the site thoroughly.

Throne Room

Sir Arthur Evans, who began excavating the Palace of Knossos in 1900, imagined the mythical King Minos himself holding court seated on the alabaster throne of this beautifully proportioned room. However, the lustral basin and griffin frescoes suggest a religious purpose, possibly under a priestess.

North Entrance

Bulls held a special status in Minoan society, as evidenced by the famous relief fresco of a charging beast gracing the columned west bastion of the north palace, which harboured workshops and storage rooms.

Grand Staircase

The royal apartments in the eastern wing were accessed via this monumental staircase sporting four flights of gypsum steps supported by columns. The lower two flights are original. It's closed to the public.

Piano Nobile

Central Court

Royal Apartments

Queen's Megaron

The queen's room is among the prettiest in the residential eastern wing thanks to the playful Dolphin Fresco. The adjacent bathroom (with clay tub) and toilet are evidence of a sophisticated drainage system.

Giant Pithoi

These massive clay jars are rare remnants from the Old Palace period and were used to store wine, oil and grain. The jars were transported by slinging ropes through a series of handles.

been the queen's **bathroom** with some sort of toilet. Continue to the king's quarters in the **Hall of the Double Axes** that takes its name from the double axe marks (*labrys*) on its light well, a sacred symbol to the Minoans and the origin of our word 'labyrinth'.

Beyond you can admire the Minoans' surprisingly sophisticated **water and drainage system**, pop by a stone mason's workshop and check out more giant storage jars before jogging around to the palace's north side for a good view of the partly reconstructed north entrance, easily recognised by the **Charging Bull Fresco**. Walking towards the exit, you pass the **theatral area**, a series of shallow steps whose function remains unknown. It could have been a theatre where spectators watched acrobatic and dance performances, or the place where people gathered to welcome important visitors arriving by the **Royal Road**, which leads off to the west and was flanked by workshops and the houses of ordinary people.

ℹ Getting There & Away

Getting to Knossos is easy. City bus 2 runs from Iraklio's city centre – from Bus Station A or from outside Hotel Capsis Astoria – every 15 minutes. Tickets cost €1.70 if purchased from a kiosk or vending machine and €2.50 from the bus driver. If driving, from Iraklio or the coastal road there are signs directing you to Knossos. There is free parking across from the souvenir shops, but the spaces fill quickly.

Iraklio Wine Country

About 70% of wine produced in Crete comes from the Iraklio Wine Country, which starts just south of Knossos and is headquartered in Peza. Almost two dozen wineries are embedded in a harmonious landscape of round-shouldered hills, sunbaked slopes and lush valleys. Winemakers cultivate many indigenous Cretan grape varietals, such as Kotsifali, Mandilari and Malvasia; many estates now offer tours, wine museums and wine tastings. Check www.winesofcrete.gr for details and look for the burgundy-red road signs directing you to local wineries.

⚹ Activities

Domaine Gavalas   WINE
(☑28940 51060, 6974642006; www.gavalascrete wines.gr; Vorias; ⊙8am-4pm Mon-Fri) The Gavalas family has been making wine since 1906. It went fully organic in 2001 and today is one of the largest organic wineries in Crete. Try its award-winning Efivos reds and whites. It's in Vorias, about 20km south of Peza.

Minos-Miliarakis Winery   WINE
(☑28107 41213; www.minoswines.gr; Main St, Peza; tasting €2; ⊙10am-4pm Mon-Sat Apr-Oct & by appointment) This massive winery was the first, in 1952, to bottle wine in Crete. It makes very respectable vintages, especially under its Miliarakis label, including a full-bodied single-vineyard organic red and a fragrant Blanc de Noirs. The tasting room is vast and doubles as a museum featuring historic winemaking equipment. The shop also sells local olive oil and raki (Cretan firewater).

Boutari Winery   WINE
(☑2810 731617; www.boutari.gr; Skalani; tours & tasting €5-12.50; ⊙9am-5pm Mon-Fri, by appointment Sat & Sun) Near Skalani, about 8km from Iraklio, Boutari was founded in 1879 and is one of Greece's biggest wine producers today. Visits of its Crete winery (one of six in the country) start with a short tour to learn about local grapes and winemaking followed by a 15-minute video on the island and the chance to sample the product in the vast and airy tasting room overlooking the vineyard.

🛏 Sleeping & Eating

Arhontiko   APARTMENT €€
(☑2810 752985; www.arhontikoarhanes.gr; Ano Arhanes; apt €55-85; P❄🖥) An air of rustic sophistication pervades this old-timey 1893 garden villa that also saw incarnations as a military barracks and an elementary school. No hint of either survives in the four fully renovated apartments with traditional decor and furnishings. All are bi-level with a fairly dark beamed-ceiling bedroom and bathroom downstairs and a kitchen and sitting room upstairs.

Eliathos   APARTMENT €€€
(☑6951804929, 2810 751818; www.eliathos.gr; Ano Arhanes; loft €105, villas €130-200; P❄🖥🏊) Tucked into the hillside south of Arhanes and with grand views of Mt Yiouhtas, this cluster of four villas is a haven of peace and quiet wrapped around a swimming pool. Each villa is divided into breezy apartments and lofts sleeping up to six and sporting a design that is sleek and contemporary, but also loaded with nods to the local setting.

The owners can help you get immersed in the local culture through cooking classes, excursions and olive oil, raki- or wine-making workshops.

★**Elia & Diosmos** CRETAN €€
(✉ 2810 731283; www.olive-mint.gr; Dimokratias 263, Skalani; mains €8-13; ⊙ noon-5pm Mon, noon-10pm Tue-Sun; 🐾) ✔ At this foodie destination, market-fresh ingredients shine in flavour-intense and progressive Cretan dishes. The menu chases the seasons, but classic choices include a *mousakas* (baked layers of eggplant or zucchini, minced meat and potatoes topped with cheese sauce) with cubed beef, a fluffy fennel pie and pork shank paired with wine, honey and citrus. It's only a short drive from Iraklio and an excellent post-Knossos recuperation stop.

Kritamon CRETAN €€
(✉ 2810 753092; www.kritamon.gr; Archanes; mains €8.50-15; ⊙ 5pm-1am Tue-Sat, noon-1am Sun; P ✱ 🐾) Send your taste buds on a wild ride at this foodie outpost in a street off the main square and set attractively around a garden courtyard with walnut trees. Ancient Cretan and creative modern recipes result in a small but soulful menu with such signature dishes as rooster with aniseed and cinnamon. Ingredients come mostly from the family farm.

Zaros Ζαρός
POP 2120

At the foot of Mt Psiloritis, Zaros is famous for its natural spring water, which is bottled here and sold all over Crete. But Zaros also has some fine Byzantine monasteries, excellent walking and delicious farm-raised trout served up in tavernas around town and on emerald-green Lake Votomos (actually a reservoir). The lake is also the kick-off point for the 5km trail through the mighty Rouvas Gorge, a major lure for hikers, birders and naturalists.

🏃 Activities

★**Rouvas Gorge** HIKING
(Agios Nikolaos Gorge; Lake Votomos) Part of the E4 European Path, the Rouvas Gorge leads to the protected Rouvas Forest, home to some of the oldest oak trees in Crete. It's an especially lovely walk in springtime when orchids, poppies, irises and other wildflowers give the landscape the vibrancy of an Impressionist painting. It's a 10km round-trip trek from the main trailhead at Lake Votomos north of Zaros village.

The trail starts at the Limni taverna but doesn't enter the gorge for another 1km, just past Moni Agios Nikolaos, a modern monastery that wraps around a historic church rife with icons and fresco fragments. The vegetation becomes increasingly lush with oak trees, lilies, orchids, sage and other mountain flora. At the end is a little chapel of Agios Ioannis where benches and tables invite a leisurely picnic. Starting at Moni Agios Nikolaos shortens the hike by 2km. Wear sneakers or hiking boots.

🛏 Sleeping & Eating

★**Eleonas Country Village** COTTAGE €€
(✉ 28940 31238, 6976670002; www.eleonas.gr; cottage incl breakfast €98-130, 3-night minimum; P ✱ @ 🛜 ☀) ✔ Owner Manolis has poured heart and soul into this charming retreat of stone cottages cradled by olive groves and built into a stunning terraced garden hillside. It's a '*this* is Crete' kind of place, such is the fresh air and tranquil feel. Fuel up for a day of hiking, exploring, biking or poolside chilling with a sumptuous breakfast of homemade Cretan treats.

It's about 1.5km northwest of Zaros. Just follow the signs. Three-night minimum.

★**Vegera** CRETAN €
(✉ 28940 31730; Main St; multicourse meal €9-12; ⊙ 8am-late; 🐾) The vivacious Vivi has a knack for turning farm-fresh local produce into flavourful and creative dishes based on traditional recipes. Her philosophy is to 'cook the way we cook in our house' and indeed her cute place quickly feels like home. Make sure you have ample time to savour the generous spread of fresh bread, salad, cheese and olives, cooked mains, pastries and raki.

❶ Getting There & Away

Zaros is about 46km southwest of Iraklio. The most scenic approach is by turning west off the main road at Agia Varvara. There's also a smaller road heading north from Kapariana just east of Mires (turn north at the small road between a bakery and Kafeneio i Zariani Strofi; look for the small sign). One daily bus heading from Iraklio's Bus Station B to Kamares passes through Zaros (€5.20, one hour). Alternatively, take one of the more frequent buses to Mires (€6, 75 minutes) and cab it to Zaros from there (around €16).

Matala   Μάταλα

POP 70

In mythology, Matala is the place where Zeus swam ashore with the kidnapped Europa on his back before dragging her off to Gortyna and getting her pregnant with the future King Minos. The Minoans used Matala as their harbour for Phaestos and under the Romans it became the port for Gortyna.

In more recent times, Matala became legendary thanks to the scores of hippies flocking here in the late 1960s to take up rent-free residence in cliffside caves once used as tombs by the Romans. Joni Mitchell famously immortalised the era in her 1971 song 'Carey'.

On summer days, the village feels anything but peaceful thanks to coachloads of day trippers. Stay overnight or visit in the off-season, though, and it's still possible to discern the Matala magic: the setting along a crescent-shaped bay flanked by headlands is simply spectacular, especially at sunset.

◉ Sights

Matala Caves   CAVE

(Roman Cemetery; Matala beach; adult/concession/under 18yr €2/1/free; ⊙10am-7pm Apr-Sep, 8am-3pm Oct-Mar) Matala's sightseeing credentials are limited to these famous caves where hippies camped out in the 1960s and 1970s. Hewn into the porous sandstone cliffs in prehistoric times, they were actually used as tombs by the Romans under whom Matala was the port town for Gortyna.

⌷ Sleeping & Eating

Hotel Nikos   HOTEL €

(☑28920 45375; www.matala-nikos.com; Matala; d €60; ❋☎) A standout on hotel row, family-run Nikos has 17 rooms, many with small kitchens and a terrace, on two floors flanking a flower-filled courtyard. The nicest is the top-floor No 24 with cave views. Breakfast is €6.

Matala Valley Village Hotel   RESORT €€

(☑28920 45776; www.valleyvillage.gr; d/bungalow €50/75; ⊙May-Oct; P❋☎⊠) This family-friendly garden resort consists of low-lying buildings with fairly basic rooms and two dozen spiffier whitewashed two-bedroom bungalows with Jacuzzi tubs and patio. Frolicking grounds include a lawn, a small playground and two pools (one for kids). Being located right by the village entrance puts it about 1km from the beach.

Giannis Family Grill House   GREEK €

(☑6983619233, 28920 45719; www.giannis family.com; mains €6-13.50; ⊙noon-4pm & 6pm-midnight; ☝) A refreshing change from the run-of-the-mill waterfront tavernas, this been-there-forever family place just past the central square exudes cheer with its turquoise furniture, potted flowers and no-nonsense homemade Greek food, including an excellent mixed grill with salad and potatoes. It serves organic wines from the Domaine Zacharioudakis in nearby Plouti as well as its own raki.

ℹ Information

Matala's main drag has a couple of ATMs and there's an excellent bookshop with lots of English-language novels and periodicals right on the central square.

ℹ Getting There & Away

Up to three KTEL buses daily leave Iraklio's Bus Station B for Matala (€8.50, two hours). There's free roadside parking and a beach parking lot that charges €2.

Rethymno   Ρέθυμνο

POP 34,300

Basking between the commanding bastions of its 15th-century fortress and the glittering azure waters of the Mediterranean, Rethymno is one of Crete's most enchanting towns. Its Venetian-Ottoman quarter is a lyrical maze of lanes draped in floral canopies and punctuated with graceful wood-balconied houses, ornate monuments and the occasional minaret.

Crete's third-largest town has lively nightlife thanks to its sizeable student population, some excellent restaurants and a worthwhile sandy beach right in town. The busier beaches, with their requisite resorts, line up along a nearly uninterrupted stretch all the way to Panormo, some 22km away.

◉ Sights

Rethymno is fairly compact, with most sights, accommodation and tavernas wedged within the largely pedestrianised old quarter off the Venetian Harbour. The long sandy beach starts just east of the harbour.

★ Fortezza   FORTRESS

(adult/concession/family €4/3/10; ⊙8am-8pm Apr-Oct, 10am-5pm Nov-Mar; P) Looming over Rethymno, the star-shaped Venetian fortress

GORTYNA ΓΟΡΤΥΝΑ

Gortyna (☎ 28920 31144; www.interkriti.org/crete/iraklion/gortyn.html; Iraklio-Phaestos Rd; adult/senior/under 18yr & EU student €6/3/free; ☉ 8am-8pm Apr-Oct, 8am-3pm Nov-Mar), also called Gortyn or Gortys, has been inhabited since Neolithic times but reached its pinnacle after becoming the capital of Roman Crete from around 67 BC until the Saracens raided the island in AD 824. At its peak, as many as 100,000 people may have milled around Gortyn's streets.

There are two sections, bisected by the highway. Most people only stop long enough to investigate the fenced area on the north side of the road past the ticket gate. However, several more important temples, baths and other buildings are actually scattered south of the road.

The first major monument visible within the **fenced area** is the 6th-century Byzantine **Church of Agios Titos**, the finest early-Christian church in Crete. Probably built atop an even older church, its only major surviving feature is the soaring apse flanked by two side chapels. It was under restoration at the time of writing, but should reopen in 2018.

A few steps away is the **Odeon**, a Roman theatre from the 1st century BC, which was levelled by an earthquake and rebuilt by Trajan in the 2nd century AD. The covered, arched structure on the far side of the theatre shelters Gortyna's star attraction: the massive stone tablets inscribed with the 6th-century-BC **Laws of Gortyna**. The 600 lines written in a Dorian dialect represent the oldest law code in the Greek world and provide a fascinating insight into the social structure of pre-Roman Crete. It turns out that ancient Cretans were preoccupied with the same issues that drive people into court today – marriage, divorce, property transfers, inheritance and adoption, as well as criminal offences. Behind the Odeon is an evergreen **plane tree** that, according to mythology, was Zeus and Europa's 'love nest'.

Excavations are still in full swing in the **area south of the highway** and all the sites can only be seen through a chain-link fence. Still, it's fun to wander around aimlessly and just stumble upon the ruins. If you prefer to explore in a more organised fashion, walk 300m east along the highway from the parking lot to a double sign pointing to the Temple of Apollo and the **Temple of the Egyptian Gods**. A narrow stone path leads to the latter after about 70m. Dedicated to Isis, Serapis and Anubis, there actually isn't much to see today. The same cannot be said of the **Temple of Apollo**, reached by continuing on the path past the sign pointing left to the Praetorium. The main sanctuary of pre-Roman Gortyna was built in the 7th century BC, expanded in the 3rd century BC and converted into a Christian basilica in the 2nd century AD. You can still make out its rectangular outline and the base of the main altar.

Backtrack and turn right at the sign to shortly reach the **Praetorium**. The palace of the Roman governor of Crete, it served both as an administrative building, a church and a private residence. Most of the ruins date from the 2nd century AD and were repaired in the 4th century. To the north is the 2nd-century **Nymphaeum**, a public bath supplied by an aqueduct bringing water from Zaros. It was originally adorned with statues of nymphs.

For a bird's-eye view of Gortyna, climb up to the hilltop **Acropolis**, which also features impressive sections of the pre-Roman ramparts. The trailhead is on the north side of the highway, about 100m west of the ticket booth; it takes about 20 to 30 minutes to get up here.

Gortyna is near Agia Deka, about 46km southwest of Iraklio. It's a stop on the Iraklio–Matala and Iraklio–Agia Galini bus routes. In Iraklio, buses leave from Bus Station B.

cuts an imposing figure with its massive walls and bastions but was nevertheless unable to stave off the Turks in 1646. Over time, an entire village took shape on the grounds, most of which was destroyed in WWII. Views are fabulous from up here and it's fun to poke around the ramparts, palm trees and remaining buildings, most notably the **Sultan Bin Ibrahim Mosque** with its huge dome.

The mosque hosts occasional musical events, while other buildings (like the twin buildings of the Bastion of Agios Nikolaos) are used to showcase art exhibits.

Rethymno

Rethymno

◉ Top Sights
1 Fortezza	A1

◉ Sights
2 Archaeological Museum	B3
3 Historical & Folk Art Museum	B3
4 Museum of Contemporary Art	B2
5 Rimondi Fountain	B2
6 Venetian Harbour	C2

✈ Activities, Courses & Tours
7 Eco Events	C3
8 Happy Walker	C4

🛏 Sleeping
9 Atelier Frosso Bora	B1

10 Casa dei Delfini	A3
11 Casa Vitae	A3
12 Rethymno Youth Hostel	B4

✦ Eating
13 Avli	B2
14 Castelvecchio	B1
15 En Plo	B1
16 Raki Baraki	B2
17 Taverna Knossos	C2

🍷 Drinking & Nightlife
18 Chalikouti	A2
19 Livingroom	D4

Venetian Harbour   LANDMARK
Rethymno's compact historic harbour is chock-a-block with tourist-geared fish tavernas and cafes. For a more atmospheric perspective, walk along the harbour walls, past the fishing boats to the prominent lighthouse, built in the 19th century by the Egyptians.

Archaeological Museum
MUSEUM

(☑28310 27506; Argiropoulon; adult/concession €2/1; ◉10am-6pm Tue-Sun) After its former digs in a Venetian prison near the fortress had become unstable, Rethymno's archaeological collection moved to the Venetian-built former Church of St Francis in May 2016. Tightly curated, but beautifully arranged, it features highlights from major archaeological digs around Rethymno province, including the cemetery at Armeni. Collection highlights include a 4500-year-old chalice, a figure of a Minoan goddess, a Roman bronze lamp and a miniature donkey from the Hellenistic period.

Agios Spyridon Church
CHAPEL

(Kefalogiannidon) FREE Built right into the cliff beneath the Venetian fortress, tiny Agios Spyridon has enough atmosphere to fill a cathedral. This Byzantine chapel is filled with richly painted icons, swinging bird candleholders and the sound of the nearby pounding surf. You'll see pairs of slippers, baby shoes and sandals in crevices in the rock wall, left as prayer offerings for the sick. Find the chapel at the top of a staircase on the western side of the fortress. Opening hours are erratic.

Rimondi Fountain
FOUNTAIN

(Plateia Petihaki; ⊞) Pride of place among the many vestiges of Venetian rule goes to this fountain with its spouting lion heads and Corinthian capitals, built in 1626 by city rector Alvise Rimondi.

Water spouts from three lions' heads into three basins flanked by Corinthian columns. Above the central basin you can make out the Rimondi family crest.

Museum of Contemporary Art
MUSEUM

(☑28310 52530; www.cca.gr; Mesologhiou 32; adult/concession/student €3/1.50/free, Thu free; ◉9am-2pm & 7-9pm Tue-Fri, 10am-3pm Sat & Sun May-Oct, 9am-2pm Tue-Fri, 6-9pm Wed & Fri, 10am-3pm Sat & Sun Nov-Apr) The cornerstone of the permanent collection of this art museum, founded in 1992, is the oils, drawings and watercolours of local lad Lefteris Kanakakis, but over time it has amassed enough works to present the arc of creative endeavour in Greece since the 1950s. Temporary exhibits further keep things dynamic. Entrance is off Mesologhiou.

Historical & Folk Art Museum
MUSEUM

(☑28310 23398; Vernardou 28; adult/concession €4/2; ◉10am-3pm Mon-Sat) In a lovely 17th-century Venetian mansion, the five-room permanent exhibit documents traditional rural life on Crete with displays of clothing, baskets, weavings, pottery, weapons and farming tools. Labelling is also in English.

Paleontological Museum
MUSEUM

(☑28310 23083; Temple of Mastaba, Satha & Markellou; adult/child €4/free; ◉9am-3pm daily May-Oct, 9am-3pm Tue, Thu & Sat Nov-Apr; ℗) Dwarf Cretan elephants and hippopotami aren't likely to start a ticket stampede, but it's well worth swinging by this museum for its setting in the restored 17th-century Temple of Mastaba (aka Veli Pasha Mosque) surrounded by gardens. Nine domes shape its silhouette, overlooked by the city's oldest minaret, while the once-communal gardens are steeply scented with thyme and oregano. The permanent exhibit displays tusks and fossils from hippos hunted to extinction 10,700 years ago.

Kara Musa Pasha Mosque
HISTORIC SITE

(Arkadiou & Hugo) This building actually began life as a monastery but was turned into a mosque by the Turks who added the domes and a minaret, of which only bits remain. It is named after the Ottoman admiral instrumental in the capture of Rethymno. It is not open to the public.

WORTH A TRIP

MUSEUM OF CRETAN ETHNOLOGY

Well worth a quick detour to Vori, the private, nonprofit **Museum of Cretan Ethnology** (☑28920 91110; www.cretanethnologymuseum.gr; Voroi Pirgiotissis, Vori; adult/concession €3/1.50; ◉11am-5pm Apr-Oct) peels away the curtain on how rural people lived on the island until well into the 20th century. The English-labelled exhibits are organised around such themes as food production, war, customs, architecture and music. Although most of the items are rather ordinary – hoes, olive presses, baskets, clothing, instruments etc – they're engagingly displayed in darkened rooms accented with spotlights. It's well signposted from the main Mires–Tymbaki road.

CRETE RETHYMNO

🏃 Activities

★ Happy Walker HIKING
(📞 28310 52920; www.happywalker.com; Tombazi 56; guided day walks €32; ⏱ 5-8.30pm daily Sep-Jun, 5-8.30pm Mon-Fri Jul & Aug) In operation for over a quarter of a century, this congenial outfit takes up to 16 global ramblers on day hikes to gorges, ancient shepherd trails and traditional villages. It's ideal for solo travellers. Rates include transport to and from trailheads and an English-speaking guide, but coffee and vegetarian lunch with wine is an extra €12. Book the evening before.

Multiday tours are also available.

Paradise Dive Centre DIVING
(📞 28310 26317; www.diving-center.gr; Petres Geraniou; 2 dives incl equipment €100, open-water certification €400) Runs diving trips for all grades of diver from its base at Petres, 14km west of Rethymno. Offers cave dives, night dives and various PADI courses. Book through travel agencies, by phone or via the website.

Mountaineering Club
of Rethymno CLIMBING
(📞 28310 57766; www.eosrethymnou.gr; Dimokratias 12; ⏱ 9-11pm Tue) Offers advice on local hikes along with the possibility to join excursions. It's best to make contact via the website.

Eco Events TOURS
(📞 28310 50055, 6946686857; www.ecoevents.gr; Eleftherios Venizelou 39; tours €18-70; ⏱ 10am-2pm & 5-9pm) This outfit specialises in small-group English-language tours that get you in touch with land, people and culture. Options include the Eco Tour where you'll meet a baker, weaver and woodcarver before sampling charcoal-grilled lamb in a traditional shepherd shelter in the mountains. Cooking classes, wine and olive oil tastings and hiking trips are also part of the line-up.

🛌 Sleeping

★ Atelier Frosso Bora PENSION €
(📞 28310 24440; www.frosso-bora.com; Himaras 25; d €45-60; ❄ 🤙) Run by local artist Frosso Bora and located above her pottery studio, these four spotless, ambience-laden rooms with exposed stone walls, small flat-screen TVs, modern bathrooms and kitchenettes are a superb budget pick. Two units have small balconies facing the old town while the other two sport Venetian architectural features and a beamed ceiling.

Rethymno Youth Hostel HOSTEL €
(📞 28310 22848; www.yhrethymno.com; Tombazi 41; dm late Sep-May €12, Jun–mid-Sep €14; ⏱ reception 8am-1pm & 5-11pm Sep-May, 8am-midnight Jun-Aug; 🤙) This cheerful, well-run hostel sleeps six to eight people in recently upgraded dorms (one for women only) with comfy mattresses and good-sized lockers. In a quiet street, yet within stumbling distance of sights and bars, it has a private, sociable patio, bar and a flowering garden to relax in. Facilities include a washing machine, a communal kitchen and hot showers.

Camping Elizabeth CAMPGROUND €
(📞 28310 28694, 6983009259; www.camping-elizabeth.net; Ionias 84, Missiria; campsites per adult/child €8.50/4.50, tent/car/caravan €5/4/6; ⏱ year-round; @ 🤙) The closest campground to Rethymno is 4km east of the old city on beautiful Missiria beach. Bamboo, palm and olive trees provide plenty of shade, and there's a taverna, snack bar and minimarket, plus a communal fridge, laundry facilities and free beach umbrellas and sun lounges. It also rents out simple bungalows and caravans from €26.50 and tents with bedding from €18.50. An Iraklio-bound bus can drop you nearby.

Sohora BOUTIQUE HOTEL €€
(📞 28313 00913; www.sohora.gr; Plateia Iroön Politechniou 11; studio/d/apt €60/80/100; ❄ 🤙) Extremely comfortable and slightly quirky,

---

THE ORIGINAL CYCLOPS

The Rethymno region seems to have had more than its share of fossil-filled caves. In fact, it's the richest area in the Mediterranean for endemic fossils, including those of the dwarf elephant. Some scientists believe that when ancient Greeks entered the shore caves and discovered the skulls of dwarf elephants, they were taken aback by what they saw. About twice the size of a human skull, the large, central nasal cavity for the trunk may well have been interpreted as an enormous, single eye-socket. The possible result? The birth of the Cyclops. Visit Rethymno's Paleontological Museum (p459) to see the skeletons for yourself.

the four rooms with kitchenette in this 200-year-old home are named after the seasons and incorporate original architectural features alongside vintage, upcycled furnishings. A solar-water heater, organic bath products and a hearty, homemade breakfast provide eco-cred. Service is both friendly and professional.

It's set on a bar-lined square popular with locals and just a short walk from the heart of the old town.

Casa Vitae BOUTIQUE HOTEL €€
(✆6973237897, 28310 35058; www.casa-vitae.gr; Patealarou 3; r €95-150; ❄️🅿️🛜) This charismatic Venetian-era building has eight quietly elegant rooms mixing exposed stone and wood and wrapping around a fountain-anchored courtyard where home-cooked breakfast is served beneath the bamboo-and-vine-shaded pergola. Romance rules in the larger suites with iron four-poster beds, whirlpool tubs and a private terrace.

Casa dei Delfini BOUTIQUE HOTEL €€
(✆6937254857, 28310 55120; www.casadeidelfini.com; Nikiforou Foka 66-68; studio €55-85, maisonette €110; ❄️🛜) The four individual rooms in this elegant mansion orbit a small courtyard and exude historic character galore. In one, the bathroom used to be a *hammam* (Turkish bath), in another the bed is tucked into an arched stone alcove. All have kitchenettes. The two-storey maisonette comes with a large private terrace.

✖️ Eating

⭐**Raki Baraki** GREEK €
(✆28310 58250; Arabatzoglou 17; meze €3-11; ⏰noon-midnight or later; ❄️🛜🎵) Rustic, colourful and lively, this is a fantastic place to while away the evening over mezedhes (appetisers) like sardines stuffed with herbs, sausage with grilled vegetables, or mussels steamed with sage. The fried feta with caramelised figs and mint is divine. Comfort food at its finest. All ingredients are sourced from small farmers around Greece.

Castelvecchio GREEK €€
(✆28310 55163; Himaras 29; mains €9-27; ⏰lunch Sep-May, dinner year-round; ❄️🛜) In a Venetian-era building a bone toss from the fortress, chic yet chilled Castelvecchio is perfect for date night – especially if your date is a plate of tender boneless lamb, done up in numerous creative ways, including a foil-cooked version with creamy tomato and feta sauce. For dessert, go for the walnut cake – it'll have you pining for seconds!

Taverna Knossos GREEK €€
(✆28310 25582; Nearhou 40; mains €12-18; ⏰noon-midnight; ❄️🛜) Most tout-fronted tavernas in the Venetian Harbour focus more on folkloric ambience than on food quality. Owned by the amiable Stavroulaki family for half a century, Knossos is a happy exception. When Mama Anna is in the kitchen, you can be sure that dishes are loaded with flavour, the fish is outstanding and the service swift and gracious.

En Plo GREEK €€
(✆28310 30950; Kefalogiannidon 28; mains €7.50-12; ⏰11am-midnight or later; 🛜🎵) One of several tavernas right at the water's edge below the fortress, En Plo does dependable faves like shrimp spaghetti and grilled salmon, but shows its most creative side when it comes to such mezedhes as feta in pastry with caramelised figs. For the younger buccaneers of your party, there's a Little Pirates' Menu.

Avli CRETAN €€€
(✆28310 58250; www.avli.gr; Xanthoudidou 22; mains €12-28; ⏰11am-midnight; ❄️🛜) This well-established Venetian villa serves creative Cretan food with a side of romance. Farm-fresh fare steers the menu, resulting in dishes with bold flavour pairings such as *creatotouria* (ravioli filled with lamb, cheese, mint and lime) or fried grouper with handpicked greens. Be sure to reserve a table in the bewitching garden.

🍷 Drinking & Nightlife

Rethymno's young and restless are mostly drawn to the cafe-bars along Eleftherios Venizelou. The area around the Rimondi Fountain and Plateia Petihaki is popular with tourists. Wander the side streets to find quieter places.

Chalikouti BAR
(✆28310 42632; Katehaki 3; ⏰9am-1am; 🛜) In the alt-flavoured quarter below the Fortezza, this cooperative-run cafe draws chatty locals keen on coffee from Mexican Zapatistas, sugar from landless workers in Brazil, and organic raki from Cretan producers. A selection of mezedhes and desserts provides sustenance.

Livingroom BAR
(✆28310 21386; www.livingroom.gr; Eleftherios Venizelou 5; ⏰9am-3am; 🛜) No matter where

the handles are on the clock, the comfy lounge sofas of this stylish hang-out are always packed with hip town folk. Mellow in the daytime, the vibe gets progressively more high-octane after dark. A good place to ease into the nightlife scene.

ℹ Information

There are free public wi-fi hotspots at the town hall, Plateia Iroön Polytechniou, the Venetian Harbour and the Municipal Garden, all within the old town.

Cool Holidays (☑ 28310 35567; www.cool holidays.gr; Melissinou 2; ☺ 9am-9pm) Helpful office that handles boat and plane tickets, hires out cars and motorcycles, and books excursions.

General Hospital of Rethymno (☑ 28313 42100; Triandalydou 19-21; ☺ 24hr)

Post Office (☑ 28310 22303; Moatsou 19; ☺ 7.30am-8.30pm Mon-Fri) Accepts letters and parcels.

Regional Tourist Office (☑ 28310 29148; www.rethymnon.gr; Sofokli Venizelou; ☺ 8am-2pm Mon-Fri) Has local maps and offers regional information.

Tourist Police (☑ 28310 28156, emergency 171; Iroön Polytechniou 29; ☺ on call 24hr)

ℹ Getting There & Away

The **bus station** (☑ 28310 22212; www.e-ktel. com; Kefalogiannidon; 🛜) is on the western edge of the centre. Services are reduced at weekends and outside high season. Check KTEL (www.e-ktel.com) for the latest schedule.

ℹ Getting Around

Rethymno's centre is wonderfully compact and best explored on foot. When visiting outlying areas, a taxi is your best bet.

Auto Moto Sports (☑ 28310 24858, 6945771933; www.automotosport.com.gr; Sofokli Venizelou 48; bicycle/car per day from €10/32; ☺ 7am-10pm) Hires out bicycles, cars and motorbikes.

Moni Arkadiou
Μονή Αρκαδίου

★ **Moni Arkadiou** HISTORIC SITE
(Arkadi Monastery; ☑ 28310 83136; €3; ☺ 9am-8pm Jun-Sep, to 7pm Apr, May & Oct, to 5pm Nov, to 4pm Dec-Mar) The 16th-century Arkadi Monastery, some 23km southeast of Rethymno, has deep significance for Cretans. As the site where hundreds of cornered locals massacred both themselves and invading Turks, it's a stark and potent symbol of resistance and considered a spark plug in the island's struggle towards freedom from Turkish occupation.

In November 1866, massive Ottoman forces arrived to crush island-wide revolts. Hundreds of Cretan men, women and children fled their villages to find shelter at Arkadiou. However, far from being a safe haven, the monastery was soon besieged by 2000 Turkish soldiers. Rather than surrender, the entrapped locals blew up stored gunpowder kegs, killing everyone, Turks included. One small girl miraculously survived and lived to a ripe old age in a village nearby. A bust of this woman and another of the abbot who lit the gunpowder are outside the monastery not far from the old windmill – now an ossuary with skulls and bones of the 1866 victims neatly arranged in a glass cabinet.

Arkadiou's impressive Venetian church (1587) has a striking Renaissance facade

BUSES FROM RETHYMNO

DESTINATION	DURATION	FARE (€)	FREQUENCY
Agia Galini (via Spili)	1½hr	6.80	up to 5 daily
Anogia	1¼hr	6	2 daily Mon-Fri
Argyroupoli	40min	3.60	2 daily Mon-Fri
Hania	1hr	6.80	hourly
Hora Sfakion (via Vrysses)	2hr	8.30	2 daily
Iraklio	1½hr	8.30	hourly
Margarites	30min	3.80	2 daily Mon-Fri
Moni Arkadiou	40min	2.80	up to 3 daily
Omalos (Samaria Gorge)	1¾hr	17.10	2 daily
Plakias	1hr	5	up to 5 daily
Preveli	1¼hr	4.90	2 daily

topped by an ornate triple-belled tower. The grounds include a small museum and the old wine cellar where the gunpowder was stored.

Three buses daily arrive here (two on weekends) from Rethymno (€3, 40 minutes), leaving you about 90 minutes for your visit before returning.

Anogia Ανώγεια

POP 2380

Perched aside Mt Psiloritis, 37km southwest of Iraklio, Anogia has a legacy of rebellious spirit and determination to express its undiluted Cretan character. During WWII, it was a centre of resistance and suffered heavily for it. The Nazis burned down the town and massacred all the men in retaliation for their role in sheltering Allied troops and aiding in the kidnapping of a Nazi general.

Anogia is also famous for its stirring music and has spawned many of Crete's best-known musicians such as Nikos Xylouris. Locals cling to time-honoured traditions and it's not rare to see men gossiping in the *kafeneia* dressed in traditional black shirts with baggy pants tucked into black boots. Elderly women, meanwhile, keep busy flogging traditional woven blankets and embroidered textiles. Though beautiful and well-priced, not all are actually produced locally, so *caveat emptor.*

⊙ Sights

Nikos Xylouris' Home HISTORIC SITE

(⊗9am-9pm) **FREE** Crete's most famous musician, the *lyra* (lyre) player and singer Nikos Xylouris, was born in a modest house on the lower village square. Until her death in 2016, his sister Zouboulia ran a *kafeneio* here and presided over an endearing collection of posters, letters and other memorabilia related to her brother.

🛏 Sleeping & Eating

Hotel Aristea HOTEL €

(☑28340 31459; www.hotelaristea.gr; Michaeli Stavrakaki; d/apt €35/85; 🅿🛜) Run by the chatty and charming Aristea, this small inn offers sweeping valley views from balconies attached to five fairly basic but spotless and comfortable-enough rooms. The four split-level apartments in a next-door annex are more modern and come with kitchens and a wood-burning fireplace for those chilly mountain nights.

★ Ta Skalomata CRETAN €

(☑28340 31316; 31 August 1944 St; mains €5-12; ⊗9am-midnight; 🛜) In the upper village, Skalomata has provided sustenance to locals and travellers for about 40 years. When you peel your eyes away from the view through panoramic windows, train your focus on the great grilled meats (the lamb is tops!), homemade wine and bread, and tasty meatless fare such as zucchini with cheese.

The owners are charming and will welcome you with open arms on your return visit.

Arodamos CRETAN €

(☑28340 31100; www.arodamos.gr; Tylisos-Anogia Rd; mains €6-10.50; ⊗10.30am-10pm) This big restaurant in a modern stone house in the upper village is held in high regard for its hearty Cretan mountain fare and gracious hospitality. Local specialities include the flame-teased lamb or goat *(ofto)* and the deceptively simple but tasty local dish of spaghetti cooked in stock and topped with *athotiros* (white cheese).

Can accommodate tour groups.

ℹ Information

An ATM and the post office are in the upper village.

ℹ Getting There & Away

There are up to three buses daily from Iraklio (€4.10, one hour) and two buses Monday to Friday from Rethymno (€6, 1¼ hours).

Mt Psiloritis Ορος Ψηλορείτης

At 2456m, Mt Psiloritis, also known as Mt Ida, is Crete's highest mountain. At its eastern base is the Nida Plateau (1400m), a wide, fertile expanse reached via a paved 21km-long road from Anogia. It passes several round stone *mitata* (traditional shepherd's huts used for cheese-making and shelter) as well as the turn-off to the highly regarded (but rarely open) Skinakas Observatory.

From the Nida Plateau, it's a short walk to the Ideon Cave where, according to legend, the god Zeus was reared (although Dikteon Cave in Lasithi claims the same). Also on the plateau is Andartis, an impressive landscape sculpture honouring the Cretan WWII resistance.

⊙ Sights

Skinakas Observatory
OBSERVATORY

(📞 28103 94238; http://skinakas.physics.uoc.
gr; ⊙ 6-11pm around full moon May-Sep) FREE
Near the top of Mt Psiloritis, at 1750m, the
Skinakas Observatory is operated by the
University of Greece and is the country's
most significant stargazing vantage point
with two powerful telescopes. From May
to September, the site opens to the public
once a month around the full moon (see the
website for exact dates). There are tours of
the site, presentations and a chance to look
through the telescope.

Ideon Cave
CAVE

(Mt Psiloritis; P) FREE Although just a huge
and fairly featureless hole in the ground,
Ideon has sacred importance in mythology
as the place where Zeus was reared by his
mother Rhea to save him from the clutches of
his child-devouring father Cronos. (Inciden-
tally, the Diktaeon Cave in the Lasithi Plateau
makes the same claim.) Ideon is on Mt Psiloritis about 15km from Anogia; it's a 1km uphill
walk from the parking lot to the entrance.

Ideon was a place of worship from the
late 4th millennium BC onward and many
artefacts, including gold jewellery and
bronze shields, statuettes and other offerings to Zeus, have been unearthed here.

Andartis – Partisan of Peace
MONUMENT

(Nida Plateau, Mt Psiloritis) FREE Right on the
Nida Plateau, high on Mt Psiloritis, you can
make out this sprawling landscape sculpture created by German artist Karina Raeck

---

WORTH A TRIP

ENAGRON

The working farm **Enagron Ecotourism Village** (📞 28340 61611; www.
enagron.gr; Axos Mylopotamou; studio/apt
incl breakfast from €87/108; P ❄ � 🛜) offers
an immersion in the traditional Cretan
way of life. Lodging is in elegantly rustic
rooms with beamed ceilings, stone walls
and fireplaces as well as kitchenettes.
The restaurant serves dishes prepared
with farm-foraged ingredients and also
runs cooking classes and cheese-
making workshops. Minimum three-
night stay on most dates.

It's also possible to visit the farm and
eat at the restaurant without checking
in, but do book ahead.

---

in 1991 to commemorate the Cretan resistance in WWII. The monument itself is a pile
of local rocks arranged in such a way that it
looks like an angel when seen from above.
Ask the taverna staff to point it out if you
can't spot it on your own. It's a flat and easy
1.25km walk out there.

Spili
Σπίλι

POP 630

Spili is a pretty mountain village and shut-
terbug favourite thanks to its cobbled
streets, big old plane trees and flower-
festooned whitewashed houses. Most people
just stop for lunch on a coast-to-coast trip,
but it's well worth staying a day or two to
explore the trails weaving through the local
mountains. The rugged Kourtaliotiko Gorge,
which culminates at the famous palm grove
of Preveli Beach, starts not far south of town.

In town, a restored **Venetian fountain**
spurts potable water from 25 stone lion
heads into a long trough. Minor attractions include a **folk museum** and the vast
modern **monastery** at the northern end of
town.

⊨ Sleeping & Eating

★ Hotel Heracles
PENSION €

(📞 6973667495, 28320 22111; www.heracles-hotel.
eu; Main St; s/d €35/40; ❄ 🛜) These five balconied rooms are quiet, spotless and simply
furnished, but it's the charming and softly
spoken Heracles himself who makes the
place so special. Intimately familiar with the
area, he's happy to put you onto the right
hiking trail, birdwatching site or hidden
beach. Optional homemade breakfasts start
at €4.50. He also rents two apartments in a
traditional Cretan house (€70 to €90).

Stratidakis
GREEK €

(Main St; dishes €3.50-6; ⊙ noon-9pm or later) At
the oldest taverna in town, the owner-chef will
likely invite you to inspect whatever dishes
are stewing in his kitchen that day before you
make your selection. Upon request, you can
also have local rabbit, lamb, pork and other
local meats prepared on the outdoor charcoal
grill. It's a simple, local place, so don't expect
any culinary flights of fancy.

❶ Information

There are two ATMs and a post office on the main
street. Some of the cafes near the fountain offer
free wi-fi.

❶ Getting There & Away

Spili is on the Rethymno–Agia Galini bus route (€3.80, 30 to 40 minutes), which has up to five services daily.

Plakias   Πλακιάς

POP 300

Set beside a sweeping sandy crescent and accessed via two scenic gorges – Kotsifou and Kourtaliotiko – Plakias gets swarmed with package tourists in summer (when it can be very windy), but otherwise remains a laid-back indie travellers' favourite. While the village itself isn't particularly pretty, it's an excellent launch pad for regional excursions and hikes through olive groves, along seaside cliffs and to some sparkling hidden beaches.

🏃 Activities

There are well-worn walking paths to the scenic village of Selia, Moni Finika, Lefkogia, and a lovely walk along the Kourtaliotiko Gorge to Moni Preveli. An easy 30-minute uphill path to Myrthios begins just before the youth hostel.

Several diving operators run shore and boat dives to nearby rocky bays, caves and canyons, and also certification courses.

Captain Lefteris Boat Cruises   BOATING
(📞 6936806635, 28320 31971; lbfinikas@gmail.com; Waterfront; tours €15-39) In summer, Baradakis Lefteris, owner-chef of the Smerna Bar, runs entertaining boat trips to nearby beaches like Preveli (€15), Frangokastello and Loutro (€39), and to Agios Pavlos, Triopetra and Preveli (€30).

🛏 Sleeping

★Plakias Youth Hostel   HOSTEL €
(📞 28320 32118; www.yhplakias.com; dm €10-12; ☉mid-Mar–early Nov; 🅿@🛜) This charismatic pad and 'Hoscar' winner for best Greek hostel in 2015 and 2016 is set in an olive grove 500m from the beach. Serene and lazy, it fosters an atmosphere of inclusiveness and good cheer that appeals to people of all ages and nationalities. There are six eight-bed dorms with fans, communal facilities and an outdoor kitchen.

Hotel Livikon   HOTEL €
(📞 28320 31216; www.hotel-livikon-plakias.com; Beach Rd; d/tr €45/50; 🅿✳🛜) This family-run affair was one of the first hotels in Plakias back in the 1970s, but the 10 impeccably kept, spotless and comfortable rooms hardly reveal their age. All have a small kitchen and a balcony (get a beach-facing one). It's upstairs from an all-day cafe that also serves breakfast (€4 to €6).

Plakias Suites   APARTMENT €€
(📞 28320 31680, 6975811559; www.plakiassuites.com; Beach Rd; ste €120-170; ☉Apr–mid-Nov; 🅿✳🛜) This stylish outpost has six two- and three-room apartments with contemporary aesthetics and Zeitgeist-compatible touches such as large flat-screen TVs, supremely comfortable mattresses, a chic kitchen and a private balcony or patio. Staying here puts you within a whisker of the best stretch of local beach, albeit about 1km from the village centre.

🍴 Eating & Drinking

To Xehoristo   GREEK €
(📞 28320 31214; Waterfront; sandwiches €2.50, mains €7-14; ☉noon-midnight) If the picture menu doesn't get you salivating, then the aroma emanating from the charcoal grill will likely do the trick. No matter, whether you grab a quick kebab pita during a beach session or tuck into a full platter of *gyros* (meat slithers cooked on a vertical rotisserie; usually eaten with pitta bread) or shrimp for dinner, you're in for a simple, but tasty, treat.

Tasomanolis   SEAFOOD €€
(📞 28320 31229; www.plakiasboattours.gr; Waterfront; mains €7-16; ☉noon-10pm or later; 🛜🍴) Tasos and his Belgian wife Lisa preside over this nautical-themed family taverna towards the far end of town. Park yourself on the colourful patio to tuck into classic Greek grills and inspired daily specials like anchovy bruschetta, ouzo shrimp or the daily catch with wild greens. Portions are not the biggest, but the quality is tops. Kids menu available.

Ostraco Bar   CAFE-BAR
(📞 28320 32249; Waterfront; ☉9am-late; 🛜) This downstairs waterfront cafe is a handy place to hang for breakfast, a cold beer or a snack any time of day, while the upstairs balconied bar kicks into gear after 9pm and keeps going until even the hardiest night owls are ready to roost.

❶ Information

Plakias has two ATMs on the central waterfront. The post office is on the first side street coming from the east.

ⓘ Getting There & Around

There are up to five buses daily to Rethymno (€5, one hour) and four to Preveli (€1.80, 30 minutes).

Alianthos Cars (✐28320 32033; www.alianthos-group.com; Waterfront; per day car/scooter from €36/23; ☺8am-10pm) Reliable car-hire outlet.

Anso Travel (✐6944755712; per day €10-25; ☺9am-2pm & 6-10pm) Rents out mountain bikes, speed bikes and even electric bikes for taking to the mountains around town. Multiday rates available.

Around Plakias

About 11km east of Plakias, the historic **Moni Preveli** (Μονή Πρεβέλης; ✐28320 31246; www.preveli.org; Koxaron-Moni Preveli Rd; €2.50; ☺9am-6pm Apr & May, 9am-1pm & 3.30-7pm Jun-Oct; Ⓟ) cuts an imposing silhouette high above the Libyan Sea. Like most Cretan monasteries, it was a centre of resistance during the Turkish occupation and also played a key role in WWII when hiding trapped Allied soldiers from the Nazis until they could escape to Egypt by submarine.

On the road to the monastery, a **memorial** showing a gun-toting abbot and an Allied British soldier commemorates this heroic act, as does a **fountain** on the right as you enter the monastery. To the left is a small **museum** with some exquisite icons, richly embroidered vestments and two silver candelabra presented by grateful soldiers after the war.

Dazzling **Preveli Beach** (Παραλία Πρεβέλης), also known as Palm Beach, is located below Moni Preveli and is one of Crete's most celebrated strands. At the mouth of the Kourtaliotiko Gorge, where the river Megalopotamos empties into the Libyan Sea, the palm-lined river banks have freshwater pools good for a dip. The beach is backed by rugged cliffs and punctuated by a heart-shaped boulder at the water's edge.

A steep path leads down to the beach (10 minutes) from a car park (€2), 1km before Moni Preveli. In summer, two daily buses come in from Rethymno (€4.90, 1¼ hours) and four from Plakias (€1.80, 30 minutes).

Plakias to Agia Galini

Triopetra   Τριόπετρα

Triopetra is a big beach named after three giant rocks jutting out of the sea. A headland divides the sandy strip into 'Little Triopetra' and 'Big Triopetra' – both have tavernas with rooms. Because of submerged sand shelves, the former is not ideal for swimming, so head to the 'big' beach for that. The area is popular for yoga retreats.

Triopetra can be reached via a 12km winding asphalt road from the village of Akoumia on the Rethymno–Agia Galini road. It's also linked to Agios Pavlos (about 300m is driveable dirt road). Ask about road conditions locally before setting out on the latter.

Pavlos' Place   PENSION €
(✐28310 25189, 6945998101; www.triopetra.com.gr; d €38-43; ☺Apr-Oct; ❋🤶) Right above Little Triopetra beach, dreamy Pavlos is the perfect chill spot and a popular yoga retreat. Rooms are down to earth (no TV), with kitchenettes and balconies that catch the sea breeze. The attached taverna does home-grown fare (mains €5 to €12). Wi-fi is intermittent and available in public areas only – great for digital detox.

Agios Pavlos   Αγιος Παύλος

Cradled by cliffs, Agios Pavlos is little more than a couple of small tavernas with rooms

---

WORTH A TRIP

MYRTHIOS   ΜΥΡΘΙΟΣ

The postcard-pretty village of Myrthios, draped across the hillside above Plakias, makes for a quieter and more village-like alternative to staying beachside. You might also be lured by great food and good deals on accommodation. Myrthios is a short drive (about 4km) or 30-minute walk (about 2km) from Plakias.

Taverna Panorama (✐28320 31450; mains €7-12; ☺9am-11pm Apr–mid-Nov; 🤶) is one of the oldest restaurants in the Plakias area and could not be more aptly named. On the shaded terrace, intoxicating views out towards Libya compete with the Cretan soul food prepared with passion and know-how by women from the village using impeccably fresh ingredients from Terpsi's family's own farm. If there's freshly baked apple pie, don't miss it!

and a beach bar set around a picture-perfect crescent with dark, coarse sand and the distinctive silhouette of Paximadia Island looming offshore. Its beauty and tranquillity have made it a popular destination for yoga retreats. A steep staircase on the bay's western end leads up Cape Melissa to some intricately pleated multihued rock formations.

The bay gets busy in summer when excursion boats arrive from Agia Galini, but it's possible to escape the crowds by heading to the beaches behind Cape Melissa. Beware that getting there involves a scramble down (and up) a steep sand dune; bring water and snacks since there are no facilities. The furthest cove is the least busy and is popular with nudists.

There is no public transport to Agios Pavlos. Drivers need to look for the turn-off to Saktouria on the Rethymno–Agia Galini road and follow the winding road 13km down to the sea.

Agios Pavlos Hotel   HOTEL €
(✍ 28320 71104; www.agiospavloshotel.gr; d €37-45, apt €45-60; ✆ Apr-Oct; 🅿❋🛜) Hugging a rugged and remote sandy bay, this place offers small but updated rooms, some with gorgeous bay views, below a trad taverna, and larger apartments with kitchens and balconies in a modern building about 1km uphill. The taverna dishes up fresh fish and Cretan standards while the palm-thatched cafe with hammocks does breakfast and drinks.

Agia Galini   Αγια Γαλήνη
POP 630

Agia Galini is an erstwhile picturesque fishing village where package tourism and overdevelopment have diluted much of the original charm. With ageing hotels and restaurants clinging densely to a steep hillside and hemmed in by cliffs, small beaches and a fishing harbour, the town can feel claustrophobic in high season, but it definitely has its charms at other times. It's a convenient base for visits to Phaestos, Agia Triada and the remote beaches west of here. The town all but shuts down in winter.

🛏 Sleeping & Eating

Camping No Problem   CAMPGROUND €
(✍ 28320 91386; per person/tent/car/caravan €6/4/3/4; ✆ year-round; 🅿🛜🏊) With shady spots to pitch a tent, this well-maintained campground is about 100m from a pebbly

beach and a 10-minute walk from the port and town centre. A small supermarket meets basic needs, but there's also an excellent taverna overlooking a big swimming pool. The turn-off is on the main road near the Shell petrol station.

Palazzo Greco   BOUTIQUE HOTEL €€
(✍ 28320 91187; www.palazzogreco.com; Main Rd; d incl breakfast €95-130; 🅿❋🛜🏊) A passion for design is reflected in the stylish details at this breezy hotel overlooking the sea. Match your mood to the wall colours – pale green, blue or red – in tranquil modern rooms with view-filled decks, flat-screen TVs, fridges and fabulous showers. Breakfast on the beautiful patio above the pool.

It's right on the main road before it descends down into the village.

Faros Fish Tavern   SEAFOOD €€
(✍ 6944773702; Port; mains €7-13; ✆ 11am-11pm) This no-frills family-run fish taverna is usually packed to the gills, and for good reason: the owner himself drops his nets into the Med, so you know what's on the plate that night was still swimming in the sea in the morning. It's in the first lane coming from the port. Squid cooked in its own ink, lobster spaghetti and fish soup are specialities (available on request only).

ⓘ Getting There & Away

In high season there are six buses daily to Iraklio (€8.70, two hours), up to five to Rethymno (€6.70, 1½ hours) and to Phaestos (€2.10, 30 to 45 minutes), and up to five to Matala (€3.50, 45 minutes) with a change in Tymbaki. Buses stop down in the village near the port.

Galini Express (✍ 6936923848; www.galini express.com) has direct buses to the airport in Iraklio (€25) and Hania (€35).

NORTHWEST CRETE

Hania   Χανιά
POP 54,000

Hania (also spelled Chania) is Crete's most evocative city, with its pretty Venetian quarter, criss-crossed by narrow lanes, culminating at a magnificent harbour. Remnants of Venetian and Turkish architecture abound, with old townhouses now transformed into atmospheric restaurants and boutique hotels.

Hania

Although all this beauty means the old town is deluged with tourists in summer, it's still a great place to unwind. The Venetian Harbour is super for a stroll and a coffee or cocktail. Plus it's got a university and a modern portion to the city, which means that it retains its charm in winter. Indie boutiques and an entire lane (Skridlof) dedicated to leather products provide good shopping and, with a multitude of creative restaurants, you'll likely have some of your best meals on Crete here.

Hania

◉ Top Sights

◉ Sights

⊕ Activities, Courses & Tours

⊟ Sleeping

✕ Eating

◉ Drinking & Nightlife

⊕ Entertainment

⊟ Shopping

◉ Sights

From Plateia 1866, the Venetian Harbour is a short walk north up Halidon. Zambeliou, once Hania's main thoroughfare, is lined with craft shops, small hotels and tavernas. The slightly bohemian Splantzia quarter, running from Plateia 1821 between Daskalogianni and Halidon, brims with atmospheric restaurants and cafes, boutique hotels and traditional shopping. The headland near the lighthouse separates the Venetian Harbour from the crowded town beach in the modern Nea Hora quarter.

★ **Venetian Harbour**　　　HISTORIC SITE
(⊙24hr) **FREE** There are few places where Hania's historic charm and grandeur is

more palpable than in the old Venetian Harbour. It's lined by pastel-coloured buildings that punctuate a maze of narrow lanes lined with shops and tavernas. The eastern side is dominated by the domed **Mosque of Kioutsouk Hasan** (Mosque of the Janissaries) **FREE**, now an exhibition hall. At sunset, join locals and tourists on a stroll out to the **lighthouse** that stands sentinel over the harbour entrance.

★**Hania Archaeological Museum**   MUSEUM

(✉28210 90334; http://chaniamuseum.culture. gr; Halidon 28; adult/concession/child €4/2/free; ⊙8am-3pm Tue-Sun) The setting alone in the beautifully restored 16th-century Venetian Church of San Francisco is reason to visit this fine collection of artefacts from Neolithic to Roman times. Late-Minoan sarcophagi catch the eye as much as a large glass case with an entire herd of clay bulls (used to worship Poseidon). Other standouts include Roman floor mosaics in back, Hellenistic gold jewellery, clay tablets with Linear A and Linear B script, and a marble sculpture of Roman emperor Hadrian.

Also particularly impressive are the statue of Diana and, in the pretty courtyard, a marble fountain decorated with lions' heads, a vestige of the Venetian tradition. A Turkish fountain is a relic from the building's days as a mosque. To the north of the church, three small rooms display choice finds from a private collection of Minoan pottery, jewellery and clay models.

The church itself was a mosque under the Turks, a movie theatre in 1913, and a munitions depot for the Germans during WWII.

---

❶ HANIA FOR KIDS

If your five-year-old has lost interest in Venetian architecture, head to the **public garden** between Tzanakaki and A Papandreou, where there's a playground and a shady cafe. Eight kilometres south of town, the giant water park **Limnoupolis** (✉28210 33246; www.limnoupolis. gr; Varypetro; day pass adult/child 4-12 €25/18, afternoon pass €17/14; ⊙10am-6pm mid-May–Aug, shorter hours Sep) has enough slides and pools to keep kids amused, and cafes and pool bars for adults. Buses leave regularly from the KTEL bus station.

★**Maritime Museum of Crete**   MUSEUM

(✉28210 91875; www.mar-mus-crete.gr; Akti Koundourioti; adult/concession €3/2; ⊙9am-5pm Mon-Sat, 10am-6pm Sun May-Oct, 9am-3.30pm daily Nov-Apr) Part of the hulking Venetian-built Firkas Fortress at the western port entrance, this museum celebrates Crete's nautical tradition with model ships, naval instruments, paintings, old photographs, maps and memorabilia. One room is dedicated to historical sea battles while upstairs there's thorough documentation on the WWII-era Battle of Crete.

Byzantine & Post-Byzantine Collection   MUSEUM

(✉28210 96046; Theotokopoulou 78; adult/concession/child €2/1/free; ⊙8am-3pm Tue-Sun) In the impressively restored Venetian Church of San Salvatore, this small but fascinating collection of artefacts, icons, jewellery and coins spans the period from AD 62 to 1913. Highlights include a segment of a mosaic floor for an early-Christian basilica and a prized icon of St George slaying the dragon. The building has a mixed bag of interesting architectural features from its various occupiers.

Church of Agios Nikolaos   CHURCH

(Plateia 1821; ⊙7am-noon & 2-7pm) One of Hania's most intriguing buildings is this Venetian-era church with both a bell tower and a double-balconied minaret – the latter replaced a second bell tower during its stint as a mosque under Turkish rule. Inside, the massive bronze chandeliers dangling from a barrel-vaulted coffered ceiling will likely draw your attention. The church was originally part of a Dominican monastery founded in 1320. The only section left from this era is the cross-vaulted arcade on the north side (off Vourdouba).

Etz Hayyim Synagogue   SYNAGOGUE

(✉28210 86286; www.etz-hayyim-hania.org; Parodos Kondylaki; ⊙10am-6pm Mon-Thu, to 3pm Fri) Crete's only remaining synagogue (dating from the 15th century) was badly damaged in WWII and reopened in 1999. It sports a *mikve* (ritual bath), tombs of rabbis and a memorial to the local Jews killed by the Nazis. Today it serves a small congregation and is open to visitors. Find it on a small lane accessible only from Kondylaki street.

Firkas Fortress
FORTRESS

(⊘ 8am-2pm Mon-Fri) The Firkas Fortress at the western tip of the harbour heads the best-preserved section of the massive fortifications that were built by the Venetians to protect the city from marauding pirates and invading Turks. The Turks invaded anyway, in 1645, and turned the fortress into a barracks and a prison. Today, parts of it house the Maritime Museum of Crete. There's a great view of the harbour from the top.

Municipal Art Gallery
GALLERY

(☑ 28210 92294; www.pinakothiki-chania.gr; Halidon 98-102; adult/child €2/free; ⊘ 10am-2pm & 7-10pm Mon-Sat) Hania's modern art gallery evokes the interior of a boat and presents temporary exhibitions of contemporary works by local and national artists on three elegant, well-lit floors.

🏖 Beaches

The town beach 2km west of the Venetian Harbour at Nea Hora is crowded but convenient if you just want to cool off and get some rays. Koum Kapi is less used (and less clean). For better swimming, keep heading west to the beaches (in order) of Agioi Apostoli, Hrysi Akti and Kalamaki, which are all served by local buses heading towards Platanias.

🏃 Activities

Blue Adventures Diving
DIVING

(☑ 28210 40403; www.divingchania.com; Chrysanthou Episkopou 39; 1-/2-tank dive €55/90; ⊘ 9.30am-10pm Apr-Nov) This established outfit offers a host of dive options, including discover courses, PADI open-water certification, and diving trips around Hania, including beginner dives in PADI training standards. There are also snorkelling trips and cruise options for those who just want to go along for the ride.

Nea Hora Beach
BEACH

(Akti Papanikoli) Hania's in-town beach is only a 10-minute walk west of the Venetian Harbour. The 500m-long yellow-sand strip is backed by tavernas, small markets and holiday apartment rentals. Fairly shallow, it's good for kids and popular with locals on weekends.

Greek Mountaineering Association
OUTDOORS

(EOS; ☑ 28210 44647; www.eoshanion.gr; Tzanakaki 90; ⊘ 8.30am-6pm Mon-Fri) For all your hiking and mountaineering needs on Crete, this is the go-to organisation. Check the

website or swing by the local EOS chapter to get the full scoop, including climbing in the Lefka Ori (White Mountains), mountain refuges and the E4 European Path.

🛏 Sleeping

Ifigenia Rooms & Studios
GUESTHOUSE €

(☑ 28210 94357; www.ifigeniastudios.gr; Gamba 23; r €50-130; ❈ 🛜) This network of refurbished buildings around the Venetian Harbour has a bed for every budget, from basic rooms to luxurious bi-level suites with Jacuzzis and sea views. Most of the 25 units brim with such old-timey touches as wrought-iron canopy beds and beamed ceilings. The pricier ones have kitchens and can sleep up to four. Specify your arrival time when booking.

Pension Theresa
PENSION €

(☑ 28210 92798; www.pensiontheresa.gr; Angelou 8; d €50-60; ❈ 🛜) This creaky old Venetian house with a steep (and narrow!) spiral staircase and antique furniture delivers snug rooms with character aplenty. The location is excellent, the ambience rustic and convivial, and the views lovely from the rooftop terrace with communal kitchen stocked with basic breakfast items. It's close to plenty of bars and restaurants.

Palazzo Duca
BOUTIQUE HOTEL €€

(☑ 28210 70460; www.palazzoduca.gr; Douka 27-29; d €85-155; ❈ 🛜) In a backstreet off the harbour, this protected building with Byzantine origins was meticulously restored and turned into a pint-sized luxury hotel with eight elegantly furnished rooms spread over three floors (there's a lift). The best is the vast top-floor suite with kitchenette and a private patio with Jacuzzi. Optional breakfast is €7.50.

★ Serenissima
BOUTIQUE HOTEL €€€

(☑ 28210 86386; www.serenissima.gr; Skoufon 4; d incl breakfast from €170; ❈ 🛜) This tranquil Venetian townhouse, renovated to impeccable standards, packs plenty of design cachet into its historic walls. The elegant rooms feature the gamut of mod cons along with period touches like stone walls, wooden beams and candlelit niches. Rates include an à la carte breakfast in the downstairs restaurant-bar.

Elia Daliani Suites
GUESTHOUSE €€€

(☑ 28215 04684; www.eliahotels.com; Chatzimichali Daliani 57; d €100; ❈ 🛜) These four spacious, stylish suites fill a restored Venetian townhouse on pedestrianised Daliani, just behind the town market. The look is edgy contemporary with all-white furniture, but you get a sense of place from the wall-sized retro black-and-white photographs of scenes from rural Crete. A small balcony looks out over the quiet street. No on-site reception.

Splanzia Hotel
BOUTIQUE HOTEL €€€

(☑ 28210 45313; www.splanzia.com; Daskalogianni 20; d incl breakfast from €130; ❋@🖤) This smartly renovated hotel in a Venetian mansion in the lively Splantzia quarter has eight stylish rooms, each different but all outfitted with custom-made wooden furniture, huge beds – some of them canopied – and the gamut of tech touches. The back rooms overlook a bougainvillea-festooned courtyard with a Turkish well.

It's run by friendly folk with a knack for hospitality. In peak season, a two- or three-night minimum stay may be required.

✖ Eating

★ Bougatsa Iordanis
CRETAN €

(☑ 28210 88855; www.iordanis.gr; Apokoronou 24; bougatsa €3; ⊙ 6am-2.30pm Mon-Sat, to 1.30pm Sun; 🖤) Locals start salivating at the mere mention of this little bakery-cafe dedicated to making the finest *bougatsa* since 1924. The flaky treat, filled with sweet or savoury cheese, is cooked fresh in enormous slabs and carved up in front of your eyes. Pair it with a coffee and you're set for the morning. There's nothing else on the menu!

Mesogiako
MEDITERRANEAN €

(☑ 28210 57992; www.mesogiako.com; Chatzimichali Daliani 36; mains €10-16; ⊙ 7pm-12.30am Mon-Sat, noon-5pm Sun; ❋🖤) Opposite the minaret in the Splantzia quarter, this trendily cosy eatery with cheerful tangerine walls and modern country-style furniture sits among a group of similarly popular eateries. The menu is most creative when it comes to the mezedhes – Moroccan roll, salmon croquettes and wild mushroom risotto are all winners.

Kouzina EPE
CRETAN €

(☑ 28210 42391; Daskalogianni 25; mains €4-9.50; ⊙ noon-7.30pm Mon-Sat) This cheery lunch spot gets contemporary designer flair from the cement floor, country-white tables and dangling silver origami boats. It's a local favourite away from the crowds, serving blackboard-listed *mayirefta* that can be inspected in the open kitchen.

★ Pallas
INTERNATIONAL €€

(☑ 28210 45688; www.pallaschania.gr; Akti Tombazi 15; mains €8-16; ⊙ 8.30am-4am; 🖤) This much buzzed-about hipster cafe-bar has a sweet location in an impeccably renovated former customs house from 1830 right in the Venetian Harbour. Grab a high chair, sofa or table to linger over the three-tiered breakfast, a crisp salad for lunch or a juicy steak dinner – or pop by just for coffee or cocktails.

To Maridaki
SEAFOOD €€

(☑ 28210 08880; www.tomaridaki.gr/en; Daskalogianni 33; mezhedes €3-14; ⊙ noon-midnight Mon-Sat) This modern seafood *mezedhopoleio* (restaurant specialising in mezedhes) is often packed to the gills with chatty locals. Dishes straddle the line between tradition and innovation with to-die-for fried calamari and crisp and delicious house white wine. The complimentary panna cotta is a worthy finish.

Tamam Restaurant
MEDITERRANEAN €€

(☑ 28210 96080; www.tamamrestaurant.com; Zambeliou 49; mains €8-13; ⊙ noon-12.30am; 🖤🖤) This convivial taverna in a converted Turkish bathhouse has captured people's attention since 1982 with strong-flavoured Cretan dishes that often incorporate Middle Eastern spices and touches. The boneless lamb in tomato sauce with raisins and mint is a winner. Tables spill out onto the narrow alleyway.

Well of the Turk
MIDDLE EASTERN €€

(☑ 28210 54547; www.welloftheturk.com; Sarpaki 1-3; mains €8-15; ⊙ 6pm-midnight Wed-Mon; ❋🖤) In an age-old stone building that used to house a *hammam*, and flanking a quiet square, this romantic taverna specialises in richly textured dishes with a strong French and Moroccan identity, yet prepared with the finest Cretan ingredients. The cheesecake with rosewater and orange makes an imaginative culinary coda.

To Karnagio
GREEK €€

(☑ 28210 53366; Plateia Katehaki 8; mains €8-18; ⊙ noon-midnight May-Oct; 🖤) Mamba-green tables spill onto a harbourside plaza next to the Grand Arsenal in this mainstay restaurant that serves a modest selection of grilled meat and seafood alongside some flaky *boureki* (pies) and fresh salads.

★ Thalassino Ageri
SEAFOOD €€€

(☑ 28210 51136; www.thalasino-ageri.gr; Vivilaki 35; fish per kg €55; ⊙ 7pm-midnight Apr–mid-Oct) This solitary fish taverna among the vestiges of Hania's old tanneries in Halepa, some 2km east of the centre, is one of Crete's top eateries. Take in the sunset from the superb setting and peruse the changing menu, dictated by the day's catch. Dishes like squid with crushed fennel and green olives hum with creativity while others (like the melt-in-your-mouth calamari) shine through their transcendent simplicity.

Drinking & Nightlife

The cafe-bars around the Venetian Harbour are nice places to sit, but charge top euro. For a more local vibe, head to Plateia 1821 in the Splantzia quarter, the interior streets near Potie, or to alt-flavoured Sarpidona on the eastern end of the harbour.

★ Sinagogi   BAR
(☑ 28210 95242; Parodos Kondylaki 15; ⊙ 1pm-3am Jun-Sep; 🛜) Housed in a roofless Venetian building on a small lane next to the synagogue, this popular summer-only lounge bar has eclectic decor and is a laid-back place to relax and take it all in. After dark, it's bathed in a romantic glow while DJs play soft electro and the bartenders whip up mojitos and daiquiris.

Kleidi   BAR
(☑ 28210 52974; Plateia 1821; ⊙ 9am-late; 🛜) By day locals fill the shady plaza tables and sip iced coffee, and by night the place buzzes with party life. There's no written sign, just the image of a keyhole (*kleidi* means key).

☆ Entertainment

★ Fagotto Jazz Bar   LIVE MUSIC
(☑ 28210 71877; Angelou 16; ⊙ 9pm-5am) Established in 1978, this Hania institution in a Venetian building offers smooth jazz, soft rock and blues (sometimes live) in a setting brimming with jazz paraphernalia, including a saxophone beer tap. Great cocktails too! The action picks up after 10pm.

🔒 Shopping

Hania offers top shopping, especially in the backstreets. Theotokopoulou is lined with souvenir and handicraft shops. Skrydlof offers a vast array of local and imported sandals, belts and bags. Find some of the most authentic crafts in the Splantzia quarter, along Chatzimichali Daliani and Daskalogianni. The *agora* (central market hall) is touristy but still worth a wander.

Agora   MARKET
(Covered Market; Chatzimichali Giannari; ⊙ 7.30am-2pm Mon, Wed & Sat, 9am-9pm Tue, Thu & Fri; ♿) Hania's cross-shaped market hall opened in 1913 and bustles mostly with souvenir-hunting tourists, though a few stands selling traditional Cretan produce and products (herbs, honey, baked goods, raki, cheese) – along with cafes – are still part of the mix.

ⓘ Information

Free wi-fi is widely available in public spaces, including the harbour, around the central market and at Plateia 1866, as well as at most hotels, restaurants, cafes and bars.

Banks cluster around Plateia Markopoulou in the new city, but there are also ATMs in the old town on Halidon.

Municipal Tourist Office (☑ 28213 36155; chania@ofcrete.gr; Kydonias 29; ⊙ 8.30am-2.30pm Mon-Fri) Modest selection of brochures, maps and transport timetables at the town hall. Open some Saturdays.

Post Office (☑ 28210 28444; Peridou 10; ⊙ 7.30am-8.30pm Mon-Fri)

Tellus Travel (☑ 28210 91500; www.tellus travel.gr; Halidon 108; ⊙ 8.30am-10pm)

Tourist Police (☑ 28210 25931, 28210 53333, 171; ⊙ 24hr)

ⓘ Getting There & Away

AIR

Hania's **airport** (☑ 28210 83800; www.chania-airport.com) is 14km east of town on the Akrotiri Peninsula, and is served year-round from Athens and Thessaloniki and seasonally from throughout Europe. Carriers include Aegean Airlines and Ryanair. A taxi anywhere in Chania costs €24. Public buses into town stop right outside the terminal (€2.50, 30 minutes).

BOAT

Hania's port is at Souda, 7km southeast of town (and the site of a NATO base). The port is linked to town by bus (€2, or €2.50 if bought aboard) and taxi (€11). Hania buses meet each boat, as do buses to Rethymno.

Anek Lines (☑ 28210 24000; www.anek.gr; Leoforos Karamanlis 70; ⊙ 7.30am-3.30pm Mon-Fri) Nightly overnight ferry between Piraeus and Hania (from €38, nine hours). Buy tickets online or at the port; reserve ahead for cars.

BUS

Hania's **KTEL bus station** (☑ info 28210 93052, tickets 28210 93306; www.e-ktel.com; Kelaidi 73-77; 🛜) has a cafeteria, minimarket and left-luggage service. Check the excellent website for the current schedule.

BUSES FROM HANIA

DESTINATION	DURATION	FARE (€)	FREQUENCY
Elafonisi	2¼hr	11	daily
Falasarna	1¾hr	8.30	3 daily
Hora Sfakion	1¾hr	8.30	3 daily
Iraklio	2¾hr	15.10	hourly
Kissamos (Kastelli)	1hr	5.10	15 daily
Kolymbari	40min	3.60	6 daily
Moni Agias Triadas	30min	2.60	2 daily
Omalos (for Samaria Gorge)	1hr	7.50	3 daily
Paleohora	1¾hr	7.60	4 daily
Rethymno	1¼hr	6.80	hourly
Sougia	1¾hr	7.80	3 daily
Stavros	40min	2.30	7 daily

ⓘ Getting Around

TO/FROM THE AIRPORT

KTEL (www.e-ktel.com) buses link the airport with central Hania roughly every 30 minutes (€2.50, 25 minutes). Taxis between any place in the city and the airport cost €24.

BUS

Local buses are operated by **Chania Urban Buses** (☑ 28210 98115; http://chaniabus.gr). Zone A/B tickets cost €1.20/1.70 if bought from a kiosk or vending machine and €2/2.50 from the driver.

A handily central stop for Souda port, Halepa, Nea Hora and other local destinations is on Giannari, near the *agora* market hall.

CAR

Major car-hire outlets are at the airport or on Halidon. Most of the old town is pedestrianised. There's free parking just west of Firkas Fortress and along the waterfront towards Nea Hora beach, or by the eastern edge of the harbour off Kyprou; but avoid areas marked residents-only.

TAXI

Taxi (☑ 28210 98700; www.chaniataxi.gr)

Kissamos (Kastelli)
Κίσσαμος (Καστέλλι)

POP 4275

Kissamos exudes an unpolished, almost gritty, air compared to other north-coast towns. This is not a place given entirely over to tourism. There are two beaches in town, separated by a waterfront promenade: the sandy Mavros Molos in the west and the pebbly Telonio beach to the east.

The largest town and capital of Kissamos province, it is referred to interchangeably as Kissamos or Kastelli (though the official name is the former).

🛏 Sleeping & Eating

Thalassa APARTMENT €
(☑ 28220 31231; www.thalassa-apts.gr; Drapanias Beach, Mithimna; studio from €40; P✳@🛜🏊) The isolated Thalassa complex is ideal for a quiet retreat about 5km east of Kissamos at Drapanias beach. The immaculate studios are airy and well fitted. There's a barbecue on the lawn, a small playground and a salt-water swimming pool with massage jets. It's helpful to have a car.

Nautilus Bay Hotel APARTMENT €€
(☑ 28220 22250; www.nautilusbay.gr; Plaka Beach; apt €110-160; P✳🛜🏊) Well-proportioned and modern apartments with streamlined furniture, small kitchenettes and black-tiled bathrooms fill this modern complex right on the sandy beach and in the centre of town. Balconies have sweeping water views and there's a restaurant and bar and a large pool area.

Taverna Sunset TAVERNA €
(☑ 28220 83478; Paraliaki; mains €7-10; ☺noon-1am; 🛜) Locals mix with in-the-know visitors at this quintessential family taverna presided over by Giannis, who's usually ensconced behind the grill coaxing meat and fish into succulent perfection. It's right on the waterfront, so you can feel the breezes coming offshore.

❶ Getting There & Away

BOAT

From the port 3km west of town, **Lane Sea Lines** (☎27360 37055; www.lane-kithira.com) has two weekly ferries to Piraeus (13 hours), four to Kythira (four hours), two to Antikythira (2¼ hours) and one to Gythion (eight hours). In summer, a bus meets ferries; otherwise taxis into town cost around €7. Schedules change seasonally.

BUS

Bus schedules change seasonally – check www.e-ktel.com. There are as many as 14 daily buses to Hania (€5.10, one hour); change in Hania for Paleohora, Rethymno and Iraklio. There are also two to three daily buses to Falasarna (€3.80, 15 minutes) in summer only and one daily to Elafonisi (€6.90, 1¼ hours) from May to October.

CAR

Kissamos is about 40km west of Hania. **Kissamos Rent a Car** (☎28220 23740; www.kissamosrentacar.com; Iroön Polytechniou 210; car per week from €159) is one of several car-hire agencies along Iroön Polytechniou, the main drag.

Around Kissamos

Polyrrinia   Πολυρρηνία

Polyrrinia   ARCHAEOLOGICAL SITE

FREE The wonderful mountaintop ruins of the ancient city of Polyrrinia (pol-ee-ren-*ee*-a) lie about 7km south of Kissamos, above the village of the same name. Sea, mountain and valley views from this defensible spire are stunning and the region is blanketed with wildflowers in spring. The site's most impressive feature is the acropolis built by the Byzantines and Venetians. There's also a church built on the foundations of a Hellenistic temple from the 4th century BC.

Polyrrinia was founded by the Dorians in the 6th century BC and was constantly at war with the Kydonians from Hania. Coins from the period depict the warrior-goddess Athena, who was evidently revered by the warlike Polyrrinians.

Unlike their rivals the Kydonians, the Polyrrinians did not resist the Roman invasion and thus the city was spared destruction. It was the best-fortified town in Crete and the administrative centre of western Crete from the Roman through to the Byzantine period. The Venetians used it as a fortress. Many of the structures, including an aqueduct built by Hadrian, date from the Roman period. Near the aqueduct is a cave dedicated to the nymphs; it still contains the niches for nymph statuettes.

There is no public transport to the site.

Gramvousa Peninsula   Χερσόνησος Γραμβούσα

Northwest of Kissamos (Kastelli) is the beautifully wild and remote Gramvousa Peninsula, whose main attraction is the stunning lagoon-like beach of Balos, on Cape Tigani on the west side of the peninsula's narrow tip. Kalyviani village is a good base for visiting the peninsula.

◉ Sights & Activities

★ Balos   LAGOON

(cruises adult/concession €27/13) The rugged Gramvousa Peninsula cradles the lagoon-like white powdery beach of Balos, whose shallow, shimmering turquoise waters will undoubtedly bring a giggle to your holiday-hungry throat. The beach is gorgeous, with lapping translucent waters dotted with tiny shellfish and darting fish. Balos overlooks two islets, the larger one (Imeri) being crowned by the ruins of a humongous Venetian fortress built to keep pirates at bay.

Cretan Daily Cruises   BOATING

(☎28220 24344; www.cretandailycruises.com; adult/child €27/13; ⊙late Apr-Oct) The easiest way to get to Gramvousa and Balos lagoon is by boat cruise from the port of Kissamos. There are three departures daily but check ahead to make sure they haven't been cancelled because of strong winds. Reasonably priced food and drink is available on board. Summer-only KTEL buses from Hania are timed to boat departures. Tickets are sold online, by phone or at the port.

🛏 Sleeping & Eating

The best base for touring this region is the village of Kalyviani, 6km west of Kissamos (Kastelli). There is no lodging at Balos.

★ Gramboussa   CRETAN €€

(☎28220 22707; http://gramvousarestaurant.com; Kalyviani; mains €8-16; ⊙10am-1pm; 🅿) 🍃 In Kalyviani village, about 6km west of central Kissamos, Gramboussa serves fine traditional Cretan cuisine in an elegantly rustic stone building set in a superb garden. It's a cut above other restaurants and offers the chance to sample the freshest regional cuisine Crete has to offer, as well as wood-oven specials like suckling pig or lamb with honey.

❶ Getting There & Away

From May to October, day trippers arriving by cruise boat from Kissamos (with a two-hour stop at Imeri) deluge Balos between 11am and 4pm. The only way to avoid the crowds is to get there by car before or after the boats arrive. The approach is via a scenic corduroy road that picks up near the village of Kalyviani. It ends 12 axle-shaking kilometres later at a parking lot from where a 1.2km trail leads down to the lagoon. Nondrivers could try hitching a ride or walk, although you'll be eating a lot of dust from passing vehicles.

Falasarna · Φαλάσαρνα
POP 25

Some 16km west of Kissamos, Falasarna is little more than a blotch of habitations on a long sandy beach – but what a beach! This broad sweep of pink-cream sand is considered among Crete's finest and is famous for its superbly clear teal waters, stunning sunsets and rolling waves. Spread your towel on the Big Beach (Megali Paralia) at the south end or pick a spot in one of the coves separated by rocky spits further north.

Falasarna has no centre as such, although there are hotels and several tavernas, bars and small supermarkets.

◉ Sights

Aside from its stunning beach, Falasarna is famous as the site of a 4th-century city-state and trading centre with its own harbour. It's possible to wander among the ancient ruins.

⌂ Sleeping

Magnolia Apartments · APARTMENT €
(☑ 28220 41407, 6945605438; www.magnolia-apartments.gr; studio/apt from €45/55; P✳❄) Just a five-minute walk back from a sparkling beach, Magnolia is a quiet holiday retreat with 12 well-equipped studio apartments whose decor is pleasant but plays it safe. Enjoy a leisurely breakfast or sunset drinks from your sea-facing balconies or in the neatly groomed garden.

Sunset Rooms & Apartments · APARTMENT €€
(☑ 28220 22155, 28220 41204; www.sunset.com.gr; d/apt/villa €40/70/160; P❄) In an enviable location steps from one of Crete's finest sandy beaches, Sunset has 13 rooms and six apartments above a convivial taverna with

fig trees and a natural spring. Rooms are snug, but tastefully decked out with apricot-coloured walls, wrought-iron beds, tile floors and sea-facing balconies.

Families should enquire about the four nearby two-floor stone villas with full kitchens.

❶ Getting There & Away

Bus schedules vary seasonally (check www.e-ktel.com). In summer, at least three daily buses make the trip out to Falasarna from Hania (€8.30, 1¼ hours) via Kissamos-Kasteli (€3.80, 40 minutes). A taxi costs about €15 from Kissamos and €65 from Hania.

SOUTHWEST COAST

The stark and muscular Lefka Ori (White Mountains) meet the sea along Crete's corrugated southwestern coast, which is indented with a handful of laid-back coastal villages, some of them accessible only by boat and therefore completely untouched by mass tourism. You can walk to perfectly isolated little beaches or soak up the majestic scenery and fragrant air on a scramble through wildy romantic gorges away from the busy Samaria Gorge, which ends in Agia Roumeli.

Frangokastello
Φραγγοκαστέλλο
POP 148

Dominated by a mighty 14th-century Venetian fortress, Frangokastello is a low-key resort with a fabulous wide and sandy beach that slopes gradually into shallow warm water, making it ideal for kids. There's no actual village, just a smattering of tavernas, small markets and low-rise holiday apartments and rooms scattered along the main street.

✖ Eating

Oasis Taverna · CRETAN €
(☑ 28250 83562; www.oasisrooms.com; Frangokastello Beach; mains €5-13; ⊙ 9am-10pm or later; P❄♿) Part of an excellent family-run studio and apartment complex at the western end of the beach, about 1km from the fortress, this is the best place to eat not only for the well-executed Cretan home-cooked meals but also for the stunning view from the flower-festooned stone-floor terrace.

Also a good place for breakfast before a day on the beach.

❶ Getting There & Away

KTEL buses stop at several spots along the main road. In summer, there are three daily buses from Hora Sfakion to Frangokastello (€2.30, 30 minutes).

Hora Sfakion
Χώρα Σφακίων

POP 212

The more bullet holes you see in the passing road signs, the closer you are to Hora Sfakion, long renowned in Cretan history for its rebellious streak against foreign occupiers. But don't worry, the pint-sized fishing village is an amiable, if eccentric, place that caters well to today's foreign visitors – many of whom are Samaria Gorge hikers stumbling off the Agia Roumeli boat on their way back to Hania. Most pause just long enough to catch the next bus out, but some are tempted into staying by the area's isolated beaches and hiking trails.

◉ Sights & Activities

Sweetwater Beach BEACH
(Glyka Nera) West of Hora Sfakion, lovely Sweetwater Beach is accessible by a small daily ferry (May to October, per person €4), by taxi boat (one-way/return €25/50) or on foot via a stony and partly vertiginous 3.5km coastal path starting at the first hairpin turn of the Anopoli road. A small cafe rents umbrellas and sun chairs.

Vrissi Beach BEACH
Abutting the western edge of the village, this tiny grey-sand cove is the closest beach for unfolding your towel or a quick dip. There's a taverna on the bluff above for snacks and refreshments.

Notos Mare Marine Adventures DIVING
(☏ 6947270106; www.notosmare.com; New Harbour; 1/2 dives €49/85) In addition to PADI certification and dives for beginners and advanced divers, this long-running professional outfit also rents boats, organises charter boat and fishing trips, and operates taxi boats to secluded beaches along the south coast.

🛏 Sleeping & Eating

Be sure to try the local *Sfakiani pita* – this thin, circular pancake filled with sweet *myzithra* and flecked with honey makes a great breakfast when served with a bit of Greek yoghurt on the side.

> ### FRANGOKASTELLO: THE 'GHOST' CASTLE
>
> Frangokastello was built by the Venetians to guard against pirates and feisty local Sfakian rebels. On 17 May 1828, during the War of Independence, many Cretan fighters were killed here by the Turks. According to legend their ghosts – the *drosoulites* – can be seen marching past the fortress in the early dawn on the battle's anniversary.

Xenia Hotel HOTEL €
(☏ 28250 91490; www.sfakia-xenia-hotel.gr; Old Harbour; d incl breakfast €55; P ❋ 🛜) Well positioned overlooking the water, this hotel has been around since the early 1960s but has since been modernised numerous times and now sports mod cons such as air-con, satellite TV and a fridge in each of the 24 rooms. Ring in the evening by toasting the waves on your sea-facing balcony.

Hotel Stavris HOTEL €
(☏ 28250 91220; www.hotel-stavris-sfakia-crete.com; s/d/apt €31/36/52; ❋ 🛜) Up the hill overlooking the old harbour, the Perrakis clan has welcomed guests since 1969. Rooms and apartments vary by size, configuration and amenities, although all are clean and come with air-con, fridge and balcony. The nicer ones have kitchenettes and harbour-facing views. Cash only.

Taverna Nikos TAVERNA €
(☏ 28250 91111; Old Harbour; mains €5-12; ⊗ 7am-midnight) At the beginning of the gauntlet of harbour-front tavernas, family-run Nikos is a reliable standby for Greek staples, grilled fish and meat and Cretan specialities like smoked pork or sautéed snails. Don't get up from the table without sampling the local speciality *Sfakiani pita*.

❶ Getting There & Away

BOAT
Hora Sfakion is the eastern terminus for the south-coast **Anendyk** (☏ 28210 95511; www.anendyk.gr; New Harbour) ferry route to/from Paleohora via Loutro, Agia Roumeli and Sougia, and also runs boats to Gavdos Island. Schedules vary seasonally, so always check ahead. Often boats only run as far as Agia Roumeli, where you must change for another ferry to Sougia and Paleohora.

DESTINATION	FARE (€)	FREQUENCY
Agia Roumeli	7.50	up to 3 daily
Loutro	6	up to 7 daily
Paleohora	20.70	daily
Sougia (via Agia Roumeli)	16.20	daily

There are also two to three boats per week to/ from Gavdos Island via Loutro and Agia Roumeli (€21.20, four hours).

BUS

KTEL buses leave from the square up the hill above the municipal car park. Schedules change seasonally; check online. In summer there are three daily services to/from Hania (€8.30, 1¾ hours); coming from Rethymno, change in Vryses (€8.30, two hours). There are also three daily buses to Frangokastello (€2.30, 30 minutes).

Loutro Λουτρό

POP 56

The pint-sized fishing village of Loutro is a tranquil crescent of flower-festooned white-and-blue buildings hugging a narrow pebbly beach between Agia Roumeli and Hora Sfakion. It's only accessible by boat and on foot and is the departure point for coastal walks to isolated beaches, such as Finix, Marmara and Sweetwater.

🏃 Activities

Loutro Canoes　　　　　　　CANOEING

(📞 28250 91433; per day €16) Hotel Porto Loutro hires out small canoes.

🛏 Sleeping & Eating

Given the captive market, the tavernas that line the waterfront in Loutro are surprisingly good. Most offer the usual array of fresh fish, local grills and traditional *mayirefta*.

Villa Niki　　　　　　　　　APARTMENT €

(📞 6972299979; www.loutro-accommodation.com; studio/apt from €55/80; 🌐 🖥 🛜) These elegantly rustic studios with beamed ceilings and stone floors accommodate up to four people and come with a kitchenette with basic equipment. Since Niki is located just above the village, you get great views over the water from the balconies.

Hotel Porto Loutro　　　　　　HOTEL €€

(📞 28250 91433, 28250 91001; www.hotelporto loutro.com; s/d incl breakfast €70/95; 🕐 Apr-Oct; 🌐 @ 🛜) The classiest hotel in the village has rooms and studios furnished in smartly contemporary island style and spread across two buildings, all with spacious furnished balconies perfect for counting the waves or chilling with a beer. Days start with a lavish breakfast spread served at the on-site restaurant. No credit cards.

ⓘ Information

There's no bank, ATM or post office, and many places do not accept credit cards. Bring plenty of cash (the nearest ATM is in Hora Sfakion).

ⓘ Getting There & Away

Loutro is on the Paleohora–Hora Sfakion boat route operated by Anendyk (www.anendyk.gr). There are seven boats daily to Hora Sfakion and three to Agia Roumeli with connections to Sougia and Paleohora. Boats from Hora Sfakion to Gavdos Island also stop in Loutro.

Sougia Σούγια

POP 136

Sougia, 67km south of Hania and on the Hora Sfakion–Paleohora ferry route, is one of the most chilled-out and refreshingly undeveloped southern beach resorts. Cafes, bars and tavernas line a tamarisk-shaded waterfront promenade along a grey pebble-and-sand beach. Most pensions and apartments enjoy a quieter inland setting. There is little to do other than relax or explore the local trails, including the popular Agia Irini Gorge.

🏃 Activities

Sougia has a pleasant 1km-long grey sand-and-pebble beach, but its drop-off is quick, so it's not ideal for families with small children.

★ Agia Irini Gorge　　　　　　HIKING

(www.agia-irini.com; €1.50; ⊙ year-round) Pretty Agia Irini Gorge starts some 13km north of Sougia. The well-maintained, mostly shaded 7.5km trail (with a 500m elevation drop) follows the river bed, is shaded by oleander, pines and other greenery, and passes caves hidden in the gorge walls. You'll emerge at a taverna where you can call a taxi (€15) or continue on foot for another 7km via a quiet, paved and sunny road to Sougia.

Of course, it's also possible to do the hike in reverse. To get to the trailhead, take the bus to Hania and ask the driver to drop you off or take a taxi.

IMBROS GORGE ΦΑΡΑΓΓΙ ΤΗΣ ΙΜΠΡΟΥ

Half the length of the more famous Samaria Gorge (p480), the 8km-long **Imbros Gorge** (€2; ☺year-round), 130km east of Sougia, is no less beautiful and a lot less busy, especially in the afternoon. Most people start in the mountain village of Imbros and hike down to the southern coastal village of Komitades. Going the other way provides a bit more of a workout as you'll be walking up a gentle grade. A taxi between the two (about €20) can be arranged by tavernas at either end.

The hike takes you past 300m-high walls buttressed by cypresses, holm oaks, fig and almond trees, and redolent sage. Landmarks include a **giant arch** at the 2km mark (coming from the south) and the **narrowest point** of the ravine (near the 4.5km mark), which is just 2m wide.The track is easy to follow as it traces the stream bed past rock-slides and caves. Sturdy shoes are essential.

🛏 Sleeping & Eating

Aretousa Studios & Rooms APARTMENT €
(📱28230 51178; studio €55-65; ☺Apr-Oct; P❄🛜) This lovely pension on the road to Hania, 200m from the sea, has 10 bright and comfortably furbished studios with tile floors, balconies and well-stocked kitchens. The tranquil relaxing garden is a nice post-tanning chill zone and there's even a playground for kids out back.

Hotel Santa Irene APARTMENT €€
(📱28230 51342; www.santa-irene.gr; Beach Rd; apt €60-80; ☺late Mar-early Nov; P❄🛜) This smart hotel in a traditional building on the beach has 14 roomy and balconied studios sleeping two to five people. Whip up breakfast or a small meal in the kitchenette or grab a snack at the attached snack bar.

Taverna Oasis TAVERNA €
(📱28230 51121; mains €6-10; ☺11am-9pm Apr-Oct) Restore energies with a cold beer and classic Greek snacks after tackling the lovely Agia Irini Gorge. From here it's another 7km walk or a €15 taxi ride back to Sougia.

Polyfimos TAVERNA €
(📱28230 51343; www.polifimos.gr; Main Rd; mains €7-13.50; ☺1pm-midnight Apr-Oct; 🛜) Hidden in a grapevine-shrouded courtyard off the Hania road, this charismatic lair specialises in charcoal-tickled local meats, hearty stews like rabbit *stifadho* (cooked with onions in a tomato purée) and lamb *tsigariasto* (sautéed). It's run by ex-hippie Yiannis who also makes his own oil, wine and raki.

★**Omikron** INTERNATIONAL €€
(📱28230 51492; Beach Rd; mains €7-15; ☺8am-late; 🛜📱) At this elegantly rustic beachfront lair, Jean-Luc Delfosse has forged his own culinary path in a refreshing change from

taverna staples. Mushroom crêpes to *Flammekuche* (Alsatian-style pizza), seafood pasta to pepper steak – it's all fresh, creative and delicious.

ℹ Information

There is one ATM but no petrol station. Visit www.sougia.info for area information.

ℹ Getting There & Around

BOAT

From May to October, ferries on **Anendyk's** (📱28230 51230; www.anendyk.gr) Paleohora–Agia Roumeli route stop in Sougia. The trip to either Paleohora or Agia Roumeli takes about 40 minutes and costs €11.20 and €11, respectively. In Agia Roumeli, you can continue east to Hora Sfakion via Loutro. There are also two or three weekly ferries to Gavdos via Agia Roumeli.
Captain George's Water Taxi (📱6947605802, 28230 51133; www.sougia.info/taxi-boats) Serves the coast near Sougia.

BUS

Two to three buses operate between Sougia and Hania (€7.80, 1¾ hours) with a stop in Agia Irini to drop off gorge hikers. The bus departing Sougia at 6.15pm waits for the Agia Roumeli boat. There are also daily buses to Omalos (for Samaria Gorge) in summer only (€5.30, one hour).

TAXI

Local **taxi** (📱28230 51403, 69777445160, 6972370480; www.taxi-selino.com) drivers have a central kiosk on the waterfront.

Paleohora Παλαιόχωρα

POP 1900

Appealing, laid-back and full of character, Paleohora lies on a narrow peninsula flanked by a long, curving tamarisk-shaded sandy beach (Pahia Ammos) and a pebbly beach

SAMARIA GORGE ΦΑΡΑΓΓΙ ΤΗΣ ΣΑΜΑΡΙΑΣ

Hiking the 16km-long **Samaria Gorge** (☑ 28210 45570; www.samaria.gr; Omalos; adult/child €5/free; ⊙ 6am-4pm May–mid-Oct), one of Europe's longest canyons, is high on the list of must-dos for many Crete visitors. There's an undeniable raw beauty to the canyon with its soaring cliffs and needle-nose passageways. The hike begins at an elevation of 1230m just south of Omalos and ends in the coastal village of Agia Roumeli. It's also possible to do it the 'lazy way' by hiking a shorter distance, starting at Agia Roumeli. The only way out of Agia Roumeli is by taking the boat to Sougia or Hora Sfakion, which are served by bus and taxi.

The best time for the Samaria trek is in April and May when wildflowers brighten the trail. Keep your eyes peeled for the endemic kri-kri, a shy endangered wild goat.

Hiking the Gorge

The trail begins at **Xyloskalo**, a steep and serpentine stone path that descends some 600m into the canyon to arrive at the simple cypress-framed **Agios Nikolaos chapel**. Beyond here the gorge is wide and open for the next 6km until you reach the abandoned settlement of **Samaria**, whose inhabitants were relocated when the gorge became a national park. Just south of the village is a 14th-century **chapel** dedicated to St Maria of Egypt, after whom the gorge is named.

Further on, the gorge narrows and becomes more dramatic until, at the 11km mark, the walls are only 3.5m apart. These are the famous **Sideroportes** (Iron Gates), where a rickety wooden pathway leads hikers the 20m or so across the water.

The gorge ends at the 12.5km mark just north of the almost abandoned village of Palea (Old) Agia Roumeli. From here it's a further 2km hike to the seaside village of **Agia Roumeli**, whose fine pebble beach and sparkling water are a most welcome sight.

Few people miss taking a refreshing dip or at least bathing sore and aching feet. The entire trek takes from about four hours for the sprinters to six hours for the strollers.

The Low-Down

➡ An early start (before 8am) helps to put you ahead of the crowd. Sleep over in Omalos to be first. During July and August even the early bus from Hania can be packed. Or start after noon, and plan to sleep over in Agia Roumeli.

➡ Hikers starting after about 2pm are only allowed to walk a distance of 2km from either end. Spending the night in the gorge is a no-no – time your trip to be out by sunset.

➡ There's a 1200m elevation drop going north to south. Wear sturdy shoes and take sunscreen, sunglasses, some food, a hat and a water bottle, which you can refill from taps with potable water along the way. Drink plenty!

➡ There are several rest stops with toilets, water, trash bins and benches along the trail.

➡ Falling rocks occasionally lead to injuries but generally it's the heat that's a far bigger problem. Check ahead as park officials may close the gorge on rainy or exceptionally hot days (generally, over 40°C), and the gorge season can end early if the rains have started.

(Halikia). Shallow waters and general quietude make the village a good choice for families with small children. The most picturesque part of Paleohora is the maze of narrow streets below the castle. Tavernas spill out onto the pavement and occasional cultural happenings inject a lively ambience. In spring and autumn, Paleohora attracts many walkers.

◉ Sights & Activities

There are several great **walking trails** nearby. From Paleohora, a six-hour walk along a scenic **coastal path** (p482) leads to Sougia, passing ancient Lissos. An easier inland loop goes to Anydri then through small, lush **Anydri Gorge** to the sea.

When a stiff summer breeze is blowing, **windsurfing** off sandy Pahia Ammos is excellent. Private dolphin-spotting trips are also run from Paleohora.

Venetian Fort FORT
(Kastro Selino; ⊙ 24hr) **FREE** There's not much left of the 13th-century Venetian castle looming above Paleohora, but it's worth the

➡ Early in the season it's sometimes necessary to wade through the stream. Later, as the flow drops, the stream-bed rocks become stepping stones.

➡ If the idea of a 16km hike does not appeal, get a taste of Samaria by doing it 'the easy way', ie starting in Agia Roumeli and heading north for as long as you feel like before doubling back. The Sideroportes, for instance, can be reached in about an hour. Or consider some of the other gorges in the area, like Agia Irini or Imbros.

Sleeping & Eating

It is forbidden to camp in the gorge. Stay at Omalos on the north end, or Agia Roumeli in the south.

There are tavernas in Omalos, including one right by the gorge entrance. A clutch of refreshment stands sell souvenirs, snacks, bottled water and the like, when the gorge is open. Agia Roumeli has several tavernas.

Agriorodo (☑ 28210 67237; 2-/3-bedroom cottage from €60/80; ☺ year-round; P ☎) These lovely modern stone cottages are a comfy base camp for expeditions to Samaria Gorge, whose entrance is a mere 15 minutes on foot away. Decorated with rustic style, each sleeps four to five people and is kitted out with satellite TV, wi-fi, kitchens and a living room with plush sofas and fireplaces.

Hotel Neos Omalos (☑ 28210 67269; www.neos-omalos.gr; Chania-Omalos Rd; s/d/tr incl breakfast €38/49/59; P ☎) This rustic mountain lair has welcomed generations of nature lovers since opening in 1954. A convivial feel pervades the public areas leading to basic, but comfortable, rooms with balcony views that will get you in the mood for hiking. The owners are a fount of information on local hikes and other outdoor activities and can also shuttle you to Samaria Gorge some 4km away.

Xyloskalo (☑ 28210 67237; mains €6-10; ☺ 10am-6pm; ☎) Perched just over the spectacular drop of Samaria Gorge, with eagles occasionally circling outside its wraparound windows, this cosy restaurant dishes up classic Cretan and Greek meals, and offers that last chance to use indoor plumbing and wi-fi.

Getting There & Away

Most people hike Samaria one way going north–south on an organised day trip from every sizeable town and resort in Crete. Confirm that tour prices include the €5 admission to the gorge or the boat ride from Agia Roumeli to Sougia or Hora Sfakion.

With some planning, it's possible to do the trek on your own. There are early-morning public buses to Omalos from Hania (€7.50, one hour), Sougia (€5.30, one hour) and Paleohora (€7, one hour), once or twice daily in high season. Check www.e-ktel.com for the seasonally changing schedule. Taxis are another option.

At the end of the trail, in Agia Roumeli, ferries operated by Anendyk (www.anendyk.gr) go to Sougia or Hora Sfakion; some are met by public buses to Hania.

---

clamber for splendid views of the sea and mountains, especially at sunset.

Built to monitor the southwestern coast from its commanding hilltop position, it was repeatedly destroyed by Cretan rebels, the pirate Barbarossa and the Ottomans.

🛏 Sleeping & Eating

Homestay Anonymous　　PENSION €
(☑ 28230 42098; www.anonymoushomestay.com; d/apt €30/55; ✳☎) This simple but good-value pension with private bathrooms and shared cooking facilities in the courtyard garden is an excellent budget pick. Friendly, well-travelled owner Manolis cultivates a welcoming atmosphere and is a mine of information on local activities. The nine units are in two quaint stone buildings and furnished in charming country style.

Corali　　APARTMENT €
(☑ 6974361868; www.corali-studios.com; Pebble Beach; studio €50-55; ✳@) A friendly Greek-Italian family runs these three immaculate studios kitted out with kitchenettes, upmarket modern furniture, large

pristine bathrooms and waterfront balconies. The central location and sea views are excellent.

Joanna's Place APARTMENT €

(☏ 28230 41801; www.joanna-place.com; studio €50-60; ☉ Apr-Nov; ᴾ ❋ ⎙) This charmer sits in a quiet spot across from a small stone beach at the southeastern tip of the peninsula. The 10 spacious and spotless studios are outfitted with functional locally made furniture, and there's a kitchenette for preparing breakfast to enjoy on your balcony.

Third Eye VEGETARIAN €

(☏ 28230 41234, 6986793504; www.thethirdeye-paleochora.com; mains €6-7; ☉ noon-3pm & 6-11pm; ⎙ ⎘) A local institution and community gathering spot since 1990, the Third Eye knew what to do with beetroot, quinoa and hummus long before meatless fare went mainstream. The globally inspired menu features delicious salads, rotating mains and snacks like samosas or guacamole. Sit on the streetside patio or in the tranquil garden.

★ **Taverna Methexis** CRETAN €€

(☏ 28230 41431; www.facebook.com/Methexis Taverna; Waterfront; mains €7-12; ☉ 12.30-11.30pm; ᴾ ⎙ ⎘) It's well worth the short saunter to the peninsula's southeastern tip to sample the authentic comfort food and warm hospitality at this locally adored taverna across from a small beach. All the classics are accounted for along with such tasty surprises as salt cod with garlic sauce and delicious pies filled with fennel or local *myzithra*.

ℹ Information

There are a couple of ATMs on the main drag, Eleftherios Venizelou.

Post Office (☉ 7am-2.30pm Mon-Fri) Just across from Pahia Ammos (sandy beach).

Selino Travel (☏ 28230 42272; selino2@ otenet.gr; Kondekaki; 3hr trip €18; ☉ 8am-1.30pm & 6-9.30pm Mon-Sat Apr-Oct, shorter hours rest of year)

ℹ Getting There & Around

Notos Rentals (☏ 6976436044; www.notoscar. gr; Eleftherios Venizelou 53; ☉ 9am-2pm & 6-10pm) has cars, motorcycles and bicycles for hire. There are two petrol stations in town. Gas up before heading on longer drives in the region, where petrol stations are rare to nonexistent.

BOAT

Boats leave from the old harbour at the far pebbly beach's southern end. Buy tickets at Selino Travel.

There is a daily morning ferry to Sougia (€11.20, 40 minutes) and Agia Roumeli (€17.20, 1½ hours) where the boat stops for 90 minutes before continuing to Loutro (€19.70, 40 minutes) and Hora Sfakion (€20.70, 20 minutes from Loutro). Some boats can transport cars and scooters.

From May to October, there are also two or three weekly ferries to Gavdos Island (€23.30, four hours) via Sougia and Agia Roumeli. One ferry daily except Sunday goes out to the west-coast beach of Elafonisi (€10, one hour).

BUS

KTEL runs four daily buses to Hania (€8.30, two hours) and one bus daily except Sunday at 6.15am to Omalos (€6.40, two hours) for Samaria Gorge. Buses also stop in Sougia and, on request, at the Agia Irini Gorge trailhead. There

---

PALEOHORA–SOUGIA COASTAL WALK

Following a portion of the E4 European Path, this hike connects two charming coastal towns via a 13km path that runs mostly along the coast.

From Paleohora, follow signs to the campsites to the northeast and turn right at the sign for Anydri. After a couple of kilometres, the path climbs steeply for a beautiful view back to Paleohora. You'll pass **Anydri Beach** and several inviting **coves** where people may be getting an all-over tan. Take a dip because the path soon turns inland to pass over **Cape Flomes**. You'll walk along a plateau carpeted with brush that leads towards the coast and some breathtaking views over the Libyan Sea. About 10km into the hike, you'll reach the Dorian site of **Lissos** from where the path weaves through a pine forest before spilling out at Sougia.

Allow five to six hours for the nearly shadeless walk and take plenty of water, a hat and sunblock. From June through August, it's best to start at sunrise in order to get to Sougia before the heat of the day. The boat back to Paleohora runs around 6pm (check the schedule, www.anendyk.gr).

are also thrice-weekly Elafonisi-bound buses (€5.50, 1½ hours).

Elafonisi   Ελαφονήσι

POP 15

If much of life in Crete is like a beach, remote Elafonisi *is* a beach and a stunning one at that. Tucked into Crete's southwest corner, this symphony of fine pinkish-white sand, turquoise water and gentle dunes looks as though lifted from the Caribbean. Off the long, wide strand lies Elafonisi Islet, easily reached by wading through 50m of knee-deep water. The entire area is part of Natura 2000, the environmental protection program of the European Union.

Alas, this natural gem is hardly a secret and less than idyllic in high summer when floods of sun seekers put pressure on its delicate ecosystem. Come early or late in the day or, better yet, stay overnight to truly sample Elafonisi's magic.

🛏 Sleeping & Eating

Restaurants at the Elafonisi hotels are basic but dependable, while a few beachfront snack bars satisfy daytime munchies.

Elafonisi Village Rooms & Taverna   HOTEL €
(📲 28220 61548, 6942872384; www.elafonisi-village.gr; Beach Rd; d €50-65; ☺ Apr-Oct; ❄ 🛜) Just 250m from Elafonisi Beach, these 10 spacious rooms with tiled floors, wooden furniture and private terraces string across an arid courtyard with sea views for catching the sunset. Four units can sleep up to four people and have a kitchenette.

Elafonisi Resort   HOTEL €
(📲 28250 61274, 6983516137; www.elafonisi-resort.com; s/d €35/45; 🅿 ❄ 🛜) This cluster of low-rise whitewashed buildings dotted around a peaceful olive grove has 21 spacious rooms with fridges; all but one have a balcony, a few come with a kitchen. The affiliated restaurant serves the catch of the day and classic Greek fare.

ℹ Getting There & Away

Elafonisi is about 75km southwest of Hania – budget about 1½ to two hours for the nonstop drive. From Paleohora, one boat (€10, one hour) and one bus daily (€5.50, one hour) make the trip out here from June to September when there is one daily bus from Hania (€11, two hours) via Kissamos (Kastelli; €6.90, 1¼ hours). Check the schedule at www.e-ktel.com.

OFF THE BEATEN TRACK

GAVDOS ISLAND
ΝΗΣΙ ΤΗΣ ΓΑΥΔΟΥ

In the Libyan Sea, 65km from Paleohora and 45km from Hora Sfakion, Gavdos is Europe's most southerly point and as much a state of mind as it is an island. It's a blissful spot with only a few rooms, tavernas and unspoilt beaches, some accessible only by foot or boat. There's little to do here except swim, walk and relax. Gavdos attracts campers, nudists and free spirits happy to trade the trappings of civilisation for an unsullied nature experience. The island is surprisingly green, with almost 65% covered in low-lying pine and cedar trees and vegetation. Most of the electricity is supplied by generators, which are often turned off at night and in the middle of the day. Note that the ferry schedule does not make it possible to visit Gavdos on a day trip.

EASTERN CRETE

Head east from Iraklio past the rocking package-tourist resorts of Hersonisos and Malia and you enter the prefecture of Lasithi, a more relaxed Cretan world that is never short of surprises. Looking for a charming resort town with a buzzy after-dark vibe? There's none better than Lasithi's main tourist draw of Agios Nikolaos. Ancient sites and culture? Lasithi has Minoan and Mycenaean sites aplenty. The fertile Lasithi Plateau offers cycling opportunities through tranquil villages and the Dikteon Cave where Zeus himself was born. Outdoor types can also look forward to walking the dramatic Valley of the Dead at Zakros Gorge. Added value comes with such unique attractions as the historic monastery of Toplou and Vaï's famous palm-backed beach. Scores of smaller towns and villages, meanwhile, maintain a rich undertow of Cretan history and spirit.

Agios Nikolaos
Αγιος Νικόλαος

POP 27,100

Lasithi's capital, Agios Nikolaos has an enviable location on hilly terrain overlooking the shores of the sensuously curving Mirabello Bay. It may feel less Cretan than other towns,

Agios Nikolaos

Agios Nikolaos

partly because of its resort-style flair, tree-lined avenues and largely modern architecture. However, there's also a strong local character to Agios Nikolaos that imbues it with charismatic, low-key flair.

A narrow channel separates the attractive harbour from the circular Voulismeni Lake, whose pedestrianised shore is lined with tourist cafes and restaurants. At night a lively ambience descends on the harbour as lounge-bars fill with stylish young Greeks and holidaymakers from the nearby resorts.

◉ Sights & Activities

In town, the beaches of sandy **Ammos** and pebbly **Kytroplatia** are small and overcrowded. Let your feet take you 1km north and south respectively to **Ammoudi** and **Almyros** beaches, for longer stretches of finer sand to call your own. Almyros is quieter than the other beaches around town with fine sand and beautiful clear water. All have umbrellas and sun chairs to rent.

Archaeological Museum MUSEUM

(☎28410 24943; Konstantinou Paleologou 74) Crete's most significant Minoan collection (after the Heraklion Archaeological Museum) includes clay coffins, ceramic musical instruments and gold from Mohlos. Closed for renovation at the time of writing, it may reopen in 2018.

Nostos Cruises BOATING

(☎28410 22819; www.nostoscruises.com; 30 Rousou Koundourou; trips to Spinalonga without/with barbecue €16/25, fishing trips from €50) Runs boat trips to Spinalonga, including a swim at Kolokytha, from the harbour in Agios Nikolaos. Also offers Spinalonga trips including a barbecue, and fishing trips with food, including anything you catch.

🛏 Sleeping

Doxa Hotel HOTEL €

(☎28410 24214; www.doxahotel.gr; Idomeneos 7; s/d/tr incl breakfast €65/75/85; ❄🖤) This 24-room hotel within a stone's throw of Ammos Beach is well cared for, albeit a bit long in the tooth. Rooms are twee and come with chocolate-brown quilts, marble floors and clean bathroom. Some rooms have a balcony.

★ Villa Olga APARTMENT €€

(☎28410 25913; www.villa-olga.gr; Anapafseos 18, Ellinika; studio €40, villa €50-90; P❄🖤📶) Halfway to Elounda, these charismatic self-catering studios and villas (sleeping up to six) enjoy serene views of the Bay of Mirabello from terraced gardens scattered with stone urns, terracotta pots and other curios of yesteryear collected by owner Michalis. His knack for details and colour also shines through in the traditional chic interiors with tiled floors and waterfront patios.

Villa Olga is reached by following the waterfront road, Akti Koundourou, northeast from the centre of Agios Nikolaos. At a junction above Ammoudi beach, take the right-hand branch towards Elounda for about 500m and look out for the Villa Olga sign on the left.

Du Lac Hotel HOTEL €€

(☎28410 22711; www.dulachotel.gr; 28 Oktovriou 17; d with lake view €50; ➔❄🖤) Smack dab in the town centre, this aging city hotel has fine views over Voulismeni Lake from its generic but comfortable rooms and studios decked out in shades of vanilla to chocolate. It's

well worth the extra money for a unit with lake-facing balcony. The downstairs cafe serves breakfast, snacks and drinks all day and gets quite buzzy.

Minos Beach Art Hotel BOUTIQUE HOTEL €€€

(☎28410 22345; www.minosbeach.com; Akti Ilia Sotirchou; r incl breakfast from €280; P❄🖤📶🏊) In a superb waterfront location just north of town, this resort is a neat fusion of substance and style with plenty of original artwork and a cluster of sea-facing rooms and bungalows kitted out in comfy modern style. With four restaurants and three bars, plus a gym and spa, you'll be tempted to linger.

🍴 Eating

Faros GREEK €

(☎28410 83168; Kitroplatia Beach; mains €5.50-19; ⏲noon-midnight; 📶) One of several tavernas fringing tiny Kitroplatia beach, family-run Faros (lighthouse) sends signals to empty stomachs with aromas wafting from the brazier out front. Sit at linen-draped tables under a blue-and-white awning next to the sand or soak up the old-school atmosphere inside. Meals are usually capped with free baklava and raki.

Sarris GREEK €

(☎28410 28059; Kyprou 15; mains €10; ⏲10.30am-midnight) This tiny rustic taverna in a residential area has just a few tables out on the street beneath a shady pergola and serves up honest-to-good Cretan home cooking. Check the blackboard for the daily specials, order a carafe of wine and chill.

Pelagos MEDITERRANEAN €€

(☎28410 25737; Koraka 11; mains €8.50-25; ⏲noon-midnight; 📶) Pelagos is not for the indecisive. First you must choose whether to sit in the elegantly rustic historic house or in the romantic, lantern-festooned garden. Tough one, but perhaps not as tough as finding your top menu pick from the big selection of fresh fish, grilled meats, inventive salads and homemade pastas.

🍷 Drinking & Nightlife

The harbour-facing lounge-bars along Akti Koundourou are busy from mid-morning until the wee hours. For dance and music clubs, try 25 Martiou, just up from the harbour.

★ Arodo Cafe CAFE-BAR

(☎28410 89895; Kantanoleontos & Akti Koundourou; ⏲11am-2am) This low-lit lair buzzes with the conversation of earnest boho locals, offering a cocktail of cool tunes, a sea-facing terrace and an eclectic and handpicked selection of beers and wine. The entrance is up the steep stairs.

Peripou Cafe
CAFE-BAR

(☑28410 24876; 28 Oktovriou 13; ⊙10am-midnight or later; 🛜) This boho cafe-bar with a narrow verandah overlooking the lake has a bijou bookstore, plays indie tunes, and sells toasties and cold beer. It gets a somewhat alternative local crowd, especially in winter when there's the occasional acoustic concert.

ℹ Information

There's free wi-fi in the harbour area and its surrounds. There are several banks with ATMs on Koundourou.

General Hospital (☑28413 43000; Knosou & Paleologou) OK for broken bones and X-rays, but for anything more serious you'll need to head to Iraklio.

Byron Travel (☑28410 24452; www.byron travel.gr; Akti Koundourou 4; ⊙8am-9pm) Well-run travel agency; books plane and boat tickets and also rents cars.

Municipal Tourist Office (☑28410 22357; www.agiosnikolaos.gr; Akti Koundourou 21; ⊙8am-10pm Apr-Nov) One of the few remaining tourist offices on Crete, this small outfit has helpful staff, a city map and a few brochures.

Tourist Police (☑28410 91409, emergency 171; Erythrou Stavrou 47)

Post Office (28 Oktovriou 9; ⊙7.30am-2.30pm Mon-Fri)

ℹ Getting There & Away

BUS

Local buses for Elounda (€1.90, 20 minutes, 14 daily) leave from stops around town, including the one on Koundourou opposite the tourist office.

The main **bus station** (☑28410 22234; Epimenidou 59) is about 1.5km north of the city centre. Check www.ktelherlas.gr for the current schedule.

DESTINATION	DURATION	FARE	FREQUENCY
Ierapetra	1hr	€4.10	9 daily
Iraklio	1½ hr	€7.70	20 daily
Kritsa	30min	€1.80	3 daily
Sitia	1½ hr	€8.30	8 daily

CAR

Club Cars (☑28410 25868; www.clubcars. net; Agios Nikolaos-Vrouchas Rd; per day/week from €50/220; ⊙8am-9pm) Has cars for hire from €50 per day in high season.

TAXI

The most central **taxi rank** (Paleologou) is behind the tourist office down by the lake. Typical fares are €14 for Elounda, €21 for Plaka, €14 for Kritsa and €18 for Ancient Lato.

ℹ Getting Around

A local bus links the main bus station with the harbour and the two in-town beaches. The centre itself is compact enough for walking. Buses also go out to Elounda at least once hourly.

Around Agios Nikolaos

Elounda
Ελούντα

POP 2200

There are fine mountain and sea views along the 11km road north from Agios Nikolaos to Elounda. It centres on a handsome fishing harbour, where you can board a boat to Spinalonga Island, an erstwhile leper colony. There is a refreshing down-to-earth feel to the town centre, which also has some pleasant waterfront bars and eateries. The beach, a short walk north of the harbour, is adequate, if nothing special, and can get crowded.

🛏 Sleeping & Eating

Dolphins Apartments
APARTMENT €

(☑28410 41641; www.pediaditis.gr/dolphins-apart ments; Papandreou 51; studio/apt €40/50; P🌢🛜🌊) These apartments with pleasingly rustic furniture and tile floors pack a lot of features into a compact frame, including a kitchenette with microwave and a furnished balcony overlooking the sea. Guests may use the pool at the nearby Milos Apartments run by the same family.

Portobello Apartments
APARTMENT €

(☑28410 41712; http://coralistudios.com/apart ments_portobello.htm; Akti Poseidonos; apt €45-75; 🛜🌊) These 15 spacious apartments can easily accommodate families or groups up to four people. Balconies offer front-row views of the sea, the beach is mere steps away and a swimming pool with bar beckons from out the back.

Corali Studios
APARTMENT €€

(☑28410 41712; www.coralistudios.com; Akti Poseidonos; r €45-75; P🌢🛜🌊) Set amid lush lawns with a shaded patio and overlooking the sandy town beach, Corali is run by a friendly family and has 20 stucco-walled rooms with waffle quilts, balcony, basic kitchenette and woodsy furniture. At the back, there's a good-sized pool with sun loungers and a bar that serves snacks and cold drinks.

★ **Hope** CRETAN €€
(Rakadiko Tou Kamari; ☑ 6972295150; Mavrikiano; mains €6-18; ⊙ 11am-11.30pm) Clinging to a steep hillside in the ancient hamlet of Mavrikiano above Elounda, Hope has been a local lair since 1938. The terrace where fishermen once gathered nightly to suss out the next day's weather is now packed with people getting giddy on wine, raki, homemade mezedhes, succulent lamb chops and the stupendous view. Since 2012, it's been run by a charming young couple, Dimitris and Amalia.

❶ Information

Olous Travel (☑ 28410 41324; www.oloustravel.gr; Plateia Sfakianaki; ⊙ 9am-11pm) Full-service agency handles air and boat tickets, finds accommodation and organises car rentals and excursions.

❶ Getting There & Away

There are 14 buses daily from Agios Nikolaos to Elounda (€1.90, 20 minutes). The bus stop is on the main square where you can buy tickets at the kiosk next to Nikos Taverna.

The taxi stand is also on the square. The fare to Agios Nikolaos is €14.

Cars, motorcycles and scooters can be hired at **Elounda Travel** (☑ 28410 41800; www.eloundatravel.gr; Sfakianaki 3; car per day/week from €47/175; ⊙ 8am-9pm), with a central office on, you guessed it, the main square, which also doubles as a (fee-based) parking lot.

Spinalonga Island
Νήσος Σπιναλόγκα

Spinalonga Island HISTORIC SITE
(☑ 28410 41773; adult/concession return €8/4; ⊙ 9am-6pm) Tiny Spinalonga Island became a leper colony in 1903 and was catapulted into pop-cultural consciousness thanks to Virginia Hislop's 2005 bestselling novel *The Island* and the subsequent Greek TV series spin-off, *To Nisi*. Boats departing from Elounda, Plaka and Agios Nikolaos drop visitors at Dante's Gate, the 20m-long tunnel through which patients once arrived. From here, a 1km trail takes you past such 'sights' (mostly ruined) as a church, the disinfection room, the hospital and the cemetery.

Kritsa
Κριτσά
POP 1296

Clinging to the craggy foothills of the Dikti range, Kritsa is one of the oldest and prettiest of the mountain villages in eastern Crete and a popular stop for tour buses. The upper village especially is redolent with romantic decay and the ghosts of the past. Many of Kritsa's older women still practise the art of traditional embroidery, although these days the doilies and blankets sold at the souvenir shops are most likely commercially produced.

◎ Sights

★ **Church of Panagia Kera** CHURCH
(☑ 28410 51806; Main Rd; adult/concession €2/1; ⊙ 8am-3pm Tue-Sun; ℗) The tiny triple-aisled Church of Panagia Kera shelters the best-preserved Byzantine frescoes in Crete. The oldest part of the church is the 13th-century central nave, but most of the frescoes date from the early to mid-14th century. The dome and nave are decorated with four gospel scenes: the Presentation, the Baptism, the Raising of Lazarus and the Entry into Jerusalem. On the western wall is a portrayal of the Crucifixion and grimly realistic depictions of the Punishment of the Damned.

The vault of the southern aisle recounts the life of the Virgin; the northern aisle is an elaborately worked-out fresco of the Second Coming. Nearby is an enticing depiction of Paradise next to the Virgin and the Patriarchs – Abraham, Isaac and Jacob. Judgement Day is portrayed on the western end, with the Archangel Michael trumpeting the Second Coming.

Ancient Lato ARCHAEOLOGICAL SITE
(Λατώ; ☑ 28410 22462; http://odysseus.culture.gr; off Kritsa-Lakonion Rd; adult/concession €2/1; ⊙ 8am-3pm Tue-Sun) Worth the wheeze for the rural serenity alone – the mountain a silvery sheen of wildflowers, the nearby peaks tipped with snow – the ancient hilltop city-state of Lato is one of Crete's few non-Minoan ancient sites. Founded by the Dorians in the 7th century BC, Lato was one of Crete's most powerful cities until it was abandoned when the administrative centre moved to its port in present-day Agios Nikolaos in the middle of the 2nd century AD.

The surviving ruins sprawl over the slopes of two acropolises in a lonely mountain setting, commanding stunning views down to the Bay of Mirabello. At a little elevation

GOURNIA ΓΟΥΡΝΙΑ

The Late Minoan settlement of **Gournia** (☑ 28420 93028; Agios Nikolaos-Sitia Rd; adult/concession €2/1; ⊘ 8am-3pm Tue-Sun; Ⓟ) lies 19km southeast of Agios Nikolaos. Comprising a small palace and residential areas, it was built between 1600 and 1500 BC, destroyed in 1450 BC and reoccupied from 1375 to 1200 BC. There are streets, stairways and houses with walls up to 2m high. Domestic, trade and agricultural implements discovered here suggest that Gournia might have been fairly prosperous. Agios Nikolaos buses bound for Sitia and Ierapetra can drop you at the site.

Snap a picture of the overview map just past the entrance, then follow a narrow ancient road as it curves uphill to the palace ruins, skirting **workshops and storage rooms**, including one where a clay wine press was found. The trail ends at the palace's **central courtyard** with steps on your right indicating the main entrance. On the opposite (west) side of the courtyard, smaller stairs lead down to an upright slab considered a 'sacred stone'. Basic explanatory panels scattered around the site provide additional information.

they begin to take form as you look down and imagine the bustling *agora*.

Enter via the **city gate** and follow a long, stepped street. On your left is a wall with two towers that doubled as residences. The street culminates at the **agora**, which embraced a deep square cistern and a rectangular temple where numerous 6th-century-BC figurines were unearthed. The circle of stones behind the cistern was a threshing floor. West of the *agora* was a **stoa** (colonnaded walkway) with stone benches. Nearby, you can spot remaining bits and pieces of a pebble mosaic.

Between the two towers on the *agora's* north end steps lead to the vast theatre-like **prytaneion** (administrative centre). At its centre, a hearth burning 24/7 was surrounded by stepped benches where the city leaders held their meetings. South of the *agora,* you can spot what's left of a large temple, and east of here and at a lower level, a semicircular theatre that could seat about 350 people next to a bench-lined **exedra** (stage).

Nearchus, one of Alexander's generals, is believed to hail from Lato, whose name derives from the goddess Leto. It was Ieto's union with Zeus that produced Artemis and Apollo.

There are no buses to Lato. The nearest stop is in Kritsa, from where it's a 3km walk north.

Mohlos Μόχλος

POP 121

At the end of a narrow road winding past massive quarries, tranquil Mohlos is an off-the-radar gem along Crete's northern shore. In this authentic fishing village time moves as gently as the waves lapping onto the pebble-and-grey-sand beach.There's little to do but relax and soak in the peacefulness. Mohlos was once a thriving Early Minoan community, traces of which still exist on the small island that is now 200m offshore. If you want to visit, ask around in the village for someone to take you there in a boat. Swimmers should be wary of strong currents.

🛏 Sleeping & Eating

Hotel Sofia PENSION €

(☑ 28430 94554; sofia-mochlos@hotmail.com; d €35-45; Ⓟ✳🛜) Right by the sea, this amiably old-school taverna has small, low-frill rooms upstairs with wine-coloured bedspreads, trad furniture, modern bathrooms and a fridge.

You pay a little extra for a sea view. The owners also have spacious apartments (€40 to €55) 200m east of the harbour, where longer stays are preferred.

★ **Petra Nova Villas** VILLA €€

(☑ 28430 94080, 6984365277; www.petranovavillas.gr; villa €95-135; Ⓟ✳🛜) These five bi-level stone villas blend seamlessly into the hillside and are just a few minutes' walk up the road from the waterfront. Sleeping up to five people, the tranquil units all come with plenty of privacy, chic interiors and stunning bay views from the patio – all ingredients for a soothing and mindful getaway. Minimum stay requirement during peak season.

Ta Kochilia GREEK €€

(☑ 28430 94432; mains €4.50-16; ⊘ 10.30am-midnight; 🛜) The oldest among several waterfront tavernas, Ta Kochilia has cooked up a storm since 1902 and is still a place for fanciers of fish and traditional Cretan dishes like spinach pies, lamb with artichokes in lemon sauce, and oven-baked feta. It's easily recognised by its cheerful white and blue trim.

❶ Getting There & Away

There is no public transport to Mohlos. Buses between Sitia and Agios Nikolaos can drop you off at the Mohlos turn-off, from where you'll need to hitch or walk the 6km down to the village.

Sitia   Σητεία

POP 9900

Sitia is an attractive seaside town that hasn't sold its soul to mass tourism. Whitewashed houses cling to a hillside laced by steep staircases and topped with a ruined Venetian castle. Below, a promenade lined with tavernas and cafes hems in the fishing harbour. It's a slow-paced, friendly place where agriculture is the mainstay of the local economy.

A long, sandy beach skirts a wide bay to the east of town.

◎ Sights

Sitia Archaeological Museum   MUSEUM
(☑ 28430 23917; Kokefalou; adult/concession €2/1; ⊙ 8am-3pm Tue-Sun) This is a compact showcase of archaeological finds from eastern Crete spanning the arc from Neolithic to Roman times, with an emphasis on Minoan artefacts. Pride of place goes to the *Palekastro Kouros* – a statue carved from hippopotamus tusks that was once fully covered in gold leaf. Finds from the palace at Zakros include a wine press, a bronze saw and cult objects scorched by the fire that destroyed the palace.

Other notable finds are fragments of Linear A tablets found at Petras and Zakros as well as Minoan *larnakes* (clay coffins).

Venetian Fort   FORT
(Kazarma; ☑ 28430 27140; Neas Ionias; ⊙ 8am-3pm) FREE Strategically perched atop a hill near the port, this structure is locally called *kazarma* (from the Venetian *casa di arma*) and was built as a garrison by the Venetians. These are the only remains of the fortifications that once protected the town from marauders. The site is now used as an open-air venue.

☐ Sleeping

Hotel El Greco   HOTEL €
(☑ 28430 23133; www.elgreco-sitia.gr; Arkadiou 13; d incl breakfast €40-45; ✳ ☎) This old-school hotel has smart and impeccably clean rooms

with tiled floors, nice but dated furniture, plasma TV, fridge and balcony (most with sea views). It's a good city hotel and a convenient base for short stays.

Sitia Bay Hotel   HOTEL €€
(☑ 28430 24800; www.sitiabay.com; Beach Rd, Patriarhou Vartholomaiou 27; d €85-125; ⊙ reception 8am-8pm; P ✳ ☎ ☀) This modern beachfront hotel has friendly service and comfortable and tastefully done-up studios and family apartments, all with kitchens, modern furniture and sea views. If the sand with loungers doesn't beckon, perhaps the pool does. At sunset, grab a drink at the bar and head to the rooftop terrace.

✖ Eating

★ Mitsakakis   BAKERY €
(☑ 28430 20200; Karamanli 6; galaktoboureko €2.90; ⊙ 6am-late; ▣) This cafe and pastry shop is a Sitian institution (since 1965) and famous for its sugar-rush-inducing *galaktoboureko* (custard-filled pastry), *loukoumades* (ball-shaped doughnuts) and *kataifi* (angel hair pastry). Totally worth the calories!

★ Rakadiko Inodion   GREEK €
(☑ 28430 26166; El Venizelou 157; mains €7.50-12; ⊙ noon-late; ☎) The best among the row of waterfront tavernas, this unpretentious family place offers a recognisable array of Greek dishes, but it's the local specials that truly shine. Anything with rabbit or goat is tops and best paired with the local wine. Many ingredients, including the oil, bread and raki, are produced by the Garefalakis family themselves.

Zorbas Taverna   TAVERNA €€
(Kazantzaki 3; mains €5.50-14; ⊙ noon-late; ☎) Gregarious owner Zorba, with his sailor's roll, sea captain's cap and bushy moustache, lays on the Greek clichés with a trowel and a wink. Bouzouki music accompanies the rich aromas of home-cooked food and grilled meats served at blue tables and chairs in his waterfront lair. Good for kids.

❶ Information

There are lots of ATMs and places to change money around the central square and side streets.

Police (☑ 28430 22259, 28430 24200; Therisou 31) Has a special tourist police unit during the summer months.

Post Office (☑ 28430 22283; Dimokritou 10; ⊘7.30am-2pm Mon-Fri)

Tzortzakis Travel (☑ 28430 29211; www. tzortzakistravel.com; Alexandrou & Papanastasiou Sts; ⊘9am-9pm Mon-Fri, to 5pm Sat) This full-service travel agency books rooms, flights and ferries and can also organise car hire.

❶ Getting There & Away

AIR

The small communal **airport** (☑ 28430 24424) about 1km north of the town centre got a new terminal in 2016 and handles flights to Athens, Iraklio, Kassos, Karpathos and Rhodes as well as seasonal charter flights from northern Europe. A taxi into town costs €6 to €8.

BOAT

Ferries dock about 600m north of Plateia Iroön Polytechniou. **Anek/Aegeon Pelagos Sea Lines** (EP; ☑ Hania 28210 24000; www.anek.gr) has ferries serving Anafi (€20, eight hours), Chalki (€20, 8¼ hours), Diafani (€18, six hours), Iraklio (€16, three hours), Karpathos (€19, 4½ hours), Kasos (€12, 2½ hours), Milos (€26, 14¼ hours), Piraeus (€44, 21½ hours), Rhodes (€28, 10½ hours) and Santorini (€28, 10 hours) on a seasonally changing schedule. Prices quoted are for deckchair seating.

BUS

Connections from Sitia's **bus station** (☑ 28430 22272; Sitias-Palekastro-Vai Rd) include five buses daily to Ierapetra (€6.90, 1¾ hours), six buses to Iraklio (€16, three hours), seven to Agios Nikolaos (€8.30, 1¾ hours) and two to Zakros (€4.50, one hour).

Around Sitia

Moni Toplou   Μονή Τοπλού

Moni Toplou   MONASTERY
(☑ 28430 61226; Toplou; €3; ⊘8am-6pm Apr-Oct) In splendid isolation on a windswept bluff, 15th-century Moni Toplou is one of the most historically significant monasteries in Crete whose defences were tested by everyone from pirates to crusading knights and the Turks. Its star attraction is the stunningly intricate *Lord Thou Art Great* icon by celebrated Cretan artist Ioannis Kornaros. Dozens of scenes from the Old and New Testaments are depicted here; look for Noah's Ark, Jonah and the Whale and Moses parting the Red Sea.

The fact that Moni Toplou looks more like a fortress than a monastery stems from the necessity imposed by the dangers it faced

at the time of its construction. The monks defended themselves with all the means at their disposal, including a heavy gate, cannons (the name Toplou is Turkish for 'with a cannon') and small holes for pouring boiling oil onto the heads of their attackers.

Moni Toplou has repeatedly been active in the cause of Cretan independence. Under the Turkish occupation, a secret school operated in the monastery, and its reputation for hiding rebels led to severe reprisals. During WWII, Abbot Silingakis was executed after sheltering resistance leaders operating an underground radio transmitter. A small exhibit in the museum recalls this period with rifles, helmets and a field telephone. The adjacent main room displays engravings.

Moni Toplou is about 18km east of Sitia. Buses drop you at the junction of the Sitia–Palekastro road, from where it's a 3km walk.

Vaï   Βάι

The beach at Vaï, 24km northeast of Sitia, is famous for its large grove of *Phoenix theophrasti* (Cretan date) palms. With calm, clear waters, it is one of Crete's most popular strands and its rows of umbrellas and sunbeds (€9) often fill by 10am in July and August. Jet skis kick into gear shortly thereafter.

If you want a nice beach without the crowd (or the palms), take the 1km scramble south over the rocky headland. The trail starts just past the gazebo lookout reached via stone steps leading up from the reasonably priced taverna on the south end of Vaï beach. Another trail leads north to Itanos beach in about 30 minutes, which is also often practically deserted and overlooked by Dorian ruins.

✖ Eating

Vai Restaurant & Cafe   GREEK €
(☑ 28430 61129; www.vai-restaurant.gr; mains €8-12; ⊘9am-late Apr-Oct) There are lovely views of the palms and the white sand of Vaï beach from the covered terrace of this waterfront restaurant serving classic Greek fare, including fish and grilled meats. The cafe below has cold drinks, coffee and ice cream.

❶ Getting There & Away

There are two daily buses to Vaï from Sitia (€3.30, one hour) from May to October. Parking costs €2.50.

Zakros & Kato Zakros
Ζάκρος & Κάτω Ζάκρος

POP 770

Zakros, 45km southeast of Sitia, is the starting point for the trail through Zakros Gorge, also known as the Valley of the Dead because of the Minoan burial caves that honeycomb the canyon cliffs. Zakros, however, is a mere prelude to coastal Kato Zakros, 7km down a winding road. Shortly before reaching the village, you can see the huge jaw of Zakros Gorge breaching the cliffs. Look closely and you can also make out the ruins of the Minoan palace just up from Kato Zakros' pebbly, narrow beach and row of tavernas. Add to all of this the isolated tranquillity and sense of peace, and you have the perfect recipe for escapism.

⊙ Sights & Activities

Zakros Palace   ARCHAEOLOGICAL SITE
(☑ 28410 22462; Kato Zakros; adult/concession €6/3; ⊙ 8am-8pm May-Sep, to 3pm Oct-Apr) Ancient Zakros, the smallest of Crete's four Minoan palatial complexes, was a major port, trading with Egypt, Syria, Anatolia and Cyprus. And, like the other three, it comprised royal apartments, shrines, storerooms and workshops grouped around a central courtyard. The exquisite rock-crystal vase and stone bull's head now in Iraklio's archaeological museum were among the treasure trove of antiquities found here. While the ruins are sparse, the wildness and remoteness of the setting make it an attractive place to explore.

Pelekita Cave   HIKING
(www.sitia-geopark.gr/en/activities/geotourism/hiking-trails/georoute-12.aspx) A 3.5km trail along the coast leads to this extraordinary 310m-long cave with magnificent views of the sea 100m below and signs of Neolithic habitation within its stalactite- and stalagmite-rich interior. To explore it bring a torch and trainers. It can only be reached on foot or by boat.

Near the cave is a limestone quarry that was used as building material for the Minoan palace at Kato Zakros. About 2km past the cave is the isolated Karoumes Beach.

Zakros Gorge   WALKING
(Gorge of the Dead; www.sitia-geopark.gr/en/activities/geotourism/hiking-trails/georoute-10.aspx) This easy-to-moderate 4km walk starts just below Zakros village and follows a dry riverbed through a narrow and (at times) soaring canyon with a riot of vegetation and wild herbs before emerging close to Zakros Palace right above the beach at Kato Zakros. For a shorter walk, pick up one of two trailheads on the road to Kato Zakros. 'Entrance A' is about 3km along, while 'Entrance B' is another 500m further on from there. A taxi back to Zakros costs about €12.

The canyon is also named Gorge of the Dead or Valley of the Dead because the Minoans used to buried their dead in caves on the rugged cliffs. The hike marks the final section of the more than 10,000km-long E4 European Path, which kicks off in Portugal.

🛏 Sleeping & Eating

Zakros is but a footnote to Kato Zakros and you should head to the latter for a spectrum of accommodation, from simple rooms to downright beautiful villas with a view. Rooms in Kato Zakros fill up fast in high season, so it is best to book.

Katerina Apartments   APARTMENT €
(☑ 28430 26893, 6974656617; www.kato-zakros.gr/_en/katerina.php; Kato Zakros; apt €50-60; P ✳ 🛜) These four stone-built studios and maisonettes can sleep up to four and enjoy a lovely setting in the hillside above Kato Zakros, with easy access to the beach, hiking trails and Minoan palace ruins. Units exude family-style hominess accented by the occasional lace doily and framed sunset photograph. All have kitchens and balconies.

★ Terra Minoika Villas   APARTMENT €€
(☑ 28430 23739; www.terraminoika.com; Kato Zakros; villa €100-150; ⊙ mid-Jan–20 Dec; P ✳ 🛜) On the hillside high above the surf, these arty cube houses built of local stone are architectural symphonies of wood-beamed ceilings, widescreen views from balconies, chic rustic furniture, urns mounted on walls, and stone floors. Every villa is individual and has a fully equipped kitchenette.

Akrogiali Taverna   GREEK €
(☑ 28430 26893; Kato Zakros; mains €5-16; ⊙ 8am-midnight; 🛜) The food gods have been smiling upon Kato Zakros' oldest taverna that does a brisk business in fresh-off-the-boat fish and Cretan classics, all prepared with locally sourced ingredients, including oil made from the owner's trees. The cheerful blue and white furniture and the beachfront setting add two more notches to its appeal.

ⓘ Getting There & Away

Two buses shuttle between Sitia and Zakros on Monday, Tuesday and Friday only (€4.50, one hour). A taxi costs about €50.

Ierapetra   Ιεράπετρα

POP 16.150

Ierapetra is a laid-back seafront town and the commercial centre of southeastern Crete's substantial greenhouse-based agribusiness. Hot and dusty in summer, it offers a low-key, authentic Cretan experience and is also the jumping-off point to the semitropical Gaïdouronisi Island (also called Hrysi).

The city's grey-sand beaches are backed by tavernas and cafes where the nightlife is busy in summer. Though little is left, Ierapetra has an impressive history with interludes as a Roman port and as a Venetian stronghold, as attested to by the harbour fortress. The narrow alleyways of the Turkish quarter recall its Ottoman period.

◉ Sights & Activities

There are usually a couple of departures in the morning to Gaïdouronisi (Hrysi Island), giving you 4½ hours on the island before returning to Ierapetra late afternoon (€25).

Archaeological Collection of Ierapetra   MUSEUM
(☑ 28420 28721; Plateia Kanoupaki; adult/concession €2/1; ☉ 8am-3pm Tue-Sun) A rectangular Ottoman-era school building shelters three rooms of dug-up treasures from regional archaeological sites. The first focuses on Minoan artefacts, including vases and jugs found at Episkopi. Room 2 features ornately decorated *larnakes*, including one with 12 panels of hunting scenes and a chariot procession. The last room is lined with headless Roman statues, which is why all eyes are on an intact 2nd-century-AD statue of the goddess Persephone.

Kales Fortress   FORTRESS
(Stratigou Samouil 10; ☉ 8am-3pm Tue-Sun) FREE South along the waterfront, the crenellated Venetian fort was built in the 13th century to protect the harbour, and in 1626 by Francesco Morosini. Climb up to the ramparts and the single tower for grand views of the bay and the mountains.

🛏 Sleeping & Eating

★ Cretan Villa Hotel   HOTEL €
(☑ 28420 28522; www.cretan-villa.com; Lakerda 16; d €47-56; ❅ 🛜) A heavy wooden door gives

way to a vine-shaded courtyard at this restful, friendly space that's a happy coupling of historic touches and the gamut of mod cons. Beautiful rooms boast brick walls, elegantly rustic furniture, stone-tiled showers, wood-beamed ceilings, small fridges and satellite TV. A central city hotel with country flair.

Akrolithos Apartments   APARTMENT €€
(☑ 28420 28522; www.ierapetra-apartments.net; Mparitaki 22; apt €55-68; ❅ 🛜) Oozing ambience and comfort, these cosy apartments orbit a central courtyard and have such lovely traditional touches as fireplaces, well-equipped kitchenettes and loads of space. It's all in a great central location. Note that there is usually a three-night minimum stay.

Napoleon   GREEK €
(☑ 28420 22410; Stratigou Samouil 26; mains €5-12; ☉ noon-midnight; 🛜 ✏) This capacious traditional place looks just like any of the many tavernas lining Ierapetra's waterfront, but the quality of the home-cooking as well as the service are actually a cut above. Sit on the covered terrace flanked by palm trees and pick from the tasty line-up of fresh fish and Cretan specialities, including dolmadhes (vine leaves stuffed with rice and sometimes meat), snails, spinach pies and squid risotto.

🍷 Drinking & Nightlife

Ierapetra has the most lively after-dark scene in the region. The waterfront tavernas often bustle until the wee hours, and if you want to bust a move on the dance floor, look for the latest music lairs in the streets around the Archaeological Collection.

ⓘ Information

There are ATMs around Plateia Kanoupaki and along Koraka and Kothri.

Ierapetra Express (☑ 28420 22411; Kothri 2; ☉ 9am-9pm)

Post Office (Koraka 25; ☉ 7.30am-2.30pm Mon-Fri)

ⓘ Getting There & Away

BUS

KTEL operates eight buses per day to Iraklio (€12, 2½ hours) via Agios Nikolaos (€4.10, one hour), four to Sitia (€6.90, 1½ hours) and six to Myrtos (€2.40, 30 minutes).

TAXI

The **central taxi stand** (☑ 28420 26600; Kothri & Plateia Kanoupaki) with fixed fares posted on a board is outside the town hall. Sample fares:

Iraklio (€100), Agios Nikolaos (€50), Sitia (€83) and Myrtos (€20).

Myrtos   Μύρτος

POP 600

Tiny Myrtos, 14km west of Ierapetra, is a positively delightful little community: cheerful, trim and fringed by an apron of grey pebble-and-sand beach and bright-blue water. It has a devoted clientele that cherishes its slow boho pulse, flower-festooned guesthouses and a cluster of tavernas on its languid seafront. In short, it's a traveller's jewel, the perfect antidote to noise and haste.

🛏 Sleeping & Eating

Big Blue   APARTMENT €

(☑28420 51094; www.big-blue.gr; studio €60-85; P ❄ 🐾 🛜) Modern amenities meet trad-Greece in these breezy sea-facing studios decorated with plenty of imagination and attention to detail. Apartment 'Blue Eye', for instance, has a neat display of *mati* (evil eye); in fact, every room is different. Balconies boast expansive views and the fragrant garden out front is a good spot for sundowners.

Villa Mertiza   APARTMENT €€

(☑28420 51208, 6932735224; www.mertiza.com; studio/apt €61/81; ❄ 🛜) Owned by a friendly Dutch guy, these boho-chic and generously dimensioned studios and apartments with small kitchen are an excellent launch pad for days on the beach or in the mountains. Framed photographs, Moroccan wall hangings and colourful pillows provide cheerful accents. There's also a book exchange.

Thalassa Taverna   GREEK €

(☑28420 51301; www.facebook.com/Taverna thalassa; Waterfront Promenade; mains €8-16; ☺10am-midnight; ❄ 🛜) This powder-blue, hole-in-the-wall waterfront restaurant has an interior festooned with coral and shells, and a few tables outside to tuck into mussels, calamari, cuttlefish, shrimps, octopus... Enough seafood to keep a shoal of mermaids quiet.

★Katerina   CRETAN €€

(☑6948325739; mains €9-19.50; ☺6pm-midnight; 🍴) Your taste buds will do somersaults at Katerina, where Yiannis is the kind of chef who puts a creative mark on even the most classic dishes. Sit back in the flower-filled alleyway to tuck into such flavour-bombs as lamb *kleftiko* (slow oven-baked), ouzo-

flambéed *saganaki* (fried cheese) and gooey chocolate cake. Foodies should enquire about Yiannis' herb-collecting tours and cooking classes.

ℹ Information

The nearest ATM is in Ierapetra.

ℹ Getting There & Away

There are six buses daily from Ierapetra (€2.40, 30 minutes). A taxi costs €20.

Lasithi Plateau

Οροπέδιο Λασιθίου

The tranquil Lasithi Plateau, 900m above sea level, is an arrestingly beautiful expanse of green fields interspersed with almond trees and orchards. Offering a sense of secluded rural Crete, it's really more of a plain than a plateau, sitting as it does in a huge depression amid the rock-studded mountains of the Dikti range. It's sparsely inhabited with just a few villages dotting the windswept expanse. The one that gets the most visitors is Psyhro, the gateway to the Dikteon Cave, where – so the myth goes – Zeus was hidden as an infant to protect him from his voracious father.

Lasithi must have been a stunning sight in the 17th century when it was dotted with some 20,000 windmills with white canvas sails, put up by the Venetians for irrigation purposes. The skeletal few that remain are an iconic (and much photographed) sight.

ℹ Getting There & Away

The plateau is not served by public buses. A taxi to Tzermiado or Psyhro costs about €60 from Heraklion and €50 from Agios Nikolaos. To cut costs, take a bus to Malia and a taxi from there (about €25).

Tzermiado   Τζερμιάδο

POP 635

The largest of Lasithi's 20 villages, Tzermiado is still a bucolic place and the gateway to the small Kronios Cave. There is only one main road running through town, plus a couple of ATMs and a post office on the main square.

◎ Sights

Kronios Cave   CAVE

(Trapeza Cave) FREE As you approach Tzermiado from the south, a sign directs you to the small Kronios Cave. Follow the path to a series of stairs leading to the cave's narrow entrance. Excavations have yielded objects going back to Neolithic times when the cave was likely used as a shelter. During the Minoan period, it served as a burial site. Bring a torch and wear sneakers when exploring the two chambers with their stalagmites and stalactites, many of which have been tampered with by humans.

🛏 Sleeping & Eating

Argoulias   APARTMENT €€
(☑ 28440 22754; www.argoulias.gr; Tzermiado; apt €50-80; ❄) Built into the hillside above the main village and constructed of exposed local stone, these self-catering apartments sleep up to five and have sweeping views across the Lasithi Plateau to the mountains. Traditional decor and furnishings exude comfort and a fireplace keeps things cosy in winter. Optional breakfast is €6 per person.

The owners also run an excellent restaurant across the road. Ask about use of bicycles. Look for signs to Argoulias at the entrance to Tzermiado coming from the east.

Taverna Kourites   GREEK €
(☑ 28440 22054; Tzermiado; mains €6-10; ⊙ 9am-9pm) This spacious taverna on the outskirts of Tzermiado does a brisk lunchtime business with coaches full of day trippers. At other times, it's a peaceful spot where menu options include lamb and suckling pig roasted in a wood-fired oven. There are clean and simple rooms above the taverna and in a nearby hotel (doubles €40, breakfast €5).

Agios Georgios   Άγιος Γεώργιος

POP 490

Dusty, wind-blown and faintly ghostly, Agios Georgios is a tiny village on the southern side of the Lasithi Plateau and one of the more pleasant places to stay in a fairly colourless bunch. If you have your own bicycle, you can base yourself here and explore the plateau at leisure.

◉ Sights

Folklore Museum   MUSEUM
(☑ 6948501457, 28440 31382; adult/concession €3/2; ⊙ 10.30am-5pm Mon-Sat May-Oct) This five-room museum opens up a window on Crete's rural past with an eclectic collection of farming tools, wooden furniture, textiles, faded black-and-white photographs and WWII relics. There are also displays of traditional workshops of a carpenter or blacksmith. A separate building has great valley views but houses a rather turgid exhibit on political legend Eleftherios Venizelos.

🛏 Sleeping & Eating

Hotel Maria   HOTEL €
(☑ 28440 31774; http://mariahotelagiosgeorgios. blogspot.de; d incl breakfast €40; ⊙ May-Oct) These pleasantly quirky rooms on the northern side of the village are in a building fronted by a leafy garden. The traditional mountain beds are rather narrow and are on stone bases. Local furnishings and woven wall hangings add to the cheerful atmosphere.

Taverna Rea   GREEK €
(☑ 28440 31774; Main St; mains €6-8; ⊙ 10am-9pm) This cheerful little restaurant has stone walls decorated with Cretan artefacts. The owner-chef does a mean souvlaki and if there's lamb on offer, it'll likely be excellent as well. Upstairs are four rooms (€30) with twin beds and bathroom.

Psyhro & Dikteon Cave   Ψυχρό & Δικταίον Αντρον

Psyhro is the closest village to the Dikteon Cave and is often clogged with tour buses. It has one main street, a sword-waving memorial statue, a few tavernas and plenty of souvenir shops. Buses stop at the northern end of town, from where it's about a 1km walk uphill to the cave.

◉ Sights

Dikteon Cave   CAVE
(Cave of Psyhro; ☑ 28410 22462; http://odysseus. culture.gr; adult/concession €6/3; ⊙ 8am-8pm Apr-Oct, 8am-3pm Nov-Mar) According to legend, Rhea hid in this cave to give birth to Zeus, far from the clutches of his offspring-gobbling father Cronos. A slick and vertiginous staircase corkscrews into the damp dark, passing overhanging stalactites and ethereal formations. It's a steep 800m walk to the cave entrance, either via a rocky but shaded natural trail or the sunny paved path starting near the car park.

The most famous formation is a stalactite nicknamed 'the mantle of Zeus' in the larger chamber on the right side. Votives found in the cave indicate that it was a place of cult worship from Minoan to Roman times. Some are now on display at the Archaeological Museum in Iraklio.

Dodecanese

Best Places to Eat

➡ Marco Polo Cafe (p505)

➡ Taverna Mylos (p556)

➡ To Ellenikon (p517)

➡ Tholos (p527)

➡ Pote Tin Kyriaki (p541)

Best Places to Stay

➡ Marco Polo Mansion (p502)

➡ Harry's Paradise (p555)

➡ Archontariki (p563)

➡ Old Markets (p527)

➡ In Camera Art Boutique Hotel (p503)

Why Go?

Ever pined for the old Greece, where timeless islands beckon modern-day adventurers just as they did Odysseus and Alexander? Enter the far-flung Dodecanese (Δωδεκάνησα; do-de-*ka*-ni-sa) archipelago, curving through the southeastern Aegean parallel to the ever-visible shoreline of Turkey. The footprints of everyone from Greeks and Romans to crusading medieval knights, and Byzantine and Ottoman potentates to 20th-century Italian bureaucrats, are found here. Beyond better-known Rhodes and Kos, enigmatic islands beg to be explored.

Hikers and naturalists flock to Tilos, while climbers scale the limestone cliffs in Kalymnos. Aesthetes adore the neoclassical mansions of Symi, Halki and Kastellorizo, divers explore underwater caves and ancient wrecks, and kitesurfers blow in to Karpathos for its legendary winds. Archaeologists and history buffs let their imaginations loose on a bevy of ancient sites, while sybarites can worship Helios on myriad beaches, far from the package crowds.

When to Go
Rhodes

Apr & May Prices are low, few tourists are around and the sea is warming up.

Jul & Aug Peak season for accommodation and visitors – book ahead.

Sep & Oct Great time to come: low prices, warm seas and perfect hiking weather.

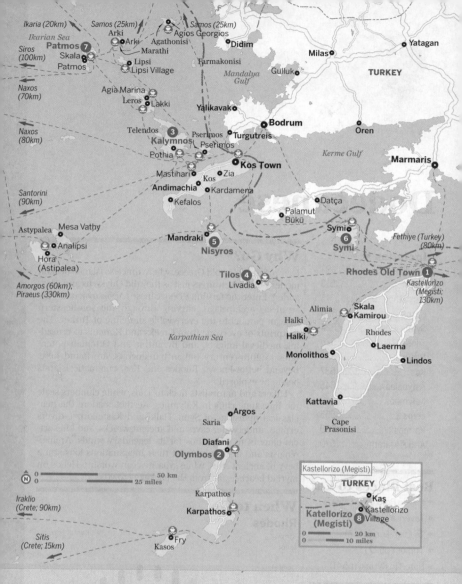

Dodecanese Highlights

1 Rhodes Old Town (p498) Wandering beneath Byzantine arches and along ancient cobbled alleyways.

2 Olymbos (p519) Following the winding road up to this timeless village.

3 Kalymnos (p549) Testing your mettle diving for wrecks or climbing limestone cliffs.

4 Tilos (p529) Hiking or birdwatching on this postcard-perfect island.

5 Nisyros (p533) Entering its fabled volcano, home to an imprisoned Titan.

6 Symi (p524) Feeling your pulse quicken as your boat pulls into the gorgeous Italianate harbour.

7 Patmos (p560) Making the pilgrimage to where St John experienced his 'Revelations'.

8 Kastellorizo (Megisti) (p522) Gasping in awe at the largest and most dramatic of blue caves in the Mediterranean.

History

The Dodecanese islands have been inhabited since pre-Minoan times. After the death of Alexander the Great in 323 BC, they were ruled by Ptolemy I of Egypt. The islanders later became the first Greeks to convert to Christianity, thanks to the tireless efforts of St Paul, who made two journeys to the archipelago during the 1st century, and St John the Divine, who was banished to Patmos, where he had his revelation and added a chapter to the Bible.

The early Byzantine era saw the islands prosper, but by the 7th century AD they were being plundered by a string of invaders. The Knights of St John of Jerusalem, who arrived during the 14th century, eventually ruled almost all the Dodecanese. Their mighty fortifications have proved strong enough to withstand time, but failed to keep out the Turks in 1522.

The Turks were in turn ousted in 1912 by the Italians, who made Italian the official language and banned the Orthodox religion. Inspired by Mussolini's vision of a vast Mediterranean empire, they also constructed grandiose public buildings in the fascist style, the antithesis of archetypal Greek architecture. More beneficially, they excavated and restored many archaeological monuments.

After the Italian surrender of 1943, the islands (particularly Leros) became a battleground for British and German forces, inflicting much suffering upon the population. The Dodecanese were formally returned to Greece in 1947.

RHODES ΡΟΔΟΣ

POP 115,000

By far the largest and historically the most important of all the Dodecanese islands, Rhodes (ro-dos) abounds in sandy beaches, wooded valleys and ancient history. Whether you arrive in search of buzzing nightlife, languid sun worshipping, diving in crystal-clear waters or to embark on a culture-vulture journey through past civilisations, it's all here. The atmospheric Old Town of Rhodes is a maze of cobbled streets that will spirit you back to the days of the Byzantine Empire and beyond. Further south is the picture-perfect town of Lindos, a soul-warming vista of sugar-cube houses spilling down to a turquoise bay.

History

The Minoans and Mycenaeans were among the first to have outposts on Rhodes, but only with the arrival of the Dorians in 1100 BC – settling in Kamiros, Ialysos and Lindos – did the island begin to make itself felt. Switching allegiances like a pendulum, Rhodes was allied to Athens when the Persians were defeated in the Battle of Marathon (490 BC), but had shifted to the Persian side by the time of the Battle of Salamis (480 BC).

After the unexpected Athenian victory at Salamis, Rhodes hastily aligned itself with Athens once more, joining the Delian League in 477 BC. Following the disastrous Sicilian Expedition (416–412 BC), Rhodes revolted against Athens and hooked up with Sparta instead, aiding it in the Peloponnesian Wars. In 408 BC the cities of Kamiros, Ialysos and Lindos consolidated their powers, co-founding the city of Rhodes. Rhodes became Athens' ally again to defeat Sparta at the Battle of Knidos (394 BC). Rhodes then joined forces with Persia to fight against Alexander the Great, only to attach itself to Alexander when he proved invincible.

In 305 BC Antigonus, a rival of Ptolemy, sent his formidable son, Demetrius Poliorketes – Besieger of Cities – to conquer Rhodes. When the city repelled Demetrius it built a 32m-high bronze statue of Helios Apollo to celebrate. Known as the Colossus of Rhodes, it was later hailed as one of the Seven Wonders of the Ancient World.

Rhodes then built the biggest navy in the Aegean, and its port became a principal Mediterranean trading centre. The arts also flourished. When Greece became the arena in which Roman generals fought for leadership of the empire, Rhodes allied itself with Julius Caesar. After Caesar's assassination in 44 BC, Cassius besieged the city, destroying its ships and carting its artworks off to Rome. Rhodes went into decline and became part of the Roman Empire in AD 70.

Rhodes eventually joined the Byzantine province of the Dodecanese and was granted independence when the Crusaders seized Constantinople. Later, the Genoese gained control. The Knights of St John arrived in 1309, and ruled Rhodes for 213 years until being ousted by the Ottomans. They were in turn kicked out by the Italians nearly four centuries later. In 1947, after 35 years of Italian occupation, Rhodes became part of Greece, along with the other Dodecanese islands.

ℹ Getting There & Away

AIR

Diagoras Airport (p756) is near Paradisi on the west coast, 16km southwest of Rhodes Town.

Aegean Airlines (☑ 22410 98345; www.aegeanair.com; Diagoras Airport; ☉ 4.30am-9pm) flies to Astypalea, Athens, Heraklion, Kalymnos, Kastellorizo and Karpathos, as well as Leros and Thessaloniki.

Olympic Air (☑ 22410 24571; www.olympicair.com; Ierou Lohou 9) has connections with Athens and destinations throughout Greece, including several Dodecanese islands. Flights to the nearby islands of Kassos, Karpathos and Kastellorizo are more frequent than the corresponding ferries and, with fares starting at less than €65, only slightly more expensive.

Sky Express (☑ 28102 23800; www.skyexpress.gr) flies up to six days a week to Heraklion on Crete (€80, one hour) and once weekly to Samos (€72, 45 minutes).

BOAT

Domestic

Rhodes is the main port in the Dodecanese. Two inter-island ferry companies operate from immediately outside the walls of Rhodes Old Town. **Dodekanisos Seaways** (☑ 22410 70590; www.12ne.gr; Afstralias 3, Rhodes Town) runs daily high-speed catamarans north up the chain, while **Blue Star Ferries** (☑ 22410 22461; www.bluestarferries.com; 111 Amerikis; ☉ 9am-8pm) provides slower and less frequent services to several of the same islands, continuing west to Astypalea and Piraeus. It also heads southwest to Karpathos, Kasos and Crete. Tickets are available at the dock and from travel agents in Rhodes Town.

The tiny port at **Skala Kamirou**, 45km southwest of Rhodes Town, has a daily ferry service to the island of Halki, operated by **Nissos Halki** (☑ mobile 6946519817, 6973460968) and **Nikos Express** (☑ mobile 6946826905). There's an hour-long connecting bus service with Rhodes Old Town.

In addition, daily excursion boats head to Symi from Mandraki Harbour in summer (day trips only, €25) while **catamarans** to Turkey leave from Kolona Harbour. Check out the boats at the harbour before you decide which to take.

International

Catamarans connect Rhodes' Commercial Harbour with Marmaris, Turkey (50 minutes), with two daily services in summer and two weekly in winter. Tickets cost €36 each way. Same-day returns cost €39, and longer-stay returns, €70. For schedules and bookings, visit www.rhodesmarmarisinfo.com.

Boat Services from Rhodes

DESTINATION	DURATION	FARE (€)	FREQUENCY
Agathonisi*	5hr	49	1 weekly
Astypalea	9hr	24	1 weekly
Halki	2hr	8	2 weekly
Halki*	1¼hr	17	2 weekly
Kalymnos	6hr	20	3 weekly
Kalymnos*	3hr	39	1 daily
Karpathos	5hr 40min	21	3 weekly
Kasos	8hr	25	3 weekly
Kastellorizo	4hr 40min	19.50	2 weekly
Kastellorizo*	2hr 20min	37	1 weekly
Kos	5hr	24.50	4 weekly
Kos*	2½hr	32	1 daily
Leros	8hr	32.50	3 weekly
Leros*	3½hr	42	6 weekly
Lipsi	9hr	24.50	1 weekly
Lipsi*	5½hr	47	6 weekly
Nisyros	4hr	13.50	2 weekly
Nisyros*	2¾hr	27	2 weekly
Patmos	10hr	37.50	3 weekly
Patmos*	5hr	49	5 weekly
Piraeus	18hr	63.60	1 daily
Samos	6hr 40min	39	3 weekly
Sitia	11hr	28	1 weekly
Symi	1hr 40min	14	2 weekly
Symi*	50min	18	1-4 daily
Tilos	2½hr	13.50	2 weekly
Tilos*	2hr	26	2 weekly

All services are from Commercial Harbour.
* high-speed services

Rhodes Town   Ρόδος

POP 86,000

Rhodes Town is really two distinct and very different towns. The **Old Town** lies within but utterly apart from the New Town, sealed like a medieval time capsule behind a double ring of high walls and a deep moat. Nowhere else in the Dodecanese can boast so many layers of architectural history, with ruins and relics of the Classical, medieval, Ottoman and Italian eras entangled in a mind-boggling maze of twisting alleys. Strolling its hauntingly pretty cobbled lanes, especially at night, is an experience no traveller should miss.

Rhodes

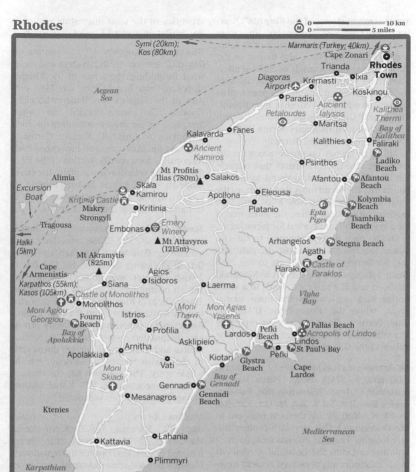

Symi (20km);
Kos (80km)

Marmaris (Turkey; 40km);
Cape Zonari

Trianda

**Rhodes
Town**

Diagoras
Airport

Kremasti

Ixia

Koskinou

Paradisi

*Aegean
Sea*

Petaloudes

*Ancient
Ialysos*

Maritsa

*Kalithea
Thermi*

Kalavarda

Fanes

Kalithies

*Bay of
Kalithea*

Faliraki

*Ancient
Kamiros*

Psinthos

Ladiko
Beach

Alimia

Mt Profitis
Ilias (780m)

Salakos

Afantou

Afantou
Beach

*Excursion
Boat*

Skala
Kamirou

Apollona

Eleousa

Kolymbia
Beach

Kritinia Castle

Makry
Strongyli

Kritinia

Platanio

*Epta
Piges*

Tsambika
Beach

Embonas

*Emery
Winery*

Arhangeios

Stegna Beach

*Halki
(5km)*

*Mt Attavyros
(1215m)*

Agathi

Tragousa

Mt Akramytis
(825m)

Haraki

*Castle of
Faraklos*

*Cape
Armenistis*

Agios
Isidoros

*Karpathos (55km);
Kasos (105km)*

Siana

Laerma

*Vlyha
Bay*

Castle of Monolithos

Monolithos

*Moni
Tharri*

*Moni Agias
Ypsenis*

*Moni Agiou
Georgiou*

Fourni
Beach

Istrios

Lardos

Pefki
Beach

Pallas Beach

*Bay of
Apolakkia*

Profilia

Asklipieio

Lindos

Acropolis of Lindos

Arnitha

Pefki

Apolakkia

Kiotari

Glystra
Beach

St Paul's Bay

*Moni
Skiadi*

Vati

*Bay of
Gennadi*

Cape
Lardos

Gennadi

Ktenies

Mesanagros

Gennadi
Beach

*Mediterranean
Sea*

*Karpathian
Sea*

Kattavia

Lahania

Plimmyri

Cape Prasonisi

Cape
Germata
Prasonisi Beach

Prasonisi

Half the fun is letting yourself get lost. The **New Town**, to the north, boasts upscale shops and waterfront bars servicing the package crowd, along with the city's best beach, while bistros and bars lurk in the backstreets behind.

Inter-island ferries and catamarans use the **Commercial Harbour**, immediately outside the walls east of the Old Town, while excursion boats and private yachts are based at **Mandraki Harbour**, further north beside the New Town.

◉ Sights

◉ Old Town

A glorious mixture of Byzantine, Turkish and Italian architecture, erected atop far more ancient and largely unidentifiable remains, the Old Town is a world of its own. In theory, it consists of three separate sections, though casual visitors seldom notice the transition from one to the next. To the north, sturdy stone mansions, known as inns, housed knights from various countries and line the arrow-straight streets of the **Knights' Quarter**. These fabulously austere buildings were laid out by the medieval Knights of St John. South of that, the **Hora**, also known as the Turkish Quarter, is a tangle of cobbled alleyways that's now the main commercial hub, packed with restaurants and shops as well as derelict mosques and Muslim monuments. The **Jewish Quarter** in the southeast, which lost most of its inhabitants during WWII, is now a sleepy residential district.

Although there's no public access to the imposing 12m-thick ramparts that encircle the Old Town, you can descend at various points into the broad moat that separates the inner and outer walls. Now filled with lush gardens rather than water, the moat makes for a great stroll and is ideal for picnickers.

Of the nine *pyles* (gateways) to the Old Town, the busiest and most dramatic are the northernmost two, closest to the New Town. Liberty Gate, the nearest to Mandraki Harbour and the taxi rank, leads to a small bridge and on towards the main tourist areas, while the atmospheric D'Amboise Gate, further inland, crosses an especially attractive section of the moat en route to the Palace of the Grand Master.

★ **Archaeological Museum**   MUSEUM
(Map p502; ☑22413 65200; Plateia Mousiou; adult/child €8/free; ⊙9am-3pm Mon, 8am-8pm Tue-Fri, 8am-3pm Sat & Sun Apr-Oct, 9am-4pm Tue-Sat Nov-Mar) By far the best museum in the Dodecanese, this airy 15th-century former Knights' Hospital extends from its main building out into the beautiful gardens. It holds magnificently preserved ancient treasures, excavated from all over the island and ranging over 7000 years. Highlights include the exquisite 'Aphrodite Bathing' marble statue from the 1st century BC, a pavilion of wall-mounted mosaics, and a reconstructed burial site from 1700 BC that held not only a helmeted warrior but also his horse.

Palace of the Grand Master   HISTORIC BUILDING
(Map p502; ☑22413 65270, 22410 23359; €6; ⊙8am-8pm May-Oct, 8am-4pm Tue-Sun Nov-Apr) From the outside, the magnificent Palace of the Grand Master looks much as it did when erected by the Knights Hospitaller during the 14th century. During the 19th century, however, it was devastated by an explosion, so the interior is an Italian reconstruction, completed in the '18th year of the Fascist Era' (1940). The dreary magisterial chambers upstairs hold haphazard looted artworks, so the most interesting section is the exhibit on ancient Rhodes downstairs.

Street of the Knights   HISTORIC SITE
(Map p502; Ippoton; ⊙24hr) Austere and somewhat forbidding, the Street of the Knights (Ippoton) was home from the 14th century to the Knights Hospitaller who ruled Rhodes. They were divided into seven 'tongues', or languages according to their birthplace – England, France, Germany, Italy, Aragon, Auvergne and Provence – each responsible for a specific section of the fortifications. As wall displays explain, the street holds an 'inn', or palace, for each tongue. Its modern appearance, though, owes much to Italian restorations during the 1930s.

Jewish Synagogue Museum   MUSEUM
(Map p502; ☑22410 22364; www.rhodesjewish museum.org; Dosiadou; ⊙10am-3pm Sun-Fri May-Oct) FREE During the 1920s, the Old Town's Jewish Quarter was home to a thriving Jewish community of around 4000 people. Tragically, 1673 Rhodian Jews were deported to Auschwitz in 1944 and it's now a time-forgotten neighbourhood of sleepy streets and dilapidated houses. Early-20th-century photos and intricately decorated documents in the Jewish Synagogue Museum tell the whole story. The museum adjoins Greece's oldest synagogue, the 1577 Kahal Shalom Synagogue. Donations welcomed.

Muslim Library   LIBRARY
(Map p502; Sokratous; ⊙9.30am-3pm Mon-Sat May-Oct) FREE This peaceful little library, founded in 1794, sits opposite the pink-domed **Mosque of Süleyman** (Sokratous), and houses over 2000 books in Persian, Arabic and Turkish. Among its treasures are a couple of handwritten and beautifully illustrated copies of the Quran dating back to the 15th and 16th centuries. Donations welcomed.

◎ New Town

The so-called New Town of Rhodes has existed for 500 years, since Ottoman conquerors drove the local Greek population to build new homes outside the city walls. Almost nothing in the area, north of the Old Town and centred on Mandraki Harbour and the casino, though, holds any historic interest. Instead the New Town is a modern resort area, alive with guesthouses and restaurants, from gleaming hotel monoliths to tiny tavernas, along with banks, boutiques and the businesses that keep Rhodes ticking along.

The town **beach**, starting north of Mandraki Harbour, stretches around the island's northernmost point and down the west side of the New Town. The best spots tend to be on the east side, where there's usually calmer water and more sand and facilities.

Modern Greek Art Museum GALLERY
(Map p506; ☑ 22410 43780; www.mgamuseum. gr; Plateia Haritou; €3; ⊙8am-8pm Tue-Sat) The main gallery of the Modern Greek Art Museum, near the New Town's northern tip, holds paintings, engravings and sculptures by Greece's greatest 20th-century artists, including Gaitis Giannis, Vasiliou Spiros and Katraki Vaso. The museum's other three sites – the Nestoridi Building and the Centre of Modern Art, both in the New Town, and the original Art Gallery, in the Old Town – are currently closed because of a lack of available funding.

Rhodes Aquarium AQUARIUM
(Map p506; ☑ 22410 27308; www.rhodes-aquarium. hcmr.gr; Kos 1; adult/child €5.50/3.50; ⊙9am-8.30pm Apr-Oct, to 4.30pm Nov-Mar) The New Town's modest aquarium is housed in an art deco building constructed by the Italians in the 1930s. Its interior is imaginatively kitted out like an underwater cave, and there are touch tanks where you can lay hands on rays, starfish and other squirming sea beasts. All the sea life featured here can be found in the Aegean, including the most recent acquisition – a lionfish caught by a fisherman just a few miles from here.

Acropolis of Rhodes ARCHAEOLOGICAL SITE
(⊙24hr) FREE The site of the ancient Hellenistic city of Rhodes, now known as the Acropolis of Rhodes, stretches up the slopes of Monte Smith, 2km southwest of the Old Town. Restored structures include a tree-lined stadium from the 2nd century BC and the adjacent theatre, originally used for lectures by the Rhodes School of Rhetoric. Steps climb from there to the Temple of Pythian Apollo. Get here on city bus 5, or a stiff half-hour hike.

🏃 Activities & Tours

The quay along Mandraki Harbour, on the east side of the New Town, is lined with boats offering all sorts of excursions, including day trips to island beaches, the island of Symi and to Turkey. There are also glass-bottomed boats for kids' rides around the harbour, and well-established PADI-licensed diving operators who advertise their businesses from their moored boats. New to the town is 9D: Throne of Helios (p507), a terrific multi-sensory cinema experience.

Rhodes Segway Tours HISTORY
(Map p502; ☑ 6983245246, 22411 12409; www. rhodessegwaytours.com; Miltiadou 8, Old Town; €59; ⊙9am-8pm; 🚻) 🖉 A sightseeing experience like no other, this is a brilliant way to spare your energy and see more of the Old Town, rolling soundlessly past ancient buildings on your Segway with your expert guide chatting away as if it was perfectly normal! Tours last two hours. Training provided. Helmets required! Also does night tours (€85).

Rhodes Mystery Escape Room ESCAPE ROOM
(Map p502; ☑ 22410 34660; www.rhodesmystery. com; Sofokleous 222; for two €40, for five €50; ⊙10am-10pm; 🚻) Can you solve the mystery of the Grand Master's diamond? Or find the missing Italian pilot? It's hugely popular and great fun: you must find the clues to escape from one of two themed rooms – the Medieval Room or the Italian Room. There's a maximum of five sleuths per room, you have an hour to solve the mystery. Hidden down an alleyway beside Sofokleous.

Waterhoppers Diving Centre DIVING
(☑ 22410 38146; www.waterhoppers.com) Operating out of Mandraki Harbour and several other bases on the island, Waterhoppers offers an 'experience scuba' one-day program (€85) and a range of diving courses, including two- and three-day PADI open-water certifications. Choose from night, wreck and cave dives if you're an advanced diver.

Trident Scuba Diving School DIVING
(Map p506; ☑ 22410 29160; www.tridentdiving school.com; Mandraki Harbour; 🚻) Trident offers a range of diving courses and dive spots around the north of the island. It also runs beginner classes and two- and three-day PADI-certified courses. Look out for Trident's boat, *Armonia*, on Mandraki Harbour for more info.

🛌 Sleeping

The most magical sleeping options are all in the Old Town. In summer it's essential to reserve ahead. In winter, most budget options close altogether. Be warned, too, that most Old Town hotels are not accessible by taxi, so you'll have to haul your luggage along the narrow, cobbled lanes. Some hotels have golf carts in which to pick you up.

DODECANESE RHODES

Rhodes Old Town

Old Town

Minos Pension
PENSION €

(Map p502; ☑ 22410 31813; www.minospension. com; 5 Omirou St; d/ste €46/80; ﹡@🛜) Family-run Minos, perched beside a disused windmill on a quiet lane on the south side of the Old Town, has well-appointed, if slightly old-fashioned, studio rooms with gleaming kitchenettes and fridge. The compelling attraction, though, is the fabulous rooftop cafe, a lovely spot offering superb Old Town views. Downstairs there's a cosy communal lounge and book exchange.

★ Marco Polo Mansion
BOUTIQUE HOTEL €€

(Map p502; ☑ 22410 25562; www.marcopolo mansion.gr; Agiou Fanouriou 40; d incl breakfast €80-260; ☉ Apr-Oct; ﹡🛜) With its stained-glass windows, dark-wood furniture, wood floors and raised beds, Marco Polo lovingly recreates an Ottoman ambience with verve and style, and is unlike anything in the Old Town. This former 15th-century pasha's house, complete with its own harem (now a magical suite), is like a journey back in time. Breakfast is served in the stunning flowering courtyard.

Catamarans
to Turkey

Commercial
Harbour
(Kolona)

Akti Sahtouri

Virgin
Mary's
Gate

St Catherine's
Gate

Pindarou

Thiseos

Kisthiniou

Promitheos

Dosiadou

Alhadef

Fidiou

Akandia
Gate

Perikleous

Tavriska

Gavala

Dionisou

Tipolemou

Ekatonos

Vyronos

0   200 m
0   0.1 miles

The Andreas   HOTEL **€€**
(Map p502; ☑ 22410 34156; www.hotelandreas.
com; Omirou 28d; ste incl breakfast €80; ☺ May-
late Oct; ❄@🛜) Nicely described by its Cal-
ifornian owner as a 'four-star hotel trapped
in the soul of a small Greek pension', this
former pasha's house has three suites each
with two rooms. Best is the Tower Suite
where you wake each morning in your traditional raised bed to a view of the Aegean
below, while the Terrace Suite has its own
private sun terrace. Five-night minimum
stay.

Antifanou Apartments   APARTMENT **€€**
(Map p502; ☑ 22410 34561; Antifanouapartments@
gmail.com; Antifanous 5-9; apt €90; ❄🛜) These
two well-equipped apartments and single
studio are stylish and serenely cool courtesy of the original stone walls and arches.
Also, for larger families, two of them can be
interconnected. Each apartment has two
separate bedrooms, a communal area in the
kitchen and an outside communal terrace
which, chances are, you'll have to yourself.

Evdokia Hotel   BOUTIQUE HOTEL **€€**
(Map p502; ☑ 22410 77077; www.evdokiahotel.com;
Evdoxou 75; s/d/tr €70/85/150; ❄🛜) Situated
in a 13th-century building, this peaceful
hotel has welcoming rooms with wrought-
iron beds, cream walls, satellite TV, minibar
and safety deposit boxes, based around a
stunning high-ceiling lobby and breakfast
room. The best of the rooms is a triple with
its own staircase and roof terrace. Traditional
Rhodian breakfast with homemade marmalade, zucchini and fruit costs €8 extra.

Hotel Cava d'Oro   B&B **€€**
(Map p502; ☑ 22410 36980; www.cavadoro.com;
Kisthiniou 15; s/d/tr incl breakfast €110/130/160;
🅿❄🛜) Originally a storage building dating
from the era of the Knights of St John, this
small family-run hotel offers characterful
rooms of varying sizes, with canopied beds,
exposed stone walls and high arching ceilings.
Breakfast is served in a cool garden courtyard,
and guests can even walk on the hotel's own
short stretch of the Old Town walls.

★ Spirit of the Knights   BOUTIQUE HOTEL **€€€**
(Map p502; ☑ 22410 39765; www.rhodesluxuryhotel.
com; Alexandridou 14; s/d incl breakfast from
€160/200; � ❄🛜) This gorgeously finished
boutique hotel has six stunning suites dripping with medieval atmosphere. Imagine
thick rugs, dark woods, stained-glass windows and a sense of tranquillity. Perfectly isolated down a sidestreet close to the Old Town
walls, this fine hotel is a work of passion and
vision. There's a library and a fragrant garden
courtyard to read in and take breakfast.

**★ In Camera Art
Boutique Hotel**   BOUTIQUE HOTEL **€€€**
(Map p502; ☑ 22410 77277; www.incamera.gr;
Sofokleous 35; r/ste/villa incl breakfast €142/
270/380; ➣ ❄🛜) Sixteen years in the making, this stunning design hotel looks out on
ancient ruins, and has four very different
suites and two rooms, named after the exhibitions of the hotel's owner, a famous Greek

photographer. The highlight is the 'Forms of Light' suite with three levels, stained-glass windows, beautifully finished bedrooms and two roof terraces. There's also a breakfast cafe and garden with Jacuzzi.

New Town

Hotel Anastasia
PENSION €€

(Map p506; ☑ 22410 28007; www.anastasia-hotel.com; 28 Oktovriou 46; s/d/tr €55/65/85; ❋ @ ☎) The New Town's friendliest and most peaceful accommodation option is found in a handsome villa set back from the road, with ochre-coloured rooms with wooden shutters, tiled floors and traditional furnishings. Some have private balconies and there's an inviting breakfast bar in the lush garden. Owner Mihalis is welcoming.

Florida Hotel
HOTEL €€

(Map p506; ☑ 22410 22111; www.florida-rhodes.com; Amarandou 5; r from €50) Small, simple, modern hotel in a quiet little pedestrian street towards the New Town's northern tip. Crisp, clean, whitewashed rooms have kitchenettes and air-con, and each has its own flower-bedecked terrace or balcony. Yvonne, the owner, is helpful and offers you her own hand-drawn maps of the area. A short walk to the beach.

✖ Eating

✗ Old Town

★ Taverna Kostas
GREEK €

(Map p502; ☑ 22410 26217; Pythagora 62; mains €7-10; ☺ 10am-late; ❋) Run by grandfather Kostas, this is not only the friendliest and best-value restaurant in the Old Town but also one of the best. Forget the bare lime-washed walls and simple decor, eating here is like taking a place at the table of a friend – indeed, regulars set their own places! Serves succulent octopus salad, calamari, sea bream.

Old Town Corner Bakery
BAKERY €

(Map p502; ☑ 22410 38494; Omirou 88; snacks €2-6; ☺ 8am-9pm; ☎) With jazz and aromatic arabica coffee drifting through this tiny bakery cafe and out onto street where there a few stools, this is an Old Town residents' favourite. Has amazing pastries – dawn-fresh croissants sell out very quickly – club sandwiches, baklava (filo pastry with nuts and honey), apple pie and a host of healthy juices.

To Marouli
GREEK €

(Map p502; ☑ 22413 04394; Platonos 22; mains €8-10; ☺ noon-10pm; ❋☎☑) ✔ 'Marouli' means lettuce, and in this stylish, veggie-only restaurant, that's exactly what you can expect: plenty of greens. But for the pasta, which comes from Italy, the menu changes daily, dependent on the availability of locally grown food. Some examples include vegan Thai pineapple and fried rice, and mushroom and zucchini strudel with salad.

Yianni's
GREEK €

(Map p502; ☑ 22410 36535; yianis.restaurant@ gmail.com; Socratous Platonos 41; mains €7-10; ⊙ 10am-late; 🐾) Follow the songbird to the old lady dressed in colourful Karpathian garb and settle indoors, or sit al fresco to experience some of the best authentic Greek food in town. Alongside the usual favourites are dishes like *youvesti* (fried pork in tomato and wine sauce), and *makarounes* (Karpathian buttered pasta fried with onion).

Fournariko
BAKERY €

(Map p502; ☑ 22410 43057; Platonos; mains €7-12; ⊙ 7am-late; 🐾🐾) While the main dining room serves up tasty Italian dishes, including pizza straight from the brick-bake oven, Fournariko is first and foremost a bakery, with alluring trays of sweet and savoury pies and filo pastries. Get here early morning for super-fresh bakes, grab a table outside and enjoy a spot of people-watching over coffee.

★ Marco Polo Cafe
MEDITERRANEAN €€

(Map p502; ☑ 22410 25562; www.marcopolo mansion.gr; Agiou Fanouriou 40-42; mains €12-25; ⊙ 7-11pm) 🐾 Don't be surprised if you are asked to taste a new wine or culinary creation, a possible new addition to the menu of regulars, such as skewered lamb with rosemary and pistachio, pork loin with figs, Greek risotto with sea bream, or octopus in sea-urchin sauce. It's served up with sincerity and style in a lemon-fragrant garden courtyard.

Nireas
SEAFOOD €€

(Map p502; ☑ 22410 21703; Sofokleous 45-47; mains €8-16; ⊙ lunch & dinner; 🐾) Nireas' status as one of Rhodes' favourite seafood restaurants owes much to the sheer verve of genial owner Theo – that and the beautifully prepared food, served beneath a vine-shaded canopy, or in the candlelit, lemon-walled interior. Be sure to sample the Symi shrimp, salted mackerel and, if you're in the mood, the 'Viagra' salad of small shellfish.

Petaladika
GREEK €€

(Map p502; ☑ 22410 27319; Menakleous 8; mains €8-15; ⊙ noon-late) Petaladika might look like just another tourist trap, tucked into a corner just off the main drag, but with its fresh, white, wood interior and chic tables and chairs out front, it's a hot favourite with locals, and a mainstay of the Old Town dining scene. Try the deep-fried baby squid, zucchini balls and freshly grilled fish.

Hatzikelis
SEAFOOD €€

(Map p502; ☑ 22410 27215; www.hatzikelis.gr; Alhadef 9; mains €10-25; 🐾🐾🐾) With its candelabra and velvet finery, Hatzikelis is patronised by gourmands and Hollywood Grecophiles who return to savour the sea urchin, scallops, lobster, swordfish and freshly caught grouper. Ask to see the catch, bathed in ice in huge silver refrigerators. There's also terrific cutlets and steak, and a vast wine selection. Surprisingly good value.

✕ New Town

Koykos
GREEK €

(Map p506; ☑ 22410 73022; http://koukosrodos. com; Mandilana 20-26; mains €3-10; ⊙ breakfast, lunch & dinner; 🐾🐾) This inviting complex, off a pedestrian shopping street, consists of several antique-filled rooms – a couple hold vintage jukeboxes – along with two courtyards and a floral roof terrace. Best known for fabulous homemade pies, it also serves all the classic mezedhes (small plates), plus meat and fish dishes, or you can drop in for a coffee or sandwich.

Niohori
TAVERNA €

(Map p506; ☑ 22410 35116; I Kazouli 29; mains €8-12; ⊙ noon-midnight) This simple, great-value taverna – the open courtyard is basically a garage – delivers with a meat-accented menu. The owner is a butcher, with a shop across the street, so he selects the best cuts. Tuck into veal liver with oil and oregano, *stifadho* (meat with onions in a tomato purée), steak and meatballs, seasoned with organ music from the nearby church.

★ Meltemi
TAVERNA €€

(Map p506; ☑ 22410 30480; Kountourioti 8; mains €10-15; ⊙ noon-late; 🅿🐾🐾) It's unspectacular from the outside, but step into its nautically themed interior and try to resist its seafood treasures: octopus, jumbo prawns, lobster, huge portions of calamari as well as feisty salads, all delivered with gusto. Add to this wide-screen sea views and you can see why it's one of best seafront spots in the New Town.

Kerasma
GREEK €€

(Map p506; ☑ 2241302410; www.kerasmarestaurant. com; George Leontos 4-6; mains €15; ⊙ noon-

DODECANESE RHODES

Rhodes New Town

11.30pm; ❄ 🛜) This contemporary restaurant has an open, stylish setting and offers Greek fusion food with dishes like grilled octopus dipped in honey and beef fillet with purple gnocchi. There's also an impressive cellar of 60 different Greek wines. An injection of taste for the New Town.

Balsamico FUSION €€
(📞 22410 75967; Akti Miaouli 4-6; mains €10; ⊙11am-11pm; ❄ 🛜) Expect well-executed Greek dishes and Italian numbers like pizza and pasta at this sea-facing restaurant with an eclectic twist; think orange and

blue walls, a ceiling of suspended bottles and reclaimed driftwood sculptures. Spiro makes a great host and there's live music some nights.

🍷 Drinking & Nightlife

🍷 Old Town

⭐**Raxati Cafe** BAR
(Map p502; 📞 22410 363651; Sofokleous 1-3; ⊙10am-late; 🛜) Overlooking stunning Ibrahim Pasha Mosque, this high-ceilinged free-spirited bar and coffee house is as pretty

Rhodes New Town

◎ Sights
1 Modern Greek Art Museum B2
2 Mosque of Murad Reis C3
3 Rhodes Aquarium B1

☉ Activities, Courses & Tours
4 Trident Scuba Diving School D5

⊜ Sleeping
5 Florida Hotel B3
6 Hotel Anastasia A4

⊗ Eating
7 Kerasma A4
8 Koykos A3
9 Meltemi C3
10 Niohori B3

◎ Drinking & Nightlife
11 Christos Garden A4

☉ Entertainment
12 9D: Throne of Helios C4

as it is friendly. Its stone walls are peppered with vintage ad posters, there are recycled Singer sewing machine tables, and graceful chandeliers cast light across the stunning bar of glass spirits. Snacks, cocktails, easy tunes and good conversation.

Rogmi Tou Chronou BAR
(Map p502; ☑ 22410 25202; Plateia Arionos 4; ☉6pm-5am; ☎) If Dracula developed a taste for rock music and opened a bar it might look something like Rogmi Tou Chronou. Imagine purple velvet drapes, a handsomely crafted wood bar lit with fairy lights, stained-glass windows, and the odd candle to stop you bumping into the furniture in the darkness. Live rock on Friday and Saturday evenings.

Macao Bar BAR
(Map p502; ☑ 6936400305; www.macaobar.gr/en; Pl Arionos; ☉8pm-6am Fri & Sat) Uber-stylish bar hidden in the Old Town; expect moody, low-lit ambience, polished concrete floors and the occasional guest DJ spinning the decks to a well-heeled crowd of fashionistas. Try the herb flavoured cocktails (€8).

Rock & Roll BAR
(Map p502; ☑ 22410 25202; Plateia Arionos 2; mains €8; ☉9am-late; ☎☖) Cool diner-style haunt with metro-tiled walls and '50s songs playing as you plant yourself at the bar and tuck into a burger. It doubles as a juice bar during the day. Great balls of fire!

♀ New Town

While there's a very lively drinking scene in the New Town, centred on bar-lined I Dragoum, there's no great reason to recommend any of its many tourist-dominated hangouts over their identical neighbours.

Methexi BAR
(Akti Miaoúli 12; ☉10am-late; ☎) Methexi means 'theatrical event' in Ancient Greek, and this boho, fiercely indie haunt honours its namesake with live music on a Friday night from 9.30pm onwards. Sit outside on the terrace for watching sunsets or within the burnt-peach interior graced with retro typewriters, antique piano and musical miscellany.

Christos Garden BAR
(Map p506; ☑ 22410 32144; Griva 102; ☉10pm-late) With its grotto-like bar and pebble-mosaic courtyard, Christos offers New Town visitors a tranquil escape. During the day it doubles as an art gallery; after dark the fairy lights twinkle. Perfect for a cocktail.

☆ Entertainment

★9D: Throne of Helios FILM
(Map p506; ☑ 22410 76850; www.throneofhelios. com; Martiou 2; adult/child €13/9; ☉11am-7pm Mon-Fri, to 10pm Sat & Sun; ☎☖) Journey back to the birth of Rhodes in this 3D experience. History is brought to life with the aid of hydraulic chairs, falling rain, snow and bubbles. Amazing visuals recreate the Colossus of Rhodes' construction, the citadel's creation under the Knights of St John, and more – up to the present day.

Cafe Chantant LIVE MUSIC
(Map p502; ☑ 22410 32277; Dimokratou 3; ☉11pm-late Fri & Sat) Locals flock to the long wooden tables here and listen to live traditional Greek music while drinking ouzo or beer. It's dark inside and you won't find snacks or nibbles, but the atmosphere is warm-hearted and friendly and the band is always lively.

🔒 Shopping

Amid the typical souvenir tat, the Old Town is fillled with quality keepsakes: Moorish lamps, icons, anthracite busts, leather sandals, belts and bags, silver jewellery, olive wood chopping boards, Rhodian wine, and local thyme honey. The New Town is more prosaic with general stores and a clutch of big-name fashion and style brands.

DODECANESE RHODES

★ **Rodoscope Creative Gallery**　CERAMICS
(Map p502; ☏ 6972202138; Ippodamou 39;
☺ 10am-10pm) This tasteful boutique has a
collection of one-off bracelets, beach-bum-
chic jewellery, driftwood sculpture, handmade T-shirts and fine ceramics. Only the
work of Rhodian artists features here. Out
back there's a peaceful courtyard to admire
your gifts over a cool drink from the cafe.
Ask about the courses run here.

Antique Gallery　ARTS & CRAFTS
(Map p502; ☏ 22414 00126; Omirou 45; ☺ 9am-
9pm) Best viewed by night, this Aladdin's
cave of a shop conjures up thoughts of the
Arabian Nights, with its shiny brass lamps,
ornate antique rings and Eastern mosaic
lights glowing like clusters of fireflies.

ℹ Information

MEDICAL SERVICES
Euromedica General Hospital (☏ 22410
45000; www.euromedica-rhodes.gr; Koskinou)
The largest private health facility on the island,
with English-speaking staff. It's 6km south of
the Old Town, in Koskinou.

General Hospital (☏ 22413 60000; Andreas
Papandreou; ☺ 24hr) State-of-the-art hospital,
but bear in mind public hospital funding –
waiting times have been severely affected by
the Greek economic crisis.

Rhodes Medical Care Private Clinic (☏ 22410
38008; www.rmc.gr; Krito Building, Ioannou
Metaxa 3) Will treat you for any emergency
provided you have health insurance. Excellent
staff and facilities.

MONEY
You'll find plenty of ATMs throughout Rhodes
Town, with useful ATM-equipped branches of
Alpha Bank next door to the Old Town tourist
office and on Plateia Kypriou in the New Town.
The National Bank of Greece has a conveniently
located office in the **New Town** (Plateia Kyprou,
New Town), as well as a branch on Plateia Mous-
iou in the Old Town.

POLICE
Emergencies & Ambulance (☏ 166)
Port Police (☏ 22410 22220; Mandraki
Harbour)
Tourist Police (☏ 22410 27423; ☺ 24hr)

POST
Main Post Office (☏ 22410 35560; Mandraki
Harbour)

TOURIST INFORMATION
EOT (Greek Tourist Information Office; ☏ 22410
44335; www.ando.gr/eot; cnr Makariou &
Papagou; ☺ 8am-2.45pm Mon-Fri) National
tourism information, with brochures, maps and
transport details.

Rhodes Tourism Office – New Town (☏ 22410
35495; www.rhodes.gr; Plateia Rimini;
☺ 7.30am-3pm Mon-Fri) Conveniently poised
between Mandraki Harbour and the Old Town;
efficiently run with lots of free brochures and
helpful staff.

Rhodes Tourism Office – Old Town (☏ 22410
35945; www.rhodes.gr; cnr Platonos & Ippoton;
☺ 7am-3pm Mon-Fri) In an ancient building
at the foot of the Street of the Knights, this
helpful office supplies excellent street maps,
leaflets and brochures.

TRAVEL AGENCIES
Skevos Travel Agency (☏ 22410 22461; www.
skevostravel.gr; 111 Amerikis; ☺ 9am-8pm) For
help with airline and ferry tickets throughout
Greece.

Triton Holidays (☏ 22410 21690; www.
tritondmc.gr; Plastira 9, Mandraki Harbour;
☺ 9am-8pm) Air and sea travel, hire cars,
accommodation and tours throughout the
Dodecanese, as well as tickets to Turkey.

ℹ Getting Around

BICYCLE
Bicycles are available for rent from Margaritis in
the New Town.

BOAT
The quay at Mandraki Harbour is lined with
excursion boats offering day trips to east-coast
towns and beaches, including Faliraki and Lindos, and also to the island of Symi.

Several islands can be visited as day trips on
Dodekanisos Seaways (p498) catamarans,
departing from the Commercial Harbour. These
include Symi and Kos (both daily), Halki and
Tilos (both twice weekly), and Kastellorizo (once
weekly).

BUS
Two bus terminals, a block apart in Rhodes
Town, serve half the island each. There is regular
transport across the island all week, with fewer
services on Saturday and only a few on Sunday.
Pick up schedules from the kiosks at either ter-
minal, or from the EOT (Greek National Tourist
Organisation) office.

The **Eastern Bus Terminal** (☏ 22410 27706;
www.ktelrodou.gr) has frequent services to
the airport (€2.40), Kalithea Thermi (€2.20),
Salakos (€4.30), Ancient Kamiros (€5.20) and
Monolithos (€5.20). From the **Western Bus
Terminal** (☏ 22410 26300) there are services
to Faliraki (€2.40), Tsambika Beach (€3.90),
Stegna Beach (€4.40) and Lindos (€5.20).

In Rhodes Town, local buses leave from the **urban bus stop** (Mandraki) on Mandraki Harbour. Bus 11 makes a circuit around the coast, up past the aquarium and on to the Acropolis. Bus 2 goes to Analipsi, bus 3 to Rodini, bus 4 to Agios Dimitrios and bus 5 to the Acropolis. Buy tickets on-board.

CAR & MOTORCYCLE

All the major car-rental chains are represented at Rhodes airport, and plenty more car- and motorcycle-rental outlets are scattered throughout Rhodes Town and the resorts. Competition is fierce, so shop around. Several agencies will deliver vehicles to renters.

Drive Rent A Car (☑ 22410 81011, 22410 68243; www.driverentacar.gr; 1st Km Tsairi-Airport; ☺ 8am-9pm) Sturdier, newer scooters and cars.

Margaritis (☑ 22410 37420; www.margaritis rentals.gr; I Kazouli St 17; ☺ 24hr) Reliable cars, scooters and bicycles in the New Town.

Orion Rent a Car (☑ 22410 22137; www. orioncarrental.com; Leontos 38) A wide range of small and luxury cars.

TAXI

Rhodes Town's main **taxi rank** is east of Plateia Rimini, on the northern edge of the Old Town. There are two zones on the island for taxi meters: zone one is Rhodes Town and zone two (for which rates are slightly higher) is everywhere else. Rates double between midnight and 5am. Set taxi fares are posted at the rank.

You can also phone for a **taxi** (☑ in Rhodes Town 22410 69800, outside Rhodes Town 22410 69600; www.rhodes-taxi.gr) or **disabled-accessible taxi** (☑ 22410 77079).

Note that taxis cannot access most locations in the largely pedestrianised Old Town; expect to be dropped at the gate nearest your destination. A few upscale hotels have golf buggies to pick you up in.

Northeastern Rhodes

Most of the sandiest beaches on Rhodes lie along the island's northeastern coast, between Rhodes Town and Lindos. As a result, this stretch is now punctuated by a long succession of resorts, filled with package holidaymakers in summer and holding endless strips of tourist bars.

Ladiko Beach, 15km south of Rhodes Town, just beyond Faliraki, is touted locally as 'Anthony Quinn Beach'. Back in the 1960s, the star of *Zorba the Greek* actually bought the beach from the Greek government, but according to his family the authorities failed to honour the sale. It consists of two back-to-back coves, with a pebbly beach on the north side that's better for swimming, and volcanic rock platforms on the south side.

Two fine beaches, **Kolymbia** and **Tsambika**, are located either side of the massive Tsambika promontory, 10km further south. Both are sandy but get crowded in summer. Not far beyond, the coast road curves inland, but a short detour seawards brings you to the low-key little resort of Stegna, arrayed along sandy, idyllic **Stegna Beach**.

The headland that marks the start of the final curve towards Lindos, 40km south of Rhodes Town, is topped by the ruins of the 15th-century **Castle of Faraklos**. Once a prison for recalcitrant knights, this was the last stronghold on the island to fall to the Turks and now offers fabulous views. A footpath climbs from the appealing little resort of **Haraki**, immediately south, where the neat horseshoe bay is lined by a pebbly beach.

⊙ Sights

Kalithea Thermi — ARCHITECTURE
(☑ 22410 65691; www.kallitheasprings.gr; Kalithea; €3; ☺ 8am-8pm Apr-Oct, to 5pm Nov-Mar; 🅿) Italian architect Pietro Lombardi constructed this opulent art deco spa, on the site of ancient thermal springs, in 1929. Its dazzling white-domed pavilions, pebble-mosaic courtyards and sweeping sea-view colonnades have appeared in movies such as *Zorba the Greek* and *The Guns of Navarone*, and have now been restored after years of neglect. In peak season its small sandy bathing beach and cafe get impossibly crowded.

Just 9km south of Rhodes Town, it can be accessed by driving directly along the coast.

Epta Piges — SPRING
(Seven Springs; Kolymbia; ☺ 24hr; 🅿) FREE
Seven natural springs at this beauty spot, in the hills 4km inland from Kolymbia, feed a river that's channelled into a narrow tunnel, exactly the size of an adult. Thrill-seeking visitors can walk a few hundred metres in pitch darkness, ankle-deep in fast-flowing water, to reach the shaded lake at the far end.

Lindos   Λίνδος

POP 3600

Your first glimpse of the ancient and unbelievably pretty town of Lindos is guaranteed to steal your breath away: the towering Acropolis radiant on the cypress-silvered hill, and the sugar-cube houses of the whitewashed town tumbling below it towards the aquamarine bay. Entering the town itself, you'll find yourself in a magical warren of hidden alleys, packed with the ornate houses of long-vanished sea captains that now hold appetising tavernas, effervescent bars and cool cafes. Pick your way past donkeys as you coax your calves up to the Acropolis and one of the finest views in Greece.

Lindos has been enjoying its wonderful setting for 4000 years, since the Dorians founded the first settlement at this excellent harbour and vantage point. Since then it has been successively overlaid with Byzantine, Frankish and Turkish structures, the remains of which can be glimpsed all around.

◉ Sights & Activities

Two magnificent beaches line the crescent harbour that curves directly below the village. The larger, logically known as **Main Beach**, is a perfect swimming spot – sandy with shallow water – for kids. Follow a path north to the western tip of the bay to reach the smaller, taverna-fringed **Pallas Beach**. Don't swim near the jetty here, which is home to sea urchins, but if it gets too crowded you can swim from the rocks beyond.

Ten minutes' walk from town on the other, western, side of the Acropolis, sheltered **St Paul's Bay** is similarly caressed by turquoise waters.

★ **Acropolis of Lindos**   ARCHAEOLOGICAL SITE
(☑ 22413 65200; adult/concession/child €12/6/free; ☉ 8am-7.40pm Tue-Fri, 8am-3pm Sat-Mon Apr-Oct, 8.30am-3pm Tue-Sun Nov-Mar) A steep footpath climbs the 116m-high rock above Lindos to reach the beautifully preserved Acropolis. First walled in the 6th century BC, the clifftop is now enclosed by battlements constructed by the Knights of St John. Once within, you're confronted by stunning ancient remains that include a **Temple to Athena Lindia** and a 20-columned **Hellenistic stoa**. Silhouetted against the deep blue sky, the stark white columns are dazzling, while the long-range coastal views are out of this world.

Be sure to pack a hat and some water, as there's no shade at the top, and take care to protect young kids from the many dangerous drop-offs. Donkey rides to the Acropolis from the village entrance only spare you around three minutes of exposed walking on the hillside, and you should note that animal-rights groups urge people to consider the treatment of the donkeys before deciding to take a ride.

★ **Lepia Dive**   DIVING
(☑ 6937417970; www.lepiadive.com; ♿) This brilliantly inclusive dive company has a range of options including PADI courses for kids, beginners and those already at an advanced level. The centre's facilities are adapted for wheelchairs and there are expertly designed dives certified by DDI (Disabled Divers International) for people with additional needs. Choose from reef, wreck and cave dives. Free pick-up.

🛏 Sleeping

Accommodation in Lindos is very limited, so be sure to book in advance. And check carefully, as most hotels that include 'Lindos' in their names and/or addresses are in fact located not in the town, but along the coast nearby.

Electra Studios   PENSION €
(☑ 22440 31266; www.electra-studios.gr; studios €50; ☉ Apr-Oct; ❄ 🛜) Simple family-run pension, where the plain, but very pleasant, whitewashed rooms have varnished wooden twin beds, fridges and air-con. Some have balconies and there's also a lovely communal roof terrace overlooking a lemon grove and the sea.

Anastasia Studios   APARTMENT €€
(☑ 22440 31417, 6970977696; www.lindos-studios. gr; d & tr €60; P ❄ 🛜) Focused around a geranium-filled courtyard on Lindos' eastern side, these six split-level apartments enjoy soaring Acropolis views. Each has a tiled floor, sofa bed, well-equipped kitchen and separate bedroom, while room 6 has its own private balcony.

★ **Melenos**   BOUTIQUE HOTEL €€€
(☑ 22440 32222; www.melenoslindos.com; ste incl breakfast from €370; ❄ @ 🛜) 🍴 Magical Moorish-style palace with bougainvillea walkways, pebble-mosaic floors, verandas festooned in lanterns and bauble lights casting a glow on Ottoman furniture. Staff glide discreetly around as you soak up the stunning bay view. Rooms are lovingly re-created in traditional Lyndian style, with raised beds, wooden ceilings and private balconies, and there's a superb restaurant.

F Charm Hotel   BOUTIQUE HOTEL €€€
(☑ 22440 32080, 6944339937; www.lindosfine staying.com; r incl breakfast from €140; ❄ 🛜) This enclosed courtyard accommodation holds half a dozen heavenly white rooms and family-sized suites. All have shabby-chic

distressed furniture, wood-beamed ceilings and traditional raised-platform beds with Cocomat mattresses, plus fridge and kitchenette. It's next to the police station, at the south end of town.

✕ Eating

Most tavernas serve their customers on roof terraces high above the tangle of streets. These give fabulous views up to the Acropolis and over the bay, but mean you can't always tell whether there's anyone in your chosen venue until you've already committed to eat there.

Captain's House
CAFE €
(snacks €7; ⊘ 8am-midnight; �// 🛜) Soaked in Lyndian atmosphere, this nautically themed, 16th-century sea captain's house is perfect for a juice on your way down from the Acropolis. Grab a pew in the pebble-mosaic courtyard and ponder the fabulous carved stone reliefs in the courtyard.

Village Cafe
BAKERY €
(☑ 22440 31559; www.lindostreasures.com; mains €8; ⊘ 8.30am-7pm; �//🛜🐾) Near the start of the path up to the Acropolis, this whitewashed bakery-cafe has an enticing vine-covered pebble-mosaic courtyard and comfortable couches in its cool interior. Drop in for hot or frozen coffee, juice or ice cream, and a mouthwatering array of cheese cakes, cherry pies, salads, wraps and freshly prepared sandwiches. Don't miss the delectable *bougatsa* (vanilla custard pie).

★ Calypso
TAVERNA €€
(☑ 22440 32135; www.kalypsolindos.gr; mains €13; ⊘ 11am-midnight; �//🛜) This former sea captain's residence with its beautiful stone relief is perfect for lunch or dinner on the roof terrace or inside. Sea bass, octopus, *makarounes* (homemade pasta served with fresh onions and melted local cheese) and grilled lamb chops are but a few of the delights.Try the 'Kalypso bread' with feta and tomato.

Melenos
MEDITERRANEAN €€€
(☑ 22440 32222; www.melenoslindos.com; mains €26; ⊘ 8am-midnight; 🛜) Gorgeous sea view terrace restaurant overlooking Pallas Beach. The menu features salmon marinated in ouzo, steamed sea bass with mussels in asparagus sauce, and grilled beef fillet with mushrooms, wine and caramelised onions. Round things off with a sumptuous dessert.

ⓘ Information

Lindos Tourist Office (☑ 22440 31900; Plateia Eleftherias; ⊘ 9am-3pm) Small information kiosk at the entrance to central Lindos.

Island Of The Sun Travel (☑ 22440 31264; Acropolis; ⊘ 9am-5pm) Local excursions, rental cars and accommodation.

Southeastern Rhodes

As you continue south of Lindos along the east coast, the island takes on a windswept appearance and sees less tourist traffic. Villages here seem to have a slower pace.

Just 2km south of Lindos, sandy **Pefki Beach** is deservedly popular. If it's too crowded, try **Glystra Beach**, just down the road and a great spot for swimming.

Sleepy one-street **Gennadi** consists of a few *kafeneia* (coffee houses), friendly locals and a cluster of whitewashed buildings set back a few hundred metres from the pebbled beach. You'll find a fruit market, bakery, supermarket and a couple of tavernas.

An almost uninterrupted beach of pebbles and sand dunes extends down from Gennadi as far as **Plimmyri**, 11km south. Watch for a signposted turning to **Lahania**, 2km inland off the main highway, and head downhill into the centre to find an old village of winding alleyways and traditional buildings.

The coast road continues south past countless chapels to the village of **Kattavia**, a friendly place that doesn't see a lot of tourists. Beyond that, a windswept 10km road snakes south to remote **Cape Prasonisi**, the island's southernmost point. Joined to Rhodes by a tenuously narrow sandy isthmus in summer months, it's cut off completely when water levels rise in winter. The Aegean Sea meets the Mediterranean here, creating ideal wind and wave conditions for kitesurfers and windsurfers. Outfitters stand ready to help with everything from rental equipment and lessons to overnight accommodation in surfer-dude-style hostels, but it all closes down in winter. To get here direct from the airport by taxi costs around €120 and takes 1½ hours.

✦ Activities

Pro Center
Kristof Kirschner ADVENTURE SPORTS
(☑ 22400 91045; www.facebook.com/procenterc. kirschner; ⊘ May-Oct; 🐾) Specialising in windsurfing equipment rental and classes.

DODECANESE RHODES

Sleeping & Eating

★ Four Elements
APARTMENT €€

(☑6939450014, 22440 46001; www.thefour
elements.be; Lahania; apt €110-165; 🅿❄@🛜🏊) Four exceptionally homey and spacious apartments, perfect for taking a rural holiday in comfort. All have full kitchens, one is adapted for wheelchair users, and there's a divine pool, outdoor barbecue and garden. Minimum two nights. The friendly Belgian owners run an on-site cafe-bar named the Fifth Element (beer being the fifth element after earth, air, fire and water).

Taverna Platanos
TAVERNA €

(☑6944199991; www.lachaniaplatanos.com; Lahania; mains €6-8; ❄🛜) Classic village taverna, tucked behind the church in Lahania's tiny main square and famed throughout the island. With its traditional decor and flower-filled patio, it's a great place to take a break. Hearty lamb, beef or chicken stews cost well under €10, with salads and dips less than half that.

Mama's Kitchen
PIZZA €

(Gennadi; mains €7-10; ❄) Check out the murals of ancient myths as you munch Olympian portions of grilled meat like lamb and beef.

Western Rhodes & the Interior

Western Rhodes is redolent with the scent of pine, its hillsides shimmering with forests. More exposed than the east side, it's also windier – a boon for kitesurfers and windsurfers – so the sea tends to be rough and the beaches mostly pebbled. If you're cycling, or have a scooter or car, the hilly roads that cross the interior are well worth exploring for their wonderful scenery.

For sightseers, the most significant potential stopoffs are the ruined ancient cities of Ialysos and Kamiros. Otherwise, once past the airport, settlements are few and far between. Skala Kamirou, 45km southwest of Rhodes Town, is a small port with direct ferries to the nearby island of Halki. Although it does have a couple of tavernas, and a twice-daily bus service, it's so isolated that it's much more use to locals than independent travellers.

The ruins of 16th-century Kritinia Castle stand proudly on a headland immediately south of Skala Kamirou. Detour off the main road for awe-inspiring views along the coast and across to Halki, in a magical setting where you half expect to encounter Romeo or Rapunzel.

Continuing south, the road is sublimely scenic. Vast mountainous vistas open up as you approach Siana, a picturesque village below Mt Akramytis (825m), and the village of Monolithos, 5km beyond. The spectacularly sited 15th-century castle that's perched on a sheer 240m-high rock above Monolithos can be reached on a dirt track. To enter, climb through the hole in the wall.

⊙ Sights & Activities

★ Petaloudes
FOREST

(Valley of the Butterflies; ☑22410 82822; €5; ⊙9am-5pm; ♿) Petaloudes, 7km up from the coast, is better known as the Valley of the Butterflies. Visit in June, July or August, when these colourful insects mature, and you'll quickly see why. They're actually tiger moths *(Callimorpha quadripunctarea)* drawn to the gorge by the scent of the resin exuded by storax trees. In summer the whole place is choking with tour buses. Out of season, you'll likely have the gorgeous forest path, streams and pools to yourself – but no butterflies.

Ancient Kamiros
ARCHAEOLOGICAL SITE

(☑22410 40037; €6; ⊙8am-7.40pm May-Oct, 8.30am-3pm Nov-Apr; ♿) The extensive remains of the Doric city of Kamiros stand above the coast, 34km southwest of Rhodes Town. Known for its figs, oil and wine, Kamiros was at its peak in the 7th century BC, but was swiftly superseded by Rhodes and devastated by earthquakes in 226 BC and 142 BC. Visible ruins include a Doric temple, with one column still standing, a temple to Athena and a 3rd-century great stoa. Come in the afternoon, when fewer visitors are around.

Ancient Ialysos
ARCHAEOLOGICAL SITE

(☑22410 92202; €6; ⊙8.30am-8pm May-Oct, 8.30am-3pm Nov-Apr; ♿) Constructed in the 3rd century BC, atop what's now Filerimos Hill, 10km southwest of Rhodes Town, the Doric city of Ialysos was repeatedly conquered. The resultant hotchpotch of Doric, Byzantine and medieval remains is now barely intelligible to casual visitors. Stairs from the entrance lead to the ruined foundations of the Temple of Athena Ialysia and the peaceful restored 14th-century Chapel of Agios Georgios. Follow the path left from the entrance to reach another 12th-century chapel, filled with frescoes.

Emery Winery
WINERY

(☑ 22460 41208; Embonas; ☺ 9.30am-4.30pm Apr-Oct) **FREE** Perched on the flanks of Mt Attavyros (1215m), the island's highest mountain, the village of Embonas is the wine capital of Rhodes. This cottage winery, on the town's eastern edge, offers tours of its facility and provides a good opportunity to taste and buy top-quality tipples such as the red Cava Emery or Zacosta and the white Villare.

✗ Eating

Mylos
CAFE €

(☑ 6940641475; Kritinia; snacks €5-7; ☺ 9am-late) Set beside the main road, with tremendous views down to Kritinia Castle, this welcoming little cafe serves coffee, drinks and snacks such as salads, omelettes and sandwiches. Best of all, though, it has its own **folklore museum**, filled with local costumes and alarming farming implements.

To Stolidi Tis Psinthoy
TAVERNA €

(☑ 22410 50009; Psinthos; mains €8-10; ☺ lunch & dinner) The pick of several appealing lunch spots in lively Psinthos, 10km southeast of Petaloudes, To Stolidi has a deeply rural feel with wooden beams, chequered tablecloths and family photos on the walls. Try the spicy pork, grilled eggplant, dolmadhes and fresh-baked country bread.

HALKI ΧΑΛΚΗ
POP 310

Thanks to the gorgeous Italianate mansions that surround its harbour, the former sponge-diving island of Halki makes an irresistible first impression. Stepping off the ferry, you enter a composite of all that's best about Greece: an old fisherman shelling prawns under a fig tree, an Orthodox priest flitting down a narrow alley, brightly painted boats bobbing along the quay. There's little to do except relax and indulge in the sleepy splendour, venturing out to tempting little beaches lapped by aquamarine waters and, in cooler months, hiking along the island's spectacular high-mountain spine.

ⓘ Getting There & Away

The **Dodekanisos Seaways** (p498) catamaran stops at Halki on Tuesday and Thursday as it heads from Rhodes to Tilos, Nisyros, Kos and Kalymnos in the morning, and back to Rhodes in the evening. On those days, you can visit the island as a day trip from Rhodes. **Blue Star Ferries** (p498) connects Halki with Rhodes up to three times weekly, and with Karpathos, Kasos, Crete, Santorini and Piraeus twice weekly.

Two boats, **Nissos Halki Halki** (☑ mobile 6946519817, 6973460968) and **Nikos Express** (☑ mobile 6946826905) link Halki daily with the tiny port of Skala Kamirou on the west coast of Rhodes; there's an hour-long connecting bus service with Rhodes Old Town. **Stelios Kazantzidis** (☑ mobile 6944434429) runs an on-demand water-taxi service to Skala Kamirou.

Boat Services from Halki (Emborios)

DESTINATION	DURATION	FARE (€)	FREQUENCY
Kalymnos*	3hr	36	2 weekly
Karpathos	4hr	13	3 weekly
Kos*	2¼hr	26	2 weekly
Nisyros*	1½hr	24	2 weekly
Piraeus	24hr	44	2 weekly
Rhodes	2hr	8	3 weekly
Rhodes*	1¼hr	18	2 weekly
Rhodes (Skala Kamirou)	1¼hr	11	1-2 daily
Santorini (Thira)	12hr	26	1 weekly
Tilos*	40min	24	2 weekly

*high-speed services

ⓘ Getting Around

Most visitors get around Halki on foot. In summer, regular minibuses connect Emborios with Pondamos, Ftenagia and Kalia beaches (€1.50 each way), while on Friday evenings there's also a round trip to Moni Agiou Ioanni monastery (€5). A water taxi also serves the main beaches, while **Zifos Travel** (☑ 22460 45028; www.zifostravel.gr; ☺ 10am-8pm) can provide details of summer-only excursion boats, for example to the uninhabited island of Alimia (€30), with its fields of wild herbs.

Emborios Εμπορειός
POP 300

Halki's one tiny town curves luxuriantly around a sheltered turquoise bay. The waterfront is a broad expanse of flagstones, almost entirely pedestrianised, populated by as many cats as humans and lined with enticing tavernas and cafes. Climbing in tiers up a low ridge, the cream, ochre, stone and rose-hued homes of 19th-century fishermen and sea captains form a magnificent backdrop. There's no town beach, but here and there ladders enable swimmers to enter the water.

Sights

The neoclassical mansions of Emborios are a visual feast. A few have crumbled into complete ruination, but most have been restored to their original glory and many now serve as rental properties.

The impressive central **clock tower** was donated by the expat Halki community in Florida; the clock itself hasn't worked for over 20 years. Nearby, the **Church of Agios Nikolaos** has the tallest belfry in the Dodecanese, incorporating stones from an ancient temple of Apollo, and boasts a picturesque mosaic-pebbled courtyard.

Traditional House of Chalki   HISTORIC BUILDING
(☑22460 45284; €3; ☉11am-3pm & 6-8pm)
Perched on the hillside, not far up from the harbour (signed to the right off the road to Pondamos Beach), the Traditional House of Chalki – an alternative transliteration of Halki – is a two-storey family home, built a century ago. It's now meticulously preserved as a museum, displaying authentic furniture, tableware and costumes, old photos – and even the underwear of the owner's grandmother, neatly framed.

Sleeping & Eating

Halki holds little accommodation, so book ahead in summer. Most visitors stay in self-catering villas and apartments; contact Zifos Travel or Nissia Holidays (www.nissia holidays.com) for details.

Captain's House   PENSION €
(☑6932511762, 22460 45201; capt50@otenet.gr; d €40; ❄☎) Attractive white-painted 19th-century house just up from the sea, near the church, featuring antique clocks and model schooners. Two lovely rooms have high ceilings, wood floors, air-con and good bathrooms, and the relaxing garden courtyard holds a sun terrace with great harbour views.

★**Aretanassa Hotel**   HOTEL €€
(☑22460 70927; www.aretanassahotel.cosmores.com; Harbour; d/tr incl breakfast €90/115; ❄☎) This wine-coloured former sponge factory has 19 gloriously sunny, sea-facing rooms with powder-blue walls, large beds and spotless tiled floors. Some rooms have balconies. There's a lovely restaurant and bar, and a sun terrace over your very own azure Mediterranean swimming pool. There's also a lift and access for those with additional needs.

Taverna Lefkosia   TAVERNA €
(☑6946978151; mains €7-12; ☉lunch & dinner) Much-loved taverna, where the check-clothed tables and blue chairs spread out onto the quay and the menu abounds in hom-made island specialities such as baked pasta. The fried cheese balls are a crispy, chewy delight, and fresh-caught fish comes in generous portions.

Black Sea   TAVERNA €
(☑22460 45021; Harbour; mains €8-14; ☉lunch & dinner; ❄☎) ✐ Sitting peacefully on the left side of the harbour, metres from bobbing boats, this brightly coloured haunt is run by a charming Georgian family. It's a great spot for fresh fish, from octopus and little shrimp to grilled bream, but the vegetable dishes, including fried mushrooms, are also good.

Dimitri's Bakery   BAKERY €
(Harbour; mains €3; ☉breakfast, lunch & dinner) Generations of Halki residents and visitors have stocked up on Dimitri's delicious sweet and savoury pies and pastries, available from early morning. Cheese, spinach and apple pies, plus croissants and – in the evening – slices of pizza.

Information

The only ATM is often out of action, so bring plenty of spare cash.
Police & Port Police (☑22460 45220) On the harbour.
Post Office (☉9am-1.30pm Mon-Fri) On the harbour, with an ATM.
Zifos Travel (☑22460 45028; www.zifostravel.gr; ☉10am-8pm) The best source of help with accommodation, boat tickets, excursions and currency exchange.

Around Halki

A broad concrete road crosses the low hill above Emborios harbour to reach Pondamos Beach, the most popular of Halki's handful of tiny shingle beaches, after 500m. Beyond that, it climbs to the abandoned village of Horio, 3km along, then continues west to the hilltop monastery of **Agiou Ioanni**. That's a total one-way hike of 8km, recommended in the cooler months only.

Two more pebble beaches, both equipped with decent tavernas and served by buses in summer, lie within walking distance of Emborios. **Ftenagia Beach** is beyond the headland 500m south of the harbour, while **Kania Beach** is an enjoyable but unshaded 2.5km hike north, signposted off the main road halfway to Pondamos.

◉ Sights

Pondamos Beach   BEACH

Pretty little Pondamos Beach is lapped by the turquoise waters of a crescent bay 10 minutes' walk up and over the hill west of Emborios. The only way to get a comfortable shaded spot is to rent a €3 sunbed alongside **Nick's Taverna** (mains €6-15; ☻breakfast, lunch & dinner; 奈), where separate sections serve good seafood meals, and drinks and snacks.

Horio   ARCHAEOLOGICAL SITE

A stiff switchback climb along the road from Pondamos Beach leads up through Halki's fertile central valley to Horio. This picturesque ruin was originally the island's main village, hidden away to escape the eyes of roving pirates. A freshly cobbled footpath heads up to the battlements of the **Knights of St John Castle** that once protected it. Pass through its forbidding gateway to see a restored chapel and amazing long-range views.

KARPATHOS ΚΑΡΠΑΘΟΣ

POP 6200

Celebrated for its wild mountains and blue coves, this long craggy island is among the least commercialised in Greece. Legend has it Prometheus and his Titans were born here, and with its cloud-wrapped villages and rugged beauty, there's still something undeniably primal in the air. Homer, never a man to mince his words, called it 'Krapathos', but actually it's a lovely island.

Popular with adrenaline junkies, southern Karpathos is in the spotlight each summer when it hosts an international kitesurfing competition. Meanwhile, the fierce wind that lifts the spray from the turquoise waves blows its way to the mountainous north, battering pine trees and howling past sugar-cube houses. Karpathian women at this end of the island still wear traditional garb, especially in the time-forgotten village eyrie of Olymbos, perched atop a perilous mountain ridge.

❶ Getting There & Away

AIR

The airport at the very southern tip of Karpathos is linked by Olympic Air (www.olympicair.com) two to four times daily with Athens (€70, one hour).

Sky Express (☑ 28102 23800; www.skyexpress.gr) has daily links between Karpathos and Rhodes (€68, 40 minutes), and once daily with Kasos (€56, 15 minutes) and Sitia (€87, one hour) on Crete.

BOAT

The island's main port, Pigadia, is served by **Blue Star Ferries** (p498), with all sailings also calling at the northern village of Diafani either before Pigadia (when southbound) or after it (when northbound). Ferries head three times weekly to Halki and Rhodes, and three times weekly to Kasos, with two continuing to Crete and one to Santorini.

Boat Services from Karpathos

The following services all depart from Pigadia

DESTINATION	DURATION	FARE (€)	FREQUENCY
Halki	4hr	13	3 weekly
Kasos	1½hr	8	3 weekly
Milos	16hr	38	1 weekly
Piraeus	17hr	44	2 weekly
Rhodes	5hr 40min	21	3 weekly
Santorini (Thira)	8hr	27	1 weekly
Sitia	4hr	19	2 weekly

❶ Getting Around

TO/FROM THE AIRPORT

The airport is 14km south of Pigadia. From late July to September, an 11.30am bus on Thursday and a 10.30am bus on Saturday go to the airport (€2.50), making the return journey on both days at 5pm. A taxi will cost €22. Given the size of the island it makes sense to rent a car. All major car-rental chains have outlets at the airport.

BOAT

Day trips head from Pigadia up to Diafani, where they connect with buses to Olymbos, or continue north to remote beaches.

BUS

KTEL (www.karpathosbus.wordpress.com) runs buses all over the island from the **bus station** (☑ 22450 22338; M Mattheou, Pigadia) in Pigadia, just up from the harbour. Only two a week go all the way north to Olymbos.

Karpathos

N
0 — 5 km
0 — 2.5 miles

Karpathos Strait
Cape Paraspori

Saria

Excursion
Boat

Tristomo
Cape
Vroukounda
Vroukounda
Moni Agiou Ioanni
Vananda
Beach
Avlona
Halki
(50km);
Rhodes
(132km)
Moni Agiou Konstantinou
Diafani
Mt Profitis
Ilias (716m)
Olymbos

Sea of
Crete

Papa
Mina
Bay

Agios Minas

Spoa

Mesohori
Agios Nikolaos
Apella
Beach
Roman Cistern
Excursion
Boat
Lefkos Beach
Mertonas
Kyra Panagia
Beach
Lefkos
Kali Limni
(1215m)
Kato Lakos
Beach
Volada
Aperi
Ahata
Beach
Adia
Othos
Cape
Proni
Pyles
Vrondi
Bay
Flaskia Gorge
Menetes
Pigadia
Basilica of
Agia Sophia
& Acropolis
Finiki
Ammoöpi
Arkasa
Cape
Volakas
Agios
Nikolaos
Beach
Cape Agios
Theodoros
Afiartis
Bay
Cape
Akrotiri
Cape
Lingi
Cape
Kastello
Kasos (10km);
Crete (80km)

DODECANESE KARPATHOS

CAR

All major car-rental chains have outlets at the airport, and there are local agencies all over the island. Recommended operators include **Europcar** (📱22450 23238; www.europcar.com), **Pegasus Motorbikes** (📱mobile 6979794727;

per day from €18.50; ⏱9am-1pm & 5-8pm), **Rent A Car** (📱22450 22911, 22450 22690; 28 Oktovriou) and **Lefkos Rent A Car** (📱mobile 6984466346, mobile 6977918774, office 22450 71030; www.lefkosrentacar.com; Lefkos).

TAXI

Taxi prices are posted at Pigadia's central **taxi rank** (📱22450 22705; Dimokratias). Fares are prohibitively high, with trips to Lefkos costing €50 and Olymbos €75.

Pigadia   Πηγάδια

POP 1690

Karpathos' capital and main ferry port, Pigadia sprawls beside a long bay on the southeast shore of the island. Decent beaches stretch away to the north, but the town itself lacks the photogenic good looks and geometrically pleasing whitewashed houses of other islands. Give it a little time, though, wandering its harbour and among waterfront bars and backstreet bakeries, and the place may grow on you. Determinedly Greek, it barely looks up from its afternoon retsina to acknowledge your arrival. But isn't that what travellers sometimes long for?

🛏 Sleeping

Budget options are concentrated in the hillside streets that rise from central Pigadia, while newer and more luxurious options spread northwards around the curve of the bay.

Rose's Studios   APARTMENT €
(📱22450 22284; www.rosesstudios.com; r €35; ❄🛜) For good-value budget lodgings, it's well worth trudging 300m up from the port to reach these eight simple but fresh rooms. They have clean bathrooms, large sea-view balconies and decent fittings, including minimal kitchenettes.

Nereides Hotel   HOTEL €€
(📱22450 23347; www.nereideshotel.gr; Nereidon St; d incl breakfast €130; 🅿❄🛜🏊) This charming little hotel has been open a few years, but everything, from the paintwork to its up-to-the-minute bathrooms, still gleams like new. Set on the hillside, five minutes' walk from the beach and 10 minutes from the harbour, it offers 30 stylish rooms with sea-view balconies, plus a good pool. There's a snack bar, but no restaurant.

Atlantis Hotel   HOTEL €€
(📱22450 22777; www.atlantishotelkarpathos.gr; s/d incl breakfast €50/55; 🏊) Friendly, long-

established, family-run hotel across from the Italian-era town hall just above the west end of the harbour. The pleasant, no-frills rooms are nicely maintained – it's well worth paying a little extra for one with a balcony facing the sea rather than the (decent-sized) pool.

✗ Eating

Both the quay and the pedestrian streets just behind it are lined with seafood tavernas, all-purpose brasseries, cafes and cocktail bars. Look out, too, for the two Italian gelaterias on Apodimon Karpathion, parallel to the harbour.

★ To Ellenikon   TAVERNA €
(☑ 22450 23932; Apodimon Karpathion; mains €10-17; ⊙ lunch & dinner; ✷ 🛜 ☑) If you're looking for typical Karpathian food cooked the way it should be then 'the Greek' is your place. Try *saganaki* (fried cheese), meatballs, shrimp and calamari, eat within the wood-accented traditional interior or outside on the narrow terrace. The owner is a lovely guy and will happily show you the kitchen.

Orea   TAVERNA €
(☑ 22450 22501; Harbour; mains €7-15; ⊙ noon-midnight) Quayside taverna near the ferry jetty, serving authentic Karpathian specialities such as *makarounes* (homemade pasta with caramelised onions and cheese). Most meat mains cost under €10, and a whole grilled fish is more like €12 to €14.

Akropolis   BRASSERIE €€
(☑ 22450 23278; Apodimon Karpathion; mains €15-25; ⊙ breakfast, lunch & dinner; ✷ 🛜) This welcoming harbour-front cafe/-restaurant is as suited to breakfast or a sunset cocktail as it is to a full dinner. Most customers are drawn here for steak rather than Greek food, with the menu ranging through T-bone, fillet, sirloin and rib-eye up to a delectable chateaubriand for two (€50).

🍷 Drinking & Nightlife

Caffe Karpathos   CAFE
(☑ 21022 87383; www.cafekarpathos.com; Apodimon Karpathion; ⊙ 8am-late; 🛜) Enjoying a morning coffee or evening glass of local wine in the wicker chairs outside this cosy little cafe, a few steps from the waterfront on a pedestrian street that climbs away near the jetty. You feel as though you're relaxing in the front room of a friend's house. The owners lived for years in Italy, hence the Italian touches.

En Plo   COCKTAIL BAR
(cocktails €6; ⊙ 8am-late) Low-lit En Plo is a quiet place to read and sip on special coffee made with honey and whipped cream.

ℹ Information

Pigadia's ferry quay juts out from the eastern end of the broad harbour. Walk east to reach the town centre within five minutes. Follow the main street, Apodimon Karpathion, which climbs from the waterfront then runs parallel to the sea, and in 500m you'll reach Plateia 5 Oktovriou, home to the Italian-era municipal buildings. The sandy beaches of Pigadia Bay begin not far beyond.

Both the **National Bank of Greece** on Apodimon Karpathion, and **Alpha Bank**, a block higher on Dimokratias, have ATMs.

Police (☑ 22450 22224) Near the hospital at the western end of town.

Possi Travel (☑ 22450 22235; Harbour; ⊙ 8am-1pm & 5.30-8.30pm) The main travel agency for ferry and air tickets, excursions and accommodation. The helpful staff speak excellent English.

Post Office (Ethnikis Andistasis) Near the hospital.

Tourist Office (www.karpathos.org; ⊙ Jul & Aug) Summer-only kiosk, in the middle of the seafront.

Southern Karpathos

Thanks to their sandy beaches, several appealing villages in the southern half of Karpathos have reinvented themselves as small-scale resorts. Peaceful villages nestle amid the hills inland, an area that's crisscrossed by scenic walking tracks.

Menetes   Μενετές

Buffeted by mountain gales, the tiny village of Menetes sits high in the cliffs above Pigadia. Climb to the church at its highest point before exploring its narrow whitewashed streets.

⊙ Sights

Folklore Museum   MUSEUM
(☑ 6985847672; Menetes; ⊙ 9am-1pm & 5-8pm) FREE Spend a few minutes walking around Menetes and you're sure to run into Irini, custodian of the keys to the ancient chapel that houses this two-room museum. Having unlocked it, she'll talk you through its haphazard treasures and point you towards the tunnels in the hillside nearby, used by German troops in WWII. Donations welcomed.

✕ Eating

Dionysos Fiesta TAVERNA €
(☎ 22450 81269; mains €6-10; ☺ breakfast, lunch & dinner; ✱ 🛜) Set in a restored traditional house, in the twisting village lanes just up from the main road, this relaxed and welcoming taverna spreads onto a raised garden terrace. Local specialities to savour include goat stew, lemon chicken, artichoke omelettes and succulent Karpathian sausages.

Arkasa   Αρκάσα

Arkasa, on the southwest coast 9km from Menetes, is one of the oldest settlements on Karpathos. The original village centre, just up from the water, is now complemented by a burgeoning beach resort below. A waterside track leads 500m to the remains of the 5th-century **Basilica of Agia Sophia**, where two chapels stand amid mosaic fragments and columns, and to an ancient **acropolis** on the headland beyond.

The best beach hereabouts, sandy **Agios Nikolaos Beach**, stretches south from the acropolis, but to reach it by road you have to turn left from the village itself.

🛏 Sleeping

★**Glaros Studios** APARTMENT €
(☎ 22450 61015; www.glarosstudios-karpathos.com; Agios Nikolaos Beach, Arkasa; apt €50-55; 🅿🛜) This well-managed and ever-expanding garden-set complex pretty much has Agios Nikolaos Beach to itself. There are spotless white studios, decorated in traditional Karpathian style with raised platform beds and small kitchenettes, plus a relaxed and good-value adjoining restaurant.

Eleni Studios APARTMENT €
(☎ 22450 61248; www.elenikarpathos.gr; Arkasa; apt €60; 🅿✱🛜✉) On the road to Finiki, Eleni Studios has fully equipped and very tidy powder-blue apartments with appealing bedrooms, built around a relaxing garden. There's an on-site bar, too, for sunset drinks and breakfast, and a tempting pool. Great sea views.

Arkasa Bay Hotel HOTEL €€
(☎ 22450 61410; www.arkasabay.com; Arkasa; d €100; ✱🛜✉) Plush Arkasa has fine rooms with kitchenette, flat-screen TVs and, best of all, a great swimming pool.

Finiki   Φοινίκι

Arrayed along a neat little south-facing crescent bay, picturesque Finiki stands just 2km north of Arkasa. White-and-blue houses, interspersed with a peppering of tavernas, front its sleepy harbour and small grey-sand beach. The best local swimming is at **Agios Georgios Beach**, a short way south towards Arkasa.

🛏 Sleeping & Eating

Pine Tree Studios APARTMENT €
(☎ 6977369948; www.pinetree-karpathos.gr; Adia; apt €50-70; ✱) Some 9km north of Finiki, just before the road winds uphill to Lefkos, are the secluded Pine Tree Studios. These comfortable studios with views over to Kasos make for a quiet rural retreat and include an excellent restaurant specialising in dishes cooked in a wood oven. Taste the *katsiki stifadho* (goat in red-wine sauce). The studios are equipped with fridge and kitchenette. There's also free shaded camping.

Marina Taverna TAVERNA €
(☎ 22450 61100; Finiki; mains €6-16; ☺ breakfast, lunch & dinner; ✱🛜) Laid-back taverna with an expansive terrace surveying the gentle turquoise bay just metres from the waterfront. Enjoy inexpensive breakfasts, snack lunches and an enjoyable seafood-accented evening menu featuring squid, crab and grilled meats.

Lefkos   Λευκός

This is the largest but also the prettiest of the low-key west-coast resorts, 20km north of Finiki and a 5km detour down from the main road. Lefkos is here for a very good reason – its curving sandy beach is absolutely delightful. This is the kind of place where two weeks can vanish in gentle wanderings between beach and brunch.

While Lefkos is connected by bus with Pigadia, it's definitely worth renting a car or scooter through Lefkos Rent a Car while here.

🛏 Sleeping & Eating

Le Grand Bleu HOTEL €€
(☎ 22450 71009; www.karpathos-legrandbleu.com; Lefkos; studio/apt €85/120; 🅿✱🛜) Very nicely equipped studios and two-bedroom apartments beside the graceful main beach, kitted out with crisp fresh linen, tasteful art and sumptuous balconies with cushioned armchairs. The recommended on-site tavern closes at 10pm to let guests sleep.

OLYMBOS   ΟΛΥΜΠΟΣ

Few moments can beat rounding a curve in the mountain road to receive your first glimpse of this mist-blown eyrie of pastel-coloured houses. Olymbos clings precariously to the summit of Mt Profitis Ilias (716m), as if flung there by a Titan's paw. Thread your way along its wind-tunnel alleys, passing old ladies in vividly coloured traditional dress, and you may feel as though you've strayed onto a film set. Many locals even speak with a dialect that still contains traces of ancient Dorian Greek.

It's considered to be the most traditional of all places in Greece; Olymbos' local ladies still wear their stunning hand-spun jackets and floral headgear. And the views – 'jaw-dropping' just doesn't cover it – will leave you spellbound as the earth plunges dramatically metres from your feet. Try and arrive in late afternoon or early morning to have the place to yourself.

Sleeping & Eating

Hotel Olymbos (☑ 22450 51009; r incl breakfast €45) Hidden away beneath the owners' excellent street-level restaurant, these three little studios have raised beds and traditional furnishings. Tread carefully; the walls are festooned with delicate decorated plates. Ask to see the family's carefully preserved blacksmith shop alongside.

Hotel Aphrodite (☑ 22450 51307; www.discoverolympos.com; d €45; 🛜) This hotel is located just beyond the central square at the far end of Olymbos. It has two rooms with two single beds, and two rooms with three. All are bright, airy and attractively decorated, but above all – literally – they have astonishing west-facing sea views.

Edem Garden (mains €6-9) Village taverna with a broad mountain-view terrace, check-cloth tables and a menu featuring delicious rural specialities such as *makarounes*, country sausage and local goat *stifadho*, along with pizzas and salads. And yes, maybe the name should really be 'Eden', but it isn't.

Dramountana   TAVERNA €
(☑ 22450 71373; Lefkos; mains €6-15; ⊙ breakfast, lunch & dinner) Part of a cluster of similar places with waterside tables at the northern end of Lefkos harbour, this all-day cafe serves everything from fresh juices and coffee to fish soup, grilled squid, roast lamb and souvlakia.

Northern Karpathos

Locals often describe Karpathos as being two distinct islands, with its rugged, mountainous and astonishingly beautiful northern half in stark contrast to the fertile, low-lying south. That said, the east-coast road starts to climb as soon as you head north from Pigadia and the scenery turns ever more spectacular. Only within the last decade has the route been sealed all the way to the north, meaning that the once-isolated village of Olymbos has become swamped with day trippers in summer. Olymbos is still a magnificent place, though, most memorably reached by boat to Diafani from Pigadia, then a connecting bus. And it's worth spending a few nights here, especially if you fancy some hiking, or swimming at remote beaches.

Diafani   Διαφάνι

POP 250

Diafani is an intimate, wind-blasted huddle of white houses fronted by cobalt-blue water, with a mountain backdrop. Bar the crash of the waves and old men playing backgammon, nothing else stirs. Most travellers simply pass through Diafani, so if you stay you'll likely have the beaches and trails to yourself. There's no bank, post office, petrol station or ATM, so bring cash and fuel.

Activities

Hiking trails from Diafani village are way-marked with red or blue markers or stone cairns. The most popular route heads inland, straight up the valley to **Olymbos**. That takes around two hours – though inevitably some prefer to catch a bus uphill and walk back down. Alternatively, a 50-minute track leads 4km north along the coast, through the pines, to **Vananda Beach**, which has a seasonal taverna.

A more strenuous three-hour walk takes you 11km northwest to the Hellenistic site of **Vroukounda**, passing the agricultural village of Avlona along the way. There are no facilities, so carry food and water with you.

Anyone planning serious walking should get hold of the 1:60,000 *Karpathos-Kasos* map, published by Terrain Maps (www.terrain maps.gr) and available in Pigadia. For advice on current conditions, call in at the Environment Management Office on Diafani's seafront before you set off.

Sleeping & Eating

Balaskas Hotel   HOTEL €
(22450 51320; www.balaskashotel.com; s/d from €35/45;) You have a choice here of either 'economy' rooms (essentially pension-style minimalism with white walls and wood beds) or 'standard', which feature more colour and flair – think romantic mozzie nets and wrought iron beds. Some have kitchenettes, all have fridges. It's a five- to ten-minute walk from the seafront.

The owners operate two excursion boats and offer a free beach trip for each guest.

La Gorgona   ITALIAN €
(Harbour; mains €7-10; 9am-late) If you're looking for a breezy spot to gaze at the sea, listen to cool tunes, drink quality coffee and digress from Greek to Italian food, La Gorgona may tick all your boxes. Owners Gigi and Sofia prepare tasty pasta dishes like carbonara and seafood spaghetti as well as a selection of pizza. Don't miss the desserts either: tiramisu and chocolate strudel.

Corali   TAVERNA €
(22450 51332; mains €7-12; breakfast, lunch & dinner) Run by Popi and Mihalis, this is probably the best spot for fresh, tasty traditional fare. Try their delicious *stifadho* or eggplant salad. Vegetables are sourced locally. Service is slow but the quality of the food and *filoxenia* (hospitality) make up for it.

Information

Environment Management Office (10am-4pm Mon-Fri) Advice on current conditions for anyone planning some serious walking on the island.
Orfanos Travel (mobile 6974990394; at Nicos Hotel; 8am-1pm & 5.30-8.30pm;) Runs boat trips and sells ferry and air tickets.

Getting There & Away

Blue Star Ferries (p498) calls in at Diafani's small jetty three times weekly heading for Halki and Rhodes, and three times weekly en route towards Pigadia and Kasos (two of which continue to Crete and one to Santorini). There are also day trips by boat to Pigadia in summer, as well as assorted excursions. Tourist coaches carry day trippers from the jetty up to Olympos. There are two scheduled buses on weekdays, one of which continues to Pigadia on Friday only, and one on weekends.

Buses run to Olympos then on to Pigadia every other day at 3.45pm.

KASOS   ΚΑΣΟΣ
POP 1080

Kasos, the southernmost Dodecanese island, looks like the Greece that time forgot. Deceptively inviting in summer, it can feel very isolated in winter, when it's battered by winds and imprisoned by huge turquoise waves. Most of its visitors are rare seabirds; most of the human returnees are Kasiots on fleeting visits. Come here, though, and you may well succumb to its tumbledown charm.

In 1820, under Turkish rule, Kasos was home to 11,000 inhabitants. Tragically, Mohammad Ali, the Turkish governor of Egypt, saw its large merchant fleet as an impediment to his plan to establish a base in Crete. On 7 June 1824, therefore, his men landed on Kasos and killed around 7000 of its people. The island never really recovered, but each year Kasiots return from all over the world to commemorate the massacre.

Getting There & Away

There are daily flights to Karpathos (€56, 10 minutes), Sitia (€61, 40 minutes) and Rhodes (€74, one hour) with **Sky Express** (p498). The only ferry service is with **Blue Star Ferries** (p498), en route between Rhodes and Karpathos, and Crete and Piraeus.

Boat Services from Kasos (Fry)

DESTINATION	DURATION	FARE (€)	FREQUENCY
Heraklion	6hr	20	1 weekly
Karpathos	1½hr	8	3 weekly
Piraeus	19hr	44	2 weekly
Rhodes	8hr	24	3 weekly
Santorini	9hr	27	2 weekly

Getting Around

The airport is 1km west of Fry. Either walk for 10 minutes along the coast road – yes, it's exposed, but you won't half feel pleased with yourself –

or call a **taxi** (☑ mobile 6973244371, mobile 6977904632). In theory, a bus connects all the island's villages, but it hasn't been working for years. Cars and scooters can be hired from **Oasis Rent-a-Car** (☑ 22450 41746; Kasos Airport).

Fry

Φρυ

POP 350

The capital, Fry (pronounced *free*), is on the north coast. The valley behind it is the only fertile land on Kasos, so the only other villages are dotted across the surrounding hillside. Although Fry is more a working port than a tourist destination, the tiny old harbour, known as **Bouka**, is impossibly photogenic. Pretty white houses with navy-blue trim line the quay, a few cafes sit waiting for customers, grizzled fishermen patiently mend their nets, and the pastel-blue church of Agios Spyridon surveys the scene. Even as late as June, though, Fry still has the feel of a ghost town.

The nearest beach is 10 minutes' walk east along the shoreline, in the tiny satellite port of **Emborio**. There are patches of gravel amid the sand, but the sea is clear and sheltered, so it's a good place for a quick dip.

◉ Sights & Activities

Archaeological Museum

MUSEUM

(◷ 9am-3pm Jul-Sep) **FREE** Housed in a grand 19th-century villa above the harbour, this seasonal museum displays objects pulled from ancient shipwrecks, assorted Greek oil lamps and Hellenistic finds, including inscribed stone slabs.

Excursion Boat

BOATING

(☑ 22450 41047, 6977911209; ⌖) When they can round up 10 or more passengers, two boats, *Athina* and *Kasos Princess,* offer summer-afternoon excursions (€10) to the uninhabited islet of Armathia, which has superb sandy beaches. The *Kasos Princess* also runs full-day trips to Pigadia on Karpathos, on summer Wednesdays only.

🛏 Sleeping & Eating

Hotel Anagennissis

HOTEL €

(☑ 22450 41495; www.anagennisishotel.gr; s/d €45/50; ✳ 🛜) Old-fashioned hotel, close to the waterfront in the village centre, where the plain but perfectly adequate rooms have comfy beds, fridges, bathrooms and sea-view balconies. Staff are seldom present in the hotel itself; the owners run the Kasos Maritime & Travel Agency (p522) next door.

DODECANESE KASOS

Kasos

0 — 5 km
0 — 2.5 miles

Karpathos (10km) →

Sea of Crete

Makra

Peronisi

Cape Akti

Lytra

Armathia

Excursion Boat

Pondikonisia   Marmara   Karavostasi
                 Beach   Beach

Emborio

Agia
Marina   Fry
          Panagia   Agia
                      Kyriaki
                      (418m)

Ammounda
Beach

Agios
Konstandinos   Arvanitohori   Poli

Andiperatos
Beach

Ellinokamara
Caves

Mt Kapsalo
(583m)

Moni Agiou
Mamma

Sitia
(80km)

Moni Agiou
Georgiou Hadion

Platy

Kourika

Cape
Trousoulas

Mediterranean
Sea

Kasos
Strait   Avlaki   Helatros   Cape Helatros

Angelica's
APARTMENT €€

(✆22450 41268; www.angelicas.gr; apt €60-80; ❄🐕) Attractive, traditionally furnished apartments in a fine old village home five minutes' walk up from the harbour. Two are on the ground floor, with private courtyards, and two upstairs, with sea-view verandas. All have painted floors and stencils on their white walls. The largest apartment sleeps up to five.

★Taverna Emborios
TAVERNA €

(✆22450 41586; Emborio Beach; mains €6-13; ☉lunch & dinner; 🐕) Crisp, beautifully neat beachfront restaurant, 10 minutes' walk from Fry. It's unquestionably the best place to eat on Kasos. The friendly owner, who lived in New York for many years, serves up wonderful local specialities, including delicious octopus, tiny home-grown olives and his own salty preserved fish.

Orea Bouka
TAVERNA €

(✆22450 41053; mains €7-10) There's no menu at this simple little taverna, which sets out tables on the sea wall on the west side of Bouka harbour. Sophia, the owner, just shows or tells you whatever she happens to be cooking. In summer, expect a choice of dolmadhes, fresh fish, baked meats and vegetable stews.

Mylos
TAVERNA €

(✆22450 41825; Plateia Iroön Kasou; mains €7; ☉lunch & dinner; 🐕🍴) Overlooking the commercial port (as opposed to Bouka), this conspicuous taverna has unbroken sea views and serves a reliable menu of local favourites such as 'mountain grass roots' – village sausage and pot-roast rabbit – along with fresh fish. Almost everything costs less than €10.

ℹ Information

Both the Commercial Bank beside the harbour and Alpha on Plateia Iroön Kasou have ATMs.

Kasos Maritime & Travel Agency (✆22450 41495; www.kassos-island.gr; Plateia Iroön Kasou) For all travel tickets.

Police (✆22450 41222) On a narrow sealed street running south from Fry's main road.

Port Police (✆22450 41288) Behind the Agios Spyridon church.

Post Office (☉7.30am-2pm Mon-Fri) Diagonally across from the police.

Around Kasos

None of the beaches on Kasos offer shade. The best is the isolated pebbled cove of **Helatros**, near Moni Agiou Georgiou Hadion, 11km southwest of Fry, but you'll need your own transport to reach it, and it has no facilities. There's another small but decent beach, **Avlaki**, in walking distance.

Agia Marina, 1km southwest of Fry, is a pretty village with a gleaming white-and-blue church that celebrates a festival on 17 July. Beyond it, the road continues to verdant **Arvanitohori**, with abundant fig and pomegranate trees. **Poli**, 3km southeast of Fry, is the former capital, built on the ancient acropolis.

KASTELLORIZO (MEGISTI)
ΚΑΣΤΕΛΛΟΡΙΖΟ (ΜΕΓΙΣΤΗ)
POP 275

So close to the Turkish coast – Kaş is just 2km away – that you can almost taste the East, the tiny, far-flung island of Kastellorizo is insanely pretty. Sailing into its one village (of the same name), past the ruined castle, minaret and pastel-painted neoclassical houses huddled around the turquoise bay, is soul enriching, and reminds a little of Symi without the super yachts and swank. 'Megisti', as Kastellorizo was once called (meaning 'great'), is the largest of a small archipelago, and despite being less than 10 sq km, enjoys more hours of sunshine than any other Greek island and boasts the most dramatic blue cave in the Med. And while it may lack powder-fine beaches, there are floating platforms and satellite idylls you can reach by boat.

Arid Kastellorizo is not easy to reach, but rewards with beauty, tranquillity and locals who welcome your custom.

History

Home to the best harbour between Beirut and Piraeus, Kastellorizo was successively a prosperous trading port for the Dorians, Romans, Crusaders, Egyptians, Turks and Venetians. Under Ottoman control, from 1552 onwards, it had the largest merchant fleet in the Dodecanese. A 1913 revolt against the Turks briefly resulted in it becoming a French naval base, and it subsequently passed into the hands of the Italians. The island progressively lost all strategic and economic importance, especially after the 1923 Greece–Turkey population exchange. Many islanders emigrated to Australia, where around 30,000 continue to live.

After Kastellorizo suffered bombardment during WWII, English commanders ordered the few remaining inhabitants to abandon the island. Most fled to Cyprus, Palestine and Egypt and those that later returned found their houses in ruins. While the island has never regained its previous population levels – the village alone was once home to 10,000 people – more recent returnees have finally restored almost all the waterfront buildings, and Kastellorizo is looking better than it has for a century.

The island has found itself in recent years in the migration path of thousands of fleeing refugees, though numbers have recently fallen to only a few; given their grandparents' experiences as refugees, the islanders acted, not surprisingly, with great compassion.

❶ Getting There & Away

AIR
Olympic Air (www.olympicair.com) flies daily from Rhodes to Kastellorizo (return €132, 40 minutes).

BOAT
Kastellorizo has a very limited ferry service. **Blue Star Ferries** (p498) calls in twice a week to and from Piraeus via Rhodes. On summer Saturdays, **Dodekanisos Seaways** (p498) sails from Rhodes to Kastellorizo and back; used as a day trip, it gives you four hours on the island.

❶ Getting Around

Kastellorizo's tiny airport is up on the central plateau, 2.5km above the village. There's no bus, so you'll have to take the island's only **taxi** (☑ mobile 6938739178) to and from the harbour (€5).

The main destinations for boat trips are Kaş in Turkey and the spectacular **Blue Cave** (€9), famous for its mirror-like blue water, on Kastellorizo's remote southeast shore. Try **Nikos Sea Wolf Taxi** (☑ mobile 6934523917; per person €8).

Kastellorizo Village
Καστελλόριζο

POP 250

Kastellorizo Village is the island's main settlement. Its harbour is its lifeblood and where the limited action gathers: mounds of yellow nets, stretching cats, youths on mobile phones and sleepy fishermen sit outside *kafeneia*, backdropped by smartly shuttered, brightly coloured mansions. Make sure you explore the labyrinthine cobbled backstreets behind.

An amazing 80% of the villagers are returned Aussie expats, which adds a definite upbeat energy to the community. Come August, thousands of 'Kassies' return to see their families.

◉ Sights & Activities

A coastal pathway around the headland below passes precarious steps that climb to a rock-hewn **Lycian tomb** from the 4th century BC, which boasts an impressive Doric facade. There are several such tombs along Turkey's Anatolian coast, but they are very rare in Greece.

It's also possible to walk the 1km up to **Paleokastro**, the island's ancient capital. Follow the concrete steps that start just past a soldier's sentry box on the airport road. The old city's Hellenistic walls enclose a tower, a water cistern and three churches.

Archaeological Museum MUSEUM
(€2; ☉ 7am-2pm Tue-Sun; ♿) Holds an assortment of ancient finds, costumes and photos as well as a documentary about Kastellorizo as told by the islanders.

Megisti Museum MUSEUM
(€2; ☉ 8.30am-3pm Tue-Sun; ♿) In a former mosque near the ferry jetty, this museum devotes itself largely to display panels telling the island's story.

Knights of St John Castle CASTLE
(☉ 7am-2pm Tue-Sun; ♿) FREE At the top of the hill, a rickety stairway leads to the ruins of the Knights of St John Castle, which gave the island its name – thanks to the red cliff on which it stood, this was the 'Castello Rosso'. It offers splendid views of Turkey.

🛏 Sleeping

★**Mediterraneo** PENSION €€
(☑ 22460 49007; www.mediterraneo-kastelorizo.com; s/d/ste €70/80/180; ☉ May-Oct; ☏) If Picasso was a hotel, he'd be the Mediterraneo. With its lime, mango and smurf-blue exterior, this revamped mansion has romantic rooms tastefully scattered with art and traditional raised-platform beds. Breakfast on the terrace amid a confection of fruit and homemade jams, read in the shaded arbour, or flop on loungers by the sea.

Megisti Hotel HOTEL €€
(☑ 22460 49220; www.megistihotel.gr; d/ste incl breakfast €144/228; ✳ @ ☎ ☑) On the harbour's western extremity, it's impossible to

miss the most imposing hotel on the island. Megisti's four suites and 15 stylish rooms have rain showers, DVD players, tiled floors, standard lamps, safety deposit boxes and private balconies. Outside on the chequerboard waterfront terrace, you can climb easily into the sea from Megisti's iron-hoop steps (like a giant swimming pool).

Poseidon HOTEL €€

(☑22460 49212, 6956617585; www.kastelorizoposeidon.gr; Plateia Australias; studio/apt €135/150; ❄☎) Set in five beautifully restored neoclassical villas, a block from the corner of the west side of the harbour, Poseidon offers comfortably finished studios and apartments with grey shabby-chic furniture offset by sugar-white walls and contemporary lighting. Add to this private verandas, big sea views, a great breakfast in the main hotel, plus a relaxing roof terrace.

✖ Eating & Drinking

Tables spill out onto the narrow harbour, cats entwine themselves around diners' legs and, by night, the atmosphere is magical. Just don't tip into the water, for the *kordoni* (walkway) that is the village's main thoroughfare, is narrow.

★ Alexandra's TAVERNA €

(☑22460 49019; mains €7-15; ⊙lunch & dinner; ❄☎) 𝒫 With bouzouki music and salt breeze wafting over its thyme-topped tables, the friendliest of Kastellorizo's quayside restaurants also serves the best food. Everything from the squid-ink risotto and calamari stuffed with feta is prepared by Alexandra herself. Mezedhes (appetisers) are full of vim and super fresh. Treat yourself to lamb on the spit.

Lazarakis GREEK €

(mains €8-15; ⊙lunch & dinner; ❄☎) This central waterfront restaurant is great for seafood – grilled octopus, lobster spaghetti, baby shrimp, grouper and succulent calamari – and also has grilled meat dishes. Eat under the vine canopy, or better still out on the jetty where you can sometimes see giant turtles in the water.

Faros Bar BAR

(☑22460 49509; mains €6; ⊙9am-late; ☎) Occupying an enviable location in the former lighthouse, beyond the ferry jetty and beside the mosque, this bar offers a wonderful opportunity to swim in turquoise shallows before taking breakfast and drinking in wide-screen views of Turkey. It even has its own quayside loungers. Salads and snacks all day, then tapas from 6pm.

❶ Information

Medical Centre (☑22460 70659 22460 49267; ⊙Mon & Fri 9am-1pm) on the eastern side of the harbour.

Papoutsis Travel (☑22460 70630, 22460 49356; ⊙9am-2pm & 5pm-8pm) Ferry and air tickets, bike and scooter rental and yachting services.

Police Station (☑22460 49333) On the bay's western side.

Port Police (☑22460 49333) At the eastern tip of the bay.

Post Office (☑22460 49298; ⊙9am-2pm Mon-Fri) Next to the police station.

SYMI ΣΥΜΗ

POP 2610

Beautiful Symi is guaranteed to evoke oohs and aahs from ferry passengers before they even get off the boat. The first sight of Gialos harbour, framed against an amphitheatre of pastel-coloured houses rising on all sides, is unforgettable. It's all thanks to the Italians, who ruled the island almost a century ago and established the neoclassical architectural style that Symi has followed ever since.

Although Symi is far from small, it's mostly barren and the only settlements are Gialos, the old village of Horio, and Pedi, down in the valley beyond. One road runs all the way to the monastery at Panormitis, near Symi's southern tip. The rest of this spellbinding island is largely deserted, but it's surrounded by blue coves and beaches, and aglitter with crystal-clear water so transparent that boats can look as if they're floating on thin air.

History

Symi has long traditions of both sponge diving and shipbuilding and is mentioned in the 'Iliad' as sending ships to assist Agamemnon's siege of Troy. In ancient legend, Glaucus, one of the island's sons, was the master builder of *Argo*, the ship that would take Jason and his compadres to distant Colchis in search of the Golden Fleece. During Ottoman times it was granted the right to fish for sponges in Turkish waters. In return, Symi supplied the sultan with first-class boat builders. This exchange enriched the island – gracious

Symi

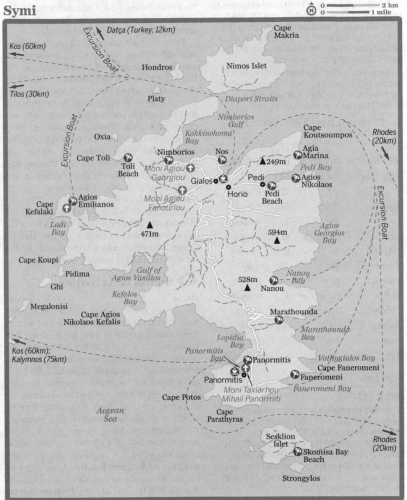

mansions were built and culture and education flourished. By the early 20th century, the population was 22,500 and Symi was launching around 500 ships a year. But the Italian occupation, the advent of the steamship and the decline of the sponge industry put an end to prosperity, obliging Symi to reinvent itself as a tourist destination.

ℹ Getting There & Away

Dodekanisos Seaways (p498) runs catamarans to and from Rhodes at least once daily – four each week stop at Panormitis en route – and also offers frequent sailings northwest, to Kos and beyond. Blue Star Ferries (p498) calls in twice weekly heading towards Rhodes, and also en route for Tilos, Nisyros, Kos, Kalymnos, Astypalea and Piraeus. Symi fills up every morning with day trippers from Rhodes, with several Rhodes-based excursion boats complementing the high-speed catamaran.

Look out for summer day trips from Gialos to Datça, Turkey (€40 including Turkish port taxes).

ℹ Getting Around

BOAT

Water taxis (☏ 22460 71423) lined up along the inner side of Gialos harbour run regular trips to the island's beaches. Most head either north to Nimborios (€6) or south to Agia Marina, Agios Nikolaos, Nanou and Marathounda (€6 to €14). In high season there's at least one departure an hour, from 9am onwards, with the last boat back usually at 5pm or 6pm.

Larger boats offer day trips further afield to remote west-coast beaches, the monastery at Panormitis, or complete island-circuit tours (up to €40) that include a barbecue lunch.

Boat Services from Symi (Gialos)

DESTINATION	DURATION	FARE (€)	FREQUENCY
Kalymnos*	2hr 20 min	32	1 daily
Kos	3hr	12	2 weekly
Kos*	1½hr	24	1 daily
Leros*	3hr	41	4 weekly
Lipsi*	3hr 10min	41	1 daily
Nisyros	3hr 20min	11.50	1 weekly
Patmos*	4hr	46	daily
Piraeus	15hr	56.50	2 weekly
Rhodes	1hr 40 min	8	2 weekly
Rhodes*	50min	18	1-4 daily
Rhodes*	1hr	16	1 daily
Samos	5hr	49	1 weekly
Tilos	2hr	8	1 weekly

*high-speed services

BUS & TAXI

The island **bus** makes hourly runs between the south side of Gialos harbour and Pedi Beach, via Horio (flat fare €1.50). There's also a service to Panormitis two to three times daily (€1.50). **Taxis** (☑ 22460 71311, mobile 6974623492; Southside of Gialos Harbour) depart from a rank 100m west of the bus stop, and cost €25 (each way) to Panormitis.

CAR

Glaros (☑ 22460 71926, mobile 6948362079; www.glarosrentacar.gr; ☺9am-9pm), near the clock tower, rents cars and scooters.

Gialos   Γιαλός

POP 2200

Your first view of Gialos is unforgettable, with its neoclassical biscuit- and ochre-hued buildings gathered aristocratically around what is perhaps the world's prettiest harbour. Fishing boats bob in water so perfectly clear they look as if they're floating on thin air, sponge salesmen hawk their weird-shaped treasures of the deep, while a few world-class boutique hotels and restaurants invite the attention of the occasional Hollywood star arriving in a gleaming super-yacht.

Plant yourself at one of the many tavernas and cafes along the quayside, making sure you try the island's celebrated shrimps. The basilica and clock tower punctuate the edge of the harbour where you catch and disembark from the ferry. Wander away from the sea to find backstreets spilling with fruit stores, ice-cream parlours and aromatic bakeries.

Head north along the seafront from the clock tower, away from the centre, and you're immediately in smaller **Harani Bay**. Traditionally a base for shipbuilding, it still holds assorted beached boats, along with its own crop of bars and tavernas.

The closest beach to Gialos, **Nos**, lies around the next headland, 500m from the clock tower. Access to this narrow strip of gravel is controlled by a taverna and bar, but it's a great spot for a swim, nonetheless.

◉ Sights & Activities

Horio   VILLAGE

Climbing calf-crunching, knee-knobbling Kali Strata, the broad stair path that sets off from the alleyways behind the harbour, will bring you in a mere 500-or-so steps to the hilltop village of Horio. En route you'll pass a succession of majestic villas built for long-gone Symi sea captains – some are utterly dilapidated, others restored to splendour.

Constructed to deter marauding pirates, Horio is an absolute warren of a place. All its tavernas and bars, though, are clustered around the top of Kali Strata. Most of the houses beyond are in ruins, and so is the **Knights of St John Kastro** at the very top, thanks to an explosion of German munitions during WWII. The island's **Archaeological Museum** is up here too, but is currently closed for restoration.

Nautical & Folklore Museum   MUSEUM

(€2; ☺9.30am-9pm) The two upper floors of a colourfully painted villa on Gialos' main square hold the separate halves of this freshly restored museum. Crammed with relics of Symi's sponge-diving era, including a pair of bulky helmets, the nautical section at the top is more interesting than the rather-haphazard folklore part below, but both contain fascinating old photos of the island.

Symi Tours   BOATING, WALKING

(☑ 22460 71307) Symi Tours organises daily excursions by boat to explore Symi's beautiful coves, bays and secluded beaches. Daily departures from Gialos harbour at 10.30am, returning at 5pm. Find it on the south side of Gialos harbour. Also offers multilingual guided walks (€12) around the island (every Tuesday at 8am), often ending with a boat ride back to Gialos.

🛏 Sleeping

⭐Hotel Fiona
HOTEL €

(☑22460 72088; www.fionahotel.com; Horio; r incl breakfast €55; ❇🛜) Offering Symi's best-value accommodation, this simple but charming family-run hotel perches on the edge of Horio (turn left at the top of Kali Strata). The views across the harbour are truly astonishing, both from the balconies of its spacious and attractively decorated rooms, kitted out with turquoise furniture, and from the breakfast area downstairs. There's also a peaceful courtyard.

Hotel Aliki
BOUTIQUE HOTEL €€

(☑22460 71655; www.hotelaliki.gr; d/ste incl breakfast €130/220; ❇🛜) Dainty Aliki is Symi's oldest hotel and evokes old-world charm with its traditionally painted wood-beamed lobby, flower-shaded lamps and vintage leather armchairs. Rooms are elegant and simple, with antique iron beds, fragrant linen and serene views of the sea lapping a few metres below. There's also a roof terrace. Check out its its sister restaurant next door, La Vaporetta.

Albatros Hotel
HOTEL €€

(☑22460 71707; www.albatrosymi.gr; s/d incl breakfast €50/65; ⊙Apr-Nov; ❇🛜) With its turquoise and biscuit-hued exterior, Albatros has a sunny breakfast room and five whitewashed air-con bedrooms with tiled floors, traditional wood ceilings and little balconies giving side-on sea views. Just a block back from the harbour in the heart of Gialos, it's clean and welcoming.

Iapetos Village
APARTMENT €€

(☑22460 72777; www.iapetos-village.gr; d/apt €135/155; ❇@🛜⛱) Set around a leafy courtyard, a short walk inland from the main square, Iapetos holds 28 high-class rooms, studios and apartments, newly built in traditional style. All have lovely wooden high ceilings and private patios or balconies, and most have fully fitted kitchens. There's also a beautiful pool, tucked under the arches, plus a sauna and bar.

⭐Old Markets
BOUTIQUE HOTEL €€€

(☑22460 71440; www.theoldmarkets.com; r/ste incl breakfast €220/395; ❇🛜) Symi's finest hotel stands a few steps up Kali Strata. The old market space has four stunningly individual rooms and one suite, while the newly opened adjoining mansion has five more contemporary suites. All rooms enjoy a pillow library, iPhone docking station and use of an honesty bar, as well as the roof terrace, pool and optional spa treatments.

🍴 Eating & Drinking

🍴 Gialos

⭐Meraklis
SEAFOOD €

(☑22460 71003; www.tavernaomeraklis.com; mains €10-13; ⊙10am-late; ❇🛜) This old-school taverna, with Santorini-blue walls decked in vintage diving photos and antique mirrors, is as pretty as it is friendly. And while its souvlakia, meatballs and roast lamb are tasty, most diners come here to feast on fresh octopus, sea bream, Symi shrimp and swordfish. Why not try the lot, with a mixed seafood plate for two (€35)?

⭐Tholos
TAVERNA €€

(☑22460 72033; Harani Bay; mains €8-14; ⊙lunch & dinner May-Oct) There's no more romantic restaurant in the Dodecanese than this lovely taverna, poised at the tip of Harani Bay, along the quay from central Gialos. The sunset views from its waterfront tables are stupendous, and so too is the food, which includes local meat and vegetables as well as fresh fish. Be sure to sample the succulent, bright-red Symi shrimp.

⭐Muses
FUSION €€

(☑6958734503; www.muses-symi.com; Gialos; mains €24; ⊙7pm-late May-Oct) Admittedly it's a little overpriced, but this wine-red bijou restaurant run by two Argentinian brothers is Symi's most exciting restaurant. A modern Mediterranean menu changes daily, combining signature dishes like octopus with fava purée and orange, or pork with pears and retsina. Seating is on a flowery terrace, beside the town square just back from the harbour.

To Spitiko
TAVERNA €€

(☑22460 72452; Harani Bay; mains €10-18; ⊙breakfast, lunch & dinner; 🛜) Owners Eruala and Fortes make their food with great care and zest, and while the place on the tip of Harani Bay harbour might not look spectacular, the cuisine most definitely is. Lemon potatoes, country sausage, Symi shrimps, grilled octopus in lemon sauce, and last but not least, mouthwatering *portoka-lopita* (orange cake). Ask to sit by the sea.

★ **Tsati** BAR
(☑ 22460 72498; Harani Bay; ⏰ 11am-late) Ultra-welcoming quayside bar, 100m along Harani Bay beyond the clock tower. As well as tables on a tree-shaded terrace, it offers stone benches carved into the sea wall. Cushioned and whitewashed, they're perfect for a sunset cocktail, served with free snacks.

✕ Horio

Olive Tree CAFE €
(☑ 22460 72681; www.olivetreesymi.eu; Horio; light meals €3-8; ⏰ 8.30am-3.30pm; 🛜 ✏ ⏺) 🏠 English-run cafe that's a favourite morning rendezvous for the island's expats. Sit yourself down on its vine-shaded terrace at the top of Kali Strata and tuck into a wide array of smoothies, juices, cakes, locally sourced salads and sandwiches.

Taverna Giorgo & Maria TAVERNA €
(☑ 22460 71984; Horio; mains €10; ⏰ lunch & dinner; 🛜) Bouzouki music piping across its

---

MONI TAXIARHOU MIHAIL PANORMITI

Near Symi's southern tip, beyond the scented pine forests of the high interior, spectacular Panormitis Bay is home to **Moni Taxiarhou Mihail Panormiti** (☑ 22460 72414; ⏰ dawn-dusk). Monasteries have stood here since the 5th century, but the present building dates from the 18th century. The principal church contains an intricately carved wooden iconostasis, frescoes and an icon of St Michael, protector of sailors and patron saint of Symi.

Pilgrims who ask the saint for a favour leave an offering; you'll see piles of these, plus prayers in bottles that have been dropped off boats and found their own way here. The large complex comprises a Byzantine museum and folkloric museum, a bakery with excellent bread, and a basic restaurant-cafe. Visitors should dress modestly. Buses come here from Gialos, and some ferries call in, too.

---

breezy courtyard and veranda, soaring views of the gas-blue bay below, and a selection of Symi shrimp, braised rabbit, pork casserole, swordfish, lobster and bream. Live music from 9pm on Friday and Saturday.

ℹ Information

Ferries and catamarans dock beside the clock tower on the north side of the harbour entrance. Excursion and taxi boats dock along the south side, near its inland end. All activity in Gialos focuses on the quay, while the Kali Strata stairway sets off up to Horio from the southeast corner.

Both the National and Alpha Banks have ATM-equipped branches on the northern side of the harbour.

Kalodoukas Holidays (☑ 22460 71077; www.kalodoukas.gr; ⏰ 9.30am-2pm & 6.30-9pm) In the absence of an official tourist office, this helpful agency, at the foot of Kali Strata, is the next best thing. It also rents houses, sells tickets, organises excursions and offers yachting services.

Police (☑ 22460 71111) By the ferry quay.

Port Police (☑ 22460 71205) By the ferry quay.

Post Office By the ferry quay.

Symi Tours (☑ 22460 71307; www.symitours. com) This agency, just behind the southeast side of the harbour, organises excursions, including island bus tours and boat trips to Datça in Turkey. Also provides yachting services and sells ferry tickets.

Symi Visitor (☑ 22460 71785; www.symi visitor.com) Very friendly agency, just off the southeast side of the quay, with a fine roster of rental properties and a full-service laundry.

Around Symi

Apart from the monastery at Panormitis, the only tourist destinations on Symi are the beaches scattered along its coastline.

Nimborios Νιμπόρειος

Nimborios is a pebble beach 3km west of Gialos, reached by walking or driving all the way around the harbour and simply continuing along the exposed but utterly beautiful shorefront road beyond. It's a peaceful spot, with a good little taverna that allows its customers to spend the day on sun loungers beneath the tamarisk trees alongside.

🛏 Sleeping

Niriides Apartments APARTMENT €€
(☑ 22460 71784; www.niriideshotel.com; Nimbo-rios; apt €140) Adjacent to Gialos is the quiet

little village of Nimborios where you'll find Niriides Apartments, sitting by peaceful Symi Bay. Pleasant, traditional decor with kitchenettes, fridges and balconies with sea views. There's a snack bar to take breakfast at and also a library.

Pedi   Πέδι

Once a village, now more of a yachting marina and low-key resort, Pedi stretches along the inner end of a large bay south of Gialos, immediately below Horio. The gentle valley behind it has always been the agricultural heartland of Symi.

Two beaches, to either side of the mouth of the bay, can be reached on foot from Pedi or water taxi from Gialos; both have appealing tavernas. **Agia Marina** to the north is a lagoon-like bay, facing a delightful chapel-topped islet across turquoise waters, which gets very crowded in summer. **Agios Nikolaos**, on the south side, is broader and sandier, with decent tree cover and idyllic swimming.

🛏 Sleeping

Pedi Beach Hotel   HOTEL €€
(☎ 22460 71981; www.pedibeachhotel.gr; Pedi; r from €117; ❄) Fresh with their aquamarine-striped beds and cobalt-blue curtains, these simple cool-tiled rooms are pleasant, with unblemished sea-view balconies. There's a beach bar and snack bar.

Nanou & Marathounda
Νανού & Μαραθούντα

Two large bays south of Pedi, Nanou and Marathounda, hold large beaches and tavernas and make great destinations for water-taxi day trips. Goat-roamed Marathounda, backed by a lush valley and also accessible via a rough road, is especially recommended.

🍴 Eating

★ Marathounda Taverna   TAVERNA €€
(☎ 22460 71425; Marathounda; mains €10-12; ☺breakfast, lunch & dinner) Quintessential beach taverna, where the owner's goats – responsible for the delicious homemade cheese and, whisper it, the goat stew, too – nuzzle up to the tables. Be sure to sample the Symi shrimp and grilled fish, along with herbs and vegetables from the organic gardens alongside. For those who can't bear to leave, it also has plush beachfront studios for rent (€125).

TILOS   ΤΗΛΟΣ

POP 550

With its russet gold mountains, lack of people, and wildflowers blooming at every turn, Tilos has a charm that will salve your busy mind. Here you can hike through meadows, mountains and valleys on shepherds' paths before flopping onto a deserted beach. The azure waters hold monk seals and sea turtles, and the island also draws birdwatchers and wildlife buffs from across the globe.

History

Amazingly, ancient Tilos is best known for its population of midget elephants. Full-sized elephants are thought to have found their way here six million years ago, when the island was still attached to Asia Minor. When cut off by the rising waters of the Mediterranean, the elephants were left with no natural predators and a diminished food supply, and shrank in size. They became extinct around 4000 BC. A large cache of their bones was discovered in 1974 in Harkadio Cave, just off the Livadia–Megalo Horio road.

ℹ Getting There & Away

Tilos has no airport and only a minimal ferry service. The Dodekanisos Seaways (p498) catamaran stops at Tilos on Tuesday and Thursday, heading from Rhodes and Halki to Nisyros, Kos and Kalymnos in the morning, and back to Rhodes in the evening. On those days, you can visit the island as a day trip from Rhodes or Halki. In addition, Blue Star Ferries (p498) sails twice each week to Piraeus via Nisyros, Kos and Kalymnos, and twice to Rhodes, one of which stops at Symi.

Boat Services from Tilos (Livadia)

DESTINATION	DURATION	FARE (€)	FREQUENCY
Halki*	40min	13	2 weekly
Kalymnos	3hr 20min	13	2 weekly
Kalymnos*	2¼hr	29	2 weekly
Kos	3hr	10	2 weekly
Kos*	1½hr	22	2 weekly
Nisyros	1½hr	7.50	2 weekly
Nisyros*	45min	13	2 weekly
Piraeus	16hr	54	2 weekly
Rhodes	2½hr	13	3 weekly
Rhodes*	1½hr	28	2 weekly
Symi	2hr	9	1 weekly

*high-speed services

ⓘ Getting Around

Five buses each day connect Livadia with Megalo Horio, Eristos Beach and Agios Antonios (€1.50). There is no taxi, but you can rent a car or scooter from **Drive Rent A Car** (☑22460 44173; www.drivetilos.gr; ☒9am-6pm) or Tilos Travel (p532).

Livadia   Λιβαδειά

POP 470

Livadia is a photogenic jumble of white-washed houses huddled around the northern end of Agios Stefanos Bay. Little happens here – a cat yawns, a fisherman falls asleep over his glass of ouzo... And that's precisely its charm: tranquillity. A narrow girdle of pebbled beach, perfect for sun worshipping, stretches some 2km from the village down the turquoise-laced bay, while the village's central square is hugged by cafes, old-time tavernas and Italian-era municipal buildings.

◎ Sights & Activities

Mikro Horio   ARCHAEOLOGICAL SITE
(☒24hr) When pirates prowled the Dodecanese, this medieval settlement was Tilos' main population centre. Its last inhabitants only left around 50 years ago and it now stands empty, 45 minutes' walk up from Livadia. In various states of ruin – one house opens as a music bar in summer – it's a fascinating place to wander. Linger until the light fades and it turns downright eerie. If you can stay awake long enough, visit Mikro Horio nightclub, in the middle of the village.

Tilos Trails   HIKING
(☑22460 44128, 6946054593; www.tilostrails. com) Tour company offering guided hikes all over the island, geared to suit individual abilities. Introductory walks last three hours. Talk to Iain and Lyn.

Tilos Heritage Tours   HIKING
(☑22460 44379, 6942061912; www.apollostudios. gr) British-run walking tours of the island. Talk to Charlie.

⏹ Sleeping

Hotel Irini   HOTEL €
(☑22460 44293; www.tilosholidays.gr; r incl breakfast €60; ❄☒☒☒) Irini has stunning white rooms with flat-screen TVs, shabby chic furniture, colourful quilts, tasteful ceramics, fridges and pool-facing balconies. Behind are great mountain views to admire over breakfast.

Apollo Studios   APARTMENT €
(☑6942061912, 22460 44379; www.apollostu dios.gr; d €50, apt €65-80; ❄☒) Fresh, well-appointed studios, run by a pleasant couple and set a few streets back from the harbour, with spotless kitchenettes, modern bathrooms, private balconies and a great communal roof terrace. They also offer roomy apartments with tiled floors and sofa beds – ask for number 3.

★Ilidi Rock Hotel   HOTEL €€
(☑22460 44293; www.tilosholidays.gr; studio/apt incl breakfast €90/130; ❄@☒) This superior hotel cascades down the cliff to two tiny aquamarine-laced inlets beside the harbour. Fully equipped studios and apartments with private balconies and four-poster beds, plus a minimalist style focusing your attention on the ravishing bay views beyond your window. Air-con costs €6 extra. There's also a great cafe-bar. Free pick-ups from the boat and complimentary use of kayaks.

✕ Eating & Drinking

★Omonoia Cafe   CAFE €
(☑22460 44287; breakfast €3-5, mains €8-11; ☒8am-late; ☒☒) Shaded by a mature fig tree on Livadia's main square, just up from the

---

BIRDWATCHING PARADISE

The landscape of Tilos is much gentler than other Dodecanese islands. Rather than forbidding mountains, the interior is characterised by fertile valleys carved into agricultural terraces. It's criss-crossed by trails laid out by farmers that now serve as perfect footpaths. With small-scale ancient fortifications and medieval chapels scattered in profusion, Tilos makes a wonderful hiking destination.

What's more, thanks to the island's low population – and long-standing ban on hunting – it's also a favourite haunt for rare birds. More than 150 species have been recorded. Some are residential, some migratory. An estimated 46 species are threatened. As you hike, keep your eyes peeled for the Bonelli's eagle, Eleonora's falcon, long-legged buzzard, Sardinian warbler, scops owl and Mediterranean black shag.

Tilos

quay, this much-loved all-day cafe is ideal for breakfast, light lunch or dinner. Its delightful elderly owners prepare everything from grilled meats and seafood to simple juices and salads, but you'll probably lose your heart – and your waistline – to their sponge cake.

Gorgona

GREEK €

(☑ 22460 70755; mains €10; ☺ 9am-11pm; ❄ 🛜 🚾) 🍴 Enjoying sweeping views of Agios Stefanos Bay, this rooftop restaurant serves olives and vegetables grown at its own farm. Following special recipes from the owner's grandmother, there's a wealth of choice from Tilos goat, lamb chops and pasta, to shrimps and octopus salad.

To Mikro Kafé

CAFE €

(snacks €5-7, mains €7-12; ☺ 6.30pm-late Mon-Fri, from 4pm Sat & Sun; ❄ 🛜 🍴 🚾) Micro in size it may be, but there's nothing diminutive about this cosy nook's appeal. With its exposed stone walls and nautically themed decoration, Micro is great for the kids, offering porthole windows, board games and little corners to play in while you nurse a sundowner on the beach-view patio (there's also a roof terrace). Offers salads, seafood, pies and sandwiches.

Armenon

TAVERNA €€

(☑ 22460 44134; www.tilosarmenon.gr; mains €8-18; ☺ breakfast, lunch & dinner; ❄ 🛜) 🍴 Open-fronted taverna on the beach with unbroken turquoise views and a menu spanning *taramasalata* to souvlakia, calamari and local favourites like lentil and anchovy salad. The charming couple who run it are so committed to home-grown ingredients they keep their own bees. Customers get a free sun lounger for the day. Look for the blue and yellow parasols.

Mikro Horio Nightclub

BAR

(☑ 6932086094, 22460 44204; Mikro Horio Village; ☺ 11am-late Jul-Sep; 🛜) Set in the creepy abandoned village of Mikro Horio, just 10 minutes' free shuttle bus from central Livadia, this place has a delightful veranda bar with amazing views of the bay and stars above. A great place for night owls.

Spitiko

CAFE

(☺ 7am-late) Overlooking the square, this cosy cafe is a popular stop-off for its great coffee, cheese and/or spinach pies, baklava and local sweets. The sign is in Greek, but everybody knows the place.

TRAIL BLAZING ON TILOS

There are 54km of trails in Tilos, and the mayor's office has made an effort to mark them with clear signage to aid keen walkers. One well-maintained and very scenic 3km walk leads north from Livadia to Lethra Beach, an undeveloped pebble-and-sand cove with limited shade. Follow the tarmac behind the Ilidi Rock Hotel, at the northwestern end of the port, to find the start of the trail. Returning via the picturesque Potami Gorge brings you to the main island highway.

A longer walk leads to the small abandoned settlement of Yera and its accompanying beach at Despoti Nero. Simply follow the road south from Livadia around the bay and keep going beyond the Church of Agios Ioannis at the far eastern end. Allow half a day for the full 6km round trip.

Two operators, Tilos Heritage Tours (p530) and Tilos Trails (p530), offer guided hikes tailored to all levels of difficulty.

❶ Information

All ferries arrive at Livadia's small quay, at the west end of the bay, just below the main square, which holds the post office and an Alpha bank with ATM.

Clinic (☑ 22460 44219; ☺ noon-5pm) Behind the church.

Police (☑ 22460 44222) In the white Italianate building on the quay.

Port Police (☑ 22460 44350) On the harbour.

Tilos Park Association (☑ 22460 70883; ☺ 10am-12.30pm Mon-Fri May-Oct) Tilos has no official tourism office, but this beachfront centre, aimed at promoting ecological conservation, has displays and brochures on local wildlife and trails.

Tilos Travel (☑ 22460 44360; www.tilos-travel.com; ☺ 9am-10pm) Helpful agency at the port, also known as Stefanakis Travel, which sells ferry tickets, rents out cars and motorbikes and offers credit-card cash withdrawals.

Megalo Horio

Μεγάλο Χωριό

Megalo Horio, the tiny 'capital' of Tilos, is a hillside village where the narrow streets hold sun-blasted cubic houses and teem with battle-scarred cats.

A taxing one-hour hike from the northern end of Megalo Horio takes you to the Knights Castle, passing the island's most ancient settlement en route.

The principal focus at the one-room museum (☑ 6984378079; ☺ 9am-2pm Jun-Sep) FREE on the main street is the island's ancient population of dwarf elephants. Expert volunteers bring their story to life.

The comfortable Miliou Studios (☑ 22460 44204, 6932086094; Megalo Horio; d €50; ✸ 🛜) 🏊 has rooms and self-catering studios with sweeping views of Eristos Bay. It's located in the centre of sleepy Megalo Horio; there's a supermarket close by, and free barbecue facilities in the grounds, plus you can also buy fruit and veg from Miliou's organic garden.

It's owned by the same people who run Mikro Horio nightclub and To Mikro Kafé.

The best taverna in the village, with a glorious hillside terrace commanding a fabulous panorama of the bay, is Kastro Cafe (☑ 22460 44232; mains €8-12; ☺ lunch & dinner). Everything on the menu is good, from the organic spit-roasted goat and locally raised pork, to the fresh little dolmadhes and tiny red shrimps.

Northwest Tilos

The northwestern end of Tilos is home to several attractive beaches. The best beach for swimming is long, broad Eristos Beach, lapped by sapphire-hued waters, 2.5km south of Megalo Horio. Generally deserted but for the odd local line-fishing, its greyish sands are fringed by tamarisk trees.

The quiet settlement of Agios Antonios, in the large bay 1.5km northwest of Megalo Horio, is a narrow strip of shingle with a taverna at either end. Much prettier Plaka Beach, in a cove another 3km west, is completely undeveloped. The water is slightly warmer, there's shade in the afternoon and, once you wade in a little, the rock shelves are good for snorkelling.

Beyond Plaka, the coast road climbs the sheer hillside, skirting 3km of alarming drop-offs to reach cliff-edge Agiou Panteleimona monastery.

🛏 Sleeping & Eating

Nitsa Apartments
APARTMENT €

(☑22460 44093; www.nitsa-tilosapartments.com; Eristos Beach; r/ste incl breakfast €50/70) Smart, modern studio block, 100m inland from Eristos Beach and holding simple rooms plus one- or two-bedroom self-catering apartments. It's attached to the all-day En Plo snack bar.

Eristos Beach Hotel
HOTEL €€

(☑22460 44025; www.eristosbeachhotel.gr; Eristos Beach; d/ste €60/90; P❄🖥🏊) Just off the beach, this large hotel is set in lush gardens crowded with hibiscus, orchids and lemon trees. Fresh rooms with tiled floors have balconies that look out to the sea beyond, while larger studios have kitchenettes and sleep four. There's also a lovely swimming pool and kid's pool, plus a restaurant and a bar.

En Plo
APARTMENT €€

(☑22460 44176; Eristos Beach; mains €10-15; ⊙10am-late; 🖥) Close to the beach, this welcoming snack bar has excellent slow-cooked food like goat stew, and regulars like squid *saganaki* (stuffed with fried cheese), souvlakia and super-fresh vegetables. Breakfast, lunch and dinner can be eaten under the vine-shaded canopy in a lovely garden.

NISYROS ΝΙΣΥΡΟΣ

POP 950

Thanks to its lack of beaches, Nisyros is very much off the tourist radar – apart from the day trippers from nearby Kos who come to witness the magnificent volcano. Yet for those seeking an island of natural beauty, goats wandering meadows stippled with beehives, soaring mountain views and wildlflowers, intimate Nisyros is just the ticket.

The main settlement, Mandraki, is a sleepy little fishing village garlanded with chic cafes, while hilltop villages Nikea and Emborios are stunning. Hike, wine-taste, immerse yourself in agrotourism... Those who chance a visit often return, again and again.

ℹ Getting There & Away

Catamarans run by Dodekanisos Seaways (p498) call in at Nisyros onTuesday and Thursday, heading to and from Kos and Rhodes. Blue Star Ferries (p498) also stops twice in each direction, en route to either Kos, Kalymnos, Astypalea and Piraeus, or Tilos, Symi and Rhodes.

There are also daily links with Kos. The *Panagia Spyliani* sails to either Kos Town or Kardamena (€8), while the smaller *Agios Konstantinos* runs to and from Kardamena (€6).

Nisyros

Boat Services from Nisyros (Mandraki)

DESTINATION	DURATION	FARE (€)	FREQUENCY
Halki*	1½hr	24	2 weekly
Kalymnos	2½hr	8	2 weekly
Kalymnos*	1½hr	21	2 weekly
Kos	1¼hr	8.50	daily
Kos*	45min	16	2 weekly
Piraeus	14hr	55	2 weekly
Rhodes	5hr	14	2 weekly
Rhodes*	2¾hr	26	2 weekly
Tilos*	40min	14	2 weekly

*high-speed services

❶ Getting Around

BOAT

Summer-only excursion boats leave Mandraki harbour for the pumice-stone, sandy beach islet of Giali (€8 to €12), returning at around 6pm.

BUS

Up to 10 bus tours run by Enetikon Travel visit the volcano each day (€6), allowing around 40 minutes at the crater. Catch them outside the office at Mandraki port. Three daily buses run from outside the port to Nikea via Pali.

CAR & MOTORCYCLE

In Mandraki, **Diakomihalis** offers good-value car rental and **Manos** (✆ 22420 31029; ◷ 9am-6pm) has a wealth of scooters and cars.

TAXI

A taxi from Mandraki to the volcano costs €20 return; call **Irini** (✆ 22420 31474).

Mandraki   Μανδράκι

POP 660

This pretty whitewashed town stretches languidly along the northern shore of Nisyros, lapped by gentle waters and lined with cafes and tavernas. Mandraki is almost completely pedestrianised, so its maze of winding backstreets is tranquil and timeless, with a fertile valley sloping up towards the rim of the volcano behind. The ferry jetty is 500m northeast of Mandraki proper. Simply walk straight along the coast to reach the centre.

❍ Sights

The major landmark is at the far western end, where the ruins of a 14th-century **Knights Castle** tower atop a cliff face. Its lower levels are occupied by an equally old

monastery, **Moni Panagias Spilianis** (Virgin of the Cave; ◷ 10.30am-3pm), accessed by climbing a short but steep stairway.

With Nisyros being very short on beaches, tiny but sandy **Mandraki Beach**, at the eastern end of town, is a popular swimming spot, despite being sometimes covered in seaweed. There's also an exposed black-stone beach to the west, **Hohlaki**, reached by following a dilapidated and precarious footpath around the headland below the monastery. Don't attempt this walk in bad weather.

Paleokastro   ARCHAEOLOGICAL SITE

(◷ 24hr) **FREE** Best reached by a lovely 20-minute hike through the fields, along a trail that starts southwest of the monastery, this astonishing Mycenaean-era acropolis was founded 3000 years ago. Its restored cyclopean walls are a little newer, from the 4th century BC – what looks like modern graffiti is in fact ancient dedications. Pass through the forbidding gateway and you can climb atop the massive blocks of volcanic rock for breathtaking views. Good explanatory signs in English are scattered throughout.

Archaeological Museum   MUSEUM

(✆ 22420 31588; €4; ◷ 8.30am-3pm Tue-Sun; ♿) This showpiece modern museum, on Mandraki's main pedestrian street, displays a fascinating collection of Hellenistic and Roman pottery and sculpture, as well as earlier artefacts made of obsidian quarried on neighbouring Giali. One ancient Greek inscription records a then-recent influx of migrants from Syria and Palestine.

Church Museum   MUSEUM

(€1; ◷ 10am-3pm Mon-Sat May-Sep) Despite its name, this small museum, just up from the seafront below the monastery, is not exclusively ecclesiastic. Besides its icons, vestments, votive offerings and memorabilia of long-deceased monks, it's crammed with oddments ranging from coins and banknotes to dolls.

🛏 Sleeping

Hotel Porfyris   HOTEL **€**

(✆ 22420 31376; www.porfyrishotel.gr; s/d/tr incl breakfast €46/54/59; ❄ ⊛ ☎) The only hotel in Mandraki town itself stands on a hillside, set above a citrus orchard five minutes' walk from the sea. If you're arriving from the ferry, fork left at Piccolo Bar. Beyond the elegant marble lobby, expect simple, cosy en-suite rooms with comfy beds and terrace or balcony. There's also a very welcome pool. Nice breakfast.

Hotel Romantzo
PENSION €

(☑ 22420 31340; www.nisyros-romantzo.gr; s/d/tr incl breakfast €35/45/55; ❋ ☎) Set just up from the ferry on the road to the volcano, this three-tiered stone building throws off a welcome glow come evening. Rooms are on the small side with fridge and flat-screen TV. Best of all, there's a communal sun-trap terrace up on the 2nd floor. The nearest restaurants are in town, 10 minutes' walk away. Generous-sized breakfast.

★ Ta Liotridia
B&B €€

(☑ 22420 31580; www.nisyros-taliotridia.com; r incl breakfast €140; ❋ ☎) Two large and very lovely B&B rooms (sleeping up to four) at the heart of the waterfront, on the upper floor of a smart wood-panelled bar. Each is furnished in comfortable traditional style, without being at all cluttered, and has a double bed in an alcove, another box bed, polished floors, stone walls and a sea-view balcony. Room 2 has the largest balcony.

✖ Eating

Pali Bakery
BAKERY

(€3; ⊙ 8am-2.30pm Tue-Sat) You can smell the delicious doughy aroma before you turn the corner to this bijou bakery on Mandraki's waterfront. Fresh brioche, cream pie, doughnuts, sweetbread with chocolate, and *tiropita* (cheese pie) are a few of the highlights in this calorific oasis.

To Kazanario
GREEK €

(☑ 6972240556; snacks €1.50-8; ⊙ noon-late; ❋ ☎) Escape the day trippers in this garden *ouzerie*, tucked off the pedestrian lane a block from the sea. A dark staircase drops from its inconspicuous doorway to a friendly old drinking den and garden beyond, where amazingly cheap snacks include souvlakia, sausages and tender calamari.

Irini
TAVERNA €

(☑ 22420 31365; Plateia Ilikiomenis; mains €9-12; ⊙ lunch & dinner; ❋ ☎ ☑ ❖) Sitting in the corner of a pebble-mosaic square in the shade of mature fig trees, Irini dishes up a mouthwatering menu of traditional fare like dolmadhes, goat in tomato sauce, souvlakia and *saganaki* (fried cheese). Try the heavenly baklava for dessert.

☕ Drinking & Nightlife

Mandraki's waterfront is lined with cafes and bars, with terraces perfectly aligned for watching the sun set over Kos.

Rythmos Bar
BAR

(⊙ 9am-late; ☎) Whether you choose a seat on its sun-soaked roof terrace or within its modish interior, this is a cool spot for a mid-day frappé or sunset glass of vino. Curiously it draws in the old boys as well as a young crowd – and it still works!

Ta Liotrida Bar
BAR

(⊙ 10am-late; ☎) Wood floors, stone walls and low-lit interior at this atmospheric bar that plays nostalgic tunes and is the perfect spot to unwind over a coffee to escape the sun. Look out for the traditional olive press inside.

❶ Information

Visit www.nisyros.gr for information on sights, history and local services.

Alpha Bank has an ATM at the harbour and a branch in Mandraki, and there's another ATM in town.

Diakomihalis (☑ 22420 31459; www.visitnisyros.gr; ⊙ 9.30am-1pm & 5pm-8pm) Ferry and air tickets, car rental and bus tours.

Enetikon Travel (☑ 22420 31180; www.enetikontravel.com; ⊙ 9.30am-2pm & 6.30pm-9pm) Run by the ever-helpful Michelle. 100m from the quay towards Mandraki, Enetikon runs boat trips and bus tours, dispenses free advice and sells tickets.

Police (☑ 22420 31201) and **Port Police** (☑ 22420 31222) both face the quay.

DODECANESE NISYROS

Around Nisyros

The Volcano   Το Ηφαίστειο

Nisyros sits on a volcanic fault line that curves around the southern Aegean. While 25,000 years have passed since the volcano that formed it last erupted, it's officially classified as dormant rather than extinct. Its summit originally stood around 850m

---

LOCAL KNOWLEDGE

EXPERIENCING NISYROS

Anaema (☑ 22420 31459; www.anaema.gr) is a brilliant new cooperative of island guides who can offer you culturally immersive experiences from one to six days – including hiking the volcano, wine-tasting trips, cookery and embroidery classes, and the chance to get involved with agrotourism.

tall, but three violent eruptions 30,000 to 40,000 years ago blew off the top 100m and caused the centre to collapse. White-and-orange pumice stones can still be seen on the northern, eastern and southern flanks of the island, while a large lava flow covers the entire southwest around Nikea.

The islanders call the volcano Polyvotis. Legend has it that during the battle between the gods and Titans, Poseidon ripped a chunk off Kos and used it to trap the giant Polyvotis deep beneath the rock of Nisyros. The roar of the volcano is his angered voice.

Visitors keen to experience the power of the volcano head by bus, car or on foot into the island's hollow caldera, a vast and otherworldly plain that was home to thousands of ancient farmers. Ruined agricultural terraces climb the walls, while cows graze amid sci-fi-set rocks.

A fenced-off area at the southern end encloses several distinct **craters** (€3; ⊙9am-8pm; P ♿). Get there before 11am and you may have the place to yourself. A path descends into the largest crater, **Stefanos**, where you can examine the multicoloured 100°C fumaroles, listen to their hissing and smell the sulphurous vapours. The surface is soft and hot, making sturdy footwear essential. Don't stray too far out, as the ground is unstable and can collapse.

An obvious track leads to the smaller and wilder crater of **Polyvotis** nearby. You can't enter the caldera itself, and the fumaroles are around the edge here, so take great care.

Emborios   Εμπορειός

Largely ruined but for a few restaurants and some very appealing accommodation, the village of Emborios is perched high on the jagged northern rim of the caldera, 9km up from Mandraki. Tumbledown houses cling to the steep flanks of the rocky ridge. A few are freshly whitewashed, but most are in stark disarray and overgrown with bougainvillea. Apart from a few yawning cats, almost no one lives here permanently.

🛏 Sleeping & Eating

★**Melanopetra**   APARTMENT €€€
(📞6978060289; www.melanopetra.gr/en; €170; ❄🛜) With its ubiquitous white and bare-wood floors flooded in natural light, Melanopetra is pure zen minimalism. Two apartments with gorgeous bedrooms and kitchens enjoy dual views of both the cal-

dera and Aegean on the other side. It's as if the rooms have been carved from the mountain itself with rough adobe walls and contemporary fittings.

Balcony Restaurant   GREEK €
(📞22420 31607; Emborios; mains €7; ⊙9am-10pm Mon-Sat; ❄🛜♿) The streetside terrace, facing the church, may look inviting, but opt if you can for a table on the namesake balcony at the back for an unforgettable panorama of the vast hollow crater. The menu is meat-heavy, with mouthwatering chops and steaks, but it also serves various vegetable fritters.

Nikea   Νικαία

The village of Nikea is 4km south along the crater's edge. No vehicles can penetrate this tight warren of dazzling white houses, so every visitor experiences the thrill of walking along the narrow lane from road's end to reach the tiny central square. Less a square than a circle, actually, it's among the most jaw-droppingly beautiful spots in the Dodecanese, with geometric pebble-mosaic designs in the middle, whitewashed benches around the edges, and the village church standing above.

Throughout Nikea, signposted overlooks command astonishing views of the volcano, laid out far below. The challenging trail down into the crater drops from behind the Volcanological Museum.

◉ Sights

Volcanological Museum   MUSEUM
(📞22420 31400; Plateia Nikolaou Hartofyli, Nikea; €2.50; ⊙11.30am-6.30pm Mon-Thu, 10.30am-2.30pm Fri & Sat May-Sep; ♿) Set beside the end of the road, this kid-friendly modern museum does a good job of explaining the history and mythology of the volcano and its impact on the island. There's also an interesting documentary worth a watch.

🍴 Eating

Porta   CAFE €
(📞22420 31832; Nikea; snacks €5-7; ⊙8.30am-late; ❄🛜) Located in Nikea's pretty central square, Porta is a wonderfully relaxing place to enjoy a cool drink, toasted sandwich, juice or beer. It looks out not to the caldera but the Aegean.

Pali   Πάλοι

This wind-buffeted seaside village sits 5km east of Mandraki, just beyond the turn-off to the volcano. Now primarily a yachting marina, it has a handful of tavernas among the sun-beaten buildings on the quay.

The coast road continues another 5km to Lies, Nisyros' most usable beach. Walking 1km along a precarious track from here brings you to Pahia Ammos, a shadeless expanse of coarse volcanic sand.

Sleeping & Eating

Mammis' Apartments APARTMENT €€
(☎ 22420 31824; www.mammis.com; Pali; d €60; ❄ 🖥) Set 100m up from the marina in gardens that are a riot of flowers, this peaceful complex holds 12 simple but imaginatively decorated apartments with kitchenettes, separate sofa beds for kids, and private balconies with sea views.

Captain's House TAVERNA €
(☎ 2242031016; Pali; mains €7-10; ⊗ 8am-midnight; ❄ 🖥) Festooned with yellow nets and so close to the water that you can taste the salt, this taverna attracts yachties and wizened fishermen alike with a menu that's packed to the gills with octopus, calamari, baby shark and cuttlefish.

KOS ΚΩΣ

POP 33,300

Fringed by the finest beaches in the Dodecanese, dwarfed beneath mighty crags, and blessed with lush valleys, Kos is an island of endless treasures. Visitors soon become blasé at sidestepping the millennia-old Corinthian columns that poke through the rampant wildflowers – even in Kos Town, the lively capital, ancient Greek ruins are scattered everywhere you turn, and a mighty medieval castle still watches over the harbour.

Visitors to Kos naturally tend to focus their attention on its beaches. In addition to those around Kos Town, there are three main resort areas. Kardamena, on the south coast, is very much dominated by package tourism, but Mastihari, on the north coast, and Kamari, in the far southwest, are more appealing. Away from the resorts, the island retains considerable wilderness, with the rugged Dikeos mountains soaring to almost 850m just a few kilometres west of Kos Town.

History

So many people lived on this fertile island in Mycenaean times that Kos was rich enough to send 30 ships to the Trojan War. In 477 BC, after suffering an earthquake and subjugation to the Persians, it joined the Delian League and again flourished. Hippocrates (460–377 BC), the Greek physician known as the founder of medicine, was born and lived on the island. After his death, the Sanctuary of Asclepius and a medical school were built, which perpetuated his teachings and made Kos famous throughout the Greek world.

That Ptolemy II of Egypt was also born on Kos secured the island the protection of Egypt. It became a prosperous trading centre, but fell under Roman domination in 130 BC and was administered by Rhodes from the 1st century AD onwards. Kos has shared the same ups and downs of fortune ever since, including conquest and/or occupation by the Knights, the Ottomans and the Italians and, much like Rhodes, its economy is now heavily dependent on tourism.

Getting There & Away

AIR

Kos' **airport** (KGS; ☎ 22420 56000; www.kosairportguide.com) is located in the middle of the island, 24km southwest of Kos Town. Olympic Air (www.olympicair.com) offers up to four daily flights to Athens (from €50, 55 minutes) and three weekly to Rhodes (€79, 30 minutes), Kalymnos (€72, 20 minutes), Leros (€79, 55 minutes) and Astypalea (€91, one hour 40 minutes).

BOAT
Domestic

From the island's main ferry port, in front of the castle in Kos Town, **Dodekanisos Seaways** (p498) runs catamarans up and down the archipelago, southeast to Rhodes via Nisyros, Tilos, Halki and Symi, and north to Samos, with stops including Kalymnos, Leros and Patmos. **Blue Star Ferries** (p498) also sails to Rhodes, as well as west to Astypalea and Piraeus.

The **Panagia Spiliani** (☎ 22420 31015), which also runs day trips from Nisyros to Kos in summer, carries passengers to Nisyros on sailings that leave from Kos Town at 2.30pm four days a week, and from Kardamena at 6.10pm on the other three days.

Eight daily ferries also connect Mastihari with Kalymnos (€4.50, 50 minutes); see www.anekalymnou.gr and www.anemferries.gr.

International

High-speed catamarans connect Kos Town with both Bodrum (two daily) and Turgutreis in Turkey (one daily). Both journeys take 20 minutes. Tickets cost €20 each way, with same-day returns €24 and longer-stay returns €36. For schedules and bookings, visit www.rhodes.marmarisinfo.com.

❶ Getting Around

TO/FROM THE AIRPORT

The airport is served by several daily buses to and from Kos Town's bus station (€3.20). A taxi to Kos Town costs around €30. Note that Kefalos-bound buses stop at the big roundabout near the airport entrance.

The airport is so far from Kos Town that if you're planning to rent a car anyway, it's worth doing so when you first arrive. All the international chains have airport offices.

BICYCLE

Cycling is very popular, so you'll be tripping over bicycles for hire. Prices range from as little as €5 per day for a boneshaker, up to €20 for a decent mountain bike. In Kos Town, **George's Bikes** (p543) offers reasonable rates.

Kos Mountainbike Activities (☑ mobile 6944150129; www.kosbikeactivities.com; Psalidi; mountain bike per day €30; ⊙ 9am-12.30pm & 5.30pm-7.30pm) offers bike rentals and guided tours.

BOAT

Several boats moored in Kos Town offer excursions around Kos and to nearby islands. A 'three island' day trip to Kalymnos, Pserimos and Platy costs around €30, including lunch, while you can find day trips to Bodrum for as little as €10.

Boat Services from Kos

DESTINATION	DURATION	FARE (€)	FREQUENCY
Astypalea	4hr	14.50	1 weekly
Kalymnos	50min	4.50	8 daily
Kalymnos	1hr 20min	6.50	3 daily
Kalymnos*	40min	16	1-2 daily
Leros	3¼hr	15	1 weekly
Leros*	1½hr	23	1-2 daily
Lipsi*	2hr	29	1-2 daily
Nisyros*	55min	16	2 weekly
Patmos*	3hr	31	1-2 daily
Piraeus	11hr	55	3 weekly
Rhodes	3hr	25	1 daily
Rhodes*	2½hr	32	1 daily
Samos	4hr	44	4 weekly
Symi	3hr	12	2 weekly
Symi*	1½hr	24	5 weekly

*high-speed services

All depart from Kos Town except the Kalymnos ferry, which departs from Mastihari.

BUS

The island's main **bus station** (☑ 22420 22292; Kleopatras 7) is located well back from the waterfront in Kos Town. It is the base for **KTEL** (☑ 22420 22292; www.ktel-kos.gr), which has services to all parts of the island, including the airport and south-coast beaches.

CAR

A recommended local operator is Auto Bank Car Rental, with outlets at the **airport** (☑ 22420 23397; www.autobank-carrentalkos.com), Kos Town and Mastihari.

Kos Town Κως
POP 14,750

A handsome harbour community, fronted by a superb medieval castle and somehow squeezed amid a mind-blowing array of ancient ruins from the Greek, Roman and Byzantine eras, Kos Town is the island's capital, main ferry port and only sizeable town. While some central streets tend to be overrun by partying tourists, most remain stylish and attractive. The port is the most appealing area of all, lined by cafes and tavernas and with an unbroken row of excursion boats, fishing vessels and fancy yachts bobbing and bristling against each other along the waterfront.

Popular beaches stretch in either direction from the harbour. Long sandy **Kritika Beach**, running northwest and in easy walking distance of the town centre, is lined with hotels and restaurants. Southeast of the harbour the thin strip of sand known as **Kos Town Beach** is dotted with parasols in summer and offers deep water for swimming. Both beaches fill with guests from adjacent hotels.

The nearest beach to Kos Town, crowded **Lambi Beach** begins just 2km northwest and has its own strip of hotels and restaurants. Further west along the coast, a long stretch of pale sand is fringed by two more resorts – **Tingaki**, 10km from Kos Town, and the slightly less crowded **Marmari Beach** beyond. Windsurfing is popular at all three beaches, while the island of Pserimos is only a few kilometres offshore and served by excursion boats from Marmari in summer.

Heading south from Kos Town along Vasileos Georgiou, on the other hand, brings you to the three busy beaches of **Psalidi** (3km from Kos Town), **Agios Fokas** (8km),

Kos & Pserimos

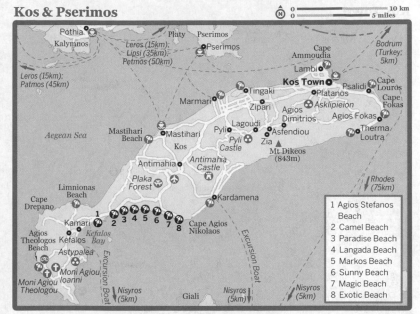

1 Agios Stefanos Beach
2 Camel Beach
3 Paradise Beach
4 Langada Beach
5 Markos Beach
6 Sunny Beach
7 Magic Beach
8 Exotic Beach

and **Therma Loutra** (12km). At Therma Loutra, hot mineral springs warm the sea.

◉ Sights & Activities

Castle of the Knights   CASTLE
(☑ 22420 27927; Harbour; €4; ⊙ 8am-8pm Apr-Oct, 8am-3pm Tue-Sun Nov-Mar) Kos' magnificent 15th-century castle was constructed not on a hilltop, but right beside the entrance to the harbour. Access it by the bridge from Plateia Platanou, crossing what was once a seawater-filled moat but is now a road. Visitors can stroll atop the intact outer walls, surveying all activity in the port and keeping a watchful eye on Turkey across the strait. The precinct within, however, is now largely overgrown, with cats stalking through a wilderness of wildflowers.

Plateia Platanou   SQUARE
The warm, graceful charm and sedate pace of Kos Town is experienced at its best in this lovely cobblestone square, immediately south of the castle. Sitting in a cafe here, you can pay your respects to **Hippocrates' plane tree** (Plateia Platanou). Hippocrates himself is said to have taught his pupils in its shade. The ancient sarcophagus beneath it was converted into a fountain by the Ottomans, while the 18th-century **Mosque of Gazi Hassan Pasha**, now sadly boarded up, stands opposite.

Ancient Agora   ARCHAEOLOGICAL SITE
(⊙ dawn-dusk) **FREE** Exposed by a devastating earthquake in 1933, Kos' ancient centre occupies a vast area south of the castle. Back in the 4th century BC, this was the first town ever laid out in blocks, and you can still discern the original town plan, even though it's very overgrown. Landmarks include a massive columned **stoa** and the ruins of a **Shrine of Aphrodite, Temple of Hercules** and Christian basilica.

The site is fenced, but usually open all day. Locals use it as a shortcut.

Western Excavation Site   ARCHAEOLOGICAL SITE
(⊙ dawn-dusk) **FREE** This open site, south of the centre, holds fascinating ancient ruins uncovered by an earthquake in 1933. Its real treasures are the mosaics of the **House of Europa**, dating from the 2nd century and protected by rudimentary shelters. In front of them, there's a section of the **Decumanus Maximus**, the Roman city's main thoroughfare, while the site also holds the **Nymphaeum**, the **Xysto** and the overgrown but evocative **Temple of Dionysos**. Across the street stands an impressive 2nd-century **theatre**.

Kos Town

Lambi
(2.5km)

Kritika Beach
(200m)

Averof

Navarinou

Themistokleous

Kanari

Amerikis

Salaminos

Alikarnasou

Akti Koundourioti

Harbour

Panagia
Spiliani

Spetson

Pindou

Megalou

Tsaldari

El Venizelou

Keovoulou

Veriopoulou

Irodotou

Alexandrou

31 Martiou

25 Martiou

Riga Fereou

Finikon

Akti Miaouli

Plateia
Platanou

Nafklirou

Alexandrou
Diakou

Plateia
Eleftherias

Xanthou

Ippokratous

El Venizelou

G Ioannidi

Korai

Ap Pavlou

Kolokotroni

Appelou Ifestou

Nisiriou

Pisandrou

Vasileos Pavlou

Ag Nikolaou

Vyronos

Mitropolis

Pisandrou

Bus
Station

Grigoriou

Makrygianni

Askiepieion (3km);
(22km);
Kefalos (37km)

Archaeological Museum   MUSEUM

(Plateia Eleftherias; €8; ☺8am-8pm Tue-Sun)
Housed in an Italian-era building in the
central square, the small archaeological
museum is finally open after restoration
and possesses a wealth of sculptures from
the Hellenistic to late Roman eras, with a
statue of Hippocrates and a 3rd-century-AD
mosaic as the star attractions. There are
information panels for many of the rooms.

Eva   BOAT

(☏6955581116, 694369300; www.facebook.com/
Eva.Boat.Kos; Akti Koundourioti; €40; ☺departs
10.30am; 🖘) Treat yourself to a boat trip on
bee-coloured *Eva*; a twin-masted wooden
caïque with a finely crafted crow's nest and
gunwales. You'll (often) see dolphins, swim
in a turquoise cove and stop at Pserimos
island for a beach flop. With Captain Savvas
and his friendly family. Returns around 6pm.

🛏 Sleeping

★**Hotel Afendoulis**   HOTEL €
(☏22420 25321; www.afendoulishotel.com; Evrip-
ilou 1; s/d/tr €35/50/60; ☺Mar-Nov; 🌡@🖘)
This family-run hotel has sparkling rooms
with TVs, balconies, hairdryes, quick internet
and comfy beds. Downstairs, the open break-

There are also pools for kids and adults and a snack bar on the roof. While it's clean and functional, it can be rather impersonal.

Hotel Sonia HOTEL €€
(☑ 22420 28798; www.hotelsonia.gr; Irodotou 9; s/d/tr incl breakfast €45/60/75; ❋ 🕏) A block from the waterfront on a peaceful backstreet, this pension offers a dozen sparkling rooms with parquet floors, fridges, smart bathrooms and an extra bed if required. Room 4 has the best sea view. Breakfast is served on a relaxing communal veranda, there's a decent book exchange, and it plans to open up the garden to visitors.

Kos Aktis Art Hotel HOTEL €€€
(☑ 22420 47200; www.kosaktis.gr; Vasileos Georgiou 7; s/d/tr from €190/200/278; ❋ @ 🕏 ⊠) Aktis' beautiful hotels are scattered across the Dodecanese and its representative here in Kos is stunning. Bedrooms are minimalist affairs of glass, light and wood. The view of the Aegean and, by night, Bodrum glittering like a giant chandelier, is romantic. There's a gym, fine restaurant and bar.

✕ Eating

★ **Pote Tin Kyriaki** TAVERNA €
(☑ 6930352099, 22420 27872; Pisandrou 9; ⊙ 7pm-2am) Named for Melina Mercouri's Oscar-winning 1960 song, 'Never on Sunday' is not the sort of place you expect to find in modern Kos – and it takes a *lot* of finding! This traditional *ouzerie* serves delicious specialities such as stuffed zucchini flowers, dolmadhes and steamed mussels.

Aegli CAFE €
(☑ 22420 30016; www.aiglikos.gr; Plateia Eleftherias; snacks €3-5; ⊙ breakfast, lunch & dinner) This bakery-cafe is run by a cooperative supporting low-income women and employs only female staff. The speciality is *marmarites* – translated as 'crumpets', but more like sourdough flatbread – with sweet or savoury toppings, but it also serves pies, juices, coffee and gigantic breakfasts (for two €16).

★ **Elia** GREEK €€
(☑ 22420 22133; Appelou Ifestou 27; mains €8-15; ⊙ 12.30pm-late; ❋ 🕏 ✎ 🖐) ✿ With its traditional wood-beamed ceiling and partly exposed stone walls covered in murals of the gods of the pantheon, Elia is earthy and friendly, while its small and focused menu is fit for a hard-to-please deity. Mezedhes (appetisers), shrimp, steamed mussels and grilled octopus are a few of your soon-to-be

fast room and breezy terrace have wrought-iron tables and chairs for reading or enjoying their memorable breakfast of homemade jams. There may be plusher hotels in Kos, but none with the soul of the Afendoulis, where nothing is too much trouble.

Kosta Palace HOTEL €€
(☑ 22420 22855; www.kosta-palace.com; cnr Akti Kountourioti & Averof; s/d/apt €65/95/135; ❋ @ 🕏 ⊠) This swanky harbour-front edifice, facing the castle across the port, holds 160 rooms with kitchenettes and private balconies. Apartments have separate rooms.

favourite things. Staff are warm and welcoming whatever the weather.

Petrino Meze Restaurant MEZEDHES €€
(☑ 22420 27251; www.petrino-kos.gr; Plateia Theologou 1; mains €9-28; ⊗ lunch & dinner; ❋ ⑤) Peaceful and balmy, this graceful restaurant has a leafy garden shaded by bougainvillea, overlooking Kos Town's western group of archaeological ruins. Highlights on its upscale menu include hearty meat concoctions such as beef stuffed with blue cheese and pork with plums, but it also serves lighter dishes such as steamed swordfish or pasta, as well as mixed mezedhes (appetisers) platters.

Nick the Fisherman SEAFOOD €€
(Averof 21; mains €10-14; ⊗ 1pm-1am; ❋ ⑤) This side-street seafood taverna is bedecked with nets and dangerous-looking fish on the walls. Try the sardines, red snapper, striped mullet and grouper.

🍸 Drinking & Nightlife

Kos Town has a very lively party scene. Aimed squarely at tourists bussed in from the coastal resorts, it centres a block south of the harbour and along the waterfront on Kritika Beach. Locals congregate on weekends to drink coffee and gossip in the cafes on Plateia Eleftherias (Freedom Sq).

Global Cafe BAR
(☑ 22420 26003; Ifestou 1; ⊗ 8.30am-late; ⑤) With its modern interior, Global Cafe bags a youthful crowd who come to chat and play backgammon over a coffee or juice. There's a lovely atrium area full of light and a long bar to perch yourself at. Salads and burgers are on the menu and the cocktails are worth a look. Can be a bit smoky.

Aenaos CAFE
(☑ 22420 26044; Plateia Eleftherias; ⊗ 8am-late; ⑤) Tucked beneath an exquisite, still-active mosque, this well-shaded cafe is popular with locals who come to people-watch – or be seen – in its smart interior, or outside on the terrace in the corner of the *plateia*. Treat yourself to its delectable spectrum of sweet confections (from €3.50), coffees and juices.

🔒 Shopping

For high-street-style shops, head to the eastern end of Ioannidi and the pedestrian streets south of Ippokratous.

Dimotiki Agora MARKET
(☑ 22420 22900; Plateia Eleftherias; ⊗ 8am-late) 🖉 Fragrant with spices, this lively open-arched market has a cornucopia of locally made honeys, natural soaps, bonbons, sandalwood spoons, mythological curios and Kalymnian sponges.

ℹ Information

Kos Town has several ATMs, including at the branches of Alpha Bank on El Venizelou and the National Bank of Greece on Riga Fereou.

Fanos Travel & Shipping (☑ 22420 20035; www.kostravel.gr; Akti Koundourioti 11; ⊗ 9am-9pm) Tickets for the hydrofoil service to Bodrum and other ferries, plus yachting services.

Kentrikon Travel (☑ 22420 28914; Akti Kountouriotou 7; ☺ 9am-9pm) The official agent for Blue Star Ferries also sells all other ferry and air tickets.

Police (☑ 22420 25462; Eparhio Bldg, Akti Miaouli)

Port Police (☑ 22420 26594; cnr Akti Koundourioti & Megalou Alexandrou)

Post Office (Vasileos Pavlou)

Tourist Police (☑ 22420 22444; Akti Miaouli)

ℹ Getting Around

BICYCLE

Cycle lanes thread all through Kos Town, with the busiest route running along the waterfront to connect the town with Lambi to the north and Psalidi to the south. Many hotels have bikes for guests, or you can rent one from **George's Bikes** (☑ 22420 24157; Kanari 8; cycle/scooter per day €4/15).

BUS

Local buses, run by **DEAS** (☑ 22420 26276; flat fare €2), operate within Kos Town, but have little relevance to visitors. Buses to the rest of the island, including the airport, depart from the KTEL **bus station** (p538).

TAXI

Taxis (☑ 22420 23333, 22420 22777) congregate on the south side of the port.

TOURIST TRAIN

One way to get your bearings in summer is to take a 20-minute city tour on the **tourist train** (☑ 22420 26276; €5), which departs frequently from Akti Kountouriotou on the harbourfront.

Around Kos

Asklepieion   Ασκληπιείον

The island's most important ancient site, **Asklepieion** (☑ 22420 28763; adult/child €8/ free; ☺ 8am-7pm Tue-Sun, 8am-3pm Nov-Mar), stands on a pine-covered hill 3km southwest of Kos Town, commanding lovely views across towards Turkey. A religious sanctuary devoted to Asclepius, the god of healing, it was also a healing centre and a school of medicine. It was founded in the 3rd century BC, according to legend by Hippocrates himself, the Kos-born 'father' of modern medicine. He was already dead by then, though, and the training here simply followed his teachings. Until the sanatorium was destroyed by an earthquake in AD 554, people came from far and wide for treatment.

The ruins occupy three levels, with the propylaeum (approach to the main gate), Roman-era public baths and remains of guest rooms on the first level. The second holds an **altar of Kyparissios Apollo**, with the 1st-century-BC **Temple to Apollo** to the east and the first **Temple of Asclepius**, built in the 4th century BC, to the west. The remains of its successor, the once-magnificent 2nd-century-BC **Temple of Asclepius**, are on the third level. Climb a little further, to the cool pine woods above, for the best views of all.

A modern museum on the path down preserves ancient inscriptions and shows films explaining the site.

Bus 3 runs hourly from Kos Town to the site. It's also a pleasant bike ride.

Mountain Villages

The villages scattered on the green northern slopes of the Dikeos mountains make ideal destinations for day trips.

Kos' prettiest mountain village – Zia, 14km west of Kos Town – is now essentially a one-street theme park. The views down to the sea are as wonderful as ever, but coachloads of tourists are deposited every few minutes to stroll along its gauntlet of souvenir shops and competing tavernas.

Continuing 6km west beyond Zia brings you to the less commercialised village of **Pyli**. Even better, just before the village a left turn leads to the extensive remains of its medieval predecessor, **Old Pyli**, scattered amid the towering rocks and pine trees of a high and very magical hillside. The summit here is crowned by the stark ruins of Pyli Castle and the whole place is so wild you half expect Pan to pop up. A well-marked trail climbs from the roadside parking area, forking left to the castle and right to the old village, where the only building still in use is a tavern hidden in the woods.

Buses connect Kos Town with Pyli itself (€2, two to three daily), but not Old Pyli.

✖ Eating

✖ Zia

The Watermill   CAFE €
(mains €8; ☺ breakfast, lunch & dinner;)
🍴 It's worth the brief climb up the hill just to sate your thirst with their delicious homemade lemonade. With its vine-covered arbour and relaxing patio giving stunning

mountain views, this former watermill exudes a serenity that will still your pulse to that of a freediver. The menu includes crêpes, fruit salad and pasta dishes.

Taverna Oromedon GREEK €€
(22420 69983; www.oromedon.com; Zia; mains €9-15; ⊙ lunch & dinner) Zia's finest restaurant is justly acclaimed for its vine-laced sun terrace, unbroken sea views and traditional Greek menu of shrimp *saganaki* (shrimp in fried cheese), dolmadhes and *stifadho*. Meat-eaters should be sure to spare some room for the chunky local sausages.

✕ Pyli

★ Oria Taverna GREEK €
(6981764991; Old Pyli; mains €7-10; ⊙9am-9pm; P) 🚶 Idyllic taverna, only accessible by hiking up the hillside facing the 1000-year-old Pyli Castle and enjoying what is certainly the best rural view on Kos. It's open all day for snacks and cooling drinks, but you can't beat a sunset dinner here, tucking into the seasonal, locally sourced menu of steaks, meatballs, zucchini and tzatziki.

Mastihari   Μαστιχάρι

Hardly more than a village, this delightful old-fashioned beach resort holds everything you need for a straightforward family holiday. There's a lovely broad strip of powder-fine sand scattered with tamarisk trees, a clutch of whitewashed rental studios and small hotels, and a row of appetising waterfront tavernas and bars. There's no historic core and nothing of any architectural interest, but as a place to spend a day or a week in the sun, Mastihari has it all.

Mastihari's tiny port is served by frequent **ANE Kalymnou** (22420 29900; www.anekalymnou.gr) and ANEM (www.anemferries.gr) ferries to Pothia on Kalymnos, as well as excursion boats to the islet of Pserimos in summer.

🛏 Sleeping & Eating

Studios Diana APARTMENT €
(22420 59116; Mastihari; apt €40) Clean and basic studios opening onto the sea, with private balconies and very tiny kitchens. Turning on the air-con costs €5 extra.

Athinas Studios APARTMENT €
(6974180326; www.athinas-studios.gr; Mastihari; d/tr €40/50) Super-fresh studio rooms

with Aegean-blue trim and spotless kitchenettes. They're a block back from the seafront, but the upper-level rooms have private seaview terraces and there's also a roof garden. One room has bunk beds, double bed and a large balcony.

El Greco TAVERNA €
(Mastihari; mains €8-12; ⊙ breakfast, lunch & dinner; ☷) Beachside taverna – follow the blue-painted walkway up from the sand – that consistently pleases with its fresh salads, zucchini, souvlakia and lamb with rosemary, as well as grilled sardines, cod and octopus. Only the very fanciest fish dishes cost more than €10, and it also serves breakfast all day.

Kali Kardia SEAFOOD €€
(22420 59289; Mastihari; mains €6-15; ⊙ breakfast, lunch & dinner) Atmospheric taverna right on the harbour, with tables out on the footpath and a wooden interior that's patronised by older folk staring out to sea. Piping aromas of squid, shrimp and souvlakia emerge from the kitchen, and large mixed platters cost €10 per person.

Kamari & Kefalos Bay
Καμάρι & Κέφαλος

Enormous Kefalos Bay, a 12km stretch of high-quality sand, lines the southwest shoreline of Kos. For most of its length the beach itself is continuous, but the main road runs along a crest around 500m inland, so each separate section served by signposted tracks has its own name. Backed by scrubby green hills and lapped by warm water, these are the finest and emptiest beaches on the island. Kamari, at the western extremity of this black-pebbled beach, is a low-key resort with plenty of cafes, tavernas and accommodation, as well as decent water sports. High above Kamari, perched on a bluff, the touristy village of Kefalos has a few spots to eat and stay. If you're determined to escape the crowds, continue on to the island's southern peninsula beyond.

The most popular stretch of sand is **Paradise Beach**, while the least developed is **Exotic Beach. Langada Beach** (which you may also see referred to as Banana Beach) makes a good compromise, but the best of the lot is **Agios Stefanos Beach**, at the far western end. A small beachfront promontory here is topped by a ruined 5th-century basilica, while the absurdly photogenic islet of **Kastri** stands within swimming distance immediately offshore.

On the west coast, **Agios Theologos Beach** is backed by meadow bluffs carpeted in olive groves, and feels far removed from the resort bustle.

🛏 Sleeping & Eating

Affordable studios and apartments are the order of the day, with an emphasis on package holiday accommodation in Kamari.

Anthoula Studios APARTMENT €
(📞 22420 71904; studios €40; 🅿✺) Perched on the hill, this yellow eyrie is set on well-kept grounds and has a great pool to cool off in, with decent rooms with safety deposit box and fridge, plus air-con for an extra €5 per night. A minibus runs to and from the beach on Kefalos Bay several times a day. Owner Anthoula is lovely.

Albatross Apartments APARTMENT €€
(📞 22420 71981; albatross@hotmail.com; Kamari Beach; apt €70; 🅿✺🛜✺) Eleven simple, spotless and identical kitchenette studios, so freshly maintained they might have been built yesterday. All have sea views, there's a good swimming pool, and the beach is just across the road, with the jetty a short walk away. There's an on-site bar but no restaurant. Airport pick-up for stays of three nights or more.

★ Restaurant Agios Theologos TAVERNA €€
(📞 6974503556; Agios Theologos Beach; mains €8-15; ⏱ lunch & dinner, Sat & Sun only Nov-Apr; ✺🛜) Set in dreamy sand dunes above Agios Theologos Beach, this much-loved seasonal taverna enjoys the best sunsets in Kos. Its zesty homemade cheese, courtesy of its inquisitive goats, is at its most flavoursome fried, while a fresh grilled bream costs around €15. There are fantastic mezedhes (appetisers) too. Pure romance.

ASTYPALEA
ΑΣΤΥΠΑΛΑΙΑ
POP 1300

Swathed in silky aquamarine waters, far-flung, butterfly-shaped Astypalea is richly rewarding for walkers, campers and history buffs. For any island hunter, this is the ultimate escape – think mountainous meadows straight from the pages of Homer, and rugged beaches fringed in vivid blue water. Chance of sighting a mermaid: fair to middling.

The island's main settlement, hilltop Hora, is a tumble of bleached-white houses cascading down from a medieval fortress to the fishing port of Skala. Although boutique hotels have been sprouting here in recent years, the tourist infrastructure – and ferry service – remains minimal, and most visitors are Greek, with the rest largely French and Italian. Fed up with the package crowds, Irish bars and fish and chips? You've come to the right place.

ℹ Getting There & Away

AIR
Olympic Air (www.olympicair.com) has three flights a week from Leros (€62, 25 minutes), Kalymnos (€62, one hour 40 minutes) and Kos (€74, one hour 40 minutes), and three per week from Athens (€134, one hour). Buy tickets online, or via Astypalea Tours (p547).

BOAT
Only two ferry operators serve Astypalea. Blue Star Ferries (p498) arrive, inconveniently, in the dead of night at the isolated little port of Agios Andreas, 6.5km north of Skala. A bus is scheduled to meet each boat, but don't bank on it. One ferry arrives four times weekly, having sailed from Piraeus via Paros, Naxos and Amorgos, and sets off back along the same route a couple of hours later. The other stops once in each direction en route between Piraeus and Rhodes, calling also at Kalymnos, Kos, Tilos and Nisyros.

Nisos Kalymnos (www.anekalymnou.gr) connects Skala's small harbour once weekly with Kalymnos.

Boat Services from Astypalea

DESTINATION	DURATION	FARE (€)	FREQUENCY
Kalymnos	2½hr	12.50	1 weekly
Kalymnos*	3½hr	15	1 weekly
Kos	4hr	15	1 weekly
Naxos	4hr	20	4 weekly
Paros	5½hr	34	4 weekly
Piraeus	8½hr	35	5 weekly
Rhodes	9hr	24	1 weekly

Unless otherwise marked, services depart from Agios Andreas.
* departs from Skala

ℹ Getting Around

Astypalea's airport is on the flat, narrow 'neck' of the island, 8km northeast of Skala. Buses connect with flights in summer, while taking either of the island's two **taxis** (📱 mobile 6975706365) to Skala costs around €10. Summer buses also link Skala with Hora and Livadi to the west, and Analipsi/Maltezana to the east, stopping at beaches en route (€2). Of the island's three vehicle-rental agencies, **Vergoulis** (📞 22430 61351; www.rent-a-car-astypalaia. com; per day scooters €15, cars €30-60; ⏰ 8am-10pm) is particularly recommended.

In July and August, boats head out for the day from Skala to the remote western beaches of Agios Ioannis, Kaminakia and Vatses, as well as to the islets of Koutsomytis (with ethereal, emerald-green water) and Kounoupa. They also make complete circuits around the island. Contact Astypalea Tours in Skala for details.

Skala & Hora
Σκάλα & Χώρα

POP 1036

Astypalea's main town, Skala, lies on the southern shore of the island's western half, curving around an attractive bay that's too shallow for large inter-island ferries. Little more than a village, with aromatic odours drifting from its bakery, Skala holds a small sand-and-pebble beach that's popular with locals. Bars and tavernas punctuate the quay, which is the sole preserve of old sea dogs in low season, but surprisingly lively on summer evenings.

Modern visitors delight in the sheer beauty of the old settlement of Hora looming above, its white houses spilling down the hillside beneath its impressive *kastro* (castle). For the original inhabitants of Skala, however, the upward migration was prompted by the endless threat of marauding pirates. These days Hora is a delightful maze to explore. Stroll around the hushed tangle of streets and climb up to the fort. Suitably exhausted, you can then relax in the clutch of inviting *kafeneia* and tavernas alongside the restored Cycladic-style windmills that mark the village entrance.

◉ Sights & Activities

Kastro
CASTLE
(Hora; ⏰ dawn-dusk) **FREE** Astypalea's imposing castle was built by the Venetian Quirini family early in the 15th century. For the next 300 years, up to 4000 people lived within this ever-expanding precinct, sheltered from pirate attacks. Its last inhabitants left in 1956, after an earthquake caused the stone houses integrated into its walls to collapse. The only entrance is through a gateway that burrows beneath the **Church of the Virgin of the Castle**; the magical **Church of Agios Georgios** lies beyond.

Archaeological Museum
MUSEUM
(📞 22430 61500; Skala; €2; ⏰ 9am-1pm & 6-8.30pm Tue-Sun Jun-Sep) Skala's small archaeological museum, at the start of the road up to Hora, holds treasures found across the island, from earliest times up to the Middle Ages. Highlights include grave offerings from two Mycenaean chamber tombs and a bronze Roman statue of Aphrodite.

Thalassopouli
BOATING
(📞 6974436338; Pera Gialos, Skala; per person €15; ⏰ Jun-Sep; 🚢) Run by Captain Yiannis, Thalassopouli leaves Skala at 11am and returns you glowing and salty at 6pm after a day's swimming around two uninhabited neighbouring islands: Kounoupi, with its golden isthmus of sand, and Kousomyti, outlined in purest aquamarine. Food is available (€7).

🛏 Sleeping

Reservations are essential in July and August. The finer boutique options are in Hora.

★ Studios Kilindra
BOUTIQUE HOTEL €€
(📞 22430 61131; www.astipalea.com.gr; Hora; d/ apt incl breakfast €130/150; ❄@🅿🏊) 🅿 Just below the *kastro*, this enchanting boutique hotel has a swish pool with a terrace overlooking the mouthwash-green bay. The lobby is scattered with eclectic antiques as well as a grand piano, while studios and larger maisonettes fuse the contemporary with the traditional, featuring split-level floors, raised beds, sofas and kitchenettes. Massage, acupuncture and herbal treatments are also available.

Mariakis Studios
APARTMENT €€
(📞 22430 62072; www.mariakis.gr; Hora; s/d from €60/70; ❄🅿) Four attractive, spotlessly white apartments adjoin a family home just steps from the heart of Hora. Island-style touches include traditional furnishings and exposed stone walls, while the spacious terraces enjoy great sea views. The breakfasts are superb.

Akti Rooms
APARTMENT €€
(📞 22430 61114; www.aktirooms.gr; Skala; d/ studio incl breakfast €80/85; ❄🅿) Waterside Akti, facing Hora from the east side of Skala,

Astypalea

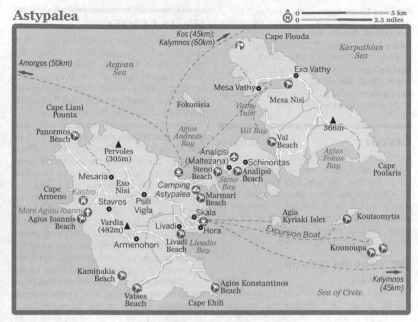

has traditionally themed rooms with ornate lights, dark-wood chests and traditional crockery. Most but not all have sea views, and the studios have kitchenettes. Swim from the private platform or chill in the stylish cafe.

Hotel Paradissos HOTEL €€
(☑ 22430 61224; www.astypalea-paradissos.com; Skala; d/tr from €80/95; ✸ 🖥) Stately and peaceful, Paradissos is so close to the harbour you can taste salt on your lips. Its 18 dazzling-white sea-view rooms hold desks and private balconies. There's also a great cafe and attached travel agency.

✖ Eating

Barbarossa TAVERNA €
(☑ 22430 61577; Hora; mains €10; ⊙ lunch & dinner; ✸ 🖥 🍴) 🖉 You can't miss this friendly taverna, serving food with soul along the main approach to Hora, with a buzzing terrace near the town hall. Inside are exposed stone walls covered with antique Greek poster girls, and there are amazing views to the rear. Menu highlights like pork fillet with prunes, mussels and grilled shrimps ensure you won't be disappointed.

Agoni Grammi TAVERNA €
(☑ 22430 61988; Hora; mains €8-12; ⊙ lunch & dinner) It's the outdoor terrace that first

catches the eye here, close to Hora's landmark windmills, but the whitewashed interior is equally appealing at night, stippled by stone flags and lit with red pendant lights. As well as homemade pasta and pizza, this island favourite is renowned for its fish soup and traditional *kokoretsi* (kebab of lamb innards).

Maïstrali TAVERNA €
(☑ 22430 61691; Skala; mains €8-12; ⊙ 10am-late; ✸ 🖥 🍴) Tucked one street back from the harbour, near the stairway to heaven (well, Hora, anyway), this stylish restaurant dishes up everything from zucchini balls, lamb chops and eggplant salad, to grilled shrimp *saganaki* (shrimp in fried cheese) and rabbit in tomato sauce.

❶ Information

Astypalea Tours (☑ 22430 61571; www.astypaleatours.gr; Skala; ⊙ 6-9pm) For air and ferry tickets and boat excursions.

Emporiki Bank (☑ 22430 59890; Skala) The island's only bank, with an ATM, is on the waterfront.

Municipal Tourist Office (☑ 22430 61412; www.astipalea.org; Hora; ⊙ 6-9pm Jun-Sep)

For history, pictures, facilities and sights go to www.astypalaia.com.

Paradise Travel Agency ([✆] 22430 61224; paradisostravel@yahoo.gr; at Hotel Paradissos, Skala) Books ferry tickets.

Police ([✆] 22430 61207, 22430 61206; Skala) In an Italianate building on the waterfront.

Port Police ([✆] 22430 61208; Skala) Shares premises with the police.

Post Office ([✆] 22430 61223; Hora) At the top of the Skala–Hora road.

Livadi Λειβάδι

Astypalea's most popular beach, Livadi Beach stands at the mouth of a lush valley in the first bay south from Hora. An easy 20-minute walk down from the old town, it's also served by local buses. In summer it's effectively transformed into a buzzing little resort, with a string of funky restaurants and bars lining the waterfront.

🛏 Sleeping & Eating

Villa Barbara　　　　　　　APARTMENT €
([✆] 22430 61448; www.villabarbara.gr; Livadia; s/d €40-45; 🅿) Set in flowering gardens, these mint-fresh white studios have tiled floors and balconies with sea views. The sea is less than a 100m away.

Fildisi Hotel　　　　　BOUTIQUE HOTEL €€
([✆] 22430 62060; www.fildisi.net; Livadi; studios from €140; 🅿🛜⛱) Split into terraces, this boutique dream has for its centrepiece an infinity pool accompanied by a juice bar and marvellous view of the sea. The breakfast/chill room is chic, while the 10 rooms, each named for a precious gem, enjoy private balconies, kitchenettes and sea views, as well as mini-bar, fridge, and flat-screen TVs with cable.

Mouras Studios　　　　　　APARTMENT €€
([✆] 22430 61127; www.mourastudios.gr; Livadi; studio/apt €75/85; 🗓 May–mid-Oct) Radiating off a beachfront courtyard, these seven stunning whitewashed studios vary in size, but all have stylish dark-wood furniture, kitchenettes and private balconies. Full-on sea views cost a few euros extra.

Astropelos　　　　　　　　　GREEK €€
([✆] 22430 61473; Livadi; mains €10-15; 🗓 8am-midnight; 🅿🛜🍴) First-class dining by the beach, on a decked verandah with chic white tables and a menu that includes octopus salad, breaded crab's pincers and lobster. French lounge tunes under the shade of tamarisk trees accompany the view of Hora on the hilltop horizon.

West of Skala

West of Skala, you swiftly hit the Astypalea outback – gnarled, bare rolling hills, perfect for a Cyclops. There's scarcely a sealed road to speak of, but it's just about possible to drive. Cross the western massif by heading directly inland from Hora and, from the point where the road finally peters out after 8km, where the **Kastro** ruins and **Moni Agiou Ioanni** stand proudly cheek by jowl above the shoreline, energetic walkers can hike down to **Agios Ioannis Beach**. Alternatively, follow the track that branches northwards shortly before road's end and you'll probably have **Panormos Beach** to yourself.

The rough track that winds along the southern coast west of Livadi, on the other hand, leads through mountainous meadows to several remote beaches. First along the way, reached on a brief detour, is the pretty, tree-shaded **Agios Konstantinos Beach** on the south side of Livadi Bay. This beach and **Kaminakia Beach** in the far west, where the track reaches its terminus, hold excellent seasonal tavernas. Book-ended by granite boulders, Kaminakia is Astypalea's best altar to sun worshipping, boasting water so clear you can see the pebbles through the turquoise.

🍴 Eating

Sti Linda　　　　　　　　　　GREEK €
([✆] 6932610050; Kaminakia Beach; mains €5-10; 🗓 Jul-Sep) 🚗 From the Stavros junction a rough track winds upwards to a shepherd's hut on the mountain spine and then an *extremely* rough track (take care) winds downwards to Kaminakia Beach, lapped by stunning turquoise water. Here there's a good seasonal restaurant, Sti Linda, which rustles up hearty fish soups, oven-baked goat and homemade bread. Make it a day trip.

East of Skala

The slender isthmus that links Astypalea's two 'wings' holds some of the island's most popular beaches. Each of the three bays at **Marmari**, just 2km northeast of Skala, has its own pebble-and-sand beach, right beside the road. **Steno Beach**, another 2km along, is sandy, shady and conveniently shallow for kids. The name means 'narrow', with the isthmus being a mere 100m wide near this spot.

The only resort area away from Skala, **Analipsi** is a pleasantly laid-back place that spreads through a fertile valley alongside the airport, 8km northeast of Skala. Also known as Maltezana, having once been the lair of Maltese pirates, it's grown recently thanks to long **Analipsi Beach** to the southeast, which offers sand, pebbles, shade and clean, shallow water. Nearby the remains of the Tallaras Roman baths still hold some mosaics.

Almost no one lives on Astypalea's eastern half. The only settlement is the remote hamlet of **Mesa Vathy**, tucked into the shelter of an enormous bottleneck bay and home to barely half a dozen families. A summer yacht harbour, it doesn't have a decent beach.

🛏 Sleeping & Eating

Camping Astypalea   CAMPGROUND €
(☑ 6973037710, 22430 61900; www.astypalaia camping.gr; Marmari; campsites per adult/tent €7/2; ⊙ Jun–early Sep; P 🔊) Shaded by tamarisk trees and shielded by bamboo groves, this summer-only campground is located next to Marmari beach, which unfortunately means it's also right beside the road, although there are hardly any cars. It has 24-hour hot water, safety deposit boxes, kitchen, barbecue, cafe and minimarket, and provides free transport from the port to the campground.

Hotel Maltezana Beach   APARTMENT €€
(☑ 22430 61558; www.maltezanabeach.gr; Analipsi; s/d incl breakfast €75/90; P ❄ 🔊 🏊) Ideal for families, this welcoming hotel stands amid manicured gardens a few metres from the beach. There are spacious rooms with balconies, set around a fine pool, plus good home cooking in the restaurant. Sea-view rooms are an extra €10.

Galini Cafe   CAFE €
(☑ 22430 61201; Mesa Vathy; mains €3-7; ⊙ Jun–Oct) At remote Mesa Vathy hamlet you can dine at the laid-back Galini Café, which offers meat and fish grills and the odd oven-baked special.

KALYMNOS ΚΑΛΥΜΝΟΣ

POP 16,000

Rugged Kalymnos is characterised by its dramatic mountains that draw hardy climbers from all over the world. Its west-

ern flank is particularly spectacular with skeletal crags towering above dazzling blue waters. The island is also greener than most of its neighbours, cradling fertile valleys dotted with beehives and bursting with oleander blooms. Add to this the enticing, car-free islet of Telendos, immediately offshore, and you will begin to see why the island is fast becoming a must-visit destination.

While its sponge-fishing heyday is long past, Kalymnos remains inextricably entwined with the sea, particularly in its capital and main ferry port, Pothia, where you'll still find stalls piled high with unearthly looking sponges, and a statue of Poseidon surveying the harbour. As Pothia is a working town, it's more restful to stay in the smaller west-coast settlements such as Emborios and Myrties, or over on Telendos.

❶ Getting There & Away

AIR

Kalymnos's airport, 6km northwest of Pothia, is served by daily Olympic Air (www.olympicair. com) flights to and from Athens (€140, one hour), Leros (€55, 15 minutes) and Kos (€55, 20 minutes). Connecting buses meet flights in summer.

BOAT

Kalymnos's main ferry port, Pothia, is linked by daily Dodekanisos Seaways (p498) catamarans with Kos, Rhodes, Leros, Patmos and other nearby islands. Blue Star Ferries (p498) connects Pothia with Piraeus, Kos and Rhodes three times weekly, and with Astypalea and Symi once or twice weekly.

Nisos Kalymnos (www.anekalymnou.gr) runs three to four times weekly to and from Leros, Lipsi, Patmos and the islets to the north, and also connects Kalymnos once weekly with Skala on Astypalea.

The Kalymnos Star and Kalymnos Dolphin (www.anekalymnou.gr) run several times daily between Pothia and Mastihari on the north shore of Kos, as does ANEM (www.anemferries.gr). Several excursion boats offer day trips from Kos Town to Pothia.

In addition, the little resort of Myrties on Kalymnos' west coast is connected three times weekly with Lipsi and Agia Marina on Leros by Anna Express (www.annaexpress.eu), and five times weekly with either Xirokambos (€10) or Pandeli (€15) on Leros by **Captain Yiannis** (☑ mobile 6944819073; Myrties Pier; €2; ⊙ 11am Tue & Thu; ♿).

Boat Services from Kalymnos

DESTINATION	DURATION	FARE (€)	FREQUENCY
Astypalea	2hr 40min	12	2 weekly
Kos	1hr 20min	6.50	3 daily
Kos*	35min	16	1-2 daily
Leros**	35min	10-15	18 weekly
Leros	1½hr	9	4 weekly
Leros*	45min	20	1-2 daily
Lipsi**	1¼hr	9	3 weekly
Lipsi*	1hr	20	1 daily
Patmos	4hr	12	4 weekly
Patmos*	1hr 40min	28	6 weekly
Piraeus	11hr	52	3 weekly
Rhodes	6hr	20.50	3 weekly
Rhodes*	3hr	39	1-2 daily
Samos*	3¾hr	39	5 weekly

Unless marked, services depart from Pothia.
* high-speed service
** departs from Myrties

❶ Getting Around

BOAT

In summer, excursion boats run from Pothia to destinations including Kefalas Cave (€20), where an impressive 103m corridor is filled with stalactites and stalagmites; and the island of Pserimos, with its big, sandy beach and tavernas. Frequent **water taxis** (☑ 22430 31316, mobile 6947082912; one way €2; ☺ 8am-midnight) also connect Myrties with Telendos Islet year-round.

BUS

Buses from Pothia harbour serve Myrties, Masouri and Armeos (€1.50, seven daily), Emporio (€2, two daily) and Vathys (€2, three daily). Check timetables at www.kalymnos-isl.gr.

CAR & MOTORCYCLE

Vehicle-hire companies along the harbour in Pothia include the friendly, good-value **Auto Market** (☑ 22430 24202, mobile 6927834628; www.kalymnoscars.gr; Harbour, Pothia), **Rent-a-Bike** (☑ mobile 6937980591; www.kalymnos rent.com; Harbour, Pothia) and **Suzuki Rentals** (☑ mobile 6937980591; Harbour, Pothia; scooter/car €8/20). Expect to pay €20 to €40 per day for a car, and €12 to €15 for a scooter.

TAXI

Shared taxis, based at Pothia's **taxi stand** (☑ 22430 50300; Plateia Kyprou), cost little more than buses. Private taxis cost around €10 to Myrties, €10 to the airport, €17 to Vathys and €30 to Emborios.

Pothia   Πόθια

POP 12,300

Kalymnos' capital, Pothia has a low-slung harbourfront of cream and white facades, and backs up the hill in a labyrinth of streets, beneath hulking mountains. If arriving by boat, this is most likely your first taste of the island. You may find some Kalymnians a little gruff, but don't be offended – these rugged islanders have been known throughout history for their toughness and terse manner. Pothia is not a resort, but there's an excellent museum and tourist office. Wander the quayside peppered with old mansions and seagod statues, past nut-brown fishermen and ex-divers in *kafeneia* and bars.

⊙ Sights & Activities

Archaeological Museum   MUSEUM

(☑ 22430 23113; €3; ☺ 8am-3pm Tue-Sun Jul & Aug, 8.30am-2.30pm Wed-Fri Sep-Jun) Kalymnos' modern Archaeological Museum is hard to find, hidden in the backstreets behind the right end of Pothia's waterfront. It's worth the effort to enjoy beautifully displayed ancient artefacts dating as far back as 5300 BC. There's some remarkable glassware and gold jewellery, but the highlight is an exquisite, larger-than-life bronze statue of a woman from the 2nd century BC. Swathed in a chiton (tunic), she was discovered underwater off Kalymnos in 1994.

Nautical & Folklore Museum   MUSEUM

(☑ 22430 51361; €3; ☺ 9am-5pm mid-Jun–mid-Sep) The two parts of the Nautical and Folklore Museum, on the central waterfront, are not always open simultaneously. The folklore section holds costumes and furniture, while the nautical museum focuses on sponge fishing, displaying mighty stone weights used by ancient divers and haunting photos of their 20th-century counterparts wearing early-model diving suits. Many suffered terrible injuries before the bends (decompression sickness) was understood.

Kalymnos Scuba Diving Club   DIVING

(☑ 6974646413, 22430 47253; www.kalymnos diving.com) One-day dives (€50) to wrecks, underwater volcanoes, reefs and caves. Owner Dimitris also runs boat trips explaining the history of sponge diving and can demonstrate the ancient art of *skandalopetra* (stone and rope freediving). Three-day PADI open-water certification €350.

Kalymnos

🛌 Sleeping

⭐ Villa Melina
BOUTIQUE HOTEL €

(☎ 22430 22682; www.villa-melina.com; d/tr incl breakfast €65/70; ❋ 🛜 ▦) Set in a colourful walled garden, this rose-pink 1930s villa exudes old-world charm, its wood-panelled rooms featuring stucco ceilings, lilac walls, mahogany armoires and huge beds. Don't expect luxury – it's all slightly faded – but owner Antonios and his cats provide a homey welcome, the bathrooms are spotless, the chandeliered library extensive, and the sparkling swimming pool irresistible.

Archontiko Hotel
PENSION €

(☎ 6942838524; www.apxontiko-hotel.com; s/d €35/50; ❋ 🛜) Overlooking the harbour, five minutes' walk from the ferry, this custard-coloured mansion is one of the most handsome in town. Under new management, its airy, white-walled rooms with balconies, have enjoyed a refurb. By night the place is decked in candles, the antique sepia photos of the Karafilis family (who originally lived here), magically animated. It's behind Magos Travel (p552).

Hotel Panorama
HOTEL €

(☎ 22430 23138; www.panorama-kalymnos.gr; Agios Nikolaos; s/d incl breakfast €35/50; ❋ 🛜) Named in honour of the breathtaking rooftop views from its hilltop eyrie, this friendly, family-run hotel offers 13 rooms with private balconies, contemporary furniture and a communal sun terrace where the basic breakfast is served. It's a stiff climb from the ferry dock – ask for free pick-up.

🍴 Eating

There are many eating options lining the quayside.

Stukas Taverna
GREEK €

(☎ 6970802346; mains €6-12; ⏱ lunch & dinner; 🛜) Tiny Stukas has linen-topped tables and a wharfside terrace, serving hearty fare. Three-course set menus cost €9 for vegetarians and €10 for fish- or meat-eaters. Towards the far end of the harbour, heading away from the ferry dock.

Barba Yiannis
GREEK €

(mains €8-12; ⊗ 9am-midnight) Smart, mercifully breezy and enjoying fine harbour views from its pretty decked terrace, Yiannis is a great spot to head for traditional Greek dishes such as *stifadho* and souvlakia, and offers a daily two-course lunch for €8. There's also swordfish, shrimp *saganaki* (shrimp in fried cheese), calamari and lobster.

Pantelis Restaurant
GREEK €€

(☑ 22430 51508; mains €7-14; ⊗ noon-midnight; ☎☑) Homey taverna, set slightly back off a corner of the harbour near the ferry dock, where island specialities include goat in red-wine sauce and homemade dolmadhes. Be sure to try the 'Ancient Greek' salad with apple and walnuts, and the fresh fish of the day. There's a good wine selection, too.

ℹ Information

Pothia's ferry dock is at the southern, left-hand end of the port. The entire quay is commercialised, but the real centre of activity is around the Italian-era municipal buildings in the middle, 600m from the ferry dock. Several banks close to the waterfront hereabouts offer ATMs. Stay alert; traffic can be hectic on the narrow, footpath-less roads behind the waterfront, so be careful of speeding scooters.

Magos Travel (☑ 22430 28777; www.magos tours.gr) The island's main travel agency, near the ferry dock, sells ferry and catamaran tickets and has a 24-hour ticket machine outside. It also offers round-island bus tours, and boat excursions in summer.

Main Post Office (Venizelou) A 10-minute walk inland, northwest of the centre.

Municipal Tourist Information (☑ 22430 29299; www.kalymnos-isl.gr; ⊗ 8am-3pm Mon-Fri) An excellent, well-organised source of info for buses and ferries, climbing and diving, festivals and general island practicalities. At the entrance to the ferry dock.

Police (☑ 22430 29301; Venizelou)

Port Police (☑ 22430 24444; 25 Martiou)

Western Kalymnos

The former capital of Kalymnos, **Horio**, stands atop the brow of the low ridge behind Pothia, around 4km up from the sea. A steep, stony and unshaded old stairway that's a little hard to find climbs up from its eastern edge to the pirate-proof village of Pera Kastro, which was inhabited until the 18th century. Beyond its forbidding walls and stern gateway, it now lies almost entirely in ruins and is overgrown with wildflowers, but amid the wreckage it's well worth seeking out nine tiny 15th-century churches that still hold stunning frescoes.

A tree-lined road drops for 2km beyond Horio to reach the pretty village of Panormos. Two neighbouring beaches are within walking distance: Linaria and the more attractive cove of Kandouni, surrounded by mountains and holding a small sandy beach where cafes, bars and hotels overlook the water.

Directly facing Telendos Islet, across 800m of generally placid sea, **Myrties** and **Masouri** have attractive beaches, with the strand at **Masouri** being larger and sandier. Beyond the Telendos ferry quay in Myrties, the west-coast road is a one-way loop. To continue any further north, you have to double back and follow a largely empty stretch higher up the hillside. Only if you're heading south do you see the main commercial strip that connects the two resorts in a seamless row of restaurants, rental studios, bars, souvenir shops and minimarkets, one block up from sea level.

North of Masouri, the road becomes two-way once more and swiftly leads into **Armeos**, perched above the coast without a beach. Smarter and newer than its neighbours, it consists almost entirely of larger hotels and apartment complexes targeted at climbers.

North of Armeos, Kalymnos' west-coast road leaves civilisation behind. Its final stretch, skirting the deep inlet that cradles tiny **Arginonda**, is utterly magnificent, cut into the flanks of mighty cliffs and bordered with flowering oleander. It comes to an end 20km from Pothia at sleepy little **Emborios**, where sugar-white houses cluster around a long, narrow pebble beach.

◉ Sights & Activities

Kalymnos Adventure Center
OUTDOORS

(☑ 6984933327, 22480 48160; www.climbersnest. com; Masouri; ⊗ 9am-noon & 4-8pm Mar-Nov) This brilliant shop sells and rents climbing equipment, maps and guidebooks. Activities include: half-day beginners and leaders climbing courses (per person from €70),

CLIMBING, HIKING & DIVING IN PARADISE

Steep crags, stark cliffs and daredevil overhangs have turned Kalymnos into Greece's premier destination for rock climbers. It now boasts more than 80 designated climbing sites, holding almost 3000 marked routes. Most are located above the island's west-coast road, especially around and north of Armeos – white roadside markers identify the precise spots – though several of the finest ascend the flanks of **Telendos Islet** (p554), just across the water.

Climbing season runs from March to mid-November, with the busiest period from mid-September until the end of October. An annual climbing festival takes place during the first 10 days of October.

The man largely responsible for the boom is Aris Theodoropolous, who along with Katie Rousseau writes the astonishingly detailed and comprehensive *Kalymnos Rock Climbing Guidebook* and maintains the useful www.climbkalymnos.com website, which includes a climbers' forum. Head to Kalymnos Adventure Center for equipment and information.

Kalymnos is also increasingly popular with hikers. Established routes are detailed on the excellent 1:25,000 *Kalymnos* map published by Terrain Maps (www.terrainmaps.gr). Serious hikers may want to undertake all or part of the highly demanding, multiday **Kalymnos Trail**, a 100km route that circles the island and also goes around Telendos for good measure. Carl Dawson published a useful guide to that and other island trails in 2015; see www.thekalymnostrail.co.uk.

Kalymnos is also becoming known as a diving island. For the beginner looking to qualify as a PADI open-water diver, as well as for the seasoned diver, there are plenty of hidden treasures in Poseidon's realm awaiting your inspection, including wreck dives, sea caves and diving with dolphins. There are four main outfits:

Kalymnos Diving (✉ 6942062215; www.scubakalymnos.com; Agios Nikolaos; ⊙ 8am-7pm)

Kalymnos Scuba Diving Club (p550)

Diver's Island (✉ 22430 48287; www.diversisland-kalymnos.gr; Kalydna Hotel, Panormos; 🖭)

Diver's Island Kalymnos Scuba Diving Club (p550)

caving (€40), hiking (€20) and horse riding (€30), plus yoga on the centre's roof three times per week (€10) and massage (€65) for 50 minutes. Run by friendly Brigitte, it's efficient and full of information.

🛏 Sleeping & Eating

Hotel Philoxenia
HOTEL €
(✉ 22430 59310; www.philoxenia-kalymnos.com; Armeos; s/d €40/50; 🅿 🕏 ⊠) Somewhat isolated up the road from the main climbers' haven of Masouri, this spacious modern hotel, below some enticing crags at Armeos, makes an ideal base for climbers. Each of its plain tile-floored rooms has its own sea-view balcony and there's a decent pool with snack bar.

Myrties Boutique Apartments
APARTMENT €€
(✉ 6986285888; www.myrtiesboutiqueapartments.gr; Myrties; €106) Two delightful, dazzling rental studios, a couple of minutes' walk up from the beach, each with two rooms, sleeping up to five guests and equipped with kitchenette and broad sea-view patio. They're cleaned daily and linen includes robes and beach towels.

⭐Fatolitis Snack Bar
CAFE €
(✉ 22430 47615; Masouri; snacks €5; ⊙ 9am-late; 🛜) A favourite with the apres-climbing gang, this lively roadside cafe has a vine-shaded terrace and cosy interior spattered with rock posters. The menu is carb-focused – think waffles, omelettes and toasties. Opposite Kalymnos Adventure Center, it's also known as 'Climbers' Station'. Swap your stories over breakfast, lunch or an evening beer.

Smuggler's Restaurant
TAVERNA €
(✉ 22430 48508; Myrties; mains €9-12; ⊙ 8am-late; 🅿 🛜 🍽) This lovely seafront taverna, close to the jetty at the south end of Myrties, is built to resemble an old fishing boat. The perfect spot, then, to enjoy fresh tuna steaks, mussels, lobster or shrimps in garlic and other deep-sea treasures, all at very reasonable prices. Look out for the sign of the Kraken outside.

VATHYS & RINA   ΒΑΘΥΣ & ΡΙΝΑ

Follow the barren coast road northeast from Pothia, instead of heading straight over to the west coast, and, after winding for 13km along the cliffs, it enters a long, lush, east-facing valley that was historically the agricultural heartland of Kalymnos. Narrow roads here thread between citrus orchards, bordered by high stone walls known as *koumoula*.

The valley takes its name from the inland settlement of Vathys, but the attraction for visitors is the little harbour of Rina. From the sea, it's accessed by a slender twisting inlet that's more like a fjord than anything you'd expect to find on a Greek island. In summer, large excursion boats bring troupes of day trippers here from Kos for lunch, keeping a clutch of competitive quayside tavernas busy, but it's a lovely spot at quieter times. Easy walks lead to 1500-year-old chapels on the hillside to either side of the bay.

Inland, beyond Vathys, a windswept road switchbacks up and over the mountains to reach the island's northwest coast, providing a speedier way to reach Emborios from Pothia than the built-up route through Myrties and Masouri.

Telendos Islet
Νήσος Τέλενδος

The bewitching islet of Telendos looms from the Aegean just off the west coast of Kalymnos. Crowned by a mountainous ridge that soars 450m high, it's thought to have been set adrift from the rest of Kalymnos by an earthquake in AD 554. It now makes a wonderful, vehicle-free destination for a day trip or longer stay.

Daily life on Telendos focuses on the short line of tavernas, cafes and whitewashed guesthouses that stretches along the pretty waterfront to either side of the jetty. Head right to reach the ruins of the early Christian basilica of **Agios Vasilios** and a footpath that climbs to the similarly dilapidated basilica of **Palaiopanayia**. Head left, on the other hand, and you can either cross a slender ridge, rich in colourful oleander, to access windswept, fine-pebbled **Hohlakas Beach**, or explore the islet's low-lying southern promontory, which holds some tiny early-Christian tombs now inhabited by goats, and a gloriously tranquil little swimming cove.

The cliffs along the northern flanks of Telendos hold several hugely popular **rock-climbing routes**, which can be reached by walking for an hour or so along a rough, exposed footpath.

🛏 Sleeping & Eating

★ On The Rocks   PENSION €
(📞 6932978142, 22430 48260; www.otr.telendos.com; r incl breakfast €60; 🕸 @ 🕸) Behind its seafront garden restaurant, open bar and terrace strung with nautical knick-knacks, 200m right from the jetty, this welcoming complex is a haven for active climbers and indolent beach bunnies alike. The spacious studios have kitchenettes, private balconies, foot massage and washing machines. Airport transfers available.

Hotel Porto Potha   HOTEL €
(📞 6949028564, 22430 47321; portopotha@klm.forthnet.gr; d incl breakfast €52; 🕸 🕸 🕸) Telendos' only hotel is located a five-minute walk out of the village heading north – look out for the smart sugar-cube complex up on the hill. Rooms are airy and bright, and there's a large lobby where guests come to relax and watch TV over a drink. There are additonal separate apartments.

Zorba's   TAVERNA €
(📞 22430 48660; www.telendos.net; mains €8-12; 🕸 🕸) Traditional cafe, a short walk from the jetty, with great sea views. The owner fishes for the seafood himself – guests can go with him – bringing up squid, octopus, tuna and swordfish. It also has three small but pleasant pink-walled en-suite rooms (€30). Arguably the best food on the island.

Emborios   Εμπορειός

In sleepy little Emborios, sugar-white houses cluster around a long, narrow pebble beach. This is the best place to swim on the island, with its crystal-clear waters sheltered by the tiny island of Kalavros offshore, and the mountains on Telendos and above Armeos dominating the horizon. Daily buses connect Emborios with Pothia, and in summer excursion boats come here for the day from Myrties – they have no fixed schedule.

🛏 Sleeping & Eating

★ Harry's Paradise APARTMENT €
(📞 22430 40062; www.harrys-paradise.gr; Emborios; d/q €50/90; 🌐 🛜) ✈ A true island favourite, set in its own garden of Eden, bursting
with jasmine, roses, hibiscus and aromatic
herbs. Fantastic-value accommodation incorporates charming shabby-chic elements,
rocking chairs, kitchenettes and large balconies – if possible, opt for the garden-facing
studios rather than the separate sea-view
block – while the divine home-cooking gives
locally sourced, quintessentially Kalymnian
ingredients a modern twist.

★ To Kyma TAVERNA €
(📞 22430 40012; www.tokyma-kalymnos.gr; Emborios; mains €8; ⊙ breakfast, lunch & dinner)
Despite its humdrum laminated menu
board, this extremely friendly beach taverna
serves truly exceptional food, including a
delicious barley-bread salad, red mullet,
salted mackerel and swordfish souvlakia.
Its name, 'The Wave', refers to the swell
whipped up by late summer's *meltemi* dry
northerly wind.

LEROS ΛΕΡΟΣ

POP 8210

Leros is said to have been the original home
of Artemis the Huntress. There's certainly
something alluringly untamed and beautiful about the island, which is scattered with
stunning Orthodox churches, dazzling blue
coves and whitewashed villages. The capital, Platanos, with its stark windmills and
ancient fortress towering above, makes a
striking centrepiece, while down below, the
busy little harbour of Agia Marina pulses
with enterprise. Leros is less about chas-
ing activities and more about worshipping
Helios, seeking out your favourite beach and
allowing the magic of the place to slowly
unfold.

ℹ Getting There & Away

AIR

Leros airport (📞 22470 22777) is at the
northern end of the island about 6km from
Agia Marina. It's serviced by Olympic Air (www.
olympicair.com), which offers daily flights to
Athens (€80, one hour) and thrice-weekly flights
to Rhodes (€74, 1¾ hours), Kalymnos (€55, 15
minutes), Kos (€62, 55 minutes) and Astypalea
(€63, 25 minutes).

BOAT

High-speed catamarans operated by Dodekanisos Seaways (p498) call in at Leros between
two and four times daily as they ply their way
to and from Kos, Kalymnos, Patmos, Samos,
Rhodes and other nearby islands. Generally they
stop at Agia Marina on the island's east coast,
but when there's bad weather they may stop at
Lakki on the west coast, so always check the
relevant port when you buy tickets, and double-
check on the day you're due to depart and be
prepared for a last-minute taxi dash across the
island.

Blue Star Ferries (p498) makes late-night
stops at Lakki twice weekly, heading once
towards Rhodes via Kos and Kalymnos, and
once towards Piraeus via Patmos and Lipsi.

Patmos Star (📞 22470 32500; www.patmos-
star.gr) sails between Agia Marina and the
islands of Lipsi and Patmos with varying frequency, increasing to daily in peak season.

Nisos Kalymnos (www.anekalymnou.gr) connects Lakki with Kalymnos to the south, and
Lipsi, Patmos and assorted islets to the north,
three to four times weekly.

Anna Express (www.annaexpress.eu) connects
Agia Marina three times weekly with Lipsi and
with Myrties on the west coast of Kalymnos.

Boat Services from Leros

DESTINATION	DURATION	FARE (€)	FREQUENCY
Agathonisi *	1hr 50min	18	1 weekly
Kalymnos	2hr	9.50	4-5 weekly
Kalymnos *	50min	20	1-2 daily
Kos	3¼hr	9.50	1 weekly
Kos *	1hr	23	1 weekly
Lipsi	1hr	9	3-4 weekly
Lipsi*	20min	13	1 daily
Patmos	2hr	10	3-4 weekly
Patmos*	45min	20	1 daily
Piraeus	10hr	42	4 weekly
Rhodes	8hr	32.50	1 weekly
Rhodes*	3½hr	41	3 weekly
Samos*	2hr 50min	30.50	5 weekly

These Dodekanisos Seaways catamarans may
dock at either Agia Marina or Lakki. Other services depart from Lakki.

*high-speed services.

ℹ Getting Around

A **taxi** (📞 mobile 6974316421, mobile
6972014531) to Agia Marina from the airport will
cost around €20.

Green-and-beige-striped buses travel the length of Leros between three and six times daily (€4 flat fare), including calling at the airport. They'll usually stop anywhere if you flag them down.

Outlets in all resort areas rent cars, scooters and bikes; **Motoland** (☑ 22470 24584, 22470 24103; www.motoland.gr; at Panteli Beach Hotel; ⊙ 9am-7pm) in Alinda and Pandeli is recommended.

The *Agios Georgios* and *Barbarosa* excursion boats make assorted day trips in summer, around the island and north to islets such as Arki and Marathi, typically costing €25.

Platanos & Agia Marina
Πλάτανος & Αγια Μαρίνα
POP 3000

Arriving at the bijou port of Agia Marina, with its yawning cats, yellow fishing nets and cluster of taverna is a delight, the biscuit- and wine-coloured Italianate buildings are as if drawn from an artist's palette. And rising behind them are the white sugar-cube houses of Platanos. Stately mansions still pepper the slopes of Platanos (a 10-minute uphill walk) and the row of renovated windmills that marches up towards its imposing clifftop castle makes a magnificent spectacle.

Heading right from the ferry quay, following the shoreline, will take you to Krithoni and Alinda.

◉ Sights & Activities

Pandeli Castle
CASTLE
(☑ 22470 23211; €1; ⊙ 8.30am-12.30pm & 4-8pm; ⛵) A steep, stony stepped path zigzags up from Platanos to reach the hilltop ruins of Pandeli Castle. The castle's oldest, innermost sections date back 1000 years, but the outer ramparts were added by the Knights of St John during the 14th and 15th centuries. Few structures now survive, but the 360-degree views from the walls are breathtaking. You can also drive here, along an exposed road that winds up from Pandeli past the windmills where you'll find a cafe in summertime.

Archaeological Museum
MUSEUM
(☑ 22470 24775; Agia Marina; €3; ⊙ 9am-2.30pm Tue-Sun Jul-Sep; ⛵) A 19th-century building on the edge of Agia Marina, at the start of the climb up to Platanos, holds Leros' small Archaeological Museum. Well-chosen artefacts collected on and around the island trace its varied history and include ancient masks and Byzantine mosaics.

Agios Georgios
BOATING
(☑ 6945551731, 22470 23060; agiosgeorgiosnl54@gmail.com; cruise incl food & drink €20; ⊙ departs 11am) Captain Manolis and his boat leave from Agia Marina harbour, taking in the islands of Arki, Marathi, Arhangelos, Tiganakia, Lipsi and Aspronisia, allowing you to stop and swim in the best spots. Returns at 7pm.

Barbarosa
BOATING
(☑ 6978048715; www.leros.org/lerostourist/barbarosa-leros; incl food & drink €25; ⊙ departs 11am; ⛵) *Barabarosa* is a traditional caïque that motors out from Agia Marina harbour to the islands of Arki, Marathi, Arhangelos, Tiganakia, Lipsi and Aspronisia on day trips, allowing you to stop and swim in the best spots. Returns at 7pm.

⛱ Sleeping

There's no accommodation in Agia Marina, and very little in Platanos. The closest alternative options are in Pandeli to the south, and Krithoni and Alinda to the north.

Maison des Couleurs
BOUTIQUE HOTEL €€
(☑ 22470 23341; www.maisondescouleurs.com; Platanos; r incl breakfast €100-150; ⛵) Delightfully peaceful little hotel set in a nostalgic wine-coloured villa that holds five spacious, high-ceilinged, antique-furnished rooms. Breakfast – and dinner, on request – is served on an idyllic flower-filled terrace. Look for a steep flight of yellow steps just west of the bus stop and taxi rank in Platanos.

✗ Eating & Drinking

Smoked mackerel and thyme honey are specialities of Leros.

★ To Paradosiakon
BAKERY €
(Agia Marina; snacks €2-5; ⊙ 7am-11.30pm; ⛵) ⌀ This Italianate patisserie and ice-cream bar provides a sweet-toothed experience like no other. Owner Harris is an alchemist confectioner using his grandmother's old recipes to create cheese cake, chocolate gateau, baklava, strawberry tart, cookies, spinach pie and homemade made ice cream. Try the yoghurt cake with ice cream and mastiha (liqueur made from the resin of mastic trees).

★ Taverna Mylos
SEAFOOD €€
(☑ 22470 24894; www.mylosexperience.gr; Agia Marina; mains €12-18; ⊙ 1pm-late; ⛵) ⌀ Lapped by turquoise waves, beside an old

Leros

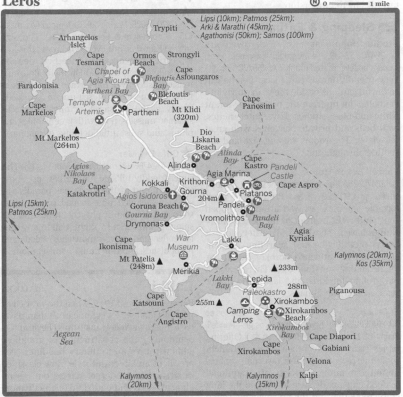

windmill at the far end of the pebbled beach that curves north from the ferry dock, Mylos infuses classic recipes with a modern twist. Go for the octopus carpaccio, the peppery basil squid, or the fabulous mixed-seafood spaghetti. The waterfront terrace is perfect for romantic sunset dinners.

Faros Bar BAR

(Agia Marina; ☉7pm-late; 🛜) Tumbledown haunt, partly hollowed into a cave beneath the lighthouse at the promontory beyond the ferry dock. With wall-mounted accordions and dim-lit ambience, it's great fun. Come evening, you can sit by the open windows and watch quicksilver fish swimming in the aquamarine water. Live music and DJs at weekends.

🛈 Information

For information on local history and facilities, visit www.leros.org.uk or www.lerosisland.com.

Kastis Travel (☑22470 22140) Useful agency, facing the quay in Agia Marina, which sells ferry tickets and organises boat trips to nearby beaches and islets.

Leros Active (☑22470 24590; www.leros active.com; Agia Marina) Agency and tour operator specialising in alternative tourism. It arranges activities including diving and hiking, as well as tours of wartime sites, and can provide information on accommodation.

Police (☑22470 22221) In Agia Marina.

Post Office Right of the quay in Agia Marina.

Pandeli Παντελή

The village of Pandeli, arrayed around a crescent bay 800m south of Platanos, is as peaceful as it is pretty. Overlooked by a clutch of hilltop windmills, its white houses tumble down the valley towards the sand-and-shingle beach and bobbing fishing boats in the harbour. There are some great tavernas by the water, too.

🛏 Sleeping & Eating

Studios Happiness
APARTMENT €

(📞22470 23498; www.studios-happiness-leros.com; Pandeli; d/studio/apt €45/55/70; 🅿️❄️📶) Very friendly family-run place, perched in colourful gardens beside the road down into Pandeli, 50m up from the beach. Its vibrant white-and-blue studios have kitchenettes, twin beds and private balconies with great sea views. The rooms vary in size and are spotless throughout.

Panteli Beach Hotel
APARTMENT €€

(📞22470 26400; www.panteli-beach.gr; Pandeli; studio/apt €90/120; 🅿️❄️📶) Pretty, very comfortable complex, arrayed around an open courtyard right in front of the beach. All 14 studios have fresh white walls, safety deposit boxes, nice duvets and sparkling kitchenettes, and the attached Sorokos beach bar offers all-day sun loungers. There's also a playground for kids, and lastly, the owner rents scooters and quads.

El Greco
SEAFOOD €€

(📞22470 25066; www.elgrecoleros.gr; Pandeli; mains €8-12; ⏱lunch & dinner; 🅿️📶) Offering tables right on the beach or on a thatch-roofed terrace, this stylish taverna prepares up-to-the-minute versions of traditional seafood cuisine. Be sure to sample the king crab croquettes and the lip-smacking salted mackerel served on buttered toast.

Apostolis
GREEK €€

(📞22470 25200, 6972821770; mains €8-12; ⏱9am-late; 🅿️📶) The cosy interior of turquoise tables matches the same colour of the waves lapping at the pebbled beach a few metres away. Eat outside on the terrace. Choose from spinach pie, calamari, mussels, octopus and a good selection of cheeses.

Vromolithos   Βρωμόλιθος

Accessible only by walking or driving over the headland immediately south of Pandeli – there's no coastal footpath – Vromolithos consists of a long, narrow beach caressed by waters of a perfect shade of Aegean blue, scattered with turquoise. Forget the ugly village, this is all about the water.

🍴 Eating & Drinking

⭐ Dimitris O Karaflas
GREEK €€

(📞22470 25626; Marcopoulo St, Vromolithos; mains €15; ⏱noon-4pm & 6pm-late; 🅿️📶) The sign says 'O Karaflas', but everyone knows this hilltop eyrie (enjoying one of the best views in the Dodecanese) as 'Bald Dimitri's'. Bouzouki music washes over the terrace, where diners feast on an array of sea-urchin spaghetti, hearty island sausages, octopus carpaccio, steamed mussels, pork with green apples and plums, and substantial helpings of calamari.

⭐ Cafe Del Mar
BAR

(📞22470 24766; Vromolithos; ⏱9am-late; 📶) This super-friendly hillside lounge bar just above the north end of the beach has paradisiacal sea views, chilled pine-shaded patios, white sofas and deckchairs, plus cool tunes and DJs spinning the decks by night. Call in any time for coffee and juice, sandwiches, salads and pasta dishes, and don't miss a sunset mojito.

Lakki   Λακκί

Between 1912 and 1948, when the west-coast port of Lakki was a significant Italian naval base, the town was transformed beyond recognition by the construction of grandiose administrative and military buildings. The prevalent architectural style, now classified as streamline moderne, started out resembling art deco and ended up distinctly more fascist. Lakki these days is ghostly quiet. Larger ferries and some catamarans dock at its jetty, a long walk from the centre of town, but there's no reason to linger.

⊙ Sights

War Museum
MUSEUM

(📞22470 22109; Merikia; €3; ⏱9.30am-1.30pm) Who remembers now that a major WWII battle was fought on this remote little island? After British troops forced the Italians to surrender in September 1943, a massive German air onslaught recaptured the island in the Battle of Leros. A network of tunnels dug by the Italians beneath the woods west of Lakki now serves as a museum, housing countless relics of the conflict. There's an explanatory video.

🍴 Eating

Petrino
GREEK €€

(Lakki; mains €10; ⏱7am-11pm; 🅿️📶) 🌿 Hands down the most succulent meat on the island is to be found at smart Petrino. Aside from delicious steaks there's octopus salad, stewed rabbit, and beef in lemon sauce. OK, so Lakki itself might be a little dull, but there's nothing ordinary about this place.

Xirokambos Ξηρόκαμπος

At the southern end of Leros, Xirokambos Bay holds a pebble-and-sand beach with some good spots for snorkelling. As well as a few village houses, it's home to a good beach taverna and is served by small excursion boats from Kalymnos. Up the hill, 1km inland towards Lakki, a signposted path climbs to the ruined **Paleokastro** fortress, which offers tremendous views.

🛏 Sleeping & Eating

Camping Leros   CAMPGROUND €
(☑ 6944238490, 22470 23372; www.campingleros. com; Xirokambos; campsites adult/tent €8/4; ⊙ Jun-Sep) Set 500m up from the beach, and 3km south of Lakki, the island's campground stands in a 400-year-old olive grove and holds a welcoming cafe that puts on evening barbecues. There are plenty of pitches shaded by said olive trees. It's also a centre for scuba diving, and owner Lefteris offer introductory dives, day dives (€60) and CMAS-certified week-long open-water courses (€500).

To Aloni   TAVERNA €
(☑ 22470 26048; Xirokambos; mains €9-15; ⊙ lunch & dinner; P ❋ 🛜 🛗) You can't miss this prominent taverna literally so close to the sea it adds a little salt seasoning to your octopus croquettes, shrimp *saganaki* (shrimp in fried cheese), swordfish, lobster, or liver in wine sauce; with tables al fresco and within its pleasant interior. Great desserts, too, if you have room.

Krithoni & Alinda
Κριθώνι & Αλιντα

POP 750

Starting just beyond the first headland north of Agia Marina, the twin resorts of Krithoni and Alinda sit next to each other on Alinda Bay, running parallel to the beach and bordered by *kafeneia* and restaurants. Leros' longest beach is at Alinda – although narrow, it's shaded and sandy with clean, shallow water. Set just back from the sea, a poignant war cemetery holds British casualties from the 1943 Battle of Leros.

For the best sun-worshipping in these parts, continue through Krithoni and Alinda to **Dio Liskaria Beach** (a few minutes' scooter ride). Bookended by rocks and with its own taverna, it's lapped by aquamarine waves.

⊙ Sights

Historic & Folklore Museum   MUSEUM
(☑ 22470 24775; Alinda; €3; ⊙ 9am-1pm & 6-8pm Tue-Sun; 🛗) Housed in an incongruous castellated villa on the seafront, this museum covers several aspects of local history. The upstairs rooms are given over largely to weapons, helmets and photos relating to WWII, while downstairs you'll find displays of traditional costumes and an emotive gallery devoted to artworks created by political prisoners incarcerated on the island during the colonels' dictatorship of the 1960s and 1970s.

🛏 Sleeping

★ To Archontiko Angelou   HOTEL €€
(☑ 6944908182, 22470 22749; www.hotel-angelou-leros.com; Alinda; r incl breakfast from €95; P ❋ 🛜) 🐾 Spilling with oleander and jacaranda, this incurably romantic, 19th-century rose-coloured villa, five minutes' walk from the beach, is like stepping into a vintage Italian film. Think wood floors, Viennese frescoes, antique beds and old-world-style rooms. Breakfast on the sun-dappled terrace is divine: a mouthwatering array of homemade bread, jams and marmalades. One of the finest hotels in the Dodecanese.

To Archontiko Angelou is Leros' first dairy-free vegan hotel.

Nefeli Hotel   APARTMENT €€
(☑ 22470 24611; www.nefelihotels.com; Krithonia; studio/apt incl breakfast from €90/110; P ❋ 🛜) Run by friendly Eva, Nefeli has beautiful sugar-white apartments with vividly coloured lavender and pink trim. These are beautifully finished spaces with stone floors, gleaming kitchens, moulded-stone couches and swallow-you-up beds. All have private balconies and there's a tempting cafe in the herb-fragrant courtyard. It's 10 minutes' walk beyond the northern edge of Agia Marina.

🍸 Drinking & Nightlife

Nemesis Cafe   BAR
(☑ 22470 22070; Krithoni; ⊙ 10am-late; 🛜) There's piping jazz and happy vibes at this well-stocked waterfront bar with a nautical theme. Perfect spot for a sundowner.

PATMOS ΠΑΤΜΟΣ

POP 3040

Patmos is known as the 'Holy Island' or, less appealingly, 'the island of the Apocalypse' after St John the Divine who, exiled some 2000 years ago, envisioned the end of the world in a cave and recorded this in the disturbing Book of Revelation: 'And I stood upon the sand of the sea, and saw a beast rise up out of the sea, having seven heads and 10 horns...'

In the Greek myths Patmos was referred to as 'Latmos', a sunken mountain which Artemis and Poseidon persuaded Zeus to resurface. You'll be glad they did, for this hourglass-shaped island has no sizeable towns, just the picturesque harbour community of Skala, and labyrinthine village of hillside Hora. Patmos still abounds in barely disturbed bays lined with sand and pebble beaches, lulled by limpid waters and overlooked by pine- and heather-coated hillsides. They say the island's strange energy either embraces or repels you; what will it do for you?

History

St John the Divine was banished to Patmos by the pagan Roman Emperor Domitian in AD 95. Living as a hermit in a cave above what's now Skala, St John heard the voice of God issuing from a cleft in the rock and transcribed his terrifying visions as the Book of Revelation. Around 1000 years later, in 1088, the Byzantine Emperor Alexis I Komninos gave the Blessed Christodoulos permission to erect a monastery in John's memory. Pirate raids necessitated powerful fortifications, so the monastery took the form of a mighty hilltop castle. In the centuries that followed, Patmos became a semi-autonomous monastic state and achieved such wealth and influence that it was able to resist Turkish oppression.

ⓘ Getting There & Away

All Patmos ferries dock in Skala. **Dodekanisos Seaways** (p498) catamarans connect Patmos with Lipsi, Leros, Kalymnos, Kos, Rhodes and other islands to the south, and also with Arki, Agathonisi, Ikaria, Fourni and Samos to the north.

Blue Star Ferries (p498) calls in twice each week, once heading south through the Dodecanese chain towards Rhodes, and once towards Piraeus.

The Nisos Kalymnos (www.anekalymnou. gr) connects Patmos with Kalymnos, Lipsi and Leros to the south, and the islets to the north, three to four times weekly.

The Patmos Star (p555) sails between Patmos and Lipsi and Leros, daily in peak season and less frequently otherwise.

Boat Services from Patmos (Skala)

DESTINATION	DURATION	FARE (€)	FREQUENCY
Agathonisi*	55min	16	1 weekly
Kalymnos	4hr	12.50	4 weekly
Kalymnos*	1hr 40min	30	6 daily
Kos*	3hr	31	1-2 daily
Leros	2hr	10	4-5 weekly
Leros*	40min	17	1-2 daily
Lipsi	50min	8	4 weekly
Lipsi*	25min	12	4 weekly
Piraeus	7hr	36	1 weekly
Rhodes	10hr	37.50	3 weekly
Rhodes*	5hr	49	5 weekly
Samos*	1hr	30	6 weekly
Symi*	4¼hr	46	1 daily

*high-speed services

ⓘ Getting Around

BOAT

Patmos Daily Cruises (p564) offers summer boat excursions to beaches around the island, including Psili Ammos, and also to nearby islets.

BUS

Buses (flat fare €2) connect Skala with Hora seven times daily, and with Grikos and Kambos four times daily, and more frequently in July and August.

CAR & MOTORCYCLE

The main seafront street in Skala holds several car- and motorcycle-hire outlets, including **T & G Automoto** (☑ 22470 33066; Skala) and **Avis** (☑ 22470 31900, 22470 33025; Skala; ☺ 9am-9pm). Demand often exceeds supply in high season, so book ahead if possible. The best scooter shop, **Moto Rent Faros** (☑ 22470 34400; www. patmos-motorentfaros.com; ☺ 8am-8.30pm), is behind the harbour on the road to Hora, and has quick, regularly serviced bikes.

TAXI

You can catch a **taxi** (☑ 22470 31225) from Skala's taxi rank, opposite the police station.

Skala   Σκάλα

POP 3000

Skala, Patmos' photogenic ferry port, is set on a huge bay on the eastern shore of the island. Apart from those moments when mighty cruise ships suddenly obliterate the entire harbour, it's a laid-back little place. There's even a tiny patch of sandy beach – albeit covered with restaurant tables – a few hundred metres from the dock.

Skala's waterfront is an unbroken string of tavernas, cafes and fading Italian buildings from the 1930s, while whitewashed houses, stylish clothing and jewellery boutiques, geletaria, and cafes fill the maze of backstreets stretching inland. The island is barely 700m wide at this point, so a 10-minute walk will take you all the way to stony, windswept **Hohlakas Beach** on its western side.

◉ Sights & Activities

Skala has a couple of religious sites, including the place where St John first baptised locals in AD 96, just north of the beach. To find out more and to see religious objects from across the island, visit the Orthodox Culture & Information Centre (p563) in the harbourside church.

If you feel like a workout, climb to the remains of an ancient **acropolis** on the hillside to the west of town. The route is not well signposted – head for the prominent chapel then follow the dirt trail across the fields. The views from the top are stunning.

☰ Sleeping

Hotel and studio owners often meet boats at the port, but it's best to call ahead and arrange a pick-up to avoid the scrum. Outside of high season (August) expect dramatically reduced rates.

Kalderimi Apartments   BOUTIQUE HOTEL €€
(☑ 22470 33008, 6972008757; www.kalderimi.com; apt incl breakfast €120; ☺ late May–early Oct; ⊛ ��) This inland whitewashed place at the start of the footpath up to Hora is pure tranquillity, with a shaded courtyard overflowing with palms, bougainvillea and Moorish lanterns. The five spacious apartments have a traditional feel, featuring wooden beams and stone walls, plus sparkling kitchens.

Captain's House   HOTEL €€
(☑ 22470 31793; www.captains-house.gr; d/apt incl breakfast €70/80; ⊛ �� ⊛) Delightful wharfside digs, 100m walk left from the quay,

holding high-spec rooms and apartments with en-suite bathrooms and crisp white lines. Five have their own sea-facing balconies. There's also a lovely swimming pool out back with sun loungers, along with a great breakfast terrace. Perfect family option.

Blue Bay Hotel   HOTEL €€
(☑ 22470 31165; www.bluebaypatmos.gr; s/d/tr incl breakfast €70/90/120; ⊛ @ �) Small hotel perched above the road immediately south of Skala, 250m walk from the harbour beyond the first headland. Basic air-con rooms are redeemed by having great seaview balconies; it's an unbeatable spot to enjoy the breakfast buffet.

✖ Eating

Tzivaeri   SEAFOOD €
(☑ 22470 31170; mains €10; ☺ 5pm-late) Skala's best option for a romantic feast spreads over a balcony terrace at the north end of the harbour. With its walls covered in shells, sponges and black-and-white photos, and the air thick with bouzouki music, it makes a memorable stop for Cretan-style sardines, shrimp or octopus, though you can also get a burger or kebab. Live music on Fridays.

Pantelis   TAVERNA €
(☑ 22470 31230; mains €10; ☺ lunch & dinner) Long-standing taverna, with locals and visitors alike packed onto tables on the narrow pedestrian street that runs parallel to the port. If you're not feeling adventurous enough to try the smoky sea-urchin salad or the *fouskes* (sea figs – definitely an acquired taste), you can always get staples such as meatballs, *moussaka* (baked layers of eggplant or zucchini, minced meat and potatoes topped with cheese sauce), grilled lamb chops and calamari.

Chiliomodi   TAVERNA €
(☑ 22470 34080; Skala; mains €12; ☺ lunch & dinner) Hidden in a back alley not far from the waterfront, Chiliomodi has been keeping travellers happy for over two decades with mouthwatering sea bream, salted cod, succulent sausages and various mezedhes to name a few. The restaurant has its own fishing boat so the seafood couldn't be fresher.

AigaionEsti AigaionEsti   GREEK €€
(☑ 6942813044; mains €15; ☺ 11am-12pm; ⊛ �) Skala's newest restaurant has wide-screen sea views, a smart interior of exposed stone and white walls, plus a menu featuring baby goat stew, wild boar, and squid with chilli

Patmos

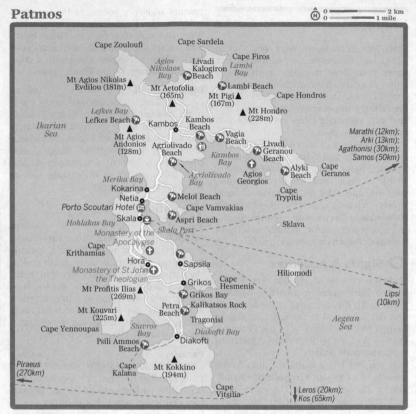

and coriander. There's a wood-fired oven for pizzas and you can also eat al fresco beside the water. To reach it, walk through the glass gauntlet of giant lobsters skulking in tanks.

Drinking & Nightlife

★ Koukoumavla Bar   CAFE

(☎ 22470 31321; ☉ 10am-late Tue-Sun; ☎) Imagine the love child of Tim Burton and Frida Kahlo opening a coffee house and you're getting close – interesting art spattered across green and orange walls, cool tunes, cocktails and excellent coffee. The 'owl' also sells crafts, books and toys and has a little garden terrace as well as tables on the alleyway, just back from the sea.

★ Art Café   BAR

(☎ 22470 33092; ☉ 7pm-late; ☎) Escape the harbour hubbub by climbing to a fabulous panoramic roof terrace then blissing out over sunset cocktails (€7 to €9) amid plump pillows and white-cushioned benches. The friendly German owner also serves great homemade hummus and there's often live music in the indoor lounge below.

Arion   BAR

(☎ 22470 31595; ☉ 9am-late; ☎) Over 100 years old, this venerable, high-raftered, wood-panelled bar, at the heart of the waterfront, is a major local landmark and rendezvous point for locals. Travellers generally prefer to sit outside, watching the world and the waves go by as they hook up to the wi-fi. Snacks include toasties and crêpes.

Meltemi   CAFE

(☎ 22470 31839; ☉ 9am-late; ☎) Irresistible beach bar at the far end of the harbour that curves 500m north from the ferry dock. Sit on the sand savouring a cocktail as the sun sinks into the sea, or come earlier for breakfast, a midday sandwich, fruit salad or milkshake under the shade of a tamarisk tree.

ⓘ Information

All Patmos ferries dock in the heart of Skala. Taxis wait at the quay, and the bus terminal is close by, as are three ATM-equipped banks. From the roundabout straight ahead, a road climbs inland towards Hora. Skala stretches away to the right, with the road skirting a narrow beach and the yacht port as it heads north.

Both www.patmos-island.com and www. patmosweb.gr provide copious information. You can also pick up a free copy of the pocket-sized *Patmos Guide* in shops and hotels.

Apollon Travel (☑22470 31324; apollon travel@stratas.gr; ☉9.30am-2pm & 6.30-9pm) and **Astoria Travel** (☑22470 31205; www. astoriatravel.com) Best for ferry tickets, along with all practical aspects of visiting Patmos, including accommodation.

Health Centre (☑22473 60000; ☉8am-2pm) Located 2km along the road to Hora; you'll find it next to the Monastery of the Apocalypse.

Municipal Tourist Office (☑22470 31666; ☉Mon 9am-5pm, Tue-Sun 9am-9-pm Jun-Sep) Has useful tips on things to see and do on the island.

Orthodox Culture & Information Centre (☑22470 33316; ☉9am-1pm & 6-9pm Mon, Tue, Thu & Fri, 9am-1pm Sat & Sun) This quayside office provides details on the island's religious sites, including current opening hours.

Police (☑22470 31303) On the main waterfront.

Port Police (☑22470 31231) Behind the quay's passenger-transit building.

Hora Χώρα

POP 800

With gorgeous views of the island from its hilltop eyrie, enchanting Hora is more than just a whitewashed mountain settlement. As you wander its incense-scented warren of 17th-century houses, the Boschian forms of St John's demons scuttling behind in your imagination, it's easy to see why Hora draws people back again and again. Allegedly there are more monasteries per square metre in Hora than anywhere else in the world. Aside from the sanctity of the place there are some lovely fashion boutiques and a couple of interesting galleries and upscale bars.

◎ Sights

★**Monastery of the Apocalypse** MONASTERY
(Cave of the Apocalypse; ☑22470 31398; €2; ☉8am-1.30pm, also 4-6pm Tue, Thu & Sat) Nestled amid the pines halfway to Hora, the Monastery of the Apocalypse focuses on the cave where St John lived as a hermit and received his revelation. Pilgrims and less-than-devout cruise passengers alike stream into the chapel built over the recess, to see the rocky pillow where the saint rested his head, the handhold with which he'd haul himself up from his prayers and the stone slab that served as his writing desk.

★**Monastery of St John the Theologian** MONASTERY
(☑22470 31223; €4; ☉8am-1.30pm daily, also 4-6pm Tue, Thu & Sat) As this immense 11th-century monastery-fortress remains active, only a small portion is open to visitors. The entrance courtyard leads to a sumptuously frescoed chapel, fronted by marble columns taken from an ancient temple. Don't expect to attend a service; daily worship is at 3am! The museum of church treasures upstairs displays the original edict establishing the monastery, signed by the Byzantine emperor in 1088.

Holy Monastery of Zoödohos Pigi CONVENT
(☑22470 31991; ☉9am-1pm daily & 5-8pm Mon-Sat, 9am-1pm Sun) FREE The Orthodox convent known as the Holy Monastery of Zoödohos Pigi is tucked away in the back alleys of Hora. You can't go beyond its pretty little courtyard, where a small church holds remarkable 17th-century frescoes. One of the 40 resident nuns will cheerfully point out Jesus on Judgement Day dispatching assorted bishops and clerics down a river of fire that flows into the maw of the beast.

🛏 Sleeping & Eating

★**Archontariki** B&B €€€
(☑22470 29368; www.archontariki-patmos.gr; ste €200; ☉Easter-Oct; ❈🅿) Hidden in a little alley near the Zoodohos Pigi monastery, these heavenly suites in a 400-year-old home are equipped with every convenience, traditional furnishings and plenty of plush touches. Relaxing under the fruit trees in the cool, quiet garden courtyard, you'll never want to leave. Suites 'Wisdom' and 'Joy' are capacious, while 'Love' and 'Hope' are smaller, traditional split-level affairs.

★**Pantheon** GREEK €
(☑22470 31226; mains €7-12; ☉5pm-midnight; ❈🍴) Look for the octopus drying outside – hence its local moniker 'the octopus place' – this whitewashed belle with Aegean-blue chairs and soaring village views is pure

Greek fare at its best. Seafood and meatballs, homemade sweets and warm crinkly smiles from its gentle owners. Located at the start of the approach to the Monastery of St John the Theologian (p563).

Jimmy's Balcony
GREEK €

(🖉 22470 32115; mains €7-12; ⏱ 10am-11pm; 🛜🖉) Perched above the road, on the principal lane through the village to the monastery, the shaded terrace of this welcoming all-day cafe-restaurant commands regal views across Skala to the islands to the north. Drop in for a cooling drink, or to enjoy its delicious salads, breakfast, *mousakas* (baked layers of eggplant or zucchini, minced meat and potatoes topped with cheese sauce) and veggie dishes.

Vaggelis
TAVERNA €€

(🖉 22470 31967; Pl Agias Lesvias; mains €10-15; ⏱ lunch & dinner; ❄🛜) With chi-chi grey chairs and tables, Vaggelis sits in one of the most intimate squares in the world. Foamy cream octopus, seafood *mousakas* and impeccably prepared traditional dishes such as baked Patmos goat are a few of the delights on offer in this contemporary restaurant. Sit in the square, or for jaw-dropping views, under the carob tree in the garden out back.

🛍 Shopping

Andreas Kalatzis Gallery
ART

(🖉 6988024890; ⏱ 8am-3pm & 8pm-late) Byzantine icon artist and Che Guevara looka-like, Andreas Kalatzis lives and works in a 1740s traditional home just east of the St John monastery. There's a beguiling mix of abstract oils, sculpture and quirky photography on show in his gallery.

North of Skala

The most popular and readily accessible beach in northern Patmos is wide, sandy **Kambos Beach**, which lies 5km northeast of Skala, just downhill from the village of Kambos. Crowded with local families in summer, it's a perfect spot for kids, with safe swimming and plenty of water-based activities.

Remoter and, with luck, quieter beaches can be reached by driving a little further. Fork inland (left) immediately after Kambos Beach and you'll soon find yourself winding down green slopes to **Lambi Beach**, an impressive expanse of multicoloured pebbles on the north shore. Stick to the coast road

east of Kambos Beach, on the other hand, to reach **Vagia Beach**, a sheltered little cove that offers good snorkelling in the island's coldest though highest-visibility water, and beyond it the pebbled, tamarisk-shaded and stunningly turquoise-laced **Livadi Geranou Beach**, where a tiny whitewashed chapel beckons from the islet just offshore.

🏃 Activities

⭐ Patmos Daily Cruises
BOAT

(🖉 6977035231, 22470 31425; www.patmosdaily cruises.com; Skala; incl wine, water & watermelon €23; ⏱ departs 10.15am) Daily excursions to islands Makronisi, Aspronisa, Marathi and Arki. You can also charter the company's three boats. Moored opposite Apollon Travel.

Kambos Beach Watersports
WATER SPORTS

(🖉 6972123541; www.patmoswatersports.com; Kambos Beach; 🛶) This outfit can take you wakeboarding and waterskiing, set loose you on a pedalo or, for the less athletically inclined, simply rent you a sun lounger and leave you in peace. There are also kayaks available.

🛏 Sleeping & Eating

Stefanos Camping
CAMPGROUND €

(🖉 22470 31821, 6945067206; www.facebook. com/pg/Stefanos-Camping-Patmos; campsites per person/tent €7/2; ⏱ May-Sep; 🛜) Clean and very friendly with bamboo-shaded pitches and a stunning view of the beach metres away. There are bikes, a minimarket, and an excellent grill cafe all run by the family. Also has cosy studios which sleep four (€90).

Porto Scoutari Hotel
HOTEL €€

(🖉 22470 33123; www.portoscoutari.com; d incl breakfast €145-235; 🅿❄@🛜🏊) Focused around a lavish swimming pool and spa centre, this was the first luxe hotel on the island and in many ways is still the grandest. It surveys the Aegean from a rural spot 3km north of Skala. Enjoy palace-sized rooms with nautical frescoes, sofas, spotless bathrooms, private balconies and antique beds plus, above all, stunning sea views. Check for amazing low-season rates.

George's Place
CAFE €

(🖉 22470 31881; Kambos Beach; snacks €6-10; ⏱ breakfast, lunch & dinner; 🅿❄🛜🛶) 🌿 Super-chilled beach bar, accessed straight off the sand, with an enticingly shaded, sun-dappled terrace facing the peacock-blue bay. Easy tunes, wi-fi, toilets that can double as changing rooms, and a simple menu of salads, homemade pies, chocolate cake, milkshakes and pastries keep the customers happy.

Livadi Geranou Taverna
TAVERNA €

(☑ 22470 32046; Livadi Geranou Beach; mains €9-12; ⊙ 10am-late) With its flower-bedecked terrace perched on the heather-clad hillside at road's end, a few metres above the beach, this hugely popular taverna benefits from heavenly sea views. Feast on a seafood spread of whitebait and octopus, or opt for a simple platter of meatballs or souvlakia.

Leonidas
TAVERNA €

(Lambi; mains €10; P ❄ ☑) ♦ Sitting on the crest of the hill overlooking Lambi Beach, Leonidas has a flower-filled terrace with food to match the serene view. Dine on souvlakia, *stifadho*, calf's liver, as well as the catch of the day.

South of Skala

The southern half of Patmos is scattered with small, tree-filled valleys and picturesque beaches. The first settlement south of Skala is tiny, peaceful **Sapsila**. **Grikos**, 1km further along over the hill, has a long, sandy beach that holds a handful of tavernas and is dominated by a plush resort hotel. St John is believed to have baptised islanders here during the 1st century AD, at a spot now marked by the chapel of **Agios Ioannis Theologos**.

South again, **Petra Beach** is peaceful and has plenty of shade, while a spit leads out to the startling **Kalikatsos Rock**. Both a rough coastal track from the beach and a longer paved road from Hora continue as far as **Diakofti**, the island's southernmost community. From there, a demanding half-hour hiking trail scrambles over the rocky hillside to reach the fine, tree-shaded stretch of sand known as **Psili Ammos Beach**, which holds a seasonal taverna. It's bewitchingly pretty and utterly isolated; if you've got kids with you, it's safer for you to hire a boat from Skala to get here.

🛏 Sleeping & Eating

Mathios Studios
APARTMENT €€

(☑ 22470 32583; www.mathiosapartments.gr; Sapsila; studio/apt €70/80; ❄ @ ☎) Located 2.5km south of Skala in sleepy Sapsila, Mathios has five studios and two apartments fully equipped with kitchen, fridge,

bathroom and balcony, with lush views of the gas-blue bay below. The style is rustic-chic complemented by quirky driftwood sculptures scattered about the grounds, while the owners do their best to make you feel at home. Also available in winter.

★ Patmos Aktis Suites
DESIGN HOTEL €€€

(☑ 22470 32800; www.patmosaktis.gr/en; Grikos Bay; r from €390; P ❄ ☎ ☎) Sitting upon Grikos Beach, Patmos' newest design hotel leaps from a David Hockney painting with its sleek geometric aesthetic and cube-white suites. Expect rain showers and private terraces giving onto a swimming pool metres from your bed. There's a great restaurant serving up contemporary Greek food, plus facilities ranging from massage treatments in the sumptuous spa to gym and boutique.

Flisvos Restaurant
SEAFOOD €

(☑ 22470 31380; mains €8; ⊙ 9am-7pm) Simple family-run taverna a short walk from Petra Beach, with zesty Greek salads, super-fresh seafood, souvlakia, homemade pies and a peaceful setting to tie it all together. If you're lucky there may be some live bouzouki music in the evening.

Benetos
GREEK €€

(☑ 22470 33089; www.benetosrestaurant.com; Sapsila; mains €10-27; ⊙ 7.30pm-late Tue-Sun Jun-Sep; ☑) ♦ Dropping down to the sea from the coast road, a couple of kilometres south of Skala, this romantic boutique restaurant, and recently added tapas bar, is set on a working farm. The menu draws its inspiration from all over the Mediterranean; think stuffed zucchini blossoms with turmeric sauce, octopus confit with eggplant salad, and calamari with red pepper sauce.

LIPSI
ΛΕΙΨΟΙ

POP 700

Lipsi might be small, at just 8km in length, but what a powerful impact it has on the traveller, with its low-slung harbour bunched with crayon-yellow nets and the whitewashed, church-crowned village of Lipsi climbing the hill behind. If rugged hills, serene blue coves and deserted beaches are what you seek, you may have just found heaven. In the 'Odyssey', Lipsi was where the nymph Calypso waylaid Odysseus for several years. Abandon yourself to sun-worshipping and wandering the backstreets, and you may fare the same.

1. Symi (p524)
The island abounds with Italian-influenced architecture.

2. Olymbos (p519), Karpathos
A woman uses a communal oven to bake bread in Greece's most traditional village.

3. Mandraki (p534), Nisyros
Stroll through this peaceful, almost traffic-free town.

4. Rhodes Old Town (p498)
Explore this incredible medieval fortress town.

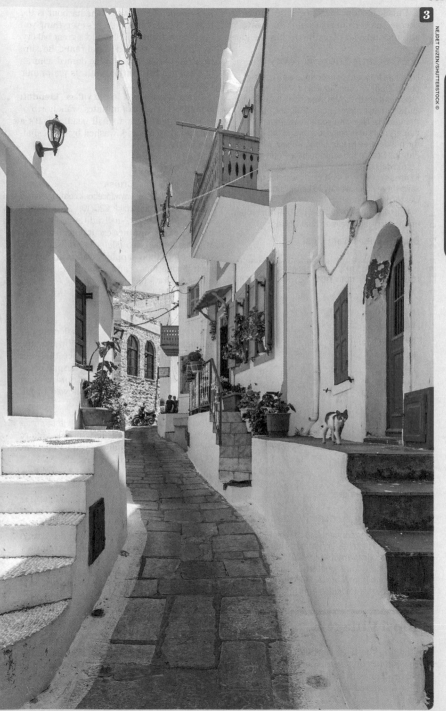

Check too the local speciality, *myzithra* cheese, made from goat's milk and seawater, and pick up a jar of distinctive thyme honey.

ℹ Getting There & Away

Lipsi has frequent connections with its neighbours. Dodekanisos Seaways (p498) catamarans head north to Arki, Agathonisi and Samos, and south to Patmos, Leros, Kos and other islands. The Nisos Kalymnos (www.anekalymnou.gr) runs to Patmos, Leros and the islets to the north three to four times weekly, while the Patmos Star (p555) sails to both Patmos and Leros, daily in summer. The Lipsi-based **Anna Express** (☑ 22479 41382; www.annaexpress.eu) sails three times weekly to Leros and Myrties on western Kalymnos.

A small **office** (☑ 22470 41290; ⊗ 8am-4pm) on the ferry jetty sells all boat tickets.

Boat Services from Lipsi

DESTINATION	DURATION	FARE (€)	FREQUENCY
Agathonisi	3hr	8	4 weekly
Agathonisi*	1hr 25min	13.50	1 weekly
Kalymnos	3hr	8	4 weekly
Kalymnos*	1½hr	22	1 daily
Kos*	4½hr	29	1 daily
Leros	50min	8.50	3 weekly
Leros*	20min	15	1 daily
Patmos	1hr	6	1 weekly
Patmos*	25min	13.50	1 daily
Piraeus	10hr	41	1 weekly
Rhodes*	5½hr	47	1 daily
Samos*	1½hr	32	1 daily except Tue

*high-speed services

ℹ Getting Around

Frequent buses connect Lipsi Village with the main island beaches in summer. There are also two **taxis** (☑ mobile 6942428223, mobile 6942409679). Hire scooters and bicycles in Lipsi Village from **Maria & Marcos** (☑ 22479 41358), next to Poseidon Apartments.

Lipsi Village   Λειψοί

POP 600

Hugging the deep harbour, Lipsi Village – the island's only settlement – is a cosy, intimate affair, with an atmospheric old town of blue-shuttered houses radiating up the hill

in a tangle of alleyways. The harbour is the hub of the action and there's everything you need here, from an ATM and a great bakery, to delectable seafood restaurants. Be sure to visit the beautiful blue-domed church of **Panagia tou Harou**, with its panoramic harbour-view terrace.

The closest beach to the village, **Liendou Beach** is a couple of minutes' walk north of the ferry port over a small headland. It's a narrow strip of sand, washed by calm, shallow water.

🏃 Activities

Rena Five Island Cruise   BOATING
(☑ 694733 9141; www.facebook.com/pg/Rena5IslandCruise; adult/child €25/10; 🖐) Sailing since 1980, *Rena,* a traditional wooden caïque, offers summer excursions from Lipsi's smaller jetty to islets Aspronisia, Makronisi (with their sapphire waters and weird rock formations), and Tiganakia, Marathi and Arki, for a picnic and swim.

✨ Festivals & Events

Panagia tou Harou   RELIGIOUS
Each year on 22 August, visitors flock to pay homage to a famous icon of the Virgin in the village church. They come to see the lilies inside its glass cabinet, which, despite being rootless and unwatered, burst miraculously into bloom. A procession is followed by all-night revelry in the lower square.

Wine Festival   FOOD & DRINK
(⊗ Aug) This Dionysian festival takes place for three days with dancing and free wine. Check locally for precise dates.

🛏 Sleeping

⭐ **Nefeli Hotel**   APARTMENT €€
(☑ 22470 41120; www.lipsinefelihotel.com; studio/apt incl breakfast €90/110; 🅿 ❄ 🛜) Stylish, welcoming boutique hotel in splendid isolation above lovely Kambos Beach, 10 minutes' walk north of the village. The apartments are spacious, with comfy beds, kitchenettes, sofa beds and private sea-view patios. Prepare to be lulled to sleep by the call of owls. There's also an opulent bar, lounge and dining area, bedecked in lavender and purples.

⭐ **Rizos Studios**   APARTMENT €€
(☑ 6976244125; www.facebook.com/rizosstudios; d €70; ❄ 🛜) Rizos' rooms have Aegean-blue and white, and biscuit and powder-blue colour themes, and are bursting with chi-chi

panache. Flagstone floors, shabby-chic furniture, fine views from private balconies and fully equipped kitchens. It's 10 minutes' walk up from the dock; call ahead to be picked up, and book ahead in high season as, unsurprisingly, it sells out quickly.

Angela Studios APARTMENT €€
(☑ 22470 41177, 6983666611; www.lipsiangela.eu; Waterfront; studio/apt €70/80; ❄ ☎) Angela has wrought-iron beds, sparkling kitchenettes, fridge and microwave, plus a dividing curtain to allow for privacy. Add to this balconies with sea views and a delicious little cafe and you need look no further. Close to the ferry dock.

✗ Eating

★ **Manolis Tastes** TAVERNA €
(☑ 22470 41065; www.manolistastes.com; mains €8-10; ⊙ noon-4pm & 5.30pm-late; ☎) ✐ In a handsome 19th-century neoclassical building (and former Italian Police station), Manolis Tastes has a roof terrace and upstairs lounge, and fine dining in a cream-and-wood interior. The real draw is Chef Manolis, his culinary flair recognised as far away as Athens. Mussels with ouzo, and pork with mustard and honey, are just a few of the splendid dishes served here.

Angela Cafe CAFE €
(☑ 6983666611; Harbour; snacks €4; ⊙ 8am-late; ❄ ☎) This new and decidedly chic little cafe with lavender and white trim has an intimate interior for snacks, coffee and cocktails, and a breezy sea-facing outside terrace.

Kairis Lipsi Bakery Shop BAKERY €
(☑ 22470 41050; sweets €1-3; ⊙ 24hr; ❄ ☎ ♿) ✐ This lively bakery-gelateria-cafe, beside the steps up to the village centre, is the social hub of the island and stays open all night. It's a veritable treasure trove of fresh-baked cookies, croissants, sausage rolls, pies, sandwiches, baklava, alcohol and some very fancy cakes, presided over by its charming and gregarious owner. Fight your way through the locals for a seat.

Cafe du Moulin CAFE €
(☑ 22470 41316; mains €9; ⊙ 8am-late; ❄ ☎) ✐ Tucked in the cool shadows of a little square by the church of Panagia tou Harou, this restaurant is run by a house-proud French, English and Italian speaking lady. It serves up great-value, tasty food: Lipsi goat with mustard, souvlakia, *saganaki* (fried cheese)

and octopus salad. You can also get breakfast here.

ⓘ Information

The main ferry jetty is at the northern, left-hand end of the port; there's an Alpha Bank with ATM nearby. Following the quay towards the village centre, up on the hill ahead, you'll pass the smaller excursion-boat jetty, while the Anna Express docks immediately below the church. The post office is up in the old town.

Lipsi Bookings (☑ 22470 41130; www.lipsibookings.com; ⊙ 9am-1pm & 3pm-7pm) Very helpful agency alongside Poseidon Studios by the port, selling tickets for all ferries and organising activities including camping, hiking, horse riding, sailing, snorkelling and visits to a winery and eco-farm.

Police (☑ 22470 41222) At the port.

Port Police (☑ 22470 41133) At the port.

Tourist Office (⊙ 10am-3pm Jul-Sep)

Around Lipsi

Lipsi is remarkably green for a Greek island. Walking to its further-flung beaches leads you through countryside dotted with olive groves, cypress trees and endless views. A minibus also services the main beaches.

Just 1km north of Lipsi Village, around the headland beyond Liendou Beach, **Kambos Beach** is narrower but sandier than its neighbour and somewhat shaded by tamarisk trees. The water is also deeper and rockier underfoot.

Fork inland at Kambos and a delightful 2.5km hike over the low-lying spine of the island will lead you to the shallow and child-friendly **Platys Gialos Beach**. Ringing with goat bells and shelving gently into crystal-clear water, it's home to an excellent summer-only taverna. Be warned: it closes at 6pm.

Just 2km south of Lipsi Village, sandy **Katsadia Beach** is wilder, especially if it's windy. There's a certain amount of shade and another good summer-only taverna, which stays open late as a bar.

The beaches at Lipsi's eastern end are harder to reach, with the roads being too rough for taxis or buses.

✗ Eating

Platis Gialos Restaurant TAVERNA €
(☑ 6944963303; Platys Gialos Beach; grills €10; ⊙ 8am-6pm Jul & Aug) Sitting on the island's best beach for swimming in unbelievable

turquoise water, this pleasant little taverna has decent grilled food and fresh salads.

Dilaila Cafe Restaurant
TAVERNA €

(☑ 22470 41041; Katasadia Beach; mains €9; ☺ Jun-Sep; P 🛜 🖊 🛖) 🍴 Tucked behind the beach at Katasadia, this inviting restaurant with colourful decor and split levels has intimate as well as communal areas to take in the stunning sea. Dishes include lentil salad with octopus, feta in honey, pork in mustard sauce, grilled tuna and many more. It costs €4 each way in a taxi from Lipsi Village.

ARKI & MARATHI
ΑΡΚΟΙ & ΜΑΡΑΘΙ

POP 55 (ARKI)

Only 5km north of Lipsi, tiny Arki has rolling hills and secluded, sandy beaches. Away from its only settlement – a little west-coast port also called Arki – the peace and stillness verges on the mystical.

The Church of Metamorfosis stands on a hill behind the settlement, while several sandy coves can be reached along a path skirting the north side of the bay.

Tiganakia Bay, on the southeast coast, has a good sandy beach. To walk there from Arki village, follow the road heading south and then the various goat tracks down to the water. Keep an eye out for dolphins.

Marathi, the largest of Arki's satellite islets, has a superb sandy beach. The old settlement, with an immaculate little church, stands on a hill above the harbour. While just three people remain on Marathi year-round, local families return each summer to reopen their seasonal tavernas.

🛏 Sleeping & Eating

Arki holds a handful of tavernas with comfortable, well-maintained rooms. Bookings are essential in July and August.

Taverna Nikolas
PENSION €

(☑ 22470 32477; Arki; d €50; ✳🛜) Simple central taverna, where the spacious, white-walled, twin-bedded rooms have sunset views. As well as whatever seafood the boats have brought in, the kitchen (mains €8 to €10) dishes up potatoes au gratin, stuffed peppers with cheese, and the local goat cheese called *sfina,* resembling a mild form of feta.

Pantelis Taverna
PENSION €

(☑ 22470 32609; www.marathi-island.gr; Marathi; d €50; ✳🛜) The closest Marathi comes to having a fully fledged beach resort, at the northern end of the sands. As well as spacious and attractively furnished rooms in a white-painted studio block, it also rents a larger maisonette. The taverna itself serves a fine menu of home-cooking (mains €8 to €12), from octopus croquettes to goat stew.

Taverna Mihalis
GREEK €

(☑ 22470 31580; Marathi; mains €8; 🛜) Set on the beach, Mihalis has a simple menu of mezedhes and seafood-oriented dishes depending what the day's catch might be. Calamari, octopus, decent salads and a nice atmosphere. Also has rooms (d €40).

ℹ Getting There & Away

Three ferry companies stop off at Arki, but not Marathi, as they sail up and down the island chain. All call at Patmos, Leros, Lipsi and Agathonisi. Weekly **Dodekanisos Seaways** (p498) catamarans run south as far as Kos and north to Samos. Anna Express (www.annaexpress.eu) also goes to Samos (two weekly), and Nisos Kalymnos (www.anekalymnou.gr) starts from Kalymnos (three to four weekly). For Marathi, a local caïque runs from Arki on Monday, Tuesday and Wednesday.

In summer, Lipsi-based excursion boats and Patmos-based caïques offer frequent day trips (€20) to Arki and Marathi.

Boat Services from Arki & Marathi

DESTINATION	DURATION	FARE (€)	FREQUENCY
Arki*	1¼hr	7	3 weekly
Kos	3hr	31	1 weekly
Lipsi	45min	13.50	6-7 weekly
Patmos	1hr	14	6-7 weekly

* Departs from Marathi. Services to other desinations depart from Arki.

AGATHONISI ΑΓΑΘΟΝΗΣΙ

POP 160

Arriving in Agathonisi's harbour – enclosed by a fjord-like formation and holding so few buildings you could count them in a breath – is pure magic. So far off the tourist radar its neighbours barely acknowledge it, Agathonisi is quiet enough to hear a distant Cyclops break wind. There's little to do here but read, swim and explore the caves where islanders once hid from pirates... and then do it again!

Keep an eye out too for the *klidonas* ritual of jumping through fire to cleanse your spirit.

❶ Getting There & Away

Three ferry companies connect Agathonisi with Patmos, Lipsi and points south. Both Dodekanisos Seaways (p498) catamarans (weekly) and Anna Express (www.annaexpress.eu, two weekly) continue north to Samos; Nisos Kalymnos (www.anekalymnou.gr) only goes as far north as Pythagoreios (three to four weekly). Buy your tickets 20 minutes before departure from **Savvas Kamitsis** (☑ 22470 29003), based by Mary's Rooms.

Boats dock at Agios Georgios, from where roads ascend right to Megalo Horio and left to Mikro Horio.

Boat Services from Agathonisi (Agios Georgios)

DESTINATION	DURATION	FARE (€)	FREQUENCY
Arki	45min	5	6-7 weekly
Kalymnos*	2hr	25	1 weekly
Kos*	3¼hr	29	1 weekly
Lipsi	1hr	8	4 weekly
Patmos	2hr	16	1 weekly
Samos	1hr	8	6-7 weekly

Agios Georgios
Αγιος Γεώργιος

The port village of Agios Georgios, the island's primary settlement, holds a few tavernas and simple sugar-cube pensions. The high point of a day is sitting on the harbour beach pondering the turquoise and watching the fishermen roll in with their catches. **Spilia Beach**, 900m southwest beyond the headland, along a track around the far side of the bay, is quieter and better for swimming. A further 1km walk will bring you to **Gaïdouravlakos**, a small bay and beach where water from one of the island's few springs meets the sea.

🛏 Sleeping & Eating

Mary's Rooms   PENSION €
(☑ 22470 29003; www.maryroomsagathonisi.com; Agios Georgios; s/d €30/40) Very simple but spic-and-span rooms in the middle of the waterfront, offering kitchenettes, fridges and tiny balconies with sea views. There's also a flower-filled courtyard.

Glaros Restaurant   TAVERNA €
(☑ 22470 29062; Agios Georgios; mains €9-12; ⊗ lunch & dinner; 🖥 ☑) Of the few harbourside tavernas, the bougainvillea-draped terrace of the 'Seagull' is probably the best place to dine. Owners Voula and Giannis are very engaging and serve *markakia* (feta fingers in vine leaves with a special sauce), along with standard oven-cooked meals, grills and fish dishes, all made from predominantly organic produce.

Megalo Horio
Μεγάλο Χωριό

The tiny hamlet of Megalo Horio is a steep and sweaty 1.5km trek uphill from the harbour, but the effort is rewarded by the stupendous views from the cliff. The village barely stirs until June, and the ideal times to come are for the festivals of **Agiou Panteleimonos** (26 July), **Sotiros** (6 August) and **Panagias** (22 August), when Megalo Horio celebrates with abundant food, music and dancing.

A series of accessible beaches lie within easy walking distance to the east: **Tsangari Beach**, **Tholos Beach**, **Poros Beach** – the only sandy option – and **Tholos (Agios Nikolaos) Beach**, close to the eponymous church.

🛏 Sleeping & Eating

Studios Ageliki   APARTMENT €
(☑ 22470 29085; Megalo Horio; s/d €35/45; ❄🖥) If you prefer an even quieter stay than at the port, these four basic but quite comfortable studios will serve you very well. All of them have stunning views over a small vineyard and down to the port, and come equipped with kitchenette, fridge and bathroom.

Restaurant Irini   GREEK €
(☑ 22470 29054; Megalo Horio; mains €7; ⊗ lunch & dinner; 🖥) Welcoming taverna on Megalo Horio's central square, renowned for its rich lamb stew and meaty *stifadho*.

Northeastern Aegean Islands

Best Places to Eat

➜ Marymary (p584)

➜ Thea's Restaurant & Rooms (p583)

➜ AAA Taverna (p594)

➜ Kechribari Ouzerie (p598)

➜ Spitalia (p605)

Best Places to Stay

➜ Rooms Dionysos (p581)

➜ Archipelagos Hotel (p586)

➜ Hotel Kyma (p614)

➜ Ino Village Hotel & Restaurant (p589)

➜ A for Art (p629)

Why Go?

The northeastern Aegean Islands (τα νησιά του Βορειοα-νατολικού Αιγαίου) are notable for their proximity to the Turkish mainland. Influences from Asia Minor abound in old-fashioned island cuisines, traditional village culture, dramatic celebrations and even the language.

Eccentric Ikaria is marked by jagged landscapes, pristine beaches and a famously long-lived, left-leaning population. Nearby Chios provides fertile ground for the planet's only gum-producing mastic trees. Other islands range from rambling Lesvos, producer of half the world's ouzo, to midsized islands such as semitropical Samos and workaday Limnos, and bright specks in the sea such as Inousses and Psara. Samothraki is home to the ancient Sanctuary of the Great Gods, while well-watered Thasos seems an extension of the mainland.

Lesvos, Chios and Samos offer easy connections to Turkey's coastal resorts and historic Hellenic sites.

When to Go
Vathy (Samos)

| Apr & May Wild red poppies adorn the backroads and Greek Easter livens up every village. | Jul & Aug Beach bars and village councils (in Ikaria's case) throw wild parties for holidaying revellers. | Oct & Nov Summer crowds evaporate, and hearty soups return to the tavernas. |

Northeastern Aegean Islands Highlights

1 Hristos Rahes (p582) Getting post-midnight coffee and spoon sweets in the nocturnal capital of Ikaria.

2 Psarotaverna O Miltos (p587) Enjoying sunset and the Aegean's best lobster spaghetti dish.

3 Potami Beach (p593) Finding a secret taverna above

the wooded waterfalls after lazing on a marble gravel beach.

4 Teriade Museum (p607) Discovering a treasure trove of top-notch art in Mytilini Town.

5 Blue Fox (p612) Watching yachts sailing through a turquoise bay while sipping *cezve* (Turkish) coffee in charming Molyvos.

6 Mastiha House (p602) Lodging in castle-like apartments in Pyrgi.

7 Sanctuary of the Great Gods (p626) Contemplating the cult of ancient gods who preceded the Olympians.

8 Mineral Baths of Eftalou (p611) Daydreaming in an ancient thermal pool on Lesvos.

1. Mineral Baths of Eftalou (p611), Lesvos

A serene location for those seeking tranquillity.

2. Teriade Museum (p607), Mytilini Town, Lesvos

A surprising collection of artworks by masters such as Picasso and Matisse.

3. Pyrgi (p602), Chios

Artists in this village use cement, volcanic sand, lime and bent forks to create intricate patterns.

4. Sanctuary of the Great Gods (p626), Samothraki

Top-secret ceremonies took place at this Thracian temple to the fertility deities..

IKARIA IKAPIA

If Greek islands were humans, then magical Ikaria would be the most charismatic, and weirdest. Its outlandish terrain, largely untamed by agriculture, comprises dramatic forested gorges, rocky moonscapes and hidden beaches with aquamarine waters. Ikaria's independent spirit and unique culture – characterised by dwellings pretending to be rocks – a nocturnal lifestyle and rave-like *panigyria* village festivals, grew over centuries out of isolated life under the constant threat of pirates and foreign invaders.

Supposedly named after Icarus, said to have crashed here after flying with wax wings too close to the sun, Ikaria is also honoured as the birthplace of Dionysos, god of wine. Ikarian villages famously throw wild parties with loads of food, wine and traditional dance. The island gets packed with Athenians and foreign visitors at the height of August's *panigyria*, but at all times you can enjoy Ikaria's serenity and the locals' sybaritic attitude to life, which results in extraordinary longevity.

ℹ Getting There & Away

AIR

Ikaria is served by **Olympic Air** (www.olympicair. com), **Aegean Airlines** (www.aegeanair.com) and

Astra Airlines (www.astra-airlines.gr). Tickets are available at agencies in Agios Kirykos and Evdilos, and at the **airport** (☑ 22750 32216; Faros).

BOAT

Get tickets in Agios Kirykos at Ikariada Travel (p578) or Dolihi Tours Travel Agency (p578). In Evdilos, try **Amfitriti Travel** (☑ 22750 32757, 6940430526; www.amfitrititravel. gr), or the Hellenic Seaways agent, **Roustas Travel** (☑ 22750 23441, 22750 32931), both on the waterfront. In addition to regular ferries, there are also weekly day-trip excursion boats between Agios Kirykos and Patmos (€32, 55 minutes, one to two per week), 20km south.

ℹ Getting Around

BOAT

In summer, a daily caïque (water taxi) goes from Agios Kirykos to Therma (€3). Another boat on Ikaria's south coast links Manganitis with the idyllic Seychelles Beach, 2.5km away, for swimming and sunbathing. Weekly day-trip excursion boats to Fourni depart from Agios Kirykos (€25).

BUS

A daily bus makes the winding route from Agios Kirykos to Hristos Rahes, via Evdilos and Armenistis. It also calls at the Ikaria airport on the way. A local bus makes the 10-minute trip to Therma every half-hour.

Ikaria & the Fourni Islands

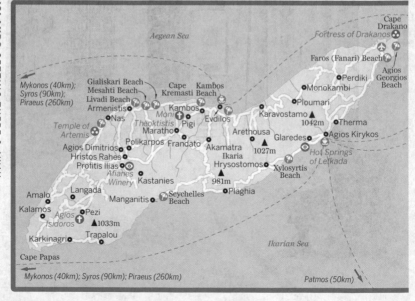

CAR & MOTORCYCLE

It's a good idea to hire a car or scooter for travel beyond the main towns. Hitchhiking is very common and considered safe by locals, but we don't recommend it.

For cars, try Dolihi Tours Travel Agency (p578) or Ikariada Travel (p578) in Agios Kirykos; **Mav Cars** (☑ 6932908944, 22750 31036; mav-cars@hol.gr; ☺ 9am-10pm) in Evdilos; and **Aventura** (☑ 22750 31140, 6972284054; aventura@otenet.gr; ☺ 9am-9pm) in Evdilos and Armenistis. Most car-hire offices can arrange for airport pick-up or drop-off, too, generally at no extra charge.

You can rent good motorbikes from **Pamfilis Bikes** (☑ 6979757539), up the steps from Alpha Bank in Agios Kirykos.

TAXI

A taxi between Agios Kirykos and Evdilos costs around €55.

Agios Kirykos
Αγιος Κήρυκος

POP 1880

Ikaria's capital is an easygoing and dependable Greek port, with clustered old streets, hotels and domatia (rooms in private homes), tasty restaurants and a lively waterfront cafe scene. Although beaches are nicer in Ikaria's north, the area's renowned hot radioactive

springs, scattered along the coast, attract aching bodies from around Europe. The main cluster is located 2km east at **Therma**, which also has a nice pebble beach.

★☆ Festivals & Events

Frikaria Music Festival   MUSIC

(☺ Jul & Aug) The hip Frikaria Music Festival attracts music freaks and free spirits alike to various locations. The three-day event, held in late July or early August, features Greek rock bands and DJ sets. Programs are available from cafes in Evdilos (try Rififi; p581) and Agios Kirykos.

Ikaria International Chess Tournament   SPORTS

(☑ 6977730286, 6947829772; www.ikaroschess.gr; ☺ Jul) This traditional annual event in Agios Kirykos, organised by local chess aficionado Kosmas Kefalos, draws chess players of all types from around Europe and beyond. The tournament celebrates its 40th anniversary in 2017 and retains a distinctly local flavour (one event features local children enacting chess moves at the square during a live grand-master match). This battle of wits takes place in mid-July, lasting about a week.

🛏 Sleeping

Pension Plumeria Flowery   PENSION €

(☑ 22750 22742, 6945139021; www.therma-ikaria.com; Therma; r incl breakfast €50) Big-hearted host Kiriaki runs these immaculate rooms – with names such as Bougainvillea, Anemone and Hyacinth – in the centre of Therma. In addition to being as helpful as one possibly can, she also makes great cakes for breakfast.

★ Hotel Akti   HOTEL €

(☑ 22750 23905; www.pensionakti.gr; s/d from €35/50; ❄ 🛜) A fine budget choice in a prime spot, Akti has cosy and attractive modern rooms with fridges, TVs, overhead fans and mosquito netting, plus friendly, English-speaking owners. A modern and locally popular cafe-bar overlooks the sea and port below. Follow the steps just right of Alpha Bank.

Agriolykos Pension   PENSION €

(☑ 22750 22433, 6944907023; www.agriolykos.gr; Therma; s/d/tr incl breakfast from €40/50/60; ❄ 🛜) This exceedingly charming lodging is the work of Mrs Voula Manolarou, who oversees every detail of the budget jewel. It sits on its own little perch, with stairs to the small bay that it overlooks.

DOMESTIC FLIGHTS FROM IKARIA

DESTINATION	DURATION	FARE (€)	FREQUENCY
Athens	35min	70-95	1-2 daily
Limnos	45min	44	6 weekly
Thessaloniki	1½hr	65-106	6 weekly

Hotel Maria-Elena   HOTEL €
(☑22750 22835; www.mariaelena.gr; s/d €40/50;
✳✹@🌐) Charming, welcoming and quiet,
the Maria-Elena enjoys a garden setting and
offers 21 simple and spotless rooms, all with
balconies overlooking the sea, plus a few
larger suites. It's open year-round, and lies
about 500m from the port, near the hospital.

✖ Eating

Filoti   TAVERNA €
(mains €5-7; ☺lunch & dinner) This tasty eatery
30m from the square, up the first alleyway,
offers Agios Kirykos' best-value meals, including tasty grills, salads and excellent pizza.

Stou Tsouris   TAVERNA €
(mains €7-10; ☺lunch & dinner) On the waterfront facing the square, this busy and traditional eatery serves tasty grills and several
very good *mayirefta* (ready-cooked meals)
and fresh fish (fairly priced by the kilo).
Open year-round.

Legouvisi Souvlakia   DELI €
(snacks €2.50-4; ☺lunch & dinner) A snappy
delicatessen next to the post office, serving
good snacks, coffee, beer and quick grills.

Taverna Klimataria   TAVERNA €
(mains €6-10; ☺lunch & dinner) An inviting
backstreet taverna, behind the National
Bank, with a lovely shaded courtyard. Strong
on grilled meats and *pastitsio* (layers of buttery macaroni and seasoned minced lamb)
with generous salads.

🍷 Drinking & Nightlife

Ambariza Bistro   CAFE
(☑22750 31721; Agios Kirykos) A convivial little
cafe-cum-bar with some tables in a romantic
bougainvillea-filled lane behind the National
Bank. In addition to coffee and alcohol, it
serves great desserts and breakfasts.

Kazino Cafe   CAFE
(☑22750 23290; Agios Kirykos; ☺8am-midnight)
One of several decent waterfront cafes, Kazino
occupies an 1850s-era building and serves coffee and fresh juices, made-to-order chocolate
milkshakes and fresh *tyropita* (cheese pie), all
managed by the philosophical Makis.

ℹ Information

Banks with ATMs are at the *plateia* (square).

Dolihi Tours Travel Agency (☑22750 23230;
dolichi@otenet.gr) Full-service agency, next to
Alpha Bank.

Hospital (☑22753 50201)

Ikariada Travel (☑22750 23322; www.ikari
ada.gr) Full-service waterfront travel agency
next to Diagonios souvlaki shop.

Island Ikaria (www.island-ikaria.com) is a
handy online guide.

Naftiliako Praktoreio (☑22750 22426)
Behind the waterfront, in the first alleyway, this
helpful hole-in-the-wall specialises in ferry tickets to Fourni and Patmos, and has local tips.

Police (☑22750 22222) Above Alpha Bank.

Port Police (☑22750 22207)

Post Office On the street above the *plateia*.

Around Agios Kirykos

Aching bodies and perfectly healthy pleasure seekers from all over Europe flock to hot
radioactive springs in the vicinity of Agios
Kirykos. Some of the springs discharge hot
water into the sea, providing for a unique
bathing experience. Most are located in
Therma, 2km from Agios Kirykos.

⊙ Sights & Activities

Fortress of Drakanos   FORTRESS
(☺8am-3pm Tue-Sat) FREE This 4th-century-
BC fortress sponsored religious rites dedicated to Eilythia, a fertility deity. A 13m-high
lookout tower anchors the site, which features informative signboards. A path from a
small chapel here leads to tiny Agios Georgios Beach.

Hot Springs of Lefkada   HOT SPRINGS
These hot sea-springs 2.5km southwest of
Agios Kirykos are therapeutic, relaxing and
free. Although it's a designated radioactive
saltwater spring, in truth it's just a beautiful
spot on the beach, identifiable by an irregular circle of rocks. You'll know you're in the
right spot when you feel the now-it's-hot,
now-it's-not intermingling of spring and
seawater.

To find the springs, drive 2km southwest and look for a small blue-and-white sign (marked 'Hot Springs' in English) next to a path leading to the rocky beach below. You'll want shoes or walking sandals for the 50m path down to the water.

★ Spilio Baths
HOT SPRINGS

(To Spilio; ☑ 22750 24048; Therma; €3.50-4.50; ☺ to dusk daily) Spilio means 'cave', but this steamy gem is an authentic thermal sauna and bath that draws on a hot underground spring. It's clean, natural and refreshing, and lures a younger clientele than its more-established thermal neighbours. Showers and lockers are included, but bring a towel. It's past the kiosk at the end of the waterfront, to the right as you face the sea.

Asklipios Bathhouse
HOT SPRINGS

(☑ 22750 50400; €3; ☺ 8am-1pm & 5-8pm Jun-Oct) Sample the effects of the area's radio-active saltwater springs at this simple beachfront bathhouse, named for the mythical Greek god of healing. The springs are famed for their beneficial effects on ailments such as arthritis and rheumatism. Hot water is piped in from a spring in the sea, and an average bath takes about 30 minutes.

Therma Hot Springs
HOT SPRINGS

(Apollon Spa; ☑ 22750 22665, 22750 24049; Therma; €4.50; ☺ 8-11am) The most traditional of Therma's hot springs is Apollon, the village's municipal spa, touted for the curative properties of its pure mineral waters.

🛏 Sleeping

★ Evon's Rooms
APARTMENT €

(☑ 6977139208, 22750 32580; www.evonsrooms. com; Faros; studios/ste from €45/120; P ❄ @ ☎) Less than 100m from Faros Beach, friendly Greek-Australian Evon Plakidas rents high-quality suites, some with spiral stairs, all with kitchenettes. The studios hold up to six people. An adjoining cafe serves breakfast, delicious crêpes, sweet *loukoumadhes* (ball-shaped doughnuts served with honey and cinnamon), fresh juices and salads.

Aleksandros Studios
GUESTHOUSE €

(☑ 22750 32030, 6986757316; www.ikariastudios. com; Manganitis; r €45) Should you decide to overnight in Manganitis, head to the naval-themed Aleksandros Studios. Brightly coloured rooms are equipped with kitchenettes, and the balcony on the 2nd floor looks like a ship's deck.

BOAT SERVICES FROM IKARIA

DESTINATION	PORT	DURATION	FARE (€)	FREQUENCY
Chios	Agios Kirykos	5½hr	15	2 weekly
Fourni	Agios Kirykos	1hr	7	3 weekly
Fourni*	Agios Kirykos	20min	14	2-3 weekly
Kalymnos	Agios Kirykos	2hr 50min	32	1 weekly
Kavala	Agios Kirykos	18hr	40	2 weekly
Lesvos (Mytilini Town)	Agios Kirykos	9½hr	23	2 weekly
Limnos	Agios Kirykos	14hr	32	2 weekly
Mykonos	Evdilos	3hr	20	4-5 weekly
Naxos	Agios Kirykos	2hr	20	1 daily
Patmos	Agios Kirykos	1½hr	13	3 weekly
Patmos*	Agios Kirykos	1hr	22	1 weekly
Piraeus	Agios Kirykos	9½hr	38	3 weekly
Piraeus	Evdilos	8½hr	38	3 weekly
Samos (Karlovasi)	Evdilos	1½hr	13	4 weekly
Samos (Pythagorio)*	Agios Kirykos	50min	25	2 weekly
Samos (Vathy)	Agios Kirykos	3hr	10	4 weekly

* hydrofoil service

✗ Eating & Drinking

O Karakas
TAVERNA €

(Karkinagri; mains €6-9; ⏱ lunch & dinner) On a bamboo-roofed seafront patio, this excellent family-run taverna serves up good fresh fish and salads. Try Ikaria's speciality *soufiko*, a tasty vegetable stew. Domatia are available, should you linger.

Sto Gialo
BAR

(☑ 22750 32636; www.stogialokaneifourtouna.gr; Manganitis) A popular seaside bar and music venue, famous for its full-moon parties.

Evdilos   Εύδηλος
POP 460

Ikaria's second port, Evdilos skirts a small semicircular bay and rises in tiers up a hillside. It features stately old houses on winding streets, and a relaxed and appealing waterfront. Evdilos is 41km northwest of Agios Kirykos, to which it's connected by Ikaria's two main roads. The memorable trip takes in high mountain ridges, striking sea views and slate-roof villages.

🛏 Sleeping

Kerame Studios
APARTMENT €

(☑ 22750 31434; www.keramehotel.gr; studio/apt/ ste from €35/45/60; ⓟ❄🛜🌊) These studio

apartments 1km before Evdilos feature kitchens and spacious decks with views. Prices are as variable as the quarters. A breakfast cafe is built into a windmill. Kerame is the sister establishment of Hotel Atheras near the port.

Hotel Atheras
HOTEL €

(☑ 22750 31434; www.atherashotel.gr; s/d/tr from €30/45/55; ⓟ❄🛜🌊) The friendly and modern Atheras has an almost Cycladic feel due to its bright-white decor contrasting with the blue Aegean beyond. There's an outdoor bar by the pool. The hotel is in the backstreets, 200m from the port.

✗ Eating & Drinking

RakoStroto
TAVERNA €

(☑ 22750 32266; mains €6-10; ⏱ dinner) Up on the hill, at the bend in the street that connects with the main road to Kambos, this newish taverna occupies a kind of natural balcony with bay views. Competently made grill and vegetable dishes are served, and musicians come for impromptu concerts in summer.

Giro Giro
GRILL €

(☑ 22750 32480; mains €2.50-7; ⏱ lunch & dinner) Serves a variety of meat – souvlaki, steaks, kebabs, sausages – to take away or to eat on the spot, from simple *gyros* (meat slithers cooked on a vertical rotisserie;

RELIGIOUS REVELRY ON THE ISLAND OF WINE

Pagan god Dionysos may no longer reign over Ikaria's vineyards, but his legacy lives on in Christianised form in the summertime *panigyria* (all-night festival celebrations held on saints' days across the island). There's no better way to dive head first into Greek island culture than drinking, dancing and feasting while honouring a village's patron saint. Bring your wallet, however: *panigyria* are important fundraisers for the local community. Use this fact to explain any overindulgence as well-intended philanthropy.

Panigyria occur across the island on the following dates:

Kambos 5 May

Armenistis 40 days after Orthodox Easter

Agios Isidoros (Pezi) 24 June

Agios Giannis (Hristos Rahes) 24 June

Platani 29 June

Karavostamo 1 July

Agios Kirykos & Ikarian Independence Day 17 July

Arethousa 17 July

Agios Panteleinonas (Fidos) 27 July

Hristos Rahes & Dafni 6 August

Akamatra 15 August

Evdilos 15–20 August

Agios Sofia & Monokambi 17 September

usually eaten with pitta bread) to large platters for two (€15).

Restaurant Koralli
TAVERNA €

(Plateia Evdilou; mains €7-9; ⊙ lunch & dinner) A local favourite among the waterfront tavernas, Koralli specialises in fresh fish and chips, excellent meat grills, veggie salads and oven-ready *mayirefta*.

Sta Perix
GREEK €€

(⌨ 22750 31056; Akamatra; mains €5-11; ⊙ lunch & dinner) Classy eatery in Akamatra, 6km south of Evdilos, that's well regarded for its traditional Ikarian recipes, a variety of local cheeses, and even its own wine.

★ Café-Bar Rififi
CAFE

(⌨ 22750 33060; Plateia Evdilou; ⊙ all day) This snappy port-side bar, with great pitta snacks, draught beer and good coffee, owes its name to the bank next door, with which it shares an interior wall. Rififi in Greek is a nickname for bank robber, and the servers are happy to point out where the serious money is stashed.

✱ Information

The waterfront has two ATMs.

Amfitriti Travel (⌨ 22750 32745; www.amfitriti-travel.gr) Helpful full-service travel office, 20m from the post office.

Medical Center (⌨ 22750 33030, 22750 32922) Around 2km east of Evdilos, with English-speaking doctor and staff.

Pharmacy (⌨ 22750 31394; Evdilos waterfront)

Police (⌨ 22750 31222)

Port Police (⌨ 22750 31007)

West of Evdilos

Kambos
Κάμπος

POP 250

Kambos, 3km west of Evdilos, was once mighty Oinoe (derived from the Greek word for wine), Ikaria's capital. Traces of this ancient glory remain, compliments of a ruined Byzantine palace, Ikaria's oldest church and a small museum. Kambos' other main attractions are its sand-and-pebble beach and scenic hill walks.

◎ Sights

Entering Kambos from Evdilos, you'll pass the modest ruins of a **Byzantine palace**, which served as a parliament and theatre during Hellenistic times. To find it, take the short path leading from Agia Irini Church.

Agia Irini Church
CHURCH

Built on the site of a 4th-century basilica, this 12th-century church contains some columns from the original. Alas, many of Agia Irini's frescoes remain covered with protective whitewash because funds for its removal are scarce.

Archaeological Museum
MUSEUM

(⌨ 22750 32935; ⊙ 8.30am-3pm Wed) FREE Kambos' small museum displays Neolithic tools, geometric vases, classical sculpture fragments, figurines and ivory trinkets. If it's closed, ask Vasilis Kambouris at Rooms Dionysos to open it.

🛏 Sleeping & Eating

★ Rooms Dionysos
PENSION €

(⌨ 22750 31688, 6944153437; www.ikaria-dionysosrooms.com; d/tr/q from €25/35/45; ℗ 🛜) The many happy guests who return every year attest to the magical atmosphere of this pension run by the charismatic Vasilis 'Dionysos' Kambouris, his Australian-born wife Demetra and Italian-speaking brother Yiannis. Rooms are simple, with private bathrooms, while the rooftop beds are a summer steal at €10. There's a communal kitchen, a book exchange and you'll get great tips on exploring Ikaria.

Balcony
PENSION €€

(⌨ 22750 31604; d/tr €60/70; ❄) There are fantastic views from the six apartments at family-run Balcony, which is a bit of a hike to reach. Classic wrought-iron furniture distinguishes the studios, each of which has a kitchen and a loft-sleeping area with twin mattresses.

★ Ikaros
GREEK €

(mains €3.50-7; ⊙ 11am-late) Ikaros is a classic village *ovelistirio,* or grill house, referring to the upright grill for making *gyros.* Excellent food, lively atmosphere, snappy service. Opposite the pharmacy.

THE WILD SOUTH

You can now drive on a fairly good paved coastal road all around the island, except for a 15km section between **Manganitis** and **Karkinagri**, located in Ikaria's southwestern corner. Both are serene end-of-the-universe places, with quaint fishing ports and a few tavernas, where hikers wind up after descending from the desolate moon-like plateau south of Hristos Rahes.

Connected by a paved road to Agios Kirykos and Evdilos, Manganitis draws crowds from elsewhere on the island every lunar month in summer when the popular Sto Gialo (p580) bar and restaurant holds its Fool Moon Party. Check out its website and advertisements around the island for other live and DJ music events. People also flock to the small and stunning Seychelles Beach, 3km east of Manganitis. Its marble pebbles, emerald water and giant rocks polished by the waves make you feel you've been teleported into the middle of the Indian Ocean – hence the name. Should you decide to sleep in Manganitis, head to naval-themed and well-equipped Aleksandros Studios (p579).

Karkinagri is now connected by a brand-new road that gives mind-blowing vistas up to the tourist clusters of Nas and Armenistis in Ikaria's northwest. Life in Karkinagri revolves around the bamboo-roofed seafront patio of taverna O Karakas (p580). It's the best place on the island to try the local speciality *soufiko,* a tasty vegetable stew.

East from Karkinagri, the dirt track in the direction of Manganitis is OK for a good car until Trapalou, which has a very nice beach. Beyond that, the road is pretty atrocious and often gets completely blocked by falling rocks. Check with locals about its current condition.

Pashalia
TAVERNA €

(mains €6-10; ⊙lunch & dinner) A family-run taverna with tradition, the Pashalia offers tasty homemade mezedhes (appetisers), such as wild mushrooms, fresh wild asparagus and goat's cheese, and is frequented by the locals.

Hristos Rahes   Χριστός Ραχών

At night the heart of Ikaria beats in the cool highlands above Armenistis, where a cluster of picturesque villages comes to life after dark, with children playing in the streets and adults drinking coffee or ouzo. These nocturnal habits hark back to the times when, fearing pirates based on nearby Fourni, Ikaria pretended to be an uninhabited island. An occasional roof covered with stone slabs is another vestige of that epoch, when people tried to camouflage their dwellings as piles of rocks. By day, Hristos Rahes is the departure point for many exciting hikes through Ikaria's highlands, covered in pine forest and fruit orchards.

◉ Sights

Afianes Winery
WINERY

(☑22750 40008, 6977893731; www.afianeswines.gr; ⊙noon-8pm Thu-Tue) **FREE** Call for directions to this excellent small family-run winery in the hills above Hristos Rahes. It has won several recent awards in Europe. In addition to the offered tastings and small

personal tours of the operation, an exhibition room features vintage winemaking equipment, gourd vessels and 19th-century wedding dresses.

🛏 Sleeping & Eating

Estia
GUESTHOUSE €€

(☑22750 41007, 6979835757; evgeniaporis@gmail.com; r from €65) Simply but tastefully decorated rooms, up the road from Hristos Rahes, with fully equipped kitchens, and balconies that face the sea and the cascade of Rahes villages descending to Armenistis.

★Taverna Platanos
TAVERNA €

(☑22750 42395; Agios Dimitrios; mains €5-9.50; ⊙lunch & dinner) Nestled under the shade of a rambling plane tree, a 500m stroll from Hristos Rahes, Platanos offers authentic Ikarian dishes, including *soufiko,* a summer favourite of stewed veggies, generally featuring whatever is picked fresh that morning. Great grills, hearty salads and local wine round out the table.

CousinA
GREEK €

(☑22750 41374; mains €6-11; ⊙lunch & dinner) A short walk from the main square, this tiny but outstanding eatery ventures well beyond the Ikarian mainstream, upgrading traditional Greek food to the level that would earn the acclaim of world food critics. Serves a superb aubergine salad with walnuts and *dakos* (Cretan rusks), an Ikarian version of bruschetta.

Armenistis   Αρμενιστής

Armenistis, 15km west of Evdilos, is Ikaria's humble version of a resort. It boasts two long, sandy beaches separated by a narrow headland; a fishing harbour; and a web of hilly streets to explore on foot. Cafes and tavernas line the beach. Moderate nightlife livens up Armenistis in summer with a mix of locals and Greek and foreign tourists.

◉ Sights

Nas Beach   BEACH
Westward 3.5km from Armenistis lies the pebbled beach of Nas, lying below the road and the few tavernas. A nudist-friendly beach, it has an impressive location at the mouth of a forested river, behind the trace ruins of an ancient **Temple of Artemis**, easily viewed from Taverna O Nas.

Livadi Beach   BEACH
Just 500m east of Armenistis is Livadi Beach, where currents are strong enough to warrant a lifeguard service and waves are sometimes big enough for surfing. Beyond Livadi are two other popular beaches, **Mesahti** and **Gialiskari**.

⌂ Sleeping

★ Pension Astaxi   PENSION €
(☑ 6982446227, 22750 71318; www.island-ikaria. com/hotels/PensionAstaxi.asp; d/tr incl breakfast from €35/50; P@🖥) This excellent and attractive budget gem is tucked back 30m from the main road, just above the Carte Postal cafe and Baido Taverna. The gracious owner, Maria, has created a relaxing and welcoming lodging, with a dozen brightly outfitted rooms with fans and balcony views to the sea.

Atsachas Rooms   HOTEL €
(☑ 22750 71226; www.atsachas.gr; Livadi Beach; d from €40; ❄🖥) Right on Livadi Beach, the Atsachas has clean, well-furnished rooms, some with fully equipped kitchens. Most have breezy sea-view balconies. The cafe spills onto a flowery garden, where a stairway descends to a nice stretch of beach.

Koimite   GUESTHOUSE €€
(☑ 22750 71545, 6974893877; www.ikariarooms. gr; d/q from €60/110; ❄🖥) Cascading down a rocky cliff, these pastel-coloured rooms come with balconies so huge you might be tempted to sell tickets to watch the spectacular sunset. Some rooms are equipped with kitchenettes; others have fridges; and there are kerosene heaters. Super-nice staff leave homemade cookies when they finish cleaning.

Villa Dimitri   APARTMENT €€
(☑ 22750 71310; www.villa-dimitri.eu; 2-person apt €50-70; ☉ Mar-Oct; ❄@🖥) This assortment of six secluded, balconied apartments, each one blue and white with wood and stone touches and set on a cliff amid colourful flowers, is managed by a welcoming Greek–German couple. It's 800m west of Armenistis and requires a minimum stay of one week.

✕ Eating

★ Thea's Restaurant & Rooms   TAVERNA €
(☑ 22750 71491, 6932154296; www.theasinn.com; Nas; mains €5-9; ☉ lunch & dinner) There are a few fine tavernas in Nas, but Thea's excels,

---

WORTH A TRIP

MOUNTAIN WALKS

With its solitude and rugged natural beauty, Ikaria is perfect for mountain walks. The most popular starting point is Hristos Rahes, where you will find a useful walking map, *The Round of Rahes on Foot* (€4), sold at most shops; proceeds go to maintaining the trails. For inexpensive guided treks all over the island, approach **Discover Ikaria** (☑ 6974042417, 6907547342; www.discoverikaria.com; Hristos Rahes).

Achievable as an independent walk, and not too hard on the bones, is the one-day circular walk along dirt roads from **Kambos**, south through **Dafni**, the remains of the 10th-century Byzantine **Castle of Koskinas** and picturesque **Frandato** and **Maratho** villages.

When you reach **Pigi**, look for the Frandato sign; continue past it for the unusual little Byzantine **Chapel of Theoskepasti**, tucked into overhanging granite. You must clamber up to reach it, and duck to get inside. The rows of old monks' skulls have been retired, but the chapel makes for an unusual visit, along with nearby **Moni Theoktistis**, with frescoes dating from 1686. The adjacent *kafeneio* (coffee house) is good for a coffee or juice with Maria, the kindly owner.

A VILLAGE BAKERY

In the village of Karavostomo, on Ikaria's north coast, everything you need to know about island values can probably be found at the village bakery, where Stephanos Kranas bakes long loaves of bread in his wood oven, along with crunchy *paximadia* (rusks) and sweet *koulouria* (fresh pretzel-style bread).

The bakery makes deliveries each morning by motorbike to village homes. But villagers can also drop by, grab a loaf from the wicker basket on the counter and, if no one's around, leave money in a counter cup. If the bakery appears to be closed, they may simply go upstairs and knock on the owner's door to enquire if there's any bread. The system has worked for years, one reason perhaps why Ikarians don't get too excited about fluctuations in the global price of oil. Olive oil, maybe.

serving up outstanding mezedhes, meat grills and a perfect veggie *mousakas* (baked layers of eggplant or zucchini, minced meat and potatoes topped with cheese sauce). Good barrel wine and local *tsipouro* firewater complete the deal. An outdoor patio overlooks the sea. Thea (aka Dorothy) also has five bright and cosy rooms (€35 including breakfast) above the restaurant.

★Taverna Baido TAVERNA €
(☑6982331539; mains €6-10) Past the bridge towards Nas, this interesting taverna is the work of Marianthi, who serves well-priced dishes using local products, fresh fish and Ikarian wine. Exceptional *soutzoukakia* (meat rissoles in tomato sauce) and *taramasalata* (a thick pink or white purée of fish roe, potato, oil and lemon juice).

Syntages tis Giagias DESSERTS €
(☑22750 71150; desserts €2-3; ☉lunch & dinner) Occupying a terrace on the 2nd floor of the main shopping compound in Armenistis, this small confectioners makes exemplary *galaktobourekia* (goat's-milk pudding), *kataïfi* (angel-hair pastry) and ice cream with local fruit flavours. Shelves are filled with jars containing spoon sweets (caramelised seasonal fruit and vegetables).

Kelaris Taverna SEAFOOD €
(☑22750 71227; Gialiskari; mains €6-11; ☉lunch & dinner) Kelaris serves its own fresh-caught

fish, cooked over coals, along with midday *mayirefta* dishes from the oven. Look for the landmark church on the point, 1.5km east of Armenistis.

★Marymary MEDITERRANEAN €€
(☑22750 71595; mains €8-12; ☉lunch & dinner) Marrying traditional island cuisine with cosmopolitan culinary fashion, this upmarket eatery in the heart of Armenistis has a small army of devoted regulars raving about its *mayierefta* dishes, such as rooster with *sioufitha* pasta or clay-pot stews. The seaview terrace is inviting for sundowners and a bottle or two of local Ikarian wine.

Drinking & Nightlife

Mythos BAR
(☉10am-late) Cosy, atmospheric bar managed by Dimitiros and Mariza, who deliver good drinks, fresh juices and live music in the summer. Walk down the street descending to the sea to find it.

Carte Postale BAR
(☑6981719567, 22750 71031; ☉10am-2am) This hip cafe-bar, 100m west of Armenistis' church, sits high over the bay. It has a mellow ambience, signalled by an eclectic music mix, from world beat to Greek fusion. Snacks range from small pizzas and salads to breakfast omelettes and evening risotto, all managed by the welcoming Myrto; her father makes the olives.

ⓘ Information

Aventura (☑22750 71117; aventura@otenet. gr) Full-service travel agency located by the patisserie just before the bridge. Offers car and motorbike rentals, and is one of the few places that hires out mountain bikes. Also does airport pick-ups and drop-offs.

Dolihi Tours & Lemy Rent-a-Car
(☑6983418878, 22750 71122; lemy@otenet. gr) Efficient travel agency next to the village market. Rents cars and organises walking tours and 4WD safaris.

East of Evdilos

Karavostamo   Καραβόσταμο

POP 550
Karavostamo is one of Ikaria's largest and most beautiful coastal villages, 6km east of Evdilos. From the main road, the village cascades down winding paths scattered with flowering gardens, village churches, veggie patches, chickens and goats, finally

reaching a cosy square and a small fishing harbour. Here you'll find nothing more than a bakery, a small general store, and a few domatia, tavernas and coffee houses where villagers congregate each evening to chat, argue, eat, play backgammon, drink and tell stories. To reach the square, take the signed road off the main road.

Sleeping & Eating

Despina Rooms   PENSION €
(21066 13999, 6977080808; www.rooms despina.gr; r €40-60; P✳❂) Well-appointed two-storey studios in the heart of the village, with kitchens and laundry facilities, about 200m from the sea and village square.

To Steki   MEZEDHES €
(meals €2-4; ⊙lunch & dinner) Join the regulars for good grills and salads, fresh chips, beer or *tsipouro* at this small and unpretentious *mezedhopoleio* (place serving mezedhes) on the square. Summer evenings find half the village at the outdoor tables.

★ Mandouvala   GREEK €€
(22750 61204; mains €7-12; ⊙lunch & dinner) Karavostamo's most upmarket eatery is at the end of the small waterfront, along a narrow cobbled lane 50m from the square. Excellent fish, grills, top wines and service add to the breezy seaside ambience.

FOURNI ISLANDS
ΟΙ ΦΟΥΡΝΟΙ
POP 1500

The Fourni archipelago is one of Greece's great unknown island gems. Its low-lying vegetation clings to gracefully rounded hills that overlap, forming intricate bays of sandy beaches and little ports. This former pirates' lair is especially beautiful at dusk, when the setting sun turns the terrain shades of pink, violet and black.

A clue to the area's swashbuckling past can be found in the name of the archipelago's capital, Fourni Korseon. The Corsairs were French privateers with a reputation for audacity, and their name became applied generically to all pirates and rogues then roaming the eastern Aegean.

Nowadays, Fourni Korseon offers most of the accommodation and services, plus several beaches. Other settlements include little Hrysomilia and Kamari to the north, plus another fishing hamlet on the islet of Thymena. In the south of the main island, the monastery of Agios Ioannis Prodromos stands serene over the far horizon.

❶ Getting There & Away
Fourni is connected to Ikaria (Agios Kirykos) and Samos by ferry and hydrofoil services. **Fourni Travel** (6975576584, 22750 51019; Fourni Korseon; ⊙10am-2pm & 6-9pm Mon-Sat, 11.30am-7pm Sun) provides information and sells tickets. **Dodecanese Seaways** (www.12ne. gr) provides faster and more expensive catamaran services.

❶ Getting Around
Gleaming new sealed roads, all 20km of them, connect Fourni Korseon with Hrysomilia and Kamari. Everyone seems to walk everywhere in Fourni, and then walk some more.

Rental cars are a recent addition to the Fourni transport scene. Hire a small car or scooter at **Escape Car & Bike Rental** (22750 51514; www.fourni-rentals.com; Fourni Korseon) on the waterfront.

Hitching is common and considered quite safe, and there's also the island's lone **taxi** (6970879102), commanded by the ebullient Georgos.

Alternatively, weekly caïques serve Hrysomilia, while another two to three go daily to Thymena.

◉ Sights & Activities
The island's rolling hills are ideal for **hiking**, and trails inevitably find a beach.

BOAT SERVICES FROM THE FOURNI ISLANDS

DESTINATION	DURATION	FARE (€)	FREQUENCY
Ikaria (Agios Kirykos)	1hr	7-14	4-5 weekly
Patmos	1½hr	13.50-25	4 weekly
Piraeus	8hr	35	3 weekly
Samos (Vathy)	2hr	13.50	2 weekly
Samos (Pythagorio)	1hr	20	3 weekly

ℹ TURKISH CONNECTIONS

Visiting Turkey's Aegean coastal resorts and historical sites from Samos, Chios and Lesvos is easy. Visas aren't usually necessary for day trips. While boat itineraries, prices and even companies change often, the following explains how things generally work.

From Samos, the Kuşadası Express leaves daily from either Vathy or Pythagorio for the 80-minute trip to Kuşadası (€40/60 one way/return), a coastal resort near ancient Ephesus (Efes). Daily excursions run from May through to October, with the option to also visit Ephesus. For tickets and information in Vathy, contact ITSA Travel, opposite the old ferry terminal, or adjoining By Ship Travel. In Pythagorio, contact By Ship Travel (p593) at the main junction entering town. Additionally, a Turkish boat connects from Karlovasi in northern Samos to Sığacık (one way/return €30/40, five weekly), which is between Kuşadası and the airport at İzmir. None of these ferries has space for cars.

From Chios, daily departures year-round connect Chios Town with Çeşme, a port near İzmir; services are most frequent in summer and some carry vehicles on board. Boats depart morning and evening for the 40-minute journey (€20/30 one way/return). Tour agencies on the seafront also sell package day trips to İzmir. Get information and tickets from Hatzelenis Tours (p599) or Sunrise Tours (p599).

From Lesvos, boats operated by Turkish company Turyol leave Mytilini Town for Ayvalık twice daily in summer and daily in winter (one way/return €15/25, 1½ hours). Thursday departures are especially popular for market day in Ayvalık. Vehicles are carried on board. Most Mytilini Town travel agencies sell Turkish tours; try Olive Groove Travel (p610), Mitilene Tours (p610) or Tsolos Travel (p610).

The nearest beach to Fourni Korseon, **Psili Ammos Beach**, waits 600m north on the coast road, with umbrellas and a beach bar that hums all night.

Along the coast road heading south, **Kampi Beach** is excellent, with its own beach bar and a small taverna. A further 2km along, **Elidaki Beach** has a gentle sandy bottom, followed by the small-pebbled **Petrokopio Beach**.

Near Fourni's southernmost tip, near the Monastery of Agios Ioannis Thermastis, the fine, sandy **Vlyhada Beach** lies before the more secluded **Kasidi Beach**.

Fourni's other main settlements, **Hrysomilia** and **Kamari**, are 17km and 10km from Fourni Korseon respectively (approximately a 30-minute drive on winding roads). Both are tranquil fishing settlements with beaches, but limited services. The trip from Fourni Korseon to these villages is spectacular, opening onto myriad views of sloping hills and hidden coves.

🛏 Sleeping

Most accommodation is in Fourni Korseon, though sleeping in the smaller settlements is possible, as is free beach camping.

★ Archipelagos Hotel   HOTEL €
(☑ 6973494967, 22750 51250; www.archipelagos hotel.gr; Fourni Korseon; s/d incl breakfast from €40/50; 🅿 ❄ 🛜) This elegant and welcoming small hotel on the harbour's northern edge comprises Fourni's most sophisticated lodgings. From the patio restaurant, set under stone arches bursting with geraniums and roses, to the well-appointed rooms and cafebar, the Archipelagos combines traditional architecture with modern luxuries.

Toula Studios   PENSION €
(☑ 22750 51332, 6976537948; info@fournitoula studio.gr; Fourni Korseon; s/d from €30/40; ❄ 🛜) Look for the Aegean-blue balconies at this friendly seafront standby near shops and tavernas. It has clean and simple selfcatering rooms, 10 of them with sea views, surrounding a large courtyard and with overhead fans.

Bilios Studios & Apartments   PENSION €€
(www.hotelbilios.com; Fourni Korseon; d/tr/q from €60/75/85) Brightly coloured and exquisitely furnished apartments on the hill overlooking the port and the bay, and similarly attractive rooms down on the seafront. All come with either kitchenettes or full kitchens. We guess this is what should be called a boutique domatia.

🍴 Eating

Fourni is famous for seafood, especially *astakomakaronadha* (fresh lobster with pasta).

★ Psarotaverna O Miltos SEAFOOD €

(☑ 22750 51407; Fourni Korseon; mains €7-10; ☺ lunch & dinner) Fourni lobster and fresh fish are expertly prepared at this iconic waterfront taverna. Excellent mezedhes and traditional salads, and fish and lobster are fairly priced by the kilo.

Psarotaverna Nikos SEAFOOD €

(Fourni Korseon; mains €7-10; ☺ lunch & dinner) This is a very reliable seafood option, next door to sibling restaurant O Miltos. Look for daily specials on the chalkboard.

🛍 Shopping

Melanthi Shop FOOD

(☑ 22750 51037; Fourni Korseon) An inviting shop on the main street selling nicely packaged fresh herbs (thyme, lavender, oregano and the unique *throubi*), along with honey, cheeses, oils, balms and salves, all from Fourni.

ℹ Information

Fourni Fishermen & Friends (www.fourni.com) The online guide to Fourni.

Health Centre (☑ 22750 51202)

Pharmacy (☑ 22750 51188)

Police (☑ 22750 51222)

Port Police (☑ 22750 51207)

SAMOS ΣΑΜΟΣ

POP 32,820

Lying just off the Turkish coast, Samos is one of the northeastern Aegean Islands' best-known destinations, yet beyond its low-key resorts and the lively capital, Vathy, there are numerous off-the-beaten-track beaches and quiet spots in the cool, forested inland mountains where traditional life continues.

Famous for its sweet local wine, Samos is also historically significant. It was the legendary birthplace of Hera, and the sprawling ruins of her ancient sanctuary, the Heraion, are impressive. Both the great mathematician Pythagoras and the hedonistic father of atomic theory, the 4th-century-BC philosopher Epicurus, were born here. Samos' scientific genius is also affirmed by the astonishing 524 BC Evpalinos Tunnel, a spectacular feat of ancient engineering that stretches for more than 1km deep underground.

ℹ Getting There & Away

AIR

Samos' airport is 4km west of Pythagorio. **Aegean Airlines** (www.aegeanair.com), **Astra Airlines** (www.astra-airlines.gr), **Olympic Air** (www.olympicair.com) and **Sky Express** (www.skyexpress.gr) all serve Samos and have offices at the airport. Charters serve Chios from Holland, Oslo and Vienna.

BOAT

Samos is home to three ports – Vathy (aka Samos), Pythagorio and Karlovasi.

ITSA Travel (☑ 22730 23605; www.itsatravel samos.gr; Themistokleous Sofouli 5; ☺ 8am-8pm), directly opposite Vathy's old ferry terminal, provides detailed information, offers free luggage storage and sells tickets, including to Turkey. The helpful staff will also pick you up at the new terminal for free. Tickets to Turkey are also available next door from **By Ship Travel** (☑ 22730 27337; www.byshiptravel.gr).

In Pythagorio, check ferry and hydrofoil schedules with the tourist office (p593), the port police (p593) or By Ship Travel (p593).

In Karlovasi, **By Ship Travel** (☑ 22730 35252; www.byshiptravel.gr) will help you with travel tickets.

ℹ Getting Around

TO/FROM THE AIRPORT

Buses run to/from the airport three to four times daily (€2). Taxis from the airport cost €25 to Vathy, or €6 to Pythagorio, from where there are local buses to Vathy.

DOMESTIC FLIGHTS FROM SAMOS

DESTINATION	DURATION	FARE (€)	FREQUENCY
Athens	45min	56	3 daily
Chios	35min	86	3 weekly
Lesvos	2hr	106	2 weekly
Limnos	2hr	86	2 weekly
Rhodes	45min	92	3 weekly
Thessaloniki	55min	55	1 daily

Samos

Siğacık (Turkey; 20km)
Fourni (30km);
Ikaria (40km)
Karlovasi
Potami Beach
Palio Karlovasi
Leka
Drakeï
Kosmadeï
Kondakeïka
Ydhrousa
Church of Profitis Ilias
Kastanea
Platanos
Kallithea
Cape Kanthario
Mt Kerkis (1434m)
Votsalakia (Kampos)
Psili Ammos Beach
Marathokampos
Ormos Marathokambou
Cape Agios Domenikos
Bay of Marathokambos
Aegean Sea
Kampos Beach
Pefkos
Skoureïka
Platanaki Beach
Chios (80km)
Agios Konstantinos
Stavrinides
Valiondates
Vourliotes
Manolates
Mt Ambelos (Karvouni; 1150m)
Avlakia
Avlakia Beach
Lemonaki & Tsamadou Beaches
Tsambou Beach
Kokkari
Moni Panagias Vrondianis
Pandhros os
Mavratzeï
Mytilinii
Pyrgos
Koumaradeï
Hora
Moni Megalis Panagias
Ireon
Pagondas
Ireon
Pappa Beach
Tigani Bay
Samiopoula
Cape Asprokavos

Boat

Daily excursion boats go from Pythagorio to Samiopoula islet (€20, including lunch).

Bus

From Vathy **bus station** (☑ 22730 27262; www.samospublicbusses.gr; Themistokleous Sofouli), frequent daily buses serve Kokkari (20 minutes), Pythagorio (25 minutes), Agios Konstantinos (40 minutes), Karlovasi (one hour), the Ireon (25 minutes), Mytilinii (20 minutes) and Portrokali (20 minutes). Tickets cost €1.50 to €4 depending on distance.

From Pythagorio, five daily buses reach the Ireon (15 minutes), while four serve Mytilinii (20 minutes) and Marathokampos (one hour). Buy tickets on the buses. Services are reduced on weekends. Tickets cost €1.50 to €7 depending on distance.

Car & Motorcycle

In Vathy, **Pegasus Rent-a-Car** (☑ 6978536440, 22730 24470; www.samos-car-rental.com; Themistokleous Sofouli 5) has good rates on car, 4WD and motorcycle hire. In Pythagorio, try **John's Rentals** (☑ 6972338103, 22730 61405; www.johns-rent-a-car.gr; Lykourgou Logotheti) on the main road near the waterfront.

Taxi

The **taxi rank** (☑ 22730 28404) in Vathy is by the National Bank of Greece. To the airport, the fare is €25, to Pythagorio €10.

In Pythagorio the **taxi rank** (☑ 22730 61450) is by the waterfront at the bottom of Lykourgou Logotheti.

Vathy (Samos) Βαθύ (Σάμος)

POP 2030

The island's capital, Vathy (also called Samos) enjoys a striking setting within the fold of a deep bay, where its curving waterfront is lined with bars, cafes and restaurants. The historic quarter of Ano Vathy, filled with steep, narrow streets and red-tiled 19th-century hillside houses, brims with atmosphere. The town centre boasts two engaging museums and a striking century-old church.

Vathy has two pebble beaches, the best being **Gagos Beach**, about 500m north from the old quay. Along the way you'll pass a string of cool bars clinging to the town's northeastern cliff.

◉ Sights

Museum of Samos Wines WINERY
(☑ 22730 87551; www.samoswine.gr; €2; ⊙ 8am-8pm Mon-Sat; ℗) FREE Look for this handsome stone building opposite the new ferry quay to find one of Samos' best vintners. Winery tours usually take place when you show up, and conveniently include a free

tasting, with several reasonably priced wines for sale.

Church of Agios Spyridonas
CHURCH

(Plateia Dimarheiou; ⊙8-11am & 6.30-7.30pm) Built in 1909, this ornate church features icons, impressive pillars hewn of marble from İzmir and, unusually, a silver candelabra from India. Decorative columns on the iconostasis are inspired by Ancient Greek and Byzantine motifs.

Archaeological Museum
MUSEUM

(☑22730 27469; Plateia Dimarheiou; adult/child €4/free, free 1st Sun of month Nov-Mar; ⊙8am-3pm Tue-Sun) One of the best museums in the islands, housed in two adjacent buildings, this handsome complex contains finds starting from the rule of Polycrates (6th century BC). The most famous item is the imposing *kouros* (male statue of the Archaic period), plucked from the Heraion (Sanctuary of Hera) near Pythagorio. At a height of 5.5m, it's the largest-known standing *kouros*. A shaded museum cafe awaits outside.

★Livadaki Beach
BEACH

🏊 Follow the north-coast road out of Vathy for 10km and look for a signposted dirt road to the left leading to Livadaki Beach. Here, tropical azure waters lap against soft sand in a long sheltered cove with facing islets. The water is warm and very shallow for a long way out, and Livadaki's mellow summer beach parties easily spill into it.

🛏 Sleeping

Pension Dreams
PENSION €

(☑6976425195, 22730 24350; Areos 9; d/tr €50/60; 🅿✳🛜) This small, quiet and central pension, 100m up from the waterfront, claims a hilltop view of the harbour. All seven rooms are bright and very well kept, some with large balconies and garden views, and all feature screened bath windows. The owner speaks English and French.

Cleomenis Hotel
HOTEL €

(☑22730 23232; Kallistratous 33; d incl breakfast from €50) Good-value rooms within walking distance of the beach and the port. Friendly owners make it a great place to stay.

★Ino Village Hotel & Restaurant
HOTEL €€

(☑22730 23241; www.inovillagehotel.com; Kalami; d incl breakfast €60-125; 🅿✳🛜⊠) With its courtyard pool flanked by ivy-clad, balconied white buildings, Ino Village, just 500m above Vathy, feels remote and elegant. While this mini-resort is sometimes booked by small tour groups, walk-in travellers can expect reasonable rates and a welcoming atmosphere. The hotel also boasts the popular **Elea restaurant** and cocktail bar, which serves fine Samian wines.

🍴 Eating

★Taverna Artemis
TAVERNA €

(Kefalopoulou 4; mains €5-9; ⊙noon-late) The Vathy Greek crowd relies on Artemis for fresh fish and well-prepared mezedhes and *mayirefta* dishes, though it is perhaps best known for *sardeles pandremenos*. In Greek, *pandremenos* means 'married', and the sardines are served open-faced, in pairs, like a couple. Open year-round; it's about 20m up from the port police at the northwest end of the port.

My Falasophy
MIDDLE EASTERN €

(☑22734 00835; Plateia Pythagorou; mains €2-5; ⊙noon-11pm) A guest from the Levant, this little fast-food joint in the main square serves large portions of artfully prepared hummus and falafel, as well as great salads. Healthy food is complemented by freshly squeezed tropical juices.

Vathy (Samos)

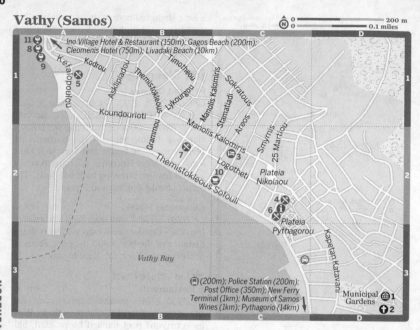

Ino Village Hotel & Restaurant (150m); Gagos Beach (200m); Cleomenis Hotel (750m); Livadaki Beach (10km)

Vathy Bay

(200m); Police Station (200m); Post Office (350m); New Ferry Terminal (1km); Museum of Samos Wines (1km); Pythagorio (14km)

Municipal Gardens

Telion　　　　　　　　　　　　　GREEK €
(☎ 22730 27526; mains €6-12; ⊙ lunch & dinner)
An outstanding grill house on the waterfront near the main square, with snappy service and a good choice of pork, chicken and lamb *gyros,* pitta souvlaki, plus dinner specials – deliveries included.

To Steki　　　　　　　　　　　TAVERNA €
(Aogotheti 61; mains €6.50-8; ⊙ lunch & dinner)
Unpretentious and welcoming back-alley eatery with generous grills, *gavros* (marinated small fish), salads and homemade soups.

🍷 Drinking & Nightlife

Of the plentiful waterfront cafes, the best for quality and service is **Joy** (☎ 22730 89770; ⊙ 8am-midnight).

Nightlife in Vathy is more Hellenic than in the island's tourist clusters, where the scene is dominated by northern European tourists. While most cafes and bars cling to the waterfront, the coolest ones, such as **Escape** (☎ 22730 28345; Kefalopoulou 9; ⊙ 10pm-6am), **Ble** (Kefalopoulou 7; ⊙ 11am-4am) and **Mezza Volta** (Kefalopoulou; ⊙ 9pm-dawn), hang over the water along Kefalopoulou 100m beyond the quay. Music and dancing is usually in full swing by midnight.

ℹ Information

Banks with ATMs line Plateia Pythagorou and the waterfront.

There is free wi-fi at Plateia Pythagorou and all along the waterfront.

Municipal Tourist Office (☎ 22730 28582; ⊙ Jun-Sep)

Police (☎ 22730 27404; Presveos Dim Nikolareïzi 2)

Port Police (☎ 22730 27890)

Post Office (Plateia Nikolaou; ⊙7.30am-2pm)
Samos General Hospital (☑22730 27407)
Efficient regional hospital for the surrounding
islands; opposite Pythagoras Hotel, north of
the port.

Pythagorio   Πυθαγόρειο

POP 1330

On the southeastern coast, opposite Turkey,
pretty Pythagorio has a yacht-lined harbour
and Samos' main archaeological finds. All
boats departing south from Samos leave
from Pythagorio, including day trips to
Samiopoula islet.

◉ Sights

Pythagorio Town Beach   BEACH
A short walk west of Pythagorio brings you
to a pristinely clean beach with umbrellas
and toilets. It's an easy stroll (less than 1km)
from town and there's decent swimming,
but pack your own food and drinks.

**Archaeological
Museum of Pythagorio**   MUSEUM
(☑22730 62811; Polykratous; €6; ⊙9am-3pm Tue-
Sun) This sparkling and renovated museum
contains well-displayed finds from Pythagorio and the 6th-century-BC Heraion, less
than 5km away, plus striking pottery pieces
spanning from the 9th century BC through

Greece's golden age. Museum labels are in
Greek, English and German.

Evpalinos Tunnel   ARCHAEOLOGICAL SITE
(☑22730 61400; adult/child €6/3; ⊙8am-3pm
Tue-Sun) In 524 BC, when Pythagorio (then
called Samos) was the island's capital and a
bustling metropolis of 80,000, the securing
of sources for drinking water became crucial. To solve the problem, ruler Polycrates
put his dictatorial whims to good use, ordering labourers to dig into a mountainside
according to the exacting plan of his ingenious engineer, Evpalinos. Many workers died
during the dangerous dig, but the result was
the 1034m-long Evpalinos Tunnel. In medieval times, locals used it to hide from pirates.

Moni Panagias Spilianis   MONASTERY
(Monastery of the Virgin of the Grotto; ☑22730
61361; ⊙9am-8pm) FREE About 1.5km northwest of Pythagorio, the road forks right, past
traces of an ancient theatre, before reaching
this grotto monastery. The walk meanders
up through old olive groves and, despite
tourist kiosks, it's a welcome respite from
the summer heat, and gives clear views to
the nearby Turkish coast.

Castle of Lykourgos Logothetis   CASTLE
(⊙9am-dusk Tue-Sun) Samians took the lead
locally in the 1821 War of Independence,
and this castle, built in 1824 by resistance
leader Logothetis, is the major relic of that

BOAT SERVICES FROM SAMOS

DESTINATION	PORT	DURATION	FARE (€)	FREQUENCY
Chios	V/K*	3-4hr	14	2-3 weekly
Fourni	Pythagorio	1hr	20	3 weekly
Fourni	Vathy	2½hr	13.50	4 weekly
Ikaria (Agios Kirykos)**	V/K*	2-3½hr	10-19	4 weekly
Ikaria (Evdilos)**	Karlovasi	4hr	13-23	6 weekly
Kavala	V/K*	15hr	53-60	2 weekly
Lesvos (Mytilini)	V/K*	6hr	29.50	2 weekly
Limnos	V/K*	12hr	30-47	2 weekly
Mykonos	Karlovasi	3½-5½hr	40-50	5 weekly
Naxos	Vathy	5hr	41-47	2 weekly
Patmos	Pythagorio	1hr	30	6 weekly
Piraeus	V/K*	12hr	38-57	1 daily
Rhodes	V/K*	6½hr	39	1 weekly

*Vathy or Karlovasi

**via Fourni

NORTHEASTERN AEGEAN ISLANDS SAMOS

turbulent time. It's situated on a hill at the southern end of Metamorfosis Sotiros, near the car park. The **city walls** once extended from here to the Evpalinos Tunnel.

🏃 Activities

Try scuba diving with **Samos Dive Center** (📞6972997645; www.samosdiving.com; Konstantinou Kanari 1). Professional instructors lead dives in search of moray eels, sea stars, octopuses, lobsters and other critters lurking in the sponge-covered crevices around Pythagorio. A two-dive half day for beginners costs around €50; a full-day dive, including open-water options, starts at around €85. Snorkelling (€20) is also offered.

🛏 Sleeping

★ Pension Despina   PENSION €
(📞22730 61677, 6938120399; www.samosrooms.gr/despina/more.html; A Nikolaou; r/studios €35/40; ❄️🌐) An impeccably well-kept and quiet pension on the small and central Plateia Irinis, the Despina offers attractive rooms and studios with overhead fans and balconies, some with kitchenettes, plus a relaxing back garden. Owner Athina is very friendly.

Polyxeni Hotel   HOTEL €
(📞22730 61590; www.polyxenihotel.com; s/d/tr incl breakfast from €40/55/70; ❄️🌐) In the middle of the port, turn inland away from the main road to find this well-managed seafront lodging with several balconied harbour-view rooms, fitted with overhead fans and double-glazed windows. Polyxeni also has a popular lobby cocktail bar, an adjacent gift shop and cheerful staff. Garden-view rooms are very quiet.

Philoxenia Pension   PENSION €
(📞22730 61055, 6973768371; www.pensionphiloxeniasamos.blogspot.com; r from €55; ❄️@🌐) Opposite the archaeological museum (p591), look

for the small courtyard bursting with flowers. Rooms are spotless and comfortable, with overhead fans and balcony views of the hills, and there's a common kitchen and laundry facilities. The owner's family lives in an adjacent apartment, so help is never far off.

🍴 Eating

★ Kafeneio To Mouragio   CAFE €
(📞2273062390; mezedhes €3-6; ⏰8am-midnight; 🛜) The warm ambience and predominantly Greek clientele hint at the fact that this place delivers the goods, with snacks such as chickpea croquettes and assorted mezedhes. Enjoy coffee in the morning and, later, iced ouzo, wine and beer. Customers are welcome to leave their luggage for free.

Faros   TAVERNA €
(📞22730 62464; mezedhes €4-7, mains €7-13; ⏰11am-midnight; 🛜) This eastern harbour eatery sits on the bay, beyond Elia Taverna. Faros is a minimalist, contemporary Mediterranean bistro serving huge bowls of salad and excellent versions of traditional Greek dishes, including Samos-style small fish fried with caramelised onions into a pie-like shape.

Genteki   MEDITERRANEAN €€
(📞6972220786; Despoti Kyrillou; mains €9-16; ⏰9am-11.30pm) In a quaint side street, this slightly upmarket place fuses taverna standards with other Mediterranean, notably Italian, fare. Smyrna-style *soutsoukakia* meatballs are outstanding and so are mushrooms *a la Greco*. Bread is served fresh from the oven.

To Tigani tis Platias   TAVERNA €€
(📞6971673770; Plateia Irinis; mains €7.50-17; 🖊️) Beautiful Greek standards, popular with both locals and visitors. It's especially great for veggie choices, such as baked feta, *gigantes* (white beans) and zucchini balls,

---

A MATTER OF MEASUREMENTS

While the obsession with the 'proper pint' may seem modern, the Ancient Greeks also fixated on measuring their alcohol. Pythagoras, a great Samian mathematician (and, presumably, drinker), created an invention that ensured party hosts and publicans could not be deceived by guests aspiring to inebriation. His creation was dubbed the *Dikiak-oupa tou Pythagora* (Just Cup of Pythagoras). This mysterious, multi-holed drinking vessel holds its contents perfectly, unless filled past the engraved line, at which point the glass drains completely from the bottom, punishing the glutton!

Today, faithful reproductions, made of colourful, glazed ceramic, are sold in Samos gift shops, and are tangible reminders of the Apollon Mean: 'Everything in moderation'.

all a cut above average. Meat grills here are also superb, and there's a shady setting, cheerful service and good wine. It's opposite Pension Despina.

Drinking & Nightlife

Katoi OUZERIE

(Lykourgou Logotheti) In the main street, this smallish modern place combines the virtues of a deli and an *ouzerie*. Ouzo and *tsipouro* are served with local cheeses and ham (€5 for the combo), which are also available for sale from the shop inside. Fresh juices are available, too.

Notos BAR

(☑ 22730 62351; Tarsanas Beach; ☺ noon-late; ☏) From the main road, turn right (south) at the port to find this popular late-night music bar and taverna, opposite a public car park. Live music most Tuesdays and Saturdays.

ⓘ Information

By Ship Travel (☑ 22730 80768; www. byshiptravel.gr) Helpful full-service travel agency, offering car hire, accommodation, air and ferry tickets. At the junction entering town.

Port Police (☑ 22730 61225)

Post Office (Lykourgou Logotheti; ☺ 7.30am-2pm)

Tourist Office (☑ 22730 61389; Lykourgou Logotheti; ☺ 8am-9.30pm, reduced hours winter)

Tourist Police (☑ 22730 61100; Lykourgou Logotheti)

Around Pythagorio

The coast road continues west from Vathy through flowery **Agios Konstantinos** before coming to workaday **Karlovasi**, Samos' third port, home to several hotels and tavernas. **Rhenia Tours** (☑ 22730 62280; Karlovasi) is good for ferry tickets and reliable information. The town's blue-collar history is on display at the the **Karlovasi Folk Art Museum** (☑ 22730 62286; Karlovasi; ☺ 9am-1pm Tue-Sun) FREE.

The old village, **Palio Karlovasi**, above the port is well worth the short drive up the hill. From the small car park, a 500m walk brings you to the chapel of **Agia Triada**, which has panoramic views.

Just 3km beyond Karlovasi lies the sand-and-pebble **Potami Beach**, blessed with good swimming and a reggae beach bar. It's complemented by nearby **forest waterfalls**;

ⓘ BUY ONE, GET THREE

If you want to visit the Archaeological Museum of Pythagorio (p591); the intriguing Evpalinos Tunnel (p591), just north of Pythagorio; and the Heraion, the outdoor temple honouring Hera (heart-throb of Zeus), just west of the airport, you can save by asking for a combination ticket (adult/child €13/7) for all three at any of the sites.

head west 50m from the beach and look for the signpost on the left. Entering the forest you'll first encounter the centuries-old **Metamorfosis Sotiros chapel**, where the devout light candles. Continuing about 1.5km through the wooded trail along the river brings you to a river channel, where it's necessary to wade or swim before enjoying a splash under the 2m-high waterfalls. Wooden stairs going up from the canyon will bring you to the excellent **Archontissa Potami Adventure Cafe** (www.facebook.com/pg/ArchontissaPotamiWaterfalls; Potami; mains €8-10).

◉ Sights

Heraion ARCHAEOLOGICAL SITE

(adult/child €6/3; ☺ 8.30am-3pm Tue-Sun) It's hard to imagine the former magnificence of this ancient sanctuary of the goddess Hera, 4km west of Pythagorio, from these scattered ruins. The 'Sacred Way', once flanked by thousands of marble statues, led from the city to this World Heritage–listed site, built at Hera's legendary birthplace. However, enough survives to provide a glimpse of a sanctuary that was four times larger than the Parthenon.

Built in the 6th century BC, the Heraion was constructed over an earlier Mycenaean temple. Plundering and earthquakes have left only one column standing, though extensive foundations remain. Other remains include a stoa, a 5th-century Christian basilica, and the headless, and unsettling, statues of a family, the Geneleos Group. Archaeologists continue to unearth treasures.

🛏 Sleeping

★Hotel Restaurant Cohyli HOTEL €

(☑ 22730 95282, 6977809389; www.hotel-cohyli.com; Ireon; s/d/tr incl breakfast from €35/45/55; P ❄ ☏) You'll sleep and eat well at this welcoming hotel-taverna gem. Rooms are cosy and clean, and equipped with fridges and fans. When you're hungry, just relocate to the shaded courtyard next door to sample excellent mezedhes, *saganaki* (fried cheese), fresh fish and breakfast with 'sunshine eggs'. There's a small beach across the road, and live acoustic music many summer evenings.

Kokkari & Mountain Villages

From Vathy, the coast road west passes a number of beaches and resorts. The first, **Kokkari** (Κοκκάρι), 10km from Vathy, was once a fishing village, but is now a rather crowded resort. Windsurfers test the waves from its long pebble beach in summer, and the nearby beaches of **Lemonaki**, **Tsamadou**, **Tsambou** and **Livadhaki** draw swimmers and sunbathers.

Continuing west, the landscape becomes more forested and mountainous. Take the left-hand turn-off after 5km for the lovely mountain village of **Vourliotes**. The village's multicoloured, shuttered houses cluster around a *plateia* (square). Walkers can enjoy an 8km loop trail between Vourliotes and Kokkari through olive groves and lofty woodlands – it's one of those magical *monopati* (footpath) routes where you hardly realise you've been climbing. Find the free walking map in Vourliotes.

Back on the coast road, look for the signposted turn-off for another fragrant village, **Manolates**, 5km further up the lower slopes of Mt Ambelos (Karvouni; 1150m). Set amid thick pine and deciduous forests, and boasting gorgeous traditional houses, Manolates is nearly encircled by mountains and offers a cooler alternative to the sweltering coast. The village is home to a fledgling artisan community, and has some excellent jewellery and souvenir shops.

Good tavernas are plentiful and, despite the more touristy patina of Manolates, both it and Vourliotes are worth visiting for a glimpse of old Samos.

🛏 Sleeping

Kerkis Bay Hotel   HOTEL €
(☑ 22730 37202; http://kerkisbayhotel.com; Ormos Marathokambou; d €30-50) It is a surprise to find such a serious multistorey establishment in such a quaint place, but here it is, complete with elevators and a popular waterfront taverna. The owner is an old-worldish gentleman and a former sea captain.

Pension Mary's House   PENSION €
(☑ 22730 93291; www.marys-house-samos.com; Vourliotes; d/tr €50/60; ❋ 🛜) Superb location in the village, with amazing balcony views, decent furnishings and a lovely garden and orchard setting. Follow the painted wooden signs 200m from the village square.

★ **Studios Angela**   APARTMENT €
(☑ 22730 62198; www.studiosangela.com; Manolates; d €30-40; ❋) A great budget choice, these five studios near the church in Manolates, built into a hillside overlooking the sea, are traditionally furnished, with modern kitchenettes and views to the sea. Owner Angela is hospitable.

🍴 Eating

★ **AAA Taverna**   TAVERNA €
(Tria Alpha; ☑ 22730 94472; Manolates; mains €7-17; ⊙ 9am-midnight) Sample homemade dishes, such as rabbit in wine sauce, sausages or grilled sardines, are served at this small, classy courtyard taverna in the heart of the village. The piped music is often avant-garde Greek jazz-folk.

★ **Hippy's Restaurant Café**   TAVERNA €
(☑ 6976770021, 22730 33796; Potami Beach; mains €7-15; ⊙ 9am-after sunset; 🅿 🛜) This cool open-air cafe-bar is a family affair, combining Greek and South Seas decor with jazz, reggae, classical, trip hop and ambient sounds. Good omelettes, pasta, grilled fresh fish and skewers are served, as well as owner Apolstolis' naturally fermented wine and assorted drinks and juices. The place has a relaxing and rambling end-of-the-road feel to it, with hospitality and character to spare.

Taverna Bira   TAVERNA €
(☑ 22730 92350; Kokkari; mains €5-9; ⊙ lunch & dinner) Opposite the bus stop, Bira is an elegant, old-fashioned taverna, offering local favourites such as *ladhera* – traditional olive-oil-rich veggie dishes that are the mainstay of religious fasting. *Horta* (wild greens) and *anthoi* (stuffed zucchini flowers) also appear among the tasty offerings.

CHIOS   ΧΙΟΣ

POP 53,820

While no Greek island is like another, Chios has one of the most distinctive faces, thanks to the unique fortress-like architecture of its

Chios

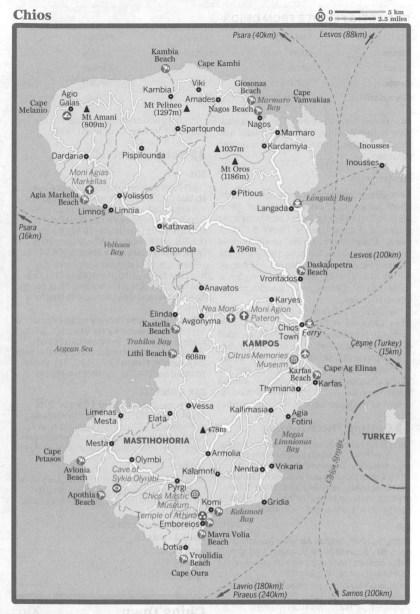

villages that makes them look so different to their sugar-cube cousins on other islands. That style stems from the island's history as the ancestral home of shipping barons and the world's only commercial producer of mastic.

Its varied terrain ranges from lonesome mountain crags in the north, to the citrus-grove estates of Kampos, near the island's port capital in the centre, to the fertile Mastihohoria in the south, where generations of mastic growers have turned their villages

DOMESTIC FLIGHTS FROM CHIOS

DESTINATION	DURATION	FARE (€)	FREQUENCY
Athens	45min	50-85	3-4 daily
Lesvos	35min	63	3 weekly
Samos	30min	63-83	3 weekly
Thessaloniki	3hr (via Athens)	75-90	1-2 daily

into decorative art gems. The intriguing, little-visited satellite islands of Psara and Inousses share Chios' legacy of maritime greatness.

History

As with northeastern Aegean island neighbours Samos and Lesvos, geographic proximity to Turkey has brought Chios both great success and great tragedy. Under the Ottomans, Chios' monopolistic production of mastic – the sultan's favourite gum – brought Chians wealth and privilege. However, during the 1821–29 War of Independence, thousands of Chians were slaughtered by Ottoman troops.

In 1922, a military campaign launched from Chios to reclaim lands with Greek-majority populations in Asia Minor ended disastrously, as waves of refugees from Asia Minor (Anatolia) flooded Chios and neighbouring islands. The following year saw the 'population exchange', in which two million ethnic Greeks and Turks were forced to return to the homelands of their ancestors.

ⓘ Getting There & Away

Chios is connected by air and also enjoys regular boat connections throughout the northeastern Aegean Islands. Between them, the ports of Chios Town in the east and Volissos in the north-west offer regular ferries to the satellite islands of Psara and Inousses and to the lively Turkish coastal resorts just across the water.

AIR

During summer, **Aegean Air** (www.aegeanair.com), **Sky Express** (www.skyexpress.gr) and **Astra Airlines** (www.astra-airlines.gr) serve Athens and surrounding islands.

The airport is 4km from Chios Town. There's no bus; an airport taxi costs €8. Tickets are available from Hatzelenis Tours (p599) in Chios Town and at the airport counters.

BOAT

In addition to regular ferry service to nearby Inousses, daily **water taxis** (☑ 6944168104, 6945361281) travel between Langada and Inousses (€65; shared between up to eight passengers).

Buy ferry tickets from Hatzelenis Tours or Michalakis Travel in Chios Town (p599).

ⓘ Getting Around

BUS

Chios Town's waterfront **long-distance bus station** (☑ 22710 27507; www.ktelchios.gr) is well organised, and has a cafe and coin lockers. From there, daily green buses serve Pyrgi (€3), Mesta (€4.20), Lithi Beach (€2.70), Kardamyla (€3.30), and Kambia (€5.80) via Langada (€2). Twice-weekly buses serve Volissos (€4.50).

From June to September, various bus day tours head around the island (€8 to €15). One tour takes in Volissos to the north, stopping at Agia Markela and then Limnos, with time for a swim.

Blue city buses on Plateia Vounaki (Vounakiou Sq) also serve nearby Karfas Beach (€1.50), just south of Chios Town, and Vrontados (€1.50), just north of town. Schedules are posted at both the **local bus station** (☑ 22710 22079; Plateia Vounaki) and the long-distance bus station.

CAR & BICYCLE

The reliable **Chandris Rent a Car** (☑ 22710 27194, 6944972051; info@chandrisrentacar. gr; Porfyra 5) is Chios Town's longest-running agency, and owner Kostas Chandris gladly provides island information and reasonable rates.

TAXI

Taxis are plentiful in Chios Town; red taxis serve Chios Town only, and grey taxis are good for the rest of the island. Sample costs from Chios Town:

Avgonyma/Anavatos €25
Chios Airport €8
Lagkada €22
Mesta €45
Pyrgi €35

Chios Town   Χίος

POP 23.780

Chios' main port and capital on the central east coast is home to almost half the island's inhabitants. Behind the busy port area lies a quieter, intriguing old quarter, where some lingering traditional Turkish houses and an old *hammam* (Turkish bathhouse) stand enclosed by the walls of a Genoese castle. There's also a busy market area behind the waterfront, and spacious public gardens (Vounaki) where an open-air cinema operates on summer evenings. The nearest decent beach is popular **Karfas**, 6km south.

◉ Sights

★Korais Library & Philip Argenti Museum
MUSEUM

(☑22710 44246; www.koraeslibrary.gr; Korai 3; €2; ⊙7am-4pm Mon-Sat) On the upper floor of the remarkable Korais Library, the Philip Argenti Museum contains a 19th-century birthing chair, along with shepherds' tools, embroidery, traditional costumes and portraits of the wealthy Argentis family. The place is a touching tribute to Greek cultural renaissance figure Adamantios Korais, who set up the library in 1792 and replenished it after the massacre of Chios. Philip Argentis is a French-born benefactor and researcher of Chian history.

Archaeological Museum
MUSEUM

(☑22710 44239; Mihalon 10; €2; ⊙8am-3pm Tue-Sun) Along with prehistoric and archaic treasures from the excavations of the British School at Emporios, this collection includes impressive Neolithic and Classical finds (coins, sculptures and pottery) from Agios Galas and Fana.

Giustiniani Palace Museum
MUSEUM

(☑22710 22819; €2; ⊙8am-3pm Tue-Sun) Near the main gate of the *kastro* (castle), this tiny museum (or 'Palataki') still looks like the 15th-century fortress it once was. Of particular interest are 12 Byzantine frescoes of the prophets, dating from the 13th century, along with an 18th-century full-length icon of the archangel Michael.

Byzantine Museum
MUSEUM

(☑22710 26866; Plateia Vounaki; €4; ⊙8.30am-3.30pm Tue-Sun) Housed in a 19th-century Ottoman mosque, the Medjitie Djami, this museum contains relics from the Byzantine, post-Byzantine, Genoese and Islamic periods, including old canons, fine icons, and Jewish, Muslim and Armenian tombstones.

🛌 Sleeping

★Chios Rooms
PENSION €

(☑22710 20198; www.chiosrooms.gr; Aigaiou 110; s/d/tr from €30/35/45; 🖲) An eclectic, hostel-like neoclassical house on the waterfront, Chios Rooms is the inspiration of its owner, native New Zealander Don. Marked by handsome vintage furnishings, traditional rugs and lofty ceilings, the place has character to spare. Most rooms have private bathrooms; other rooms share. Fresh spring water is provided for guests.

Rooms Alex
PENSION €

(☑6979535256; roomsalex@hotmail.gr; Livanou 29; r €30) Host and former sea captain Alex Stoupas' handmade model ships decorate each of the simple but clean rooms here. The *kapetanios* (captain) is '100% helpful', as he'll happily tell you; he picks up guests from the ferry and speaks English, French and Spanish.

BOAT SERVICES FROM CHIOS

DESTINATION	PORT	DURATION	FARE (€)	FREQUENCY
Ikaria (Agios Kirykos)	Chios	4½hr	15	2 weekly
Inousses	Chios	1hr	5	1 daily
Kavala	Chios	12hr	33.50	1 weekly
Lavrio	Mesta	8hr	28.50	1 weekly
Lesvos (Mytilini Town)	Chios	2½hr	21	1 daily
Limnos	Chios	8hr	24	1 weekly
Piraeus	Chios	6-9hr	32	1-2 daily
Psara	Chios	3hr	7-14	1 daily
Psara	Volissos	1¼hr	7-14	2 weekly
Samos (Karlovasi)	Chios	2hr	17.50	1-2 weekly
Samos (Vathy)	Chios	2½hr	14	2 weekly

Chios Town

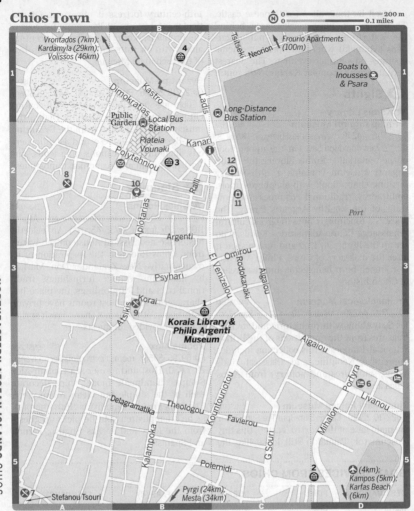

N 0 — 200 m
0 — 0.1 miles

NORTHEASTERN AEGEAN ISLANDS CHIOS

Vrontados (7km);
Kardamyla (29km);
Volissos (46km)

Frourio Apartments
(100m)

Boats to
Inousses
& Psara

Dimokratias

Kastro

Ladis

Tsitseki

Neorion

Public
Garden

Local Bus
Station

Long-Distance
Bus Station

Plateia
Vounaki

Kanari

Polytehniou

4

3

8

10

12

11

Ralli

Aplotarias

Argenti

Port

El Venizelou

Omirou

Psyhari

Rodokanaki

Aigalou

Korai

Atsikis

9

1

**Korais Library &
Philip Argenti
Museum**

Aigalou

Portyra

5

6

Livanou

Delagramatika

Theologou

Kountouriotou

Favierou

Mihalon

Kalampoka

G Souri

Polemidi

2

(4km);
Kampos (5km);
Karfas Beach
(6km)

7

Stefanou Tsouri

Pyrgi (24km);
Mesta (34km)

Frourio Apartments
APARTMENT €€

(☑ 22710 42476, 6945408464; www.chiosfrourio.
gr; d/tr/q from €60/70/80) After the hustle
and bustle of traffic-filled Chios Town, it
is a pleasure to find yourself in the serene
neighbourhood inside the *kastro*, where
the greatest noise is produced by singing
canaries and church bells. There is enough
equipment in the large modern apartment
to sustain a nuclear winter. Crucially, that
includes a washing machine.

Eating & Drinking

★ Kechribari Ouzerie
GREEK €

(☑ 6942425459; Agion Anargyron 7; mains €5-10;
☺ lunch Jun-Sep) This cosy gem of an *ouzerie*,
a 10-minute walk up from the waterfront,
offers a variety of small plates in addition to
excellent fish, mussels, baked potatoes and
grilled meats. The choice is between two set
menus – meat or fish; beyond that, you don't
know exactly what you'll get. But indeed
that's part of the appeal.

Chios Town

Kronos
ICE CREAM €

(☑22710 82982; Filippou Argenti 2; ☺8am-late)
This historic parlour has been treating visitors and locals to great mastic-flavoured and dried-fruit ice creams since 1929.

Hotzas Taverna
TAVERNA €

(☑22710 42787; Kondyli 3; mains €5.50-9; ☺dinner Mon-Sat) This comfortable and attractive taverna above Chios Town serves fine Greek standards with a twist, such as lamb kebab with yoghurt and rocket, white beans with tomato and mandarin, and dolmadhes with lemon. There's a variety of great veggie dishes, including risotto. Everything is *herisia* (handmade), from the pasta to the dessert.

Kubrick All Day Bar
BAR

(☑22711 02744; Anelastou 11; ☺8am-4am) Filling at night with a bohemian clientele, this tiny bar has stills from Stanley Kubrick films adorning its walls, and opens into a quaint bougainvillea-filled courtyard where patrons pass their time in mellow conversations over cocktails and coffee.

🔒 Shopping

Mastihashop
COSMETICS

(☑22710 81600; www.mastihashop.com; Aigaiou 36; ☺8.30am-10pm) Efficient and attractive shop with a range of mastic-based products such as lotions, toothpastes, soaps and condiments. Ask for a sample of pure mastic to chew on.

Sarandis Tourist Shop
SOUVENIRS, BOOKS

(☑22710 24224; www.saranti.gr; cnr Aigaiou & Roïdi) Rambling Sarandis carries a little bit of everything, from cold drinks and wine to mastic-style lotions and good maps of the island.

❶ Information

Banks with ATMs can be found along the waterfront and in Plateia Vounaki.

Chios General Hospital (☑22710 44302; El Venizelou 7)

Chios Tourist Office (☑22713 51726; www.chios.gr; Kanari 18; ☺7am-3pm & 6-10pm Jul & Aug) Island transport and accommodation info, plus a useful free booklet, *Cultural Routes of Chios*.

Hatzelenis Tours (☑22710 20002; www.infochios.com; Aigaiou 2) Opposite the port, this dependable full-service travel agency arranges ferry and air tickets, excursions (including to nearby Inousses), accommodation and reasonable car hire.

Michalakis Travel (☑22710 40070; www.michalakistravel.gr; Neorion)

Police (☑22710 44427; cnr Polemidi 1 & Kountouriotou)

Port Authority (☑22710 44432; Neorion)

Post Office (☑22710 44350; Kontoleontos Sgouta 8; ☺7.30am-2pm)

Sunrise Tours (☑22710 41390; www.sunrisetours.gr; Kanari 28) Chios tours and tickets for Inousses Island and Çeşme (Turkey).

Tourist Police (☑22710 81539; Polemidi)

Central Chios

The stonewall maze of wealthy centuries-old suburbs in Chios Town and the blood-soaked sites of 19th-century massacres along the road towards the western coast mean central Chios is a magnet for history buffs; less so for beach-goers and other pleasure seekers. That said, the aesthetic pleasure of mountain landscapes and singular endemic architecture compensate for the relative lack of hedonism.

◎ Sights

Roughly 4km north of Chios Town, **Vrontados** is the site of Homer's legendary stone chair, the **Daskalopetra** (in Greek, teacher's stone), a rock pinnacle close to the sea that's an obvious choice for holding class.

Immediately south of Chios Town is **Kampos**, a lush area with citrus trees where wealthy Genoese and Greek merchant families summered from the 14th century onwards. You can see elaborate gardens and high-walled mansions, some restored, others crumbling.

A road leading west from Chios Town will bring you to **Avgonyma**, a scenic mountain-top village and a convenient base for exploring desolate historic sites that witnessed some of the most tragic events in the island's history. Beyond Avgonyma lies a string of quiet beaches, the most popular of which is picturesque **Lithi**, which has several inviting tavernas next to the small bay.

Anavatos
VILLAGE

At the end of a silent stretch of road that branches off the main road near Avgonyma, this solemn site serves as a reminder of the island's brutal history. The abandoned village of grey-stone houses and narrow stepped pathways is perched on a precipitous cliff over which villagers hurled themselves to avoid capture during Turkish reprisals in 1822. Nowadays, it's referred to as the 'ghost village'.

Citrus Memories Museum
MUSEUM

(☑ 22710 31513; www.citrus-chios.gr; Kampos; ⊙ 10am-9pm Jun-Sep, to 6pm Oct-Apr) **FREE** This museum has attractive and well-signed historical displays of Kampos-area citrus, the Chian mandarin in particular. Also has a shaded courtyard cafe with – voila – fresh orange juice.

Nea Moni
MONASTERY

(New Monastery; ⊙ 9am-1pm & 4-7pm) **FREE** At the island's centre, Nea Moni is a World Heritage–listed 11th-century Byzantine monastery. Once one of Greece's richest monasteries, it attracted pre-eminent Byzantine artists to create the mosaics in its *katholikon* (principal church). Disastrously, during the Greek War of Independence (1821–29), the Turks torched the monastery and massacred its monks. Their skulls are now kept in a glass cabinet inside a chapel to the left of the main entrance.

🛏 Sleeping & Eating

Spiti Elaionas
APARTMENT €

(☑ 22710 20002; mano2@otenet.gr; Kampos; d from €50) Two traditional and tastefully decorated stone houses, 300m from Karfas Beach in a quiet hillside setting, with great views across to the Turkish coast.

Mouzaliko Traditional Hotel
GUESTHOUSE €€

(http://mouzalikohotel.gr; Zanis & Marias Chalkousi 52, Kampos; r incl breakfast €50-80; ❋ 🛜) If you wonder what might be hiding behind the tall stone walls of Kampos, here is your chance to find out. Rooms in this typically introverted stone mansion all face the handsome courtyard, where the Greek–Quebecoise owners serve hearty breakfasts with yummy honey buns. A citrus version of a Chekhovian cherry orchard, also inside the enclosure, adds to the idyll.

Perleas Mansion
HISTORIC HOTEL €€

(☑ 22710 32217; www.perleas.gr; Vitiadou, Kampos; s/d/tr incl breakfast from €105/130/160; 🅿 ❋ 🛜) Restored Perleas Mansion offers seven elegant and well-appointed apartments, and a restaurant serving traditional Greek cuisine. The relaxing estate, built in 1640, exemplifies high Genoese architecture.

★ Pyrgos
TAVERNA €

(☑ 22710 42175; www.chiospyrgosrooms.gr; Avgonyma; mains €5-10; ⊙ breakfast, lunch & dinner) Excellent setting, service and food. This traditional hilltop stone taverna serves up superb mezedhes plus spit-roasted lamb and pork. Upstairs are five classy rooms (from €40) with names such as Mary, Irene and Ben.

Northern Chios

The craggy peaks of Mt Pelineo, Mt Oros and Mt Amani mark the drive north from Chios Town across the island's boulder-strewn lunar interior.

◉ Sights

Near to Chios Town and the scattered settlements of Vrontados, **Langada** is a relaxed cove of pine trees, homes, domatia and tavernas, and a launching point for water taxis to nearby Inousses. The most noise you're likely to hear might be a few caged birds entertaining the taverna tables. The octopus you see drying in the sun may be on the grill come evening time.

The main villages of **Marmaro** and **Kardamyla** follow as you head north, containing the ancestral homes of many wealthy ship-owning families. At **Nagos**, the road continues northwest, skirting **Mt Pelineo** (1297m), then winding and twisting its way through **Kambia**, high on a ridge overlooking the sea. In the northwest, wild camping is allowed around **Agio Galas**, also home to **Agio Galas Cave** (②22740 22004), the island's largest and most impressive.

The central road will lead you south via Fita and Diefha to **Volissos**, Homer's legendary birthplace, now crowned with the impressive ruins of its hilltop Genoese fort. Down below, the working port of **Limnia**, from where boats depart to Psara Island, is flanked by a couple of pretty coves with pebble beaches. It has a few tavernas and domatias.

Driving 5km northeast will get you to **Moni Agias Markellas**, named for Chios' patron saint. From Volissos the coastal road continues south until **Elinda**, then heads eastward towards Chios Town.

✖ Eating

El Sueño GREEK €
(②22740 22122; Limnos Beach; ⊙10am-11pm)
Veering from the taverna mainstteam, this beach cafe features a good variety of salads and unusual appetisers, such as spicy mussels with beer and ginger, as well as standard Greek seafood and meat dishes.

★**Taverna Fabrika** TAVERNA €
(②22740 22045, 6976255829; fabrika_chios@yahoo.com; Volissos; mains €6-8.50; ⊙lunch & dinner; ℗) This cheerful traditional eatery nestled in the trees of Volissos occupies a century-old olive-and-flour mill, where some of the vintage equipment is displayed. Top off excellent grills, *mayirefta* and good barrel wine with homemade custard or sweet *loukoumadhes*. Above the taverna are six handsome rooms, with fireplaces and wi-fi (triples €50).

Southern Chios

Unique southern Chios is arguably the island's best destination. Though it grows elsewhere in the Aegean, the gum-producing mastic tree of Chios has for centuries been the sole commercial producer of mastic gum. The tree thrives in a fertile, reddish territory known as the **Mastihohoria** (Mastic villages). This region of rolling hills, crisscrossed with elaborate stone walls running through olive and mastic groves, is highly atmospheric.

The Ottoman rulers' penchant for mastic made the Mastihohoria wealthy for centuries. Some architectural wonders remain in the villages of Pyrgi (p602) and **Mesta**. The former features houses decorated in unusual

MASTIC: SOMETHING TO CHEW ON

Mastic gum is a resin that drips from the lentisk tree, which flourishes in southern Chios' gentle climate. Mastic gum has been around at least since the golden age of Greece when Hippocrates touted its pharmaceutical benefit, and for centuries it supported the local economy. Modern research indicates that it contains antioxidants.

During Ottoman rule, Chios received preferential treatment from the sultans who, along with the women of the harem, were quite fond of chewing mastic gum. You can find samples in Mesta and Chios Town shops.

For a comprehensive story of mastic production in Chios, head to the Chios Mastic Museum near Pyrgi.

colourful patterns, while the latter is a car-free, walled fortress settlement built by the Genoese in the 14th century.

The sad and dramatic story of mastic production in Chios is celebrated in the brand-new **Chios Mastic Museum** (②22710 72212; www.piop.gr; Pyrgi, Rachi Site; €3; ⊙10am-6pm Wed-Mon, to 5pm winter), halfway between Pyrgi and **Emboreios**, which was the Mastihohoria's port back when mastic producers were high rollers. Today it's much quieter, though it does boast Mavra Volia Beach, named for its black volcanic pebbles. Domatia and tavernas are available, and the archaeological ruins of an Early Bronze Age temple to Athena are signed nearby.

The west-coast workaday port of **Limenas Mesta** (also called Limenas) is home to a couple of decent port tavernas and is a short drive from Mesta. For swimming, head to **Apothia Beach** (7km south of Olymbi), a curving, sandy cove where the water is a stunning turquoise, backed by two *almiriki* (tamarisk) shade trees and a canteen in summer.

Around 3km southeast of Mesta, **Olymbi** – like Mesta and Pyrgi – is a mastic-producing village characterised by its defensive architecture. A well-maintained 3km **trail** connects Olymbi and Mesta. A popular side trip takes you 5km south to the splendid **Cave of Sykia Olymbi** (②22710 93364; €5; ⊙9am-3pm Tue-Sun), signposted as 'Olympi Cave'.

PYRGI ΠΥΡΓΙ

The Mastihohoria's largest village, 24km southwest of Chios Town, Pyrgi looks like a magic jewellery box, with its facades decorated in intricate grey-and-white patterns, some geometric and others based on flowers, leaves and animals. The technique, called *xysta*, uses equal amounts of cement, volcanic sand and lime as well as bent forks and a fine eye.

Pyrgi's central square is flanked by tavernas, shops and the little 12th-century **Church of Agios Apostolos** (⊙8am-3pm Tue-Sun). East of the square, note the house with a plaque attesting to its former occupant – one Christopher Columbus, who was also a fan of mastic gum, though he apparently preferred it as a sealant in boat construction. There are several tavernas and cafes in the main square. Should you wish to stay, the castle-like apartments at **Mastiha House** (☑22710 72900, 6944604870; www.mastiha house.gr; r €50) offer fantastic value for money.

🏃 Activities

★Masticulture
Ecotourism Activities ECOTOUR
(☑6976113007, 22710 76084; www.masticulture. com; tours from €18) To participate in traditional cultural activities such as Chian farming, contact Vassilis and Roula, who provide unique ecotourism opportunities that introduce visitors to the local community, its history and culture. Activities include mastic cultivation tours, stargazing, and bicycle and sea-kayak outings. They can help find area accommodation and offer tips for visiting nearby Psara Island.

🛏 Sleeping & Eating

Despina Karabela
Traditional Apartments APARTMENT €
(☑22710 76065; www.taste-mesta.gr; s/d €40/50; ❄️🐾) A short walk from the square, outside the walled village, these lovely apartments are cosy and tastefully decorated. Exposed stone highlights the interiors, while loft 'bedrooms' are on raised platforms. Despina also promotes the local food scene; ask for a wander to the nearby family fields.

Medieval
Castle Suites ACCOMMODATION SERVICES €€
(☑22710 76025; www.medievalcastlesuites.com; d/tr/f from €60/80/110) The Castle Suites is a collection of 20 rooms spread throughout the village, all with traditional stone touches, modern bathrooms and a few with fireplaces and even computers. Rooms vary considerably in size and proximity to the square.

★Meseonas TAVERNA €
(☑22710 76050; Plateia Taxiarhon; mains €6-9; ⊙lunch & dinner) With tables spread across Plateia Taxiarhon, this relaxed and reliable eatery appeals to locals and visitors alike, and serves hearty portions of *mayirefta*, beef *keftedhes* (rissoles) and grills. Everything is local, right down to the friendly host family's *souma* (mastic-flavoured firewater).

INOUSSES ΟΙΝΟΥΣΣΕΣ
POP 400

Just northeast of Chios Town, serene Inousses is the ancestral home of nearly a third of Greece's shipping barons (the *arhontes*), whose wealthy descendants return here annually for summer vacations from their homes overseas.

Inousses was settled in 1750 by ship-owning families from Kardamyla in northeastern Chios, some of whom amassed huge fortunes during the 19th and early 20th centuries. Traces of this history linger in Inousses' grand mansions and ornate family mausoleums high above the sea.

Although Inousses is little visited, it does get lively in summer, with an open-air cinema, friendly residents and a buzzing nighttime waterfront. The island's port attests to its seafaring identity. Arriving by ferry, you'll see a small, green sculpted mermaid watching over the harbour. In the port, the striking statue of **Mitera Inoussiotissa** (Mother of Inoussa), a village woman waving goodbye to seafaring men, is incredibly photogenic at sunset.

◉ Sights & Activities

Inousses has numerous opportunities for hill walking, and pristine beaches. Just a 10-minute walk from the port you'll find pretty and swimmable **Kakopetria Beach**. Another five to 10 minutes will bring you to **Bilali Beach**, set on a tranquil bay with a not-quite-tranquil beach cantina that buzzes all night in summer.

Nautical Museum of Inousses MUSEUM
(☑ 6973412474, 22710 55182; Stefanou Tsouri 20; €1.50; ⊙ 9am-1pm) Created in 1965, this handsome museum showcases the collection of local shipping magnate Antonis Lemos. Many of the models on display (some intentionally half-completed then set flush against a mirror so that you 'see' the whole vessel) were made by French prisoners of war during the Napoleonic Wars. There's also a swashbuckling collection of 18th-century muskets and sabres, a WWII-era US Navy diving helmet, a hand crank from a 19th-century lighthouse and paintings of Nazi submarines attacking Greek sailing vessels.

Mausoleum of Inousses CEMETERY
(Nekrotafion Inouson) In the leafy courtyard of the Church of Agia Paraskevi stands the Mausoleum of Inousses, where the island's ship-owning dynasties have endowed the tombs of their greats with huge chambers, marble sculptures and miniature churches. It's a melancholy, moving place and speaks volumes about the worldly achievements and self-perception of the extraordinary natives of these tiny islands.

🛌 Sleeping

Rooms Bilali ACCOMMODATION SERVICES €
(☑ 6944677882; d €45-70; ❋) Contact Kostas at Bilali Beach Bar for information on well-appointed one- and two-bedroom apartments in the upper village.

Rooms Tsouri ACCOMMODATION SERVICES €€
(☑ 6946286791; oinoussesstudios@ymail.com; d incl breakfast from €60; ❋ 🛜) For help with finding attractive rooms, you can contact the resourceful Despina Tsouri, in the upper village.

🍴 Eating

Aignothiotiko TAVERNA €
(☑ 6971663746; upper village; mains €4-7; ⊙ 9am-11pm) Next to the church in the upper village, this friendly taverna serves great mezedhes, including exemplary fava, and attracts a mostly Greek clientele. Tasteful retro soundtracks fit neatly into the old village ambience.

Palio Teloneío TAVERNA €
(Old Customs; mains €5-9; ⊙ lunch & dinner) This excellent eatery on the waterfront has a bit of everything Greek, but is proudest of its daily fresh catch of *barbounia* (red mullet) and crispy *gavros*.

To Pateroniso TAVERNA, CAFE €
(mains €5-8; ⊙ lunch & dinner) A reliable taverna near the square, with good grills and seafood, including the Inousses/Chios speciality of *atherinopita*, a scrumptious heads-and-all pan-fry of onions and fresh anchovies.

🍷 Drinking & Nightlife

Bilali Beach Bar BAR
(☑ 6944677882; ⊙ until sunset) Cool spot on the small and shallow swimming bay at Bilali Beach, with shady tables, thumping music, good drinks, juices, smoothies and snacks. Very popular summer hang-out, from morning till the wee hours.

Naftikos Omilos Inousson BAR
(Yacht Club; ☑ 22720 55596; ⊙ 9am-3am; 🛜) Towards the end of the waterfront, the Inousses Yacht Club's long bar and outdoor patio are filled mostly with young Greeks and their vacationing diaspora relatives, and not a few day trippers from Chios.

⭐ Entertainment

A summertime **open-air cinema** (tickets €3; ⊙ 9.30pm) near the central waterfront brings Hollywood hits to Inousses.

ℹ️ Information

The bank (with ATM) is next to the nautical museum.
Dimarhio (Town Hall; ☑ 22713 51314, after hours 6973412474; ⊙ 8am-3pm) Free brochures and accommodation help, opposite the ferry dock. Ask for Kostas Lignos.
Doctor (☑ 22710 55300)
Police (☑ 22710 55222)
Post Office Next to the nautical museum.

ℹ️ Getting There & Away

The little *Oinoussi III* (€5 one way, one hour, daily) leaves from Chios in the afternoon and returns from Inousses the next morning, warranting overnight stays. Purchase tickets onboard or from Sunrise Tours (p599) in Chios Town. There are weekend summertime excursions (€20) available.

Daily **water taxis** (☑ 6944168104, 6938370129, 22710 55329) travel to/from Langada (20 minutes), 15km north of Chios Town. The one-way fare is €65, split among up to eight passengers.

ℹ Getting Around

Inousses has neither buses nor car hire; ask at the port for its one semitaxi. You can also bring a bicycle or scooter on the ferry from Chios.

PSARA ΨΑΡΑ

POP 420

Celebrated Psara is one of maritime Greece's true oddities. A tiny speck in the sea 16km northwest of Chios, this island of scrub vegetation, wandering goats and weird red-rock formations has one settlement (also called Psara), a remote monastery and pristine beaches.

History

Psara looms inordinately large in modern lore. The Psariot clans became wealthy through shipping, and their participation in the 1821–29 War of Independence is etched into modern Greek history, particularly the exploits of Konstantinos Kanaris (1793–1877), whose heroic stature propelled him, six times, to the position of prime minister.

Kanaris' most famous operation occurred on the night of 6 June 1822. In revenge for Turkish massacres on Chios, the Psariots destroyed the Turkish admiral's flagship while the unsuspecting enemy was holding a post-massacre celebration. Kanaris' forces detonated the ship's powder keg, blowing up 2000 sailors and the admiral himself. However, as on Chios, their involvement sparked a brutal Ottoman reprisal, assisted by Egyptian and French mercenaries, that decimated the island in 1824.

ISLAND FLAG: SEEING RED

Throughout Psara village you will notice the island's memorable red-and-white flag waving proudly in the breeze. Emblazoned with the revolutionary slogan 'Eleftheria i Thanatos' (Freedom or Death), it features a red cross at its centre, with an upturned spear jutting from one side, and an anchor apparently impaling a green snake on the other. As if the reference to the Islamic rule of the Turks wasn't apparent enough, it features an upside-down crescent moon and star for good measure. The yellow dove of freedom flutters patiently at one side.

Over the next century, many Psariots resettled in America and other foreign lands. Their descendants still return every summer, so don't be surprised if the first Greek you meet speaks English with a New York accent.

⊙ Sights & Activities

Psara village is tucked within a long bay on the island's southwest. When you disembark the ferry, you can't miss the jagged Mavri Rachi, or 'Black Shoulder', the rock from which thousands of Psariots are said to have hurled themselves during the 1824 Ottoman assault.

Psara's main cultural attraction, the **Monastery of Kimisis Theotokou** (Monastery of the Dormition of the Virgin; ☉ Sun), 12km north of town, is a smallish chapel surrounded by protective walls; it contains rare hieratic scripts from Mt Athos and a sacred icon that is paraded through the village on the night of 4 August. In all, there are 67 chapels across the island, each cared for by a local family.

In the centre of Psara village is the **Monument to Konstantinos Kanaris**, where Greeks honour their national hero, who is actually buried in Athens while his heart is kept in the Naval Museum in Piraeus. The hyper-photogenic wall of a ruined **Ottoman-era mansion** on the waterfront looks like a stone version of Edvard Munch's *Scream*, or a web-chat emoticon.

Hiking

Visitors should take the splendid introductory walk along the **Black Shoulder** (aka Black Rock) to the little chapel of **Agios Ioannis** and the **lookout memorial**. The views are impressive from the top, especially at sunset.

A further three relatively short and documented hiking trails can also be tackled. The first one takes you to the **cannon emplacements** at the northwestern tip of Psara (2km each way); the second takes you to remote **Limnonaria Beach** (900m each way) on the south coast; and the third is a circular route (3km) taking in **Adami** and **Kanalos Bays**. All three hikes are detailed on the Terrain Maps (www.terrainmaps.gr) map of Psara.

🐾 Beaches

A number of clean pebble-and-sand beaches stretch themselves along Psara's jagged edges. The closest to the village are **Kato Gialos** and **Katsouni**. The former is on the west side of the headland and is pebbled; the latter is a short walk north of the harbour, and is sandy with shallow water, ideal for kids. Both beaches have tavernas nearby.

Further afield, and just over 1km northeast, are the twin beaches of **Lazareta** and **Megali Ammos**, consisting of fine pebbles. **Lakka Beach**, 2.5km up the west coast, is the next option, followed by **Agios Dimitrios**, 3.5km from Psara.

🛏 Sleeping

Village accommodation consists primarily of rooms and studios. Contact Psara Travel, or Michalakis Travel (p596) or Masticulture Ecotourism Activities (p602) on Chios, to book ahead for rooms.

Kato Gialos Apartments　　　APARTMENT **€**
(☑ 6945755321, 22740 61178; Kato Gialos Beach; studios from €40; ❄) Spyros Giannakos rents out clean, bright rooms and kitchenette apartments overlooking Kato Gialos Beach. Enquire at English-speaking Psara Travel.

Studios Psara　　　APARTMENT **€**
(☑ 22740 61386; studios €50; ❄ 🛜) At the edge of the village, in a palm-tree garden, you'll find these clean and airy rooms with kitchenettes, plus a popular *kafeneio* (coffee house) attached.

✖ Eating & Drinking

★ Spitalia　　　TAVERNA **€**
(Katsounis Beach; mains €7-12; ⊙ 11am-1am) Formerly a seaside Ottoman quarantine station, this excellent eatery is great for a lazy beachside lunch or dinner. Stuffed pork or goat is the signature dish.

To Iliovasilema　　　TAVERNA **€**
(☑ 22740 61121; Kato Gialos Beach; mains €4.50-9; ⊙ lunch & dinner) Sit under the outdoor canopy at the village's newest fish taverna and *ouzerie*.

To Petrino　　　BAR
A relaxed bar with arguably the most romantic setting on the whole island – amid the ruins of an ancient house and facing the beautiful harbour.

ℹ Information

There's an ATM on the waterfront square.

Diana Katakouzinou of **Psara Travel** (☑ 22740 61351, 6932528489; www.psaratravel.gr/en) is ever-helpful and conducts a 90-minute morning tour of Psara (€6). There's also a summer **tourist kiosk** (⊙ 9am-11pm) at the port.

Doctor (☑ 22740 61277; Medical Centre)

Police (☑ 22740 61222)

ℹ Getting There & Away

Ferries reach Psara from Chios Town (€12 return, three hours, Monday to Friday), Volissos (€7, 1½ hours, weekends only) and Piraeus (€31, five hours, weekly).

Buy tickets to Psara from Hatzelenis Tours or Michalakis Travel in Chios Town (p599).

ℹ Getting Around

Neither car nor motorbike hire is available on Psara, and there's no taxi, so consider ferrying a rental car or motorbike from Chios.

Hitchhiking is common on the island. (Hitching is never entirely safe, of course, and we don't recommend it. Travellers who hitch should understand that they are taking a small but potentially serious risk.)

LESVOS (MYTILINI)
ΛΕΣΒΟΣ (ΜΥΤΙΛΗΝΗ)

POP 95,330

Greece's third-largest island, Lesvos is marked by long sweeps of rugged, desertlike western plains that give way to sandy beaches and salt marshes in the centre. To the east are thickly forested mountains and dense olive groves – around 11 million olive trees are cultivated here.

The port and capital, Mytilini Town, is a lively place year-round, filled with exemplary *ouzeries* and good accommodation, while the north-coast town of Molyvos (aka Mythimna) is an aesthetic treat, with old stone houses clustered on winding lanes overlooking the sea.

Along with hiking and cycling, Lesvos is a mecca for birdwatching; more than 279 species, from raptors to waders, are often sighted. The island's therapeutic hot springs gush with some of the warmest mineral waters in Europe.

Despite its undeniable tourist appeal, Lesvos' chief livelihood is agriculture. Its olive oil is highly regarded, and the island's farmers produce around half the ouzo sold worldwide.

Lesvos (Mytilini)

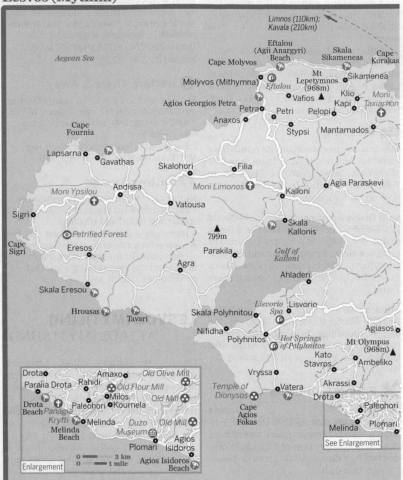

Limnos (110km);
Kavala (210km)

Aegean Sea

Cape Molyvos

Eftalou
(Agii Anargyri)
Beach

Skala
Sikameneas

Cape
Korakas

Molyvos (Mithymna)

Eftalou

Mt
Lepetymnos
(968m)

Sikamenea

Agios Georgios Petra

Vafios

Klio

Kapi

*Moni
Taxiarhon*

Petra

Petri

Pelopi

Anaxos

Stypsi

Mantamados

Cape
Fournia

Lapsarna

Gavathas

Skalohori

Filia

Moni Limonos

Kalloni

Agia Paraskevi

Moni Ypsilou

Andissa

Vatousa

Sigri

799m

Skala
Kallonis

*Gulf of
Kalloni*

Cape
Sigri

Petrified Forest

Eresos

Parakila

Agra

Ahladeri

Skala Eresou

Hrousas

Tavari

Skala Polyhnitou

*Lisvorio
Spa*

Lisvorio

Agiasos

Nifidha

Polyhnitos

*Hot Springs
of Polyhnitos*

Mt Olympus
(968m)

Kato
Stavros

Ambeliko

Vryssa

Vatera

Akrassi

*Temple of
Dionysos*

Drota

Cape
Agios
Fokas

Paleohori

Melinda

Plomari

See Enlargement

Drota

Amaxo

Old Olive Mill

Paralia Drota

Rahidi

Old Flour Mill

Milos

Drota
Beach

Panagia

Paleohori

Kournela

Old Mill

Kryfti

Melinda

*Ouzo
Museum*

Old Mill

Melinda
Beach

Plomari

Agios
Isidoros

Agios Isidoros
Beach

0 — 2 km
0 — 1 mile

Enlargement

History

Lesvos' great cultural legacy stretches from the 7th-century-BC musical composer Terpander to 20th-century figures such as Nobel Prize–winning poet Odysseus Elytis and primitive painter Theophilos.

Ancient philosophers Aristotle and Epicurus also led a philosophical academy here. Most famous, however, is Sappho, one of Ancient Greece's greatest poets. Her sensuous, passionate poetry has fuelled a modern-day following and draws lesbians from around the world to the village of Skala Eresou, where she was born (c 630 BC).

❶ Getting There & Away

AIR

The **airport** (☐ 22510 38700, 22510 61212) is 8km south of Mytilini Town. A taxi to town costs €10 and a bus €1.60.

Aegean Air (www.aegeanair.com), **Olympic Air** (www.olympicair.com), **Sky Express** (www.sky express.gr), **Astra Airlines** (www.astra-airlines. gr) and **Air Minoan** (www.minoanair.com/en) have offices at the airport. Mytilini Town travel agents also sell tickets. At the time of writing, Spanish no-frills newcomer **Volotea** (www.volo tea.com) was offering dirt cheap fares (from €9 on flights to/from Athens).

Sigri €10.70, 2½ hours, one daily

Skala Eresou €11.20, 2½ hours, one to two daily, via Eresos

Vatera €6.80, 1½ hours, three daily, via Polyhnitos.

Travelling between smaller places often requires changing in Kalloni, which receives three to four daily buses from Mytilini (€4.90, 45 minutes).

Three to four daily buses also go north from Mytilini Town to Mantamados (for Moni Taxiarhon; €4.50, one hour).

Mytilini's **local bus station** (KTEL; 22510 46436; Pavlou Kountourioti), near Plateia Sapphou, serves in-town destinations and nearby Loutra, Skala Loutron and Tahiarhis.

CAR & MOTORCYCLE

Local companies **Discover Rent-a-Car** (6936057676, 22510 20391; www.discover1.gr; Aristarhou 1) and **Billy's Rentals** (6944759716, 22510 20006; www.billys-rentacar.com; Kountourioti 87; 7.30am-10pm) have newish cars and flexible service. Billy's also has motorbikes, as do others along Pavlou Kountourioti in Mytilini Town. In Molyvos, hire vehicles from **Kosmos Rent-a-Car** (22530 71710; www.lesvosrentals.com).

BOAT

In Mytilini Town, buy ferry tickets from Mitilene Tours (p610), Olive Groove Travel (p610), and Tsolos Travel (p610).

❶ Getting Around

BUS

From Mytilini Town's **long-distance bus station** (KTEL; 22510 28873; El Venizelou), near Agias Irinis Park, buses serve the following:

Agiasos €3.20, 45 minutes, three daily

Molyvos (Mithymna) €7.50, 1½ hours, two to three daily, via Petra

Plomari €5, 1¼ hours, three daily

Mytilini Town Μυτιλήνη

POP 29,650

Lesvos' port and capital, Mytilini is a lively student town with great eating and drinking options, plus eclectic churches and a set of grand 19th-century mansions and museums. Indeed, its remarkable Teriade Museum boasts paintings by Picasso, Chagall and Matisse, along with home-grown painter Theophilos. In fact, the island is known in equal parts for its poets and painters and for its olive oil and ouzo.

Ferries dock at the northeastern end of the curving waterfront thoroughfare, Pavlou Kountourioti, where most of the action is centred. Handmade ceramics, jewellery and traditional products are sold on and around the main shopping street Ermou, and there are many fine *ouzeries* and student-fuelled bars to enjoy.

◉ Sights & Activities

★**Teriade Museum**   MUSEUM
(22510 23372; http://museumteriade.gr; Varia; €3; 9am-2pm Tue-Sun) Varia, 4km south of Mytilini, is the unlikely home of the Teriade Museum and its astonishing collection of paintings by artists such as Picasso, Chagall, Miro, Le Corbusier and Matisse.

Mytilini Town

The museum honours the Lesvos-born artist and critic Stratis Eleftheriadis, who brought the work of primitive painter and Lesvos native Theophilos to international attention.

Fortress
FORTRESS

(Kastro; €2; ⊙8am-3pm Tue-Sun) Mytilini's imposing early Byzantine fortress was renovated in the 14th century by Genoese overlord Francisco Gatelouzo, and then the Turks enlarged it again. Flanked by pine trees, it's popular for a stroll, with great views included.

Theophilos Museum
MUSEUM

(☎22510 41644; Varia; €3; ⊙8.30am-2pm Mon-Fri) This humble structure contains 86 paintings by the primitive painter Theophilos, who remains a folk hero among Greek literati. During his life he barely scratched out an existence, moving frequently and painting coffee-house walls for his daily bread, depicting the people he met at work and at play. A year after his death in 1934, his work was exhibited at the Louvre.

Archaeological Museum
MUSEUM

(☎22510 40223; 8 Noemvriou; €4; ⊙8am-3pm Tue-Sun) This handsome and refurbished

Mytilini Town

museum, about 500m above the eastern quay (and the now-closed Old Archaeological Museum), portrays island life from the 2nd century BC to the 3rd century AD, including striking floor mosaics with a walking 'trail' across the protective glass surface.

Church of Agios Therapon   CHURCH
(Arionos; ⊘ 9am-1pm) The bulbous dome of this church crowns Mytilini's skyline. Its ornate interior boasts a huge chandelier, an intricately carved iconostasis, a priest's throne and a frescoed dome. Within the church courtyard, you'll find the icon-rich **Byzantine Museum** (⊉ 22510 28916; www. immyt.net/museum; Arionos; ⊘ 9am-1pm) **FREE**.

Therma Spa   HOT SPRINGS
(http://thermaspalesvos.com/en; Km 7 Mytilini-Kalloni road; €8; ⊘ 9am-9pm) Hikers and cyclists can give their muscles a well deserved rest at this newly renovated spa, which now combines an old Ottoman-styled indoor thermal pool with a new open-air pool next to a large sundeck facing the Bay of Gera. A range of massage and other treatments is available (€20 to €40). There's also an on-site cafe.

⊨ Sleeping

★**Alkaios Rooms**   PENSION €
(⊉ 22510 47737, 6981314154; www.alkaiosrooms. gr; Alkaiou 16; s/d/tr incl breakfast €35/45/55;

※ ⊜) This collection of 30 spotless and well-kept rooms nestled discreetly in two renovated traditional buildings is Mytilini's most attractive budget option. It's a two-minute walk up from the west side of the waterfront (and Kitchen 19 cafe). The reception is in a restored mansion, where breakfast is served in a flowery courtyard.

Porto Lesvos Hotel   HOTEL €
(⊉ 22510 41771; www.portolesvos.gr; Komninaki 21; s/d €30/40; ※ ⊜) Back behind the far end of the waterfront, this efficient and friendly lodging offers good value, and has a decent breakfast buffet. Rooms are a tad snug, but clean and comfortable. Upper rooms overlook either the sea or the old castle.

Theofilos Paradise Boutique Hotel   BOUTIQUE HOTEL €€
(⊉ 22510 43300; www.theofilosparadise.gr; Skra 7; d/ste/f incl breakfast from €90/105/130; ℙ ※ @ ⊜ ⊜) This smartly restored 100-year-old mansion is elegant, cheerful and good value, with modern amenities and a traditional *hammam*. The 22 swanky rooms (plus two luxe suites) are spread among three adjacent buildings surrounding an inviting courtyard.

Hotel Lesvion   HOTEL €€
(⊉ 22510 28177; www.lesvion.gr; Pavlou Kountourioti 27a; s/d incl breakfast from €50/70; ※ ⊜) The modern and well-positioned Lesvion, smack on the harbour, has friendly service, and attractive and spacious rooms, some with excellent port-view balconies. A breakfast bar overlooks the harbour.

⋇ Eating

Averoff Restaurant   TAVERNA €
(⊉ 22510 22180; Pavlou Kountourioti; mains €4.50-9; ⊘ 10am-10pm) No-frills old-fashioned eatery with waiters in ties. It specialises in generous *mayirefta* plates such as chicken and potatoes, stuffed tomatoes and *briam* (mixed veggies). It's on the central waterfront.

Cafe P   CAFE €
(⊉ 22510 55594; Samou 2; mains €2-5; ⊘ 11am-3am) This hip back-alley bistro draws a crowd mostly from the university for its unusual and well-priced small plates, slight menu, eclectic music mix and all-round chilled atmosphere. Oven-cooked pork with leeks or baked feta in a fig balsamic, served with a draught beer, costs €6. It's about 50m in from Plateia Sapphou (Sappho Sq). Look for a sign with a single Greek letter, 'Π'.

DOMESTIC FLIGHTS FROM LESVOS (MYTILINI)

DESTINATION	AIRPORT	DURATION	FARE (€)	FREQUENCY
Athens	Mytilini Town	40min	9-89	3-4 daily
Chios	Mytilini Town	30min	80	3 weekly
Crete (Iraklio)	Mytilini Town	50min	80	2 weekly
Limnos	Mytilini Town	30min	86	3 weekly
Rhodes	Mytilini Town	70min	117	3 weekly
Samos (via Chios)	Mytilini Town	40min	86	3 weekly
Thessaloniki	Mytilini Town	55min	38-70	2-3 daily

Polytechnos
FAST FOOD €

(☑ 22510 44128; Fanari; mains €2-5.50; ☉ lunch & dinner) A hands-down favourite for excellent *gyros*, pitta souvlaki and snappy service. Great for picnic lunches, too. Find it on the waterfront at the south end of the harbour.

Jimmy's Hodros
TAVERNA €

(☑ 22510 42614; Fanari; €7-10; ☉ lunch & dinner) Best translated as 'Fat Jimmy's'. Look for excellent grills and fresh fish, served alongside low-key mandolin and guitar duos on summer weekends.

★ Taverna Efkaliptos
SEAFOOD €€

(☑ 22510 32727; Old Harbour, Panagiouda; mains €8-18; ☉ lunch & dinner) You might be sitting closer to the fishing boats than the kitchen at this first-class fish taverna in Panagiouda; it's just 4km north of Mytilini Town but has a distinctly remote feel. Excellent mezedhes and well-priced fresh fish, great service and white wine from nearby Limnos.

🍸 Drinking & Nightlife

Mytilini's loud waterfront cafes are inevitably busy; the best watering holes are found in the backstreets.

★ Mousiko Kafenio
CAFE

(cnr Mitropoleos & Vernardaki; ☉ 7.30am-2am) This hip student favourite is filled with eclectic paintings, old mirrors and well-worn wooden fixtures, giving it a relaxed, arty vibe. Mix in some great music and it's one of the most fun places in town. Great drinks, fresh juices and coffee, and even homemade iced tea on hot summer days.

Cartel
BAR

(☑ 22510 41143; Komninaki) A busy bar with a convivial atmosphere, lots of dressed-up folks, cocktails, and refreshing nonalcoholic concoctions such as sour cherry with almond, and pomegranate with green tea.

Bobiras
BAR

(Komninaki; ☉ 11am-3am) Bobiras fills up as the night goes on. Great small plates, ouzo and atmosphere to spare.

🛍 Shopping

Book & Art
BOOKS

(☑ 22510 37961; Komninaki 5) Unusual and inviting side-street bookshop, gallery and toy store.

Sfetoudi Bookshop
BOOKS

(☑ 22510 22287; Ermou 41) Carries good island maps and stocks books on Lesvos.

ℹ️ Information

Bostaneio General Hospital (☑ 22510 57700; E Vostani 48)

EOT (Greek National Tourist Organisation; ☑ 22510 42512; Aristarhou 6; ☉ 9am-2pm Mon-Fri)

Lesvos – More Than Just Another Greek Island (www.lesvos.com) Online guide to Lesvos; useful despite the PR.

Mitilene Tours (☑ 22510 54261; www.mitilene tours.gr; Kountourioti 87) Full-service agency on the east side of the port. Helps with accommodation, car rentals, and trips and tours to Turkey.

Municipal Tourist Office (EOT; ☑ 22510 43255; Gate B, Port; ☉ 9am-3pm Mon-Sat) Near the quay.

Olive Groove Travel (☑ 22510 37533; www. olive-groove.gr; 11 Pavlou Kountourioti; ☉ 7.30am-10pm) All-purpose travel agency on the central waterfront, selling tickets, including to Turkey, and helpful with local info.

Port Authority (☑ 22510 40827) On the quay.

Port Police (☑ 22510 28827; waterfront) On the waterfront.

Post Office (Vournasson; ☉ 7.30am-2pm)

Tourist Police (☑ 22510 22776) On the quay.

Tsolos Travel (☑ 22510 25346; www.flytsolos. com; Fanari) Full-service agency on the south side of the port. Sells ferry tickets to Turkey.

Zoumboulis Tours (☑ 22510 37755; Kountouri-oti 69; ◷ 8am-8pm) Sells ferry and air tickets, and runs boat trips to Turkey.

South of Mytilini

The small olive-groved peninsula south of Mytilini has several unique attractions. Following the coast road 7km south, opposite the airport you'll find the long, pebbled **Neapoli Beach**; it hosts a few chilled-out beach bars, popular with swimsuited students, and usually pulsates with reggae and Greek sounds.

Around 9km further south, the peninsula wraps around to the popular sand-and-pebble **Agios Ermogenis Beach**, and **Haramida Beach**, which has toilets and showers under pine trees on the bluff above the beach.

Northern Lesvos

Home to rolling hills covered in pine and olive trees, peaceful beaches and the aesthetically harmonious town of Molyvos (also called Mithymna), northern Lesvos offers both solitude and low-key resort action. Traditional seaside hot springs and intriguing Byzantine monasteries round out the region's offerings.

Lying 5km south of Molyvos, **Petra** is mostly a crowded beach village. Its one cultural site, situated above the giant overhanging rock for which the village was named, is the 18th-century **Panagia Glykofilousa** (Church of the Sweet-Kissing Virgin), accessible on foot up 114 rock-hewn steps. Note the mysterious figurines, looking like relatives of Easter Island stone heads, on top of the main gate. It's possible to stay overnight, but the village lacks the character of

Molyvos or nearby Eftalou Beach – it's barely a strip of souvenir shops and restaurants, though its small square can be relaxing.

Eftalou Beach (also called Agii Anargyri Beach), 2km northeast of Petra, is the place for solitude seekers. Backed by a cliff, the serene, narrow pebbled beach has pristine waters and also boasts the charming **Mineral Baths of Eftalou** (☑ 22530 71245; Eftalou Beach; old/new bathhouse €4/6; ◷ 10am-6pm). Beyond the baths, the beachfront **Hrysi Akti** (☑ 22530 71879; Eftalou Beach; s/d €30/35) offers simple rooms with bathrooms in an idyllic pebbled cove, complete with the friendly owners' small **restaurant** (☑ 22530 71947; mains from €5-8; ◷ breakfast, lunch & dinner) overlooking the sea.

From Eftalou, a coastal road continues for 9.5km to **Skala Sikameneas**, an exceedingly pretty fishing port with some domatia and two popular tavernas, including **I Mouria tou Mirivili** (☑ 22530 55319; Skala Sikameneas; €7-15; ◷ breakfast, lunch & dinner). Both eating options specialise in *astakomakaronadha*.

Above the port, its parent village of **Sikamenea** is where the main road from Molyvos turns south towards **Mantamados**, home to **Moni Taxiarhon** (◷ 8am-dusk) FREE monastery. Further south, **Agia Paraskevi** houses the excellent **Museum of Industrial Olive Oil Production** (☑ 22530 32300; www.piop.gr; €3; ◷ 10am-6pm Wed-Mon Mar-Oct, to 5pm Nov-Feb).

Molyvos   Μόλυβος

POP 1500

Molyvos, also known as Mithymna, is a well-preserved Ottoman-era town of narrow cobbled lanes and stone houses, with jutting wooden balconies wreathed in flowers, overlooking a sparkling pebble beach below. Its grand 14th-century Byzantine castle, some

NORTHEASTERN AEGEAN ISLANDS LESVOS (MYTILINI)

BOAT SERVICES FROM LESVOS (MYTILINI)

DESTINATION	DURATION	FARE (€)	FREQUENCY
Agios Efstratios	1½hr	7.50	5-6 weekly
Ikaria (Agios Kirykos)	13hr	40-50	2 weekly
Kavala	4½hr	16-27	6 weekly
Lavrio	9hr	31-38	4 weekly
Lesvos (Mytilini)	6hr	20-31	3 weekly
Piraeus	20hr	60	3 weekly
Samos (Karlovasi)	10½hr	38	1-2 weekly
Samos (Vathy)	11hr	40	1 weekly

good nearby beaches and its north-central island location make it a great launch pad from which to explore Lesvos.

◉ Sights & Activities

Beach lovers can take an excursion boat for Skala Sikameneas village (10km) and nearby Eftalou (from €20, 10.30am daily). It's also possible to hike one way and catch the excursion boat back to Molyvos. Sunset cruises are available. Enquire at the portside Faonas Travel Agency, inside the Sea Horse Hotel, or Lesvorama on the main road.

A popular **yoga retreat** (www.angela-victor. com) is organised by Angela Farmer at the Yoga Hall. Workshop dates vary through the year.

Byzantine-Genoese Castle   CASTLE
(☑ 22530 71803; €2; ☺ 8am-3pm Tue-Sun) This handsome 14th-century castle stands guard above Molyvos. A steep climb is repaid by sweeping views over the town and sea – even across to Turkey, shimmering on the horizon. In summer the castle hosts several festivals.

⌷ Sleeping

More than 50 registered, good-quality domatia are available in Molyvos. Ask at the municipal tourist office or Molyvos Tourism Association on upper Agora.

★ Lela's Studios   APARTMENT €
(☑ 22530 71285, 6942928224; www.eftalouolive grove.com/lelas_studios.htm; studios from €40; ❇☁) Two handsome studios are set in a courtyard of roses and geraniums. Each comes with a fully outfitted kitchen and sunset sea views from a relaxing stone verandah.

★ Nassos Guest House   GUESTHOUSE €
(☑ 6942046279; www.nassosguesthouse.com; d/ tr without bathroom from €30/40; ☁) Head up to the Old Town's only blue house to reach this former Turkish mansion. It has a small enclosed garden and a homey atmosphere throughout. There are seven rooms and two communal kitchens, along with two full bathrooms, one on each floor. Friendly Dutch manager Tom runs a refugee relief project of his own and seeks volunteers.

Nadia Apartments & Studios   PENSION €
(☑ 22530 71345; www.apartments-molivos.com; Molyvos; d/tr €43/60; ❇☁) On the road to Sikamenea and a short walk from the Old

Town, these large motel-styled rooms surrounding an expansive shady courtyard are owned by the humorous Nadia. Her trademark cakes and teasing are complimentary.

Schoolmistress with the Golden Eyes   PENSION €
(☑ 22530 71390; www.molivos.gr; r €40) With a name that refers to the mysterious protagonist from a book by Stratis Myrivilis, this pension has a surprisingly hipster lumberjack owner, who will readily explain that the author actually lived at these premises. Clean and simple, the rooms come with breathtaking views of St Panteleimonas Church and the bay.

The unsigned place is located in Kastro (Castle) St, above the church and next to a grocery shop. Carrying heavy luggage up the hill can be a challenge.

Sea Horse Hotel   HOTEL €€
(☑ 22530 71630; www.seahorse-hotel.com; s/d/tr incl breakfast from €50/60/80; ℙ❇☁) In the heart of the port area, you'll find modern and comfortable rooms, all with balconies overlooking the harbour, along with the family's restaurant and travel agency. Three family-friendly studios have kitchenettes with partial sea views.

✗ Eating

★ Betty's   TAVERNA €
(☑ 22530 71421; 17 Noemvriou; mains €8; ☺ 8.30am-11pm) This restored Turkish pasha's residence on the upper street, overlooking the harbour below, offers a tasty variety of excellent *mayirefta* dishes such as *mousakas* (meat or veggie), baked fish, lamb souvlaki and *kotiropitakia* (small cheese pies), plus tasty breakfast specials. Betty also has two spacious and well-appointed studio apartments occupying a quiet and shady corner near the restaurant.

★ Blue Fox   DESSERTS €
(☑ 22530 72347; Agora; desserts €1-4; ☺ breakfast, lunch & dinner) Turkish-styled *cezve* coffee, delicious cream cakes and traditional Greek desserts, such as baklava and *kataïfi*, are served on a terrace with bay views that will take your breath away. The place looks so immaculately retro that it's hard to believe it is actually brand new.

To Hani   TAVERNA €
(☑ 22530 71618; Agora; mains €7-11; ☺ lunch & dinner) Snappy family taverna in the busy *agora* (market) above the waterfront. Great

for well-priced fresh fish and grills, and stellar views of the sea.

Marjoran   MEDITERRANEAN €€
(📞 6948830700; mains €9-20; ⊗ lunch & dinner)
Lovely location, perched slightly above the main road along the seafront. This is one of the town's few upmarket eateries, with a Mediterranean menu of well-prepared pasta, meat and veggie dishes. Service and atmosphere excel.

🍷 **Drinking & Nightlife**

★ **Molly's Bar**   BAR
(📞 22530 71772; ⊗ 6pm-late; 🛜) With its painted blue stars, beaded curtains and bottles of Guinness, this whimsical British-run bar on the harbour waterfront's far eastern side is always in shipshape condition. Molly's caters to a lively local, international and expat crowd. The small balcony is perfect at sunset.

Conga's   BAR
Rocking beach bar with music by day, dancing by night, burgers, cocktails, smoothies and breakfast the next morning.

ℹ️ **Information**

There's a reliable ATM at the National Bank.
Com.travel (📞 22530 71900; www.comtravel.
gr) Efficient full-service agency in a converted olive-oil factory on the main road.
Faonas Travel Agency (📞 22530 71630;
tekes@otenet.gr) Adjacent to the Sea Horse Hotel, this helpful agency handles trips to Turkey, along with boat and land excursions around Lesvos.
Lesvorama (📞 22530 72291; www.lesvorama.
gr; ⊗ 9am-10pm) Travel agency specialising in Lesvos excursions and sightseeing trips.

Medical Centre (📞 22530 71333; Agora)
Molyvos Tourism Association (📞 22510
71990; Agora; ⊗ 8am-3pm) Tourist office on upper Agora, near the pharmacy.
Post Office (Kastrou; ⊗ 7.30am-2pm)

Western Lesvos

Western Lesvos was formed by massive, primeval volcanic eruptions that fossilised trees and all other living things, making it an intriguing site for prehistoric-treasure hunters. Its striking, bare landscape, broken only by craggy boulders and the occasional olive tree, is dramatically different to that in the rest of Lesvos. Heading far to the southwest, however, a grassier landscape emerges, leading to the coastal village of Skala Eresou, birthplace of one of Greece's most famous lyric poets, Sappho, who was dubbed the 10th muse by Plato.

Heading west from Skala Kallonis towards Sigri, a stark and ancient volcanic landscape awaits, home to the scattered remains of a **petrified forest** (📞 22510
47033; www.petrifiedforest.gr; ⊗ park 8am-4pm Tue-Sun Jul-Sep, museum 9.30am-5.30pm Jul-Sep, 9am-5pm Tue-Sun Oct-Jun). A fascinating and rare monument of geological heritage, the forest is a product of intense volcanic activity in the northern Aegean during the Miocene period. Sadly, the main visitors' area in the centre of this Unesco-nominated geopark was off limits at the time of research, due to acute underfunding. Check its current status with the **museum** (📞 22530 54434;
www.lesvosmuseum.gr; €5; ⊗ 9am-6pm Jul-Sep, 8.30am-4.30pm Oct-Jun; 🅿️🚻) in Sigri, which has a little patch of the forest in its premises.

NORTHEASTERN AEGEAN ISLANDS LESVOS (MYTILINI)

BIRDER TIPS

Just south of agricultural Kalloni, coastal **Skala Kallonis** turns from sleepy fishing village to birdwatching mecca every spring and autumn. During the spring migration, unrivalled across Europe, Lesvos' wetland reserves become home to more than 130 species of bird, from flamingos and raptors to woodpeckers and marsh sandpipers. It's a spectacular show that has grabbed the attention of European birdwatchers, who flock to the island during the peak viewing season of mid-April to mid-May, and again from mid-September to October. Skala Kallonis shares the enthusiasm, with the Pasiphae Hotel (p614) serving as an unofficial centre, where birdwatchers gather to compare notes (or brag) at the lobby bar. Bring your binoculars.

If you can't tell the difference between a blue-eyed hawker dragonfly and a crested grebe, pick up Steve Dudley's *A Birdwatching Guide to Lesvos*. Steve leads birdwatching tours around the island. There are also 50 species of butterfly and dragonfly flitting about, as well as myriad marsh frogs filling the air with their croaky crooning.

Sleepy **Sigri** is a fishing port, with narrow streets lined with pretty whitewashed houses descending towards an impressive Ottoman castle. The village has beautiful sea views, especially at sunset, and there are idyllic, little-visited beaches just southwest.

Coming back from Sigri, stop for a lunch break or coffee at **Andissa**, a jovial, rustic village of narrow streets kept cool by the two enormous plane trees that stand over its square. Listen to the crickets and the banter of old-timers over a Greek coffee or frappé. Don't leave before trying the 'sweet spoons' at To Kati Allo.

🛏 Sleeping & Eating

Pasiphae Hotel
HOTEL €

(☑ 22530 23212; www.pasiphaehotel.com; Skala Kollonis; s/d incl breakfast from €40/45; P ❄ @ 🛜 🛝) A well-managed and welcoming hotel in a shady setting at Skala Kollonis, about 300m from the sea and village square. It's a favourite for returning visitors, including the birdwatchers who gather at the lobby bar to compare notes in spring and autumn. Managed by the informative Vasillis Vogiatzis, with exceptional service and spotless rooms.

To Kati Allo
CAFE

(Something Else; Andissa) Sweet in every sense of the word, this cafe in the main square of Andissa is a wonderful place to stop for a cup of Greek coffee with a spoon sweet.

Skala Eresou   Σκάλα Ερεσού
POP 1560

Skala Eresou is part traditional fishing village, part laid-back bohemian beach town, and part lesbian mecca, especially during September when a lively two-week festival honours the great lyrical poet Sappho, born here in 630 BC. The small seaside community has an easygoing, end-of-the-road ambience, with little cafes and tavernas hugging the shore and wispy tamarisk trees swaying in the breeze.

⊙ Sights

Near the town market, the remains of the early **Christian Basilica of Agios Andreas** include partially intact 5th-century mosaics.

Eresos Archaeological Museum   MUSEUM
(€2; ⊙ 8.30am-3pm Tue-Sun) FREE A small museum with irregular hours, but the outside (and fenced) mosaics are of great interest. The museum is located on a quiet street in the southeast part of the village, two blocks away from the sea.

🛏 Sleeping

★ Hotel Kyma
GUESTHOUSE €

(☑ 22530 53555; Skala Eresou; d €45; ❄ 🛜) You can almost plunge into the deep blue sea from your private balcony at this lovely guesthouse perched above the narrow beach at the eastern edge of Skala Eresou. Rooms are simple yet stylish, and sunset views are to die for.

Hotel Gallini
HOTEL €

(☑ 22530 53138; www.hotel-galinos.gr; Alkaiou; s/d incl breakfast from €35/45; P ❄ 🛜) This budget gem, about 80m back from the waterfront, has tile floors and small balconies overlooking the hillside. Breakfast, with homemade jams and cheeses, is served on the flowery verandah.

INTERNATIONAL ERESSOS WOMEN'S FESTIVAL

The **International Eressos Women's Festival** (☑ 22530 52130; www.womensfestival. eu; Skala Eresou; tickets €30-65; ⊙ Sep), with a local atmosphere, involves two weeks of partying. Activities range from live music, open-air cinema, poetry and Greek dancing to beach volleyball, water sports, yoga and meditation, all in a gay-friendly atmosphere under the sun and stars.

Highlights include an LGBT film festival, live Greek, Turkish and Mediterranean folk music, 4WD safaris, an alternative fashion show (featuring festival participants), photography workshops and tattooing demonstrations. Live performances cover comedy and spoken word to burlesque and rock and roll.

The crystal waters offer swimming near cocktail bars or, for those who prefer things clothing-optional, a beach further on. For avid walkers and hikers, the area is threaded with inland and coastal routes. Nearby there are also thermal spas, archaeological remains, water sports, boat trips, birdwatching excursions and mountain biking.

Aumkara Apartments
APARTMENT €

(☑6948131032, 22530 53190; www.aumkara.eu; Skala Eresou; d/tr/q from €35/60/80; P❄🛜) Smart and spotless apartments near the centre of the village, managed by the welcoming Maria and her crew. Self-caterers will like the handy kitchenettes, and rooms range from small studios to two-bedroom apartments. About 50m from the beach.

Heliotopos
APARTMENT €

(☑6948510527; www.heliotoposeressos.gr; apt €55-70; P❄🛜) A leisurely 15-minute walk from the village, this flowery garden lodging features five studios and three two-bedroom apartments, all with full kitchens. Free bikes are available for pedalling around.

Sappho the Eresia
HOTEL €€

(Sappho Hotel; ☑22530 53233; www.sappho-hotel.com; waterfront; s/d/tr €45/70/85; P❄🛜) The friendly 18-room Sappho is what passes for a big hotel in laid-back Skala Eresou. Its modest position on the quieter west end of the beach is appealing, as are its overhead fans and an easygoing cafe-bar. The best rooms overlook the sea and the island of Psara. Breakfast is available for €8.

✗ Eating

Skala Eresou's restaurants and bars line the beach, as do its tamarisk trees. Fresh fish is a speciality. Look for the hanging squid and octopus. On clear days Chios emerges on the horizon.

★Soulatso
SEAFOOD €

(fish €6-12; ⊙lunch & dinner) This busy beachfront *ouzerie*-taverna along the boardwalk has a large outdoor patio and specialises in fresh fish, reasonably priced by the kilo; it's also known for its excellent mezedhes. Good service, ample portions and worthy wines.

Sam's Café-Restaurant
TAVERNA €

(Eresos; mains €6.50-9; ⊙lunch & dinner) Don't let the five-minute drive from Skala Eresou up to little Eresos keep you from trying this excellent Lebanese-Greek patio taverna for a taste of Sam and Niki's excellent home cooking.

Taverna Karavogiannos
TAVERNA €

(mains €6-12; ⊙lunch & dinner) A fine seaside taverna overlooking the beach along the boardwalk, with fresh fish, grills, several veggie dishes (such as *horta*) and a variety of salads.

SAPPHO: ANCIENT POET, MODERN VOICE

The classical Greek poet Sappho is renowned for her lyrical verse. Her words speak of passion and love for both sexes, but her emotion is balanced by clarity of language and a simple style. Though only fragments of her work remain, we do know that she married, had a daughter and was exiled for a period to Sicily, most likely for her political affiliation. Her surviving poems and love songs seem to have been addressed to an inner circle of female devotees. She was certainly an early advocate for women's voices, and hers continues to resonate.

🍷 Drinking & Nightlife

Skala Eresou's low-key nightlife consists of a contiguous series of small cafe-bars strung along the eastern end of the short waterfront.

★Parasol
BAR

(☑22530 52050; ⊙9am-2am) With its orange lanterns and super-eclectic music mix, little Parasol does cocktails to match its South Seas decor. As the day rolls on, Christos and Anastasia's made-to-order breakfasts and cappuccinos give way to lunch specials, fresh juices, noodles and handmade pizza.

★Portokali
BAR

(Eresos) Tiny and convivial cafe-bar 3km up the hill in Eresos, and the village favourite for coffee and conversation, sweets and *tsipouro*.

Notia Jazz Bar
BAR

(Plateia Anthis) Come for the drinks and stay for the tunes at this hip music bar. There's live jazz on summer weekends. Good cocktails, Greek wine, draught beer, plus Miles and Monk.

🛍 Shopping

Thalassaki
ARTS & CRAFTS

(☑6973525421; ⊙11am-11pm) Despina Iossifelli makes the handmade ceramics and jewellery at this bright and inviting waterfront gift shop.

Leather Workshop FASHION & ACCESSORIES

Check out the old sewing machines at this friendly little leather and accessories shop. In his spare time, owner Kiriakos teaches kung fu to the village kids. It's located on the main road, a short walk from the square.

ⓘ Information

Full-service **Sappho Travel** (☑ 22530 52130; www.sapphotravel.com) arranges car hire, accommodation and provides information about the **International Eressos Women's Festival** (p614).

Doctor (☑ 22530 53947; ⊘ 24hr)

Pharmacy (☑ 22530 53844)

Southern Lesvos

Interspersed groves of olive and pine trees mark southern Lesvos, from the flanks of Mt Olympus (968m), the area's highest peak, right down to the sea, where the best beaches lie. This is a hot, intensely agricultural place where the vital olive oil, wine and ouzo industries overshadow tourism.

⊙ Sights

Just south of the Mytilini–Polyhnitos road, **Agiasos** is the first point of interest. On the northern side of Mt Olympus, it's a quirky, well-kept, traditional hamlet of narrow cobbled streets where fishers sell their morning catch from the back of old pick-up trucks; village elders sip Greek coffee in the local *kafeneia* (coffee houses); and cheesemakers and ceramic artisans hawk their wares. It's a relaxing, leafy place, and boasts the exceptional **Church of the Panagia Vrefokratousa**.

The road south along the western shore of the Gulf of Gera reaches **Plomari**, the centre of Lesvos' ouzo industry. It's an attractive, if busy, seaside village with a large, palm-lined square and waterfront tavernas.

The popular beach settlement of **Agios Isidoros**, 3km east, absorbs most of Plomari's summertime guests. **Tarti**, a bit further east, is less crowded. West of Plomari, **Melinda** is a tranquil fishing village with a beach, tavernas and domatia.

From Melinda, the road less taken to the beach resort of **Vatera** passes through tranquil mountain villages, richly forested hills and steep gorges. Driving north, you'll pass the picturesque villages of **Paleohori**, **Akrassi** and **Ambeliko**, from where a signposted, rental-car-friendly dirt road

descends through serene olive and pine forests with great views to the coast. The total driving time from Melinda to Vatera is about an hour.

Despite its 10km-long sandy beach, Vatera remains a low-key getaway destination, with only a few small hotels and domatia operating, and even fewer bars.

On its western edge, at **Cape Agios Fokas**, the sparse ruins of an ancient **Temple of Dionysos** occupy a headland overlooking the sea. In the cove between the beach and the cape, evidence indicates an ancient military encampment. Indeed, some historians believe this is the place Homer was referring to in his epic poem 'Iliad' as the resting point for Greek armies besieging Troy.

Vatera's ancient history includes fossils dating back 5.5 million years, including remains of a tortoise as big as a Volkswagen, and fossils of a gigantic horse and gazelle. The inviting **Vrisa Natural History Museum** (☑ 22520 61890; €1; ⊘ 9am-9pm Jun-Sep, 9.30am-3.30pm Wed-Sun Oct-May) in nearby **Vryssa** displays these and other significant remains.

About 5km northwest of Polyhnitos, the little fishing port of **Skala Polyhnitou** lies on the Gulf of Kalloni, where caïques bob at the docks and fishers untangle their nets. It's great for low-key seafood dinners at sunset. If you want lower-key yet, head 6km west to the seaside village of **Nifidha**.

Varvagianni Ouzo Museum MUSEUM

(☑ 22520 32741; www.barbayanni-ouzo.com; Plomari; ⊘ 9am-4pm Mon-Fri Apr-Oct, 10am-2pm Mon-Fri Nov-Mar, by appointment Sat & Sun) **FREE** Plomari is ouzo central for Greece. This museum, where the family has made ouzo for five generations, gives you the chance to tour its copper distillery and compare different ouzo tastes. When sampling ouzo, look for '100%' written on the label, indicating the quality of the distillate.

Ouzo Plomariou MUSEUM

(Arvaniti Isidorou; ☑ 22520 31450; www.theworldof ouzo.gr; Kampos Plagias; €2; ⊘ 10am-3pm Mon-Sat, 9am-2pm Sun May-Oct) Up the main road from Agios Isidoros, this famous distillery offers tours and tastings.

Vrana Olive-Press Museum MUSEUM

(☑ 22510 82007; Papados; €1; ⊘ 9am-7pm Tue-Sun) Modestly tucked away in the village of Papados, between Mytilini and south-coast Plomari, the little Vrana Olive-Press Museum showcases 19th-century steam-powered presses and vintage paintings of a bygone era. It also occupies a bit of Greek literary history – it was built by Nicholas Vranas, grandfather of Greek Nobel Prize–winning poet Odysseus Elytis.

🏃 Activities

Hikers here can enjoy southern Lesvos' **olive trails**, which comprise paths and old local roads threading inland from Plomari and Melinda. The **Melinda–Paleohori trail** (1.2km, 30 minutes) follows the Selandas River for 200m before ascending to Paleohori, passing a spring with potable water along the way. The trail ends at the village's olive press.

Another appealing trail from Melinda leads to **Panagia Kryfti**, a cave church near a **hot spring** (built for two), and the nearby **Drota Beach**; or take the **Paleohori–Rahidi trail** (1km, 30 minutes), which is paved with white stone and passes springs and vineyards. Rahidi, which was only connected to electricity in 2001, has charming old houses and a coffee house.

Other, more complicated hiking trail can get you directly from Melinda to Vatera; consult the EOT (p610) or the tourist office (p610), both in Mytilini Town.

Agricultural **Polyhnitos**, 10km north of Vatera on the road to Mytilini Town, is known for its two nearby hot springs, among the hottest in Europe. The more popular of the two, the **Hot Springs of Polyhnitos** (Polyhnitos Spa; ☑22520 41229, 6977592991; www.hotsprings.gr; €4; ⊙2-8pm Mon-Sat, 11am-8pm Sun), await just 1.5km east of the village.

🛏 Sleeping

★Hotel Vatera Beach   HOTEL €
(☑22520 61212; www.vaterabeach.com; Vatera Beach; s/d incl breakfast from €35/50; P❋@🐾) This peaceful beachfront hotel regards its guests, many of whom return annually, as old friends. The congenial brother-and-sister team of Takis and Jeannie Ballis provides great service and comfortable rooms, just opposite the beach. The hotel's excellent restaurant uses mostly local and organic ingredients to supply the small daily menu.

Pano Sto Kyma   PENSION €
(☑22520 33160, 6942906124; www.panostokyma. gr; Agios Isidoros; studios from €42) Eleven sparkling-clean rooms come with wooden furniture painted in the lightest shade of blue – the same colour as the sea, just 30m from the front door. No breakfast is served, but village cafes open early and rooms come with kitchenettes.

🍴 Eating

Psarotaverna O Stratos   SEAFOOD €
(Skala Polyhnitou; fish €6-9; ⊙10am-1am) Look for the fishing boats moored beside this popular fish taverna on Skala Polyhnitou's waterfront. Enjoy inexpensive fresh seafood, plus salads such as *vlita* (wild greens) and tasty mezedhes such as *taramasalata*.

★Sunset   GREEK €€
(☑22520 32740; Agios Isidoros; mains €8-13; ⊙noon-1am) Perched above the main road, this is not your average taverna but a fully fledged restaurant, with attentive service and a very competent chef-manager, Dimitris, whose advice about what's best on the day should be taken seriously. The lamb chops alone are worth the drive. Beautiful sunsets are free of charge.

LIMNOS   ΛΗΜΝΟΣ

POP 16,700

Isolated Limnos, alone in the northeastern Aegean save for neighbouring Agios Efstratios, appeals to those looking for Greek island life that's relatively unaffected by modern tourism. Limnos' capital, Myrina, has retained its classic Greek fishing-harbour feel, while a grand Genoese castle provides a dramatic backdrop.

The island's eastern lakes are visited by spectacular flocks of flamingos and its central plain is filled with spring wildflowers. Superb sandy beaches lie near the capital and in more distant corners of the island.

ℹ️ Getting There & Away

AIR

The airport is 22km east of Myrina, and has offices for **Aegean Air** (www.aegeanair.com), **Sky Express** (www.skyexpress.gr) and **Astra Airlines** (www.astra-airlines.gr). Taxis to/from Myrina cost about €25.

BOAT

Ferries depart the New Port in Myrina. Buy tickets at Atzamis Travel (p620), Petrides Travel (p620), or **Aegean Travel** (☑22540 25936; www.aegeantravel.eu; waterfront), all in Myrina.

Limnos

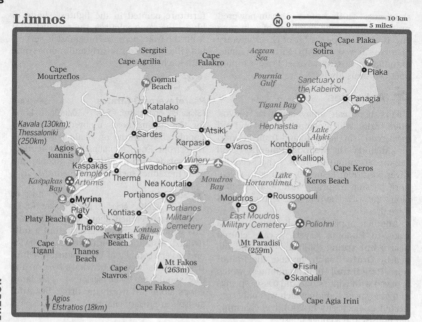

ℹ️ Getting Around

BUS
Limnos' bus service has one purpose: to bring villagers to town for their morning shopping and to get them home by lunch. From Myrina, buses serve Moudros, via the airport (€3, 30 minutes, five daily), with the last return bus leaving at 12.15pm. However, buses do not coordinate with flight departures. For other destinations around the island, buses are not particularly useful.

Myrina's **bus station** (☎22540 22464; Plateia Eleftheriou Venizelou) displays schedules – handwritten in Greek to complicate matters.

CAR & MOTORCYCLE
Petrides Travel (p620), **Holiday Car Rental** (☎22540 23280; Myrina) and **Aegean Travel** (p617), all located near the waterfront in Myrina, rent cars from €30 per day. Motorcycle-hire outlets are on Kyda-Karatza.

TAXI
There's a **taxi rank** (☎22540 23820; Myrina) on Myrina's central square.

Myrina   Μύρινα
POP 5110

Backed by volcanic rock and a craggy Genoese castle, Limnos' capital is strikingly old-fashioned. Here you'll see fishers sipping

Greek coffee while unfolding their nets, and colourful caïques dotting the harbour.

In summer Myrina comes to life, with shops selling traditional foods, handicrafts and more in its bustling *agora*. White-washed stone houses, old-fashioned barber shops and *kafeneia* (coffee houses), sitting among weather-worn neoclassical mansions, create a relaxed old-world charm.

The town, like Limnos in general, is mostly frequented by Greek tourists, lending a distinct Hellenic flavour to the waterfront nightlife. Above the town, on the castle's overgrown slopes, it's a different story: here, shy, fleet-footed deer dart about after dark, and even venture down to the *agora* on winter nights.

👁 Sights & Activities

Castle of Myrina   CASTLE
FREE Myrina's lonely hilltop *kastro* dates from the 13th century and occupies a headland that divides the town from its popular beach. The ruins of the Venetian-built fortress are imposing, but deserted, except for the deer that roam here freely. It's worth the 20- to 25-minute walk up the hill for the sea views alone, which extend to Mt Athos and, come evening, the twinkling cafe lights below.

Archaeological Museum
MUSEUM

(☑22540 22990; €2; ⊙8.30am-3pm Tue-Sun)
Myrina's fine neoclassical mansion-museum
overlooks Romeïkos Gialos Beach and contains 8th- and 7th-century-BC finds from
Limnos' three major sites of: Poliohni, the
Sanctuary of the Kabeiroi and Hephaistia.
Worth seeing are the earthenware lamp
statuettes of sirens, along with details of
the mandated Greek–Turkish population
exchange of 1923.

Boat & Bus Tours

From June to September, travel agencies
organise round-the-island sightseeing tours
by boat (half-/full day €20/25) and bus (full
day €20). Boat tours stop for lunch and
swimming, and take in the archaeological
sites, usually ending at sunset. Bus tours can
additionally visit the military cemeteries at
Moudros and Portianos. Contact Petrides
Travel (p620) or Atzamis Travel (p620).

🏖 Beaches

The town's beaches include the wide and
sandy **Rea Maditos**, and the superior
Romeïkos Gialos, beyond the harbour;
further on, the beach becomes **Riha Nera**
(Shallow Water), named for its gently shelving sea floor. Waterfront cafes and restaurants stay open late through summer.

Five minutes south, on the road towards
Thanos Beach, **Platy Beach** is a shallow,
sandy crescent with cantinas, tavernas and
a few lodgings.

🛏 Sleeping

Vicky Studios
APARTMENT €

(☑22540 22137; www.vickystudios.com; Maroulas
5; studios from €30; P❄⊙) This immaculate
and friendly budget gem is a five-minute
walk from shops and the beach at Riha Nera.
Rooms face a lovely garden and feature

kitchenettes, desks and fridges. Also has
accommodation in Platy.

Apollo Pavilion
HOTEL €

(☑22540 23712; www.apollopavilion.gr; Garoufal-
lidhou; d/tr incl breakfast from €52/60; P❄⊙)
Tucked behind the port in a charming neoclassical house, these large high-ceilinged
rooms come with kitchenettes and balconies. Located near the police station, 150m
above the port.

Hotel Lemnos
HOTEL €

(☑22540 22153; www.lemnoshotel.com; s/d/tr
from €40/45/60; ❄⊙) The middle-of-the-
waterfront Lemnos, under new management, is a decent budget choice with friendly
staff and modern, if smallish, rooms, plus
balconies overlooking the harbour or castle.

To Arhontiko
BOUTIQUE HOTEL €€

(☑22540 29800; www.arxontikohotel.gr; cnr
Sahtouri & Filellinon; r from €60; P❄⊙) This
restored mansion (and Myrina's first hotel)
dating from 1851 impresses with swanky
boutique rooms, fireplaces, helpful staff,
a cosy bar, classic charm throughout and
a classic Greek breakfast to last the day.
It's on a quiet alleyway near the *plateia* of
Romeïkos Gialos.

🍴 Eating

★Ouzeri To 11
SEAFOOD €

(Glinou 6; seafood mezedhes €6-12; ⊙noon-
midnight) This unassuming little *ouzerie* by
the bus depot is the local favourite for seafood. From *kydonia* (mussels with garlic
and Venus clams) to sea urchins, crayfish
and more, 'To *En*-dheka' (as it's pronounced)
serves all the stranger stuff, along with plenty
of ouzo to help you forget what you're eating.

To Limanaki
TAVERNA €

(mains €7-15; ⊙lunch & dinner) Near the end
of the waterfront, To Limanaki serves up

(Vertical right margin:) NORTHEASTERN AEGEAN ISLANDS LIMNOS

DOMESTIC FLIGHTS FROM LIMNOS

DESTINATION	DURATION	FARE (€)	FREQUENCY
Athens	50min	98	1 daily
Chios	1½hr	56	2 weekly
Ikaria	45min	43	6 weekly
Lesvos	40min	69	3 weekly
Rhodes	3hr	88	5 weekly
Samos	2hr	69	4 weekly
Thessaloniki	45min	71	5 weekly

well-priced fresh seafood and late-night meat grills, along with cheery service and good Limnos wine.

O Platanos Restaurant TAVERNA €
(Kyda-Karatza; mains €5-8) Homemade pasta, good Limni wine and excellent *mayirefta* dishes, with an emphasis on meat, are served at this iconic place under two majestic plane trees, halfway along the *agora's* main street.

Drinking & Nightlife

Manos Bar BAR
(☑ 6932411134; Argonafton 20; ☺ 9am-2am) Lively open-air beach bar at Riha Nera, open all day and most of the night, with decent drinks and an all-ages clientele.

Karagiozis BAR
(Romeïkos Gialos; ☺ 9am-5am) On a leafy terrace near the sea, Karagiozis morphs from snazzy frappé-cafe by day to a drink-till-you-drop bar under the stars. Sturdy, fair-priced drinks.

ⓘ Information

There are three ATMs around Myrina's central square, Plateia Eleftheriou Venizelou, which sits midway along the main thoroughfare of Kyda-Karatza (aka the *agora*). Another ATM is on the quay.

Atzamis Travel (☑ 22540 25690; atzamisk@otenet.gr; waterfront) Arranges ferry and air tickets, accommodation, excursions and bicycle rentals. Can arrange visits to the wetlands on Limnos' east coast.

Information kiosk (Old Port; ☺ hours vary) Very useful brochures, plane and ferry schedules as well as helpful English-speaking staff. Opposite the main pier in the Old Port.

Karaiskaki Travel (☑ 22540 22900, 22540 22460; hrissa5a@otenet.gr; Myrina waterfront) Specialises in trips to Agios Efstratios island. Formerly known as Myrina Travel.

Petrides Travel (☑ 22540 22039; www.petridestravel.gr; Kyda-Karatza 116) Helpful and informed staff arranges island sightseeing tours, boat trips, car hire, transfers and accommodation.

Police Station (☑ 22540 22200; Nikolaou Garoufallidou)

Port Police (☑ 22540 22225)

Post Office (Nikolaou Garoufallidou; ☺ 7.30am-2pm)

Pravlis Travel (☑ 22540 24617; www.pravlis.gr) Efficient and helpful full-service agency at the port.

Western Limnos

A densely populated area around Myrina boasts a few nice beaches and plenty of accommodation – especially at **Platy**, a scenic bay 3km south of the capital. The island's main road heads southeast, passing villages with quirky museums and interesting historic sites. North of Myrina, the road left after Kaspakas village accesses the appealing **Agios Ioannis Beach**, set nicely beneath an overhanging volcanic slab. Hidden away in the mountainous hinterland, a cluster of villages around Sardes serve as a convenient pit stop on the way to the seldom visited sand dunes of **Gomati Bay** on the northern coast.

Immediately south of Myrina, **Plati** is a long sandy beach with plenty of decent hotels, but virtually no restaurants. The nearest are up the hill at Plati village or in Myrina.

Tucked into a giant rock cavity on top of a hill, the **Church of Panagia Kakaviotissa** is totally worth the 20-minute hike from the village of Thanos, 4km south of Myrina. Further along the southwest coast, Kontias is a charming village of windmills and stone houses, and home to the celebrated **Kontias Gallery of Modern Balkan Art**. Sadly closed at the time of research, it might be open when you visit, so ask locally.

From Kontias, the main road continues east to the village of **Portianou**. The chair Winston Churchill sat on while commanding the Allied offensive at Gallipoli is the most venerated item at the village's lovely **Folklore Museum** (☑ 22543 50000; www.laografiko-limnos.gr; ☺ hours vary). Victims of the man's strategic gaffes lie at **Portianos Military Cemetery** nearby. Four kilometres away, the **Old Russian Cemetery** at Cape Punda is the final resting place for more than 300 White Russians; they were interned on the islands by Allied troops, living in terrible conditions and dying of hunger and disease.

The road north leads to a cluster of mountain villages around **Sardes**, which boasts an outstanding taverna. Beyond them, lies a desolate coast famous for its **dunes**, an unusual sight for Greek islands.

North of Myrina, the road left after **Kaspakas** village accesses the appealing **Agios Ioannis Beach**, with a few tavernas and beach houses set nicely beneath an overhanging volcanic slab.

🛌 Sleeping & Eating

Panorama Plati　　　　　　GUESTHOUSE €
(🖉6947718755, 22540 24118; www.panorama
plati.com; Plati Beach; studios from €40; 🅿🛜)
Standing on a hillock, 500m away from Plati
Beach, these tidy and well-equipped studios
complete with kitchens indeed offer panoramic views of the scenic bay below. The
charming host goes out of her way to help.

Villa Victoria　　　　　　　APARTMENT €€
(🖉6942906120, 22540 29077; www.villa-victoria.
gr; Platy Beach; d/apt €80/100; 🅿🅿🛜🅿)
These attractive stone buildings are just
metres from the beach, set on a rambling
kid-friendly green with a pool. Rooms have
smart wood and stone motifs, with kitchenettes. Several two-storey apartments can
sleep four.

★Mantella Taverna　　　　　　TAVERNA €
(🖉22540 61349; Sardes; mains €5-9.50; 😊lunch
& dinner) A popular and well-managed taverna, 20 minutes' drive from Myrina in the
village of Sardes. Traditional country dishes
include rooster, goat and pork stews, along
with excellent local cheeses and crisp Limni
wines. Although listed as a main course, the
sweet *moustoukoulika* pasta makes a great
calorie-bomb dessert.

Eastern Limnos

Eastern Limnos' flat plateaus are dotted with
wheat fields, small vineyards and sheep.
Limnos' second-largest town, Moudros,
occupies the eastern side of muddy Moudros
Bay, famous for its role as the principal base
for the ill-fated Gallipoli campaign in 1915.
The rugged northeastern coast is sparsely
populated, which was not the case in Trojan
War times when Lemnians founded what's
believed to be Europe's first constituted
democracy. Three large and scenic archaeological sites in the area are related to that
golden age of Limnos. The region also hosts
the Greek Air Force's central command, and
so large parts are off limits to tourists.

👁 Sights

Chapel of Zoodochos Pigi　　　　　CHURCH
(Kotsinas) This hilltop late-Byzantine church
built next to a holy-water spring wouldn't be
such an outstanding attraction if not for its
scenic observation point with a striking statue
of Maroula, a fierce sword-wielding female
figure looking defiantly in the direction of

nearby Turkey. A local heroine, Maroula is
said to have taken her dying father's sword
during the battle with the Ottomans in 1478.
The site is a short walk from the beach in
Kotsinas.

East Moudros Military Cemetery　　CEMETERY
(near Moudros) As if taken from the middle
of England, this grassy patch is dotted with
memorials to 800 Anzac and other British
Empire soldiers who died of wounds in a
nearby military hospital and were laid to
rest here, when Limnos served as the headquarters of the ill-fated Gallipoli operation
during WWI. In 1921 the island also served
as an internment camp for thousands of
White Russians, escaping the Red Terror;
around 20 of them are also buried here.

The site is located right outside Moudros,
on the road to Roussopoli and Poliohni.

Poliohni　　　　　　　　　ARCHAEOLOGICAL SITE
(€2; 😊8am-3pm Tue-Sun) On the southeast
coast, Poliohni is considered the first prehistoric settlement in the Aegean and –
allegedly – the first example of constituted
democracy in the whole of Europe. It has
the remains of four ancient settlements, the
most significant being a pre-Mycenaean city
that predated Troy VI (1800–1275 BC). The
site, with its tiny museum, is fascinating, but
remains are few.

**Sanctuary of
the Kabeiroi**　　　　　　ARCHAEOLOGICAL SITE
(Ta Kaviria; €2; 😊8am-3pm Tue-Sun) A beautifully desolate clifftop site, the Sanctuary
of the Kabeiroi lies at the northern tip of
remote Tigani Bay. The worship of the
Kabeiroi gods here actually predates that
which took place on nearby Samothraki.
The major attraction is a Hellenistic **sanctuary** with 11 partial columns.

A trail leads down the cliff to the legendary **Cave of Philoctetes**, supposedly where
the eponymous Trojan War hero was abandoned while his gangrenous, snake-bitten
leg healed. A marked path from the site
leads to the sea cave.

Hephaistia　　　　　　　ARCHAEOLOGICAL SITE
(Ta Ifestia; €2; 😊8am-3pm Tue-Sun) Reconstructed and occasionally serving its original purpose after 2500 years of oblivion,
this late-5th-century-BC theatre sits on the
site of an earlier, Mycenaean-age city. As the
story goes, Hephaistia is where Hephaestus,
god of fire and metallurgy, was hurled down
from Mt Olympus by Zeus.

🛏 Sleeping & Eating

Varos Village
RESORT €€

(Varos; ☑22540 31728; www.varosvillage.com;
ste & houses from €85; ❈ ☎ ⚟) This unusual
resort has taken over a semi-abandoned
hamlet, with suites located in windmills in
the reception/pool area and restored village houses scattered around the village.
Although self-sufficient, the place is quite
isolated, with the nearest beach and tavernas at Kotsinas, 2km away. It's best to rent
a car if you do chose to stay here.

Galazio Limani
TAVERNA €

(☑22540 71041; Moudros; mains €7-10; ⊙ breakfast, lunch & dinner) The large taverna on the
seafront in Moudros cooks outstanding
fish soup in addition to Aegean seafood
standards.

Giannakaros
GREEK €

(☑22540 41744; Limanaki Kotsina; mains €6-10;
⊙11am-noon) Popular with visiting Greeks
and airbase personnel, this upmarket seafront taverna is heaving at weekends when it
roasts a whole lamb or goat. Seafood dishes
are excellent any day of the week.

AGIOS EFSTRATIOS
ΑΓΙΟΣ ΕΥΣΤΡΑΤΙΟΣ

POP 370

You can't get any further from holidaying crowds than this little speck of land
between Limnos and continental Greece.
Abbreviated by locals as 'Aï-Stratis', the
island attracts visitors for its isolation,
remote beaches and quiet beauty. Here
is your chance to plunge into the micro-
cosm of a close-knit island community.
For the curious, it is also the place to learn
about the country's complicated history,
since Agios Efstratios was the place where
right-wing governments would exile pro-
communist intelligentsia until the 1970s.
The island's only museum relates that story.

The sparsely populated island has domatia, good seafood tavernas, relaxing hill
walks and fine beaches. The main village,
also called Agios Efstratios, is often just
called 'the village'. Entirely rebuilt after
a catastrophic earthquake that virtually
flattened it in 1968, it is a serene getaway
for those who need to escape from the big
noisy world.

History

Archaeological evidence from the island's
northeast, opposite Limnos, points to Early
Bronze Age (2800–1900 BC) settlements.
Later civilisations recognised the island as a
strategic central point in the Aegean, and it
was colonised frequently, first by the Mycenaeans, then in succession by the Athenians, Romans and, during the Middle Ages,
the Byzantine Empire, which was based in
Constantinople (modern-day İstanbul). The
island is named from that period for a St
Efstratios, who arrived here in 813 as a political exile.

Like the island's namesake saint, political prisoners were exiled here for decades
in the early 20th century, especially by the
divisive and dictatorial Metaxas regime of
the 1930s, and again during the 'time of
the colonels', as Greeks refer to the military junta that ruled from 1967–74. Many
dissidents and suspected communists were
banished to the island, including renowned
composer Mikis Theodorakis and poets
Kostas Varnalis and Yiannis Ritsos.

◉ Sights & Activities

The 1968 earthquake left little of the old village. A single Byzantine monument has survived: **Agios Vassilios church**, dating from
1727, with a domed basilica.

Just south of the village are the sea caves
of **Trypia Spilia**. Agios Efstratios' pristine
beaches include the **village beach**, which
has dark volcanic sand and warm waters,
Agios Dimitrios beach (5km south) and
Ftelio beach (8km south). The latter pair
are best reached by local boat, 4WD or
motorbike. Enquire with Mr Aris at Taverna
Artemonas, near Agios Nikolas church.

Well-worn paths and trails criss-cross
the island's meadows, which are covered
with daffodils, fennel, thistles, amaranth,
blackberries, poplars and willows. On
the island's northeast corner, a 2.2km
trail explores the hills of Avlakia, passing
through a dense **oak forest**. On the east
coast, you'll find graceful **sand dunes** at
Alonitsi Beach.

On any walk, you're sure to see goats,
sheep, cows and horses, which all tend to
roam freely on the small island, along with
migratory and resident birds, including
herons, owls and kingfishers.

Democracy Museum
MUSEUM

(☑ 21032 40645) FREE Up the main road from the port, this little museum tells the story of Greek left-wingers, mostly urban intellectuals, who were exiled to various Aegean islands by a succession of pro-Western right-wing regimes throughout the second part of the 20th century. Left to their own devices on a barren island, the prisoners were greatly helped by generous villagers, who in turn benefited from the presence of the country's best doctors and lawyers on the island.

Across the road, Julia Balaska at An-Strati guesthouse has the key for the museum.

Sleeping & Eating

An-Strati
GUESTHOUSE €

(☑ 6945563325, 22540 93329; balaskajulia2000@yahoo.gr; d €30-40) English-speaking Julia Balaska runs this lovely guesthouse, which has a large common balcony facing the harbour and science-book images of fish adorning the walls.

Taverna Artemonas
TAVERNA €

(☑ 22540 93333; ⊙ 9am-midnight) Traditional and convivial Greek taverna at the port.

Drinking & Nightlife

Veranta
CAFE

(☑ 22540 93442) The entire male population of the island seems to converge at this cafe by the port in the evenings to watch basketball and play backgammon.

ⓘ Getting There & Away

The small *Aeolis* ferry runs between Limnos and Agios Efstratios five times a week (€8, 1½ hours, Monday to Saturday). Buy tickets at Karaiskaki Travel (p620) in Myrina on Limnos. The ferry leaves Limnos at about 2.30pm, and returns from Agios Efstratios at 6am, so unless you're going for dinner, plan on staying at least two nights. However, weekend day trips (€20) are available in the summer; contact Petrides Travel (p620) in Myrina.

There are also four ferries a week from both mainland Lavrio (€26, eight hours) and Kavala (€25, seven hours).

SAMOTHRAKI
ΣΑΜΟΘΡΑΚΗ

POP 2860

Overlooked by most island-hoppers, Samothraki sits alone in the northeastern corner of the Aegean, accessible only from the

AUGUST FULL-MOON HIKE

The August full-moon hike to the summit of Mt Fengari (1611m), the highest peak on the island, is a beloved annual event organised by the Hellenic Trekking Association. It sees scores of enthusiastic young hikers climb to an open field at 1200m on the day of the full moon, drink in the sight of the peak during a night-time party, sleep on the mountain and continue to the summit the next morning for sunrise. Stragglers are welcome. Enquire at Kafeneio Ta Therma (p627) in Loutra or Samothraki Travel (p625) in Kamariotissa.

mainland port of Alexandroupouli. This lush, forested island boasts one of the most important archaeological sites in Greece: the ancient Thracian Sanctuary of the Great Gods. Also here stands the Aegean's loftiest peak, Mt Fengari (1611m), from where, according to Homer, Poseidon, god of the sea, watched the Trojan War unfold.

Samothraki's mountainous interior, filled with massive oak and plane trees, is ideal for hiking and mountain biking, and the island's waterfalls, plunging into deep pools, provide cool relief on hot summer days. Remote southeastern beaches are pristine, while the north offers hot baths at Loutra (Therma). Inland from the main fishing port of Kamariotissa lies the former capital, Hora, bursting with flowers and handsome homes, all overlooking the distant sea.

ⓘ Getting There & Away

SAOS Lines (www.saos.gr) ferries connect Samothraki with Alexandroupoli – twice daily in summer, less frequently out of season, and vary in price (from €9.60 to €14.50, two hours). Purchase tickets at the port kiosk.

ⓘ Getting Around

BUS

From Kamariotissa, there are six buses daily to Hora and Palepoli, five to Profitis Ilias via Alonia and Lakkoma, and two to Loutra.

CAR & MOTORCYCLE

Kyrkos Rent-a-Car (☑ 6972839231, 25510 41620; Kamariotissa) rents cars and small Jeeps. Motorcycles and scooters are offered by **Rent-a-Motor-Bike** (☑ 25510 41057; Kamariotissa). Both are opposite the ferry quay in Kamariotissa.

TAXI

One of only three cabbies on the island, friendly **Evdohia Brahiolia Taxi** (📞 6976991270, 6976991271), serves all the popular destinations from Kamariotissa, with the longest trips costing under €20.

Kamariotissa Καμαριώτισσα

POP 960

Samothraki's port, largest town and transport hub, Kamariotissa is home to the island's main services. A nearby pebble beach has bars and decent swimming. While most visitors don't linger here, it's a likeable and attractive port filled with flowers and fish tavernas.

Further south, the 800m-long Pahia Ammos is a superb sandy beach along an 8km winding road from a cluster of serene villages, including Profitis Ilias and Lakkoma. Both of these villages are easily accessible from Kamariotissa and have some of the island's best tavernas.

🛌 Sleeping

Most domatia and hotels are out of town and, unlike many Greek isles, you won't find locals hawking rooms to arriving ferry passengers. Rooms are available at Lakkoma Beach.

Hotel Aeolos　　　　　　　HOTEL €
(📞 25510 41595; d/tr from €45/55; ❄🛜🏊) Up behind Niki Beach Hotel, the comfortable Aeolos stands on a hill overlooking the sea. Front rooms face a swimming pool and garden, while back rooms overlook Mt Fengari.

Niki Beach Hotel　　　　　HOTEL €€
(📞 25510 41545; www.nikibeach.gr; s/d/tr incl breakfast €35/55/105; ❄🛜🏊) This handsome and well-managed hotel with large, modern rooms is just opposite the town beach. Balconies face the sea, while flowers and poplar trees fill an interior garden. Owners Elena and Vasillis manage to give it a boutique feel, despite the 37 rooms.

🍴 Eating & Drinking

⭐**I Synantisi**　　　　　　　TAVERNA €
(📞 25510 41308; fish €6-12; ⏱lunch & dinner) Excellent fresh fish and *gavros* – the owner is a spear diver – as well as fine meat dishes such as roasted goat and rice pilaf. The place is cosy and welcoming, with a small open kitchen, and it often serves up *chaslamas,* a Turkish-named dessert unique to Samothraki.

Vrahos　　　　　　　　　　TAVERNA €
(📞 25510 95264; Profitis Ilias; mains €4.50-9; ⏱lunch & dinner) This popular grill house in Profitis Ilias heaves during the weekends when a whole animal is grilled – either a goat or a sheep.

Fournello　　　　　　　　　ITALIAN €
(mains €5-10; ⏱lunch & dinner) Fournello makes for a nice change of pace, serving good pizza and spaghetti. It's one of the few places where you can dine by the sea. Close to Niki Beach Hotel.

Klimataria Restaurant　　　TAVERNA €
(mains €6-9; ⏱lunch & dinner) Highly regarded waterfront eatery serving the unusual *gianiotiko,* an oven-baked dish of diced pork, potatoes and egg, along with excellent *mousakas* and other *mayirefta* standbys.

Samothraki

Kafeneio Panagiotis Makris CAFE
Voted one of the most traditional coffee shops in Greece. Step into little Panagiotis for a sip of *tsipouro* with saffron, accompanied by mezedhes, of course. No wi-fi now, or ever.

ⓘ Information

Port Police (☏ 25510 41305)
Samothraki Travel (☏ 6984908254, 25510 89444; www.samothrakitravel.gr) Excellent tour and travel operation offering information on lodgings, and outdoor adventures from boating, diving and horse riding to trekking and canyoning.

Hora (Samothraki)
Χώρα (Σαμοθράκη)

Set within a natural fortress of two sheer cliffs, and with a commanding view of the sea, Hora (also called Samothraki) was the obvious choice for the island's capital. In the 10th century the Byzantines built a **castle** on its northwestern peak, though today's substantial remains mostly date from the 15th-century Genoese rule.

Marked by twisting and colourful cobbled streets wreathed in flowers, and vintage traditional houses with terracotta roofs, Hora is perfect for enjoying a leisurely lunch or coffee, and on summer evenings there's easygoing nightlife in the small lanes and rooftop bars.

◉ Sights

Kastro CASTLE
(Hora; ⊙ 11am-2pm Wed & Fri-Sun) FREE Freshly converted into a fully fledged tourist sight complete with helpful English-language signs, the picturesque castle was built in 1431–33 by Genovese noble Palamede Gattilusio, who received the island in exchange for assisting the Byzantine emperor in a fratricidal war. Both men's coats-of-arms appear on a marble plaque at the castle entrance. In addition to sweeping views, the ruins feature a large stone cistern used to collect rainwater and a murder hole for people whose company the Italian gentleman didn't enjoy.

⌂ Sleeping & Eating

Hotel Axieros HOTEL €
(☏ 25510 41416, 25510 41294; www.axieros.gr; d/tr/q from €50/60/65; ❄️ 🛜) Friendly and welcoming, with handsomely furnished

ⓘ OUTDOOR ADVENTURE

With its beaches, craggy peaks, lush jungle rivers and waterfalls, Samothraki is ideal for outdoor adventure activities. However, paths are poorly marked and rushing mountain waters can turn torrential, making a good guide essential. Samothraki Travel offers guided trekking (€15) on hard-to-find mountain trails, as well as canyoning (from €40) along 10 spectacular routes. Both are guided by experienced Georgos Andreas, usually in August and September. The same agency offers **diving** trips that include equipment (€50 for two).

traditional rooms featuring well-equipped kitchenettes and views of the village.

Trapeza me Thea CAFE €
(crêpes €4.50-5.50; ⊙ all day) Ex-urbanites Elias and Theodora have taken over Hora's old bank building and transformed it into a wonderful coffee shop, with a director's desk turned into a bar. Take a seat on the balcony overlooking the valley below and enjoy your coffee with 'submarine' (sweet mastic paste submerged in water) or a 'spoon sweet'.

O Lefkos Pyrgos SWEETS €
(desserts €4-6; ⊙ 9am-late Jul & Aug) The summer-only Lefkos Pyrgos is an excellent, inventive and all-natural sweets shop run by master confectioners Georgios and Dafni. Try lemonade with honey and cinnamon, or Greek yoghurt with bitter almond, along with exotic teas, coffees and mixed drinks.

Café-Ouzeri 1900 TAVERNA €
(mains €3.50-9; ⊙ breakfast, lunch & dinner) Start your day at this flower-filled taverna with yoghurt and honey, or sample the house *tzigerosarmades* (goat with onion, dill and spearmint). The large, colourful menu, printed to look like a newspaper, is a take-home memento.

Loutra
Λουτρά

Loutra (also called Therma), 14km east of Kamariotissa near the coast, is Samothraki's most popular place to stay. This relaxing village of plane and horse-chestnut trees, dense greenery and gurgling creeks comes to life at night when people of all ages gather in its outdoor cafes.

👁 Sights & Activities

Paradeisos Waterfalls
WATERFALL

About 500m past Kafeneion Ta Therma, a lush wooded path (100m) leads to a series of rock pools and waterfalls, the most impressive being 30m in height. This is gorgeous, *Lord of the Rings*–like terrain, where gnarled 600-year-old plane trees covered in moss loom out of fog over a forest floor of giant ferns and brackish boulders. Get ready for an ice-cold dip on a hot summer's day.

Ghria Vathra Canyon
HIKING

Running roughly parallel with the Paradeisos Waterfalls, but further east along the coast road, this lush canyon is known for its shimmering series of rock pools and waterfalls, and is an easy and enjoyable hike-and-splash if going inland from the waterfront road.

Thermal Baths
HOT SPRINGS, BATHHOUSE

(📞 25513 50800; €4-6; ⏰ 7-10am & 6-9pm Jun-Sep) Loutra village's other name, Therma, refers to its warm, therapeutic, mineral-rich springs, reportedly able to cure everything

---

DON'T MISS

SANCTUARY OF THE GREAT GODS   ΤΟ ΙΕΡΟ ΤΩΝ ΜΕΓΑΛΩΝ ΘΕΩΝ

About 6km northeast of Kamariotissa, the **Sanctuary of the Great Gods** (📞 25510 41474; €6; ⏰ 8am-3pm) is one of Greece's most mysterious archaeological sites. The Thracians built this temple to their fertility deities around 1000 BC. By the 5th century BC, the secret rites and sacrifices associated with the cult had attracted famous pilgrims, including Egyptian queen Arsinou, Philip II of Macedon (father of Alexander the Great) and Greek historian Herodotus. Remarkably, the sanctuary operated until paganism was forbidden in the 4th century AD.

The principal deity, the fertility goddess Alceros Cybele (Great Mother), was later merged with the Olympian female deities Demeter, Aphrodite and Hecate. Other deities worshipped here were the Great Mother's consort, the virile young Kadmilos (god of the phallus), later integrated with the Olympian god Hermes; and the demonic Kabeiroi twins, Dardanos and Aeton, the sons of Zeus and Leda. Samothraki's great gods were venerated for their immense power – in comparison, the bickering Olympian gods were considered frivolous.

Little is known about what actually transpired here, though archaeological evidence points to two initiations, a lower and a higher. In the first, the great gods were invoked to grant the initiate a spiritual rebirth; in the second, the candidate was absolved of transgressions. This second confessional rite took place at the sacred **Hieron**, whose remaining columns are easily the most photographed ruin of the sanctuary.

We do know that the rituals at the sanctuary were open to all – men, women, citizens, servants and slaves – and since death was the penalty for revealing the secrets of the sanctuary, the main requirements seem to have been showing up and keeping quiet.

The **Archaeological Museum** at the Sanctuary of the Great Gods provides a helpful overview of the entire site. Pick up the free museum map before exploring the area. Museum exhibits include a striking marble frieze of dancing women, terracotta figurines and amphorae, jewellery, and clay lamps indicative of the nocturnal nature of the rituals. A plaster cast stands in for the celebrated **Winged Victory of Samothrace** (now in the Louvre), looted in 1863 by French diplomat and amateur archaeologist Charles Champoiseau.

About 75m south of the museum stands the **Arisinoeion** (rotunda), a gift from Queen Arisinou of Egypt. The sanctuary's original rock altar was discovered nearby. Adjacent are the rectangular **Anaktoron**, where lower initiations took place; the **Temenos**, a hall where a celebratory feast was held; and the Hieron, site of higher initiations.

Opposite the Hieron stand remnants of a **theatre**. Nearby, a path ascends to the **Nike monument**, where once stood the magnificent Winged Victory of Samothrace ('*nike*' means 'victory' in Greek), which faced northward overlooking the sea – appropriate since it was likely dedicated to the gods following a victorious naval battle.

from skin problems to infertility. The prominent white building by the bus stop houses the official bath, though there is **free bathing** at two small outdoor baths 75m up the hill.

Theodora BOATING
(☑ 6945392089, 25510 89444; €25) In summer this tour boat embarks on circular day trips of the island, departing from Loutra at noon and returning by 6pm. The boat passes the Byzantine Tower of Fonias, the Panias rock formations and Kremasto Waterfall, stopping mid-way at Vatos Beach for swimming. Snacks are available on board and (sometimes) a beach BBQ is offered.

🛏 Sleeping

Aleka Studios APARTMENT €
(☑ 6977739264, 25510 98272; www.alekastudios. com; d from €40) High-quality private rooms and bungalows in a flower-filled garden setting. Rooms are spacious and striking, with splendid sea or mountain views.

Mariva Bungalows BUNGALOW €
(☑ 25510 98230; www.mariva.gr; d incl breakfast €55; P ❄ 🐾) These secluded vine-covered stone bungalows, with breezy modern rooms, sit on a lush hillside near a waterfall. To reach them, turn from the coast road inland towards Loutra and follow the signs.

Municipal Camping CAMPGROUND €
(☑ 25513 50800; campsites free) Free and attractive shaded municipal campground behind the beach at Loutra (Therma), with basic facilities.

★ Archondissa BOUTIQUE HOTEL €€
(☑ 25510 98098, 6942210527; www.archondissa. gr; d/tr €75/95; ❄ 🐾) This Cycladic-styled sugar cube contains brightly coloured apartments with kilim rugs and ergonomic kitchenettes camouflaged as wardrobes. The sea is 30m away across a pretty flower garden.

🍴 Eating

★ Kafeneio Ta Therma CAFE €
(☑ 6984994856; mains €3-5; ⏱ 8am-2am; 🐾) Run by the jovial Iordanis Iordaninis for more than 20 years, this is the centre of the action in Loutra, with live music, impromptu vendors, artists and dancers in the surrounding open areas, plus coffee, beer and sweets. It's near the baths and several trails.

WORTH A TRIP

FONIAS RIVER
ΠΟΤΑΜΙ ΦΟΝΙΑΣ

Heading east from Loutra on the northeast coast takes you to the Fonias River and the famous **Fonias Rock Pools**. The walk starts at the bridge 4.7km east of Loutra, by the (summer-only) ticket booths. The first 40 minutes are along an easy, well-marked track leading to a large and swimmable rock pool fed by a dramatic 12m-high waterfall. The river is known as the 'Murderer', and in winter rain can transform the waters into a raging torrent. The real danger, however, is getting lost – though there are six waterfalls, marked paths are few. For hiking here and near Mt Fengari, consult Samothraki Travel (p625).

Taverna O Paradisos TAVERNA €
(☑ 25510 98271; mains €4-8.50; ⏱ lunch & dinner) A popular summer-evening meeting place under a huge plane tree, serving excellent fish. Ask Andreas to see the day's catch.

THASOS ΘΑΣΟΣ
POP 13,770

One of Greece's greenest and most gentle islands, Thasos lies 10km from mainland Kavala. Its climate and vegetation make it seem like the island is an extension of northern Greece, yet it boasts enviable sandy beaches and a forested mountain interior. Quite inexpensive by Greek-island standards, it's popular with families and students from Bulgaria and the ex-Yugoslav republics. Frequent ferries from the mainland allow independent travellers to get here quickly, and the excellent bus network makes getting around easy.

The island's main sources of wealth are its natural beauty, beaches, inland villages and historic attractions. The excellent archaeological museum in the capital, Thasos (Limenas), is complemented by the Byzantine Moni Arhangelou, with its stunning clifftop setting, and the Ancient Greek temple at Alyki on the serene southeast coast.

History

Over its long history, Thasos has benefited from its natural wealth. The Parians, who founded the ancient city of Thasos

Thasos

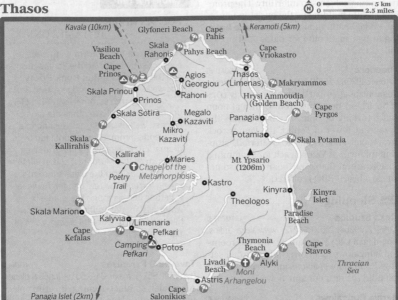

Thasos

(Limenas) in 700 BC, struck gold at Mt Pangaion, creating an export trade lucrative enough to subsidise a naval fleet. While the gold is long gone, Thasos' white Parian marble is still being exploited, though scarring a mountainside in the process.

❶ Getting There & Away

Thasos is only accessible from the mainland ports of Keramoti and Kavala. Hourly ferries run between Keramoti and Thasos (Limenas; €3.50, 40 minutes), and two to three a day between Kavala and Skala Prinou (€5, 1¼ hours).

Get ferry schedules at the **ticket booths** (☑ 25930 22318) in Thasos (Limenas) and the **port police** (☑ 25930 22106) at Skala Prinou.

❶ Getting Around

BICYCLE

Basic bikes can be hired in Thasos (Limenas). Top-of-the-line models and detailed route information are available in Potos, on the southwest coast, from Velo Bike Rental (p630).

BUS

Frequent buses serve the entire island coast and inland villages, too. Buses meet arriving ferries at Skala Prinou and Thasos (Limenas), the island's transport hub. The two port towns are connected by eight daily buses (€2.80, 20 minutes).

Frequent buses run throughout the day from Thasos (Limenas) to west-coast villages such as Limenaria (€4.50), Potos (€4.70) and Theologos (€5.90). Buses from Limenas also reach the east-coast destinations of Hrysi Ammoudia (Golden Beach; €2), Skala Potamia (€1.70) via Panagia (€1.60) and Potamia (€1.60), Paradise Beach (€2.90) and Alyki (€3.70).

A full circular tour (about 100km) runs six to eight times daily (€10.60, 3½ hours) – three clockwise and three anticlockwise. This round-the-island ticket is valid all day, so you can jump on and off without paying extra. The **bus station** (☑ 25930 22162) on the Thasos (Limenas) waterfront provides timetables.

CAR & MOTORCYCLE

Potos Car Rentals (☑ 25930 52071; www.rentacarpotos.gr; Hotel Potos, Potos) is reliable and reasonable. **Avis Rent-a-Car** (☑ 25930 22535) is in Thasos (Limenas), Potamia and Skala Prinou.

Crazy Rollers (☑ 6978937536; crazyrollers@gmail.com) in Thasos (Limenas) and **Moto Zagos** (☑ 25930 53340; www.motozagos.gr; Limenaria) in Limenaria rent motorbikes and bicycles.

TAXI

The Thasos (Limenas) **taxi rank** (☑ 25930 22394, 6944170373) is on the waterfront, next to the main bus stop. Sample destinations and fares: Skala Prinou €20, Panagia €12, Skala Potamia €20, Alyki €40 and Potos €50.

In Potos, there's a taxi rank with listed prices beside the bus stop on the main road.

Thasos (Limenas)
Θάσος (Λιμένας)

POP 2610

Thasos (also called Limenas) has the island's main services and year-round activity. It sports a picturesque fishing harbour, a sandy beach, shopping, a few ancient ruins and an archaeological museum. If you're exploring the eastern side of town, note the signpost for historical sites, beginning a five-minute walk up a shaded trail to the lovely chapel of Agioi Apostoli, where there are views over the seafront.

◉ Sights

Archaeological Museum   MUSEUM
(☑25930 22180; €2; ☉8.30am-3pm Tue-Sun) Looking like an alien creature from the sci-fi movie *Avatar,* a 5m-tall 6th-century-BC *kouros* carrying a ram greets visitors at this large and modern archaeological museum. Statues and other artefacts from the Classical and Roman periods are on display. The museum is located about 100m from the Old Harbour's waterfront.

Ancient Agora   RUINS
Next to the archaeological museum stand the foundation ruins of the ancient *agora,* the commercial centre in ancient times. About 100m east of the *agora,* the ancient **theatre** stages performances of ancient dramas and comedies during the Philippi Thasos Festival. The theatre is signposted from the harbour. A path connects the *agora* to the **acropolis**, where substantial remains of a medieval fortress stand, with commanding views of the coast. Carved rock steps descend to the foundations of the ancient town.

✯ Festivals & Events

Philippi Thasos Festival   CULTURAL
(www.philippifestival.gr; ☉Jul & Aug) This lively festival takes place in on Thasos and in mainland Kavala in late July and August. Classical drama, painting exhibitions and contemporary Greek music are featured. Programs are available at hotels, cafes and tourist agencies. The Kavala **tourist information centre** (☑25102 31011; www.kavala

greece.gr; Eleftherias Sq, Kavala), the Thasos (Limenas) tourist police (p630) and the Visit North Greece (p630) travel agency have ticket information.

⌸ Sleeping

★A for Art   DESIGN HOTEL €€
(☑25930 58405; www.aforarthotel.gr; Theogenous & 18 Oktovriou; d €90-135; ❋ ⬚ ☎) Dreamed up in a psychedelic haze, this fanciful hotel is filled with Dalí-esque furniture and whimsical sculpture. If you don't mind the decadent decor, it is a very comfortable place to spend a few nights, and has an excellent garden bar where you can meet fellow travellers (and a purple flamingo).

Hotel Galini   HOTEL €€
(☑6945443322, 25930 22195; Theogeneous; s/d incl breakfast €90/110; P ❋ ☎) This small and smartly updated hotel, next to Euro Bank and a short block inland from the waterfront, has 16 attractive and comfortable rooms (four with sea views) and a flowery back garden.

✗ Eating & Drinking

Masabuka   GRILL €
(☑25930 23651; 18 Oktovriou; mains €2-4; ☉4pm-midnight) Visitors rave about this exceptionally friendly 21st-century souvlaki joint, where meat skewers are served with a variety of mouthwatering dips. It's located in the pedestrianised street connecting the centre with the harbour area.

★Simi   TAVERNA €€
(☑25930 22517; Old Harbour; mains €7-12; ☉9.30am-midnight) Locals agree that this year-round eatery at the Old Harbour serves Limenas' best fish, along with fine fish soup, *stifadho* (meat, game or seafood cooked with onions in a tomato purée) and grilled sardines. There's a kids' menu, good wines and spicy mezedhes, including hot peppers that can change your life.

Karnagio   BAR
(☑25930 23170) Stroll past the Old Harbour for a quiet sunset drink at Karnagio, where outdoor seating straddles a rocky promontory lapped by waves. You can also clamber up the rocks to a small, candlelit chapel.

ⓘ Information

ATMs can be found near the central square.
Billias Travel Service (☑25930 24003; Pavlou Mela 6) Full-service travel agency.

INLAND VILLAGES

Two interior villages warrant a day trip inland. About 6km from Skala Marion, forested **Maries** rewards visitors with cool highland air and a handsome monastery, Agios Taxiarchis.

Thasos' medieval and Ottoman capital, **Theologos**, is only accessible from Potos, where the road leads inland to the forested hamlet of 400 souls, notable for its white-washed slate-roofed houses. Find the 1803 Church of Agios Dimitrios, distinguished by its grand slate roof, exquisite polished wood interior and white-plastered clock tower. Relax at one of the local cafes or tavernas to soak it all up.

Visit North Greece (☑ 25106 20566, 6942524337; www.visitnorthgreece.com; Pavlou Mela 17) Well-managed and unique tour operator offering hiking, walking and cycling excursions, along with 4WD safaris and sailing trips. The helpful owners, Chrisoula and Stelios, can also handle transfers and suggest accommodation.

Thassos Island Nature (www.gothassos.com) Useful online resource.

Tourist Police (☑ 25930 23111)

Western Coast

Thasos' west coast has been assailed by package tours for years, though there are still a few idyllic spots and quiet sandy beaches. Better still, the inland mountain villages preserve a traditional pace of life and some fine stone architecture.

Following the coast west from Thasos (Limenas), two sandy beaches emerge: decent **Glyfoneri** and the superior **Pahys Beach**.

Continuing west, the port of **Skala Prinou** has ferries to Kavala, though little else to warrant a stop. But 6km inland, past the town of Prinos, the hillside villages of **Mikro Kazaviti** and **Megalo Kazaviti** (aka the Prinou villages) offer a lush break from the touristed coast, with undeniable character and a few places to stay and eat, including Menir Luxury Apartments. An easy-to-follow trail network branches off from the pretty square in Megalo Kazaviti, with a sign marking the routes.

The next real point of interest, the whimsical fishing port of **Skala Marion**, lies further south. Its few canopied tavernas overlooking the sea are faithfully populated by village elders shuffling backgammon chips while children scamper about. The village has a few domatia and a bakery on the northern jetty. On the village's feast day (24

June), church services are followed by folk dancing around the square.

The coast road south passes more beaches until reaching **Limenaria**, Thasos' second-largest town, which is followed quickly by **Pefkari** and **Potos**, two fishing villages turned package resorts, both with long sandy beaches lined with cafes and tavernas.

From the Theologos–Potos corner of the main road, head southeast round the coast for views of the stunning bays. The last southwestern settlement, **Astris**, has a good beach with tavernas and the **Astris Sun Hotel** (☑ 25930 51281; www.astrissunhotel.gr; r from €60; ❉ ❆ ❆).

🏃 Activities

★ **Velo Bike Rental**   CYCLING
(☑ 6946955704, 25930 52459; www.velobikerental.com; Potos) Hires out bikes year-round and also runs guided biking and hiking tours to Mt Ypsario. Inspired owner Yiannis Reizis also organises a number of international cycling events and races on the island.

Thassos Horse Club   HORSE RIDING
(☑ 6999391777; www.thassoshorseclub.snadno.eu; Skala Prinou) Runs riding lessons and tailor-made horseback trips out of Skala Prinou.

Panagia Islet   BIRDWATCHING, BOATING
(☑ 6973209576; www.gothassos.com; trips €25) The rocky, uninhabited Panagia Islet, southwest of Potos, is home to the country's largest colony of shags (www.yrefail.net/Thasos/habitats.htm). Local environmentalist Yiannis Markianos at Aldebran Pension arranges birdwatching boat trips, weather permitting.

Diving Club Vasiliadis   DIVING
(☑ 6944542974; www.scuba-vas.gr; Potos) Diving for beginners and open-water divers is offered in Potos by Vasilis Vasiliadis, including to Alyki's submerged ancient marble quarry.

🛏 Sleeping

★ Aldebran Pension PENSION €
(☑ 6973209576, 25930 52494; www.gothassos. com; Potos; d from €40; ❋ ⬚) Well-informed and attentive owners Elke and Yiannis make Aldebran the best value in southern Thasos. Along with a leafy courtyard and table tennis, it boasts modern baths, a well-equipped communal kitchen, and all-day coffee and tea. Resident ornithologist Yiannis offers birdwatching tours for guests in spring and autumn, and offers info on local hiking trails and more.

Hotel Menel – The Tree House DESIGN HOTEL €
(☑ 6944578954, 25930 51396; www.dhotels.gr; Limenaria; d incl breakfast from €45) This funky edifice stands out among Limenaria's seafront hotels thanks to its Scandinavian ecodesign, with wooden facade and 16 airy modern rooms, all with sea-view balconies. A great rooftop terrace with sunbeds comes as a bonus.

Camping Pefkari CAMPGROUND €
(☑ 25930 51190; www.camping-pefkari.gr; campsites per adult/tent €6.70/7.30; ⊙ Jun-Sep) Wooded spot above Pefkari Beach that's popular with families and features spotless bathrooms, laundry and cooking facilities.

Menir Luxury Apartments APARTMENT €€
(☑ 25930 58270; www.menir-thassos.gr; Mikro Kazaviti; r incl breakfast from €80; ❋ ⬚) Some of the most handsome and spacious digs in this rustic area. There are five apartments, two with spa and all with fireplaces, open year-round.

🍴 Eating

★ Armeno TAVERNA €
(Skala Marion; mains €5-9; ⊙ lunch & dinner) Well-regarded waterfront taverna, in offbeat Skala Marion, where you can have a look at the day's catch of fish. The organic produce here is from the gardens of the friendly Filaktaki family, who also rent **rooms** (☑ 25930 52634, 6977413789; r from €35; ❋ ⬚) and can help with local information.

Piatsa Michalis TAVERNA €
(Potos; mains €7-12; ⊙ 9am-1am) Potos' 50-year-old beachfront taverna was operating well before mass tourism came to town, and continues to stick to the recipe with specialities such as stewed rabbit and octopus in red-wine sauce, plus a full menu of taverna fare.

Psarotaverna To Limani SEAFOOD €
(Limenaria; mains €6.50-10; ⊙ lunch & dinner) Limenaria's best seafood is served at this waterfront restaurant opposite the National Bank of Greece. Prices can be steep.

Taverna Giatrou TAVERNA €
(Theologos; mains €7-11; ⊙ lunch & dinner) Set 800m on the right side when entering Theologos, this big taverna has great balcony views of village roofs and verdure below. Run by Kostas Giatrou ('the Doctor') and family, the place offers specialities including local roast lamb.

ℹ Information

There are ATMs in Skala Prinou, Limenaria and Potos.

Eastern Thasos

Thasos' east-coast beaches are beautiful in summer and less crowded than the more-developed west coast. The dramatic coastal landscape features thick forests that run from mountains to sea. There are fewer organised activities here, but the warm, shallow waters are excellent for families.

Tiny **Alyki** may be the most overlooked spot on the southeast coast. The village is great for unwinding, with a few shops, domatia and tavernas, and there are two fine sandy beach coves, separated by a small olive grove dotted with ancient ruins comprising the archaeological site of Alyki.

OFF THE BEATEN TRACK

POETRY TRAIL

One of Thasos' inland delights is a short steep path at Kallirahi. Dubbed the Poetry Trail, it's an 800m-long path starting at the eastern edge of the village and ending at the Chapel of the Metamorphosis. Along the way, the poetry and writings of Herman Hesse, Rainer Maria Rilke and Goethe, along with the riddle of the Sphinx, among others, are inscribed on marble slabs.

From the chapel, a circular hike of 11km, known as the Kallirahi Circuit, ascends to one of the best viewpoints on Thasos.

◉ Sights & Activities

★ Archaeological
Site of Alyki   ARCHAEOLOGICAL SITE

FREE Alluring and easily accessible, the island's crown gem includes the considerable and photogenic remains of an ancient temple where the gods were once invoked to protect sailors. By all means enter the site through the back door by following a beautiful trail that skirts the headland, passing a partially submerged marble quarry that remained operational from the 7th century BC to the 6th century AD. The path starts at the far end of the beach lined by tavernas.

Moni Arhangelou   MONASTERY
(⊙9am-2pm & 5pm-sunset) FREE West from Alyki, past Thymonia Beach, is the clifftop Moni Arhangelou, an Athonite dependency and working convent, notable for its 400-year-old church (with some ungainly modern touches) and stellar sea views. Those improperly attired will get shawled up for entry by the friendly nuns. Archangel Michael, whose name the monastery bears, happens to be venerated as the patron of Greek armed forces, so don't be surprised to see a room filled with sabres and uniforms attached to the main church.

Mt Ypsario   HIKING
Potamia makes a good jumping-off point for climbing Thasos' highest peak, Mt Ypsario (1206m). A tractor trail west from Potamia continues to the valley's end, after which arrows and cairns point the way up a steep path. The three-hour Ypsario hike is classified as moderately difficult.

🏖 Beaches

Panagia and Potamia are 4km west of the east coast's most popular beaches: sand-duned **Hrysi Ammoudia (Golden Beach)**, tucked inside a long bay; and gentle **Skala Potamia**, on its southern end. Both have accommodation, restaurants and a bit of nightlife.

Further south from Skala Potamia is the deservedly popular and nudist-friendly **Paradise Beach**, 2km after tiny Kinyra village.

Beautiful **Livadi Beach** is 2.5km from Moni Arhangelou on the southeast coast.

🛏 Sleeping

There's some accommodation at Kinyra, Alyki and Paradise Beach, but more at Hrysi Ammoudia (Golden Beach) and Skala Potamia.

Thassos Inn   HOTEL €
(🖉25930 61612; www.thassosinn.gr; Panagia; d from €45; P 🕸) Just follow the sound of rushing spring water to this rambling hotel by the church for great views of Panagia's slate-roofed houses. The welcoming owners, Toula and Tasos, can also advise hikers who want to stay close to the Mt Ypsario trailhead.

Hotel Theo   HOTEL €
(🖉25930 61284; www.hotel-theo.gr; Panagia; d from €45; P ✳🕸) Very welcoming 14-room lodging with spotless rooms and a leafy courtyard overlooking the village. Breakfast €3 per person.

★ Hotel Kamelia   HOTEL €€
(🖉698898767, 25930 61463; www.hotel-kamelia. gr; Skala Potamia; s/d incl breakfast from €68/88; P ✳🕸) This beachfront gem is the best in town – understated, with cool jazz in the garden bar and friendly service throughout. The gracious owners, Eleni, Stavros and family, serve a fine Greek breakfast overlooking the sea and provide plenty of tips about the area. It's 500m north of the busier main beach, over a very small bridge.

🍴 Eating

Taverna Krambousa   SEAFOOD €
(Skala Potamia; mains €6-10; ⊙lunch & dinner) Relaxing, popular and well-priced fish taverna on the beach, just before Hotel Kamelia, in Skala Potamia.

Arhontissa Alyki   GREEK €
(🖉25930 31552; Alyki; mains €6-11; ⊙lunch & dinner) The friendly Anastasios Kuzis and family run this tranquil taverna with great sea views. It serves excellent fare, with fresh fish and mezedhes among the star offerings. Find it east of the village car park, signposted up a steep drive.

Evia & the Sporades

Best Places to Eat

➡ Dina's Amfilirion Restaurant (p638)

➡ Taverna-Ouzerie Kabourelia (p643)

➡ To Perivoli Restaurant (p648)

➡ Hayiati (p654)

➡ Stefanos Taverna (p660)

Best Places to Stay

➡ Hotel Nefeli (p657)

➡ Atrium Hotel (p645)

➡ Pension Sotos (p648)

➡ Liadromia Hotel (p653)

➡ Perigiali Hotel & Studios (p659)

Why Go?

Evia (Εὐβοια) and the four Sporades islands (Οι Σποράδες) remain largely off the beaten island path. Although Evia is Greece's second-largest island, it seems hidden in plain view, separated from the mainland by the narrow Evripos Channel at Halkida. Away from this workaday hub, the pace slows as the landscape stretches out, dotted by hilltop monasteries, small farms, vineyards, hidden bays and curious goats.

Most visitors will use Evia as a jumping-off point for the gorgeous Sporades ('scattered ones'). They seem like extensions of the forested Pelion Peninsula and, in fact, they were joined in prehistoric times. Skiathos, easily the most developed, claims the sandiest beaches in the Aegean. Low-key Skopelos kicks back with a postcard-worthy harbour and forest meadows, while remote Alonnisos anchors a national marine park. Southerly Skyros is known for culinary and artistic traditions dating from Byzantine times, when these islands were home to rogues and pirates.

When to Go
Skiathos Town

Feb & Mar Carnival season keeps things warm with plenty of merrymaking.

Apr & May Spring is in the air and Easter festivities linger long into the night.

Jun & Sep Perfect temperatures and clear skies – ideal hiking and swimming conditions.

Evia & the Sporades Highlights

1 **Manos Faltaïts Folk Museum** (p657) Delving into the artistic traditions and unique architecture of Skyros.

2 **Bouzouki music** (p648) Hearing live music at Ouzerie Anatoli, above the *kastro* overlooking Skopelos Town.

3 **Dimosari Gorge** (p641) Hiking this lush spot in south Evia, then cooling off in the sea near trail's end.

4 **Alonnisos** (p651) Watching for dolphins while sailing around Greece's only national marine park.

5 **Skopelos** (p645) Hiking the inland meadows among poppies and butterflies.

6 **Skyros** (p655) Nuzzling up with one of the gentle and rare Skyrian horses.

7 **Loutra Edipsou** (p638) Swimming year-round in this thermal-fed bay on Evia.

8 **Moni Evangelistrias** (p645) Sampling the monks' wine on Skiathos, where Greek independence was first declared in 1807.

EVIA   EYBOIA

POP 200,000

Evia, Greece's second-largest island after Crete, is mostly off the tourist map, with many visitors using it to nip off to smaller and more obviously enticing islands. Take some time here, though, and you'll find it offers glorious mountain roads, challenging treks, major archaeological finds and many uncrowded beaches. A north–south mountainous spine divides the island's eastern cliffs from the gentler and resort-friendly west coast.

Ferries link the island to the mainland, along with two bridges at humdrum Halkida. One of these bridges is a sliding drawbridge (the original span dates from 410 BC) over the narrow Evripos Channel, which reverses direction about seven times daily, an event whose full explanation has eluded observers since Aristotle, and was dreaded by ancient mariners.

ℹ Getting There & Away

There are regular buses between Halkida and Athens (€8, 1¼ hours, half-hourly), Ioannina (€45, seven hours, one to two daily) and Thessaloniki (€45, 6¼ hours, one to two daily).

There is also a regular train service between Halkida and Athens (€6.50, 1½ hours, 11 daily) and an express service between Halkida and Thessaloniki (€46, 5½ hours, six daily).

Five ports on Evia serve the mainland; one serves the island of Skyros; and another serves Skopelos and Skiathos.

Central Evia

Central Evia is forested, lush and graced with beaches on both coasts, though the more remote eastern beaches facing the Aegean Sea have finer sand and even clearer waters.

Beyond the mainland bridge entry to Evia at busy **Halkida**, the road veers south, following the coastline to **Eretria**, a bustling local resort and archaeological site that's of moderate interest.

Further on, a string of hamlets and fishing villages dot the route until the junction at Lepoura, where the road forks north towards **Kymi**, and south towards **Karystos**. A rough dirt road winds west from Kymi to a rock-enclosed arc of beach at **Paralia Hiliadou**.

Halkida   Χαλκίδα

POP 78,900

Mentioned in 'Iliad', once powerful Halkida (aka Halkis or Chalkis) spawned several colonies around the Mediterranean. The name derives from the bronze that was manufactured here in antiquity ('halkos' means bronze in Greek). Today there's little to detain tourists, but it's a lively commercial centre, and the gateway to Evia. As evening approaches, the waterfront promenade by the old bridge comes to life.

◉ Sights

To glimpse Halkida's diverse religious history, head up Kotsou towards the *kastro* (castle) to find a striking 15th-century mosque and 19th-century synagogue, adjacent to Plateia Tzami. About 150m south is the Byzantine church of Agia Paraskevi, and a Venetian aqueduct.

Archaeological Museum   MUSEUM
(☏ 22210 15131; Leoforos Venizelou 13; €2; ⊙ 8.30am-3pm Tue-Sun) Houses 7th-century-BC artefacts from both Halkida and nearby Eretria, including a headless torso of Apollo. Other remarkable finds from this former powerhouse city include a Hellenistic-era beak-mouthed jug and two golden wreaths.

BOAT SERVICES FROM EVIA

DESTINATION	PORT	FARE (€)	DURATION	FREQUENCY
Agia Marina	Nea Styra	4	45min	6-9 daily
Alonnisos	Paralia Kymis	26	3½hr	3 weekly
Arkitsa	Loutra Edipsou	4	40min	8-14 daily
Glyfa	Agiokambos	3	20min	5-7 daily
Rafina	Marmari	9	1hr	3-4 daily
Skala Oropou	Eretria	2.50	25min	half-hourly
Skopelos (Glossa)	Mantoudi	19	1½hr	3 weekly
Skyros	Paralia Kymis	12	1¾hr	1-2 daily

Kokkino Spiti ARCHITECTURE

(Red House; cnr Tziarntini & Dimitrou Karaoli; €2; ⊙ 9am-4pm Tue-Sun) Halkida's 19th-century grandeur just about endures at waterfront Kokkino Spiti. Carved into the rock, it became headquarters for the occupying Germans in WWII.

🍴 Sleeping & Eating

Hotel Paliria BUSINESS HOTEL €€

(☑ 22210 28001; www.paliria-hotel.gr; Eleftheriou Venizelou 2; s/d incl breakfast €60/80; P ✳ @ 🕏) The waterfront Paliria bears more than a passing resemblance to a modern seven-storey cruise ship, and occupies a prime spot near the old bridge, with spacious and plain carpeted rooms. It's not a thriller, but it is quiet and comfortable.

Pantheon 1900 TAPAS €

(Voudouri; €3-7; ⊙ 9am-1am) Nestled in a handsome neoclassical building on the waterfront, this smart tapas bar features Greek wines, tasty small plates and snappy service.

ℹ️ Information

Several ATMs cluster at the waterfront near the corner of Venizelou and Voudouri.

Post Office (cnr Karamourtzouni & Kriezotou; ⊙ 8am-2pm Mon-Fri)

ℹ️ Getting There & Away

From Halkida, buses serve Athens (€6.50, 1¼ hours, half-hourly), Ioannina (€39, seven hours, four to six daily) and Thessaloniki (€40, 6¼ hours, eight to 10 daily). Regular trains also connect Halkida with Athens, and an express service runs to Thessaloniki.

From **Halkida KTEL bus station** (☑ 22210 20400; cnr Styron & Arethousis), 3km east of the old bridge (taxi fare €4), buses also connect to the following destinations on Evia:

DESTINATION	DURATION	FARE (€)	FREQUENCY
Eretria	25min	2.20	hourly
Karystos	3hr	14.20	3 daily
Kymi Town & Paralia Kymis	2hr	9.20	3 daily
Limni	2hr	8	3 daily
Loutra Edipsou	3½hr	14.20	2 daily
Mantoudi	2hr	8.20	3 daily
Steni	50min	3.70	3 daily

Eretria Ερέτρια

POP 3600

Eretria, about 20km southeast from Halkida, is the first place of interest on Evia for travellers coming from the mainland. It has a small fishing harbour, substantial archaeological remains, and a touristy boardwalk of lively tavernas, open-air cafes and beach bars.

👁️ Sights

Ancient Eretria was a major maritime power with an eminent school of philosophy. The city was destroyed in AD 87 by the Roman commander Sylla. West of the ancient acropolis are the remains of a theatre with a subterranean passage used by actors to reach the stage, as well the remnants of baths, a gymnasium, a house with mosaics and a hilltop temple to Athena. Visit the Archaeological Museum for a map to tour these scant but fascinating sights.

Archaeological Museum of Eretria MUSEUM

(☑ 22290 62206; www.gtp.gr/archaeological museumoferetria; Archaiou Theatrou & Isidos; €2; ⊙ 8.30am-3pm Tue-Sun) The signature piece at the museum is a terracotta depiction of the mythical Medusa, whose tresses were turned into live serpents by the goddess Athena as revenge for Medusa's dalliance with Poseidon.

🍴 Sleeping & Eating

Milos Camping CAMPGROUND €

(☑ 22290 60420; www.camping-in-evia.gr; campsites per adult/tent €6/4) This well-managed and shaded campground, 1km northwest of Eretria, has a small restaurant, bar and 200m-long pebble beach.

Diamanto Rooms PENSION €

(☑ 22290 62214, 6946836529; www.diamanto rooms.gr; Varvaki 2; s/d €35/45; P ✳ @ 🕏) Ten sparkling but old-fashioned rooms with balconies, cheerful service, a common kitchen and a plant-wreathed entrance way. Ask for a room with a sea view.

Villa Belmar Apartments APARTMENT €€

(☑ 6971588424; www.villabelmar.gr; s/d/f incl breakfast from €45/65/90; P ✳ @ 🕏) Southwest of the port, these stylish apartments with a private waterfront deck are managed by welcoming sisters Lina and Renia.

Primavera TAVERNA €

(☑ 22290 64051; mains €6-12) A stand-out along the scenic but touristy seafront strip of restaurants, serving decent pizza, seafood, *mousakas* (baked layers of eggplant or zucchini, minced meat and potatoes topped with cheese sauce) and the like. Round it off with a slab of watermelon.

❶ Getting There & Away

Ferries travel daily between Eretria and Skala Oropou (€2, 25 minutes, half-hourly). Purchase tickets from the dock kiosks. There are regular buses to and from Halkida (€2.20, 25 minutes, hourly), which decant passengers in the centre of town.

Steni   Στενή

POP 1200

From Halkida, it's 31km to the picturesque mountain village of Steni, with its gurgling springs, and shady plane and chestnut trees. Steni is also the starting point for hikers tackling Mt Dirfys.

A twisting road continues from Steni to Paralia Hiliadou on the north coast, where a grove of maple and chestnut trees borders a beach, along with a few domatia (rooms in private homes) and tavernas.

🏃 Activities

Steni is the starting point for hiking up Mt Dirfys (1743m), Evia's highest mountain. The **Dirfys Refuge** (☑ 22210 85760, 22210 25230, mobile 6974057517; www.eoschalkidas.gr; per person €12), at 1120m, can be reached along a 9km dirt road. From there, it's a steep 7km to the summit. Experienced hikers should allow about six hours from Steni to the summit. For refuge lodging information (and key), as well as current hiking conditions, contact **Minas Patsourakis** (☑ 22210 85760, mobile 6974057517; www.facebook.com/groups/eoschalkidas) and the EOS-affiliated **Halkida Alpine Club** (☑ 22210 25230, 22210 25279; www.eoschalkidas.gr; Angeli Gouviou 22; ⊘ 9am-5pm Mon-Sat). See the Anavasi Topo 25 map, *Mt Dirfys 5.11 1:25,000*.

🛏 Sleeping

Hotel Dirfys   HOTEL €
(☑ 6972319451, 22280 51270; dirfis@otenet.gr; s/d incl breakfast €40/50; P 🐾) This is the most appealing of Steni's three hotels. All rooms have balcony views of the surrounding forest, sparkling bathrooms, and the hotel taverna draws in locals come evening.

O Neromylos   TAVERNA €
(Agia Kyriaki; mains €5-10; ⊘ lunch & dinner) The Watermill shares the lush landscape of Agia Kyriaki, signposted 3km southeast of Steni.

Kitchen favourites include roasted mushrooms and homemade sausages.

Kymi & Paralia Kymis
Κύμη & Παραλία Κύμης

POP 3250

The workaday town of Kymi perks up at dusk when the town square comes to life. Kymi is a prosperous agricultural centre surrounded by vineyards and fruit orchards. The port of Paralia Kymis, 4km downhill, is the departure point for ferries to Skyros, Alonnisos and, in summer, Skopelos.

◎ Sights

Folklore Museum   MUSEUM
(☑ 22220 22011; Kymi; €2; ⊘ 10.30am-1.30pm & 6-8pm Jul & Aug, 10.30am-2pm Wed, Sat & Sun rest of year) The Folklore Museum, 30m downhill from the main square of Kymi, includes a display honouring Kymi-born Dr George Papanikolaou, inventor of the Pap smear test and pioneer in the early diagnosis of cancer. There are also exhibits on traditional homes and clothing.

🛏 Sleeping & Eating

In Paralia Kymis, a string of tavernas lines the waterfront. Just 3km south in tiny Platana, there are a couple of excellent choices.

Corali Hotel   HOTEL €
(☑ 69794 45548; www.coralihotel.gr; Paralia Kymis; r from €40; ❄ 🐾) Much the best stop if you're waiting for a ferry. Corali is located just 500m from the port. The stylish modern building contains 21 plain, but comfortable, rooms. Farm fresh eggs and homemade pastries and jam feature on the breakfast menu.

Koutelos   TAVERNA €
(☑ 22220 71272; Platana; mains €7-11; ⊘ lunch & dinner) This century-old taverna is known for well-priced standards such as fish soup, *taramasalata* (a thick pink or white purée of fish roe, potato, oil and lemon juice), and crunchy *gavros* (a marinated small fish). Splurge on a half kilo of fresh lobster with salad and wine (about €40 for two), and look out at the sea view.

🛍 Shopping

Figs of Kymi   FOOD
(☑ 22220 31722; Platana; ⊘ 9am-9pm Sep-Nov) FREE Platana, located 3km south of Paralia Kymis, is home to Figs of Kymi, a lively agricultural co-op supporting local fig

farmers and sustainable production. Preservative-free fresh and dried figs and jams are on sale. Also open by appointment outside usual hours.

Northern Evia

From Halkida a road threads north into the mountainous interior of northern Evia, reaching the beautiful village of **Prokopi**, whose inhabitants are descended from refugees who came from Prokopion in Turkey's Cappadocia region in 1923. They established the substantial pilgrimage church of St John the Russian, named for the saint who remains central to the town's identity and livelihood to this day, and is celebrated with a festival on 27 May.

At Strofylia, the road heads southwest to picturesque **Limni**, which clusters around a bay, then north to the little thermal resort of Loutra Edipsou.

Loutra Edipsou   Λουτρά Αιδηψού

POP 3700

The sedate spa resort of Loutra Edipsou is the most visited spot in northern Evia. Its therapeutic sulphur waters have been celebrated since antiquity, and continue to draw a stream of medical tourists. Famous skinny-dippers have included Aristotle, Strabo, Plutarch, Plinius and Sylla.

Today, the town has Greece's most up-to-date hydrotherapy and physiotherapy centres, and several hotels have their own modern facilities. The town beach (Paralia Loutron) heats up year-round thanks to the thermal waters that spill into the bay.

🏃 Activities

EOT Hydrotherapy-
Physiotherapy Centre   SPA
(☑ 22260 23501; 25 Martiou St 37; ⏰ 7am-1pm & 5-7pm Jun-Oct) The more affordable of the resort's two big spas, the welcoming and attractive EOT Hydrotherapy-Physiotherapy Centre is speckled with palm trees and has a large outdoor pool that mixes mineral and sea water. Hydromassage bath treatments start at a very reasonable €8.

Thermae Sylla Hotel & Spa   SPA
(☑ 22260 60100; www.thermaesylla.gr; Posidonos 2; ⏰ 9am-8pm) This ultra-posh spa styles itself a 'thermal palace', with a late-Roman ambience befitting its name. It offers assorted health and beauty treatments, from

thermal mud baths to seaweed body wraps, and an outdoor pool with curving edges makes a dramatic centrepiece.

🛏 Sleeping

★ Hotel Kentrikon   HOTEL €
(☑ 22260 22302; www.kentrikonhotel.com; 25 Martiou 14; s/d/tr incl breakfast €40/50/60; ✹ ❀ ☏ ✸) Managed by Greek-Irish Konstantinos and Una, the Kentrikon is equal parts kitsch and old-world charm, with modern rooms and balcony views. A free thermal pool awaits, along with a professional massage therapist.

Hotel Irini   HOTEL €
(☑ 22260 22634; www.hotelirini.gr; Byzantinon Aftokratoron 1; s/d from €25/35; ✹ @ ☏) The cheerful and affordable Irini, tucked into a side street opposite the port, offers clean, snug rooms, most with sea views. It also has spa treatments and a *hammam* (Turkish baths), from €25.

Thermae Sylla Hotel & Spa   HOTEL €€€
(☑ 22260 60100; www.thermaesylla.gr; Posidonos 2; s/d/ste incl breakfast from €110/170/260; P ✹ @ ☏ ✸) This posh, in-your-mud-masked-face seaside resort offers elegant luxury accommodation as well as countless beauty treatments. Day visitors can sample the outdoor thermal pool (€35).

🍴 Eating

★ Dina's Amfilirion Restaurant   GREEK €
(28 Octovriou 26; mains €8-12; ⏰ lunch & dinner) Daily specials, no menu, await at this simple eatery 20m north of the ferry dock. A tasty grilled cod with oven potatoes, tomato-cucumber salad and wine runs to €12 per person. Look for the small wooden sign with green letters.

Deux Amis   BAKERY €
(28 Octovriou & Miaouli 1; items from €1.50) This friendly, expansive bakery-cafe on the waterfront is a good bet for tasty and filling *tyropita* (cheese pie), *bougatsa* (creamy semolina pudding wrapped in a pastry envelope and baked), and all kinds of cakes and ice cream.

Ouzerie Ta Kohilia   GREEK €
(☑ 22260 23478; 28 Octovriou 20; mains €4-7; ⏰ lunch & dinner) Look for the blue chairs outside to find the best mezedhes (appetisers) on the waterfront, next to the Avra Hotel.

❶ Getting There & Away

BOAT

Regular ferries run between Loutra Edipsou and mainland Arkitsa (€3.70, 40 minutes), and also between nearby Agiokambos and mainland Glyfa (€2.30, 20 minutes). Purchase tickets at the dock kiosks.

BUS

From the **KTEL bus station** (📞 22260 22250; Thermopotamou), 200m from the port, buses run to Halkida (€14.20, 3½ hours, twice daily), Athens (€14.20, three hours, three to four daily) via Arkitsa, and Thessaloniki (€24, four hours, daily) via Glyfa.

Limni   Λίμνη

POP 2300

Picturesque Limni's maze of whitewashed houses and narrow lanes spill onto a cosy harbour speckled with cafes and tavernas.

◉ Sights

Convent of Galataki   CONVENT
(📞 22270 31489; ⊙9am-noon & 5-8pm) The 16th-century Convent of Galataki lies 9km southeast of Limni, following a narrow road that hugs a picturesque shoreline (with plenty of stops for a swim) and then climbs steeply uphill. It is home to a coterie of six gently welcoming nuns and a fine fresco, *Entry of the Righteous into Paradise*, in its *katholikon* (principal church).

Museum of History & Folk Art   MUSEUM
(📞 22270 31335; www.gtp.gr/historicalandfolklore museumoflimni; Anagnosti Goviou 7; €2; ⊙9am-1pm Mon-Sat, 10.30am-2pm Sun) The town's quaint folk museum, 50m from the waterfront, houses handsome village costumes and domestic items.

✯ Festivals & Events

Skyllias Swimming Marathon   SPORTS
(https://sites.google.com/site/skylliaslimni; ⊙Jul) Limni's midsummer Elimnia Festival kicks off with the 14.5km Skyllias swimming marathon between mainland Theologos and Limni. It was named for the long-distance swimmer who, in 480 BC, warned the Greeks of the approaching Persian fleet.

🛏 Sleeping & Eating

Rovies Camping   CAMPGROUND €
(📞 22270 71120; campsites per adult/tent €7/6.50; 🄿🛜) Attractive, well-managed Rovies borders a pebble beach and a grove of olive and pine trees, 12km northwest of Limni. A restaurant and mini-market are open all day. There are 150 pitches, of which an increasing number are used by dive enthusiasts.

Home Graegos   APARTMENT €€
(📞 22270 31117; www.graegos.com; apt from €65; 🄿❄🛜) Graegos has four simple, but decent, apartments with modern kitchenettes and sweeping verandah sea views at the centre of the waterfront. The front two apartments have big balconies and sea views.

O Platanos   TAVERNA €
(mains €5-9; ⊙lunch & dinner) Tucked inside Limni's inner lanes, near the village museum, this popular local standby does excellent grills and hearty salads and serves great local wines.

Southern Evia

East of Eretria, the road branches south at Lepoura as the north's rich vegetation gives way to sparse and rugged mountains. A turn-off leads to **Lake Dhistos**, a shallow lake bed favoured by migrating egrets: water levels have been diminished by local agriculture. You'll pass high-tech windmills and catch views of both coasts as the island narrows before reaching **Karystos**, the only really enticing resort here, where friendly locals enjoy life at a pace that makes you forget how close you are to Athens.

Karystos   Κάρυστος

POP 5300

Set on wide Karystos Bay below Mt Ohi (1398m), and flanked by two sandy beaches, this low-key coastal resort is the starting point for treks to Mt Ohi and Dimosari Gorge. Karystos' lively Plateia Amalias faces the harbour, which glitters come evening with lights and bobbing boats.

◉ Sights

Archaeological Museum of Karystos   MUSEUM
(📞 22240 29218, 22240 25661; €2; ⊙8.30am-3pm Tue-Sun) Karystos, mentioned in Homer's 'Iliad', was a powerful city-state during the Peloponnesian Wars. The displays at the museum range from tiny Neolithic clay lamps to temple carvings and votive objects to an exhibit on the 6th-century-BC *drakospita* (dragon houses) of Mt Ohi and Styra. The museum sits opposite the castle.

WORTH A TRIP

WHISTLING VILLAGE OF ANTIA

East of Karystos, the 'whistling village' of Antia is famous for its linguistically talented villagers who speak in whistles. One of a small global group of whistling languages, this one was devised during Byzantine times to warn of danger and invasion from pirates, with each tone corresponding to a letter of the alphabet. Until the early 1980s the language was still widely used, but today it's mostly the old-timers who still put their lips together and blow. The good news involves a resurgence of interest in the whistling among the kids of Antia. Stay tuned.

Bourtzi   CASTLE

FREE Karystos' striking 14th-century Venetian castle is a remnant of the town's former fortifications. The low, bulky tower sits on the waterfront.

★☆ Festivals & Events

Wine & Cultural Festival   CULTURAL

(☑ 22240 22246) Karystos hosts a lively summer wine and cultural festival during the last week of August and the first week of September, which includes theatre performances, traditional dancing to the tune of local musicians, and exhibits by local artists. The summer merrymaking features local wines, free for the tasting.

🛏 Sleeping & Eating

★ Hotel Karystion   HOTEL €

(☑ 22240 22391; www.karystion.gr; Kriezotou 3; s/d incl breakfast from €40/50; P ❄ 🖙) The handsome Karystion sits above the beach just beyond the Bourtzi castle, and features modern, well-appointed rooms, a filling breakfast with homemade yoghurt and a helpful multilingual staff. A stairway leads to a sandy beach, great for swimming.

★ Cavo d'Oro   TAVERNA €

(mains €5-8; ☉ lunch & dinner) 🥗 Join the locals in this cheery alleyway restaurant off the main square for well-prepared Greek mainstays such as octopus in red wine sauce and country salads featuring local produce and olive oil. The genial owner, Kyriakos, is a regular at the summer wine festival, bouzouki in hand.

🍷 Drinking & Nightlife

Aeriko   BAR

(☑ 22240 22365; ☉ 8am-1am; 🖙) Aeriko is the pick of the harbour beach bars with a gorgeous sandy setting, live music on summer weekends, sun beds, decent drinks and an all-ages clientele.

❶ Information

Alpha Bank and Piraeus Bank ATMs are on the main square.

South Evia Tours (☑ 22240 26200; www.eviatravel.gr; Plateia Amalias; ☉ 10am-10pm)

❶ Getting There & Away

BOAT

There is a regular ferry service from Marmari (10km west of Karystos) to Rafina (€8.50, one hour), and from Nea Styra (35km north of Karystos) to Agia Marina (€3.80, 45 minutes).

Purchase tickets from either the dock kiosk or South Evia Tours.

BUS

From the **Karystos KTEL bus station** (☑ 22240 26303) opposite Agios Nikolaos church, buses run to Halkida (€14.20, three hours), Athens (€19, three hours) and Marmari (€1.80, 20 minutes). A taxi to Marmari costs €18.

Around Karystos

The ruins of Castello Rosso (Red Castle), a 13th-century Frankish fortress, are a short walk from Myli, a well-watered village 4km inland from Karystos. The aqueduct behind the castle once carried water from the mountain springs to the Bourtzi in Karystos. A 3km walk from Myli brings you to a 2nd-century-AD Roman quarry (Kylindroi, meaning 'cylinder') strewn with marble columns, abandoned during the time of Caesar.

With your own transport you can explore the pristine Cavo d'Oro villages nestling in the southern foothills of Mt Ohi. Highlights include Platanistos, Potami and the walled ruins of an ancient settlement at Helleniko.

◉ Sights & Activities

In addition to Dimosari Gorge and Mt Ohi, worthy day hikes above Karystos include ambles through the natural springs of **Agios Dimitrios Gorge**, where a branch trail ascends to scenic **Boublia Peak** (1127m). From tiny **Thymi**, a narrow dirt track reaches beautiful **Archampoli Beach**, about an hour's walk.

South Evia Tours can help organise hiking excursions to Mt Ohi's and Styra's *drakospita*, as well as bicycle and kayak rentals, and cruises around the Petali Islands (€38). Owner Nikos and staff also arrange transport for hikes to the summit of Mt Ohi and back, and four-hour guided walks through Dimosari Gorge (€25).

Mt Ohi   MOUNTAIN

From Myli, it's a four-hour hike up Mt Ohi (1398m) for magnificent Aegean views. It's possible to stay overnight at a refuge at 1000m, then hike up to catch sunrise. The summit (Profitis Ilias peak) is home to the ancient *drakospita,* Stonehenge-like dwellings or temples dating from the 7th century BC, hewn from rocks weighing several tonnes and joined without mortar.

The dragon houses' commanding position near marble quarries suggest that they were guard posts; another theory holds that they honoured mythological deities that roamed Mt Ohi, in particular the goddess Hera. Another dragon house near the road to Styra (30km north of Karystos) is equally fascinating.

★Dimosari Gorge   HIKING

A beautiful and well-maintained 10km trail that can be covered in four hours (including time for a swim). It begins in Petrokanalo village at 950m, descending through Lenosei village to the sea. Much of this stunning trek follows a cobbled path, splashing through shady creeks, ponds, giant ferns and forest before ending at the sand-and-pebble beach of Kallianos.

THE SPORADES

The Sporades (Οι Σποράδες) are home to four unique islands. Skiathos and its 60-odd beaches draws the most visitors by far, while handsome Skopelos strikes a cooler pose with its hidden bays and inland trails. Alonnisos, with one bus, four taxis and 27 churches, is the most remote and pristine of this northern group, while Skyros is home to wild horses and a lively arts scene.

Skiathos   Σκιάθος

POP 6450

Skiathos is blessed with some of the Aegean's most beautiful beaches, so it's little wonder that in July and August the island can fill up with sun-starved northern Europeans, as prices soar and rooms dwindle.

Skiathos Town, the island's major settlement and port, lies on the southeast coast. The rest of the south coast is interspersed with walled-in holiday villas and pine-fringed sandy beaches.

❶ Getting There & Away

AIR

Skiathos airport (JSI; ☑ 24270 29100) is 2km northeast of Skiathos Town. In summer there are daily flights to/from Athens with **Olympic Air** (☑ 24270 22200; www.olympicair.com), in addition to numerous charter flights from northern Europe. **Aegean Air** (☑ 24270 29100; https://en.aegeanair.com) has an office at the airport.

BOAT

Skiathos' main port is Skiathos Town, which has links to Volos and Agios Konstantinos on the mainland, and to island destinations Skopelos and Alonnisos. Tickets can be purchased from **Hellenic Seaways** (☑ 24270 22209; www.skiathosoe.com; cnr Papadiamantis).

❶ Getting Around

BOAT

Water taxis depart hourly from the old port for Achladies Bay (€2.70, 15 minutes), Kanapitsa (€3.20, 20 minutes) and Koukounaries (€5.30, 30 minutes).

Boat Services from Skiathos

DESTINATION	DURATION	FARE (€)	FREQUENCY
Agios Konstantinos	2½hr	32	1 daily
Agios Konstantinos*	1½hr	38	1-2 daily
Alonnisos	2hr	11	1 daily
Alonnisos*	1½hr	18	2 daily
Skopelos (Glossa)	30min	6.50	1 daily
Skopelos (Glossa)*	20min	11	2 daily
Skopelos (Skopelos Town)	1½hr	10.50	1 daily
Skopelos (Skopelos Town)*	45min	18	2 daily
Volos	2½hr	24	1-2 daily
Volos*	1½hr	38	1-2 daily

* hydrofoil services

Skiathos

BUS

Buses leave Skiathos Town for Koukounaries Beach (€2.20, 30 minutes, half-hourly) between 7.30am and 11pm. The buses stop at 26 numbered beach access points along the south coast.

CAR & MOTORCYCLE

Reliable motorbike and car-hire outlets in Skiathos Town include **Europcar/Creator Tours** (☑ 24270 22385; www.europcar.co.uk), which also rents bicycles, and Heliotropio Tourism & Travel (p644). Both are located at the new port.

TAXI

Taxis (☑ 24270 21460) leave from the stand opposite the ferry dock. A taxi to/from the airport costs €8, to Koukounaries €18 and to Moni Evangelistrias €9.

Skiathos Town   Σκιάθος

POP 5000

The town is a major tourist centre, with hotels, souvenir shops, galleries, travel agents, tavernas and bars spread along the

waterfront and Papadiamanti, the cobbled pedestrian thoroughfare. Away from the main drag, though, things quieten down quickly and you can catch more of a local flavour. Opposite the waterfront via a 15m causeway lies shady and inviting **Bourtzi Islet**, where you'll find a maritime museum and restaurant.

◉ Sights & Activities

Papadiamantis House Museum   MUSEUM
(☑ 24270 22240; Plateia Papadiamanti; €1.50; ◷10am-1pm & 5-7pm Tue-Sun) Skiathos was the birthplace of famous 19th-century Greek novelist and short-story writer Alexandros Papadiamantis, who is looked on as the father of modern Greek literature, and whose writings draw upon the hard lives of the islanders he grew up with. His plain whitewashed 1860 house is now a small and charming museum with books, paintings and photos of the author and his family. Bleak and ballad-like novella *The*

Murderess, set on Skiathos, is Papadiamantis' most famous work.

Maritime and Culture
Tradition Museum
MUSEUM

(€2; ⊙11am-1pm & 6.30-10.30pm) A former school on Bourtzi Islet houses a one-room local history museum. Staff will point out exhibits, which are signed in Greek and consist mostly of 20th-century paraphernalia relating to shipbuilding and navigation. The open-air theatre behind the museum is used for summer concerts.

★ Argo III Yacht
BOATING

(☑6932325167; www.argosailing.com; per person €65, sunset cruise €45) For a splendid sailing tour of the island waters between Skiathos and Alonnisos, climb aboard the *Argo III*, managed by husband-and-wife team George and Dina.

🛏 Sleeping

Skiathos House
PENSION €

(☑24270 22733; www.skiathoshouse.gr; off Papadiamanti; r from €30; ❉☎) Comfortable modern rooms and self-catering apartments at bargain prices, and with an amazingly central location in a small palm-shaded garden. Proprietor Denis is very welcoming and helpful. You'll find Skiathos House behind the post office, one street away from Papadiamanti.

Hotel Mouria
HOTEL €

(☑24270 21193; www.mouriahotel.com; Papadiamanti; d/tr/f incl breakfast from €40/60/80; ❉@☎) The handsome Mouria hides just behind the National Bank, set back in a flowery courtyard. There's a common kitchen for guests, though a full breakfast awaits, plus bright rooms and vintage photos all around. The taverna was once a regular haunt of Alexandros Papadiamantis.

★ Bourtzi Boutique
Hotel
BOUTIQUE HOTEL €€

(☑24270 21304; www.hotelbourtzi.gr; Moraitou 8, cnr Papadiamanti; d incl breakfast from €90; Ⓟ❉☎❄) On upper Papadiamanti, the swanky Bourtzi features austere-modern rooms, contrasted with warmly attentive staff, and an inviting garden and pool. They also provide a welcome cocktail, and a beach bag for your stay – with towel. Good online rates for three-night stays.

✖ Eating

★ Taverna-Ouzerie Kabourelia
TAVERNA €

(☑24270 21112; Old Harbour; mains €6-11; ⊙noon-midnight; ☎) Poke your nose into the open kitchen to glimpse the day's catch at this popular year-round taverna at the old port. Perfect fish grills and house wine are served at moderate prices. Grilled octopus and *taramasalata* are just two of several standout mezedhes.

★ Foodie
CAFE €

(Igloo; ☑24270 24076; Papadiamanti; snacks €1.50-3; ⊙6am-11pm) This is a great, quick and super-friendly stop for baguettes, cold drinks, ice cream and fresh juice, and breakfast goodies before early ferry departures.

O Batis
TAVERNA €

(☑24270 22288; Old Harbour; mains €4-9; ⊙noon-midnight) This popular fish taverna on the path above the old port is a local standby for reliable and well-priced fresh fish, *gavros,* and fine mezedhes. Cosy atmosphere and a good selection of island wines, year-round.

Taverna Hellinikon
TAVERNA €

(mains €7-10; ⊙lunch & dinner) Opposite the church above the old port, little Hellinikon is a mother-and-daughter affair, with well-prepared taverna standards like slow-roasted lamb. Good house wines, along with live Greek music on summer evenings.

Lo & La
MEDITERRANEAN €

(☑24270 29070; mains €7-12; ⊙lunch & dinner) Perched above the old port, Lo & La shows off an Italian-Greek couple's kitchen favourites. Pastas are handmade, and the risotto with local mushrooms excels.

★ La Cucina di Maria
RISTORANTE €€

(☑24270 24168; Plateia Trion Ierarhon; €8-15; ⊙dinner) Excellent thin-crust pizza twirled in the air is just the beginning at this popular spot above the old port. Fresh pasta, fine meat and fish grills in a colourful setting under the mulberry tree: look out for the bright plates embedded in the outside walls.

Bourtzi
TAPAS €€

(☑24270 23900; www.facebook.com/Bourtzi; mains €13-20; ⊙9am-2am) This chilled-out and elegant tapas joint and wine bar enjoys a sublime and secluded location on Bourtzi Islet. Come here for morning coffee, or to watch the sun set on the harbour.

🍸 Drinking & Entertainment

Kentavros
BAR

(🗹24270 22980; off Plateia Papadiamanti; ☉10am-late) Handsome Kentavros promises rock, jazz and blues, and has been getting the thumbs-up from locals and expats since 1978 for its mellow ambience, artwork and sturdy drinks.

Portobello
BAR

(🗹24270 29051; www.portobelloskiathos.gr; Papadiamanti; ☉8.30am-12.30pm; 🛜) Portobello eschews cocktail bling in favour of a fan-cooled terrace shaded by an olive tree and climbing plants. There's an epically long wooden bar and a laid-back vibe.

Cinema Attikon
CINEMA

(🗹24720 22352, 6972706305; tickets €7) Catch current English-language movies – mostly, if not exclusively, *Mamma Mia!* – at this open-air cinema. Sip a beer and practise speed-reading your Greek subtitles.

🛍 Shopping

★ Galerie Varsakis
ANTIQUES

(🗹24270 22255; www.varsakis.com; Plateia Trion Ierarhon; ☉10am-2pm & 6-11pm) Browse for unusual antiques, such as 19th-century spinning sticks made by grooms for their intended brides – the collection rivals the best Greek folklore museums. Upstairs is a dazzling display of the owner's paintings, in oil on gold leaf, begun in the 1970s. They depict Greek myths and predatory contemporary politicians. Downstairs there's an original 1830s kitchen.

Loupos & His Dolphins
ANTIQUES

(🗹24270 23777; Plateia Papadiamanti; ☉10am-1.30pm & 6-10.30pm) Find delicate hand-painted icons, handsome ceramics and an array of jewellery at this quality bougainvillea-framed gallery shop, in the courtyard by Papadiamantis House Museum (p642).

Blue House Art Gallery
ARTS & CRAFTS

(🗹24270 21681; Nikotsara St; ☉10am-10pm) Handmade jewellery, ceramics and vintage pieces stand out at this intimate and lovely shop behind the old port.

Efimeris
GIFTS & SOUVENIRS

(www.facebook.com/efimeris.skiathos; Papadiamanti 39; ☉10am-10pm) Among many identikit boutiques, this one stands out for its focus on handmade Greek products, from striped fabric towels to turquoise rings to elegant woven clutch bags.

ℹ Information

The bus terminus is at the northern end of the new harbour with departures to the island beaches. Regular water taxis leave from the old port for Achladies Bay, Kanapiitsa and Koukounaries. You'll find car-hire outlets and taxis at the new port.

Numerous ATMs are on Papadiamanti and the waterfront.

Creator Tours (🗹24270 22385; www.creator tours.com; New Harbour; ☉10am-9pm)
Heliotropio Tourism & Travel (🗹24270 22430; www.heliotropio.gr; ☉7.30am-11pm)
Port Police (🗹24270 22017; New Harbour)
Post Office (Papadiamanti; ☉8am-2pm)
Tourist Police (🗹24270 23172; Ring Rd; ☉8am-9pm)

Around Skiathos

🏖 Beaches

With 65 beaches to choose from, beach-hopping on Skiathos can become a full-time occupation. Buses ply the south coast, stopping at 26 numbered beach access points. The first long stretch of sand worth stopping at is wide and pine-fringed **Vromolimnos Beach**. The road then continues to the white sands of **Koukounaries Beach**, which is backed by pine trees and a small wetland. Come the busy midsummer period, it's best viewed at a distance, from where the 1200m-long sweep of pale gold sand does indeed sparkle.

West of Koukounaries, **Big Banana Beach**, known for its curving shape, soft sand and beach-bar buzz, lies across a narrow headland. Skinny-dippers prefer to hang at equally frenetic **Little Banana Beach** (also popular with gay and lesbian sunbathers) around the rocky corner, though current building works are impeding access.

About 400m north, the narrow arc of **Agia Eleni Beach** is a favourite with windsurfers. Soft-sand **Mandraki Beach**, a 1.5km walk along a pine-shaded path, is distant enough to keep it clear of the masses, while sporting a good taverna. From Troulos, it's 4km to **Megalos Aselinos Beach**, a long and lovely stretch of sand, with tiny rock-enclosed **Mikros Aselinos** and secluded **Kehria Beach** hidden down a steep track a few kilometres further on.

The northwest coast's beaches are less crowded but are subject to summer *meltemi* (dry northerly winds). **Lalaria Beach** is a tranquil strand of pale grey, egg-shaped pebbles on the northern coast with a scenic rock arch, but can only be reached by excursion boat from Skiathos Town.

◎ Sights

★Moni Evangelistrias MONASTERY
(☑24270 22012; museum €2; ☺10am-dusk) This famously historic monastery was a hilltop refuge for freedom fighters during the War of Independence, and the Greek flag was first raised here in 1807. Today, two monks do the chores, which include winemaking. You can sample the tasty results in the museum shop. An adjacent shed of vintage olive and wine presses recalls an earlier era, before the satellite dish appeared above the courtyard.

Kastro RUINS
(☺24hr) FREE Perched dramatically on a rocky headland above the north coast, Kastro was the fortified pirate-proof capital of the island from 1540 to 1829. An old cannon remains at the northern end, along with four restored churches, including Christos, home to several fine frescoes. Excursion boats come from the old port in Skiathos Town to the beach below Kastro, from where it's an easy clamber up to the ruins.

Moni Panagias Kounistras MONASTERY
(☺dawn-dusk) From Troulos, a road winds 4km inland to the serene 17th-century Moni Panagias Kounistras, worth a visit for the fine frescoes adorning its *katholikon*.

⚒ Activities

Diving
The small islets off the south shore of Skiathos make for great diving and snorkelling. The dive-instructor team of Theofanis and Eva of **Octopus Diving Centre** (☑6944168958, 24270 24549; www.odc-skiathos.com; New Harbour; half-day dives €50-60) leads dives around Tsougria and Tsougriaki islets for beginners and experts alike. Enquire at their boat on the new harbour in Skiathos Town. **Dolphin Diving** (☑6944999181; www.ddiving.gr; Hotel Nostos, Tzaneria Beach; half-day dives €50-60) and **Skiathos Diving Centre** (☑6977081444; www.skiathosdiving.gr; Koukounaries; from €49) also have strong reputations.

Hiking
A 6km-long hiking route begins at Moni Evangelistrias and eventually reaches **Cape Kastro** before circling back through **Agios Apostolis**. Kastro is a spring mecca for

birdwatchers, who may spot long-necked Mediterranean shags or blue rock-thrushes skimming the waves.

🛏 Sleeping & Eating

Achladies Apartments APARTMENT €
(☑24270 22486; www.achladiesapartments.com; Achladies Bay; d/tr/f incl breakfast €60/75/80; P🔊) This welcoming gem, 5km south of Skiathos Town, features comfortable kitchenette rooms with ceiling fans, plus an eco-friendly tortoise sanctuary and a rambling succulent garden (complete with an aviary) winding down to a sandy beach. From here, water taxis connect with Skiathos Town and Koukounaries Beach.

Camping Koukounaries CAMPGROUND €
(☑24270 49250; Koukounaries Beach; campsites per adult/tent €11/free; P🔊) Shaded by fig and mulberry trees opposite Koukounaries Beach, with spotless bathroom, cooking facilities, washing machines, a minimarket and taverna. Cash only.

★Atrium Hotel HOTEL €€
(☑24270 49345; www.atriumhotel.gr; Paraskevi Beach; s/d/ste incl breakfast from €105/140/200; P🅿◉🔊🏊) Traditional architecture and soothing modern decor make this hillside perch the best in its class. Elegant rooms feature private sinks and private balconies overlooking the sea. Amenities include a sauna, a children's pool, billiards, ping-pong and a lavish breakfast buffet to start the day. Two-night rates available online.

Panorama Pizza PIZZA €
(www.skiathospanorama.gr; Ring Rd; pizzas €8-12; ☺noon-4pm & 7pm-late; 🕿) Hilltop retreat off the Ring Rd for brick-oven pizza and perfect views.

Salt & Pepper INTERNATIONAL €€
(☑24270 49329; Troulos; mains €8-14; ☺lunch & dinner) This popular upscale eatery features innovative fish and meat grills and traditional salad and veggie dishes. A full bar anchors the outdoor garden. Opposite the Troulos turn-off.

Skopelos Σκόπελος
POP 6000
Skopelos is a handsome island of pine forests, vineyards, olive groves, and orchards of plums and almonds, which find their way into many local dishes.

EVIA & THE SPORADES SKOPELOS

Like neighbouring island Skiathos, the high cliffs of the northwest coast are exposed, while the sheltered southeast coast harbours several sand-and-pebble beaches. There are two settlements: the wonderfully attractive main port of Skopelos Town on the east coast and the northwest village of Glossa, 2km north of Loutraki, the island's second port.

ⓘ Getting There & Away

Skopelos has two ports, Skopelos Town and Glossa (aka Loutraki). Both link to Volos and Agios Konstantinos on the mainland, and the islands of Skiathos, Alonnisos and Skyros.

Tickets are available from **Hellenic Seaways** (🕿 24240 22767; ⏱ 9am-10pm) in Skopelos Town and the port of Glossa; and from Madro Travel (p649) on the waterfront in Skopelos Town.

ⓘ Getting Around

BOAT

A water taxi departs Skopelos Town late morning for Glysteri Beach (€6 each way).

BUS

In summer there are four to six buses per day from Skopelos Town to Glossa/Loutraki (€5.60, 55 minutes) and Neo Klima (Elios; €4, 45 minutes); and three more that go to Panormos

(€3.20, 25 minutes), Milia (€3.80, 35 minutes), Agnontas (€1.80, 15 minutes) and Stafylos (€1.70, 15 minutes).

CAR & MOTORCYCLE

For car and motorcycle hire, head to **Magic Cars** (🕿 24240 23250, 6973790936; http://skopelos. net/magiccars; Potoki) in the town centre.

TAXI

Taxis wait by the bus stop in Skopelos Town. A taxi to Stafylos is €8, to Limnonari €14 and to Glossa €34.

Skopelos Town Σκόπελος

POP 4800

Skopelos Town skirts a semicircular bay and rises in picturesque tiers up a hillside of dazzling white houses with bright shutters and flower-adorned balconies, ending at an old fortress and a cluster of four gleaming whitewashed churches.

The town's waterfront is flanked by two quays. The old quay wraps around the western end of the harbour; the new quay at the eastern end is used by all ferries and hydrofoils.

Strolling around town and sitting at the waterside cafes might be your chief occupations in Skopelos, but there are also two small museums.

BOAT SERVICES FROM SKOPELOS

DESTINATION	PORT	DURATION	FARE (€)	FREQUENCY
Agios Konstantinos	Skopelos Town	4hr	36	1 daily
Agios Konstantinos*	Skopelos Town	2½hr	54	1 daily
Agios Konstantinos**	Glossa	2½hr	47	1 daily
Alonnisos	Glossa	1hr	9	1 daily
Alonnisos*	Skopelos Town	30min	6	2-3 daily
Alonnisos**	Skopelos Town	20min	9.50	2 daily
Skiathos (via Glossa)	Skopelos Town	1½hr	10.50	2-3 daily
Skiathos*	Skopelos Town	45min	18	2 daily
Skiathos**	Glossa	30min	11	2 daily
Evia (Mantoudi)	Glossa	1¾hr	19.80	3 weekly
Evia (Paralia Kymis)	Skopelos Town	4hr	26	4-6 weekly
Volos	Skopelos Town	3¾hr	25.70	2 daily
Volos*	Skopelos Town	3hr	26.50	2-3 daily
Volos**	Glossa	2½hr	40	1 daily

*fast-ferry services/**hydrofoil services

EVIA & THE SPORADES SKOPELOS

Skopelos

Skiathos (1.5km);
Volos (55km);
Agios Konstantinos (67km)

Cape
Gourouni

Aegean
Sea

Perivoliou
Beach

Church of
Agios Ioannis
Kastri

Glossa
Loutraki
Mahalas

Roman
Baths
▲383m
Palio
Klima
Kaloyeros

Skiathos (10km);
Evia (Mantoudi; 35km);
Volos (50km);
Agios Konstantinos
(62km)

Glysteri
Beach

Alonnisos Strait

Alonnisos (12km);
Skyros (Summer Only);
80km)

Agios
Georgios

▲
690m

Neo Klima
(Elios)

Karia

Skopelos
Bay
Moni
Varvaras

Moni
Prodromou
Moni Metamorfosis

Skopelos Town
Ring Rd

Moni
Evangelistras
Moni
Sotiros
567m
▲

Cape
Kiourto

Skopelos
Strait

Kastani Beach
Dasia
Milia
Beach
Andrines Beach
Panormos
Beach

Limnonari
Rooms
258m
▲

Aegean
Sea

Cape
Myti

Limnonari
Beach

Stafylos
Agnontas

Velanio
Beach

Agnontas
Bay
Taverna
Pavlos
Cape
Amarandos

Stafylos Beach
Mando
Rooms

Cape Velona

Sights & Activities

Vakratsa Mansion Museum   MUSEUM
(24240 23494; €3; 10am-2pm & 6-9pm)
Housed in what was a doctor's 18th-century
mansion, this museum displays medical
instruments of the era as well as traditional
clothing for married and unmarried men
and women, and is well worth seeing for
the window it offers onto middle-class
Greek life in the 19th century. It's near
the middle of the waterfront, 100m inland
from Ploumisti Shop, housed behind a high,
white wall.

Folklore Museum   MUSEUM
(24240 23494; Hatzistamati; €3; 10am-2pm
& 7-10pm Mon-Fri) This handsome museum
features a Skopelean wedding room, complete with traditional costumes and bridal
bed. It's a block west of Agios Nikolaou
Church.

Skopelos Cycling   CYCLING
(24240 22398, 6947023145; skopeloscycling@
yahoo.gr; per 24hr €10-18; 10am-2pm & 6-10pm
Mon-Fri, 10am-2pm Sat) High-quality trekking
and mountain bikes, and bike tours, are available from Panos Provias at Skopelos Cycling,
who will lend you maps and advise on routes.
It's located near the post office (p649).

SkopArt   ART
(Skopelos Foundation for the Arts; 24240 24143;
www.skopartfoundation.org; Raches) Perched
high above Skopelos Town, SkopArt offers
popular residential classes, ranging from
painting and drawing to ceramics and
paper-making.

Sleeping

★ Thea Home Hotel   PENSION €
(24240 22859; www.theahomehotel.com; Ring
Rd; d/apt from €40/80) Fresh and modern
rooms with sea views that are well worth

the steep walk up from town. There's a small pool, and breakfast includes thick Greek yoghurt, fruit and homemade pastries.

★ Pension Sotos
PENSION €

(☑ 24240 22549; www.skopelostravel.net/sotos; s/d from €30/45; ❄ � 🛜) The pine-floored rooms at this charming waterfront pension are each a bit different; an old brick oven serves as a handy shelf in one. There's a relaxing interior courtyard, a flowery terrace and a communal kitchen, all managed by the welcoming and resourceful Alexandra. Amazingly secluded feel, despite the super-central location.

Ionia Hotel
HOTEL €€

(☑ 24240 22568; www.ioniahotel.gr; s/d/tr/f incl breakfast from €65/75/55/95; 🅿 ❄ @ 🛜 🌊) Stylish and quiet, the Ionia is tucked away, a five-minute stroll from the Skopelos Town waterfront. Service is excellent and rooms surround a spacious courtyard with a pool.

✕ Eating

To Rodi
GREEK €

(☑ 24240 24601; Chimou; mains €4.50-10; ⊙ 7pm-midnight) Classy and comfortable courtyard eatery with a pomegranate tree; just follow the signs for Hidden Door bar and you'll find it further up and on the right. Pork in wine sauce is a speciality.

Ta Kymata
TAVERNA €

(☑ 24240 22381; mains €5-9.50) The oldest tavern on the island, at the end of the old port, has had a steady local following for its hearty grills and classic *mayirefta* (ready-cooked meals) since 1896. They have a veggie-specific menu, as well as swordfish, lobster and humbler dishes including shrimps cooked with sundried tomatoes and ouzo.

O Michalis
CAFE €

(8am-late; snacks €3-5) The red door and hand-painted signs give away this snappy hole-in-the-wall serving superb *tyropita*. At night the place morphs into a mellow wine bar. It's mid-waterfront, a block inland from Pension Sotos.

★ Anna's Restaurant
GREEK €€

(☑ 24240 24734; Gifthorema; mains €7-17; ⊙ 7pm-midnight) A lone palm tree marks this handsome and upscale alleyway bistro that serves authentic Skopelean dishes such as sautéed veal with plums. There's a good Greek wine list and healthy salads with ingredients such as goji berries and seaweed. Live traditional music on Saturday nights.

★ To Perivoli Restaurant
GREEK €€

(☑ 24240 23758; mains €7-14; ⊙ 7.30pm-midnight) Perivoli delivers excellent Greek cuisine in an elegant and secluded courtyard setting just above Plateia Platanos. Specialities include rolled pork with *koromila* (local plums) in wine sauce, plus fine Greek wines.

🍷 Drinking & Nightlife

★ Cafe Bar Thalassa
CAFE

(☑ 6978929975; ⊙ 10am-9pm) Clamber above the churches at the far end of the old quay to this divine sea-view terrace. It's friendly and efficient, with coffees, fresh fruit and cocktails served from a tiny blue-shuttered kitchen.

★ Platanos Jazz Bar
BAR

(☑ 24240 23661) Near the end of the old quay under a vast spreading tree, this is the hippest spot for a coffee or a quiet drink. No touts, no fuss and a great soundtrack of jazz, Beatles and Dylan.

Pablo's Bar
COCKTAIL BAR

(☑ 24240 24804; Old Port; ⊙ 6pm-3am) Owner-bartender Christos serves up mellow jazz and mellower cocktails; there's a breezy roof terrace above it all. Far southwest end of the waterfront, above Ta Kymata taverna.

Hidden Door
BAR

(☑ 6978252848; ⊙ 7pm-late) Mellow bar on a quieter lane behind the waterfront, in a converted 100-year-old house where a side, or hidden, door once led to the kitchen. Three blocks inland from Agios Nikolaos Church.

Oionos Blue Bar
BAR

(☑ 6942406136) Cosy and cool, little Oionos serves up blues and soul plus a good selection of single malt whiskies.

☆ Entertainment

★ Ouzerie Anatoli
TRADITIONAL MUSIC

(⊙ 8pm-2am summer) Wait till at least 11pm, then head to this breezy outdoor *ouzerie* (place that serves ouzo and light snacks), high above the *kastro* near the southeast corner of the waterfront, to hear traditional *rembetika* (blues songs) sung by Georgos Xindaris, Skopelos' own exponent of the Greek blues and a bouzouki master.

🛍 Shopping

The waterfront hosts some wonderful shops selling quality ceramics, small paintings, icons and handmade jewellery.

★**Skopelos Sandals**   SHOES
(⊙10am-10pm) Classic handmade leather sandals and belts, adjusted to fit by the genial owner. The leather stretches, so wear your sandals around town for a few days and go back to have them readjusted if need be. Prices are great – around €20 to €30 for sandals. You'll find the shop a couple of blocks uphill from Pension Sotos.

★**Ploumisti Shop**   ARTS & CRAFTS
(☑24240 22059; Waterfront; ⊙9am-midnight) The same couple have been running this wonderful shop for 40 years, selling linen shirts and scarves, paintings, jewellery and ceramics. You can hear the owner play *rembetika* every Saturday night at Anna's Restaurant.

ⓘ Information

There are four ATMs along the waterfront.
Dolphin Tours (☑6977468190, 24240 29191; www.dolphinofskopelos.com; Waterfront; ⊙10am-9pm)
Health Centre (☑24240 22222; Ring Rd; ⊙10am-8pm)
Madro Travel (☑24240 22300; www.madro travel.com; Waterfront; ⊙9am-10pm)
Police (☑24240 22235; New Quay)
Port Police (☑24240 22180; Old Quay)
Post Office (opposite Panagia Church; ⊙7.30am-2pm)
Thalpos Holidays (☑24240 29036; www.holidayislands.com; Waterfront; ⊙10am-8pm)

Glossa & Loutraki
Γλώσσα & Λουτράκι
POP 950

Glossa, Skopelos' second settlement, is a whitewashed cluster of shops and eateries. A 2km road winds down from the small square to the laid-back port of Loutraki ('Glossa' in ferry timetables). A shorter *kalderimi* (cobblestoned path) connects both villages as well. Fans of the 2008 movie *Mamma Mia!* can start their pilgrimage in Glossa to reach the film's little church, Agios Ioannis Kastri (St John of the Castle).

Loutraki means 'small bath' and you can see the remains of ancient Roman baths at the archaeological kiosk on the port.

🤿 Activities

Kayaking Greece   KAYAKING
(Sea Kayak Center; ☑24240 33805, 6983211298; www.kayakinggreece.com) This well-managed kayaking outfit based in Glossa offers everything from full-day trips (€65) and simple sunset outings (€35) to six-day adventures (€590) and customised island expeditions led by CUB-qualified guides.

🛏 Sleeping & Eating

Pension Platana   PENSION €
(☑24240 33188, 6973646702; pensionplatana@hotmail.com; Glossa; r from €35; P ❋ 🕸) This cosy and welcoming domatia has overhead fans, kitchenettes and balcony views overlooking the port of Loutraki. Welcoming Greek-Australian owner Eleni provides tea and tips. About 30m past the Shell petrol station on the left.

★**Flisvos Taverna**   TAVERNA €
(☑24240 33856; Loutraki; mains €4-9; ⊙lunch & dinner) With simple Greek fare at its best, friendly beachfront Flisvos offers fresh fish at reasonable prices, along with traditional standards, such as *mousakas* and *stifadho* (meat, game or seafood cooked with onions in a tomato purée). Appetisers such as tzatziki (sauce of grated cucumber, yoghurt and garlic) and *taramasalata* excel.

Around Skopelos

Visitors to Skopelos can see several monasteries via a scenic drive or day-long trek above Skopelos Town. Begin by following Monastery Rd, which skirts the bay and then climbs inland to 18th-century convent **Moni Evangelistrias**, home to a solitary nun. The monastery's prize, aside from superb views, is a gilded iconostasis containing an 11th-century icon of the Virgin Mary.

Further on, 16th-century **Moni Metamorfosis Sotiros** is the island's oldest monastery. From there a narrow road continues to 17th-century **Moni Varvaras** overlooking the bay below, and 18th-century convent **Moni Prodromou**, 8km from Skopelos Town.

🏖 Beaches

Most of Skopelos' best beaches are on the sheltered southwest and west coasts; a good way to reach them is by hiring a bike from Skopelos Cycling (p647).

The first beach you come to is sand-and-pebble **Stafylos Beach**, 4km southeast of

Skopelos Town. From its eastern end, a path leads over a small headland to the quieter **Velanio Beach**, the island's official nudist beach and coincidentally a great snorkelling spot. Lovely **Agnontas**, 3km west of Stafylos, has a pebble-and-sand beach from where caïques depart to sheltered and sandier **Limnonari Beach**.

You could easily lose a day to picnicking and hidden-cove swimming at **Cape Amarandos**. Around 75m before you reach Agnontas, take the left-hand turn, following a steep rocky track at the bend. The track provides umpteen private rocky beach stops, but if you keep going to a sharp left turn you'll see a dramatic cleft in the rocks. Follow the faint path here along the cliff to the water's edge, where a sea cave and pine shade provides a wonderfully spectacular stop.

From Agnontas, the road cuts inland through pine forests before re-emerging at pretty **Panormos Beach**, which has tavernas and domatia. The next two bays, **Milia** and **Kastani**, are excellent for swimming. On the island's northeast coast, serene **Perivoliou Beach** is a 25-minute drive from Glossa.

🏃 Activities

★**Heather Parsons' Guided Walks** WALKING

(📞6945249328; http://skopelos-walks.com; tours €20-25) If you can't tell a twin-tailed pascha butterfly from a leopard orchid, join one of island resident Heather Parsons' guided walks. Her four-hour Panormos walk follows a centuries-old *kalderimi* path across the island, ending at a beach taverna, with wonderful views to Alonnisos and Evia along the way. Her book *Skopelos Trails* contains graded trail descriptions.

Heather and a loyal band of volunteers continue to clear, signpost and GPS the trails across the island. She also offers *Mamma Mia!* jeep tours to most of the movie's filming locations.

🛏 Sleeping & Eating

Limnonari Rooms & Taverna APARTMENT €

(📞24240 23046, 6946464515; www.skopelos. net/limnonarirooms; Limnonari Beach; d/tr/ste from €35/60/80; P🅿❄🛜) This cluster of 10 well-equipped apartments faces beautiful Limnonari Bay. The family's garden taverna serves vegetarian *mousakas,* fish and meat grills, and homemade olives and feta.

★**Guesthouse Mando Beachfront** APARTMENT €€

(📞24240 23917, 6936131316; mando_skopelos@ yahoo.gr; Stafylos; d/tr/f incl breakfast from €75/85/115; P🅿❄🛜) Nestled behind a cove on Stafylos Bay, this well-managed, family-oriented lodging offers modest rooms alongside luxe villas, plus an outdoor communal kitchen and a solid platform over the rocks from which to enter the sea for swimming and snorkelling.

★**Taverna Pavlos** TAVERNA €€

(📞24240 22409; Agnondas; mains €9-15; ⊙lunch & dinner) Locals think nothing of driving over to Agnontas for beautifully prepared fresh fish and excellent mezedhes at this shaded taverna steps from the beach. Octopus *stifadho* (cooked with onions in a tomato purée) and fava dip are just two of the star offerings.

Alonnisos   Αλόννησος

POP 3500

Alonnisos rises from the sea in a mountain of greenery, with stands of Aleppo pine, kermes oak, mastic and arbutus bushes, vineyards, olive and fruit trees, threaded with perfumy patches of wild herbs. The west and north coasts are steep and rocky, while the east is speckled with bays and pebble-and-sand beaches.

Alonnisos has had its share of bad luck; in 1952, a thriving wine industry collapsed when vines imported from California were infested with phylloxera insects. Robbed of their livelihood, many people moved away. Then, in 1965, an earthquake destroyed the hilltop capital of Old Alonnisos. Inhabitants were rehoused at Patitiri, which has since evolved into a quaint island port; 11km to the north is the seaside village of Steni Vala. The most recent trouble was in early 2017, when storms destroyed a third of the island's trees; many inhabitants decamp to Athens for the surprisingly harsh winter season.

❶ Getting There & Away

Alonnisos' main port of Patitiri has links to mainland Volos and Agios Konstantinos; to Paralia Kymis on Evia; and to nearby Skopelos, Skiathos and (summer only) Skyros.

Tickets can be purchased from Alkyon Travel (p653), Albedo Travel (p653) and Alonnisos Travel (p653) in Patitiri.

Boat Services from Alonnisos

DESTINATION	DURATION	FARE (€)	FREQUENCY
Agios Konstantinos*	2½hr	54	4 weekly
Agios Konstantinos**	3½hr	36	1 daily
Evia (Paralia Kymis)	2½hr	25	2-3 weekly
Skiathos	2hr	11.50	4 weekly
Skiathos*	1½hr	18	4-5 daily
Skopelos	40min	6	1 daily
Skopelos*	20min	9.50	2-3 daily
Skopelos (Glossa)*	45min	14	3-4 daily
Volos*	2½hr	52	1-2 daily
Volos**	3½hr	30	1-2 daily

*hydrofoil services
**fast-ferry services

❶ Getting Around

BUS

A bus plies the route between Patitiri and Old Alonnisos (€1.70), and then heads to Steni Vala (€1.80). Additionally, a summer **beach bus** (☑ 6973805610; round trip €5) leaves Patitiri around 10.30am for points to the north and returns after 4pm.

CAR & MOTORCYCLE

Several motorcycle-hire outlets cluster near the waterfront in Patitiri, including reliable **I'm Bike** (☑ 24240 65010). For cars, try Albedo Travel (p653) or Alonnisos Travel (p653), also in Patitiri.

TAXI

A few taxis congregate opposite the Alykon Hotel on the waterfront in Patitiri. It costs €6 to Old Alonnisos, €10 to Leftos Gialos and €13 to Steni Vala.

Patitiri   Πατητήρι

POP 1800

Patitiri (meaning Wine Press) sits between two sandstone cliffs at the southern end of the east coast. The quay is in the centre of the waterfront, from where two roads lead inland; the main road is the one closest to the harbour. There are no road signs: people simply refer to the left-hand or right-hand road.

◉ Sights

★National Marine Park of
Alonnisos Northern Sporades   NATIONAL PARK
(www.alonissos-park.gr) In a country not noted for ecological foresight, the National Marine Park of Alonnisos (the largest marine park in Europe) is a welcome innovation. Created in 1992, its prime aim has been the protection of the endangered Mediterranean monk seal and several rare seabirds. In summer, licensed boats from Alonnisos and Skopelos conduct excursions through the pristine park. Though it's unlikely you'll find the shy monk seal, chances of spotting dolphins are fairly good. Buy excursion tickets from waterfront agencies.

★**Alonnisos Museum**   MUSEUM
(☑ 24240 66250; www.alonissosmuseum.com; adult/child €4/free; ☺ 11am-6pm May & Sep, to 8pm Jun-Aug) This town museum includes antique nautical maps, a well-signed collection of pirates' weapons and boarding equipment, and an absorbing display on wartime resistance. Downstairs there's a recreated farmhouse interior, and artefacts relating to traditional crafts and industries. Go down Bar St on the beach and follow the signs up to the museum.

MOM Information Centre   MUSEUM
(☑ 24240 66350; www.mom.gr; Waterfront; ☺ 10am-10pm Jun-Sep) FREE Don't miss this excellent waterfront info centre, all about the protected and extremely appealing Mediterranean monk seal. It has good displays, videos with English subtitles and helpful multilingual staff on hand. They are campaigning to ban the ubiquitous plastic bags handed out by local shopkeepers.

☗ Activities

Boat Trips

Sea-kayaking excursions around Alonnisos, from half-day to overnight cove camping, are arranged by Albedo Travel (p653).

Both Albedo Travel and Alonnisos Travel (p653) hire out four-person 15HP to 25HP motorboats (from €53 to €77 per day).

Diving

A few ancient sailing vessels have been discovered at the bottom of the shallow sea around Alonnisos. Efforts are under way to open these sites to guided dives. Contact **Alonissos Triton Center** (☑ 24240 65804; http://bestdivingingreece.com; scuba dives from €65) or Ikion Diving (p655).

Alonnisos

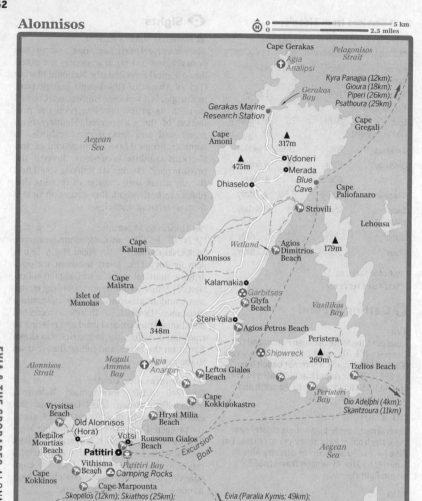

Hiking

A 2.5km *kalderimi* path winds up through shrubbery and orchards to Old Alonnisos. Albedo Travel can help arrange guided walks.

Tours

Two full-service travel agencies on the waterfront, Albedo Travel and Alonnisos Travel, provide maps, run popular marine-park trips, and organise snorkelling and swimming excursions to Skantzoura and nearby islands.

Popular round-the-island excursions (€40) aboard the classic *Gorgona,* captained by charming island local **Pakis Athanasiou** (☑ 6978386588), visit the **Blue Cave** on the northeast coast and the islets of **Kyra Panagia** and **Peristera** in the marine park. There are lunch and swimming breaks along the way.

Sleeping

Camping Rocks　　　　　CAMPGROUND €
(☑ 6973230977, 24240 65410; www.campingrocks.
eu; Marpounta; campsites per adult/tent €7.50/3)
Follow the signposts 800m south of the port

to this clean and pine-shaded coastal spot with a cafe and grocery store.

★ **Liadromia Hotel** HOTEL €
(☑ 24240 65521; www.liadromia.gr; d/tr/ste incl breakfast from €40/60/75; P❄@�) This welcoming and impeccably maintained hotel overlooking the harbour was Patitiri's first. All rooms have character to spare, from hand-embroidered curtains to period furnishings. The gracious owner, Maria, takes obvious delight in making it all work. Their upstairs breakfast room has a grand harbour view and quirky touches such as an antique gramophone.

Ilias Studios HOTEL €
(☑ 24240 65451; www.ilias-studios.gr; Pelasgon 27; r from €35; ❄�) Just 100m from the port, owners Ilias and Magdalini provide a genuine welcome in this jaunty-looking blue-and-white building. Rooms are spotless, airy and light, and a common kitchen awaits self-caterers.

★ **Paradise Hotel** HOTEL €€
(☑ 24240 65160; www.paradise-hotel.gr; s/d/tr incl breakfast from €65/70/77; P❄�❄) Wood ceilings and stone-tiled floors give a rustic feel to these quiet, comfortable rooms, along with modern bathrooms and shuttered balconies that overlook the bay. Beyond the pool bar, a stairway leads to a small cove for swimming. They also have the only hotel pool in town.

🍴 Eating & Drinking

★ **Ouzerie Archipelagos** GREEK €
(mains €6-10; ☉ lunch & dinner) To get a feel for this very Greek establishment on the harbourfront, pick a table towards the back where locals gather to order round after round of fine mezedhes, always-fresh grilled fish and local firewater favourite *tsipouro* as the night rolls on.

Cafe Bistro Helios BISTRO €
(☑ 24240 65667; snacks €3-7; ☉ 6pm-midnight) Snappy bistro hidden in plain view, via the stepped path located a few doors down from the National Bank. Well-priced small plates, a superb high harbour view, plus an international twist.

To Kamaki Ouzerie TAVERNA €€
(mains €5-15; ☉ dinner) This long-time local favourite, next to the National Bank on the main road, offers well-priced fresh fish and

tasty vegetarian plates. Weekends often feature a family bouzouki player.

Drunk Seal BAR
(☉ 10am-late) One of several cheery dives serving unique cocktails at the port, tilting in the direction of the town museum. Globes hang from the awning and there's a tropical, hippie feel.

🛍 Shopping

Ikos Traditional Products GIFTS & SOUVENIRS
(Women's Cooperative Shop; ☑ 24240 66270; Ikion Dolopon; ☉ 9am-2pm & 6-9pm) This delightful women's cooperative is a combination bakery, nuts-and-island-herbs, jams-and-honey shop, open year-round.

ℹ Information

Albedo Travel (☑ 24240 65804; www.alonissosholidays.com; Waterfront; ☉ 9am-10pm)
Alkyon Travel (☑ 24240 65220; http://alkyontravel.gr; Waterfront; ☉ 9am-10pm)
Alonnisos Travel (☑ 24240 65188, 24240 66000; www.alonnisostravel.gr; Waterfront; ☉ 9am-10pm)
Pharmacy (☑ 24240 66096)
Police (☑ 24240 65205)
Port Police (☑ 24240 65595)
Post Office (☉ 7.30am-2pm)

Old Alonnisos Παλιά Αλόννησος
POP 500
Old Alonnisos (aka Palia Alonnisos and Hora) is an enchanting place with panoramic views and winding stepped alleys. From the village, a 2km donkey path leads down to Mikros Mourtias Beach or, from just outside the village, take the steep road down to Megalos Mourtias, a beautiful enclosed stony curve with a cluster of small restaurants and a bar. At the bus stop, you'll find a blue noticeboard that details several area walks.

◉ Sights & Activities

Church of the Birth of Christ CHURCH
A 17th-century rough-hewn stone church sits on the village square. Inside you'll see a tiny wooden gallery, and an ornate screen depicting the lives of the Apostles.

Kali Thea YOGA
(☑ 24240 65513, 6975930108; www.kalithea.org; from €10; ☉ May-Oct) Hatha yoga and massage, courtesy of Bibi and Lee, on the outskirts of Old Alonnisos. Drop-in group classes plus private tuition.

🛏 Sleeping

Elma's Houses
APARTMENT €

(☑ 24240 66108, 6945466776; www.elmashouses. com; studio/apt from €45/75; ❋ 🛜) Families will appreciate either of Elma's two roomy stone houses, each traditionally decorated and with full kitchen, comfy beds and great views from the courtyard. Interior walls are rugged and whitewashed, and there are wooden beams and staircases. It's located near the old school in the village.

Pension Chiliadromia
PENSION €

(☑ 24240 65814; www.chiliadromia.gr; Plateia Hristou; r/studio from €35/50; ❋ 🛜) Tucked into the heart of the old village, this homey pension is a budget gem, with small balconies, comfortable beds, well-equipped kitchens and traditional decorations. There's a morning cafe downstairs.

★ Konstantina Studios
APARTMENT €€

(☑ 24240 66165, 6932271540; www.konstantinastudios.gr; d/ste/apt incl breakfast from €96/106/130; P ❋ 🛜) Among the nicest accommodation on Alonnisos, these handsome and quiet studios with fully equipped kitchens, power showers and fluffy bathrobes come with balcony views of the southwest coast. The resourceful owner, Konstantina, fetches her guests from the dock and serves wonderful breakfasts consisting of fruit plus homemade baking, jam and omelettes.

🍴 Eating & Drinking

★ Hayiati
CAFE €

(☑ 24240 66244; snacks €4-11.50; ⊘ 9am-2am) Hayiati is a *glykopoleio* (sweets shop) by day and a piano bar by night, with sweeping views from its descending outdoor terraces. Morning fare includes made-to-order *tyropita*. Later, you'll find homemade pastas along with the gracious hospitality of owner-cooks Meni and Angela. It's located in the upper part of the village.

Taverna Megalos Mourtias
TAVERNA €

(Megalos Mourtias; mains €4-8; ⊘ breakfast, lunch & dinner) A stone's throw from the surf, this laid-back taverna and beach bar 2km down the hill from the Hora prepares fine salads, *gyros* (meat slithers cooked on a vertical rotisserie), fish soup and several veggie dishes.

★ Astrofegia
GREEK €€

(mains €7-15; ⊘ dinner) There's a stunning view from this outdoor dining spot, with its cheery red-checked tablecloths, friendly family welcome and grape vines. Choose from well-prepared Greek standards, rare veggie *mousakas*, mixed seafood souvlakia and good house wines. Or go straight for the *galaktoboureko* (custard slice). It's opposite the small car park at the village entrance.

Aerides Cafe-Bar
BAR

(⊘ 9am-5pm & 7pm-2am; 🛜) Maria and Yiannis make the drinks, pick the music and scoop the ice cream at this hip hole-in-the-wall on the village square. It's a good spot for breakfast and fresh juices.

Around Alonnios

From Patitiri, Alonnisos' main road reaches 19km to the northern tip of the island at Gerakas; turtles nest on the beach here, though, sadly, the water isn't the cleanest.

North of Patitiri, though, several roads descend to small fishing bays and some lovely secluded beaches. Along the east coast, the first bay from town is **Rousoum Gialos**, an easy 1km walk from town: the beautiful stony curve of the bay provides great swimming, and it's backed by tavernas. Next is **Votsi**, which is more of a fishing port while, 3km on, **Hrysi Milia** is a gently shelving sandy strand with a beach bar and pine-tree shade. The next point north is the gorgeous arc of **Cape Kokkinokastro**, site of the ancient and submerged city of Ikos. Continuing, the road reaches **Leftos Gialos**, home to a pebble beach dotted with raffia sun shades.

Steni Vala, an attractive little fishing village and deep-water yacht port, has 50-odd rooms in domatia and tavernas overlooking the small marina. Small and pebbly **Agios Petros Beach** sits just 500m south of the village.

Kalamakia, 2km further north and the last village of note, comprises a small harbour, a few domatia and fine dockside fish tavernas. It's not ideal for swimming, so it's best to press on for 3km on the sealed road to a wetland marsh and **Agios Dimitrios Beach**, where a truck-canteen and domatia sit opposite a graceful stretch of white pebbles. A 5km circular walk to the wetland at Kastanorema takes two hours. Beyond Agios Dimitrios, the road narrows to a footpath heading inland.

🏃 Activities

Hiking opportunities abound on Alonnisos and more than a dozen trails have been way-marked. Popular trails are highlighted on

---

THE MONK SEAL

Once populating hundreds of colonies in the Black Sea, the Mediterranean Sea and along Africa's Atlantic coast, the Mediterranean monk seal has been reduced to about 700 individuals. Half of these live in the seas around Greece.

One of the earth's rarest mammals, the monk seal is now one of the 20 most endangered species worldwide. Major threats include decreasing food supplies and destruction of habitat. Thankfully, the once-common killings by fishers – who saw the seal as a pest that tore holes in nets and robbed their catch – have diminished with the recognition that protecting the seal also promotes recovery of fish stocks.

For more information about monk seals and to see infra-red film of their impossibly adorable pups, visit MOM Information Centre (p651).

---

the Terrain and Anavasi maps of Alonnisos. Albedo Travel (p653) in Patitiri can help arrange guided walks, which start in town and explore either the coasts or the heart of the island. The routes generally end at a beach, so bring swimming gear.

Ikion Diving   DIVING
(☑ 24240 65158, 6984181598; www.ikiondiving.gr; Steni Vala) Offers both shore and boat dives, plus snorkelling (from €270).

🛏 Sleeping & Eating

Lithea Studios   VILLA €€
(☑ 24240 66435, 6932586001; www.lithea.gr; Agios Petros; studios/villas from €60/90; ℗✻🛜) Nestled into the coastal hamlet of Agios Petros, this traditional stone complex impresses with a rambling garden of olive and citrus trees hung with hammocks, handsome rooms, kitchenettes and hospitable owners Panayioti and Maria. Wander through the trees to take a dip in the sea.

Ilya Suites   APARTMENT €€
(☑ 21032 49209, 6938327401; www.ilyasuites.gr; Glyfa Beach; ste/villa from €80/160; ℗✻🛜) Get away from it all at these elegant well-appointed suites and villas on Glyfa Beach facing Peristera Island. From the geranium- and rose-filled courtyard to the spacious low-key luxe rooms, everything feels soothingly elegant. Apartments sleep two to four people.

Taverna Eleonas   TAVERNA €
(☑ 69450 81006; Leftos Gialos; mains €5-11; ☺ lunch & dinner) Fine outdoor taverna on the bay at Leftos Gialos with hearty spinach and feta *pites* (pies), and heartier homemade wine. You sit in the shade of olive trees with views of the beach.

Taverna Fanari   TAVERNA €
(Waterfront, Steni Vala; mains €4-9) Stuffed squid and seafood linguine are two of the offerings at this great harbour taverna, rounded off with a small pudding on the house.

Skyros   Σκύρος
POP 3000

Skyros, the largest of the Sporades group, can seem like two separate islands: the north has small bays, rolling farmland and pine forests while the south features arid hills and a rocky shoreline. In Greek mythology, Skyros was the hiding place of the young Achilles, who is thought to have ridden a Skyrian horse into Troy: the endangered small-bodied horses can still be seen in the wild on the island.

These days, the island has somewhat of a hip but off-the-radar feel thanks to the alternative arts and wellness courses run by the Skyros Centre (p657). It's also popular with birders, in search of the slender Eleonora's falcon which migrates between here and Madagascar. Skyros Town, perched on its high rock, is a tranquil car-free base.

❶ Getting There & Away

AIR

In addition to domestic flights, Skyros airport, 11km north of Skyros Town at the far tip of the island, has occasional charter flights from Oslo, Amsterdam and destinations in France. Domestic flights from Skyros head to Athens (€28, 25 minutes) and Thessaloniki (€50, 45 minutes) three times a week.

For tickets, contact **Sky Express** (☑ 22220 91876, 28102 23500; www.skyexpress.gr; Skyros Airport), **Aegean Airlines** (☑ 22220 91684; www.aegeanair.com; Skyros Airport) or visit Skyros Travel Agency (p658) in Skyros Town.

EVIA & THE SPORADES SKYROS

BOAT

Skyros' main port is Linaria. Ferries link to Evia (Paralia Kymis; €12.10, 1¾ hours, one to two daily), and Alonnisos and Skopelos in summer (€26, 4½ to five hours, three weekly).

Purchase tickets from Skyros Travel (p658) in Skyros Town or from the ticket kiosk at the dock in Linaria or in Paralia Kymis (Evia).

❶ Getting Around

BUS & TAXI

A bus links up with ferry arrivals and runs from Linaria to Skyros Town, Magazia and Molos (€1.80); and from Skyros Town to the airport (€2.70). A **taxi** (☑ 6972894088) from Skyros Town to Linaria costs €15; to the airport it's €25.

CAR & MOTORCYCLE

Cars, motorbikes and bicycles can all be hired in Skyros Town from **Martina's Rentals** (☑ 22220 92022, 6974572380; Machairas 1; ⊙ 9am-9pm), or from **Europcar Skyros** (☑ 22220 92092; www.europcar.com; Molos 340) on the way down to Magazia. **Vayos Motorbikes** (☑ 22220 92957) – also for bicycles – is located near the bus station in Skyros Town.

Skyros Town   Σκύρος

POP 2000

Skyros' capital is draped over a high rocky bluff. It's topped by a 13th-century Venetian fortress, and is laced with labyrinthine, smooth cobblestone streets that invite wandering, but were designed to keep out the elements, and also pirates.

Agoras, the main thoroughfare, is a lively jumble of tavernas, bars and shops flanked by winding alleyways. About 100m past Plateia (the main square), the main drag of Agoras forks left and zigzags to two small museums adjacent to Plateia Rupert Brooke, marked by a bronze nude in his honour, from where a wide stone path descends 1km to Magazia Beach.

Skyros

☉ Sights

★ **Manos Faltaïts Folk Museum** MUSEUM
(🖃 22220 91232; www.faltaits.gr/english/museum.
htm; Plateia Rupert Brooke; €2, incl tour €5;
☉ 10am-2pm & 6-9pm) This not-to-be-missed
gem details the mythology and folklore
of Skyros. The 19th-century mansion is a
multilevel labyrinth of Skyrian costumes,
embroidery, antique furniture, ceramics,
daggers, cooking pots and vintage photographs; among the wealth of items is a goat
mask and heavy bells worn by revellers at
carnival time. There's also an excellent gift
shop selling bespoke ceramics, fabrics,
books and prints.

Monastery of St George MONASTERY
(☉ 10am-1.30pm) FREE Keep heading uphill
in Skyros Town, and eventually all the winding alleys lead to the Byzantine Monastery
of St George, founded in 962. This working monastery (whose bells might wake
you early if you're staying in the town) was
out of bounds until recently due to earthquake damage. You can now visit its chapel,
which features an ornate gilded screen and
faded frescoes. Beyond are the ruins of the
13th-century Venetian fortress, which are
being restored and may reopen.

Archaeological Museum MUSEUM
(🖃 22220 91327; Plateia Rupert Brooke; €2;
☉ 8.30am-3pm Tue-Sun) Along with Mycenaean pottery found near Magazia and
artefacts from the Bronze Age excavation at
Palamari, this attractive courtyard building
contains a traditional Skyrian house interior, transported in its entirety from the
benefactor's home.

🏃 Activities & Tours

★ **Feel Ingreece** CULTURAL
(🖃 22220 93100; www.feelingreece.gr; off upper
Agoras; from €20; ☉ 9.30am-1.30pm & 7-10pm)
Owner Chrysanthi Zygogianni is dedicated
to helping sustain the best of Skyrian culture.
The focus is on local arts and the island's natural environment. The office arranges hiking
excursions to glimpse wild Skyrian horses,
wetland birdwatching trips, pottery, wood-
carving, Skyrian cooking and Greek dance
lessons, and various boat trips. To get here,
turn right opposite Ammos jewellers.

Skyros Centre COURSE
(🖃 in UK 44(0)1983 865566; www.skyros.com)
Established in 1979, the Skyros Centre fosters alternative living and learning, with residential courses in writing, music, well-being
and the arts. Each day starts with morning
yoga. There's another centre in Atsitsa.

Niko Sikkes TOURS
(🖃 22220 92707, 69769 83712; nikonisi@hotmail.
com) Contact the well-informed and resourceful Niko Sikkes for his impromptu
tours of the island and the town.

✯ Festivals & Events

Skyros Carnival CARNIVAL
(☉ Jan/Feb) In this wild pre-Lenten festival,
which takes place on the last four weekends
before Lent and Orthodox Easter, young
men don goat masks, hairy jackets and dozens of copper goat bells. They then proceed
to clank and dance through Skyros Town,
each with a male partner dressed up as a
Skyrian bride but also wearing a goat mask.

The overtly pagan revelries include much
singing, dancing, drinking and feasting.
Local lore is that the event derives from the
story of a shepherd, who went mad when his
goats died in the snow and took to wearing
their skins; the transvestism evident in the
carnival is anyone's guess.

More than 2000 visitors arrive for the
final weekend, so book early, or go during
one of the earlier weekends when you'll
catch more of a local flavour of the festival.

Rembetika Music Festival MUSIC
(🖃 22220 91232; www.rebetikoseminar.com/index.
php) For one week in mid-July, the Manos
Faltaïts Folk Museum in Skyros Town is host
to a *rembetika* music festival. The festival
includes daily instrument and voice workshops, films and seminars. The evening
hours are filled with music and dinners at
local tavernas, and the week concludes with
a Saturday-night concert, open to the public.

🛏 Sleeping

Pension Nikolas PENSION €
(🖃 22220 91778; www.nicolaspension.gr; Playia; s/d/
tr €40/50/60; 🅿 ❄ 🛜) Set back on a quiet road
on the edge of town, this friendly pension and
budget gem is only a five-minute walk to busy
Agoras. Upper rooms have air-conditioning
and balconies; the lower rooms have fans and
open onto a shady garden.

★ **Hotel Nefeli
& Skyrian Studios** BOUTIQUE HOTEL €€
(🖃 22220 91964; www.skyros-nefeli.gr; d/studio/
ste incl breakfast from €75/95/245; 🅿 ❄ @ 🛜 ❄)
This smart and welcoming hotel on the

edge of town has an easy minimalist-meets-Skyrian feel to it, with handsome furnishings and swanky bathrooms. Some studios are replicas of Skyrian houses, with internal wooden galleries. The hotel and adjacent studios share a saltwater swimming pool and outdoor bar. Breakfast includes savoury and sweet Greek favourites.

✕ Eating & Drinking

⭐ O Pappous Kai Ego   TAVERNA €
(☑22220 93200; Agoras; mains €6-9; ⊘lunch & dinner) The name of this small taverna means 'my grandfather and me' and it's easy to see how one generation of family recipes followed another. It's well known for the Skyrian dolmadhes made with a touch of goat milk. A lovely corner location on Agoras, on a raised outdoor terrace.

Maryetis Restaurant   GREEK €
(☑22220 91311; Agoras; mains €6-9; ⊘lunch & dinner) The local favourite in town for grilled fish and octopus *stifadho,* great grills and mezedhes. Wines and service are excellent.

⭐ Kalypso   BAR
(Agoras; ⊘noon-late; 🔊) Classy Kalypso occupies a historic pharmacy building, and with its gleaming wood and marbled floors makes the best spot for a coffee in town: grab a breakfast pastry from the simple bak-ery right next door. Owner-bartender Hristos plays lots of jazz and blues and makes a fine straight-up margarita along with home-made sangria.

ⓘ Information

National Bank of Greece (Agoras) Has an ATM.

Police (☑22220 91274; Agoras)

Post Office (Plateia; ⊘7.30am-2pm) On the main square.

Skyrian Horse Society (☑22220 92345, 6974694023; www.skyrianhorsesociety.gr)

Skyros Travel Agency (☑22220 91600, 6944884588; www.skyrostravel.com; Agoras; ⊘9.30am-1.30pm & 6.30-9.30pm) Helpful full-service agency that arranges accommodation; transfers and onward travel; car and motorbike hire; and 4WD and boat excursions around Skyros.

Magazia & Molos
Μαγαζιά & Μώλος

POP 400

The resort of Magazia is a compact and colourful maze of winding alleys that skirts the southern end of a long, sandy beach beneath Skyros Town. The name 'Magazia' comes from the Greek word for shop; the original buildings were storehouses for olive oil, produce and dry goods.

SKYROS' ARTISTIC HOMES

Skyros has a flourishing community of working artists, from potters and painters to sculptors and weavers. The island artistry dates from Byzantine times when passing pirates collaborated with rogue residents, whose houses became virtual galleries for stolen booty looted from merchant ships, including ceramic plates and copper ornaments from Europe, the Middle East and Asia Minor. Today, similar items adorn almost every Skyrian house, shown to best advantage on locally carved wooden shelves.

The best places to see Skyrian domestic interiors are the Manos Faltaïts Folk Museum (p657) and the Archaeological Museum (p657), both of which contain atmospheric recreated homesteads. A key feature is the dramatic *boulmes*, a carved screen often decorated with the Byzantine two-headed eagle, cockerels and pomegranates. Stone hearths are embellished with embroidery, and shelves display glass and clayware. The *krevatsoula* is a low wooden bed with fabric drapes and embroidered cushions, which might depict gorgons, ships or weddings, and small wooden chairs and shelves are carved with more emblems and patterns. The overall effect is rich and sophisticated, as are the dashing 18th- and 19th-century traditional costumes which both museums display.

To see the legacy of Skyrian traditions, check out the work of ceramicist Stamatis Ftoulis and embroiderers and woodcarvers **Olga Zacharaiki** (☑6974666113; Agoras; ⊘11am-10pm), **Andreou Stamatiou** (☑22220 92827; Agoras; ⊘11am-10pm) and **Amersa Panagiotou** (☑22220 92827; Agoras; ⊘10am-10pm). Several artisans display their work between the Plateia and upper Agoras; Chrysanthi at Feel Ingreece (p657) can fill you in on the local scene.

ENDANGERED: A RARE BREED

The small-bodied Skyrian horse (*Equus caballus Skyriano*) is valued for its intelligence, beauty and gentleness. Common across Greece in ancient times – the horses on the Parthenon frieze are thought to be Skyrian – today there are fewer than 300 of these diminutive creatures, with a population living on the southern slopes of Mt Kochilas on Skyros.

Several Skyrians are working to conserve this endangered species. In 2006 Amanda Simpson and Stathis Katsarelias started **Friends of the Skyrian Horse** (☑ 6986051678; http://skyrosislandhorsetrust.com; Trachi; ☺ by appointment) with just three horses. Their modest facilities have expanded to accommodate around 40 horses as they seek to re-establish a herd of wild, pure-bred Skyrian horses. Visitors are welcome at the small ranch near Skyros Town.

Each summer in late June, the free three-day **Skyrian Horse Festival** features two parades (one for mares, another for stallions) complete with live music and traditional dance. Participants can get close to the horses in their natural habitat, and children can ride the horses safely at **Mouries Farm** (☑ 6947465900; www.skyrianhorses.org), opposite Taverna Mouries in Kalamitsa. The farm is engaged in pure-breeding the horses, and runs an excellent volunteer program.

For information about breeding efforts and other farms on the island, visit the **Skyrian Horse Society** at the Skyros Life Project office located near the bus station in Skyros Town.

Near the northern end of the beach, once-sleepy Molos now has its own share of tavernas, bars and rooms. Its landmark windmill (now a bar) and adjacent rock-hewn church of Agios Nikolaos are easy to spot. Skinny-dippers can leave it all behind at nude-friendly **Papa Houma** near the southern end of Magazia.

◉ Sights

Agios Nikolaos CHURCH
A huge rectangular free-standing rock forms the sacred space of Agios Nikolaos; the area was a quarry in ancient times. The turquoise door opens into the candelit sanctuary with its altar and icons.

Stamatis Ftoulis GALLERY
(☑ 22220 92220, 22220 91559; Magazia; ☺ 11am-9pm) Intimate ceramics workshop on the narrow boardwalk at Magazia; also has a showroom in Skyros Town.

🛏 Sleeping

★**Antigoni Studios** APARTMENT €
(☑ 6945100230, 22220 91310; www.antigoni studios.com; d/f from €55/85; ᴾ✳🛜) Out-standing addition to the Magazia sleep scene, with 20 large studios, each with handsome furnishings, kitchens, modern bathrooms – all just a three-minute walk to the beach. Managed by the hospitable Katarina,

it's located at the southern edge of Magazia. Book well in advance.

★**Perigiali Hotel & Studios** HOTEL €
(☑ 22220 92075; www.perigiali.com; Magazia; d/tr/apt incl breakfast from €55/80/115; ᴾ✳@🛜🏊) Leafy Perigiali feels secluded despite being only 60m from the beach. Skyrian-style rooms overlook a garden with pear and apricot trees, while an upscale wing sports a pool with luxe apartments; includes a great buffet breakfast. Owner Amalia is full of ideas for travellers.

Ariadne Apartments HOTEL €
(☑ 22220 91113; www.ariadnestudios.gr; Magazia; d/apt from €60/85; ✳@🛜) Just 50m from the beach, these inviting studios and two-room apartments enclose a small courtyard and breakfast cafe (with great pastries). Spacious rooms have fully equipped kitchens and are decorated with original artwork and Skyrian woodwork.

Ammos Hotel HOTEL €€
(☑ 22220 91234, 6974354181; www.skyrosammos hotel.com; Magazia; d/t incl breakfast from €80/110; ᴾ✳🛜🏊) This strikingly well-designed lodging is low-key and inviting, with soothing pale-hued rooms, handsome bathrooms, overhead fans and made-to-order Skyrian breakfasts to start the day, plus a rooftop terrace to catch the sunset.

WORTH A TRIP

PALAMARI ΠΑΛΑΜΑΡΙ

At the northeast end of the island, uncrowded Palamari occupies a graceful stretch of sandy beach, and is the site of a fascinating **archaeological dig** (http://geomorphologie.revues.org/668; Palamari; ⊗8am-2pm) **FREE** located down a dirt road, where a Bronze Age town dating from between 2500 BC and 1650 BC has been excavated. Work began in 1981, uncovering artefacts relating to fishing and hunting, stone walls, even drainpipes and paved walkways. The excavation provided evidence of a powerfully fortified prehistoric coastal settlement near the heart of early Mediterranean trade routes, and you can now follow walkways around it.

A small well-organised visitor centre opened in 2014, and more findings from Palamari are on display at the Archaeological Museum (p657) in Skyros Town.

An adjacent wetland is the remnant of an ancient lagoon, which supported this fishing and hunting community. Today it remains a major birdwatching attraction, notable for long-legged waders like herons and ibises.

✗ Eating & Drinking

★**Stefanos Taverna** TAVERNA €
(☑6974350372; Magazia; mains €5.50-9.50; ⊗breakfast, lunch & dinner) Sit on the terrace overlooking the beach and choose from a range of baked dishes such as *yemista* (stuffed tomatoes), juicy grills and locally made sausage, wild greens and fresh fish. Breakfast omelettes start at €3.

★**Oi Istories Tou Barba** TAVERNA €
(☑22220 91453; Molos; mains €4-10; ⊗lunch & dinner) Look for the light-blue railing above the beach in Molos to find this excellent cafe-taverna with handwritten menus and delicious lobster spaghetti.

★**Anenomulos** BAR
(☑22220 93656; www.anemomulos.gr; Cape Pouria; ⊗9am-3am) Gorgeous conversion of a windmill, perched on the sea by the rock-cut church of Agios Nikolaos. They serve snacks, wines and cocktails, and the sundowner location is sublime. A couple of tables perch on little wooden platforms on the surrounding rocks, where you can watch the sun set on distant Skyros Town.

Northwest Coast

The picturesque port village of **Atsitsa** on the island's west coast occupies a woody shoreline setting. There's an outpost of the alternative learning Skyros Centre (p657) here, and the organic **Sunset Cafe** (snacks €1.50-4; ⊗breakfast-sunset) overlooks the bay. Two kilometres north, find the excellent roadside taverna **Cook-Nara** (☑22221 00005; Kyra Panagia; mains €5-9.50; ⊗lunch & dinner).

At azure-blue **Cape Petritsa**, 1.5km south of Atsitsa, the coastal road turns inland, finding the sea again at sandy **Agios Fokas Bay**, with a taverna and great swimming.

A beautiful horseshoe-shaped beach graces **Pefkos Bay**, 10km southeast of Atsitsa, where you can lunch at **Stamatia's Taverna** (mains €7-11; ⊗noon-midnight). Nearby, the beach at **Aherounes** has a gentle kid-friendly sandy bottom, along with two tavernas and domatia.

Tris Boukes Bay
Όρμος Τρεις Μπούκες

The southernmost corner of the island is a windswept landscape partly restricted by a Greek naval station. Many come here to visit English poet Rupert Brooke's grave, just inland from Tris Boukes Bay. It's signed with a wooden sign in Greek. The gravestone is inscribed with Brooke's most famous sonnet, 'The Soldier'. When Brooke's fellow naval officers buried him, they erected a simple wooden cross (now in England) with an inscription originally in Greek: 'Here lies the servant of God, sub-lieutenant in the English Navy, who died for the deliverance of Constantinople from the Turks.'

From Tris Boukes Bay, a rough dirt road (4WD recommended) leads to Renes Bay, from where a 5km hiking trail skirts a coastal plateau, ending at the lighthouse at Cape Lithari. Small herds of wild Skyrian horses are often glimpsed here, along with rare Eleonora's falcons that nest in the steep cliffs nearby from April to October.

Ionian Islands

Best Places to Eat

➡ White House (p674)

➡ Carnayo (p677)

➡ Nissi (p682)

➡ Prosilio (p699)

➡ O Platanos (p706)

Best Places to Stay

➡ Perantzada 1811 (p694)

➡ Petani Bay Hotel (p690)

➡ El Sol Hotel (p704)

➡ Levant Hotel (p675)

➡ Torri E Merli (p678)

Why Go?

With their cooler climate, abundant olive and cypress trees, and forested mountains, the Ionians (Τα Ιόνια Νησιά) are a lighter, greener variation on the Greek template. Venetian, French and British occupiers have all helped to shape the islands' architecture, culture and (excellent) cuisine, and contributed to the unique feel of Ionian life.

Though the islands lie linked in a chain along the west coast of mainland Greece, each has its own distinct landscape and history. Corfu Town holds Parisian-style arcades, Venetian alleyways and Italian-inspired delicacies. Lefkada boasts some of Greece's finest turquoise-lapped beaches, while Kefallonia is adorned with soaring mountains and vineyards. Paxi's Italianate harbour villages are impossibly pretty, and soulful Ithaki preserves wild terrain and a sense of myth. Zakynthos has sea caves and waters teeming with turtles, and Kythira offers off-the-beaten-track walks. The Ionians hold something new for adventure seekers, food lovers, culture vultures and beach bums alike.

When to Go
Corfu Town

May Life is still quiet while the wildflowers are in bloom everywhere.

Jul Escape the heat elsewhere in Greece by heading to the country's coolest islands.

Sep Leaves change colour, and the *robola* grapes are harvested in Kefallonia.

Ionian Islands Highlights

1 Corfu Town (p665) Exploring world-class museums, fortresses and restaurants, as well as Venetian, French and British architecture.

2 Paxi (p676) Hopping from one gorgeous harbour to another on this tiny pastoral island.

3 Fiskardo (p691) Savouring the flavours in the waterfront restaurants of Kefallonia's best-preserved historic village.

4 Kefallonia (p685) Diving and kayaking in the myriad magnificent bays that pepper Kefallonia's coastline.

5 Beaches Ranking your favourite strips of sand, from the busiest on Corfu (p674) and Zakynthos (p699) to the quieter joys of Paxi (p676) and Lefkada's west coast (p683).

6 Ithaki (p693) Walking in the footsteps of epic poet Homer.

7 Kythira (p701) Discovering tiny villages, waterfalls and remote coves.

History

The origin of the name 'Ionian' is obscure, but may derive from the goddess Io. A paramour of Zeus, she passed through what's now known as the Ionian Sea while fleeing the wrath of Hera.

According to the writings of Homer, the Ionian Islands were important during Mycenaean times, but to date only tombs, not villages or palaces, have been identified. By the 8th century BC the islands belonged to mighty city-state Corinth, but Corfu staged a successful revolt a century later. The Peloponnesian Wars (431–404 BC) left Corfu as little more than a staging post for whoever happened to be controlling Greece.

By the end of the 3rd century BC, the Romans ruled the Ionians. Anthony and Cleopatra dined on Paxi the night before the Battle of Actium (31 BC), and the emperor Nero holidayed on Corfu in the 1st century AD. Later, the islands suffered waves of invaders: the Byzantine Empire, Venice, Napoleon (in 1797), Russia (from 1799 to 1807), and then Napoleon again.

In 1815 the Ionians became a British protectorate. Although the British improved infrastructure, developed agriculture and industry, and even taught the Corfiots cricket, nationalists campaigned against their oppressive rule, and by 1864 Britain relinquished the islands to Greece.

WWII was rough on the Ionians, under occupation first by the Italians and then the Germans. Further mass emigration followed devastating earthquakes in 1948 and 1953. But by the 1960s foreign holidaymakers were visiting in increasing numbers, and tourism has flourished ever since.

CORFU (KERKYRA)
KEPKYPA

POP 102,070

Still recognisable as the idyllic refuge where the shipwrecked Odysseus was soothed and sent on his way home, Corfu continues to welcome weary travellers with its lush scenery, bountiful produce and pristine beaches.

Since the 8th century BC the island the Greeks call Kerkyra has been prized for its untamed beauty and strategic location. Ancient armies fought to possess it, while in the early days of modern Greece it was a beacon of learning. Corfiots remain proud of their intellectual and artistic roots, with vestiges of the past ranging from Corfu Town's Venetian architecture to British legacies such as cricket and ginger beer.

While certain regions of the island have succumbed to overdevelopment, particularly those close to Corfu Town, Corfu is large enough to make it possible to escape the crowds. Venture across cypress-studded hills to find vertiginous villages in the fertile interior, and sandy coves lapped by cobalt-blue waters.

❶ Getting There & Away

AIR

Corfu's **airport** (📞 26610 89600; www.corfu-airport.com) is on the southwestern fringes of Corfu Town, just over 2km southwest of the Old Town.

Domestic

Aegean Air (www.aegeanair.com) Direct flights to Athens and Thessaloniki.

Astra Airlines (www.astra-airlines.gr) Direct flights to Thessaloniki.

Sky Express (www.skyexpress.gr) Operates a thrice-weekly island-hopping route to Preveza, Kefallonia and Zakynthos.

DESTINATION	DURATION	FARE	FREQUENCY
Athens	1hr	€65	3 daily
Kefallonia	75min	€73	3 weekly
Preveza	30min	€73	3 weekly
Thessaloniki	55min	€76	3 weekly
Zakynthos	2hr	€79	3 weekly

International

Both **EasyJet** (www.easyjet.com) and **Ryanair** (www.ryanair.com) offer direct flights in summer between Corfu and the UK, and several other European destinations, while **British Airways** (www.ba.com) also flies from the UK to Corfu. Between May and September, many charter flights come from northern Europe and the UK.

BOAT

Ferries depart from Neo Limani (New Port), west of Corfu Town's Old Town.

Domestic

Ticket agencies line Ethnikis Antistaseos in Corfu Town, facing the Neo Limani.

Two ferry operators connect Corfu Town with Paxi:

Ilida (📞 Corfu 26610 49800, Paxi 26620 32401; Ethnikis Antistaseos 1) High-speed hydrofoil, from mid-March to mid-October.

Kamelia Lines (📞 Corfu 26610 40372, Paxi 26620 32131; www.kamelialines.gr) Runs the *Despina* ferry; advance bookings are essential.

No ferries sail directly to Zakynthos; fly with **Sky Express** (www.skyexpress.gr) instead.

Some international ferries from Corfu also call in at Igoumenitsa and Kefallonia. For schedules, see www.openseas.gr. If you're heading to Patra, catch the ferry to Igoumenitsa first.

ROUTE	DURATION	FARE	FREQUENCY
Corfu–Igoumenitsa	1¼hr	€10	hourly
Lefkimmi–Igoumenitsa	1hr 10min	€7	6 daily
Corfu–Paxi (high-speed)	55min	€25	1-3 daily

Italy

ANEK Lines (www.anek.gr) ferries connect Corfu with Bari (€60, eight hours, two weekly) and Ancona (€85, 14½ hours, one to two daily) in Italy, and Igoumenitsa on the Greek mainland, where you can pick up other connections.

BUS

Green Buses (www.greenbuses.gr) goes to Athens (€48, 8½ hours, three daily, from Monday to Thursday; one via Lefkimmi), Thessaloniki (€38.50, eight hours, twice daily) and Larisa (€30.40, 5½ hours, daily).

Corfu

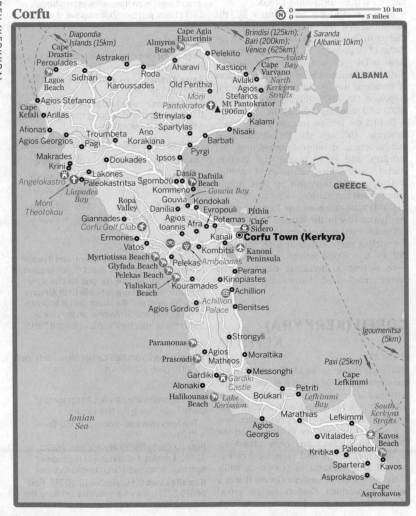

ⓘ Getting Around

TO/FROM THE AIRPORT

Taxis between the airport and Corfu Town cost around €12, while local bus 15 runs to both Plateia G Theotoki (Plateia San Rocco) in town and the Neo Limani (New Port) New Port beyond.

BUS

Long-distance Green Buses radiate out from Corfu Town's **long-distance bus station** (☑ 26610 28900; www.greenbuses.gr; I Theotoki) in the New Town. Fares cost €1.50 to €4.80; services are reduced on Saturday, and may be nonexistent on Sundays and holidays.

DESTINATION	DURATION	FREQUENCY
Agios Gordios	45min	8 daily
Agios Stefanos	2hr	4 daily
Aharavi (via Roda)	1¼hr	7 daily
Arillas (via Afionas)	1¼hr	2 daily
Barbati	45min	10 daily
Ermones	30min	7 daily
Glyfada	45min	6 daily
Kassiopi	1¼hr	8 daily
Kavos	1½hr	10 daily
Messonghi	35min	15 daily
Paleokastritsa	1hr	11 daily
Pyrgi	30min	5 daily
Sidhari	1¼hr	8 daily
Spartera	1½hr	2 daily

Local blue buses depart from the **local bus station** (☑ 26610 31595; www.astikoktelkerkyras.gr; Plateia G Theotoki) in Corfu Old Town. Journeys cost €1.20 or €1.70. Buy tickets at the booth on Plateia G Theotiki, or on the bus itself if heading to Achillion, Benitses or Kouramades. All trips are less than 30 minutes. Service is reduced on weekends.

CAR & MOTORCYCLE

Car- and motorbike-hire outlets (Alamo, Hertz, Europcar etc) abound at the airport, in Corfu Town and the resorts. Prices start at around €50 per day.

Corfu Town · Κέρκυρα

POP 30,000

Imbued with Venetian grace and elegance, historic Corfu Town (also known as Kerkyra) stands halfway down the island's east coast. The name Corfu, meaning 'peaks', refers to its twin hills, each topped by a massive fortress built to withstand Ottoman sieges. Sitting between the two, the Old Town is a tight-packed warren of winding lanes, some bursting with fine restaurants, lively bars and intriguing shops, others timeless back alleys where washing lines stretch from balcony to balcony. It also holds some majestic architecture, including the splendid Liston arcade, and high-class museums, along with no fewer than 39 churches.

During the day, cruise passengers and day trippers bustle through the streets; come evening, everyone settles down to enjoy themselves. When it comes to drinking, dining and dancing, this is the hottest spot in the Ionian Islands.

⊙ Sights

The Old Town's most eye-catching feature is the grand French-built **Liston** arcade, facing the Old Fort across the lawns of the **Spianada**, and lined with packed cafes. At its northern end, the neoclassical **Palace of St Michael & St George** contains the excellent Corfu Museum of Asian Art. Head inland and you can lose yourself for a happy hour or two amid the maze-like alleyways, seeking out sumptuous Orthodox churches or cosy cafes as the mood takes you.

Continue southwest, skirting the mighty Neo Frourio (New Fort; p666), to reach the **New Town**, busy with everyday shops and services and centring on Plateia G Theotoki (also known as Plateia San Rocco). To the south, around curving Garitsa Bay, the ruin-strewn Mon Repos Estate (p666) marks the site of the ancient settlement of Palaeopolis.

★**Corfu Museum of Asian Art**   MUSEUM
(☑ 26610 30443; www.matk.gr; Palace of St Michael & St George; adult/child €6/3; ⊗ 8am-8pm) Home to stunning artefacts ranging from prehistoric bronzes to works in onyx and ivory, this excellent museum occupies the central portions of the Palace of St Michael & St George. One gallery provides a chronological overview of Chinese ceramics, while showcasing remarkable jade carvings and snuff bottles. The India section opens with Alexander the Great, 'When Greece Met India', and displays fascinating Graeco-Buddhist figures, including a blue-grey schist Buddha. A new Japanese section incorporates magnificent samurai armour, Noh masks and superb woodblock prints.

Municipal Art Gallery
GALLERY

(☑ 26610 48690; www.artcorfu.com; Palace of St Michael & St George; €2; ☺ 9am-4pm Tue-Sun) Make the effort to find this gallery – it's entered via a staircase that climbs from the wide patio on the palace's eastern side – and you'll be rewarded with a handful of high-quality Byzantine icons, including 16th-century works by the Cretan Damaskinos, plus a more extensive array of canvases by Corfiot painters. Look out for the Italian-influenced 19th-century father and son artists, Spyridon and Paul Prossalendis.

★ Palaio Frourio
FORTRESS

(Old Fort; ☑ 26610 48310; adult/concession €6/3; ☺ 8am-8pm Apr-Oct, 8.30am-3pm Nov-Mar) The rocky headland that juts east from Corfu Town is topped by the Venetian-built 14th-century Palaio Frourio. Before that, already enclosed within massive stone walls, it cradled the entire Byzantine city. A solitary bridge crosses its seawater moat.

Only parts of this huge site, which also holds later structures from the British era, are accessible to visitors; wander up to the lighthouse on the larger of the two hills for superb views, or down to reach small gravelly beaches.

Vidos Island
ISLAND

Hourly boats from the Old Port make the 10-minute crossing to tiny, thickly wooded Vidos Island (€5 return), immediately offshore. There's a taverna at the jetty, but the big attraction is to walk the 600m across the island to reach a couple of lovely beaches on its northern shore.

Antivouniotissa Museum
MUSEUM

(Byzantine Museum; ☑ 26610 38313; www.antivouniotissamuseum.gr; off Arseniou; adult/child €4/€2; ☺ 8.30am-3pm Tue-Sun) Home to an outstanding collection of Byzantine and post-Byzantine icons and artefacts, the exquisite, timber-roofed Church of Our Lady of Antivouniotissa doubles as both church and museum. It stands atop a short, broad stairway that climbs from shore-front Arseniou, and frames views out towards the wooded Vidos island.

Mon Repos Estate
PARK

(Kanoni Peninsula; ☺ 7.30am-7.30pm May-Oct, to 5pm Nov-Apr) FREE This park-like wooded estate 2km around the bay south of the Old Town was the site of Corfu's most important ancient settlement, Palaeopolis. More recently, in 1921, the secluded neoclassical villa that now holds the Museum of Palaeopolis was the birthplace of Prince Philip of Greece, who was to marry Britain's Queen Elizabeth II. Footpaths lead through the woods to ancient ruins, including sanctuaries to Hera and Apollo, and a more complete Doric temple atop a small coastal cliff.

It takes half an hour to walk to Mon Repos from town, or you can catch bus 2a from the Spianada (€1.70, every 20 minutes). Bring a picnic and plenty of water; there are no shops nearby.

Corfu Living History
HOUSE

(Casa Parlante; ☑ 26610 49190; www.casaparlante.gr; N Theotoki 16; €5; ☺ 10am-6pm) Corfu Living History is a town house that has been remodelled to illustrate the daily lives of a fictitious merchant family from the mid-19th century. Enthusiastic tour guides make the whole experience fun and informative, while in each room waxworks make small, endlessly repeated movements.

Neo Frourio
FORTRESS

(New Fort; ☺ 9am-3.30pm) FREE The forbidding Neo Frourio is in fact little younger than the Old Fort across town. Surrounded by massive walls that crown the low hill at the western edge of the Old Town, it too dates from the Venetian era. Climbing the stairway at the western end of Solomou brings you to the entrance, where dank tunnels and passages lead through the walls. The ramparts beyond enjoy wonderful views.

Church of Agios Spyridon
CHURCH

(Agios Spyridonos; ☺ 8am-9pm) Pilgrims and day trippers alike throng this Old Town landmark. As well as magnificent frescoes, the small 16th-century basilica holds the remains of Corfu's patron saint, Spyridon, a 4th-century Cypriot shepherd. His body, brought here from Constantinople in 1453, lies in an elaborate silver casket, and is paraded through the town on festival days.

Corfu Philharmonic Society
MUSEUM

(☑ 26610 39289; www.fek.gr; N Theotoki 10; €2; ☺ 9.30am-1.30pm Mon-Sat) Via battered old instruments, photos and scores, this entertaining little museum tells the story of Greece's first-ever marching band, which performed at the first modern Olympics in 1896, and still plays regularly. Founded in 1840 by Nikolaos Mantzaros, composer of the Greek national anthem, the Corfu Philharmonic Society offers free music lessons for local kids in the afternoons.

Corfu Reading Society
HISTORIC BUILDING

(📞26610 39528; www.anagnostikicorfu.com; Kapodistriou 120; ⊙9.30am-1.30pm Mon-Sat) **FREE** Although there's no obvious sign on this grand cream-and-white villa, anyone is welcome to climb its external staircase and settle down with a book in the library of the Corfu Reading Society. Founded in 1836, the oldest cultural institution in modern Greece holds 30,000 volumes in several languages, mostly devoted to the Ionian Islands.

Banknote Museum
MUSEUM

(📞26610 41552; www.alphanumismatics.gr; Plateia Agios Spyridon; ⊙9am-2pm & 5.30-8.30pm Wed & Fri, 9am-3pm Thu, 8.30am-3pm Sat & Sun) **FREE** Somewhat specialist, but oddly fascinating, the Banknote Museum occupies the upper floors of what was in 1840 the first-ever all-Greek bank. It traces the story of the drachma until it was replaced by the euro in 2002, and includes the largest denomination note ever issued: a 100-billion-drachma note from the inflationary era of 1944.

👉 Tours

All sorts of tours can help you explore in and around Corfu Town, whether on foot with **Corfu Walking Tours** (📞6980140160; www.corfuwalkingtours.com), by bus with **Corfu Sightseeing** (www.corfusightseeing.gr; €15), or in the **toy-train** and **horse-drawn carriage** tours that start from the Spianada. Cruises along the coast or to neighbouring islands start from the New Port, with operators including **Ionian Cruises** (📞26610 31649; www.ionian-cruises.com; Ethnikis Antistaseos 4) and **Sarris Cruises** (📞26610 25317; www.sarriscruises.gr; Mouriki 1), while if you fancy learning to sail, contact **Corfu Sea School** (📞26610 97628; www.corfuseaschool.com; Gouvia Marina) at Gouvia marina not far northwest.

Venturing further afield, you can go **horse riding** with **Trailriders** (📞6946653317; www.trailriderscorfu.com; Ano Korakiana) in the village of Ano Korakiana, 18km northwest of Corfu Town, or enjoy a round on one of Greece's finest courses at the **Corfu Golf Club** (📞26610 94220; www.corfugolfclub.com) not far from Ermones, 15km west.

The entire island has excellent walking. The **Corfu Trail** (www.thecorfutrail.com) traverses the island from north to south and takes between eight and 12 days to complete. You can organise a trip through Aperghi Travel (p672), or simply arrange a day's guided hiking with **Corfu Walks & Hikes** (www.walking-corfu.blogspot.co.uk).

🛏 Sleeping

As most island visitors head straight to the beaches and resorts, Corfu Town holds fewer accommodation options than you might expect. Those that do exist tend to be relatively pricey, even in low season.

★ Bella Venezia
BOUTIQUE HOTEL €€

(📞26610 46500; www.bellaveneziahotel.com; N Zambeli 4; s/d incl breakfast from €120/135; ❋🛜) From the instant you enter this neoclassical villa, set in a peaceful central street, you'll be seduced by its pure old-world charm. Previously both a bank and a girls' school, it features an elegant lobby decked in candelabras, with velvet chairs and a grand piano. The plush, high-ceilinged rooms (some with balconies) have fine city views, while the garden breakfast room is delightful.

Dalia Hotel
HOTEL €€

(📞26610 32341; www.daliahotel.com; Plateia Etikou Stado 9; d/tr incl breakfast €95/103; ❋🛜) This friendly, family-run, neighbourhood hotel is set back from the sea, 15 minutes' walk south of the Old Town and just 800m from the airport. The rooms are comfortable but small, and there are bikes available.

Folies Corfu
HOTEL €€

(📞26610 49300; www.foliescorfu.com; s/d €68/81; ❋🛜) Bright self-catering studios and one- or two-bedroom apartments, all with balconies or terraces, arrayed around a lush garden pool in a residential neighbourhood. It's well priced thanks to the away-from-it-all location, 2km west of the New Town – a half-hour walk from the centre. Breakfast costs €5 extra.

Arion Hotel
HOTEL €€

(📞26610 37950; www.arioncorfu.gr; Sxerias 6, Mon Repo Anemomylos; s/d/tr incl breakfast €75/90/125; ❋🛜) Set 15 minutes' walk south of Corfu Town down waterfront Dimokratias, this large hotel has pleasant rooms with small balconies and clean bathrooms. Avoid cheaper corner rooms and those facing the road, and plump for one with a sea view. There's a handsome lobby, a pool, a great bar and a terrific breakfast smorgasbord. Good value and tranquil.

★ Siorra Vittoria
BOUTIQUE HOTEL €€€

(📞26610 36300; www.siorravittoria.com; Stefanou Padova 36; d incl breakfast from €200; 🅿❋🛜) Expect luxury and style at this quiet 19th-century Old Town mansion, where restored traditional architecture meets

Corfu Old Town

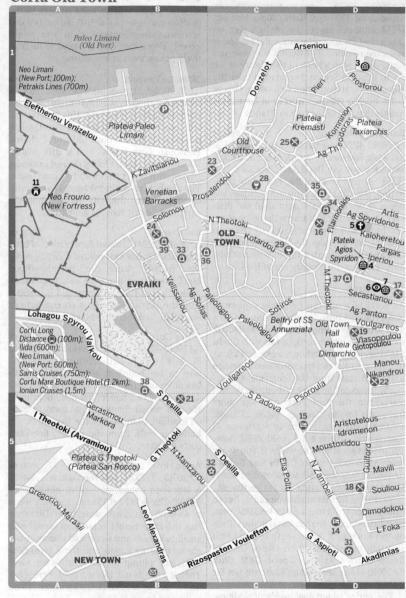

modern amenities; marble bathrooms, crisp linens and genteel service make for a relaxed stay. Breakfast is served either in your room or beneath an ancient magnolia in the peaceful garden.

Corfu Mare Boutique Hotel HOTEL €€€
(☏ 26610 31011; www.corfumare.gr; Nikolau Zervou 5; d/tr incl breakfast €175/235; ✳ ☎ ⊠) Palatial villa-like hotel, just up from the New Port and open to adults only. While larger than 'boutique' might suggest, it's every bit as

Corfu Old Town

⊚ Top Sights
1	Corfu Museum of Asian Art	E2
2	Palaio Frourio	F4

⊚ Sights
3	Antivouniotissa Museum	D1
4	Banknote Museum	D3
5	Church of Agios Spyridon	D3
6	Corfu Living History	D3
7	Corfu Philharmonic Society	D3
8	Corfu Reading Society	E2
9	Liston	E3
10	Municipal Art Gallery	E2
11	Neo Frourio	A2
12	Palace of St Michael & St George	E2
13	Spianada	E4

⊨ Sleeping
14	Bella Venezia	D6
15	Siorra Vittoria	C5

⊗ Eating
16	Anthos	D3
17	Chrisomalis	D3
18	Il Vesuvio	D5
19	Pane & Souvlaki	D4
20	Rex	E3
21	Rouvas	B5
22	Starenio	D4
23	To Alato Pipero	C2
24	To Tavernaki tis Marinas	B3
25	Venetian Well	C2
26	Veranda	E1

⊙ Drinking & Nightlife
27	Josephine	E4
28	Kourdisto Portokali	C2
29	Mikro Café	C3
30	NAOK Azur	E6

✪ Entertainment
31	Cine Orfeas	D6
32	Municipal Theatre	C5

🛍 Shopping
33	Ceramic Art	B3
34	Corfu Bookbinding	D3
35	Corfu Sandals	D2
36	Handiworks Hierotechnima	B3
37	Papagiorgis	D3
38	Public Market	B4
39	Sweet'n'Spicy Bahar	B3

stylish and modern. Each room has its own tasteful decor, with huge prints and striking wallpaper on themes such as pop art and art deco. There's also a bar, a restaurant and a pool.

Corfu Palace Hotel   HOTEL €€€
(☎26610 39485; www.corfupalace.com; Dimokratias 2; s/d/tr incl breakfast €168/195/280; ❄🐾) A grand resort-style hotel on the seafront immediately south of the Old Town. All its bright, floral rooms have views across the

bay, and polished-wood floors or carpets, and there's a large sea-view pool in the gardens.

✕ Eating

Corfiot cuisine shows the delicious influences of many cultures, especially Italian. Great restaurants and tavernas are scattered throughout the Old Town.

★ Pane & Souvlaki   GRILL €

(🖉26610 20100; www.panesouvlaki.com; Guilford 77; mains €5-9; ⊗noon-1am) Arguably the Old Town's best-value budget option, with outdoor tables on the Town Hall square, this quick-fire restaurant does exactly what its name suggests, serving up three skewers of chicken or pork with chunky chips, dipping sauce and warm pitta in individual metal trays. The salads and burgers are good, too.

★ Starenio   BAKERY €

(🖉26610 47370; Guilford 59; sweets & pastries from €2; ⊗8.30am-11pm Mon-Sat) Magical little bakery, dripping with bougainvillea, where in-the-know locals linger at little tables on the sloping pedestrian street to savour cakes, coffee, pastries, and delicious fresh pies with vegetarian fillings such as mushrooms or nettles.

To Alato Pipero   TAVERNA €

(🖉69422 63873; Dhona 17; mains €7-9; ⊗noon-1am) Welcoming all-day taverna–*ouzeri* (place that serves ouzo and light snacks) with outdoor tables in a pedestrian alley. Grilled specialities include local sausages and pork steaks, squid and anchovies, and vegetarian alternatives such as thinly sliced eggplant.

Chrisomalis   TAVERNA €

(🖉26610 30342; N Theotoki 6; mains €7-13; ⊗noon-midnight) Going strong for more than 150 years, this traditional little taverna was a haunt of Lawrence Durrell and family and actor Anthony Quinn. Follow your nose to the traditional grill for souvlaki, pork chops and swordfish. Warm service and pavement tables make it ideal for people-watching.

Rouvas   TAVERNA €

(🖉26610 31182; www.facebook.com/taverna rouvas; S Desilla 13; mains €7-9; ⊗10am-5pm Mon-Sat) Festooned in flowers and as Greek as it gets, this earthy, lunch-only delight is a Corfiot institution. With its menus of standout dishes such as beef stew with tomatoes and fried salt cod, as well as plenty of veggie

options, even celebrity chef Rick Stein is impressed.

★ To Tavernaki tis Marinas   TAVERNA €€

(🖉26611 00792; 4th Parados, Agias Sofias 1; mains €8-18; ⊗noon-midnight) Restored stone walls, hardwood floors and cheerful staff lift the ambience of this taverna. Check the daily specials or choose anything from *mousakas* (baked layers of eggplant or zucchini, minced meat and potatoes topped with cheese sauce) or grilled sardines to steak. Accompany it all with a dram of ouzo or *tsipouro* (distilled spirit similar to raki).

Rex   MEDITERRANEAN €€

(🖉26610 39649; www.rexrestaurant.gr; Kapodistriou 66; mains €9-18; ⊗noon-9pm) A favourite local rendezvous, especially for leisurely lunches, this stately cafe-restaurant set a block back from the Liston serves a Mediterranean-leaning menu of pasta, salads and specialities such as veal *sofrito* (cooked in wine and garlic) and Corfiot rooster (cooked in tomato sauce).

Anthos   GREEK €€

(🖉26610 32252; www.facebook.com/anthos restaurant; Maniarizi-Arlioti 15; mains €10-21; ⊗noon-midnight Mon-Sat, 6pm-midnight Sun; 🖻) Much-loved little back-alley restaurant, with a handful of outdoor tables. Most diners are here for the seafood, savouring dishes such as squid carpaccio, octopus with fava mousse, and grilled sea bass, but it also serves standard Greek meat favourites.

Veranda   GREEK €€

(🖉26610 81716; Arseniou 19; mains €8-15; ⊗noon-midnight) Lovely waterfront restaurant, with a shaded terrace jutting over the turquoise waters that's often packed at lunchtime. Diners relish Greek classics, from cheesy shrimp to grilled chicken skewers.

Il Vesuvio   ITALIAN €€

(🖉26610 21284; Guilford 16; mains €9-18; ⊗noon-late; 🖻) A classy Italian place, with outdoor tables on both sides of the pedestrian street, that's won awards for its moreish home-made gnocchi, cannelloni and pizzas. Leave room for the silky-smooth panna cotta, so fresh it will make your taste buds sing.

★ Venetian Well   GREEK €€€

(🖉26615 50955; www.venetianwell.gr; Plateia Kremasti; mains €15-34; ⊗7pm-midnight, closed winter; ❋🖻) Corfu Town's finest special-occasion restaurant has a beautifully faded square to itself, hidden away near the cathedral and complete with a genuine Venetian well. The exquisite contemporary approach to cuisine adorns local meats, fish and vegetables with all sorts of foams, mousses and gels; even if you can't always tell what it is you're eating, it's invariably delicious.

Drinking & Nightlife

Perhaps the best place to kick-start the evening is on the stylish Liston arcade, where Corfiots go to see and be seen; after that, the choices are legion.

For dance venues, head after 11pm to Corfu's disco strip, starting west beyond the New Port, along Ethnikis Antistaseos; take a taxi, as it's a busy, unlit road without walkways. A €10 admission fee usually includes one drink.

★ Mikro Café   BAR
(☑26610 31009; www.mikrocafe.com; N Theotoki 42) Whether your favoured beverage is coffee, wine or beer, the Old Town holds no finer spot for drinking and people-watching than the delightful, multilevel vine-shaded terrace of the convivial 'little cafe'.

54 Dreamy Nights   CLUB
(☑6940645436; www.54dreamynights.com; Ethnikis Antistaseos 54; ⊗10pm-late; ☎) Gleaming, bright-white nightspot, west along the New Port, with a minimalist aesthetic, spectacular night shows and a retractable roof. Open-air DJ parties and live gigs by big-name Greek music stars attract up to 3000 clubbers.

Kourdisto Portokali   BAR
(☑6933291188; www.facebook.com/kourdisto.gr; Alypiou 5; ⊗9.30am-3pm & 6pm-6am) A cool haven for the Old Town's retro rockers, on a hilly alleyway just south of the cathedral; the name means 'Clockwork Orange', hence the splendid hanging sign. There's always a rocking vinyl soundtrack.

NAOK Azur   CAFE
(☑26610 80700; www.naokazur.com; Dimokratias 1; ⊗9am-late) Chic, split-level venue across from the Spianada, with an all-day beach bar on its own little gravel beach, and several higher tiers incorporating a restaurant, a cafe and, after sundown, a fully fledged nightclub.

Josephine   CAFE
(☑26610 27275; www.josephinecafe.com; Liston 4; ⊗9am-2am; ☎) Emulate Napoleon's namesake empress by lounging for a languid hour,

over coffee or fine French wine, on the plush seats of the Liston arcade's grandest cafe.

☆ Entertainment

Corfu Town has a lively cultural life; check www.corfuland.gr (in Greek) for current listings.

Cine Orfeas   CINEMA
(☑26610 39769; www.cineorfeas.gr; Aspioti 1) Hidden beneath an apartment block, the Old Town's only cinema screens the latest big movies in their original languages.

Municipal Theatre   PERFORMING ARTS
(☑26610 33598; G Theotoki 68) This brutalist modern edifice, on the edge of the Old Town, serves as Corfu's cultural powerhouse, putting on classical music, opera, dance and drama; some productions are also staged at the theatre next to Mon Repos (p666).

Shopping

The Old Town is crammed with shopping opportunities. The heaviest concentration of souvenir shops, which sell everything from 'evil eye' amulets and olive-wood carvings to pashminas and perfume, is along narrow Filarmonikis between the two main churches, while N Theotoki is good for idiosyncratic boutiques.

★ Sweet'n'Spicy Bahar   SPICES
(☑26610 33848; www.sweetnspicy.gr; Agias Sofias 12; ⊗9am-8.30pm) Gloriously aromatic spice and condiment shop, run by an ever-so-enthusiastic Greek-Canadian-Lebanese woman with a palpable love for devising her own enticing mixes of Greek and imported spices.

Papagiorgis   FOOD & DRINKS
(☑26610 39474; www.papagiorgis.gr; N Theotoki 32; ⊗9am-midnight) Irresistible old-fashioned patisserie that's an Old Town landmark thanks to its 40 different flavours of ice cream, plus a mouthwatering array of homemade tarts, biscuits and honey.

Corfu Sandals   SHOES
(☑26610 47301; www.facebook.com/corfusandals; Philhellinon 9; ⊗9am-11pm) This standout shoe store, on the narrow lane that holds Corfu Town's heaviest (and tackiest) concentration of souvenir shops, sells well-priced handmade leather sandals in all styles and sizes, many with ergonomic bubble soles.

WORTH A TRIP

SOUTHERN CORFU

The first resort that you reach as you head south on the coast road from Corfu Town is sleepy **Benitses**, 14km along. This pleasant old village backs a sand-and-gravel beach and is home to a ruined Roman villa, with footpaths ascending the wooded slopes.

Further south again, beyond the popular but uninspiring beach resorts of **Moraïtika** and **Messonghi**, the coastal road winds through sun-dappled woods, passing prettier and much less developed little coves. Tiny **Boukari** cradles an attractive little harbour, while the fishing port of **Petriti**, where the road finally turns away from the shoreline, holds a row of welcoming seafood tavernas. Nearing the southern tip of Corfu, **Lefkimmi** is an elongated little town where everyday life simply carries on as usual, untroubled by visitors.

Sights

Achillion Palace (☑ 26610 56210; www.achillion-corfu.gr; Gastouri; €8; ☉ 8am-8pm Apr-Oct, to 4pm Nov-Mar) Set atop a steep coastal hill 12km south of Corfu Town, the Achillion Palace was built during the 1890s as the summer palace of Austria's empress Elizabeth, the niece of King Otto of Greece. The palace's two principal features are its intricately decorated central staircase, rising in geometrical flights, and its sweeping garden terraces, which command eye-popping views.

Eating

Klimataria (☑ 26610 71201; www.klimataria-restaurant.gr; Benitses; mains €8-15; ☉ 6.30-11.30pm Mon-Sat, noon-4.30pm Sun) This tiny, old-fashioned taverna, in a custard-coloured villa facing the main road, is worth a pilgrimage in its own right – every dish is delicious and superbly fresh, from the tender octopus or various mezedhes (appetisers) to the feta and olive oil. Call for reservations in summer.

Spiros Karidis (☑ 26620 51205; Boukari; mains €8-22; ☉ lunch & dinner) At this seafront taverna facing a tumbledown jetty, just beyond Boukari's harbour, you can feast on locally caught mullet, bass, grouper or octopus beneath the shade of giant eucalyptus trees. Celeb chef Rick Stein has stopped by to pick up a few tips from the excellent owner.

Ceramic Art   CERAMICS
(☑ 26610 95069; www.ceramicart.gr; Agias Sofias 23; ☉ 10am-10pm, reduced hours in winter) This light, appealing Old Town gallery sells affordable pottery ranging from colourful homewares, ornaments and toys to striking wood-fired pieces made using the ancient terra sigillata technique. You can also visit the artists in their workshop, which faces the waterfront near the Old Port.

Handiworks Hierotechnima   ARTS & CRAFTS
(Paleologlou 60; ☉ 8am-8pm Mon-Sat) Backstreet shop selling one-of-a-kind, mostly wooden ornaments and souvenirs, hand-crafted on the premises by the friendly owner. The star attractions are ships made of driftwood, fully rigged with cotton sails.

Corfu Bookbinding   BOOKS
(☑ 26610 31566; www.ionianbookstore.com; Maniarizi-Arlioti 27; ☉ 10am-9pm Mon-Fri) For souvenir hunters, this old bookshop near the cathedral is of most interest for its hand-made notebooks and unusual framed prints, old and new; serious bibliophiles can join regular bookbinding workshops.

Public Market   MARKET
(north of Plateia G Theotoki; ☉ 6.30am-2pm Mon-Sat) Forming an alleyway between the newer part of town and the New Fort, Corfu Town's fresh-produce market sells fruit and vegetables, mostly local and often organic, plus the daily fisher's catch, and is also home to decent cafes.

ⓘ Information

All Ways Travel (☑ 26610 33955; www.allways travel.com.gr; Plateia G Theotoki 34) Helpful English-speaking staff in the New Town's main square.

Aperghi Travel (☑ 26610 48713; www.aperghi travel.gr; I Polyla 1) Handles tours and accommodation, especially for walkers on the Corfu Trail (www.corfutrail.com).

Corfu General Hospital (☑ 26613 60400; Kontokali) About 8km west of the town centre.

Municipal Tourist Kiosk (Spianada; ☉ 9am-4pm Mon-Sat Jun-Sep) Helps with accommodation, transport and things to do around Corfu.

Pachis Travel (☑ 26610 28298; www.pachis travel.com; Guilford 7; ☉ 9am-2.30pm & 5.30-9pm Mon-Sat) Busy little agency that's useful for hotels, ferry and plane tickets, and excursions to Paxi.

Post Office (Leoforos Alexandras 26; ☉ 7.30am-8.30pm Mon-Fri)

Tourist Police (☑ 26610 29168; I Andreadi 1) In the New Town, off Plateia G Theotoki (Plateia San Rocco).

ℹ️ Getting Around

Most Corfu Town rental companies are based along the northern waterfront.

Budget (☑ 26610 24404; www.budget.gr; Eleftheriou Venizelou 29)

Sunrise (☑ 26610 44325; www.corfusunrise. com; Ethnikis Antistaseos 16)

Top Cars (☑ 26610 35237; www.carrental corfu.com; Donzelot 25)

Northern Corfu

Immediately north of Corfu Town, the coastline consists of an all-but-continuous strip of busy beach resorts, including **Gouvia**, **Dasia**, **Ipsos** and **Pyrgi**. These offer all you need for a family holiday, but are otherwise unremarkable.

Continue north, though, and the coast road begins to wind and undulate around the massif formed by the island's highest peak, **Mt Pantokrator** (906m). The scenery becomes much more attractive, and each of the pretty little coves that pepper the seafront seems to hold a delightful village, or at least a taverna.

An exhilarating drive – or hike, for those with calves of steel – can take you up either the northern or southern slopes of Mt Pantokrator. Coming from the south, look for a turning just beyond Pyrgi. A narrow road from there switchbacks its way up, passing through the picturesque villages of **Spartylas** and **Strinylas**, then climbs through stark terrain – transformed by wildflowers in spring – to reach the very summit. Sadly, the venerable monastery of **Moni Pantokrator** there is now straddled by a huge and ugly telecommunications tower. The all-round views are as superb as ever, though, stretching as far as the mountains of Albania and the Greek mainland. Alternatively, approaching from the north, the direct ascent starts in Aharavi, while another route from Pelekito stops short of the summit, but enables you to visit the magnificent, beautifully restored Venetian village of **Old Perithia**.

Staying on the coast road north of Pyrgi brings you to **Barbati**, where a large straight beach of flat white pebbles fills a wooded inlet. Further on, in the exquisite bayside village of **Kalami**, down below the road, the former home of Lawrence Durrell now holds a delightful restaurant, White House (p674). North again, **Agios Stefanos** is another attractive fishing village, nestled in a sheltered bay, and flanked by a shingle beach to the north and an olive grove to the south. On the other side of a wooded headland beyond, gorgeous and minimally developed little **Avlaki** lines a popular windsurfing beach.

Still no more than a village despite a history stretching back to the Romans – Nero holidayed outrageously here – charming **Kassiopi** spreads between a sheltered harbour and a thin strip of stony beach. It's home to some excellent restaurants and hotels, as well as shops selling the renowned local embroidery. Steps climb up from the main street to the overgrown, but enticing, ruins of a Venetian castle immediately above; walk around the headland instead to reach secluded **Battaria** and **Kanoni** beaches.

Beyond Kassiopi, the coast road heads west past the resorts of **Aharavi**, **Roda** and **Sidhari**, hugely popular with British families drawn by the broad, crowded beaches and inexpensive tavernas. Look out in Aharavi for the **Folklore Museum** (☑ 26630 63479; www.museum-acharavi.webs.com; Aharavi; adult/child €3/1.50; ☉ 10am-2pm Mon-Sat), an enjoyable mishmash of everything from accordions and olive presses to puppets and phones. Confusingly, Corfu holds another resort named **Agios Stefanos**, on the far northwest coast and fronted by a large sandy beach. From either there or Sidhari, excursion boats head in summer to the **Diapondia Islands**, a little-known cluster 40 minutes offshore; reserve through **San Stefano Travel** (☑ 26630 51910; www.san-stefano. gr; Agios Stefanos, northeast coast).

🛏️ Sleeping

Dionysus Camping Village   CAMPGROUND € (☑ 26610 91417; www.dionysuscamping.gr; Dafnila Bay; campsites per adult/car/tent €7.10/4.40/4.50, huts per person €14; 🐾🖥) What better setting for a campsite than a shaded, tiered 400-year-old olive grove? Located near Dasia

THE DURRELLS

British writers Gerald and Lawrence Durrell lived on Corfu for the four years preceding WWII. Gerald, then a child but later a prominent naturalist, chronicled his eccentric family's island idyll in several charming and hilarious books. The three houses where they lived, north of Corfu Town, are not open to visitors. The White House (p674) at Kalami, however, which was home to Lawrence and his wife Nancy while he wrote his lyrical nonfiction account of Corfu, *Prospero's Cell*, is now a lovely restaurant.

As for the hit TV series *The Durrells*, its principal shooting location is **Danilia**, a restored, once-abandoned village that is only accessible to guests staying at the **Grecotel Corfu Imperial** (☑26610 88400; www.corfuimperial.com; Kommeno; d incl breakfast €463; ☺May-Oct; ❈☏❉) resort down on the coast.

Beach, 10km north of Corfu Town (on bus route 7), it also has rondavel huts and a pool.

★ Manessis Apartments
APARTMENT €€

(☑6973918416; www.manessiskassiopi.com; Kassiopi; 4-person apt €80-100; ❈☏) Bougainvillea-draped two-bedroom apartments, some with sea-facing balconies, set in flower-filled gardens towards the far end of Kassiopi's picturesque harbour. The friendly Greek-Irish owner makes sure everything goes smoothly.

Casa Lucia
APARTMENT, BUNGALOW €€

(☑26610 91419; www.casa-lucia-corfu.com; Sgombou; studios & cottages €70-120; ☺Apr-Oct; ℗❧) 🌿 This attractive garden complex of studios and cottages, 3km up from Gouvia towards Paleokastritsa, has a strong artistic and community ethos and offers yoga, t'ai chi and Pilates.

Bella Mare
HOTEL €€€

(☑26630 81997; www.belmare.gr; Avlaki; s/d €139/187; ❈☏) If you've come to Corfu to relax, look no further than this away-from-it-all resort hotel, overlooking stunning Avlaki Beach from the olive groves at its western end. It has spacious contemporary rooms and suites, plus a pool, spa treatments and yoga classes.

✖ Eating

To Fagopotion
GREEK €€

(☑26630 82020; Agios Stefanos, northeast coast; €11-19; ☺noon-1am) Of the procession of similar tavernas that serve up seafront dining at Agios Stefanos, Fagopotion, presided over by the genial Christos, has to be the best for its inventive Greek seafood and meat cuisine.

Cavo Barbaro
SEAFOOD €€

(☑26630 81905; Avlaki; mains €10-22; ☺9.30am-late) With widescreen views of the beach, and sea breezes wafting through the garden, this pretty and very spacious restaurant makes a charming spot for a leisurely meal of octopus, calamari, *saganaki* (fried cheese), *mousakas* or swordfish.

Taverna Galini
GREEK €€

(☑26630 81492; www.galinitaverna.gr; Agios Stefanos, northeast coast; mains €15-21; ☺lunch & dinner) Shaded by vines by day, lit by hurricane lamps by night, this olive-and-cream gem spreads across a semi-al fresco seafront terrace. Enjoy *stifadho* (meat, game or seafood cooked with onions in a tomato purée), *kleftiko* (slow oven-baked lamb or goat), souvlaki and fresh local fish.

★ White House
MEDITERRANEAN €€€

(☑26630 91040; www.corfu-kalami.gr; Kalami; mains €10-23; ☺9am-midnight) Utterly ravishing waterfront restaurant in the former home of writer Lawrence Durrell, with tables quayside – many diners arrive by motorboat – as well as on a vine-shaded terrace. The appetisers are predominantly Greek, and the mains and desserts Italian, such as delicious mixed seafood risotto or linguine for €20. Offers boat rentals and apartments, too.

Western Coast

Corfu's western shoreline boasts some of the island's most spectacular scenery, its prettiest villages and finest beaches. No coastal road connects the many sandy coves that nibble into the towering cliffs along its central stretch, so sightseers have to choose their targets wisely. **Paleokastritsa** in the north has a great beach, a beautiful monastery and fine hiking; **Pelekas** is a delightful hilltop village; and **Agios Gordios** in the south is a backpackers' haven with a superb beach.

The popular resort area of Paleokastritsa, 23km northwest of Corfu Town, stretches for nearly 3km through a series of small, picturesque bays. Craggy mountains swathed in cypress and olive trees tower above. The real treat comes at the resort's end, where an exquisite little beach is said to be where the weary Odysseus washed ashore. Boat trips from the little jetty here include **Paradise Sunset** (☑6972276442; per person €10-20) cruises to nearby grottoes and the glass-bottomed **Yellow Submarine** (☑6977409246; www.yellowsubmarine.gr; €10; ☉10am-6pm, night cruises 9pm).

Set amid splendid gardens on the rocky promontory above, an easy 10-minute walk from the beach, the **Moni Theotokou** (☉7am-1pm & 3-8pm) **FREE** monastery dates back to the 13th century, and is home to an interesting little **museum** (☉Apr-Oct) **FREE** and a shop selling oils and herbs.

A circuitous hike or drive west from Paleokastritsa will take you along a high winding road through the unspoiled villages of **Lakones** and **Krini**. A minor track that drops west of Krini dead-ends far above the waves at a mighty isolated crag, where a broad stone stairway climbs up to the impregnable Byzantine fortress of **Angelokastro**. Though its ramparts remain largely intact, rampant wildflowers now fill its interior; the views back to Paleokastritsa are unforgettable.

Further north, the coastline becomes much flatter, and the low-key resorts of **Agios Georgios** and **Arillas** line their own long beaches.

South of Paleokastritsa, the pebbly beach at **Ermones** has become overdeveloped, but sleepy little **Pelekas**, atop wooded cliffs 6km southeast, is a confection of biscuit-cream-hued buildings. Kalimera Bakery (p676) here sells fresh pastries, while the frog-green **Witch House** (☑6974525376; ☉10am-10pm), almost opposite, is perfect for offbeat gifts. Kaiser Wilhelm rode his horse to get 360-degree island views from the peak immediately above the village, now known as the **Kaiser's Throne**.

Sandy beaches within easy reach of Pelekas include **Kontogialos** (also called Pelekas) and **Glyfada**, both now fully fledged resorts with large hotels and other accommodation. Lawrence Durrell hailed **Myrtiotissa Beach**, further east, as arguably the best in the whole world. Now dominated by nudists, it remains relatively pristine because it's so hard to reach – it requires a long slog down a steep and only partly surfaced road (drivers should park on the hilltop).

The rambling old vineyard estate at **Ambelonas** (☑6932158888; http://ambelonas-corfu.gr; ☉7-11pm Wed-Fri Jun-Oct, 1-6pm Sun Dec-May), 5km east of Pelekas (and only 8km west of Corfu Town), produces and sells enticing products ranging from wine and vinegar to olive oil and sweets.

Continuing south, the resort of **Agios Gordios** is set below a stupendous verdant hillside, with a long sand-and-pebble beach that can accommodate any crowd. Another 12km south, just off the main road, the Byzantine **Gardiki Castle** makes an impressive spectacle, but is largely ruined. Beyond it lies vast **Lake Korission**, separated from the sea by a narrow spit that's fronted by long, sandy **Halikounas Beach**.

🛏 Sleeping

The main overnight destinations in western Corfu are Paleokastritsa, which holds a large crop of medium-range hotels, and Agios Gordios, which has long been a favourite with backpackers but is now moving increasingly upmarket.

Paleokastritsa Camping CAMPGROUND €

(☑26630 41204; www.paleokastritsa-bliss.com; campsites 1/2 adults €18.50/22.90; ☉mid-May–late Oct; P🐶🛜🏊) Well-organised camping ground, set in the shade of olive terraces above the main road 1km east of town, with a pool and ready access to great walks.

Pink Palace HOSTEL, HOTEL €

(☑26610 53103; www.thepinkpalace.com; Agios Gordios Beach; dm/d/tr incl breakfast & dinner from €24/56/84; ✳@) You can't miss Corfu's major rendezvous for partying backpackers – not only is it bright pink, it's enormous, sprawling down the steep hillside towards the sea. Breakfast and dinner are served in the beachfront restaurant, a hundred steps down from the basic hostel rooms (wi-fi in communal areas only) and the fancier apartments. Activities include quad biking and booze cruises. Two-night minimum.

Jimmy's Restaurant & Rooms PENSION €

(☑26610 94284; www.jimmyspelekas.com; Pelekas village; s/d/tr €35/45/55; ☉May-Oct; ✳🛜) Simple but perfectly decent rooms, with views over the rooftops, set above a lively village restaurant that's only open for breakfast (€8) and dinner (mains €7 to €14).

★Levant Hotel HOTEL €€

(☑26610 94230; www.levantcorfu.com; Pelekas village; s/d incl breakfast €80/100; ☉May–mid-Oct;

P ✱ 🛜 💻) A creamy neoclassical hotel, up in the gods just below the Kaiser's Throne, with pastel-blue rooms, wooden floors, belle-époque lights and balconies. Throw in a refined restaurant serving shrimp, risotto and *stifadho* on a terrace with sublime sunset views. Tempted?

Hotel Zefiros
HOTEL €€

(📋 26630 41244; www.hotel-zefiros.gr; Paleokastritsa; d/tr/q from €90/130/145; ✱ 🛜 💻) Set slightly askew of Paleokastritsa's pretty beach, with a cool olive-grey terrace cafe at lobby level, wine-coloured Zefiros offers attractive rooms with balconies and contemporary flourishes. Room 107 has the finest view.

Rolling Stone
PENSION €€

(📋 26610 94942; www.pelekasbeach.com; Pelekas Beach; r/apt €70/98; @ 🛜) Close to the beach, this funky travellers' oasis has new two-bedroom family apartments, with fresh rooms, bathrooms and kitchenettes. The original apartments are also spotless, and encircle a shaded terrace where people gather to chat. Laid-back and friendly.

✗ Eating & Drinking

Elia Restaurant
TAVERNA €

(📋 6982316598; www.eliamirtiotissa.com; Myrtiotissa; mains €7-14; ⏱ noon-late May-Oct) An irresistible taverna, perched above the track down to breathtaking Myrtiotissa Beach, serving an enticing menu of Corfiot specialities and much-needed cold drinks.

To Stavrodromi
TAVERNA €

(📋 26610 94274; www.tostavrodromi.com; Pelekas; mains €7-12; ⏱ 6-11pm) A homey dinner-only joint at the main crossroads just east of Pelekas. Delicious local specialities include Corfu's finest *kontosouvli* (spit-roast pork with paprika and onions), as well as rabbit *stifadho* and pepper steak.

Kalimera Bakery
BAKERY €

(Pelekas village; pastries from €2; ⏱ 7am-late) Put a spring in your morning step by savouring the wood-fired bread, *pastelli* (sesame biscuits), baklava and heavenly coffee at this mustard-coloured bakery in the village square.

★ Alonaki Bay
TAVERNA €€

(📋 26610 75872; Alonaki; mains €10-15; ⏱ lunch & dinner; 🛜) Follow the dirt roads out to the headland northwest of Lake Korission to find this simple, family-run taverna, perched on dramatic cliffs. It serves a small menu of home-cooked meat and *mayirefta* (ready-cooked meals), and also offers clean rooms (€50) and apartments (€55), overlooking the garden.

Nereids
TAVERNA €€

(📋 26630 41013; Paleokastritsa; mains €12-19; ⏱ lunch & dinner) Just below a huge curve in the road as you enter Paleokastritsa, this romantic spot is best experienced at night, when its terrace of ornamental rock pools and urns is softly lit. Try dolmadhes (vine leaves stuffed with rice, and sometimes meat), meatballs in tomato sauce, *kleftiko* and *stifadho*.

La Grotta
CAFE

(📋 26630 41006; www.lagrottabar.com; Paleokastritsa; ⏱ 10am-late mid-May–mid-Oct) Tucked away in a rocky cove, immediately above the sea and replete with sunbeds and a diving board, this decked terrace makes an ideal chill-out escape. Follow the steep steps opposite the Hotel Paleokastritsa driveway.

PAXI
ΠΑΞΟΙ
POP 2300

Measuring a mere 13km from tip to toe, and spared overdevelopment by its lack of an airport, Paxi packs a lot of punch into its tiny frame. Facilities are concentrated in three delightful harbour villages tucked into its eastern shores – Lakka, Loggos and the ferry port of Gaïos. Each has its own crop of tasteful little hotels, rental apartments and seafront tavernas, and its own devoted fans.

All make wonderful bases for exploring the rolling hills and centuries-old olive groves of the interior, and the wilder scenery of the west coast. Unspoiled coves can be reached by motorboat, while former mule trails lead to sheer limestone cliffs that plunge into the azure sea. Great hikes lead out to majestic Tripitos Arch in the south, and down to Erimitis Beach in the west, beneath a vast wall of crumbling rock, with a potential pause at Erimitis Bar & Restaurant (📋 6977753499; www.erimitis.com; mains €12-24; ⏱ 4pm-2am; 🛜) en route.

❶ Getting There & Away

BOAT

Busy passenger-only Ilida (p663) hydrofoils links Paxi's ferry port at Gaïos with Corfu Town (€25, 55 minutes, three to eight daily, May to mid-October) and, occasionally, Igoumenitsa. A slower but cheaper service on the Corfu Town route (€10.30, 90 minutes, one to three daily,

April to October) is provided by **Kamelia Lines** ([☑] Corfu 26610 40372, Paxi 26620 32131; www.kamelialines.gr), while car ferries also link Paxi with Igoumenitsa (per passenger/vehicle €11/42.30, one to three daily, April to October). Buy ferry tickets from **New Plans** (Bouas Tours; [☑] 26620 32088; www.newplans.gr; Gaïos) or **Zefi Travel** ([☑] 26620 32114; www.zefitravel. com; Gaïos; ⊙8.30am-3pm & 6-11pm).

Fast sea taxis are available on demand; Corfu to Paxi costs €330 with **Paxos Sea Taxi** ([☑]6932232072, 26620 32444; www.paxossea taxi.com; Gaïos).

Regular excursion boats run from Gaïos to Antipaxi (€10 return) from June onwards through summer.

BUS

A direct bus connects Athens with Paxi (€71 including Paxi–Igoumenitsa ferry, seven hours) once a week in high season. On Paxi, get tickets from New Plans.

❶ Getting Around

Buses link Gaïos and Lakka via Loggos twice daily (€2.50); they're not convenient for day trips.

Taxis between Gaïos and Lakka or Loggos cost about €15; Gaïos' taxi rank is by the inland car park.

Many agencies rent small boats (from €50 to €100, depending on engine capacity).

Daily car rental with **Alfa Hire** ([☑] 26620 32505; Gaïos) starts at €40 in high season.

Gaïos   Γάιος

POP 500

Gaïos is a supremely peaceful harbour village. Arrayed in a lazy, gentle curve along a narrow, fjord-like channel, it's caressed by beautiful teal water and faces across to the wooded islet of Agios Nikolaos. A long row of rose- and biscuit-hued neoclassical villas line the waterfront promenade, many of them housing cafes and tavernas, while yachts and excursion boats bob at the quayside.

🛏 Sleeping & Eating

Paxos Beach Hotel   HOTEL €€
([☑] 26620 32211; www.paxosbeachhotel.gr; d incl breakfast €105-180, ste €200-280; ❉ 🛜 ⊠) Nestling into a tiny cove, a pleasant 1.5km walk southeast along the waterfront from Gaïos, this family-run hotel has its own beach, plus a jetty, a swimming pool, a tennis court and a seaside restaurant. With rooms in separate villas on the terraced hillside, you can expect a lot of steps. Ferry transfers and rental boats available.

Paxi & Antipaxi

Theklis-Clara Studios   PENSION €€
([☑] 26620 32313, 6972923838; www.theklis-studios. com; studios €100; ❉) Lovely Thekli, a free-diver with her own boat, rents out four beautiful two-person studios, furnished with shabby-chic flair, in a handsome house set 100m up from the quayside. All have well-equipped kitchenettes and bathrooms, and balconies with serene sea views. Ferry transfers possible on request.

Water Planet Rooms   APARTMENT €€
([☑] 6972111995; www.waterplanet.gr; d €60; ❉ 🛜) Attractive and well-priced rooms, some with sea views, in a fine old villa tucked slightly back from the waterfront. Guests share use of a kitchen and a courtyard garden. The friendly and very helpful owners run the adjoining dive shop.

Capriccio Creperie   CAFE €
([☑] 26620 32065; crêpes €3-6; ⊙9am-2am) Pretty little lilac villa, with a handful of quayside tables, slightly southeast of the centre. The waffles and crêpes are superfresh, while the delicious homemade ice cream, including flavours such as *kaimaki* (mastic and cinnamon), is a tonic for the soul.

★**Carnayo**   MEDITERRANEAN €€
([☑] 26620 32376; www.carnayopaxos.gr; mains €10-22; ⊙lunch & dinner Tue-Sun) Paxi's finest

restaurant serves local food that's head and shoulders above the harbour-front tavernas, for much the same price. Set 400m up from central Gaïos, it features a refined indoor dining room and a romantically lit garden courtyard. For €8 you can get a mixed plate of starters. Mains range from slow-roasted pork to homemade burgers and crispy-skin bream.

Dodos TAVERNA €€
(☑26620 32265; http://dodos-paxos.blogspot.co.uk; mains €7-15; ⊙noon-midnight) Dodos is a friendly little taverna hidden away in a colourful and very quirky secret garden (follow the signs from the southern end of the waterfront). Come for traditional dishes such as lamb cooked with honey or pork stuffed with cheese; and linger for live music. It's all presided over by the genial Dodo. There are also simple studios for rent (from €60).

❶ Information

Gaios' main street, Panagioti Kanga, stretching inland from the central seafront square, holds assorted banks and ATMs.

Gaios has no tourist office but travel agencies, such as **Paxos Magic Holidays** (☑26620 32269; www.paxosmagic.com), organise excursions, book tickets and arrange accommodation.

Loggos Λόγγος

Bookended by white cliffs and the hulk of an old olive-oil factory, breathtaking little Loggos, 6km northwest of Gaïos, consists of a cluster of pretty Venetian houses huddled around a tiny bay of crystal-clear water. Bars and restaurants overlook the sea, while wooded slopes climb steeply above.

🛏 Sleeping & Eating

Arthur House APARTMENT €€
(☑26620 31330; http://paxos-arthur.blogspot.gr; 1-/2-bedroom apt €70/120; ℗) Simple, but spacious, and very clean apartments, with kitchenettes, washing machines and balconies, set in a pleasant garden 50m from the waterfront.

O Gios TAVERNA €
(☑26620 31735; mains €7-12; ⊙noon-midnight; ☎) Sturdy little stone-built taverna at the heart of the harbour, preparing home-cooked, good-value grills, seafood and baked dishes at bargain prices.

Vasilis MEDITERRANEAN €€
(☑26620 31587; www.vassilisrestaurant.com; mains €13-27; ⊙lunch & dinner) In a low-slung terracotta cottage on the paved harbourfront,

Vasilis serves local specialities including pan-fried cuttlefish, sea urchin and *bourdeto* (fresh fish cooked in tomato and paprika sauce). Reserve ahead in summer.

❶ Information

Paxos Thalassa Travel (☑26620 31662; www.paxos-thalassatravel.com) Rental motorboats of all shapes and sizes, plus local accommodation and boat trips to Antipaxi.

Lakka Λάκκα

So languid it seems forever on the point of slipping into the yacht-flecked waters, Lakka is sure to slow your pulse and make you smile. Wander the quayside to savour the tempting aromas and gentle music that waft from the tavernas, or venture westward to reach sandy **Harami Beach**, or the **lighthouse** atop the headland beyond.

🛏 Sleeping & Eating

Yorgos Studios APARTMENT €€
(☑26620 31807; www.routsis-holidays.com; d €80; ✳☎) Immaculate and comfy two-person studios, next door to and run by Routsis Holidays, which represents several other local studios and apartments.

★ **Torri E Merli** BOUTIQUE HOTEL €€€
(☑26212 34123; www.torriemerli.com; ste from €420; ⊙May-Oct; ℗✳☎🏊) Constructed in 1750, its towers designed to repel pirates, this beautiful boutique property complements its original Venetian elements with contemporary decor – exposed-stone walls, white-wood floors – to create what's arguably the Ionians' loveliest hotel. Set in the olive groves 800m south of Lakka, it holds just seven suites, along with a restaurant and a kidney-shaped pool.

★ **Arriva Fish Restaurant** SEAFOOD €€
(☑26620 33041; mains €10-17; ⊙lunch & dinner) Waterfront taverna with little tables perched on the very brink of the quayside. Check out the blackboard for an amazing list of freshly caught fish and seafood, from lobster to scorpion fish, prepared every imaginable way – grilled, barbecued, or in risotto or pasta dishes. The octopus *krasato* (in red-wine sauce) is delectable.

❶ Information

Helpful **Routsis Holidays** (☑26620 31807; www.routsis-holidays.com) rents out well-appointed apartments and villas to suit all budgets, and arranges transport and excursions. Harbourside **Sun & Sea** (☑ 26620 31162; www.paxossunandsea.com; Lakka; ⊗ 8.30am-2.30pm & 5.30-11pm) also offers accommodation, as well as boat rental (from €50).

ANTIPAXI ΑΝΤΙΠΑΞΟΙ

POP 25

The ravishing and barely inhabited little island of Antipaxi is a favourite day trip destination from Paxi, just 2km north, and Corfu. While very few visitors stay overnight, the two superb beach coves near the island's northern tip are thronged every day in summer with boats large and small. Sandy **Vrika Beach**, the closest to Paxi, and longer but stonier **Voutoumi Beach** further south, hold a couple of tavernas each. Both lie cradled beneath densely wooded slopes, and shelter dazzlingly clear waters.

Footpaths from both beaches and from the island's totally undeveloped harbour, 600m south of Voutoumi, climb to Antipaxi's central spine, where the 'village' of Vigla consists of a few scattered villas, with no centre or commercial activity. Keep walking to reach the wilder and beach-less western coast within a few minutes, or head for the lighthouse at the island's southernmost tip; take plenty of water and allow at least 1½ hours each way.

Rental properties on Antipaxi are generally available by the week only.

Beach tavernas cater to day trippers but close at night, and Antipaxi has no shops, so anyone staying overnight needs to be self-sufficient.

❶ Getting There & Away

Between June and September boats to Antipaxi typically leave Gaïos on Paxi (return €10) at 10am and return around 4.30pm, with increased services in July and August. **Ionian Cruises** (☑ 26610 31649; www.ionian-cruises.com; Ethnikis Antistaseos 4) and other operators offer day trips to Paxi and Antipaxi from Corfu Town.

LEFKADA ΛΕΥΚΑΔΑ

POP 22,650

Despite being connected to the mainland by a narrow causeway, making it one of the few Greek islands that you can drive to, Lefkada remains surprisingly unaffected by tourism.

Laid-back Lefkada Town is a charming place to spend a day or two, while the hills of the interior still conceal timeless villages and wild olive groves, and the rugged west coast holds some amazing beaches, albeit in some cases badly damaged by recent earthquakes. Only along the east coast are there some overdeveloped enclaves; if you continue all the way south you'll find stunning little bays and inlets, as well as windy conditions that attract kitesurfers and windsurfers from all over the world.

Lefkada was originally a peninsula, not a true island. Corinthian colonisers cut a canal through the narrow isthmus that joined it to the rest of Greece in the 8th century BC.

❶ Getting There & Away

AIR

Lefkada's closest airport is near Preveza (Aktion; PVK), on the mainland 20km north. **Sky Express** (www.skyexpress.gr) connects it with Corfu (€73, 30 minutes), Kefallonia (€67, 30 minutes), Zakynthos (€73, 1½ hours) and Sitia (Crete; €117, 1½ hours, June to September only). **Olympic Air** (www.olympicair.com) flies from Preveza to Athens, with connections throughout Greece. In summer, **Easyjet** (www.easyjet.com) flies to Preveza from the UK, as do charter flights from all over northern Europe.

BOAT

Two ferry companies connect Vasiliki to Kefallonia in high season; **West Ferry** (www.westferry.gr) runs daily to Fiskardo, while **Ionion Pelagos** (www.ionionpelagos.com) sails via Piso Aetos in Ithaki to Sami. For bookings contact **Samba Tours** (☑ 26450 31520; www.sambatours.gr; Vasiliki).

Between July and mid-September, the **Meganisi II** (☑ 26450 92528; www.ferryboatmeganisi.gr) ferry runs twice daily between Nydri and Frikes in Ithaki.

The following services from Lefkada all cost €10:

DESTINATION	DURATION	FREQUENCY
Fiskardo (Kefallonia)	1hr	2 daily
Frikes (Ithaki)	2hr	2 daily, seasonal
Piso Aetos (Ithaki)	1hr	1-2 daily
Sami (Kefallonia)	1¾hr	1 daily

BUS

Lefkada Town's **KTEL Bus Station** (☑ 26450 22364; www.ktel-lefkadas.gr; Ant Tzeveleki), opposite the marina 1km from the centre, serves Athens (€35.80, 5½ hours, five daily), Patra (€17.60, three hours, two weekly), Thessaloniki (€38.50, eight hours, daily) and Igoumenitsa (€13.30, two hours, daily).

ℹ️ Getting Around

TO/FROM THE AIRPORT

There's no direct bus between Lefkada Town and Preveza airport, but buses connect Lefkada Town with Preveza itself (€2.90, 30 minutes, six daily), from where you can take a taxi to the airport (€15).

Taxis from the airport to Lefkada Town cost from €40.

BUS

Frequent buses from Lefkada Town serve the island in high season; Sunday services are greatly reduced. Destinations include the following:

Agios Nikitas €1.80, 30 minutes, three daily

Karya €1.80, 30 minutes, six daily

Nydri €1.80, 30 minutes, 13 daily

Vasiliki €3.70, one hour, three daily

Vlicho €2, 40 minutes, 10 daily

CAR

Rentals start at €40 per day; there are car-, scooter- and bicycle-hire companies in Lefkada Town, Nydri and Vasiliki.

It's possible to pick up a hire car at Preveza's Aktion Airport and return it in Vasiliki, if you are catching a ferry south (or vice versa).

Lefkada Town Λευκάδα

POP 8670

Unusually broad and flat for a Greek-island town, Lefkada's bustling capital faces the mainland across a salty lagoon from its northeastern tip. After losing its historic Venetian architecture in earthquakes in 1948 and 1953, Lefkada Town was rebuilt in a distinctively quake-proof and attractive style. It now resembles a Caribbean port, with wooden buildings in faded pastel colours whose upper storeys are adorned with brightly painted corrugated iron.

A relaxed, cheerful place, it's all very logically laid out, with shops and restaurants concentrated along its central pedestrian street (initially Dorpfeld, then Ioannou Mela further west); cafes and bars on the marina to the south; and banks and businesses closest to the causeway.

◎ Sights

Archaeological Museum MUSEUM

(☑ 26450 21635; Ang Sikelianou; €2; ☉ 8am-3pm Tue-Sun) This excellent museum, west along the waterfront in the modern cultural centre, illuminates island history from the Palaeolithic era to the Romans. Prize exhibits include terracotta ensembles from the 6th century BC, depicting a flute player surrounded by dancing nymphs, seen as evidence that a Pan cult once flourished on Lefkada.

Fortress of Agia Mavra FORTRESS

(€2; ☉ 8am-3pm Tue-Sun) Guarding Lefkada at the start of the causeway, 1.4km from town, Agia Mavra fortress was constructed in the 14th century and later expanded by the Venetians. While its lichen-covered walls remain intact, surrounded by a saltwater moat, the interior now lies in ruins. You can enter the occasional bare chamber as you stroll among the wildflowers.

Collection of Post-Byzantine Icons MUSEUM

(☑ 26450 22502; Rontogianni 11; €2; ☉ 11am-9pm Tue, 8.30am-2.30pm Wed-Fri, 8.30am-1.30pm Sat) Upstairs in the local library, and unlocked on demand, this small gallery displays icons from the Ionian school and Russia that date back to 1500. The two finest, often on loan elsewhere, are believed to have influenced El Greco.

Moni Faneromenis MONASTERY

(☑ 26450 21305; ☉ 8am-2pm & 4-8pm) **FREE** Set in beautiful hilltop gardens, 3km west of town towards Agias Nikitas, the Moni Faneromenis monastery was founded in 1634 and rebuilt following a fire in 1886. The ascent is rewarded with magnificent views over both town and lagoon.

🛏️ Sleeping

★ Boschetto Hotel BOUTIQUE HOTEL €€

(☑ 26450 20244; www.boschettohotel.com; Dorpfeld 1; d incl breakfast €114; ❋ ⏦) This attractive century-old building on the seafront square holds four large, tasteful rooms and a single suite, all with wooden floors, fine linen, marble bathrooms, and balconies looking across the cafe below to the bright-blue waters of the lagoon.

Hotel Santa Maura HOTEL €€

(☑ 26450 21308; www.santamaurahotel.gr; Sp Vlanti 2; s/d/tr incl breakfast €70/90/120; ❋ ⏦) Pastel-pink 19th-century hotel on the main pedestrian street, with green shutters and wraparound street-view balconies, divided between the 18 fresh, sizeable rooms. Breakfast is served in your room or in the garden courtyard.

Pension Pirofani HOTEL €€

(☑ 26450 25844; www.pirofanilefkada.com; Dorpfeld 10; d €125-150; ❋ ⏦) Very friendly and

Lefkada & Meganisi

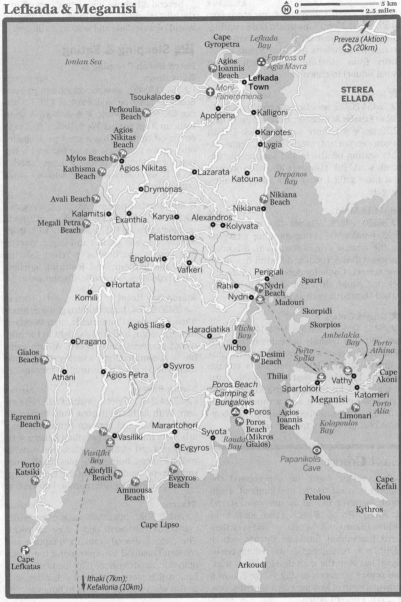

0   5 km
0   2.5 miles

Ionian Sea

Cape Gyropetra
Lefkada Bay
Fortress of Agia Mavra
Preveza (Aktion) (20km)
Agios Ioannis Beach
Lefkada Town
Moni Faneromenis
STEREA ELLADA
Tsoukalades
Apolpena
Kalligoni
Pefkoulia Beach
Kariotes
Agios Nikitas Beach
Lygia
Mylos Beach
Agios Nikitas
Lazarata
Katouna
Drepanos Bay
Kathisma Beach
Drymonas
Nikiana Beach
Avali Beach
Nikiana
Kalamitsi
Exanthia
Karya
Alexandros
Megali Petra Beach
Platistoma
Kolyvata
Englouvi
Vafkeri
Perigiali
Sparti
Hortata
Rahi
Nydri Beach
Komili
Nydri
Madouri
Skorpidi
Agios Ilias
Haradiatika
Vlicho Bay
Skorpios
Ambelakia Bay
Porto Athina
Dragano
Vlicho
Desimi Beach
Porto Spilia
Gialos Beach
Syvros
Thilia
Vathy
Cape Akoni
Athani
Agios Petra
Spartohori
Katomeri
Poros Beach Camping & Bungalows
Meganisi
Porto Alia
Egremni Beach
Marantohori
Poros
Limonari
Syvota
Agios Ioannis Beach
Kolopoulos Bay
Vasiliki
Poros Beach (Mikros Gialos)
Porto Katsiki
Evgyros
Rouda Bay
Vasiliki Bay
Papanikolis Cave
Agiofylli Beach
Evgyros Beach
Ammousa Beach
Cape Kefali
Petalou
Kythros
Cape Lipso
Ithaki (7km); Kefallonia (10km)
Cape Lefkatas
Arkoudi

central family-run hotel, where the rooms themselves, furnished in bland contemporary style and equipped with immaculate bathrooms, are less stylish than the plush lobby.

✖ Eating & Drinking

Brisk year-round trade ensures that Lefkada Town holds some genuinely good restaurants, competing to attract customers browsing along the main street.

Ciao ICE CREAM €

(📞 26450 25557; Mitropoleos 8; per scoop from €1.50; 🕐 6-11.30pm) This bright little evening-only gelateria, just off the pedestrian drag, scoops up delicious fresh ice cream in flavours from *mastiha* (a stomach-settling sweet liquor) to chocolate.

★ Nissi MEDITERRANEAN €€

(📞 26454 00725; www.facebook.com/nissilefkada; Plateia Ethnikis Antistaseos; mains €8-16; 🕐 1pm-12.30am; 🕸🅼) Truly superb Greek–Italian fusion restaurant, with stylish, comfortable seating on the inland square; the jet-black squid-ink risotto (€10), with octopus and huge grilled prawns, is an astonishing bargain.

Frini Sto Molo TAVERNA €€

(📞 26450 24879; Golemi 12; mains €8-15; 🕐 10am-midnight) Long-standing taverna on the marina side of town, with a homely enclosed dining room and a wind-free quayside terrace. Come for dependable seafood – octopus, squid, shrimp and fresh fish – plus baked standards such as *mousakas*.

★ Gogos Gefsis BAR

(📞 26453 00509; Ioannou Mela 149; 🕐 noon-2am; 🅼) Very friendly bar-cafe on the main pedestrian street, with pavement tables plus a quirky interior kitted out like a vintage grocery. The Greek sign is fiendishly hard to read; look for the hammer-and-sickle flag flying above. While it sells a short menu of grilled snacks and cheesy shrimp, just buying a beer gets you a free hot snack.

East Coast

Lefkada's east coast has experienced the island's heaviest tourist development. Head south, however, to find the unspoiled strand at lovely **Poros Beach** (also known as Mikros Gialos) and the relaxed and very sheltered harbour at fjord-like **Syvota**, where yachts now bob alongside the fishing boats. **Nydri** has seen the most development; what was once a gorgeous fishing village is now a crowded strip of kiss-me-quick tourist shops, without a decent beach.

Boat excursions from Nydri head out to Meganisi (€12 to €20), often including swimming stops at lesser islets en route; some venture further afield to Ithaki and Kefallonia (€20 to €25). Borsalino Travel (📞 26450 92528; www.borsalinotravel.gr; Nydri) can make all arrangements.

Several attractive hiking trails set off into the hills inland from Nydri, entering another world of waterfalls and scattered villages.

🛏 Sleeping & Eating

Poros Beach Camping & Bungalows CAMPGROUND €

(📞 26450 95452; www.porosbeach.com.gr; Poros Beach; campsite per adult/car/tent €10/3/5, studios €70-95; 🕐 May-Sep; 🅿🕸@🅼🏊) A short walk up from perfect Poros Beach, this well-equipped campsite has a great pool, shaded olive-grove tent sites, a nice bar and a restaurant stretching across a huge wooden deck. It also offers attractive studios – some family-sized.

Galini Sivota Apartments PENSION €

(📞 26450 31347; www.galinistudiossivotalefkada.gr; Syvota; studios €45, 4-person apt €70; 🕸🅼) Simple sea-view studios and larger, smarter four-person apartments, perched 15m up from the harbour, and featuring kitchenettes, balconies and spotless bathrooms.

Rouda Bay Hotel HOTEL €€

(📞 26450 95634; http://roudabay.gr; Poros Beach; d from €70; 🕸🅼) Comfortable, high-standard, modern rooms and studios, right in the middle of gorgeous Paros Beach. All are capable of accommodating a family of four, and there's also a good waterfront restaurant.

Sivota Bakery BAKERY €

(📞 6972432497; Syvota; mains €6-12; 🕐 8am-2am) With its harbour-front walls hung with antique bikes and carriage lamps, this cool arbour is much more cafe than bakery, serving pizzas and waffles, cocktails and wine, as well as juices, homemade pies, fresh croissants, crêpes and ice cream. No extra charge for the swallows whistling around the ceiling.

Stavros TAVERNA €

(📞 26450 31181; http://tavernastavros.gr; Syvota; mains €7-14; 🕐 breakfast, lunch & dinner Easter-Oct) The pick of several similarly tempting and colourful seafood tavernas along the pretty quayside, Stavros offers a full menu of freshly caught fish along with local delicacies such as fish soup and leg of lamb in honey.

Minas Taverna TAVERNA €€

(📞 26450 71480; www.tavernaminas.gr; Nikiana; mains €8-18; 🕐 dinner daily, lunch Sat & Sun, reduced hours in low season) Top-notch taverna that's equally good for everything from seafood pasta to grilled meat and fish. It's above the main road 5km north of Nydri, and just south of Nikiana.

Vasiliki   Βασιλική

As well as being a handy ferry hub for Kefallonia and Ithaki, this friendly harbour village, complete with stony beach, is one of the top places to learn windsurfing in Greece, thanks to its breezy conditions. A tasty clutch of eucalyptus-shaded tavernas fringes the waterfront, while boutique shops line the short street that connects the harbour with the main road.

🏃 Activities

Caïques take visitors to nearby beaches and coves. The big attraction for boating day trips is Egremni Beach, especially since earthquake damage means it's no longer accessible by road.

Helpful Samba Tours (p679) sells tickets for ferries and excursion boats, including to Egremni, and can arrange car and bicycle hire.

Along the quayside, water-sports outfits stake their claims with flags and equipment; some have their own hotels for clients.

Club Vassiliki   WATER SPORTS
(☑ 26450 31588; www.clubvass.com) Long-established club specialising in all-inclusive learn-to-windsurf packages, including flights and accommodation. Also offers windsurf hire, private lessons and a wide range of other activities, from diving to mountain biking.

Nautilus Diving Club   DIVING
(☑ 6936181775; www.underwater.gr) Single dives (€60) and PADI open-water courses (€410), plus snorkel trips and sea-kayak hire.

🛏 Sleeping & Eating

Vasiliki Blue   APARTMENT €€
(☑ 26450 31602; www.vasilikiblue.gr; d €75; ❄ 🛜) Bright, scrupulously clean kitchenette apartments, perched on the hillside a few metres up from the harbour, with sea-view balconies draped in bougainvillea.

Pension Holidays   HOTEL €€
(☑ 26450 31426; s/d incl breakfast €65/70; ❄ 🛜) Simply furnished, great-value kitchenette apartments, around the corner beyond the main bay, just above the newly expanded marina. Friendly Spiros and family offer Greek hospitality, plus sea-view breakfasts on the balcony.

Vagelaras   TAVERNA €€
(☑ 26450 31224; mains €7-16; ⊙ 8am-late; 🛜) Sitting at the end of the harbour, just short of the ferry dock, this century-old taverna serves great salads, mezedhes, pasta and fresh seafood at waterfront tables. Its upper floor has had a modern makeover and now holds the cool Acqua bar.

Dolphin   TAVERNA €€
(☑ 26450 31430; mains €8-17; ⊙ breakfast, lunch & dinner) Seafood taverna with quayside tables, enticing customers with aromatic grilled seafood and souvlaki, and proud of the fact that Ernest Hemingway once ate here. Be sure to sample the tasty little local prawns.

🍷 Drinking & Nightlife

155   BAR
(☑ 26450 31868; www.155cocktailbar.com; ⊙ 6pm-late May-Oct) Welcoming watering hole on the main street, slightly back from the harbourfront, serving top cocktails (€8) and simple snacks.

West Coast

The dazzling white beaches that line Lefkada's west coast have long been ranked among the finest in the world. Sadly, the best known were seriously damaged by a 2015 earthquake, but others remain intact, and there's still plenty of scope for explorations.

The one resort on the west coast, the ever-expanding village of **Agios Nikitas**, stands 13km southwest of Lefkada Town along the coast road. A short street of inviting tavernas leads down to a curving white-sand beach that's lapped by aquamarine water. Head across the headland to the west, following the footpath from the Poseidon taverna, and you'll come to broad, straight and utterly delightful **Mylos Beach**. White-pebbled **Pefkoulia Beach** is a five-minute drive north and similar **Kathisma Beach** is the same distance south.

Further south, beyond the village of **Athani**, where stalls sell olive oil, honey and wine, two of Lefkada's most famous beaches, **Egremni Beach** and **Porto Katsiki**, were devastated by the 2015 earthquake. Both were submerged in debris, as the white cliffs above them came crumbling down, though geologists believe they will eventually be washed clean and restored to their former glory. Porto Katsiki is in slightly better shape, and remains accessible by car, but both the 720-step stairway that led to Egremni, and the road by which it is reached, were obliterated and are unlikely to be rebuilt. Now the only way to see what's left of Egremni, and to bathe in its magical turquoise waters, is on a boat excursion from ports elsewhere on the island, such as Vasiliki.

Sleeping

★ Mira Resort
APARTMENT €€

(☑ 6977075881, 26450 24967; www.miraresort.com; Tsoukalades; maisonettes incl breakfast from €145; ☺ May-Oct; P ✳ ⚑ ⚐) Perfectly positioned on the mountainside 6km southwest of Lefkada Town, with panoramic views of the glittering sea, Mira has cosy and immaculate maisonettes, plus a large pool and a cafe-bar.

Hotel Agatha
HOTEL €€

(☑ 6948620615; www.agatha-hotel.com; Agios Nikitas; studios/apt €70/90; ✳ 🛜) Beside the coast road, a few minutes' walk up from the beach's eastern end, Agatha offers lovely, cool kitchenette studios and two-room apartments that are flooded with sunlight and ring with birdsong. Number 1 is our favourite.

Olive Tree Hotel
HOTEL €€

(☑ 26450 97453; www.olivetreehotel.gr; Agios Nikitas; s/d/studios incl breakfast €80/90/100; ☺ May-Sep; ✳ 🛜) Modest rooms, just above the village centre, managed by friendly Greek-Canadians. Each has its own terrace, with side-on sea views, and there's a good buffet breakfast.

Eating

★ Lefkatas
TAVERNA €

(☑ 26450 33149; www.lefkatas.gr; Athani; mains €7-12; ☺ brunch, lunch & dinner May-Sep; 🛜) ⚐ This delightful terrace restaurant, on a corner along the main road in the heart of Athani village, has inspiring views down the mountainside to the sea beyond. Sit in the shade of a cedar tree to enjoy breakfast, salads or seafood, and look out for daily specials such as hornbeam fish with garlic and tomato.

T'Agnantio
TAVERNA €

(☑ 26450 97383; www.tagnantio.gr; Agios Nikitas; mains €7-15; ☺ lunch & dinner Easter-Oct) The vine-shaded terrace of Agios Nikitas' finest taverna sits slightly up from the beach and offers sweeping views out to sea. Feast on seafood fresh off the boat – including swordfish, shrimp and octopus – as well as souvlaki, meatballs and local cheese.

Bilvi
GREEK €

(☑ 6973309604; www.bilvi.gr; Porto Katsiki; snacks €6-10; ☺ 9am-late; ✳ ⚑) The closest restaurant to dazzling but earthquake-ravaged Porto Katsiki beach is 600m uphill from the

sea. Relax on the terrace, grab a swim in the pool, and then tuck into a club sandwich or a host of snacks and desserts. And the good news: Bilvi delivers down to the beach itself.

Central Lefkada

Replete with traditional farming villages, lush green peaks, fragrant pine trees, olive groves and vineyards, Lefkada's dramatic central spine is hugely rewarding to explore.

The small village of **Karya** has a pretty central square with plane trees and tavernas, but attracts crowds in high season. It's famous for its embroidery, introduced by a remarkable one-handed local woman, Maria Koutsochero, during the 19th century, and commemorated by a small museum.

The island's highest village, **Englouvi**, a few kilometres south of Karya, is renowned for producing honey and lentils. Book ahead for a guided **herbal walk** (☑ 6934287446; www.lefkas.cc; Kolyvata) near quaint **Alexandros**.

Eating

★ Maria's Tavern
TAVERNA €

(☑ 26450 41228, 6984056686; www.facebook.com/MariasTavern; Kolyvata; mains €6-9; ☺ breakfast, lunch & dinner Apr-Oct) In the tiny hamlet of Kolyvata, which enjoys idyllic views over the hills, the gregarious Kiria Maria opens her home to culinary adventurers. Using whatever's ready in her garden, she serves fresh, perfectly cooked treats. Call ahead to check she's there. Kolyvata is signposted between Alexandros and Nikiana.

MEGANISI   ΜΕΓΑΝΗΣΙ

POP 1040

The elongated island of Meganisi, off Lefkada's southeast corner, is an easy boat ride from Nydri (Lefkada). Most visit on a day trip, but with its verdant hills and turquoise bays, fringed by pebbled beaches, it's well worth considering for a longer, more relaxed stay. From the ferry dock at **Porto Spilia**, climb the steep road or stairway to reach the narrow lanes and bougainvillea-bedecked houses of **Spartohori**, on the plateau above. The next inlet to the east holds pretty **Vathy**, the island's second harbour, 1km below the village of **Katomeri**.

Hotel Meganisi (☑ 26450 51240; www.hotelmeganisi.gr; Katomeri; d incl breakfast €77; ✳ 🛜 ⚐) offers simple rooms with sea views.

The much-loved fish taverna **Errikos** (Porto Vathy; ☑ 26450 51125; mains €7-15; ⊙ lunch & dinner; 🐾) stands beside a small jetty in Vathy.

ⓘ Information

Asteria Holidays (☑ 26450 51107; www. asteria.gr; Porto Spilia) can help with accommodation and travel arrangements.

ⓘ Getting There & Around

Ferries from Nydri sail to both Porto Spilia and Vathy on Meganisi (per person/car €2/13, 25 to 40 minutes, four daily); buy tickets from **Borsalino Travel** (☑ 26450 92528; www. borsalinotravel.gr; Nydri).

Local buses connect Spartohori and Vathy five to seven times daily, via Katomeri, but bringing your own vehicle is recommended.

KEFALLONIA
ΚΕΦΑΛΛΟΝΙΑ

POP 35,800

Kefallonia is a place where it's easy to lose yourself, amid air thick with oleander and the bells of wandering goats. The largest of the Ionian Islands, its convoluted coastline conceals all sorts of captivating coves and beach-lined bays. Despite the devastating earthquake of 1953 that razed much of its historic Venetian architecture, ravishing harbour-front villages such as Fiskardo and Assos still show off Italianate good looks, while the lush and mountainous interior, dotted with wild meadows and vineyards, invites endless exploration.

ⓘ Getting There & Away

AIR

The **airport** (☑ 26710 29900; http://kefalonia airport.info) is 9km south of Argostoli. From May to September, **Easyjet** (www.easyjet.com) flies from London, and many charter flights come from northern Europe and the UK. In addition,

Olympic Air (www.olympicair.com) serves Athens, and **Sky Express** (www.skyexpress.gr) serves Corfu, Preveza and Zakynthos.

DESTINATION	DURATION	FARE	FREQUENCY
Athens	55min	€88	2 daily
Corfu	1hr	€73	3 weekly
Preveza	20min	€67	3 weekly
Zakynthos	25min	€73	3 weekly

BOAT
Domestic

Up to five daily **Ionian Group** (www.ioniangroup. com) ferries connect Poros with Kyllini in the Peloponnese in summer, where you can catch onward ferries to Zakynthos.

Ionian Pelagos (www.ionionpelagos.com) runs up to three daily ferries between Sami and Piso Aetos in Ithaki, of which one or two continue to Astakos in the Peloponnese; connects Sami to Vasiliki in Lefkada twice weekly in summer; and also runs twice daily in summer between the remote and not readily accessible port of Pesada in southern Kefallonia and similarly isolated Agios Nikolaos in northern Zakynthos.

West Ferry (www.westferry.gr) runs between Fiskardo and Vasiliki (Lefkada); buy tickets at Nautilus Travel (p693).

International

Between mid-July and mid-September, **Ventouris Ferries** (http://ventourisferries.com) offers once-weekly connection between Sami, Zakynthos, Igoumenitsa on the mainland, and Bari, Italy. **Red Star Ferries** (www.directferries. co.uk/red_star_ferries.htm) goes to Brindisi from Sami once a week on Fridays during the same period (seat from €95, bunk from €115, 16 hours).

Buy tickets from **Blue Sea Travel** (☑ 26740 23007; www.samistar.com; Posidonos 16, Sami), or **Vassilatos Shipping** (☑ 26710 22618; A Tritsi 54, Argostoli).

BUS

Three daily buses from the **KTEL Bus Station** (☑ 26710 22276; www.ktelkefalonias.gr; A Tritsi 5) in Argostoli use the ferry from Poros to make

BOAT SERVICES FROM KEFALLONIA

DESTINATION	PORT	DURATION	FARE (€)	FREQUENCY
Agios Nikolaos (Zakynthos)	Pesada	1½hr	8	2 daily (May-Sep)
Astakos (mainland)	Sami	3hr	11	1-2 daily
Kyllini (Peloponnese)	Poros	1½hr	9	4-5 daily
Piso Aetos (Ithaki)	Sami	30min	3	2-3 daily
Vasiliki (Lefkada)	Fiskardo	1hr	9	2-3 daily
Vasiliki (Lefkada)	Sami	1¾hr	9	2 weekly (seasonal)

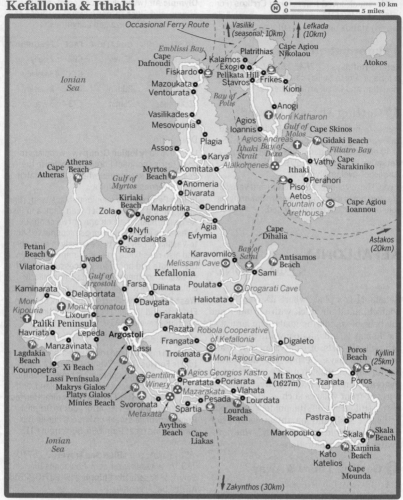

the journey to Athens (€40, seven hours, three daily). You can also buy tickets to Poros itself (€37, four hours, one daily) and Lixouri (€45, seven hours, one daily).

❶ Getting Around

TO/FROM THE AIRPORT

There's no airport bus; taxis to Argostoli cost around €20.

BOAT

Car ferries (☑ 26710 23560) connect Argostoli and Lixouri on the island's western Paliki Peninsula.

BUS

KTEL buses (p685) connect Argostoli with all the island's major towns. In addition, one or two daily services run along the east coast, linking Katelios with Skala, Poros, Sami, Agia Evfyma and Fiskardo. Buses run on Sundays in high season only.

CAR & MOTORCYCLE

Car- and motorbike-hire companies fill major resorts, while **Europcar** (☑ 26710 41008), **Hertz** (☑ 26710 42142) and other operators have offices at the airport. Sami-based **Kefalonia2Ride** (☑ 26740 22970; www. kefalonia2ride.rentals; Maiouli 29, Sami; ⊙ 9.30am-9pm) offers scooters (from €23 per day) and ATVs.

Argostoli   Αργοστόλι

POP 9750

Shielded from the open sea, its waterfront stretching along the landward side of a short peninsula, Argostoli was once renowned for its elegant Venetian-era architecture. Almost all of that was destroyed by earthquake in 1953, however, and it's now a lively, forward-looking town. The main focus of activity is just inland, centred on charming, freshly pedestrianised **Plateia Valianou**, where locals come to chat and eat at the many restaurants. In summer, musicians stroll the streets singing *kantades,* traditional songs accompanied by guitar and mandolin. **Lithostroto**, the pedestrian shopping street immediately south, is lined with stylish boutiques and cafes.

◉ Sights

Platys Gialos   BEACH

This little 'pocket' beach, just beyond Makrys Gialos, has plenty of shade and very clear water, as well as a few places to eat.

Cephalonia Botanica   GARDENS

(✔26710 26595; www.focas-cosmetatos.gr; ⊙9am-2.30pm Tue-Sat) **FREE** This lovely botanical garden, designed to study, preserve and display plants and herbs from the island, is located 2km south of central Argostoli. It also holds a small artificial lake.

Korgialenio History &
Folklore Museum   MUSEUM

(✔26710 28835; www.corgialenios.gr; Ilia Zervou 12; €3; ⊙9am-noon & 6-9pm Mon, 9am-2pm & 6-9pm Tue-Fri, 10am-2pm Sat) Dedicated to preserving Kefallonian art and culture, this fine museum houses icons, assorted furniture, clothes and artwork, taken from the homes of gentry and farm workers.

Makrys Gialos   BEACH

Blessed with enticing turquoise water, just 3km southwest of Argostoli, Makrys Gialos tends to be rammed to the gills in summer with holidaying Brits.

Focas-Cosmetatos Foundation   MUSEUM

(✔26710 26595; www.focas-cosmetatos.gr; Valianou; adult/child €3/free; ⊙10am-2pm Mon-Fri May-Oct) One of the few historic buildings in Agostoli to survive successive earthquakes now holds displays on Kefallonia's cultural and political history, including lithographs by Edward Lear and other British artists. The same family also runs the Cephalonia Botanica.

Archaeological Museum   MUSEUM

(✔26710 28300; Rokou Vergoti; €3) Kefallonia's archaeological museum, which holds treasures from all over the island, including Mycenaean finds, sustained serious damage in a 2014 earthquake, and has yet to reopen.

🛏 Sleeping

⭐**Vivian Villa**   APARTMENT €

(✔26710 23396; www.kefalonia-vivianvilla.gr; Deladetsima 11; d/studios €55/60; ❋🐾) Exquisitely tasteful villa on a quiet inland street, overlooking a garden fragrant with thyme and basil. As well as hotel-style rooms, some with balconies, it offers larger apartments with well-stocked kitchenettes and separate bedrooms for the kids. The stunning loft apartment – which has a lift – sleeps five. Everything runs like clockwork.

Camping Argostoli   CAMPGROUND €

(✔26710 23487; www.campingargostoli.gr; campsites per adult/car/tent €6.50/3/5; ⊙May-Sep; 🅿) This pleasant and hugely welcoming family-run campsite, 2km beyond Argostoli near

---

IONIAN ON THE VINE

The Ionian Islands would not be the same without wine, and Kefallonia is especially famed for its vintages. The most notable derive from the unique *robola* grape (VQRPD; Vin de Qualité Produit dans une Région Déterminée), thought to have been introduced by the Venetians, while other varieties include *mavrodaphni* (AOC; Appellation d'Origine Contrôlée) and *muscat* (AOC).

Nestled at the heart of verdant Omala Valley, in the hilly country southeast of Argostoli, the winery of the **Robola Cooperative of Kefallonia** (✔26710 86301; www.robola.gr; Omala; ⊙9am-8pm daily May-Oct, to 3pm Mon-Fri Nov-Apr) transforms grapes from 300 independent growers into a dry white wine of subtle yet lively flavour. Visitors can take a self-guided tour and enjoy free tastings. Smaller yet similarly distinguished **Gentilini** (✔26710 41618; www.gentilini.gr; Minies), 5km south of Argostoli on the airport road, has a charming setting and produces a range of superb wines, including the scintillating Classico.

Argostoli

Argostoli

◉ **Sights**
- 1 Archaeological Museum...........................B3
- 2 Focas-Kosmetatos Foundation.........B3
- 3 Korgialenio History & Folklore
  Museum..B4

🛏 **Sleeping**
- 4 Hotel Ionian Plaza................................B2
- 5 Mouikis Hotel.......................................C4
- 6 Vivian Villa...A1

✕ **Eating**
- 7 Arhontiko..B2
- 8 Ladokolla..B1

🍷 **Drinking & Nightlife**
- 9 Bass Club..C3

the lighthouse on the northernmost point of the peninsula, can hardly have changed in years – and it's all the better for it. It also has its own tavern.

Mouikis Hotel
HOTEL €€
(☎26710 23032; http://mouikis.com.gr; Vyronos 3; d incl breakfast €133; ❄🐾) Clean, modern hotel, near the market at the southern end of the town centre, with a smart but rather anonymous decor targeted mainly at business travellers. Most of the small but very well-equipped rooms have balconies; some have sea views. The buffet breakfast is substantial.

Hotel Ionian Plaza
HOTEL €€
(☎26710 25581; www.ionianplaza.gr; Plateia Valianou; s/d incl breakfast €137/147; P❄🐾) Imposing hotel in an unbeatable location, with a stylish marble-trimmed lobby and small but comfortable rooms, all with balconies overlooking the central pedestrian square.

✕ Eating

★ **Ladokolla**
GREEK €
(☎26710 25522; Harbouri 13; dishes €2-8; ⏱12.30pm-2am) Lively and hugely popular grill house, where piping-hot and irresistibly

flavourful chicken, pork or lamb kebabs and pittas are served up straight onto tabletop covers (no plates). It also delivers.

Tzivras GREEK €
(☑ 26710 24259; Vandorou 1; mains €7-9; ☺ noon-5pm) A veteran restaurant, a block inland from the waterfront market, where locals lunch on hearty, great-value baked standards such as veal with okra, goat with potatoes, or cod pie. Everything on the menu is less than €10.

Kiani Akti SEAFOOD €€
(☑ 26710 26680; A Tritsi; mains €8-20; ☺ 1pm-2am; ☏) For Argostoli's finest views, follow the waterfront north to the cruise-ship dock, where this huge wooden deck stretches out into the harbour. The wide-ranging menu includes a range of tasty Greek appetisers, along with daily seafood specials of all kinds and meaty classics. You can also just drop in for a drink.

Arhontiko TAVERNA €€
(☑ 26710 27213; Risospaston 5; mains €9-18; ☺ breakfast, lunch & dinner; ☏) Wood-ceilinged and stone-walled, this friendly taverna offers local seafood such as squid, grilled shrimp and octopus, plus carnivore favourites Kefallonian meat pie and *exohiko* (pork stuffed with tomatoes, onions, peppers and feta). Good house wines, helpful service and a cosy atmosphere – no wonder it's always busy.

🍸 Drinking & Nightlife

Cafes line Plateia Valianou and Lithostroto, and are buzzing by late evening. **Bass Club** (☑ 26710 25020; www.bassclub.gr; cnr S Metaxa & Vergoti; ☺ noon-7am; ☏) in town draws the younger set, while club-restaurant **Katavothres** (☑ 26710 22221; www.katavothres.gr; Mikeli Davi 10; ☺ 5pm-10am Mon-Thu & Sun, 24hr Fri & Sat; ☏) at the tip of the peninsula combines strange geological formations with iconic futuristic furnishings, and puts on top-name DJs. Beach bar **Stavento**, in Makrys Gialos (p687), hops in summer.

ℹ️ Information

Banks with ATMs line the northern waterfront and Lithostroto.

EOT (Greek National Tourist Organisation; ☑ 26710 22248; ☺ 7am-2.30pm Mon-Fri)

Post Office (Lithostroto)

Around Argostoli

◉ Sights

Agios Georgios Kastro FORTRESS
(Castle of St George; Peratata; ☺ 8.30am-3pm Tue-Sun) FREE This 16th-century Venetian castle enjoys stellar views from atop a conspicuous pyramid-shaped hill 7km southeast of Argostoli. Kefallonia's capital for 200 years, it is now in ruins, and approached via a short pedestrian street from the adjoining village. Strolling around the unshaded, wildflower-strewn site takes around 20 minutes; relax afterwards over a coffee or snack in the gardens of the neighbouring Kastro Cafe.

Moni Agiou Gerasimou MONASTERY
(☑ 26710 86045; Omala; ☺ 9am-1pm & 3.30-8pm) FREE Dedicated to Kefallonia's patron saint, the large Moni Agiou Gerasimou monastery is maintained by nuns. Its chapel encloses the cave to which St Gerasimos withdrew to escape the rigours of monastic life. The monastery is located in Omala Valley, alongside the Robola Cooperative of Kefallonia winery.

🍴 Eating

★ Kastro Cafe CAFE €
(☑ 26710 69367; Peratata; mains €6-10; ☺ 10am-7pm; ☏) Relaxed garden cafe, just before the gateway to Agios Georgios Kastro, that's a wonderfully peaceful spot for coffee, cake, cold drinks or lunchtime snacks.

☆ Entertainment

Astraios LIVE MUSIC
(☑ 6997210687; Peratata; ☺ 9pm-late; ☏) Lively bar with a panoramic sea-view terrace near Agios Georgios Kastro. It's owned by venerated musician Dionysos Frangopoulos and puts on live Greek music.

Paliki Peninsula
Χερσόνησος Παλική

Anchored by the bustling gulf-side town of **Lixouri**, the Paliki Peninsula is an under-explored region of spectral white, cream and red clay cliffs; verdant farmland and vineyards; and hilltop villages. **Petani Beach** to the northwest is a spectacular strand of white sand that's enough to entice a jaded mermaid, while red-sand **Xi Beach** to the south also has its appeal, but can feel overcrowded in summer. Between the two in the far west,

IONIAN ISLANDS KEFALLONIA

overlooking stark cliffs, azure seas and robust vineyards, the **Moni Kipouria** monastery was built by a lone, solitude-loving monk.

🛏 Sleeping & Eating

★ Ksouras
APARTMENT €€

(📞 26710 97458; www.facebook.com/ksouras; Petani; d €85; P ✱ ❄ 🛜) Very pleasant rooms in a blue villa immediately above the owners' beachfront taverna. It's a sublimely tranquil spot in the evenings, once the crowds have gone and the sunset is in full swing. The taverna is open for all meals, and serves uniformly excellent and inexpensive Greek classics.

Xi Village
PENSION €€

(📞 26710 93830; www.xi-village.gr; Xi; d/tr/q €70/80/90; P ✱ 🛜 ❄ 🏊) Basic, wood-accented, white-walled apartments, all with balconies and kitchenettes, right on long Xi Beach. There's also a pool. It's not luxurious, but it's a good budget choice.

★ Petani Bay Hotel
HOTEL €€€

(📞 26710 97701; www.petanibayhotel.gr; Petani; d incl breakfast €175-275; P ✱ 🛜 ❄ 🏊) Boasting one of the finest infinity pools in Greece, this adults-only boutique eyrie overlooks the cobalt-blue bay far below. There are just 13 romantic suites, with marble floors, wood-blade fans and kitchenettes. It's all about peace here; the only sound is the bleating of goats and the chink of chilled wine glasses.

Mavroeidis
BAKERY €

(📞 26710 22021; Lixouri; baked goods from €1.50; ⏱ 8am-late; ✱ 🛜) Large bakery-cafe in the heart of Lixouri, with outdoor tables at the inland end of the main pedestrian square, and a panoply of sweet-smelling delights inside. Buying a coffee gets you a free taster of the island's best *amygdalopita* (sweet almond cake).

Akrogiali
TAVERNA €

(📞 26710 92613; Lixouri; mains €6-13; ⏱ 11am-midnight; 🛜) Low-slung, old-fashioned taverna on Lixouri's seafront street, serving a mouthwatering menu of local favourite dishes, including plenty of vegetarian options as well as baked meat and fish.

Erasmia
TAVERNA €

(📞 26710 97372; Petani Beach; mains €6-10; ⏱ lunch & dinner May-Sep) Buzzing beachfront taverna, right at the foot of the road, where the no-nonsense seafood cooking has a devoted local following. A pleasant spot for lunch, it's even better in the face of a glowing, fiery sunset.

Sami & Around
Σάμη

POP 1030

Cheerful Sami, Kefallonia's main port, stands across the island 25km northeast of Argostoli. Nestled in a bright bay and flanked by steep hills, it consists of a waterside strip, which stares across to Ithaki and is loaded with tourist-oriented cafes. Nearby monasteries, castle ruins and natural features, including the busy but rather overrated **Drogarati Cave** (📞 26740 23302; adult/child €5/3; ⏱ 8am-8pm Jun-Sep, shorter hours low season), offer enticements to linger. Quieter alternative bases with better beaches, such as **Karavomilos** and **Agia Evfymia**, line the bay as you head further north.

🛏 Sleeping & Eating

Karavomilos Beach Camping
CAMPGROUND €

(📞 26740 22480; www.camping-karavomilos.gr; Sami-Karavomilos road; adult/car/tent €8.50/3.50/6.50; ⏱ mid-Apr–Sep; 🛜 🏊) Large family-oriented camping ground, with well-shaded sites stretching back from a decent pebble beach just 800m west of central Sami. Good facilities include excellent washrooms.

Hotel Athina
HOTEL €€

(📞 26740 22779; www.athinahotel.gr; Karavomilos; d incl breakfast €99, apt €130; ⏱ May-Oct; ✱ @) Bright, spotless resort hotel, where simple rooms and larger apartments have balconies overlooking the bay. Guests can use the pool at the swankier neighbouring **Ionian Emerald Resort** (📞 26740 22708; www.ionian emerald.gr; Karavomilos; d incl breakfast from €300; ✱ 🛜 🏊), which has the same owner.

Melissani Hotel
HOTEL €€

(📞 26740 22464; www.melissanihotel.gr; Dihalion 23, Sami; s/d/tr €50/65/75; ⏱ May-Oct; ✱ 🛜) Melissani is a welcoming little hotel, two blocks up from the Sami waterfront. Small and rather basic rooms have sea-view balconies plus retro quirks such as orange 1970s phones and old-fashioned showers. There's also a spacious roof terrace.

Odyssey Hotel
HOTEL €€€

(📞 26740 61089; www.hotelodyssey.gr; Agia Evfymia; d from €216; P ✱ 🛜 🏊) Plush resort hotel, just around the corner north of the harbour, with very comfortable balcony suites looking across to Ithaki, as well as a spa, gym, restaurant and two bars.

MYRTOS BEACH ΠΑΡΑΛΙΑ ΜΥΡΤΟΥ

One of the most breathtaking beaches in all Greece, Myrtos Beach is a stunning expanse of broad white sand 10km northeast of Kefallonia's narrow central isthmus. The only road access drops for 3km in sweeping switchbacks from Divarata, on the main road. Halfway down, a viewing area offers a first glimpse of the shimmering blue water far below. There are no facilities at the beach itself, which drops off sharply, but once you're in the sea it's heavenly.

The limestone cliffs to either side are scarred by landslides from recent earthquakes, which have also for the moment blocked the road north from Divarata towards Assos.

★ **Paradise Beach** GREEK €€
(☑26740 61392; www.paradisebeachtaverna.com; Agia Evfymia; mains €7-22; ⊙lunch & dinner mid-May–mid-Oct; 🛜) At the end of the coast road 700m beyond the harbour, this much-loved taverna has a vine-shaded terrace overlooking a little beach where turtles bob in the water below. Thanks to its locally reared meat – in dishes such as exceptionally tender lamb chops, Kefallonian meat pie or braised rabbit – and seafood delights, it's an island institution. You'll be coming back, believe us!

❶ Information

Sami has all necessary facilities, including a post office and banks.
Port Authority (☑26740 22031)

Fiskardo Φισκάρδο

POP 190

The little port of Fiskardo curves serenely beside coral-blue waters, gazing out towards Ithaki. Thanks to its colourful crop of Venetian villas, spared from earthquake damage by resting on a sturdy bed of flat rock, Fiskardo is the island's most exclusive resort, home to upmarket restaurants and choice accommodation. There's no real dock or jetty here; ferries from Lefkada arrive unceremoniously at the northern end, while yachts jostle for space along the rest of the harbour. While it can get very crowded in summer, it has a cosmopolitan buzz unmatched elsewhere on the island.

There's no beach in Fiskardo itself, but pretty little coves lie both to the north, where the gorgeous sand at **Emblissi** is shaded by olive trees, and to the south, where **Foki Bay** is home to an attractive taverna.

The ultra-clear waters hereabouts make Fiskardo a perfect place to learn to dive. **Fiskardo Divers** (☑6970206172; www.fiskardo-divers.com; 3hr beginners courses €55, open-water 4-day

PADI courses €430) offers PADI courses, plus dives to caves, wrecks, reefs and a downed Bristol Beaufort WWII bomber.

🛏 Sleeping

As well as holding hotels to suit all budgets, Fiskardo and the adjacent bays are peppered with rental villas and apartments. Several are available via **Ionian Villas** (www.ionian-villas.co.uk).

Regina Studios APARTMENT €
(☑26740 41125; www.regina-studios-boats.gr; d/tr €55/75; 🗱🛜) A pink villa, beside the village car park up the steps from the waterfront, which holds great-value 'en-suite' economy rooms, larger studios with sea-view balconies and shared kitchens, and larger two-bedroom apartments. The owner also rents out boats of all sizes.

Kiki Apartments APARTMENT €€
(☑26710 22754; www.kiki-apartments.gr; studios/apt €110/130; 🗱🛜🌊) Six scrupulously maintained apartments lie 300m along the waterfront south of the village. Chunky wood-top tables and a green-and-cream colour scheme, give them a chic Provençal feel, and they include gleaming kitchenettes, private balconies and stunning bedrooms. There's also a pool with a spacious terrace.

Stella Hotel Apartments HOTEL €€
(☑26740 41261; www.stella-apartments.gr; studios/apt from €82/160; 🗱🛜) Welcoming hillside hotel, just above the coast road 10 minutes' walk south of the village, where the comfortable rooms have large bay-view balconies.

Villa Romantza PENSION €€
(☑26740 41322; www.villa-romantza.gr; r/studios/apt €60/80/100; 🗱🛜) Excellent budget option, near the central car park, where simple, spacious and well-maintained rooms, studios and apartments share a communal terrace; some have two bedrooms and kitchenettes.

Emelisse Hotel
RESORT €€€

(📞26740 41200; www.arthotel.gr; Emblissi Bay; d/ste incl breakfast from €363, 4-person apt from €870; ⏱mid-Apr–mid-Oct; 🅿🌀@🛜🏊) This luxury hotel is set in magnificent seclusion on a headland overlooking superb Emblissi Beach, 1.5km north of Fiskardo along the winding coast road. Its beautifully appointed rooms are laid out on immaculately groomed terraces, leading down to a lavish swimming pool and a restaurant with fantastic views to Lefkada, Ithaki and beyond.

✗ Eating & Drinking

Fiskardo's restaurants are among the best – and most expensive – in the Ionian Islands.

Lagoudera
GREEK €€

(📞26740 41275; mains €10-17; ⏱noon-2am; 🌀🛜) Fiskardo's largest restaurant, spreading across open squares between separate quayside and backstreet dining rooms, is a friendly, unhurried but very efficient operation. It's very dependable for well-cooked local classics such as a rich, chunky octopus *stifadho* or herby crab fritters.

Café Tselenti
MEDITERRANEAN €€

(📞26740 41344; mains €8-26; ⏱breakfast, lunch & dinner May-Oct) Owned by the Tselenti family since 1893, this popular restaurant serves Italian-influenced dishes such as a terrific linguine with prawns, mussels and crayfish, as well as local specialities such as lamb shank, beef *stifadho* and grilled swordfish. It has a romantic terrace on the village square as well as quayside tables.

Tassia
TAVERNA €€

(📞26740 41205; www.tassia.gr; mains €9-19; ⏱noon-2am May-Oct) Down-to-earth seafront taverna run by well-known Kefallonian chef Tassia, who delights diners with her homemade pies, mezedhes and zucchini croquettes. Try the 'fisherman's pasta', incorporating finely chopped squid, octopus, mussels and prawns in a magical combination with a dash of cognac.

★ Irida
GREEK €€€

(📞26740 41343; mains €9-35; ⏱9am-late; 🌀🛜) Whether you dine in the shadowy boho interior or out on the waterfront, there's something for everyone at this 200-year-old salt store. Dishes include meatballs, stuffed aubergine, and the much pricier lobster risotto or spaghetti, and it's all scrupulously prepared and presented.

Vasso's
SEAFOOD €€€

(📞26740 41276; mains €9-48; ⏱lunch & dinner May-Oct; 🛜) Vasso's is widely renowned for its high-quality seafood, with highlights

---

KEFALLONIA'S GREAT OUTDOORS

While the EOT occasionally stocks excellent leaflets with walking routes around the island, it's well worth enlisting an experienced local to guide you off the beaten path.

Sea Kayaking Kefalonia (📞6934010400; www.seakayakingkefalonia-greece.com) Offers a full range of day-long kayak tours, with lunch and snorkelling gear included (€65), plus multiday excursions and certified courses.

Bavarian Horse Riding (📞6977533203; www.kephalonia.com; Koulourata; 1/4hr €25/80) Ride sturdy Bavarian horses through the Kefallonian countryside. Day trips range from one to four hours, with your choice of route. One longer trek leads across Mt Enos and down to the sea, where you can take the horses for a swim. Multiday itineraries also possible.

Outdoor Kefalonia (📞6979987611; http://outdoorkefalonia.com) All manner of trips, from coasteering (€35), hiking (€60) and canyoning (€60), to sea kayaking (€60) and Jeep safaris (from €50).

Donkey Trekking (📞6980059630; www.donkeytrekkingkefalonia.com; per hr from €25) Slow-paced donkey treks, exploring ruined villages and evergreen valleys in the hilly country south of Sami. Bring sturdy footwear.

Pyrgos House (📞6989863140; www.pyrgoshouse.com; walking tours €15; ⏱9.30am-1.30pm & 5-8pm) Highly recommended outdoor activities, including €15 guided walks of Hora's *kastro* (fortress; 10am Wednesday), Arionadika (6pm Wednesday), Potamos (6pm Friday) and Mylopotamos (9am Saturday). Also offers six-hour sea-kayaking expeditions (€45); canyoning (€25, 3.30pm Thursday); and evening bike tours from Potamos (€35). A nine-day walking tour of the island costs €450 per person including accommodation.

ASSOS ΑΣΣΟΣ

Almost too photogenically perfect for words, pint-sized Assos (population 88) is a confection of Italianate cream- and ochre-coloured houses, with a pretty crescent-shaped cove that's protected by a wooded peninsula. The fortress atop the headland makes a great hike, while the bay is eminently swimmable.

A mouthwatering array of tasty tavernas, plus a pace so slow you can palpably feel your pulse dropping, are compelling reasons to visit. It's also possible to stay overnight.

Note that the main coastal highway is currently closed between Assos and Myrtos Beach to the south, so drivers are directed along back routes higher up the mountainside.

Sleeping & Eating

Apartment Linardos (☑26740 51563; www.linardosapartments.gr; d/tr/q €80/90/120; ☉May-Sep; ✴☎) Tastefully finished kitchenette studios, perched on the isthmus a stone's throw from the beach, with postcard-perfect balcony views of both harbour and fortress. Let the waves lull you to sleep.

Platanos (☑26740 51143; mains €7-15; ☉breakfast, lunch & dinner Easter-Oct; ☎☑) Platanos is admired island-wide for its fresh, locally sourced ingredients, and especially for its meat dishes. There are also fish and vegetarian options such as vegetable *mousakas*. It adjoins an attractive shady plaza just back from the waterfront, but has no sea views.

Molos (☑26740 51220; mains €7-14; ☉9.30am-late; ☎) At the far northern end of the curving bay, this custard-hued taverna has tables right on the quayside that catch the late-afternoon 'golden hour'. Molos serves everything from breakfast omelettes to fresh grilled tuna.

including honeyed octopus with mashed fava, mussels, *saganaki* and *sofigado* (veal in tomato sauce).

ℹ Information

Nautilus Travel (☑26740 41440; Fiskardo) and **Pama Travel** (☑26740 41033; www.pamatravel.com; ☉9am-2pm & 5.30-9pm) can make all travel and ferry arrangements.

ITHAKI ΙΘΑΚΗ

POP 3230

Every bit as rugged, romantic and all-round epic as its role in Homeric legend would suggest, Ithaki (Map p686) is something special. The hilly, sea-girt homeland to which Odysseus struggled to return for 10 heroic years continues to charm and seduce travellers with its ancient ruins, breathtaking harbour villages and wilderness walks. Squeezed between Kefallonia and the mainland, it's the kind of island where time seems to slow down and cares slip away.

Cut almost in two by the huge gulf that shields **Vathy**, its main town, Ithaki effectively consists of two separate islands linked by a narrow isthmus. Vathy is the only significant settlement in the south, while the mighty northern massif holds delightful

villages such as **Stavros** and **Anogi**, and is peppered with little coves holding pocket-sized resorts such as **Frikes** and **Kioni**.

ℹ Getting There & Away

Ionian Pelagos (www.ionionpelagos.com) runs two or three times daily in high season between Piso Aetos and Sami (Kefallonia), and once or twice from Piso Aetos to Astakos (on the mainland).

Between July and mid-September, the **Meganisi II** (☑26740 33120; www.terryboatmeganisi.gr) ferry runs twice daily between Frikes and Nydri on Lefkada.

Buy tickets from **Polyctor Tours** (☑26740 33120; www.ithakiholidays.com) or **Ithaca Tours** (☑26740 33336; www.ithacatours.gr) in Vathy.

West Ferry (www.westferry.gr) has in the past connected Frikes with Fiskardo (Kefallonia) and Vasiliki (Lefkada); that service has not run in recent years, but it's worth checking the website to see whether it has resumed.

ℹ Getting Around

Piso Aetos, the port on Ithaki's west coast, has no settlement. **Taxis** (☑6946552397, 6945700214) often meet boats, as does the municipal bus in high season. Bus services are very limited, though, so it's well worth renting a car – easiest in Vathy – for at least one day of your stay.

Vathy   Βαθύ

POP 1820

Set around a superbly sheltered natural harbour, and fringed with sky-blue and ochre villas holding lively bars and restaurants, pretty Vathy is Ithaki's main commercial hub. The quayside buzzes with activity, while narrow lanes wriggle away inland.

◉ Sights & Activities

Other than the **archaeological museum** (☑26740 32200; Anastasiou Kallinikou; ⊙8.30am-3pm Tue-Sun) FREE, Vathy holds few sights to see, but there's some wonderful walking nearby. Follow the line of the harbour all the way east, until the road finally peters out, and a spectacular coastal footpath leads in another half-hour to the whitewashed waterfront chapel of **Agios Andreas**. Alternatively, stay on the road as it climbs away at the eastern end of the harbour; cross the brow of the hill, and you'll come to a succession of increasingly wonderful, secluded beaches – first Mnimata, then Skinos, and finally, after a total of 4km, the magnificent white sands of **Gidaki**.

Albatross (☑6973467977) and **Mana Korina** (☑6976654351) offer boat excursions from Vathy in high season to outlying beaches and unpopulated islets.

★ **Island Walks** WALKING
(☑6944990458; www.islandwalks.com; walks €15-18) Charming expat artist Ester runs guided walks of varying lengths, all over the island. Her most popular route, the three-hour Homer Walk, winds up the hillside near Stavros to the ruins where the real Odysseus may have lived 2800 years ago, and also takes in the village museum.

🛌 Sleeping

★ **Perantzada 1811** BOUTIQUE HOTEL €€
(☑26740 33496; www.arthotel.gr/perantzada; Odyssea Androutsou; d/q incl breakfast from €110/345; ⊙Easter–mid-Oct; ❋🐾🕙) Centred on a 19th-century neoclassical villa, hovering above the harbour, this self-styled 'art hotel' holds large balconied rooms as minimal as white clouds, replete with granite-and-wood bathrooms. Cheaper rooms lack sea views and share balconies, while larger suites in the new wing have baths you could free-dive in. The breakfast buffet is pure decadence, and there's an enticing infinity pool.

Hotel Familia BOUTIQUE HOTEL €€
(☑26740 33366; www.hotel-familia.com; Odysseos 60; s/d incl breakfast from €130/145; ❋🕙) Converted from an old olive press, juxtaposing chic slate with soft tapestries and gentle lighting, this charming boutique hotel has a real 'wow' factor. It's family-run and family-friendly – but although it's only 50m from the southwestern corner of the harbour, there are no sea views, and only one room has a courtyard.

Grivas View APARTMENT €€
(☑26740 33328; Odyssea Androutsou; d/tr €75/85; ❋🕙) Bright, spacious, good-value studios, with flower-draped terraces overlooking the bay; for the best views, ask for one upstairs. They're on the eastern side of the harbour just before it broadens, on the street parallel to the waterfront.

Odyssey Apartments APARTMENT €€
(☑26740 33400; www.odysseyapartments.gr; studios €105, 1-/2-bedroom apt €135/175; 🅿❋🕙) Perched on a hillside 600m beyond the eastern end of the harbour, a 20-minute walk from the centre, these spotless studios and apartments (some sleeping five people) have balconies with magical views of the bay. There's a simple cafe by the pool.

🍴 Eating

Trehantiri TAVERNA €
(☑26740 33444; http://trehantiri.ithakionline.com; mains €7-12; ⊙lunch & dinner; ❋🕙) Traditional taverna with blue tables set up off the square in the heart of town. Every day the kitchen cooks up something different, from goat stew to stuffed tomatoes, *saganaki* to *kleftiko*. Look out for *savoro,* marinated local fish.

Karamela Cafe CAFE €
(☑26740 33580; mains €5-8; ⊙6.30am-late; ❋🕙) A laid-back, bright-orange cafe as you enter town at the western end of the harbour; its quayside tables are usually thronged with sailors moored alongside. Come for wholesome breakfasts, lunchtime pizzas or salads, or sunset cocktails.

★ **O Batis** SEAFOOD €€
(☑26740 33010; mains €8-18; ⊙lunch & dinner; ❋🕙) Vathy's top pick for ultra-fresh seafood sits amid a row of similar-looking places along the harbour. Tourists flock to the waterfront tables, while local fishers, who've had quite enough sea views for one day, prefer the no-frills interior. For €15 you'll get a whole grilled fish plus salad and wine or beer.

Sirenes　　　　　　　　GREEK €€
(📞26740 33001; http://sirenes.eu; mains €8-15; ⊙lunch & dinner; ❋🛜) A smart little restaurant, a block back from the waterfront, with a cool front terrace and a swanky bar in its elegant wood-panelled dining room. Distinctive local dishes include *strapatsada* (clay pot lamb) and slow-cooked rabbit, plus fresh seafood.

Around Ithaki

Cross the slender isthmus to reach Ithaki's northern half and you face an immediate choice of onward routes, along either flank of the island's towering (809m) central spine. Following the eastern road brings you after 5.5km to the somewhat dilapidated hilltop monastery of **Katharon**, which commands astonishing views back down to Vathy. Another 4km along this fabulously scenic mountain road, you'll reach sleepy **Anogi**, once the island's capital. Ask in the village *kafeneio* (coffee house) for the keys to the restored church of **Agia Panagia**, which holds incredible Byzantine frescoes.

Further north again, the east- and west-coast roads rejoin at the larger village of **Stavros**, above the Bay of Polis. A lovely rural walk up the nearby hillside leads to a site long known as the **School of Homer**, but is suggested by recent archaeological digs to be the long-lost palace of Odysseus himself. It's all in ruins, and smaller than you might expect, but wonderfully evocative nonetheless. Artefacts associated with the legendary hero are on show in Stavros' one-room **archaeological museum** (📞26740 31305; ⊙8.30am-3.15pm Tue-Sun) FREE.

Dropping back seawards northeast of Stavros takes you to the tiny ferry port of **Frikes**, clasped between windswept cliffs and home to a cluster of waterfront restaurants and bars. The beautiful and sinuous coast road beyond ends at pretty little **Kioni**, a hamlet of mustard-and-cream Venetian houses tumbling down to an irresistibly bijou harbour.

🛏 Sleeping

Ourania Apartments　　　　APARTMENT €
(📞26740 31027; www.ithacagreece.com/ourania/ourania.htm; Stavros; studios/apt €45/70; P❋) A romantic shuttered villa, two minutes' walk from Stavros, festooned in flowers and rejoicing in amazing views over the olive groves to the sea. Two homey studios, with kitchenettes and balconies, plus a

---

ODYSSEUS UNCOVERED

It took 10 long years of fighting before the wily Odysseus devised the stratagem – the Trojan Horse – that finally breached the walls of Troy. The war over, he was free to return to his beloved Ithaki and his queen Penelope. How long could the 910-km voyage home possibly take?

According to Homer, another 10 years. Blown off course while passing Kythira, and buffeted thereafter by winds unleashed by Poseidon the Earth Shaker, Odysseus was subjected to an appalling series of perils and misadventures. En route he was imprisoned by the nymph Calypso on Ogygia, possibly modern-day Gozo; encountered the Lotus-Eaters in North Africa; blinded the Cyclops Polyphemus somewhere near Sicily; resisted the seductive song of the sirens in the Bay of Naples; and braved the straits between Scylla, a man-eating sea monster, and Charybdis the deadly whirlpool. Eventually, the gods allowed him to escape another long period of captivity, in the arms of the enchantress Circe. Shipwrecked on the shores of Scheria, commonly identified as Corfu, he returned at last to Ithaki, and wrought his vengeance on the suitors harrying the long-suffering Penelope.

Many of modern-day Ithaki's most popular hiking trails lead to sites associated with Homer's epic poem 'Odyssey'. Finding them, though, can be an epic journey of its own, as signposts are few and far between. Targets include the **Fountain of Arethousa**, an exposed and isolated three-hour round-trip south of Vathy, which is said to be the spot where Odysseus' swineherd, Eumaeus, brought his pigs to drink.

As for Odysseus' palace, the German archaeologist Heinrich Schliemann, who rediscovered Troy itself, thought he'd found it at **Alalkomenes**, near Piso Aetos. More recent excavations have led modern archaeologists to identify ruins on Pelikata Hill outside Stavros as the scene of the poem's bloody climax.

larger apartment that sleeps four. The owners are warmth itself.

Captain's Apartments
APARTMENT €€

(☑26740 31481; www.captains-apartments.gr; Kioni; 2-/4-person apt €65/90; ✳🛜) Clean, simple studios with pine fittings and well-stocked kitchenettes; some have wrap-around balconies with views in all directions. Turn right just before you reach the harbour on the winding road down the hill.

Kioni Apartments
APARTMENT €€

(☑26740 31144; www.ithacagreece.eu; Kioni; apt €100; ☉May-Oct; ✳🛜) A handsome Italianate building in the corner of the harbour, drowning in bougainvillea, and holding welcoming apartments with wooden ceilings and large balconies. Stylish but homey, central but quiet. In a word: perfect.

✘ Eating

En Plo
CAFE €

(☑26740 31520; Kioni; mains €6-8; ☉8am-midnight; ✳🛜) Chic, laid-back waterfront cafe, where the upstairs terrace is a lovely spot for watching sunsets and the lights as they come on in the windmills across the bay. Open all day, for bites ranging from yoghurt or omelettes for breakfast to salads and burgers, and, of course, cocktails later on.

★ Yefuri
TAVERNA €€

(☑26740 31131; www.facebook.com/Yefuri; Platrithias; mains €7-17; ☉dinner Tue-Sat, brunch & dinner Sun, reduced hours low season; ✳🛜) This eclectic, very popular little restaurant, 2km north of Stavros, is renowned island-wide for its fresh produce and rotating Italian-influenced menu, which ranges from eggs Benedict for Sunday brunch to stir-fried chicken and roast pork for dinner.

Ithaki Restaurant
GREEK €€

(☑26740 31081; Stavros; mains €8-15; ☉lunch & dinner) Smart restaurant on the corner of the village square, serving succulent meaty specialities such as local sausages, charcoal-grilled veal or pork, and lamb souvlaki. The terrace of the attached Sunset Café has sumptuous views in the early evening.

Mythos
TAVERNA €€

(☑26740 31122; Kioni; mains €8-14; ☉lunch & dinner; ✳🛜) This unpretentious traditional taverna sitting by the waves in Kioni dishes up tasty and substantial helpings of local favourites, such as *pastitsio* (layers of buttery macaroni and seasoned minced lamb),

veal *stifadho,* homemade chicken pie and prawns *saganaki.*

ZAKYNTHOS ΖΑΚΥΝΘΟΣ

POP 40,760

Beautiful Zakynthos, also known by its Italian name Zante, has become dominated along its southern and southeastern shoreline by package tourism. Once you leave the long sandy beaches of those regions behind, however, and set off to explore the rest of the island, you'll discover plenty of wilderness and traditional rural villages. Some attractive lower-key bases lie just beyond the larger, run-of-the-mill resorts, including **Keri** and **Limni Keriou** in the remote southwest, and **Agios Nikolaos** and **Cape Skinari** in the far north, but it's the spectacular scenery of the rugged west coast, where mighty limestone cliffs plummet down to turquoise waters, that's the true highlight.

ⓘ Getting There & Away

AIR

Zakynthos Airport (☑26950 29500; www.zakynthos-airport.com) is 5km southwest of Zakynthos Town.

Domestic

Olympic Air (www.olympicair.com) Flies to Athens.

Sky Express (www.skyexpress.gr) Flies to Corfu via Kefallonia and Preveza.

International

Between May and September, charter flights connect Zakynthos with northern Europe and the UK.

Air Berlin (www.airberlin.com) Flies to Düsseldorf in Germany.

EasyJet (www.easyjet.com) Flies to London (Gatwick and Stansted), Liverpool, Bristol and Milan in high season.

BOAT

Domestic

Ionian Group (www.ionian-group.com) runs between four and seven ferries daily, depending on the season, between Zakynthos Town and Kyllini in the Peloponnese. Occasional international ferries call in on the way to/from Igoumenitsa, Sami (Kefallonia), and Bari and Brindisi (Italy).

From the isolated northern port of Agios Nikolaos, **Ionian Pelagos** (www.ionionpelagos.com) ferries sail to Pesada in southern Kefallonia twice daily from mid-May to October; **Chionis Tours** (☑26950 48996; Lomvardou 8; ☉9am-11.30pm) sells tickets. Neither port has good

Zakynthos

bus connections, however, so most travellers find it easier and cheaper to cross to mainland Kyllini from Zakynthos Town, and catch another ferry from there to Kefallonia.

International

Ventouris Ferries (http://ventourisferries.com) connects Zakynthos Town with Bari (Italy) in high season, with a stop in Kefallonia (Sami) en route.

BUS

The **KTEL Bus Station** (☎ 26950 22255; www. ktel-zakynthos.gr) is on the hillside bypass in Zakynthos Town, 500m up from the waterfront and 15 minutes' walk southwest of Plateia Solomou. Long-distance routes include Athens (€28.60, six hours, four daily), Patra (€8.70, 3½

hours, four daily) and Thessaloniki (€54.40, 10 hours, two weekly). Budget an additional €8.90 for the ferry to Kyllini.

ⓘ Getting Around

Zakynthos Town is the centre of an extensive local bus network.

Rental cars (from €40 per day in high season) and motorcycles are available at the airport and in larger resorts.

Europcar (☎ 26950 43313; www.europcar -greece.com; Zakynthos Airport) At the airport.

Hertz Locations at the **airport** (☎ 26950 24287; www.hertz.gr; Zakynthos Airport) and in **Zakynthos Town** (☎ 26950 45706; www.hertz. gr; Lomvardou 38; ⊙ 8am-2pm & 5.30-9pm).

BOAT SERVICES FROM ZAKYNTHOS

DESTINATION	PORT	DURATION	FARE (€)	FREQUENCY
Kyllini (Peloponnese)	Zakynthos Town	1hr	8.90	4-7 daily
Pesada (Kefallonia)	Agios Nikolaos	1½hr	8	2 daily, seasonal

Zakynthos Town Ζάκυνθος

POP 9770

Sandwiched between steep wooded slopes topped by a ruined Venetian fortress and a huge harbour cradled between two long jetties, Zakynthos Town is the pulsating capital of the island. Famous for its glorious ensemble of Italianate architecture until an earthquake struck in 1953, it was subsequently reconstructed in fine style, with arcaded streets and gracious neoclassical public buildings. Recent years have seen the restoration of its showpiece waterfront square, the dazzling **Plateia Solomou**. The hubbub of everyday life centres on the newly pedestrianised streets behind it, leading to smaller **Plateia Agiou Markou**.

⊙ Sights & Activities

★ Byzantine Museum   MUSEUM
(☑ 26950 42714; Plateia Solomou; €3; ⊙ 8am-3pm Tue-Sat) This magnificent museum of ecclesiastical art is housed in a beautifully restored building on the central waterfront plaza. Almost everything here was rescued – by volunteer sailors! – in the immediate aftermath of the 1953 earthquake, with displays including entire church interiors, and frescoes arranged in a replica of the 16th-century monastery of St Andreas.

Kastro   FORTRESS
(☑ 26950 48099; €4; ⊙ 8am-3pm Tue-Sun) A ruined Venetian fortress sits atop the wooded slope that looms over the town centre. Reached by a steep, enjoyable 15-minute hike, or a circuitous 2.5km drive, it's now essentially a peaceful forest park, enclosed within sturdy ramparts and affording tremendous views. Tumbledown churches lie scattered through the woods, along with a 19th-century British football pitch and a cafe.

Church of St Dionysios   CHURCH
(museum €1; ⊙ 9am-1pm & 4.30-9pm) Devoted to Zakynthos' patron saint, the rebuilt Church of St Dionysios (1948) stands at the south end of the waterfront, near the ferry jetty. Its interior holds opulent gilt work and impressive frescoes, while its museum, entered around the back, is a major centre for restoration. Exhibits include ecclesiastical trappings and vestments, including those of Dionysios himself.

Museum of Solomos   MUSEUM
(☑ 26950 48982; Plateia Agiou Markou 15; adult/child €4/free; ⊙ 9am-2pm) To give it its full name, the Museum of Solomos and Eminent Zakynthian People houses not only the archives of island-born poet Dionysios Solomos (1798–1857), but even his tomb. He's best known for his 'Hymn to Liberty', now the Greek national anthem. Neither his memorabilia nor the sombre portraits of other famous Zakynthians – mostly 19th-century generals – have English captions.

🛌 Sleeping

Diana Hotel   HOTEL €€
(☑ 26950 28547; www.dianahotels.gr; Mitropoleos; s/d/q incl breakfast €95/115/140; ❄ 🛜 🏊) A long-standing hotel just north of the main square, traditionally targeted at business travellers but spruced up by the addition of an unexpected delight – a rooftop garden with swimming pool and bar. The rooms themselves vary, from small and faded to more luxurious balcony suites with swish bathrooms.

Hotel Strada Marina   HOTEL €€
(☑ 26950 42761; www.stradamarina.gr; Lombardou 14; s/d/q incl breakfast €55/81/171; ❄ 🛜 🏊) This large waterfront hotel that set the luxe standard for Zakynthos a century ago retains an elegant appeal, thanks to recent renovations. Its delightful rooftop terrace holds a restaurant and a pool that command the best views in town. Half the rooms have marina-view balconies.

Plaza Hotel   HOTEL €€
(☑ 26950 45733; www.plazazante.gr; Kolokotronis 2; s/d €85/100; ❄ 🛜) Across from the small town beach, this presentable four-storey hotel has a lift to carry guests up to its nicely modernised rooms, which have good bathrooms and sea-view balconies.

Alba Hotel   PENSION €€
(☑ 26950 26641; www.albahotel.gr; L Ziva 38; s/d/tr €54/66/108; ❄ 🛜) Simple but very central budget hotel, where the clean, smallish, marble-accented rooms have old-fashioned bathrooms, plus balconies and fridges.

✗ Eating

Fresh Pies   PIES €
(☑ 26951 01649; Koliva 101; pies & sandwiches from €3; ⊙ 8am-late; 🛜) Who could resist the name of this hugely popular student hang-out, just off the main pedestrian shopping street? Order at the counter, then sit at tables on the open square opposite. It's not just hot pies and sandwiches, either; it also whips up fabulous fresh juices and smoothies, from just €2.

Mesathes　　　　　　　　　　　　GREEK €

(☑ 26950 49315; Plateia Dimokratia 4; mains €8-14; ☉ lunch & dinner; ☎) A prime spot for people-watching, this welcoming taverna spreads through a broad and breezy terrace on the open pedestrian precinct behind the Byzantine Museum, and offers a well-priced menu of beautifully presented dishes such as rabbit *stifadho*, grilled shrimp, and panna cotta that melts on your tongue. The owner plays a mean tune on the guitar.

Malanos　　　　　　　　　　　　TAVERNA €

(☑ 26950 45936; www.malanos.gr; Agiou Athanasiou, Keri; mains €7-13; ☉ noon-4pm & 7pm-late) This much-loved family-run taverna, set amid the fields on the southern outskirts of town 2km from the centre, is renowned island-wide for serving huge portions of rich local favourites such as rooster, rabbit and wild boar at its simple, plaid-covered tables.

★Prosilio　　　　　　　　MEDITERRANEAN €€

(☑ 26950 22040; www.prosiliozakynthos.gr; A Latta 15; mains €9-19; ☉ 6pm-late Tue-Sat summer, Fri & Sat winter; ❋ ☎) Gourmet dinner-only restaurant, with a boutique interior and a romantic garden courtyard. The hushed atmosphere may be unusual, but the service is relaxed and friendly, and if you love Greek food you're sure to relish the inventive take on dishes such as *taramasalata* (a thick pink or white purée of fish roe, potato, oil and lemon juice), served with crispy prawns. The wine list abounds in well-priced local wines.

★Avli　　　　　　　　MEDITERRANEAN €€

(Yard of Taste; ☑ 26950 29815; www.avlizante. gr; Rizospaston 15; mains €8-15; ☉ noon-1am; ❋ ☎ ☑) Delicious and wholesome Italian-influenced food, much of it organic and/or vegetarian, served in an enticing setting, with comfortable seating, vibrant linens and upholstery. As well as pasta and Greek staples, it prepares huge salads using unusual grains and pulses.

Drinking & Nightlife

Base　　　　　　　　　　　　　　BAR

(☑ 26950 42409; www.basecafe.gr; L Ziva 3; ☉ 9am-late; ☎) Down at street level, Base surveys the flow through Plateia Agiou Markou, dispensing coffees, drinks and music to a hip local crowd. The stylish rooftop bar, open from late afternoon, is a fabulous venue for knockout cocktails.

Around Zakynthos

Prosperous and lively Zakynthos Town, home to the island's airport and ferry port, makes a bustling point of arrival. Package tourism is concentrated both along the shoreline to the north and, especially, along the southern coast, between **Laganas** and **Kalamaki**. The **Vasilikos Peninsula**, poking south from the southeast corner, is a little less developed, though long, narrow **Banana Beach** on its northern side is awash with crowds, water sports and parasols. Keep going right to the tip to reach **Gerakas Beach**; a strand of fine sand that faces into Laganas Bay, it's the island's best. It's also a crucial turtle-nesting site, so visitor numbers are restricted, and all access is forbidden between dusk and dawn from May to October; conservation advice is displayed near the access path.

ENDANGERED LOGGERHEADS

The Ionian Islands are home to one of Europe's most endangered marine species, the **loggerhead turtle** (*Caretta caretta*). Zakynthos hosts the largest density of loggerhead nests, with an estimated 1500 along the Bay of Laganas, an area protected as the **National Marine Park of Zakynthos** (NMPZ; ☑ 26950 29870; www.nmp-zak.org).

Unfortunately, the extended tracts of clean, flat sand on which the turtles lay their eggs are also the favoured habitat of basking beach lovers. Strict regulations limit building, boating, fishing and water sports in designated zones. During breeding season (from May to October), nesting beaches are barred to visitors between dusk and dawn, and as the eggs start to hatch, from July onwards, conservation agencies place frames with warning notes over buried nests. Many are still destroyed by visitors, however, and countless hatchlings fail to reach the water after becoming disoriented by sunbeds, noise and lights.

Volunteers from **Archelon** (www.archelon.gr) and the park run education and volunteer programs, including a visitor centre at Gerakas Beach. Advice includes to not use umbrellas on dry sand (use the wet part of the beach), and to not take boating trips in the Bay of Laganas, as these have been known to torment and even kill turtles.

Beyond Laganas, the rugged terrain of the far southwest starts to unfold. Follow a tiny road from the pretty village of **Keri** to reach lighthouse-topped **Cape Keri**, and a high viewpoint surveying the endless cliffs that stretch away up the west coast; a converted van sells snacks.

There's no shoreline road north, but a happily confusing tangle of highland routes threads through the wooded hill country parallel to the coast. Here and there, spur roads either drop to coves such as **Limnionas** or climb to the clifftops, as at **Kambi**. Detouring inland brings you to villages such as **Kiliomeno**, where the Church of St Nikolaos features an unusual roofless campanile, and gorgeous little **Louha**, which tumbles down a valley surrounded by woodlands and pastures. Locals sell honey and seasonal products pretty much everywhere, but it's **Volimes** in the north that's the major sales centre for traditional products such as olive oil, tablecloths and rugs.

The most dramatic sight along the west coast is magnificent **Shipwreck Beach**, home to a stranded cargo ship that ran aground in the 1960s. It's only accessible on boat trips – in summer, the waters immediately offshore are choc-a-bloc with sightseeing cruises – but you can admire it from above, and get fabulous photos, from a precariously perched lookout platform signposted between Anafonitria and Volimes.

On the east coast, resorts immediately north of Zakynthos Town are generally humdrum, but the further north you go the more dramatic the scenery becomes. The road narrows at the little ferry village of **Agios Nikolaos**, which holds a nice crop of restaurants and accommodation, while the majestic headland of **Cape Skinari** marks the end of the road at the northern tip.

🏃 Activities

Boat trips, run by Karidis and Potamitis Trips, head from both Agios Nikolaos and Cape Skinari to the **Blue Caves** and **Shipwreck Beach**; smaller vessels can enter these sea-level caverns, where the water inside turns a translucent blue in the morning sunlight, between roughly 9am and 2pm.

Potamitis Trips   BOATING
(📩26950 31132; www.potamitisbros.gr; Cape Skinari) Glass-bottom boats leave every 15 minutes to the Blue Caves (€10), or to Shipwreck Beach (€15).

Karidis   BOATING
(📩6977275463; Agios Nikolaos) Frequent boat trips to the Blue Caves (€10), some of which continue to Shipwreck Beach (€20).

🛏 Sleeping

The huge curve of the Bay of Laganas, along the south coast, is lined with hotels catering to package holidaymakers, while the beach resorts immediately northwest of Zakynthos Town are a bit more sedate. More upmarket options are hidden away on the Vasilikos Peninsula in the southeast, and in Agios Nikolaos in the north.

Panorama   APARTMENT €
(📩26950 31013; Agios Nikolaos; studios €50; 🅿❄🛜) Excellent studios with sea views, managed by a friendly English-speaking family and set back in a lovely garden from the main road, a 700m uphill walk south of Agios Nikolaos.

Joanna's Stone Villas   APARTMENT €€
(📩6955497431; www.joannasvillas.com; Vasilikos; d/q €124/152; ❄🛜🏊) Very stylish modern apartments, maisonettes and entire villas, in a peaceful rural complex near the southeast corner of the island. All have kitchens, and share separate kids' and adults' pools.

Zakynthos Windmills   APARTMENT €€
(📩2695031132;www.potamitisbros.gr;CapeSkinari; apt from €60, windmills from €130; ❄🛜) Two converted windmills – one dazzling white, the other with exposed stone walls, each sleeping two guests – plus two- and four-person apartments in a stone house have a fantastic clifftop location in Cape Skinari. Rooms have cool tiled floors and boutique flourishes, and there's a taverna alongside. Steps lead to a lovely swimming area.

Villa Christina   APARTMENT €€
(📩26950 49208; www.villachristina.gr; Limni Keriou; studios €65, apt €75-90, 5-person maisonettes €160; ⏲Apr-Oct; 🅿❄🛜🏊) Clay-coloured studios, set amid flowering gardens within an idyllic olive grove near Zakynthos' southwest corner. The clean, pine-accented apartments of various sizes, with balconies and kitchenettes, share barbecue areas and a sparkling pool. There's also a small shop.

🍴 Eating

Zakynthos Town has a lively dining scene, and the beach resorts hold plenty of tavernas. The most distinctive local food is served in the hill villages of the interior.

★ **Stavros** GREEK €
(Cross Tavern; ☑ 26950 48481; Kambi; mains €6-16; ⊙ lunch & dinner; ❋ ☎) Perched above the west-coast cliffs at the far end of the road that climbs beyond Kambi, and marked by a huge white cross, this top-notch taverna extends over multilevel terraces, so diners can enjoy the stunning views. The menu covers all bases, from omelette and chips to baked standards and grilled fish, all accompanied by wonderful fresh-baked bread.

Allegro GREEK €
(☑ 6979261627; Keri; mains €6-10; ⊙ lunch & dinner; ❋ ☎) This delightful, very welcoming taverna-cafe on Keri's village square has a changing daily menu of home-cooked Greek specialities, usually including *mousakas* and stuffed aubergines. Drinks range from iced coffee to local wine, and there's often live music on summer evenings.

Nobelos Bio Restaurant MEDITERRANEAN €€
(☑ 6944148283; www.nobelos.gr; Agios Nikolaos; mains €7-27; ⊙ breakfast, lunch & dinner; ❋ ☎) Although it's accessed from the hillside road, 300m up from Agios Nikolaos, this exquisitely romantic restaurant is down at sea level beside the private beach of its namesake boutique hotel. The irresistible setting is the main reason to come here, along with the sunset cocktail menu, but the Italian Greek food is reliably good, with lots of seafood pasta options and meaty stews.

KYTHIRA ΚΥΘΗΡΑ
POP 3530

Poised between the Aegean and Ionian Seas, the gloriously time-forgotten island of Kythira lies just 12km off the southern tip of the Peloponnese's Lakonian Peninsula. Despite its distinctly Cycladic sugar-cube architecture, both historic and modern, Kythira is officially regarded as belonging to the Ionian Island group.

With its population spread between 40 villages, Kythira feels for much of the year like a ghost land; it's an unspoiled wilderness of lush valleys, overgrown gorges, and flower-speckled cliffs tumbling into the vivid blue sea.

Apart from July and August, when Italians especially swoop in to enjoy the fine sandy beaches, tourism remains very low-key. Visiting outside these months, however, brings huge rewards, whether you fancy hiking to scenic wonders and intriguing ancient settlements, or simply relaxing in the old-style tavernas and *kafeneia* (coffee houses) that pepper its village squares.

❶ Getting There & Away

AIR
Kythira Airport, 10km southeast of Potamos, is connected to Athens in summer by both **Olympic Air** (www.olympicair.com; €65, 50 minutes, one daily) and **Sky Express** (www. skyexpress.gr; €88, 50 minutes, twice daily except Tuesdays and Wednesdays). **Ellinair** (http://en.ellinair.com) flies to Kythira from Thessaloniki (€89, 75 minutes, twice weekly). There are far fewer flights in low season.

BOAT
Kythira's ferry port is at sleepy little Diakofti, halfway up the east coast. Buy tickets at the port just before departure, or via Kithira Travel (p704).

Boats from Neapoli in the Peloponnese come to Diakofti twice daily in summer, and once daily otherwise; two each week continue to Antikythira.

LANE Lines (www.lane-kithira.com) operates an intricate, seasonally changing schedule of ferries that connect Diakofti with Piraeus, Antikythira, Kissamos (Kastelli; Crete) and Gythio (Peloponnese); in summer there are usually two weekly services to and from each of those destinations.

TO	DURATION	FARE	FREQUENCY
Gythio	2½hr	€12	2 weekly
Kissamos (Kastelli)	2½-4hr	€22	2 weekly (2 via Antikythira; €9)
Neapoli	1¼hr	€12	12 daily
Piraeus	6½hr	€26	2 weekly

❶ Getting Around

Occasional buses operate in August. **Taxis** (☑ 6977991799, 6944305433) are pricey and charge around €25 between Hora (Kythira) and the airport. Your best bet is to pick up a hire car at the airport, or have one dropped off at your hotel.
Drakakis Tours (☑ 27360 31160; www. drakakistours.gr; Livadi) Rental cars, vans and 4WDs, with airport pick-up; airport transfers; buses to Athens (€45, one to two weekly); and sightseeing tours.
Panayotis Rent A Car (☑ Hora 27360 31004, Kapsali 27360 31600, airport 6944263757; www.panayotis-rent-a-car.gr; car/scooter per day from €45/15) A fleet of 120 cars – including 4WDs, small cars, motorbikes and scooters – with branches at the airport and across the island, including at Diakofti and Kapsali.

Kythira & Antikythira

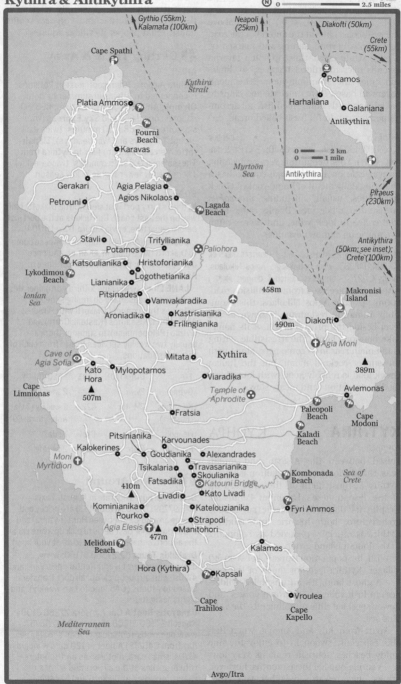

0 ____ 5 km
0 ____ 2.5 miles

Gythio (55km);
Kalamata (100km)

Neapoli
(25km)

Cape Spathi

*Kythira
Strait*

Platia Ammos

Fourni
Beach

Karavas

*Myrtoön
Sea*

Gerakari

Agia Pelagia

Petrouni

Agios Nikolaos

Lagada
Beach

Stavli

Trifyllianika

Potamos

Paliohora

Katsoulianika

Hristoforianika

Lykodimou
Beach

Logothetianika

Lianianika

Pitsinades

458m

*Ionian
Sea*

Vamvakaradika

Aroniadika

Kastrisianika

Frilingianika

490m

Diakofti

Makronisi
Island

Cave of
Agia Sofia

Mitata

Kythira

Agia Moni

Kato
Hora

Mylopotamos

Viaradika

389m

Cape
Limnionas

507m

*Temple of
Aphrodite*

Avlemonas

Fratsia

Paleopoli
Beach

Cape
Modoni

Pitsinianika

Karvounades

Kaladi
Beach

Kalokerines

Goudianika

Alexandrades

*Moni
Myrtidion*

Tsikalaria

Travasarianika

Fatsadika

Skoulianika

Kombonada
Beach

*Sea of
Crete*

410m

Livadi

Kato Livadi

Katouni Bridge

Kominianika

Katelouzianika

Pourko

Fyri Ammos

Agia Elesis

Strapodi

477m

Manitohori

Melidoni
Beach

Kalamos

Hora (Kythira)

Kapsali

Vroulea

Cape
Trahilos

Cape
Kapello

*Mediterranean
Sea*

Avgo/Itra

Piraeus
(230km)

Antikythira
(50km; see inset);
Crete (100km)

Inset (Antikythira)

Diakofti (50km)

Crete
(55km)

Potamos

Harhaliana

Galaniana

Antikythira

0 ____ 2 km
0 ____ 1 mile

Antikythira

Hora (Kythira)
Χώρα (Κύθηρα)

POP 270

Hora (itself also known as Kythira), the island's small capital, consists of a Cycladic-style cluster of white-and-blue cubes, stretching south along a slender ridge towards a 14th-century Venetian *kastro* perched on a separate craggy hilltop. Most of the action is based around the open square at its northern end, while tasteful little shops line the way to the *kastro,* ranging from fine antiques to bespoke jewellery.

◉ Sights

★ Kastro
FORTRESS

(⊗ 8am-8pm, shorter hours winter) **FREE** Crowning the rocky headland that soars at the southern end of Hora, this majestic 14th-century fortress was built by Kythira's first Venetian governor. Within its ramparts the fort is now largely in ruins, but the site is stupendous, drenched in wildflowers and commanding stunning views down to Kapsali and out as far as Antikythira. Only the unenthralling **Coat of Arms Collection** (adult/child €2/1; ⊗ 9am-2pm & 5-8pm Tue-Sun), in a former powder magazine, charges an admission fee.

Archaeological Museum of Kythira
MUSEUM

(✐ 27360 31739; adult/child €4/2; ⊗ 8am-8pm Tue-Sun) Hora's impressive archaeological museum, beside the main road at the north end of town, traces the history of 'this small island' in two rooms. Among artefacts from the ancient settlements of Palaiopolis and Palaiokastro, pride of place goes to the white marble statue known as the Lion of Kythira.

⬛ Sleeping & Eating

Castello Rooms
PENSION €

(✐ 27360 31069; www.kythera-castelloapts.gr; Spyridonos Staï; d from €45; ❄☎) Eight cosy white-walled rooms and kitchenette apartments, with balconies facing the *kastro,* set in a garden of flowers and fruit trees. It's just off the far end of the main street. The owners are super-friendly.

★ Hotel Margarita
PENSION €€

(✐ 27360 31711; www.hotel-margarita.com; off Spyridonos Staï; s/d/tr incl breakfast €60/90/110; ⊗ Easter-Oct; ❄☎) Set in an impeccably restored, white-walled 19th-century villa, just off the main alleyway not far beyond the main square, this charming hotel offers 12 simple antique-furnished rooms accessed via a quirky old spiral staircase. A wonderful terrace, used for the good buffet breakfast and afternoon drinks, affords fantastic *kastro* and sea views.

Corte O
APARTMENT €€

(✐ 27360 39139; www.corteo.gr; room/2-bedroom apt incl breakfast €90/170; ⊗ Apr-Oct; ❄☎) Three beautiful two-bedroom apartments set in a late-18th-century house just a spit away from the *kastro*. All have modern, minimal decor plus full kitchens, private terraces and sea or valley views; one can be divided to create two en-suite rooms.

Zorba's
TAVERNA €

(✐ 27360 31655; mains €9; ⊗ dinner Tue-Sun; ❄) Hora's only year-round restaurant, on the main alleyway not far off the square, is a very simple affair serving succulent grilled meats – pork, lamb chops, beef or chicken – either in the plain, old-fashioned dining room or out on the terrace.

Veranda Cafe
CAFE

(✐ 27360 31316; ⊗ 8am-late; ☎) A smart, cool and very aptly named cafe on the corner of the main square. The elegant interior holds a well-stocked bar, while the adjoining balcony terrace has comfy sofa seating and astonishing long-range views. Perfect for coffee, juices and ice cream, and for long sunset-gazing sessions.

🛍 Shopping

Yfanda
FASHION & ACCESSORIES

(www.facebook.com/borse.gr; ⊗ 9am-9pm) Intriguing one-room, one-woman workshop on the pedestrian alleyway south of the main square. All the colourful and very distinctive hand-woven shoulder and clutch bags on sale are created on the loom in the middle of the floor.

THE BIRTH OF APHRODITE

Kythira was famous in antiquity as the birthplace of Aphrodite. As described by Hesiod and painted by Botticelli, the goddess of love, desire and beauty rose resplendent from the foam upon a giant scallop, possibly off the islet of Avgo ('egg') off Kapsali. Confusingly, she's also said to have re-emerged near Pafos in Cyprus, so both islands haggle over the claim.

Aquarium
JEWELLERY

(☑6977287741; www.facebook.com/pg/aquarium kythira; ⊙10am-9pm) Exquisite one-off pieces of bespoke jewellery, in a boutique overseen by the eponymous fish tank, on the street that leads down the hill to the main square of Hora. It's not always open and hours vary, but it's worth persevering.

ℹ Information

The central square holds banks with ATMs, and the post office.

Kithira Travel (☑Hora 27360 31390, Potamos 27360 31848; www.kithiratravel.gr; ⊙9am-2pm & 6-8pm Mon-Sat) Helpful staff; sells flights and boat tickets.

Police Station (☑27360 31206) Near the *kastro*.

Kapsali   Καψάλι
POP 35

Down by the sea 2km east of Hora (Kythira), pretty little Kapsali was the island's main port during the Venetian era. These days, in summer at least, it's a bustling resort, with its two languidly curving bays lined by a necklace of tavernas, chic cafes and studios, and the sandy, ochre-coloured beach offering sheltered swimming. It's a superb spectacle when viewed from Hora's clifftop *kastro*.

The rocky islet offshore is known by two names. **Avgo** ('egg'), referring to its legendary role as the birthplace of Aphrodite, and **Itra** ('cooking pot') referring to its resemblance when topped by clouds to a steaming cauldron.

🏃 Activities

Panayotis
BOATING

(☑27360 31600; www.panayotis-rent-a-car.gr) Waterfront outlet that rents canoes and pedal boats (as well as cars and mopeds).

Kythera Dive
DIVING

(☑27360 37400; www.kytheradive.gr) PADI open-water courses start from €400, and reef or cave dives from €50.

Captain Spiros
BOATING

(☑6974022079; per person from €12) Daily cruises in a glass-bottomed boat; destinations include Itra, where you can swim.

🛏 Sleeping

Vassili Studios
PENSION €

(☑27360 31125; http://kithira.biz; d/tr incl breakfast from €55/65; 🅿✳🛜) This tree-lined complex has a perfect setting overlooking Kapsali

Beach. Rooms are light and welcoming, with wooden ceilings and floors, shabby-chic furniture and wrought-iron beds; the larger and more expensive options have bay views.

★El Sol Hotel
HOTEL €€

(☑27360 31766; www.elsolhotels.gr; d incl breakfast €120, 5-person apt €170; 🅿✳🛜🏊) Striking white-cube apartments, perched high above the Hora–Kapsali road, with Olympian views of the sea and across to Hora's *kastro*. Immaculate, minimalist rooms have private terraces, and there's a terrific pool, plenty of sun loungers, and a breakfast room packed with board games for rainy days.

Aphrodite Apartments
APARTMENT €€

(☑27360 31328; www.hotel-afrodite.gr; d/tr/q from €60/75/80; ✳🛜) On the coast road, barely a minute up from the beach, the gleaming white Aphrodite offers a choice between simple but spacious tiled-floor rooms or apartments with kitchenettes and balconies. For the best views, choose the top floor. Irene and Yiannis are great hosts.

🍴 Eating & Drinking

Goldfish
CAFE €

(☑27360 31032; www.facebook.com/chrysopsaro; mains €6-9; ⊙noon-11pm Tue-Sun; 🛜) The coolest cafe along Kapsali Beach, with nicely padded seats, baby-blue tables and a very laid-back vibe. Settle down over juices or shakes, coffee or beer, or order from an eclectic fusion menu that includes Japanese-, Indian- or Argentinian-style chicken; burgers; omelettes; and waffles soaked in ice cream.

Hytra
TAVERNA €

(☑27360 37200; mains €7-11; ⊙lunch & dinner; 🛜) Slap-bang in the middle of the waterfront – look for the green awning – this traditional joint dishes up casseroles, tasty spinach pies, fire-grilled lamb chops, veal steak and plenty of fresh seafood.

Magos
SEAFOOD €€

(☑27360 31407; mains €7-13; ⊙lunch & dinner; ✳🛜) Long-standing and very dependable seafood specialist, surveying the Kapsali scene from the far eastern end of the waterfront. Choose a fish from the day's fresh catch, displayed in the kitchen, or opt for standards such as grilled squid or shrimp.

Fox Anglais
BAR

(☑27360 31458; ⊙noon-late Jun-Sep; 🛜) This veteran bar-club on the waterfront, with outdoor tables and a cosy interior, is the epicentre of Kythira's nightlife in summer, with acoustic music on the beach on Tuesdays, and DJs every other night.

Potamos Ποταμός
POP 395

The attractive hillside village of Potamos, at the heart of the island, serves as Kythira's social hub. Its flower-filled central square hosts a Sunday-morning flea market, and is great for people-watching any day of the week.

✗ Eating & Drinking

Panaretos TAVERNA €€
(☑27360 34290; www.facebook.com/taverna Panaretos; mains €7-14; ⊙ lunch & dinner daily Mar-Oct, Thu-Sun Nov-Feb; 🖜) One of five tavernas that amiably share the main village square for al fresco dining at cream-coloured tables and chairs, Panaretos excels with dishes based on home-grown produce, such as wild goat with olive oil and oregano sauce, pork fillet with thyme, and assorted mezedhes.

★ Kafe Astikon CAFE
(☑27360 33141; www.facebook.com/astikon; ⊙7am-late; 🖜) Very charming old cafe–music bar, near the main square. The high-ceilinged and shadowy interior oozes atmosphere, with its coral-green walls, leather 'egg' chairs and a penny-farthing. Expect live music on the little stage nightly (late) in July and August, and impromptu jam sessions at other times. It also serves breakfast, pizza and pasta.

Agia Pelagia Αγία Πελαγία
POP 280

Kythira's northernmost resort, Agia Pelagia is a simple seafront village backed by swooping cliffs and wooded valleys. Vibrant azure waters lick against its sand-and-pebble beaches, while some magnificent volcanic beaches lie south beyond the headland. Red, pink and tawny along to Lagada Beach, they make a great target for coastal hikers.

⌂ Sleeping & Eating

Hotel Pelagia Aphrodite HOTEL €€
(☑27360 33926; www.pelagia-aphrodite.com; s/d/tr incl breakfast €90/100/140; ⊙ Easter-Oct; P❋❋🖜) Right on the beach at the southern end of town, and run by returning Aussie-Kythirans, this lovely hotel has 13 terrific rooms with wooden ceilings and huge, sea-facing balconies. The older rooms,

whitewashed and simple, are closest to the waves, and there's a pleasant breakfast room downstairs.

Pantonia Apartments APARTMENT €€
(☑27360 39112; www.pantonia-apartments.com; 1-/2-bedroom apt incl breakfast €81/138; ❋❋🖜) Smart, modern kitchenette apartments, 200m up from the sea, with separate sleeping and dining rooms. All have sweeping sea views – those higher up from private balconies and some from a shared terrace.

Maneas Beach Hotel HOTEL €€
(☑27360 33503; www.maneashotel.com; d with/without sea views incl breakfast €110/85; P❋❋🖜) Upmarket beach hotel, right on the waterfront south of the jetty, with a contemporary feel. Rooms boast modern fittings and large balconies with awesome sea views.

★ Kaleris GREEK €
(☑27360 33461; www.facebook.com/kaleris; mains €7-11; ⊙ lunch & dinner Apr-Oct; 🖜) Renowned for its creative cuisine, romantic little Kaleris has a waterfront pavilion and tables on the beach itself, shaded by tamarisk trees. Trust the charismatic owner Yiannis to advise on handwritten daily advertised specials such as yoghurt salad with smoked aubergine, filo parcels with feta drizzled with thyme-infused honey, braised lamb shank or grilled prawns.

Akrogiali SEAFOOD €
(☑27360 34314; mains €7-12; ⊙ 11am-late; 🖜) Fresh seafood, served up on the beach; look out for the painted sign showing a mermaid riding a dolphin. As well as mullet, mackerel, bream and shrimp, Akrogiali does chicken in red-wine sauce and a simple tomato pie.

Sempreviva CAFE
(☑27360 33390; ⊙8.30am-late; 🖜) Very appealing little beachfront cafe-bar, with cosy, breezy seats out on the sand. It's the ideal spot for morning coffee, evening cocktails, and anything in between.

Around Kythira

You'll need your own transport to explore the backroads that thread between Kythira's scattered villages, which pass orchards and vineyards, olive groves and stands of cypress.

In the south, the small **Museum of Byzantine & Post-Byzantine Art** (☑27360 31731; adult/child €2/free; ⊙8.30am-2.30pm Tue-Sun) in Kato Livadi, 6km north of Hora, houses icons

WORTH A TRIP

MYLOPOTAMOS ΜΥΛΟΠΟΤΑΜΟΣ

The delightful little village of **Mylopotamos** nestles into a small valley 13km north of Hora (Kythira). The tables of an utterly charming *kafeneio* (coffee house), **O Platanos** (☑ 27360 33397; mains €5-10; ☺ lunch & dinner; ☏), fill its tiny central square, which is flanked on one side by the walled channel of a babbling stream, populated by tame ducks and geese. As it flows away northwest towards the sea, that stream cuts ever deeper into the wooded hillside, along a gorge that once held 22 separate **watermills**. Only one now survives – Mylopotamos means 'Mill on the River' – but a ravishing little footpath still follows the river, leading through luxuriant greenery to the aquamarine pool of the **Neraïda ('water nymph') waterfall**.

A separate hike, signposted along the left-hand fork in the road north of the village square, takes 15 minutes to reach the older village of **Kato Hora**. Make your way behind a castellated 19th-century villa here and you'll find the extraordinary ruins of Mylopotamos' Venetian-era **kastro**, a quite magical warren of abandoned churches and fortified houses, liberally overgrown with colourful flowers.

and frescoes salvaged from churches all over the island. Spanning a shallow stream bed just north, incongruous **Katouni Bridge**, built by the British in the 19th century, is the largest stone bridge in Greece. Head southeast, following spectacular twisty roads, to reach the mauve-grey stone beach at **Fyri Ammos**.

Avlemonas, further up the coast, is a former fishing village turned exquisite resort. A spotless vision of blue and dazzling white, with footpaths leading across the rocks to ladders that drop into the pristine lagoon, it's idyllic, if a little unreal. The closest beaches lie to the west: first comes broad, pebbled **Paleopoli Beach**, and then **Kaladi Beach**, in a separate cove and accessed via a staircase.

Few traces survive of ancient **Paleopoli**, just inland, but you can spend an enjoyable hour hiking up and around the hill that once held the **Temple of Aphrodite**, marking the birthplace of the goddess of beauty.

Much more substantial ruins survive of Kythira's medieval capital, **Paliohora**, in the north. It's a totally magnificent spot, set on a craggy pinnacle at the confluence of two deep-cut gorges. In theory, it was safely hidden from enemy ships, but it was destroyed by a Turkish fleet in 1537. Strewn with the tumbledown remains of chapels and mansions, the isolated hill top can now be reached by driving a 4km dead-end road east of Potamos, the last 2km of which is unsurfaced, or following the delightful parallel hiking trail.

🛏 Sleeping & Eating

★ Maryianni APARTMENT €€
(☑ 27360 33316; www.maryianni.gr; Avlemonas; 3-person studios €110, apt €130; ℗ ❋ ☏) Rather wonderful white-and-blue studios, stacked

Cycladic-style above the Avlemonas shoreline, with kitchens and sumptuous sea-view terraces. Even the smaller options are well above average, with boutique flourishes such as terracotta tiles, wrought-iron beds, classical art and choice furniture.

★ Filio TAVERNA €
(☑ 27360 31549; http://filio.net; Kalamos; mains €8-12; ☺ 4pm-midnight; ☏) Acclaimed local taverna, far off the beaten track 1km beyond Kalamos en route towards Fyri Ammos (look for signs), offering island classics such as slow-cooked lamb in lemon sauce, eggplant stuffed with meat and Kythiran sausages, in a well-shaded terrace garden. The owners also rent out attractive apartments nearby.

Pierros GREEK €
(☑ 27360 31014; www.pieros.gr; Livadi; mains €6-11; ☺ lunch & dinner; ❋ ☏) For almost a century, this family-run favourite has been serving up no-nonsense staples such as *mousakas, pastitsio,* and baked chicken or veal. The main road through Livadi is hardly a beautiful setting, but for an authentic Greek experience this is hard to beat.

Skandeia TAVERNA €€
(☑ 27360 33700; www.skandeia.gr; Paleopoli; mains €8-15; ☺ 1-11pm; ☏) A delightful taverna on the hillside at the northwestern end of Paleopoli Beach, Skandeia places a major emphasis on wholesome, freshly sourced local produce in preparing its definitive Greek cuisine, which ranges from grilled fish and fish soup to roasted eggplant. Relax beneath the spreading elm trees, away from the madding crowd.

Understand Greece

Greece Today

Greek resilience has been stretched thin, leaving many disillusioned and apprehensive of a future in the European Union. The continued deterioration of the Greek economy is taking its toll on virtually every aspect of society. Few have been unaffected by savage wage and pension cuts, new taxes and record joblessness. Meanwhile, thousands of refugees who hoped to cross through Greece to other areas of Europe are trapped by closed borders, causing a humanitarian crisis that Greece is struggling to deal with.

Best in Print

Something Will Happen, You'll See (Christos Ikonomou; 2016) Moving short stories of characters caught in the financial crisis.

Odyssey (Homer; 8th century BC) Plagued by Poseidon, Odysseus struggles to return home to Ithaca.

Zorba the Greek (Nikos Kazantzakis; 1946) A spiritual bible to many; one man's unquenchable lust for life.

The Magus (John Fowles; 1966) Creepy mind games set on fictional Phraxos.

Falling for Icarus: A Journey among the Cretans (Rory MacLean; 2004) A travel writer builds a plane in Icarus.

Best on Film

300 (2007) Testosterone-fuelled retelling of the Spartans' epic stand against the Persians in the Battle of Thermopylae, 480 BC.

Mamma Mia (2008) The island of Skopelos shines to an Abba soundtrack.

Guns of Navarone (1961) Allied soldiers enter Nazi-occupied Greece in this compelling thriller.

Shirley Valentine (1989) Classic Greek-island romance on Mykonos.

Captain Corelli's Mandolin (2001) Lavish retelling of Louis de Bernières' novel set in occupied Greece.

Austerity Measures

The numerous multi-billion-euro bailouts loaned to Greece by its EU and International Monetary Fund (IMF) creditors since 2009 have come with strong strings. To secure them, the Greek government was forced to implement austerity measures that saw severe wage and pension cuts and increased taxes while living costs soared at an unpalatable rate. At the same time, unemployment reached around 23%.

Austerity measures and declining living standards have also widened Greece's stark economic and social disparities – the hedonistic lifestyles of Athenians taking weekend jaunts to Mykonos bear no resemblance to struggling pensioners whose pensions have been cut by 40%. Homelessness, suicides and once-rare violent crime have risen. Growing anger and social unrest has sparked mass strikes, demonstrations and violent clashes with police. Disillusioned young Greeks are bearing the brunt of years of economic mismanagement – the country's most educated generation faces bleak prospects as the level of youth unemployment sits at 46%. There is a feeling of despair that is decidedly un-Greek.

Immigration & Asylum

The primary entry point for immigrants to Europe, Greece has seen 1.3 million people arrive in the country since 2015 in search of safety and a better life, often hoping to reunite with family in other European countries. Most come from Afghanistan, Iraq, Syria and Africa via the porous Turkish border and Greece's outlying islands.

In 2016 a deal between the EU and Turkey brought the closure of European borders with Greece and a plan to return illegal migrants to Turkey, in an attempt to discourage migrants from crossing the ocean to reach Greece. In exchange, the EU committed to giving Turkey €6 billion to deal with their own refugee crisis. The numbers of refugees reaching the islands dropped drastically; some islands that saw up to 5000 arrivals daily in 2015 saw as few as 100 arrivals a day in 2017. Consequently, the number of drownings in the dangerous crossing has also declined greatly.

Nevertheless, many NGOs and humanitarian groups believe the deal has not only been unsuccessful but has increased human suffering. To date, less than 1000 refugees have been returned to Turkey. For many refugees who fled persecution and risked perilous boat journeys to reach Greece, Turkey is not considered a safe option. The alternative is to be trapped in Greece where, at the time of writing, 62,000 refugees waited for processing. Over 14,000 of these are on the southeastern islands and more than half are women and children, many unaccompanied. Conditions in overflowing camps have deteriorated drastically, with widespread crime and abuse. Increased trauma and depression have also brought a rise in suicide attempts. Many refugees have been trapped for over a year and have run out of money and hope.

European press coverage of the crisis led to a slight decline in tourism on some southeastern islands in 2016, despite little evidence that refugees had any interaction with or impact on tourists. Within Greece, economic decline has fuelled xenophobia, sparking anti-immigrant rallies and growing hostility, yet deep-rooted Greek hospitality has reared its noble head, particularly on the islands. Despite their own financial struggles, many Greeks independently offer food and clothing to immigrants while local doctors volunteer to care for them.

Brain Drain

Greece's once-shrinking villages are welcoming a new wave of nouveau-poor Greeks. Families of out-of-work professionals and tradespeople, along with unemployed university graduates, are returning to ancestral homes on the islands and to help with family businesses, often in tourism or farming. An increase in agricultural employment is one of the byproducts of the times, going back to Greece's traditional strength and way of life. An increasing number of educated under-30s are also migrating to other parts of Europe, America and Australia to find employment.

POPULATION: **10.9 MILLION**

GDP: **€175 BILLION (US$195 BILLION)**

EXTERNAL DEBT: **€337 BILLION (US$376 BILLION)**

INFLATION: **1.6%**

PER CAPITA INCOME: **€18,138 (US$20,270)**

UNEMPLOYMENT: **26.5%**

if Greece were 100 people

89 would be Greek
11 would be other

belief systems
(% of population)

Greek Orthodox   Muslim   Other

population per sq km

= 35 people

History

A doorstep between Asia Minor and Europe, Greece has always been tied to the rising and waning fortunes of its neighbours. In the 5th century BC Greece was almost devoured by the unstoppable spread of the Persian Empire, only reversed by Alexander. Later the Roman Empire overwhelmed old Hellas, but the nation revived once more under Byzantine rule. However, the Greeks' genius was their ability to adapt elements of other cultures' architecture and craft, taking it to new heights.

Early Days

The discovery of a Neanderthal skull in a cave on the Halkidiki peninsula of Macedonia confirmed the presence of humans in Greece 700,000 years ago. People from the Palaeolithic times (around 6500 BC) left bones and tools in the Pindos Mountains, while pastoral communities emerged during Neolithic times (7000–3000 BC), primarily in the fertile region that is now Thessaly. Agriculturally sophisticated, they grew crops, bred sheep and goats, and used clay to produce pots, vases and stylised representations of idols as figures of worship.

Homer's classic work, the 'Iliad', written in the 8th century BC, relates in poetic epithet a mythical episode of the Trojan War. Its sequel, the 'Odyssey', recounts the epic adventures of Odysseus and his companions in their journey home from the Trojan War.

Artistic & Cultural Legacies

Ancient Civilisations

By 3000 BC, settlements had developed into streets, squares and mudbrick houses. Indo-European migrants introduced the processing of bronze into Greece and from there began three remarkable civilisations: Cycladic, Minoan and Mycenaean.

The Cycladic civilisation was a cluster of fishing and farming island communities with a sophisticated artistic temperament. The most striking legacy is the carving of statuettes from Parian marble – the famous Cycladic figurines. Cycladic sculptors are also renowned for their impressive, life-sized *kouroi* (marble statues).

The Minoans were Europe's first advanced civilisation, named after King Minos, the mythical ruler of Crete (and stepfather of the Minotaur). Around 1900 BC, the splendid complex of Knossos was first built with its frescoes, ventilation shafts and sewerage systems marking an abrupt acceleration

TIMELINE	7000–3000 BC	3000–1100 BC	2000 BC
	For 4000 years, inhabitants of the Greek peninsula live a simple agrarian life, growing crops and herding animals. Communities with housing and planned streets appear around 3000 BC.	The discovery of blending copper and tin into a strong alloy heralds the Bronze Age. Trade gains traction; increased prosperity births the Cycladic, Minoan and Mycenaean civilisations.	Minoan civilisation reaches its peak in Crete: architectural advances lead to the first palaces in Knossos, Phaestos, Malia and Zakros, while pottery-making improves and Crete's first script emerges.

from Neolithic life. Using bronze, the Minoans were able to build great sea vessels and their reach extended across Asia Minor and North Africa.

The jury is out on what triggered the demise of this great civilisation. Was it the tsunami and ash fallout caused by the volcanic eruption in Thira, Santorini, in 1500 BC? Or perhaps the invading force of Mycenae?

The decline of the Minoan civilisation coincided with the rise of Mycenae (1600–1100 BC), which reached its peak between 1500 and 1200 BC with mainland city-states such as Corinth, Tiryns and Mycenae. Warrior kings, who measured their wealth in weapons, now ruled from heavily fortified palaces. Commercial transactions were documented on tablets in Linear B (a form of Greek language 500 years older than the Ionic Greek used by Homer). The Mycenaean's most impressive legacy is their magnificent gold masks, refined jewellery and metal ornaments, the best of which are in the National Archaeological Museum in Athens.

Geometric & Archaic Ages

The Dorians were an ancient Hellenic people who settled in the Peloponnese by the 8th century BC. In the 11th or 12th century BC, these warrior-like people fanned out to occupy much of the mainland, seizing control of the Mycenaean kingdoms and enslaving the inhabitants. The following 400-year period is often referred to as Greece's dark age; however, the Dorians introduced iron and developed a new, intricate style of pottery, decorated with striking geometric designs. Significantly they were to introduce the practice of *polytheism* (the worship of many gods), paving the foundations for Zeus and his pantheon of 12 principal deities.

During the following Archaic period, about 1000–800 BC, Greek culture developed rapidly; many of the advancements in literature, sculpture, theatre, architecture and intellectual endeavour began. This revival overlapped with the Classical period (the two eras are often classified as the Hellenic period). Advances included the Greek alphabet, the verses of Homer (the 'Odyssey' was possibly the world's first epic work of literature), the founding of the Olympic Games and central sanctuaries such as Delphi. These common bonds gave Greeks a sense of national identity and intellectual vigour.

By about 800 BC, Greece had been divided into a series of independent city-states, the most powerful being Argos, Athens, Corinth, Elis, Sparta and Thiva (Thebes). Most abolished monarchic rule and aristocratic monopoly, establishing a set of laws that redistributed wealth and allowed the city's citizens to regain control over their lands.

Classical Age

Greece's golden age, from the 6th to 4th centuries BC, saw a renaissance in cultural creativity. Literature and drama blossomed as many city-states enjoyed increased economic reform, political prosperity and a surge in

Philip II engaged the philosopher Aristotle to tutor the teenage Alexander, who was greatly inspired by Homer's 'Iliad'. Alexander retained a strong interest in the arts and culture throughout his life.

Scholars divide the Cycladic civilisation into three periods: Early (3000–2000 BC), Middle (2000–1500 BC) and Late (1500–1100 BC).

HISTORY ARTISTIC & CULTURAL LEGACIES

1700–1550 BC	1500–1200 BC	1400 BC	1200–800 BC
Santorini erupts with a cataclysmic volcanic explosion, causing a Mediterranean-wide tsunami that scholars suggest contributed to the destruction of Minoan civilisation.	The authoritarian Mycenaean culture from the Peloponnese usurps much of the Cretan and Cycladic cultures. Goldsmithing is a predominant feature of Mycenaean life.	The Mycenaeans colonise Crete, building cities such as Kydonia (Hania) and Polyrrinia. Weapons manufacturing flourishes; fine arts fall into decline. Greek gods replace worship of the Mother Goddess.	The Dorians herald 400 years of obscurity in international trade, but excel in the use of iron weaponry and ironwork in architecture, and develop striking geometric designs on pottery.

DEMOCRACY

The seafaring city-state of Athens was still in the hands of aristocrats when Athens' greatest reformist, Solon, was appointed chief magistrate in 594 BC. His mandate was to defuse the mounting tensions between the haves and have-nots by cancelling all debts and liberating those who'd become enslaved because of them. Declaring all free Athenians equal by law, Solon abolished inherited privileges and restructured political power, establishing four classes based on wealth. Although only the first two classes were eligible for office, all four could elect magistrates and vote on legislation. Solon's reforms have become regarded as a blueprint of the ideological democratic system.

The Trial of Socrates by IF Stone frames in a contemporary investigative light Plato's version of events surrounding the philosopher Socrates' life and death.

mental agility, led by the noble works of Aeschylus, Euripides and Sophocles who contributed dramatic tragedies, and Aristophanes who inspired political satire with his comedies. Today the potency of this fertile era still resonates – many ideas discussed today were debated by these great minds. And that's not forgetting the journalistic blogs of historians Herodotus – widely regarded as the father of history – and Thucydides.

Athens reached its zenith after the monumental defeat of the Persians at the Battle of Marathon in 490 BC, founding the Delian League, a naval alliance formed to liberate city-states still occupied by Persia. Many Aegean and Ionian city-states swore an allegiance to Athens, making an annual contribution to the treasury of ships, bringing it fantastic wealth unrivalled by its poor neighbour, Sparta, and also turning it into something of an empire.

When Pericles became leader of Athens in 461 BC, he moved the treasury from Delos to the Acropolis, reappropriating funds to construct grander temples upon it, including the majestic Parthenon, and elsewhere, including the Temple of Zeus at Olympia. It was also during this classical period that sculptors developed a more naturalistic, aesthetic style for marble pieces and bronze casts, such as the enduring marble friezes of the Parthenon and the sculpture of the city's patroness, Athena.

Persian Fire by Tom Holland is a compelling account of the warring city-states of Athens and Sparta and how they had to finally pull together to face the Persian threat.

With the Aegean Sea safely under its wing, Athens began to look westward for further expansion, bringing it into conflict with the Sparta-dominated Peloponnesian League. A series of skirmishes and provocations subsequently led to the Peloponnesian Wars.

War & Conquest
The Persian Wars

Athens' rapid growth as a major city-state also meant heavy reliance on food imports from the Black Sea; and Persia's imperial expansion westward threatened strategic coastal trade routes across Asia Minor. Athens' support

1100 BC	800–650 BC	700–500 BC	594 BC
The Dorians overrun the Mycenaean cities in Crete. They reorganise the political system, dividing society into classes. A rudimentary democracy replaces monarchical government.	Independent city-states emerge in the Archaic period as the Dorians develop. Aristocrats rule these ministates while tyrants occasionally take power by force. Greek alphabet emerges from Phoenician script.	Having originated around 1000 BC in the Peloponnese, the Spartans come to play a decisive role in Greek history. Politically and militarily, the Spartans dominate for around 200 years.	Solon, a ruling aristocrat in Athens, introduces rules of fair play to his citizenry. His radical rule-changing – in effect creating human and political rights – is credited as being the first step to real democracy.

for a rebellion in the Persian colonies of Asia Minor sparked the Persian drive to destroy the city. Persian Emperor Darius spent five years suppressing the revolt and remained determined to succeed. A 25,000-strong Persian army reached Attica in 490 BC, but was defeated when an Athenian force of 10,000 outmanoeuvred it at the Battle of Marathon.

When Darius died in 485 BC, his son Xerxes resumed the quest to conquer Greece with a massive land and sea invasion in 480 BC. Some 30 city-states met in Corinth to devise a defence, forming the Hellenic League with an army and navy under Spartan command. The army held at the pass at Thermopylae, near present-day Lamia, the main passage into central Greece from the north. Despite the Greeks being greatly outnumbered, this bottleneck was easy to defend until a traitor showed the Persians another way over the mountains, from where they turned to attack the Greeks who retreated.

The Greeks fell back on their second line of defence, an earthen wall across the Isthmus of Corinth, while the Persians advanced upon Athens and razed it to the ground. The Persian naval campaign, however, was not successful. By skilful manoeuvring, the smaller, more agile Greek warships trapped the larger Persian ships in the narrow waters off Salamis. Xerxes returned to Persia in disgust, leaving his general Mardonius to subdue Greece. The result was quite the reverse: a year later, the Greeks obliterated the Persian army at the Battle of Plataea.

> The Histories, written by Herodotus in the 5th century BC, chronicles the conflicts between the Ancient Greek city-states and Persia. The work is considered to be the first narrative of historical events ever written.

The Peloponnesian Wars

The Peloponnesian League was a military coalition governed by the iron hand of Sparta, who maintained political dominance over the Peloponnesian region. Athens' growing imperialism threatened Spartan hegemony; the ensuing power struggle was to last almost 30 years.

Athens' support for Corcyra (present-day Corfu) against Sparta's powerful ally Corinth sparked the first Peloponnesian War (431–421 BC). Athens knew it couldn't defeat the Spartans on land, so withdrew behind its mighty walls and blockaded the Peloponnese with its navy. Athens suffered badly during the siege; plague broke out killing a third of the population but the defences held firm. The blockade of the Peloponnese eventually began to hurt and the two cities negotiated an uneasy truce.

> In The Peloponnesian War, Thucydides sets out a historical narrative of the quarrels and warfare between Athens and Sparta.

The truce lasted until 413 BC, when the Spartans went to the aid of the Sicilian city of Syracuse, which the Athenians had been besieging for three years. The Spartans ended the siege, destroying the Athenian fleet and army. Athens fought on for a further nine years before it finally surrendered to Sparta in 404 BC. Corinth urged the total destruction of Athens, but the Spartans felt honour-bound to spare the city that had saved Greece from the Persians. Instead, they crippled it by confiscating its fleet, abolishing the Delian League and tearing down the walls between the city and Piraeus.

490 BC	480 BC	477 BC	461–32 BC
Athens invokes the ire of the Persians by supporting insurgencies within Persian territorial domains. Seeking revenge, the Persian King Darius sends an army to teach Greece a lesson but is defeated at Marathon.	Darius' son Xerxes seeks revenge for the Marathon defeat and sacks Athens. The Greeks retaliate by smashing the Persian army at the decisive Battle of Plataea. The Persian Wars are over.	Seeking security while building a de facto empire, the Athenians establish a political and military alliance called the Delian League. Many city-states and islands join the new club.	New Athenian leader Pericles shifts power from Delos to Athens and uses the treasury wealth of the Delian League to fund massive works, including the construction of the magnificent Parthenon, an enduring legacy.

The Rise of Macedon & Alexander the Great

By the late 4th century BC, the Greeks were engineering their own decline. Sparta began a doomed campaign to reclaim the cities of Asia Minor from Persian rule, bringing the Persians back into Greek affairs where they found willing allies in Athens and an increasingly powerful Thebes (Thiva). The rivalry between Sparta and Thebes culminated in the decisive Battle of Leuctra in 371 BC, where Thebes inflicted Sparta's first defeat. Spartan influence collapsed and Thebes filled the vacuum. In a surprise about-turn, Athens now allied itself with Sparta, and their combined forces battled the Theban army in the Peloponnese in 362 BC. Thebes won the battle, but their leader was killed and Theban power soon crumbled.

The political influence of the major city-states had by now been significantly eroded and they were unable to combat the new power in the north, Macedon (modern Macedonia), which was gathering strength under its aggressive monarch, Philip II. In 338 BC, Philip II marched into Greece and defeated a combined army of Athenians and Thebans at the Battle of Chaeronea. Philip persuaded all the city-states (except Sparta) to swear allegiance to Macedonia by promising to campaign against Persia. Before the campaign began, Philip was assassinated and his 20-year-old son, Alexander, became king in 336 BC.

Philip II's death sparked rebellions throughout the empire, but Alexander quickly crushed them, making an example of Thebes by razing it to the ground. Upon his black stallion he was always the first into battle ahead of his men, and was renowned for his valour, cunning and recklessness. After restoring order in Thebes, he turned his attention to the Persian Empire and marched his seasoned army of 40,000 men into Asia Minor in 334 BC. After a few bloody battles with the Persians, Alexander succeeded in conquering Syria, Palestine and Egypt – where he was proclaimed pharaoh and founded the city of Alexandria. To minimise future resistance from his new subjects, he interbred them with his soldiers.

Alexander continued his reign east into what is now Uzbekistan, Balkh in Afghanistan and northern India. His ambition was to conquer the world, which he believed ended at the sea beyond India, but his now-aged soldiers grew weary and in 324 BC forced him to return to Mesopotamia, where he settled in Babylon. The following year, at age 33, he fell ill suddenly and died. His generals swooped like vultures on the empire and, when the dust settled, Alexander's empire was carved up into fractious, independent kingdoms. Macedonia lost control of the Greek city-states to the south, which banded together into the Aetolian League, centred on Delphi, and the Achaean League, based in the Peloponnese. Athens and Sparta joined neither.

Alexander the Great is considered to be one of the best military leaders of all time. He was never beaten in battle and by the age of 30 reigned over one of the largest ancient empires, stretching from Greece to the Himalayas.

413–404 BC	399 BC	359 BC	334–23 BC
A second war between Sparta and Athens breaks out over the distant colony of Sicily, ending an eight-year truce. The Spartans break the Athenian siege and Sparta assumes total dominance.	Socrates stands trial, accused of corrupting the young with pedagogical speeches. A jury condemns him to death. Rather than appealing for voluntary exile, Socrates defiantly accepts a cup of hemlock.	In Macedonia, King Philip II seizes power. He seeks alliances with Sparta and Athens on a promise to wage war again on Persia. Following Phillip's untimely murder, his son Alexander assumes leadership.	Alexander the Great sets out to conquer the known world. Thebes (Thiva) is the first victim, followed by the Persians, the Egyptians and finally the peoples of today's central Asia. He dies in 323 BC.

Foreign Rule

Roman Era

While Alexander the Great was forging his vast empire in the east, the Romans had been expanding theirs to the west, and now they were keen to start making inroads into Greece. After several inconclusive clashes, they defeated Macedon in 168 BC at the Battle of Pydna.

The Achaean League was defeated in 146 BC and the Roman consul Mummius made an example of the rebellious Corinthians by destroying their city. In 86 BC Athens joined an ill-fated rebellion against the Romans in Asia Minor staged by the king of the Black Sea region, Mithridates VI. In retribution, the Roman statesman Sulla invaded Athens and took off with its most valuable sculptures. Greece now became the Graeco-Roman province of Achaea. Although officially under the auspices of Rome, some major Greek cities were given the freedom to self-govern to some extent. As the Romans revered Greek culture, Athens retained its status as a centre of learning. During a succession of Roman emperors, namely Augustus, Nero and Hadrian, Greece experienced a period of relative peace, the Pax Romana, which was to last until the middle of the 3rd century AD.

The Byzantine Empire & the Crusades

The Pax Romana began to crumble in AD 250 when the Goths invaded Greece, the first of a succession of invaders spurred on by the 'great migrations' of the Visigoths and then the Ostrogoths from the middle Balkans.

In AD 324, in an effort to resolve conflict in the region, Roman Emperor Constantine I transferred the capital of the empire from Rome to Byzantium, a city on the western shore of the Bosphorus, which was renamed Constantinople (present-day İstanbul). While Rome went into terminal decline, the eastern capital began to grow in wealth and strength as a Christian state. In the ensuing centuries, Byzantine Greece faced continued pressure from the Persians and Arabs, but managed to retain its stronghold over the region.

It is ironic that the demise of the Byzantine Empire was accelerated by fellow Christians from the west – the Frankish Crusaders. The stated mission of the Crusades was to liberate the Holy Land from the Muslims, but in reality they were driven as much by greed as by religious zeal. The first three Crusades passed by without affecting the area, but the leaders of the Fourth Crusade (in the early part of the 13th century) decided that Constantinople presented richer pickings than Jerusalem and struck a deal with Venice, who had helped prop up the Crusades.

Constantinople was sacked in 1204 and much of the Byzantine Empire was partitioned into fiefdoms ruled by self-styled 'Latin' (mostly Frankish or western-Germanic) princes. The Venetians, meanwhile, had also

86 BC–AD 224	AD 63	324	394
Roman expansion includes Greek territory. First defeating Macedonia at Pydna in 168 BC, the Romans ultimately overtake the mainland and establish the Pax Romana. It lasts 300 years.	Christianity emerges after St Paul visits Crete and leaves his disciple, Titus, to convert the island. St Titus becomes Crete's first bishop.	The AD 250 invasion of Greece by the Goths signals the decline of the Pax Romana and in 324 the capital of the Roman Empire is moved to Byzantium (later renamed Constantinople). Christianity gains traction.	Christianity is declared the official religion. All pagan worship of Greek and Roman gods is outlawed. Christian theology supplants classical philosophy.

secured a foothold in Greece. Over the next few centuries they acquired all the key Greek ports, including Methoni, Koroni and Monemvasia in the Peloponnese (then known as the Morea), and the island of Crete, and became the wealthiest and most powerful traders in the Mediterranean.

Despite this sorry state of affairs, Byzantium was not yet dead. In 1259 the Byzantine Emperor Michael VIII Palaeologos recaptured the Peloponnese and made the city of Mystras his headquarters. Many eminent Byzantine artists, architects, intellectuals and philosophers converged on the city for a final burst of Byzantine creativity. Michael VIII managed to reclaim Constantinople in 1261, but by this time Byzantium was a shadow of its former self.

Ottoman Rule

Constantinople soon faced a much greater threat from the east. The Seljuk Turks, a tribe from central Asia, had first appeared on the eastern fringes of the empire in the middle of the 11th century. The Ottomans (the followers of Osman, who ruled from 1289–1326) supplanted the Seljuks as the dominant Turkish tribe. The Muslim Ottomans began to rapidly expand the areas under their control and by the mid-15th century were harassing the Byzantine Empire on all sides.

On 29 May 1453, Constantinople fell under Turkish Ottoman rule (referred to by Greeks as *turkokratia*). Once more Greece became a battleground, this time fought over by the Turks and Venetians. Eventually, with the exception of the Ionian Islands (where the Venetians retained control), Greece became part of the Ottoman Empire.

Ottoman power reached its zenith under Sultan Süleyman the Magnificent, who ruled from 1520–66. His successor, Selim the Sot, added Cyprus to their dominions in 1570, but his death in 1574 marked an end to serious territorial expansion. Although they captured Crete in 1669 after a 25-year campaign, the ineffectual sultans that followed in the late 16th and 17th centuries saw the empire go into steady decline.

Venice expelled the Turks from the Peloponnese in a three-year campaign (1685–87) that saw Venetian troops advance as far as Athens. During this campaign, Venetian artillery struck gunpowder stored inside the ruins of the Acropolis and badly damaged the Parthenon.

The Ottomans restored rule in 1715, but never regained their former authority. By the end of the 18th century, pockets of Turkish officials and aristocrats had emerged throughout Greece as self-governing cliques that made cursory gestures of obligation to the sultan in Constantinople. Also, some Greeks had gained influence under the sultan's lax leadership or enjoyed privileged administrative status; they were influential church clerics, wealthy merchants, landowners or governors, ruling over the provincial Greek peasants. But there also existed an ever-increasing group of Greeks, including many intellectual expatriates, who aspired to emancipation.

The Green Line separating Greece and Turkey in modern-day Cyprus is a ghost town, a desert of silence where the clock stopped in 1974. Greeks still peer through the barb-wire partition to the place they were born and banished from, and are unlikely to return to live.

529	1204	1453	1460
Athens' cultural influence is dealt a fatal blow when Emperor Justinian outlaws the teaching of classical philosophy in favour of Christian theology, by now regarded as the ultimate form of intellectual endeavour.	Marauding Frankish Crusaders sack Constantinople. Trading religious fervour for self-interest, the Crusaders strike a blow that sets Constantinople on the road to a slow demise.	Greece becomes a dominion of the Ottoman Turks after they seize control of Constantinople, sounding the death knell for the Byzantine Empire.	By 1460, the Venetian stronghold of Morea (Peloponnese) falls to the Turks and centuries of power struggles between the Turks and Venetians follow.

Independence

In 1814 businessmen Athanasios Tsakalof, Emmanuel Xanthos and Niko-laos Skoufas founded the first Greek independence party, the Filiki Eteria (Friendly Society). The underground organisation's message spread quick-ly. Supporters believed that armed force was the only effective means of lib-eration, and made generous financial contributions to the Greek fighters.

On 25 March 1821, the Greeks launched the War of Independence. Up-risings broke out almost simultaneously across most of Greece and the occupied islands. The fighting was savage and atrocities were committed on both sides; in the Peloponnese, 12,000 Turkish inhabitants were killed after the capture of the city of Tripolitsa (present-day Tripoli), while the Turks retaliated with massacres in Asia Minor, most notoriously on the island of Chios.

The campaign escalated, and within a year the Greeks had captured the fortresses of Monemvasia, Navarino (modern Pylos) and Nafplio in the Peloponnese, and Messolongi, Athens and Thebes. The Greeks pro-claimed independence on 13 January 1822 at Epidavros.

Regional differences over national governance escalated into civil war in 1824 and 1825. The Ottomans took advantage and by 1827 the Turks (with Egyptian reinforcements) had recaptured most of the Peloponnese, as well as Messolongi and Athens. The Western powers intervened and a combined Russian, French and British naval fleet sunk the Turkish-Egyptian fleet in the Battle of Navarino in October 1827. Sultan Mahmud II defied the odds and proclaimed a holy war, prompting Russia to send troops into the Balkans to engage the Ottoman army. Fighting continued until 1829 when, with Russian troops at the gates of Constantinople, the sultan accepted Greek independence with the Treaty of Adrianople. In-dependence was formally recognised in 1830.

The Modern Greek Nation

The Greeks, meanwhile, had been busy organising the independent state they had proclaimed several years earlier. In April 1827 the Greeks elect-ed Ioannis Kapodistrias, a Corfiot and former diplomat of Russian Tsar Alexander I, as the first president of the republic. Nafplio, in the Pelopon-nese, was chosen as the capital.

There was, however, much dissension within Greek ranks. Kapodistri-as was assassinated in 1831 after he had ordered the imprisonment of a Maniot chieftain, part of a response to undermine rising rebellion among the many parties whose authority had been weakened by the new state.

Amid the ensuing anarchy, Britain, France and Russia declared Greece a monarchy. They set on the throne a non-Greek, 17-year-old Bavarian Prince Otto, who arrived in Nafplio in January 1833. The new kingdom (established by the London Convention of 1832) consisted of the Pelo-ponnese, Sterea Ellada, the Cyclades and the Sporades.

Greece is home to the oldest mosque in Europe. The Bayezit's Mosque at Didymotiho was built by Ottoman Sultan Bayezit I in the late 14th century.

Eugène Delacroix' oil canvas *The Massacre at Chios* (1824) was inspired by the events in Asia Minor during Greece's War of Independence in 1821. The painting hangs in the Louvre Museum in Paris.

1541	1684–87	1770s & 1780s	1814
Dominikos Theot-okopoulos, later known as 'El Greco', is born in Candia; his subsequent creations in Italy and Spain are marked by both Cretan School influence and bold personal innovation.	The Venetians expel the Turks from the Pelo-ponnese in a campaign that sees Venetian troops advance as far as Athens.	Catherine the Great of Russia dislodges the Turks from the Black Sea coast and assigns several towns Ancient Greek names. She offers Greeks financial incentives and free land to settle the region.	The underground Hellenic Independence organisation known as the Filiki Eteria (Friendly Society) is established in the town of Odessa on the Black Sea coast. Its influence spreads throughout Greece.

After moving the capital to Athens in 1834, King Otto proved to be an abrasive ruler who had alienated the independence veterans by giving the most prestigious official posts to his Bavarian court. By the end of the 1850s, most of the stalwarts of the War of Independence had been replaced by a new breed of graduates from Athens University.

The Great Idea

Greece's foreign policy (dubbed the 'Great Idea') was to assert sovereignty over its dispersed Greek populations. Set against the background of the Crimean conflict, British and French interests were nervous at the prospect of a Greek alliance with Russia against the Ottomans, especially after 1862 when Otto was ousted in a bloodless coup.

British influence in the Ionian Islands had begun in 1815 (following a spell of political ping pong between the Venetians, Russians and French). The British did improve the islands' infrastructure and many locals adopted British customs (such as afternoon tea and cricket). But Greek independence put pressure on Britain to give sovereignty to the Greek nation, and in 1864 the British left. Meanwhile, Britain simultaneously eased on to the Greek throne the young Danish Prince William, crowned King George I in 1863. His 50-year reign eventually brought some stability to the country, beginning with a new constitution in 1864 that established the power of democratically elected representatives.

In 1881 Greece acquired Thessaly and part of Epiros as a result of a Russo-Turkish war. But Greece failed miserably when, in 1897, it tried to attack Turkey in the north in an effort to reach *enosis* (union) with Crete (who had persistently agitated for liberation from the Ottomans). The bid drained much of the country's resources and timely diplomatic intervention by the great powers prevented the Turkish army from taking Athens.

Crete was placed under international administration, but the government of the island was gradually handed over to the Greeks. In 1905 the president of the Cretan assembly, Eleftherios Venizelos, announced Crete's union with Greece, recognised by international law in 1913. Venizelos went on to become prime minister of Greece in 1910.

WWI & Smyrna

In March 1913 King George was assassinated and his son Constantine became the monarch. King Constantine, who was married to the sister of the German emperor, insisted that Greece remain neutral when WWI broke out in August 1914. As the war dragged on, the Allies (Britain, France and Russia) put increasing pressure on Greece to join forces with them against Germany and Turkey, promising concessions in Asia Minor in return. Prime Minister Venizelos favoured the Allied cause, placing him at loggerheads with the king. The king left Greece in June 1917, replaced by his second-born son, Alexander, who was more amenable to the Allies.

Poet Lord Byron was one of a large group of philhellenic volunteers who played an active role in fanning the Independence cause. Byron's war effort was cut short when he died in 1824.

1821	1822–29	1827–31	1833
On 25 March, Bishop Germanos of Patra (a member of the Filiki Eteria) signals the beginning of the War of Independence on the mainland. Greece celebrates this date as its national day of Independence.	Independence is declared at Epidavros on 13 January 1822, but fighting continues for another seven years. The Ottomans capitulate and accept the terms of the Treaty of Adrianople.	Ioannis Kapodistrias is appointed prime minister of a fledgling government with its capital in the Peloponnesian town of Nafplio. Discontent ensues and Kapodistrias is assassinated.	The powers of the Triple Entente (Britain, France and Russia) decree that Greece should be a monarchy and dispatch Prince Otto of Bavaria to Greece to be the first appointed monarch in modern Greece.

BALKAN WARS

Although the Ottoman Empire was in its death throes at the beginning of the 20th century, it had still retained Macedonia. This was a prize coveted by the newly formed Balkan countries of Serbia and Bulgaria, as well as by Greece, and led to the outbreak of the Balkan Wars (1912 and 1913). The outcome was the Treaty of Bucharest (August 1913), which greatly expanded Greek territory (and with it, its fertile agricultural resources). Its borders now took in the southern part of Macedonia, including Thessaloniki, the vital cultural centre strategically positioned on the Balkan trade routes; part of Thrace; another chunk of Epiros; and the northeastern Aegean Islands.

Greek troops served with distinction on the Allied side, but when the war ended in 1918 the promised land in Asia Minor was not forthcoming. Venizelos led a diplomatic campaign to further the case and, with Allied acquiescence, landed troops in Smyrna (present-day İzmir in Turkey) in May 1919, under the guise of protecting the half a million Greeks living in the city. With a seemingly viable hold in Asia Minor, Venizelos ordered his troops to march ahead, and by September 1921 they had advanced as far as Ankara. By this stage foreign support for Venizelos had ebbed and Turkish forces, commanded by Mustafa Kemal (later to become Atatürk), halted the offensive. The Greek army retreated but Smyrna fell in 1922, and tens of thousands of its Greek inhabitants were killed.

The outcome of these hostilities was the Treaty of Lausanne in July 1923, whereby Turkey recovered eastern Thrace and the islands of Imvros and Tenedos, while Italy kept the Dodecanese (which it had temporarily acquired in 1912 and would hold until 1947).

The treaty also called for a population exchange between Greece and Turkey to prevent future disputes. Almost 1.5 million Greeks left Turkey and almost 400,000 Turks left Greece. The exchange put tremendous strain on the Greek economy and caused great bitterness and hardship. Many Greeks abandoned a privileged life in Asia Minor for one of extreme poverty in emerging urban shanty towns in Athens and Thessaloniki.

The Republic of 1924–35

The arrival of the Greek refugees from Turkey coincided with, and compounded, a period of political instability unprecedented even by Greek standards. In 1920 King Alexander died from a monkey bite and his father Constantine was restored to the throne. But the ensuing political crisis deepened and Constantine abdicated (again) after the fall of Smyrna. He was replaced by his first son, George II, who was no match for the group of army officers who seized power after the war. A republic was proclaimed in March 1924 amid a series of coups and countercoups.

1862–63	1863–64	1883	1896
The monarchy takes a nosedive and King Otto is deposed in a bloodless coup. The British return the Ionian Islands (a British protectorate since 1815) to Greece in an effort to quell Greece's expansionist urges.	The British engineer the ascension to the Greek throne of Danish Prince William, later crowned King George I. His 50-year reign begins with a new constitution in 1864.	Greece completes construction of the Corinth Canal that cuts through the Isthmus of Corinth. The engineering feat opens a link between the Aegean and Ionian Seas.	The staging of the first modern Olympic Games in Athens marks Greece's coming of age. Winners receive a silver medal and olive crown, and second and third places receive a bronze medal and a laurel branch respectively.

A measure of stability was attained with Venizelos' return to power in 1928. He pursued a policy of economic and educational reform, but progress was inhibited by the Great Depression. His antiroyalist Liberal Party faced a growing challenge from the monarchist Popular Party, culminating in defeat at the polls in March 1933. The new government was preparing for the restoration of the monarchy when Venizelos and his supporters staged an unsuccessful coup in March 1935. Venizelos was exiled to Paris, where he died a year later. In November 1935 King George II reassumed the throne and installed the right-wing General Ioannis Metaxas as prime minister. Nine months later, Metaxas assumed dictatorial powers with the king's consent, under the pretext of preventing a communist-inspired republican coup.

> On 25 November 1942, a coalition of Greek resistance groups, aided by the British, blew up the Gorgopotamos railway bridge near Lamia in Sterea Ellada, sabotaging for weeks German supply routes through the country.

WWII

Metaxas' grandiose vision was to create a utopian Third Greek Civilisation, based on its glorious ancient and Byzantine past, but what he actually created was more like a Greek version of the Third Reich. He exiled or imprisoned opponents, banned trade unions and the recently established Kommounistiko Komma Elladas (KKE, the Greek Communist Party), imposed press censorship and created a secret police force and fascist-style youth movement. But Metaxas is best known for his reply of *ohi* (no) to Mussolini's ultimatum to allow Italians passage through Greece at the beginning of WWII, thus maintaining Greece's policy of strict neutrality. The Italians invaded Greece, but the Greeks drove them back into Albania.

A prerequisite of Hitler's plan to invade the Soviet Union was a secure southern flank in the Balkans. The British, realising this, asked Metaxas if they could land troops in Greece. He gave the same reply as he had given the Italians, but then died suddenly in January 1941. The king replaced him with the more timid Alexandros Koryzis, who agreed to British forces landing in Greece. Koryzis committed suicide when German troops invaded Greece on 6 April 1941. The Nazis vastly outnumbered the defending Greek, British, Australian and New Zealand troops, and the whole country was under Nazi occupation within a few weeks. The civilian population suffered appallingly during the occupation, many dying of starvation. The Nazis rounded up more than half the Jewish population and transported them to death camps.

> *Inside Hitler's Greece: the Experience of Occupation, 1941–44*, by Mark Mazower, is an intimate and comprehensive account of Greece under Nazi occupation and the rise of the resistance movement.

Numerous resistance movements sprang up. The dominant three were Ellinikos Laïkos Apeleftherotikos Stratos (ELAS), the left-wing Ethnikon Apeleftherotikon Metopon (EAM) and the right-wing Ethnikos Dimokratikos Ellinikos Syndesmos (EDES). These groups fought one another with as much venom as they fought the Germans, often with devastating results for the civilian Greek population.

The Germans began to retreat from Greece in October 1944, but the communist and monarchist resistance groups continued to fight one another.

1900	1912–13	1914	1919–23
Sir Arthur Evans begins excavations at Knossos, quickly unearthing the palace and stunning the archaeological world with the discovery of the advanced Minoan civilisation.	The Balkan Wars erupt when Greece and Serbia initially side with Bulgaria against Turkey over Macedonia. Then Greece and Serbia fight for the same territory against Bulgaria. Greece's territory expands.	The outbreak of WWI sees Greece initially neutral but eventually siding with the Western Allies against Germany and Turkey on the promise of land in Asia Minor.	Greece embarks on the 'Great Idea' to unite former Hellenic regions, including those in Asia Minor. It fails and leads to a population exchange between Greece and Turkey in 1923 (aka the Asia Minor catastrophe).

Civil War

By late 1944 the royalists, republicans and communists were polarised by interparty division and locked in a serious battle for control. The British-backed provisional government was in an untenable position: the left was threatening revolt while the British were pushing to prevent the communists from further legitimising their hold over the administration and vying to reinstate the Greek monarchy.

On 3 December 1944, the police fired on a communist demonstration in Plateia Syntagmatos (Syntagma Sq) in Athens, killing 28 people. The ensuing six weeks of fighting between the left and the right, known as the Dekemvriana (events of December), marked the first round of the Greek Civil War. British troops intervened and prevented an ELAS-EAM coalition victory.

In February 1945 formal negotiations for reconciliation between the government and the communists fell flat, and the friction continued. Many civilians on all political sides were subjected to bitter reprisals at the hands of leftist groups, the army or rogue right-wing vigilantes. The royalists won the March 1946 election (which the communists had unsuccessfully boycotted), and a plebiscite (widely reported as rigged) in September put George II back on the throne.

In October the left-wing Democratic Army of Greece (DSE) was formed to resume the fight against the monarchy and its British supporters. Under the leadership of Markos Vafiadis, the DSE swiftly occupied a large swath of land along Greece's northern border with Albania and Yugoslavia.

In 1947 the US intervened and the civil war developed into a setting for the new Cold War theatre. Communism was declared illegal and the government introduced its notorious Certificate of Political Reliability (remaining valid until 1962), which declared that the document bearer was not a left-wing sympathiser; without this certificate Greeks could not vote and found it almost impossible to get work. US aid did little to improve the situation on the ground. The DSE continued to be supplied from the north (by Yugoslavia, Bulgaria and indirectly by the Soviets through the Balkan states), and by the end of 1947, large chunks of the mainland were under its control as well as parts of the islands of Crete, Chios and Lesvos. The fighting dragged on until October 1949, when Yugoslavia fell out with the Soviet Union and cut the DSE's supply lines.

The civil war left Greece politically frayed and economically shattered. More Greeks had been killed in three years of bitter civil war than in WWII, and a quarter of a million people were homeless. The sense of despair became the trigger for a mass exodus. Almost a million Greeks headed off in search of a better life elsewhere, primarily to Australia, Canada and the US.

The bestseller *Eleni*, written by Nicholas Gage, tells the gripping personal account of his family's life in the village of Lia, and the events leading to the execution of Gage's mother by communist guerrillas during the Greek Civil War.

HISTORY THE MODERN GREEK NATION

1924–34	1935	1940	1941–44
Greece is proclaimed a republic and King George II leaves Greece. The Great Depression counters the nation's return to stability. Monarchists and parliamentarians under Eleftherios Venizelos tussle for control.	The monarchy is restored and King George II is reappointed to the throne. Right-wing General Ioannis Metaxas adopts the role of prime minister while introducing dictatorial measures of governance.	On 28 October Metaxas famously rebuffs the Italian request to traverse Greece at the beginning of WWII. The Italians engage Greek forces and are driven back into Albania.	Germany invades and occupies Greece. Monarchists, republicans and communists form resistance groups that, despite infighting, drive out the Germans after three years.

Reconstruction

After a series of unworkable coalitions, the electoral system was changed to majority voting in 1952 – which excluded the communists from future governments. The November 1952 election was a victory for the right-wing Ellinikos Synagermos (Greek Rally). The leader, General Alexander Papagos (a former civil-war field marshal), remained in power until his death in 1955, when he was replaced by Konstantinos Karamanlis.

Greece joined NATO in 1952, and in 1953 the US was granted the right to operate sovereign bases. Intent on maintaining support for the anticommunist government, the US gave generous economic and military aid.

In 1958 Georgios Papandreou founded the broadly based Centre Union (EK), but elections in 1961 returned the National Radical Union (ERE), Karamanlis' new name for Greek Rally, to power for the third time in succession. Papandreou accused the ERE of ballot rigging, and the political turmoil that followed culminated in the murder, in May 1963, of Grigoris Lambrakis, the deputy of the communist Union of the Democratic Left (EDA). All this proved too much for Karamanlis, who resigned and went to live in Paris.

The EK finally came to power in February 1964 and Papandreou wasted no time in implementing a series of radical changes. He freed political prisoners and allowed exiles to come back to Greece, reduced income tax and the defence budget, and increased spending on social services and education.

Prince Philip, Duke of Edinburgh, was part of the Greek royal family – born on Corfu as Prince Philip of Greece and Denmark in 1921. Former king of Greece, Constantine, is Prince William's godfather and Prince Charles' third cousin. Constantine and his family were exiled in London for 46 years, returning to Athens in 2013.

Colonels, Monarchs & Democracy

The political right in Greece was rattled by Papandreou's tolerance of the left, and a group of army colonels, led by Georgios Papadopoulos and Stylianos Patakos, staged a coup on 21 April 1967. They established a military junta with Papadopoulos as prime minister. King Constantine tried an unsuccessful countercoup in December, after which he fled to Rome, then London.

The colonels declared martial law, banned political parties and trade unions, imposed censorship and imprisoned, tortured and exiled thousands of dissidents. In June 1972 Papadopoulos declared Greece a republic and appointed himself president.

On 17 November 1973, tanks stormed a building at the Athens Polytechnio (Technical University) to quell a student occupation calling for an uprising against the US-backed junta. While the number of casualties is still in dispute (more than 20 students were reportedly killed and hundreds injured), the act spelled the death knell for the junta.

The junta dictatorship collapsed. Karamanlis was summoned from Paris to take office and his New Democracy (ND) party won a large

The 1963 political assassination of Grigoris Lambrakis is described in Vassilis Vassilikos' novel *Z*, which later became an award-winning film.

1944–49	1967–74	1974	1981
The end of WWII sees Greece descend into civil war, pitching monarchists against communists. The monarchists recover in 1946, but the civil war takes its toll and many Greeks emigrate in search of a better life.	Right- and left-wing factions continue to bicker, provoking in April 1967 a right-wing military coup d'état by army generals who establish a junta. They impose martial law and abolish many civil rights.	A botched plan to unite Cyprus with Greece prompts the invasion of Cyprus by Turkish troops and results in the fall of the military junta. This acts as a catalyst for the restoration of parliamentary democracy in Greece.	Greece joins the EU, effectively removing protective trade barriers and opening up the Greek economy to the wider world for the first time. The economy grows smartly.

majority at the November elections in 1974, against the newly formed Panhellenic Socialist Union (PASOK), led by Andreas Papandreou (son of Georgios). A plebiscite voted 69% against the restoration of the monarchy and the ban on communist parties was lifted.

The 1980s & 1990s

When Greece became the 10th member of the EU in 1981, it was the smallest and poorest member. In October 1981 Andreas Papandreou's PASOK party was elected as Greece's first socialist government. PASOK ruled for almost two decades (minus 1990–93). PASOK promised ambitious social reform, to close the US air bases and to withdraw from NATO. US military presence was reduced, but unemployment was high and reforms in education and welfare were limited. Women's issues fared better: the dowry system was abolished, abortion legalised, and civil marriage and divorce were implemented.

Economic scandal, a series of general strikes and fundamental policy wrangling over the country's education system damaged PASOK, and in 1990 Konstandinos Mitsotakis led the ND back to office. Intent on redressing the country's economic problems – high inflation and high government spending – the government imposed austerity measures, including a wage freeze for civil servants and steep increases in public-utility costs and basic services.

By late 1992, corruption allegations were being levelled against the government. By mid-1993 Mitsotakis supporters had abandoned the ND for the new Political Spring party; the ND lost its parliamentary majority and an early election in October returned Andreas Papandreou's PASOK party.

Papandreou stepped down in early 1996 due to ill health and died on 26 June. His departure produced a dramatic change of direction for PASOK, with the party abandoning Papandreou's left-leaning politics and electing experienced economist and lawyer Costas Simitis as the new prime minister, who won a comfortable majority at the October 1996 polls.

The 21st Century

The new millennium saw Greece join the eurozone in 2001, amid rumblings from existing members that it was not economically ready – its public borrowing was too high, as was its inflation level. In hindsight, many look back on that year and bemoan the miscalibration of the drachma against the euro, claiming Greece's currency was undervalued, and that, overnight, living became disproportionately more expensive. That said, billions of euros poured into large-scale infrastructure projects across Greece, including the redevelopment of Athens – spurred on largely by its hosting of the 2004 Olympic Games. However, rising unemployment,

1981–90	1999	2001	2004
Greece acquires its first elected socialist government (PASOK) under the leadership of Andreas Papandreou. The honeymoon lasts nine years. The conservatives ultimately reassume power.	Turkey and Greece experience powerful earthquakes within weeks of each other that result in hundreds of deaths. By pledging mutual aid and support, the two nations initiate a warming of diplomatic relations.	Greece adopts the euro, joining the first wave of European countries to introduce the new currency on 1 January 2002.	Greece successfully hosts the 28th Summer Olympic Games amid much muffled rumour that infrastructure would not be complete in time. Greece also wins the European football championship.

ballooning public debt, slowing inflation and the squeezing of consumer credit took their toll. Public opinion soured further in 2007 when the conservative government (who had come to power in 2004) was widely criticised for its handling of severe summer fires, responsible for widespread destruction throughout Greece. Nevertheless, snap elections held in September 2007 returned the conservatives, albeit with a diminished majority.

In the following years, a series of massive general strikes and blockades highlighted mounting electoral discontent. The backlash against the government reached boiling point in December 2008, when urban rioting broke out across the country, led by youths outraged by the police shooting of a 15-year-old boy in Athens following an alleged exchange between police and a group of teenagers. Concern continued over political tangles in investigations regarding alleged corruption among state executives (on both sides of the political fence) in connection with the Siemens Hellas group. This followed another controversy that involved land-swap deals between a monastery and the government, which some commentators believe to have gone heavily in the monastery's favour, at the expense of taxpayers. A general election held in October 2009, midway through Karamanlis' term, saw PASOK (under Georgios Papandreou) take back the reins in a landslide win against the conservatives.

Sink or Swim

In 2009 a lethal cocktail of high public spending and widespread tax evasion, combined with the credit crunch of global recession, threatened to cripple Greece's economy. In 2010 Greece's fellow eurozone countries agreed to a €125-billion package (half of Greece's GDP) to get the country back on its feet, though with strict conditions: the ruling government, PASOK, still lead by Georgios Papandreou, would have to impose austere measures of reform. Huge cuts followed, including 10% off public workers' salaries, but it was too little too late and foreign creditors continued to demand ever-higher interest rates for their loans.

Greece was stuck between a real-life Scylla and Charybdis – to receive yet another bailout, which was absolutely essential to stop them toppling the euro as a credible currency, they had to effect reforms that penalised the average Greek even further, pushing formerly nonpolitical citizens towards revolution.

Georgios Papandreou asked the people for a referendum on the EU bailout, then failed to form a coalition government and stepped down from office. In November 2011 Lucas Papademos – a former vice-president of the European Central Bank – became prime minister. Antonis

Greek is Europe's oldest written language, second only to Chinese in the world. It is traceable back to the Linear B script of the Minoans and Mycenaeans. For more on Linear B script, visit www.ancientscripts.com/linearb.html.

The web portal www.ancientgreece.com is great for all things ancient and Greek. Want to check out a family tree of the ancient Greek gods, read all about the first Olympics or exactly who Archimedes was? It's all there.

2007	2009	2011	2012
Vast forest fires devastate much of the western Peloponnese as well as parts of Evia and Epiros, causing Greece's worst ecological disaster in decades. Thousands lose their homes and 66 people perish.	Eurozone countries approve a €110-billion rescue package for the country's economic crisis, in exchange for tougher austerity laws.	Protesters march on parliament to oppose government efforts to pass new austerity laws. Prime Minister Papandreou resigns and a coalition government is formed by Antonis Samaras of the New Democracy party.	Parliament passes a €13.5-billion austerity plan to secure a second €130-billion EU and IMF bailout. Cuts include 22% off minimum wage, 15% off pensions, 15,000 public-sector jobs. The bailout would expire 30 June 2015.

Samaras, leader of the New Democracy party, succeeded him the following year and assembled a coalition with third-placed PASOK and smaller groups to pursue the austerity program. A second bailout of €130 billion brought further austerity requirements and Athens again saw major strikes aimed at the massive cuts – 22% off minimum wage, 15% off pensions and the axing of 15,000 public-sector jobs. Suicide rates in the capital were up by 40%. Also up was support for the far-right fascist organisation, the Golden Dawn, bringing with them a rising tide of racism aimed squarely at Greece's immigrant population.

These were indeed brutal times for the average Greek, with wage cuts of around 30% and up to 17 'new' taxes crippling monthly income. While the EU and IMF initially predicted that Greece would return to growth in 2014, the inability of many Greeks to pay their taxes at the end of the year meant that growth was a mere 0.4%. In January 2015 the New Democrat party lost at the polls to left-wing Syriza. The new Prime Minister, 40-year-old Alexis Tsipras, won the election with an antiausterity platform.

This was the first-ever election win for radical left-wing Syriza. To reach a majority, Syriza established a coalition with right-wing Independent Greeks (ANEL), unlikely bedfellows united by their mutual condemnation of the bailout program.

Initially, Tsipras stuck to his guns and June 2015 saw Greece become the first first-world nation to go into arrears with the EU and IMF. Attempts to negotiate a new bailout and avoid default were unsuccessful as Tsipras took the offer back to Greece and held a referendum. Over 61% of voters were not willing to accept the bailout conditions.

The week that followed was one of turmoil. Greek banks closed and began running out of cash, and markets around the world fell as the EU produced a detailed plan for a possible Grexit – Greece's removal from the EU.

At the 11th hour, Tsipras secured an €86-billion bailout loan – but the austerity measures attached were even more vigorous than those proposed before the referendum and many felt that, with Greek banks on the brink of collapse, Tsipras had been bullied into accepting the terms.

Dissent within Syriza and ANEL, brought on by hardliners opposed to the bailout, led Tsipras to resign in August 2015 and return to the polls in September. This was Greece's fourth election in just over three years. The outcome was an unexpectedly large victory for Tsipras, just six seats short of an absolute majority. Nevertheless, voter turnout was 57%, the lowest recorded in Greece. For many Greeks, choosing between the austerity measures and Grexit had become akin to rearranging deck chairs on the Titanic.

In June 2013 the 70-year-old Hellenic Broadcasting Corp (ERT) was closed in government cost-cutting attempts to axe 2500 workers due to demands by creditors. Journalist unions staged a 24-hour strike in solidarity, creating a nationwide news blackout. It was reopened six days later, following intervention by Greece's high court.

2013	2015	2016	2017
Unemployment rises to 26.8% – the highest rate in the EU. Youth unemployment climbs to almost 60%.	Greece defaults on its bailout loans and is threatened with Grexit – removal from the eurozone.	A deal between the EU and Turkey closes European borders to refugees arriving in Greece, effectively trapping them in Greece or returning them to Turkey.	Number of refugees in Greece reaches 62,000 (over half of them women and children), mainly from Syria, Afghanistan and Iraq.

Ancient Greek Culture

When the Roman Empire assimilated Greece it did so with considerable respect and idealism. The Romans in many ways based themselves on the Ancient Greeks, absorbing their deities (and renaming them), literature, myths, philosophy, fine arts and architecture. So what made the Ancient Greeks so special? From thespians to philosophers, from monster-slewing heroes to agoddess born of sea foam, the Ancient Greeks were captivating.

The Golden Age

Two of Socrates' most famous quotes are: 'The only true wisdom consists of knowing that you know nothing' and 'The unexamined life is not worth living'.

In the 5th century BC, Athens had a cultural renaissance that has never been equalled – in fact, such was the diversity of its achievements that modern classical scholars refer to it as 'the miracle'. The era started with a vastly outnumbered Greek army defeating the Persian horde in the battles of Marathon and Salamis, and ended with the beginning of the inevitable war between Athens and Sparta. It's often said that Athens' 'Golden Age' is the bedrock of Western civilisation, and had the Persians won, Europe today would have been a vastly different place. Like Paris in the 1930s, Athens was a hotbed of talent. Any artist or writer worth their salt left their hometown and travelled to the great city of wisdom to share their thoughts and hear the great minds of the day express themselves.

Drama

The great dramatists such as Aeschylus, Aristophanes, Euripides and Sophocles redefined theatre from religious ritual to become a compelling form of entertainment. They were to be found at the Theatre of Dionysos at the foot of the Acropolis, and their comedies and tragedies reveal a great deal about the psyche of the Ancient Greeks.

Across the country, large open-air theatres were built on the sides of hills, designed to accommodate plays with increasingly sophisticated backdrops and props, choruses and themes, and to maximise sound so that even the people in the back row might hear the actors on stage. The dominant genres of theatre were tragedy and comedy. The first known actor was a man called Thespis, from whose name we derive the word 'thespian'.

Philosophy

The World of the Ancient Greeks (2002), by archaeologists John Camp and Elizabeth Fisher, is a broad and in-depth look at how the Greeks have left their imprint on politics, philosophy, theatre, art, medicine and architecture.

While the dramatists were cutting their thespian cloth, late-5th and early-4th-century-BC philosophers Aristotle, Plato and Socrates were introducing new trains of thought rooted in rationality, as the new Greek mind focused on logic and reason. Athens' greatest, most noble citizen, Socrates (469–399 BC), was forced to drink hemlock for allegedly corrupting the youth by asking probing, uncomfortable questions, but before he died he left behind a school of hypothetical reductionism that is still used today.

Plato (427–347 BC), Socrates' star student, was responsible for documenting his teacher's thoughts, and without his work in books such as the *Symposium,* they would have been lost to us. Considered an idealist,

Plato wrote *The Republic* as a warning to the city-state of Athens that unless its people respected law and leadership, and educated its youth sufficiently, it would be doomed.

Plato's student Aristotle (384–322 BC), at the end of the Golden Age, focused his gifts on astronomy, physics, zoology, ethics and politics. Aristotle was also the personal physician to Philip II, King of Macedon, and the tutor of Alexander the Great. The greatest gift of the Athenian philosophers to modern-day thought is their spirit of rational inquiry.

Sculpture

Classical sculpture began to gather pace in Greece in the 6th century BC with the renderings of nudes in marble. Most statues were created to revere a particular god or goddess and many were robed in grandiose garments. The statues of the preceding Archaic period, known as *kouroi,* had focused on symmetry and form, but in the early 5th century BC artists sought to create expression and animation. As temples demanded elaborate carvings, sculptors were called upon to create large reliefs upon them.

During the 5th century BC, the craft became yet more sophisticated, as sculptors were taught to successfully map a face and create a likeness of their subject in marble busts. Perhaps the most famous Greek sculptor was Pheidias, whose reliefs upon the Parthenon depicting the Greek and Persian Wars – now known as the Parthenon Marbles – are celebrated as among the finest of the Golden Age.

No original works by the celebrated classical sculptor Pheidias survive, though copies were made by Roman sculptors. Pheidias' colossal chryselephantine (gold and ivory) statue of Zeus was one of the Wonders of the Ancient World.

The Heroes

Some of the greatest stories of all time – and some say the wellspring of story itself – are to be found in the Greek myths. For many of us, the fantastical stories of Heracles and Odysseus we heard as kids still linger in our imagination, and contemporary writers continue to reinterpret these stories and characters for books and films. Standing in the ancient ruins of an acropolis and peering across the watery horizon, it's not difficult to picture the Kraken (Poseidon's pet monster) rising from the Aegean, nor to imagine that fishing boat you see heading into the sunset as Jason's Argo en route to Colchis for the Golden Fleece.

The average Greek is fiercely proud of their myths and will love entertaining you with a list of the gods, but they'll love it even more if you know a few of them yourself.

ISLANDS IN MYTHOLOGY

Greece is steeped in mythology and its many islands provided dramatic settings for its legends and interactions between gods and mortals.

Myrina, Lemnos Believed to have been founded by Myrina, queen of the Amazons.

Crete Zeus' mother allegedly gave birth to him in a cave to prevent him from being eaten by his father, Cronos. Crete was also home of the dreaded minotaur.

Lesvos When Orpheus was killed and dismembered by the Maenads, the waves brought his head here and it was buried near Antissa.

Kythira Aphrodite is said to have been born out of the waves surrounding Kythira.

Delos This island rose up from the waves when the goddess Leto was looking for a place to give birth to Apollo and Artemis.

Mykonos Zeus and the Titans battled it out on this island and Hercules slew the Giants here.

Rhodes The island given to Helios the sun god after Zeus' victory over the Giants.

Theseus

The Athenian hero volunteered himself as one of seven men and maidens in the annual sacrifice to the Minotaur, the crazed half-bull, half-man offspring of King Minos of Crete. Once inside its forbidding labyrinth (from which none had returned), Theseus, aided by Princess Ariadne (who had a crush on him induced by Aphrodite's dart), loosened a spool of thread to find his way out once he'd killed the monster.

Icarus

Along with Daedalus (his father), Icarus flew off the cliffs of Crete pursued by King Minos and his troops, using wings made of feathers and wax. His father instructed him to fly away from the midday sun, but Icarus became carried away with the exhilaration of flying...the wax melted, the feathers separated and the bird-boy fell to his death.

Perseus

Perseus' impossible task was to kill the gorgon, Medusa. With a head of snakes Medusa could turn a man to stone with a single glance. Armed with an invisibility cap and a pair of flying sandals from Hermes, Perseus used his reflective shield to avoid Medusa's stare. He cut off her head and secreted it in a bag, but it was shortly unsheathed to save Andromeda, a princess bound to a rock and about to be sacrificed to a sea monster. Medusa's head turned the sea monster to stone and Perseus got the girl.

Oedipus

Oedipus was the Ancient Greeks' gift to the Freudian school of psychology. Having been abandoned at birth, Oedipus learned from the Delphic oracle that he would one day slay his father and marry his mother. On the journey back to his birthplace, Thiva (Thebes), he killed a rude stranger and then discovered the city was plagued by a murderous Sphinx (a winged lion with a woman's head). The creature gave unsuspecting travellers and citizens a riddle: if they couldn't answer it, they were dashed on the rocks. Oedipus succeeded in solving the riddle, felled the Sphinx and so gained the queen of Thiva's hand in marriage. On discovering the stranger he'd killed was his father and that his new wife was in fact his mother, Oedipus ripped out his eyes and exiled himself.

Mythology

Ancient Greece revolved around careful worship of 12 central gods and goddesses, all of whom played a major role in the *mythos* (mythology), and none of whom can be commended for their behaviour. They frequently displayed pettiness, spitefulness, outright cruelty and low self-esteem that led to unworthy competitions with mortals which were always rigged in the gods' favour. Each city-state had its own patron god or goddess to appease and flatter, while on a personal level a farmer might make sacrifice to the goddess Demeter to bless his crops, or a fisherman to Poseidon to bring him fish and safe passage on the waves.

The Ancient Pantheon

Here's a quick guide to the 12 central gods and goddesses of Greek mythology – their Roman names are in brackets.

➡ **Zeus (Jupiter)** The fire-bolt-flinging king of the gods, ruler of Mt Olympus, lord of the skies and master of disguise in pursuit of mortal maidens. Wardrobe includes shower of gold, bull, eagle and swan.

Marcel Camus' film *Black Orpheus* (1959) won an Oscar for its reimagining of the Orpheus and Eurydice tale, set in a favela in 1950s Brazil to a bossa nova soundtrack. The lovers flee a hitman and Orfeu's vindictive fiancée.

The Greek tragedy *Medea*, by Euripides, is about the sun god Helios' granddaughter who takes revenge on her husband by killing her children and finds new life in the dark. It was turned into a fatalistic namesake film (1988) by Lars von Trier.

TOP FIVE MYTHICAL CREATURES

Of the grotesque and fantastical creatures whose stories are dear to Greek hearts, these five are the most notorious.

Medusa The snake-headed one punished by the gods for her inflated vanity. Even dead, her blood is lethal.

Cyclops A one-eyed giant. Odysseus and his crew were trapped in the cave of one such cyclops, Polyphemus.

Cerberus The three-headed dog of hell, he guards the entrance to the underworld – under his watch no one gets in or out.

Minotaur This half-man, half-bull mutant leads a life of existential angst in the abysmal labyrinth, tempered only by the occasional morsel of human flesh.

Hydra Cut one of its nine heads off and another two will grow in its place. Heracles solved the problem by cauterising each stump with his burning brand.

➡ **Hera (Juno)** Protector of women and family, the queen of heaven is both the embattled wife and sister of Zeus. She was the prototype of the jealous, domineering wife who took revenge on Zeus' illegitimate children.

➡ **Poseidon (Neptune)** God of the seas, master of the mists and younger brother of Zeus. He dwelt in a glittering underwater palace.

➡ **Hades (Pluto)** God of death and also brother of Zeus, he ruled the underworld, bringing in the newly dead with the help of his skeletal ferryman, Charon. Serious offenders were sent for torture in Tartarus, while heroes enjoyed eternal R&R in the Elysian Fields.

➡ **Athena (Minerva)** Goddess of wisdom, war, science and guardian of Athens, born in full armour out of Zeus' forehead. The antithesis of Ares, Athena was deliberate and, where possible, diplomatic in the art of war. Heracles, Jason (of Jason and the Argonauts fame) and Perseus all benefited from her patronage.

➡ **Aphrodite (Venus)** Goddess of love and beauty who was said to have been born of sea foam. When she wasn't cuckolding her husband, Hephaestus, she and her cherubic son Eros (Cupid) were enflaming hearts and causing trouble (cue the Trojan War).

➡ **Apollo** God of music, the arts and fortune-telling, Apollo was also the god of light and an expert shot with a bow and arrow. It was his steady hand which guided Paris' arrow towards Achilles' only weak spot – his heel – thus killing him.

➡ **Artemis (Diana)** The goddess of the hunt and twin sister of Apollo was, ironically, patron saint of wild animals. By turns spiteful and magnanimous, she was closely associated with the sinister Hecate, patroness of witchcraft.

➡ **Ares (Mars)** God of war, bloodthirsty and lacking control. Zeus' least favourite of his progeny. Not surprisingly, Ares was worshipped by the bellicose Spartans.

➡ **Hermes (Mercury)** Messenger of the gods, patron saint of travellers and the handsome one with a winged hat and sandals. He was always on hand to smooth over the affairs of Zeus, his father.

➡ **Hephaestus (Vulcan)** God of craftsmanship, metallurgy and fire, this deformed and oft-derided son of Zeus made the world's first woman of clay, Pandora, as a punishment for man. Inside her box were the evils of mankind.

➡ **Hestia (Vesta)** Goddess of the hearth, she protected state fires in city halls from where citizens of Greece could light their brands. She remained unmarried, inviolate.

From the Greek stories of Oedipus and the castration of Uranus by Cronos, Sigmund Freud drew the conclusion that myths often reflect strong, taboo desires that are otherwise unable to be expressed in society.

The Greek Way of Life

Visitors may be forgiven for wondering about the state of the nation when they see Athens' bustling cafes and what appears to be business as usual on the Greek islands. The Greek way of life took a major hit as austerity measures further sunk the country into recession, but it's not in the Greeks' nature to retreat into the gloom.

National Psyche

Showing solidarity in the face of austerity, enterprising locals in Volos have developed an alternative currency unit to the euro (the TEM), establishing a novel informal bartering system for goods and services, where participants exchange anything from olive oil to car repairs.

Greeks have always shared good and bad times in the company of family and friends; they've danced when sad or defiant and sought solace in their country's rich culture and simple pleasures. Someone will always buy an unemployed youth a coffee, or their *yiayia* (grandmother) will give them *hatziliki* (pocket money) from her shrunken pension.

Greek values and the national character have come under attack during the crisis – with Greeks universally characterised as lazy, leisure-loving, corrupt tax-evaders recklessly bringing Europe to the brink of economic collapse. The realities are far more complex – for every 'lazy' Greek there are hard-working people juggling two jobs to provide for their families.

Greeks pride themselves on their *filotimo*, a hard-to-translate Greek concept that underpins society's cultural norms. It encompasses personal and family honour, respect and loyalty to parents and grandparents, sacrifice and help for friends and strangers alike, pride in country and heritage, and gratitude and hospitality. Though some would argue it has been eroded, the concept remains an important part of Greek identity.

The Greeks also generously extend their *filoxenia* (hospitality). Despite the current fiscal problems, the average Greek will still lavish you with free drinks, fresh cake from their kitchen and the warmth they have always been famous for. Curious by nature, as well as passionate, loyal and fiery, Greeks engage in animated personal and political discussions rather than polite small talk. Nothing is off limits for conversation, and you may find yourself quizzed as to why you don't have children, why you're not married and how much you earn. They can be fervently

SPORTING PASSIONS

If the streets are quiet, you can't get a taxi or you hear a mighty roar coming from nearby cafes, chances are there's a football (soccer) game underway. Greece's most popular spectator sport inspires local passions and often unedifying fan hooliganism.

Football's first division is dominated by the big clubs: Olympiakos of Piraeus and arch-rivals Panathinaikos of Athens, along with AEK Athens and Thessaloniki's PAOK.

While the top clubs have won European championships, Greece has remained in the shadow of Europe's soccer heavyweights since its 2004 European Cup win.

Greece is also one of the powerhouses of European basketball. Panathinaikos has won six Euroleague championships, while Olympiakos claimed its third title in 2013. Nigerian-born Greek basketballer Giannis Antetokounmpo became the poster boy for Greece's immigrants in 2013 when he was picked for the Milwaukee Bucks in the NBA draft (having had his Greek citizenship fast-tracked).

patriotic, nationalistic and ethnocentric. Issues are debated with strong will. Greeks are unashamed about staring and blatantly observing (and commenting on) the comings and goings of people around them. They prefer spontaneity to making plans and are notoriously unpunctual (turning up on time is referred to as 'being English').

Today's Greeks cherish the achievements of their ancient forbears, and so they should. Without the Golden Age of Ancient Greece (about 500–300 BC) the world would arguably not have developed its classical sculpture, mathematics, geometry, philosophy, democracy, drama and politics. Not to mention the rich tapestry that Greek myths brought to the well of story and imagination. Show just a little appreciation of this to the average Greek and they will love you for it.

Social & Family Life

Greek life has always taken place in the public sphere, whether it's men talking politics at the local *kafeneio* (coffee house) or the elderly gathering in neighbourhood squares while their grandchildren play into the evening. While entertainment spending has been seriously curtailed, the gregarious Greeks nonetheless enjoy a vibrant social and cultural life and infamously lively nightlife.

Rather than living to work, Greeks work to live. People of all ages take their afternoon *volta* (outing) along seafront promenades or town centres, dressed up and refreshed from a siesta (albeit a dying institution). On weekends they flock to the beach and seaside tavernas, and summer holidays are the highlight of the year – traditionally, the capital virtually shuts down mid-August as people take off for the islands, beach towns or their ancestral villages. A peculiarly Greek social talking point is how many swims you've had that summer.

Greek society remains dominated by the family, and while many men may appear soaked with machismo, the matriarchal domestic model is still very much commonplace, with women subtly pulling the strings in the background. These strong family ties and kinship are helping Greeks survive testing times. Greece's weak welfare system means Greeks rely on families and social groups for support. Most Greek businesses are small, family-run operations and parents strive to provide homes for their children when they get married. Greeks rarely move out of home before they marry, unless they go to university or work in another city. While this was changing among professionals and people marrying later, low wages and rising unemployment have forced many young people to stay – or return – home.

Greeks retain strong regional identities and ties to their ancestral villages. Even the country's most remote villages are bustling during holidays. Greece's large diaspora plays a significant role in the life of many islands and villages, returning each summer in droves.

The State

Personal freedom and the right to protest and protect their democratic rights are sacrosanct to Greeks. Trade-union activism, mass demonstrations and crippling general strikes are a routine part of life in Athens and other major cities, with police and property normally bearing the brunt of antiestablishment sentiment. This rebellious spirit came to the fore during antiausterity protests, as Greeks resisted economic reforms crucial to help curb Greece's soaring national debt.

The nation's capacity to overcome its economic woes has been stifled by systemic problems with Greece's political and civil life, aspects of society that Greeks have long criticised and perpetuated. A residual mistrust of the state and its institutions is a legacy of years of foreign occupation, while political instability fostered a weak civil society based

Best Blogs

Greece Is (*www. greece-is.com*) Nearly daily blogs on top beaches, wineries, sights, activities...virtually everything under the Greek sun.

Greece by a Greek (*www. greecebyagreek. com*) Regular blogs about local customs, culture and traditions.

Life Beyond Borders (*www. lifebeyond bordersblog.com*) The experiences and insight of a travel writer who gave up her nine-to-five life and moved to Greece.

Debunking the myth of the lazy Greek, Organisation for Economic Cooperation and Development (OECD) research suggests Greeks actually work longer hours than their European and US counterparts, though they have lower productivity and labour-participation rates. Greek wages are among Europe's lowest and living costs among the highest.

THE NEW GREEKS

Greece has long been a magnet for foreigners seeking an idyllic island lifestyle and an escape from the rat race. Apart from those owning holiday houses, the small resident population of disparate *xenoi* (foreigners) have largely been somewhat-eccentric or retired Europeans, ex-hippies and artists or people married to locals. In recent years there has also been a steady stream of Americans, Australians and others with Greek heritage returning to their ancestral islands.

The Greek year revolves around saints' days and festivals of the Orthodox Church calendar. Easter is bigger than Christmas, and name days (celebrating your namesake saint) are more important than birthdays. Most people are named after a saint, as are boats, suburbs and train stations.

on tax evasion, political patronage and nepotism, and a black-market economy. Merit has long taken second place to political interests when allocating coveted public-sector jobs or EU funds. Making headway with Greece's bloated and inefficient bureaucracy required *meson* (the help of someone working in the system). The infamous *fakelaki* (envelope of cash) became a common way to cut red tape. At its worst, the system fed corruption and profiteering.

Aversion to the perceived over-regulated approach of Western nations is also part of the national psyche. An undercurrent of civil disobedience extends to lax attitudes to road rules or parking restrictions (you will see motorcyclists carrying their helmets as they chat on their mobile phones).

Faith & Identity

Families flock to church for lively Easter celebrations, weddings, baptisms and annual festivals, but it's largely women and the elderly who attend church services regularly. While most Greeks aren't devout, the Orthodox faith – the official religion of Greece – remains an important part of their identity and culture.

Religious rituals are part of daily life. You will notice taxi drivers, motorcyclists and people on public transport making the sign of the cross when they pass a church; compliments to babies and adults are followed by the *'ftou ftou'* (spitting) gesture to ward off the evil eye; and people light church candles in memory of loved ones. Hundreds of privately built small chapels dot the countryside, while the tiny roadside *iconostases* (chapels) are either shrines to road-accident victims or dedications to saints.

During consecutive foreign occupations the Church was the principal upholder of Greek culture, language and traditions, and it still exerts significant social, political and economic influence, though recent scandals have taken their toll.

The word *xenos* means both 'stranger' and 'guest', and Greeks see *filoxenia* (hospitality, welcome, shelter) almost as a duty and matter of personal pride and honour.

The Arts

Greece is revered for its artistic and cultural legacy, and the arts remain a vibrant and evolving element of Greek culture, identity and self-expression. Despite, or because of, Greece's current economic woes, it has seen a palpable burst of artistic activity and creativity. While savage cuts in meagre state-arts funding have some sectors reeling, an alternative cultural scene is fighting back with low-budget films, artist collectives, and small underground theatres and galleries popping up in the capital.

Modern Greek Art

Until the start of the 19th century, the primary art form in Greece was Byzantine religious painting. There was little artistic output under Ottoman rule, during which Greece essentially missed the Renaissance.

Byzantine church frescoes and icons depicted scenes from the life of Christ and figures of the saints. The 'Cretan school' of icon painting, influenced by the Italian Renaissance and artists fleeing to Crete after the fall of Constantinople, combined technical brilliance and dramatic richness. Cretan-born Renaissance painter El Greco ('The Greek' in Spanish), née Dominikos Theotokopoulos, got his grounding in the tradition of late-Byzantine fresco painting before moving to Spain in 1577.

Modern Greek art per se evolved after Independence, when painting became more secular, focusing on portraits, nautical themes and the War of Independence. Major 19th-century painters included Dionysios Tsokos, Theodoros Vryzakis, Nikiforos Lytras and Nicholas Gyzis, a leading artist of the Munich School (where many Greek artists of the day studied).

Early-20th-century artists such as Konstantinos Parthenis, Fotis Kontoglou, Konstantinos Kaleas and, later, the expressionist George Bouzianis, drew on their heritage and incorporated developments in modern art.

Leading 20th-century artists include cubist Nikos Hatzikyriakos-Ghikas, surrealist artist and poet Nikos Engonopoulos, Yiannis Tsarouhis, Panayiotis Tetsis, Yannis Moralis, Dimitris Mytaras and pioneer of the Arte Povera movement, Yiannis Kounellis.

The Athens National Gallery has the most extensive collection of Greek 20th-century art, with significant collections at the New Art Gallery on Rhodes and the Museum of Contemporary Art on Andros.

Modern and contemporary sculpture is shown at the National Sculpture Gallery in Athens. Greece's marble sculpture tradition endures on Tinos, birthplace of foremost modern sculptors Dimitrios Filippotis and Yannoulis Halepas, as well as Costas Tsoclis, whose work fills the island's new museum.

Contemporary Greek Art Scene

Contemporary Greek art has been gaining exposure in Greece and abroad, with a growing number of Greek artists participating in international art events. The Greek arts scene has become more vibrant, less isolated and more experimental, and Athens' street art is gaining

Athens' metro stations feature an impressive showcase of Greek art from prominent artists including Yannis Gaitis (Larisa), Giorgos Zongolopoulos (Syntagma) and Alekos Fassianos (Metaxourgio), whose work fetches record prices for a living Greek artist.

GREECE ON THE SCREEN

Greece's new-generation filmmakers have been gaining attention for what some critics have dubbed the 'weird wave' of Greek cinema. The award-winning films of Yorgos Lanthimos (Alps; The Lobster; The Killing of a Sacred Deer) and Athina Rachel Tsangari (Attenburg; Chevalier), at the weirder end of the scale, represent a new style of independent films emerging from Greece.

While Ektoras Kygizos' extraordinary Boy Eating Bird Food is an allegory for Greece's current plight, other notable recent films are a product of it – small, creative collaborations largely produced in the absence of state or industry funding.

The focus on Greek film comes in the wake of the loss of Greece's most critically acclaimed filmmaker, Theo Angelopoulos, who was hit by a motorcycle during a film shoot in 2012. Angelopoulos was renowned for his epic, dreamlike cinematic style and long takes, and his melancholy symbolism and commentary on modern Greek history and society.

International festivals may be lauding art-house Greek films, but domestic audiences prefer comedies such as box-office hits Nisos (2009), Sirens in the Aegean (2005) and What If (2011), a film set amid the country's economic crisis.

Few Greek films get commercial releases abroad. Exceptions include Tasos Boulmetis' A Touch of Spice (2003), Pantelis Voulgaris' Brides (2004) and Yannis Smaragdis' big-budget El Greco (2007). Greece's most internationally acclaimed film remains the classic 1964 Oscar-winner Zorba the Greek.

recognition. Many Greek artists have studied and made their homes and reputations abroad, but a new wave is returning or staying put, contributing to a fresh artistic energy. Watch for work by street artist, Cacao Rocks, the collages of Chryssa Romanos, painter Lucas Samaras, kinetic artist Takis, and sculptor Stephen Antonakos.

Greeks have had unprecedented exposure to global art through major international exhibitions held in impressive new art venues, small private galleries and artist-run initiatives such as the annual Hydra School Project. Since 2007, Biennales in Athens have put the capital on the international contemporary-arts circuit.

Modern Greek Literature

Greek literature virtually ceased under Ottoman rule, and was then stifled by conflict over language – Ancient Greek versus the vernacular Demotic or katharevousa, a compromise between the two (dimotiki won in 1976).

One of the most important works of early Greek literature is the 17th-century 10,000-line epic poem 'Erotokritos', by Crete's Vitsenzos Kornaros. Its 15-syllable rhyming verses are still recited in Crete's famous mantinadhes (rhyming couplets) and put to music.

Greece's most celebrated (and translated) 20th-century novelist is the controversial Nikos Kazantzakis, whose novels are full of drama and larger-than-life characters, such as the magnificent title character in Alexis Zorbas (Zorba the Greek). Another great novelist of the time, Stratis Myrivilis, wrote the classics Vasilis Arvanitis and The Mermaid Madonna.

Eminent 20th-century Greek poets include Egypt-born Constantine Cavafy and Nobel-prize laureates George Seferis and Odysseus Elytis, awarded in 1963 and 1979 respectively.

Greece's literary giants include Iakovos Kambanellis, Alexandros Papadiamantis, Kostis Palamas and poet-playwright Angelos Sikelianos. The plays of Yiorgos Skourtis and Pavlos Matessis have been translated and performed abroad.

The quirky, Rebus-like Inspector Haritos in Petros Markaris' popular crime series provides an enjoyable insight into crime and corruption in Athens. Che Committed Suicide (2010), Basic Shareholder (2009), The Late Night News (2005) and Zone Defence (2007) have been translated into English.

Contemporary Writers

Greece has a prolific publishing industry but scant fiction is translated into English.

Contemporary Greek writers have made small inroads into foreign markets, such as Apostolos Doxiadis with his international bestseller *Uncle Petros and Goldbach's Conjecture*, and award-winning children's writer Eugene Trivizas.

Greek publisher Kedros' modern-literature translation series includes Dido Sotiriou's *Farewell Anatolia*, Maro Douka's *Fool's God* and Kostas Mourselas' bestselling *Red-Dyed Hair*, which was made into a popular TV series. Other prominent writers in translation include Ersi Sotiropoulou, Thanassis Valtinos, Rhea Galanaki, Ziranna Ziteli, Petros Markaris and Ioanna Karystiani. Christos Ikonomou's *Something Will Happen, You'll See* was a recent bestseller in Greece.

Bypassing the translation issue, London-based Panos Karnezis *(The Maze; The Birthday Party; The Convent; The Fugitives)* and Soti Triantafyllou *(Poor Margo; Albatross; Rare Earths)* write in English. Other notable contemporary authors available in translation include Alexis Stamatis *(Bar Flaubert; American Fugue; The Book of Rain)* and Vangelis Hatziyannidis *(Four Walls; Stolen Time)*.

Music

For most people, Greek music and dance evoke images of spirited, high-kicking laps around the dance floor to the tune of the bouzouki (a musical instrument in the lute family). Greece's strong and enduring music tradition, however, is a rich mosaic of musical influences and styles.

While many leading performers draw on traditional folk, *laïka* (popular urban folk) and *rembetika* (blues), Greece's vibrant music scene is also pumping out its share of pop, club dance music, jazz, rock and even hip-hop.

Traditional Folk Music

Traditional folk music was shunned by the Greek bourgeoisie after Independence, when they looked to Europe – and classical music and opera – rather than their Eastern or 'peasant' roots.

Greece's regional folk music is generally divided into *nisiotika* (the lighter, upbeat music of the islands) and the more grounded *dimotika* of the mainland – where the *klarino* (clarinet) is prominent and lyrics refer to hard times, war and rural life. The spirited music of Crete, dominated by the Cretan *lyra* (a pear-shaped, three-string, bowed instrument) and

THE ARTS MUSIC

The memorable opening-credits track from the 1994 film *Pulp Fiction* was based on surf-guitar legend Dirk Dale's 1960s version of *Misirlou* – originally recorded by a Greek *rembetika* (blues) band around 1930.

GREEK GIG GUIDE

In summer Greece's leading acts perform in outdoor concerts around the country. In winter they perform in clubs in Athens and large regional towns.

Authentic folk music is harder to find. The best bet is at regional *panigyria* (open-air festivals) during summer. Look for posters, often around telephone and power poles, or ask around.

Athens' live-music scene includes intimate *rembetika* (blues) clubs and glitzy, expensive, cabaret-style venues known as *bouzoukia*. Second-rate *bouzoukia* clubs are referred to as *skyladhika* (doghouses) – apparently because the crooning singers resemble a whining dog. *Bouzoukia* are the venues for flower-throwing (plate-smashing is rare these days), wanton (and expensive) displays of exuberance, excess and *kefi* (good spirits or mojo). *Opa!*

REMBETIKA: THE GREEK BLUES

Known as the Greek 'blues', *rembetika* emerged in Greece's urban underground and has strongly influenced the sound of Greek popular music.

Two styles make up what is broadly known as *rembetika*. *Smyrneika* or Cafe Aman music emerged in the mid- to late-19th century in the thriving port cities of Smyrna and Constantinople, which had large Greek populations, and in Thessaloniki, Volos, Syros and Athens. With a rich vocal style, haunting *amanedhes* (vocal improvisations) and occasional Turkish lyrics, its sound had more Eastern influence. Predominant instruments were the violin, *outi* (oud), guitar, mandolin, *kanonaki* and *santouri* (a flat multistringed instrument). The second style, dominated by the six-stringed bouzouki, evolved in Piraeus.

After the influx of refugees from Asia Minor in Piraeus following the 1922 population exchange (many also went to America, where *rembetika* was recorded in the 1920s), the two styles somewhat overlapped and *rembetika* became the music of the ghettos. Infused with defiance, nostalgia and lament, the songs reflected life's bleaker themes and *manges* (streetwise outcasts) who sang and danced in the *tekedhes* (hash dens that inspired many songs).

In the mid-1930s, the Metaxas dictatorship tried to wipe out the subculture through censorship, police harassment and raids on *tekedhes*. People were arrested for carrying a bouzouki. Many artists stopped performing and recording, though the music continued clandestinely. After WWII, a new wave of *rembetika* emerged that eliminated much of its seedy side.

Rembetika legends include Markos Vamvakaris, who became popular with the first bouzouki group in the early 1930s, composer Vasilis Tsitsanis, Apostolos Kaldaras, Yiannis Papaioannou, Giorgos Mitsakis and Apostolos Hatzihristou, and the songstresses Sotiria Bellou and Marika Ninou, whose life inspired Costas Ferris' 1983 film *Rembetiko*.

Interest in genuine *rembetika* was revived in the late 1970s to early 1980s – particularly among students and intellectuals – and it continues to be rediscovered by new generations.

Rembetika ensembles perform seated in a row and traditionally play acoustically. A characteristic feature is an improvised introduction called a *taxim*.

lute, remains a dynamic musical tradition, with regular performances and recordings by new-generation exponents.

Laïka & Entehna

Laïka (popular or urban folk music) is Greece's most popular music. A mainstream offshoot of *rembetika, laïka* emerged in the late 1950s and '60s, when clubs in Athens became bigger and glitzier, and the music more commercial. The bouzouki went electric and the sentimental tunes about love, loss, pain and emigration came to embody the nation's spirit. The late Stelios Kazantzidis was the big voice of this era, along with Grigoris Bithikotsis.

Classically trained composers Mikis Theodorakis and Manos Hatzidakis led a new style known as *entehni mousiki* ('artistic' music). They drew on *rembetika* and used instruments such as the bouzouki in more symphonic arrangements, and created popular hits from the poetry of Seferis, Elytis, Ritsos and Kavadias.

Composer Yiannis Markopoulos later introduced rural folk music and traditional instruments such as the *lyra, santouri,* violin and *kanonaki* into the mainstream, and brought folk performers such as Crete's legendary Nikos Xylouris to the fore.

During the junta years the music of Theodorakis and Markopoulos became a form of political expression (Theodorakis' music was banned and the composer jailed).

The sound of the bouzouki, immortalised in Mikis Theodorakis' 1960s soundtrack to *Zorba the Greek,* has become synonymous with Greece. The long-necked lute-like instrument became central to *rembetika* and dominates *laïka*.

Contemporary & Pop Music

While few Greek performers have made it big internationally – 1970s genre-defying icons Nana Mouskouri and Demis Roussos remain the best known – Greece has a strong local music scene, from traditional and pop music to Greek rock, heavy metal, rap and electronic dance.

Some of the most interesting music emerging from Greece fuses elements of folk, *laïka* and *entehna* with Western influences. One of the most whimsical examples was Greece's tongue-in-cheek 2013 Eurovision contender, in which *rembetika* veteran Agathonas Iakovidis teamed up with the ska-Balkan rhythms of Thessaloniki's kilt-wearing Koza Mostra.

Big names in contemporary Greek music include Dionysis Savopoulos, dubbed the Bob Dylan of Greece, and seasoned performers George Dalaras and Haris Alexiou.

Standout performers include Cypriot-born Alkinoos Ioannides, Eleftheria Arvanitakiis, Savina Yannatou, and ethnic-jazz-fusion artists Kristi Stasinopoulou, Mode Plagal and the Cretan-inspired Haïnides.

Headline *laïka* performers include Yiannis Ploutarhos, Antonis Remos and Thanos Petrelis while the pop scene sees a steady stream of performers creating a uniquely Greek sound. Listen for Στella, Kid Moxie, Sarah P and Keep Shelley in Athens.

Classical Music & Opera

Despite classical music and opera appealing to an (albeit growing) minority of Greeks, this field is where Greece has made the most significant international contribution, most notably composers Mikis Theodorakis and Manos Hatzidakis and opera diva Maria Callas.

Dimitris Mitropoulos led the New York Philharmonic in the 1950s, while composers include Stavros Xarhakos and the late Yannis Xenakis. Leading contemporary performers include pianist Dimitris Sgouros, tenor Mario Frangoulis and sopranos Elena Kelessidi and Irini Tsirakidou.

The country's concert halls and major cultural festivals such as the Hellenic Festival offer rich international programs, while opera buffs have the Greek National Opera and Syros' Apollo Theatre.

Greek Dance

Greeks have danced since the dawn of Hellenism. Some folk dances derive from the ritual dances performed in ancient temples – ancient vases depict a version of the well-known *syrtos* folk dance. Dancing was later part of military education; in times of occupation it became an act of defiance and a covert way to keep fit.

Regional dances, like musical styles, vary across Greece. The slow and dignified *tsamikos* reflects the often cold and insular nature of mountain life, while the brighter islands gave rise to light, springy dances such as the *ballos* and the *syrtos*. The Pontian Greeks' vigorous and warlike dances such as the *kotsari* reflect years of altercations with their Turkish neighbours. Crete has its graceful *syrtos*, the fast and triumphant *maleviziotiko* and the dynamic *pentozali*, with its agility-testing high kicks and leaps. The so-called 'Zorba dance', or *syrtaki*, is a stylised dance for two or three dancers with arms linked on each other's shoulders, though the modern variation is danced in a long circle with an ever-quickening beat. Women and men traditionally danced separately and had their own dances, except in courtship dances such as the *sousta*.

Folk-dance groups throughout Greece preserve regional traditions. The best place to see folk dancing is at regional festivals and the Dora Stratou Dance Theatre in Athens.

Contemporary dance is gaining prominence in Greece, with leading local troupes taking their place among the international line-up at the Athens International Dance Festival.

Byzantine music is mostly heard in Greek churches these days, though Byzantine choirs perform in concerts in Greece and abroad, and the music has influenced folk music.

Men dance the often spectacular solo *zeïmbekiko* (whirling, meditative improvisations with roots in *rembetika*). Women do the sensuous *tsifteteli*, a svelte, sinewy show of femininity evolved from the Middle Eastern belly dance.

THE ARTS GREEK DANCE

Architecture

Cast your eyes around most major Western cities and you'll find a reinterpretation of classical Greek architecture. The Renaissance was inspired by the ancient style, as was the neoclassical movement and the British Greek Revival. For those with an eye to the past, part of the allure of Greece is the sheer volume of its well-preserved temples. Stand in the ruins of the Parthenon and with a little imagination it's easy to transport yourself back to classical 5th-century Greece.

Minoan Magnificence

Most of our knowledge of Greek architecture proper begins at around 2000 BC with the Minoans, who were based in Crete but whose influence spread throughout the Aegean to include the Cyclades. Minoan architects are famous for having constructed technologically advanced, labyrinthine palace complexes. The famous site at Knossos is one of the largest. Usually characterised as 'palaces', these sites were in fact multifunctional settlements that were the primary residences of royalty and priests, but housed some plebs too. Large Minoan villages, such as those of Gournia and Palekastro in Crete, also included internal networks of paved roads that extended throughout the countryside to link the settlements with the palaces. More Minoan palace-era sophistication exists in Crete at Phaestos, Malia and Ancient Zakros, and at the Minoan outpost of Ancient Akrotiri on the south of Santorini.

Several gigantic volcanic eruptions rocked the region in the mid-15th century BC, causing geological ripple effects that at the very least caused big chunks of palace to fall to the ground. The Minoans resolutely rebuilt their crumbling palaces on an even grander scale, only to have more natural disasters wipe them out again. The latter effected an architectural chasm that was filled by the emerging Mycenaean rivals on mainland Greece.

Grandeur of Knossos

According to myth, the man tasked with designing a maze to withhold the dreaded Minotaur was famous Athenian inventor Daedalus, father of Icarus. He also designed the Palace of Knossos for King Minos.

First discovered by a Cretan, Milos Kalokirinos, in 1878, it wasn't until 1900 that the ruins of Knossos were unearthed by Englishman Sir Arthur Evans. The elaborate palace complex at Knossos was originally formed largely as an administrative settlement surrounding the main palace, which comprised the main buildings arranged around a large central courtyard (1250 sq metres). Over time the entire settlement was rebuilt and extended. Long, raised causeways formed main corridors; narrow labyrinthine chambers flanked the palace walls (this meandering floor plan, together with the graphic ritual importance of bulls, inspired the myth of the labyrinth and the Minotaur). The compound featured strategically placed interior light wells, sophisticated ventilation systems, aqueducts, freshwater irrigation wells and bathrooms with extensive plumbing and drainage systems. The ground levels consisted mostly of workshops, cylindrical grain silos and storage magazines.

Thanks to its restoration, today's Knossos is one of the easiest ruins for your imagination to take hold of.

Mycenaean Engineering

The Mycenaeans had a fierce reputation as builders of massive masonry. These war-mongering people roamed southern mainland Greece, picking off the choice vantage points for their austere palaces, fenced within formidable citadels. The citadels' fortified Cyclopean-stone walls were on average an unbreachable 3m to 7m thick. The immense royal beehive tomb of the Treasury of Atreus (aka Tomb of Agamemnon) at Mycenae was constructed using tapered limestone blocks weighing up to 120 tonnes. The palace at Tiryns has stupendous corbel-vaulted galleries and is riddled with secret passageways; the incredibly well-preserved Nestor's Palace, near modern Pylos, also illustrates the Mycenaeans' structural expertise.

Classical Compositions

The classical age (5th to 4th centuries BC) is when most Greek architectural clichés converge. This is when temples became characterised by the famous orders of columns, particularly the Doric, Ionic and Corinthian.

The mother of all Doric structures is the 5th-century-BC Parthenon, the ultimate in architectural bling: a gleaming, solid marble crown. To this day, it's probably *the* most obsessively photographed jewel in all of Greece.

In the meantime, the Greek colonies of the Asia Minor coast were creating their own Ionic order, designing a column base in several tiers and adding more flutes. This more graceful order's capital (the head) received an ornamented necking, and Iktinos fused elements of its design in the Parthenon. This order is used on the Acropolis' Temple of Athena Nike and the Erechtheion, where the famous Caryatids regally stand.

Towards the tail end of the classical period, the Corinthian column was in limited vogue. Featuring a single or double row of ornate leafy scrolls (usually the very sculptural acanthus), the order was subsequently adopted by the Romans and used only on Corinthian temples in Athens. The Temple of Olympian Zeus, completed during Emperor Hadrian's reign, is a grand, imposing structure. Another temple design,

THE COLUMNS OF ANCIENT GREECE

Columns are columns are columns, right? Recognising the differences between them is, in fact, the easiest way to differentiate between the three distinct architectural orders of Ancient Greece.

Doric The most simple of the three styles. The shaft (the main part of the column) is plain and has 20 sides, while the capital (the head) is formed in a simple circle. Also there's no base. An obvious example of this is the Parthenon.

Ionic Look out for the ridged flutes carved into the column from top to bottom. The capital is also distinctive for its scrolls, while the base looks like a stack of rings.

Corinthian The most decorative and popular of all three orders. The column is ridged; however, the distinctive feature is the capital's flowers and leaves, beneath a small scroll. The base is like that of the Ionic.

the graceful, circular temple *tholos* (dome) style, was used for the great Sanctuary of Athena Pronea at Delphi.

The Greek theatre design is a hallmark of the classical period (an example is the 4th-century-BC theatre at Epidavros) and had a round stage, radiating a semicircle of steeply banked stone benches that seated many thousands. Cleverly engineered acoustics meant every spectator could monitor every syllable uttered on the stage below. Most ancient Greek theatres are still used for summer festivals, music concerts and plays.

Hellenistic Citizens

In the twilight years of the classical age (from about the late 4th century BC), cosmopolitan folks started to weary of temples, casting their gaze towards a more decadent urban style. The Hellenistic architect was in hot demand for private homes and palace makeovers as wealthy citizens, dignitaries and political heavyweights lavishly remodelled their abodes in marble, and striking mosaics were displayed as status symbols (read *more* bling). The best Hellenistic ancient-home displays are the grand houses at Delos.

Byzantine Zeal

Church-building was particularly expressive during the time of the Byzantine Empire in Greece (from around AD 700). The original Greek Byzantine model features a distinctive cross shape; essentially a central dome supported by four arches on piers and flanked by vaults, with smaller domes at the four corners and three apses to the east. Theologian architects opted for spectacular devotional mosaics and frescoes instead of carvings for the stylistic religious interiors. In Athens, the very appealing 12th-century Church of Agios Eleftherios incorporates fragments of a classical frieze in Pentelic marble; the charming 11th-century Church of Kapnikarea sits stranded, smack-bang in the middle of downtown Athens – its interior flooring is of coloured marble, and the external brickwork, which alternates with stone, is set in patterns. Thessaloniki's 8th-century Church of Agia Sofia, with its 30m-high dome, is a humble version of its namesake in İstanbul. There are numerous Byzantine chapels in Mystras, many of which were originally private chapels, attached to enchanting 17th- and 18th-century *arhontika* (mansions once owned by *arhons,* wealthy bourgeoisie merchants).

Several Byzantine monastic sites have made it to the Unesco World Heritage register, including the *katholikon* (main churches) of Osios Loukas, significant for their late-Byzantine multidomed style, and the

11th-century Moni Dafniou, which stands on the site of an ancient Sanctuary of Apollo.

Frankish Keeps & Venetian Strongholds

After the sacking of Constantinople by the Crusaders in 1204, much of Greece became the fiefdoms of Western aristocrats. The Villehardouin family punctuated the Peloponnesian landscape with Frankish castles, such as at Kalamata and at Mystras, where they also built a palace that ended up a court of the Byzantine imperial family for two centuries. When the Venetians dropped by to seize a few coastal enclaves, they built the impenetrable 16th-century Koules fortress in Iraklio, the very sturdy fortress at Methoni and the imposing 18th-century Palamidi fortress at Nafplio. The rambling defence at Acrocorinth is studded with imposing gateways, and the rock-nest protecting the enchanting Byzantine village at Monemvasia commands spectacular ocean views.

Ottoman Offerings

Interestingly, remarkably few monuments are left to catalogue after four centuries of Ottoman Turkish rule (16th to 19th centuries). Though many mosques and their minarets have sadly crumbled or are in serious disrepair, some terrific Ottoman-Turkish examples still survive. These include the prominent pink-domed Mosque of Süleyman in Rhodes' Old Town. The Fethiye Mosque and Turkish Baths are two of Athens' few surviving Ottoman reminders, and the architect for the 16th-century Koursoun Tzami in Trikala also designed the Blue Mosque in İstanbul. The Turkish quarter of Varousi in Trikala, and the streets of Thessaloniki and of Didymotiho, near the Turkish border, showcase superb Turkish-designed homes with stained-glass windows, wooden overhangs on buttresses, decorated plasterwork and painted woodwork.

Neoclassical Spendour

Regarded by experts as the most beautiful neoclassical building worldwide, the 1885 Athens Academy reflects Greece's post-Independence yearnings for grand and geometric forms, and Hellenistic detail. Renowned Danish architect Theophile Hansen drew inspiration from the Erechtheion to design the Academy's Ionic-style column entrance (guarded over by Apollo and Athena); the great interior oblong hall is lined with marble seating, and Austrian painter Christian Griepenkerl

---

THE CAPTAIN'S HOUSE

During the 17th century, Greek ship captains grew increasingly prosperous. Many of them poured their new-found wealth into building lofty homes that towered over the traditional village houses. These captains' houses are now dotted throughout the islands and many have been given a new lease on life as boutique hotels or restaurants.

While the size of the house often reflected the wealth of a captain, some of the smallest of these 400-year-old homes are the most grand. Captain's houses didn't need to be large as they spent so much time at sea. Whitewashed walls stretch upward to the soaring resin ceiling, often intricately painted with elaborate, colourful patterns. The windows are sea-facing and placed very high, often with wooden lofts to reach them. This was to let the heat out in summer and also so the captain's wife could watch the sea for the arrival of her husband's ship. The traditional *pyliones* (stone doorways) are hand-carved with symbolic pictures. Corn means good harvest, birds mean peace, the cross brings safety and the sunflowers sunlight. The number of ropes carved around the perimeter of the door shows how many ships the captain had.

Some of the finest examples of these houses are found in Lindos, on Rhodes.

BEST FUTURISTIC ATHENS

Despite its massive contribution to ancient architecture, Athens is not stuck in the past. Its modern architects are innovative and fearless.

Acropolis Museum (p73) This relatively new space houses Greece's antiquities. Designed by Bernard Tschumi, the museum features an internal glass *cella* (inner room) mirroring the Parthenon with the same number of columns (clad in steel) and a glass floor overlooking excavated ruins in situ.

Stavros Niarchos Foundation Cultural Center (p118) The Pritzker Prize–winning architect Renzo Piano designed the SNFCC, which opened in 2016. A multifunctional arts and entertainment venue, it houses the National Library of Greece and the National Opera amid natural surroundings that link the centre's park (at the old horse-racing tracks in Faliro) with the sea.

Planetarium (p88) This is one of the world's largest digital hemispherical domes, with a dome diameter of 25m. It provides 360-degree 3D virtual rides through the galaxy in a space the size of 2.5 basketball courts.

Athens Olympic Complex (p93) Designed by well-known Spanish architect Santiago Calatrata to house the 2004 Olympics, this complex has a striking, ultramodern glass-and-steel roof, which is suspended by cables from large arches. The laminated glass, in the shape of two giant leaves, is capable of reflecting 90% of the sunlight.

National Museum of Contemporary Art (p76) The abandoned FIX brewery in central Athens has been hollowed out and renovated to create 20,000 sq metres of space to house the gallery. Built in the 1950s, the building retains much of its postwar industrial architecture, including the horizontal feel achieved with lateral linear glass, while one side of the facade has been covered in stone reminiscent of the riverbed that was once here. Inside, it's all about glass and light, with a sculpture garden on the roof.

was commissioned to decorate its elaborate ceiling and wall paintings. In a similar vein, the Doric columns of the Temple of Hephaestus influenced Theophile's solid-marble National Library, while Christian Hansen (Theophile's brother) was responsible for the handsome but more sedate Athens University, with its clean lines.

Meticulously restored neoclassical mansions house notable museums such as the acclaimed Benaki Museum in Athens.

Many provincial towns also display beautiful domestic adaptations of neoclassicism. In Symi, the harbour at Gialos is flanked by colourful neoclassical facades (still striking even if a little derelict) and Nafplio is also embellished with neoclassical buildings.

The distinctive blue-and-white Cycladic-style architecture most associated with the Greek islands was pragmatic and functional. The cuboid flat-roofed houses, huddled together along labyrinthine alleys, were designed to guard against the elements: strong winds and pirates.

Modern Ideas

Athens today is embracing a sophisticated look-both-ways architectural aesthetic by showcasing its vast collection of antiquities and archaeological heritage in revolutionary buildings, and by beautifying landscapes for pedestrian zones to improve the urban environment. Examples include the well-designed facelift of the historic centre, including its spectacular floodlighting (designed by the renowned Pierre Bideau) of the ancient promenade, and the cutting-edge spaces emerging from once-drab and derelict industrial zones, such as the Technopolis gasworks arts complex in Gazi.

Nature & Wildlife

While Greece is a perfect place to rub shoulders with ancient statues, it's equally ideal for getting up close to nature. Hike through wildflowers, come eye to eye with a loggerhead turtle or simply stretch out on a beach. Greece has something for everyone who wants to get out and explore.

Experiencing the Outdoors

Greek Geography

No matter where you go in Greece, it's impossible to be much more than 100km from the sea. Rugged mountains and seemingly innumerable islands dominate the landscape, which was shaped by submerging seas, volcanic explosions and mineral-rich terrain. The mainland covers 131,944 sq km, with an indented coastline stretching for 15,020km. Mountains rise over 2000m and occasionally tumble down into plains, particularly in Thessaly and Thrace. Meanwhile, the Aegean and Ionian Seas link together the country's 1400 islands, with just 169 of them inhabited. These islands fill 400,000 sq km of territorial waters.

> Greece is the most seismically active country in all of Europe, with more than half of the continent's volcanic activity.

During the Triassic, Jurassic, Cretaceous and even later geological periods, Greece was a shallow, oxygen-rich sea. The continuous submerging of land created large tracts of limestone through the whole submarine land mass. Later, as the land emerged from the sea to form the backbone of the current topography, a distinctly eroded landscape with crystalline rocks and other valuable minerals began to appear, marking the spine that links the north and south of the mainland today. Limestone caves are a major feature of this karst landscape, shaped by the dissolution of a soluble layer of bedrock.

Volcanic activity once regularly hit Greece with force – one of the world's largest volcanic explosions was on Santorini around 1650 BC. Today earthquakes continue to shake the country on a smaller scale, but with almost-predictable frequency. In 1999 a 5.9-magnitude earthquake near Athens killed nearly 150 people and left thousands homeless. Since 2006, the country has had six quakes ranging from 6.4 to 6.9 in magnitude. None caused major damage. To check out Greece's explosive past, visit the craters of Santorini, Nisyros and Polyvotis.

Greece is short on rivers, with none that are navigable, although they've become popular locations for white-water rafting. The largest rivers are the Aheloös, Aliakmonas, Aoös and Arahthos, all of which have their source in the Pindos Mountains of Epiros.

The long plains of the river valleys, and those between the mountains and the coast, form Greece's only lowlands. The mountainous terrain, dry climate and poor soil leave farmers at a loss, and less than 25% of the land is cultivated. Greece is, however, rich in minerals, with reserves of oil, manganese, bauxite and lignite.

Wildflowers & Herbs

Greece is endowed with a variety of flora unrivalled in Europe. The wildflowers are spectacular, with more than 6000 species, including more than 100 varieties of orchid. They continue to thrive because most of the land is inadequate for intensive agriculture and has therefore escaped the ravages of chemical fertilisers.

The regions with the most wildflowers are the Lefka Ori (White Mountains) in Crete and the Mani area of the Peloponnese. Trees begin to blossom as early as the end of February in warmer areas and the wildflowers start to appear in March. During spring, hillsides are carpeted with flowers, which seem to sprout even from the rocks. By summer the flowers have disappeared from everywhere but the northern mountainous regions. Autumn brings a new period of blossoming.

Herbs grow wild throughout much of Greece and you'll see locals out picking fresh herbs for their kitchen. Locally grown herbs are also increasingly sold as souvenirs and are generally organic.

Herbs in Cooking is an illustrative book by Maria and Nikos Psilakis that can be used as both an identification guide and a cookbook for Greek dishes seasoned with local herbs.

Forests

The lush forests that once covered ancient Greece are increasingly rare. Having been decimated by thousands of years of clearing for grazing, boatbuilding and housing, they've more recently suffered from severe forest fires. Northern Greece is the only region that has retained significant areas of native forest – there are mountainsides covered with dense thickets of hop hornbeam *(Ostrya carpinifolia)*, noted for its lavish display of white-clustered flowers. Another common species is the Cyprus plane *(Platanus orientalis insularis)*, which thrives wherever there's ample water.

Watching for Wildlife

On the Ground

In areas widely inhabited by humans, you're unlikely to spot any wild animals other than the odd fox, weasel, hare or rabbit. The more remote mountains of northern Greece continue to support a wide range of wildlife, including wild dogs and shepherds' dogs, which often roam higher pastures on grazing mountains and should be given a wide berth.

The brown bear, Europe's largest land mammal, still manages to survive in very small numbers in the Pindos Mountains, the Peristeri Range that rises above the Prespa Lakes and in the mountains that lie along the Bulgarian border. It's estimated that only around 200 survive; your best bet for seeing one is at the Arcturos Bear Sanctuary (p281) in Macedonia.

The Greek Orthodox Church is the second-largest landowner in Greece.

The protected grey wolf is officially classified as stable with an estimated 200 to 300 surviving in the wild. It's believed up to 100 are killed annually by indiscriminate (and illegal) use of poison baits in retaliation for the occasional marauding of flocks. The Greek government and insurance companies pay compensation for lost livestock but it doesn't appear to slow the killings. The surviving wolves live in the Pindos Mountains and the Dadia Forest Reserve area. Head to the Arcturos Wolf Sanctuary in Agrapidia, near Florina, which houses wolves rescued from illegal captivity.

The golden jackal is a strong candidate for Greece's most misunderstood mammal. Although its diet is 50% vegetarian (the other 50% is made up of carrion, reptiles and small mammals), it has traditionally shouldered much of the blame for attacks on stock and has been hunted by farmers as a preventative measure. Near the brink of extinction, it was declared a protected species in 1990 and now survives only in the Fokida district of central Greece and on the island of Samos.

Once roaming across all of mainland Greece, the graceful red deer is now restricted to the Sithonia peninsula, the Rhodope Mountain bordering Bulgaria and Mt Parnitha north of Athens. As the largest herbivore in Greece, its population is under constant threat from illegal hunters, making attempts at population redistribution unsuccessful.

Originally brought to the island of Skyros in the 5th century BC by colonists, the diminutive Skryrian horses are an ancient breed that became wild once they had been replaced by agricultural mechanisation. Around

NATIONAL PARKS

National parks were first established in Greece in 1938 with the creation of Mt Olympus National Park. There are now 10 national parks and two marine parks, which aim to protect Greece's unique flora and fauna.

Facilities for visitors are often basic, abundant walking trails are not always maintained and the clutch of refuges is very simple. To most, the facilities matter little when compared to nature's magnificent backdrop. It's well worth experiencing the wild side of Greece in one of these settings.

Mt Olympus National Park (p273) Home to Greece's tallest mountain, rich flora and considered the home of the gods.

Mt Parnitha National Park (p134) Very popular wooded parkland north of Athens; home to the red deer.

National Marine Park of Alonnisos Northern Sporades (p651) Covers six islands and 22 islets in the Sporades and is home to monk seals, dolphins and rare birdlife.

Parnassos National Park (p209) Towering limestone and scenic views to Delphi.

Prespa Lakes (p279) One of Europe's oldest lakes, steeped in wildlife and tranquillity.

Samaria Gorge (p480) Spectacular gorge in Crete and a refuge for the *kri-kri* (Cretan goat).

Cape Sounion (p134) A cape with panoramic views and home to the Temple of Poseidon.

Vikos-Aoös National Park Excellent hiking with caves, canyons and dense forest.

National Marine Park of Zakynthos (p699) An Ionian refuge for loggerhead turtles.

Iti National Park (p217) Tranquil stretches of forest, meadows and pools; home to eagles, deer and boars.

Valia Calda National Park (p293) Beech and black pine forest, alpine meadows and home to the brown bear, wolf, otter and golden and king eagles, in the Epiros region.

190 survive on the island, approximately 70% of their population. You'll also see these horses featured in the Parthenon friezes.

Greece has an active snake population and in spring and summer you will inevitably spot them on roads and pathways around the country. Fortunately the majority are harmless, though the viper and the coral snake can cause fatalities. Lizards are in abundance too.

The Hellenic Wildlife Hospital (p755) is the oldest and largest wildlife rehabilitation centre in southern Europe.

In the Air

Birdwatchers hit the jackpot in Greece as much of the country is on north–south migratory paths. Lesvos (Mytilini) in particular draws a regular following of birders from all over Europe, who come to spot some of more than 279 recorded species that stop at the island annually. Storks are more visible visitors, arriving in early spring from Africa and returning to the same nests year after year. These are built on electricity poles, chimney tops and church towers, and can weigh up to 50kg. Keep an eye out for them in northern Greece, especially in Thrace in Macedonia. Thrace has the richest colony of fish-eating birds in Europe, including species such as egrets, herons, cormorants and ibises, as well as the rare Dalmatian pelican. The wetlands at the mouth of the Evros River, close to the border with Turkey, are home to two easily identifiable wading birds: the avocet, which has a long curving beak, and the black-winged stilt, which has extremely long pink legs.

Upstream on the Evros River in Thrace, the dense forests and rocky outcrops of the 72-sq-km Dadia Forest Reserve play host to Europe's

Wildlife Websites

Pelicans and pygmy cormorants (www.spp.gr)

Birdlife (www. ornithologiki.gr)

Wildflowers (www.greek mountain flora.info)

Sea turtles (www. archelon.gr)

GREEN ISSUES

Environmental awareness is beginning to seep into the fabric of Greek society, leading to slow but positive change. Environmental education happens in schools, recycling is common in cities, and even in the smallest villages you may find organic restaurants and environmentally sustainable businesses. However, problems such as deforestation and soil erosion date back thousands of years. Live cultivation, goats, construction and industry have all taken their toll.

Illegal development of mainly coastal areas, and building in forested or protected areas, has gained momentum in Greece since the 1970s. Despite attempts at introducing laws, and protests by locals and environmental groups, corruption and the lack of an infrastructure to enforce the laws means little is done to abate the land-grab. The issue is complicated by population growth and increased urban sprawl. Developments often put a severe strain on water supplies and endangered wildlife. While a few developments have been torn down, in more cases illegal buildings are legalised as they offer much needed, affordable housing.

In 2014 NATO's plan to decommission 700 tonnes of Syria's chemical weapons off the southern coast of Crete was protested by over 10,000 islanders. Scientists claimed seawater would neutralise the chemicals within 90 days, but after Albania, Thailand, Belgium, Germany and Norway refused to have the process take place in their waters, the UN approved the international waters between Crete and Malta. Protesters claimed the effectiveness of hydrolysis was unclear, as was the impact of the discharge on the Mediterranean's marine ecosystems and tourism. Sadly, only time will tell if they were right.

Greece's economic troubles have also impacted the environment. The lifting of the diesel ban in Athens and Thessaloniki in 2012 decreased air quality as people opted for cheaper transport. As heating oil tripled in price, people turned to burning wood, often treated, as well as garbage to keep warm. Wintertime particle pollution increased by 30% on some evenings, with lead and arsenic particles found in the air.

largest range of birds of prey. Thirty-six of the 38 European species can be seen here and it is a breeding ground for 23 of them. Permanent residents include the giant black vulture, whose wingspan reaches 3m, the griffon vulture and the golden eagle. Europe's last 15 pairs of royal eagle nest on the river delta.

Over 350 pairs of the rare Eleonora's falcon (60% of the world's population) nest on the island of Piperi in the Sporades and on Tilos, which is also home to the very rare Bonelli's eagle and the shy, cormorant-like Mediterranean shag.

Under the Sea

As Europe's most endangered marine mammal, the monk seal (Monachus monachus) ekes out an extremely precarious existence in Greece. Approximately 200 to 250 monk seals, about 50% of the world's population, are found in both the Ionian and Aegean Seas. Small colonies also live on the island of Alonnisos and there have been reported sightings on Tilos.

Loggerhead-turtle hatchlings use the journey from the nest to the sea to build up their strength. Helping the baby turtles to the sea can actually lower their chances of survival.

The waters around Zakynthos are home to the last large sea-turtle colony in Europe, that of the endangered loggerhead turtle (Caretta caretta). Loggerheads also nest in smaller numbers in the Peloponnese and on Kefallonia and Crete. Greece's turtles have many hazards to dodge: entanglement in fishing nets and boat propellers, consumption of floating rubbish, and the destruction of their nesting beaches by sunloungers and beach umbrellas that threaten their eggs. It doesn't help that the turtles' nesting time coincides with the European summer-holiday season.

There is still the chance that you will spot dolphins from a ferry deck, though a number of the species are now considered vulnerable. The number of common dolphins (Delphinus delphis) has dropped from 150 to less than 20 in the past decade. The main threats to dolphins are a diminished food supply and entanglement in fishing nets.

Survival Guide

Directory A–Z

Accommodation

Greece's plethora of accommodation means that, whatever your taste or budget, there is somewhere to suit your needs. All places to stay are subject to strict price controls set by the tourist police. By law, a notice must be displayed in every room, stating the category of the room and the price charged in each season. It's difficult to generalise accommodation prices in Greece as rates depend entirely on the season and location. Don't expect to pay the same price for a double room on one of the islands as you would in central Greece or Athens.

When considering hotel prices, take note of the following points:

➡ Prices include community tax and VAT (value-added tax).

➡ A 10% surcharge may be added for stays of fewer than three nights, but this is not mandatory.

➡ A mandatory charge of 20% is levied for an additional bed (although this is often waived if the bed is for a child).

➡ During July and August accommodation owners will charge the maximum price, which can be as much as double the low-season price. In spring and autumn prices can drop by 20%.

➡ Rip-offs are rare; if you suspect that you have been exploited make a report to the tourist police or the regular police, and they will act swiftly.

Camping

Camping is a decent option, especially in summer. There are almost 350 campgrounds in Greece, found on the majority of islands (with the notable exception of the Saronic Gulf Islands). Standard facilities include hot showers, kitchens, restaurants and minimarkets – and often a swimming pool.

Most campgrounds are open only between May and October although always check ahead; particularly in the north, some don't open until June. The **Panhellenic Camping Association** (☏21036 21560; www.greece camping.gr) website lists all of its campgrounds and relevant details.

If you're camping in the height of summer, bring a silver fly sheet to reflect the heat off your tent (dark tents become sweat lodges). Between May and mid-September the weather is warm enough to sleep out under the stars. Many campgrounds have covered areas where tourists who don't have tents can sleep in summer; you can get by with a lightweight sleeping bag. It's a good idea to have a foam pad to lie on, a waterproof cover for your sleeping bag and plenty of bug repellent.

➡ Camping fees are highest from mid-June through to the end of August.

➡ Campgrounds charge €6 to €12 per adult and €3 to €5 for children aged four to 12. There's no charge for children under four.

➡ Tent sites cost from €5 per night.

➡ You can often rent tents for around €5.

➡ Caravan sites start at around €7; car costs are typically €4 to €5.

Domatia

Domatia (literally 'rooms') are the Greek equivalent of the British B&B, minus the breakfast. Once upon a time, domatia were little more than spare rooms in the family home; nowadays, many are purpose-built appendages with fully equipped kitchens. Standards of cleanliness are generally high.

Domatia remain a popular option for budget travellers. Expect to pay from €30 to €60 for a single, and €40 to €80 for a double, depending on whether bathrooms are shared or private, the season and how long you plan to stay. Domatia are found throughout the mainland (except in large cities) and on almost every island that has a permanent population. Many domatia are open only between April and October.

From June to September, domatia owners are out in force, touting for customers. They meet buses and boats, shouting 'room, room!' and often carry photographs of their rooms. In peak season it can prove a mistake not to take up an offer – but be wary of owners who are vague about the location of their accommodation.

Hostels

Most youth hostels in Greece are run by the **Greek Youth Hostel Organisation** (www. athensyhostel.com/index. php/g-y-h-o). There are affiliated hostels in Athens, Olympia, Patra and Thessaloniki on the mainland, and on the island of Crete.

Hostel rates vary from around €10 to €20 for a bed in a dorm and you don't have to be a member to stay in them. Few have curfews.

Hotels

Hotels in Greece are divided into six categories: deluxe, A, B, C, D and E. Hotels are categorised according to the size of the rooms, whether or not they have a bar, and the ratio of bathrooms to beds, rather than standards of cleanliness, comfort of beds and friendliness of staff – all elements that may be of greater relevance to guests.

Prices listed here refer to the high season:

➡ **A and B class** Full amenities, private bathrooms and

---

constant hot water; prices range from €60 to €85 for a single and upwards of €100 for a double.

➡ **C class** A snack bar and rooms with private bathrooms, but not necessarily constant hot water; prices range from €40 to €70 for a single in high season and €50 to €90 for a double.

➡ **D class** Generally have shared bathrooms and they may have solar-heated water, meaning hot water is not guaranteed; prices range from €30 to €50 for a single and €40 to €70 for a double.

➡ **E class** Shared bathrooms and hot water may cost extra; prices are around €25 for a single and €35 for a double.

Mountain Refuges

There are 55 mountain refuges dotted around the Greek mainland, Crete and Evia. They range from small huts with outdoor toilets and no cooking facilities to very comfortable modern lodges. They are run by the country's various mountaineering and skiing clubs. Prices start at around €10 per person, depending on the facilities. The EOT (Greek National Tourist Organisation; www. visitgreece.gr) publication *Greece: Mountain Refuges & Ski Centres* has details about

---

each refuge; copies are available at all EOT branches.

Pensions

Pensions are indistinguishable from hotels. They are categorised as A, B or C class. An A-class pension is equivalent in amenities and price to a B-class hotel, a B-class pension is equivalent to a C-class hotel, and a C-class pension is equivalent to a D- or E-class hotel.

Rental Accommodation

A practical way to save money and maximise comfort is to rent a furnished apartment or villa. Many are purpose-built for tourists while others – villas in particular – may be owners' homes that they are not using. Some owners may insist on a minimum stay of a week. A good site to spot prospective villas is www. greekislands.com.

Customs Regulations

There are no longer duty-free restrictions within the EU. Upon entering Greece from outside the EU, customs inspection is usually cursory for foreign tourists and a verbal declaration is generally all that is required. Random

GOVERNMENT TRAVEL ADVICE

The following government websites offer travel advisories and information on current hotspots.

➡ Australian Department of Foreign Affairs (dfat.gov.au)
➡ British Foreign Office (www.fco.gov.uk)
➡ Canadian Department of Foreign Affairs (travel.gc.ca)
➡ US State Department (travel.state.gov)

searches are still occasionally made for drugs. Import regulations for medicines are strict; if you are taking medication, make sure you get a statement from your doctor before you leave home. It is illegal, for instance, to take codeine into Greece without a doctor's certificate.

It is strictly forbidden to export antiquities (anything more than 100 years old) without an export permit. This crime is second only to drug smuggling in the penalties imposed. It is an offence to remove even the smallest article from an archaeological site. The place to apply for an export permit is the Antique Dealers and Private Collections section of the **Athens Archaeological Service** (Map p78; http://nam.culture.gr; Polygnotou 13, Plaka).

Vehicles

Cars can be brought into Greece for six months without a carnet; only a green card (international third-party insurance) is required. If arriving from Italy, your only proof of entry into the country may be your ferry ticket stub, so don't lose it. From other countries, a passport stamp will be ample evidence.

Discount Cards

Camping Card International (CCI; www.campingcardinternational.com) Gives up to 25% savings in camping fees and third-party liability insurance while in the campground. Valid in over 2900 campsites across Europe.

European Youth Card (www.eyca.org) Available for anyone up to the age of 26 or 30, depending on the country. You don't have to be a resident of Europe. It provides discounts of up to 20% at sights, shops and for some transport. Available from the website or travel agencies in Athens and Thessaloniki for €10.

International Student Identity Card (ISIC; www.isic.org) Entitles the holder to half-price admission to museums and ancient sites, and discounts at some budget hotels and hostels. Available from travel agencies in Athens. Applicants require documents proving their student status, a passport photo and €10. Available to students aged 12 to 30.

Seniors cards Card-carrying EU pensioners can claim a range of benefits such as reduced admission to sites and museums, and discounts on bus and train fares.

Electricity

Type C
220V/50Hz

Type F
230V/50Hz

Embassies & Consulates

All foreign embassies in Greece are in Athens and its suburbs, with a few consulates in Thessaloniki.

Albanian Embassy (210 687 6200; embassy.athens@mfa.gov.al; Vekiareli 7, Filothei)

Australian Embassy (210 870 4000; www.greece.embassy.gov.au; 6th fl, Thon Bldg, cnr Leoforos Alexandras & Leoforos Kifisias, Ambelokipi)

Bulgarian Embassy (210 674 8105; www.mfa.bg/embassies/greece; Stratigou Kalari 33a, Psychiko)

Canadian Embassy (210 727 3400; www.greece.gc.ca; Ethnikis Antistaseos 48, Halandri)

Cypriot Embassy (210 373 4800; Xenofontos 2a, Syntagma; ⊙8am-3.30pm Mon-Fri)

French Embassy (210 339 1000; www.ambafrance-gr.org; Leoforos Vasilissis Sofias 7, Syntagma)

German Embassy (210 728 5111; www.athen.diplo.de; Dimitriou Karaoli 3, Kolonaki)

Irish Embassy (☎210 723 2771; www.embassyofireland.gr; Leoforos Vasileos Konstantinou 5-7, Pangrati)

Italian Embassy (☎210 361 7260; www.ambatene.esteri.it; Sekeri 2, Kolonaki)

Netherlands Embassy (☎210 725 4900; www.nederland wereldwijd.nl/landen/grieken land; Leoforos Vasileos Konstantinou 5-7, Pangrati)

Turkish Embassy (☎210 726 3000; http://athens.emb.mfa. gov.tr; Vasileos Georgiou II 11, Syntagma) Has an additional branch in **Athens** (☎210 672 9830; Vasileos Pavlou 22, Psyhiko) and one in **Thessaloniki** (☎2310 248 452; turkbaskon@ kom.forthnet.gr; Agiou Dimitriou 151).

UK Embassy (☎210 727 2600; www.ukingreece.fco.gov.uk; Ploutarhou 1, Kolonaki) Also has a branch in **Thessaloniki** (☎2310 278 006; www.british-consulate.net/Thessaloniki; Tsimiski 43).

US Embassy (☎210 721 2951; http://athens.usembassy.gov; 91 Vasilissis Sofias, Ilissia) Also has a branch in **Thessaloniki** (☎2310 242 905; https:// gr.usembassy.gov; 7th fl, Tsimiski 43).

Gay & Lesbian Travellers

In a country where the Church still plays a prominent role in shaping society's views on issues such as sexuality, it comes as no surprise that homosexuality is generally frowned upon by many locals – especially outside major cities. While there is no legislation against homosexual activity, it pays to be discreet.

Some areas of Greece are, however, extremely popular destinations for gay and lesbian travellers. Athens has a busy gay scene, but most gay and lesbian travellers head for the islands. Mykonos has long been famous for its bars, beaches and general hedonism, while

Skiathos also has its share of gay hang-outs. The island of Lesvos (Mytilini), birthplace of the lesbian poet Sappho, has become something of a place of pilgrimage for lesbians.

The *Spartacus International Gay Guide* (www.spart acusworld.com), published by Bruno Gmünder (Berlin), is widely regarded as the leading authority on gay travel. The Greece section contains a wealth of information on gay venues everywhere from Alexandroupoli to Xanthi.

Health
Availability & Cost of Healthcare

Although medical training is of a high standard in Greece, the public health service is badly underfunded. Hospitals can be overcrowded, hygiene is not always what it should be, and relatives are expected to bring in food for the patient – which can be a problem for a tourist. Conditions and treatment are much better in private hospitals, which are expensive. All this means that a good health-insurance policy is essential.

➡ If you need an ambulance in Greece call ☎166.

➡ There is at least one doctor on every island, and larger islands have hospitals.

➡ Pharmacies can dispense medicines that are available only on prescription in most European countries.

➡ Consult a pharmacist for minor ailments.

Environmental Hazards

➡ Dangerous snakes include the adder and the less common viper and coral snakes. To minimise the possibilities of being bitten, always wear boots, socks and long trousers when walking through undergrowth where snakes may be present.

➡ Mosquitoes can be an annoying problem, though there is no danger of contracting malaria. The electric mosquito-repellent devices are usually sufficient to keep the insects at bay at night. Choose accommodation that has flyscreen on the windows wherever possible. Some mosquitoes in northern Greece can provoke a severe reaction.

➡ The Asian tiger mosquito (*Aedes albopictus*) may be encountered in mountainous areas. It can be a voracious daytime biter and is known to carry several viruses, including Eastern equine encephalitis, which can affect the central nervous system and cause severe complications and death. Use protective sprays or lotion if you suspect you are being bitten during the day.

Insurance

If you're an EU citizen, a European Health Insurance Card (EHIC) covers you for most medical care but not emergency repatriation or nonemergencies. Citizens from other countries should find out if there is a reciprocal arrangement for free medical care between their country and Greece. If you do need health insurance, make sure you get a policy that covers you for the worst possible scenario, such as an accident requiring an emergency flight home. Find out in advance if your insurance plan will make payments directly to providers or reimburse you later for overseas health expenditures.

Worldwide travel insurance is available at www. lonelyplanet.com/travel-insurance. You can buy, extend and claim online any-time – even if you're already on the road.

Water

Tap water is drinkable and safe in much of Greece but not always in small villages and on some of the islands. Always ask locally if the water is safe and, if in doubt, drink boiled or bought water. Even when water is safe, the substances and bacteria in it may be different from those you are used to and can cause vomiting or diarrhoea. Bottled water is widely available.

Internet Access

There has been a huge increase in the number of hotels and businesses using the internet, and free wi-fi is available in most cafes, restaurants and hotels. Some cities even have free wi-fi zones in shopping and eating areas. There are fewer and fewer internet cafes or computers for guests to use as people increasingly carry their own smartphone or tablet.

Legal Matters

It is a good idea to have your passport with you at all times in case you are stopped by the police and questioned. This is particularly true if you are travelling in border areas. Greek citizens are presumed always to have identification on them and the police presume foreign visitors do too. If you are arrested by police insist on an interpreter (*diermi̱néas;* say "*the*-lo dhi-ermi-*nea*") and/or a lawyer (*diki̱góros;* say "*the*-lo dhi-ki-*go*-ro").

Drugs

Greek drug laws are the strictest in Europe. Greek courts make no distinction between possession and pushing. Possession of even a small amount of marijuana is likely to land you in jail.

Maps

Unless you are going to hike or drive, the free maps given out by the EOT and larger hotels will probably suffice,

although they are not 100% accurate.

Anavasi (www.mountains.gr) Athens-based company publishing maps with excellent coverage. Hikers should consider its *Topo* series, which has durable, waterproof paper and detailed walking trails for many of the Aegean islands.

Terrain (www.terrainmaps.gr) Maps published in Athens and offering equally good coverage. All maps can be bought online or at major bookstores in Greece.

Money
ATMS

ATMs are found in every town large enough to support a bank and in almost all the tourist areas. If you have MasterCard or Visa, there are plenty of places to withdraw money. Cirrus and Maestro users can make withdrawals in all major towns and tourist areas. Be aware that many ATMs on the islands can lose their connection for a day or two at a time, making it impossible for anyone (locals included) to withdraw money. It's useful to have a backup source of money.

Automated foreign-exchange machines are common in major tourist areas. They take all major European currencies, Australian and US dollars and Japanese yen, and are useful in an emergency, although they charge a hefty commission.

Be warned that many card companies can put an automatic block on your card after your first withdrawal abroad, as an antifraud mechanism. To avoid this happening, inform your bank of your travel plans.

Cash

Nothing beats cash for convenience – or for risk. If you lose cash, it's gone for good and very few travel insurers will come to your rescue.

Those that will normally limit the amount to approximately US$300. That said, in the current financial climate, many businesses are requesting cash only. It's best to carry no more cash than you need for the next few days. It's also a good idea to set aside a small amount, say US$100, as an emergency stash.

Note that Greek shopkeepers and small-business owners have a perennial problem with having small change. When buying small items it is better to tender coins or small-denomination notes.

Credit Cards

Credit cards are an accepted part of the commercial scene in Greece, although they're often not accepted on many of the smaller islands or in small villages. In larger places, credit cards can be used at top-end hotels, restaurants and shops. Some C-class hotels will accept credit cards, but D- and E-class hotels very seldom do.

The main credit cards are MasterCard and Visa, both of which are widely accepted. They can also be used as cash cards to draw cash from the ATMs of affiliated Greek banks. Daily withdrawal limits are set by the issuing bank and are given in local currency only.

Tipping

Restaurants If a service charge is included, a small tip is appreciated. If there's no service charge, leave 10% to 20%.

Taxis Round up the fare by a couple of euros. There's a small fee for handling bags; this is an official charge, not a tip.

Bellhops Bellhops in hotels and stewards on ferries expect a small gratuity of €1 to €3.

Travellers Cheques

The main reason to carry travellers cheques rather than cash is the protection they offer against theft.

They are, however, losing popularity as more and more travellers opt to put their money in a bank at home and withdraw it at ATMs as they go. American Express, Visa and Thomas Cook cheques are available in euros and are all widely accepted and have efficient replacement policies.

Opening Hours

Opening hours vary throughout the year. We've provided high-season opening hours; hours decrease significantly in the shoulder and low seasons, when many places shut completely.

Banks 8.30am–2.30pm Monday to Thursday, 8am–2pm Friday

Restaurants 11am–3pm and 7pm–1am

Cafes 10am–midnight

Bars 8pm–late

Clubs 10pm–4am

Post Offices 7.30am–2pm Monday to Friday (rural); 7.30am–8pm Monday to Friday, 7.30am–2pm Saturday (urban)

Shops 8am–3pm Monday, Wednesday and Saturday; 8am–2.30pm and 5–8pm Tuesday, Thursday and Friday

Photography

➡ Digital memory cards are readily available from camera stores.

➡ Never photograph a military installation; some are less than obvious and close to wildlife viewing areas.

➡ Flash photography is not allowed inside churches and it's considered taboo to photograph the main altar.

➡ Greeks usually love having their photos taken, but always ask permission first.

➡ At archaeological sites you will be stopped from using a tripod as it marks you as a 'professional'.

PRACTICALITIES

Weights & Measures The metric system is used.

Post To send post abroad, use the yellow post boxes labelled *exoteriko* (for overseas).

Newspapers Greek current affairs are covered in the daily English-language edition of *Kathimerini* (www. ekathimerini.com) within the *New York Times International Edition*.

DVDs Greece is region code 2 if buying DVDs to watch back home.

Public Holidays

All banks and shops and most museums and ancient sites close on public holidays.

Many sites (including the ancient sites in Athens) offer free entry on the first Sunday of the month, with the exception of July and August. You may also gain free entry on other locally celebrated holidays, although this varies across the country.

National public holidays:

New Year's Day 1 January

Epiphany 6 January

First Sunday in Lent February

Greek Independence Day 25 March

Good Friday March/April

Orthodox Easter Sunday 8 April 2018, 28 April 2019, 19 April 2020, 2 May 2021

May Day (Protomagia) 1 May

Whit Monday (Agiou Pnevmatos) 50 days after Easter Sunday

Feast of the Assumption 15 August

Ohi Day 28 October

Christmas Day 25 December

St Stephen's Day 26 December

Safe Travel

Drinks

Adulterated drinks (known as *bombes*) are served in some bars and clubs in Athens and at resorts known for partying. These drinks are diluted with cheap illegal imports that leave you

feeling worse for wear the next day.

At many of the party resorts catering to large budget-tour groups, spiked drinks are not uncommon; keep your hand over the top of your glass. More often than not, the perpetrators are foreign tourists rather than locals.

Tourist Police

The *touristikí astynomía* (tourist police) work in cooperation with the regular Greek police and are found in cities and popular tourist destinations. Each tourist police office has at least one member of staff who speaks English. Hotels, restaurants, travel agencies, tourist shops, tourist guides, waiters, taxi drivers and bus drivers all come under the jurisdiction of the tourist police. If you have a complaint about any of these, report it to the tourist police and they will investigate. If you need to report a theft or loss of passport, go to the tourist police first, and they will act as interpreters between you and the regular police.

Smoking

In July 2009 Greece brought in antismoking laws similar to those found in most of Europe. Smoking is now banned inside public places, with the penalty being fines placed on the business owners. Greece is home to some of the heaviest smokers in

Europe, so enforcement is a challenge. The laws are often imposed in only a nominal way in remote locations where proprietors fear they would lose business.

Telephone

The Greek telephone service is maintained by the public corporation OTE (pronounced o-*teh*; Organismos Tilepikoinonion Ellados). There are public telephones just about everywhere, including in some unbelievably isolated spots. The phones are easy to operate and can be used for local, long-distance and international calls. The 'i' at the top left of the push-button dialling panel brings up the operating instructions in English.

Note that in Greece the area code must always be dialled when making a call (ie all Greek phone numbers are 10-digit).

Mobile Phones

Local SIM cards can be used in European and Australian phones. Most other phones can be set to roaming. US/Canadian phones need to have a dual- or tri-band system.

There are several mobile service providers in Greece, among which Cosmote, Vodafone and Wind are the best known. Of these three, Cosmote tends to have the best coverage in remote areas. All offer 2G connectivity and pay-as-you-talk services for which you can buy a rechargeable SIM card and have your own Greek mobile number. If you're buying a package, be sure to triple-check the fine print. There are restrictions on deals such as 'free minutes' only being available to phones using the same provider.

The use of a mobile phone while driving in Greece is prohibited, but the use of a Bluetooth headset is allowed.

Phonecards

All public phones use OTE phonecards, known as *telekarta*, not coins. These cards are widely available at *periptera* (street kiosks), corner shops and tourist shops. A local call costs around €0.30 for three minutes.

It's also possible to use payphones with the growing range of discount-card schemes. This involves dialling an access code and then punching in your card number. The OTE version of this card is known as 'Hronokarta'. The cards come with instructions in Greek and English and the talk time is enormous compared with the standard phonecard rates.

Time

Greece maintains one time zone throughout the country. It is two hours ahead of GMT/UTC and three hours ahead on daylight-saving time – which begins on the last Sunday in March, when clocks are put forward one hour. Daylight saving ends on the last Sunday in October.

Toilets

➡ Most places in Greece have Western-style toilets, especially hotels and restaurants that cater to tourists. You'll occasionally come across Asian-style squat toilets in older houses, *kafeneia* (coffee houses) and public toilets.

➡ Public toilets are a rarity, except at airports and bus and train stations. Cafes are the best option if you get caught short, but you'll be expected to buy something for the privilege.

➡ The Greek plumbing system can't handle toilet paper; apparently the pipes are too narrow and anything larger than a postage stamp seems

to cause a problem. Toilet paper etc should be placed in the small bin provided next to every toilet.

Tourist Information

The **Greek National Tourist Organisation** (www.visitgreece.gr) is known as GNTO abroad and EOT within Greece. The quality of service from office to office varies dramatically; in some you'll get information aplenty and in others you'll be hard-pressed to find anyone behind the desk. EOT offices can be found in major tourist locations, though they are increasingly being supplemented or even replaced by local municipality tourist offices (such as in the Peloponnese).

The tourist police also fulfil the same functions as the EOT and municipal tourist offices, dispensing maps and brochures, and giving information on transport. If you're really stuck, the tourist police may be able to help find accommodation.

Travellers with Disabilities

Access for travellers with disabilities has improved somewhat in recent years, though mostly in Athens where there are more accessible sights, hotels and restaurants. Much of the rest of Greece remains inaccessible to wheelchairs, and the abundance of stones, marble, slippery cobbles and stepped alleys creates a further challenge. People who have visual or hearing impairments are also rarely catered to.

Careful planning before you go can make a world of difference.

Travel Guide to Greece (www.greecetravel.com/handicapped) Links to local articles, resorts and tour groups catering to tourists with physical disabilities.

Sailing Holidays (www.charter ayachtingreece.com/dryachting/index.html) Two-day to two-week sailing trips around the Greek islands in fully accessible yachts.

Sirens Resort (☎27410 91161; www.disableds-resort.gr; Skalouma) Family-friendly resort with accessible apartments, tours and ramps into the sea.

Visas

The list of countries whose nationals can stay in Greece for up to three months without a visa includes Australia, Canada, all EU countries, Iceland, Israel, Japan, New Zealand, Norway, Switzerland and the USA. Other countries included are the European principalities of Monaco and San Marino and most South American countries. The list changes though – contact Greek embassies for the latest.

If you wish to stay in Greece for longer than three months within a six-month period, you require a visa from the Greek embassy in your country of residence. You are unable to apply for this in Greece. Unlike student and work visas, tourist visas are rarely granted for more than three months.

Volunteering

Hellenic Wildlife Hospital (www.ekpazp.gr) Volunteers head to Aegina (particularly during winter) to this large wildlife rehabilitation centre.

Mouries Farm (☎6947465900; www.skyrianhorses.org; Kalamitsa) Help with the breeding and care of rare Skyrian horses.

Sea Turtle Protection Society of Greece (☎21052 31342; www.archelon.gr) Includes monitoring sea turtles in the Peloponnese.

WWOOF (World Wide Opportunities on Organic Farms; www.wwoofgreece.org) Offers opportunities for volunteers at one of more than 50 farms in Greece.

Women Travellers

Many women travel alone in Greece. The crime rate remains relatively low and solo travel is probably safer than in most European countries. This does not mean that you should be lulled into complacency; bag snatching and sexual assault do occur, particularly at party resorts on the islands.

The biggest nuisance to foreign women travelling alone is the guys the Greeks have nicknamed *kamaki*. The word means 'fishing trident' and refers to the *kamaki's* favourite pastime: 'fishing' for foreign women. You'll find them wherever there are lots of tourists: young (for the most part), smooth-talking guys who aren't in the least bashful about approaching women in the street. They can be very persistent, but they are usually a hassle rather than a threat. The majority of Greek men treat foreign women with respect.

Working

EU nationals don't need a work permit, but they need a residency permit and a Greek tax-file number if they intend to stay longer than three months. Nationals of other countries require a work permit.

English Tutoring

If you're looking for a permanent job, the most widely available option is to teach English. A TEFL (Teaching English as a Foreign Language) certificate or a university degree is an advantage but not essential. In the UK, look through the *Times* educational supplement or Tuesday's edition of the *Guardian* newspaper for opportunities; in other countries, contact the Greek embassy.

Another possibility is to find a job teaching English once you are in Greece. You will see language schools everywhere. Strictly speaking, you need a licence to teach in these schools, but many will employ teachers without one. The best time to look around for such a job is late summer.

The noticeboard at the Compendium bookshop (www.compendium.gr) in Athens sometimes has advertisements looking for private English lessons.

Transport

GETTING THERE & AWAY

Greece is easy to reach by air or sea – particularly in summer when it opens its arms (and schedules) wide. Getting to or from Greece by train or vehicle takes more planning but isn't impossible.

Entering the Country

Visitors to Greece with EU passports are rarely given more than a cursory glance, but customs and police may be interested in what you are carrying. EU citizens may also enter Greece on a national identity card.

Visitors from outside the EU may require a visa. Be sure to check with consular authorities before you arrive.

Air

Greece has four main international airports that take chartered and scheduled flights.

Other international airports across the country

include Santorini (Thira), Karpathos, Samos, Skiathos, Hrysoupoli, Aktion, Kefallonia and Zakynthos. These airports are most often used for charter flights from the UK, Germany and Scandinavia.

Eleftherios Venizelos International Airport (ATH; ☎210 353 0000; www.aia.gr) Athens' Eleftherios Venizelos International Airport lies near Spata, 27km east of Athens. It has all the modern conveniences, including 24-hour luggage storage in the arrivals hall and a children's playroom – even a small archaeological museum above the check-in hall for passing time.

Nikos Kazantzakis International Airport (HER; ☎general 2810 397800, info 2810 397136; www.heraklion-airport. info) About 5km east of Iraklio (Crete). Has a bank, ATM, duty-free shop and cafe-bar.

Diagoras Airport (RHO; ☎22410 88700; www.rhodes-airport.org) On the island of Rhodes.

Makedonia International Airport (SKG; ☎2310 985 000; www. thessalonikiairport.com) About 17km southeast of Thessaloniki. Served by local bus 78 (half-hourly); a taxi costs around €15 to €20.

Airlines

Aegean Airlines (A3; ☎801 112 0000; www.aegeanair.com) and its subsidiary, **Olympic Air** (☎801 801 0101; www. olympicair.com), have flights between Athens and destinations throughout Europe, as well as to Cairo, İstanbul, Tel Aviv, New York and Toronto. They also operate flights throughout Greece, many of which transfer in Athens. Both airlines have exemplary safety records.

Tickets

If you're coming from outside Europe, consider a cheap flight to a European hub (eg London) and then an onward ticket with a charter airline such as **easyJet** (U2; ☎210 967 0000; www.easyjet.com). Some airlines also offer cheap deals to students. If you're planning to travel between June and September, it's wise to book ahead.

Departure Tax

Most airports levy a €13 departure tax for airport improvement; however, it's included in the price of the ticket.

CLIMATE CHANGE & TRAVEL

Every form of transport that relies on carbon-based fuel generates CO_2, the main cause of human-induced climate change. Modern travel is dependent on aeroplanes, which might use less fuel per kilometre per person than most cars but travel much greater distances. The altitude at which aircraft emit gases (including CO_2) and particles also contributes to their climate change impact. Many websites offer 'carbon calculators' that allow people to estimate the carbon emissions generated by their journey and, for those who wish to do so, to offset the impact of the greenhouse gases emitted with contributions to portfolios of climate-friendly initiatives throughout the world. Lonely Planet offsets the carbon footprint of all staff and author travel.

OVERLAND FROM WESTERN EUROPE

If you're keen to travel without flying and enjoy the independence of a road trip, you can reach Greece by heading overland to an Italian port and hopping on a ferry. A high-speed ferry from Venice to Patra takes around 26 hours. Patra to Athens is a 3½-hour drive.

Fancy a bit more convenience and speed than a bus or a car? Overland enthusiasts can reach Greece by rail through the Balkan peninsula, passing through Croatia, Serbia and the Former Yugoslav Republic of Macedonia. Or head to the western coast of Italy (there are connections throughout most of Europe) and then take a ferry to Greece. Not only will you be doing your bit for the earth, but you'll see some gorgeous scenery from your window.

A sample itinerary from London would see you catching the Eurostar to Paris and then an overnight sleeper train to Bologna in Italy. From there, a coastal train takes you to Bari, where there's an overnight boat to Patra in the Peloponnese. From Patra, it's a 4½-hour train journey to Athens. You'll be in Athens within two days of leaving London. See www.raileurope.com for routes and tickets.

Greece is part of the Eurail network (www.eurail.com). Eurail passes can be bought only by residents of non-European countries; they should be purchased before arriving in Europe, but can be bought in Europe if your passport proves that you've been there for less than six months. Greece is also part of the Inter-Rail Pass system (www.interrail.eu), available to those who have resided in Europe for six months or more, and the Rail Plus Balkan Flexipass (www.raileurope.com), which offers unlimited travel for five, 10 or 15 days within a month. See the websites for full details of passes and prices.

Land

If you travel by land you can really appreciate the landscape, as well as the many experiences that go along with train or bus travel. International train travel, in particular, has become much more feasible in recent years, with speedier trains and better connections. You can now travel from London to Athens by train and ferry in less than two days. By choosing to travel on the ground instead of the air, you'll also be reducing your carbon footprint.

Border Crossings

Due to the ongoing refugee crisis, make sure you have all of your visas sorted out before attempting to cross land borders into or out of Greece. At the time of writing, all migrants were being denied access to the borders while EU passport holders were allowed across. As the situation is volatile, it's worth checking with the relevant embassies before travelling.

ALBANIA

The main crossing at Kakavia can have intensely slow queues.

Albatrans (☑+355 42 259 204; www.albatrans.com.al) runs buses between Greece and Albania.

Kakavia 60km northwest of Ioannina

Krystallopigi 14km west of Kotas on the Florina–Kastoria road

Mertziani 17km west of Konitsa

Sagiada 28km north of Igoumenitsa

BULGARIA

As Bulgaria is part of the EU, crossings are usually quick and hassle-free.

Exohi A 448m-tunnel border crossing 50km north of Drama

Ormenio 41km from Serres in northeastern Thrace

Promahonas 109km northeast of Thessaloniki

FORMER YUGOSLAV REPUBLIC OF MACEDONIA (FYROM)

Doïrani 31km north of Kilkis

Evzoni 68km north of Thessaloniki

Niki 16km north of Florina

TURKEY

Kipi is more convenient if you're heading for İstanbul. The route through Kastanies goes via Soufli and Didymotiho in Greece, and Edirne (ancient Adrianoupolis) in Turkey.

Kastanies 139km northeast of Alexandroupoli

Kipi 43km east of Alexandroupoli

Train

The Greek railways organisation **OSE** (Organismos Sidirodromon Ellados; ☑14511; www.trainose.gr) runs daily trains from Thessaloniki to Sofia and to Belgrade (via Skopje), with a weekly onward train to and from Budapest.

Sea

Ferries can get very crowded in summer. If you want to take a vehicle across it's wise to make a reservation beforehand. Please note that tickets for all ferries to Turkey must be bought a day in advance – and you will almost certainly be asked to turn in your passport the night before the trip. It will be returned the next day before you board the boat. Port tax for departures to Turkey is around €15.

Another way to visit by sea is to join one of the many cruises that ply the Aegean.

Ferry Routes

100 km
50 miles

Black
Sea

TURKEY

Sea of Marmara

TURKEY

BULGARIA

Thracian
Sea

Alexandroupoli

Keramoti

Kavala

Skala
Prinou

Thasos
(Limenas)

Thasos

THRACE

Samothraki

Gökçeada
(Imvros)

Limnos

Myrina

Agios
Efstratios

Sigri

Lesvos

Mytilini
Town

Aegean Sea

Northeastern
Aegean Islands

Skyros

SERBIA

MACEDONIA
(FYROM)

MACEDONIA

Thessaloniki

Gulf of
Thessaloniki

Thessaloniki

Sporades

Loutraki

Skiathos (Glossa Port)

Prasouda

Alonnisos

Skopelos

THESSALY

Volos

Glyfa

Agiokambos

Loutra Edipsou

Agios
Konstantinos

Arkitsa

Evia

Kymi

STEREA
ELLADA

ALBANIA

EPIROS

Igoumenitsa

Preveza

Meganisi

Mytikas

Corfu
Town

Lefkimmi

Corfu

Paxi

Antipaxi

Lefkada

Vasiliki

IONIAN
ISLANDS

Italy

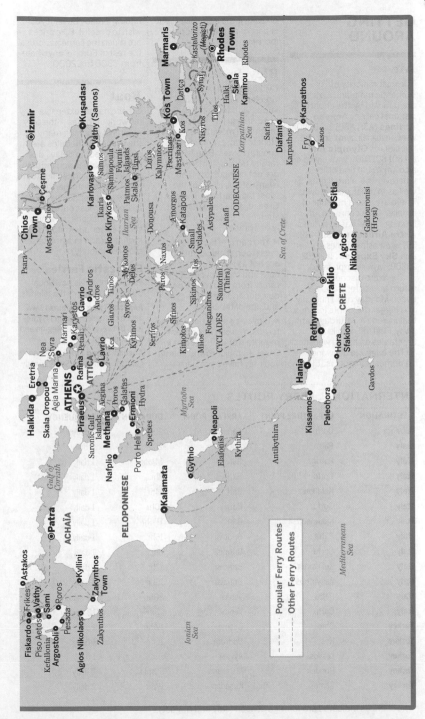

GETTING AROUND

Air

The vast majority of domestic mainland flights are handled by the country's national carrier **Aegean Airlines** (A3; ☎801 112 0000; www.aegeanair.com) and its subsidiary, **Olympic Air** (☎801 801 0101; www.olympic air.com). You'll find offices wherever there are flights, as well as in other major towns. There are also a number of smaller Greek carriers, including Crete-based airlines **Astra Airlines** (☎2310 489 391; www.astra-airlines.gr) and **Sky Express** (☎28102 23800; www.skyexpress.gr).

There are discounts for return tickets for travel between Monday and Thursday, and bigger discounts for trips that include a Saturday night away. Find full details and timetables on airline websites.

The baggage allowance on domestic flights is 15kg,

or 20kg if the domestic flight is part of an international journey.

Bicycle

Cycling is not popular among Greeks – but it's gaining kudos with tourists. You'll need strong leg muscles to tackle the mountains; or just stick to some of the flatter coastal routes. Bike lanes are rare to nonexistent; helmets are not compulsory. The island of Kos is about the most bicycle-friendly place in Greece, as is anywhere flat, such as the plains of Thessaly or Thrace.

➡ You can hire bicycles in most tourist places, but they are not as widely available as cars and motorcycles. Prices range from €10 to €15 per day, depending on the type and age of the bike.

➡ Bicycles are carried free on ferries. You can buy decent mountain or touring bikes in Greece's major towns, though you may have a problem

finding a ready buyer if you wish to onsell it. Bike prices are much the same as across the rest of Europe: anywhere from €300 to €2000.

Boat

Greece has an extensive network of ferries – the only means of reaching many of the islands. Schedules are often subject to delays due to poor weather and industrial action, and prices fluctuate regularly. In summer, ferries run regular service between all but the most out-of-the-way destinations; however, services seriously slow down in winter (and in some cases stop completely).

Domestic Ferries

Ferry companies have local offices on many of the islands.

Aegean Flying Dolphins (www. aegeanflyingdolphins.gr) Hydrofoils between Athens, Aegina and the Sporades.

Aegean Speed Lines (www.ae geanspeedlines.gr) Superspeedy

INTERNATIONAL FERRY ROUTES

DESTINATION	DEPARTURE POINT	ARRIVAL POINT	DURATION	FREQUENCY
Albania	Corfu	Saranda	25min	1 daily
Italy	Patra	Ancona	20hr	3 daily
Italy	Patra	Bari	14½hr	1 daily
Italy	Corfu	Bari	8hr	1 daily
Italy	Kefallonia	Bari	14hr	1 daily
Italy	Corfu	Bari	10hr	1 daily
Italy	Igoumenitsa	Bari	11½hr	1 daily
Italy	Patra	Brindisi	15hr	1 daily
Italy	Corfu	Brindisi	6hr	1 daily
Italy	Kefallonia	Brindisi	12hr	1 daily
Italy	Zakynthos	Brindisi	15hr	1 daily
Italy	Patra	Venice	30hr	12 weekly
Italy	Corfu	Venice	25hr	12 weekly
Turkey	Chios	Çeşme	1½hr	1 daily
Turkey	Kos	Bodrum	1hr	1 daily
Turkey	Lesvos	Ayvalik	1hr	1 daily
Turkey	Rhodes	Marmaris	50min	2 daily
Turkey	Samos	Kuşadası	1½hr	2 daily

*The services indicated are for high season (July and August).

boats between Athens and the Cyclades.

Aegeon Pelagos (www.anek.gr) A subsidiary of ANEK Lines.

ANEK Lines (www.anek.gr) Crete-based long-haul ferries. Its Igoumenitsa–Patra route is now jointly operated by Superfast Ferries.

ANES (www.anes.gr) Old-style ferries servicing Evia and the Sporades.

Anna Express (www.annaexpress. eu) Small, fast ferry connecting the northern Dodecanese.

Blue Star Ferries (www.bluestar ferries.com) Long-haul, high-speed ferries and Seajets catamarans between the mainland, the Cyclades, the north-eastern Aegean Islands, Crete and the Dodecanese.

Dodekanisos Seaways (www. 12ne.gr) Runs large, high-speed catamarans in the Dodecanese.

Fast Ferries (www.fastferries. com.gr) Comfortable ferries from Rafina to the Cyclades islands of Andros, Tinos, Naxos and Mykonos.

Glyfa Ferries (www.ferriesglyfa. gr) Comfortable short-haul ferry services between Glyfa on the mainland and Agiokambos in northern Evia.

Hellenic Seaways (www.hellenic seaways.gr) Conventional long-haul ferries and catamarans from the mainland to the Cyclades and between the Sporades and Saronic islands.

Ionian Ferries (www.ionian ferries.gr) Large ferries serving the Ionian Islands.

LANE Lines (www.ferries.gr/lane) Long-haul ferries serving the Ionians, Dodecanese and Crete.

Minoan Lines (www.minoan. gr) High-speed luxury ferries between Piraeus and Iraklio, and Patra, Igoumenitsa and Corfu.

Patmos Star (www.patmos-star. com) Small, local ferry linking Patmos, Leros and Lipsi in the Dodecanese.

SAOS Lines (www.saos.gr) Big, slow boats calling in at many of the islands.

Seajets (www.seajets.gr) Catamarans calling at Athens, Crete, Santorini (Thira), Paros and many islands in between.

Skyros Shipping Company (www.sne.gr) Slow boat between Skyros and Kymi on Evia.

Superfast Ferries (www.super fast.com) As the name implies, speedy ferries from the mainland to Crete, Corfu and Patra.

Ventouris Ferries (www.ventour issealines.gr) Big boats from the mainland to the Cyclades.

Zante Ferries (www.zanteferries. gr) Older ferries connecting the mainland with the western Cyclades.

Bus

The bus network is comprehensive. All long-distance buses, on the mainland and the islands, are operated by regional collectives known as KTEL (www.ktelbus.com). Details of interurban buses throughout Greece are available by dialling ☑14505. Bus fares are fixed by the government and bus travel is very reasonably priced. A journey costs approximately €5 per 100km.

Services

Every prefecture on the mainland has a KTEL, which operates local services within it and to the main towns of other prefectures. With the exception of towns in Thrace, which are serviced by Thessaloniki, all major towns on the mainland have frequent connections to Athens. The islands of Corfu, Kefallonia and Zakynthos can also be reached directly from Athens by bus – the fares include the price of the ferry ticket.

Most villages have a daily bus service of some sort, although remote areas may have only one or two buses a week. They operate for the benefit of people going to town to shop, rather than for tourists, and consequently leave the villages very early in the morning and return early in the afternoon.

Practicalities

➡ It is important to note that big cities like Athens, Iraklio, Patra and Thessaloniki may have more than one

bus station, each serving different regions. Make sure you find the correct station for your destination. In small towns and villages the 'bus station' may be no more than a bus stop outside a *kafeneio* (coffee house) or taverna that doubles as a booking office.

➡ In remote areas, the timetable may be in Greek only, but most booking offices have timetables in both Greek and Roman script and many bus stations are now posting them online.

➡ It's best to turn up at least 20 minutes before departure to make sure you get a seat – buses have been known to leave a few minutes before their scheduled departure.

➡ When you buy a ticket you may be allotted a seat number, printed on the ticket. The seat number is indicated on the *back* of each seat of the bus, not on the back of the seat in front; this causes confusion among Greeks and tourists alike. Often, the seat numbers are simply ignored.

➡ You can board a bus without a ticket and pay on board, but on a popular route or during high season, you may have to stand.

➡ The KTEL buses are safe and modern, and these days most are air conditioned – at least on major routes. In more remote, rural areas they tend to be older and less comfortable. Buses on less-frequented routes do not usually have toilets on board and stop about every three hours on long journeys.

➡ Smoking is prohibited on all buses in Greece.

Car & Motorcycle

No one who has travelled in Greece will be surprised to hear that the country's road fatality rate is one of the highest in Europe. More than 1000 people die on the roads every year, with 10 times that number of people injured. Overtaking is listed as the greatest cause of accidents.

TRANSPORT CAR & MOTORCYCLE

ROAD DISTANCES (KM)

	Alexandroupoli	Athens	Corinth	Edessa	Florina	Igoumenitsa	Ioannina	Kalamata	Kastoria	Kavala	Lamia	Larisa	Monemvasia	Nafplio	Patra	Pyrgos	Sparta	Thessaloniki	Trikala	Tripoli
Athens	854																			
Corinth	884	84																		
Edessa	427	569	596																	
Florina	497	592	251	353																
Igoumenitsa	816	473	393	380	353															
Ioannina	702	447	364	298	320	96														
Kalamata	1055	284	175	767	763	501	467													
Kastoria	535	489	519	108	67	286	204	690												
Kavala	177	682	655	250	320	615	525	878	358											
Lamia	643	214	244	355	360	353	263	415	274	466										
Larisa	493	361	389	218	231	309	209	561	239	323	151									
Monemvasia	1156	350	266	869	855	613	579	156	756	976	505	655								
Nafplio	947	165	63	659	664	482	427	163	582	770	307	455	215							
Patra	828	220	138	567	513	281	247	220	483	664	193	341	332	201						
Pyrgos	924	320	234	636	643	367	347	119	542	747	284	432	275	208	96					
Sparta	1025	225	145	737	759	517	483	60	660	848	385	533	96	119	236	180				
Thessaloniki	349	513	544	89	159	452	362	715	220	169	303	154	807	610	488	584	711			
Trikala	554	330	356	227	233	247	148	520	159	377	115	62	597	419	310	400	501	216		
Tripoli	964	194	110	713	681	457	430	90	639	820	324	472	157	81	176	155	61	624	466	
Volos	556	326	355	278	293	371	271	518	301	383	115	62	620	417	308	408	524	214	124	435

Heart-stopping moments aside, your own car is a great way to explore off the beaten track. The road network has improved enormously in recent years; many roads marked as dirt tracks on older maps have now been asphalted and many of the islands have very little traffic. There are regular (if costly) car-ferry services to almost all islands.

AUTOMOBILE ASSOCIATIONS

Greece's domestic automobile association is **ELPA** (Elliniki Leschi Aftokinitou kai Periigiseon; ☎210 606 8800, 24hr roadside assistance 10400; Leoforos Mesogion 541, Agia Paraskevi, Athens).

ENTRY

EU-registered vehicles enter free for up to six months without road taxes being due. A green card (international third-party insurance) is required, along with proof of date of entry (ferry ticket or your passport stamp). Non-EU-registered vehicles may be logged in your passport.

DRIVING LICENCES

EU driving licences are valid in Greece. Drivers from outside the EU may require International Driving Permits; while rental agencies will rarely ask for one, local authorities may if you're stopped. International Driving Permits can only be obtained in the country where your driving licence was issued.

FUEL

Available widely throughout the country, though service stations may be closed on weekends and public holidays. On the islands, there may be only one petrol station; check where it is before you head out. Self-service and credit-card pumps are not the norm in Greece. Petrol is cheaper here than in many European countries, but expensive by American or Australian standards.

Petrol types:

➡ *super* (leaded)

➡ *amolyvdi* (unleaded)

➡ *petreleo kinisis* (diesel)

Hire

CARS

➡ All the big multinational companies are represented in Athens; most have branches in major towns and popular tourist destinations. The majority of islands have at least one outlet.

➡ By Greek law, rental cars have to be replaced every six years, so most vehicles you hire will be relatively new.

➡ The minimum driving age in Greece is 18 years, but most car-hire firms require you to be at least 21 (or 23 for larger vehicles).

➡ High-season weekly rates with unlimited mileage start at about €280 for the smallest models (eg a Fiat Seicento), dropping to about €200 per week in winter. These prices don't include local tax (known as VAT).

➡ You can often find great deals at local companies. Their advertised rates can be up to 50% cheaper than the multinationals and they are normally open to negotiation, especially if business is slow.

➡ On the islands, you can rent a car for the day for around €35 to €60, including all insurance and taxes.

➡ Always check what the insurance includes; there are often rough roads or dangerous routes that you can only tackle by renting a 4WD.

➡ If you want to take a hire car to another country or on to a ferry, you will need advance written authorisation from the hire company, as the insurance may not cover you.

➡ Unless you pay with a credit card, most hire companies will require a minimum deposit of €120 per day.

The major car-hire companies in Greece:

Avis (www.avis.gr)

Budget (www.budget.gr)

Europcar (www.europcar.gr)

MOTORCYCLES

➡ Mopeds, motorcycles and scooters are available for hire wherever there are tourists to rent them. Most machines are newish and in good condition. Nonetheless, check the brakes at the earliest opportunity.

➡ You must produce a licence that shows proficiency to ride the category of bike you wish to rent; this applies to everything from 50cc up. British citizens must obtain a Category A licence from the Driver & Vehicle Licensing Agency (www.dft.gov.uk/dvla) in the UK (in most other EU countries separate licences are automatically issued).

➡ Rates start from about €20 per day for a moped or 50cc motorcycle, ranging to €35 per day for a 250cc motorcycle. Out of season these prices drop considerably, so use your bargaining skills.

➡ Most motorcycle hirers include third-party insurance in the price, but it's wise to check this. This insurance will not include medical expenses.

➡ Helmets are compulsory and rental agencies are obliged to offer one as part of the hire deal.

Road Conditions

➡ Main highways in Greece have been improving steadily over the years but many still don't offer smooth sailing.

➡ Some main roads retain the two-lane/hard-shoulder format of the 1960s, which can be confusing and even downright dangerous.

➡ Roadworks can take years and years in Greece – especially on the islands, where funding often only trickles in. In other cases, excellent new tarmac roads may have appeared that are not on any local maps.

Road Hazards

➡ Slow drivers – many of them unsure and hesitant tourists – can cause serious traffic events on the roads.

➡ Road surfaces can change rapidly when a section of road has succumbed to subsidence or weathering. Snow and ice can be a serious challenge in winter,

and drivers are advised to carry snow chains. In rural areas, keep a close eye out for animals wandering on to roads.

➡ Roads passing through mountainous areas are often littered with fallen rocks, which can cause extensive damage to a vehicle's underside or throw a motorbike rider.

Road Rules

➡ In Greece, as throughout Continental Europe, you drive on the right and overtake on the left.

➡ Outside built-up areas, traffic on a main road has right of way at intersections. In towns, vehicles coming from the right have right of way. This includes roundabouts – even if you're in the roundabout, you must give way to drivers coming on to the roundabout to your right.

➡ Seatbelts must be worn in front seats, and in back seats if the car is fitted with them.

➡ Children under 12 years of age are not allowed in the front seat.

➡ It is compulsory to carry a first-aid kit, fire extinguisher and warning triangle, and it is forbidden to carry cans of petrol.

➡ Helmets are compulsory for motorcyclists if the motorcycle is 50cc or more. Police will book you if you're caught without a helmet.

➡ Outside residential areas the speed limit is 120km/h on

MOTORCYCLE WARNING

Greece is not the best place to initiate yourself into motorcycling. There are still a lot of gravel roads, particularly on the islands, and dozens of tourists have accidents every year. Scooters are particularly prone to sliding on gravelly bends. Try to hire a motorcycle with thinner-profile tyres. If you plan to use a motorcycle or moped, check that your travel insurance covers you: many insurance companies don't cover motorcycle accidents. Another option on the islands is to rent quad bikes – they're slightly more expensive but don't require a motorcycle licence.

highways, 90km/h on other roads and 50km/h in built-up areas. The speed limit for motorcycles up to 100cc is 70km/h; for larger motorcycles, 90km/h. Drivers exceeding the speed limit by 20% are liable to receive a fine of €60; exceeding it by 40% costs €150.

➡ A blood-alcohol content of 0.05% can incur a fine of €150, while over 0.08% is a criminal offence.

➡ If you are involved in an accident and no one is hurt, the police will not be required to write a report, but it is advisable to go to a nearby police station and explain what happened. You may need a police report for insurance purposes. If an accident involves injury, a driver who does not stop and does not inform the police may face a prison sentence.

Local Transport

Bus

Most Greek towns are small enough to get around on foot. All the major towns have local buses, but the only places you're likely to need them are Athens, Patra, Kalamata and Thessaloniki.

Metro

Athens is the only city in Greece large enough to warrant an underground system. Note that only Greek student cards are valid for a student ticket on the metro.

Taxi

Taxis are widely available in Greece, except on very small or remote islands. They are reasonably priced by European standards. Many taxi drivers have sat-nav systems in their cars, so finding a destination is a breeze as long as you have the exact address.

Yellow city cabs are metered, with rates doubling between midnight and 5am. Additional costs are charged for trips from an airport or a bus, port or train station, as well as for each piece of

luggage over 10kg. Grey rural taxis do not have meters, so you should always settle on a price before you get in.

Some taxi drivers in Athens have been known to overcharge unwary travellers. If you have a complaint about a taxi driver, take the cab number and report your complaint to the tourist police. Taxi drivers in other towns in Greece are, on the whole, friendly, helpful and honest.

Tours

Tours are worth considering if your time is very limited or if you prefer someone else do the planning. In Athens, you'll find countless day tours, with some agencies offering two- or three-day trips to nearby sights. For something on a larger scale, try Intrepid Travel (www.intrepidtravel.com; offices in Australia, the UK and the USA). Encounter Greece (www.encounter greece.com) offers a plethora of tours; a 13-day tour across the country costs €1445 while seven days on the mainland is €885.

More adventurous tours include guided activities such as hiking, climbing, white-water rafting, kayaking, canoeing or canyoning.

Also worth considering:

Alpin Club (www.alpinclub.gr) For kayaking, rafting, canyoning and mountain biking – just to name a few. In Athens but operates out of Karitena in the Peloponnese.

Robinson Expeditions (www.robinson.gr) For hiking and mountain biking. Run tours from the centre and north of Greece.

Trekking Hellas (www.trekking.gr) An outfit that runs trekking, kayaking and rafting tours from the centre and north of Greece.

Train

Trains are operated by the Greek railways organisation **OSE** (Organismos Sidirodromon Ellados; ☎14511; www.trainose.gr). The Greek railway network is limited; its northern line is the most substantial.

Standard-gauge service runs from Athens to Dikea in the northeast via Thessaloniki and Alexandroupoli. There are also connections to Florina and the Pelion Peninsula. The Peloponnese network runs only as far as Klato, with bus services to Plata for ferry connections.

Due to financial instability, prices and schedules are very changeable. When you can, double-check on the OSE website. Information on departures from Athens or Thessaloniki are also available by calling ☎1440.

Classes

There are two types of service: regular (slow) trains that stop at all stations, and faster, modern intercity (IC) trains that link most major cities. The slow trains represent the country's cheapest form of public transport: 2nd-class fares are absurdly cheap, and even 1st class is cheaper than bus travel.

The IC trains that link the major Greek cities are an excellent way to travel. The services are not necessarily fast – Greece is far too mountainous for that – but the trains are modern and comfortable. There is a cafe-bar on board. On some services, meals can be ordered and delivered to your seat. The night service between Athens and Thessaloniki also offers a choice of couchettes, two-bed compartments and single compartments.

Train Passes

➡ Eurail, Inter-Rail and Rail Plus Balkan Flexipass cards are valid in Greece, but they're generally not worth buying if Greece is the only place where you plan to use them. For IC and sleeper cars, a costly supplement is required.

➡ On presentation of ID or passports, passengers more than 60 years old are entitled to a 25% discount on all lines, except in July and August and over the Easter week.

➡ Whatever pass you have, you must have a reservation to board the train.

Language

The Greek language is believed to be one of the oldest European languages, with an oral tradition of 4000 years and a written tradition of approximately 3000 years. Due to its centuries of influence, Greek constitutes the origin of a large part of the vocabulary of many Indo-European languages (including English). It is the official language of Greece and co-official language of Cyprus (alongside Turkish), and is spoken by many migrant communities throughout the world.

The Greek alphabet is explained on the following page, but if you read the pronunciation guides given with each phrase in this chapter as if they were English, you'll be understood. Note that dh is pronounced as 'th' in 'there'; gh is a softer, slightly throaty version of 'g'; and kh is a throaty sound like the 'ch' in the Scottish 'loch'. All Greek words of two or more syllables have an acute accent (´), which indicates where the stress falls. In our pronunciation guides, stressed syllables are in italics.

In this chapter, masculine, feminine and neuter forms of words are included where necessary, separated with a slash and indicated with 'm', 'f' and 'n' respectively. Polite and informal options are indicated where relevant with 'pol' and 'inf'.

BASICS

Hello.	Γειά σας.	ya·sas (pol)
	Γειά σου.	ya·su (inf)
Goodbye.	Αντίο.	an·di·o

WANT MORE?

For in-depth language information and handy phrases, check out Lonely Planet's *Greek Phrasebook*. You'll find it at **shop.lonelyplanet.com**, or you can buy Lonely Planet's iPhone phrasebooks at the Apple App Store.

Yes./No.	Ναι./Οχι.	ne/o·hi
Please.	Παρακαλώ.	pa·ra·ka·lo
Thank you.	Ευχαριστώ.	ef·ha·ri·sto
You're welcome.	Παρακαλώ.	pa·ra·ka·lo
Excuse me.	Με συγχωρείτε.	me sing·kho·ri·te
Sorry.	Συγγνώμη.	sigh·no·mi

What's your name?
Πώς σας λένε;   pos sas le·ne

My name is ...
Με λένε ...   me le·ne ...

Do you speak English?
Μιλάτε αγγλικά;   mi·la·te an·gli·ka

I don't understand.
Δεν καταλαβαίνω.   dhen ka·ta·la·ve·no

ACCOMMODATION

campsite	χώρος για κάμπινγκ	kho·ros yia kam·ping
hotel	ξενοδοχείο	kse·no·dho·khi·o
youth hostel	γιουθ χόστελ	yuth kho·stel
a ... room	ένα ... δωμάτιο	e·na ... dho·ma·ti·o
single	μονόκλινο	mo·no·kli·no
double	δίκλινο	dhi·kli·no
How much is it ...?	Πόσο κάνει ...;	po·so ka·ni ...
per night	τη βραδυά	ti·vra·dhya
per person	το άτομο	to a·to·mo
air-con	έρκοντίσιον	er·kon·di·si·on
bathroom	μπάνιο	ba·nio
fan	ανεμιστήρας	a·ne·mi·sti·ras
window	παράθυρο	pa·ra·thi·ro

GREEK APLHABET

The Greek alphabet has 24 letters, shown below in their upper- and lower-case forms. Be aware that some letters look like English letters but are pronounced very differently, such as **B**, which is pronounced v; and **P**, pronounced r. As in English, how letters are pronounced is also influenced by the way they are combined, for example the **ου** combination is pronounced u as in 'put', and **οι** is pronounced ee as in 'feet'.

Α α	a	as in 'father'	**Ξ ξ**	x	as in 'ox'
Β β	v	as in 'vine'	**Ο ο**	o	as in 'hot'
Γ γ	gh	a softer, throaty 'g', or	**Π π**	p	as in 'pup'
	y	as in 'yes'	**Ρ ρ**	r	as in 'road',
Δ δ	dh	as in 'there'			slightly trilled
Ε ε	e	as in 'egg'	**Σ σ, ς**	s	as in 'sand'
Ζ ζ	z	as in 'zoo'	**Τ τ**	t	as in 'tap'
Η η	i	as in 'feet'	**Υ υ**	i	as in 'feet'
Θ θ	th	as in 'throw'	**Φ φ**	f	as in 'find'
Ι ι	i	as in 'feet'	**Χ χ**	kh	as the 'ch' in the
Κ κ	k	as in 'kite'			Scottish 'loch', or
Λ λ	l	as in 'leg'		h	like a rough 'h'
Μ μ	m	as in 'man'	**Ψ ψ**	ps	as in 'lapse'
Ν ν	n	as in 'net'	**Ω ω**	o	as in 'hot'

Note that the letter **Σ** has two forms for the lower case – **σ** and **ς**. The second one is used at the end of words. The Greek question mark is represented with the English equivalent of a semicolon (;).

DIRECTIONS

Where is ...?
Πού είναι …;   pu *i*·ne …

What's the address?
Ποια είναι η διεύθυνση;   pia *i*·ne i dhi·*ef*·thin·si

Can you show me (on the map)?
Μπορείς να μου δείξεις   bo·*ris* na mu *dhik*·sis
(στο χάρτη);   (sto *khar*·ti)

Turn left.
Στρίψτε αριστερά.   *strips*·te a·ri·ste·*ra*

Turn right.
Στρίψτε δεξιά.   *strips*·te dhe·*ksia*

at the next corner
στην επόμενη γωνία   stin e·*po*·me·ni gho·*ni*·a

at the traffic lights
στα φώτα   sta *fo*·ta

behind | πίσω | *pi*·so
far | μακριά | ma·kri·*a*
in front of | μπροστά | bro·*sta*
near (to) | κοντά | kon·*da*
next to | δίπλα | *dhi*·pla
opposite | απέναντι | a·*pe*·nan·di
straight ahead | ολο ευθεία | o·lo ef·*thi*·a

EATING & DRINKING

a table for ... | Ενα τραπέζι | e·na tra·*pe*·zi
| για … | ya …

(eight) o'clock | στις (οχτώ) | stis (okh·*to*)
(two) people | (δύο) άτομα | (*dhi*·o) a·to·ma

I don't eat ... | Δεν τρώγω … | dhen tro·gho …
fish | ψάρι | psa·ri
(red) meat | (κόκκινο) | (ko·ki·no)
| κρέας | kre·as
peanuts | φυστίκια | fi·*sti*·kia
poultry | πουλερικά | pu·le·ri·*ka*

What would you recommend?
Τι θα συνιστούσες;   ti tha si·ni·*stu*·ses

What's in that dish?
Τι περιέχει αυτό το   ti pe·ri·e·hi af·*to* to
φαγητό;   fa·ghi·*to*

Cheers!
Εις υγείαν!   is i·*yi*·an

That was delicious.
Ήταν νοστιμότατο!   *i*·tan no·sti·*mo*·ta·to

Please bring the bill.
Το λογαριασμό,   to lo·ghar·ya·zmo
παρακαλώ.   pa·ra·ka·*lo*

Key Words

appetisers	ορεκτικά	o·rek·ti·ka
bar	μπαρ	bar
beef	βοδινό	vo·dhi·no
beer	μπύρα	bi·ra
bottle	μπουκάλι	bu·ka·li
bowl	μπωλ	bol
bread	ψωμί	pso·mi
breakfast	πρόγευμα	pro·yev·ma
cafe	καφετέρια	ka·fe·te·ri·a
cheese	τυρί	ti·ri
chicken	κοτόπουλο	ko·to·pu·lo
coffee	καφές	ka·fes
cold	κρύο	kri·o
cream	κρέμα	kre·ma
delicatessen	ντελικατέσεν	de·li·ka·te·sen
desserts	επιδόρπια	e·pi·dhor·pi·a
dinner	δείπνο	dhip·no
egg	αυγό	av·gho
fish	ψάρι	psa·ri
food	φαγητό	fa·yi·to
fork	πιρούνι	pi·ru·ni
fruit	φρούτα	fru·ta
glass	ποτήρι	po·ti·ri
grocery store	οπωροπωλείο	o·po·ro·po·li·o
herb	βότανο	vo·ta·no
high chair	καρέκλα για μωρά	ka·re·kla yia mo·ra
hot	ζεστός	ze·stos
juice	χυμός	hi·mos
knife	μαχαίρι	ma·he·ri
lamb	αρνί	ar·ni
lunch	μεσημεριανό φαγητό	me·si·me·ria·no fa·yi·to
main courses	κύρια φαγητά	ki·ri·a fa·yi·ta
market	αγορά	a·gho·ra
menu	μενού	me·nu
milk	γάλα	gha·la
nut	καρύδι	ka·ri·dhi
oil	λάδι	la·dhi
pepper	πιπέρι	pi·pe·ri
plate	πιάτο	pia·to
pork	χοιρινό	hi·ri·no
red wine	κόκκινο κρασί	ko·ki·no kra·si
restaurant	εστιατόριο	e·sti·a·to·ri·o
salt	αλάτι	a·la·ti
soft drink	αναψυκτικό	a·na·psik·ti·ko

spoon	κουτάλι	ku·ta·li
sugar	ζάχαρη	za·kha·ri
tea	τσάι	tsa·i
vegetable	λαχανικά	la·kha·ni·ka
vegetarian	χορτοφάγος	khor·to·fa·ghos
vinegar	ξύδι	ksi·dhi
water	νερό	ne·ro
white wine	άσπρο κρασί	a·spro kra·si
with/without	με/χωρίς	me/kho·ris

SIGNS

ΕΙΣΟΔΟΣ	Entry
ΕΞΟΔΟΣ	Exit
ΠΛΗΡΟΦΟΡΙΕΣ	Information
ΑΝΟΙΧΤΟ	Open
ΚΛΕΙΣΤΟ	Closed
ΑΠΑΓΟΡΕΥΕΤΑΙ	Prohibited
ΑΣΤΥΝΟΜΙΑ	Police
ΓΥΝΑΙΚΩΝ	Toilets (Women)
ΑΝΔΡΩΝ	Toilets (Men)

EMERGENCIES

Help!	Βοήθεια!	vo·i·thya
Go away!	Φύγε!	fi·ye
I'm lost.	Έχω χαθεί.	e·kho kha·thi
Where's the toilet?	Πού είναι η τουαλέτα;	pu i·ne i tu·a·le·ta
Call ...!	Φωνάξτε ...!	fo·nak·ste ...
a doctor	ένα γιατρό	e·na yi·a·tro
the police	την αστυνομία	tin a·sti·no·mi·a

I'm ill.
Είμαι άρρωστος.   i·me a·ro·stos

I'm allergic to (antibiotics).
Είμαι αλλεργικός/   i·me a·ler·yi·kos/
αλλεργική   a·ler·yi·ki (m/f)
(στα αντιβιωτικά)   (sta an·di·vi·o·ti·ka)

QUESTION WORDS

How?	Πώς;	pos
What?	Τι;	ti
When?	Πότε;	po·te
Where?	Πού;	pu
Who?	Ποιος;	pi·os (m)
	Ποια;	pi·a (f)
	Ποιο;	pi·o (n)
Why?	Γιατί;	yi·a·ti

KEY PATTERNS

To get by in Greek, mix and match these simple patterns with words of your choice:

When's (the next bus)?
Πότε είναι | po·te i·ne
(το επόμενο | (to e·po·me·no
λεωφορείο); | le·o·fo·ri·o)

Where's (the station)?
Πού είναι (ο σταθμός); | pu i·ne (o stath·mos)

Do you have (a local map)?
Έχετε οδικό | e·he·te o·dhi·ko
(τοπικό χάρτη); | (to·pi·ko khar·ti)

Is there a (lift)?
Υπάρχει (ασανσέρ); | i·par·hi (a·san·ser)

Can I (try it on)?
Μπορώ να | bo·ro na
(το προβάρω); | (to pro·va·ro)

Could you (please help)?
Μπορείς να | bo·ris na
(βοηθήσεις, | (vo·i·thi·sis
παρακαλώ); | pa·ra·ka·lo)

Do I need (to book)?
Χρειάζεται | khri·a·ze·te
(να κλείσω θέση); | (na kli·so the·si)

I need (assistance).
Χρειάζομαι | khri·a·zo·me
(βοήθεια). | (vo·i·thi·a)

I'd like (to hire a car).
Θα ήθελα (να | tha i·the·la (na
ενοικιάσω ένα | e·ni·ki·a·so e·na
αυτοκίνητο). | af·to·ki·ni·to)

How much is it (per night)?
Πόσο είναι (για | po·so i·ne (yia
κάθε νύχτα); | ka·the nikh·ta)

SHOPPING & SERVICES

I'd like to buy ...
Θέλω ν' αγοράσω ... | the·lo na·gho·ra·so ...

I'm just looking.
Απλώς κοιτάζω. | ap·los ki·ta·zo

Can I see it?
Μπορώ να το δω; | bo·ro na to dho

I don't like it.
Δεν μου αρέσει. | dhen mu a·re·si

How much is it?
Πόσο κάνει; | po·so ka·ni

It's too expensive.
Είναι πολύ ακριβό. | i·ne po·li a·kri·vo

Can you lower the price?
Μπορείς να κατεβάσεις | bo·ris na ka·te·va·sis
την τιμή; | tin ti·mi

ATM | αυτόματη | af·to·ma·ti
| μηχανή | mi·kha·ni
| χρημάτων | khri·ma·ton

bank | τράπεζα | tra·pe·za
credit card | πιστωτική | pi·sto·ti·ki
| κάρτα | kar·ta
internet cafe | καφενείο | ka·fe·ni·o
| διαδικτύου | dhi·a·dhik·ti·u
mobile phone | κινητό | ki·ni·to
post office | ταχυδρομείο | ta·hi·dhro·mi·o
tourist office | τουριστικό | tu·ri·sti·ko
| γραφείο | ghra·fi·o

TIME & DATES

What time is it?
Τι ώρα είναι; | ti o·ra i·ne

It's (two) o'clock.
Είναι (δύο) η ώρα. | i·ne (dhi·o) i o·ra

It's half past (10).
(Δέκα) και μισή. | (dhe·ka) ke mi·si

morning | πρωί | pro·i
(this) | (αυτό το) | (af·to to)
  afternoon | απόγευμα | a·po·yev·ma
evening | βράδυ | vra·dhi

yesterday | χθες | hthes
today | σήμερα | si·me·ra
tomorrow | αύριο | av·ri·o

Monday | Δευτέρα | dhef·te·ra
Tuesday | Τρίτη | tri·ti
Wednesday | Τετάρτη | te·tar·ti
Thursday | Πέμπτη | pemp·ti
Friday | Παρασκευή | pa·ras·ke·vi
Saturday | Σάββατο | sa·va·to
Sunday | Κυριακή | ky·ri·a·ki

January | Ιανουάριος | ia·nu·ar·i·os
February | Φεβρουάριος | fev·ru·ar·i·os
March | Μάρτιος | mar·ti·os
April | Απρίλιος | a·pri·li·os
May | Μάιος | mai·os
June | Ιούνιος | i·u·ni·os
July | Ιούλιος | i·u·li·os
August | Αύγουστος | av·ghus·tos
September | Σεπτέμβριος | sep·tem·vri·os
October | Οκτώβριος | ok·to·vri·os
November | Νοέμβριος | no·em·vri·os
December | Δεκέμβριος | dhe·kem·vri·os

TRANSPORT

Public Transport

boat	πλοίο	pli·o
city bus	αστικό	a·sti·ko
intercity bus	λεωφορείο	le·o·fo·ri·o
plane	αεροπλάνο	ae·ro·pla·no
train	τρένο	tre·no

Where do I buy a ticket?
Πού αγοράζω εισιτήριο; pu a·gho·ra·zo i·si·ti·ri·o
I want to go to ...
Θέλω να πάω στο/στη ... the·lo na pao sto/sti...
What time does it leave?
Τι ώρα φεύγει; ti o·ra fev·yi
Does it stop at (Iraklio)?
Σταματάει στο sta·ma·ta·i sto
(Ηράκλειο); (i·ra·kli·o)
I'd like to get off at (Iraklio).
Θα ήθελα να κατεβώ tha i·the·la na ka·te·vo
στο (Ηράκλειο). sto (i·ra·kli·o)

I'd like (a) ...	Θα ήθελα (ένα) ...	tha i·the·la (e·na) ...
1st class	πρώτη θέση	pro·ti the·si
2nd class	δεύτερη θέση	def·te·ri the·si
one-way ticket	απλό εισιτήριο	a·plo i·si·ti·ri·o
return ticket	εισιτήριο με επιστροφή	i·si·ti·ri·o me e·pi·stro·fi
cancelled	ακυρώθηκε	a·ki·ro·thi·ke
delayed	καθυστέρησε	ka·thi·ste·ri·se
platform	πλατφόρμα	plat·for·ma
ticket office	εκδοτήριο εισιτηρίων	ek·dho·li·ri·o i·si·ti·ri·on
timetable	δρομολόγιο	dhro·mo·lo·gio
train station	σταθμός τρένου	stath·mos tre·nu

Driving & Cycling

I'd like to hire a ...	Θα ήθελα να νοικιάσω ...	tha i·the·la na ni·ki·a·so ...
4WD	ένα τέσσερα επί τέσσερα	e·na tes·se·ra e·pi tes·se·ra
bicycle	ένα ποδήλατο	e·na po·dhi·la·to
car	ένα αυτοκίνητο	e·na af·to·ki·ni·to
jeep	ένα τζιπ	e·na tzip
motorbike	μια μοτοσυκλέττα	mya mo·to·si·klet·ta

NUMBERS

1	ένας	e·nas (m)
	μία	mi·a (f)
	ένα	e·na (n)
2	δύο	dhi·o
3	τρεις	tris (m&f)
	τρία	tri·a (n)
4	τέσσερεις	te·se·ris (m&f)
	τέσσερα	te·se·ra (n)
5	πέντε	pen·de
6	έξη	e·xi
7	επτά	ep·ta
8	οχτώ	oh·to
9	εννέα	e·ne·a
10	δέκα	dhe·ka
20	είκοσι	ik·o·si
30	τριάντα	tri·an·da
40	σαράντα	sa·ran·da
50	πενήντα	pe·nin·da
60	εξήντα	ek·sin·da
70	εβδομήντα	ev·dho·min·da
80	ογδόντα	ogh·dhon·da
90	ενενήντα	e·ne·nin·da
100	εκατό	e·ka·to
1000	χίλιοι	hi·li·i (m)
	χίλιες	hi·li·ez (f)
	χίλια	hi·li·a (n)

Do I need a helmet?
Χρειάζομαι κράνος; khri·a·zo·me kra·nos
Is this the road to ...?
Αυτός είναι ο af·tos i·ne o
δρόμος για ... ; dhro·mos ya ...
Where's a petrol station?
Πού είναι ένα πρατήριο pu i·ne e·na pra·ti·ri·o
βενζίνας; ven·zi·nas
(How long) Can I park here?
(Πόση ώρα) Μπορώ να (po·si o·ra) bo·ro na
παρκάρω εδώ; par·ka·ro e·dho
The car/motorbike has broken down (at ...).
Το αυτοκίνητο/ to af·to·ki·ni·to/
η μοτοσυκλέττα i mo·to·si·klet·ta
χάλασε (στο ...). kha·la·se (sto ...)
I need a mechanic.
Χρειάζομαι μηχανικό. khri·a·zo·me mi·kha·ni·ko
I have a flat tyre.
Έπαθα λάστιχο. e·pa·tha la·sti·cho
I've run out of petrol.
Έμεινα από βενζίνη. e·mi·na a·po ven·zi·ni

Behind the Scenes

SEND US YOUR FEEDBACK

We love to hear from travellers – your comments keep us on our toes and help make our books better. Our well-travelled team reads every word on what you loved or loathed about this book. Although we cannot reply individually to your submissions, we always guarantee that your feedback goes straight to the appropriate authors, in time for the next edition. Each person who sends us information is thanked in the next edition – the most useful submissions are rewarded with a selection of digital PDF chapters.

Visit **lonelyplanet.com/contact** to submit your updates and suggestions or to ask for help. Our award-winning website also features inspirational travel stories, news and discussions.

Note: We may edit, reproduce and incorporate your comments in Lonely Planet products such as guidebooks, websites and digital products, so let us know if you don't want your comments reproduced or your name acknowledged. For a copy of our privacy policy visit lonelyplanet.com/privacy.

OUR READERS

Many thanks to the travellers who used the last edition and wrote to us with helpful hints, useful advice and interesting anecdotes:

Alex Jasper, Andrew Trotter, Chris Docker, Craig Wood, Daniel Kolodrubetz, Daria Fireman, Eric Poscher, Felix Widmer, George and Linda Moss, Indivar Kamtekar, Javier López, Louise Eckhardt, Marian Smith, Michael Williamson, Patrick Barfield, Robert Femenella, Sabine Gerull, Sain Alizada, Sonja Carter, Steven Tagle

WRITER THANKS

Korina Miller

A warm *efharisto* to all of the people in Greece who shared their stories, knowledge and enthusiasm for their country. Thank you to Brana at LP for bringing me on board and to my coauthors for their insights. Thank you to my fabulous daughters, Monique and Simone, for letting me work and also encouraging me to take breaks. Thanks to Kirk for being my rock and to Bing, the loyal coonhound, for keeping me company while I burned the midnight oil.

Kate Armstrong

Efharisto poli to Brana, editor extraordinaire. And of course, my information-sharing Greek friends whose genuine love of both country and visitors is so humbling: the entire Zotos family in Nafplio; Apostolos in Attica; Mina in the Mani; Nena and Koula in

Stemnitsa; Aggela and Yiannis in Kardamyli. Finally, a huge thanks to my very own Christos who shared my love for everything from *horta* to the Taygetos Mountains. And who finally heard me say *ta ellinika mu telionu ado* in person.

Alexis Averbuck

Boundless gratitude to Alexandra Stamopoulou for her INSPIRATION. She travels with me everywhere. Ryan is a peachy companion, on the road and off. Boundless thanks to Anthy, Costas and Matthew who first introduced me to Greece, and then to Hydra, the other love of my life. *Efharisto poli* to Oren who made researching Poros a blast, and to Rachel, Jenny and Timothy for their enthusiastic companionship. Margarita, Kostas, Zisis and Okeanida also make Greece home for me.

Michael Stamatios Clark

A hearty ευχαριστω to the generous, good-natured and persevering Greeks who shared their stories and tables with me. Among many friends and friendly strangers, special gratitude to Lena Spiliotopoulou (Amfissa), Nikos Petrochilos (archaeologist, Delphi), Jenny Panourgia (Nafpaktos), Jill Sleeman (Mouressi), Julia and Sofia (Loutra Ipatis), Yiannis Karkantas (Kalambaka), Angelina Srebric (Meteora) and Anastasia Koutzouradi (Volos). A huge thanks for Brana Vladisavljevic's unflappable help and common sense throughout. And to my Janet, Melina and Alexandros, couldn't do it without you!

Anna Kaminski

A big thank you to Brana, for entrusting me with half of the Cyclades, and to everyone who helped me en route. In particular: Edd and Meg for research input in Mykonos and Delos; Aristoteles in Kea, Konstantinos in Syros for aiding a stranded travel writer; Alexander and Eleni in Kythnos; Spiros in Andros; Giorgios in Milos; Sofia and Dimitris in Tinos; and the good people in Milos who rented me a scooter that coped with sand, gravel and cobblestones.

Vesna Maric

I would like to thank Tania, Stamathios and Maria in Thessaloniki, for their excellent gastronomic guidance, and to Nana for setting me up with great people. Big thanks to Damir Ugljen. Warmest thanks to my editor, Brana Vladisavljevic.

Craig McLachlan

A hearty *efharisto* to everyone who helped out during my research trip, but especially to my exceptionally beautiful wife, Yuriko, who kept me on track, focused and constantly smiling. The Greek islands are a joy to island-hop through, and a big part of that joy comes from meeting and talking to happy Greeks! – thanks to you all.

Zora O'Neill

Many thanks to Georgia Lale, Annia Ciezadlo, Ioanna Theodorou, Maria Papadimitriou, Rod Ben Zeev, Polycarpe Nana Toukam, Dora Papagiannou and everyone else who shared their knowledge of and affection for wonderful Athens. At Lonely Planet, thanks to editor Brana Vladisavljevic for being calm and collected, and to Alexis Averbuck for her work in previous years. And special thanks to Peter Moskos, who got me to Athens in the first place.

Leonid Ragozin

Huge thanks of all the wonderfully friendly Greek people – domatia and taverna owners, travel agents, ferry attendants, gas station employees, taxi drivers – for giving invaluable tips and helping out in all sorts of situations. You've once again reinforced my long-standing opinion that

Greece is possibly the best place to travel on Earth. I would also like to thank my wife, Maria Makeeva, for accompanying me on this journey, driving thousands of miles and helping with the research.

Andrea Schulte-Peevers

Big heartfelt thank yous to all the wonderful people I met during my travels around Crete who so generously and patiently shared their knowledge, insights, wisdom and passion, and made me once again feel connected with the island.

Helena Smith

Thank you to Chara Stavropoulou and Manolis Avgerinos on Skyros for sharing their local knowledge, to Alexandra on Skopelos and to Amy on Alonnisos. And to everyone who was so generous and welcoming throughout Evia and the Sporades.

Greg Ward

Thanks to the many wonderful people who helped me on my way around the Ionian Islands; without Greek hospitality I'd have learned a whole lot less and had a lot less fun into the bargain. And thanks as ever, with all my heart, to my dear wife Sam.

Richard Waters

Special thanks to Fokas, Maria Cristofi, Skevos Travel, Marianna, George at GNTO, and all the Greek friends who helped me along the way with my research.

ACKNOWLEDGEMENTS

Climate map data adapted from Peel MC, Finlayson BL & McMahon TA (2007) 'Updated World Map of the Köppen-Geiger Climate Classification', Hydrology and Earth System Sciences, 11, 163344.

Illustrations pp70-1, pp452-3 by Javier Martinez Zarracina; pp202-3 by Michael Weldon.

Cover photograph: Naoussa Harbour, Paros; Maurizio Rellini/4Corners ©

THIS BOOK

This 13th edition of Lonely Planet's *Greece* guidebook was researched and written by Korina Miller, Kate Armstrong, Alexis Averbuck, Michael Stamatios Clark, Anna Kaminski, Vesna Maric, Craig McLachlan, Zora O'Neill, Leonid Ragozin, Andrea Schulte-Peevers, Helena Smith, Greg Ward and Richard Waters. This guidebook was produced by the following:

Destination Editor
Brana Vladisavljevic

Product Editor Vicky Smith

Senior Cartographer
Anthony Phelan

Book Designer Clara Monitto

Assisting Editors Carolyn Bain, Judith Bamber, Carolyn Boicos, Kate Chapman, Andrea Dobbin, Bruce Evans, Shona Gray, Carly Hall, Sandie Kestell, Kellie Langdon, Lou McGregor, Anne Mulvaney, Kristin Odijk, Charlotte Orr, Susan Paterson, Monique Perrin, Christopher Pitts, Sam Wheeler

Assisting Cartographers
Corey Hutchison, Hunor Csutoros, Rachel Imeson, James Leversha

Cover Researcher
Naomi Parker

Thanks to Ronan Abayawickrema, Hannah Cartmel, Elizabeth Jones, Kate Kiely, Anne Mason, Marissa Tejada, Gina Tsarouhas, Tony Wheeler, Amanda Williamson

Index

Map Legend

Sights

- Beach
- Bird Sanctuary
- Buddhist
- Castle/Palace
- Christian
- Confucian
- Hindu
- Islamic
- Jain
- Jewish
- Monument
- Museum/Gallery/Historic Building
- Ruin
- Shinto
- Sikh
- Taoist
- Winery/Vineyard
- Zoo/Wildlife Sanctuary
- Other Sight

Activities, Courses & Tours

- Bodysurfing
- Diving
- Canoeing/Kayaking
- Course/Tour
- Sento Hot Baths/Onsen
- Skiing
- Snorkelling
- Surfing
- Swimming/Pool
- Walking
- Windsurfing
- Other Activity

Sleeping

- Sleeping
- Camping
- Hut/Shelter

Eating

- Eating

Drinking & Nightlife

- Drinking & Nightlife
- Cafe

Entertainment

- Entertainment

Shopping

- Shopping

Information

- Bank
- Embassy/Consulate
- Hospital/Medical
- Internet
- Police
- Post Office
- Telephone
- Toilet
- Tourist Information
- Other Information

Geographic

- Beach
- Gate
- Hut/Shelter
- Lighthouse
- Lookout
- Mountain/Volcano
- Oasis
- Park
- Pass
- Picnic Area
- Waterfall

Population

- Capital (National)
- Capital (State/Province)
- City/Large Town
- Town/Village

Transport

- Airport
- Border crossing
- Bus
- Cable car/Funicular
- Cycling
- Ferry
- Metro station
- Monorail
- Parking
- Petrol station
- S-Bahn/Subway station
- Taxi
- T-bane/Tunnelbana station
- Train station/Railway
- Tram
- Tube station
- U-Bahn/Underground station
- Other Transport

Routes

- Tollway
- Freeway
- Primary
- Secondary
- Tertiary
- Lane
- Unsealed road
- Road under construction
- Plaza/Mall
- Steps
- Tunnel
- Pedestrian overpass
- Walking Tour
- Walking Tour detour
- Path/Walking Trail

Boundaries

- International
- State/Province
- Disputed
- Regional/Suburb
- Marine Park
- Cliff
- Wall

Hydrography

- River, Creek
- Intermittent River
- Canal
- Water
- Dry/Salt/Intermittent Lake
- Reef

Areas

- Airport/Runway
- Beach/Desert
- Cemetery (Christian)
- Cemetery (Other)
- Glacier
- Mudflat
- Park/Forest
- Sight (Building)
- Sportsground
- Swamp/Mangrove

Note: Not all symbols displayed above appear on the maps in this book

Vesna Maric

Northern Greece Vesna has been a Lonely Planet author for more than a decade, covering places as far and wide as Bolivia, Algeria, Sicily, Cyprus, Barcelona, London and Croatia, among others. Her latest work has been updating the Burkina Faso and Ivory Coast chapters for the *West Africa* and *Africa* guides.

Craig McLachlan

Cyclades Craig has covered destinations all over the globe for Lonely Planet for two decades. Based in Queenstown, New Zealand, for half the year, he runs an outdoor activities company and a sake brewery, then moonlights overseas for the other half, leading tours and writing for Lonely Planet. Describing himself as a 'freelance anything', Craig has an MBA from the University of Hawai'i and is also a Japanese interpreter, pilot, photographer, hiking guide, tour leader, karate instructor and budding novelist. Check out www.craigmclachlan.com.

Zora O'Neill

Athens & Around A freelance writer since 2000, Zora speaks Arabic with the accent of an Egyptian soap-opera queen. She has written more than a dozen guidebooks to many of her favourite places, from Amsterdam to Yucatán. She is the author of *All Strangers Are Kin,* a travel memoir about studying Arabic in the Middle East.

Leonid Ragozin

Northeastern Aegean Islands Leonid Ragozin studied beach dynamics at Moscow State University, but for want of decent beaches in Russia, he switched to journalism and spent 12 years voyaging through different parts of the BBC, with a break for a four-year stint as a foreign correspondent for *Russian Newsweek.* Leonid is currently a freelance journalist focusing largely on the conflict between Russia and Ukraine, which prompted him to leave Moscow and find a new home in Rīga.

Andrea Schulte-Peevers

Crete Born and raised in Germany and educated in London and at UCLA, Andrea has travelled the distance to the moon and back in her visits to some 75 countries. She has earned her living as a professional travel writer for more than two decades and authored or contributed to nearly 100 Lonely Planet titles as well as to newspapers, magazines and websites around the world. She also works as a travel consultant, translator and editor. Andrea's destination expertise is especially strong when it comes to Germany, Dubai and the UAE, Crete and the Caribbean Islands.

Helena Smith

Evia & the Sporades Helena is an award-winning writer and photographer covering travel, outdoors and food – she has written guidebooks on destinations from Fiji to northern Norway. Helena is from Scotland but was partly brought up in Malawi, so Africa always feels like home. She also enjoys global travel in her multicultural home area of Hackney and wrote, photographed and published *Inside Hackney,* the first guide to the borough (https://insidehackney.com).

Greg Ward

Ionian Islands Besides covering the Ionian islands for Lonely Planet *Greece,* Greg has also written the New Mexico chapter for Lonely Planet *Southwest USA,* and has been writing for many years about other destinations including France, Spain, Japan, Australia, Hawaii and Belize. See his website, www.gregward.info, for his favourite photos and memories.

Richard Waters

Dodecanese Richard is an award-winning writer who first cut his travelling teeth in Guatemala, stumbling unprepared into the last days of the Civil War whilst trying to nurse his camper van back to life. He writes for the *Telegraph* and *Sunday Times* on subjects including wildlife and adventure travel. For Lonely Planet he's cowritten more than 25 books. He lives with his family in the Cotswolds. Greece has been in his blood since he visited Corfu as a kid in the first wave of British tourists. His spiritual home is Greece. You can read some of his stories for the *Independent* at: www.independent.co.uk/author/richard-waters

OUR STORY

A beat-up old car, a few dollars in the pocket and a sense of adventure. In 1972 that's all Tony and Maureen Wheeler needed for the trip of a lifetime – across Europe and Asia overland to Australia. It took several months, and at the end – broke but inspired – they sat at their kitchen table writing and stapling together their first travel guide, *Across Asia on the Cheap*. Within a week they'd sold 1500 copies. Lonely Planet was born.

Today, Lonely Planet has offices in Franklin, London, Melbourne, Oakland, Dublin, Beijing and Delhi, with more than 600 staff and writers. We share Tony's belief that 'a great guidebook should do three things: inform, educate and amuse'.

OUR WRITERS

Korina Miller

Curator, Greece, Greek Islands Korina grew up on Vancouver Island and has been exploring the globe independently since she was 16, visiting or living in 36 countries and picking up a degree in Communications and Canadian Studies, an MA in Migration Studies and a diploma in Visual Arts en route. Korina has worked on nearly 60 titles for Lonely Planet and has also worked with LP.com, BBC, the *Independent*, the *Guardian*, BBC5 and CBC, covering travel, art and culture.

Kate Armstrong

Peloponnese Kate Armstrong has spent much of her adult life travelling and living around the world. A full-time freelance travel journalist, she has contributed to around 40 Lonely Planet guides and trade publications and is regularly published in Australian and worldwide publications. She is the author of several books and children's educational titles. You can read more about her on www.katearmstrongtravelwriter.com and @nomaditis.

Alexis Averbuck

Saronic Gulf Islands Alexis Averbuck has travelled and lived all over the world, from Sri Lanka to Ecuador, Zanzibar and Antarctica. In recent years she's been living on the Greek island of Hydra and exploring her adopted homeland; sampling oysters in Brittany and careening through hilltop villages in Provence; and adventuring along Iceland's surreal lava fields. A travel writer for more than two decades, Alexis has lived in Antarctica for a year, crossed the Pacific by sailboat and written books on her journeys through Asia, Europe and the Americas.

Michael Stamatios Clark

Central Greece Michael's Greek roots go back to the village of Karavostamo on the Aegean island of Ikaria, home to his maternal grandparents. He first travelled to Greece as a deckhand aboard a Greek freighter. For this journey, he drove over alpine passes, sea-kayaked in the Aegean, and walked the cobbled paths of Pelion villages, marvelling at the resiliency of Greeks in austere times. He has worked on Lonely Planet guides to Myanmar (Burma), New York, Hawaii and Japan.

Anna Kaminski

Cyclades Originally from the Soviet Union, Anna grew up in Cambridge, UK. She graduated from the University of Warwick with a degree in Comparative American Studies, a background in the history, culture and literature of the Americas and the Caribbean, and an enduring love of Latin America. Her wanderings led her to settle briefly in Oaxaca and Bangkok and her flirtation with criminal law saw her volunteering as a lawyer's assistant in the courts, ghettos and prisons of Kingston, Jamaica. Anna has contributed to almost 30 Lonely Planet titles.

OVER PAGE
MORE WRITERS

Published by Lonely Planet Global Limited
CRN 554153
13th edition – Mar 2018
ISBN 978 1 78657 446 6
© Lonely Planet 2018   Photographs © as indicated 2018
10 9 8 7 6 5 4 3 2 1
Printed in Singapore